THE OXFORD HANDBOOK OF

SPORT AND SPECTACLE IN THE ANCIENT WORLD

THE OXFORD HANDBOOK OF

SPORT AND SPECTACLE IN THE ANCIENT WORLD

Edited by

ALISON FUTRELL

and

THOMAS F. SCANLON

OXFORD
UNIVERSITY PRESS

OXFORD
UNIVERSITY PRESS

Great Clarendon Street, Oxford, OX2 6DP,
United Kingdom

Oxford University Press is a department of the University of Oxford.
It furthers the University's objective of excellence in research, scholarship,
and education by publishing worldwide. Oxford is a registered trade mark of
Oxford University Press in the UK and in certain other countries

First Edition published in 2021
Impression: 1

Published in the United States of America by Oxford University Press
198 Madison Avenue, New York, NY 10016, United States of America

British Library Cataloguing in Publication Data
Data available

Library of Congress Control Number: 2020952433

ISBN 978–0–19–959208–1

DOI: 10.1093/oxfordhb/9780199592081.001.0001

Printed and bound by
CPI Group (UK) Ltd, Croydon, CR0 4YY

In memoriam
Wolfgang Decker and Garrett G. Fagan
collegis doctissimis

CONTENTS

PART III FORMS OF CONTESTS AND DISPLAY

PART VI BODY AND INDIVIDUAL

Section 1 Health and Training

Section 2 Gender and Sexuality

FIGURES

Journal Titles and Abbreviations

Journal titles have routinely been abbreviated following the standards of *L'Année Philologique*. The abbreviations for the names of ancient authors and their works and for standard reference works are in general accordance with those found in the Oxford Classical Dictionary, available online at: https://classics.oxfordre.com/staticfiles/images/ORECLA/OCD.ABBREVIATIONS.pdf.

A&R	*Atene e Roma: rassegna trimestrale dell'Associazione Italiana di Cultura classica*
AAA	*Archaiologika Analekta ex Athenon/Athens Annals of Archaeology*
AAP	*Atti dell'Accademia Pontaniana*
AArchHung	*Acta Archaeologica Academiae Scientiarum Hungaricae*
ABSA	*Annual of the British School at Athens*
ABull	*The Art Bulletin: A quarterly published by the College Art Association of America*
ABV	*Attic Black-figure Vase Painters.* J. D. Beazley, ed. Oxford. 1956
ARV²	*Attic Red-Figure Vase Painters.* 2nd edn. J. D. Beazley, ed. Oxford. 1963
AC	*L'Antiquité classique*
AClass	*Acta classica: Proceedings of the Classical Association of South Africa*
AE	*L'Année épigraphique.* Paris. 1888–
AEA	*Archivo Español de Arqueología*
AEph (*AEphem*)	*Archaiologike ephemeris*
AH	*Ancient History*
AHB	*The Ancient History Bulletin*
AJA	*American Journal of Archaeology*
AJN	*American Journal of Numismatics*
AJPh (*AJP*)	*American Journal of Philology*
AK	*Antike Kunst, hrsg. von der Vereiningung der Freunde antiker Kunst*
AM	see *MDAI(A)*
AncW	*The Ancient World*
AntAfr	*Antiquités africaines*
ArchClass	*Archeologia classica: rivista della Scuola naz. di Archeologia, pubbl. a cura degli Ist. Di Archeologia e Storia dell'arte greca e romana e di Etruscologia e antichità italiche dell' Università. di Roma*
AS	*Anatolian Studies: Journal of the British Inst. of Archaeology at Ankara*
BA	*Bollettino d'arte del Ministero per i beni culturali e ambientali*
BASP	*Bulletin of the American Society of Papyrologists*
BCH	*Bulletin de correspondance hellénique*

BEFAR	*Bibliothèque des Écoles françaises d'Écoles and Athènes et de Rome*
BIAO	*Bulletin de l'Institut français d'archéologie orientale*
BICS	*Bulletin of the Institute of Classical Studies of the University of London*
BMC	*British Museum Catalogue*
ByzF	*Byzantinische Forschungen: internationale Zeitschrift für Byzantinistik*
ByzZ (BZ)	*Byzantinische Zeitschrift*
CB	*The Classical Bulletin*
CEG	*Carmina epigraphica Graeca saeculorum VIII-V a. Chr. n.* Vol. 1. P. A. Hansen, ed. Berlin and New York. 1983; *Carmina epigraphica graeca saeculi IV a. Chr. n.* Vol. 2. P. A. Hansen, ed. Berlin and New York. 1989
CID	*Corpus des inscriptions de Delphes. Tome I: Lois sacrées et règlements religieux.* C. Rougemont, ed. Paris. 1977
CIL	*Corpus Inscriptionum Latinarum.* Berlin. 1863–
CJ	*The Classical Journal*
ClAnt (CA; Clas. Ant.)	*Classical Antiquity*
CMS	*Corpus der minoischen und mykenischen Siegel.* I. Pini and W. Müller, eds. Berlin. 1960–2009
CPh (CP)	*Classical Philology*
CPJ	*Corpus papyrorum Judaicarum.* A. Tcherikover, A. Fuks., M. Stern, eds. Cambridge, MA. 1895–1978
CQ	*Classical Quarterly*
CR	*Classical Review*
CRAI	*Comptes rendus de l'Académie des Inscriptions et Belles-Lettres*
CSCA	*California Studies in Classical Antiquity* (continued as *Classical Antiquity* [*ClAnt*])
CVA	*Corpus Vasorum Antiquorum.* 1925–
CW	*The Classical World*
Dar.–Sag.	C. Daremberg and E. Saglio, *Dictionnaire des antiquités grecques et romaines d'après les textes et les monuments.* 1877–1919
DHA	*Dialogues d'histoire ancienne*
DK	*Fragmente der Vorsokratiker.* 6th edn. H. Diels and W. Kranz, eds. 1952
DNP	*Der Neue Pauly. Enzyklopädie der Antike.* H. Cancik and H. Schneider, eds. Stuttgart. 1996–
EA	*Epigraphica Anatolica: Zeitschrift für Epigraphik und historische Geographie Anatoliens*
EAOR	P. Sabbatini Tumolesi, et al. *Epigrafia anfiteatrale dell'Occidente Romano,* Rome. 1989–2009
EMC	*Échos du monde classique (Classical Views)*
EuGeSta	*Journal of Gender Studies in Antiquity*
FD	*Fouilles de Delphes, III. Épigraphie.* Paris. 1929
FGrH	*Fragmente der griechischen Historiker.* F. Jacoby, ed. Berlin. 1923–
G&R	*Greece and Rome*

GRBS	*Greek, Roman and Byzantine Studies*
HSPh (HSCP; HSCPh)	*Harvard Studies in Classical Philology*
ICos	*Iscrizioni di Cos.* Mario Serge, ed. Rome. 1993
IG	*Inscriptiones Graecae.* 1873–
IGBulg	*Inscriptiones graecae in Bulgaria repertae*, ed. Georgi Mihailov. 5 vols. Sofia 1958–1970, 1997. Vol. 1. *Inscriptiones orae Ponti Euxini.* 1970²
IGR (IGRR)	*Inscriptiones Graecae ad res Romanas pertinentes.* René Cagnat et al., eds. 3 vols. Paris. 1901–1927
I.Histria	*Inscriptiones Scythiae Minoris Graecae et Latinae* I. *Inscriptiones Histriae et viciniae.* M. Pippidi, ed. Bucarest. 1983
IJHS	*International Journal of the History of Sport*
IK	*Inschriften griechischer Städte aus Kleinasien.* 1972–
IMagnesia	*Die Inschriften von Magnesia am Maeander.* O. Kern, ed. Berlin. 1900
IvO	*Die Inscriften von Olympia.* W. Dittenberger and K. Purgold, eds. Berlin. 1896
IPerg. (I.Pergamon)	*Die Inschriften von Pergamon.* 2 vols. Max Fränkel, ed. Berlin. 1890–1895
I. Priene	*Inschriften von Priene.* F. F. Hiller von Gaetringen et al., eds. Berlin. 1906
JAH	*Journal of Ancient History*
JDAI (JdI)	*Jahrbuch des Deutschen archäologischen Instituts*
JECS	*Journal of Early Christian Studies*
JHS	*Journal of Hellenic Studies*
JHSex	*Journal of the History of Sexuality*
JJS	*Journal of Jewish Studies*
JNG	*Jahrbuch für Numismatik und Geldgeschichte*
JÖAI (ÖAI)	*Jahreshefte des österreichischen archäologischen Instituts*
JÖByz	*Jahrbuch der österreichischen Byzantinistik*
JPR	*Journal of Prehistoric Religion*
JRA	*Journal of Roman Archaeology*
JRMES	*Journal of Roman Military Equipment Studies*
JRS	*Journal of Roman Studies*
JSAH	*Journal of the Society of Architectural Historians*
JSH	*Journal of Sports History*
KN	Knossos Linear B tablet prefix
LCM	*Liverpool Classical Monthly*
LIMC	*Lexicon Iconographicum Mythologiae Classicae.* Zurich. 1981–
LP	Lobel, Edgar and Denys Page. *Poetarum Lesbiorum fragmenta.* Oxford. 1955
LSJ	Liddell and Scott, *Greek-English Lexicon*, 9th edn., rev. H. Stuart Jones, ed. 1925–1940; Suppl. by E. A. Barber and others. Oxford. 1968
LTUR	M. Steinby, ed. *Lexicon Topographicum Urbis Romae.* Rome. 1993–2000

MAAL	*Monumenti Antichi della Reale Accademia dei Lincei.* 1890–1966
MAL (MemLinc)	*Memorie della Classe di Scienze morali e storiche dell'Accademia dei Lincei*
MDAI(A)	*Mitteilungen des Deutschen archäologischen Instituts (Athen. Abt.)*
MDAI(R)	*Mitteilungen des Deutschen archäologischen Instituts (Röm. Abt.)*
MedArch	*Mediterranean Archaeology: Australian and New Zealand Journal for the Archaeology of the Mediterranean World*
MEFRA	*Mélanges d'archéologie et d'histoire de l'École française de Rome, Antiquité*
MGR	*Miscellanea greca e romana: studi pubblicati dall'Ist. Italiano per la storia antica*
MH	*Museum Helveticum: revue suisse pour l'étude de l'Antiquité classique*
Milet 6.1	*Milet 6.1. Inschriften von Milet 1.* A. Rehm and P. Herrmann, eds. Berlin. 1997
MycPictVP	*Mycenaean Pictorial Vase Painting.* E. T. Vermeule and V. Karageorghis. Cambridge. 1982
NC	*Numismatic Chronicle*
NECJ	*New England Classical Journal*
NMA	National Museum, Athens
OGI (OGIS)	*Orientis Graeci Inscriptiones Selectae.* 2 vols. Wilhelm Dittenberger, ed. Leipzig. 1903–1905
P&P	*Past and Present: A Journal of Historical Studies*
PAAH	*Praktika tes en Athenais Archaiologikes Etaireias*
Page, PMG	*Poetae Melici Graeci.* D. Page, ed. Oxford. 1962
PBSR	*Papers of the British School at Rome*
PCPhS (PCPS)	*Proceedings of the Cambridge Philological Society*
PGM	*Papyri Graecae Magicae,* vol. 1. 1973. K. Preisendanz, ed. Rev. edn A. Henrichs. Stuttgart. Trans. H. D. Betz. *The Greek Magical Papyri in Translation: Including the Demotic Spells.* Chicago. 1986
PLondon	*Greek Papyri in the British Museum.* H. I. Bell, ed. London. 1910
PM	*The Palace of Minos at Knossos.* 4 vols. A. Evans. London. 1921–1935
PMG	See Page, *PMG*
RA (Rev. Arch.)	*Revue archéologique*
RAAN	*Rendiconti dell'Accademia di archeologia, lettere e belle arti di Napoli*
RAL	*Rendiconti della Classe di scienze morali, storiche e filologiche dell'Accademia dei Lincei*
RE	*Real-Encyclopädie der klassischen Altertumswissenschaft.* A. Pauly, G. Wissowa, and W. Kroll, eds. Stuttgart. 1893–1983
REA	*Revue des études anciennes*
REG	*Revue des études grecques*
RFIC	*Rivista di filologia e di istruzione classica*
RhM	*Rheinisches Museum*
RIDA	*Revue Internationale des Droits de l'Antiquité*
RPh	*Revue de philologie, de littérature et d'histoire anciennes*
RO	P. J. Rhodes and R. Osborne, *Greek Historical Inscriptions, 404–323* BC. Oxford. 2003; rev. 2007

RSP (RStPomp)	*Rivista di studi pompeiani*
RWKIL	*Repertorium der westkilikischen Inschriften nach den Scheden der Kleinasiatische Komission der Österreichischen Akademie der Wissenschaft.* S. Hagel and K. Tomaschitz, eds. Vienna. 1998
SEG	*Supplementum epigraphicum Graecum.* 1923–
SIG	See *Syll.*
Syll.	*Sylloge inscriptionum Graecarum.* W. Dittenberger, ed. Leipzig. 1883–
Syll.³	*Sylloge inscriptionum Graecarum.* Third edition. W. Dittenberger, ed. Leipzig. 1915–1924
SIMA	*Studies in Mediterranean Archaeology*
SMSR	*Studi e materiali di storia delle religioni*
T&MByz	*Travaux et Mémoires du Centre de Recherches d'hist. et civil. Byzantines*
TAM III	*Tituli Asiae Minoris, III. Tituli Pisidiae linguis Graeca et Latina conscripti, 1. Tituli Termessi et agri Termessensis.* Rudolf Heberdey, ed. Vienna. 1941
TAPhA (TAPA)	*Transactions and Proceedings of the American Philological Association*
ZPE	*Zeitschrift für Papyrologie und Epigraphik*

Contributors

Richard Beacham is Emeritus Professor of Classics at Kings College London, where he has been a leader in the creation of three-dimensional digital visualizations of ancient performance spaces. A specialist in the ancient Theatre, his books include *The Roman Theatre and Its Audience* (1992), *Spectacle Entertainments of Early Imperial Rome* (1999), *Adolphe Appia. Künstler und Visionär des Modernen Theaters* (2006) and *Living Theatre: Roman Theatricalism in the Domestic Sphere* (with Hugh Denard, forthcoming).

Shelby Brown is a Senior Education Specialist in antiquities at the Getty Villa Museum. Among other roles related to public outreach on ancient topics, she oversees lectures and programmes about the classical world and the interconnected cultures of the Mediterranean, Near/Middle East, and central Asia. Her research interests include the ways peoples marginalize other cultures and groups within their own societies and therefore deny their rights and justify violence against them.

Michael J. Carter is Professor of Classics at Brock University in Canada. He has authored several papers concerning the organization and logistics of gladiatorial *munera* and is especially interested in the diffusion of these spectacles into the eastern Greek regions of the Roman Empire.

Paul Cartledge is A.G. Leventis Senior Research Fellow, Clare College, Cambridge, and emeritus A.G. Leventis Professor of Greek Culture, University of Cambridge. He is the author, co-author, editor, or co-editor of over thirty books, most recently *Thebes: the Forgotten City of Ancient Greece* (2020). He is co-director of *The Oxford History of the Archaic Greek World* (in progress) and President of the Society for the Promotion of Hellenic Studies (UK). He is an Honorary Citizen of Sparti and holds the Commander of the Order of Honour (Hellenic Republic).

Guy Chamberland is an Associate Professor and Chair of Ancient Studies at Thorneloe University (Ontario, Canada). His research areas include Latin epigraphy and Roman social history and spectacle. His work has been published in *Zeitschrift für Papyrologie und Epigraphik, Journal of Roman Archaeology, Phoenix, Entretiens sur l'Antiquité Classique*, and other venues.

Kathryn Chew is a Professor of Classics and Religious Studies at California State University Long Beach. Her interests include ancient Greek and Latin novels, early Christian martyr accounts, and the eastern Roman Empire in the fifth century. Her research has appeared in *Historia, Phoenix, Classical Philology, Latomus*, and *Classical World*, among others.

Paul Christesen is William R. Kenan Professor of Ancient Greek History in the Department of Classics at Dartmouth College. He is the author of three books (including, most recently, *A New Reading of the Damonon Stele*) and more than thirty articles, and he is currently working with Paul Cartledge of Cambridge University on the *Oxford History of the Archaic Greek World*. His areas of expertise include ancient Greek history (with a particular focus on Sparta) and the relationship between sport and political systems. He holds a PhD from Columbia University, and he is life fellow of Clare Hall at Cambridge University.

Lucia D'Amore is a teacher of Italian Language at the Luigi Settembrini School in Rome. She is the author of *Iscrizioni Greche di Reggio Calabria* (2007), *Nel fiore dell'amabile giovinezza: Ginnasio ed efebia negli epigrammi greci* (2017), and of numerous articles on the Greek gymnasion and the history of Magna Graecia.

Lesley Dean-Jones is Associate Professor of Classics at The University of Texas at Austin. She has published on Greek literature, history, philosophy and medicine, including *Women's Bodies in Classical Greek Science* (1994). Her current major research topics are a translation and commentary on *Historia Animalium* X and the early professionalization of Greek medicine, especially the effects of literacy. She is also the editor of *Acta Hippocratica* XIII.

Wolfgang Decker (1941–2020) was Professor Emeritus of the History of Sport at the Deutsche Sporthochschule Cologne. He was a major international figure in the resurgence of research in ancient sport history in recent decades, as a co-founder in 1988 and co-editor of *Nikephoros: Journal of Sport and Culture in Antiquity*, and as prolific scholar. His works include foundational studies of sport in ancient Egypt, and numerous books, articles, and extensive bibliographies on Greek and Roman sport history, up to and including the modern Olympic movement. A select bibliography includes: *Quellentexte zu Sport und Körperkultur im alten Ägypten* (1975); *Sport und Spiel im alten Ägypten* (1987; English trans. *Sports and Games of Ancient Egypt* (1992)); *Bildatlas zum Sport im alten Ägypten* (1992); *Sport in der griechischen Antike* (2012); and *Antiken Spitzensportler* (2014). He was a guest professor at the universities of Tehran (Iran), Graz (Austria), Athens (Greece) and frequently at the International Olympic Academy, Olympia (Greece). Prof. Decker was also awarded with an Honorary doctorate of the Aristotelian University Thessaloniki (Greece), and was a Fellow of the European Committee for Sports History.

Matthew Dillon is the Professor of Classics and Ancient at the University of New England, Armidale, Australia. His books include *Girls and Women in Classical Greek Religion* (2002), and *Omens and Oracles: Divination in Ancient Greece* (2017), as well as textbooks on Greek and Roman history. He has written widely on Greek religion and society, and is particularly interested in the lived experience of ancient Greek religion in the lives of ordinary people, but especially of women and children.

Hazel Dodge is Louis Claude Purser Associate Professor in Classical Archaeology at Trinity College, Dublin. Her research focuses on Roman urbanization and building construction technology, especially on the accommodations made for ancient spectacle. Among her publications are *Spectacle in the Roman World* (2011) and *Ancient Rome: Archaeology of the Eternal City* (with J. Coulston, 2000).

Nathan T. Elkins is Associate Professor of Art History and Director of the Allbritton Art Institute at Baylor University. His research interests include political ideology communicated through Roman art and coinage, the topography of Rome, amphitheatres and their associated spectacles, and the illicit antiquities trade. He is author of *Monuments in Miniature: Architecture on Roman Coinage* (2015); *The Image of Political Power in the Reign* *of Nerva*, AD *96–98* (2017); and *A Monument to Dynasty and Death: The Story of Rome's Colosseum and the Emperors Who Built It* (2019).

Garrett G. Fagan (1963–2017) was Professor in the Department of Classics and Ancient Mediterranean Studies at Penn State University. A much-respected specialist in Roman society and culture, his publications include *Bathing in Public in the Roman World* (1999) and *The Lure of the Arena: Social Psychology and the Crowd at the Roman Games* (2011), as well as the edited and co-edited volumes *New Perspectives on Ancient Warfare* (2010); *The Topography of Violence in Classical Antiquity* (2016); and *Archaeological Fantasies: How Pseudoarchaeology Misrepresents the Past and Misleads the Public* (2006). He is missed.

Alison Futrell is Associate Professor and Head of the History Department at the University of Arizona. Her research interests focus on the discourse, performance, and imagery of power in imperial Rome, with special interest in spectacle and gender; a current project uses a digitized staging of Plautus' *Rudens* as a node for interdisciplinary analyses of Roman society, theatre, and interpretation. Her interest in manifestations of the ancient Mediterranean in modern popular culture has led to publications on *The Viking Queen*, *Spartacus*, HBO's *Rome* and *Xena: Warrior Princess*. She is the author of *Blood in the Arena* (1997) and *Roman Games* (2006) and co-editor of the present volume, *Oxford Handbook of Sport and Spectacle in the Ancient World*.

Peter J. Holliday is a Professor of the History of Classical Art and Archaeology at California State University, Long Beach, and is the author of *The Origins of Roman Historical Commemoration in the Visual Arts* (2002), *American Arcadia: California and the Classical Tradition* (2016), and articles in various scholarly journals, including the *Art Bulletin*, *American Journal of Archaeology*, and *Memoirs of the American Academy in Rome*.

Alexander Hollmann is Associate Professor in the Department of Classics and Vidalakis Professor of Hellenic Studies at the University of Washington in Seattle. He is the author of *The Master of Signs: Signs and the Interpretation of Signs in Herodotus' Histories* (2011) and several articles on Herodotean studies and on curse tablets from late-antique Antioch. He is currently writing with Robert Daniel of the University of Cologne an edition and commentary of new curse tablets from Caesarea and Antioch, *Magica Levantina*.

Valerie Hope is a Senior Lecturer in Classical Studies at the Open University and has published widely on Roman funerals, mourning rituals, and funerary monuments, including the commemorative practices of key social groups such as soldiers, freed slaves, and gladiators. Her books include *War as Spectacle: Ancient and Modern Perspectives on the Display of Armed Conflict* (2015), *Memory and Mourning: Studies on Roman Death* (2011), *Roman Death: The Dying and the Dead in Ancient Rome* (2009), and *Death in Ancient Rome: A Sourcebook* (2007).

Luciana Jacobelli is a specialist in Classics, archaeology and art history, with many years of collaboration with the Soprintendenza Archeologica di Napoli e Caserta and the Soprintendenza Archeologica di Pompei. Among her books are *Gladiators at Pompeii* (2003), *A Day in Pompeii* (2004), and *Le Pitture Erotiche delle Terme Suburbane di Pompei* (1995).

Nigel Kennell teaches at the University of British Columbia. His research interests include Spartan history and Greek civic institutions. He was a research assistant and visiting member at the Institute for Advanced Study in Princeton, New Jersey, a Chercheur Associé at le Centre de Recherche d'Histoire et Civilisation de Byzance, Collège de France, Paris, and Visiting Fellow at All Souls College, Oxford. He is the author of *The Gymnasium of Virtue: Education and Culture in Ancient Sparta* (1995), *Ephebeia: A Register of Greek Cities with Citizen Training Systems in the Hellenistic and Roman Periods* (2006), and *Spartans: A New History* (2010).

Anne Hrychuk Kontokosta is Assistant Professor/Faculty Fellow of Roman Art and Architecture at the Institute of Fine Arts, New York University. Her research is concerned with intersections between material culture, the built environment, and the socio-political history of republican and early imperial Rome. She is the co-editor of *Roman Sculpture in Context: Selected Papers in Ancient Art and Architecture* (2020) and is the author of articles on early Roman arches, Roman *horti* and *thermae*, and Roman gladiators.

Leslie Kurke is Professor of Classics and Comparative Literature at the University of California, Berkeley. She works on ancient Greek literature and cultural history, with special emphasis on archaic Greek poetry in its social context; Herodotus and early prose; ancient Greek popular culture; the constitution of ideology through material practices; and the interactions of performed poetry and architectural space. She is the author, most recently, of *Pindar, Song, and Space: Towards a Lyric Archaeology* (co-authored with Richard Neer), and *Genre in Archaic and Classical Greek Poetry: Theories and Models* (co-edited with Margaret Foster and Naomi Weiss).

Donald G. Kyle is Emeritus Professor of History at the University of Texas at Arlington and is an internationally recognized expert on ancient sport and spectacles. He is the author of *Athletics in Ancient Athens* (1993), *Spectacles of Death in Ancient Rome* (2012), and the award-winning *Sport and Spectacle in the Ancient World* (2nd edn, 2015). He has co-edited volumes, including *Sport History and Sport Mythology* and a *Companion to Ancient Sport and Spectacle* (2014), and has written numerous articles and book chapters on topics from Greek athletic prizes to Roman beast spectacles.

Michael MacKinnon is Professor of Classics at the University of Winnipeg, Canada. His research concentrates on interdisciplinary exploration of the role and use of animals in Greco-Roman antiquity. As a zooarchaeologist, he has contributed to more than sixty different projects at sites in the Mediterranean region. His honours include residencies as Rome Scholar at the British School at Rome and Malcolm Wiener Professor at the American School of Classical Studies at Athens.

Manuela Mari is Associate Professor of Greek History at the University of Bari (Italy). Her research interests include Macedonian history and institutions; Hellenistic societies and political language; Panhellenic festivals and games; and Greek historiography from the fifth century to the early Roman period. She is the author of *Al di là dell'Olimpo: Macedoni e grandi santuari della Grecia dall'età arcaica al primo ellenismo* (2002), the co-editor of *Parole in movimento: Linguaggio politico e lessico storiografico nel mondo ellenistico* (2013), and the editor of *L'età ellenistica: Società, politica, cultura* (2019). She also wrote two chapters in R. J. Lane Fox (ed.), *Brill's Companion to Ancient Macedon* (2011).

Paul Milliman is an Associate Professor in the History Department at the University of Arizona. His research and teaching focus on games and food as well as the making of Europe in the global middle ages. Recent publications have focused on sports diplomacy in late Medieval Europe and on games and governance in twelfth-century England.

Gregory Nagy is the author of *The Best of the Achaeans: Concepts of the Hero in Archaic Greek Poetry* (1979; 2nd edn 1999). Other publications include *Homer the Preclassic* (2010) and *The Ancient Greek Hero in 24 Hours* (2013). With Stephen A. Mitchell, he co-edited the second edition (2000) of Albert Lord's *The Singer of Tales* (1960), co-authoring a new introduction. Since 2000, he has been the Faculty Director of the Harvard Center for Hellenic Studies in Washington, DC, while continuing to teach at the Harvard campus in Cambridge as the Francis Jones Professor of Classical Greek Literature and Professor of Comparative Literature.

Zahra Newby is Professor of Classics and Ancient History at the University of Warwick. Her research explores the experience of Greek culture in the Roman period, with a focus on visual and material culture. She is author of *Greek Athletics in the Roman World* (2005), *Athletics in the Ancient World* (2006), and *Greek Myths in Roman Art and Culture* (2016). She is currently leading a Leverhulme Trust project exploring the importance of materiality in ancient festival culture.

Nigel Nicholson is the Walter Mintz Professor of Classics at Reed College, where he has also served as the Dean of the Faculty. His research circles around Pindar, athletics, medicine, and Sicily, and he is the author of three books: *Aristocracy and Athletics in Archaic and Classical Greece* (2005), *The Poetics of Victory in the Greek West: Epinician, Oral Tradition and the Deinomenid Empire* (2016), and *The Rhetoric of Medicine* (2019), jointly authored with Dr. Nathan Selden. In 2005, he was named Oregon's Professor of the Year by the Carnegie Foundation for the Advancement of Teaching.

Zinon Papakonstantinou is Professor of Classics at the University of Illinois at Chicago, USA and Visiting Professor of History at the University of Mannheim, Germany. From 2013 to 2016 he was Alexander von Humboldt Foundation fellow at the University of Hamburg, Germany. A cultural historian of ancient Greece, his research interests span the entire Greco-Roman antiquity (8th century BCE - 4th century CE) as well as the field of Classical reception, with a particular emphasis on sport, magic, popular culture, disputes, and legalities. He has authored *Cursing for Justice: Magic, Disputes, and the Lawcourts in Classical Athens* (2021), *Sport and Identity in Ancient Greece* (2019), and *Lawmaking and Adjudication in Archaic Greece* (2008); he has edited *Sport in the Cultures of the Ancient World: New Perspectives* (2010); and co-edited *Sport, Bodily Culture and Classical Antiquity in Modern Greece* (2011). He is also the author of more than forty articles and book chapters on sport, leisure, law, and magic in the ancient Greek world. His current book project, tentatively entitled *"First of the Greeks": Victory and Memory in Greek Sport,* examines patterns of competition, victory, and commemoration of Greek athletics in the Hellenistic and Roman Imperial eras.

Michael B. Poliakoff is the president of the American Council of Trustees and Alumni, following service as Pennsylvania Deputy Secretary of Education and as Director of Education Programs at the National Endowment for the Humanities. He is the author of *Combat Sports in the Ancient World. Competition, Violence, and Culture* and teaches Classics as an adjunct professor at George Mason University. His academic career includes appointments at Wellesley College, Georgetown University, George Washington University, and Hillsdale College, where he was the founding chairman of the Classics Department.

David Potter is Francis W. Kelsey Professor of Greek and Roman History and Arthur F. Thurnau Professor and Professor of Greek and Latin at the University of Michigan. His recent publications include *The Victor's Crown* (2011), *Constantine the Emperor* (2013), *The Roman Empire at Bay: AD 180–395* (2nd edn 2014), *Theodora: Actress, Empress, Saint* (2015), *Ancient Rome: A New History* (3rd edn 2018), and *The Origin of Empire* (2019). His forthcoming book, *Disruption: Why Things Change*, is a study of radical change in history from the Roman empire to the present.

David M. Pritchard is Associate Professor of Greek History and Department Chair of Classics and Ancient History at the University of Queensland (Australia). In 2019–20 he was also Research Fellow in l'Institut d'études avancées de l'université de Lyon (France), and has obtained thirteen fellowships in Australia, Denmark, France, the Netherlands, the United Kingdom and the United States of America. He has authored *Athenian Democracy at War* (2019), *Public Spending and Democracy in Classical Athens* (2015), and *Sport, Democracy and War in Classical Athens* (2013), and has edited *War, Democracy and Culture in Classical Athens* (2010) and co-edited *Sport and Festival in the Ancient Greek World*.

Wendy Raschke is Emerita Professor of Classics at the University of California, Riverside, where she was Director of Classical Studies. Her research areas are Greek sculpture, Greek athletics, and Roman satire. Select publications include the book *The Archaeology of the Olympics*; contributions to books: *Panhellenism and the Temple of Zeus* (2013), *Contest, Unity, and Marriage in the Sanctuary of Zeus at Olympia* (2014), *A Red-Figure Kylix in Malibu: The Iconography of Female Charioteers* (1996). She has been a Supervising Professor at a 2011 graduate seminar at the International Olympic Academy, Olympia (Greece), and professor and guest lecturer at the 2014 seminar held by Harvard University's Hellenic Center and the International Olympic Academy. Public lectures include those at conferences on War, Peace, and Panhellenism, sponsored by the International Institute for Ancient Hellenic History, in Olympia, Greece (2005), 'Body and Spirit: Sport and Christianity in History' at Universidad Católica de Murcia, Spain (2016), and Roman satire at the Freie Universität, Berlin (2008).

David Gilman Romano is the Nicholas and Athena Karabots Professor of Greek Archaeology in the School of Anthropology at the University of Arizona. His main research interests include Greek and Roman city planning, architecture, landscapes, and athletics. He has been a pioneer in several computer applications in archaeology including digital cartography, GIS and remote sensing, especially in the study of ancient cities and landscapes. At the University of Arizona he is the Director of the Archaeological Mapping Lab. He has been the Director of the Corinth Computer Project since 1988 and is the Co-Director and Field Director of the Mt. Lykaion Excavation and Survey Project, since 2004. He is the Director of the Initiative of the Parrhasian Heritage Park of the Peloponnesos, Greece's first large scale cultural heritage park. His major publications include *Athletics and Mathematics in Archaic Corinth: The Origins of the Greek Stadion* (1993), *The Catalogue of the Classical Collection of the Glencairn Museum* (1999) (with Irene Romano), and *Mapping Augustan Rome* (2002) (with Lothar Haselberger and others). He is co-editor with Mary Voyatzis of a four-volume series on the results of the excavations at the Sanctuary of Zeus at Mt Lykaion, to be published through the American School of Classical Studies at Athens.

Thomas F. Scanlon is Emeritus Professor of Classics at the University of California, Riverside. In addition to co-editing the present volume, his publications include *Greek*

Historiography (2015), *Greek Poetry and Sport, Classics@* (2015, ed.), *Oxford Readings in Sport in the Greek and Roman Worlds*, 2 vols. (2014, ed.), *Eros and Greek Athletics* (2002), *Olympia and Macedonia: Games, Gymnasia and Politics* (1997), *Spes Frustrata: Hope in Sallust* (1987), *Greek and Roman Athletics: A Bibliography* (1984), and *The Influence of Thucydides on Sallust* (1980). His research areas include Greek sport, Greek gender studies, Greek religion, and Greek and Roman historiography.

Julia L. Shear is currently (2020–22) a CHS Fellow in Hellenic Studies at the Center for Hellenic Studies of Harvard University, having previously held a NEH Fellowship at the American School of Classical Studies at Athens and positions at Boğaziçi University, Istanbul and the University of Glasgow. She is the author of *Polis and Revolution: Responding to Oligarchy in Classical Athens* (2011), which was shortlisted for the Runciman Award in 2012, and *Serving Athena: The Festival of the Panathenaia and the Construction of Athenian Identities* (2021). She is currently working on a book on creating collective memory in ancient Athens. She has excavated extensively on various sites in Greece, Cyprus, and Italy.

Ulrich Sinn is Emeritus Professor of Classics at the University of Würzburg. His research focuses on the archaeology of religion, cult and society in the Graeco-Roman world. He is the author of *Das antike Olympia, Spiel und Kunst* (2004), editor of *Thomas Völling, Olympia in Frühbyzantinischer Zeit*, and author of numerous articles on Greek art and Greek asylia.

Paola Stirpe has a PhD in Ancient History from the University of Rome (La Sapienza). Her research includes festivals and games of the Hellenistic and Roman ages, and Hellenistic poetry (more particularly, Lycophron's *Alexandra*). She contributed to the volume *Nike: Ideologia, iconografia, feste della vittoria in età antica* (Domenico Musti, ed., Rome 2005). She has been the curator of the itinerant exhibition *Images of a Legend: Iconography of Alexander the Great in Italy*, organized by the General Directorate for Cultural Promotion and Cooperation of the Italian Ministry of Foreign Affairs (2006).

Geoffrey S. Sumi is Professor of Classics at Mount Holyoke College. He is the author of *Ceremony and Power: Performing Politics in Rome between Republic and Empire* (2005) as well as articles that analyse the intersection of ceremony, ideology, and topography in ancient Rome.

Rabun Taylor is Floyd A. Cailloux Centennial Professor of Classics at the University of Texas at Austin. His recent scholarly work encompasses such topics as the architecture and cognitive history of the Hellenistic and Roman theatre, the cultural history of architecture as object, and cults of the Nymphs. He currently directs the Aqua Traiana Project. His articles have appeared in the *American Journal of Archaeology, Journal of Roman Archaeology, Journal of the Society of Architectural Historians, Memoirs of the American Academy at Rome, RES: Anthropology and Aesthetics, Arethusa, Papers of the British School at Rome* and other venues. His books include *Rome: An Urban History* (with Katherine Rinne and Spiro Kostof, 2016), *The Moral Mirror of Roman Art* (2008), *Roman Builders: A Study in Architectural Process* (2003), and Ancient Naples: A Documentary History (2021).

Jean-Paul Thuillier, long-term member of the École Française de Rome, is professor emeritus of the École normale supérieure (ENS) in Paris, where he directed the Department of Sciences of Antiquity for a long time. He has written many works and numerous articles on the Etruscan civilization and the history of ancient sport, including his recent book *Allez les Rouges! Les jeux du cirque en Étrurie et à Rome* (2018).

Steven L. Tuck is Professor of History and Classics at Miami University. He received his PhD in Classical Art and Archaeology from the University of Michigan. He is the author of *A History of Roman Art* and many articles and chapters on Roman art, especially sculpture. He also publishes on Latin epigraphy, notably his research tracing survivors from the eruption of Vesuvius in AD 79. His work, on both sculpture and inscriptions, focuses on spectacle entertainments in the Roman world. He has received numerous recognitions for pedagogy, including the Archaeological Institute of America Excellence in Undergraduate Teaching Award.

Panos Valavanis is Emeritus Professor of Classical Archaeology at the University of Athens (Greece). Author or editor of thirteen books and over sixty-five articles on ancient Greek pottery and iconography, Panathenaic amphorae, architecture and topography of Athens, ancient athletics and politics, as well as ancient Greek technology. Current programmes: open-air public spaces in ancient Greece; ancient Greek hippodromes; the topography of West Lokris.

Onno van Nijf is Professor of Ancient History at the University of Groningen. His research is mostly on Greek cities of the Hellenistic and Roman periods, with special focus on (athletic) festivals and connectivity, and the political culture, which he approaches preferably through epigraphic sources. He is currently preparing a cultural history of Greek athletics 300 BC–AD 300.

Ingomar Weiler is retired Professor of Ancient History and Sport History, Institut für Alte Geschichte und Altertumskunde (since October 2019: Institut für Antike) Universität Graz, Austria. Supervising Professor at the International Olympic Academy, Olympia (Greece); awarded with an Honorary doctorate of the University of Mainz (Germany). He is co-editor and co-founder of *Nikephoros. Zeitschrift für Sport und Kultur im Altertum*; author of *Der Agon im Mythos. Zur Einstellung der Griechen zum Wettkampf* (1974), *Der Sport bei den Völkern der alten Welt* (2nd edn 1988), *Griechische Geschichte* (2nd edn 1988), *Die Gegenwart der Antike: Ausgewählte Schriften zu Geschichte, Kultur und Rezeption des Altertums* (2004); editor of *Quellendokumentation zur Gymnastik und Agonistik im Altertum* (7 vols., 1991–2002).

John G. Younger is Professor emeritus of Classics at the University of Kansas, where he also chaired the Department of Women, Gender, and Sexuality Studies and the Program in Jewish Studies. He has a BA in History from Stanford University (with BA requirements in Music and Classics also met), and an MA and PhD in Classics from the University of Cincinnati. Younger publishes on Bronze Age Aegean art and administration and on Classical Greek architecture and sculpture (e.g. *Music in the Aegean Bronze Age* and *Sex in the Ancient World A–Z*; and 'Technical Observations on the Pedimental Sculptures from the Temple of Zeus at Olympia', *Hesperia*, Spring 2009). He now lives on a farm in eastern Kansas with cats, dogs, and chickens, and some 850 grapevines and several orchards.

PART I

INTRODUCTION

CHAPTER 1

....

OVERVIEW AND APPROACHES

....

THOMAS F. SCANLON

OVERVIEW

....

THE last few decades have seen the analysis of sport and spectacle in Greece and Rome grow from small corners of specialized or ancillary Greek and Roman studies to a vital area of broad new exploration. This handbook aims to present progressive current thought in the field and indicate directions for future work. The aim in juxtaposing Greek and Roman games is to clarify areas of convergence, to shed light on similarities and differences in the two cultures, and also to suggest parallels in other cultures, including our own. This work therefore aims to facilitate research and provoke thinking in particular aspects of Greek sport and Roman spectacle, including the following:

- fifty articles explore Greek sport and Roman spectacle, and, to a lesser extent, Bronze age precedents, Etruscan agonistic phenomena, and related issues of modern identity formation through sport and spectacle;
- the work puts an emphasis on guiding the reader to serious engagement with topical and chronological aspects of Greek and Roman contest cultures: this aspect should make the work useful not only to specialists in Classics, Ancient History, and Classical Archaeology, but also to non-specialists as well as scholars in related academic fields, and to thoughtful non-academic aficionados such as modern sport historians and scholars and students of religion, anthropology, gender studies, sexuality, violence, economics, sociology, media and cultural studies, and the modern Olympics.

This book is not intended as an encyclopaedia of the status quo, as this kind of resource is well represented elsewhere in general books. Rather it is a research tool that might provide inspiration as well as information, one which explores and exemplifies the different ways in which evidence can be used, emphasizes the breadth and potential of studies in ancient contests and spectacles, and encourages informed dialogue between disciplines.

The volume as a whole affords prominent scholars the opportunity to put their own studies in perspective, or to extend their work into sport-related studies, so as to generate new insights and encourage cross-fertilization of subfields. Importantly, the work will seek to encourage greater interdisciplinary approaches to the field. The selection of major headings indicates our plan for a hybrid approach, combining historical perspectives, contest forms, contest-related texts, civic and social aspects, and the use and meaning of the individual body. Greek and Roman topics are, however, interwoven under each heading to stimulate (and simulate) contest-like tensions and complementarities, juxtaposing, for example, violence in Greek athletics and in Roman gladiatorial events, Greek and Roman chariot events, architectural frameworks for contests and games in the two cultures, and contrasting views of religion, bodily regimens, and judicial classification related to both cultures.

The focus of the collection is to an extent on the social contexts of games, namely the evolution of sport and spectacle diachronically and geographically across cultural and political boundaries, and how games are adapted to multiple contexts and multiple purposes, reinforcing, for example, social hierarchies, performing shared values, and playing out deep cultural tensions. In addition to a dialogue between the two major cultures regarding how they defined and appropriated habits of identity construction through public contests, the work pays some attention to other directing forces in the ancient Mediterranean (e.g. Bronze Age Egypt and the Near East; Etruria; and early Christianity). The volume also aims to address themes in common with and of importance to antiquity and modern society, such as issues of class, gender, health, and the popular culture of the modern Olympics and of gladiators. Sport and spectacle are to be represented, in part at least, as media of social discourse or negotiation, as well as performances validated by the cachet of constructed tradition and elite values. Just as athletes, performers, presenters, and audiences engaged in the real historical games in each stadium, arena, or circus, the phenomenon represents a kind of 'meta-*agon*' by which the contests themselves provided structure and form for a range of regional, local, and personal contestations, venturing into political, social, commercial, and artistic realms.

SOME MODERN AND ANCIENT NAMES AND VALUES OF SPORT AND SPECTACLE

The study of sport and spectacle in the ancient Mediterranean has offered a flood of new studies in the last five decades, and it is our aim here to assemble the most recent perspectives on the very different Greek and Roman manifestations of these pastimes. Let us begin by looking back from the present and by interrogating the term 'sport', which is conventionally, and perhaps mistakenly, applied to Greek athletic contests and gymnasium culture. Mistakenly because modern connotations of 'sport' conjure up notions of global commercial enterprises as well as private and local ventures propped up by industrial interests. By one estimate these are worth US$145 billion in 2015 for event gate revenue (http://statista.com/ statistics/194122/sporting-event –gate-revenue-worldwide-by region-since-2004/), but possibly US$1.5 trillion for all sport-associated revenues (of which about $500 billion is in the US; http://www.plunkettresearch.com/statistics/sports-industry/). To put that in perspective, the estimated world total of military expenses in 2015 was US$1.56 trillion, or approximately the same as that the income for sport worldwide (https://en.wikipedia.org/wiki/List_ of_countries_by_military_expenditures). 'Sport' today includes most visibly the highly lucrative professional sports circuits such as world soccer, tennis and golf, American football, baseball and basketball, motor-racing, horse-racing, and the Olympic Games. Then there are the secondary leagues feeding the professional organizations, and the collegiate, amateur, and smaller local leagues with their own revenues and expenses. And neither least nor last there is the health and fitness industry for private individuals that does not usually, strictly speaking, include competitive sports, but is connected with it in the public imagination of tennis, golf, swimming, handball, squash, and other pastimes. Dare we include the massive industry of video-gaming, or 'eSports', played or watched by an estimated 205 million people in 2015 (http://espn.go.com/espn/story/_/id/13059210/esports-massive-industry-growing/)? Note that the above financial statistics relate to revenue, not expenditure, the figures for which are more difficult to track, but it has been noted that local governments in France today spend about US$15 billion per year on sports, while in Germany it is US$8 billion, and in the US in 2010, the Division 1 collegiate teams spent $6.2 billion on athletics (two thirds of which came from television rights and ticket sales) (Christesen 2012: 5). In sum, the massive amounts spent on sport in modern cultures raise questions of how this is justified in light of other crucial civic needs. There is some compelling social pressure among developed countries to offer a substantial menu of sports to their peoples without their objections to the expense, indeed likely in response to their ongoing need for the second half of the cliché 'bread and circuses'.

The formal dictionary and informal social meanings of the term 'sport' are fluid, highly dependent on context, and much debated by scholars of sport. We will draw a line excluding eSports, favouring here a more traditional definition of sport that includes 'serious physical training, competition for prizes and the goal of victory' (Kyle 2015: 7).

The totality of global practices of sport today cannot be simply summarized in its regional and traditional differences, of course. Suffice it to say that the modern manifestations do include the category 'spectacle', which is separately named as a term in our title to address Roman public displays, some of a contest nature such as gladiatorial bouts and chariot races by teams, and some more purely performances, such as hunts in the arena, executions by animals, and sea-battle events. The spectacular element of modern professional sport is self-evident, but the fact that it is included in our notion of 'sport' points back to a basic difference in ancient and modern notions carried by our different terms.

With those cautions of anachronistic ideas in mind, we can locate the Greek notion closest to our 'sport' in their word closest to the idea, *agōn* (pl. *agōnes*), 'contest', 'struggle', from which we have the word 'agony' in view of the suffering considered essential to successful competition. The ancient Greeks would not have understood the modern slogan popularized by ABC's *Wide World of Sports* in which the high points of sport were said to be 'the thrill of victory and the agony of defeat'. The Greeks would have preferred 'the agony of victory and the humiliation of defeat'. The Greek *agōnes* included what we call track and field events, combat sports (boxing, wrestling, and a combination of both called pancration), and equestrian events (chariot and horse racing). Nagy (this volume, Chapter 22) also reminds us that *agōn* is derived from the root *ag-* of the verb *agō* as it is used in the compound forma-tion *sun-agō*, which means 'bring together, assemble, gather', so that an *agōn* is a 'bringing together' of people; and the occasion of such a 'bringing together' is a 'competition'. Beyond the *agōn* and closely associated with it was the gymnasium and the regimes of physical edu-cation, sometimes highly institutionalized in the youth corps (ephebate), but in the Classical period and earlier entirely left to individuals and mostly to the wealthy and elite of each city state. Gymnasium is derived from Greek *gymnasion*, meaning simply 'the place where you perform naked', 'naked' in Greek being *gymnos*. Greek physical education and their contest system differ in many ways socially and practically from our supposed equivalents.

Nagy reminds us of further cultural connotations, namely

> the meanings of the ancient Greek words *āthlos* (epic *aethlos*) 'ordeal, contest', *āthlon* (epic *aethlon*) 'prize won in the course of participating in an *āthlos*', and *āthlētēs* 'athlete, one who participates in an *āthlos*'. To restate the concept of athletics in ancient Greek terms: an *āthlos* was the ritual 'ordeal' or 'contest' of an athlete engaging in athletic contests that were taking place in the historical present, but it was also the mythological 'ordeal' or 'contest' of a hero engaging in life-and-death contests that took place once upon a time in the heroic past; moreover, the ritual 'ordeals' or 'contests' of the historical present were viewed as *re-enactments* of the mythical 'ordeals' or 'contests' of the heroic past.

The athlete in one sense then, during the occasion of the *agōn*-gathering, re-enacts in a quasi-ritual the feats of the Homeric hero. The ritual ordeal of athletics mimics that of warfare, such that the *agōn* term is applied to both: for example, the expression *arēios agōn*, 'the *agōn* of Ares', as used by Herodotus (9.33.3) refers to the ritual experience of combat in war, and *āthlos* (epic *aethlos*) refers to the experience of warriors (Hdt. 1.67.1) as well as athletes (Hdt. 5.22.2).

Though Roman gladiators also overlap with warriors in appearance and in other senses, the Roman contest does not assimilate the gladiators so readily to the realm of epic heroes since they were almost always from the ranks of non-citizens, and their status was even legally and socially marked by infamy. Now, to observe Roman terminology, 'spectacle', Latin *spectaculum* (an 'event to view'; pl. *spectacula*), is generally taken as a more appropriate term than 'sport' for the regular festivals or special celebrations of the Romans that included gladiator contests (*munera*), chariot races (*ludi circenses*), animal hunts (*venationes*), execution by animals (*damnatio ad bestias*), naval battles (*naumachiae*), and dramatic performances (*ludi scaenici*). We include drama as spectacle though it does not fit our focus on (mostly) unscripted physical competitions with uncertain outcomes. Most modern commentators avoid the term 'sport' for these spectacles since the participants were generally not voluntary, and, except for the chariot races, they placed human life at risk more deliberately than do ancient Greek *agōnes* or modern contests.

Yet in the ancient Mediterranean, the audiences both in the East and in the West mutually enjoyed Greek *agônes* and Roman *spectacula*. Circus races and gladiatorial battles took place all over the East and athletic performances were regularly held in the West, especially in Italy (Remijsen 2015: 27–17). Across the Mediterranean, alongside Roman chariot races, the most popular were generally the most violent events: the gladiator matches and Greek combat sports including boxing, wrestling, and pancration. For a gladiatorial 'fight' and 'fighting' (properly in Greek *machē* and *machesthai*) the Greek terms for boxing (*pugmē* and *pukteuein*) were regularly used in inscriptions in the eastern empire (Robert 1940), a usage that points to the popular equation of gladiatorial bouts to combat sports.

The attraction to violence raises the question posed by Poliakoff (this volume, Chapter 17): 'At what point does the contest cross the line from a competitive activity bound by its own special rules and conventions, abstracted from the criteria that govern success or failure in everyday life, to an activity that more closely resembles acts of violence that are typically regarded as criminal behaviour?' Brutal as they were, Greek combat sports seem mild next to the Roman gladiatorial events. Modern concerns about the deleterious effects on the brain from concussions in US football (Chronic Traumatic Encephalopathy (CTE)) and from boxing evidence have heightened collective concerns of tolerable sanctioned violence, and the need to respect the well-being of others, current apprehensions that were far from those of Greek boxers and pancratiasts. One observation that certainly arises from comparative analysis of world sport is that the definition of what it can rightly include, and the legal and social restrictions on what it is allowed to include, are not universal, but rather defined and determined again and again over time by groups, societies, and states.

It is not straightforward to gauge the importance of ancient sport and spectacle in comparison with that of their modern counterparts. 'Following the money', as we did above, is difficult given the absence of verifiable records for Greek and Roman expenditures on these pastimes for all or part of the centuries covered in this volume. But there have been 'snapshot' estimates of funding allocated to ancient events, which give a sense of general funding priorities. For Athens, it seems, in the Classical period (c.450– c.350 BCE), the annual expenditure was about 100 talents for state sponsored festivals (including athletics in the Panathenaia and drama in the City Dionysia, accounting for thirty-five per cent of this total); the expenditure on armed forces for the 370s and 360s was about 500 talents per year (Pritchard 2012). One talent equals the salary for about eight to nine man-years of skilled labour. The economy of Greek festivals relied generally on 'festival liturgies' levied on the wealthy citizens of each polis in the Classical and Hellenistic periods, not on direct government spending or taxes imposed on all citizens. So, assuming some parity with the situation at Athens, the economic outlay for festivals in cities across Greece was a hugely significant amount of money for each polis. Festival expenditure was bigger than any other regular civic expense except the military, and at Athens it was roughly twenty per cent of the costs for the military.

Roman games (ludi) occupied about two and a half months of the Roman calendar in the first century BCE, and rose to almost six months annually by the mid-fourth century CE (Veyne 1990: 399). The spectacles were financed by the state and the magistrates who ran them, without admission charges to spectators (Dunkle 2013: 382). During the empire it was the job especially of the priests of the imperial cult to provide these costly events, and one good index of the costs is a decree of the Senate from 177 CE in which the prices of gladiators were reduced to make the games less burdensome to the magistrates (Carter 2014: 229–266). The annual cost of gladiators prior to 177 CE was anywhere from 60 to 120 million sesterces (based on Carter 2014: 232), which was reduced to roughly 40 to 90 million after the reforms. If we estimate a median cost of 90 million sesterces empire-wide for annual gladiatorial games before 177, and 65 million just after that date, we can compare that with the total annual military costs, estimated to be about 670 million sesterces in about 150 CE (Duncan-Jones 1994: 45). In short, the annual cost gladiators in the mid to late second century CE empire amounted to between ten and thirteen per cent of the cost of the military. Note that the gladiator costs are only a portion of the total annual costs for Roman spectacles, which would be much higher if we included the costs of circus events, beast hunts, and so on. Arguably, then, the cost of spectacles could have been about twenty per cent of that for the military, roughly the same as Athens' outlay for festivals compared with its military in the early fourth century BCE.

Each culture, modern global, and ancient Greek and Roman, has or had its own peculiar names and terms for pastimes which the populace participates in or delights in watching.

The events across time can be distilled in definition as public, physical, competitive, and prize-awarding contests. Greek athletes, Roman gladiators, ancient charioteers of Greece and Rome, and modern athletes of the most popular modern sports all have much in common, which suggests universal impulses over time. Contestants' aspirations to fame and the audience's adulation or devaluation of them resonate then as they do now.

Another crucial, virtually universal aspect of sport and spectacle is the massive audience appetite for these entertainment vehicles. People crave watching sport and spectacle, mostly across history in person, and today more and more over the public media of television and the Internet. The main question is why? Why is there such an enduring desire to watch these contests, such that the wealthy who can afford to sponsor them do so at such great expense? Regarding the viewers, theorists see spectatorship as therapy, either as vicarious participation through one's favourite team or player, or as a sharing in the expression of victory, machismo, or personal or team achievement to validate elevated status. In sum, the spectators, ancient or modern, delight in escaping their quotidian realities and for a time experiencing something better, feeling part of success, or being comforted by the similarity of their own setbacks to those of the loser. To this extent the experience is close to that of watching drama on stage, or, for us today, watching narratives on film, on the television, or on the Internet. Today the other part of the equation of this popular vehicle is that the sponsors do make money from revenues of all sorts. In antiquity, when revenues for benefactors were not so much of an issue, the motivation for the elite to fund contests was twofold: social obligation/pressure ('it's your turn'), and political capital (purchasing favour and popularity within the ideal of civic generosity) (for the greater complexity of this situation: Migeotte 2014; Duncan-Jones 1982; Zuiderhoek 2009). In essence the ancient motivation was simple—to gain or maintain social status. Which is essentially not much different from the modern situation with wealth from the revenue largely defining status.

As we have observed, Greek, Roman, and modern global sports also have in common the mega-investment in sport and spectacle in relation to the military expenditures of each culture. That reality across societies is a stunning confirmation of the relatively very high importance of sport and spectacle as a social element of great consequence. The comparison with the military budget in each culture illustrates a consistent, real outlay of high significance: directly or indirectly, sport and spectacle competed with the financing for efforts to defend one's own people or to acquire more land and power. There are few other pan-social undertakings that can compare with military expenditures for a given culture across history. In most cultures, civic organizations usually provide for infrastructure needs like roads, water and sewer systems, public buildings, and sometimes food (grain) and shelter. We have selected military outlay as a baseline of comparison mainly because there are ways to calculate it for ancient cultures. It may well be that civic funding for infrastructure needs was greater than for sport and spectacle, but outlay for entertainment, even in festivals, was not strictly so essential as these other needs. The comparison points up the powerful priority of games in Greece and Rome, and in the modern global economy.

We should note that this sport-and-spectacle ratio to the military has not been true of all or even most cultures in world history since the Greeks and Romans, but it is markedly true in the nineteenth and twentieth centuries for states in Europe and North and South America. In antiquity, the enormous outlay was also possibly the case for the Egyptian and the Near Eastern cultures, and for the Mesoamericans, though here the lack of accounts involves more speculation based on archaeological remains. Events of sport and spectacle have since the mid-twentieth century saturated virtually every nation in the world: for the 196 nations in the world in 2016, there are actually 206 National Olympic Committees (http://www.olympic.org); 69 nations participated in the 1952 Summer Olympics in Helsinki, and 204 at the London Olympics in 2012. The International Federation of Association Football, FIFA, founded in 1904, had 209 national association members in 2016; in 2011 their 35 administrators received total compensation of US$30 million.

A common, essential quality seems to unite us in the general yearning to put on public performances of sports contests, yet we cannot say if this is human nature or culture, DNA or social formation. The similarities across time and between Greeks and Roman contemporaries are in sharp contrast to the many different societal and personal values, class, economies, and political systems which each form of sport and spectacle reflects. For example, who may compete is telling: citizens among Greek athletes, prisoners and criminals among Roman gladiators, and ever-changing character race and gender lines among modern sportspersons admitted to different events. In the last seventy years, non-whites broke into US major league baseball in 1946, and women first boxed in the Olympics in London in 2012, while golf, tennis, yachting, horse-racing, and others remain sports almost entirely for the wealthy. The public-contest-with-prize format is a simple equation, but the interesting realities lie beneath it and invest it with meaning. The particular meanings for each culture are part of the aim of this study.

Sources

It may seem to be a startling gap between ancient and current cultures that, despite a shared mania for sport and spectacle, the Greeks and Romans left very few narrative accounts of actual contests that might echo our obsessive coverage of dramatic and cliff-hanging events in sports pages, magazines, online blogs, and non-fiction accounts like Roger Kahn's *The Boys of Summer*, Dan Jenkins's *Semi-Tough*, Norman Mailer's *The Fight*, and Franklin Foer's *How Football Explains the World*. Among the thousands of gladiatorial matches over the Roman era, the only close accounts of a contest are the few in Martial's *Liber Spectaculorum* ('Book of Spectacles'). Pausanias and other Greek writers offer a few asides that amplify descriptions of famous contests, such as that of Creugas and Damoxenus. But if a reader today is seeking for an account of a historic contest, they are not to be found in Pindar's *Odes* which simply allude to the event and the victory. The same ancient silence, and current loquacity, holds true for any extended discussion of rules, bureaucratic structures, and details of technique and training, an exception being Philostratus' *Gymnastics*.

What explains our logorrhea and antiquity's virtual silence on actual contests is a more difficult, cross-cultural and historical question. A short part of the answer is that a few works that correspond to our sport-and-spectacle narratives have been lost. Another reply is that ancient poetry filled the appetite for vicarious experience of a chariot race or wrestling match. But the best explanation is that Greeks and Romans for the most part did not see the point in close accounts of events that were not crucial to civic welfare, like wars and political coups.

And so we who delve into ancient contests are forced to be detectives that dig into scraps of evidence that does exist, and filter out from it the most telling factoids that can be pieced together to tell the bigger story. Many great works of Greek and Latin literature, and numerous less well known ones, provide information about the historical realities of ancient sport and spectacle, though these all require exegesis that appreciates the aim and context of the text, as well as (to the extent possible) an account of authorial biases. In this volume, Nagy (Chapter 22), Kurke (Chapter 23), and Chew (Chapter 24) undertake such studies of Homer, Homeric Hymns, Pindar, Bacchylides, Euripides, Ovid, Martial, and Tertullian. Greek and Roman inscriptions provide valuable insights from different perspectives that reflect the establishment of rules for contests and training (see Papakonstantionou in Chapter 45) and a record of victories by individuals (e.g. the Spartan Cynisca and by Greek athletes from the seventh century BCE onward); see Nagy, Kurke, van Nijf (Chapter 36), Poliakoff (Chapter 17), Shear (Chapter 8), Weiler (Chapter 40), Cartledge (Chapter 28, on the Spartan Damonon inscription) and others this volume.

SCOPE AND STRUCTURE

This handbook addresses competitive events over a broad period of time, seeking patterns of behaviour in a range of contexts rather than attempting complete chronological coverage. As noted above and evident in the table of contents, this work breaks down to some extent the traditional separation between the Greek and Roman worlds and between Greco-Roman antiquity and its immediate precedents. Contributors consider the development of contests and spectacles as venues of connection and as opportunities for the negotiation of status and the exchange of value, largely understood. While the political realm—the functioning of games and performance as displays of regal or imperial authority—figures strongly in these patterns, we are also interested in how, for example, early Panhellenic sanctuaries were shaped in response to economic stakeholders, and how groups and individuals in the later Roman empire forged links through their shared interest in the circus events, links that could cut across other social and political distinctions.

The section after this introduction, Development in Historical Perspective (II), primarily considers the larger structures within which sports and spectacles were organized and deployed, highlighting key phases and key systems. Narrowing our focus to the Forms of Contests (III), we hope to lay out the basic parameters of the events as well as underlying social and cultural assumptions that shape the physical actions. The next section focuses on Texts, Contexts, and Contests (IV), drawing together the scant written evidence for pre-Classical agonistic performances and considering the rise of celebratory literary genres, themselves competitive expressions of the range of meanings held by the games. Other textual forms demonstrate how individuals marshalled the power of the competitions, Ovid for seduction, Tertullian for proselytization, and many others calling upon the gods of the arena to curse rivals and performers and advantage themselves.

The Civic Contexts section (V) scrutinizes the phenomenon through a series of narrowing lenses. From discussing the regional catchment of games in the Greek world and the administration of spectacle in the Roman provinces, the focus turns to localized case studies of how games functioned in specific urban environments: how spectacle structures engaged performers, spectators, and sponsors in social and cultural discourse, crafting connections paralleled and expanded upon in public and private material representations.

These networks of social connection within the city and within the professional infrastructure of ancient sport provided opportunities for self-definition, for self-expression; the religious frameworks added yet another dimension for understanding the human experience of the games. The focus tightens to the personal level in the next section, Body and Individual (VI), as we examine how agonism worked with and upon the physical human. For some this involved the conceptual balancing of bodily extremes, from athletes as physical ideals to the perceived dangers of the gladiatorial lifestyle. Risk is likewise entailed in sexual definition and testing against the athletic body, in the sexualized allure of the performer that cut across the usual parameters of intimate contact.

BIBLIOGRAPHY AND FURTHER READING

There are currently several good, standard, and recent introductory books on Greek sport, such as those of D. Kyle (2015), S. Miller (2004a), D. Young (2004), N. Spivey (2004), and M. Golden (1998); see also W. Decker (2012) in German. For broader books on Greek, Roman, and other ancient sport, see Golden's (2010) or Scanlon's (2014a and 2014 b) collection of articles, Decker and Thuillier's overview (2004, in French), Crowther's global survey of pre-modern sports (2007), and Weiler's careful survey of Greek, Roman and other cultures (1988, in German). The need for reliable sourcebooks on Greek athletics has been filled, notably by Miller (2004b); see also W. Sweet (1987) and R. S. Robinson (1955). Roman games and spectacles have not been the subject of any recent textbook per se, but they have been treated in monographs from several different theoretical perspectives, focusing on gladiators, animal events, circuses and amphitheatres, including English-language works by J. H. Humphrey (1986), P. Veyne (1990), C. Barton (1993), P. Plass (1995), A. Futrell (1997), D. Kyle (1998), R. C. Beacham (1999), E. Köhne and C. Ewigleben (2000), and K. Welch (2007). Sourcebooks on Roman games have been recently produced by A. Mahoney (2001) and Futrell (2006). Golden (2004) and Matz (1991) provide dictionary-format treatments of special topics; these are convenient and reliable guides to fundamental information but necessarily of limited depth on each entry. Complementary to the present handbook work is the 'companion' collection of original scholarly studies edited by Christesen and Kyle (2014), organized in bipartite fashion on Greece, then Rome, with each half having, among other topics, 'People, Settings, Ideas' and some discussion of the later manifestations of sport and spectacle. Recent, individual monographs of note are two on the relation of Greek sport to democracy, with very different approaches: Christesen (2012) compares ancient Greece to modern Britain and Germany with a view to assessing the 'horizontal and vertical' aspects of sport that promote social unity and hierarchy; Pritchard (2013) assesses the contradiction in the fact that the participants in Athenian sport were primarily from the elite, and yet the phenomenon was supported by the non-elite (see also Pritchard, this volume Chapter 48). Other important recent monographs include König (2005) on the social status of sport in literature, epigraphy, and culture of the first to third centuries CE, König's edition of Philostratus' *Gymnasticus* (König and Rusten, 2014), and Golden (2008) on sport and social status.

REFERENCES

Barton, C. A. 1993. *The Sorrows of the Ancient Romans: the Gladiator and the Monster.* Princeton.

Beacham, R. C. 1999. *Spectacle Entertainments of Early Imperial Rome*. New Haven.

Carter, M. 2014. 'Gladiatorial Ranking and the *SC de Pretiis Gladiatorum Minuendis (CIL* II 6278 = *ILS* 5163)'. In *Sport in the Greek and Roman Worlds*, vol. 2. 229–266. T. F. Scanlon, ed. Oxford.

Christesen, P. 2012. *Sport and Democracy in the Ancient and Modern Worlds*. Cambridge.

Christesen, P. and D. G. Kyle, eds. 2014. *A Companion to Sport and Spectacle in Greek and Roman Antiquity*. Malden, MA.

Crowther, N. B. 2007. *Sport in Ancient Times*. Westport.

Decker, W. 2012. *Sport in der griechischen Antike: Vom minoischen Wettkampf bis zu den Olympischen Spielen*. Hildesheim.

Decker, W. and J.-P. Thuillier. 2004. *Le Sport dans l'Antiquité: Égypte, Grèce, Rome*. Cahors.

Duncan-Jones, R. 1982. *The Economy of the Roman Empire: Quantitative Studies*. Cambridge.

Duncan-Jones, R. 1994. *Money and Government in the Roman Empire*. Cambridge.

Dunkle, R. 'Overview of Roman Spectacle'. 381–94 in Christesen and Kyle 2014.

Futrell, A. 1997. *Blood in the Arena: The Spectacle of Roman Power*. Austin, TX.

Futrell, A. 2006. *The Roman Games: Historical Sources in Translation*. Oxford.

Golden, M. 1998. *Sport and Society in Ancient Greece*. Cambridge.

Golden, M. 2004. *Sport in the Ancient World from A to Z*. London.

Golden, M. 2008. *Greek Sport and Social Status*. Austin, TX.

Humphrey, J. H. 1986. *Roman Circuses: Arenas for Chariot Racing*. Berkeley.

Köhne, E. and C. Ewigleben. 2000. *Gladiators and Caesars: The Power of Spectacle in Ancient Rome*. Berkeley.

König, J. P. 2005. *Athletics and Literature in the Roman Empire*. Cambridge.

König, J. P., ed. 2010. *Greek Athletics*. Edinburgh.

König, J. P. and J. Rusten, 2014. *Philostratus, Heroicus and Gymnasticus*. Loeb Classical Library. Cambridge, MA.

Kyle, D. G. 1988. *Spectacles of Death in Ancient Rome*, London.

Kyle, D. G. 2015. *Sport and Spectacle in the Ancient World*, 2nd edn. Malden, MA.

Mahoney, A. 2001. *Roman Sports and Spectacles: A Sourcebook*. Newburyport, MA.

Matz, D. 1991. *Greek and Roman Sport*. Jefferson, NC.

Migeotte, L. 2014. *Les finances des cités grecques: aux périodes classique et hellénistique. Epigraphica*, 8. Paris.

Miller, S. G. 2004a. *Ancient Greek Athletics*. New Haven.

Miller, S. G. 2004b. *Aretê: Ancient Writers, Papyri, And Inscriptions On The History And Ideals Of Greek Athletics And Games*. 3rd edn. Berkeley.

Papkonstantinou, Z., ed. 2010. *Sport in the Cultures of the Ancient World: New Perspectives*. London.

Plass, P. 1995. *The Game of Death in Ancient Rome: Arena Sport and Political Suicide*. Madison, WI.

Pritchard, D. M. 2012. 'Costing Festivals and War: Priorities of the Athenian Democracy'. *Historia. Zeitschrift für Alte Geschichte* 61.1: 18–65.

Pritchard, D. M. 2013. *Sport, Democracy and War in Classical Athens*. Cambridge.

Remijsen, S. 2015. *The End of Greek Athletics in Late Antiquity*. Cambridge.

Robert, L. 1940. *Les gladiateurs dans l'Orient grec*. Paris.

Robinson, R. S. 1955. *Sources for the History of Greek Athletics*. Cincinnati. Repr. 1979, Chicago.

Scanlon, T. F. 2014a. *Sport in the Greek and Roman Worlds*, vol. 1: *Early Greece, the Olympics, and Contests*. Oxford.

Scanlon, T. F. 2014b. *Sport in the Greek and Roman Worlds*, vol. 2: *Greek Athletic Identities and Roman Sports and Spectacle*. Oxford.

Spivey, N. 2004. *The Ancient Olympics*. Oxford.

Sweet, W. 1987. *Sport and Recreation in Ancient Greece: A Sourcebook with Translations*. New York.

Veyne, P. 1990. *Bread and Circuses: Historical Sociology and Political Pluralism*. B. Pearce, trans. London. (French orig. *Le Pain et le cirque*, 1976. Paris.)

Welch, K. E. 2007. *The Roman Amphitheatre: From Its Origins to the Colosseum*. Cambridge.

Weiler, I. 1988. *Der Sport bei den Völkern der alten Welt: Eine Einführung*, 2nd edn. Darmstadt.

Young, D. C. 2004. *A Brief History of the Olympic Games*. Oxford.

Zuiderhoek, A. 2009. *The Politics of Munificence in the Roman Empire: Citizens, Elites and Benefactors in Asia Minor*. Cambridge.

CHAPTER 2

··

THEORIES OF GREEK AND ROMAN SPORT

··

PAUL CHRISTESEN

INTRODUCTION

IT is appropriate to begin an essay on theory with a definition of the term itself, which can take on a bewildering array of meanings. For the purposes of this essay a theory can be defined as a generalization that holds true with a specified level of certainty under specified circumstances. Perhaps the most obvious example of a theory is Marxism, a generalization about patterns of economic, social, and political development whose early adherents tended to believe always held true under all circumstances. Other theories are less ambitious: Thucydides, for example, articulated what would here be called a theory, about the effects of war on society, which he argued held true in the circumstances of the Peloponnesian War. Although confident that his theory would be valid in the future as well, Thucydides was reasonably cautious about the range of circumstances under which it would apply and the level of certainty that it conferred. As he put it, 'as different circumstances arise, the general rules will admit of some variety' (3.82).[1]

Theory has not played a central role in the study of Greek and Roman sport, though it has been applied with increasing frequency and considerable success in recent explorations of the relevant literary sources. For example, N. Nicholson has made fruitful use of New Historicism in his studies of Pindar's epinician odes, and J. König has offered insightful, theoretically informed readings of Roman-era Greek and Latin writings on sport (Nicholson 2005; Nicholson 2007; König 2005).

The paucity of theory in scholarly work on Greek and Roman sport is somewhat surprising given that in the past three decades scholars working in a variety of fields, most notably sociology and religious studies, have generated an array of theories that facilitate the study of sport in general and the relationship between sport and society in particular. These theories have been regularly used to good effect in explorations of the sport of recent centuries. It is impossible within the bounds of this essay to go through all of the reasons why they have not been applied with equal frequency to comparable material from ancient Greece and Rome, but three considerations merit brief mention.

First, scholars specializing in the study of Greek and Roman sport have typically been trained as humanists rather than social scientists. Although there is enormous variation among individual scholars, it is probably safe to say that humanists typically focus on 'the meanings of the complexity of lived experience' and have an idiographic orientation in that 'God is in the details'. Social scientists, on the other hand, 'aim to cut through the messy details that make up real life' and have a nomothetic orientation in that they seek 'to find underlying general structures and principles' (Morris 2002: 8; on idiographic and nomothetic approaches, see Windelband 1894). That is not, of course, to say that humanists are uninterested in theoretical approaches; but they tend to see theory as a means to the end of understanding the material they study, whereas many social scientists see the generation of theories as an important goal of their work. Social scientists thus tend to be more thoroughly trained in and amenable to the use of theory than humanists. The study of the sport of recent centuries has been pursued by both humanists and social scientists, and sports sociology has become a recognized sub-field with a highly theoretical orientation. Sports sociologists have, however, evinced virtually no interest in ancient Greek and Roman sport. That area of enquiry remains largely the preserve of humanists, most especially scholars trained as ancient historians, who as a group are considerably less enthusiastic than sports sociologists about the use of theory.[2]

A second factor is that historians of all kinds have been particularly wary of theory in part because it rejects or minimizes the importance of contingency and the free will of historical actors. A dyed-in-the-wool Marxist, for example, would dismiss out of hand the idea of 'historical accidents' or the ability of individual humans to alter the course of history in any fundamental fashion. Even in its less extreme forms, theory typically postulates predictable patterns in human behaviour, which in turn implies the operation of forces capable of overriding individual actions and desires. However, historians as a group—again allowing for a wide range of difference—tend to see contingency and the free will of individuals as important if not determinative factors in shaping events of all kinds.

Finally, much theory employs exceedingly dense language that can verge on the impenetrable to those not deeply versed in the relevant scholarly literature. This preference for what might be called technical language, sometimes dismissively labelled jargon, can be justified on the grounds that it makes possible more precise treatment of complex issues. However, it is probably also true that theories expressed in such a fashion can do more to obfuscate than to clarify (Morley 2004: 26–30). Indeed, in at least some cases dexterity in the use of the relevant technical language becomes an important, if implicit, truth claim, while more substantive issues, such as the closeness of fit between theory and evidence, are given short shrift.

All of these considerations are valid, but what they suggest is not that theory has nothing to offer the study of Greek and Roman sport but that it is crucial that the right kinds of theories be used, that they be expressed in appropriate language, and that the dialectic between theory and evidence be kept in the foreground at all times. Under those conditions, theory can be an invaluable 'source for new ideas and new ways of reading the ancient evidence, and thus . . . a means of developing a richer understanding of the past' (Morley 2004: 6).

The remainder of this essay is devoted to concise presentations of five different kinds of theory that have been productively applied to the study of sport: functionalism, conflict theory, the 'discipline' theory of Michel Foucault, Pierre Bourdieu's work on corporeal discipline and on the relationship between sport and social inequality, and ritual theory. This is by no means a comprehensive survey of theories that have been used in the study of sport—a task that could occupy a volume of its own. (For a broad if not quite exhaustive survey of theories used in the study of sport, see Coakley and Dunning 2000: 8–137.) The five theories discussed here were chosen because they have strong potential usefulness in the study of Greek and Roman sport. So, for instance, no mention is made of the considerable collection of feminist theory on sport, solely because the extent of female participation in ancient sport was limited, and the relevant evidence even more so. It is worth bearing in mind throughout that serious academic study of sport is a relatively recent phenomenon: neither historians nor sociologists devoted sustained attention to sport until the 1970s. Partly as a result, sports history and sports sociology remain highly dynamic fields in which methodological change continues apace.

FUNCTIONALISM

Functionalism, like theory, is a term that can take on a wide range of meanings. At the most basic level functionalism is an analytical approach that presumes 1) that norms, social practices, and institutions shape (but do not necessarily determine) individual behaviour by means of socialization and the promotion of consensus and 2) that those norms, practices, and institutions foster the well-being of individuals (individualistic functionalism) or the stability of entire social systems (societal functionalism). Societal functionalism is based on the further assumption 3) that many if not all of the constituent parts of a society contribute to the maintenance of a system of interlocking norms, practices, and institutions that is relatively stable over time. Functionalist analyses virtually always focus on the effects of social systems on individuals, rather than the reverse.

There are in practice two 'flavours' of societal functionalism, strong and weak. Strong functionalism takes societies to be nearly perfectly integrated systems in which a) all the constituent parts came into existence to ensure societal stability and persist for the same reason, and b) conflict is minimized by consistent success in the socialization of individuals and in the creation of consensus.[3] This type of functionalism, which is most closely associated with the work of Talcott Parsons in the middle of the twentieth century, has long been discredited, primarily because it could not account for change and largely ignored intra-societal conflict and individual agency. Weak functionalism assumes x) that while norms, practices, and institutions do contribute to the socialization of individuals and the creation of consensus and hence underpin societal stability, they do so in a distinctly untidy fashion and can simultaneously generate potentially destabilizing tensions; y) that some degree of intra-societal conflict is inevitable; and z) that, as a result of x) and y), societies are imperfectly integrated systems that change over time.[4] Due to lingering negative associations with strong functionalism, few scholars studying sport overtly use the term functionalism to describe their work, but weak functionalism continues to be influential in fact if not in name.

The application of individualistic functionalism to sport has typically been driven less by a thorough grounding in theory than by an intuition that participation in sport is the source of a deep-seated sense of personal fulfilment. Among the more famous works that adopt this perspective is Michael Novak's *The Joy of Sports*, a lyrical ode to sport as a spiritually uplifting activity (Novak 1988).

More overtly theoretical functionalist studies of sport understand it as a means by which individuals are socialized and reach consensus with each other. From a functionalist perspective, children who are members of a soccer team from an early age are socialized into adopting certain values, such as the importance of willingly engaging in competitive behaviour and accepting the outcome of competition, and are presented with opportunities to build social bonds that help make it possible for the members of a team to achieve consensus. Functionalist analyses typically see sport as a positive activity that contributes to the well-being of both individuals and societies. For example, H. Marsh and S. Kleitman studied the results of participation in high-school athletics in the United States and concluded that it had almost uniformly positive effects, including higher grades and improved eventual educational attainment, probably because athletic participation 'fosters identification with the school and school-related values' (Marsh and Kleitman 2003: 206).[5]

Functionalist studies of sport are frequently criticized on the grounds that they overstate the positive effects of sport, ignore the fact that sport creates not only harmony but also conflict, and underestimate the extent to which the interests of individuals and groups within a society diverge and the ability of privileged groups within a society to use sport for their own ends.

CONFLICT THEORY

Conflict theory is based on the assumptions 1) that societies are inevitably riven by conflict due to the unequal distribution of power and resources and 2) that societies are held together by means of coercive mechanisms deployed by elites acting in their own best interests. Applications of conflict theory to sport presume that it is a means by which elites impose their will on the disadvantaged members of a society. The earliest studies applying conflict theory to sport made use of a somewhat heavy-handed Marxism. For example, P. Hoch, in *Rip off the Big Game* (1972), 'argued that sport was an inherently conservative institution that not only diverted the attention of the masses from their systematic oppression, but also peddled values and ideals that supported the status quo and led blue-collar workers to conspire in their own exploitation' (Sugden and Tomlinson 2000: 314). Critics pointed out that this approach portrayed working-class athletes as passive, pliable consumers of the values and ideologies encoded in sport.

More recent applications of conflict theory to the study of sport have used a more subtle approach that is based on Antonio Gramsci's concept of hegemony. Gramsci (1891–1937) sought to understand why the oppressed working classes of Europe did not revolt. He proposed that elites maintained their dominance primarily by controlling civil society and its institutions such as schools and mass media. This enabled them to propagate ideologies that served their interests so that the disadvantaged members of a society came to accept ideas and practices that perpetuated their subordination. Those ideas and practices were more important than the actual or threatened use of force in winning control. However, Gramsci also argued that subordinate groups were always capable of effective resistance to attempts to dominate them, and that, as a result, elites needed to engage in negotiation and accommodation in order to hold onto power. Gramsci gave the name hegemony to the complex, ongoing process by means of which elites established and maintained dominance.[6]

Among the most influential applications of Gramscian hegemony theory to the study of sport is J. Hargreaves's *Sport, Power, and Culture*. Hargreaves sought to show that the bourgeoisie of nineteenth-century Britain achieved hegemony in part because participation in sport simultaneously unified the bourgeoisie (by successfully inculcating a shared set of values that served their collective interests) and fragmented the working class (by presenting and to a limited extent imposing those same values and, more importantly, by fostering divisions along the lines of income, gender, geography, etc.: Hargreaves 1986).[7] Hegemony theory has recently been applied to ancient Greek sport by T. K. Hubbard in a relatively brief article in which he argues that expansion of participation in athletics in the sixth and fifth centuries BCE was 'a continuation of elite hegemony by appropriation of the commercial and artisanal classes' (Hubbard 2008: 379).

Studies of sport based on conflict theory are frequently criticized on the grounds that they fail to recognize that sport can empower individuals and groups, underestimate the importance of socialization and consensus, do not offer clear means of separating occasions when sport serves as a control mechanism and when it becomes a site of resistance, and undervalue the importance of societal divisions that cross-cut economic and power relations, such as gender, ethnicity, and age.

The 'Discipline' Theory of Michel Foucault

Conflict theory presumes that a privileged group in society seeks to coerce one or more less privileged groups, whereas Michel Foucault, while acknowledging the existence of significant differentials in power and influence among individuals and groups, argued that all of the members of a society are subject to forms of coercion. He also argued that coercion frequently takes the form of the inculcation of a habit of docility accompanied by a constant, subtle pressure to adhere to social norms. Foucault called that type of coercion 'discipline' and labelled its operation as the 'micro-physics of power'. He described individuals who have been taught discipline as 'the obedient subject, the individual subjected to habits, rules, orders, an authority that is continually exercised around him and upon him, and which he must allow to function automatically in him' (Foucault 1977 [1975]: 128–129. For a concise introduction to Foucault's work, see Downing 2008.). From Foucault's perspective, the constrictions of discipline are something from which no one can hope to escape.

Foucault made the case that discipline was instilled and reinforced by placing individuals in specific kinds of environments in which they were subject to what he called hierarchical observation, normalizing judgement, and examination. Foucault's work was grounded in studies of psychiatric hospitals and prisons, but perhaps the best example of a disciplinary environment is a school. The activities of students are observed and supervised by their teachers, who in turn are observed and supervised by one or more school administrators, who typically themselves are subject to observation and supervision. Teachers exercise normalizing judgement, which is to say that they constantly compare the students' behaviour to norms and point out deviations large and small. The students are subject to examinations that test their knowledge of and conformity to norms and that are the basis for appropriate rewards and punishments. Individuals placed in such a system from an early age and for an extended period tend to develop into compliant adults who are 'well-behaved' in the sense that they typically do what they are expected to do, without the application of any overt forms of coercion (Foucault 1977 [1975]: 135–230).[8]

It has become close to an article of faith among sports sociologists that organized sports almost invariably and inevitably constitute a disciplinary environment. Athletes are observed by their coaches, who in many cases have assistants and who are themselves subject to observation by other coaches, athletes on other teams, and the families of the athletes. Coaches are expected to exercise normalizing judgement on the athletes for whom they are responsible, and to supervise examinations that take the form of athletic competitions. Athletes thus become disciplined individuals. A nice illustration of the resulting behaviour can be found in Peyton Manning, one of the most famous players in American professional football. When asked how he felt about being removed from a game against his will, he said, 'Until any player in here is the head coach, you follow orders and you follow them with all of your heart. That's what we've done as players. We follow orders.'[9]

The number of studies applying Foucault's work to the study of sport is large and continues to grow rapidly. To give but one example, an article by N. Barker-Ruchti and R. Tinning, with the title 'Foucault in Leotards: Corporeal Discipline in Women's Artistic Gymnastics', focuses on an elite gymnastics school in Australia. The authors describe the environment at the school as one that involves 'an extensive and elaborate process of corporeal discipline' and argue that it 'prevented the gymnasts ... from developing independence and self-determination', making them instead into 'docile athletes' (Barker-Ruchti and Tinning 2010: 299, 243).[10]

Most of the same complaints levelled against conflict theory are also relevant to Foucault's work, as it has been employed in the study of sport.

PIERRE BOURDIEU ON CORPOREAL DISCIPLINE AND ON THE RELATIONSHIP BETWEEN SPORT AND SOCIAL INEQUALITY

Pierre Bourdieu worked along the same lines as Foucault, but broke new ground by paying heed to the specifically physical dimensions of discipline and by offering a highly nuanced theory of the relationship between sport and social inequality. (Foucault, it is true, placed a great deal of emphasis on the body, but in fact tended to see discipline as something that was imposed on the body through the intermediary of the mind, and for the most part took the body as a passive entity that received but did not initiate actions. See the discussion in Lash 1991 and McNay 1999.)

Bourdieu believed that discipline could be inculcated by means of bodily training and that the disciplined body as a corporeal entity could in and of itself shape individual behaviour. Unlike Foucault, who evinced no direct interest in the subject, Bourdieu wrote at some length on sport. He made the case that:

> If most organizations—the Church, the army, political parties, industrial firms, etc.—put such a great emphasis on bodily disciplines, it is because obedience consists in large part in belief, and belief is what the body ... concedes even when the mind ... says no ... It is perhaps by

considering what is most specific in sport, that is, the ... manipulation of the body, and the fact that sport—as all disciplines in all total or totalitarian institutions, such as convents, prisons, asylums, political parties, etc.—is a way of obtaining from the body a form of consent that the mind could refuse, that one will best manage to understand the use that most authoritarian regimes make of sports. Bodily discipline is the instrument par excellence of all forms of 'domestication' (Bourdieu 1988a: 161).[11]

Hence, what Foucault believed took place through the medium of the mind in prisons and classrooms, Bourdieu believed frequently took place through the medium of the body on the playing field.

The effects of participation in sport, in Bourdieu's opinion, extended beyond the imposition of discipline to the inculcation of dispositions that contributed to the perpetuation of social inequality. There are three related concepts that require explanation. First, Bourdieu argued that individual behaviour is shaped by *habitus*, which might be thought of as learned, deeply ingrained inclinations that predispose individuals to act in certain ways in certain situations, without determining their course of action in any given instance. Second, he sought to show that the ability of individuals to achieve their goals in any given social setting was proportionate to the capital at their disposal and that capital could come in a variety of different forms, particularly economic (wealth), social (e.g. social connections) and cultural (e.g. a university degree). Third, he made the case that societies consist of collections of 'fields', or semi-autonomous spheres of social action (e.g. business and academia).

These concepts taken together provide an explanation for how societies function. Starting literally from birth and continuing throughout their lives, individuals develop *habitus* that reflect their life experiences. Although each individual's *habitus* is unique, those from the same class fraction (i.e. those who experience similar socio-economic conditions) tend to develop similar sets of dispositions. Individuals inherit and accumulate capital of different kinds, which they then deploy to achieve social standing. The kind of capital that is useful varies from field to field, so that, for instance, economic capital is highly valued in the field of business, while cultural capital is highly valued in academia. Social inequalities tend to be self-perpetuating because individuals develop *habitus* that are suited to the socio-economic conditions in which they were born, and those *habitus* shape aspirations, provide certain forms of capital, and prepare individuals to acquire particular forms of capital and to act competently in some fields rather than others.

In this schema sport plays an important role because it is a powerful means of inculcating *habitus* and offers individuals the opportunity to accumulate capital. Members of different class fractions play different sports, and in doing so learn different *habitus* and accumulate different forms of capital that are useful in different fields. So, for instance, tennis and basketball players tend to come from different class fractions, and the experience of playing these sports helps form individuals with *habitus* and competences suitable for the kinds of fields in which members of their class fraction are normally active.

Bourdieu emphasized that the repercussions of involvement in sport are easily underestimated because corporeal training has far-reaching effects that are resistant to conscious examination:

If all societies and, significantly, all the 'totalitarian institutions' in Goffman's phrase, that seek to produce a new man through a process of 'deculturation' and 'reculturation' set such store on the seemingly most insignificant details of *dress, bearing*, physical and verbal *manners*, the reason is that, treating the body as a memory, they entrust to it in abbreviated and practical, i.e. mnemonic, form the fundamental principles of the arbitrary content of the culture. The principles em-bodied in this way are placed beyond the grasp of consciousness, and hence cannot be touched by voluntary, deliberate transformation, cannot even be made explicit; nothing seems more ineffable, more incommunicable, more inimitable, and, therefore, more precious, than the values given body, *made* body by the transubstantiation achieved by the hidden persuasion of an implicit pedagogy, capable of instilling a whole cosmology, an ethic, a metaphysic, a political philosophy, through injunctions as insignificant as 'stand up straight' or 'don't hold your knife in your left hand.'... The whole trick of pedagogic reason lies precisely in the way it extorts the essential while seeming to demand the insignificant (Bourdieu 1977 [1972]: 94–95).

As a result, 'the body is in the social world but the social world is also in the body' (Bourdieu 1990: 190).

Bourdieu himself wrote quite a bit about sport, and his ideas have been used extensively by sports sociologists (Bourdieu 1978; Bourdieu 1988a; Bourdieu 1988b: 173–195). Perhaps the best known relevant work is that of Loïc Wacquant, one of Bourdieu's students, who intensively studied a boxing gym in Chicago and how involvement with the gym shaped the lives of the individuals who trained there (Wacquant 2004).[12]

Bourdieu's work has been criticized on a number of different grounds, among the most notable of which is that the criteria for identifying distinct class fractions, forms of capital and fields are so vague that an almost infinite number of types and subtypes of each can potentially be identified. That, in turn, vastly complicates any analysis conducted along the lines suggested by Bourdieu and might be understood as vitiating the results of such analyses. In addition, some scholars have argued that Bourdieu's ideas leave little room for individual agency.[13]

RITUAL THEORY

Another perspective on sport is opened up when it is seen as a form of ritualized activity, which can be understood as an iterated practice that involves performance and that is distinguished from more ordinary behaviour as a different and special way of acting.[14] Sport can easily become a ritualized activity because it is inherently performative and is frequently set apart from everyday life. Johan Huizinga, in his famous *Homo Ludens*, characterized sport as a form of play and defined play as a 'free activity standing quite consciously outside "ordinary" life' (Huizinga 1950 [1938]: 13). If other considerations, such as the provision of special playing fields and uniforms (or, in ancient Greece, nudity) are taken into account, the identification of sport as at least a potentially ritualized activity becomes almost an inevitability.

What ritualized activities do and how they do it are questions that continue to be debated. For our purposes it is sufficient to adopt a relatively simple approach and consider ritualized activities as having two distinct dimensions, communication and practice, and serving as both *models of* and *models for* society.[15]

With respect to their communicative dimension, ritualized activities are 'flexible forms of symbolic activity that reaffirm cultural values and a sense of order' (Bell 2005: 7849). The element of practice in ritualized activities has to do with the fact that they are by definition performative and hence involve both saying and doing. As models of society, ritualized activities have the capacity to present idealized and simplified visions of how society and relations between individuals could or should be. (This is a close paraphrase taken from the excellent discussion of ritual found at Kowalzig 2007: 34.) The fact that ritualized activities are by definition set apart from everyday life is particularly significant, as they are for this reason immune to many of the mundane necessities of existence that otherwise can generate a divergence between the normative and normal. As a result, ritualized activities frequently, perhaps typically, reflect social norms with a degree of faithfulness that is otherwise difficult to achieve. They also serve as models for society in that participants in them enact norms and hence reproduce idealized forms of behaviour that they are expected to manifest in some form in their daily lives. Ritualized activities thus inculcate habits of thought and behavioural dispositions that shape the actions of individuals in all settings and can serve as models for activity outside the ritualized sphere.

The element of practice in ritualized activities extends beyond performance to the creation of what C. Bell has called the 'ritualized body'. Bell, who built directly upon Bourdieu's ideas, argued that regular participation in ritualized activities *physically* inculcates the thought and behavioural patterns underlying and underpinning such activities and that 'as bodies … absorb the logic of spaces and temporal events, they then project these structural schemes, reproducing liturgical arrangements out of their own "sense" of the fitness of things' (Bell 2005: 7853; for a full discussion, see Bell 1992: 94–117).

Ritual theory has been employed with some regularity in the study of modern sport, for instance in J. MacAloon's work on the content of and reasons for the popularity of the present-day Olympic Games (MacAloon 1984). It has in recent years also been applied with increasing frequency to Greek and Roman material, to explore topics such as choral dance (Kowalzig 2007) and Roman spectacle (though not sport) (Bell 2004).

The scholars who in recent decades have generated and used ritual theory have engaged in continuing, frequently polemical discussion of its promise and limitations. There remains sharp disagreement with respect to what is and is not a ritualized activity, the effects of participation in ritualized activities, and how to account for those effects. These disagreements, which are played out in a very extensive and unusually dense body of writing, can present challenges to anyone wishing to apply ritual theory.[16]

CONCLUSION

Greek and Roman sport show every sign of offering particularly fertile ground for the judicious use of theory. Scholarship on ancient Greek and Roman sport has been largely empirical, inductive, and idiographic. The results have been impressive, but not entirely without shortcomings. Perhaps the most significant issue is that it is difficult to trace the complex relationship between sport and society solely on the basis of empiricist treatments of archaeological and literary evidence. Not only is that evidence lacunose, it is also incomplete in the sense that emic perspectives, i.e. those coming only from within the culture being studied, are inherently limited due to inevitable difficulties in tracing patterns that developed over long periods and in uncovering processes such as socialization that operated largely outside the realm of conscious thought. As Foucault put it, 'people know what they do; they frequently know why they do what they do; but what they don't know is what what they do does'.[17]

Although it is impossible in the bounds of this essay to demonstrate in detail the potentialities of theory for the study of Greek and Roman sport, it is possible to suggest a few applications. Conflict theory could be used to explore the development of sport in Greece during the archaic period, a time when elites and non-elites engaged in a prolonged struggle for political and social predominance, a struggle in which sport played a more than minor role. Bourdieu's work on the relationship between sport and social inequality might suggest new and interesting explanations for athletic nudity, in which nudity is understood as a means of creating important, corporeally based social distinctions. Foucault's discipline theory and Bourdieu's work on the effects of corporeal training could be used to explicate the confused and long-debated relationship between athletic and military activity in ancient Greece (see e.g. Poliakoff 1987: 94–103; Reed 1998; Spivey 2004: 1–29).

The growing prevalence of the use of theory in the study of classical literature, and the close, ongoing connection between scholars specializing in classical literature and in ancient history, suggest that change is imminent, and that the study of Greek and Roman sport will in the future give due consideration to theory. The results promise to be of great interest.

Notes

1. For a good introduction to theory in the specific context of the study of the ancient world, see Morley 2004, particularly 1–32, on which this paragraph draws heavily. See also Morris 2002 and Shaw 1982. On Marx and Marxism, see Rigby 1997. On Thucydides, see Hornblower 1991–6, 1: 61, 481–482 and Luce 1997: 60–98.
2. 'Within the discipline of ancient history, grown to a stunted maturity under the paternalistic aegis of classical philology, approaches to history that stress the techniques and methodologies of the social sciences (e.g. primacy of theory, model building, conceptual sophistication, quantification) rather than those of the mainstream tradition (e.g. linguistic categorization, literary source criticism, citation of authority) must expect to meet with more than a slight suspicion of illegitimacy' (Shaw 1982: 17).
3. In some cases functionalist analyses make no claims about the reasons for the origins of norms, practices, and institutions and make claims only about the reasons for their persistence. Socialization entails inculcating social norms from such an early age and so regularly that individuals accept those norms as a given and thus generally adhere to them; consensus entails individual members of a group coming to a broad, conscious agreement about the norms with which they will voluntarily comply.
4. Weak functionalism has its roots in the work of Robert Merton (Merton 1957). The extent to which societies can be understood as well-organized systems has been the subject of vigorous debate among sociologists. A good discussion can be found in Ritzer 2008: 186–222. For a concise treatment of strong functionalism and its flaws, see Holmwood 2005. For an excellent overview of functionalist approaches to the study of sport, see Coakley and Pike 2009: 35–41 and Loy and Booth 2000, with the caveat that Loy and Booth show a particular interest in strong functionalism. For incisive discussions of the strengths and weaknesses of functionalism as a methodology for social analysis, see Barnes 1995: 37–60; Kincaid 1996: 101–138; and Mouzelis 1995: 127–147.

5. Although functionalism has not been overtly applied to the study of Greek or Roman sport, it has been regularly, if implicitly, employed in the study of Greek choral dance, which has been repeatedly characterized as a powerful means of socialization. See, for instance, Clark 1996: 1177. For a functionalist reading of sport in ancient Sparta, see Christesen 2012.

6. On Gramsci's life and work, see Jones 2006. On conflict theory and its use in the study of sport, see Coakley and Pike 2009: 41–49; Rigauer 2000; and Sugden and Tomlinson 2000.

7. Another noteworthy work on sport in which hegemony theory is employed to good effect is Gruneau 1999.

8. Foucault also emphasized the significance of fine-grained control over how the activities of individuals are spatially and temporally organized and of placing individuals in an environment in which surveillance is always possible and which thus induces self-policing (what he called panopticism).

9. https://www.espn.com/nfl/recap?gameId=291227011.

10. A thoroughgoing exploration of the application of Foucault's ideas to the study of sport can be found in Markula and Pringle 2006.

11. For a concise and lucid introduction to Bourdieu's work, see Wacquant 1998.

12. On the use of Bourdieu's ideas in the study of sport, see Clement 1995.

13. Good discussions that both appreciate the merits of Bourdieu's work while also explicating its flaws can be found in Brubaker 1985 and Mouzelis 1995: 100–126.

14. On defining and demarcating ritualized activities, see Bell 1992: 37–168 and *passim*.

15. A good, brief introduction to ritual theory can be found in Bell 2005. For a longer, more detailed overview, see Bell 1997. The view of rituals as models of and for society is elucidated in Geertz 1973: 87–125.

16. A 'carefully selected' bibliography of essential scholarly work on ritual theory covering the years from 1966 to 2005 lists no fewer than 620 items (Kreinath et al. 2007).

17. Cited as a personal communication in Dreyfus et al. 1983: 187. This parallels the differentiation Merton made between manifest and latent functions, on which see Merton 1996: 87–95.

References

Barker-Ruchti, N. and R. Tinning. 2010. 'Foucault in Leotards: Corporeal Discipline in Women's Artistic Gymnastics.' *Sociology of Sport Journal* 27: 229–250.

Barnes, B. 1995. *The Elements of Social Theory*. Princeton.

Bell, A. 2004. *Spectacular Power in the Greek and Roman City*. Oxford.

Bell, C. 1992. *Ritual Theory, Ritual Practice*. New York.

Bell, C. 1997. *Ritual: Perspectives and Dimensions*. New York.

Bell, C. 2005. 'Ritual, Further Considerations.' In *Encyclopedia of Religion*, 2nd edn. 11: 7848–7856. L. Jones, ed. Detroit.

Bourdieu, P. 1977 [1972]. *Outline of a Theory of Practice*. R. Nice, trans. Cambridge.

Bourdieu, P. 1978. 'Sport and Social Class.' *Social Science Information* 17: 819–840.

Bourdieu, P. 1988a. 'Program for a Sociology of Sport.' *Sociology of Sport Journal* 5: 153–161.

Bourdieu, P. 1988b. *Questions de Sociologie*. Ed. augmentée d'un index. Paris.

Bourdieu, P. 1990. *In Other Words: Essays towards a Reflexive Sociology*. Stanford.

Brubaker, R. 1985. 'Rethinking Classical Theory: The Sociological Vision of Pierre Bourdieu.' *Theory and Society* 14: 745–775.

Christesen, P. 2012. 'Athletics in Sparta in the Classical Period.' *Classical Antiquity* 31.2: 193–255.

Clark, C. 1996. 'The Gendering of the Body in Alcman's Partheneion 1: Narrative, Sex, and Social Order in Archaic Sparta.' *Helios* 23: 143–172.

Clement, J. P. 1995. 'Contributions of the Sociology of Pierre Bourdieu to the Sociology of Sport.' *Sociology of Sport Journal* 12: 147–157.

Coakley, J. and E. Dunning, eds. 2000. *Handbook of Sports Studies*. Los Angeles.

Coakley, J. and E. Pike. 2009. *Sports in Society: Issues and Controversies*, 9th edn. London.

Downing, L. 2008. *The Cambridge Introduction to Michel Foucault*. Cambridge.

Dreyfus, H. L., P. Rabinow, and M. Foucault. 1983. *Michel Foucault: Beyond Structuralism and Hermeneutics*, 2nd edn. Chicago.

Foucault, M. 1977 [1975]. *Discipline and Punish: The Birth of the Prison*. A. Sheridan, trans. New York.

Geertz, C. 1973. *The Interpretation of Cultures*. New York.

Gruneau, R. 1999. *Class, Sports, and Social Development*, 2nd edn. Champaign, IL.

Hargreaves, J. 1986. *Sport, Power and Culture*. New York.

Holmwood, J. 2005. 'Functionalism and Its Critics.' In *Modern Social Theory: An Introduction*. 87–110. A. Harrington, ed. Oxford.

Hornblower, S. 1991–1996. *A Commentary on Thucydides*. 3 vols. Oxford.

Hubbard, T. 2008. 'Contemporary Sport Sociology and Ancient Greek Athletics.' *Leisure Studies* 27: 379–393.

Huizinga, J. 1950 [1938]. *Homo Ludens: A Study of the Play Element in Culture*. New York.

Jones, S. 2006. *Antonio Gramsci*. London.

Kincaid, H. 1996. *Philosophical Foundations of the Social Sciences: Analyzing Controversies in Social Research*. Cambridge.

König, J. 2005. *Athletics and Literature in the Roman Empire*. Cambridge.

Kowalzig, B. 2007. *Singing for the Gods: Performances of Myth and Ritual in Archaic and Classical Greece*. Oxford.

Kreinath, J., J. A. M. Snoek, and M. Stausberg. 2007. *Theorizing Rituals: Annotated Bibliography of Ritual Theory, 1966–2005*. Leiden.

Lash, S. 1991. 'Genealogy and the Body: Foucault/Deleuze/Nietzsche.' In *The Body: Social Process and Cultural Theory*. 256–280. M. Featherstone, M. Hepworth, and B. S. Turner, eds. London.

Loy, J. and D. Booth. 2000. 'Functionalism, Sport and Society.' In *Handbook of Sports Studies*. 8–27. J. Coakley and E. Dunning, eds. London.

Luce, T. J. 1997. *The Greek Historians*. London.

MacAloon, J. 1984. 'Olympic Games and the Theory of Spectacle in Modern Societies.' In *Rite, Drama, Festival, Spectacle: Rehearsals toward a Theory of Cultural Performance*. 241–280. J. MacAloon, ed. Philadelphia.

Markula, P. and R. Pringle. 2006. *Foucault, Sport and Exercise: Power, Knowledge and Transforming the Self*. London.

Marsh, H. and S. Kleitman. 2003. 'School Athletic Participation: Mostly Gain with Little Pain.' *Journal of Sport and Exercise Psychology* 25: 205–228.

McNay, L. 1999. 'Gender, Habitus, and the Field: Pierre Bourdieu and the Limits of Reflexivity.' *Theory, Culture and Society* 16: 95–117.

Merton, R. K. 1957. *Social Theory and Social Structure*, rev. edn. Glencoe, IL.

Merton, R. K. 1996. *On Social Structure and Science.* Chicago.

Morley, N. 2004. *Theories, Models and Concepts in Ancient History.* London.

Morris, I. 2002. 'Hard Surfaces.' In *Money, Labour and Land: Approaches to the Economies of Ancient Greece.* 8–43. P. Cartledge, E. Cohen, and L. Foxhall, eds. London.

Mouzelis, N. P. 1995. *Sociological Theory: What Went Wrong? Diagnosis and Remedies.* London.

Nicholson, N. 2005. *Aristocracy and Athletics in Archaic and Classical Greece.* Cambridge.

Nicholson, N. 2007. 'Pindar, History and Historicism.' *Classical Philology* 102: 208–227.

Novak, M. 1988. *The Joy of Sports: End Zones, Bases, Baskets, Balls, and the Consecration of the American Spirit,* 2nd edn. Lanham, MD.

Poliakoff, M. 1987. *Combat Sports in the Ancient World.* New Haven.

Reed, N. 1998. *More than Just a Game: The Military Nature of Greek Athletic Contests.* Chicago.

Rigauer, B. 2000. 'Marxist Theories.' In *Handbook of Sports Studies.* 28–47. J. Coakley and E. Dunning, eds. London.

Rigby, S. H. 1997. 'Marxist Historiography.' In *Companion to Historiography.* 899–928. M. Bentley, ed. London.

Ritzer, G. 2008. *Classical Sociological Theory,* 5th edn. Boston.

Shaw, B. 1982. 'Social Science and Ancient History: Keith Hopkins in *Partibus Infidelium.' Helios* 9: 17–57.

Spivey, N. 2004. *The Ancient Olympics.* Oxford.

Sugden, J. and A. Tomlinson. 2000. 'Theorizing Sport, Social Class and Status.' In *Handbook of Sports Studies.* 309–321. J. Coakley and E. Dunning, eds. London.

Wacquant, L. 1998. 'Pierre Bourdieu.' In *Key Sociological Thinkers.* 215–229. R. Stones, ed. New York.

Wacquant, L. 2004. *Body and Soul: Notebooks of an Apprentice Boxer.* Oxford.

Windelband, W. 1894. 'Geschichte und Naturwissenschaft.' In *Rektoratsreden der Universität Strassburg.* 193–208. Strassburg.

PART II

DEVELOPMENT IN HISTORICAL PERSPECTIVE

SECTION 1

PRE-GREEK MEDITERRANEAN

CHAPTER 3

....

SPORT IN ANCIENT EGYPT AND THE ANCIENT NEAR EAST

....

WOLFGANG DECKER

INTRODUCTION

....

THE sources for sport in the early high cultures of the Nile Valley and Mesopotamia go back almost 5,000 years, and owing to their great age give expectations of some evidence about the origin of sport, a topic which is difficult to investigate. For a long time research into sport in both cultures was overshadowed by the preoccupation with sport in classical antiquity; but sport in Ancient Egypt, particularly, has come out of the shadows in recent decades through the scholarly study of its written and iconographic records (Decker 1987; Decker 1992).

The central figure in Egyptian sport history is the pharaoh, whose sportsmanship exceeds his physical strength and is essentially embodied in the dogma of kingship. However, the Pharaoh as *victor perpetuus* was forbidden from taking part in sporting contests where the outcome was uncertain, yet he expresses his athletic superiority by means of impressive demonstrations of mighty achievements in archery, with copper discs as targets, supreme command of chariot-driving, and the high art of horse-training. At the jubilee, a symbolic re-enactment of his accession, the king takes renewed possession of his rule through a ritual run, which says a lot about the origin of sport. The historical reality of the feast is mirrored in the preserved track in the pyramid precinct of Djoser (Third Dynasty).

Many features of sport among the common people are modelled on the person of the king (sports festivals, foot-races); the victorious nature of the king is transferred to the Egyptian athletes who in the mortuary temple of Ramses III (Twentieth Dynasty) gain the upper hand against their foreign opponents in combat sports.

Outside the ideological canon, there are attested historic influences on the history of sport in Egypt, for example the blossoming of royal sport in the Eighteenth Dynasty, after the end of foreign rule by the Hyksos. The arsenal of 'sports equipment' such as chariots, bows, and hunting weapons from the intact grave of Tutankhamen shows what was expected from a king of this period (McLeod 1970).

In the Ancient Near East, too, where a systematic study of sources, particularly cuneiform texts, for the history of sport is yet to be undertaken, the special status of the king in the field of sport is characteristic, as is shown in hymns of the Sumerian ruler Shulgi (*c.*2000 BCE) for instance. This supreme athlete was permitted to take part in contests; his achievements, such as running more than 320 km in one single day (Hymn A), come close to being miracles. The art of seal-making has its own particular character in the early second millennium BCE in the Ancient Near East: it uses the motif of the 'athlete-warrior' who appears in combat sports (wrestling, boxing, armed combat; cf. *hoplomachia* in Mycenaean culture and the *Iliad*).

For the history of sport, rich sources may be found in the various versions of the Gilgamesh epic, which originated in ancient Babylonian times. A famous example is the wrestling match between the eponymous hero and his friend Enkidu, during which the walls trembled and the gateposts were smashed. In more recent research into the Ancient Near East, Gilgamesh is also seen as a keen player of stickball, evidence of a team sport in the Ancient Near East as early as the third millennium BCE. A later version of the epic indicates sport as part of funeral rites, and the work also gives evidence of swimming and diving.

There is a detailed training plan for chariot horses, covering a period of 184 days, in the text of the horse-trainer Kikkuli, which survives in the Hittite language and contains instructions for various racing disciplines, feeding, and hygienic measures. Training in stamina and technique seem to be compiled in the world's oldest training manual. Furthermore, the Indo-European Hittites seem in a certain way to prefigure the *agōn* in Homer. Recently, evidence of bull-leaping has been found in this civilization; it was also practised in other cultures of the Ancient Near East (and Crete).

A late ancient Eastern culture flourished in Persia and was admired by the Greeks; it might be the model for the present-day institution of the *surkahne* ('house of strength'), which *mutatis mutandis* may be compared to the Greek gymnasium.

After the deciphering of cuneiform script (1802) and Egyptian hieroglyphs (1822), the study of sport in Ancient Egypt and the Ancient Near East was not undertaken for a long time. For decades it was overshadowed by the interest in sport in Greek antiquity, especially after the founding of the modern Olympic Games (1896). Only in the last generation have we seen the beginnings of systematic attempts to shed light on Ancient Egyptian sport (Decker 1975; Decker and Herb 1994). Only recently has sport in the Ancient Near East been given an entry in the *Reallexikon der Assyriologie* (Rollinger 2011), the foremost publication in this field.

Sport in Ancient Egypt

Ancient Egyptian sports culture has a few unique characteristics which distinguish it clearly from other sports cultures of the ancient world, and indeed give it a special role in the universal history of sport. It offers numerous iconographic sources (Decker and Herb 1994) and written ones (these being relatively less numerous) (Decker 1975) for a phenomenon for which there is no attested general term used by the Egyptians. An important partial term which appears in this context is the word *šḥmḥ-ib*, 'amusement' (literally: 'make the heart forget'; Cannuyer 2002), present semantically in the late Latin root of the contemporary term *sport* which is understood internationally. Nearly 2,000 instances from iconographic sources alone have been listed in a relevant handbook (Decker and Herb 1994). This wealth of sources, though varying in density, extends over a continuous period of three millennia, where the oldest examples go back to the beginnings of written Egyptian history at the end of the fourth millennium BCE.

The Sporting Kings

The Egyptian cosmos was centred on the figure of the pharaoh. According to the Egyptian conception of history, he was the very guarantor of life. As the protector of the country he disarmed its enemies, who were condemned to powerlessness and defeat. This role assumed a priori an existence distinguished by power and strength, which were essential conditions of his rule. This is precisely where his sporting character originates (Decker 1971; Decker 2006: 6–11). These characteristics of the king also affect the way he appears as an athlete. Admittedly he does not fight for material prizes; his prize is the validation of his kingship, which he often proves before witnesses with his achievements as a runner, archer, or charioteer and horse-trainer. As *victor perpetuus* he cannot take part in sporting contests whose outcome is not certain. The only explicit exception is Amenophis II (1428–1397 BCE), who could be designated the 'athlete on the royal throne' on the basis of the plethora of reports (Der Manuelian 1987: 191–213; Decker 2006: 42–27) (Fig. 3.1). The pharaoh reaches the highest level of achievement in sport disciplines, yet there was a taboo on his participation in competitions with other contestants, as the mere theoretical possibility of defeat was not consistent with the dogma of kingship.

The Foot Race at the Jubilee

It is only natural that the physical superiority which is constantly stressed in royal inscriptions was also required, and particularly so, of the ageing ruler. In order to demonstrate the physical powers he retained, which were essential to exercising his rule, the king ideally celebrated the so-called *Sed* festival or jubilee thirty years after his accession, and every three years thereafter (Hornung and Staehelin 1974; and 2006). The main feature was a run with which he proved his continuing qualification to be king. There is evidence for the festival in all thirty-one dynasties, and in the Ptolemaic and Roman era as well (Decker and Herb 1994: Chapter A). A unique track for this ritual survives in the funeral precinct of Djoser (2690–2670 BCE) in Sakkara (Friedmann 1995). Even if it is only a replica, a stage for the dead king to celebrate his jubilees for all eternity, we may conclude that races of this kind were run around posts 55 metres (c.100 Egyptian ells) apart. The king's ritual run (of unknown length) took place on tracks of this kind. He celebrated it without opponents. In a magical fashion the pharaoh gathered new powers, symbolically took renewed possession of his territory, and requalified himself for his office by this running ritual (Wiedemann 1975). There are indications that this race goes back to earliest times, when the most able hunter qualified himself to be chief of his tribe.

FIGURE 3.1. Pairs of wrestlers, Beni Hasan, tomb 15, east wall (cf. P.E. Newberry, *Beni Hasan* II, London 1894, Pl. V), about 2000 BCE. Photo: Wolfgang Decker.

Pharaoh and Sport in the New Kingdom

The New Kingdom (1550–1070 BCE) is the real era of sporting kings. At the beginning of the Eighteenth Dynasty, after wars of liberation, the first foreign hegemony over Egypt by the Hyksos came to an end, but the trauma had a long-lasting effect. In the official texts the kings now emphasized in traditional manner their achievements in war and in hunting, and latterly in sport as well. It is noteworthy that the sporting character of the king can be handed down over three generations, as is the case of Thutmosis III (1479–1425 BCE), Amenophis II (1328–1197 BCE), and Thutmosis IV (1397–1388 BCE) (Hayes 1973).

Archery with Copper Targets

The special sport of the kings was now shooting at copper targets with a bow and arrow, where the achievements of predecessors were outdone, and the notion of records (Decker 1990) makes its first appearance in the history of sport. The thickness of the target and the penetration of the arrow were the objective measures. The use of copper targets derives from the ingots traded in every Mediterranean seaport (along with tin) for the production of bronze. Numerous originals have been discovered in wrecks of the Bronze Age in the depths of the Mediterranean by underwater archaeology (Yalçin et al. 2005). In other words, the copper discs that the kings of the New Kingdom allegedly penetrated with their arrows really existed, though it was of course impossible to penetrate them with arrows (Decker and Klauck 1974). Even the highly elastic composite bow made of wood, animal tendons, and horn did not produce sufficient force, leaving aside the fact that the arrows were inadequate. Only the ideal king was capable of this superhuman achievement.

The motif was so effective that it was taken up in Greek literature; there it appears in the *Odyssey*. On his return home after being thought missing in Troy, the warrior Odysseus engages in a contest with the suitors. Here too the aim was to shoot through metal objects (handle-holes in axes which resemble Egyptian copper ingots) (Burkert 1973; Decker 1977).

Charioteering and Horse-Training

The New Kingdom saw the introduction of the composite bow, which enabled huge improvements in archery; there was also the technical innovation of the light chariot with two spoked wheels, drawn by two horses, which the Hyksos also brought to Egypt (Hofmann 1989; Herold 1999). This chariot became a status symbol and was very popular at the royal court. This was firstly because of its use as a new instrument of war, though the significance of this is often overestimated, but also because of the breeding of fine horses whose skill and condition were crucial for the survival of the chariot warrior. From this high regard for horses arose the art of training horses, appropriate for the king, and attributed in great measure to Amenophis II (1428–1397 BCE) on a sphinx stele (Decker 1975 no. 17; Klug 2002: 223–234). A pharaoh as late as Ramses III (1183/1182–1152/1151 BCE) is depicted in his mortuary temple in Medinet Habu, selecting from his stable a pair of horses which 'he had trained with his own hand' (Decker and Herb 1994: I 99) (Fig. 3.2).

Even if the Egyptians were thoroughly conscious of experiencing speeds unknown until then, on the sphinx stele of Thutmosis IV (1397–1388 BCE) we read: 'His horses were faster than the wind' (Decker 1975 no. 21; Klug 2002: 298). No sources have yet been found for charioteering. In respect to the pharaoh, we must assume the taboo against contests applied.

FIGURE 3.2. Archery 'Stela' of Amenophis II (1428–1397 BCE), Luxor Museum J.129. Photo: Wolfgang Decker.

I Upper text:
The perfect god, great in strength, who acts with his two hands in the presence of his army, the mighty bowman who shoots to hit and whose arrows do not go astray. When he shoots at a target of copper, he splits it as (one splits) papyrus, without (even) considering (using) any wooden one ... on account of his strength. Strong of arm, whose equal has never existed; Mentu, when he appears in the chariot.

II Lower text:
The great target of foreign copper at which His Majesty shot (is), of three fingers in thickness. The one great of strength pierced it with many arrows; he caused three palms' (thickness) to come forth at the back of this target; one who shot to hit every time he aimed, the hero, lord of strength. His Majesty did this pleasure before the entire land. (Translation by P. Der Manuelian, *Studies in the Reign of Amenophis II*, Hildesheim 1987: 204–205.)

With the preservation of eight original chariots from the Eighteenth Dynasty, six of them from the tomb of Tutankhamen (1333–1323 BCE), ancient Egypt provides us with an inestimable corpus for the study of the technology of chariot-building, which will have an important place in the history of charioteering that is yet to be written (Littauer and Crouwel 1985).

Sport for the Pharaoh

The sport practised by individuals was also often in the service of the king, though it was not subject to the taboo against competition. This applied particularly when it occurred as part of the programme of festivals (Decker 2000). An example of this occurs as early as the middle of the third millennium BCE. Only a few years ago there were discovered on the ramp to the mortuary temple of Sahure (2496–2483 BCE) near Abusir, reliefs which commemorate the completion ceremony of his pyramid, as is shown by the hauling of the *pyramidion*, the pinnacle stone of the building, by a team of workmen. As part of this celebration, sporting contests were held with participation by those who had been engaged in the building of the burial place. The sports were wrestling (freestyle, in the presence of a referee), stick-fencing, and target-shooting with bow and arrow; a fourth component, a rowing contest, is also possible (El Awady 2009; Decker and Förster 2011).

The next example of a sporting festival is more recent, by nearly 1,200 years. It is the third jubilee of Amenophis III (1388–1351/50 BCE), which was set in the tomb of Cheriuf, who was responsible for organizing it. At the ceremony marking the erection of the *Djed*-pillar there were contests in stick-fencing (with papyrus stalks) and fist-fights (with bare fists). The inscriptions name the king as the dedicatee of the sports, 'Fights for Amenophis III', while the contestants, above all the boxers, are conspicuous for their elegant movements (Touny and Wenig 1969: table 14; Decker and Herb 1994: M 2, N 1).

From the time of his successor, Amenophis IV (1352/1–1334 BCE), comes the tomb of Merire II in Amarna, on the east wall of which the foreign peoples pay tribute to the enthroned royal couple and present typical products of their countries. The tribute given by the Nubians includes the performance of dances and pairs of men, Nubian athletes, in combat (wrestling, stick-fencing, boxing[?]) (Touny and Wenig 1969: ill. 6; Decker and Herb 1994: L 2, M 3, N 2) (Fig. 3.3).

The presence of Tutankhamen (1333–1323 BCE), whose intact tomb offers a treasure-trove of relics of the history of sport (Decker 1980), gave resplendence and an official festive character to a rowing regatta on the Nile; to prepare for it, the participating soldiers had to submit to training. Tutankhamen expresses his delight that the 'squad of youngsters' achieving their victory here are in good form. The inscription on a ceremonial staff of the king is the oldest evidence of a rowing regatta in all of sport history (Decker and Kurth 1999).

There is a particularly expressive quality in the depiction of a sporting contest between Egyptians and foreigners (Libyans, Asians, and Nubians) which is situated in the mortuary temple of Ramses III (1182/1181–1153/1152 BCE) in Medinet Habu below the window of appearances of the palace, hence in a prominent position (Touny and Wenig 1969: tables 6–11, 16–18; Decker and Herb 1994: L 34, M 9). The meeting, held before spectators, has an international character which comes about through the contests fought with Egypt's neighbours, but does not in any way prefigure the spirit of the modern Olympic Games—it aims to demonstrate Egypt's superiority; the athletes dominate their foreign opponents in sporting contests just as the pharaoh, shown nearby, defeats his enemies. The presence of foreigners among the spectators, appearing to emphasize the international atmosphere, is seen in a different light when this ideological perspective is considered: they are witnesses to the superiority of Egypt and their own feebleness, represented by the sporting defeat of their countrymen in wrestling, which is uniquely documented in the ancient valley of the Nile by the tombs of Beni Hasan from the Middle Kingdom (Wilsdorf 1939), and in stick-fencing. A referee is there to signal that in these (one-sided) contests everything is played according to the rules. The intention of dedicating the contests to the pharaoh also emerges from the speeches of the athletes which allude to the presence of the king (Wilson 1931).

International contacts are also responsible for the surprising find of a wall fresco in a palace of the early Eighteenth Dynasty in the eastern delta (Avaris). It is decorated with the

FIGURE 3.3. Wrestlers, an Egyptian and a Libyan, Medinet Habu, mortuary temple of Ramses III (1183/1182–1152/1151 BCE), first court, south, under window of appearance. Photo: Wolfgang Decker.

bull-jumping motif. The style and technique remove all doubt that it was created by Minoan artists who probably executed the theme, exotic in Egypt, by commission of the king of Knossos as a gift for his Egyptian colleague (Bietak et al. 2007).

The last example, from the sixth year of the reign of Taharka (690–664 BCE), also establishes a close connection of a sporting event with the pharaoh, when the account on the so-called running stele ends with the statement that the runners had performed for His Majesty. Previously it had been mentioned that a group of (probably 250) soldiers had undergone running training in a kind of training camp. At the end of the training process, a race of over 100 km is held, which is interrupted by a break halfway at the turning-point. The time of four hours needed for half the way for the best runners makes us conclude that the time for the whole race was close to the best times in distance running towards the end of the nineteenth century. Both the mention of the running times and the awarding of prizes (of an archaic nature, like a common banquet) are elements which are unique in the sport history of Egypt and are extremely rare for this period anywhere (Altenmüller and Moussa 1981; Decker 1984).

The examples of sporting festivals presented above, which almost always lack evidence of ongoing performance, may be seen as precursors of Greek *agōnes*, as they are sometimes also encountered in other pre-Greek sporting cultures (Decker 2004).

Once the iconographic and written sources have been assembled and the secondary literature explored (Decker 1978; Decker and Förster 2002a; 2002b), a history of sport in Ancient Egypt is highly to be desired. An encyclopaedia could meanwhile present the individual phenomena in a way that is also easily understood by scholars in related areas.

SPORT IN THE ANCIENT NEAR EAST

Mesopotamia

Situated in southern Mesopotamia, the 'land between the rivers' (Euphrates and Tigris), Sumer gives a plethora of evidence for the time of the Third Dynasty of Ur at the end of the third millennium BCE, which R. Rollinger uses as the basis for a major collection of materials relating to sport in the Ancient Near East. The rich source material, literary and archival (and to a lesser extent iconographic), has numerous examples of the key concepts *lirum/lirùm* ('wrestling') and *gešbá* ('running') (Rollinger 1994: 8–46; diverging completely: Vermaak 1994; cf. Rollinger 1994: 35 n.150). The texts from this context suggest that sports events had a firm place in the programme of festivals. Thus in the myth 'The Marriage of the god Mardu' the divine personification of the Mardu nomads appears at the town of Ninab, where he woos the daughter of the city god of Kazallu. The civilized lady is, however, warned about the rough manners of the nomad god Mardu, who during a festival honouring the god Numušda runs rampage among the young men and kills many of them in wrestling contests. The site of the contests, whose participants have apparently attended a kind of 'training camp', is a place (*kisal maḫ* = 'great court') in the temple itself (Rollinger 1994: 18–22).

Interestingly, economic documents from the Ur-III period provide us with a series of references to sporting events as part of monthly festivals, where there is mention of gifts of clothing, bullocks, lambs, beer flour, and emmer grain for wrestlers and athletes, which are to be used to sustain them. The place where the contestants reside is called a 'wrestlers' house' (è- gešbá), while the place of the contests seems to have been the temple court (kisal) (Rollinger 1994: 28–30).

Among the prizes awarded to the wrestlers is a silver ring worth 10 shekels, which is presented to Šulgigalz, son of the musician Alla, by the grand vizier. He is the first athlete identified by name in the Ancient Near East and seems to come from a high social stratum (Rollinger 1994: 30–31).

The sporting contests are held in honour of various divinities, of whom the god Nabû was associated particularly with sprinting (Weidner 1952–1953). At a ritual that was performed in the temple of Ishtar in Mari, where wrestlers, jugglers, and acrobats took part (Blocher 1992), the king was present personally (Rollinger 1994: 32).

The Sumerian royal hymns treat the king as an outstanding athlete, which applies particularly to Shulgi (2030–1983 BCE) (Vermaak 1993), who in Hymn C presents himself as mighty and bursting with strength, with nobody being his equal. (Translation of Hymn C in Vermaak 1993: 16; and Rollinger 1994: 44.) Unlike the Egyptian king, the peerless ruler is permitted by royal dogma to take part in the sporting contest in the 'great court' of the temple, the traditional site for sports in Sumer. His opponents are 'the heroes of the land of Sumer', 'the swift men of Sumer', and also 'the mighty and strong, (all of them) selected from foreign lands'. Did royal participation in the contest, conceivable according to this text, actually take place? This is another question that arises if one compares the text discussed with Hymn A, in which Shulgi boasts of having run from Nippur to Ur and back in one day (320 km altogether) and, moreover, into a thunderstorm on the second stretch (Vermaak 1993: 11–13; sceptically Rollinger 1994: 45–61; uncritically Anderson Lamont 1995). Hymn V also alludes to this race (Frayne 1983) and furthermore mentions a statue of Shulgi as a runner which was erected in Ekur, a custom in which he is followed by Ischmedagan (Rollinger 1994: 51). Depictions of wrestlers on cylindrical seals, votive tablets, and cult steles are found in Mesopotamia for the early dynastic era (c.3000– c.2440) (Eder 1994: 93–97), where the wrestling scenes are associated with a banquet and music, and may thus immediately be recognized as a part of the cultic symposium. Wrestlers and pugilists are also found on cylindrical seals of the Ancient Near East (c.1950–177 BCE); here the figure of the 'athlete warrior' regularly appears as a type (Eder 1994).

The Gilgamesh Epic

In the widely disseminated ancient Babylonian Gilgamesh epic, which in Ancient Near East culture plays a role comparable with the Homeric epics in the Greek world, the hero meets Enkidu in Uruk, a wrestling match immediately ensues, and it obviously ends with Gilgamesh's victory. One may imagine that the opponents grab each other's loincloths, as already worn by the two wrestler figures in the early dynastic wrestling group from the Nintu temple in Tutub/Hafaği (Crowther 2007: 17, fig. 2.2). Wrestling may be understood as part of hospitality ceremonies. The walls trembled and the doorposts were smashed in the violent encounter of the two heroes (Rollinger 1994: 16–18).

In the Nineveh version (from the library of the Assyrian king Assurbanipal, 668–627 BCE) there is surprisingly a scene of stickball (pukku = ball, mikkû = bat), which, owing to the Sumerian precursor of this version, may be assumed to be a sport practised in Mesopotamia as early as the second half of the third millennium BCE. It is a remarkable fact that this ball game, in which Gilgamesh naturally plays a dominant role, may be shown to belong to this early period. The hero tyrannizes the whole city of Uruk with his unbridled urge to play, and triumphs over the opposing team composed of orphaned sons, after a game lasting all day. The captain of the victorious team, in this case Gilgamesh, is carried piggyback (in a modern-looking fashion of informally honouring the victor). Women bring food and drink on to the playing field for the players (Rollinger 2006).

It is worth noting the fact that in the short Sumerian epic 'The Death of Gilgamesh' there is a passage in which sporting contests are mentioned in connection with funeral ceremonies, where a semi-circular grandstand holds the spectators (Rollinger 1994: 36–40). Disconnected from the direct context of funeral rituals, but with a hint at their origin through the mention of the month of *Abu*, contests of this kind were still known in Seleucid times, as a late cuneiform source attests (Rollinger 1994: 39, with n. 171).

Finally, the Gilgamesh epic also attests to the skill of diving and swimming, which occasionally appears in other Ancient Near Eastern sources (Rollinger 2000).

Hittites

At the beginning of the second millennium BCE the Hittites appear in Anatolia and gradually develop into the great power that could even defy mighty Egypt in the battle of Kadesh (fifth year of Ramses II = 1286 BCE), as is attested by the subsequent peace treaty which was based on notions of equality (Edel 1997). Its mere existence corrects the version, widespread in Egypt, in which the pharaoh is victorious in battle and the opposing commander nearly drowns in the Orontes river. They were the only Indo-Europeans to use cuneiform, as this form of writing was found among their neighbours on all sides in the Ancient Near East. For reasons not yet clear, their power declined around 1200 BCE, around the same time as the movements of the 'Sea Peoples' in the eastern Aegean. In their capital city Ḫattusha (150 km east of Ankara) a state archive of more than 30,000 clay tablets was discovered, which have been readable since 1915 when F. Hrozny rediscovered their language, yet it has been researched only to a small extent for what it says about sport.

The gem of Hittite sport culture (Haas 2001) is a handbook transmitted under the name of 'Kikkuli, horse-trainer from the land of Mitanni', which was written as early as the fifteenth century BCE and is preserved in a copy from the thirteenth century BCE on four clay tablets. The horse-training text is preserved without gaps for a period of 184 consecutive days, before it breaks off (presumably shortly before it ends) (Kammenhuber 1961). Despite very precise daily entries concerning various running distances and gaits, varying doses of feed and drink as well as ways of caring such as dry rubbing, salves, and plunging in water, together with the housing of the animals (mostly in a stable), the precise purpose of the training cannot be determined, as its aim is never mentioned *expressis verbis*. We must however assume that the chariot horses were not trained for chariot-races (as claimed by Potratz 1938) but for military use (which theoretically would not exclude use in racing as a spin-off activity). This is supported by the season (autumn and winter) which could have been chosen to prepare for the war season which began in spring, but also by the beginning of training at varying times of day and night, which would correspond to unforeseeable irregularity of military necessity. While Kammenhuber (1961) advocates stamina and fitness training as the main object, Starke (1995) has supported technique training, which is mainly directed at the ability of a pair of horses to perform rapid changes in direction and about-turns. The most recent editors of the tract (Raulwing and Meyer 2004) once more tend to Kammerhuber's idea, though this implies a distance of 150 km of trotting and 21 km of galloping a day, where their conversion of Hittite measures of length are clearly far too high. The Kikkuli text, which is not unique in its genre in the Ancient Near East (Ebeling 1951; Marzahn 2007), has a unique position in the history of sport: it is the oldest training handbook in world history which has as a general aim the improvement in performance, of whatever kind (in this case animal performance).

The collection of passages relevant to various sporting disciplines of the Hittite written tradition has been consolidated by J. Puhvel (1988) into the thesis that here we have palpable precursors of the world of Homeric sport. Alongside the astonishing variety of named sports (running, archery (Haas 1989), armed combat, boxing, wrestling, stone-heaving, and horse-racing; Hutter-Braunsar 2012), the connection of contests with festivals (Haas 1989; Carter 1988; Decker 2004: 18–21), and the awarding of prizes may also have led him to this conclusion. In a race of the king's bodyguards at the spring festival the victor holds the halter (Hutter-Braunsar 2008: 27–28, with n. 25; as opposed to Ehelolf 1925, who is thinking of the office of the royal bridle-holder), while the victor in another contest held on the occasion of the KI.LAM festival and the second place getter are both given a garment. According to an earlier version, the victor's prize is a mina of silver and two loaves from the hand of the king (Hutter-Braunsar 2008: 26–27). A ritual between men from Hatti armed with bronze weapons and men from Maša who are equipped only with canes is evidence of a kind of team combat among the Hittites, though the outcome was predetermined (Ehelolf 1925; Lesky 1926; Hutter-Braunsar 2008: 31–32).

A depiction of bull-leaping, which is attested not only in Minoan Crete but in many cultures of the Ancient World (Decker 2003), has been recently found in territory where Hittite culture was established (Sipahi 2000; 2001). The iconographic context suggests that the acrobatic leap over the bull took place with musical accompaniment and in the presence of women.

It is worth mentioning that sport also appears as a motif in Hittite literature. In a fragment from an epic, the (Hurrite) king Gurpazanzah defeats sixty kings and seventy heroes in archery at a banquet after a hunt in Akkad (Haas 1989: 38–39).

Persia

We have no direct sources for ancient Iranian sport, but we are informed about ancient Persian sport culture indirectly by Greek authors and later Persian literature, which is in the continuity of older traditions, as is the *Shahname* (Book of Kings). The founder of the Persian empire, Cyrus the Great (559–529 BCE), was designated as the ideal of a king by his Greek admirer Xenophon in the mirror for princes, *Cyropaedia*, as the ideal of a king. Herodotus's statement (1.136) that the Persians 'instruct boys from fifteen to twenty years of age ... [in] riding and archery and telling the truth' has become a classic notion in our conception of Iranian education. The image of the *pahlawan* ('hero') is cultivated particularly in the epic poem *Shahnameh* by Ferdowsi (939–1020 CE). His sporting prowess is prominent amongst his knightly skills, and it is particularly developed in Rustam (Knauth 1976).

There is already mention in the *Cyropaedia* of a horse-race that Cyrus holds (Xenophon, *Cyr.* 8.3.24–36), a custom which is also reported by Xerxes I (486–465 BCE), whose horses by far outdo those of the Greeks in speed (Hdt., 8.196). The art of riding is also the foundation of polo (in literature also played by young girls at court) (Knauth 1976: 44–48). Polo posts even today adorn the central *Meidan Shah* ('Royal Square') in Isfahan. It is the 'favourite and national sport of Iranian nobles' (Knauth 1976: 44), and not infrequently a participating king suffered mortal injuries in this game. It is also likely that charioteering was practised in ancient Iran (Knauth 1976: 53). Archery also has a dominant position among Persian disciplines. There is an instructive report of the Sassanid king Shapur I (241–272 CE) near Persepolis who boasts a shot that may have broken a record for distance (Knauth 1976: 56), as King Argishti of Urartu did almost 1,000 years earlier when he shot an arrow a distance of 476 metres (Haas 1989: 40). In the epic, shields and armour are penetrated by arrows, which recalls the magisterial shot by Odysseus through the 12 axes (Hom. *Od.* 21.404ff.) and ultimately the skills of the Egyptian kings of the New Kingdom (Knauth 1976: 57). Wrestling, too, is among the preferred disciplines; it is developed as a motif in literature, including wrestling on horseback (Knauth 1976: 63–65). The king was excluded from this immediate, man-to-man test of strength.

It cannot be historically established when the institution of the *surchane* ('house of strength') appeared. Even today it is a characteristic of Persian physical culture (*mutatis mutandis* similar to the Greek *gymnasion*) (Rochard 2000; Yaldai 2005). Yet there can be no doubt that it goes back to ancient pre-Islamic models, if one compares them with pictures from the Ancient Near East, in which sportsmen are accompanied by instruments (Eder 1994: 7) similar to those that still provide background music for exercises in the houses of strength in Persia.

References

Altenmüller, H. and A. M. Moussa. 1981. 'Die Inschriften auf der Taharkastele von der Dahschurstraße.' *Studien zur Altägyptischen Kultur* 9: 57–84.

Anderson Lamont, D. 1995. 'Running Phenomena in Ancient Sumer.' *Journal of Sport History* 22: 207–215.

Bietak, M., N. Marinatos, C. Palivou, and A. Brysbaert. 2007. *Taureador Scenes in Tell el-Dabca (Avaris) and Knossos.* Vienna.

Blocher, F. 1992. 'Gaukler im Alten Orient.' In *Außenseiter und Randgruppen. Beiträge zu einer Sozialgeschichte des alten Orients: Drittes Konstanzer Altorientalisches Symposion, 5.–8. Juni 1989.* 79–111. V. Haas, ed. Konstanz.

Burkert, W. 1973. 'Von Amenophis II. zur Bogenprobe des Odysseus.' *Grazer Beiträge* 1: 69–78.

Cannuyer, C. 2002. 'À propos de l'expression égyptienne śḥmḫ-ib "se divertir".' *Acta Orientalia Belgica* 16: 123–134.

Carter, C. 1988. 'Athletic Contests in Hittite Religious Festivals.' *Journal of Near Eastern Studies* 47: 185–187.

Crowther, N. B. 2007. *Sport in Ancient Times.* Westport.

Decker, W. 1971. *Die physische Leistung Pharaos.* Cologne.

Decker, W. 1975. *Quellentexte zu Sport und Körperkultur im alten Ägypten*. St. Augustin.

Decker, W. 1977. 'Zur Bogenprobe des Odysseus.' *Kölner Beiträge zur Sportwissenschaft. Jahrbuch der Deutschen Sporthochschule Köln* 6: 149–155.

Decker, W. 1978. *Annotierte Bibliographie zum Sport im alten Ägypten*. St. Augustin.

Decker, W. 1980. 'Tutanchamun und der Sport im Alten Ägypten.' *Kölner Beiträge zur Sportwissenschaft. Jahrbuch der Deutschen Sporthochschule Köln* 8/9: 77–112.

Decker, W. 1984. 'Die Lauf-Stele des Königs Taharka.' *Kölner Beiträge zur Sportwissenschaft. Jahrbuch der Deutschen Sporthochschule Köln* 13: 7–37.

Decker, W. 1987. *Spiel und Sport im Alten Ägypten*. Munich.

Decker, W. 1990. 'The Record of the Ritual: The Athletic Records of Ancient Egypt.' In *Ritual and Record: Sports Records and Quantification in Pre-Modern Societies*. 21–30. J. M. Carter and A. Krüger, eds. New York.

Decker, W. 1992. *Sports and Games of Ancient Egypt*. A. Guttmann, trans. New Haven.

Decker, W. 2000. 'Sport und Fest im Alten Ägypten.' In *Ideologie—Sport—Außenseiter. Aktuelle Aspekte einer Beschäftigung mit der antiken Gesellschaft*. 111–145. C. Ulf, ed. Innsbruck.

Decker, W. 2003. 'Zum Stand der Erforschung des "Stierspiels" in der Alten Welt.' In *Altertumswissenschaften im Dialog: Festschrift für Wolfgang Nagel zur Vollendung seines 80. Lebensjahres*. 31–79. R. Dittmann, C. Eder, and B. Jacobs, eds. Münster.

Decker, W. 2004. 'Vorformen griechischer Agone in der Alten Welt.' *Nikephoros* 17: 9–25.

Decker, W. 2006. *Pharao und Sport*. Mainz.

Decker, W. and F. Förster. 2002a. *Annotierte Bibliographie zum Sport im Alten Ägypten II: 1978–2000 nebst Nachträgen aus früheren Jahren und unter Einbeziehung der Nachbarkulturen*. Hildesheim.

Decker, W. and F. Förster. 2002b. 'Annotierte Bibliographie zum Sport im Alten Ägypten für die Jahre 2001 und 2002 (nebst Nachträgen aus früheren Jahren).' *Nikephoros* 15: 197–244.

Decker, W. and F. Förster. 2011. 'Sahures trainierte Truppe. Sporthistorische Bemerkungen zu einem Relief aus der Pyramidenanlage des ägyptischen König Sahure (2496–2483 v. Chr.).' *Nikephoros* 24: 17–70.

Decker, W. and Herb, M. 1994. *Bildatlas zum Sport im Alten Ägypten. Corpus der bildlichen Quellen zu Leibesübungen, Spiel, Jagd, Tanz und verwandten Themen*. 2 vols. Leiden.

Decker, W. and J. Klauck. 1974. 'Königliche Bogenschießleistungen in der 18. ägyptischen Dynastie. Historische Dokumente und Aspekte für eine experimentelle Überprüfung.' *Kölner Beiträge zur Sportwissenschaft. Jahrbuch der Deutschen Sporthochschule Köln* 3: 23–55.

Decker, W. and D. Kurth. 1999. 'Eine Ruderregatta zur Zeit des Tutanchamun.' *Nikephoros* 12: 19–31.

Der Manuelian, P. 1987. *Studies in the Reign of Amenophis II*. Hildesheim.

Ebeling, E. 1951. *Bruchstücke einer mittelassyrischen Vorschriftensammlung für die Akklimatisierung und Trainierung von Wagenpferden*. Berlin.

Edel, E. 1997. *Der Vertrag zwischen Ramses II. von Ägypten und Ḫattušili III. von Ḫatti*. Berlin.

Eder, C. 1994. 'Kampfsport in der Siegelkunst der Altlevante.' *Nikephoros* 7: 83–120.

Ehelolf, H. 1925. 'Wettlauf und szenisches Spiel im hethitischen Ritual.' *Sitzungsberichte der Preußischen Akademie der Wissenschaften, Philosophisch-historische Klasse*: 267–272.

El Awady, T. 2009. *Sahure—The Pyramid Causeway: History and Decoration Program in the Old Kingdom*. Prague.

Frayne, D. R. 1983. 'Šulgi, the Runner.' *Journal of the American Oriental Society*, 103: 739–748.

Friedman, F. D. 1995. 'The Underground Relief Panels of King Djoser at the Step Pyramid Complex.' *Journal of the American Research Center of Egypt* 32: 1–42.

Haas, V. 1989. 'Kompositbogen und Bogenschießen als Wettkampf im Alten Orient.' *Nikephoros* 2: 27–42.

Haas, V. 2001. 'Sport IV. Alter Orient V. Hethiter', in *Der Neue Pauly. Enzyklopädie der Antike*, vol. 11. 840–842. H. Cancik and H. Schneider, eds. Stuttgart.

Hayes, W. C. 1973. 'The Sporting Tradition.' In *The Cambridge Ancient History*, 3rd edn, vol. II. 333–338. I. E. S. Edwards, C. J. Gadd, N. G. L. Hammond, and E. Sollberger, eds. Cambridge.

Herold, A. 1999. *Streitwagentechnologie in der Ramses-Stadt. Bronze an Pferd und Wagen*. Mainz.

Hofmann, U. 1989. 'Fuhrwesen und Pferdehaltung im Alten Ägypten.' Doctoral dissertation, Rheinischen Friedrich-Wilhelms-Universität, Bonn.

Hornung, E. and E. Staehelin. 1974. *Studien zum Sedfest*. Genf.

Hornung, E. and E. Staehelin. 2006 *Neue Studien zum Sedfest*. Basel.

Hutter-Braunsar, S. 2008. 'Sport bei den Hethitern.' In *Antike Lebenswelten: Konstanz—Wandel—Wirkungsmacht. Festschrift für Ingomar Weiler zum 70. Geburtstag*. 25–37. P. Mauritsch, W. Petermandl, R. Rollinger, and C. Ulf, eds. Wiesbaden.

Hutter-Braunsar, S. 2012. 'Sports in Hittite Anatolia.' In *Nikephoros. Special Issue 2012: Youth—Sport—Olympic Games*. 35–40. W. Petermandl and C. Ulf, eds. Hildesheim.

Kammenhuber, A. 1961. *Hippologia Hethitica*. Wiesbaden.

Klug, A. 2002. *Königliche Stelen in der Zeit von Ahmose bis Amenophis III*. Turnhout.

Knauth, W. 1976. 'Die sportlichen Qualifikationen der altiranischen Fürsten.' *Stadion* 2: 1–89.

Lesky, A. 1926. 'Ein ritueller Scheinkampf bei den Hethitern.' *Archiv für Religionswissenschaft* 24: 73–82.

Littauer, M. A. and J. H. Crouwel. 1985. *Chariots and Related Equipment from the Tomb of Tut'ankhamūn*. Oxford.

Marzahn, J. 2007. 'Pferdetraining nach Keilschrifttexten.' In *Pferdestärken: Das Pferd bewegt die Menschheit*. 45–49. A. Wieczorek and M. Tellenbach, eds. Mannheim.

McLeod, W. E. 1970. *Composite Bows from the Tomb of Tut'ankhamūn*. Oxford.

Potratz, J. 1938. 'Der Pferdetext aus dem Keilschriftarchiv von Boghazköi.' Dissertation. Leipzig.

Puhvel, J. 1988. 'Hittite Athletics as Prefigurations of Greek Games.' In *The Archaeology of the Olympics: The Olympics and other Festivals in Antiquity*. 26–31. W. Raschke, ed. Madison, WI.

Raulwing, P. and Meyer, H. 2004. 'Der Kikkuli-Text. Hippologische und methodenkritische Überlegungen zum Training von Streitwagenpferden im Alten Orient.' In *Rad und Wagen: Der Ursprung einer Innovation. Wagen im Vorderen Orient und Europa*. 491–506. S. Burmeister, ed. S. Mainz.

Rochard, P. 2000. 'Le sport antique des zurkhâne de Téhéran: Forme et significations de la pratique contemporaine.' Dissertation, Université de Provence, Aix-en-Provence.

Rollinger, R. 1994. 'Aspekte des Sports im Alten Sumer.' *Nikephoros* 7: 7–64.

Rollinger, R. 2000. 'Schwimmen und Nichtschwimmen im Alten Orient.' In *Ideologie –Sport—Außenseiter. Aktuelle Aspekte einer Beschäftigung mit der antiken Gesellschaft*. 147–165. C. Ulf, ed. Innsbruck.

Rollinger, R. 2006. 'Gilgamesch als "Sportler", oder: *pukku* und *mikkû* als Sportgeräte des Helden von Uruk.' *Nikephoros* 19: 9–44.

Rollinger, R. 2011. 'Sport und Spiel.' *Reallexikon der Assyriologie* 12: 235–252.

Sipahi, T. 2000. 'Eine althethitische Reliefvase vom Hüseyindede Tepesi.' *Istanbuler Mitteilungen* 50: 63–85.

Sipahi, T. 2001. 'New Evidence from Anatolia Regarding Bull-leaping Scenes in the Art of the Aegean and the Near East.' *Anatolica* 27: 107–125.

Starke, F. 1995. *Ausbildung und Training von Streitwagenpferden: Eine hippologisch orientierte Interpretation des Kikkuli-Textes*. Wiesbaden.

Touny, A. D. and S. Wenig. 1969. *Der Sport im alten Ägypten*. Leipzig.

Vermaak, P. S. 1993. 'Šulgi as Sportsman in the Sumerian Self-laudatory Hymns.' *Nikephoros* 6: 7–21.

Vermaak, P. S. 1994. 'The Sumerian *GEŠPÚ-LIRÙM-MA*'. *Nikephoros* 7: 65–82.

Weidner, E. 1952–1953. 'Nabû, der (Gott) des Schnellaufens.' *Archiv für Orientforschung* 16: 66.

Wiedemann, D. 1975. 'Der Sinn des Laufes im alten Ägypten.' Dissertation, Vienna.

Wilsdorf, H. 1939. *Ringkampf im alten Ägypten*. Würzburg.

Wilson, J. A. 1931. 'Ceremonial Games in the New Kingdom.' *Journal of Egyptian Archaeology* 17: 211–220.

Yalçin, Ü., C. Pulak, and R. Slotta. 2005. *Das Schiff von Ulu Burun: Welthandel vor 3000 Jahren. Katalog der Ausstellung des Deutschen Bergbau-Museums Bochum vom 15. Juli 2005 bis 16. Juli 2006*. Bochum.

Yaldai, S. 2005. 'Der altiranische Sport im Surchane: Religiös-mystische Hintergründe seiner Entstehung'. *Nikephoros* 18: 241–256.

CHAPTER 4

....

SPORT AND SPECTACLE IN THE GREEK BRONZE AGE

....

JOHN G. YOUNGER

INTRODUCTION: SOCIAL AND LITERARY BACKGROUND

....

THIS study presents archaeological and literary evidence for sports, spectacles, and games in Minoan Crete and on the Mycenaean mainland in the Aegean Bronze Age (roughly 3000–1000 BCE: Ridington 1935; Putnam 1967; Laser 1987; Decker 1995). The later games at Olympia provide a useful framework (cf. Mouratidis 1989). The historian Pausanias cites games held sporadically from mythological times until their reorganization in 776 BCE (5.8–9; cf. Mouratidis 1983), after which they were held continuously until 393 CE. The first event was a foot-race of one Olympic stade (approximately 600 ft). Then the *diaulos* (two stades) was added in 724 BCE, the *dolichos* (18–24 stades; 720), wrestling and the *pentathlon* (wrestling, short foot-race, long jump, and javelin- and discus-throwing; 708), boxing (688), chariot-racing (680), and the pankration (full contact fighting) and horse-racing (648). These events had also been sporadically practised before the reorganization; afterward, new games were also instituted, like boys' foot-races and wrestling (628) and boxing (616).

In many of these events, the male athletes contested nude. Occasional public male nudity was a distinctively Greek trait (cf. Luc. *Anach.* 36–37). To Thucydides, nudity was instituted at the Olympic games 'recently', but other authors cite it as early as 720 when the athlete Orsippos of Megara dropped his loincloth (*IG* 7.52; cf. Paus. 1.44.1; Sweet 1985; Papalas 1991; McDonnell 1992).

Women also had a role at the Olympic games. The priestess of Demeter Clyméné could watch the games from her throne (still *in situ* in the stadium), and unmarried women may also have watched (Paus. 5.6.7, 6.7.2; cf. Pind. *P.* 9). Since, from mythological days, the horse owners won horse- and chariot-races (Paus. 5.8.3), women could enter their horses and win, as did Cyniska of Sparta (396 and 392), Belistiche of Macedon (286), and others. There was also a separate athletic event for women at Olympia, the Heraia games, a shorter foot-race in the stadium perhaps taking place just before the men's games (Paus. 5.16.2–3; Scanlon 2002: 98–120; Serwint 1993).

Panhellenic games had several purposes: they showcased athletes and provided a peaceful venue for competition, and the festival-like atmosphere provided entertainment and opportunities for socializing, conducting politics and business (cf. German 2007), and contracting marriages (Instone 1990). Cleisthenes of Sikyon announced the eligibility of his daughter Agariste at the Olympic games *c.*576.

Local games, especially those focusing on adolescent contestants, often marked age grades. Foot-races again were important (cf. Plat. *Laws* 833c–834d). Young females ran foot-races in the Heraia games, in honour of Dionysos Colonatas at Sparta, and at the Arkteia for Artemis in Attica. Foot-races were also common for young men. At Sparta, boys ran the *staphylodrómos* (running with grapes) during the festival of Apollo Carneus (Paus. 3.14.6); compare the Oschophoria at Athens. In Crete, the verb *ekdromeín*, 'to complete the race course', meant 'to become a citizen'.

Homer (late eighth century BCE) also describes early sports. *Odyssey* book 8 briefly mentions games among the Phaiacians (boxing, wrestling, foot-races, and hurling a lump of iron [*sólos*], as well as singing and dancing). The *Iliad* describes the funeral games for Patroklos in detail: chariot-racing, boxing, wrestling, foot-races, spear-throwing to wound, *sólos*-hurling, archery, and spear-throwing for distance. Prizes included, for the winners, skilled women worth several oxen, mares, fat oxen, tripod cauldrons, silver mixing bowls, and gold talents—losers got two-handled bowls. For archery (the target is both a leashed dove and the leash), there are special prizes, double and single axes.

Such funeral games were common. For instance, Hesiod (contemporary with Homer) won a singing contest at the funeral games for Amphidamas of Chalcis (*Op.* 655–660). And in front of the Dipylon Gate in Athens, the road (*drómos*) to the Academy widens to accommodate the crowds attending the funeral games for those buried in the public cemetery; these included foot-races, and horse- and chariot-races from the Academy to the Dipylon, a distance of some six stades (Paus. 1.30.2; Ar. *Ran.* 129; Knigge 1988: 158).

THE ARCHAEOLOGICAL EVIDENCE

Venues and Prizes

Spectator Areas

Minoan palaces consist of buildings that surround a large, central, rectangular court about a quarter to a third of a stade long. Malia's central court is surrounded by columns and pillars, in between which are cuttings for wooden barricades. We can imagine people watching bull-leaping (see section below on Bull-Sports) from behind the barricades and in the upper balconies supported by the colonnade.

More formal are the theatral areas to the north-west of the palaces. At Phaistos, nine broad steps front the West Court. At Knossos (*PM* II 578–587), two sets of steps intersect at right angles with a platform between, and these look down the long, paved Royal Road (total length, one stade). Excavations in 1971 (*AR* 1972–73: 26–28) revealed a long wall on the south side of the west end of the road that could have supported bleachers. The Royal Road, therefore, may have been a *drómos* for races.

Prizes

Skilled women, given out as prizes at the Patroklos games, were also a concern of the Minoan administration, whose clay tablets, written in Mycenaean Greek (Linear B), distinguish between newly and already trained women (KN Ak 781, 783). The tablets also mention tripod cauldrons (PY Ta 641) and oxen to be fattened (PY Cn 418). And, for the losers, a Mycenaean pictorial *krater* fragment (*MycPictVP* XI.66; cf. III.21/22) depicts a two-handled bowl on the ground.

Events Involving Only People

Foot-Races

Mycenaean pictorial vases, mostly *kraters*, were painted in the thirteenth and twelfth century and many have been found at tombs where they were smashed after a feast (Wright 2004: 8–9; Steele 2004).

More interesting is the contemporary gold ring from the sanctuary of Hermes and Aphrodite at Syme in south Crete (Fig. 4.1; Lembessi et al. 2004). We see (right to left on the ring) a man, a male runner, and a woman in court dress, all on a pavement (*drómos*?). The

FIGURE 4.1. 'Runner' ring from Syme, the Sanctuary of Hermes and Aphrodite (fifteenth century BCE; Lembessi et al. 2004). By permission of the excavators.

runner is in an energetic pose: legs wide apart and off the ground, head tilted back, arms flung out. Above his waist we see the top of a belt, and against his far thigh the edge of a loincloth. The woman raises her arms as if in encouragement. The man wears a hide skirt common in processions (cf. *CMS* II 6.9–11), and he carries an object not well understood ('Snake Frame'? *phórminx*, a type of lyre?). The occasion in any case seems religious—compare Pharaoh's run at the Heb Sed ceremony (e.g. Decker and Herb 1994: A47; Decker, Ch. 3, this volume).

Boxing

Boxing is also depicted on pictorial *kraters*: *MycPictVP* V.29 and 32A show two men facing each other, legs apart, arms out for sparring. A unique depiction occurs on V.14: a belt around the waist of two men forces them to fight at close quarters.

From Akrotiri, Thera, comes a late seventeenth-century fresco (Immerwahr 1989: 185–186 AK 4) that presents two life-size boxing boys, ages 6–10 (Chapin 2007). From their distinctive hairstyle we know they are in transition to adolescence. They both wear a belt, a loincloth, and a glove on one hand only (cf. terracotta figurines from Kophinas: Rethemiotakis 2001: 126–127 figs. 137, 138). The left boy may be the intended victor; he is taller and wears more jewellery (Marinatos 1984: 109–111).

Contemporary with the Boxing Boys fresco is a fragmentary stone funnel (*rhyton*) from Ayia Triada in south Crete (Fig. 4.2; Koehl 2006: 164–166, frontispiece, fig. 29). At the top, zone 1 presents pairs of boxers, zone 2 bull-leapers, zone 3 more boxers, and zone 4 wrestlers. The boxers wear belts with a backflap and penis sheath, tall boots, gloves, necklaces, and an elaborate helmet. This uniform is more protective than that of the Boxing Boys. Perhaps we are seeing a Minoan pankration.

Wrestling

The Boxer Rhyton also appears to depict pairs of wrestlers, although the combatants are not actually shown wrestling. Instead, the left figure stands aggressively, while the right figure lies supine on the ground, feet in the air to parry another attack. Life-size plaster relief frescoes from Knossos may depict other wrestlers, especially the fragment showing a man's torso with an opponent's thumb against his chest (*PM* III 497–504, fig. 342A).

Discus

Homer's hurled *sólos* has not been identified in the archaeological record. Mythology remembers similar throws of a discus from before the Trojan War, but only when it kills: Perseus kills his grandfather Akrisios with a discus, and Peleus and Telamon kill their half-brother Phokos. Stone-casting is known archaeologically from the sixth century (Crowther 2007). Bubon threw a massive stone (315 lbs) over his head at Olympia (*SIG* 3.1071), while Eumastos budged an even heavier stone on Thera (1056 lbs; *IG* 12.3.449).

Dance

In the *Iliad*, the shield of Achilles (*Il*. 18.590–605) relates how youths and girls as valuable as cattle (cf. 23.730) hold each other by the wrist and dance on a dancing-floor like the one

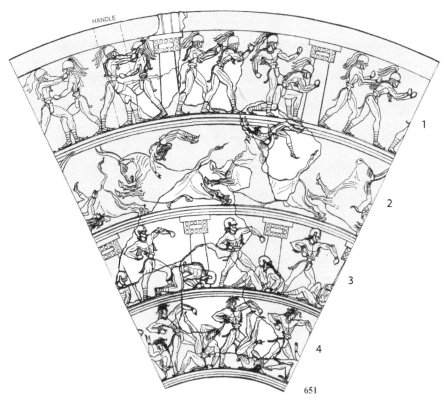

FIGURE 4.2. The Boxer Rhyton from Ayia Triada (*c*.1500 BCE). Drawing adapted from R. Koehl 2006, fig. 29 by Ray Porter, with permission.

Daidalos created for Ariadne at Knossos (cf. the theatral area there). They run lightly in circles or in rows; spectators look on as two acrobats whirl in the air. During the festivities of the Phaiacians (*Od.* 8.260–264, 370–380), boys dance while Demodokos sings, and then two youths toss a purple ball into the air and leap up to catch it while spectators beat time.

There are few sure representations of Bronze Age dance. From Knossos, the 'Dance in the Grove' fresco shows at least ten women dancing freely across a court (the West Court?); their arms make expressive gestures (Immerwahr 1989: 173 Kn 16). A similar group of women move across the Tylissos fresco (Immerwahr 1989: 184 Ty no. 1), while men may dance and sing on a fresco from Ayia Irini, Kea (Immerwahr 1989: 189 A.I. 4 pl. 33). Another Knossos fresco preserves a woman from the chest up; her flung-out arms and flying hair testify to a whirling movement (Immerwahr 1989: 175 Kn 24).

Circle dances are depicted in two terracotta groups. From the Kamilari *tholos*, four women dance (HMp 15073; Rethemiotakis 2001: 112–113 fig. 126), placing their hands on each other's shoulders and moving on a circular platform. Another terracotta group from Palaikastro (HM 2634/3903; Bosanquet and Dawkins 1923: 88 fig. 71; Younger 1998: 75) presents three women (originally six?) dancing in a circle; a separate figure (probably a man) plays the lyre.

Dance depictions are fairly common in Late Geometric vase-painting (late eighth century). Women and men usually dance separately, holding hands or wrists, while a lyre-player accompanies them. The interior of a bowl in Athens (NMA 874; Sweeney et al. 1987: 80–1) depicts several lines of dancers, each headed by a lyre-player. One line, however, consists of four men and three women holding hands. Between each figure is a column of chevrons and above the joined hands there is another column of chevrons, representing the sprig held by dancing pairs. A late eighteenth-century seal impression from Phaistos (*CMS* II 5.324) carries a man and a woman, the man moving towards her, their hands possibly touching; and above their hands is a vertical line, perhaps another sprig—are they dancing?

Acrobats

Acrobats (Deonna 1953) are mentioned in both Homeric dance passages. Rare Cycladic marble figurines (*c*.2300) have a small figure standing on the head of a larger figure or two figures carrying a third between them (Getz-Preziosi 1987: pl. 1); these may be acrobats, but none comes from an excavated context. Four sealstones (*c*.1700– *c*.1500) depict acrobats. Two of these (*CMS* I 131, VI 184) carry a pair of acrobats executing handstands, back to back (the men on the second seal wear plumes on their head); since large stemmed flowers grow between the acrobats, they are outside. Two other seals carry a single acrobat in the arch-position (body supine and curved up, hands and feet on the ground; *CMS* I Supp. 169a, III 166a); the first seal has the acrobat arched around a *lotos* flower (therefore also outside), while the second seal shows the acrobat with a backlock or plume on his head. A Minoanizing fresco from Tel el Dab'a in the eastern Nile delta (late fifteenth century? Bietak et al. 2007: 149–150 fig. 138) depicts another acrobat with a lily on his head executing an arch position; he is also outside, next to a palm tree.

A gold disk from Malia was found with a sword and its ivory pommel (*c*.1700; Chapouthier 1938; Pelon 1985). The disk is decorated with an arched male acrobat in a short skirt. Since the disk decorated the underside of the sword's pommel, the acrobat is arched literally around the sword.

The vigorous Phaiacian dance includes a ball-game. On the beach, princess Nausicaa plays ball with her handmaidens (*Od.* 6.100–102, 115–117). Archaeologically, however, there is scant evidence for Aegean ball-games: two seals (*CMS* VIII 147, IX 146) depict a man juggling balls next to a bull—perhaps juggling occurred during bull-games.

Music

There are no depictions of musical contests until the Classical period (West 1992; Bundrick 2005). In the Bronze Age (Younger 1998) musical performances were depicted in a wide variety of media and actual instruments have survived. The harp was preferred until about 1700, replaced by the lyre. A pair of lyre-players is attested on a Linear B tablet from Thebes (Av 106), and Homer's Demodokos plays the concert lyre (*phórminx*). In Homer the sound of the *phórminx* rushes, probably because the instrument was mostly strummed. The other major instrument is the double oboe (*aúlos*), whose raucous sound suited animal sacrifices and military processions. There are few depictions of singing. For most of antiquity choral singing was in octaves, but on the Harvester Vase (sixteenth century) the three singers stretch out their throats at different angles, as if they were singing parts. Homer and other early authors prefer a clear and thin singing voice, like that in the 'Old European' style (nasal with the throat stretched). In the Bronze Age and in Homer only men sing and play musical instruments.

Archery

We first see depictions of men with bows on sealstones dating to about 1700 (e.g. *CMS* III 163, VIII 12 with hound). Archery contests may be implied on a Mycenaean *krater* (*MycPictVP* V.28B: two men with bows follow two runners). The most notable archery contests are those in Homer: the funeral games for Patroklos (*Il.* 23.850–883) and the archery contest in the *Odyssey* (19.572–580, and 21). The latter has two goals, to string Odysseus's bow (only he can do it) and to use it to shoot through twelve bronze axes set upright in the earth. Exactly how, in reality, this feat might have been accomplished has exercised scholars. Brain and Skinner (1978) suggest axes with rings at the end of their handles (cleavers, not axes, have such handles [NMA 443, 445, 447 from Mycenae ShGr IV]); Wace and Stubbings (1962: 534–535 fig. 62) suggest axes laid so low in the ground as to be impossible to shoot through their handle sockets; Myres (1948) suggests shooting through fenestrated axes—one is extant (from the Vapheio *tholos*; *PM* IV 413–419) and others appear on sealstones (e.g. *CMS* I 225, II 3.98, II 8.258). But the whole contest is a fantasy about power: consider pharaohs Thutmose III and Amenhotep II, who reportedly shot several arrows at once through a row of thick copper ingots spreading over some 30 feet (Pritchard 1969: 243–244; Decker, Ch. 3, this volume; also depicted on reliefs from Karnak and Giza and on scarabs).

A new thirteenth-century fresco fragment from Pylos shows a woman archer (Brecoulaki et al. 2008), and others appear on a sealstone (*CMS* XI 26) and a gold ring (*CMS* XI 29), both dating to the fifteenth century.

Board-Games

'Pavement'-games are found everywhere throughout the ancient world and in all periods, usually scratched on stone steps and floors; these seem to be simple board-games like checkers or tic-tac-toe (Bell 2007; Bell and Roueché 2007).

More sophisticated games arose from the East, like *go* from China and chess from India, and, from Egypt, *mehen* (with a spiral game-board like a 'coiled' snake) and *senet*; these had a long life (Laser 1987: 126–184; Purcell 2007; Rieche 2007). The rectangular *senet*-board is divided into three rows of ten squares each. The two players sit opposite each other and move their pieces onto the end of one of the outside rows. Two-sided sticks coloured white on one side and black on the other were thrown to determine moves (for example, with two sticks, both white up = 1 point; white and black = 2 points, both black = 3 points). According to the throws, the players move their pieces down the squares of the outside row, back up the middle row, and back down the other outside row, all the while jumping on or over (and removing) their opponent's pieces.

Board-games also existed in Bronze Age Greece (Hillbom 2005). An early seal (*c.*2000) comes from Ayia Triada (*CMS* II 1.64a); one side depicts what looks like a *senet*-board and pieces. A slightly later seal (*CMS* VI 45a) portrays a seated man apparently moving a large piece on a game-board table. And a miniature fresco at Knossos may show boys playing a pavement-game (Immerwahr 1989: 174 Kn 19).

An elaborate game-board (*c.*1600) with four ivory pieces comes from Knossos (Fig. 4.3; *PM* I 470–486, figs. 338–340, 342, colour pl. V). Pieces were probably moved (right to left in the photo) from the bottom of the game-board through safe side-squares to the central four squares where pieces could be taken; a throw of three might have been necessary to cross a 'bridge' in order to contest again in a final 'citadel' of four squares (Brumbaugh 1975; Hillbom 2005: 201–65).

Kernoi (Hillbom 2005: 45–200) consist of flat circular stones with a circle of shallow depressions on the surface surrounding a central depression. They range from casual, crude examples found throughout the Aegean to several elaborate ones. They have been variously interpreted as, for instance, offering tables (food samples placed in the depressions to be 'taken' by the gods) or gaming-boards. If the latter, the game must have been simple, rather like pavement-games and the Egyptian *mehen* where players move their pieces along in a linear direction, jumping over or on their opponent's to remove them.

Events Involving People and Animals

Horses

Horses may have been domesticated *c.*4000 in southern Russia, spreading to Mesopotamia, Anatolia and Greece by 3000 (Davis 1987: 33, 130–131). The introduction of the chariot follows in the seventeenth century (Crouwel 1981).

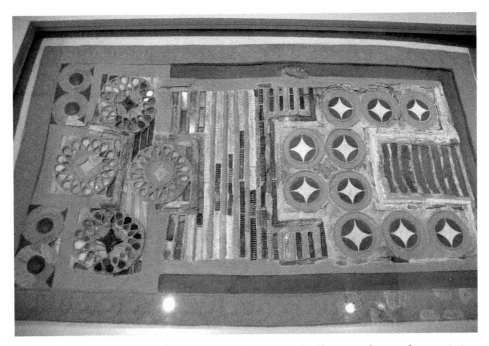

FIGURE 4.3. Game board from Knossos (*c.*1500 BCE). Photo: author with permission from the Herakleion Museum and the Greek Ministry of Education, Religion, Culture, and Athletics - TAP.

Horse-riding is depicted on some Mycenaean pictorial *kraters*. On two, the rider stands on the back of his horse (*MycPictVP* V.17, 26). Four other *kraters* from Mycenae are more fragmentary: on IX.8, a man accompanies his horse; IX.5 and IX.7 preserve only horses, but they are galloping; and on IX.7 the hooves of two galloping horses overlap. The riders have not survived, but it is difficult to imagine galloping horses riderless.

Horse-driven chariots are depicted on sealstones and gold finger rings, in frescoes, and on pictorial vases (Crouwel 1981). Most representations show men riding in chariots, usually in pairs (e.g. *MycPictVP* IV.21, IX.1.1). Most scenes are calm, but there can be further interest: charioteers hunt deer (*CMS* I 15), or warriors and dogs accompany them (*MycPictVP* X.1), or a beaked fish-monster chases them (V.18).

One *krater* shows a man and a woman driving a chariot (*MycPictVP* III.18); other depictions show only women. On the west, short, end of the Ayia Triada sarcophagus (Long 1974), a pair of women ride in a chariot drawn by two horses with the upswept horns of a Cretan wild goat. On the east end, two griffins draw a chariot driven by two women (goddesses?). A fresco from Tiryns shows a procession of women driving chariots (Immerwahr 1989: 202 Ti 6a) through what Rhys Carpenter once called a forest of 'upended pingpong rackets' (1959: 2). Similar forests using the common 'Mycenaean flower' (Furumark 1972, 1: 284–298, motif 18) occur with chariots on pictorial *kraters* (e.g. *MycPictVP* IV.26, 50).

Finally, one chariot *krater* (*MycPictVP*, p. 230, XI.19.1) depicts a race in connection with a *krater* sitting on a stand and an enthroned woman lifting a *kylix*. The enthroned woman, the chariot-race, the implied feasting (*kylix* and the actual *krater*), and the possible prize *krater* may imply funeral games.

Bull-Sports

Bull-sports consisted of several major events (Younger 1995): capturing a huge wild bull (the *bos primigenius*, extinct in 1627 CE), leaping it, baiting it with darts (e.g. *CMS* V 497), slaughtering it (*CMS* I 80), and eating it at a feast (Stocker and Davis 2004).

There were two ways of leaping the bull. In Evans's schema the leaper took hold of the bull's horns and, with the bull tossing its head up, executed a somersault to land feet-first on the bull's back before jumping off onto the ground. In the Diving Leaper schema the leaper dived onto the bull's neck from an elevated position and executed a somersault off the bull's back to land on the ground. The representations in Evans's schema mostly date to the period before the Mycenaean takeover of Knossos (c.1400 BCE), while most Diving Leaper representations date later.

A third set of representations shows a figure floating above the bull's back, holding onto the horns with one hand; these date exclusively to the Mycenaean period. There is no sequence in these 'floating' representations, so it is impossible to know how the floating leaper got there or what the leaper was meant to do next. Perhaps this was a simple vault from side to side over the bull's back.

In Evans's schema, to grab a bull by its horns would be dangerous, potentially fatal (Boxer Rhyton zone 2 depicts a gored leaper). In the Diving Leaper schema, it is difficult to imagine a bull charging toward a platform. There is, however, further archaeological evidence for both schemata. In the north-west corner of Malia's central court there is a small oval boulder with a depression in its north-west side as if to provide a toehold for a leaper to use as a kind of springboard for throwing himself over the bull's head (Evans's schema). A sealstone (*CMS* VI 181) depicts a leaper diving from a platform decorated with zigzags onto a bull's neck; in the north-west corner of Phaistos' central court there is a stepped platform next to niches similarly decorated.

Scholars have also debated the place of women in bull-leaping (cf. Scanlon 1999). In the Taureador frescoes from Knossos (Immerwahr 1989: 175 Kn 23), persons with white-painted flesh act as frontal or rear assistants. According to the colour convention inherited from Egypt, these should be women. But some scholars feel that women would not be participating in bull-leaping; they point out that the white-painted figures wear the man's kilt and penis sheath, and display no breast development (Indelicato 1988; Marinatos in Bietak et al. 2007: 127–128).

I maintain that these white-painted figures are indeed female, and the lack of breast development can be paralleled in modern gymnastics where rigorous training has delayed the onset of secondary sexual characteristics. Bull-leaping may also have been gendered male, which could require the male costume.

Marinatos states that no white-painted figure is shown actually executing the somersault over the back of the bull. This is not exactly true. A fresco from Knossos shows a white-painted figure grasping the horns of a bull (Younger 1995 no. 47), and another seems to depict two women with long hair flying over the back of a bull (Younger 1995 no. 106; cf. *CMS* V, Supp. IB 135); another comes from Tel el Dab'a (Bietak et al. 2007: 89–91 no. A6). And, finally, a fresco from Tiryns shows a white-painted Floating Leaper (Immerwahr 1989: 202 Ti 1).

I feel therefore that it is possible to maintain that these white-painted athletes were women.

Bull-sports are found most commonly at Knossos. Outside Crete such scenes are found in far fewer numbers, and if we count just bull-leaping scenes on the Greek mainland, we find one fresco each at Orchomenos, Pylos, and Tiryns, one stone vase fragment from the Athens Acropolis, three fresco panels and one pictorial *krater* from Mycenae, and a painted *larnax* from Tanagra. It seems that, apart from Mycenae, most mainland sites referred to bull-leaping only once.

Bull-leaping was not, however, confined to the Aegean. From Tel el Dab'a (Bietak et al. 2007) comes a series of bull-leaping scenes (including one white-painted leaper) all apparently following the Diving Leaper schema (Younger 2009). The frescoes are in the Minoan *buon fresco* technique and in a Minoanizing style, but may not have been painted by Minoan artists (Shaw 2009).

Bull-sports also appear in the Near East. On a Hittite vase (1565–1540 BCE; Sipahi 2001; Decker 2003 fig. 21), an acrobat executes an arch on the bull's back. On Near Eastern cylinder seals (*c.*1700; Collon 1987 nos. 707 and 708; Collon 1994; Nys and Åström 2003), two acrobats execute handstands on a single bull's back, and, on another cylinder (Collon 1987 no. 710), a would-be leaper is caught on the bull's horns. A wooden box (eighteenth dynasty) from Lisht, Egypt (Smith 1965 fig. 139), depicts a Floating Leaper over the bull's back. None of these examples conveys Minoan bull-leaping precisely.

Hunting

Like bull sports, hunting is seen on a variety of media, especially seals, frescoes and pictorial vase painting. Men are usually depicted alone, hunting with spear or lance, occasionally with bow and arrow; the favourite prey include deer, boar, and lion (whose occasional presence in the Aegean is assured; Thomas 2014). Often, the hunter is accompanied by his hound (*MycPictVP* XI.70, 71, 73). On XI.80 he kneels behind the dogs while they corner a stag. Deer- and boar-hunting occupies frescoes from Orchomenos, Pylos, and Tiryns (Immerwahr 1989: 195 Or 3, 197 Py 11, 202–203 Ti 6, 7). At Pylos, Hall 64 has a frieze depicting an 'overlapping (and yapping) pack of life-size hunting dogs' (Lang 1969: 214–15; Immerwahr 1989: 199 PY 20). At Tiryns, there were at least two friezes of hunters, one with hounds, horses and stags, and another with hounds, boars and nets (Immerwahr 1989: 202–3 Ti 6, 7). For both friezes there are fragments of white-painted legs and hands testifying to the presence of women hunters (Rodenwaldt 1976: 111–112 nos. 141–142, 120–122 nos. 156–160 pl. XIV nos. 1, 10, 12). Two Linear B tablets may also refer to hunters (Hiller 1998–1999): on PY Na 248 hunters (*ku-na-ke-ta-i*) get free flax, while TH Av 100.2 authorizes grain *ku-na-ki-si*, either 'to women' or 'to women hunters' (Aravantinos et al. 2001: 167).

Boar-hunting had special significance. When approaching manhood (15–16 years old?), Odysseus visits his maternal grandfather Autolykos near Delphi (*Od.* 19.392–466); they go hunting on Parnassos where a boar gashes Odysseus' leg. This is a classic coming-of-age story: separation, pain, and return home (cf. van Gennep 1960). Boar-hunting was obviously dangerous: Croesus' son Atys was killed in a boar-hunt (Hdt. 1.34–45), and so also might have been the Minoan youth (*c.*1600) found at Anemospilia high on Mt Juktas with a boar's lance in his chest (Sakellarakis and Sapouna-Sakellarakis 1981). Dangerous though boar-hunting may have been, it was necessary if one wanted a boar's tusk helmet (*Il.* 10.261–265; Korres 1969; Morris 1990). Since a boar's tusk helmet uses over sixty-five half-tusks (representing over thirty male boars killed, Varvaregos 1981: 48), it signals the prowess of the wearer. We should keep this in mind when contemplating the two women wearing boar's tusk helmets in frescoes from Mycenae and Thebes (Immerwahr 1989: 192 MY 9, 201 TH 2).

Fishing

In the late eighteenth century we first see men carrying the fish they caught (Powell 1992). A sealstone (*CMS* II 2.174a) shows a man holding a large fish by the tail, and a clay stand from Phylakopi depicts four men in a similar scene (Atkinson et al. 1904: 123–125 fig. 95 pl. XXII). A late-seventeenth-century sealstone (*CMS* VI 183) presents a man carrying a string of fish in one hand and an octopus in the other. From Akrotiri, Thera, come two contemporary frescoes that show fisherboys holding strings of dolphin fish and small tuna (Immerwahr 1989: 187 Ak 11; Doumas 1992 pls. 18–23; Economides 2000; Mylona 2000). Both boys are nude except for a knotted string around their neck, and they have shaved heads with short side- and front-locks. From their physique, Chapin estimates their age at mid-adolescence (2007: 241–242). Perhaps catching numbers of fish was a rite of passage.

CONCLUSIONS

Almost all Greek sports had their origin in the Bronze Age; both had foot-racing, boxing, wrestling, chariot- and horse-races, and board- and pavement-games. Bull-sports are confined to the Aegean Bronze Age, especially Crete, though there are (poorly understood) references to bull-leaping throughout the eastern Mediterranean. If we trust Homer, Aegean *solos*-hurling developed into the Greek discus-throw.

The major difference between Bronze Age and Early Iron Age sports may be their social purpose—or the social theorizing of Aegean scholars. Aegean foot-racing, boxing and bull-sports may have been practised more within the context of (theoretical) coming of age ceremonies; and these, plus horse- and chariot-races, may have functioned more within the context of funeral games. Greek games similarly had such purposes, but they also functioned as purely athletic events.

Aegean women participated in sport, perhaps in different ways than their later Greek counterparts; while we have no Aegean evidence for women's foot-races or for women riding horses, they did leap bulls, drive chariots, and hunt boar with dogs. And though they are not represented playing music, they did dance.

ABBREVIATIONS

CMS = Pini and Müller 1960–2009
MycPictVP = Vermeule and Karageorghis 1982
PM = Evans 1921–1935

REFERENCES

Aravantinos, V. L., L. Godart, and A. Sacconi. 2001. *Thèbes: Fouilles de la Cadmée*, I: *Les tablettes en Linéaire B de la 'Odos Pelopidou.' Édition et commentaire*. Pisa.

Atkinson, T. D. et al. 1904. *Excavations at Phylakopi in Melos Conducted by the British School at Athens*. Society for the Promotion of Hellenic Studies Supp. 4. London.

Bell, R. C. 2007. 'Notes on Pavement Games of Greece and Rome.' In Finkel. 98–99. London.

Bell, R. C. and C. M. Roueché. 2007. 'Graeco-Roman Pavement Signs and Game Boards: A British Museum Working Typology.' In Finkel. 106–109. London.

Bietak, M., N. Marinatos, and C. Palyvou. 2007. *Taureador Scenes in Tell El Dab'a (Avaris) and Knossos*. Vienna.

Bosanquet, R. C., and R. M. Dawkins. 1923. *The Unpublished Objects from the Palaikastro Excavations 1902–1906, Part 1*. ABSA Supp. Paper 1. London.

Brain, P. and D. D. Skinner. 1978. 'Odysseus and the Axes: Homeric Ballistics Reconstructed.' *G&R* 25: 55–58.

Brecoulaki, H., C. Zaitoun, S. R. Stocker, and J. L. Davis. 2008. 'An Archer from the Palace of Nestor: A New Wall-Painting Fragment in the Chora Museum.' *Hesperia* 77: 363–397.

Brumbaugh, R. S. 1975. 'The Knossos Game Board.' *AJA* 79: 135–137.

Bundrick, S. 2005. *Music and Image in Classical Athens*. Cambridge.

Carpenter, R. 1959. 'Archaeology Now and Then.' *Phoenix* 13: 1–12.

Chapin, A. 2007. 'Boys Will Be Boys: Youth and Gender Identity in the Theran Frescoes.' In *Constructions of Childhood in Ancient Greece and Italy* (*Hesperia* Supp. 41). 229–255. A. Cohen and J. B. Rutter, eds. Princeton.

Chapouthier, F. 1938. *Deux épés d'apparat découvertes en 1936 au palais de Mallia au cours des fouilles exécutées au nom de l'École Française d'Athènes* (*EtCrét* 5). Paris.

Collon, D. 1987. *First Impressions, Cylinder Seals in the Ancient Near East*. Chicago.

Collon, D. 1994. 'Bull-Leaping in Syria.' *Ägypten und Levante* 4: 81–88.

Crouwel, J. 1981. *Chariots and Other Means of Land Transport in Bronze Age Greece.* Amsterdam.

Crowther, N. B. 2007. 'The Ancient Olympic Games through the Centuries.' In Schaus and Wenn 2007. 3–13.

Davis, S. J. M. 1987. *The Archaeology of Animals*. London.

Decker, W. 1995. *Sport in der griechischen Antike: vom minoischen Wettkampf bis zu den Olympischen Spielen*. Munich.

Decker, W. 2003. 'Zum Stand der Erforschung des "Stierspiels" in der Alten Welt.' In *Altertumswissenschaften im Dialog. Festschrift für Wolfram Nagel zur Vollendung seines 80. Lebensjahres*. Alter Orient und Altes Testament 306. 31–79. R. Dittmann, C. Eder, and B. Jacobs, eds. Münster.

Decker, W. and M. Herb. 1994. *Bildatlas zum Sport im alten Ägypten: Corpus der bildlichen Quellen zu Leibesübungen, Spiel, Jagd, Tanz und verwandten Themen*. Leiden.

Deonna, W. 1953. *Le symbolisme de l'acrobatie antique*. Collection Latomus 9. Brussels.

Doumas, C. 1992. *The Wall Paintings of Thera*. Athens.

Economides, P. S. 2000. 'The "Little Fisherman" and the Fish He Holds.' In *The Wall Paintings of Thera: Proceedings of the First International Symposium, Petros M. Nomikos Conference Centre, Thera, Hellas, 30 August–4 September 1997*. 555–560. S. Sherratt, ed. Athens.

Evans, A. J. 1921–1935. *Palace of Minos*. London.

Finkel, I., ed. 2007. *Ancient Board Games in Perspective*. London.

Furumark, A. 1972. *Mycenaean Pottery, I: Analysis and Classification (SkrAth 4°, XX:1)*. Stockholm.

German, S. C. 2007. 'Politics and the Bronze Age Origins of Olympic Practices.' In Schaus and Wenn. 15–25.

Getz-Preziosi, P. 1987. *Sculptors of the Cyclades: Individual and Tradition in the Third Millennium B.C.* Ann Arbor.

Hillbom, N. 2005. *Minoan Games and Game Boards*. Lund.

Hiller, S. 1998–1999. 'KU-NA-KE-TA-I.' *Minos* 33–34: 191–196.

Immerwahr, S. A. 1989. *Aegean Painting in the Bronze Age*. University Park, PA.

Indelicato, S. D. 1988. 'Were Cretan Girls Playing at Bull-Leaping?' *Cretan Studies* 1: 39–47.

Instone, S. 1990. 'Love and Sex in Pindar: Some Practical Thrusts.' *BICS* 37: 30–42.

Knigge, U. 1988. *Der Kerameikos von Athen. Führung durch Ausgrabungen und Geschichte*. Athens.

Koehl, R. 2006. *Aegean Bronze Age Rhyta*. Prehistory Monographs 19. Philadelphia.

Korres, G. S. 1969. 'I megaloprepeia ton mukenaïkon kranon.' ['The Splendour of Mycenaean Helmets.'] *AAA* 2.3: 446–462.

Lang, M. L. 1969. *The Palace of Nestor at Pylos in Western Messenia*. II. *The Frescoes*. Princeton.

Laser, S. 1987. *Sport und Spiel (ArchHom T)*. Göttingen.

Lembessi, A., Muhly, P. and Papasavvas, G. 2004. 'The Runner's Ring: A Minoan Athlete's Dedication at the Syme Sanctuary, Crete.' *AM* 119: 1–31.

Long, C. R. 1974. *The Ayia Triadha Sarcophagus: A Study of Late Minoan and Mycenaean Funerary Practices and Beliefs*. SIMA 41. Gothenburg.

Marinatos, N. 1984. *Art and Religion in Thera: Reconstructing a Bronze Age Society*. Athens.

McDonnell, M. 1992. 'The Introduction of Athletic Nudity: Thucydides, Plato, and the Vases.' *JHS* 102: 182–193.

Morris, C. E. 1990. 'In Pursuit of the White Tusked Boar: Aspects of Hunting in Mycenaean Society.' In *Celebrations of Death and Divinity in the Bronze Age Argolid: Proceedings of the Sixth International Symposium at the Swedish Institute at Athens, 11–13 June, 1988 (SkrAth 4°, XL)*. 149–156. R. Hägg and G. C. Nordquist, eds. Stockholm.

Mouratidis, J. 1983. 'Greek Sports, Games and Festivals before the 8th Century B.C.' PhD Dissertation, Ohio State University.

Mouratidis, J. 1989. 'Are there Minoan Influences on Mycenaean Sports, Games and Dances?' *Nikephoros* 2: 43–63.

Mylona, D. 2000. 'The "Fisherman" Frescoes in the Light of the Fish Bone Evidence.' In *The Wall Paintings of Thera: Proceedings of the First International Symposium, Petros M. Nomikos Conference Centre, Thera, Hellas, 30 August–4 September 1997*. 561–567. S. Sherrat, ed. Athens.

Myres, J. L. 1948. 'The Axes Yet Again.' *CR* 62: 113.

Nys, K., and Åström, P. 2003. 'Evidence of Bull-Riding in the Cypriote Bronze Age.' *JPR* 16–17: 4–15.

Papalas, A. J. 1991. 'Boy Athletes in Ancient Greece.' *Stadion* 17: 165–192.

Pelon, O. 1985. 'L'acrobate de Malia et l'art de l'époque protopalatiale en Crète.' In *L'Iconographie minoenne. BCH* Supp. 11: 35–40.

Pini, I. and W. Müller. 1960–2009. *Corpus der minoischen und mykenischen Siegel.* Berlin.

Powell, J. 1992. 'Archaeological and Pictorial Evidence for Fishing in the Bronze Age: Issues of Identification and Interpretation.' In *EIKON. Aegean Bronze Age Iconography: Shaping a Methodology. 4th International Aegean Conference, University of Tasmania, Hobart, 6–9 April 1992 (Aegaeum 8)*. 307–316. R. Laffineur and J. Crowley, eds. Liège.

Pritchard, J. B., ed. 1969. *Ancient Near Eastern Texts Relating to the Old Testament with Supplement.* Princeton.

Purcell, N. 2007. 'Inscribed Imperil Roman Gaming-Boards.' In Finkel. 90–97.

Putnam, B. J. 1967. 'Concepts of Sport in Minoan Art.' PhD Dissertation, University of Southern California.

Rethemiotakis, G. 2001. *Minoan Clay Figures and Figurines from the Neopalatial to the Subminoan Period.* Archaeological Society at Athens Library 219. Athens.

Ridington, W. R. 1935. *The Minoan-Mycenaean Background of Greek Athletics.* Philadelphia.

Rieche, A. 2007. 'Board Games and Their Symbols from Roman Times to Early Christianity.' In Finkel. 87–89.

Rodenwaldt, G. 1976. *Tiryns* II: *Die Fresken des Palastes.* Mainz.

Rystedt, E. 1988. 'Mycenaean Runners – Including Apobatai.' In *Problems in Greek Prehistory: Papers Presented at the Centenary Conference of the British School of Archaeology at Athens, Manchester, April 1986*. 437–442. E. B. French and K. A. Wardle, eds. Bristol.

Sakellarakis, Y. and E. Sapouna-Sakellaraki. 1981. 'Drama of Death in a Minoan Temple.' *National Geographic Magazine* 159.2: 205–222.

Scanlon, T. F. 1999. 'Bull Sports, Cults, and Women's Status in Minoan Crete.' *Nikephoros* 12: 33–70.

Scanlon, T. F. 2002. *Eros and Greek Athletics.* New York.

Schaus, G. P. and S. R. Wenn, eds. 2007. *Onward to the Olympics: Historical Perspectives on the Olympic Games.* Waterloo, Ont.

Serwint, N. 1993. 'Female Athletic Costume at the Heraia.' *AJA* 97: 403–422.

Shaw, M. C. 2009. Review Article: 'A Bull-Leaping Fresco from the Nile Delta and a Search for Patrons and Artists.' Review of Bietak, Marinatos, and Palyvou 2007. *AJA* 113: 471–477.

Sipahi, T. 2001. 'New Evidence from Anatolia Regarding Bull Leaping Scenes in the Art of the Aegean and the Near East.' *Anatolica* 27: 107–125.

Smith, W. S. 1965. *Interconnections in the Ancient Near East: A Study of the Relationships between the Arts of Egypt, the Aegean, and Western Asia.* New Haven.

Steele, L. 2004. 'A Goodly Feast ... A Cup of Mellow Wine: Feasting in Bronze Age Cyprus.' In Wright. 161–180.

Stocker, S. and J. Davis. 2004. 'Animal Sacrifice, Archives, and Feasting at the Palace of Nestor.' In Wright. 59–75.

Sweeney, J., T. Curry, and Y. Tzedakis, eds. 1987. *The Human Figure in Early Greek Art.* Athens.

Sweet, W. E. 1985. 'Protection of the Genitals in Greek Athletics.' *AncWorld* 11: 43–52.

Thomas, N. 2014. A Lion's Eye View of the Greek Bronze Age" In *PHYSIS: L'environnement naturel et la relation homme-mieu dans le monde Égéen protohistorique (Aegaeum 37).* 375–389. G. Touchais, R. Laffineur, and F. Rougemont, eds. Leuven.

Van Gennep, A. 1960. *The Rites of Passage.* Chicago.

Varvaregos, A. P. 1981. 'To odontophrakton mykenaïkon kranos: hos pros ten techniken tes kataskeues tou.' ['The Mycenaean boar's tusk helmet: the techniques of its manufacture.'] PhD Dissertation, University of Athens.

Vermeule, E. T., and V. Karageorghis. 1982. *Mycenaean Pictorial Vase Painting.* Cambridge.

Wace, A. J., and F. Stubbings. 1962. *A Companion to Homer.* London.

West, M. L. 1992. *Ancient Greek Music.* Oxford.

Wright, J. C., ed. 2004. *The Mycenaean Feast.* Princeton.

Younger, J. G. 1995. 'Bronze Age Representations of Aegean Bull-Games, III.' In *Politeia. Society and State in the Aegean Bronze Age. Proceedings of the 5th International Aegean Conference/ 5e Rencontre égéenne internationale, University of Heidelberg, Archäologisches Institut, 10–13 April 1994 (Aegaeum 12).* 507–545. R. Laffineur and W.-D. Niemeier, eds. Liège.

Younger, J. G. 1998. *Music in the Aegean Bronze Age.* SIMA pocket book 96. Jonsered.

Younger, J. G. 2009. 'The Bull-Leaping Scenes from Tell el-Dab'a.' Review of Bietak, Marinatos, and Palyvou 2007. *AJA* 113: 479–480.

SECTION 2

EARLY COMPETITIONS AND EVENTS

CHAPTER 5

ORIGINS OF THE OLYMPICS TO THE SIXTH CENTURY BCE

ULRICH SINN

WE have two ways of crossing the gap of over three thousand years to gain access to the early history of Olympia: in antiquity, of course, many authors wrote about the beginnings of the cult at Olympia, and further sources of information are the archaeological finds made by excavations in the modern era. Both channels provide only incomplete insight into the history of the cult site; an overall view initially yields a disparate picture, and many questions remain unanswered. However, new finds from recent excavations have extended our knowledge, and a number of puzzles have come closer to being solved.

THE ARCHAEOLOGICAL FINDS

Thanks to the most recent excavations by Helmut Kyrieleis and Jörg Rambach we can give a well-supported answer to the question of when the first gatherings occurred at Olympia for ritual festivals (Rambach 2002: 177–212; Kyrieleis 2002: 213–220; Kyrieleis 2006: 1–139). The earliest evidence of cult activity may be dated in the late eleventh century BCE. These are sub-Mycenaean drinking bowls on tall-stemmed feet (*kylikes*), and early iron-age drinking vessels which belong to the characteristic repertoire of ritual meals and symposia held in connection with religious celebrations (Eder 2006: 141–246, especially 209–210). The central place in which these pots were used for the exercise of this cult was the area close to the tumulus, which in a later phase of the sanctuary was developed as the cult site of Pelops (see the next section and Kyrieleis 2006: 55–61 and 79–83). Until a few years ago, this tumulus was considered evidence of cult activity as early as the Mycenaean era. Most recent investigations have revealed its true age: it was built around the middle of the third millennium BCE on a south-sloping spur of the Hill of Kronos. The surface was paved with rocks and slabs of light-coloured limestone. It was an element of a prehistoric settlement, of which remains of apsidal houses have been preserved to the north and east of the tumulus. This settlement was abandoned in the early part of the second millennium BCE (on the form and history of the prehistoric settlement, see Rambach 2002: 177–212). In the following centuries, the flat land at the foot of the Hill of Kronos was covered by a layer of sand which has yielded no archaeological finds. There are no traces of human presence in this precinct for almost a whole millennium. Only in the late eleventh century BCE did life reappear on the flat land south of the Hill of Kronos. There is no archaeological evidence of cultural continuity in Olympia from Mycenaean until Protogeometric times (Kyrieleis 2006: 26, 61–79; Eder 2006: 192).

The decision to found a cult on this site was doubtless based on the fact that the tumulus projected from the accumulated sand here. In the course of later digging, it could be proved that the upper zone of the prehistoric tumulus was indeed still visible in the late eleventh century BCE (Kyrieleis 2002: 215–216). This phenomenon, considered mysterious, was probably interpreted as a sign from the gods.

Who were the people who decided to establish a cult site in the precinct which had been abandoned for such a long time? Information about their origin and their cult practices is given by a massive accumulation of loose material around the tumulus, now honoured as a sacred site. This accumulation is designated in archaeological literature a 'black stratum' (the most recent and extensive characterization and evaluation of the 'black stratum': Kyrieleis 2006: 27–55). The term comes from the dark colouring of the soil through the presence of ash and charcoal. Helmut Kyrieleis associates this convincingly with the waste from the oldest altar of Zeus at Olympia (Kyrieleis 2006: 35–47). He was able to identify the structural remains of the altar, dated from the end of the eleventh century, at the northern edge of the tumulus (Kyrieleis 2006: 38–39, with fig. 1). From the 'black stratum' excavators have recovered countless animal bones, remains of spits (*obeloi*), votive statuettes, and a wide range of ceramics. We may deduce from the ceramics that the ritual meals were part of the performance of early cult ceremonies (Kyrieleis 2006: 27–55).

The origins of the people who set up the cult site and subsequently visited it regularly are revealed in the composition of the cult ceramics. The forms, decoration, and clay used in the large-format, sub-Mycenaean *kylikes* are from local potteries. They give evidence that the population of the wider environs of the Hill of Kronos and in the Alpheios Valley took part in the cult during the whole Mycenaean period (Kyrieleis 2006: 77, with n. 312; on the probable location of the Mycenaean settlement in the hilly land east of the Hill of Kronos, see Rambach 2002: 200; Eder 2006: 210). However, the pots recovered from the 'black stratum' at the tumulus also indicate contacts maintained by the inhabitants of the Alpheios Valley at the time of the founding of the sanctuary with the regions to the north of Olympia, namely Achaea, Aetolia, and Akarnania. One cannot exclude the possibility that these pots come from people migrating from the north-west of the Greek mainland and the offshore islands. The foundation of Olympia was presumably triggered or at least favoured by the shifts in population at the end of the second millennium BCE (Sinn 2004: 77, with a reference to the cult of Apollo Thermios in Olympia; Kyrieleis 2006: 77–79, with a reference to the myths surrounding Aitolos and Oxylos [Strabo 8.354–355 and 10.463–464; also Pausanias 5.3.6–4.7]; Eder 2006: 212–213, with a reference to imported ceramics). It is thus possible to attempt an answer to the question of the motivation for the establishment of the cult using the finds from Olympia, particularly those from the 'black stratum' (Himmelmann 2002: 91–107 gives an analysis in summary).

There are two dominating themes in the figurative votive offerings of the tenth to the eighth century BCE. The largest group of finds from the Geometric period are the hand-shaped statuettes. Alongside a few human figures, these are predominantly animal figures, mainly oxen, horses, sheep, rams, and goats (Heilmeyer 1972). Together with the comparatively unpretentious execution in clay, there is a more ambitious bronze version with the same themes. The diggings have brought to light a few thousand examples of this genre (Heilmeyer 1979). A further group with uniform themes are the bronze tripod kettles, which are among the votive gifts from the ninth and eighth centuries BCE. While the oldest pieces from the early ninth century still have modest dimensions, about 65 cm in height, there are examples attested from the second half of the eighth century that reach a monumental height of over 3 metres (Maass 1978). Characteristic of the later tripods are the outer edges of the legs, decorated in relief, and the ring handles at the edge of the basin, ornamented with figurative decoration. The iconography of this design reveals no connection with athletics. Mythical battle scenes and statuettes of warriors, particularly, point in the other direction, which will be examined more closely below.

From the late eighth and early seventh centuries BCE comes a remarkable assemblage of armour from central Italy, preserved as fragments (Herrmann 1984: 272–294). We shall also take a closer look at its significance below. Unlike the case of any other Greek sanctuary, votive offerings with a reference to war dominate in the finds of the first half of the first millennium BCE. As early as 1852—long before the first systematic excavations at Olympia—Ernst Curtius concluded from an analysis of the written sources: 'There was hardly one war waged in Hellas after which the victorious city did not dedicate a statue or other work of art to honour the Olympian Zeus' (Curtius 1852: 20). Compare also Herrmann (1972: 108): 'Olympia today holds in the galleries and store-rooms of its museum the largest arsenal of weapons from antiquity in existence'; and Mallwitz (1972: 24): 'Nowhere, not even in Delphi, have so many weapons been found as in Olympia.' Weapons, armour, and war material were dedicated to Olympian Zeus in great number. Amongst these are the impressive votive gifts of tripod kettles with their statuettes of warriors as ring handles (Sinn 1991: 43, with n. 46).

Two significant alterations in the topography of the sanctuary give evidence of fundamental caesuras in its history. Till the late eighth century the sacred precinct was restricted essentially to the south slope of the Hill of Kronos and the flat land adjoining the south side as far as the Alpheios. The ritual centre was the altar, situated in the immediate vicinity of the tumulus (see previous section). This layout changed around 700 BCE. In the wider vicinity of the Hill of Kronos we have evidence of levelling and earth works at this time (Schilbach 1984: 234 with n. 25; re the first constructions on the 'treasury terrace'; Heiden 1995: 12–18). In the south-east, the precinct of the sanctuary extended as far as the area occupied later by the stadium. On the south slope of the Hill of Kronos a wide terrace (the so-called treasury terrace) was built using retaining walls and rubble fill. The first small buildings were erected on it soon after. Particularly great effort was required for the development of the new sacred precinct west of the Hill of Kronos: it involved diverting the Kladeos 160 metres to the west. In order to avoid flooding of the sacred precinct by the swollen Kladeos in winter, the reclaimed land was secured by an embankment, the remains of which are still visible today (Kyrieleis 2003: 21–22, with figs. 23–24; 29–31, with figs. 34–36).

From archaeological finds we may also determine the reasons for the extension of the sacred precinct. At this time, Olympia was clearly experiencing a marked increase in visitors to the sanctuary. With his systematic analysis of all the wells so characteristic of Olympia, Alfred Mallwitz was able to demonstrate that the digging of more than 250 wells in quick succession began at the same time as the extension of the sanctuary in the early seventh century BCE. The influx of visitors had increased so much that the pilgrims' need for water required that the abundant underground water supply at Olympia be tapped. The earliest wells south-east of the sanctuary were placed in such a way that they left untouched the area which was subsequently used as the running surface of the stadium. Mallwitz comes to the convincing conclusion that a stadium was first erected at Olympia around 700 BCE (Mallwitz 1988: 79–109). We shall see below that there is a direct connection between the building of the first stadium and the extension of the sanctuary.

About one hundred years after this radical break, the layout of the sanctuary changed again. Around 600 BCE the accumulation of the 'black stratum' on the tumulus ceased. This coincides with the beginning of the building work on the Temple of Hera situated immediately north of the tumulus (Kyrieleis 2006, 79; on the temple of Hera, Mallwitz 1972: 137–149; Sinn 2001: 63–70; Moustaka 2002: 301–315). The construction of the first peripteral temple in Olympia was, according to Pausanias (5.16.1), endowed by the original masters of the sanctuary, the Triphylians. However, it is also conceivable that the construction goes back to the Eleans, who, around 600 BCE or soon after, extended their hegemony as far as the Alpheios and thus also had control of Olympia (Möller 2004: 249–270). As part of this building work, the first altar of Zeus, originally situated here, was moved further east. It was in its final position where Pausanias saw it (5.13.8): 'The altar of the Olympian Zeus is about as far from the Pelopion as from the temple of Hera, and is positioned in front of both of them.' The continued flourishing of Olympia and its constantly increasing attraction for the inhabitants of the entire Greek world is attested in an impressive manner by the closely set row of treasuries which were built in the course of the sixth century on the terrace at the south foot of the Hill of Kronos (Herrmann 1992: 25–32).

THE ANCIENT WRITTEN SOURCES ON THE EARLY HISTORY OF OLYMPIA

There are many reports from antiquity about the foundation and early history of the sanctuary at Olympia. However, the texts which are derived from corresponding 'cult legends' are full of contradictions. Most of them have in common the fact that they call the 'Olympic *agōn*' a cult-founding ritual, though the persons concerned are not identical. Zeus, the Theban Herakles, Apollo, and several mythical kings of Elis are named as founders of the contests. Scholars today agree that the disparate spectrum of cult legends was an expression of the conflicts continuing into the fifth century BCE about the domination of the renowned cult site. All the contenders strove to support their claim through their presence there from the beginning. One may therefore not expect to find authentic information in these texts, which were all written long after the founding of the cult in the late eleventh century (most recently fundamental: Ulf 1997: 9–51).

One may illustrate this interpretation using as a representative example probably the best-known cult legend, whose protagonist is Pelops. In the tenth *Olympian Ode*, Pindar (10.24–25 476 BCE) speaks of the 'place of contests' (*agōna*) which Herakles had instituted at the monument (*sāmati*) to Pelops. See also Pausanius (5.13.2) who says: 'Herakles is said to have instituted the cult precinct of Pelops, as he was a descendant of Pelops.' The discussion about the role of Pelops in the early history of Olympia has been set on a new foundation by

Helmut Kyrieleis. As mentioned above, in accordance with his convincing analysis of the 'black stratum', all the finds recovered from it dating into the early sixth century BCE were dedicated solely to the honouring of Zeus. The tumulus can only have been given its function as the heröon of Pelops around 600 BCE, in the course of the restructuring of the religious centre (Kyrieleis 2006: 55–61 and 79–83). Pindar picked up this version propounded at his time by the Eleans, vividly portrayed in the eastern pediment of the temple of Zeus, and projected it back into early times, in the form the Eleans saw it (Kyrieleis 1997: 13–27). If one wishes to trace the historical starting point at the foundation of Olympia, one cannot there-fore rely on Pindar's portrayal of the beginnings of the cult site. The archaeological findings show Zeus as lord of the sanctuary from the beginning. It is also now proven that between the establishment of the cult site in the late eleventh century and the provision of a stadium a good three centuries elapsed, during which the sanctuary to Zeus drew pilgrims without the added attraction of contests.

In the Homeric epics, Olympia is not mentioned by name. One can possibly locate in Olympia the sacrifice made on the bank of the Alpheios by Nestor to Zeus, mentioned by Homer, *Iliad* 11.727 (Scanlon 2004; Kyle 2015: 75). However, passages also exist that unargu-ably shed light on the understanding of the cult of Olympia. The Alpheios Valley was under the hegemony of Nestor, who is given a substantial role in Homer (Frame 2009). This is the source of a very graphic characterization of the landscape and the conditions of life in this region. We are told that Nestor and his fellow citizens owe their status and their affluence to rich agricultural production, particularly grazing and cattle-breeding. Nestor boasts of the wealth of flocks of sheep and herds of cattle and goats, and also success in horse-breeding (Homer, *Iliad* 11.670–682). The earliest votive offerings at Olympia all reflect this world. When the inhabitants of the Alpheios Valley established the cult site at the foot of the Hill of Kronos at the end of the second millennium BCE, their aim was clearly to obtain divine help in preserving their livelihood, which was based on agriculture and cattle-breeding. However, they probably did not direct their prayers and sacrifices to Zeus alone; they honoured Poseidon as lord of horse-breeding, and the fertility goddess Artemis as protector of cattle. Both had altars at Olympia. Several festivals were celebrated at Olympia to honour Artemis in particular (Sinn 1981: 25–43).

Among the ancient written sources on the early history of Olympia one must not neg-lect the '*Chronicle* of Hippias' (sometimes called Hippias' *Olympic Victor List*). It mentions the specific date 776 BCE as the beginning of the contests held continuously from that time onwards at Olympia. The authenticity of its reports about the initial phase of the contests was already doubted in antiquity, and today's scholars follow suit, almost unanimously (Sinn 1991: 51–54). In principle, however, Hippias' *Chronicle* agrees with the archaeological findings to the extent that in this account of the history of the sanctuary, the contests were only incorporated into cult practice after a long interval of time in relation to the founda-tion of Olympia. As one considers how Hippias might have hit upon the year 776 BCE in his reconstruction of the list of Olympian victors, which he compiled around 400 BCE, one's attention turns to the cult festival of the year 476 BCE, still remembered in Hippias' time. It was the first cult festival celebrated after the defeat of the Persians at the battle of Plataea (see the description of the festive atmosphere in Plutarch, *Themistokles* 17; Sinn 1994b: 599). This festival may have been chosen by Hippias as a point of orientation, and by adding a round number, he was taken back to the year 776 BCE (Christesen 2007).

In his description, Strabo seems to capture a glimpse of the early history of Olympia that comes closer to historical reality (Sinn 1994a: 147–166; Ulf 1997: 31–34). Strabo (8.3.30) writes in his clear and concise way about the early history of Olympia:

> The sanctuary attained its fame originally through the oracle of Zeus Olympios. As the oracle became less prominent, the eminence of the sanctuary did not suffer at all; on the contrary: as is well known, its renown increased, though this was due to the great cult festival (*tēn panēgurin*) and the Olympic Games (*ton agōna tōn Olumpiakōn*). The victor's wreath won here enjoyed the highest esteem.

According to this tradition, the beginning of the cult at Olympia is the establishment of the seat of an oracle. Pindar, too, mentions the activity of the oracle at Olympia several times. The mythical roots are the subject of his sixth *Olympian Ode* from the year 468 BCE. He describes the proceedings as follows: on the bank of the Alpheios, Apollo fathers the boy Iamos with Euadne, daughter of the king of Arcadia. Soon afterwards he bestows visionary power on the child and promises him his own oracular seat, from the time when Herakles was to come to Olympia to establish a sanctuary to Zeus with a cult festival and athletic contests. He designates the crest of the altar to Zeus as the seat of the oracle. Iamos and his successors were to read the will of Zeus from the flames of the sacrificial fire. In the eighth *Olympian Ode* Pindar first apostrophizes Olympia (*O.* 8.1-2) with the double honorific 'mother of the athletic games and mistress of the truth'. In this ode of Pindar the oracle and the athletic contests are equal elements in the cult of Olympia, without any chronological distinction. Pindar's apostrophizing in the eighth *Olympian Ode* implies that the Olympian oracle exercised its specific function in the context of the athletic contests—i.e. the oracle was asked by the athletes about their chances of victory (thus Herrmann 1972: 30; Mallwitz 1972: 65; Ebert 1980: 48). Continuing the cited apostrophizing of Olympia, Pindar (8.2-6) gives the following explanation of the exercise of the oracular function:

> where men who prophesy, interpreting burning sacrifices, ask Zeus of the dazzling thunderbolts whether he pays heed to men who strive in their hearts to attain the fame of great heroes and a respite from their toils.

'Men striving for the fame of heroes' may be equated with athletes, but this is only one way of construing the text, which may be interpreted in a different fashion (see next section). While we cannot exclude completely the notion that athletes enquired of the oracle about their chances of success in the Olympic *agōn* and swore oaths as part of the process, according to ancient historians and archaeological finds from the sanctuary of Zeus the oracle at Olympia derived its significance in the entire Greek world from an entirely different base.

THE ORACLE OF ZEUS OLYMPIOS AS AN ADVISER IN MATTERS OF WAR

Let us return to Strabo's account. We recognize how close his representation is to the archaeological findings if we examine the specific character of the oracle. There is only one historically attested case of consulting the oracle at Olympia. Xenophon (*Hellenika* 4.7.2) reports the presence of a Spartan embassy which enquires of the oracle of Zeus Olympios about the legitimacy of a planned campaign against Argos, in the fourth century BCE. And here we have a key word that describes an essential characteristic of the seers of Olympia. The successors of Iamos and the family of the Klyatids who were connected with his clan were specialized in giving counsel in matters of war. As a general rule, the Olympian seers were active outside the sanctuary. They accompanied Greek armies on to the battlefields and served on the spot as advisers to the generals (Weniger 1915: 53–115; Sinn 1991: 38–49).

Iamids or Klytiads were present at many decisive battles in Greek history. Herodotus (9.33–36) writes of the preparations by the Greek army at the beginning of the battle of Plataea: 'For the Greeks it was Teisamenus, son of Antiochus, who performed the sacrifice. He had accompanied the army as a seer (*mantis*). His origins were in Elis and he was a Klytiad from the clan of the Iamids.' And Herodotus continues: 'This Teisamenus exercised the office of seer for the Greeks at Plataea.' His interpretation of the sacrifice is also recorded: 'The sacrifice promised the Greeks success, but only on the condition that they restricted themselves to defence and did not initiate the battle by crossing the Asopos.' The Spartans' victory in the battle of Aigospotamoi in 405 BCE is also attributed to his visionary power (Pausanias 3.11.5; 10.9.7). The written reports on the activity of the Iamids and the Klytiads assembled by Ludwig Weniger reach back into the late Hellenistic era. The earliest evidence of such activity of the Olympian seers from the clan of the Iamids are the first lines of Pindar's sixth *Olympian Ode* from the year 468 BCE. Here Pindar sings of the victory of Hagesias of Syracuse. Pindar praises him not only as a victor at Olympia, but also as a member of the Iamid clan. In this connection he recalls the participation of a Iamid in the foundation of Syracuse in the year 734 BCE.

Among their earliest brilliant achievements was the successful colonization of Southern Italy and Sicily at the turn of the eighth to the seventh centuries BCE. The ancient Italic weapons and armour, mentioned above, are clearly booty from the military campaigns during colonization. The colossal bronze tripods with their statuettes of warriors (see above) may be explained as gifts of gratitude to the Olympian oracle (further evidence in Sinn 1991: 42–46).

THE DEVELOPMENT OF THE OLYMPIAN *PANĒGURIS* INTO A FESTIVAL FOR ALL GREEKS

The brilliant way in which Olympian seers proved their worth in the train of the colonizers brought more than exotic votive gifts. In the succeeding years the sanctuary was given a new role: it was the preferred meeting-point of Greeks who had emigrated abroad with their fellow countrymen who had remained at home. From this time on they celebrated the cult festival in the Alpheios valley together. Olympia's new role as the scene of the regular 'meetings in the homeland of Greeks living abroad' may be discerned in many ways. An unusually high proportion of the votive gifts was given by expatriate Greeks. This may be seen more clearly in the example of the group of the so-called treasuries on the terrace at the foot of the Hill of Kronos. At least eight of the eleven of these particularly imposing temple-like dedications were given by colonial cities in Southern Italy and in Sicily, in North Africa and

Asia Minor (Herrmann 1992: 25–32). With many participants in the festival coming from overseas, Olympia also reached the highest status in the eyes of the athletes. If someone achieved victory against this unique background, his name went 'around the whole world' as a result. So it is no coincidence that—as was mentioned earlier in this chapter—we can prove that at exactly this time the first stadium was built at Olympia. The name 'Olympia' now had such a ring in the whole Greek world that anyone who was able to make a successful appearance before the assembled masses here could use it to his advantage well into the future (more extensive treatment in Sinn 1991: 46–49).

References

Christesen, P. 2007. *Olympic Victor Lists and Ancient Greek History*. Cambridge.

Curtius, E. 1852. *Olympia: Ein Vortrag im wissenschaftlichen Vereine zu Berlin am 10. Januar gehalten*. Berlin.

Ebert, J. 1980. *Olympia: Von den Anfängen bis zu Coubertin*. Leipzig.

Eder, B. 2006. 'Die spätbronze- und früheisenzeitliche Keramik.' In H. Kyrieleis, *Anfänge und Frühzeit des Heiligtums von Olympia: Die Ausgrabungen am Pelopion 1987–1996*. Berlin.

Frame, D. 2009. *Hippota Nestor*. Hellenic Studies 34. Cambridge, MA.

Heiden, A. 1995. *Die Tondächer von Olympia*. Berlin.

Heilmeyer, W.-D. 1972. *Frühe Olympische Tonfiguren*. Berlin.

Heilmeyer, W.-D. 1979. *Frühe Olympische Bronzefiguren. Die Tiervotive*. Berlin.

Herrmann, H.-V. 1972. *Olympia. Heiligtum und Wettkampfstätte*. Munich.

Herrmann, H.-V. 1984. 'Altitalisches und Etruskisches in Olympia: Neue Funde und Forschungen.' *Annuario della Scuola Archeologica di Atene* 46: 271–294.

Herrmann, K. 1972. 'Die Schatzhäuser in Olympia.' In *Proceedings of an International Symposium on the Olympic Games, 5–9 September 1988*. 25–32. W. Coulson and H. Kyrieleis, eds. Athens.

Himmelmann, N. 2002. 'Frühe Weihgeschenke in Olympia', in *Olympia 1875–2000: 125 Jahre Deutsche Ausgrabungen. Internationales Symposion, Berlin 9.–11. November 2000*, ed. H. Kyrieleis. Mainz.

Kyle, D. 2015. *Sport and Spectacle in the Ancient World*, 2nd edn. Malden, MA.

Kyrieleis, H. 1997. 'Zeus and Pelops in the East Pediment of the Temple of Zeus at Olympia.' In *The Interpretation of Architectural Sculpture in Greece and Rome*. 13–27. D. Buitron-Oliver, ed. Hanover, NH.

Kyrieleis, H. 2002. *Olympia 1875–2000. 125 Jahre Deutsche Ausgrabungen. Internationales Symposion, Berlin 9.-11. November 2000*. Mainz.

Kyrieleis, H. 2003. *XII. Bericht über die Ausgrabungen in Olympia*. Berlin.

Kyrieleis, H. 2006. *Anfänge und Frühzeit des Heiligtums von Olympia: Die Ausgrabungen am Pelopion 1987–1996*. Berlin.

Maass, M. 1978. *Die geometrischen Dreifüße von Olympia*. Berlin.

Mallwitz, A. 1972. *Olympia und seine Bauten*. Munich.

Mallwitz, A. 1988. 'Cult and Competition Locations at Olympia.' In *The Archaeology of the Olympics: The Olympics and Other Festivals in Antiquity*. 79–109. W. J. Raschke, ed. Madison, WI.

Möller, A. 2004. 'Elis, Olympia und das Jahr 580 v. Chr. Zur Frage der Eroberung der Pisatis.' In *Griechische Archaik: Interne Entwicklungen—externe Impulse*. 249–270. R. Rollinger and C. Ulf, eds. Berlin.

Moustaka, A. 2002. 'Zeus und Hera im Heiligtum von Olympia und die Kulttopographie von Elis und Olympia.' In *Olympia 1875–2000: 125 Jahre Deutsche Ausgrabungen. Internationales Symposion, Berlin 9. –11. November 2000*. 301–315. H Kyrieleis, ed. Mainz.

Rambach, J. 2002. 'Olympia: 2500 Jahre Vorgeschichte vor der Gründung des eisenzeitlichen griechischen Heiligtums', in *Olympia 1875–2000: 125 Jahre Deutsche Ausgrabungen. Internationales Symposion, Berlin 9.-11. November 2000*. 177–212. H. Kyrieleis, ed. Mainz.

Scanlon, T. F. 2004. 'Homer, The Olympics, and the Heroic Ethos.' In *The Olympic Games in Antiquity: 'Bring Forth Rain and bear Fruit.'* 61–91. Maria Kaïla et al., eds. Athens; reprinted with footnotes added in *Classics@* 13. https://chs.harvard.edu/classics13-scanlon/ (accessed March 15, 2021).

Schilbach, J. 1984. 'Untersuchung der Schatzhausterrasse südlich des Schatzhauses der Sikyonier in Olympia.' *Archäologischer Anzeiger*: 225–236.

Sinn, U. 1981. 'Das Heiligtum der Artemis Limnatis bei Kombothekra. II: Der Kult. Zur Bestimmung der frühen "olympischen" Tonfiguren.' *Mitteilungen des Deutschen Archäologischen Instituts* 96: 25–43.

Sinn, U. 1991. 'Die Stellung der Wettkämpfe im Kult des Zeus Olympios.' *Nikephoros* 4: 31–54.

Sinn, U. 1994a. 'Die Entwicklung des Zeuskultes in Olympia bei Strabo.' In *Strabone e la Grecia*. 145–166. A. M. Biraschi, ed. Naples.

Sinn, U. 1994b. 'Apollon und die Kentauromachie im Westgiebel des Zeustempels in Olympia: Die Wettkampfstätte als Forum der griechischen Diplomatie nach den Perserkriegen.' *Archäologischer Anzeiger*: 585–602.

Sinn, U. 2001. 'Die Stellung des Hera-Tempels im Kultbetrieb von Olympia.' In *Archaische griechische Tempel und Altägypten*. 63–70. M. Bietak, ed. Vienna.

Sinn, U. 2002. *Olympia. Kult, Sport und Fest in der Antike*, 2nd edn. Munich.

Sinn, U. 2004. *Das antike Olympia: Götter, Spiel und Kunst*. Munich.

Ulf, C. 1997. 'Die Mythen um Olympia – politischer Gehalt und politische Intentionen.' *Nikephoros* 10: 9–51.

Weniger, L. 1915. *Die Seher von Olympia*. Leipzig.

CHAPTER 6

··

ETRUSCAN EVENTS

··

JEAN-PAUL THUILLIER

INTRODUCTION

It is worth remarking, first and foremost, that we have at our disposal relatively abundant evidence on Etruscan sport and spectacles. Bear in mind that Etruscan civilization, which hit its peak in central Italy in the seventh and sixth centuries BCE, has long been thought of as 'mysterious'. This 'mystery', fixated on the two questions of origins and of language, is generated in fact primarily by lacunae in our sources (Briquel 1999; Thuillier 1990; Thuillier 2003). However, as J. Heurgon observed half a century ago, 'What we know most clearly about the customs of the Etruscans, perhaps, we owe most to their games, because they loved to paint them, particularly their funerary games, on the walls of their tombs or sculpt them on their *cippi* and their sarcophagi.' (Heurgon 1961: 241–242). Though it is true that the tomb paintings of Tarquinia and Chiusi, alongside the archaic reliefs of the latter city, are certainly our principal iconographic sources, other categories of evidence should not be neglected, such as the *stelae* of Felsina (Bologna), black- and red-figure ceramics, and engraved mirrors (Camporeale 2004: 160–167). Some recent discoveries that include sports scenes likewise have allowed us to confirm and to refine our understanding on this subject.

In the second place, emphasis should be placed on the originality, usually hidden, of many aspects of Etruscan sport. Too often has there been a scholarly tendency to see Etruscan games as merely a reflection of the agonistic practices of Greece, in the *palaestra* as in the stadium and the hippodrome. Indeed, this perception often inflects the approach to Etruscan civilization in its entirety, as it is seen as a minor offshoot of Greek culture, and this habit is again reinforced by the considerable impact of Greek gymnastic culture and sport. Not that one should disclaim any Greek influence on the Etruscans in general and on the Etruscan sports universe in particular. It is, however, clear that Etruscan sports diverge from the Greek 'model' on many points. This can be seen, for example, in 'technical' aspects of equestrian competition (e.g. details of the races, equipment and practice of charioteers) (see below). This Etruscan distinctiveness holds true as well for the social status of athletes, the presence of women in public spaces, and likely the pattern of organizing these competitions. As the iconography certainly reveals this, it is likewise the whole function of spectacle which takes on another dimension. Indeed, the analysis of diverse sources, literary, epigraphic, and visual, show that Etruria exercised an essential influence on the *ludi circenses* of Rome and even on the spectacles of the *Urbs* in a larger sense, since, as we know, the *ludi scaenici* were themselves of Etruscan origin. Far from acting as a simple intermediary between Greece and Rome, Etruria played a fundamental role in this field which must be acknowledged.

THE BEGINNINGS OF ETRUSCAN SPORT SPECTACLE IN THE SEVENTH CENTURY BCE

The unique and foundational impact of the Etruscans can be traced in analysis of the oldest representations of sport. Indeed, a passage in Herodotus (1.166–167) is often invoked to note the dependence of the Etruscans on the Greeks, specifically in the matter of sports competitions, and to push the date for the origins of Etruscan games forward to the middle of the sixth century or thereabouts. According to the Greek historian, the Etruscans of Caere (modern Cerveteri) ordered the stoning of a portion of their Phocaean prisoners of war following a naval victory around 540 BCE. A whole series of prodigies followed in the wake of this action and the Caeretans went to consult the oracle of Delphi. As Herodotus says, 'The Pythia commanded them to perform something which they still are doing in our day: they offer rich sacrifices to the spirits of the Phocaeans and they established athletic and equestrian competitions in their honour.' Etruria thus immediately appears indebted to Delphi in this domain and even as a mere province of Greece. Moreover, the presence of numerous sport motifs on tomb paintings in Tarquinia dating to the second half of the sixth century seems to carry immediate confirmation of Herodotus' claim.

But the Etruscans did not need to go to Delphi to discover games and sports. Livy (1.35.7–9), in his account of the beginning of Tarquinius Priscus' reign (traditionally dated 615–578 BCE), notes that the king celebrated his victory over the Latins by organizing, in a newly constructed Circus Maximus, games more sumptuous than any of his royal predecessors. This spectacle (*ludicrum*) included on the playbill equestrian events (*equi*) and boxers (*pugiles*) 'which [Tarquin] imported mainly from Etruria' (*ex Etruria maxime acciti*). Thus, in at least some Etruscan cities, sporting events were known from the end of the seventh century: one will think for example of Veii, the city closest to Rome and its eternal rival since the foundation of the Urbs. The fact remains that an incised bucchero vase, found at Veii in the last century and dating to the last third of the seventh century, effectively illustrates this proposition. (Bucchero ware is a kind of black ceramic that one could consider the 'national' pottery of the Etruscans.) On the belly of this *olla* is a very beautiful boxing scene, with two pugilists facing off, fists up and ready, and apparently wearing tunic-trunks (Thuillier 1985a: 57–65). And Veii is not the only Etruscan city involved: at Caere (modern Cerveteri) a painted urn has been found, likewise from the seventh century, which represents a boxing match (Martelli 1987: 260). In addition, surviving from the same period and the same city (in the Tomb of San Paolo) is a bucchero *olpe* decorated in mythological scenes, with Medea, Daedalus, and possibly Jason engaged in a boxing match (Rizzo 2001: 170–171). Finally, still from the seventh century, a painted *olla* attributed to the Painter of Civitavecchia, who may have worked in the same region as Caere, portrays a boxing match, accompanied for the first time by a musician, a flute player; from this point on, such musical accompaniment would be a constant in this civilization, as we will see (Bruni 2000: 556).

It is immediately clear that boxing is the preferred sport of the Etruscans; this will also be the case for the Romans. But boxing is not the only athletic event, nor the only combat sport depicted in this early period in Etruria: two wrestlers in all-out action, under the watchful eye of a referee armed with a long rod, are represented in a small bronze sculpture group found at Murlo, also dating to the end of the seventh century. One last find comes from the same elite residence in Murlo, dating a little after 600 BCE: a series of terracotta plaques, which together form a frieze, depict a horse race, each steed mounted bareback by its jockey, heading toward the prize for the competition, a cauldron perched atop a column. Murlo is located a few kilometres to the south of Siena: we thus witness on these plaques a kind of Palio before the fact (Root 1973)! These ancient riders each wear a tall cap (*pileus*) and actually may be *desultores*, the rider-acrobats. With these numerous combatants and this horse race, Etruscan iconography seems to confirm for this period Livy's claim that seventh-century Rome could import professional resources for sporting events from contemporary Etruria. Another significant demonstration of this is discussed below.

THE SPORT SPECTACLE PROGRAMME IN THE SIXTH AND FIFTH CENTURIES BCE

Equestrian Events

If there is any area that highlights the true originality of Etruria, it is that of horse racing, especially chariot-races, which were fantastically successful there, as they would be later in Rome. We have already noted Livy's story that, around 610–600 BCE, the king Tarquinius Priscus summoned boxers and horses from Etruria. Funerary frescoes from Tarquinia and Chiusi offer even more striking attestation. One such is the assemblage of painted walls from the Tomb of the Olympic Games, dating to around 530 BCE, which was discovered in 1958 at Tarquinia, using the modern detection methods of the Foundation Carlo Lerici (Steingräber 1985: 336–337). The name of the tomb is due only to the fact that the modern Olympic Games took place in Rome in 1960; the name contributes, unfortunately, to the impression of widespread hellenization in Etruria. On the left wall of this small subterranean structure (alongside a pair of boxers) four *bigae* (two-horse chariots) hurtle toward a simple red post that marks the finish: the leading driver turns back to see where his opponents are and the trailing charioteer is felled by a *naufragium*, i.e. a spectacular crash. The specialized clothing of these drivers is extremely significant: each wears a short tunic that falls to mid-thigh and some of them have leather helmets. This outfit has no similarity to that of Greek charioteers, who wore a long tunic that fell to their feet and normally kept their head uncovered, as does, for example, the Charioteer of Delphi. The driving technique depicted is likewise distinctive: the Etruscan charioteers kept the reins tied (the painting depicts a somewhat oversized knot) around the waist, so as not to drop them; Greek drivers, however, simply held the reins in their hands—a 'bundle' of reins falling in the car of the chariot also allows for better control there. Add to this that Etruscan drivers used a whip, yet their Greek colleagues deployed the *kentron*, a long goad. This confirms the gulf between the hippic cultures of these two peoples (Bronson 1965). On the other hand, later evidence suggests that, in terms of equipment or means of managing the chariot, the Romans learned practically everything from the Etruscans ... and very little from the Greeks: thousands of documents, large and small, mosaics, bas-reliefs, terracottas, glass pieces, gemstones, corroborate this claim.

Closer examination of the type of chariot used in these equestrian competitions likewise points to Etruscan distinctiveness. *Bigae*—chariots hitched to two horses—are represented on the tomb paintings. It is strange that the Etruscans never became familiar with racing in the four-horse *quadriga*, the leading chariot type in Greece, where victory in the *quadriga* was reserved solely for the social and political elite: one knows for example that the Charioteer of Delphi is part of the victory monument of Polyzalus, a Sicilian tyrant. In contrast, the Etruscans were partial to the *triga*, the chariot drawn by three horses, with two horses on the yoke and one exterior free horse; indeed, almost half the harness races shown on the archaic reliefs of Chiusi are *trigae* events (Jannot 1984: 350–355). And here it's almost a textbook case of the Etruscan influence on Rome: in fact the Greeks never organized races of *trigae*, whereas the Romans came to take up this event for themselves, as one sees clearly in Dionysius of Halicarnassus and on several inscriptions detailing the wins of star charioteers. In fact, at Rome (on the Campus Martius along the Tiber) there was a training circus called the Trigarium, surely because of the *trigae* they produced there: it is certain that this place-name dates back to the 'Etruscan' period of Rome, under the Tarquin kings (Coarelli 1977). A final argument in this discussion: the shared importance for the Etruscans and the Romans of the rider-acrobat events (in Latin, the *desultores* and the *cursores*). These performers would leap down from their mounts at one or another moment of the race, or jump from one horse to another, although both are hardly ever depicted in straightforward races with conventional jockeys; other than the ambiguous case of Murlo (see previous section), one finds no more such representations in Etruria or in the Roman circus (Thuillier 1989). Even though the Romans adopted *quadriga* races with passion, the *trigae* and the rider-acrobats represent a new point of contact between Etruscan and Roman sports and a new divergence from the Greek reality.

Combat Sports

The prominence of boxing in Etruria is confirmed by its many representations in the sixth and fifth centuries BCE, particularly in the tomb paintings of Tarquinia. Here, boxers are occasionally the only athletes painted and often are placed in a focal location, flanking, in the Cardarelli Tomb for example, the entry door like two guards coming to menace the potential undesirable visitor (Steingräber 1985). Examination of funerary *stelae* of Felsina (Bologna) confirms the apparent popularity of boxing: to begin with, here it is the only athletic event represented, sometimes alongside *biga* racing, a combination that hearkens back to the Tarquin games program detailed by Livy. Equally, this sport occupies a privileged place even within the decoration (Sassatelli 1993: 45–67). When the artist, in effect, wanted to depict a sporting festival in a manner as complete as possible, showing both the procession as well as the hippic and gymnic *ludi*, as on a black-figure amphora by the Micali Painter at the British Museum (B 64), he nevertheless kept a focus quite particular to the boxing scene, which squeezed, by its situation and the number of people present, the rest of the competitions (Beazley 1947: 2). The *tibicen*, the flute-player whose reed instrument is close to the modern oboe or clarinet, is almost always present next to Etruscan boxers (Thuillier 1985a: 231–254). Several ancient authors for that matter picked up this habit, which is shocking to some: this used to be interpreted as a sign of softness, of that dissolute life that the Etruscans in antiquity were often reproached for, in particular among the Greek authors (Thuillier 2014: 37–44). In reality, this accusation of '*truphē*'—to go back to the Greek term—only works to betray the jealousy of these same Greeks towards an Etruscan people who enjoyed very favourable economic conditions and who (O the scandal!) even allowed women to play a not negligible role in social life (Liébert 2006: 28). To repeat this resentment about *truphē* concerning musical accompaniment for Etruscan boxing does not make much sense: as in traditional Thai boxing, which has nothing particularly soft about it, it was necessary for the musicians to punctuate the blows of the two adversaries and even to rouse their ardour for combat, should it flag too much.

Besides the chronological or numerical data, other confirmations reveal again the importance of boxing in the sports customs of the Etruscans: one can identify, on an archaic relief from Chiusi, the existence of a veritable ballet of boxing, with three athletes boxing and dancing in rhythm, under the direction of a flute-player (Jannot 1984: 329–330; Jannot 1985: 66–75). One cannot find in any case an illustration more precise than the expression of Jean Cocteau who described boxers as 'dancers who kill' (Thuillier 2018: 47–61); such choreographies are not unknown today, for that matter. Until a scene of classical boxing was discovered on a relief from Chiusi, unpublished until quite recently, one observed particularly in this city a strong interest in wrestling (Thuillier 1997: 243–260): one often witnesses, on reliefs as on the frescoes of Chiusi, a very spectacular grapple in which one of the adversaries accomplishes a veritable flying leap over the other competitor: this athletic movement, which puts an end to one of the phases of the match—if the Etruscans picked up on the Greek rule of three 'falls'—appears to be in any case a signature of the Chiusi artisans. It is necessary to take account here of the specificity of the Etruscan cities. But Tarquinia did not ignore wrestling, as is shown in a very beautiful scene with two athletes grappling in the initial phase of combat, found in the Tomb of the Augurs (around 530).

Other Events: Pentathlon

Besides these 'heavy' events, the Etruscans also were familiar with the 'light' athletic events. Thus the painted Tomb of the Olympic Games displays for us on one of its main walls a *biga* race and a boxing competition—one finds here a new example of this programme already seen above—and on the opposite wall, a collection of three events, with runners, a long-jumper, and a discus hurler. This second wall also offers the typically Etruscan game of Phersu: a hooded man, armed with a club, is attacked by a ferocious dog being driven by a masked executioner. This latter carries the name of Phersu, in other words, the 'Mask' (a word which corresponds to the Latin 'persona'). Some want to see here, wrongly, the prefiguration of Roman gladiatorial combats, which seem in reality to find their origin not in Etruria but in Campania, as the funerary paintings of Paestum show (Pontrandolfo and Rouveret 1992).

The assemblage of three athletic events cited above enables us to speculate that the Etruscans were also familiar with the Greek-style pentathlon: likewise, on certain panathenaic amphorae, it is a simple matter of choosing which events will be used to represent a victory in the pentathlon. This impression is confirmed by other evidence like the already-cited amphora B 65 of the Micali Painter, where one can see a discus thrower and a javelin thrower side by side, and especially an archaic relief from Chiusi, preserved at Palermo, on which the same athlete, at the moment of receiving his prizes, is holding both a discus and a javelin. But an uncertainty remains, on account of the absence of literary texts or inscriptions.

For the same reasons, it is difficult to know, for example, if the Etruscans competed in three races: the stadium, the *diaulos* (double-stadium distance) and the *dolichos* (the long distance). The images certainly allow us to note that the Etruscan long jumper habitually made use of the *haltēres* (hand weights) to improve his performance, and that the javelin thrower propelled his instrument with the help of a strap called, in Latin, the *amentum* (of which one can see a very nice representation on the wall paintings in the Tomb of the Monkey at Chiusi). On these points, the imitation of Greece seems to be more obvious. But there is also a small bronze from Felsina which can hardly be anything but a shot putter: did this competition exist in Etruria? And if the Greek influences were important, even there Etruscan originality must not be underestimated. The question of nudity can be at first an essential criterion, because the Greeks claimed this athletic nudity as a trait that distinguished them radically from the 'barbarians'. In fact, Etruscan society seems to evade this category: although one sees the athletes wearing a loincloth in the archaic period, one can also come across, from the sixth century, Etruscan wrestlers who are entirely naked, as in the Tomb of the Augurs at Tarquinia (Thuillier 1988). But the realism of Etruscan art—at the end of the sixth and beginning of the fifth century anyway—allows us to better understand that certain practices are almost totally hidden by the idealization of the athlete in contemporary Attic art. Thus one notes that certain Etruscan athletes were equipped with an 'athletic' belt or even more precisely with a 'jockstrap': the genitals are held lifted by a cord which is itself attached to a belt. The frescoes of the Tomb of the Monkey at Chiusi offer some particularly nice examples of this practice. Truth be told, the reality for the Greeks was no different from this. So the fact remains that, on this question, the Etruscans were not true 'barbarians'; by this we also have proof that the Etruscan artists were not content to reproduce Greek images, as is too often suggested, but that they well and truly depict local realities (Thuillier 1985a: 369–404; Thuillier 2018: 32–46).

THE PLACES FOR SPORT SHOWS

In Greece, the gymnic events took place in the stadium, while the equestrian competitions were in the hippodrome: in the archaic period, it's a question for that matter of 'places' instead of actual structures. With the Etruscans, the situation was similar to that at Rome: equestrian and athletic competitions were clearly held in the same space, as one can see, for example, in the Tomb of the Olympic Games already cited, where boxers and a race of *bigae* are situated on the same wall, without the slightest separation, and this was the case in the Roman circus during the traditional *ludi*, which follow the example of their origins: Tarquinius Priscus established the Circus Maximus, between the Palatine and the Aventine, fitted into the Murcia valley, and inaugurated the structure with a *ludicrum* that included *pugiles* and *equi*. It would not be until the end of the first century CE that Greek-style competitions would be held on the site of what is now the Piazza Navona, with the construction of the stadium of Domitian, designed to house the *certamina graeca*.

Up till now, no one has recovered an Etruscan 'circus' and this is no wonder, given the light and provisional character of the installations which needed to be put in place for the games, in particular in the sixth century. But we can hypothesize on the location of these circuses where, among other events, chariot-races took place: there is every chance that they would be found on the closest plain of the tufa plateau, on which were built the majority of the great cities of southern Etruria such as Caere, Tarquinia, Orvieto; if this plain is moreover neighbouring one of the grand necropoleis of the city, where funerals and funeral games took place, the hypothesis gains still more credibility.

Funerary archaeology leads to some other observations. From the seventh century, several orientalizing tumuli of Tarquinia (the Doganaccia, the Poggio del Forno, the Poggio Galinaro, the Infernaccio tumuli) introduce a structure that one could call 'theatriform': a very large dromos, similar to a small plaza, is often bounded on several sides with steps designed to accommodate spectators, at first those within the clan, who were thus able to watch scenic dances but also boxing matches or fights, in the setting of funerary games. No doubt some other religious ceremonies, starting with sacrifices, could be celebrated there. Later, in the sixth century, a tomb like the famous Cuccumella Tumulus at Vulci, or the cave complex of Grotta Porcina, near Blera, with an altar or a base for *cippi*, present again some structures of the same type (Colonna 1993).

But there are frescoes which offer us still very beautiful representations of installations for spectators, such as the Tomb of the Bigae in Tarquinia, dating from around 500 BCE. One can see here remarkable wooden bleachers protected by *vela* (awnings), which seem moreover to illustrate directly descriptions of the Circus Maximus from the time of the *Etruscan* king Tarquin the Elder, such as the one given by Livy or even Dionysus of Halicarnassus (Thuillier 1985a: 622–634). While young servitors, lying under the stands, give themselves up to more or less innocent games, 'noble' spectators are seated on the benches, men and women mingled: the mixing of this public is an eminently significant trait, insofar as, in this case at least, it is a woman who seems to occupy the foreground, which is the place of honour in a grandstand. One never sees an Etruscan female athlete or charioteer, contrary to what a passage of the hostile source Theopompus would let us suppose (Athenaeus 12.517d). Their presence among the public, however, is a sign, among others, of the privileged status of the Etruscan woman. All this moves us away in each case from Greek stadia, from the stadium at Olympia, for example, which never had seats for the public at large and where, with the exception of the priestess of Demeter Chamyne, no female spectator was accommodated. The presence of women connects us once more with Rome, where according to Ovid (*The Loves*, 3.2; *The Art of Love*, 1.135–162), the Circus Maximus was a favoured place for attempts at seduction!

OCCASIONS FOR SPECTACLE: RELIGIOUS AND SOCIAL ASPECTS

Funerary Games

In the quote referenced in the introduction, J. Heurgon speaks of 'funeral games' and, in spite of multiple scholarly debates, it is difficult not to think immediately that the tomb paintings were meant to evoke the games and ceremonies organized at the time of the funeral of the deceased honoree: the Etruscans obviously were familiar with a ritual like that described already by Homer for the funeral of Patroclus in book 23 of the *Iliad*. This is the location of one phase of a rite of passage which of course also includes other moments: the viewing and transport of the body, which we can reconstruct on the basis of certain images (on the archaic reliefs of Chiusi) and the analysis of the furnishings of certain major tombs; the banquet and dances associated with sports can be seen on several frescoes. In the absence of texts, however, it is difficult to establish the order of the rites, even if one could assume that the games came last (Jannot 1998: 66). All this concerns the dead, certainly, but also the living: the familial clan and, beyond them, the neighbours and the inhabitants of the city are afflicted and even temporarily broken by this bereavement that must be overcome. The competitions, the dances, the banquet allow the group to get past this psychological trial, to be restored in every sense of the term, and to recover the strength to ensure the future of their community (d'Agostino 1989: 1–10). The deceased himself was meant to find comfort in the paintings that extend the ritual effectiveness of the games; he could be delighted by this vision, if one believes that he lives a quiet life in the hereafter. The violent and dangerous character of certain Etruscan sports is also noted, sports which easily make blood flow; in some boxing scenes, such as those in the Tomb of the Olympic Games and the Tomb of the Funeral Couch at Tarquinia, one of the fighters loses a lot of blood. Perhaps it was necessary to revitalize the deceased in this manner, to provide him, ritually or symbolically, with a supplement of life force (Jannot 1998: 67).

Social History

The bloody violence of the boxers, however, or the *naufragium* of the chariots, possibly fatal for the charioteer, are not the artistic monopoly of Etruria: not only do these motifs also exist in Greece and later in Rome, but it's likely that these are absolutely realistic episodes which animated and spiced up the spectacle and its representation. Furthermore the names of fighters and boxers are painted alongside their images in two Tarquinian tombs (the Tomb of the Augurs and the rightly named Tomb of the Inscriptions, around 530 BCE): these probably indicate the favorite stars of the deceased. This parallels Trimalchio, the famous parvenu in Petronius' *Satiricon*, who, six centuries later, asks the entrepreneur in charge of building his tomb to paint on it the bouts of Petraites, his favorite gladiator, 'so as to have the good luck of living on after his death' (71.6). One can also make a connection with the first-century-CE funerary altar of T. Flavius Abascantus at Urbino, on which a relief shows Scorpus, a star of the Circus Maximus in Rome (*CIL* 6.8628). No doubt certain modern football fans would love to carry the image of Zidane or Beckham to their graves! The presence of sports stars on these frescoes of Tarquinia possibly refers to games organized by the deceased during the course of his life: in any event, it should without doubt emphasize his social status and that of his *gens*. It should be noted that in the great necropolis of Monterozzi in Tarquinia, only two per cent of the tombs are painted. This was an investment which was not within the means of common citizens; one could say the same thing about the games that constitute one of the frequent motifs on the painted walls. The Tomb of the Bigae, already cited for its exceptional depiction of wooden bleachers, lets us go further: in effect, the seats are filled with a numerous and varied public, which does not correspond to a single family. This is beyond the solely private sphere. Indeed, it is not absurd to imagine that the deceased noble was a magistrate for his city of Tarquinia and that his descendants organized the funerary games to which were invited at least some of his constituents. The fresco enhances simultaneously the social position of both the deceased and his family (Thuillier 1985a: 622–635; Massa-Pairault 1996: 131).

Sacred Games

Alongside the private or semi-private funeral games, organized in the circle of great families of the Etruscan aristocracy, there were also sacred games, public ones, offered to a range of divinities, and the gods delighted in these spectacles. The organization of games moreover appeased them, in the case of an epidemic, for example; the concept of the *ludi* as a ritual of expiation seems to be an Italic tradition, Etruscan first then largely diffused at Rome. The city of Caere thus organized equestrian and gymnic games there after the battle of Alalia and the stoning of the Phocaean prisoners. We might theorize that the majority of Etruscan cities celebrated, possibly on an annual basis, games in honour at least of their main divine patron, on the model of the Roman Ludi Magni held in September in honour of Jupiter Capitolinus. But the precise identification of the gods or goddesses to whom the Etruscan *ludi* were dedicated is more uncertain. In evoking the Dioscuri, Apollo, or Herakles, one wanted especially to find a Greek model. The most striking case is without doubt that of Turms, the Etruscan Hermes. For a long time, it was believed that the statue of Hermes Enagonios could be recognized on the mutilated frescoes of the Tomb of the Bigae at Tarquinia, an identification suited to satisfy all those who could only see Etruria through a Greek filter. The discovery of the Tomb of the Jugglers, also at Tarquinia, showed that this enigmatic figure was actually a circus acrobat holding a candelabra balanced on her head (Thuillier 1985a: 462–469).

But there is at least one more positive case. In Etruria, the games were organized in the framework of the confederation of Twelve Cities, just as the Panhellenic competitions at Olympia and elsewhere in Greece drew on resources beyond the single polis. The Etruscan dodecapolis only recognized its unity during these religious and spectacular manifestations which also were arranged to accompany a great market: in any case, this league never managed to develop a political federation and certainly this facilitated the Roman conquest. We can believe that these games had a sports and theatrical programme reflected in funerary iconography. They were dedicated to Tin(ia), the Etruscan Jupiter, the principal god (*princeps*) of the Tuscan pantheon, celebrated here under the invocation of Voltumna, which ought to reflect his role as protector of the League of Twelve Peoples. This religious situation is described to us by authors like Livy for the later period of Etruscan independence, which came to an end in 264 BCE. These Panetruscan *Ludi* were placed under the authority of a high priest, a *sacerdos*, and represent the most visible mark of a very fragile Etruscan unity. They were still celebrated long after the end of Etruscan independence: they may even be mentioned under the reign of Constantine. (Gascou 1967). The *Fanum Voltumnae*, the great Panetruscan sanctuary that Livy referenced five times, without specifying its location, must be found at the base of the rocky hill of Volsinii, modern day Orvieto.

CONCLUSION: THE STATUS OF ATHLETES

In Etruria, the iconographic portrayal of games emphasized the positive function of spectacle, and this is not without consequences for its social aspects. As is amply demonstrated by literary and epigraphic sources, as well as images of executioners and buffoons that are clearly sports-related, we do not see here the Greek agonistic model of the classical period exported to Etruria, but something distinctively Etruscan. In effect, these were not citizens carrying a *praenomen* and gentile *nomen*, nor *ephēbes*, born of some of the better families, whom we see performing on the sand of the track or the grass of the plain; these were professionals at a servile level, 'dependents' carrying a single unique name and connected in general to the troupe of a lord, or a king (of a so-called *lucumon*?), like that of the king of Veii who, at the end of the fifth century, withdrew his performers from the Panetruscan games of Volsinii, furious that he had not been elected *sacerdos* of the league by his peers. This anecdote, transmitted to us by Livy (5.1), concerns both the professionals of the circus as well as those of the theatre (*circi et scaenae artifices*, as Symmachus puts it in *Letters* 6.33) (Thuillier 2009). It seems difficult otherwise to discern a chronological evolution or profound geographical disparities that could have existed. Finally, this inferior social condition of Etruscan sportsmen makes more than problematic the hypothesis, imprudently advanced on the strength of one mutilated inscription, of an Etruscan participation in the great Panhellenic games circuit like those of Delphi (Thuillier 1985b).

REFERENCES

Beazley, J. D. 1947. *Etruscan Vase-painting*. Oxford.
Bevagna, G. 2014. 'Etruscan Sport.' In *Sport and Spectacle in Greek and Roman Antiquity*. 395–411. P. Christesen and D. G. Kyle, eds. Chichester.
Briquel, D. 1999. *La civilisation étrusque*. Paris.
Bronson, R. C. 1965. 'Chariot racing in Etruria.' In *Studi in onore di Luisa Banti*. 89–106. Rome.
Bruni, S. 2000. 'La scultura.' In *Gli Etruschi*. 365–391. M. Torelli, ed. Venice.
Camporeale, G. 2004. *Gli Etruschi: Storia e civiltà*. Turin.
Coarelli, F. 1977. 'Il Campo Marzio occidentale. Storia e topografia.' *MEFRA* 89: 807–846.
Colonna, G. 1993. 'Strutture teatriformi in Etruria.' In *Spectacles sportifs et scéniques dans le monde étrusco-italique*. 321–347. J.-P. Thuillier, ed. Rome.
D'Agostino, B. 1989. 'Image and Society in Archaic Etruria.' *JRS* 79: 1–10.
Gascou, J. 1967. 'Le rescrit d'Hispellum.' *MEFRA* 79: 609–659.
Heurgon, J. 1961. *La vie quotidienne chez les Etrusques*. Paris.
Jannot, J.-R. 1984. *Les reliefs archaïques de Chiusi*. Rome.
Jannot, J.-R. 1985. 'De l'agôn au geste rituel.' *AClass* 54: 66–75.
Jannot, J.-R. 1998. *Devins, dieux et démons : Regards sur la religion de l'Etrurie antique*. Paris.
Liébert, Y. 2006. *Regards sur la truphè étrusque*. Limoges.
Martelli, M. 1987. *La ceramica degli Etruschi. La pittura vascolare*. Novara.
Massa-Pairault, F.-H. 1996. *La cité des Etrusques*. Paris.
Pontrandolfo, A. and Rouveret, A. 1992. *Le tombe dipinte di Paestum*. Modena.
Rizzo, M. A. 2001. 'Le tombe orientalizzanti di San Paolo.' In *Veio, Cerveteri, Vulci. Città d'Etruria a confronto*. 163–176. A. M. Moretti Sgubini, ed. Rome.
Root, M. C. 1973. 'An Etruscan Horse Race from Poggio Civitate.' *AJA* 77: 121–137.
Sassatelli, G. 1993. 'Rappresentazioni di giochi atletici in monumenti funerari di area padana.' In *Spectacles sportifs et scéniques dans le monde étrusco-italique*. 45–67. J.-P. Thuillier, ed. Rome.
Steingräber, S. 1985. *Etruskische Wandmalerei*. Zürich.
Thuillier, J.-P. 1985a. *Les jeux athlétiques dans la civilisation étrusque*. Rome.

Thuillier, J.-P. 1985b. 'Mort d'un lutteur.' *MEFRA* 97: 639–646.

Thuillier, J.-P. 1988. 'La nudité athlétique (Grèce, Etrurie, Rome).' *Nikephoros* 1: 29–48.

Thuillier, J.-P. 1989. 'Les *desultores* de l'Italie antique.' *CRAI* 133: 33–53.

Thuillier, J.-P. 1990. *Les Etrusques: La fin d'un mystère?* Paris.

Thuillier, J.-P. 1997. 'Un relief archaïque inédit de Chiusi.' *RA* 2: 243–260.

Thuillier, J.-P. 2003. *Les Etrusques. Histoire d'un peuple.* Paris.

Thuillier, J.-P. 2009. 'Un pugiliste serviteur de deux maîtres: Inscriptions "sportives" d'Etrurie.' In *Etruria e Italia preromana: studi in onore di Giovannangelo Camporeale.* 877–880. S. Bruni, ed. Pisa.

Thuillier, J.-P. 2014. 'Sport et musique en Etrurie.' In *Etrusques. Les plus heureux des hommes.* 37–44. D. Frère et L. Hugot, éd. Rennes.

Thuillier, J.-P. 2018. *Allez les Rouges! Les jeux du cirque en Etrurie et à Rome.* Paris.

PANHELLENIC GAMES AND THE SPREAD OF THE TRADITION

CHAPTER 7

··

THE GREEK CROWN GAMES

··

MANUELA MARI AND PAOLA STIRPE

In ancient Greece, athletic competitions were the principal occasions for religious demonstrations of a local, regional, Panhellenic (or international) nature. The *agōnes stephanitai* ('stephanitic' or 'crown' games) were athletic, equestrian, or musical contests in which prizes were limited to wreaths (*stephanoi*) of leaves. Originally the only victors to receive a prize consisting of such a wreath were those who won at the Panhellenic games that made up the so-called *periodos*: ('cycle') the games of Olympia, Delphi, Isthmia, and Nemea. This prize, though possessing only a modest material value, assured the victor not only great prestige, which reflected on the whole community from which he came, but also concrete privileges in his homeland (a triumphal procession when he returned to the city, support at public expense, a post of honour at spectacles; cf. Pleket 1974, 1975 and 1996; Papakonstantinou 2002; for later developments see Rumscheid 2000; on the evolution of ancient terminology and on the actual ancient uses of the term *stephanitēs* see Remijsen 2011). For Athenian victors at the Olympic and Isthmian Games, for example, Solon is said to have introduced monetary prizes (Plut. *Sol.* 23.3). The *periodonikai* were those athletes who succeeded in winning competitions in a specific event at all four games of the *periodos*. Some inscriptions suggest there was special honour in winning at the four games within the four-year cycle that began with each edition of the Olympics—an achievement analogous to winning the modern 'Grand Slam' in tennis (Knab 1934; Moretti 1954; Buhmann 1972). There was no prize provided for those who came in second or third, except at local meets, which offered valuable objects or money as prizes (*thematikoi agōnes*; Crowther 1992). These minor games were widespread ever since the archaic period, and were frequented even by famous athletes, such as the illustrious pugilist Theagenes of Thasos, to whom tradition attributes victories in more than a thousand competitions (Moretti 1953 no. 21).

In the different versions that ancient authors give of the origins of the games of the *periodos*, there is a recurrent characterization of each as an *agōn epitaphios*—games established in honour of a dead person. The *Iliad*'s account of the funeral games for Patroclus (Book 23), in fact, includes most of the events that made up the programme of the Olympic Games (Yiannakis 1990).

These games, in honour of Zeus, were celebrated at Olympia in Elis every four years from 776 BCE until 393 CE, when they were ended forever by decree of the emperor Theodosius (for a fuller discussion: Remijsen 2015). Pindar (*Ol.* 1) tells us that when Pelops came to the Peloponnese he defeated King Oinomaos in a chariot-race, winning his daughter Hippodamia for his bride. The king died during the race or killed himself after being beaten. To commemorate him, Pelops established the games in his honour, and celebrations in his memory were still being held in the second century CE, according to Pausanias (5.4.4; 6.20.9; on the hero and the Olympics see Burkert 1988). According to another tradition originating with Pindar (*Ol.* 10; *Ol.* 3; cf. Strab. 8.354–355 Casaubon Paus. 5.8.3; Apollod. *Bibliot.* 2.7.2), the games underwent a reform after Herakles defeated King Augeus: Herakles decreed that they would take place every four years, dedicated them to Zeus and then went to the land of the Hyperboreans to procure the wild olive that would shade and reward the victors. But there were other versions of the origins of the Olympic Games: according to Pausanias (5.7.6–9), they began with Herakles Idaeus, one of the Curetes who had received the baby Zeus from Rhea. Herakles Idaeus is said to have urged his brothers to compete in the race and to have given the victor a branch of wild olive gathered in the land of the Hyperboreans. Because he and his brothers were five in number, he decreed that the games be held 'every fifth year', or at a penteteric interval (in modern terms, every four years, since the Greeks calculated years inclusively: the penteteric Olympic and Pythian Games were held every four years, the trieteric Isthmian and Nemean every two). According to yet another version, it was Zeus himself who established the games after defeating Cronus (Paus. 5.7.10). Later, the games are said to have been restored by a descendant of Herakles Idaeus, Clymenus, and then celebrated by other figures. On the occasion of the Heraclidae's return to the Peloponnese, Oxylus obtained Elis as a reward for having given them aid, but after his time the games were not held again until Iphitus reorganized them in 776 BCE (Paus. 5.4.5–6; 8.1–5).

From that time (one of the key dates in the ordering of the Greek historical memory) begins the list of Olympic victors attributed to Julius Africanus, who was inspired by the now-lost works of Hippias of Elis and Aristotle. Already in ancient times there was discussion of the reliability of the dates available to those who studied the history of the games; but it seems that at Olympia, and probably in all the other sanctuaries of the *periodos*, there were lists of victors and other 'archival' materials on the history of the games available from a fairly early date. Aristotle, who also wrote a history of the Pythian Games and a list of *Pythionikai*, seems to have worked directly from data kept in the sanctuary, at least in the case of Delphi; his name and that of Callisthenes, the future historian of Alexander, are recorded in a Delphic decree honouring this research activity (*CID* IV.10). Pausanias knew of rolls of the Isthmian and Nemean victors as well (6.13.8) (Christesen 2007).

For the first celebrations of the games, we find victors coming exclusively from the neighbourhood of Olympia (on the site see Kunze et al. 1937– and, for more synthetic presentations, Mallwitz 1972; Sinn 1991; 2010; Kyrieleis 2011; Sinn, Chapter 5, this volume; on the relationship between Olympia and its neighbourhood see Taita 2007; Kõiv 2013). Later, as the fame of the games grew, victors are attested from the rest of the Greek peninsula and from many other Greek cities across the Mediterranean (Moretti 1957; Bengtson 1971; Morgan 1990; Farrington 1997). Some famous Olympic victors in the equestrian contests were the Sicilian tyrants Hieron and Theron, the Athenian Alcibiades, the king of Macedonia, Philip II, and, later, various Hellenistic monarchs (Moretti 1957; 1970; 1987). In equestrian races it was the owner of the horses who was proclaimed the winner, not the jockey or the charioteer; defeat certainly posed less of a risk to the personal prestige of a sovereign in these competitions than in a footrace or a boxing match. Herodotus tells us, however (5.22), that Alexander I of Macedon competed and tied for first place in the *stadion* race at Olympia. From the first century BCE we also find victors of Roman origin at Olympia, but it was mostly emperors (for example, Tiberius and Nero) who won victories there. Nero also caused the rule to be broken by which Olympia hosted only athletic and equestrian contests, so that he might compete among the tragedians and lyre players (Lucian *Nero* 2; Suet. *Nero* 23.1).

According to Pausanias (5.8.6–11, 9.1), the programme of the Olympic games changed several times through the ages (Lee 2001). The oldest and most prestigious competition was the *stadion* footrace, whose length varied from place to place, but was generally a little less than 200 metres. There were also other races ('the double *stadion*' or *diaulos*, 'the long race' or *dolichos*, and the race in armour), along with wrestling, boxing, *pancration*, and *pentathlon*. The most prestigious of the horse races was the *tethrippon* (four-horse chariot-race). The contests and ceremonies in honour of Zeus took place in July and August, lasting five or six days, but we are not well informed about the order of the events (Miller 1975). The competitors were subdivided into at least two age classes (*paides* and *andres*), a system also attested for other crown games, where we find an additional, intermediate category of *ageneioi*, or beardless youths. The prize for victory was a crown of leaves gathered from a wild olive that grew in the sanctuary of Olympia itself; the tree was called *kallistephanos* and was kept into imperial times (Plin. *Hist. Nat.* 16.240; cf. Paus. 8.48.2–3). Seventeen boughs for the victory crowns, one for each of the Olympic events, were cut with a golden sickle by a boy who had both parents still living. Being crowned as *Olympionikēs*, 'Olympic victor', was the highest point of any athlete's career. Beyond the crown, such a victor could expect an epinician poem, such as the many that survive by the lyric poets Pindar and Bacchylides, as well as a statue. Statues of victorious athletes, which were erected within the sanctuary where their victories were won, along with the above-mentioned lists of victors compiled at the same sanctuaries, connected the history of the games with a collection of historical memories, especially at the local level, of which Pausanias *Periēgēsis* is often our only testimony (Herrmann 1988; Christesen 2007).

The Pythian Games were held in honour of Apollo at Delphi, in Phokis, every four years, at a two-year interval from the Olympic Games (Davies 2007; Fontenrose 1959; Pouilloux 1977; Rougemont 1973; Miller 2004: 95–101; on the site see Bommelaer and Laroche 1991). They differed from the other Panhellenic games in their greater emphasis on musical contests, which were connected directly with the foundation myth of the games. According to a well-known tradition, Apollo defeated the serpent Pytho and became lord of Delphi (*Hymn. Homer.* 3; Aristot. fr. 637 Rose; Schol. Pind. *Pyth. Argum.* a, p. 2, ll. 6–16; c, p. 4, ll. 3–18 Drachmann; Hygin. *Fab.* 140; Ovid, *Met.* 1.438–451; cf. Fontenrose 1959); he then performed a hymn in honour of the serpent to a lyre accompaniment, thereby founding the Pythian Games, which were thus also an *agōn epitaphios* ('funeral game').

In the beginning, the Pythian Games involved only the musical competition, which consisted of the performance of a hymn in honour of Apollo to the accompaniment of a lyre. The plan of the hymn reflected the one performed by the god and retold his exploit against Pytho (Paus. 10.7.2–4; Strab. 9.421 Casaubon Schol. Pind. *Pyth. Argum.* a, p. 2, ll. 10–16 Drachmann). In its first phase, the contest took place every eight years (Censor. *De Die Nat.* 18; Schol. Pind. *Pyth. Argum.* c, p. 4 ll. 14–15 Drachmann): this number was connected directly to the legend, which told of Apollo's eight-year exile after his killing of Pytho.

The games in honour of Apollo long retained their local character under the jurisdiction of the Phocians of Crisa and Cirrha. But the sacred league called 'Amphictyony', with its headquarters at Anthela, imposed tributes on the two centres (it is uncertain, however, that the toponyms Crisa and Cirrha indicate two separate places) and tried to usurp their admin-istration of the games; Cirrha was forbidden to impose a toll on the pilgrims to Delphi who disembarked there (Davies 1994; Dillon 1997; on the Amphictyony see Lefèvre 1998). This was the origin of the so-called First Sacred War (the designation *hieros polemos* is ancient, the numeration modern: Strab. 9.418 Casaubon; Athen. 13.560c; Plut. *Sol.* 11; Paus. 10.37; Lefèvre 1998; Skoczylas Pownall 1998). The members of the Amphictyony won the war; Crisa was taken and destroyed, and its territory was consecrated to Apollo. There followed, in cele-bration of the victory, a reorganization of the games, which became quadrennial in 586 BCE, and in 582 expanded their programme with athletic and equestrian events, additional mu-sical events (Paus. 10.7.4–8) and perhaps a contest in painting, attested for the fifth century (Plin. *Hist. Nat.* 35.58). The equestrian events were held in the plain of Cirrha (Paus. 10.37.4). The tradition of the First Sacred War is largely the fruit of successive elaborations, and it is impossible to define its historical nucleus, but archaeological data possibly suggest that Delphi was at war at the beginning of the sixth century (Davies 1994; 2007).

Only in 582 were objects of value replaced as prizes by wreaths, first of oak leaves and then of laurel, the tree sacred to Apollo (Ovid. *Met.* 1.448–451; Paus. 10.7.5; Schol. Pind. *Pyth. Argum.* b, p. 3, ll. 12–18, d, p. 4, ll. 22–25, l. 4 Drachmann). The leaves were collected in the valley of Tempe and given to the victor by a boy with both parents living (Paus. 8.48.2–3; 10.7.8; Aelian, *Var. Hist.* 3.1). Thus from being *chrematitai* ('value-prize games') the games had become *stephanitai* ('crown games'). It appears that the musical contests were held first, followed by the athletic and equestrian events (Plut. *Quaest. Symp.* 2.4; Soph. *Electr.* 698ff.), confirming the greater importance of music at Delphi (Biliński 1979).

The Isthmian Games were held in the sanctuary of Poseidon at Isthmia, near Corinth (Gebhard 1993; 2002; Morgan 2002; Miller 2004: 101–105). According to one tradition, the games were born as a consequence of the struggle between Helios and Poseidon for possession of the Corinthian territory: Briareus, chosen as arbiter, gave the Acrocorinth to Helios and the Isthmus to Poseidon (Paus. 2.1.6; Dio Chrysost. *Orat. Corinth.* 11). According to another version, the games were established in memory of Melicertes (son of Athamas and Ino-Leucothea), whom the Greeks would later call Palaemon, and who leapt into the sea with his mother (Paus. 1.44.8; Apollod. *Bibliot.* 3.4.3; Ovid, *Met.* 4.519–542; Stat. *Theb.* 6.10–14; Auson. *Eclog.* 21, 22; Schol. Pind., *Isthm. Argum.* a, b, c, d, pp. 192–195 Drachmann). A third tradition records that Sisyphus established the games in honour of Melicertes after finding his body on the shore of the Isthmus, where a dol-phin had deposited it (Paus. 2.1.3; Gebhard and Reese 2005; in this case too, therefore, a great Panhellenic festival is attributed to a 'funerary' origin). The Attic hero Theseus, after defeating Sinis (or Skiron), is said to have founded the games in honour of Poseidon that replaced those for Melicertes (Schol. Pind. *Isthm. Argum.* b, pp. 192, ll. 16–193, l. 5 Drachmann; Plut. *Thes.* 25.5–6; Hygin. *Fab.* 273; Plin., *Nat. Hist.* 7.57): this tradition is the basis of the concession to the Athenians of the privilege of *proedria* at the games (Plut. *Thes.* 25.7). While the Athenians had a place of honour at the Isthmian Games, the Eleans were forever barred from them (Paus. 5.2.1–5). Interrupted by the tyrant Cypselus, the Isthmian Games were reorganized as a Panhellenic festival by the Corinthians in 582 BCE: a Pythian year, indeed the first of the new Pythian Games, reinstituted after the First Sacred War (Solin. 7.14). The existence of Isthmian Games is attested, however, in the time of Solon, according to the above-cited Plut. *Sol.* 23.3. The games were moved to Sicyon when Corinth was destroyed in 146 BCE and returned to Corinth when the city was reborn at the wish of Julius Caesar in the middle of the first century BCE (Gebhard 1993 and 2002; Morgan 2002; Gebhard and Reese 2005).

The prize for Isthmian victors was originally a crown of pine, later replaced for some time by one of dry celery and then restored (Plut. *Quaest. symp.* 5.3.1; Paus. 8.48.2–3; Schol. Pind. *Isthm. Argum.* b, p. 193, ll. 9–18; c, p. 194, ll. 17–19 Drachmann; Lucian, *Anach.* 9, 16; Broneer 1962). The pine tree was sacred to Poseidon, because its wood was used to make vessels that plied the seas, of which Poseidon was the god, while the adoption of celery may have been inspired by the prize given in the Nemean Games. The Isthmian events were athletic, equestrian, and musical, the last being introduced at least by the third century BCE and attested with great frequency, especially in the Roman era. The dramatic contests also had great importance, as demonstrated by the existence of companies of artists of Dionysus called Isthmian and Nemean. According to Pliny the Elder (*Hist. Nat.* 35.58), there was also a competition in painting at the Isthmus.

The Nemean Games were held at Nemea in the Argolid, between the territories of Phlius and of Cleonae, then later at Corinth or Argos. They were founded, according to tradition, by Adrastus and his Argive companions during the expedition of the Seven against Thebes (Miller 2004: 105–111; Mari 2008; on the site see Miller 1990). These too are said to have been funerary games, celebrating the memory of the child Opheltes, son of Lycurgus, ruler of Nemea, whose death Adrastus and his companions involuntarily caused. Opheltes was also called Archemorus, but in some variants of the tradition the latter is a separate person to whom the games were dedicated (Apollod. *Bibliot.* 3.6.4; Schol. Pind. *Nem. Argum.* a, b, c, d, e pp. 1–5 Drachmann; Stat. *Theb.* 4, 5, 6 *passim*; Hygin. *Fab.* 74, 273; Paus. 2.15.2–3, 8.48.2; Bacchyl. 9.10 ff.). Nor are other versions lacking, one of which makes room for the role of Herakles, who is said to have founded the games after killing the Nemean Lion, or to have restored those established earlier for Archemorus giving them greater solemnity by dedicating them to Zeus (Schol. Pind. *Nem. Argum.* a, p. 1, ll. 3–4; d, p. 4, ll. 20–22; e, p. 5, ll. 16–18 Drachmann; see Doffey 1992).

The first 'historical' attestation of the Nemean Games dates from 573/572 BCE (Euseb. *Chron.* 2.94–95 Schoene). Their organization was long the subject of controversy between the cities of Cleonae and Argos (see below). The games included athletic, equestrian, and musical contests (Plut. *Philop.* 11; Paus. 8.50.3). The victors originally received a wreath of olive (as at Olympia), which was later replaced by one of fresh celery (Paus. 8.48.2–3; Schol. Pind. *Nem. Argum.* d, p. 4, ll. 22–25, l. 2 Drachmann). In addition to the summer Nemean Games there were also winter games, in the Roman era if not earlier, mentioned in literary and epigraphical sources (Paus. 2.15 3, 6.16.4; Moretti 1953 no. 85).

The literary and epigraphical sources provide evidence for the practicalities especially of the festivals of Olympia and Delphi, for the activities of the umpires, and for the duties of the organizers (Miller 2001a; Crowther 2004). To the Eleans were reserved the *agōnothesia* (presidency) of the Olympic Games, the general administration, the sacrifices, lodgings for the athletes and spectators, a general oversight and the sending of envoys (*theōroi*) charged with proclaiming the next celebration of the games and the truce (Gehrke 2013). But the Eleans, according to Pausanias (6.4.2; 6.8.3; 6.22.2–3), did not administer the eighth, thirty-fourth, and one-hundred-and-fourth Olympiads, when the organization of the games was taken from them by other peoples. These Olympiads, therefore, were considered illegal 'Anolympiads', and were not registered in the official Elean catalogue. Especially notorious were the games of 364, organized by the Arcadians and Pisatans. On the opening day of the *panēgyris*, the Eleans and Achaeans marched on Olympia to avenge the outrage, and the battle took place within sanctuary itself (Xen. *Hell.* 7.4.30–32). Moreover, there was no competition at Olympia in 80 BCE, apart from the boys' *stadion*, because Sulla had summoned all the athletes to Rome, making celebration of the event impossible (App., *Civ.* 1.99). From 580 BCE and long thereafter, the organizers of the games were two men chosen by lot from among the Eleans. In 400, according to Pausanias (5.9.5), the nine *Hellanodikai* were first appointed, though their name and functions were already known to Herodotus (5.22.1). It was the duty of these umpires to ensure that the games were held according to the rules, to check the origin, condition, age, and physical fitness of the participating athletes, and to crown the victors (Siewert 1992). Their number changed many times, and was ten in the time of Pausanias.

At Delphi, after the First Sacred War, control of the sanctuary and the *agōnothesia* of the games passed to the Amphictyony, which took care of the stadium, hippodrome, and theatre for the games, proclaimed the sacred truce by having it announced by *theōroi*, and, during the festival, provided for the sacrifices and the procession in honour of the god (Lefèvre 1998). Among the Delphic inscriptions richest in information on these details is a long accounting document perhaps datable to 247/246 BCE (*CID* II 139; Pouilloux 1977). The *hieromnēmones* (representatives of the twelve Amphictyonic peoples) were responsible for the practical administration of the contests and, like the *Hellanodikai* of Olympia, for the registration of the athletes, and they ensured respect for the rules and gave prizes to the victors (Pind., *Pyth.* 4.66; Heliod., *Aethiop.* 4.2). A blatantly 'illegal' celebration of the Pythian Games took place in 290 BCE, when Demetrius Poliorcetes held them at Athens in order to contest the legitimacy of the control exercised by the Aetolians over Delphi and the Amphictyony at that time (Plut. *Demetr.* 40).

Both the Isthmian and Nemean Games, on the other hand, were organized by a single city. Isthmia and the Isthmian Games were always under the control of Corinth, with an Argive interval connected with a moment of political union between the two cities in 390 BCE (Xen. *Hell.* 4.5.1–2). The Nemean Games were traditionally organized by the little city of Cleonae, but for long periods they fell under the control of Argos, where they were transferred in the Hellenistic period and where they took place regularly in the time of Pausanias. Other cities of the northern Peloponnese (such as Mycenae and Corinth) occasionally advanced claims to the sanctuary and its games (Mari 2008; 2013).

The great Panhellenic games reproduced, in some sense, the forms of 'exclusion' that were the basis of Greek society within every polis. Thus, neither foreigners nor women were admitted to them. The exclusion of non-Greeks is usually presumed for Olympia (Hdt. 5.22) and for the other Panhellenic Games, but this has been questioned (Remijsen 2019). The case of women is also best attested for Olympia, from whose games they were rigidly banned, even as spectators (Paus. 5.6.7–8; Dillon 2000). But here too the special status of the equestrian events, in which the victor was the owner of the horses, not necessarily present in person, allowed women to compete in the games. There is the well-known instance of the Spartan Cynisca, daughter of Archidamus II and sister of Agesilaus, who was an Olympic winner at the beginning of the fourth century BCE (Paus. 3.8.1; Plut., *Ages.* 20.1; *IvO* 160), and her example was followed by many women, especially in Hellenistic times. By the Roman era, as is shown by a Delphic inscription in honour of three athletes from Tralles (Moretti 1953 no. 63), women were competing even in footraces, at least at the Pythian, Isthmian, and Nemean Games. Previously, women, especially Spartans and other Dorians, were able to compete in footraces only at events reserved for them alone, such as the Elean *Heraia* (Paus. 5.16.2–8); here, like the men, they competed in age classes, and the winners received a crown of olive and the right to dedicate statues in commemoration of their victories (Scanlon, this volume Chapter 49). Female participation in the poetic and musical competitions was more common and started earlier.

The Greeks as a whole had no single calendar that united the different localities: each region, if not each city, had its own calendar, organized around local festivals and cults (Trümpy 1997). The four crown games therefore also represented an attempt to organize time in the Greek world in a uniform way. When a Panhellenic festival was to be celebrated, the host sanctuary sent *theōroi* to the various cities to announce the *panēgyris* and the sacred truce (*ekekheiria*) (Arist. fr. 533 Rose; cf. Daux 1967; Rougemont 1973; Perlman 2000; Gehrke 2013). The timely announcement prevented the differences among the civic calendars from affecting the success of the games by causing sparse attendance. The truce, which allowed both athletes and pilgrims to reach the sanctuary without danger, theoretically reaffirmed the moral and cultural unity of the Greek world on the occasion of the great *panēgyreis* (in reality, it was often broken).

In fact, the Panhellenic festivals created a dense fabric of religious and competitive encounters that were repeated with regularity, giving rise to the adoption of the Olympiad (the space of four years between successive celebrations of the games at Olympia) as the basis of a Panhellenic chronology. Each Olympiad was opened and closed in summer by the festival of Olympia (Miller 1975); the Pythian Games were held in late summer of the third year of each Olympiad (Davies 2007), the Isthmian Games in the spring of the first and third years of each Olympiad (Gebhard 2002), and the Nemean Games in the summer of the second and fourth year of each Olympiad (Miller 2001b). Thus no year of the four-year Olympic cycle was without its Panhellenic celebrations.

The *panēgyreis* and the competitions held at them attracted an enormous number of visitors, who could attend a variety of events: apart from the sporting and religious observances, the festivals hosted cultural events, such as readings, oratorical and rhetorical displays, lyric choruses, and exhibitions of artwork. According to the rich ancient literary tradition on this subject, Herodotus won a great success with his public reading, at Olympia, of selections from his *Histories* (Lucian, *Herod.* 1–3); famous orators used the great stage of the Panhellenic festivals for political appeals (cf. Paus. 6.17.7–8 on Gorgias; or Diod. 14.109.1–3 on Lysias); the painter Aetion brought to Olympia a famous painting of the wedding of Alexander and Roxana (Lucian, *Herod.* 4). The economic and 'mercantile' aspect of the games was no less important: the fact that each year saw at least one *panēgyris* that attracted spectators and participants from the whole Greek world guaranteed the development of a great 'fair' capable of serving the needs of an extensive area. It is no accident that the festivals of the *periodos* were concentrated in the regions of Greece with the strongest presence of urban centres (three in the Peloponnese, one in central Greece), and one can imagine the true distribution of commercial areas among the four Panhellenic centres (Davies 2007).

More generally, the Panhellenic festivals were a meeting place for the different populations of the Greek peninsula, and a useful opportunity for finalizing diplomatic negotiations, for depositing or displaying treaties and other documents of public interest in the sanctuaries, and for announcements of 'international' import. In the ancient world, which lacked modern means of mass communication, events such as the Panhellenic festivals were the best occasions for cementing political and commercial agreements, for communicating political and military news that was not merely local, and for advertising. An example is the proclamation of Cleisthenes, tyrant of Sicyon, who in seeking the best Greek as a bridegroom for his daughter Agariste (and, clearly, as a political ally), promised during the Olympic Games of 572 BCE that he would celebrate the wedding within the year, beginning from the sixtieth day from the date of the proclamation (Hdt. 6.126–131). In the sanctuary of Poseidon on the Isthmus, on the other hand, the Greeks gathered in 481 BCE to decide on a defensive strategy against the Persian invasion (Hdt. 7.172); and it was also here (if not in nearby Corinth) that they proclaimed Philip II head of the expedition against the Persians during the Panhellenic conference of 338/337 BCE (Just. 9.5; Diod. 16.89.3). Alexander the Great chose Olympia for announcing to the Greeks the order that every city recall its exiles in 324 BCE (Diod. 17.109.1; 18.8.2–7). At Isthmia, during the games of 196 BCE, T. Quinctius Flamininus proclaimed through a herald the Roman decision to 'liberate' Greece (Polyb. 18.46; Plut., *Flam.* 10), a gesture repeated by Nero at the Isthmian Games of 67 CE (Suet., *Nero* 24).

Imitation of the ancient and prestigious crown games led to the attribution of the titles 'Isolympic', 'Isopythic', etc., to many local games (Farrington 1997; Lämmer 1967; Mari 1998). The adjective indicated a contest that was 'equal' or 'like' the model in one or more respects (the name of the festival, its frequency, its religious ceremonies, the type of events and age classes, aspects of administration, prizes; Musti 2005). The wide diffusion of Greek culture, connected with the conquests of Alexander and with the kingdoms of his successors, caused, among other consequences, a flowering of local games, both in the capitals of the kingdoms (where the games sometimes took the name of the reigning sovereign) and in remoter places.

In the imperial age, especially, there was a multiplication of Olympic and Pythian festivals in the most various places, both in mainland Greece and in Asia. In some cases the name was juxtaposed with that of the imitated festival. The organizers generally avoided a perfect synchronicity between the new and ancient festivals, to prevent the failure of the newer celebrations. The epigraphical and, in some cases, the numismatic evidence is particularly instructive for the degree and aspects of imitation of the models (cf. Moretti 1953: 278–279 with the commentary on the relevant inscriptions and the synthesis of Pleket 1996: 521–523; Newby 2005: 246–255; for cases of particular interest, cf. Lämmer 1967; Frei-Stolba 1985; Gallis 1988; Spawforth 1989; Mitchell 1990; Mari 1998; and, among the many studies of Robert, at least 1938: 53–62; 1940–1965: V, 59–63; VII, 82–88; 93–104; XI–XII, 350–368; 1969–1990: I, 611–632; 644–670; II, 1125–1160; V, 347–437; 647–674; 791–839; 1970: 418–429). The birth and rapid diffusion of such a large number of games imitating the crown games of the *periodos* brought about a progressive diminution of the latter's importance, since crown games very similar to the originals of Olympia, Delphi, the Isthmus, and Nemea were being celebrated almost everywhere. Also contributing to this phenomenon was the alteration of the original *periodos*, which in the Roman era was enlarged to include other competitions of both ancient and recent establishment (Remijsen 2015).

REFERENCES

Biliński, B. 1979. *Agoni ginnici: Componenti artistiche ed intellettuali nell'antica agonistica greca.* Rome.

Bommelaer, J.-F. and D. Laroche. 1991. *Guide de Delphes. Le site.* Athens.

Broneer, O. 1962. 'The Isthmian Victory Crown.' *AJA* 66: 259–263.

Buhmann, H. 1972. 'Der Sieg in Olympia und in der anderen panhellenischen Spielen.' Dissertation, Munich.

Burkert, W. 1988. 'Heros, Tod und Sport: Ritual und Mythos der Olympischen Spiele in der Antike.' In *Körper- und Einbildungskraft*. 31–43. Berlin.

Christesen, P. 2007. *Olympic Victor Lists and Ancient Greek History*. Cambridge.

Crowther, N. B. 1992. 'Second-Place Finishes and Lower in Greek Athletics (including the Pentathlon).' *ZPE* 90: 97–102.

Crowther, N. B. 2004. *Athletika: Studies on the Olympic Games and Greek Athletics*. Hildesheim.

Daux, G. 1967. 'Théores et théarodoques.' *REG* 80: 292–297.

Davies, J. K. 1994. 'The Tradition about the First Sacred War.' In *Greek Historiography*. 193–212. S. Hornblower, ed. Oxford.

Davies, J. K. 2007. 'The Origins of the Festivals, especially Delphi and the Pythia.' In *Pindar's Poetry, Patrons, and Festivals*. 47–69. S. Hornblower and C. Morgan, eds. Oxford.

Dillon, M. P. J. 1997. *Pilgrims and Pilgrimage in Ancient Greece*. London.

Dillon, M. P. J. 2000. 'Did Parthenoi attend the Olympic Games? Girls and Women Competing, Spectating, and Carrying out Cult Roles at Greek Religious Festivals.' *Hermes* 128: 457–480.

Doffey, M.-Ch. 1992. 'Les mythes de fondation des concours Néméens.' In *Polydipsion Argos: Argos de la fin des palais mycéniens à la constitution de l'État classique. Fribourg (Suisse) 7–9 mai 1987 (BCH Suppl. 22)*. 185–193. M. Piérart, ed. Athens.

Drachmann, A. B. 1903–1927; repr. 1969. *Scholia vetera in Pindari carmina*. 3 vols. Amsterdam.

Farrington, A. 1997. 'Olympic Victors and the Popularity of the Olympic Games in the Imperial Period.' *Tyche* 12: 15–46. Repr. with addendum in *Sport in the Greek and Roman Worlds*, vol. 1: *Early Greece, the Olympics and Contests*. 158–202. T. Scanlon, ed. 2015. Oxford.

Frei-Stolba, R. 1985. 'Wirtschaft, Sport und Kultur in den römischen Provinzstädten.' *Civitas* 40: 299–302.

Fontenrose, J. 1959. *Python: A Study of Delphic Myth and its Origins*. Berkeley.

Gallis, K. J. 1988. 'Games in Ancient Larisa: an Example of Provincial Olympic Games.' In *The Archaeology of the Olympics: The Olympics and Other Festivals in Antiquity*. 217–235. W. Raschke, ed. Madison.

Gebhard, E. R. 1993. 'The Evolution of a Panhellenic Sanctuary: From Archaeology towards History at Isthmia.' In *Greek Sanctuaries*. 154–177. N. Marinatos and R. Hägg, eds. London.

Gebhard, E. R. 2002. 'The Beginnings of Panhellenic Games at the Isthmus.' In *Olympia 1875– 2000: 125 Jahre deutsche Ausgrabungen: Internationales Symposion, Berlin 9.–11. November 2000*. 221–237. H. Kyrieleis, ed. Mainz.

Gebhard, E. R. and Reese, D. S. 2005. 'Sacrifices for Poseidon and Melikertes-Palaimon at Isthmia.' In *Greek Sacrificial Ritual, Olympian and Chthonian. Proceedings of the Sixth International Seminar on Ancient Greek Cult, Göteborg University, 25–27 April 1997*. 125–154. R. Hägg and B. Alroth, eds. Stockholm.

Gehrke, H.-J. 2013. 'Theoroi in und aus Olympia: Beobachtungen zur religiösen Kommunikation in der archaischen Zeit.' *Klio* 95: 40–60.

Herrmann, H.-V. 1988. 'Die Siegerstatuen von Olympia.' *Nikephoros* 1: 119–183.

Knab, R. 1934. *Die Periodoniken: Ein Beitrag zur Geschichte der gymnischen Agone an den vier griechischen Hauptfesten*. Dissertation, Giessen (Chicago, 1980).

Kõiv, M. 2013. 'Early History of Elis and Pisa: Invented or Evolving Traditions?' *Klio* 95: 315–368.

Kunze, E. et al. 1937–. *Berichte über die Ausgrabungen in Olympia* (Berlin, 1937–).

Kyrieleis, H. 2011. *Olympia: Archäologie eines Heiligtums*. Mainz.

Lämmer, M. 1967. *Olympien und Hadrianeen im antiken Ephesos*. Cologne.

Lee, H. M. 2001. *The Program and Schedule of the Ancient Olympic Games*. Hildesheim.

Lefèvre, F. 1998. *L'Amphictionie pyléo-delphique: histoire et institutions*. Athens.

Mallwitz, A. 1972. *Olympia und seine Bauten*. Munich.

Mari, M. 1998. 'Le Olimpie macedoni di Dion tra Archelao e l'età romana.' *RFIC* 126: 137–169.

Mari, M. 2008. 'Festa mobile: Nemea e i suoi giochi nella tradizione letteraria e nell'evidenza materiale. I: l'età arcaica e classica.' *Incidenza dell'Antico* 6: 91–132.

Mari, M. 2013. 'Festa mobile. Nemea e i suoi giochi nella tradizione letteraria e nell'evidenza materiale. II: l'età ellenistica e romana.' *Incidenza dell'antico* 11: 9–62.

Miller, S. G. 1975. 'The Date of Olympic Festivals.' *MDAI(A)* 90: 215–231.

Miller, S. G. 1990. *Nemea: A Guide to the Site and Museum*, Berkeley.

Miller, S. G. 2001a. 'Organisation et fonctionnement des jeux Olympiques.' In *Olympie. Cycle de huit conférences organisé au musée du Louvre par le Service culturel du 18 janvier au 15 mars 1999. 75–125*. A. Pasquier, ed. Paris.

Miller, S. G. 2001b. *Nemea II: The Early Hellenistic Stadium*. Berkeley.

Miller, S. G. 2004. *Ancient Greek Athletics*. New Haven.

Mitchell, S. 1990. 'Festivals, Games, and Civic Life in Roman Asia Minor.' *JRS* 80: 183–193.

Moretti, L. 1953. *Iscrizioni agonistiche greche*. Rome.

Moretti, L. 1954. 'Note sugli antichi periodonikai.' *Athenaeum* 32: 115–120.

Moretti, L. 1957. 'Olympionikai. I vincitori degli antichi agoni olimpici.' *MAL* 8.8: 53–198.

Moretti, L. 1970. 'Supplemento al Catalogo degli Olympionikai.' *Klio* 52: 295–303.

Moretti, L. 1987. 'Nuovo supplemento al catalogo degli Olympionikai.' *MGR* 12: 67–91.

Morgan, C. 2002. 'The Origins of the Isthmian Festival.' In *Olympia 1875–2000: 125 Jahre deutsche Ausgrabungen: Internationales Symposion, Berlin 9.–11. November 2000. 251–271*. H. Kyrieleis, ed. Mainz.

Musti, D. 2005. Ed. *Nike. Ideologia, iconografia, feste della vittoria in età antica*. Rome.

Newby, Z. 2005. *Greek Athletics in the Roman World*. Oxford.

Papakonstantinou, Z. 2002. 'Prizes in Early Archaic Greek Sport.' *Nikephoros* 15: 51–67.

Perlman, P. 2000. *City and Sanctuary in Ancient Greece: The Theorodokia in the Peloponnese*. Göttingen.

Pleket, H. W. 1974. 'Zur Soziologie des antiken Sports.' *Mededelingen van het Nederlands Instituut te Rome* 36: 57–87. 1988. Repr. in *Lo sport in Grecia*. 31–77. P. Angeli Bernardini, ed. Rome.

Pleket, H. W. 1975. 'Games, Prizes, Athletes and Ideology: Some Aspects of the History of Sport in the Graeco-Roman World.' *Stadion* (=*Arena*) 1: 49–89.

Pleket, H. W. 1996. 'L'agonismo sportivo.' In *I Greci: Storia Cultura Arte Società*. 507–537. S. Settis, ed. Turin.

Pouilloux, J. 1977. 'Travaux à Delphes à l'occasion des Pythia.' *Études delphiques* (*BCH Suppl.* 4): 103–123.

Remijsen, S. 2011. 'The So-Called 'Crown-Games': Terminology and Historical Context of the Ancient Categories for Agones.' *ZPE* 177: 97–109.

Remijsen, S. 2015. *The End of Greek Athletics in Late Antiquity*. Cambridge.

Remijsen, S. 2019. 'Only Greeks at the Olympics? Reconsidering the Rule against Non-Greeks at 'Panhellenic' Games.' *Classica &Mediaevalia* 67: 1–61.

Robert, L. 1938. *Études épigraphiques et philologiques*. Paris.

Robert, L. 1940–65. *Hellenica: Recueil d'épigraphie, de numismatique et d'antiquités grecques*, vols. I–XIII. Limoges.

Robert, L. 1969–1990. *Opera Minora Selecta: Épigraphie et antiquités grecques*, vols. I–VII. Amsterdam.

Robert, L. 1970. *Études anatoliennes: Recherches sur les inscriptions grecques de l'Asie Mineure*. Amsterdam.

Rougemont, G. 1973. 'La hiéroménie des Pythia et les «trêves sacrées» d'Éleusis, de Delphes et d'Olympie.' *BCH* 97: 75–106.

Rumscheid J. 2000. *Kranz und Krone: Zu Insignien, Siegespreisen und Ehrenzeichen der römischen Kaiserzeit*. Tübingen.

Siewert, P. 1992. 'The Olympic Rules.' In *Proceedings of an International Symposium on the Olympic Games, 5–9 September 1988*. 113–117. W. Coulson and H. Kyrieleis, eds. Athens.

Sinn, U. 1991. 'Olympia: die Stellung der Wettkämpfe im Kult des Zeus Olympios.' *Nikephoros* 4: 31–54.

Sinn, U. 2010. *Olympia: Zeustempel und Wettkampfstätte*. Munich.

Skoczylas Pownall, F. 1998. 'What Makes a War a Sacred War?' *EMC* 42: 35–55.

Spawforth, A. J. S. 1989. 'Agonistic Festivals in Roman Greece.' In *The Greek Renaissance in the Roman Empire*. 193–197. S. Walker and A. Cameron, eds. London.

Taita, J. 2007. *Olimpia e il suo vicinato in epoca arcaica*. Milan.

Trümpy, C. 1997. *Untersuchungen zu den altgriechischen Monatsnamen und Monatsfolgen*, Heidelberg.

Yiannakis, T. 1990. 'The Relationship between the Underground–Chthonian World and the Sacred Panhellenic Games.' *Nikephoros* 3: 23–30.

CHAPTER 8

THE PANATHENAIA AND LOCAL FESTIVALS

JULIA L. SHEAR

At the Great Panathenaia of 182 BCE, wearing his armour, Kallias, the son of Thrasippos, jumped on and off his moving four-horse chariot as the team raced up the Panathenaic Way towards the Eleusinion. And the winner was … 'Kallias, the son of Thrasippos, of the tribe Aigeis', as we know from the inscribed victors' list (*IG* II² 2314 + *SEG* 41 114.36–37). The specification of Kallias' tribe Aigeis rather than his ethnic (Athenian) indicates that participation in this contest was restricted to Athenian citizens. For us, this apobatic race brings out an important aspect of regional and city festivals and their competitions: their focus on local concerns rather than the emphasis on being Greek which we find in the four Panhellenic festivals. As we shall see with the Panathenaia, how one participated demonstrated one's relationship to Athens and Athena so that both the games and the larger ritual setting served to display the city to herself and to her visitors. These dynamics are not limited to the Panathenaia and we shall see them also in the Artemisia held outside Eretria at Amarynthos. In contrast to Athena's festival, participation in the procession and the much less elaborate competitions for Artemis was unrestricted in the classical period. Such games were not static over time, as our third festival, the Delia held on Delos for Apollo, clearly brings out. The Delia also shows how such a celebration can work at the level of the region, rather than of the city. As with the other two festivals, its emphasis was not on being Greek, but on more local concerns appropriate to its participants.

THE PANATHENAIA AT ATHENS

The Panathenaia (Shear 2021) was held annually on 28 Hekatombaion, the first month of the Attic year. Every four years, it was celebrated in a grander and more elaborate form which was known as the Great Panathenaia and included an extensive series of games drawing participants from many parts of the Greek world. In contrast, the much smaller Little or Annual Panathenaia focused on Athenians and, in the late fifth and fourth centuries BCE, included only a very limited number of competitions (Tracy 2007). The Great Panathenaia, on which we shall concentrate, was instituted most probably in 566 BCE and it continued to be held until the end of the fourth century CE (Shear 2021: 5–8). This multi-day, international event provided a series of different occasions for spectacles, the most important of which were the elaborate games and the procession on 28 Hekatombaion. Different events had different rules for participation so that they provided multiple opportunities for presenting status relative to the goddess and the city.

In the classical period, the games fell into four divisions: musical contests, athletic competitions, chariot- and horse-races, and competitions for tribal teams, as the inscribed prize list from the 380s BCE makes clear (*SEG* 53 192 with Shear 2003). In the very full programme of the 380s, contestants competed in various different classes (Table 8.1). As the musical competitions show, some events might be restricted to boys or men, but others were not; very probably, the performers in this open category were adult men. While the athletic contests are divided into three classes (boys, beardless youths or *ageneioi*, and men), not all events were held for each age class: the competitions were most limited for beardless youths and most extensive for men. The divisions reflect the physical differences between boys, youths, and men and the different musical skills of boys and men. In contrast, the organization of the hippic games was rather more complicated and the divisions were determined not only by the age of the horses involved but also by the relationships of the human participants or, in the open events, the owners to the city. In the unrestricted competitions, there seems to have been one contest for racehorses, but, for the various chariot events, colts raced separately from adult horses (Shear 2003: 92–93); most, but not all, of these races were also held at this time at the Olympic and Pythian games. A large part of the Panathenaic hippic programme was taken up by contests not open to all participants/owners. The apobatic race with which we started was among the restricted events, as were a series of events 'for warriors'. Since the horse-race and processional *zeugos* reappear in the second century BCE when they are limited to Athenians (Shear 2007: 138; Tracy and Habicht 1991: 198–201), it is very likely that these fourth-century warriors were also Athenians (and members of the cavalry) who represented their tribes. In the second century, some hippic contests were also specifically limited to the cavalry and their officers (Shear 2007: 138; Tracy and Habicht 1991: 198–200). The programme was rounded off by a series of events for teams representing the Athenian tribes. Although the *purrhichē* or dance in arms and the cyclic choruses were divided into classes, the other contests will have been the province of adult men, and the *anthippasia*, the mock cavalry battle, will have been restricted to members of the city's cavalry. The four different divisions of the games were also distinguished by their prizes: musicians received gold crowns and cash, victors in the athletic and hippic events were awarded amphorae of olive oil, and the winning tribes got oxen for banquets.

The Panathenaic programme contrasts sharply with the events held at the games in the Panhellenic sanctuaries. The large number of competitions open only to Athenians representing their tribes marks out the contests at Athena's festival. Also striking is its martial flavour: contestants in the *hoplitēs* (race in armour), the apobatic race, the *purrhichē*, and the *anthippasia* all wore armour, while military weapons were used in the javelin-throw from horseback, as well as the *purrhichē* and *anthippasia*; the participants in the events for warriors may also have been clad in armour. Of these events, only the *hoplitēs* was open to all participants: all the rest were restricted to Athenian citizens or, in the case of the *purrhichē*, citizens-to-be. Participation in the tribal events of the Panathenaia, accordingly, identified the individual as a male citizen who was prepared to fight on behalf of the city. The martial competitions are particularly appropriate for a festival celebrating the victory of the gods

Table 8.1: The Panathenaic Programme in the 380s BCE

Musical Competitions

Open	Men	Boys
rhapsodes	*aulōidoi*	*aulōidoi*
kitharōidoi	*kitharistai*	*kitharistai*
aulētai		
sunaulētai		

Athletic Games

Boys	Beardless youths (*ageneioi*)	Men
dolichos	*stadion*	*dolichos*
stadion	pentathlon	*stadion*
pentathlon	wrestling	*diaulos*
wrestling	boxing	pentathlon
boxing	pankration	wrestling
pankration		boxing
		pankration
		hoplitēs (race in armour)

Hippic Games

Citizens	Open		Warriors (citizens)
apobatēs	racehorse		racehorse
	four-horse chariot	colts	*zeugos* (pair)
		adult animals	processional *zeugos* (pair)
	sunōris (racing pair)	colts	javelin-throw from horseback
		adult animals	
	zeugos (pair)	colts	
		adult animals	

Contests for Tribal Teams

purrhichē[1]	boys	
	beardless youths (*ageneioi*)	
	men	
euandria		
torch-race		
contest of ships		
anthippasia		
cyclic chorus	boys	
	men	

[1] For the *purrhichē* as tribal, see Shear 2003: 90 n. 7; Shear 2021: 357–360; cf. Parker 2005: 256.

over the Giants and founded by Erichthonios, the mythical inventor of the apobatic race and the chariot (Shear 2021: 39–66; Parker 2005: 254–256). In origin, the *purrhichē* was also closely associated with Athena: she first performed it either after her birth or in celebration after defeating the Giants (Parker 2005: 257). In addition, some versions of the apobatic race identify Athena as one of the participants (Schultz 2007: 59–60). Consequently, appearing in armour at this particular festival associated the individual closely with the occasion's origins, its founder, and the goddess. In this context, taking part in the tribal competitions not only marked the individuals as citizens, but it also positioned them more closely in relation to the goddess than the other competitors in the open contests. Citizens' participation in the tribal events was in no way neutral and it served to promulgate a very specific version of what it meant to be an Athenian. Non-Athenians were also clearly identified: they watched the citizens perform in the restricted competitions and they competed with everyone else in the contests open to all.

The importance of the tribal competitions was not limited to the early fourth century. Some, but not all, of them are attested in the late fifth century and the apobatic race and the *purrhichē* existed already by 510 and 520 BCE respectively, that is before the invention of the ten Kleisthenic tribes. Although the tribal team events are not attested after the Great Panathenaia of probably 290 BCE (*IG* II^2 3079; Shear 2021: 361–365), the preserved sections of the victors' lists from the second century BCE document an extensive array of individual hippic contests for Athenians (Shear 2007: 137–140). At the festival of 182, there were four such contests, all held on the Panathenaic Way (*IG* II^2 2314 + *SEG* 41 114.36–44), but, four years later in 178, there were eight contests on the processional route and another five in the hippodrome (*IG* II^2 2314 + *SEG* 41 114.68–83, 96–105). This distinct increase in the number of races shows that the Athenians wished to make it possible for more individuals to compete in and win these tribal competitions (Shear 2007: 139–140); for us, they bring out the importance in taking part in the games in the restricted events. Doing so in the second century continued to identify a man as a citizen prepared to fight on behalf of the city. The desirability of displaying one's Athenian status at this international occasion is further brought out by the participation of the Ptolemies and Attalids not only in the open hippic contests but also in the tribal competitions (Shear 2007). How one positioned oneself in relation to the goddess and the city continued to matter, even to the powerful Hellenistic kings.

The restrictions on participation were not limited to the games because they also extended to the procession and sacrifices. In the procession, the participants all have clear relationships to the city: they are citizens (officials, hoplites, cavalry, *thallophoroi*, *apobatai*), daughters of citizens (*kanēphoroi*), metics (*skaphēphoroi*), daughters of metics (*hudriaphoroi*, *diphrophoroi*, and parasol-bearers), colonists, and allies (Parker 2005: 258–261 and Shear 2021: 118–148, both with further references). Individuals who do not fall into these categories are not attested as marching in Athena's procession and their status as spectators will have marked them out as not being members of the community. Similarly, sacrificial animals were offered by the city, her subdivisions (demes, tribes, *genē*), colonies, and allies (Shear 2007: 140). When the sacrifices were offered and the meat subsequently distributed, these groups will have been identified as members of the sacrificial community of the Athenians and they will have been separated out from the visitors who watched them (Detienne 1989: 3–4; Shear 2010: 142–143). Not all these groups took part in all periods: metics belong to the classical period, but their daughters are attested only from the late fifth century and the allies were involved only in the second half of this century; some colonies reappear in the fourth and second centuries BCE. Nor did they participate in the same way so that their different roles marked their various relationships in and to the city. Citizens had a greater number of (more impressive) roles than other classes, but they also disproportionately represented the elite members of the community. For all these groups, how they took part in the procession and sacrifices defined in an important way what it meant to be a citizen, citizen's daughter, metic, metic's daughter, colonist, or ally (Shear 2021: 212–313). The most important status of Athenian citizen was further reinforced by the tribal contests in the games, moments when metics, colonists, and allies, as well as visitors, watched the Athenians perform for the goddess.

This differential participation and the distinct emphasis on Athenians brings out for us the local focus of the Panathenaia and they set it sharply in contrast to the four Panhellenic festivals and their games. Taking part in Athena's celebration identified one's standing in the city and one's relationship to the goddess. In this way, the reciprocal relationships created here (Parker 1998) were between the city and other select individuals and the goddess. These dynamics leave little room for individuals from other cities, who may compete in the open events, but primarily act as spectators as the city presents herself to herself and incidentally to her visitors. This decidedly local focus within the international atmosphere of this important festival had further consequences. The rich prizes, as attested by the prize list, were presumably intended to attract competitors to the games and international participation is attested already in the sixth century, but these efforts never succeeded in making the Panathenaia into the fifth event in the Panhellenic circuit. Instead, it always remained just below the other four celebrations in importance. While those festivals emphasized the division between Greeks and non-Greeks and so were broadly inclusive, the politics of the Panathenaia were more complicated: all competitors were welcome in certain contests, but other events were reserved for Athenians and only some groups could participate in the procession and sacrifices. This specific focus suggests that Athena's celebration was ultimately too local, too Athenian, to rival the truly Panhellenic games at which all Greeks were equally welcome and the international elements could never fully dominate the Athenocentric nature of the occasion. For non-Athenians, Athens was never the equivalent of Hellas.

THE ERETRIAN ARTEMISIA AT AMARYNTHOS

The focus on local concerns is not peculiar to the Panathenaia and it is typical of many other festivals, including ones with competitions which drew contestants from beyond the sponsoring community. These dynamics are clearly visible in the Artemisia which was celebrated by the people of Eretria in their extramural sanctuary at Amarynthos some 10 km east of the town (location: Knoepfler 1988). In the classical period, when the celebration is best attested, we can see both a desire to make the occasion attractive to individuals from beyond Eretria and also a focus on displaying the city to residents and visitors.

Our best evidence for the competitions comes from a decree of about 340 BCE which regulates various aspects of the festival (RO 73). The document establishes musical contests and stipulates the prizes to be awarded (Table 8.2). The programme is more restricted than the musical competitions at the Panathenaia and it includes one event, for singers of parodies of Homeric epic, not included in the games at Athens. As at the Athenian competitions, victors at the Artemisia were rewarded with cash prizes, as were the second- and third-place finishers. Although the amount of the compensation was significantly less than at the Panathenaia (Table 8.2) and victors did not receive (gold) crowns, the awards will have increased the attractiveness of the Artemisia to competitors from beyond Eretria. That such participants were desired by the Eretrians is further suggested by the maintenance given to contestants from three days before the *proagōn* until the competition itself and by the lambs sacrificed for five days before the musical events. If all competitors came from Eretria, such arrangements would not have been necessary; they also provide an additional benefit for those travelling from further away. The Eretrians, consequently, seem to have been quite intent on attracting contestants from beyond the limits of their territory.

This inscription provides further information about the festival. It included a procession and sacrifices of animals provided by the people of Eretria, by the districts (*chōroi*), and by private individuals, if they wished. The animals were conducted to the sanctuary in this order and the competitors in the musical contests were also to take part in this procession. In contrast to the Panathenaia, there are no restrictions on participation either in

Table 8.2: The Musical Contests of the Artemisia and Panathenaia

Event	Place	Prizes at Artemisia[1]	Prizes at Panathenaia[2]
rhapsodes	1	120 dr.	crown (amount not preserved)
	2	50 dr.	not preserved
	3	20 dr.	not preserved
boys' *aulōidoi*	1	50 dr.	not preserved
	2	30 dr.	not preserved
	3	20 dr.	
men's *aulōidoi*	1		crown of 300 dr.
	2		100 dr.
men's *kitharistai*	1	110 dr.	crown of 300 dr. + 200 dr.
	2	70 dr.	at least 200 dr.
	3	55 dr.	at least 100 dr.
kitharōidoi	1	200 dr.	crown of 1,000 dr. + 500 dr.
	2	150 dr.	1,200 dr.
	3	100 dr.	600 dr.
	4		400 dr.
	5		300 dr.
singers of parodies (*parōidoi*)	1	50 dr.	
	2	10 dr.	

[1] From RO 73.
[2] From *SEG* LIII 192.

the competitions or in the procession and sacrifices. Visitors who came and were prepared to compete and/or buy sacrificial animals participated as fully as Eretrian citizens, and the openness of the events will have increased its attractiveness to people from the larger region. The procession, however, also focused particularly on the people of Eretria: it included 3,000 hoplites, 600 cavalrymen, and 60 chariots, as we know from a *stēlē* described by Strabo and probably dating to the classical period (10.1.10; Knoepfler 1997: 392 with n. 299). In this way, it put the assembled Eretrians on show to themselves and their visitors and it stressed their military might, while the sacrificial animals provided by the districts presented one of the civic divisions of the city.

When the regulations for the Artemisia were passed, this display will not have been neutral because, in 341, after a period of tyranny and civil strife, the city was once again ruled by democracy (Knoepfler 1997: 377; Rhodes and Osborne 2003: 364). Indeed, the final clauses of the inscription stress that the Artemisia will happen in this way forever, 'while the people of Eretria are free and prosper and rule themselves' (RO 73.42–45). When the festival was held, it brought all the people of Eretria together irrespective of their political allegiances and their earlier divisions which will not have been visible. Consequently, the Eretrians will have shown both themselves and their visitors that they were now united and no longer divided by civil strife. The process of participating in the Artemisia will also have created a memory for the Eretrians of what it meant to be a united people, and this memory will have been reinforced at subsequent festivals. This remembering, in turn, will have helped to prevent further civil strife. Meanwhile, the addition of the new musical contests will have demonstrated the people's control of the city, because they had the power to make changes to one of Eretria's most important festivals. At this time, accordingly, the politics of inclusion, which are so clear in the inscribed regulations, work both at the level of the city and of the region, to which the city belongs. While the people of Eretria clearly wanted to welcome visitors from abroad, they were also very focused on local issues, the (re)creation of unity and the recovery from civil strife.

In view of the Artemisia's politics of inclusion in the years after 341, it is striking that no mention is made in the regulations of competitors from other types of contests. This absence suggests that, at this time, the Artemisia only included musical events. In the Hellenistic period, however, this situation certainly changed: by about 100 BCE, there was also a competition for the *purrhichē* (*IG* XII.9 236.44–46; 237.21–23; XII Suppl. 553.28–30). As at Athens, it will have been contested by teams, but, in this case, they were made up specifically of ephebes (Chankowski 1993: 19–30). Although non-Eretrians seem to have taken part in the *ephēbeia* (*IG* XII.9 234.23–28; Chankowski 1993: 22–25), the ephebes as a group represented the city and their participation in this contest made clear their close relationship to Eretria and the goddess. The ideal competitors were configured as citizens-to-be, while the spectators were either Eretrians who had taken part in this event before they became adults or foreigners without specific connections to the city. By this time, the *purrhichē* had also become the occasion for announcing honours for the city's benefactors (*IG* XII.9 236.44–46; 237.21–23; XII Suppl. 553.28–30). These announcements will have reinforced the connections between this event and citizenship, and they marked it as the most important contest at the Artemisia. By the second half of the second century BCE, there also were athletic competitions (*SEG* 28 722; Knoepfler 1988: 388) and musical events continued to be held in the first century BCE, as we know from a partially preserved victors' list (*IG* XII.9 141). Whether athletic contests existed before the second century is unclear; an ancient commentator on Pindar's *Olympian*

13 certainly thought so (schol. Pind. *O.* 13.159b), but Pindar (*O.* 13.112), in fact, only mentions Euboia, not Eretria or the Artemisia. Reference to another Euboian festival suggests that this commentator was guessing about the exact occasion to which the poet alludes. If there were athletic competitions in the fifth century, then they must have ceased by about 340 when the regulations for the Artemisia were passed.

As with the Panathenaia, the contests at the Artemisia changed over time and they seem to have become significantly larger at some point between about 340 and the late second century BCE. Throughout this period, the Amarynthian festival focused on presenting the Eretrians to themselves and their guests, but the politics involved did not remain the same. While the fourth-century regulations are striking for their inclusion, the addition of competitions for teams of ephebes in the *purrhichē* added an element of exclusion to the Artemisia: not everyone could take part in the same way on this occasion and some participants were more privileged, both in the games and in relationship to the goddess, than others. These contests kept the focus on the city and they emphasized that citizenship involved prior performance for Artemis. The martial nature of this competition will also have reinforced the military display of the Eretrians in the procession. The existence of this restricted contest by the late second century is particularly striking because our best evidence for the participation of non-Eretrians, both from elsewhere on Euboia and from further away, belongs to this century (Liv. 35.38.3, in 192 BCE; *IG* XII.9 234.24–32; cf. Knoepfler 1972: 284, 294–296). Evidently, the addition of such a competition did not make the festival unattractive to non-Eretrians who continued to attend.

The Artemisia also shows us how a festival might be used to work out extremely local issues, in this case, recovering from civil strife and responding to oligarchy. At one level, using the celebration to create and reinforce Eretrian unity was extremely appropriate because the Artemisia seems to have been one of the city's most important festivals and so many Eretrians will have been involved with it in some way. At another level, it contrasts strikingly with the Panathenaia at Athens which was not used for similar purposes after the oligarchies of 411 and of the Thirty in 404/403. Instead, unity was (re)created at the City Dionysia and the Eleusinian Mysteries, two festivals with politics and dynamics which differed significantly from those of the Panathenaia (Shear 2011: chs. 5, 7, 10). Comparison with the Artemisia suggests also that the Panathenaia may have been considered too international an occasion for working out such internal issues. Despite its visitors from elsewhere, the festival for Artemis, in contrast, was more locally oriented and so it could be used as an opportunity for addressing concerns relevant primarily to Eretria's inhabitants rather than to her visitors.

THE DELIA ON DELOS

While the Panathenaia presents us with a local festival which never quite made it to the ranks of the four Panhellenic celebrations and the Artemisia remained primarily local, despite drawing participants from beyond the city's boundaries, the Delia shows how such an occasion might work at the level of the region, which, in this case, included not just the Cyclades, but also the Ionians. It served to bring together delegations from different cities and to create for them a regional identity. The Delia also demonstrates how a festival may change over time and how its politics and development are inextricably intertwined.

In the archaic period, the Delia was an elaborate annual festival with a variety of different contests: Thucydides mentions both gymnastic and musical competitions, as well as choruses sent by cities (3.104.3). The celebration drew participants from beyond Delos itself and Thucydides specifically describes it as an occasion when the Ionians and the neighbouring islanders came together on the island to honour Apollo. Since the choruses were sent by communities rather than individuals, they will have acted as official representatives of their cities. Participation in such a chorus, consequently, ought to have identified an individual as a member of the sponsoring community. Additionally, the festival provided the Ionians with an opportunity to come together as a group, so that taking part in the Delia also functioned as a marker of Ionian status. For the cities involved, it will have confirmed their status as Ionian and the inhabitants of the neighbouring islands should have been so identified too. In this way, the Delia created identity not only for the city of Delos, but also for the region.

At some point, due to the misfortunes of the Ionians, the festivities were reduced to choruses and sacrifices (Thuc. 3.104.6), but the Athenians and islanders continued to honour Apollo. In 426/425, the Athenians introduced radical changes to the Delia: it became quadrennial, the athletic games were re-established, and horse-races were added for the first time (Thuc. 3.104.2, 6). The whole occasion was now much more elaborate and it provided additional opportunities for spectacle and participation. Although this renewal was carried out by the Athenians, other cities continued to take part in the festival (Plut. Nic. 3.5). In the immediate aftermath of 426/425, these changes will have emphasized Athens' role as leader of the Ionians and participation will now also have made clear one's relationship to Athena's city. By the 330s BCE, Athenian officials (the annual hieropoioi) took part in the festival (Aristot. Const. Ath. 54.7), which must now have seemed more like an Athenian occasion than an Ionian one. Indeed, the Delia appears to have fallen into abeyance when the island became independent in 314 and it was only restored when Athens regained control of Delos in 166 BCE (Bruneau 1970: 81–82). The celebration had become too closely connected with Athenian control to be attractive to the newly independent Delians. Participation, consequently, identified one with Athens, not the Ionians, and the festival must have ceased to serve as a gathering of the Ionians. With the restoration after 166, participation will have marked individuals' relationships with Athenian Delos and helped to define what it meant to be an Athenian on the island at that time.

While the Delia's role as a gathering place for the region does not seem to have changed during its history, the consequences of participation did not remain the same. They shifted from constructing Ionian and regional identity in the archaic period to defining relationships with Athens and her position in relation to the Ionians in the years after 426/425. By the late fourth century, Athens was so closely linked to the Delia that the independent Delians actually let the festival fall into abeyance with all the possibilities for angering the god which such a decision entailed (cf. Shear 2010: 141–147). The changes in the festival's politics literally made it disappear from the calendars of both the Delians and the region, and the focus shifted to other celebrations with their own concerns.

LOCAL FESTIVALS AND THEIR CONCERNS

These three celebrations provide us with a spectrum of festivities focusing on more local concerns than the great Panhellenic festivals. While the Panathenaia almost reached their international level, the Artemisia remained centred on the city of Eretria. Like the Panathenaia, the Delia drew participants from beyond the sponsoring community, but it concentrated on its surrounding region as the Panathenaia never did. In all three celebrations, how individuals took part both in the competitions and in the other spectacles was crucial to the dynamics of the occasion and the construction of its politics. Indeed, these principles explain both why the Panathenaia never became truly Panhellenic and why the Delia was suspended after 314: both festivals focused too closely on Athens and Athenian concerns. The Artemisia and the Delia further show how a celebration's politics might change over time. At the Artemisia, the restricted participation of the ephebes as citizens-to-be in the *purrhichē* in the Hellenistic period contrasts with the inclusiveness in the years after about 340 when the city was recovering from civil strife. The focus of the Delia shifted from creating identity for the region in the archaic period to putting on show Athens and other cities' relationships to her in the years after 426/425. While participation is crucial in all three festivals, the dynamics are specific to the particular occasion and its (local) concerns. As the Artemisia shows, the issues involved may concentrate on the sponsoring city and may be particular to a specific moment in time, but this focus also coexisted with a desire to draw contestants from beyond Eretria and inclusiveness was used for new purposes. These local festivals, accordingly, existed in tension between the needs of the particular community and its relationships to other cities and the larger region(s). These dynamics were not static and were subject to change, but participation remained the crucial element. Taking part in festivals both at home and in other cities displayed individuals and their cities in sport and spectacle to the larger world.

References

Bruneau, P. 1970. *Recherches sur les cultes de Délos a l'époque hellénistique et a l'époque impériale*. Paris.

Chankowski, A. S. 1993. 'Date et circonstances de l'institution de l'éphébie à Érétrie.' *DHA* 19.2: 17–44.

Detienne, M. 1989. 'Culinary Practices and the Spirit of Sacrifice.' In *The Cuisine of Sacrifice among the Greeks*. 1–20. M. Detienne and J.-P. Vernant, eds. Chicago.

Knoepfler, D. 1972. 'Carystos et les Artémisia d'Amarynthos.' *BCH* 96: 283–301.

Knoepfler, D. 1988. 'Sur les traces de l'Artemision d'Amarynthos près d'Érétrie.' *CRAI*: 382–421.

Knoepfler, D. 1997. 'Le territoire d'Erétrie et l'organisation politique de la cité (*dêmoi, chôroi, phylai*).' In *The Polis as an Urban Centre and as a Political Community*. 352–449. Acts of the Copenhagen Polis Centre 4. M. H. Hansen, ed. Copenhagen.

Palagia, O. and A. Choremi-Spetsieri, eds. 2007. *The Panathenaic Games: Proceedings of an International Conference held at the University of Athens, May 11–12, 2004*. Oxford.

Parker, R. 1998. 'Pleasing Thighs: Reciprocity in Greek Religion.' In *Reciprocity in Ancient Greece*. 105–125. C. Gill, N. Postlethwaite, and R. Seaford, eds. Oxford.

Parker, R. 2005. *Polytheism and Society at Athens*. Oxford.

Rhodes, P. J. and R. Osborne, eds. 2003. *Greek Historical Inscriptions, 404–323 BC*. Oxford.

Schultz, P. 2007. 'The Iconography of the Athenian Apobatic Race: Origins, Meanings, Transformations.' In Palagia and Choremi-Spetsieri. 59–72.

Shear, J. L. 2003. 'Prizes from Athens: the List of Panathenaic Prizes and the Sacred Oil.' *ZPE* 142: 87–108.

Shear, J. L. 2007. 'Royal Athenians: the Ptolemies and Attalids at the Panathenaia.' In Palagia and Choremi-Spetsieri. 135–145.

Shear, J. L. 2010. 'Demetrios Poliorketes, Kallias of Sphettos, and the Panathenaia.' In *Studies in Greek Epigraphy and History in Honor of Stephen V. Tracy*. 135–152. G. Reger, F. X. Ryan, and T. F. Winters, eds. Bordeaux.

Shear, J. L. 2011. *Polis and Revolution: Responding to Oligarchy in Classical Athens*. Cambridge.

Shear, J. L. 2021. *Serving Athena: The Festival of the Panathenaia and the Construction of Athenian Identities*. Cambridge.

Tracy, S. V. 2007. 'Games at the Lesser Panathenaia?' In Palagia and Choremi-Spetsieri. 53–57.

Tracy, S. V. and C. Habicht. 1991. 'New and Old Panathenaic Victor Lists.' *Hesperia* 60: 187–236.

CHAPTER 9

PATTERNS OF POLITICS IN ANCIENT GREEK ATHLETICS

PANOS VALAVANIS

'ONE sometimes hears people saying that politics should be kept out of sport, often combined with a plea for a return to the ancient Olympic spirit. This idealistic view, that ancient sport was non-political, rests on a misunderstanding of what athletics meant to ancient Greeks, who liked the political symbolism of winning.' These axiomatic observations of S. Hornblower (2004: 3–4) sum up modern trends of research into ancient Greek athletics, which ascertain that politics runs through its entire history from start to finish, though with a varying degree and role.

Bearing in mind the decisive role played by religion and communal worship in the collective life in antiquity, plus the fact that worship in the context of festivals was an extremely important—indeed sometimes the only—form of group self-expression, it becomes clear why these occasions held such great importance for the social and political elites, particularly in early historical times.

Moreover, throughout the course of Greek history, athletic events were directly connected with worship and the games were an integral part. For this reason we cannot separate—at least in the early period—athletics from other cult and votive practices, which took place in sanctuaries during the sacred festivals (Sinn 2000: 29; Valavanis 2006: 141–148; Davies 2007: 56–58; Douglas 2007: 407; Christesen 2007b: 67 n. 18; Murray 2014: 309–319; Kyle 2015: 71–72).

ATHLETICS AND THE INDIVIDUAL

The Greek games were patently a competition for prestige (Douglas 2007: 408); Papakonstantinou 2019, 30–33. Athletic competition thus became a type of primordial striving for eminence in early communities, and would certainly complement the striving for prominence by members of local aristocracies, which at that time was expressed chiefly by the setting up of valuable votive offerings in sanctuaries and the circulation of prestige goods (Morgan 1990: 43–48, 90–92, 194–200; Morgan 1993: 21; Kyle 1996: 111; Sinn 2000: 20–22;

Neer 2007: 226; Scott 2010: 146–147; Kyle 2015: 74–75). The most important offerings were the huge tripod cauldrons, usually decorated near the handles with attached bronze figures of horses, horsemen, or warriors, which alluded to the social class and wealth of the donors. The significance of these material remains, initially found mainly in Olympia and Delphi, lies in the fact that they constitute the first certainly documented offerings of a 'political' nature at Greek sanctuaries and portend the subsequent sharp rise of the political role of athletics in the framework of the later Panhellenic festivals (Sinn, this volume Chapter 5).

ATHLETICS AND INTERNAL RIVALRIES

The great structural changes in the Greek world during the Geometric and Archaic periods, which resulted in the creation of the city-states and colonization, brought with them the instituting of the first local celebrations and festivals, the result of which was to delineate borders and unite the people of each region as well as to reinforce their unifying elements, which led to the civic consciousness of the new communities.

Athletics and sporting competition took on a collective character and, due to the phenomena of acceptance and exclusion to which they gave rise, were used as means for creating group identities and helped in the building of intra-community status hierarchies and in the stabilization of socio-political structures (Hall 2002: 167; Scanlon 2002: 3–24; Christesen 2007b: 61–63; Papakonstantinou 2014). Athletics and Olympia played a central and continuous role in state formation during the Archaic period and considerably helped to foster civic unity and pride (Neer 2007; Kyle 2015: 78–79, 165–166).

At the same time, there was a sharp increase in athletic activity, followed by many changes in its organization. This appeared primarily at Olympia and from the first half of the sixth century BCE at the other Panhellenic sanctuaries, where the most interesting phenomena involving the political exploitation of athletics can be seen. Representatives of the political and social elite rushed to take part in the games, using their victories as springboards to rise to prominence and stand out among their rivals both at home and beyond, and the boast that a victor had raised his city to fame could be useful for all regimes. By the seventh and sixth centuries, some form of participation in Olympia was a sine qua non of elite status (Neer 2007: 227; Thomas 2007: 166; Kyriakou 2007: 149; Valavanis 2013; Kyle 2015: 123).

Emerging as an Olympic victor was a powerful means of pursuing political ambitions in the Greek city-state. The oldest recorded example is the case of the Athenian Cylon (636 BCE; Hdt. 5.71; Thuc. 1.126.3–5; Kyle 1996: 110, 156) and from this period onward, ancient history is full of cases of wealthy individuals who would invest especially in chariot-racing as a means of transforming large-scale property ownership into political power. On the other hand, many winners were themselves exploited by their own communities, in the framework of 'the economy of *kudos*', according to which the victor was seen as possessing a talismanic power or authority, 'an aura of invincibility', which was then diffused among the entire community that he led (Kurke 1993 = Kurke 2010; Hodkinson 2000: 325; Neer 2007: 231; Murray 2014: 315–316).

On the basis of this perception, the winner was an ideal person to be associated with the leadership of major state undertakings. Thus, many victors of Panhellenic games became leaders of new colonies or military commanders of their cities. In exceptional cases, particularly successful or outstanding victors could even come to be revered themselves by later generations via the institution of the hero cult (Hönle 1968: 45–48, 55; Kurke 1993 = Kurke 2010: 209–211; Hornblower 2004: 10 n. 22; Matthews 2007: 87; Kyriakou 2007: 139–147; Kyle 2009: 186 n. 10; De Polignac 2014). Recently however, the theory of *economy of kudos* and especially its talismanic authority, which had been widely accepted, was strongly disputed by Kyriakou (2007), who describes the phenomenon more simply by stating that 'such victories had the potential of being used as political capital by the victor and of being co-opted by the cities for the purposes of internal political harmony and international prestige' (Cf. Murray 2014: 315–316).

Furthermore, it was the tyrants of a number of Greek cities during the sixth century BCE who gave considerable impetus to athletic activity, always for the purpose of political exploitation. First there was Cleisthenes, tyrant of Sicyon, one of the victors of the First Sacred War, a fact that led to the reorganization of the Pythian Games. Cleisthenes won the chariot-race at the first games in 582 but then founded similar games at Sicyon (Neer 2007: 244; Scott 2010: 53–56; Kyle 2015: 81) ; Papakonstantinou 2019, 33–36. It seems also that the institution of Isthmian Games was a result of a tyrant's initiative, as the building of the temple of Poseidon was an outcome of internal rivalry between aristocratic clans of Corinth (Morgan 1990: 214; Morgan 1993: 35; Davies 2007: 62). Similarly, the Athenians (with the initiative of the 'richest and most good-looking man in Athens, Hippokleides' [Hdt. 6.127] or the soon-to-be-tyrant Peisistratus) reorganized the Panathenaea in 566 BCE, which played a leading role in reinforcing civic athletics. For they saw their value for promoting Athens in the frames of the cult of the city goddess, for anticipating aristocratic energies, and for pleasing the people (Kyle 1987: 25–31, 158–159; Neer 2007: 233; Neils 2007: 41–51).

Characteristic cases of using an athletic victory in internal political rivalry are the incidents involving some members of the Alcmaeonid family, who, having been victors in the equestrian events at Delphi and Olympia, used their successes as powerful political weapons against the tyrants, initially to promote their return to the city and subsequently for their efforts to seize power. Sometimes, however, as in the case of the Philaid Cimon I, they attempted reconciliation with the tyrant and avoidance of conflict. At the end he was killed by the Peisistratids, who saw the fame he gained from his third victory as a destabilizing factor for their regime (Hdt. 6.103–104; Davies 1971: 300; Kyle 1987: 157–158, 204; Stahl 1987: 116–120; Hodkinson 2000: 324; Mann 2001: 82–5; OKell 2004: 37; Jünger 2006: 192–202; Kyriakou 2007: 152–153; Papakonstantinou 2013; Papakonstantinou 2014: 89–90, 109–113; Kyle 2015: 164–165); Papakonstantinou 2019, 37–42, 48–49.

On the other hand, the strong participation of Athenian aristocrats in chariot-racing and its commemoration on the Acropolis and in Panhellenic Sanctuaries with wealthy dedications has been interpreted as a reaction and as an attempt to deploy property power to substitute for their declining cult authority (Davies 1981: 88–131; Hodkinson 2000: 309); Papakonstantinou 2019, 51–52. The victories of the aristocrats and their exploitation, which continued also during the period of democracy, did not conflict with the new ideology, since they were put in the service of the state's prestige (Kyriakou 2007: 154), promoted a sense of egalitarianism and unity among newly empowered members of Greek communities and thus played an important role in consolidating and extending democratization in the Greek world (Papakonstantinou 2014: 95; Kyle 2015: 200–201; Pritchard 2021).

For some Greek cities the emergence of a winner, above all of a multiple winner (*polynikēs*) was a unique opportunity for political presence (demonstration) in the international scene, as well as a unique possibility to have pride for having been victorious over greater and more important cities than their own (as is also the case today with Olympic champions from poor African countries). Who in the world of antiquity would know Skotoussa of Thessaly, if it weren't for the pancratiast Polydamas, and who would have heard of Pellana in Achaia, Keramos in Asia Minor, or the small island Astypalaia, if it weren't for the famous runners Phanas and Polites and for the boxer Kleomedes?

ATHLETICS AND INTERSTATE RIVALRIES. THE CASE BETWEEN ATHENS AND SPARTA

All the games, especially the Panhellenic ones, were highly politicized and competitions between athletes from different city-states were understood as contests for status and supremacy between them (Nielsen 2014). From as early as the sixth century BCE, there were periods in which domination of the chariot-races alternated between Athenians and Spartans (Kyle 1987: 195–228; Golden 1998: 172; Hodkinson 2000: 307–309; OKell 2004: 34). Toward the end of the century, of particular interest are the participation and victory of some Spartan(s) in the chariot-race at the Panathenaic Games, as attested by the dedication of Panathenaic amphoras at the sanctuary of Athena Chalkioikos and at the Menelaion. This is the same period when the Eurypontid king Damaratos won an Olympic four-horse chariot victory (Bentz 1998: 115–116, 132, 225; Hodkinson 2000: 307–309; Morgan 2007: 215–216). But immediately after the Persian Wars and the abatement of the external threat, the conflict between the two major powers took the form of the contemporary 'Cold War'. In this framework, the politicization of Panhellenic athletic victories, especially in the most spectacular contest, the chariot-race, was an additional weapon in the political battle between the two rivals.

Thus, after the Persian Wars, aristocratic Spartans started to breed horses with more passion (Paus. 6.2.1; Hönle 1968: 152; Mann 2001: 158–162; Kyriakou 2007: 153). Although there were no Spartan victories prior to the middle of the fifth century, they gained the ascendancy in the equestrian events at the Olympic Games, securing a series of successive victories in horse- and chariot-races from 448 to 424 BCE with only one exception (Hodkinson 2000: 320; Jünger 2006: 82–103; Christesen 2007a: 159–160). This triumphant run was abruptly interrupted in the last two decades of the fifth century BCE by events that took place at the Olympic Games in 420, held in a climate of political tension and mutual mistrust, when Elis offended and banned Sparta from Olympia and flogged the distinguished Spartan Lichas (Thuc. 5.49; Xen. Hell. 3.2.21; Paus. 6.2.2; Roy 1998; Hornblower 2004: 273–286; Miller 2004: 220–221; Scott 2010: 202–203; Gribble 2012: 51–53; Nielsen 2014: 141). Despite the political and moral injury suffered by the Spartans as a result of these events, they exercised self-restraint at the time and there were no immediate repercussions, maybe because of the Peloponnesian War (Cartledge, this volume Chapter 28, generally on Spartan athletics).

At the next Olympic Games in 416 BCE, the Athenians intervened on the initiative of Alcibiades, who with his complete triumph simultaneously 'struck' several targets at a domestic and at a foreign policy level (Plut. Alc. 2.2, 12.1; Ps.-And. 4.29–30; Isocr. 16, 34; Athen.

1.3e; Golden 1998: 169–175; Mann 2001: 102–113; Papakonstantinou 2003; OKell 2004: 36; Golden 2008: 9–12; Gribble 2012). A few months later, in the summer of 415, he used the political support gained through his victories to further his views in favour of the great expedition against Syracuse, convincing his compatriots to approve it and appoint him as one of the commanders-in-chief (Jünger 2006: 203–212; Kyriakou 2007: 149–150, 155). In the middle of the expedition he fled to Sparta, where the Athenian 'playboy politician', as M. Golden (2008: 6) has characterized him, is said to have seduced the wife of the Spartan King Agis II, Timaea, with whom he had a son, thereby causing great offence not only to the royal house but to Sparta itself (Hornblower 2004: 258–261).

Sparta's response at the level of military operations and athletics did not come before the end of the fifth century BCE, which was indeed a late reaction (Cartledge 1979: 271; Hornblower 2004: 276; Christesen 2007a: 55–56; Roy 2009; Hornblower 2011; Kyle 2015: 125). It began with an expedition under Agis II, who seized Elis in 399 BCE (Xen. *Hell.* 3.2.23–30), and was completed with two victories in the equestrian events of the Olympic Games in 396 and 392 BCE, with horses owned by Princess Cynisca, daughter of King Archidamus II of Sparta, sister of Agesilaus and half-sister of Agis II (Cartledge, this volume Chapter 28; Raschke, this volume Chapter 35).

According to a contemporary with first-hand knowledge, Xenophon, and other ancient writers, Cynisca was encouraged to participate in the games by her brother, King Agesilaus, who wished to demonstrate that an Olympic victory was not the result of manly courage but the lavish outlay of money. Some scholars believe that this action on the part of Agesilaus was provoked by his wish to discredit the sport because he personally disdained it, since he is reported by Xenophon to have said that breeding war-horses, not race-horses, was the manly thing. Others believe that it is an episode of internal political pressures in Sparta and was aimed at defaming and belittling certain victors who could pose a threat to the authority of the kings (Hodkinson 2000: 310–312, 327; Palagia 2009: 32–36). P. Cartledge (1987: 149–150, 352) believes that the reasons were of ethical origin, to boost the dedication of the Spartan society to the communal warlike ethos. The issue can also be explained in the political-psychology terms put forward by D. Kyle (Kyle 2007: 141–145; Golden 2008: 10–12, Kyle 2015: 184–185). According to his view, Agesilaus avenged the affront suffered by Sparta and its royal house some twenty years earlier. On the one hand he insulted Elis, since he undermined the prestige of the games by in effect emasculating them. On the other, he was able to insult Alcibiades himself, even though he was dead, by having a woman declared victor in the very event that he had triumphed in with such gloating!

In this same context of the conflict between Athens and Sparta during the Peloponnesian War—as a side effect—one can also place the incident with the distinguished athlete, military commander, and political leader Dorieus, son of Diagoras of Rhodes. Dorieus was a remarkable pancratiast who dominated the event from 432 BCE with thirty-seven victories in all four Panhellenic games, and four times in the Panathenaea. During the Peloponnesian War he had sided with the Spartans and in 407 BCE, with ten ships in the Aegean, supported the military operations of his allies. After some clash he was captured by the Athenians who took him to Athens, where he was sentenced to death. Realizing, however, that they had before them a great athlete who had been victorious in their own games too, the Athenians changed their minds and released him without harming him in the slightest (Paus. 6.7.5; Hornblower 2004: 131–142). In fact, athletics saves lives.

STRENGTHENING AND CONSOLIDATION
OF GREEKNESS

Anyone wishing to participate in Panhellenic games had to be Greek; through his participation, he asserted his Greek credentials (Hdt. 2.160.1; Remijsen 2019, questions this view). The first of these two elements, which can be traced through the existence of Olympic champions from a certain region, is used by current research in order to define Greek regions as well as the existence of organized city states (Hall 2002: 158–168; Nielsen 2004: 107–110; Nielsen 2014: 134–135). The second can be pointed out especially in places from the periphery of the Greek world, with typical examples the western colonials and the Macedonians. We will start with the western Greeks, and mainly with the actions of some tyrants of Sicilian cities in the late sixth and first half of the fifth century BCE, particularly at Olympia and Delphi, which were the most appropriate places for the formation and proclamation of Hellenic identity (Jünger 2006: 36–62; Antonaccio 2007: 268–270; Scott 2010: 81–88, 250–273).

Thus, the colonists from early on began to take part in Panhellenic games, the first victor being Dáippos of Croton in 672 BCE, which presaged the splendid continuation of entries and victories of his compatriots one century later. Indeed, the domination by athletes from Croton of the foot-race and wrestling events during the sixth and early fifth century BCE has been interpreted either as an attempt to 'manufacture winners' using advanced diet and training methods or that these western Greeks recruited athletes from other cities and paid them handsomely (Young 1984: 133; Kyle 1996: 131 n. 62; Miller 2004: 217–218; Kyle 2015: 79–80). This change of citizenship on the part of athletes seems to have been a not unusual practice in ancient times, judging, for example, from the large number of decisions taken by the council of Ephesus in the Hellenistic period, granting citizenship to foreign athletes. Thus it may be concluded that the purchase of young, ambitious athletes from other city-states was a standard policy of some Greek cities (Crowther 2004: 24–25; Kratzmüller and Trinkl 2005: 160; Golden 2008: 32; Kyle 2015: 236–237).

The anecdotal claim of the Crotoniates, after seven of their runners had taken the lead over all others in a race, that the last of the Crotoniates was the first among all Greeks (Strab. 6.1.12), as well as the inscription on the base of the statue of the athlete Ergoteles (a native of Knossos who became a citizen of Himera) at Olympia, which stated that he had beaten the Greeks (Hornblower 2004: 193), should be seen in the framework of the rivalry between the colonies and the motherland and as an expression of the special pride/conceit felt by the provincials of all eras when they successfully contend against city dwellers.

The impressive performance in Panhellenic games of western Greeks should be viewed overall in the context also of the general relations that they developed, particularly with the sanctuaries of Olympia and Delphi. Although it was more costly than for competitors from Greece, the colonists took part in the festivals with grand official delegations, while their participation was also marked by the erection of treasuries, the dedication of gold tripods and outstanding statues, and the commission for epinician odes (Philipp 1994; Antonaccio 2007: 276–283; Scott 2010: 88–91, 176–178). All this was 'because they wanted to demonstrate their Hellenic identity and sought to sustain their perceived right to rule by subscribing to the values of Greek elites' (Hornblower and Morgan 2007: 4–5; Neer 2007: 238–239;

Antonaccio 2014). And they were fully conscious of the value of athletics and the role that the games played in maintaining Hellenic identity.

Recent research has noted that the involvement of the rulers of colonies in the major Panhellenic games took place in periods of crisis for their regimes, when association with Greekness was politically expedient. This brings to mind modern political practices, where prior to elections many leaders seek to bolster their political profile by meeting with strong leaders (for example the US president) or hosting prominent political figures in their country.

This appears to have been the case also with the colonies of southern Italy and Sicily in the early fifth century BCE, when they faced internal instability and an external threat (Hornblower 2004: 194–195), but the case of Arkesilas IV, tyrant of Cyrene, is particularly revealing. The participation and victory of the latter in the chariot-race of the Pythian Games in 462 BCE, as well as the commissioning of a victory ode by Pindar, were part of a plan to reassert his status and his Greek credentials locally and internationally at a time of monarchical crisis. In this way, he succeeded in promoting not only his own prestige but also that of his fatherland as a powerful and independent country (Hornblower and Morgan 2007: 16; Morgan 2007: 224). In similar difficult periods of crisis, a trend can also be seen toward heroization of and reverence toward great athletes, who could become figures reintegrated into and sharing their *kudos* with the city (Kurke 1993 = Kurke 2010: 225–230; Bentz and Mann 2001: 230–240; Morgan 2007: 218).

'Thus, Olympia and Delphi became the prime venues for the proclamation of western identities, especially for the tyrants of the West, who continued the archaic link between political prominences on the one hand and athletic and equestrian success on the other' (Antonaccio 2007: 285). Sometimes, however, the extravagant delegations of the wealthy and arrogant western tyrants were confronted in a way that brought unexpected results. A characteristic example of this is the ineffectual attempt by Themistocles at the Olympics of 476 BCE to exclude the tyrant Hieron of Syracuse from the games and prevent his charioteers from racing, because the tyrant's brother, Gelon, had refused to help the Greeks in their struggle against the Persians after demanding but not being given overall military command (Hdt. 7.158; Plut. *Them.* 25; Crowther, 2004: 30).

A similar incident occurred at the Olympic Games in 388 BCE, when the orator Lysias—a metic at Athens but of Syracusan origin and a strong supporter of democracy—came to deliver his Olympian oration. He urged the crowd not to accept the emissaries of another tyrant of Syracuse, Dionysius I. Lysias' initiative was politically motivated for, on the one hand, the orator was an implacable opponent of tyranny and, on the other, Dionysius was an ally of Sparta at the time. Thus, Lysias' action was simultaneously a political move against the enemies of his new city (D.H. *Lys.* 29; Diod. 14.109.2–3; Crowther 2004: 19). Not to mention the fact that all Eleans were permanently excluded from the Isthmian Games because of political rivalry with Corinth (Paus. 5.2.2–5, 5.21.5, 6.12.2; Crowther 2004: 30; Miller 2004: 220; Kyle 2015: 138).

Lastly, although there has been much discussion of the issue, there is no doubt that from as early as the beginning of the sixth century BCE, the crown games reinforced the role of athletics in Greek ethnicity and the sense of Panhellenism, although for the Greeks Panhellenism was more a matter of cultural sharing rather than political unity (Kyle 2009). Indeed for some, the Panhellenic games were the prime manifestations of the Greek spirit (Morgan 1993; Hall 2002: 157–159; Crowther 2007: 74–76; Scott 2010: 250–273). By coming to Olympia for common worship, feasting, and athletic competition, the different Greek groups created a new community, one by definition more culturally and politically diverse than the faraway communities from which they had themselves come (Reid 2009: 32). It was no coincidence that in the late fifth and fourth century BCE, when the call for unification of all the Greeks became stronger, the great thinkers of the time came to Olympia to deliver their relevant speeches (Philostr. *VA* 4.31; Weiler 1997; Crowther 2007: 74–76; Nielsen 2014: 135–136).

THE GREEKNESS OF THE MACEDONIANS

A characteristic example of the important political role of the games for the recognition of Greekness is provided by the Macedonian royal family. At the beginning of the fifth century BCE, King Alexander I, seeking to integrate his country into the Greek world, decided to take part in the Olympic Games, a decision that provides the first firm evidence regarding relations between the Macedonians and Panhellenic sanctuaries (Hdt. 5.22; Hall 2002: 154–156; Mari 2002: 31–36, 45–46; Adams 2003: 205–217; Adams 2014; Taylor 2016); Papakonstantinou 2019, 73–75. The fact that he was accepted, despite the opposition of his rivals, was of great political significance since it was the first time that Macedonia was projected as part of the Greek world—and at that world's most important sanctuary. Kertesz (2005) and Kyle (2009: 187 n. 15) maintain that this took place at the Olympic Games of 480 or 476 BCE, setting forth various thoughts about Alexander's anti-Greek stance and his double game, since at that time Macedonia was a vassal province of the Persian empire. But this would mean Alexander would have been about 45 years old and therefore unlikely to be distinguished in a foot-race. It is more likely that he participated in the games earlier, when he was still young, perhaps in 496 BCE, shortly after ascending to the throne, or even in 500, as Mari (2002: 31–36) believes.

While some historians challenge the veracity of this story or others believe that it happened later, at the end of the fifth century BCE (Hall 2002: 154–7; Adams 2003: 205–221; Kyle 2009: 187), some finds in Macedonia have changed the picture we have: the discovery of at least two Panathenaic amphoras of the early fifth century BCE in the cemetery of Aiani, in the territory of ancient Elimeia (Upper Macedonia), proves that such vases were greatly esteemed by the Macedonians of the time, even if they were not awarded to a native (Tiverios 2000: 36–37; Kephalidou 2001).

Evidence for the interest in and esteem for the games, or even that some members of the Macedonian dynasty may have taken part in the Panathenaic and other Greek games from as early as the fifth century BCE, was provided by two finds in the cemetery at Vergina: a) a Panathenaic amphora, dating to 425–420 BCE, featuring the representation of a boys' or ephebes' race (Bentz 1998: 101–102, 236; Tiverios 2000: 36 n. 135) and b) a bronze tripod from the same period found in the so-called 'tomb of Philip II'. This latter bears the inscription: 'I am from the contests of Argive Hera', which means that it was awarded as a prize at the games of Argos. It is plausible to assume that either they were valuable gifts or that a member of the Macedonian royal family had won in these games and that, after three generations, his prize was placed in the king's tomb as an important family heirloom (Tiverios 2000: 43; Hornblower 2004: 13–14; Kottaridi 2011 figs. 6–7). It is interesting to note as well that, although the games held in Argos at the time were not Panhellenic in nature, the members of the Macedonian court still wished to take part since they traced their origins back to Argos, which served as a powerful weapon for asserting their Greekness.

Finally, another royal grave at Vergina, the tomb with the throne, which predates the so called 'tomb of Philip II', has yielded fragments of at least three Panathenaic amphoras, dating to the archonship of Lyciscus (344/343,) when, according to historical sources, a Macedonian delegation had visited Athens (Andronikos 1987: 379; Tiverios 1991: 41–42 n. 118; Morgan 2007: 256–257). Of particular importance for the role of these vessels is the fact that they were placed in the funeral pyre of the dead. Andronikos (1987: 379) believed that the tomb belonged to a woman, indeed attributing it to the mother of Philip II, Eurydice. However, the presence of the Panathenaic amphorae in the pyre of a woman does not support this assumption, all the more so since they didn't help us date this event to around 344/343 BCE, as Kottaridi (2011: 145 fig. 168) believes. They just provide a *terminus post quem*.

PANATHENAEA AND POLITICS

The discovery of Panathenaic *amphorae* in areas outside Athens is of great significance for our research. Although most often they do not attest participation in the games, everywhere and always they constituted objects endowed with considerable social status and attested to the relation of the owner with athletics, even during the Hellenistic and Roman periods (Valavanis 2001).

Panathenaic *amphorae* were also extremely important for their creators, the ancient Athenians, since they provided a powerful weapon for promoting the games and, by extension, the political presence of their city. In fact, the appearance of the vase with its iconography (Athena + the inscription + athletic images) made it typically Athenian. Thus, even the most uninformed viewer in the four corners of the Mediterranean would easily be able to recognize them. 'Games brought people to Athens, but prizes took Athens abroad' (Kyle 1996: 118–122; Kyle 2015: 152). In effect, it was a political trademark, which even today's advertisers would envy!

In tracing the political parameters of Athenian athletics, emphasis is usually placed on the participation of Athenian athletes in the Panhellenic games. Equally indicative however, despite a dearth of evidence, is the participation of members of Athenian families also in the Panathenaic Games (Mansfield 1985: 294–367; Themelis 2007: 30–31; Kyle 2015: 161–163). Most characteristic of the political power and propaganda medium of the Panathenaea both at home and beyond is the care taken by the majority of Athenian leaders (Solon, Peisistratus, Themistocles, Cimon, Pericles, Lycurgus, Micion, and Eurycleidas) to further develop and strengthen the festival and games (Kyle 1987: 155–168: Phillips 2003).

Also of particular interest is the participation in the Panathenaea, along with the Panhellenic games, of the members of royal families of the Hellenistic east, especially the Ptolemies (men and women) and to a lesser extent the Attalids, the Seleucids, and a Nubian king (who performed admirably in the equestrian events), in conjunction with the significant donations they made to the city of Athens. These were patently political actions and were connected with the very good political relations that the wealthy rulers endeavoured to maintain with Athens (Tiverios 2000: 50; Shear 2007; Bremen 2007: 360–372; Mann 2018).

These special relations stemmed from the fact that Athens still continued to be the centre of learning and culture and a pole of attraction for the Greco-Macedonian elites of the Hellenistic courts. In addition, although Athens had been superseded politically, the city functioned as a kind of intermediate pole between the Hellenistic east and Rome, which was expanding eastward at the time. Consequently, visiting Athens and participating in the Panathenaea was an action with multiple political parameters.

The Hellenistic rulers, especially the Ptolemies, used sport to reinforce their socio-political superiority and invested heavily in the symbolism of athletics as a token of Hellenic identity and an international power symbol. Kings and queens won victories in the equestrian events of the Panhellenic games and duly advertised and capitalized on their achievements, with epinician poetry, statues, and inscriptions (Paus. 10.7.8; Tiverios 2000: 41; Sinn 2000: 101–102; Crowther 2004: 24–25; Bremen 2007: 374; Golden 2008: 19–23; Remijsen 2009: 246–271; Remijsen 2014; Kyle 2015: 237–238; Mann 2018). They constructed hippodromes, stadia and gymnasia and it seems that even the palaestra and the gymnasium(?) of Olympia were the result of a Hellenistic benefaction (Sinn 2000: 101–103; Kyle 2015: 238). They also helped young promising athletes financially, as in the case of the boxer Aristonicus, who had been trained and sent by King Ptolemy IV to the Olympic Games of 216 or 212 BCE (Plb. 27.9.3–13; Paus. 6.15.3; Crowther 2004: 15; Crowther 2007: 71; Matthews 2007: 83–84; Remijsen 2009: 257; Mann 2014: 283; Kyle 2015: 238–239; Mann 2018: 456–457, 460–466). The way Aristonicus' fight unfolded, and its final outcome, revealed the latent identification and manifestations of 'nationalism' in the stadiums and hippodromes. It is also clear that athletes, as representatives of their states, were automatically regarded as exponents of the politics and ideology of the respective regimes.

Another account is characteristic of the fanatical claims of victory that were sometimes made (Plut. *De Sera* 553a–b). When the boy Teletias emerged as victor at the Pythian Games at Delphi, the spectators from Sicyon and Cleonae, two neighbouring cities of the northeast Peloponnese, began to quarrel at the awards ceremony as to which of the two should be credited with the victory. In the end, the affair developed into a violent clash to 'claim the victor', and to a beating that led to Teletias' death!

USE OF ATHLETICS IN THE POLITICAL AGENDAS OF PHILIP II AND ALEXANDER THE GREAT

Philip II was the Macedonian king who used the games as a political tool more skilfully than any other (Miller 2000; Miller 2004: 223–224; Kertesz 2007; Kyle 2015: 224–227). Seeking, as part of his expansionist policy, to become involved in the political affairs of Greek polities to the south, he chose participation in the Olympic Games as his means. He was crowned champion in three different equestrian events at three successive Olympiads from 356 to 348 BCE and immortalized his victories on gold and silver coins that circulated widely. He most probably also dedicated a bronze chariot, perhaps the work of the Athenian sculptor and painter Euphranor (Romano 1990: 63–79; Mari 2002: 80–82; Jünger 2006: 116–119; Scott 2010: 132–135).

Furthermore, after the Battle of Chaeronea (338 BCE), which ensured his domination of southern Greece, Philip embarked on large-scale construction programmes at all three

Panhellenic sanctuaries in the Peloponnese, in order to emphatically project his supremacy at the most important political centres of Hellenism. At Olympia he ordered the construction of the Philippeion (suggesting his quasi-divine aspirations) and the Echo Colonnade, at Isthmia the new stadium, while at Nemea he demanded the return of the games to their cradle after they were moved to Argos during the period 415–335 BCE approximately. Indeed, he began a massive and very costly building programme as part of his policy of renovating and embellishing sites to assert the unification and control of Greece (Miller 1988: 144–145; Miller 2000; Kertesz 2007: 331–332; Scott 2010: 210–214, 238–240; Kyle 2015: 140; Taylor 2016: 12–25).

The same political policy of exploiting athletics and games was pursued by his son, Alexander the Great, with certain differences (Miller 2004: 223–225). Philip's involvement in the Panhellenic sanctuaries was an attempt to secure recognition of the leading role of the Macedonians in the whole of Greece. Alexander, on the other hand, turned to the games of Athens, the cradle of civilization even for the ancients, to secure acknowledgement of the leading Macedonian role in the campaign of 'civilized' Greeks against the 'barbarians'. The dispatch of 300 Persian shields to the Acropolis after Alexander's first victory at the Battle of the Granicus in 334 (accompanied by the well-known inscription 'From all the Greeks except the Spartans') thus had clear political symbolism and was probably proclaimed with great pomp and ceremony at the Panathenaea of the same year. It is in this same framework that one should view the return to Athens of the statues of the Tyrannicides, which had been carried off by Xerxes in 480 BCE and were found by Alexander (or Seleucus) in the Persian palace at Sousa. In order to confirm the relations between Macedonians and Athens, Alexander also used various Athenian symbols on his coins, such as statues of Athena or Nike, adopted from Panathenaic iconography (Tiverios 2000: 42 n. 152, 54–56; Tiverios 2001: 50–52; Themelis 2003: 162–172).

In all the lands he conquered, Alexander established athletic contests to celebrate victories or honor dead companions, using them as the main vehicle for disseminating Greek culture. He organized games with valuable prizes in many places, and as a point of contact among and a means of unifying all peoples. Gymnasia, too, were a means of transmitting Greek culture to the East, and at the same time helped the Greeks preserve their identity (Miller 2004: 196–206; Adams 2014; Kyle 2015: 227–232).

All this athletics-related activity with its major or minor political parameters continued without interruption and probably intensified on the Greek mainland and in the Hellenistic and, later, Roman east, as part of the ancient legacy (Pleket 2014; Kyle 2015: 232–236, 262–263, 314–316; Mann 2018); Papakonstantinou 2019, 175–182. Despite the great changes that have taken place in the world, 'the classical language of athletic victory continued to be spoken (or at least understood) across the multi-ethnic Hellenistic world and its Roman successor' (Hornblower and Morgan 2007: 42).

References

Adams, W. L. 2003. 'Other People's Games: The Olympics, Macedonia and Greek Athletics.' *JSH* 30: 205–217.

Adams, W. L. 2014. 'Sport, Spectacle and Society in Ancient Macedonia.' In Christesen and Kyle, eds. 332–345.

Andronikos, M. 1987. Ἡ ζωγραφική στην Αρχαία Μακεδονία.' *AEphem*: 363–379.

Antonaccio, C. 2007. 'Elite Mobility in the West.' In Morgan and Hornblower, eds. 265–286.

Antonaccio, C. 2014. 'Sport and Society in the Greek West.' In Christesen and Kyle, eds. 192–207.

Bentz, M. 1998. *Panathenäische Preisamphoren*. Basel.

Bentz, M. and N. Eschbach, eds. 2001. *Panathenaika: Symposion zu den panathenaeischen Preisamphoren*. Mainz.

Bentz, M. and C. Mann. 2001. 'Zur Heroisierung von Athleten.' In *Konstruktionen von Wirklichkeit: Bilder im Griechenland des 5. und 4. Jhs v. Chr.* 225–240. R. Van den Hoff and S. Schmidt, eds. Stuttgart.

Bremen, R. van. 2007. 'The Entire House is Full of Crowns: Hellenistic Agones and the Commemoration of Victory.' In Hornblower and Morgan, eds. 345–376.

Cartledge, P. 1979. *Sparta and Laconia: A Regional History, 1300–362 BC*. London.

Cartledge, P. 1987. *Agesilaos and the Crisis of Sparta*. Baltimore.

Christesen, P. 2007a. *Olympic Victor Lists and Ancient Greek History*. Cambridge.

Christesen, P. 2007b. 'The Transformation of Athletics in Sixth-Century Greece.' In Schaus and Wenn. 59–80.

Christesen, P. and D. Kyle, eds. 2014. *A Companion to Sport and Spectacle in Greek and Roman Antiquity*. Hoboken, New Jersey.

Crowther, N. 2004. *Athletica: Studies on the Olympic Games and Greek Athletics*. Nikephoros Beih. 11. Hildesheim.

Crowther, N. 2007. 'The Ancient Olympics and their Ideals.' In Schaus and Wenn, eds. 69–80.

Davies, J. K. 1971. *Athenian Propertied Families. 600–300 B.C.* Oxford

Davies, J. K. 1981. *Wealth and the Power of Wealth in Classical Athens*. New York.

Davies, J. K. 2007. 'The Origin of the Festivals Especially Delphi and the Pythia.' In Morgan and Hornblower, eds. 47–69.

De Polignac, Fr. 2014. 'Athletic Cults in Ancient Greece: Political Topic, Mythical Discourse.' In Scanlon 2014, ed. 91–116.

Douglas, M. 2007. 'The Prestige of the Games.' In Morgan and Hornblower, eds. 391–407.

Golden, M. 1998. *Sport and Society in Ancient Greece*. Cambridge.

Golden, M. 2008. *Greek Sport and Social Status*. Austin.

Gribble, D. 2012. 'Alcibiades at the Olympics: Performance, Politics and Civic Ideology.' *Classical Quarterly* 62: 45–71.

Hall, J. M. 2002. *Hellenicity: Between Ethnicity and Culture*. Chicago.

Hodkinson, S. 2000. *Property and Wealth in Classical Sparta*. London.

Hönle, A. 1968. *Olympia in der Politik der griechischen Staatenwelt*. Tübingen.

Hornblower, S. 2004. *Thucydides and Pindar: Historical Narrative and the World of Epinician Poetry*. Oxford.

Hornblower, S. 2011. 'Thucydides, Xenophon and Lichas: Were the Spartans Excluded from the Olympic Games from 420 to 400 BC?' In *Thucydidean Themes*. 196–212. S. Hornblower. Oxford.

Hornblower, S. and C. Morgan, eds. 2007. *Pindar's Poetry, Patrons and Festivals: From Archaic Greece to the Roman Empire*. Oxford.

Jünger, F. 2006. *Gespann und Herrschaft: Form und Intention grossformatiger Gespanndenkmäler im griechischen Kulturraum von der archaischen bis in die hellenistische Zeit*. Hamburg.

Kephalidou, E. 2001. 'New Panathenaic Prize-Amphoras from Aiani in Upper Macedonia.' In Bentz and Eschbach, eds. 11–17.

Kertesz, I. 2005. 'When did Alexander I Visit Olympia?' *Nikephoros* 18: 115–126.

Kertesz, I. 2007. 'Philip II the Sportsman.' In *Ancient Macedonia, VII: Macedonia from the Iron Age to the Death of Philip II.* 327–332. D. Kaplanidou and I. Chioti, eds. Thessaloniki.

Koenig, J., ed. 2010. *Greek Athletics*. Edinburgh Readings on the Ancient World. Edinburgh.

Kottaridi, A. 2011. 'Burial Customs and Beliefs in the Royal Necropolis of Aegae.' In *Heracles to Alexander: The Great Treasures from the Royal Capital of Macedon, a Hellenic Kingdom in the Age of Democracy.* 131–152. A. Kottaridi and S. Walker, eds. Oxford.

Kratzmüller, B. and Trinkl, E. 2005. 'Von Athleten und Töpfern. Ephesische Bürgern auf der Spur.' In *Synergia: Festschrift für F. Krinzinger.* 157–167. I. B. Brandt, V. Gassner, and S. Ladstätter, eds. Vienna.

Kurke, L. 1993. 'The Economy of *Kudos*.' In *Cultural Poetics in Archaic Greece. Cult, Performance, Politics.* 131–163. C. Dougherty and L. Kurke, eds. Cambridge. = Kurke 2010: 204–237 in Koenig 2010.

Kyle, D. 1987. *Athletics in Ancient Athens*. Leiden.

Kyle, D. 1996. 'Gifts and Glory.' In *Worshipping Athena: Panathenaia and Parthenon.* 106–136. J. Neils, ed. Madison.

Kyle, D. 2007. 'Fabulous Females and Ancient Olympia.' In Schaus and Wenn. 131–152.

Kyle, D. 2009. 'Pan-Hellenism and Particularism: Herodotus on Sport, Greekness, Piety and War.' *International Journal of the History of Sport* 26: 183–211.

Kyle, D. 2015. *Sport and Spectacle in the Ancient World* (second edition). Malden, MA.

Kyriakou, P. 2007. 'Epidoxon Kydos. Crown Victory and its Rewards.' *Classica et Medievalia* 58: 119–58.

Mann, C. 2001. *Athlet und Polis im archaischen und frühklassischen Griechenland*. Göttingen.

Mann, C. 2014. 'People on the Fringes of Greek Sport.' In Christesen and Kyle, eds. 276–286.

Mann, C. 2018. 'Koenige, Poleis und Athleten in hellenistischer Zeit.' *Klio* 100 (2): 447–479.

Mansfield, J. 1985. *Prize-amphoras and Prize-oil*. M.A. University of California, Berkeley.

Mari, M. 2002. *Al Di la dell' Olimpo. Macedoni e grandi santuari de la Grecia dall' età Arcaica al primo Ellenismo.* Athens.

Murray, S. 2014. 'The Role of Religion in Greek Sport.' In Christesen and Kyle, eds. 309–319.

Matthews, V. 2007. 'Olympic Losers: Why Athletes Who Did Not Win at Olympia Are Remembered.' In Schaus and Wenn. 81–93.

Miller, S. 1988. 'Excavations at the Panhellenic Site of Nemea.' In *The Archaeology of the Olympics.* 141–54. W. Raschke, ed. Madison, WI.

Miller, S. 2000. 'Macedonians at Delphi.' in *Delphes cent ans après la grande fouille.* 263–81. A. Jacquemin, ed. Paris.

Miller, S. 2004. *Ancient Greek Athletics*. New Haven.

Morgan, C. 1990. *Athletes and Oracles. The Transformation of Olympia and Delphi in the Eighth Century B.C.* Cambridge.

Morgan, C. 1993. 'The Origins of Panhellenism' In *Greek Sanctuaries: New Approaches.* 18–44. N. Marinatos and R. Hägg, eds. London.

Morgan, C. 2007. 'Debating Patronage: Argos and Corinth.' In Hornblower and Morgan. 213–63.

Neer, R. 2007. 'Delphi, Olympia and the Art of Politics.' In Shapiro. 225–64.

Neils, J. 2007. 'Replicating Tradition: the First Celebrations of the Greater Panathenaia.' In *The Panathenaic Games.* 41–51. O. Palagia and A. Choremi-Spetsieri, eds. Oxford.

Nielsen, T. H. 2004. 'Victors in Panhellenic Games as Evidence for *polis* Identity.' In *An Inventory of Archaic and Classical Poleis*. 107–110. M. H. Hansen and T. H. Nielsen, eds. Oxford.

Nielsen, T. H. 2014. 'Panhellenic Athletics at Olympia.' In Christesen and Kyle, eds. 133–145.

OKell, E. 2004. 'Orestes the Contender: Chariot Racing and Politics in Fifth-Century Athens and Sophocles' Electra.' In *Games and Festivals in Classical Antiquity. Proceedings of the Conference held in Edinburgh, 10-12 July 2000* (BAR 1220). 33–43. S. Bell and G. Davis, eds. Oxford.

Palagia, O. 2009. 'Spartan Self-Presentation in the Panhellenic Sanctuaries of Delphi and Olympia in the Classical Period.' In *Athens-Sparta. Contributions to the Research on the History and Archaeology of the Two City-States*. 32–40. N. Kaltsas, ed. Athens.

Papakonstantinou, Z. 2003. 'Alcibiades in Olympia. Olympic Ideology, Sport and Social Conflict in Classical Athens.' *JSH* 30: 173–82.

Papakonstantinou, Z. 2013. 'Cimon the Elder, Peisistratus and the *Tethrippon* Olympic Victory of 532 B.C.' *JAH* 1 (2): 99–118.

Papakonstantinou, Z. 2014. 'Sport, Victory, Communication and Elite Identities in Archaic and Early Classical Athens.' *C&M* 65: 87–126.

Papakonstantinou, Z. 2019. Sport and Identity in Ancient Greece. London and New York.

Philipp, H. 1994. 'Olympia, der Peloponnes und die Westgriechen.' *JdI* 109: 77–92.

Phillips, D. 2003. 'Athenian Political History: A Panathenaic perspective.' In *Sport and Festival in the Ancient Greek World*. 197–232. D. Phillips and D. Pritchard, eds. Swansea.

Pleket, H. W. 2014. 'Sport in the Hellenistic and Roman Asia Minor.' In Christesen and Kyle, eds. 364–375.

Pritchard, D. 2021. 'Athletics, Democracy and War.' In *The Cambridge Companion to Ancient Athens*. 307–318. J. Neils and D. Rogers, eds. Cambridge.

Reid, H. 2009. 'Olympic Sport and its Lessons for Peace.' In *Olympic Truce. Sport as a Platform for Peace*. 25–35. K. Georgiadis and A. Syrigos, eds. Athens.

Remijsen S. 2009. 'Challenged by Egyptians: Greek Sports in the 3rd Century BC.' *International Journal of the History of Sport* 26: 246–271.

Remijsen, S. 2014 'Greek Sport in Egypt: Status Symbol and Lifestyle.' In Christesen and Kyle, eds. 349–363.

Remijsen, S. 2019. 'Only Greeks at the Olympics? Reconsidering the Rule against Non-Greeks at "Panhellenic" Games.' *C&M* 67: 1–61.

Romano, D. G. 1990. 'Philip of Macedon, Alexander the Great and the Ancient Olympic Games.' In *The World of Philip and Alexander: A Symposium on Greek Life and Times*. 61–79. C. Daniel, ed. Philadelphia.

Roy, J. 1998. 'Thucydides 5.49.1–50.4: The Quarrel between Elis and Sparta in 420 B.C. and Elis' Exploitation of Olympia.' *Klio* 80: 360–368.

Roy, J. 2009. 'The Spartan–Elean War of 400 BC.' *Atheneum* 97: 69–86.

Scanlon, T. F. 2002. *Eros and Greek Athletics*. New York.

Scanlon, T. F. ed. 2014. *Sport in the Greek and Roman Worlds* I. Oxford.

Schaus, G. P. and S. R.Wenn, eds. 2007. *Onward to the Olympics: Historical Perspectives on the Olympic Games*. Waterloo, Ont.

Scott, M. 2010. *Delphi and Olympia: The Spatial Politics of Panhellenism in the Archaic and Classical Periods*. Cambridge.

Shapiro, H. A., ed. 2007. *The Cambridge Companion to Archaic Greece*. Cambridge.

Shear, J. L. 2007. 'Royal Athenians: The Ptolemies and Attalids at the Panathenaia.' In *The Panathenaic Games*. 135–145. O. Palagia and A. Choremi Spetsieri, eds. Oxford.

Sinn, U. 2000. *Olympia: Cults, Sport and Ancient Festival*. Princeton.

Stahl, M. 1987. *Aristokraten und Tyrannen im archaischen Athen*. Stuttgart.

Taylor, E. 2016. *Athletics and the Macedonian Search for Greek Identity* (PhD Emory University).

Themelis, P. 2003. 'Macedonian Dedications on the Acropolis.' In *The Macedonians in Athens, 322–229 BC*. 162–172. O. Palagia and S. Tracy, eds. Oxford.

Themelis, P. 2007. 'Panathenaic Prizes and Dedications.' In *The Panathenaic Games*. 21–32. O. Palagia and A. Choremi Spetsieri, eds. Oxford.

Thomas, R. 2007. 'Fame, Memorial and Choral Poetry: The Origins of Epinician Poetry—An Historical Study.' In Morgan and Hornblower, eds. 141–166.

Tiverios, M. 1991. 'Παναθηναϊκοί αμφορείς από την Πέλλα.' *AEphem*: 15–44.

Tiverios, M. 2000. *Μακεδόνες και Παναθήναια. Παναθηναϊκοί αμφορείς από τον Βορειοελλαδικό χώρο*. Athens.

Tiverios, M. 2001. 'Panathenaeen und Makedonen: Panathenaeische Preisamphoren aus dem nordgriechischen Raum.' In Bentz and Eschbach, eds. 41–54.

Valavanis, P. 2001. 'Panathenäische Amphoren auf Monumenten spätklassischer, hellenistischer und römischer Zeit.' In Bentz and Eschbach, eds. 161–173.

Valavanis, P. 2006. 'Thoughts on the Historical Origins of the Olympic Games and the Cult of Pelops in Olympia.' *Nikephoros* 19: 137–152.

Valavanis, P. 2013. 'The Political and Social Role of Olympia.' In *Olympics. Past and Present*. 45–51. Qatar Olympic and Sports Museum et al., eds. Munich, London, New York.

Weiler, I. 1997. 'Olympia-Jenseits der Agonistik: Kultur und Spektakel.' *Nikephoros* 10: 191–213.

Young, D. 1984. *The Olympic Myth of Greek Amateur Athletics*. Chicago.

CHAPTER 10

....

GREEK FESTIVALS IN THE HELLENISTIC ERA

....

ZAHRA NEWBY

THE Hellenistic era witnessed a rapid expansion of the Greek world, as the areas conquered by Alexander were settled by his successors and new fusions of Greek and indigenous cultures were created. In 'old' Greece (the Greek mainland and the cities of western Asia Minor) cities jostled for prestige and position under the wider influence first of the Hellenistic monarchs and later of Rome. Further afield, new city foundations in central Asia Minor, Syria, and Egypt were set up on the model of the *polis*, while pre-existing cities and communities adopted some aspects of Hellenic culture. The old-fashioned view that Greek civic religion declined in the Hellenistic period in the face of the newer mystery religions has rightly been rejected by modern scholars (for a balanced overview see Mikalson 2006), but the role which festivals played in this new international world is only now receiving detailed study. In this chapter I will explore some of the fortunes of Greek festival culture, looking first at the festival at Olympia and then at the institution of new Panhellenic festivals, to consider the evidence for a broadening of athletic participation eastwards. Overwhelmingly the evidence is epigraphic; much of it was collated and explored by Moretti (1953; 1957; with updates 1970; 1987) and Robert (numerous articles, many reprinted in Robert 1969–90; for a brief overview see Robert 1984) but only recently have scholars begun to work in detail on how this material helps us to understand the functioning of festivals within the cultural contexts of the Hellenistic era (see especially the Connected Contests project led by Onno van Nijf and Christina Williamson at the University of Groningen, http://www.connectedcontests. org; also Wilson 2007; Pleket 2014; van Nijf and Williamson 2015; and Mann, Remijsen, and Scharff 2016, esp. van Nijf and Williamson 2016).

THE FESTIVAL AT OLYMPIA

....

Our knowledge of the changing fortunes of the Olympic Games over the course of Antiquity is patchy and limited by the nature of the evidence available (Farrington 1997: 24-30). Literary references to Olympic victors are uneven; a relatively complete list of victors in the stade race is contained in Eusebius' *Chronika* (covering 776 BCE to 217 CE) and a few fragments survive of more extensive lists. For others, however, we are heavily reliant on Pausanias' description of the athletic statues set up at Olympia, itself highly selective (Paus. 6.1.1; Herrmann 1988), and on the surviving inscriptions from Olympia and other classical sites. These epigraphic texts cannot be taken as fully representative of the total numbers and origins of victors, but rather of those who (or whose father, city or trainer) thought it worthwhile to pay for the expense of a statue or inscription, either at Olympia or in their home city. Low numbers of surviving statue bases in a particular place for a particular period might be explained by financial and political circumstances, as well as personal choices, while in other areas new archaeological excavations could still reveal more evidence.

The evidence for Olympic victors from the Hellenistic and Roman periods has been well discussed by Farrington (1997) and Scanlon (2002: 40–67). References to attested Olympic victors decline in number from the fifth century BCE to a low point in the second century BCE, to climb again in the Roman period (Fig. 10.1). A study of the victory inscriptions set up at Olympia itself (many of them inscribed on the bases to victory statues) similarly shows a pronounced dip, especially in the second half of the second century BCE, while many of those who did celebrate victories at Olympia in the fourth to first centuries BCE were from the local area, especially Elis (on these, see Crowther 1988).

However, while these statistics might seem to suggest that there was a gradual diminution in the status of, and interest in, the Olympic festival over the course of the Hellenistic period, a closer look at the attested victories suggests a more nuanced picture. Although some areas, such as Magna Graecia, became less interested in seeking or celebrating victories at the Games, other new areas began to celebrate victories here for the first time. For example, we know of twelve victories by Alexandrian athletes during the course of the third to the first centuries BCE, probably an under-representation of the total number, as well as a number of victors from western Asia Minor (Egypt: Scanlon 2002: 45; Remijsen 2009: 254–256). Here I want to explore the importance of Olympic victory in the cities of western Asia Minor in the early Hellenistic period, through a look at some of the attested victors for the fourth and third centuries BCE.

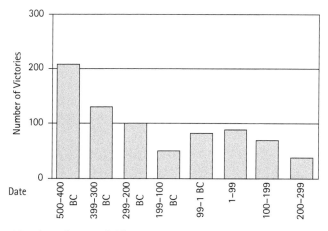

FIGURE 10.1. Number of attested Olympic victories 500 BCE–300 CE. Farrington, *Tyche* 12 (1997), fig. 1; by kind permission of Andrew Farrington and Verlag Holzhausen.

'The First of the Ionians ...': Regional and Civic Pride in Olympic Victory Monuments

In the course of his description of athletic victory monuments in the sanctuary at Olympia, Pausanias records the statue of the Milesian boy boxer, Antipatros. Whereas many of his other references to statues are brief, here Pausanias gives a full account of the circumstances surrounding Antipatros' victory, and the statue he set up:

> By the statue of Thrasyboulos stands ... the Milesian, Antipatros, son of Kleinopatros, victorious in the boys' boxing. Men of Syracuse who were bringing sacrifice to Olympia from Dionysios [II, tyrant of that city], attempted to bribe his father to have his son proclaimed as a Syracusan. But Antipatros, thinking nothing of the tyrant's gifts, proclaimed himself as Milesian and wrote on his statue that he was of Milesian descent and the first of the Ionians to set up a statue at Olympia. (6.2.6)

Dionysios' attempt to persuade a victorious athlete to declare himself a citizen of Syracuse rather than of his own home town is nothing new, with forerunners reaching back at least a century (e.g. Astylos of Kroton; Paus. 6.13.1). Yet what is interesting here is Antipatros' keen assertion on his statue of his ethnic and regional identity. He is a Milesian, whatever Dionysios might wish, but he is also the first of the Ionians to set up a statue at Olympia (though a couple of earlier victors from Ionia are identified in literary sources: Moretti 1957 nos. 29, 79, 438). He declares to the wider Greek world which assembled at Olympia that Ionia can produce victorious athletes, and also identifies his own city, Miletos, as a leading city within Ionia, implicitly setting it up in rivalry with its neighbours.

Antipatros' victory dates to the early decades of the fourth century, probably 388 BCE (Moretti 1957 no. 385), but it begins a series of declarations of primacy among athletes from the cities of Asia Minor which run into the Hellenistic period. Sometime later, the athlete Herodotos of Klazomenae was also honoured with a statue at Olympia for a victory in the boys' stade race (Moretti 1957 no. 528 suggests a date in the early third century). Pausanias tells us that the Klazomenians set up the statue because Herodotos was the first Klazomenian to be proclaimed victor at Olympia (6.17.2). Two citizens of Kolophon were also honoured with statues at Olympia, both for victories in the boys' boxing (Paus. 6.17.4; Moretti 1957 nos. 475, 557). The victory statue of the first, Hermesianax, was set up by the people of Kolophon, probably to honour the fact that he was the first citizen from here to win an Olympic victory. The later statue was of Eikasios, whom Pausanias describes as 'son of Lykinos and the daughter of Hermesianax'. The unusual reference to his mother as well as his father here can be explained by the fact that his maternal grandfather was an Olympic victor too. Eikasios' statue was set up next to that of his grandfather; the reference to his parentage suggests the desire to assert familial continuity in athletic prowess (see Day 2019: 75–81 on the Daochos group at Delphi).

While victors from the cities of Ionia can be seen already celebrating victories at Olympia in the fourth century, participation later spread to other areas of Asia Minor too. Just as Antipatros refers to himself as first of the Ionians, an epigram inscribed onto a statue base found in the sanctuary proudly identifies its subject Akestorides as 'first of the Trojans' to win an Olympic victory, as well as listing his victories at Epidauros, Nemea, and the Arcadian cities of Lusoi and

Pheneus (*IvO* 184; Moretti 1953 no. 43; 1957 no. 590 dated to *c*.212 BCE). Sometime later another citizen of the Troad, Sodamas of Assos, also set up a statue (Paus. 6.4.9; Moretti 1957 no. 597). Pausanias comments that he was 'the first of the Aeolians in this area to win the boy's stade race at Olympia', information which presumably comes from the statue's dedicatory inscription. In his account of the development of the games Pausanias also tells us that the boys' *pankration* was introduced at the 145th festival (200 BCE), and was won by Phaidimos, an Aeolian from the city of Troas (Alexandria Troas; Paus. 5.8.11; Moretti 1957 no. 603). The evidence suggests a keenness on the part of the cities of Asia Minor to participate in the festival at Olympia, and the proud assertion of their victories through statue dedications.

The majority of the evidence for these victories comes from Pausanias' account of Olympia. Yet where epigraphic evidence is also available (compare Paus. 6.17.4 and *SEG* 35.1125, both for Hermesianax), it seems that he is transcribing accurately, though pride in his own origins from Asia Minor may have influenced his selection. The evidence thus suggests a growing interest in the festival at Olympia on the part of the cities of Asia Minor, and a proud assertion of victories won there, especially when they could be claimed a first. Statues were expensive and the small number attested does not necessarily mean that other victories were not also won here by victors from the area. Where we know the identity of the dedicants, they are usually the athletes themselves or their family (Antipatros, Akestorides, probably Eikasios) or their home city (Hermesianax). Athletes were keen to assert their civic identity, and bring honour to their homelands through references to their primacy in particular events. These statements were aimed at the Greeks assembled at the festival, but also at the neighbouring cities of the victor's homeland. Victory monuments can be seen as one of the ways in which cities and individuals vied for recognition and prestige within their own smaller communities, as well as providing proof of the claim of these cities to present themselves as part of the wider Greek community (more generally on the spatial dynamics of sanctuary displays see Scott 2010).

Apart from Akestorides, an equestrian victor, all the other athletes discussed above won victories in the boys' events. There is some evidence that individual cities might sponsor some successful boy athletes in an attempt to win further victories in the men's competitions. The best examples come from two inscriptions found in Ephesos which clearly show the prestige a victorious athlete could bring to his city (*IvE* 1415–1416, 2005, *c*.300 BCE; Robert 1967: 14–32; Brunet 2003: 227–230). The first inscription contains two decrees honouring successful athletes. The first, Athenodoros, was resident in Ephesos but not originally an Ephesian citizen. However, since he had declared himself as Ephesian when he won the boys' boxing at Nemea, the Ephesians decide to make him a citizen and award him all the honours and rewards which accrued to citizens who won victories at Nemea: public proclamation in the agora and a cash reward (*IvE* 1415, ll. 6–15). The second athlete, Timonax, has also won victories at Isthmia and Nemea and is thought likely to win more, 'again crowning the city'. The text breaks off, but his father seems to be asking for some grant of favour or support to his son (*IvE* 1416, ll. 18–23). The nature of such support is clarified in another inscription, which returns to Athenodoros (*IvE* 2005; identification: Robert 1967: 29–32). Here the athlete's trainer Therippides has appeared in front of the council to request that those who provide funds for the athlete's training and travel should themselves be rewarded with citizenship. Again, the motivation for the city is the hope of future victories and the prestige they will bring; they act in the expectation that Athenodoros will be victorious in other games, and again crown his city.

These examples show the importance placed upon victories in the great Panhellenic festivals of mainland Greece, and the ways in which they could be celebrated both at the place of victory and at home. Statues in Olympia asserted a city's claims and prestige to a wider audience, while actions at home reveal the place that athletic victories played within civic pride, and a city's relations with its own and its adopted citizens. Aspiring athletes were seen as a worthwhile investment, and athletic victory was not just a matter of personal pride but of civic importance. The statues at Olympia with their claims to be 'the first of the Ionians' or 'the first of the Trojans' show athletes and cities asserting that importance on the wider Panhellenic stage, as well as to themselves and their neighbours (for further discussion of athletic self-representation see Scharff 2019). Like many aspects of Hellenistic culture, the expansion of interest in the Olympics has its roots earlier in the fourth century but continues to develop in the Hellenistic period.

A similar picture of the eastern expansion of interest in the Panhellenic festivals of Greece can also be shown for the festival at Nemea (Farrington 2010), and was probably true too elsewhere. A particularly telling example is shown by an inscription from Sidon, a Phoenician city, which acclaims one of its leading citizens, Diotimos, for a victory in the chariot-race at Nemea (Moretti 1953 no. 41; generally on the Hellenization of Phoenicia see Millar 1983):

> You were the first of our citizens to bring back from Greece the glory of a victory in the chariot race to the house of the noble sons of Agenor. The sacred city of Cadmean Thebes also exults when she sees her mother city made famous by victories. As for your father Dionysius, [his prayer] about the competition was fulfilled when Hellas raised this clear [cry]: 'Not only do you excel in your ships [Sidon], but also in your yoked [chariots which bring] victory' (trans. Austin 2006 no. 140).

The civic pride felt in Diotimos' victory is palpable. As the first citizen to win a victory at Nemea he brings the city to the attention of the whole of Greece (Hellas). This participation is a clear sign of the enthusiastic adoption of Hellenic culture in Phoenicia, while the reference to Thebes alludes to the myth whereby a hero from Sidon, Kadmos, travelled to Greece to found the city of Thebes. While Diotimos' novel victory suggests that Sidon had hitherto between outside the Greek world, this link also backdates its claims to Hellenic culture into the distant past.

KINGS, ATHLETES, AND FESTIVALS

The discussion above has shown the importance of Panhellenic victories to the cities of Asia Minor, but they were certainly not alone. Cities of mainland Greece too continued to celebrate victories here, with many of the attested victors coming from the Peloponnese. Indeed, the dominance of Elis in the attested victories for the fourth, third, and first centuries BCE suggests that Elis took advantage of times of uncertainty to dominate the Altis and its competitions, especially in the expensive equestrian contests (Crowther 1988: 303; Scanlon 2002: 45). Yet Olympic victories were not just a place for Greek cities to prove their Hellenic credentials in the face of a changing world. We also find Hellenistic dynasts using Olympia to present themselves to the wider Greek world, either through competition themselves, or the promotion of others (see esp. Remijsen 2009 and Kainz 2016 on the Ptolemies).

An epigram from the Pergamene acropolis provides a good example (*IPerg.* 10; Moretti 1953 no. 37). Inscribed upon a statue base, it celebrates a victory in the chariot-race with foals. The victor was Attalos, probably a nephew and adopted son of the founder of the Attalid dynasty, Philetairos, who died young, rather than the later King Attalos I (Moretti 1953: 97–98). The end of the epigram hails the fame which accrues to Philetairos and the city of Pergamon, as well as stressing the fact that this victory was won in the eyes of thousands of Greeks. Moretti dates the inscription to around 280–272 BCE, the early days of the Attalid dynasty. In sending his adopted son to Olympia, Philetairos can be seen as asserting his Hellenic credentials, winning fame and recognition for his newly founded dynasty (cf. Macedonian kings earlier, discussed by Valavanis, this volume Chapter 9). Chariot-racing remained the sport of the elite throughout the Hellenistic period, and other victories are attested by those associated with royal dynasties, such as Belistichē, the *hetaira* of Ptolemy II, who won the two-horse chariot-race with foals when it was introduced at Olympia in 264 BCE (Paus. 5.8.11; Athen. 13.576e–f). Yet as well as kings or members of their households gaining Olympic victories, they also took action to raise the status of their regimes through the promotion of other promising athletes (Remijsen 2009: 256–258). A good example is recorded by Polybius, in a passage which also suggests how jealously claims to Greek identity were still protected in this period. Polybius describes how King Ptolemy IV of Egypt trained the boxer Aristonikos to take on the dominant Theban pankratiast Kleitomachos at the Olympic Games. Initially the crowd favoured the underdog, Aristonikos, until Kleitomachos called upon their sense of Greek pride, reminding them that Aristonikos was fighting for the glory of Ptolemy, but he for the glory of Greece, asking 'whether they would prefer an Egyptian man carrying off the Olympic crown, having conquered the Greeks, or a Theban and Boeotian to be proclaimed victor in the men's boxing' (Plb. 27.9.12). Aristonikos has a Greek name, and was probably of Greek lineage, but in Kleitomachos' eyes (at least as represented here) he is Egyptian. The imputation is that it is shameful for the Greeks assembled at Olympia to wish to be conquered by a foreign power; instead, Kleitomachos asserts his undeniable Greekness, as a Theban from Boeotia. While much of our inscriptional evidence attests to the widening pool of those who wished to see themselves as Greek and bring home an Olympic victory, this passage suggests that Greek identity could still be contested, with some cities more 'Greek' than others. For Kleitomachos his civic, regional, and wider identities coalesce; he is Greek because he is Theban, whereas an athlete promoted by the King of Egypt will always be Egyptian, no matter what his true origins might be.

THE SPREAD OF THE TRADITION: NEW ISOLYMPIC AND ISOPYTHIAN FESTIVALS

An innovation of the Hellenistic period was the institution of new festivals or the upgrading of existing ones with a status equal to that of the most important crown games in Greece and the invitation to other Greek states to participate (see Robert 1984 with the nuanced corrections of Parker 2004, now also van Nijf and Williamson 2015; 2016). Prior to this festivals were often open to performers from outside the city, as numerous victory lists attest, and evidence for the public proclamation of a festival to cities around the Greek world is attested for festivals other than the great Panhellenic four from at least the fourth century BCE. Only from the third century BCE, however, do we begin to find the explicit institution of festivals which are said to be isolympic, isonemean or isopythian; i.e. having the same rules and rewards as those held at Olympia, Nemea, or Delphi (though see Slater 2007: 27–30 for some confusions).

The first such attested festival is the Ptolemaia festival instituted at Alexandria by Ptolemy II in honour of his father. A series of epigraphic evidence attests to the fact that Ptolemy sent out envoys to Greek cities and leagues urging them to recognize this festival as equal in rank to the Olympic Games. A decree of the League of Islanders gives the fullest account, noting that the festival includes gymnastic, equestrian, and musical contests and agreeing to recognize it as equal to the Olympic Games, to send sacred envoys, to give victors in the games the same honours as they would award victors at Olympia and to bring a gold crown to honour King Ptolemy (*Syll*³ 390; Austin 2006 no. 256).

Accepting this festival was not a simply a diplomatic nicety, but carried a real financial burden. Recognition of victors at the games as equal to those at Olympia entailed providing them with cash rewards and other honours, such as those granted to Athenodoros at Ephesos for his Nemean victory, discussed above. In addition, the league had to fund an embassy to attend the games and bring the golden crown to Alexandria. The costs such embassies entailed are indicated in other texts, which commemorate the generosity of certain individual citizens (e.g. Boulagoras of Samos, *SEG* 1.366, Austin 2006 no. 132), but they also provided crucial opportunities to meet with the King, representing the interests of one's city and often asking for help (e.g. Kallias of Sphettus for Athens, *SEG* 49.113; Austin 2006 no. 55).

Ptolemy's institution of the Ptolemaia festival was a carefully orchestrated move to place Alexandria and its court on the map of Greek festival culture. The embassies who attended the sacrifice here and the performers who took part in the competitions would be able to see the showcase of Greek culture that was Alexandria, with its vibrant intellectual culture expressed through the Library and Mouseion. Processions were an integral part of religious festivals and some idea of what the Ptolemaia festival might have looked like is given by the description preserved in Athenaeus of a procession which took place in the city under Ptolemy II, though scholars are undecided whether or not this describes the Ptolemaia festival itself (Athen. 5.197c–203b; for discussion Rice 1983; Wikander 1992).

The account is drawn from Kallixeinos' history of Alexandria and starts with the description of a lavish temporary pavilion, presumably designed to host the envoys who attended the festival. The procession itself is described in extraordinary detail, with a special concentration on a section honouring the god Dionysos. In addition to representatives of the various bodies involved in the festival, such as the poet Philiskos (priest of Dionysos and probably also head of the Mouseion) and the guild of actors, the procession also includes figures dressed up as mythological characters, such as Silenoi and satyrs, and staged tableaux representing different episodes in Dionysos' life. The legitimacy of the Ptolemaic dynasty was underlined through the presence of statues of Alexander the Great and Ptolemy I, while Egypt's military and financial strength were stressed through the display of military troops and vast quantities of gold and silver. All in all, the procession seems to have been a proud assertion of Alexandria's strength and prestige, designed to impress both citizens and foreigners, as well as positioning the Ptolemies and their city, through the references to Greek culture and gods, firmly within the Hellenic world.

Later the Attalids acted similarly, sending envoys to the Greek cities and leagues (the Aetolian League, Delphic Amphictyony, Kos, and possibly Iasos are attested) to join the celebration of the Nikephoria festival, set up by Eumenes II to Athena Nikephoros following the defeat of Prusias of Bithynia in 183 BCE (Rigsby 1996: 362–377). A request for the inviolability (*asylia*) of the sanctuary to be recognized is included in these decrees, and features in a number of other examples of the institution or upgrading of festivals, though not all (Parker 2004: 10–11; on *asylia* see Rigsby 1996).

While these two examples show Hellenistic kings instituting new Panhellenic festivals and inviting the cities of Greece to recognize and attend them, the majority of the evidence for new or upgraded festivals comes from the cities themselves, especially those of Asia Minor. The best known example is Magnesia on the Maeander, in western Asia Minor, where an extensive dossier of decrees was proudly inscribed upon the walls of the agora. This recorded the city's (eventual) success in 208 BCE in upgrading the festival of its patron goddess Artemis Leukophryene to isopythian status and gaining recognition of her sanctuary as sacred and inviolate (Rigsby 1996: 179–279 collects the texts; selected examples in Austin 2006 nos. 189–190; see also Thonemann 2007 on the city's first attempt). The responses show that Magnesia had sent out their envoys throughout the Greek world, including to the kings Antiochus III of Syria, Ptolemy IV of Egypt, and Attalos I of Pergamon. Among those who responded were the major leagues and cities of mainland Greece, the islands, cities of Asia Minor, and communities as far west as Syracuse and as far east as Antioch in Persis, who make much of their ties of kinship with the Magnesians.

This wide geographical expanse is a good illustration of how the Greek world had grown by the late third century BCE, to encompass the Greek heartland, the traditional western communities of Magna Graecia (though only Syracuse is known for certain) and newer foundations in the East, such as Antioch in Persis. By the late second century BCE, the magistrate in charge of the Klaria festival at Klaros even went as far as to invite 'all mankind' to that festival (Robert and Robert 1989: 51, 94; Parker 2004: 16–17). Invitations to participate in and recognize Panhellenic, crowned, festivals suggest the broadening geography of the Greek world and the ways in which religious festivals with their athletic and musical contests continued to play a crucial role as a means by which cities asserted their Greek culture and situated themselves within the wider Greek world.

REFERENCES

Austin, M. M. 2006. *The Hellenistic World from Alexander to the Roman Conquest*. Cambridge.

Brunet, S. 2003. 'Olympic Hopefuls from Ephesos.' *JSH* 30: 219–235.

Crowther, N. B. 1988. 'Elis and the Games.' *AC* 57: 301–310; repr. in N. B. Crowther. 2004. *Athletika: Studies on the Olympic Games and Greek Athletics. Nikephoros* Beihefte I: 99–108.

Day, J. W. 2019. 'The "Spatial Dynamics" of Archaic and Classical Greek Epigram: Conversations among Locations, Monuments, Texts, and Viewer-Readers.' In *The Materiality of Text— Placement, Perception, and Presence of Inscribed Texts in Classical Antiquity.* 73–104. A. Petrovic, I. Petrovic, and E. Thomas, eds. Leiden and Boston.

Farrington, A. 1997. 'Olympic Victors and the Popularity of the Olympic Games in the Imperial Period.' *Tyche* 12: 15–46. Revised and reprinted in Scanlon 2014: 158–205.

Farrington, A. 2010. 'The Origin of Victors in the Isthmian Games.' In *Roman Peloponnese* III. Meletemata 63. 421–429. A. D. Rizakis and C. E. Lepenioti, eds. Athens.

Herrmann, H.-V. 1988. 'Die Siegerstatuen von Olympia.' *Nikephoros* 1: 119–183.

Kainz, L. 2016. '"We are the Best, We are One, and We are Greeks!" Reflections on the Ptolemies' Participation in the *Agones.*' In Mann, Remijsen, and Scharff 2016: 331–353.

Mann, C., Remijsen, S., and Scharff, S. eds. 2016. *Athletics in the Hellenistic World.* Stuttgart.

Millar, F. 1983. 'The Phoenician Cities: a Case-study of Hellenisation.' *PCPhS* 29: 55–71.

Mikalson, J. D. 2006. 'Greek Religion: Continuity and Change in the Hellenistic Period.' In *The Cambridge Companion to the Hellenistic World.* 208–222. G. R. Bugh, ed. New York.

Moretti, L. 1953. *Iscrizioni agonistiche greche.* Rome.

Moretti, L. 1957. *Olympionikai: i vincitori negli antichi agoni olimpici.* Rome.

Moretti, L. 1970. 'Supplemento al catalogo degli Olympionikai.' *Klio* 52: 295–303.

Moretti, L. 1987. 'Nuovo Supplemento al catalogo degli Olympionikai.' *Miscellanea Greca eRomana* 12: 67–91.

Parker, R. 2004. 'New "Panhellenic" Festivals in Hellenistic Greece.' In *Mobility and Travel in the Mediterranean from Antiquity to the Middle Ages.* 9–22. R. Schlesier and U. Zellmann, eds. Münster.

Pleket, H. W. 2014. 'Sport in Hellenistic and Roman Asia Minor.' In *A Companion to Sport and Spectacle in Greek and Roman Antiquity.* 364–375. P. Christesen and D. G. Kyle, eds. Malden, MA, and Oxford.

Remijsen, S. 2009. 'Challenged by Egyptians: Greek Sports in the Third Century BC.' *The International Journal of the History of Sport* 26.2: 246–271.

Rice, E. E. 1983. *The Grand Procession of Ptolemy Philadelphus.* Oxford.

Rigsby, K. J. 1996. *Asylia. Territorial Inviolability in the Hellenistic World.* Berkeley.

Robert, L. 1967. 'Sur des inscriptions d'Éphèse: fêtes, athlètes, empereurs, épigrammes.' *Revue de Philologie, de literature et d'histoire anciennes* ser. 3, 41 [93]: 7–84.

Robert, L. 1969-1990. *Opera Minora Selecta.* 7 vols. Amsterdam.

Robert, L. 1984. 'Discours d'ouverture.' *Actes du VIIIe. Congrès international d'épigraphie grecque et latine à Athenes, 1982.* Athens, 35–45; English trans. in *Greek Athletics (Edinburgh Readings on the Ancient World).* 2010. J. König, ed. Edinburgh: 108–119.

Robert, L. and J. Robert. 1989. *Claros I.* Paris.

Scanlon, T. F. 2002. *Eros and Greek Athletics.* New York.

Scanlon, T. F. ed. 2014. *Sport in the Greek and Roman Worlds* I. Oxford.

Scharff, S. 2019. '"The Very First of the Citizens." Agonistic Cultures and the Self-presentation of Hellenistic Athletes.' Habilitationsschrift, Mannheim.

Scott, M. 2010. *Delphi and Olympia. The Spatial Politics of Panhellenism in the Archaic and Classical Periods.* Cambridge.

Slater, W. 2007. 'Deconstructing Festivals.' In Wilson 2007: 21–47.

Thonemann, P. 2007. 'Magnesia and the Greeks of Asia (*I. Magnesia* 16.16).' *GRBS* 47: 151–160.

Van Nijf, O. M. and Williamson, C. G. 2015. 'Re-inventing Traditions: Connecting Contests in the Hellenistic and Roman world.' In *Reinventing 'The Invention of Tradition'? Indigenous Pasts and the Roman Present.* 95–111. D. Boschung, A. W. Busch and M. J. Verluys eds. Paderborn.

Van Nijf, O. M. and Williamson, C. G. 2016. 'Connecting the Greeks: Festival Networks in the Hellenistic World.' In Mann, Remijsen and Scharff 2016: 43–71.

Wikander, C. 1992. 'Pomp and Circumstance: The Procession of Ptolemaios II.' *Opuscula Atheniensia* 19.12: 143–150.

Wilson, P. ed. 2007. *The Greek Theatre and Festivals. Documentary Studies.* Oxford.

SECTION 4

ROMAN GAMES AND SPECTACLES

CHAPTER 11

GAMES IN THE REPUBLIC
Performance and Space

ALISON FUTRELL

ROMAN spectacle encompasses a broad range of events, occasions, and celebrations, elaborate and formal series of actions that invited and required the participation of an expanded human audience. The organization of such events by the state apparatus began in the early republic, with the Ludi Magni or Ludi Romani, in honour of Jupiter Optimus Maximus, initially held to celebrate military victory and give thanks to the divinities responsible for that success. By the fourth century, the Ludi Romani had become an annual state-sponsored event, organized by public officials to secure the blessing of Rome's gods. To more overtly ritual elements of procession and sacrifice were added other kinds of spectacle, physical competitions or performances that likewise honoured the gods, especially *ludi circenses*, chariot-racing, and *ludi scaenici*, stage or theatrical performances. As Rome expanded into the Mediterranean, such public programming increased in intensity and frequency, becoming an important means of demonstrating Rome's growing power and legitimizing her dominance on a world stage. Events engaged the attendance and participation of a wide range of Romans, high and low, rich and poor, scions of old families and more recent immigrants, those devoted to the ways of the ancestors, and those who embraced the cosmopolitan possibilities of the Mediterranean milieu. Of particular interest here are the theatrical games, as these furnish sharp examples of the interactions of performers, elites, and those outside the leadership class in a complex dynamic, attested in some detail by surviving sources.

ONE AND THE CROWD: TENSION AND COLLABORATION

There were, in ancient Rome, a range of state rituals, religious and political, that focused the gaze on a specific leader: standing on a podium or in the chariot, clad in distinctive garb, performing authority in gesture, movement, and speech, acting as an agent for the state, entrusted with or taking on significant actions for the shared benefit of the collective. With the growth of empire and the increasing magnificence of state panoply, individual leaders expressed their leadership skills through the organization of mass spectacle. A pithy remark attributed to Aemilius Paullus, victor over King Perseus of Macedonia, asserts that a man who knows how to conquer in war was a man who knew how to organize a show and was also, apparently, a man who knew how to capitalize on that politically (Livy 45.32–33). One can see this connection made especially for Roman leaders celebrating triumphs, who, because of the extraordinary nature of their public displays, had more opportunity to direct the attention of the audience.

The gaze of spectators and supporters recognizes and honours authority and acts as assent, as agreement and co-participation, originating from those whose capacity to wield influence operated at lower levels than the leader. Rome's republic officially was a collective of power, where individuals (particularly freeborn male citizens) were organized into groups: political, social, economic, and religious. People formed voting units on the basis of where they lived or their level of wealth, the 'orders' whose '*concordia*' Cicero idealistically envisioned. Others found support and belonging in relationships of mutual benefit around a specific patron; often these loyalties were passed through generations in families. Some came together in *collegia* or voluntary associations based on occupation, or bonded through religious affiliations, or found common ground in literal common ground, as neighbourhood groups. Movement and action at rituals were at times based on these membership units, as individuals visually united and voiced their assent as a group whole. Still, tensions were inherent in the Roman political system.

There was increasing mobilization in the late republic to differentiate groups and agendas, at a time when the radical economic and cultural changes wrought by imperialism had enhanced differences within the Roman populace. That populace was itself much larger and more diversified, because of Rome's successful expansion. It was also empowered, in many ways, by the second-century shift in voting processes away from acclamation: because individual votes were no longer so visible (and subject to intimidation), voters had to be more energetically wooed for their support. Note that this was not purely a binary relationship between a singular leader and the massed sub-elite: multiple groups assert their claims to access.

There was (and had been for some time) heightened tension among the ruling elites, who competed strenuously for influence and access to power. The latter tensions simmered in the ambience of the votive games commemorating the military successes of their peers. There was mobilization and mobility within spectacles to contest the traditional hierarchy and challenge the status verification of immobile visibility.

THE CROWD SPEAKS

The Roman populace was well familiar with habits of group vocalization, deployed in multiple spheres of public activity. In religious ritual, there was reciprocal call and response in prayer, as still can be found among congregants of modern systems of belief. In politics, vote by acclamation was standard practice until the balloting laws or *leges tabellariae* routinized individual, 'secret' voting practices toward the end of the second century BCE. At games, spectators expressed gratitude to magistrates and producers or *editores*, formally welcoming them into the space of the spectacle. These habits at the shows were often engaged in 'claques', small groups who specialized in the urgent, audible, infectious expression of support or disdain, groups formed, probably, on the basis of social connections forged in the *collegia* and neighbourhood groups, as well as among the clients of notable Romans. There was regularized organization of these by political figures for public action in the late republic. This networking points to the enhanced communication this entailed. Claque members or claqueurs would chant in short bursts; brevity of message and familiarity of vocal pattern allowed those in proximity to pick it up. These snappy and familiar articulations became the ancient equivalents of memes: they were adopted and spread by those outside the claque.

Some techniques of the claques derived from a ritual context. Claqueurs could adapt phrases used to invoke the gods; they changed the name of the addressee, his notable attribute, and the verb, and a current powerbroker was made to parallel or parody the original divine honorand, spice or enhancement added by the intertextuality. Claques adapted material from other contexts as well: songs from farce and lines from drama with some aspect or catchphrase that seemed relevant to contemporary activity, paralleling the circumstances or providing a verbal echo for hot-button issues. In other cases, pithy or snarky remarks by characters were picked up and repeated for the occasion. How this worked in practice may have varied. Cicero in one instance suggests that the audience seized the initiative on the spot, having noticed a parallel between fictive stage events and contemporary actions in Rome; their response was then encouraged by the actor (*For Sestius* 118). Elsewhere, Cicero suspects claqueurs responded to specific cues with rehearsed phrases or that prepared claqueurs were positioned strategically within a larger group, to get the chanting started (*Letters to his brother Quintus* 2.3.2). Such 'spontaneous' expressions at spectacle could be redeployed at later trials and meetings by claques and by speakers. The recreated critique shifted the earlier interaction to a new purpose, to persuade and challenge and to demand specific outcomes. The claqueurs and their leaders were good at manipulating reactions of the larger crowd at the performance (Cameron 1974; Axer 1989; Potter 1996; Aldrete 1999).

The Roman public had plenty of practice in articulating their views, not only at the festivals and public events that were part of the state calendar, but also in attending 'private' events and ad hoc gatherings (Taylor 1937; Aldrete 1999; Parker 1999). Mass utterances like these could be pretty sophisticated: exchanges between opposed groups are known from late republic contexts as they are from the high empire. Dio Cassius describes one such incident in 217 CE, when the spectators bellowed their complaints about state action in Latin and the Senate responded, also in unison, in Greek (Dio Cassius 79.20).

This kind of activity worked to create and solidify group identity, to tighten the cohesion of social cadres in Rome (Edmondson 1996). Sections of the populace made use of these regular opportunities to articulate points of view, refined and nuanced as circumstances warranted. The channelling of emotion, too, could provide a valuable cathartic service in, for example, the expression of grief. At the same time, such clear expressions, magnified by the emotions of the participants, held danger. Quintilian (6.37–39) recognized peril in the laughter of the group; when the politically powerless joined in derision against their social and political betters, this tool could undermine the *dignitas* of the powerful (Bell 1997: 15–18). Others noted that mass gatherings could cause tensions simmering beneath the surface to manifest in the open: Valerius Maximus (7.4.1) references the 'battle lines' that formed in the origins of the theatre.

THE GAMES BEGIN

In 364 BCE, dramatic performances were added to the Ludi Romani, games that had originated (according to Roman tradition) in the fifth century. Dionysius of Halicarnassus asserts that Roman *ludi* incorporated a theatrical component from their earliest days (7.71–72). Ritual processions for the Ludi Magni had always had what he calls a satyrs' chorus, who chant derisively and mimic the other participants in the solemn procession, provoking laughter as a fundamental part of the ritual. He notes this choral mockery is known from a number of ritual contexts in Rome, including triumphal processions and public funerals; for both the latter contexts, a point of emphasis seems to be that the mockery is being directed at very privileged individuals in ceremonies that carry a great deal of social and political weight. The performances here integrate both verse and stylized movement accompanied by music, which Dionysius specifically identifies as theatrical, as identical to the actions of the chorus in Greek satyr plays.

Livy's take (7.2) on the origins of *ludi scaenici* places the games in a more specific historical context, connecting Rome's adoption of theatrical events to religious innovation meant to propitiate the gods during a particularly persistent plague in 364 BCE. The decision was made to bring in outside specialists: Etruscan dancers performing decorously to flutes would provide the appropriate ritual action to restore the sacred balance. Livy is careful to note that the music was wordless and that, likewise, the dancers' movements were not meant to evoke specific lyrics or narrative. This decorousness, however, was soon moderated by 'young Romans', who made this into a sung exchange of salty verses, adapting their dance movements to the ribald content. Valerius Maximus (2.4.4) parallels Livy's presentation in some key points: the religious response composed for the plague was reworked by young men with crudely humorous gestures, then refined with Etruscan dance forms and structured metre. This was Rome's pattern for *ludi scaenici* for more than a century, we are told, with performances that featured young male players and ad hoc mocking songs enhanced by suggestive but stylized movements, a model that seemingly fits with Dionysius' description of early drama.

These developments were far from isolated phenomena: Rome was in constant contact with various cultural and political groups in Italy, each with their own performance traditions, adding to the rich fusion that became Roman drama (Marshall 2006; Rawson 1985). The cities of Magna Graecia to the south of Rome had long and continuous connections to productivity in the larger Greek world, including not just the formal developments in Old and New Comedy, but the revivals and parodies of plots and specific plays, reinterpreted for new circumstances and audiences (Dearden 2012; Marconi 2012). Gnaeus Naevius was embedded in this formal dramatic practice; he came to Rome as an adult, after having fought in the First Punic War (Aulus Gellius, *Attic Nights* 17.21.45–47). Fragments at most remain of his output of comedies and tragedies, little to indicate what sort of distinctively Italian sensibility they bore. Livius Andronicus, roughly contemporary with Naevius, in one tradition came to Rome a captive from Tarentum; he also crafted *fabula palliata*, plays in Greek clothes. Other performing traditions impacted Rome, including crude Fescennine verses, that built raw and extemporized metric exchanges between players. Atellan farces, linked to the small Oscan town of Atella, deployed stock characters in improvised basic plots, laced with pratfalls, 'beatings', and exaggerated physical byplay; among the mainstay roles were

Maccus, the fool, Pappus, the old man, and Manducus, the 'jaws'. Visual representations of burlesque theatre can be found on the South Italian 'phlyax' vases; whether or not these vases represent the production of known Middle Comedy dramatists in this tradition, the images suggest the regional popularity of this kind of broad comedy there in the fourth century BCE (Dearden 2012).

Rome may have been a draw for troupes of performers in different genres from an earlier date than suggested in our sources, lured by the presence of trade emporia and seasonal celebrations. The sixth century temple complexes of Sant' Omobono on the Forum Boarium and in the Circus Maximus area certainly pulled in regional traffic and possibly from further afield in Italy.

MATTERS OF SPACE

During the republic, there were relatively few purpose-built permanent structures meant to house Roman spectacle. Early chariot-racing likely took place on tracks laid out ad hoc on expanses of flat land. The low-lying stretch between the Palatine and Aventine was configured early on for this purpose: Livy attributes the planning of the Circus Maximus to the first Tarquin, Rome's king, according to tradition, in the late seventh/early sixth century BCE (Livy 1.35). Long years would pass, however, before the space was shaped in impressive and permanent architecture. This maximized the flexible use of the space, with improvised seating to be had on the slopes nearby (Favro 1999). The Forum was also a multipurpose space; Vitruvius attributes the specific proportions of these central spaces in Italy to the long custom of holding gladiatorial matches there, enhancing public structures with wider intercolumniations and upper-storey balconies in order to enhance the visibility of the spectacle for attendees (Vitruvius 5.1.1–2). Sponsors of events thus provided temporary accommodations for specific events, erected in public spaces and dismantled after the performance (Welch 2007: 30–71). The selection of an appropriate location offered significant opportunities and challenges.

Rome's public spaces, especially the Forum and the Triumphal pathways, were a 'Memory Palace', filled with visual rhetoric that was a constant iteration of Rome's (literal) constructed historical identity, as manifested in the state-approved achievements of individuals and of the polity (Flower 2003; Sumi 2009; Holliday 2002; Hölscher 2006; Gowing 2005; Latham 2016; Favro and Johanson 2010; Popkin 2016). Structures and monuments commemorated the trajectory of Roman success in general and honoured, as well, specific historic incidents of signal import to the Romans as a whole, to the SPQR (Senatus Populusque Romanus). Visual examples abounded, in the public structures funded by individuals, acting as magistrates, as triumphant generals, and as private citizens. Monuments were officially commissioned to memorialize extraordinary actions of specific leaders, using at times representations of individuals in active association with mnemonics of their achievements: the painting of Manlius Valerius Messalla's victory over Hiero of Syracuse in the First Punic War, placed on the wall of the Curia, may have drawn on more ephemeral images carried past that very spot during the actual triumph (Pliny, *Natural History* 35.22). Other representations ventured beyond the battlefield to create visual narratives that spoke to the qualities of individual authority. Spurius Carvilius used material from helmets and breastplates, taken in defeating the Samnites in the early third century, to have a massive statue of Jupiter created for the Capitoline; he also commissioned a portrait statue of himself to be placed next to the god (Pliny, *Natural History* 34.43). Tiberius Sempronius Gracchus commemorated a victory in the Hannibalic War by ordering a painting of a post-battle victory banquet for the Temple of Libertas on the Aventine, a painting that carefully delineated different levels of battlefield commitment among Roman troops (Livy 24.16).

These figural and architectural reminders of specific careers and leading families hovered continually in the public background in spaces that housed official and mundane functions. As backdrops to key events, rituals, and performances, such monumentalized narratives offered constant comparison and contrast to present leaders: spectacles, triumphs, speeches, and meetings all were flavoured by the visual memorials of the achievements of the forebears, framing the agents of Rome's current public actions and the ongoing creation of collective memory (Gowing 2005: 13–17; Hölscher 2006: 36–41; Popkin 2016: 77–80).

Public structures were funded by individuals, as magistrates and triumphators. Temples and shrines, vowed on the field of battle, were constructed using the general's portion of the spoils, ostensibly to give thanks to the deities whose favour enabled Roman success in battle.

The Campus Martius had long been used for significant public actions: this was the site where Rome marshalled its citizen troops in times of war; here too gathered battle-weary legions, in anticipation of the triumphal celebration. This became a prime location for permanent victory monuments and temples vowed in wartime, lasting constructions that evoked and, ideally, recaptured the enthusiasms and cohesions of earlier, ephemeral celebrations. These structures framed and even created a distinctive physical space for Rome's spectacles and performances, particularly in the Circus Flaminius area, a low-lying open space in the southern part of the Campus Martius, west of the Capitoline; importantly, the Circus Flaminius had been home to plebeian impromptu and formal assemblies as early as the fifth century, as well as the Ludi Plebeii (Vanderbroeck 1987: 234–235; Coarelli 1997a; Morstein-Marx 2004: 59–60). As noted above, the Circus Maximus housed *ludi* with theatrical performances and staged animal hunts, as well as the more typical chariot-races. Temples were likely spectacle locations, accommodating dramatic performances as well as ritual, in the centuries prior to purpose-built theatres in Rome. Indeed, temple steps and sanctuary precincts were routinely deployed for theatrical performances in Italy (Hanson 1959; Goldberg 1998). The Temple of Magna Mater and that of Flora were in near proximity to the Circus; both deities were honoured by calendrical sets of games that made use of this convenient space. The Temple of Magna Mater on the Palatine was the probable original location for the theatrical events associated with the annual Megalesia; with a relatively high podium and two levels of steps, the lower one wrapped around the plaza south and west of the temple, the Great Mother's sanctuary could accommodate as many as 1,600 spectators watching performances on a temporary stage below (Goldberg 1998: 14–19). This was likely true for a range of temples in the city; a speech given by the Choragus in Plautus' comedy *Curculio* gives a verbal tour of the Roman Forum, as if its features were in the sightlines of both the character on stage and the audience (*Curculio* 462–486; Goldberg 1998: 1–3; Marshall 2006: 160). Performances for some festivals, such as the annual Compitalia organized by neighbourhoods, were likely held on local streets, near the cross-road sanctuaries for the deities honoured by the celebrations. Special arrangements to accommodate these may have been quite simple, reflective, perhaps, of the basic features found on *phlyax* vases from elsewhere in Italy: an elevated surface to make the performance more visible to a standing audience, a framing structure to delineate dramatic space and punctuate actors' movements (Beacham 1991: 7–9, 59–62; Rawson 1985; Richlin 2014). (Indeed, Rome's dramatic performances were likely enacted by troupes whose circuit served Italy broadly.)

Eventually, Roman patrons would draw on architectural traditions outside and inside Rome to commission formal and permanent purpose-built structures to house performances. But there was long-term resistance to the creation of such venues for performance, lasting over a century and delaying construction that, clearly, many in Rome wanted (North 1992; Goldberg 1998: 2; Manuwald 2011: 57–61). A controversy erupted over an attempt to formalize a performance structure in 194 BCE, when the censors told the aediles in charge of the *ludi Romani* to set aside special seats for the senators, separated from the general public, setting a standard for other performances (Livy 34.44). Valerius Maximus attributes this initiative to Scipio Africanus, as consul for the year (2.4.3). The massed unity of senatorial togas would foreground, literally, that body's *auctoritas*; some spectators were stirred to pronounce this honour was long deserved (Gruen 1990: 5–33; Moore 1994–1995: 114–120). Others, however, perceived this as an arrogant slap at the people, who were diminished by this privileging of one class after so many years of sharing a mixed audience space at such public events. Scipio's popularity was shaken. The games had long been presented by magistrates, who likewise could exert some authority over access to the shows. This change may have been meant to diminish the impact of rivalry within the senate by guaranteeing premium seating for the body as a whole.

In 179 BCE, Marcus Aemilius Lepidus and Marcus Fulvius Nobilior held the censorship, a pair with a history of tense rivalry and active factional efforts; in the previous decade, the two had competed as generals vying for prestigious postings and for priority in the award of a triumph. Nobilior accelerated his return from Aetolia to celebrate his triumph in 187, bringing with him Greek actors and athletes to lend lustre to the games associated with his success. These were votive games, vowed to Jupiter Optimus Maximus at the battle of Ambracia in 189. Nobilior's victory there was dramatized formally with the premiere of Ennius' play *Ambracia*, performed twice by the Greek *technitai*, specialists brought in for the event. The stage building created to house the performances also included an orchestra space, a feature that affected the relationship between audience and actors by stretching the distance between them (Livy 39.22; Gruen 1990: 117, 124–157; Gruen 1992: 195–196). The orchestra was where elite seating was located in Greek practice; the reserved seating for senators that was now mandated could have been accommodated here in Nobilior's structure. Nobilior soon began work on a Temple to Hercules and the Muses, combining the well-known deified hero with the goddesses that inspired Greek artistic achievement; here he would house Greek works of art he had taken as victor that may have been part of the triumphal display in 187. All reverence paid to these deities would thus simultaneously recognize Nobilior's success, not just as military leader, but as a discerning claimant to Mediterranean cultural prestige and as a host of significant, impactful public gatherings (Holliday 1997: 142; Edmondson 1999: 80; Pittenger 2008: 212).

In 179, Lepidus was preparing five days of *ludi scaenici* for the dedication of his newly completed temples to Juno Regina and Diana, structures he'd vowed as commander during the Ligurian War in 187 BCE (Jacobs and Conlin 2014: 43–45). The date set for their dedication was the anniversary of his rival Nobilior's Aetolian triumph; Lepidus thus could claim some of Nobilior's memorializing cachet by launching a new set of annual events for Rome's religious calendar. And not just Nobilior's cachet: both temples were located along the triumphal parade route and would stand as silent commentaries on all subsequent processions. While Juno Regina was located not far from Nobilior's sanctuary of Hercules and the Muses, the Aemilian Temple of Diana may have been a near neighbour of the Temple of Apollo, in the shadow of the Capitoline. Among the building projects credited to Lepidus is a *theatrum* and *proscaenium* at the Temple of Apollo (Livy 40.51; Vitruvius 3.3.4; Platner and Ashby 1929: 14–15, 290; Bruno 1999: 260–262; Coarelli 1997a: 34; Coarelli 2014: 383). The 'theatre' referenced by Livy may have been supplemental seating, in addition to the usual temple steps, which, with or without the stage structure, may have been intended as a more substantial facility to be reused each year by the aediles in charge of Apollo's games (Jacobs and Conlin 2014: 69). Nobilior, meanwhile, did some restoration work on the Temple of Apollo and built a portico for it, a covered colonnade extending as far as the Tiber and possibly intended as an amenity for the theatre-going crowds regularly to be found there during the six days of the Ludi Apollinares. The building efforts of these censors focused on public access to sacred areas that were meant to function as spectacle spaces, not just as placements for altars and images. Their renovations took into account how needs had changed since the Temple of Apollo's last renovation in 353 BCE, specifically the establishment of annual *ludi* with increasingly de luxe shows for Rome's greatly expanded population (Goldberg 1998: 10).

In 167 BCE, L. Anicius Gallus celebrated a triumph over Illyria; the votive games were elaborate and expensive, with a venue scaled up to accommodate them. An enormous stage building was erected in the 'circus', of a size that impressed even Polybius, who was familiar with contemporary theatrical structures in the Greek mainland (Polybius 30.22 = Athenaeus, *Dinner Sophists* 14.4; Livy 45.43). Gallus imported Greek tragic actors, choral dancers, and celebrated flute-players for his games. The performance that ensued was notable, although perhaps more in a notoriously negative sense; although the show began with the anticipated high quality music and movement, things then went strangely awry as the relationship between performers and audience changed. Athenaeus notes that the four flute-players were featured first on the programme, accompanying the movements of the chorus. Gallus, however, pressed them to 'show more competitive spirit'; one of the sponsor's lictors explained to the baffled performers that 'they should turn and go for each other and make a sort of fight of it'. Now understanding, those on the stage complied with Gallus' intent; as Athenaeus notes, this 'suited their own appetite for licence'. Groups of dancers moved in aggressive faux battle lines against each other and 'faced about and retreated in turn', while the flute-players likewise 'advanced towards each other in turn', their instruments resounding in 'unintelligible discord'. When one of the dancers rolled up his robe and took up a boxing stance against a flautist, the spectators broke into loud applause and cheers; thus incentivized, more musicians, dancers, and even boxers clambered into the orchestra. The fragment ends with Polybius' consternation about describing a scenario that he finds literally indescribable, so far does it range from performance norms familiar to his readers (Polybius 30.22, Paton translation; Athenaeus, *Dinner Sophists* 14.4). It's important, however, that audience and Gallus colluded in creating the impromptu mishmash of mayhem and music. We may note in a similar vein Terence's repeated difficulties with competition from other shows in the mid-160s: twice his *Hecyra* is disrupted by nearby events, such as fights and tightrope walking; the venue was also rushed by gladiatorial spectators, indicating the intensely close proximity and, possibly, a premium on performance space (Sandbach 1982; Edmondson 1999: 81–84).

A major commotion erupted in 154 (or 179/174), when Rome's censors let a contract for the construction of a stage building or theatre located along the south-west slope of the Palatine (Velleius Paterculus 1.15). Progress on the project was apparently well under way when elite resistance interfered; objections to this development seemed to focus on the seating. P. Cornelius Scipio Nasica, the moral centre in this dispute, insisted that this building was useless; indeed it was actively dangerous for public morals and should be destroyed (Livy, *Epitome* 48). Other sources emphasize traditional Roman austerity and elite concern about the growing influence of leisure on the morals of citizens, who might be tempted into lolling about all day at the theatre, as if they were decadent Greeks (Velleius Paterculus 1.15; Tacitus, *Annals* 14.21–22). Elsewhere, the focus is on how this might harm the martial strength of the Romans, who should stand upright when they attended spectacles, to maintain both Roman sinews and martial spirit (Valerius Maximus 2.4.2; Orosius, *Against the Pagans* 4.21). Appian suggests the threat is rooted in class tension, that a permanent theatre might accommodate extended popular discussion of sedition, possibly impacting senatorial domination of Rome's political discourse (*Civil Wars* 1.28, 125). The Senate voted to dismantle the unfinished structure and enacted some sort of enduring restriction on permanent accommodations for shows within the city (Mitens 1993: 98; Goldberg 1998: 2, 10; Gruen 1992: 206–210). Attending to the letter (but not the spirit) of this legislation would push the conception of 'temporary' structures to the limit. It also provoked significant reactions from the sub-elite.

A compelling disagreement over access, status, and spectacle is associated with Gaius Gracchus' activism in 122 BCE, during the final part of his second tribunate (Plutarch, *Gaius* 12). A gladiatorial show was being organized by one of his fellow tribunes, to take place in the Forum.

Wooden bleachers had been set up for spectators, but limitations were in place that excluded Rome's economically disadvantaged. In later years, tokens for the seating at such events were distributed through the regular networks of family and friends of the sponsoring magistrate, along with those in his particular patronage. If this particular tribune did not lean populist in his politics, as Gaius did, then likely the beneficiaries of his generosity would not fit the same sub-elite demographic ascribed to Gaius' radical stance. Gracchus insisted that the seats be removed from the public space; the other tribunes ignored the request. Gracchus and his ally workmen, partners in his social programmes, then dismantled the structure on the night preceding the event, thus liberating the sightlines for all Rome's spectators at this public show. Plutarch claims that Gaius' fellow magistrates were so outraged by Gaius' forceful interference that they falsified returns at the subsequent polls, ensuring that Gaius failed to achieve a third term in office and triggering the civic bloodshed of his downfall.

In time, temporary performance structures were pushed to the limits, infamously by the structure of Marcus Aemilius Scaurus, curule aedile in charge of the Ludi Magni (Romani) in September of 58 BCE, which by all accounts spared no expense in its remarkable provisions; Scaurus even provided a hippopotamus, the first seen in Rome (Valerius Maximus 2.4.6; Ammianus 22.15.24). The arrangements evoked superlatives in pleasure and criticism, for contemporaries and for future generations. Cicero (*For Sestius* 116) calls the event 'most splendid and magnificent' (*ludos apparatissimos magnificentissimosque*). For Pliny it was 'the greatest work of all' (*opus maximum omnium*) and he describes at some length the elaborate stage building, three storeys high, built of de luxe materials, its articulated columns made of marble for the ground floor, of glass on the middle level, gilded wood at the top. Indeed, there were 360 columns in all, the shortest being 38 feet tall, and 3,000 bronze statues. Scaurus' outlay was a reputed thirty million sesterces and could allegedly seat an audience of 80,000 spectators, twice that of Pompey's later theatre (*Natural History* 36.114–115). Scaurus' theatre becomes a milestone in the long tale of republican moral decline; even Cicero registers some qualms about the structure (Cicero, *On Duties* 2.5.7; Valerius Maximus 2.4.6; Bruno 1999: 264–265; Leach 2000: 384–385).

Cicero's later defence of Scaurus incorporates monuments funded by his ancestors as character witnesses, such as the cult images from the Capitoline; their visibility to the judges is meant to persuade them not to convict this worthy scion of the Aemilii (*For Scaurus* 45a). In that same defence, Cicero asserts that the marble columns relocated from the theatre to Scaurus' house are appropriate, given the family wealth and dignity; an upstart, however, would not merit such de luxe domestic decor. The defence was undertaken when Scaurus was charged with provincial extortion while running for the consulship of 54, so the appropriate use of money, in public and at home, in Rome itself or in her overseas territories, was something of an ongoing sensitivity for Scaurus. Cicero got Scaurus off in 54 BCE, but went into exile the following year, dogged by accusations of campaign violations.

Another major landmark in the competition of 'temporary' spectacle accommodations came in 52 BCE, when Gaius Scribonius Curio, a candidate for aedile, tried to surpass Scaurus' standard with a dynamic novelty structure as part of the games honouring his deceased father. Pliny describes a pair of wooden theatres mounted on pivots. In the morning, the theatres were back to back and housed two separate dramatic performances. Later in the day, they could be rotated to join the two performance spaces and thus convert to a theatre-on-two-sides, or 'amphitheatre', in which paired gladiators provided the spectacle. As Pliny notes, however, the real show was the audience's thrill-seeking proclivities, exposing themselves to danger as they careened about atop the revolving mechanism. Pliny contrasts the frenzied madness of the flighty spectators, risking death for fleeting pleasure, with the sober determination of the ancestors who faced Hannibal (*Natural History* 36.117–120).

Between Scaurus' excess and Curio's recklessness, chronologically, stands Pompey's complex, his Theatre, centred on the Temple of Venus Victrix and dedicated in 55 BCE. Its overt political messaging, however, is more usefully contextualized after a deeper dive into the period's deployment of spectacle in the service of factionalism.

Shows and Political Discourse in the 50s

We turn now to identity negotiation, to examine how public shows provided an opportunity for negotiating and disputing public alliances and ruptures: the one vs the crowd, multiple ones in groups, contested crowds; to consider as well how the voice of the people worked, or did not, or indeed how it was subverted, outraged, and corrupted in a few famous spectacles from the 50s BCE. The focus here is on populism and spectacle, with special interest in the habits of interaction between players, elites, and audiences in this period (Vanderbroeck 1987; Tatum 1990; Parker 1999). We rely heavily in this assessment on Cicero's views of how the interface took place and his delineation of the political divisions and claims being made. Cicero consistently backs the elite, who are the *boni* or 'the good men' in his narrative. He lauds the spectacles as the best of Rome's public gatherings: at *ludi* and gladiatorial games, the truest expression of the Roman People can be heard (*For Sestius* 106, 115). Cicero like-wise denounces the manipulations of Rome's populist politicians and derides their followers as 'slaves', rabble-rousers, and 'gladiators', unworthy and degraded, their support so easy to manipulate through their base impulses. He harps upon the chaos they create, with evoca-tive references to the Tiber choked with the bodies of citizens, to their blood mopped with sponges off the paving stones of the Forum (*For Sestius* 77).

P. Cornelius Lentulus Spinther sponsored a set of theatrical events as part of games he organized that took place in the early summer of 57 BCE (Cicero, *For Sestius* 116–123). Cicero's account, written not long afterward, presents the interactions between performers and audi-ence at the theatre as informed by and paralleling a Senate meeting that was taking place simultaneously at the Temple of Honour and Virtue, a venue located on the Velian Hill close to the urban centre, originally built by Gaius Marius to commemorate his victory over the invading Cimbri and Teutones (Plutarch, *Marius* 32; Valerius Maximus 1.7.5; Vitruvius 3.2.5). Both meeting and games addressed the recall of Cicero from exile; both were sponsored by Spinther, who seems to have laid considerable groundwork for each, shaping the parameters of the dialogue and crafting, as much as possible, the narrative and outcomes (Leach 2000: 385–390).

Spinther was one of the consuls for the year; though he had been both aedile and praetor, those offices were in his past, so it's unlikely that these games were part of the ordinary reli-gious calendar but, perhaps, funeral or votive games instead. The audience catchment, there-fore, would be different from that for one of the major festivals of the religious year: more reliant on locals rather than a regional draw. Some scholars have preferred to place these theatrical performances within the Floralia in May (Vanderbroeck 1987 no. 53); the Temple of Flora was in the vicinity of the Circus Maximus, a capacious potential performance venue in the shadow of the Palatine. The particular visual references made during the events, how-ever, point to a location within the Forum, whence the Aedes Libertatis or Shrine of Liberty on the northern side of the Palatine would have been visible (the shrine having replaced Cicero's house, destroyed in partisan violence) (Tatum 1999: 142–162; Roller 2010: 156–157).

Spinther made his entrance prior to the first presentation on the programme, a comedy, *Simulans* (*The Pretender*). The audience gave him a standing ovation: stretching their hands toward him, they wept for joy and chanted their gratitude, drawing perhaps upon the ac-clamation formulae of Roman religious practice. The arrival of the sponsor was typically a ceremonial moment in spectacle performances, an opportunity to initiate the sponsor-spectator connection that would play out throughout the event. No doubt the audience regularly indicated their appreciation of sponsors' generosity at that moment. Cicero's de-scription suggests that this audience was particularly demonstrative, their thanks verging on that rendered to sacred or salvific figures; Cicero hints that this intensity resonated with Spinther's current political actions on Cicero's behalf (*For Sestius* 117).

P. Clodius Pulcher, Cicero's political nemesis, was also in attendance; as a candidate for the aedileship, he would have wanted to maximize his visibility at significant events in the city. The audience response to his entrance, however, was apparently quite different from their greeting for Spinther: rhythmic prayers turned to curses and abuse, with vehement and threatening gestures conveying the hostile message visually. The chorus on stage soon added to the anti-Clodius demonstration, redirecting a line from the comedy outward to the notorious Clodius. 'This is the outcome of your vice-ridden life!' they said in loud unison; they reinforced their vocal disapproval with physical performance, leaning over Clodius and glaring directly at him, their choices meant to equate an original scripted referent to the con-temporary, 'real' correspondent that had just arrived in the elite seating section. Clodius was taken aback by this reception; Cicero notes that he was used to directing abusive chanters, not being targeted by them. Cicero claims that similar allusions were extracted from the rest of the play and performed by the actors, then picked up by the spectators in attendance, and then by the entire people (*populus universus*) of Rome (*For Sestius* 118).

Two other plays at Spinther's shows, Lucius Accius' *Eurysaces* and *Brutus*, were likewise liberally rendered metatheatrical, as key words and phrases that resonated with current tensions over Cicero's leadership were given special emphasis from within collective constructs of the legendary past (Manuwald 2011: 222–224). Claudius Aesopus, a major tragic performer of the time, took the lead in this and was credited by Cicero with pleading his cause, essentially as a public advocate (*For Sestius* 120–121). *Eurysaces* dealt with the age of legendary heroes, dramatizing the expulsion of Telamon, father of Ajax, from his home. The audience groaned and wept, as if on cue, at Aesopus' tearful reminders of an absent and beloved leader and father, at his once-great house, now fallen, now in ruins. At this point, with the line 'all this I saw in flames', the actor likely gestured toward the Palatine Hill, where until recently the house of Cicero had stood; its ceremonial destruction by Clodius' supporters had been intended to remove the owner from the collective memory of Rome, re-move his achievements from the honoured traditions of the past, and to disrupt the effective social networks that Cicero had painstakingly created within its halls (Roller 2010: 122–123). That effort had not succeeded, clearly, as the poignancy conveyed here by the absence of that house, its dramatic weight enhanced by the shared memory of the fall of other legendary houses, carried a great deal of emotional power for the audience in 57. Cicero says that even his opponents among the spectators were shedding tears (*For Sestius* 121).

Accius' *Brutus* was a *fabula praetexta* which, by definition, drew upon Rome's historic past for its content. In this case, the drama enacted legendary events leading to the foundation of the republic, focusing on the ouster of Servius Tullius, a 'just' king, by a usurping tyrant, aided by his wife, the treacherous daughter of the king. Again the original was adapted to point up the parallel to Marcus Tullius Cicero, a literal 'modern' Tullius, and his situation, looking to the resolve and righteousness of the contemporary Senate to make things right. Aesopus lingered emphatically over a line that specifically referenced Tullius as the foun-dation of citizens' *libertas*; the spectators cheered and made him repeat the line a 'thousand times', Aesopus providing fodder for pro-Cicero claques like a claqueur himself (*For Sestius* 123). This was another opportunity for explicit intervisuality, as actor and audience together performed a wrenching contrast between the visible Clodian Shrine to Libertas rising on the Palatine and the memory of both the missing *domus* and the missing Cicero, their ab-sence the cause of an alleged failure of Roman liberty. Elite houses themselves served to stage their owners' enactment of power (Q. Cicero, *Commentary on Electioneering* 34–35; Flower 1996: 217–220; Tatum 1999: 159–161; Roller 2010: 123–125). The vocalizations of performers and spectators at the theatrical games of Lentulus Spinther worked in concert to recreate the house of Cicero in public memory, playing it as an expression of the core values and allegiances of the Roman populace.

Politically expressive gladiatorial matches offered further heat in 57's warm season, as Q. Caecilius Metellus Scipio presented *munera* in honour of his long-deceased adopted father, Q. Caecilius Metellus Pius (Vanderbroeck 1987 no. 54). Metellus Scipio was curule aedile for the year, a post that normally carried responsibility for organizing the festival for

Magna Mater in April and the Ludi Magni in September. Adding several days of gladiatorial combats to this workload would maximize his share of the populace's spectacular gratitude while also fulfilling his filial duty.

The Forum was a prominent and favoured location for gladiatorial events in the republic; in the 40s (in time for his quadruple triumph), Julius Caesar would enhance the area as a performance venue by building substructures to support special effects. The Forum was *the* prestige location for politicized displays, amply supplied with a host of memory markers as well as a clear space optimal for this kind of spectacle, as we are told by Vitruvius (*On Architecture* 5.1) (Welch 2007: 38–65).

Gladiatorial combat was, of course, far less word-driven than theatrical performance, less available to the crafting of verbal referents to current political tensions. Cicero's interpretation of these games focuses on the actions around the arena, the movements of key spectators who, nevertheless, are key players in the event; responses to these movements constitute the judgement of the unified Roman people.

Cicero concentrates on Publius Sestius, tribune in 57 BCE and supporter of Cicero's recall, who was among the magistrates on show at the opening of the games. Sestius entered the performance space next to the Maenian columnar monument near the Comitium; this area would have been a prime seating location, possibly one reserved for Rome's political elites. Audience applause for Sestius immediately burst forth and resounded from the Capitoline, surrounding the event and engaging the whole of the city in expression of public support, greater and more unified than ever before in Roman history, from a crowd of spectators larger than any seen before, or so Cicero claims (*For Sestius* 124–125). (Cicero lingers on this, as one might expect, in a speech composed to defend Sestius against politically driven charges.) Cicero clarifies that this was support for Sestius as one of the *optimates*, the 'best men', the conservative supporters of senatorial dominance of Roman politics.

He contrasts Sestius' reception to that of Appius Claudius Pulcher, who, as praetor during the preceding year, had been a strong supporter and advocate of his brother Clodius' tribunate. Cicero claims that Appius Claudius was actually afraid of interaction with the 'True People' of Rome (those who support the conservative leaders, as Cicero sees it). Because of this fear, he has been avoiding the kind of entrance appropriate for someone of his rank and standing. Instead, Claudius slithered into the games from *sub tabulas*, from, apparently, the space beneath the bleachers erected as temporary seating for spectacle. His movement is thus unscripted against the monumental texts of the Forum, his passage from one meaningful backdrop to another does not tell the story of his leadership; indeed, Cicero compares him to the stage appearance of a ghost (*For Sestius* 126). The audience responded with hisses so loud they scared the gladiatorial horses.

This was not an isolated incident. Appius Claudius' seeming habitual evasion of the public eye was, Cicero sarcastically asserts, being spoken of by the people as 'the Appian Way'. The actual Appian Way, the most famous of Rome's strategic trunk roads, was a massive engineering project launched during the late fourth century censorship of Appius Claudius Caecus, hero of the Samnite Wars, who oversaw its completion stretching from Rome's city centre as far as the city of Capua. Here, the Appian Way is repurposed by the spectators, not as a pre-eminent memorial of past ancestral achievement for Appius Claudius (and for Clodius) but as a path of ignominy, of shame, taken by a leader who is avoiding the urban gaze, who is trying to hide his public self instead of doing what ruling elites are supposed to do: glory in the cheers of the populace.

Clodius himself, long experienced in the techniques of mass persuasion, had plans to marshal populist opinion at the major festivals, which came to fruition at the Games of Apollo in July of 57, held just prior to Cicero's restoration, shortly after the events sponsored by Lentulus Spinther (Vanderbroeck 1987 no. 55). L. Caecilius Rufus was the urban praetor at this time, responsible for organizing these major events in the religious calendar, which would have included dramatic performances that, like theatrical games in the second century, probably made use of space and features in the vicinity of the Temple of Apollo on the Campus Martius. Tensions in the city were running high because of ongoing issues with the regular grain supply. Asconius references how a lower-class (*infima*) multitude was driven to riot on this matter, storming the theatre and driving out those assembled for the show (*Commentaries on Five Speeches of Cicero* 48C). Asconius alludes to less spontaneity in this action than simple hunger, hinting that someone with strong connections to the urban poor may have done the necessary planning to drive the movement, gathering the warm bodies needed for effective action: someone, perhaps, like Clodius. The Ludi Apollinares, as one of the regularly scheduled games, may have been more of a regional draw than other events, with greater competition for seats and thus an audience more likely elite in its demographic. Asconius' emphasis on the sub-elite status of this group is notable here, certainly, but problems with the grain supply would affect many sectors of the population, albeit in different ways. One need not have been living on the thin edge of subsistence to find common ground for complaint. The spectators may then have been incited by the protestors and abandoned the theatre to join them in their demands for resolution of this felt need.

Later that same year, in September, Quintus Caecilius Metellus Scipio, as curule aedile, organized the Great Games that coincided with Cicero's return from exile to the city, a restoration that had been the object of much dispute. Rome was also still riled up over grain; there had been a sudden recent rise in prices that may have been the combined result of ongoing shortages and the influx of people into the city for the games and, potentially, for Cicero's homecoming (Cicero, *On His House* 11; *Letters to Atticus* 4.1; Dio Cassius 39.9; Tatum 1999; Vanderbroeck 1987 no. 60). Clodius again attempted to leverage the popular tension to his own advantage, drawing upon the skills of the claque and the cohesion engineered by spectacular timing, or so alleges Cicero.

In this episode, the people as a whole rushed first to the temporary theatre then in use, then, their numbers fortified, moved en masse to the Capitoline, where a meeting of the Senate had been called in the Temple of Concord. Bursting in on their session, the crowd demanded a solution to the crisis; Cicero claims that Clodius had incited them to blame Cicero for the problem (*Letters to Atticus* 4.1). Dio focuses on the danger to civic order, describing the crowd's threats to slaughter the senators with their own hands, to burn them to ashes and the temples around them. There are references to the advanced preparation involved, which points to the use of orchestrated chants, led by Clodius' regular operatives, along with the co-opting of spectators from the dramatic performance.

Indeed, the emphasis on planned opportunism and on 'casting' of protestors demonstrates the fluid boundaries between the politicized theatre and the theatrics of politics. Here, however, the venerated monuments of Rome's public spaces, routinely deployed by spectacle sponsors to enhance their messaging, are themselves under threat of destruction, as the hostile crowd tries to seize control of the discourse.

Cicero spins another situation that occurred at the Games of Magna Mater in April of 56 CE, when traditions were cast asunder and contested spectacle space was stained with

Roman blood. As one of the aediles for the year, Clodius was responsible for organizing this annual celebration of the Phrygian Great Mother, a cult which, since its importation to Rome in the last phase of the Hannibalic War, had preserved carefully warded elements of its dangerously ecstatic eastern origins, drawing distinctions between ritual appropriate to Roman customs and the ceremonies kept in the hands of the goddess's *galli*, the foreign-born eunuch officiants (Livy 29.14.6–12; Dionysius of Halicarnassus 2.19.4–5). Cicero's description of the events of 56, crafted a few weeks after the games, asserts that Clodius' Megalesia was an affront to Roman and divine order; he focuses particularly on the actions of organized slaves and the long-term claims to moral authority by two patrician clans.

Cicero's speech does not lay out a clear order of events, but aims to denounce the supposed sacrilege committed by Clodius over several years, actions that had a devastating personal impact on Cicero. One possible reconstruction might be that, following the ritual procession and the ceremonial enthronement of the Great Mother's image, the theatrical events were already under way in the usual venue on the Palatine. Suddenly the stage was rushed from every gate and archway by a mass of 'slaves', 'recruited' from every neighbourhood and goaded on by the aedile in charge, Clodius, who gave the signal for action. The attendees that were the targets of this attack, the senatorials, equestrians, and the 'good' men, the *boni* so favoured by Cicero, were particularly endangered by the characteristics of the space, which was constricted and tightly packed, with narrow seats, that confined them in the face of this unexpected intrusion (*On the Response of the Soothsayers* 22). (After a fire in 111, renovations in the sanctuary area raised the level of the plaza surrounding the temple, covering over several risers of steps and thus decreasing the space available for performance seating (Hanson 1959: 13–16; Goldberg 1998: 3, 7–9; Cicero, *On the Response of the Soothsayers* 22–26).) Cicero alludes to the threat represented by the action, that has replaced joy with terror, religious rites with funeral rites; the city was on the verge of murder, of massacre (23–24).

On the surface, this seems like another instance of civic disruption: Clodius' entourage and followers were practised in the appropriation of public space and were motivated by class-based inequity to action. They came from the shops and *collegia* of the neighbourhoods, whose modest *compitalia* festivals had been recently restored to them by Clodius as tribune, who had likewise tightened their communication networks as part of the grain distribution system put in place by Clodius (Laurence 1991; Laurence 1994: 68–72; Tatum 1999). In this case, they have swiftly taken control of the performance space, able to control the gaze of the spectators and demand assent from the immobilized elites, who have been made powerless by the decisive action of the Clodiani.

The tables were turned, however, by Gnaeus Cornelius Lentulus Marcellinus, consul for the year, who stood up to challenge Clodius' actions. Cicero credits him with redirecting the attention of those present, using his voice, his face, his strength of command to seize control of the discourse. Cicero cites the power of Lentulus' name, specifically, and repeatedly references the consul's great-grandfather and great-great-grandfather, as Rome's saviour in an earlier crisis and as the original steward of the goddess's migration to the city. Here Cicero may be echoing the argument used by Lentulus during the situation, asserting authority based on his descent from Cornelii Scipiones. Publius Cornelius Scipio Nasica had been chosen the 'best man' in the city, to be accorded the honour of physically transporting her sacred stone into Rome (Livy 29.14; Gruen 1992: 46–47). Recall that in the 170s, as consul, Scipio Nasica argued vehemently against the construction of a permanent theatre on moral grounds. The first *ludi scaenici* for the Great Mother were held in 194 BCE. As we have seen, that was the year that Scipio Africanus, as consul, demanded (unsuccessfully) that the Senate be granted special seats at such events; here, Cicero claims that the demand was made specifically *for* the first Megalesia (24). Lentulus' references to ancestral claims of virtue, specifically related to this cult and to spectacle, may have been chosen to counter claims by Clodius along similar lines, featuring the famed leadership of the Claudii (Littlewood 1981: 383–385). Cicero had used the family legacy against Clodius in the 'Appian Way' riposte; in this case, he archly demands whether Clodius actually wants to call attention to his birth (26), when his ancestors sustained the 'proper' hierarchical ranking of elites and citizens over slaves. As asserted by Cicero (and possibly by Lentulus as well) Clodius' present actions have betrayed his class, his city, his gods; these efforts are 'deformed', 'polluted', and 'deranged' (25) (Flower 1995: 170–176; Beacham 1999: 59–61).

An important point to be made, concerning these allegedly distorted spectacles, is the emphasis on spatial movement even in Cicero's very hostile descriptions, how the spectators take over spectacle space, how they commandeer and control a venue that has been a major site for the creation of elite political reputations for generations, and how their ability to do so clearly problematizes that space for the class in which we find its major backers, and that would include populist elites like Clodius, and Caesar, and Pompey. It is important as well that the temporary nature of the venue, be it ever so lavish, enables that kind of action.

A permanent structure, however, was soon to come: 55 BCE saw the inauguration of the Temple of Venus Victrix, a relatively modest temple set above an enormous theatre structure, serving as its podium. Cicero (*Letters to Atticus* 2.21) hints at the idea that Pompey's decision to act on his long-delayed plan to build a monumental theatre was based on the decline in his popularity in the 50s; to rebuild that support, Pompey constructed a setting in which his achievement was made concrete, quite literally so (Beacham 1999: 52–53). To carry out this plan, he had to negotiate Rome's established resistance to permanent spectacle venues. An important factor in this was that the structure would be a multi-purpose building, not destined solely for performances, but combining the colonnaded portico found in other contemporary complexes (such as Clodius' Shrine of Liberty) with a temple to Venus Victrix, Pompey's patron deity. This complex could now be claimed as an elaborate variant on the normative performance space opening off the temple's porch and podium. To some extent, Pompey's own authority also helped overcome residual qualms.

The project offered Pompey the opportunity to leave a permanent mark on the cityscape and to attach to himself some measure of acclaim for all future performances held in the structure. Importantly, this structure could create its own cityscape; this was an immersive complex that severely limited visual access to the Memory Palace of the Roman urban environment. Because of its self-contained quality, Pompey's Theatre evaded the ability of Rome's public monuments to dominate, constantly and silently, specific presentations of the Roman body politic and to provide a visual counter-argument to persuasive performances offered by Rome's magnates. Future sponsors of spectacle literally sat in Pompey's shadow, their prestige always to be compared to his. Constant visual reminders of Pompey surrounded spectators, from his patron deity overlooking the audience and stage to the sculpted representations of the nations conquered by him. Spectators sat inside a monument to Pompey (Pliny, *Natural History* 36.41; Klar 2006; Mitens 1993: 98–103; Bruno 1999: 265–266).

The layout of the complex also had some powerful implications. The 'theatre' proper— i.e. the stage building and seating/Temple—occupies only the western portion of the facility, backed against colonnades surrounding a rectangular garden area, a place that sheltered theatregoers during inclement weather as well as offering space for exhibitions and gatherings of various kinds (Kuttner 1999). A larger room, the 'Curia Pompeia', dominated the east wing of the peristyle and was apparently intended for meetings of the Senate during the reconstruction of its Forum headquarters in the 50s; an enormous statue of Pompey himself was positioned directly opposite the central 'king's' entrance on the stage. Thus every theatrical king re-enacted the authority of Pompey, just as Pompey's implicitly regal image loomed over senatorial gatherings. Pompey's reputation was deeply embedded in the structure; in his description of Tiberius' restoration, Tacitus carefully points out that 'Pompey's name was to be retained' as the building's identification (Tacitus, *Annals* 3.72; Sear 1993: 687; Coarelli 1997b: 118–122; Gagliardo and Packer 2006).

The dedicatory games in September of 55 BCE were much anticipated, Pompey's friends hailing these as unprecedented in their magnificence, scale, expenditure; nothing in Rome's past or future could compare (Cicero, *Against Piso* 65.). In addition to the theatrical performances for which, arguably, the 'temple' had been built, there were athletic competitions, *venationes*, *munera*, and music, with performance venues reaching beyond the new complex. The events did, however, reiterate the theme of the structure; Pompey presents the world to Rome: world conquest, exotic objects from far-flung reaches, exotic animals as dynamic embodiments of the stretch of empire, and the sheer scale of the theatre itself. To enter Pompey's Theatre was to enter a world, *the* world, created by Pompey, quite literally, as the complex isolated the visitor from the sight-lines to the rest of the city, recreating a cosmos dominated by Pompey's achievement, Pompey's personality, Pompey's vision (Kuttner 1999; Klar 2006; Beacham 1999: 61–71).

Even in Pompey's world, however, even during the Pompey-centric extravaganza of the dedication events, the message was clearly disrupted by other voices, as is apparent in the elephant incident. Cicero's letter to M. Marius, written shortly after the event, notes the crowd's 'astonishment' at the lavish *venationes*, but asserts they were not actually pleased, because of the way the hunt had played out (Cicero, *Letters to Friends* 7.1). We have already seen the way in which spectator response can shape how performances are received and even impact the programme's order. Here, spectators connected emotionally to the hopeless, pain-filled vocalizations and gestures of the last surviving pachyderm performers, perceiving them as suffering an undeserved fate, betrayed by their trust in the Roman handlers (Dio Cassius 39.38). A sizable portion of the audience apparently responded more profoundly to the presentation of the elephants as noble, sympathetic victims of Pompey's ambition; Pliny links their angry tears and curses to Pompey's ultimate political failure (Pliny, *Natural History* 8.20–21; Potter 1993: 53; Shelton 1999).

One could say that Pompey's own political deterioration, his leadership during the Civil War, bore some resemblance to the heroic wounded elephant remembered from these games, on its knees, snatching desperately at the weapons of the Gaetulians. But spectacle changed with the creation of the permanent venues and with the imperial monarchy. The space and the movement would be much more susceptible to control, and the emperors much more attuned to maintaining a productive dialogue with the crowds.

This volume, in its Roman sections, focuses mainly on the more familiar 'spectacles', the physical contests of chariot-racing and gladiatorial matches. The theatrical events, the *ludi scaenici*, however, were embedded in the same political and social framework and presented similar advantages and challenges for their sponsors and participants. As phenomena that were fundamentally word-driven, they have left a particular sort of textual imprint. Their relationship to dramatic traditions elsewhere in the ancient Mediterranean is complicated and, at this remove, impossible to untangle. But as spectacle, they served a vital function in the negotiation of power in Rome, a dynamic process in which performers, sponsors, and attendees of varying social and political standing laid claim to some control over the ultimate form of the event, the meaning it carried for contemporaries and for posterity. The tools available to these participants can, with some care, be extracted from the remaining evidence. The performance space was a place of contested access, with seat availability reliant on connections. In particularly volatile moments, access may have required individual audience members to participate in mass expressions of praise or contempt, rehearsed in advance. Ambitious elites were on display; visibility that conveyed authority, through movement and by placement, was key to maintaining influence and prestige. Leaders and their entourages could not, however, compel the crowd to respond with the desired positive acclaim. Creating memorable venues, redolent of sponsors' wealth and capacity to command vast resources, or that offered dizzying new sensory experiences, could work to overawe attendees and leave a lasting legacy; the tremendous cost carried a serious risk, one that, ultimately, Rome's imperial monarchs would monopolize.

REFERENCES

Aldrete, G. S. 1999. *Gestures and Acclamations in Ancient Rome.* Baltimore.

Axer, J. 1989. 'Tribunal-State-Arena: Modelling of the Communication Situation in M. Tullius Cicero's Judicial Speeches.' *Rhetorica* 7.4: 299–311.

Beacham, R. C. 1991. *The Roman Theatre and its Audience.* Exeter.

Beacham, R. C. 1999. *Spectacle Entertainments of Early Imperial Rome.* New Haven.

Bell, A. J. E. 1997. 'Cicero and the Spectacle of Power.' *JRS* 87: 1–22.

Bruno, P. 1999. 'Le théâtre de Marcellus et la sphere.' *MEFRA* 111.1: 257–272.

Cameron, A. 1974. *Bread and Circuses: The Roman Emperor and His People.* Oxford.

Coarelli, F. 1997a. *Il Campo Marzio: dalle origini alla fine della repubblica.* Rome.

Coarelli, F. 1997b. 'Le théâtre de Pompée.' *DHA* 23.2:105–124.

Coarelli, F. 2014. *Rome and Environs: An Archaeological Guide.* J. J. Clauss and D. P. Harmon, trans. Berkeley.

Dearden, C. 2012. 'Whose Line is it Anyway? West Greek Comedy in its Context.' In *Theater Outside Athens: Drama in Greek Sicily and South Italy.* 272–88. K. Bosher, ed. Cambridge.

Edmondson, J. C. 1996. 'Dynamic Arenas: Gladiatorial Presentations in the City of Rome and the Construction of Roman Society during the Early Empire.' In *Roman Theater and Society.* 69–112. W. J. Slater, ed. Ann Arbor.

Edmondson, J. C. 1999. 'The Cultural Politics of Public Spectacle in Rome and the Greek East, 167–166 BCE.' In *The Art of Ancient Spectacle.* 77–96. B. Bergmann and C. Kondoleon, eds. Washington, DC.

Favro, D. 1999. 'The City is a Living Thing: The Performative Role of an Urban Site in Ancient Rome, the Vallis Murcia.' In *The Art of Ancient Spectacle.* 205–220. B. Bergmann and C. Kondoleon, eds. Washington, DC.

Favro, D. and C. Johanson. 2010. 'Death in Motion: Funeral Processions in the Roman Forum.' *JSAH* 69.1: 12–37.

Flower, H. I. 1995. '*Fabulae Praetextae* in Context: When Were Plays on Contemporary Subjects Performed in Republican Rome?' *CQ* 45.1: 170–190.

Flower, H. I. 1996. *Ancestor Masks and Aristocratic Power in Roman Culture*. Oxford.

Flower, H. I. 2003. 'Memories of Marcellus.' In *Formen Römischer Geschichtsschreibung von den Anfängen bis Livius: Gattungen, Autoren, Kontexte*. 39–52. U. Eigler, ed. Darmstadt.

Gagliardo, M. C. and J. E. Packer. 2006. 'A New Look at Pompey's Theater: History, Documentation, and Recent Excavation.' *AJA* 110: 93–122.

Goldberg, S. W. 1998. 'Plautus on the Palatine.' *JRS* 88: 1–20.

Gowing, A. 2005. *Empire and Memory: The Representation of the Roman Republic in Imperial Culture*. Cambridge.

Gruen, E. S. 1990. *Studies in Greek Culture and Roman Policy*. Berkeley.

Gruen, E. S. 1992. *Culture and National Identity in Republican Rome*. Ithaca, NY.

Hanson, J. A. 1959. *Roman Theater-Temples*. Princeton.

Holliday, P. J. 1997. 'Roman Triumphal Painting: Its Function, Development, and Reception.' *ABull* 79.1: 130–147.

Holliday, P. J. 2002. *Origins of Roman Historical Commemoration in the Visual Arts*. Cambridge.

Hölscher, T. 2006. 'The Transformation of Victory into Power: From Event to Structure.' In *Representations of War in Ancient Rome*. 27–48. S. Dillon and K. Welch, eds. New York.

Jacobs, P. W. and D. A. Conlin. 2014. *Campus Martius: The Field of Mars in the Life of Ancient Rome*. Cambridge.

Klar, L. S. 2006. 'The Origins of the Roman *Scaenae Frons* and the Architecture of Triumphal Games in the Second Century B.C.' In *Representations of War in Ancient Rome*. 162–183. S. Dillon and K. E. Welch, eds. Cambridge.

Kuttner, A. 1999. 'Culture and History at Pompey's Museum.' *TAPA* 129: 343–373.

Latham, J. A. 2016. *Performance, Memory, and Processions in Ancient Rome*. Cambridge.

Laurence, R. 1991. 'The Urban Vicus: The Spatial Organization of Power in the Roman City.' In *Papers of the Fourth Conference of Italian Archaeology*. 145–50. E. Herring, R. Whitehouse, and J. Wilkins, eds. London.

Laurence, R. 1994. 'Rumour and Communication in Roman Politics.' *G&R* 41.1: 62–74.

Leach, E. 2000. 'The *Spectacula* of Cicero's *Pro Sestio*.' In *Rome and her Monuments: Essays on the City and Literature of Rome in Honor of Katherine A. Geffcken*. 369–397. S. K. Dickison and J. P. Hallett, eds. Wauconda, IL.

Littlewood, R. J. 1981. 'Poetic Artistry and Dynastic Politics: Ovid at the *Ludi Megalenses* (*Fasti* 4. 179–372).' *CQ* 31.2: 381–395.

Marconi, C. 2012. 'Between Performance and Identity: The Social Context of Stone Theaters in Late Classical and Hellenistic Sicily.' In *Theater Outside Athens: Drama in Greek Sicily and South Italy*. 175–207. K. Bosher, ed. Cambridge.

Manuwald, G., 2011. *Roman Republican Theatre*. Cambridge.

Marshall, C. W. 2006. *The Stagecraft and Performance of Roman Comedy*. Cambridge.

Mitens, K. 1993. 'Theatre Architecture in Central Italy.' In *Aspects of Hellenism in Italy: Towards a Cultural Unity?* 91–106. P. G. Bilde, I. Nielsen, and M. Nielsen, eds. Copenhagen.

Moore, T. J. 1994–1995. 'Seats and Social Status in the Plautine Theatre.' *CJ* 90.2: 113–123.

Morstein-Marx, R. 2004. *Mass Oratory and Political Power in the Late Roman Republic*. Cambridge.

North, J. A. 1992. 'Deconstructing Stone Theaters.' In *Apodosis: Essays Presented to Dr. W. W. Cruickshank to Mark His Eightieth Birthday*. 75–83. London.

Parker, H. 1999. 'The Observed of All Observers: Spectacle, Applause, and Cultural Poetics in the Roman Theater Audience.' In *The Art of Ancient Spectacle*. 163–179. B. Bergmann and C. Kondoleon, eds. New Haven.

Pittenger, M. R. P. 2008. *Contested Triumphs: Politics, Pageantry, and Performance in Livy's Republican Rome*. Berkeley.

Platner, S. B. and T. Ashby. 1929. *A Topographical Dictionary of Ancient Rome*. London.

Popkin, M. 2016. *Architecture of the Roman Triumph: Monuments, Memory, and Identity*. Cambridge.

Potter, D. 1993. 'Martyrdom as Spectacle.' In *Theater and Society in the Classical World*. 53–88. R. Scodel, ed. Ann Arbor.

Potter, D. 1996. 'Performance, Power, and Justice in the High Empire.' In *Roman Theater and Society*. 129–160. W. J. Slater, ed. Ann Arbor.

Rawson, E. 1985. 'Theatrical Life in Republican Rome and Italy.' *PBSR* 53: 97–113.

Richlin, A. 2014. 'Talking to Slaves in the Plautine Audience.' *CA* 33.1: 174–226.

Roller, M. B. 2010. 'Demolished Houses, Monumentality and Memory in Roman Culture.' *CA* 29.1: 117–180.

Sandbach, F. H. 1982. 'How Terence's *Hecyra* Failed.' *CQ* 32.1: 134–135.

Sear, F. B. 1993. 'The *Scaenae Frons* of the Theater of Pompey.' *AJA* 97.4: 687–701.

Shelton, J. 1999. 'Elephants, Pompey, and the Reports of Popular Displeasure in 55 BC.' In *Veritatis Amicitiaeque Causa: Essays in Honor of Anna Lydia Motto and John R. Clark*. 231–271. S. N. Byrne and E. P. Cueva, eds. Mundelein, IL.

Sumi, G. S. 2009. 'Monuments and Memory: The *Aedes Castoris* in the Formation of Augustan Ideology.' *CQ* 59: 167–186.

Tatum, W. J. 1990. 'Another Look at the Spectators at the Roman Games.' *AHB* 4: 104–107.

Tatum, W. J. 1999. *The Patrician Tribune: Publius Clodius Pulcher*. Chapel Hill, NC.

Taylor, L. R. 1937. 'The Opportunities for Dramatic Performances in the Time of Plautus and Terence.' *TAPA* 68: 284–304.

Vanderbroeck, P. J. J. 1987. *Popular Leadership and Collective Behavior in the Late Roman Republic*. Amsterdam.

Welch, K. E. 2007. *The Roman Amphitheatre from Its Origins to the Colosseum*. Cambridge.

CHAPTER 12

··

THEATRE OF CRUELTY
Games of the Flavian Emperors

··

RICHARD BEACHAM

'The crowd of people set off running, not to fly and disperse, but to reach the colonnades and elevated places of the Forum, as if to get places to view a spectacle.' (Plutarch, *Life of Galba* 26.4 on the murder of Galba, 15 January 69 CE).

'The whole populace of Rome ... with discordant shouts called for the death of Otho as if they were demanding some show in the circus or theatre' (Tacitus, *Histories* 1.32.1).

'The populace was present as spectator [at the battle in December of 69], and, as if at the theatrical contests, favoured in turn one side and another with shouts and clapping.' (Tacitus, *Histories* 3.83.1)

THE 'long year' of 69 CE witnessed the deaths of three emperors as well as the recognition by the Senate of a fourth, Vespasian, who had already been acclaimed emperor in July by the eastern legions. By the end of the year Rome suffered 'a disaster more horrible and deplorable than any since the founding of the City': on 19 December, the Capitol was stormed by the praetorian forces of Vitellius, and the great Temple of Juppiter Optimus Maximus burned to the ground, destroyed 'by the mad folly of two rival Emperors' (Tacitus, *Histories* 3.72.1).

This fearful act was followed by an orgy of pillaging and murder, in which (if Dio may be believed) as many as fifty thousand died (Dio Cassius 64.19.3). Underscoring the bizarre horror of the scene, the rape of the City took place during the *Saturnalia*, with drunken and riotous crowds viewing the carnage as an enhancement of the holiday (Tacitus, *Histories* 3.83). Tacitus' powerful representation of the terrified and chaotic City, as it experienced the bloody birth of a new dynasty displacing the Julio-Claudians, emphasizes the grotesquely theatrical quality of the situation.

On one level this phantasmagoria may be plausibly explained as a particularly stark and brutal manifestation of the now well-established fact that actual political life had been transmogrified into a form of 'spectator sport', while the games themselves, by virtue of the licence traditionally allowed that venue, had evolved into one of the few Roman institutions through which popular political concerns and grievances could still be expressed and addressed. Indeed, during the chaotic year of 69 CE, the populace had used the public shows to demand executions, especially of imperial favourites and informers (Tacitus, *Histories* 1.72–3; Suetonius, *Life of Galba* 15.2; Plutarch, *Life of Galba* 17.5). Vitellius during his brief reign had followed established imperial practice; his years as a courtier had demonstrated his capacity to share Caligula's enthusiasm for chariot-racing as well as his facility in egging on Nero's spectacle performance (Suetonius, *Life of Vitellius* 3–4, 11.2). Indeed, Vitellius intensified the centrality of spectacle for his regime: Suetonius claims that he 'regulated the greater part of his rule entirely according to the advice and whims of the commonest actors and charioteers' (*Life of Vitellius* 12.1). Tacitus adds that 'by showing himself as a spectator in the theatre, and as a partisan in the circus, he courted every breath of applause from the lowest rabble, which would have made him popular, had his motives been better'; he 'filled the Circus with gorgeous shows of gladiators and wild beasts'; and even 'gratified the rabble ... by putting up altars in the Campus Martius and holding a funeral service in honour of Nero' (*Histories* 2.91.8–9; 2.94.16; 2.95.3–5; Suetonius, *Life of Vitellius* 11.2; Dio Cassius 65.7).

Now, two days after the burning of the Capitol, the emperor provided the ultimate spectacle of his own destruction, dragged through jeering crowds into the Forum (where traditionally gladiatorial contests had been held) to watch his statues being thrown down, and stare at the site where a year earlier his rival Galba had been murdered. There he was publicly butchered (Dio Cassius 64.20–21).

'ROMA RESURGENS'

Vespasian did not return to Rome from Alexandria until October of 70 CE, to be greeted with acclamations as benefactor, saviour, and the only worthy emperor of Rome (Josephus, *Jewish War* 7.71). This was underscored most graphically and spectacularly by the 'Judean' Triumph celebrated with Titus early in June of 71 CE. Indeed, to give the spectators a better view, after assembling as usual near the Temple of Bellona on the Campus Martius, the triumph apparently diverged from the traditional route to take an extended detour through Rome's theatres in the vicinity, which must have greatly increased its length while providing viewers a degree of comfort as they contemplated the pageantry of power.

Not only were onlookers dazzled by the sight of their victorious rulers and the vast array of plunder, they also viewed veritable 'moving pictures', *tableaux vivants* on huge pageant wagons, depicting the Judean campaign's most dramatic events, not only the battlefields but also the taking of cities, soldiers in urban streets, sacking houses and burning temples (Josephus, *Jewish War* 7.122–157). This particular innovation, using theatrical space and mobile imperial displays to transform a potentate's grand procession, hearkens back to techniques deployed by Ptolemy Philadelphus in creating his public persona (Athenaeus 197C, 199A; Coleman 1996b: 51) In the Roman context, however, other resonances may have prevailed. For many its display of slaughter and destruction must have seemed almost uncomfortably close to the horrific scenes eighteen months earlier in Rome itself, in the very streets and public spaces where they now assembled to be entertained.

Vespasian ruled for ten years, during which he restored the State finances, provided efficient and stable government, secured the succession of his son, and enjoyed the privilege (rare for emperors) of dying a natural death in June 79 CE, aged 69. Moreover, he provided one extraordinary visible expression, if not of his own grandeur, then of the sentiment inscribed on his coins: 'Roma resurgens'. In 72 he authorized work to begin on the Colosseum.

Nero had confiscated private land for the building of the Domus Aurea, his hated house; Vespasian returned it to the people for their favourite pastime. The setting also acknowledged the more recent political reality of the emperor's responsibility for the provision of gladiatorial games at Rome where, moreover, 'his personal presence at *munera* was expected' (Wiedemann 1992: 171). Indeed, control of the *munera* was eventually an imperial monopoly, secured by Domitian, who forbade games unless sponsored by magistrates on his behalf.

Beyond glorifying the emperors, the activities taking place within the arena demonstrated Roman virtues of fortitude and fighting skill. Executions staged there both symbolized and demonstrated the enforcement of law and the protection and reaffirmation of social values in the face of dangerous criminality. Even the mode of execution reflected and affirmed the social order: freeborn condemned had the right to be killed by the sword (*ad gladium*), while those diminished in social prestige endured fates on a continuum of perceived degradation, such as being burnt alive, crucified, or being thrown to the beasts (*ad bestias*) (see Edmondson 1996: 96–97 and Garnsey 1970: 105–131). Arena events served not just as symbols of Roman majesty and justice but as the formal venues where the civilized world confronted and demonstrated its mastery of nature.

Gladiatorial games and animal hunts (*venationes*) were closely linked as entertainments, taking place in the same venues and, indeed, normally on the same day. 'The slaughter of exotic and fierce animals in the Emperor's presence, or exceptionally by the Emperor himself or by his palace guard, was a spectacular dramatization of the Emperor's formidable power: immediate, bloody and symbolic' (Hopkins 1983: 12). Following Augustus' example, emperors relentlessly continued both to search for novelty and to showcase visible evidence of the expansion and extent of their power over the far-flung empire and its inhabitants, both human and animal.

Emperors saw in the *venationes* an opportunity both to entertain and gratify their people and to communicate a powerful ideological and political message. Martial's contemporary account *Liber de Spectaculis* commemorates the hundred days of games staged by Titus to mark the dedication of the Colosseum, and conveys some impression of how these were construed as imperial propaganda. Permeating Martial's work is the *leitmotif* of the emperor as one who reifies the miraculous and mythical before the bedazzled eyes of the grateful subjects/spectators drawn to his City from all the races and realms of the earth (*On the Spectacles* 3).

Titus is thus a constant focus and agent of the spectacle, a miracle-making Master of Ceremonies who ordained, controlled, and was in turn honoured by the shows. A telling dichotomy, however, was set up between the emperor's majestic role and the heroic *bestiarius*, Carpophorus, the darling of the crowd. Carpophorus' feats included the slaying of a giant lion, a leopard, an arctic bear, a buffalo (probably an aurochs), a bison, and a boar. Stressing the mythic resonance, Martial claims that had such a hero lived in olden times, various monsters of mythology would have posed no threat, since Carpophorus, whose feats outnumbered those of Hercules and who could slay twenty beasts in a single performance, would have made short work of them (*On the Spectacles* 27). Titus too displayed qualities unmatched by myth. 'Let not an ancient age marvel at itself, Caesar, for whatever Fame has recited, the arena brings forth for you!' (*On the Spectacles* 5).

MYTH MADE MURDEROUS: THE STAGING OF EXECUTIONS

Titus' entertainments included a further element that provided both an improving diversion for the crowd and flattery for the emperor: the execution of criminals staged as events from mythology (Coleman 1990). At a fundamental level, this overturned the very notion of representation: here, the ostensibly theatrical was replaced by the palpably real, a paradox that seems to have fascinated the spectators. Their enjoyment, however, depended upon both the physical barrier erected between the arena and the spectacle seating, which protected them from its dangers, as well as an equally essential aesthetic barrier to shield them psychologically. The solidarity and reinforcement of being anonymously part of a vast approving crowd (and one moreover deliberately constituted as a microcosm of legitimate society) undoubtedly contributed to the effect, as too did the assurance and satisfaction that justice and retribution were publicly being delivered before the people by their responsible rulers (Coleman 1998). At the same time, 'any manifestation of popular justice in a political context could be manipulated in such a way as to allow the Emperor to pretend that it was only the execution of the will of the people' (Nippel 1995: 45–46).

Thus on the one hand any impulse towards compassion was curbed by the manner in which the arena as an institution transformed 'murder and mayhem' into 'justice', while on the other as entertainment it could still exercise both a powerful aesthetic and, according to numerous ancient assessments, even an erotic appeal. With the emperor and his people separated ideologically, socially, and physically from those 'others' who had transgressed the laws of the collective and must be expelled from it, the arena became for those present a highly charged and symbolic space in which civilization most graphically expressed and renewed itself.

The congregation arranged inside the oval of the amphitheatre exercised its power to identify, humiliate, and destroy those whose behaviour had placed them outside civilized society. The events there were framed by ritual—preceded by a formal procession and various prayers and ceremonies—and suffused by elements of traditional myth and magic. In the analogous symbolic space of the theatre, the exposition and celebration of national identity and culture had for centuries been accomplished through the medium of mythology and suggestive ritual; why should the arena not draw upon similar material, and the sentiment and emotion engendered by it, in enacting its spectacles of State?

WATER EVENTS

The accounts of Titus' games emphasize a further feature complementing the gladiatorial and animal combats, and the imaginatively staged executions. Both in the Colosseum itself and on the western side of the Tiber in the pool or *stagnum* created there by Augustus in 2 BCE, elaborate aquatic displays took place with particular prominence given to the enactment of naval engagements; the series of events ran the gamut from solo performances by individual swimmers, through various animal shows presented under unusual aquatic conditions, to a *naumachia* employing thousands of combatants.

This nautical battle provided the climax to Titus' great cycle of spectacles. In the actual historic battle evoked, the Athenians were defeated by Syracuse; at Titus' pageant, however, they were victorious. Apart from contributing to the generally topsy-turvy treatment of reality which characterized the spectacles as a whole, this confounding of history may have had some more profound purpose. Having comprehensively recreated and refashioned myth, why should the miracle-working emperor not take history too and 'remould it nearer to the heart's desire' by bestowing a victory that might emphasize for his Roman audience a flattering 'parallel between their own role and that of fifth-century Athens' (Coleman 1993: 72)?

Such an approach would surpass mere propaganda, since it in effect lifted an event from history, changed its factual basis, and then rendered it concrete and immediate as something occurring in the very presence of the spectators; just as in the other entertainments, myth had become real, and nothing feigned about the representation of death. Moreover, Titus had the satisfaction of having surpassed his predecessors; in the age-old Roman tradition of extravagant, conspicuous display and grandeur of gesture, he could claim to have 'lived up to' the Colosseum.

He seems to have been motivated by desire for personal aggrandizement and fame, and to give pleasure to his subjects, to whom 'he was second to none of his predecessors in munificence' (Suetonius, *Life of Titus* 7.2). By all accounts, Titus was a 'good' emperor during his brief reign. This was something of a surprise: when he became emperor in June of 79 CE, aged thirty-nine, 'people not only feared but openly declared that he would be a second Nero' (*Life of Titus* 8.1). Instead he was tolerant and kindly, with an aptitude for the arts and literature; in particular, he was concerned to indulge the 'whole body of the people' at games and entertainments, encouraging the customary presentation there of petitions, 'refusing nothing which anyone sought, and indeed even urging them to ask for favours'. He styled himself as a 'fan' who avidly shared popular enthusiasms, joking and bantering with the crowd. At gladiatorial combats, he good-naturedly displayed his partisanship for a particular category of fighters (the 'Thracians') 'by words and gestures, while always, however, preserving his dignity and behaving fairly' (Suetonius, *Life of Titus* 8.2).

In August of 79, Vesuvius had erupted, burying the towns of Pompeii and Herculaneum (Dio Cassius 66.21–23). Then, while Titus was absent in Campania 'attending to the catastrophe', a second disaster struck Rome itself. Fire raged for three days, consuming a great many of its most prominent buildings, including such public venues as the *Saepta Iulia*, the Baths of Agrippa, the Theatre of Balbus, and the stage building of the Theatre of Pompey (Dio Cassius 66.24). This was followed by 'a plague the like of which had hardly ever been known before' (Suetonius, *Life of Titus* 8.3). Titus, in dealing with these calamities, 'showed not merely the concern of an Emperor, but a father's surpassing love'; indeed, 'there was no aid, human or divine, which he did not employ'. This context, both of Titus' extraordinary concern for the people of Rome and of the traumatic events recently experienced, provided the backdrop for the extravagant diversions the emperor placed before his people the following summer with the three-month festival of entertainments to inaugurate the Colosseum. At the games' final conclusion, Titus broke down in tears and wept openly before the public

(Suetonius *Life of Titus* 10.1; Dio Cassius 66.26.1). In September of 81 he died, was immediately deified, and succeeded by his younger brother Domitian who took power just short of his thirtieth birthday.

PRINCES OF PERPETUAL PAGEANTRY

Titus was revered as the 'delight and darling of the human race' (Suetonius, *Life of Titus* 1.1). Domitian was far less well regarded; indeed, widely condemned as one of the worst of emperors, he would suffer *damnatio memoriae* following his assassination in September 96 CE after a reign of exactly fifteen years. He was quick to demand the pomp appropriate to such power. 'He was elected consul for ten years in succession and censor for life' (Dio Cassius 67.4.3); the formal powers of the latter office, unprecedented for an emperor to hold in perpetuity, gave him virtually total control of the Senate and its membership, as well as supervision of public conduct and morals.

Despite these and other constitutional changes, and the frank espousal of autocracy, Domitian did not make significant innovations in either the style or genre of the games and shows. He did not need to, since the existing repertoire as it had evolved under his predecessors ultimately provided everything a divine and autocratic monarch might require suitably to celebrate and signify his power and position and lend emphasis and substance to his kingly and divine aspirations. A brief review of his practice illustrates the 'state of the art' pageantry had achieved during the first century of the Principate, the legacy extensively drawn upon by subsequent emperors to the end of antiquity.

'He constantly gave grand and expensive shows' (Suetonius, *Life of Domitian* 4.1), but for the most part these were in effect 're-runs' of previous extravaganzas. Thus, after completing the Colosseum, his only innovations were to reintroduce traditional boxing into the arena and present contests between dwarves and women (Dio Cassius 67.8.4; Martial 8.80.1–4). He was avidly partisan, supporting the lightly protected, sword-bearing *myrmillones* (whose fans were called the *scutarii* for the shields of their champions), against the heavily armed, scimitar-wielding Thracians, favoured by the *parmularii* (Ville 1981: 443–445; Auguet 1972: 46–50; 78–80). A few years later, when Trajan was emperor and the danger past, Pliny recalled how under Domitian 'a spectator found himself turned spectacle, dragged off by the hook to satisfy grim pleasures' by a 'madman ... who felt himself slighted and scorned if we failed to pay homage to his gladiators ... seeing insults to his own spirit and divinity' (Pliny, *Panegyric* 33.3–4).

In the Circus Domitian established two new racing factions, the gold and purple, to join the traditional red, white, blue, and green (Suetonius, *Life of Domitian* 7.1; Dio Cassius 67.4.4). Meanwhile, according to Pliny, he arrogantly refused to sit where the public could see him. Unlike Trajan, whose audience was 'permitted to see not just the Emperor's box, but their Emperor himself seated among his people' (*Panegyric* 51.5), Domitian evidently positioned himself out of sight (possibly behind curtains) in a box placed behind the *pulvinar*, or viewed in splendid seclusion high above from his new residence on the Palatine (Bollinger 1969: 74–77; Humphrey 1986: 80; Veyne 1990: 399–401, 476). Certainly the parapets and loggia of this *Domus Augustana* afforded the emperor a superb view of the contests, while presenting to the audience below a spectacle rivalling anything in the Circus.

Martial deemed Domitian's palace more wondrous than the pyramids: 'nothing so grand in all the earth ... concealed among the twinkling stars and above the storm, its apex resounds to the thunder from the cloud below ... yet this palace [*domus*] ... is nevertheless less than its lord [*dominus*]' (*Epigrams* 8.36; also 7.56 and 9.13). Statius used similar hyperbole to describe Domitian's Palatine residence, both in its celestial scale ('the ceiling of the golden sky') and in its god-like eminence ('the nearby palace of Juppiter stares at it with awe') (*Silvae* 4.2.18–31) (Blankenhagen 1940: 66–76; Kähler 1963: 115–120; MacDonald 1982: 47–74; Jones 1992: 95–96; Steinby 1995: 40–45).

Straining for further novelty, Domitian recalculated the appropriate date for holding the *ludi Saeculares*. In the Republican tradition, these games were supposed to occur every century or so (the length of an epoch or *saeculum*) and had been held by Augustus in 17 BCE to celebrate the dawn of a new and golden age; this was followed then, aberrantly or pedantically, by Claudius' version in 47 CE (Weinstock 1971: 191–197; Jones 1992: 102–103; Galinsky 1996: 100–101). Domitian now staged them in 88 CE, probably in the early summer. Previously (in 86), taking his cue from Nero and the precedent of the discontinued *Neronia*, Domitian had established a new set of sacred games: the *Capitolia*. Domitian wanted to associate the *Capitolia* with the *lustrum*, the purification ritual traditionally celebrated by Rome's censors; Domitian had assumed the office of censor in perpetuity (Censorinus, *On the Birthday* 18.13–15). The *Capitolia* were cyclical Greek-inspired contests, celebrated every four years by Domitian and then by later emperors for centuries after his death (Lana 1951; Robert 1970: 6–7; Jones 1992: 103–105; Robert 1930: 53; Roueché 1993: 164, 167–168, 176, 181). The festival was in honour of Capitoline Jupiter—to whom Domitian credited the preservation of his life during the Battle of Rome in 69 (Tacitus, *Histories* 3.74)—and consisted of three areas of competition: musical, equestrian, and athletic, with the first prize of a sacred oak wreath awarded to the victors (Statius, *Silvae* 5.3.231). The artistic contests were similar to those instituted by Nero, in such events as Greek and Latin oratory, poetry, singing, and dramatic recitations.

Domitian presented the contests in the grand style, not only in scope (in 94 CE there were fifty-two contestants for the prize in Greek poetry alone), but in the overall *mise en scène*. Extravagant new buildings were constructed for these events, including both Rome's first odeum and stadium, located on the Campus Martius near the Baths of Nero and the Theatre of Pompey. The Odeum, an elegant roofed theatre to host the musical competitions, accommodated about seven thousand spectators; the Stadium (its shape now preserved by the Piazza Navonna) allowed twenty thousand to view the athletic contests held on its track, some seven hundred and fifty feet in length. At the festival itself, as Nero had done before him, 'Domitian maintained the Greek tenor of it all, wearing a purple toga and a golden crown bearing representations of Jupiter, Juno and Minerva', the Capitoline triad (Jones 1992: 103).

He memorably demonstrated that he was 'master' of ceremonies, by refusing to accede to the spectators' request that the winner of the prize for oratory, Palfurius Sura, be restored to the Senate from which Vespasian had expelled him. 'He *deigned* no reply, but merely had a herald bid them be silent' (Suetonius, *Life of Domitian* 13.1); this was a calculated violation of the indulgence expected by the crowd under the cherished tradition of *theatralis licentia*. Decades later, Domitian's notorious 'silence' command was still remembered as uniquely insulting, and in a most literal sense, 'unspeakable', since, as Dio warned, 'crowds should never be silenced by proclamation' (69.6.2–3).

In addition to the new public festival of the *Capitolia*, Domitian privately celebrated a second holiday at his Alban estate in honour of Minerva, his patron goddess, for whom he also instituted a new college of priests (Suetonius, *Life of Domitian* 4.4; 15.3). Long-established at Rome, this festival of the *Quinquatria* took place each year over five days beginning on the nineteenth of March, and Domitian marked and enhanced it with contests in oratory and poetry, as well as plays and displays of gladiators and animals (Dio 67.1.2; cf. 54.28.3).

While exhibiting an interest and even an aptitude in the fine arts, Domitian increasingly revealed and gratified a taste for conspicuous cruelty and violence (Suetonius, *Life of Domitian* 2.2; 10.1–5; 11.1–3; Dio Cassius 67.2.6). He was alleged to have had the pantomimus Paris murdered because his wife Domitia was in love with him (Jones 1992: 34–36). Evidently this rumoured liaison had allowed Paris to exercise considerable influence at court, allegedly making military appointments and elevating some to honorary equestrian status; Juvenal caustically claimed that 'you can get from a stage performer what no great man will give you' (Juvenal, *Satire* 7.90). Juvenal also notes Paris' extraordinary artistic influence: the poet Statius, whose poetry 'people flock to hear ... their souls charmed by his sweetness, listening to him in rapture', would have starved had he not managed to sell his pantomime the *Agave* to Paris to perform (Juvenal, *Satire* 7.84–87). Domitian also executed Helvidius Priscus the younger (a friend of both Tacitus and Pliny the younger) for a mime he composed that touched too closely upon the affair between the Empress and Paris (Suetonius, *Life of Domitian* 10.4; Jones 1992: 187).

In addition to such direct attempts to curb actors' affronts to his private life, Domitian undertook to regulate their public impact as well. He banned (once again) the pantomimes from the theatres, although they were still permitted to perform in private houses (Suetonius, *Life of Domitian* 7.1; Pliny, *Panegyric* 46). This may not have greatly helped public morals since it had become common for wealthier families to maintain whole troupes of performers. Acting again in his role as censor, and in order to maintain decorum in the theatres and amphitheatre, Domitian 'by edict of our God and Master' ordered that the seating regulations be reinforced (Suetonius, *Life of Domitian* 8.3; Juvenal, *Satire* 3.153–158), as well as the rules first laid down by Augustus stipulating appropriate clothing at the spectacles, with a white toga obligatory for all citizens.

'EVERY NOVELTY HAS LONG SINCE BEEN EXPENDED IN ADULATION'

This observation by Pliny, aptly and possibly self-consciously demonstrated by the very context in which he expressed it—a long hyperbolic speech praising the emperor Trajan—epitomizes the state of spectacle and the spectacles of State at the close of the first century CE. Domitian, employing cruelty and terror against those he feared or resented, had been equally adept at engendering awe (or its simulation) in the mass of his subjects while manipulating their gratitude to his own greater glory.

> Could any place remain ignorant of the miserable mood of adulation, when praise of the Emperors was celebrated in shows and competitions, while dancing and shrieking and every

sort of sound and gesture was expressed in effeminate buffoonery? But the greatest disgrace was that it was all praised in the Senate as well as on the stage, at the same time by actor and consul alike (Pliny, *Panegyric* 54.1–2).

The studied extravagancy of style both in the presentation and reception of the god-like monarch was itself a species of theatre, contrived and executed according to an elaborate scenario and conventions of performance from which actors or audience strayed at their peril. Yet virtually every variety of act or novelty of setting had already been employed by the current *Princeps*' imperial predecessors. Eventually the calendar became so clogged with regularly scheduled *ludi* and extraordinary *munera* that ordinary life at Rome was overshadowed by festivity; the emperor and his people might spend as much as a third of the year together at shows. Inhabitants 'no longer felt that they were masters and citizens of their own City, but rather the monarch's household' (Veyne 1990: 397).

Reality intruded long enough to remove Domitian from the scene. His bad relations with the senatorial members of the aristocracy—a great many of whom he executed or exiled, 'becoming an object of terror and hatred to all'—and his rapacious greed, exacerbated by the 'costs of his buildings and shows', encouraged a series of conspiracies. He was murdered in his bedroom in September of 96 by several conspirators, including a gladiator from the imperial troupe. 'The people received the news with indifference' (Suetonius, *Life of Domitian* 12.1, 14.1, 23.1).

Exactly four years later, in September of 100, Pliny gave his speech, the *Panegyric*, before the Senate, to assert 'the end of an era of dissimulation: against the theatricality of a bygone era ... the masklessness of the present' (Bartsch 1994: 149). But this claim of transparency was largely doublespeak. Pliny and his audience could no longer free themselves from the dramaturgical imperatives that controlled their lives.

Pliny implicitly gives the game away when he recalls how at the beginning of his consulate, Trajan had entered the Senate and 'exhorted us both individually and as a group to take back freedom, and conduct the business of state *as if* we shared it' (Pliny, *Panegyric* 66.2). From the time of Augustus the Senate had ceased to display much meaningful power; indeed, its members repeatedly disdained even to exercise the responsibilities technically still theirs. Instead, senators' idea of *libertas* was an elaborate masquerade in which they were free to express their opinion to the emperor without fear of reprisal, and in turn expected to be treated with the appearance of respect for their dignity and counsel without indulging in the dubious and dangerous honour of trying to enforce it. Domitian was hated because he refused to 'play the game' of shrouding their humiliating paralysis with polite platitudes, instead insisting, when challenged, on brutally reminding them of reality. For Pliny, his colleagues, and their successors, hypocrisy was obviously preferable to slaughter.

No more convincing was Pliny's suggestion that, because the new emperor had 'removed all the theatrical arts from your worship' (*Panegyric* 54.2), spectators could now express genuine enthusiasm at the games in place of that feigned earlier, and the occasion of the spectacles themselves was somehow transformed from make-believe to true representation (*Panegyric* 16.3; 34.3; 81.3). Under the imperial system, the emperor could not dispense with the spectacles for validating and indeed exercising a power for which such public entertainments had become an essential setting and symbol. He must use his munificence not so much to attain glory and power as to reflect it. His shows must therefore eclipse those which, vestigially, were still required from other magistrates. Under the constitutional sleight of hand through which the Principate was conjured, the emperor must have the majesty of his *auctoritas*, the quality of his *virtus*, and the splendour of his *dignitas* publicly acclaimed by the populace. The people, in turn, defined their relationship to the ruler by his benefactions and response to requests at the shows, thereby displaying himself as a good and generous father. For their part, the audience expressed their affection and desire to be the emperor's people, serving as his clients and acknowledging his patronage.

The shows had become politicized not just by the emperor and people, but by senators as well. Although flattered when emperors attended games sponsored by senatorial magistrates (Suetonius, *Life of Claudius* 12.2; *Life of Domitian* 4.2; Dio Cassius 69.7.4), they resented any emperor who, not content with making himself popular (as was appropriate for a magistrate), sought excessive adulation and heaped unseemly gifts and flattery upon the populace—the practice of a tyrant. On numerous occasions, the dignity of both senators and equestrians had been graphically diminished when 'tyrannical' emperors forced them across the barrier into the arena itself in a manner with threatened both this elite social order and by extension, that of all of Roman society (Edmondson 1996: 83–86; 107).

Because the games had assumed a central role in the political and cultural life of Rome, all the participants—the emperor, senators, and various strata of society—were caught up in a scenic symbiosis, an obsessive syndrome from which all were powerless to extricate themselves. The *Princeps* was constrained to give ever more extravagant and novel shows; the more sumptuous, successful, and frequent these were, the more the spectators expected and demanded. Quite apart from its effect on the populace, the situation undoubtedly tended to corrupt or even 'unhinge' the emperors themselves.

They had to appear in too many different roles: incarnate god, modest Senator among his peers, responsible magistrate, popular magistrate, Good King, majestic sovereign, administrator in his council, 'tormented by their contradictions to the threshold of madness... inclined to persecution mania, changeable, exhibitionistic, cultivated, moving from simple humanity to aestheticism or to ... brutality' (Veyne 1990: 413).

Contradictions abounded. Pliny asserts that instead of praising the emperor's voice or good looks—the custom in the days of Nero and Domitian—the crowds now praise Trajan's courage and self-restraint (*Panegyric* 2.6). A few paragraphs later, however, he expansively praises Trajan's good looks! He claims it is unnecessary to 'flatter you as a god or a divinity; we speak not of a tyrant, but a citizen, not a master [*Dominus*] but a father'; then proceeds to catalogue Trajan's god-like qualities and thereafter habitually addresses him as *Dominus* in his own correspondence with the emperor (*Panegyric* 4.7, 2.3).

Whatever improvement in character the new emperor might display in comparison to his predecessors, the pageantry of power continued much as before. In 108 CE Trajan gave *munera* lasting one hundred and twenty three days at which some eleven thousand animals were killed and ten thousand gladiators fought (Dio Cassius 68.15; Veyne 1990: 399). But the essential point is indisputable. The emperors and the Roman people continued to share each other's company at a great variety of festive events and venues to the end of antiquity. Indeed under Trajan and his successors the role of the spectacles if anything became even more important, since as the dominant symbol of Roman culture they played a vital part in the 'decolonization' of the empire—the process through which the provinces were in effect transformed into a multinational State united by integration and participation in a common civilization.

The spectacles were thus, even for those contemptuous of them, entirely too important to ignore. Everyone 'respectable or not, went more or less regularly to public entertainments, and the senators were particularly assiduous, out of both duty and inclination' (Veyne 1990: 396). Pliny might boast (describing the Circus audience) 'when I observe men so insatiably fond of so silly, so low, so boring and so common an entertainment, I congratulate myself that I am insensible to these pleasures' (*Letters* 9.6). In a similar vein he condemned the use of hired claques in the theatre as 'a scandal that increases daily' (*Letters* 2.14). Tacitus too might contemplate with distaste 'the dregs of the City, haunting the Circus and the theatre' (*Histories* 1.4). Yet both men are compromised by an anecdote related by Pliny in a letter in which he records:

> I never was more pleased than I was lately by a remark by Cornelius Tacitus. He told me that at the last games in the Circus there sat next to him a Roman equestrian. After much learned talk his neighbour asked him, 'are you of Italy, or from the provinces?' Tacitus replied, 'you know me, and that from your reading.' Then said the other 'Are you Tacitus or Pliny?' (*Letters* 9.23).

The incident reveals that even such high-minded critics attended the games, where they could find themselves in the most learned company.

Several decades later, Fronto succinctly analysed the prevailing condition:

> One of the highest principles of politics is that the Emperor must not ignore actors or other performers on the stage or in the Circus, since he knows that the Roman people are held fast by two things above all: the grain-dole and the shows ... An Emperor's rule depends on entertainments as much as upon more serious things; neglecting the latter is more harmful, neglecting the former causes greater unrest. Gifts of food are a weaker incentive than spectacles; by such gifts only the proletariat on the grain-register are satisfied singly and individually, whereas by the shows the whole population is kept in good spirits. (Fronto, *Prologue of History* 17)

The games and the infrastructure which sustained them were, and would remain, a vital fact of life at Rome however much Pliny and his colleagues decried the situation, or looked hopefully to future emperors to modify it. They not only reflected dominant Roman values and social norms, but beyond that had become the occasion both for validating and renewing, as well as occasionally modifying, fundamental political and cultural relationships.

It seems therefore appropriate to conclude with an eyewitness account of the state of play at the close of the first century—and thereafter. Statius records a 'day at the spectacles' given by Domitian to celebrate the *Saturnalia*—a festival which must have held particular poignancy for that emperor when he recalled the events of December 69 which almost cost the eighteen-year-old future *Princeps* his life, but ended with him acclaimed for the first time as 'Caesar'.

Statius opens his narrative (*Silvae* 1.6) of the 'glad festival of our merry Caesar' at dawn when, to get the show under way, the crowd was inundated with a 'generous profusion' of rich treats and exotic goodies (called *missilia* or *munuscula*) tumbling down upon them from the nets extended over the auditorium by 'our own Jove who sends us such showers'. But this was mere appetizer, soon followed by an entire banquet conveyed by a liveried multitude of servants bearing 'sumptuous food and abundant wine' up into the auditorium as if (to continue the 'Jovial' simile) they were 'cupbearers on Ida'. All the thousands present were fed—rich and poor, humble and grand—as if the 'golden age of primeval Jove' had returned, or indeed been surpassed. 'One table serves all: children, women, plebs, equestrians, and senators; freedom [*libertas*] has loosed the bonds of awe.' All were both made grateful by the patronage bestowed upon them, and 'blessed to be honoured as the leader's guest'. Thus, adeptly (and anticipating the similar function of carnivals, masquerade balls, and feasts of misrule down through the ages), social restraints and their attendant tensions were briefly relaxed in therapeutic theatre—an act of collective make-believe and wish-fulfilment (Barton 1993: 122–124; Edmondson 1996: 95; Ville 1981: 434–435).

These 'excitements and strange luxuries' nearly overshadow the show, despite such novelties as women—'you might take them for Amazons!'—fighting in armed combat, or a 'bold array' of deformed dwarfs—always good for 'a laugh from Father Mars and bloodstained *Virtus*'—as they engage in Lilliputian slaughter. As evening approached, more delights appeared. 'Bargains from the brothel' as well as a veritable variety show of entertainers parade about. 'Here a crowd of buxom Lydian girls clap hands, there tinkle the cymbals of Gadiz, yonder troops of Syrians make an uproar, and here are the theatre folk [*plebs scenica*]'. In the midst of all this frivolity vast numbers of rare birds are dropped down into the arena. Finally, the day was rounded off with a kind of fireworks display, when 'through the dense darkness a ball of flame fell gleaming into the centre of the arena' while 'the sky was ablaze with fire'.

Statius too was aglow. 'Who can sing of the spectacle, the unrestrained mirth, the feasting, the free bounty, the swollen streams of wine?' But then—a drowsy numbness stealing over him—he fell into a drunken sleep, murmuring praise and astonishment and gratitude. His exit lines provide our final cue. 'How many years shall this festival continue! ... It shall abide so long as the hills of Latium and Father Tiber, so long as Rome itself and the Capitol restored to the World remain.' The spectacles at Rome and throughout the empire continued for a further five centuries.

References

Auguet, R. 1972. *Cruelty and Civilization: The Roman Games*. London.
Barton, C. A. 1993. *The Sorrows of the Ancient Romans: The Gladiator and the Monster*. Princeton.
Bartsch, S. 1994. *Actors in the Audience: Theatricality and Doublespeak from Nero to Hadrian*. Cambridge.
Blankenhagen, P. H. von. 1940. *Flavische Architektur und ihre Dekoration, untersucht am Nervaforum*. Berlin.
Bollinger, T. 1969. *Theatralis Licentia: Die Publikumsdemonstrationen an den öffentlichen Spielen im Rom der früheren Kaiserzeit und ihre Bedeutung im politischen Leben*. Basel.
Coleman, K. M. 1990. 'Fatal Charades: Roman Executions Staged as Mythological Enactments'. *JRS* 80: 44–73.
Coleman, K. M. 1993. 'Launching into History: Aquatic Displays in the Early Empire'. *JRS* 83: 48–74.
Coleman, K. M. 1996b. 'Ptolemy Philadelphus and the Roman Amphitheater'. In *Roman Theater and Society*. 49–68. W. J. Slater ed. Ann Arbor.
Coleman, K. M. 1998. 'The Contagion of the Throng: Absorbing Violence in the Roman World'. *Hermathena* 164: 65–88.
Edmondson, J. C. 1996. 'Dynamic Arenas: Gladiatorial Presentations in the City of Rome and the Construction of Roman Society during the Early Empire'. In *Roman Theater and Society*. 69–112. W. J. Slater, ed. Ann Arbor.

Galinsky, K. 1996. *Augustan Culture: An Interpretive Introduction*. Princeton.

Garnsey, P. 1970. *Social Status and Legal Privilege in the Roman Empire*. Oxford.

Hopkins, K. 1983. *Death and Renewal*. Cambridge.

Humphrey, J. H. 1986. *Roman Circuses: Arenas for Chariot Racing*. Berkeley.

Jones, B. W. 1992. *The Emperor Domitian*. London.

Kähler, H. 1963. *Rome and Her Empire*. London.

Lana, I. 1951. 'I ludi Capitolini di Domiziano.' *RFIC* 29: 145–160.

MacDonald, W. 1982. *The Architecture of the Roman Empire*, I: *An Introductory Study*. New Haven.

Nippel, W. 1995. *Public Order in Ancient Rome*. Cambridge.

Ramsay, G. G. 1918. *Juvenal and Persius*. London.

Robert, L. 1930. 'Études d'épigraphie grecque.' *RPh* 56: 25–60.

Robert, L. 1970. 'Deux concours grecs à Rome.' *CRAI* 114: 6–27.

Rouché, C. 1993. *Performers and Partisans at Aphrodisias in the Roman and Late Roman Periods*. London.

Steinby, E. M. 1995. *Lexicon Topographicum Urbis Romae*. Rome.

Veyne, P. 1990. *Bread and Circuses: Historical Sociology and Political Pluralism*. London.

Ville, G. 1981. *La gladiature en Occident des origines à la mort de Domitien*. Rome.

Weinstock, S. 1971. *Divus Julius*. Oxford.

Wiedemann, T. 1992. *Emperors and Gladiators*. London.

CHAPTER 13

....

GREEK FESTIVALS IN THE ROMAN ERA

....

ZAHRA NEWBY

THE picture of Greek festival culture in the Roman era is one of both continuity and change. The Roman period saw the vast expansion of Greek festivals across the Mediterranean, especially in the Eastern provinces of the empire, but also in Italy and the western provinces, such as Gaul and North Africa. Yet at the same time the traditional centres of athletics, such as Olympia, continued to thrive, attracting increased numbers of contestants from a wide geographical area. The recognition and honours given to victors in these festivals also show both continuity and changes: while home cities continued to honour their victors, setting up statues either at home or in Panhellenic sanctuaries, the most successful athletes and performers also gained fame on a wider stage, being recognized outside their own homelands and often accumulating the rights to citizenship of a number of different cities. In this chapter I will trace some of this vibrant festival culture through a look at attested Olympic victors, the development of new festivals across the empire, and the celebration of victorious athletes.

CELEBRATING OLYMPIC VICTORY

....

Recorded Olympic victories from the Roman period paint a picture of continuing interest in Olympia, though with a changed geographical dimension (Farrington 1997; Scanlon 2002: 40–63). After a dip in total numbers in the Late Republican period, when the majority of victors come from the Peloponnese, numbers of attested victors begin to rise again with a change in their geographical origins. The proportion of victors from mainland Greece and the Peloponnese declines in favour of those from Asia Minor, with increasing numbers of victors also coming from Egypt and North Africa, especially from the later first century CE. Victors from Magna Graecia, which had already declined in number in the Hellenistic period, continue to be largely absent, though a few equestrian victories are attested from Roman citizens, especially members of the imperial family.

The apparent success enjoyed by the cities of Asia Minor versus those of mainland Greece deserves further discussion, and may in part be due to varying epigraphic habits (Farrington 1997: 26–30). It suggests a continuing keenness on the part of the cities of Asia Minor to prove their Panhellenic credentials, already seen in the boasts of primacy which feature on victory monuments of the fourth and third centuries BCE (Newby, this volume Chapter 10). In the imperial period they seem to have enjoyed greater success, in large part probably due to the greater financial resources of these cities to train promising athletes in the gymnasium (e.g. Brunet 2003). However, the small numbers of celebrated successes by athletes from mainland Greece should not be taken for lack of interest. Pausanias' account of the victory statues seen on his tour of Greece is illuminating, since he makes repeated reference to earlier statues commemorating Olympic victories, both at Olympia and within individual cities. For Pausanias, these statues seem to serve as continued proof of cities' claims to Hellenic identity and their share in the Panhellenic project; their continued survival and prominence suggests that for their cities they continued to provide proof of their membership in the wider community of Greece, even if this was achieved through the memory of past athletic victories (Newby 2005: 214–228).

The few attested imperial victors also show that mainland Greece continued to produce and celebrate Olympic victories right up until the end of the Games' history, albeit perhaps in smaller numbers. In his final book, Pausanias mentions the athlete Mnesiboulos of Elateia (in Phokis, near Delphi) who had a bronze statue in the Street of the Runner at Elateia (10.34.5). This man had met his death fighting against the Kostobokoi tribe which overran Greece *c.*170 CE. Pausanias describes his death in battle, and then tells us that he had won numerous victories in running, including the stade race and race in armour at the 235th Olympic games (161 CE), information which is corroborated by an inscription from Elateia, naming him as both *periodonikēs*, 'circuit-victor', and 'first of the Hellenes', that is with victories at four of the major Panhellenic festivals on the circuit, and in the race in armour at Plataea (*SIG* 871; Moretti 1957 nos. 868–869).

Sixty years later we find the victories of P. Aelius Alkandridas of Sparta. This man had statues at both Olympia and Sparta celebrating his victories in the stade race at Olympia in 221 and 225 CE, as well as numerous other victories (*IvO* 238, *SEG* XI.831, *IG* V.1, 556A l.5 describes him as 'twice *periodonikēs*'; Moretti 1957 nos. 917, 920). The latest known Olympic victors are also from mainland Greece, from the city of Athens; while not awarded victory statues (the latest attested is for a herald in 261 CE, *IvO* 242/3), they are recorded on a bronze plaque which was found in Olympia, listing victors from the first century BCE to the fourth century CE (Sinn et al. 1994: 238–241 [Ebert]). This lists the victories in 381 and 385 CE, respectively, of the Athenians Aurelius Eukarpides in the boys' pancration and Aurelius Zopyros in the boys' boxing. Right up until the end of the Olympic festival, athletes from mainland Greece continued to participate, though the extensive geographical scope of the festival by this time can also be seen in the victory a decade or so earlier of the Armenian boxer Varazdat (Moretti 1957 no. 944, *c.*369 CE). While the statistics show that the celebration of victories at Olympia from the first to fourth centuries CE was dominated by figures from Asia Minor and Egypt, these latest recorded victors also show both the extent to which Olympia had changed, in the broadening of participation to figures from non-Greek backgrounds, and the extent to which it remained the same, the cultural heart of Hellenic identity.

Olympia probably meant many different things to different people in the Roman era. For those on the edges of the Mediterranean world it was the pre-eminent athletic festival, victory at which was still the pinnacle of an athletic career, as its prominent place on surviving victory lists shows. However, for those seeking to understand and represent their cultural identities in a time of shifting political power it was also a place redolent of the Greek past, the centre of the Hellenic world, as Pausanias' prominent placement of it at the heart of his description of Greece clearly shows (Elsner 2001; König 2005: 158–204; Newby 2005: 202–228). These different conceptions of what Olympic victory meant help to explain the patterns of commemoration which we find in the sanctuary. Despite the number of victors from North Africa (roughly 25 percent of those attested from the late first to fourth centuries CE) no victory statues to African or Egyptian athletes are known from the surviving statue bases. Admittedly evidence is scanty, with only sixteen attested statues dating from the first century CE onwards (Herrmann 1998: list II), but it seems as though athletes from North Africa were not interested in advertising themselves here.

Instead, where known, the origins of those commemorated by statues break down as follows: Elis 4, Rome 3, Ephesos 2, Antioch on the Orontes 2, Magnesia on the Maeander 1, Sparta 1, Rhodes 1. With the exception of Rome, all of these were well-established Greek communities by the Roman era. The decision to commemorate victories at Olympia, rather than in the athletes' home town as became increasingly common, suggests a deliberate act of self-representation in this Panhellenic meeting place. Ephesos and Antioch were two of the major cities of the Mediterranean; the self-promotion of their successful athletes demonstrates their wealth and success, as well as their claims to be part of the Panhellenic community, while Rome's victories can be seen as evidence of her wider authority and of loyalty on behalf of the local community (the statue of Germanicus and an earlier one to Tiberius in 4 BCE were both set up by others to them as patrons: *IvO* 220, 221). Sparta and Magnesia were smaller cities whose citizens were commemorating major achievements (both were *periodonikēs*: see above for Alkandridas and *IvO* 211, *IMagnesia* 149 for the Magnesian athlete Demokrates who won three times at Olympia). Elis, the city in charge of the games, can be seen using the sanctuary almost as an extension of its civic space, but one with a much wider audience to which to promote itself (further Farrington 1997: 31–32; statues to Elean victors especially dominated the sanctuary in the first century BCE). While statistics can help us to sketch the broad history of the festival at this period, only a detailed examination of individual statue bases and inscriptions can provide a full understanding of what Olympic victory meant to individual victors, their families and cities (e.g. König 2005: 124–132; Mouratidis 2020).

THE EXPANSION OF GREEK FESTIVAL CULTURE

In addition to Olympia, those commemorated for Olympic victories also competed in a vastly expanded programme of festivals which spanned the Mediterranean. As well as long-standing festivals such as those of the traditional Panhellenic *periodos* (Olympic, Pythian, Isthmian, and Nemean festivals) and civic festivals such as the Panatheneia at Athens, huge numbers of new festivals were instituted in the Roman period (Robert 1984; Spawforth 1989; Mitchell 1990; on festival culture in Late Antiquity see Graf 2015 and Remijsen 2015). The traditional division between the most prestigious sacred crown games (*agōnes hieroi kai stephaneitai*) and prize games (*agones thematikoi*) still held, though in practice it seems likely that monetary rewards were also given at many sacred games, and the wreath was a visual symbol of victory regardless of the category of games at which it was won (Pleket 1975: 148–161; 2004; Dunbabin 2010; Remijsen 2011; Slater 2012). Victory at sacred games could bring athletes valuable benefits from their home cities, such as an honorific statue, freedom from taxation, and monetary pensions (Slater 2013).

In the Hellenistic period crown status was achieved through recognition by Hellenistic kings and other Greek cities that a festival was equal in rank to the Olympic or Pythian games (Newby, this volume Chapter 10), but in the Roman period it became the preserve of the emperor. The financial burden which the number of crowned festivals (now often described as 'eiselastic') imposed on cities is well shown in the correspondence of the Younger Pliny, asking the Emperor Trajan for advice in administering the benefits due to victors in eiselastic contests in the province of Bithynia (*Ep.* 10.118–119; Slater 2013: 147–149). Victors had been requesting the backdating of benefits to the time of their victory, rather than their arrival back home, and suggesting that victories won before a festival became termed eiselastic should be credited under its new status. Trajan is adamant—no backdating and no retrospective claims; the clear implication is that such generous interpretation of the rules would be far too expensive, though Hadrian later conceded the point (Petzl and Schwertheim 2006: ll. 49–50; Jones 2007: 154).

A vast number of new festivals were instituted in the Roman period, some including just athletic or musical contests and others the whole range of contests, and varying from strictly civic affairs to those with regional or international catchment areas. Prize games competed to attract high-quality athletes and musicians en route to more prestigious festivals, and smaller games also provided young athletes with the experience needed to be successful later on a wider stage (Brunet 2003) as well as offering opportunities for the expression of civic identity (van Nijf 1999; 2001; this volume Chapter 36). Many of these festivals were the product of local euergetism, especially from the second century CE onwards, when festivals appear alongside public building projects as a favoured means of self-representation (Zuiderhoek 2009: 71–112; see also Ng 2015 and Graf 2015: 36–40 for some of the tensions). Others were imperial foundations, though in many cases titles such as Hadrianeia or Commodeia may have been added to new or pre-existing festivals by the city itself, to honour the ruling emperor or commemorate a particular act of imperial euergetism (Price 1984: 101–132; Boatwright 2000: 94–104). Emperors could both grant and remove crown status from the festivals of individual cities, and such grants were eagerly sought in the struggles for prestige between neighbouring cities (e.g. Robert 1977). The vibrancy of Greek festival culture in the Roman period is well illustrated by one study, estimating the number of new or revamped festivals in the eastern provinces as high as 500 (Leschhorn 1998).

Civic coinage advertised festivals and patron gods to the wider community (Harl 1987: 63–70; Klose 2005; a comprehensive discussion will be given in Calomino, forthcoming) while festival processions could re-enact a city's history from its mythological past to its place within the contemporary Roman world (Rogers 1991 on Ephesos). Festivals were also experienced within the wider context of urban space: processions threaded through the city, contests took place in the theatre and stadium, and after the festival had ended its victors were remembered through victory statues and their inscriptions (Carless Unwin, forthcoming). Festivals could fulfil a multitude of functions. They provided a way for cities to celebrate their civic gods and assert the continuity of their local, regional, and ethnic identities as well as to communicate with the emperor, advertising both their loyalty and imperial favour (Ziegler 1985 on Cilicia). As an illustration let us look briefly at Hierapolis in Phrygia which, in the early third century CE, proudly celebrated its own Pythian games (for a fuller discussion, see Newby forthcoming).

Hierapolis' patron god was Apollo Archegetes, and an Apolloneia festival in honour of the god was probably in existence from an earlier period (Ritti 2017: 174–175). From the Severan period, however, Hierapolis started to celebrate the festival on its coinage, with types which show either a prize-crown or a wreath and the legend 'Pythia' (Johnston 1984: 63; 70, no. 41). An inscription from Tralleis dated to c.200 CE refers to the festival as the Apolloneia Isopythia in Hierapolis, showing that the festival was equated with the more famous Pythia at Delphi (*SEG* 43.732).

The festival also takes pride of place in the decoration of Hierapolis' new theatre, dedicated in 206–208 CE to the god Apollo Archegetēs, the emperor Septimius Severus, and his family (D'Andria and Ritti 1985: 9–10). The relief above the central door of the *scaenae frons* shows the emperor presiding over the festival, accompanied by his family and placed next to a large prize crown placed on a table (Fig. 13.1; Ritti 1985: 57–77). The imperial presence in the right half of this central panel is mirrored and balanced by local personifications in the left half, including the personification of the city herself, originally holding a statuette of the patron god, and Agonothesia, the 'presidency of the games', providing a shared emphasis on both the emperor and Hierapolis and its festival. Figures on the flanking panels extend the references to Hierapolis' festival presenting, on the left, the figures (all labelled) of *Sunthusia* (Joint Sacrifice), *Oikoumenē* (the inhabited world) and *Aion* (time) and, on the right, *Andreia* (courage) and *Sunodos* (the guild of actors) along with a priestess and an athlete crowning himself. The back of the left side panel shows a young boy being crowned victor, labelled above as *Pythikos*, while the back of the right side panel shows a scene of sacrifice. The reliefs at the front of the projecting side panels show (left) the president of the games (*agonothetēs*) with a female figure and (right) another athlete being crowned.

The overall message is clear. The Hierapolitans celebrate their major civic festival, held in honour of Apollo Archegetēs and bearing the title Pythian. The personifications stress the connection between the festival and the city and also show its wider impact through the personifications of world-wide sacrifice and time. To the right, both the athletic and artistic sides of the festival are represented through the martial figure of courage and the personification of the guild of actors, who holds a tragic mask. Athletic victories, in particular, are shown through the representation of a number of naked male figures either crowning themselves or being crowned. At the centre of all this is Septimius Severus, a clear sign that the festival itself is held under the auspices of the imperial power. The rest of the theatre reliefs continue this celebration of Hierapolis' religious culture; the reliefs which run along the back of the stage link the life and cult of Apollo with his famous twin sister, the goddess Artemis of Ephesos (D'Andria and Ritti 1985). The decision to put Apollo and Hierapolis' Pythian festival at the heart of this new theatre was probably prompted by a recent upgrading of the pre-existing Apolloneia festival by Septimius Severus to crown status (Ritti 1985: 73–74). It is an excellent example of the way in which civic self-representation lay claim to long-standing Greek cultural values under the wider auspices of imperial power.

FIGURE 13.1. Theatre relief at Hierapolis celebrating the Pythia festival. Photo: Carless Unwin, by kind permission of Prof Francesco D'Andrian and the Missone Archeologica Italiana a Hierapolis.

GREEK FESTIVALS IN THE
WESTERN MEDITERRANEAN

I have concentrated above on the vast explosion of festivals in the eastern half of the Mediterranean and the ways in which these provided cities with proven claims to Greek identity as well as expressing loyalty or imperial favour. Yet athletic festivals also spread to the western half of the empire, at first through the direct involvement of the emperor. Although it was not until 86 CE, during the reign of Domitian, that a permanent Greek-style festival, the *Agon Capitolinus*, was finally instituted at Rome: this can be seen as the climax in a series of moves (Robert 1970; Caldelli 1993; Newby 2005: 21–44; Mann 2014: 163–168). Ad hoc competitions involving Greek athletes had been seen at Rome during the Republican period (Arnold 1960; Crowther 1983; see also Thuillier 1982 on athletic contests in Roman *ludi*) but the moves towards permanently instituting Greek festival culture in Italy began with Augustus. In Greece, he instituted the *Actia* festival at Nikopolis in 30/28 BCE to commemorate his victory over Antony, while back at Rome Greek-style athletic events formed part of the 'games for the health of Caesar', *ludi pro valetudine Caesaris*, voted him by the senate in 28 BCE. This *gymnicus agōn* was held in a wooden stadium built on the Campus Martius and the games seem to have been repeated every four years at least until 9 CE (Dio 53.1.4–6; Suet. *Aug.* 43; Caldelli 1993: 21–37).

The first permanent Greek athletic festival in Italy took place in Naples. The *Sebasta* festival was set up by the senate and local community probably in 2 CE at Naples and followed the programme of the Olympic festival (*IvO* 56; Suet. *Aug.* 18.2; Caldelli 1993: 28–9; Leiwo 1994: 45–8). Dio Cassius links the festival to the Neapolitans' desire 'alone of the Campanians to imitate the customs of the Greeks' (55.10.9) and it seems to have acted as a symbol of the Greek origins of this vibrant town. Yet, as elsewhere, this cultural identity was embraced and supported by the rulers in Rome. Naples' public epigraphy continued to be written in Greek, and Roman emperors are recorded as attending and officiating at the games (Suet. *Cl.* 11.2; Themistius *Or.* 139a–b; Miranda De Martino 2007).

In Rome a Greek festival, the Neronia, was first instituted by the emperor Nero in 60 CE. It was held again in 65 CE but then lapsed on his death. Twenty years later, in 86 CE, the emperor Domitian instituted the Capitoline Games in honour of the Capitoline triad (Caldelli 1993). These survived the death of their founder and are attested well into the fourth century CE. From the privileged position in which it appears on victory lists we know that the festival enjoyed great prestige; victories here appear second only to those at Olympia, which continued to enjoy first place. The festival gave Rome a central place on the festival circuit, drawing athletes and performers from across the Mediterranean to compete at it. More festivals were instituted under subsequent emperors, including the *Eusebeia* festival in honour of Hadrian, set up by Antoninus Pius in Puteoli in 143 CE, and at least three festivals instituted at Rome during the third century (Ael. Sp. *Had.* 27.3; *CIL* 10.515; Robert 1970; Caldelli 1993: 43–52). Through these new institutions the festival map was redrawn. While the eastern Mediterranean still dominated in terms of the sheer number of festivals, these prestigious imperially sponsored festivals made Italy a crucial destination. Indeed, in the second century CE, the international guild of athletes set up their headquarters at Rome near the Baths of Trajan on land granted by the emperors Hadrian and Antoninus Pius (Pleket 1973; Caldelli 1992).

Literary sources suggest that the Roman response to these new festivals was mixed. Tacitus uses the institution of the Neronia festival to stage a moralizing debate in the senate, with those who oppose the festival fearing that Roman nobles will start to strip naked and take up boxing gloves (*Ann.* 14.20). Pliny the Younger is similarly hostile to the Capitoline Games, blaming them for 'corrupting the morals of all men' and encouraging similar vices around the provinces (*Ep.* 4.22.3, 7). Yet these fears seem to have been unfounded. If a few Romans did take part in the contests, they do not seem to have enjoyed much success. Italian victors are notable by their absence from the athletic victory lists, which largely feature figures from the eastern provinces, though they do appear among the musical victors (Caldelli 1993: 90–94). However, the festivals do seem to have enjoyed popularity as a spectacle, as is shown by the appearance of named athletes on floor mosaics (Newby 2002; 2005: 45–87). A mosaic decorating an inn in Ostia shows a pair of pancratiasts named above as Alexander and Helix (Fig. 13.2). They can be identified with two leading athletes of the early third century CE, Aurelius Alexander and Aurelius Helix (Jones 1998). Helix was victor in the 218 CE Capitoline games at Rome while Alexander later held the position of chief priest of the athletic synod in Rome. The mosaic may commemorate a particular contest between the men at the Capitoline festival. The same two names reappear again in a mosaic at Puteoli which commemorates the Eusebeia festival there, again attesting to widespread interest in these Greek festivals and those who competed in them (Gialanella 2001).

FIGURE 13.2. Mosaic from the Inn of Alexander Helix at Ostia, celebrating two successful pancratiasts. Photo: Archivio Fotografico della Soprintendenza Speciale per i Beni Archeologici di Rome e Ostia.

The success of the festivals at Rome and Naples seems to have encouraged the institution of other festivals in the western provinces (see Caldelli 1997 on Gaul). Two examples from Gaul and North Africa show just how widely this festival culture spread. Pliny the Younger blames the Capitoline festival for encouraging the development of similar festivals elsewhere, citing the example of an athletic festival at Vienne in Gaul, which had just been abolished at the time of his writing (*Ep.* 4.22). While that festival did not survive, there is indeed evidence for an enduring interest in athletic pursuits at Vienne and probably of a later athletic festival (Newby 2005: 76–84 pls. 2–3). Wall paintings decorating the latrines in a public bath complex at St Romaine-en-Gal, across the river from Vienne, show a series of athletic scenes, with contests in wrestling, boxing, and throwing the discus, and may reflect a local festival as well as the pursuits enjoyed in the baths. A large floor mosaic found in the centre of Vienne also shows a series of athletic vignettes around the central figure of Herakles. One possibility is that it decorated the headquarters of a local athletic guild.

A number of festivals are also attested in the cities of North Africa, including prestigious crown games such as the Pythia and Asclepieia festivals at Carthage. Over the course of time smaller cities also came to enjoy the attractions of a Greek-style festival, as is clearly shown by an exceptional mosaic discovered in Baten Zammour in Tunisia, near the ancient city of Capsa (Khanoussi 1988; Pausz and Reitinger 1992; Newby 2005: 84–86 pl. 4). Divided into four registers, this shows a series of athletic contests and the prizes awarded to the victors, including contests in the pentathlon, boxing, wrestling, pancration, and a torch-race wearing armour. Elaborate metal crowns, victory palms, and bags of money constitute the prizes awarded to the victors. The mosaic probably commemorates the generosity of a particular local notable who had funded a set of prize games for his local community, and can be likened to the displays of generosity which we find on other mosaics in North Africa, such as the famous Magerius mosaic from Smirat (Dunbabin 1978: 67–70). The mosaic seems to date to the early fourth century CE. It is an excellent example of the way that Greek festival culture gradually became part of the benefits of membership in the Roman empire, a way for elites from around the empire to advertise their cosmopolitanism and generosity to their individual cities, without necessarily laying claim to a deeply seated Greek identity.

CELEBRATING ATHLETIC VICTORY

While festivals were also embraced in the western provinces, particularly from the second century CE onwards, they continued to be a particular feature of civic life in the East, where they did continue to act as powerful assertions of a long-standing Greek cultural identity. In conclusion, to illustrate both the international nature of festivals in the Roman era and their enduring importance for local identity, I will focus on two sets of victory monuments, set up in the cities of Aphrodisias and Magnesia on the Maeander in Asia Minor. The first is a pair of boxers, commemorated in honorific statues set up at either end of the stage of the theatre at Aphrodisias in Caria, probably in the late third or early fourth century (Fig. 13.3). Inscribed statue bases identify the athletes as Candidianus and Piseas; both are labelled as *periodonikēs*, 'circuit-victor', though Candidianus also won at the Actia festival, and the statues were set up by 'the fatherland', the city of Aphrodisias (Roueché 1993 nos. 74–75; Van Voorhis 2008: 240–243 discusses the chronology noting that the statues seem to date earlier

FIGURE 13.3. Statue of Piseas of Aphrodisias, victorious boxer. Aphrodisias Museum inv. 70-508-511. Photo: New York University Excavations at Aphrodisias.

than the inscriptions). Their statues show them in their professional guise, with shaven heads and the cirrus (a lock of hair at the top of the head) often worn by athletes at this period, as well as long boxing gloves. The inscriptions are relatively brief, but convey the essential points: these are citizens of Aphrodisias, honoured with a prestigious place in the theatre for their athletic victories at the most important crown festivals.

The second set of victory monuments consists of two statue bases from the city of Magnesia on the Maeander (*IMagnesia* 180–181; Moretti 1953 no. 71). The statues themselves are lost, but the inscriptions show that they honoured Publius Aelius Aristomachus, a citizen of Magnesia, for victories in the boys' pancration. The first monument holds a prose inscription, listing Aristomachus' victories and other honours and dedicating statues of himself to his city. The second inscription is in verse and concentrates on his athletic victories. To give a flavour of the way Aristomachus represents himself, it is worth quoting the first inscription in full (*IMagnesia* 180):

> P. Aelius Aristomachus, circuit-victor (*peridonikēs*), president of the athletic synod, first and only of his generation to have been victorious at Olympia in the boys' pancration in the 224th Olympiad (117 CE), and at the next Capitolia in Rome (118 CE), the Sebasta in Naples, the Actia, the first Panathenaia after it was granted eiselastic status by the god Hadrian, the common games of Asia in Smyrna, the Isthmian games, Nemean games, the Ourania festival in Sparta and a second time at Isthmia in the youths' pancration, never being declared joint winner or agreeing to share the prize, and because of these victories having been honoured by the god Hadrian with Roman citizenship, as were also his father, mother, and brothers, and made president of the Cyzicene synod, and having served as an ambassador many times to the emperors both in royal Rome and in Pannonia, set up these statues of himself to his most sweet fatherland.

The inscription was set up after Hadrian's death around 140 CE, some twenty years after the victories recorded here, and reflects the whole of Aristomachus' career. After his early athletic victories he has continued to be involved in athletics, as the president of the athletic synod. Aristomachus seems to have become an important member of his community; his athletic victories have brought him and his family Roman citizenship, and in turn this imperial favour has made him a useful ambassador for his city. He is part of the Greek civic elite, showing the important role that athletic victories continued to play in asserting status and identity (van Nijf 1999; 2001). The victories won here encompass both the prestigious and long-standing festivals at Olympia, Isthmia, and Nemea, as well as those in Italy. The order in which they are listed may reflect the chronology of Aristomachus' victories, but it also seems to reflect a hierarchy of value, the Capitoline games coming second only to Olympia.

The victory monuments at Magnesia and Aphrodisias show the continuing importance of athletic victories for the cities of Asia Minor, both for individual athletes such as Aristomachus and for their cities, as shown in the public dedication of the statues at Aphrodisias. As in earlier periods, Olympia continued to be the pre-eminent festival at which to gain victory, but the newer festivals founded in Italy also gained a central place on the Greek festival calendar. Festival culture had become an international, empire-wide phenomenon, while still playing a crucial role in the self-identities of cities and individuals in the Greek world.

References

Arnold, I. R. 1960. 'Agonistic Festivals in Italy and Sicily.' *AJA* 64: 245–251.
Boatwright, M. T. 2000. *Hadrian and the Cities of the Roman Empire*. Princeton.
Brunet, S. 2003. 'Olympic Hopefuls from Ephesos.' *JSH* 30: 219–235.

Caldelli, M. L. 1992. 'Curia athletarum, iera xystike synodos e organizzazione delle terme a Roma.' *ZPE* 93: 75–87.

Caldelli, M. L. 1993. *L'Agon Capitolinus*. Rome.

Caldelli, M. L. 1997. *Gli agoni alla greca nelle regioni occidentali dell'impero. La Gallia Narbonensis*. Rome.

Calomino, D. Forthcoming. *Greek Festival Culture and Civic Coinages in the Roman East*. Cambridge.

Carless Unwin, N. Forthcoming. *Inscribing Festival Culture in the Graeco-Roman East*. Cambridge.

Crowther, N. B. 1983. 'Greek Games in Republican Rome.' *AC* 52: 268–273.

D'Andria, F. and T. Ritti. 1985. *Hierapolis Scavi e Ricerche II. Le Sculture del Teatro*. Archaeologica 55. Rome.

Dunbabin, K. M. D. 1978. *The Mosaics of Roman North Africa: Studies in Iconography and Patronage*. Oxford.

Dunbabin, K. M. D. 2010. 'The Prize Table: Crowns, Wreaths and Moneybags in Roman Art.' In *L'argent dans les concours du monde grec*. 301–345. B. LeGuen, ed. Paris.

Elsner, J. 2001. 'Structuring "Greece". Pausanias' *Periegesis* as a Literary Construct.' In *Pausanias: Travel and Memory in Roman Greece*. 3–20. S. E. Alcock, J. F. Cherry, and J. Elsner, eds. Oxford.

Farrington, A. 1997. 'Olympic Victors and the Popularity of the Olympic Games in the Imperial Period.' *Tyche* 12: 15–46. Repr. with addendum in *Sport in the Greek and Roman Worlds, vol. 1: Early Greece, the Olympics and Contests*. 158–202. T. Scanlon, ed. 2015. Oxford.

Gialanella C. 2001. 'Il mosaico con lottatori da una villa del suburbio orientale di Puteoli.' In *Atti dell' VIII Colloquio AISCOM, Firenze 21–23 febbraio 2001*. 599–624. F. Guidobaldi and A. Paribeni, eds. Ravenna.

Graf, F. 2015. *Roman Festivals in the Greek East: From the Early Empire to the Middle Byzantine Period*. Cambridge.

Harl, K. 1987. *Civic Coins and Civic Politics in the Roman East AD 180–275*. Berkeley.

Herrmann, H.-V. 1988. 'Die Siegerstatuen von Olympia.' *Nikephoros* 1: 119–183.

Johnston, A. 1984. 'Hierapolis Revisitied.' *Numismatic Chronicle* 144: 52–80.

Jones, C. P. 1998. 'The Pancratiasts Helix and Alexander on an Ostian Mosaic.' *JRA* 11: 293–298.

Jones, C. P. 2007. 'Three New Letters of the Emperor Hadrian.' *ZPE* 161: 145–156.

Khanoussi, M. 1988. 'Spectaculum pugilum et gymnasium: Compte rendu d'un spectacle de jeux athlétiques et de pugilat, figuré sur une mosaïque de la région de Gafsa (Tunisie).' *CRAI*: 543–561.

Klose, D. O. A. 2005. 'Festivals and Games in the Cities of the East during the Roman Empire.' In *Coinage and Identity in the Roman Provinces*. 125–33. C. Howgego, V. Heuchert, and A. Burnett, eds. Oxford.

König, J. 2005. *Athletics and Literature in the Roman Empire*. Cambridge.

König, J., ed. 2010. *Greek Athletics*. Edinburgh Readings on the Ancient World. Edinburgh.

Leiwo, M. 1994. *Neapolitana: A Study of Population and Language in Graeco-Roman Naples*. Commentationes Humanarum Litterarum 102. Helsinki.

Leschhorn, W. 1998. 'Die Verbreitung von Agonen in den östlichen Provinzen des römischen Reiches.' *Stadion* 24: 31–57.

Mann, C. 2014. 'Greek Sport and Roman Identity. The *Certamina Athletarum* at Rome.' In *Sport in the Greek and Roman Worlds*, vol. II. 151–181. T. Scanlon, ed. Oxford.

Miranda De Martino, E. 2007. 'Neapolis e gli imperatori.' *Oebalus* 2: 203–215.

Mitchell, S. 1990. 'Festivals, Games and Civic Life in Roman Asia Minor.' *JRS* 80: 183–193.

Moretti, L. 1953. *Iscrizioni agonistiche greche*. Rome.

Moretti, L. 1957. *Olympionikai: i vincitori negli antichi agoni olimpici*. Rome.

Mouratidis, G. 2020. 'Athlete and Polis. The Relationship between Athletes and Cities in the Epigraphic Record of the Late Hellenistic and Imperial Periods.' Unpublished PhD thesis, University of St Andrews.

Newby, Z. 2002. 'Greek Athletics as Roman Spectacle: the Mosaics from Ostia and Rome.' *PBSR* 70: 177–203. Repr. in König 2010. 238–262.

Newby, Z. 2005. *Greek Athletics in the Roman World. Victory and Virtue*. Oxford.

Newby, Z. Forthcoming. 'Festivals and the Performance of Community and Status in the Theatres at Hierapolis and Perge.' In *The Material Dynamics of Festivals in the Graeco-Roman East*. Z. Newby, ed. Cambridge.

Ng, D. 2015. 'Commemoration and Élite Benefaction of Buildings and Spectacles in the Roman World.' *JRS* 105: 101–123.

Pausz, R.-D. and W. Reitinger. 1992. 'Das mosaik der gymnischen Agone von Batten Zammour, Tunisien.' *Nikephoros* 5: 119–123.

Petzl, G. and E. Schwertheim. 2006. *Hadrian und die dionysischen Künstler. Drei in Alexandria Troas neugefundene Briefe des Kaisers an die Künstler*. Bonn.

Pleket, H. W. 1973. 'Some Aspects of the History of the Athletic Guilds.' *ZPE* 10: 197–227.

Pleket, H. W. 1975. 'Games, Prizes, Athletes and Ideology: Some Aspects of the History of Sport in the Greco-Roman World.' *Arena* 1 [= *Stadion* 1]: 49–89. Repr. in König 2010. 145–174.

Pleket, H. W. 2004. 'Einige Betrachtungen zum Thema "Geld und Sport".' *Nikephoros* 17: 77–89.

Price, S. R. F. 1984. *Rituals and Power: The Roman Imperial Cult in Asia Minor*. Cambridge.

Remijsen, S. 2011. 'The So-Called 'Crown Games': Terminology and Historical Context of the Ancient Categories for *Agones*.' *ZPE* 177: 97–109.

Remijsen, S. 2015. *The End of Greek Athletics in Late Antiquity*. Cambridge.

Ritti, T. 1985. *Hierapolis Scavi e Ricerche I. Fonti letterarie ed epigrafiche*. Archaeologica 53. Rome.

Ritti, T. 2017. *Storia e istituzioni di Hierapolis*. Hierapolis di Frigia IX. Istanbul.

Robert, L. 1970. 'Deux concours grecs à Rome.' *CRAI*: 6–27. English trans. in König 2010. 120–140.

Robert, L. 1977. 'La titulature de Nicée et de Nicomédia: la gloire e la haine.' *HSCP* 81: 1–39. Repr. in Robert, L. 1990. *Opera Minora Selecta* 7. 211–249.

Robert, L. 1984. 'Discours d'ouverture.' *Actes du VIIIe. Congrès international d'épigraphie grecque et latine à Athenes, 1982*. Athens. 35–45. English trans. in König 2010. 108–119.

Rogers, G. M. 1991 *The Sacred Identity of Ephesos: Foundation Myths of a Roman City*. London.

Roueché, C. 1993. *Performers and Partisans at Aphrodisias in the Roman and Late Roman Periods. JRS* Monograph 6. London.

Scanlon, T. F. 2002. *Eros and Greek Athletics*. New York.

Sinn, U., G. Ladstaetter, A. Martin, and U. Voelling. 1994. 'Bericht über das Forschungsprojekt "Olympia während der römischen Kaiserzeit und in der Spätantike" III: Die Arbeiten im Jahr 1994, mit Beiträgen von J. Ebert und M. Mathea-Förtsch.' *Nikephoros* 7: 229–250.

Slater, W. 2012. 'Stephanitic Orthodoxy?' *ZPE* 182: 168–178.

Slater, W. 2013. 'The Victor's Return and the Categories of Games.' In *Epigraphical Approaches to the Post-Classial Polis: Fourth Century BC to Second Century AD*. 139–163. P. Martzavou and N. Papazarkadas, eds. Oxford.

Spawforth, A. J. S. 1989. 'Agonistic Festivals in Roman Greece.' In *The Greek Renaissance in the Roman Empire. BICS* Supplement 55. 193–197. S. Walker and A. Cameron, eds. London.

Thuillier, J.-P. 1982. 'Le programme "Atlétique" des *Ludi Circenses* dans la Rome Republicaine.' *Rev. Ét. Lat.* 60: 105–122.

Van Nijf, O. 1999. 'Athletics, Festivals and Greek Identity in the Roman East.' *PCPhS* 45: 176–200. Repr. in König 2010. 175–197.

Van Nijf, O. 2001. 'Local Heroes: Athletics, Festivals and Elite Self-fashioning in the Roman East.' In *Being Greek Under Rome: Cultural Identity, the Second Sophistic and the Development of Empire*. 306–334. S. Goldhill, ed. Cambridge.

Van Voorhis, J. 2008. 'Two Portrait Statues of Boxers and the Culture of Athletics in the 3rd c. A.D.' In *Aphrodisias Papers* 4. JRA Supplement. 231–252. C. Ratte and R. R. R. Smith, eds. Ann Arbor.

Ziegler, R. 1985. *Städtisches Prestige und kaiserliche Politik: Studien zum Festwesen in Ostkilikien im 2. und 3. Jahrhundert n. Chr.* Düsseldorf.

Zuiderhoek, A. 2009. *The Politics of Munificence in the Roman Empire: Citizens, Elites and Benefactors in Asia Minor.* Cambridge.

CHAPTER 14

ROMAN GAMES AND SPECTACLE

Christian Identity and the Arena

DAVID POTTER

AT some point towards the end of the second or the beginning of the third century CE, one of the leading members of the Christian community at Carthage set himself the task of convincing his fellows that trips to the theatre, amphitheatre, and circus were bad for them. 'The condition of Faith, the reason of Truth,' so he wrote, 'that rule of discipline takes away the pleasures of the spectacles along with the errors of the time' (*On the Spectacles* 1.1). Not so, argued his opponents. God, they said, would not be offended if his people were happy, and asked if spectacles would be a feature of creation without his will. Tertullian, for he is the author in question, found his task complicated because nowhere in the body of text that Christians then regarded as authoritative was there explicit condemnation of athletics, chariot-racing, gladiatorial combat, or theatrical events. To make matters worse, there was a passage that Tertullian's opponents had evidently adduced in which St Paul compared his experience in the faith with that of an athlete (*On the Spectacles* 18.1):

> Do you not know that all the runners run in the *stadion* race, but that only one takes the prize? Therefore run so that you will take it. Everyone who contends (*agōnizomenos*) goes into training, but they do so that they will win an ephemeral crown, we do so to win one that is immortal. Therefore I do not run aimlessly nor do I box like one striking the air (1 Corinthians 9:24–26).

In refuting his opponents, Tertullian could do no better than to bring up a passage in Deuteronomy and launch into a generalized attack on all spectacles for being diametrically opposed to the Christian way of life (*On the Spectacles* 23.6; Jürgens 1972: 224; Sallmann 1990: 249). Christians were to live as a people apart, while attendance at any spectacle symbolized engagement with civic life. The history of the games (which Tertullian duly provides in splendid and largely fantastic form) was implicated in cult. The reality of current spectacles was that they were occasions for sacrifice and moved people to think of sex and violence. To urge on a gladiator was to be vicariously involved in murder, to appreciate the mimesis of the stage was to celebrate the violation of God's creation. In sum, spectacles should be avoided because they are idolatrous, contrary to the discipline of Christian life, and incompatible with God and Truth (Turcan 1986: 35–36).

We are unusually fortunate in the case of Tertullian to know other participants (or another participant) in the discussion at that time, for there could never, as the tenor of Tertullian's own discussion suggests, be a single Christian position on spectacle. Rather there was a continuum of behaviours and doctrines ranging from rabid fandom to absolute denunciation—divides within the Christian community that mirrored divisions in the pagan society of Tertullian's own time. Like educated members of the contemporary pagan community, Christian authors appear to have known the texts of plays that were part of the school tradition very well (Jürgens 1972: 5–146; Sallmann 1990: 246). Within a few years of the composition of *On the Spectacles*, the work in which Tertullian expressed the views adumbrated above, the emperor Septimius Severus would ban female gladiators in shows; a rowdy crowd at Rome had greeted an exhibition by female athletes with lewd suggestions offensive to distinguished women (Dio Cassius 75.16.1). Tertullian himself, in a work roughly contemporary with *On the Spectacles*, had suggested that the amphitheatre might even have a role to play in the expansion of the Christian community (*Apology* 50.13; Turcan 1986: 37–45). It was in the amphitheatre that Christians were put to death, and, as Tertullian would famously put it, 'the blood of Martyrs is seed', a view he evidently shared with no less a figure than Cornelius Tacitus. Tacitus seems to have thought that the Neronian persecution of 64 CE garnered sympathy for what he regarded as an 'execrable superstition' (*Annals* 15.44).

Neither Tacitus, now in the grave for perhaps three quarters of a century, nor Severus were the members of Tertullian's potential audience; Vibia Perpetua, a young woman of good standing, probably from the nearby city of Thuburbo Minus, could have been in that group (*The Passion of Perpetua and Felicitas* 3.1; Amat 1995: 55–66; Robert 1982; Turcan 1986: 45). At one point Tertullian allows that seeking revelations was an activity in which Christians might reasonably engage (*On the Spectacles* 29.3). In writing this, Tertullian identified himself as being in sympathy with a group of Christians who held the view that new revelation was an important aspect of their faith: Perpetua seems to have believed this with an intense passion. Something that Tertullian seems to have found annoying, again at roughly the same time, was a book telling the tale of a young woman by the name of Thecla, who supposedly became a Christian when she heard Paul preaching in what is now southern Turkey, and subsequently spurned her mother's attempts to arrange her marriage. We have no idea if there was ever a real Thecla, but the descriptions of her miraculous escapes from death, once by incineration at her home town of Iconium and a second time in Pisidian Antioch after offending a local agonothete, belong firmly in the realm of faith literature (Davis 2001: 6–8). What we do know is that the *Acts of Paul and Thecla* was written by a man who wished to justify women performing baptism. We know this much because Tertullian tells us so when he writes:

> But if certain *Acts of Paul*, which are falsely so named, claim the example of Thecla for allowing women to teach and to baptize, let men know that in Asia the presbyter who compiled that document, thinking to add of his own to Paul's reputation, was found out, and though he professed he had done it for love of Paul, he was deposed from his position. How could we believe that Paul should give a female power to teach and to baptize, when he did not allow a woman even to learn by her own right? (*Concerning Baptism* 17).

Although the fictionality of the *Acts* cannot be in doubt (as if the presence of man-eating seals in the theatre of Pisidian Antioch were not enough of a giveaway even without the improbable collection of miracles by which Thecla is saved from death), the setting is of great interest. For Thecla to prove that her faith was greater than her family obligation and that her faith would protect her from the perils of the world, she needed to appear in the amphitheatre and overcome the horror of a spectacular death. For Thecla, the legal system and its manifestation in an entertainment venue was the ultimate symbol of earthly authority, the ultimate focalizer of earthly power relationships. Seen from that perspective, how could a Christian stay away? The games were there as a test.

Perpetua seems to have felt that death in the arena was the path to salvation and that it was her task to guide her companions to their deaths, for that would seem to be the function of the dreams she reports in her prison diary. Just as her actual battle with her father defined her separation from social norms, her visionary pankration bout with an Egyptian symbolizes her victory over the Devil. At the same time it reveals a person who seems to have known a good deal about this form of all-out fighting. She knows that Egyptians are stellar pankratiasts—in her lifetime the greatest pankratiast of all was Marcus Aurelius Asclepiades from Hermopolis in Egypt—and she seems to have known many of the technical aspects of a pankration bout (Moretti 1953 n. 79; Robert 1982: 255–256). Women were not banned from athletic displays in North Africa, as far as we know, and it would certainly seem that Perpetua had seen some. Her depiction of her God as the spectacle officiant, the *munerarius*, seems to echo contemporary art of the arena, especially the famous second-century funerary relief housed in the Vatican that pictures an outsized *munerarius* who looms over a circus event in precisely the style of Perpetua's dream (*The Passion of Perpetua and Felicitas* 10.8). Her presentation of her last days, her self-conscious decision to die as she died, suggests that she might also have been a reader of the *Acts of Paul and Thecla*, whose career seems to track her own (Davis 2001: 28–29; Bremmer 1996: 43–44).

Well before Perpetua, the emergent ideology of martyrdom had drawn connections between contests athletic and spiritual that went well beyond Paul's statement and had even influenced Tertullian's prose in his own discussion of martyrdom. In the document known as the *First Letter of Clement*, probably a composition of the late first century CE, the author wrote that 'we will stop giving ancient examples, and we shall come to the athletes closest in time and we will consider the noble examples of our own time', giving Peter and Paul as examples of 'athletes' who had suffered for their faith, while the author of the letter concerning the Martyrs of Lyons had written how the use of a cross had 'given courage to those engaging in the contest (*agōnizomenois*)' (1 *Clement* 5.1; Eusebius, *The Church History* 5.1.41; Baumeister 1991: 43; 87–88). Tertullian himself wrote:

> You are about to undergo a good contest in which wherein the *agonothete* (president of the games) is the living God; the *xystarch* (official in charge of the gymnasium) is the Holy Spirit; the crown is eternity; the prize is of angelic being; the citizenship is in the heavens; the glory for ever and ever. Your trainer is Jesus Christ, who has anointed you with the spirit, and brought you into this wrestling-ground, and wished, before the day of the contest, to separate you from free living in harder training, so that your powers might be strengthened within you. For athletes are set apart for a stricter discipline, so that they will be free to build up their strength. They are kept from luxury, from the richer sorts of food, from more pleasant drink: they are driven, harassed, worn out: the harder they have worked in their training, the more hope they have for victory (*To the Martyrs* 3.3–4).

The points of contact with the real world of the games here suggest a more than passing familiarity with what went on in the athletic world than might be expected if one were to take the rhetoric of *On the Spectacles* at face value. Not only does Tertullian have the vocabulary right, but he is also familiar with the habit of athletes having themselves proclaimed citizens of different cities and the sorts of training regimes that are outlined in a work like Philostratus' *Gymnastics* (Bowersock 1995: 51; Potter 2011: 137–144).

Tertullian, the author of the *Acts of Paul and Thecla*, and Perpetua represent a wide range of attitudes towards spectacle coexisting within the early third-century Christian community. In the most negative view, Christians should stay away from events where sacrifice took place, where pagan gods were celebrated, where God's creation was held up to implicit ridicule, where sexual abstinence could be threatened by open exhibitions of sexuality or discourse on sexual themes, or where blood would be shed. On the more positive side, Christians should see themselves as athletes contending for their faith; and spectacles were splendid places to display devotion that might inspire other Christians and attract the sympathy of non-Christians. The games might even be a location where people could put their purity of spirit to the test.

SPECTACLE IN THE CHRISTIAN EMPIRE

There were major changes in the entertainment system between the time of Tertullian and the reign of Constantine (306–337) when the representatives of the Church were confronted with the possibility that their coreligionists might have to run games and that they counted an increasing number of participants as members of their communities. The two most important changes were the decline in the importance of independent athletic festivals and the increasing dominance of circus chariot-racing.

The rise in the importance of circus factions followed upon the creation of multiple imperial capitals and the perceived need for palaces to be joined to circuses as the fourth century dawned. Circuses became the primary venue for interactions between emperors and their subjects in these new capitals, and greater familiarity with circus chariot racing created a market for these events outside the ambit of imperial cities.

One thing that was not a major factor in the decline of traditional spectacle was the conversion of the Roman government to Christianity. Indeed, it is notable that there is a very little difference in the way that Christians complain about spectacles in the centuries after Constantine, a fact which suggests, in and of itself, that not much had changed. Thus Arnobius, writing in the early fourth century, described the amphitheatre as a place of blood and public impiety (*Against the Pagans* 2.41), and the North African author of another work *On Spectacles* (probably the rigorist Novatian who was a thorn in the side of Cyprian in the 250s) repeated many of Tertullian's resolutely anti-spectacle arguments. And, as the fourth century turned into the fifth, an eastern theologian, Jacob of Serugh, complained that a pantomime artist 'meditates on the stories of the gods. Who can bathe in the mud without being soiled' (Moss 1935: 109). A century later, bishop Severus of Antioch grumbled that when crowds in the circus shouted 'Fortune of the City give victory', they were invoking a pagan divinity, and that the city's Olympic games, which had outlived the original Olympic games in Greece, were a feature of pagan worship (Brière and Graffin (1974): 544–557.

Even as Christians continued to complain about traditional spectacles, there are many signs that most Christians were changing from rejectionist ideology to accomodationist behaviours (Sallmann 1990: 249–250). The most significant early evidence for this change is provided by the acts of the Council of Elvira in the first decade of the fourth century and those of Arles in 314, both with respect to men who have held official positions (including local priesthoods of the Imperial Cult) and performers. At Elvira the second canon stated that a man who held a priesthood and offered sacrifice after he had received communion might double his offence if subsequently involved in murder (*eo quod geminaverint scelera accidente homicidio*) and treble it if 'immorality' were additionally involved (*vel triplicaverint scelera, cohaerente moechia*); such a man was not to be allowed communion (*Acts of the Council of Elvira* 2 Jonkers). The use of ablatives in the Latin implies that the additional sins took place in the immediate context of the priesthood, during the games required of this official; it is thus perhaps not unreasonable to think that the 'murder' involved would be a death in the amphitheatre (sponsors of games had a choice whether to include executions and determined whether gladiatorial combats must be to the death) and that the additional 'immorality' might be a stage show that could be regarded as lewd, or a sexualized punishment like that inflicted in the arena by Lucius in his beast form in the *Ass* and the *Golden Ass*. Elvira's third canon treats men who held priesthoods but abstained from sacrifice, saying that for 'those priests who only hold games, in so far as they kept themselves from murderous sacrifices, it is decided that they may take communion after performing a suitable penance' (*Acts of the Council of Elvira* 3 Jonkers). In the *Acts of the Council of Arles* it is stated that charioteers who are Christian shall be barred from communion so long as they are driving and that actors too will be barred from communion so long as they are active (*Acts of the Council of Arles* 4–5 Jonkers). As for Christians on government service, it was decided that they should request episcopal letters of communion (certificates from their home bishop stating that they are in good standing) to show to the bishop of their assigned residence, with the proviso that they obey the local bishop and will be excluded from communion if they 'act against the discipline' (*Acts of the Council of Arles* 6 Jonkers). No one, presumably, thought that this would apply to the world's most important convert who wrote to the bishops with a crucially important statement of his faith.

The legislative record of Constantine's reign, as known through the *Theodosian Code*, is strikingly spare with respect to public entertainments. In a rescript to the *vicarius* of Africa in 315, Constantine wrote that people who were condemned (*damnati*) *ad ludum* should be sent to the amphitheatre as soon as possible so that they would not learn how to fight before they appeared there; in 325, however, faced with the general disuse of the penalty in the East, he wrote to the *vicarius* of the Diocese of the East ordering that people who might previously have been sentenced *ad ludum* should be sent to the mines instead (*Theodosian Code* 9.18.1: 15.12.1; Potter 2010: 601–604). This particular rescript went on to have an interesting history, being misquoted (or misconstrued) by Eusebius as a ban on gladiatorial combat and, later, edited down by the compilers of *The Code of Justinian* to make it into such a ban, presumably because they could not find any actual such ban on the books and because, by the mid-sixth century, gladiatorial combat had genuinely ceased to be a public entertainment (Eusebius, *Life of Constantine* 2.45.1; *Code of Justinian* 11.44). As far as the reign of Constantine goes, perhaps the most telling pieces of evidence are that Maximus, the official who received the rescript of 325, was praetorian prefect of the eastern provinces in 328 when a relative of Libanius put on gladiatorial games at the administrative capital of Antioch, and that, in Constantine's letter to Hispellum from the last year of his life, gladiatorial games are explicitly allowed even while blood sacrifice is deprecated (Libanius *Life* 5; Ville

1960: 299–301; Potter 2010: 598–599). Indeed there is ample evidence, though more from the West than the East, for the continuation of gladiatorial games: complaints are made about gladiators fighting around the time of the Saturnalia well into the fourth century, and there is the extensive correspondence of Symmachus on the subject of his son's aedilician games (Ausonius, *Book of Eclogues* 16.33–36; Ville 1960: 278–285, 298–299; Symmachus, *Letters* 2.47; 76; 77; 5. 20; 22; 46; 59; 62; 7.76; 9.117; 119; 120). Augustine famously visited the amphitheatre with his friend Alypius in 385; he elsewhere states he had 'gone mad' at gladiatorial exhibitions in his youth (Augustine, *Confessions* 6.8; *Expositions on the Psalms* 147.7; O'Donnell 1992: 365). The editors of the *Theodosian Code* treat gladiatorial games as events that need to be regulated (although references are far less frequent than those linked with the circus and theatres), which should mean that some gladiatorial exhibitions were continuing in the fifth century, but the sixth-century rewriting of Constantine's 325 rescript on *damnati ad ludum* to make it the abolition of gladiatorial combat suggests that gladiatorial exhibitions had largely ceased by that point (Potter 2010: 604). What seems to have continued a good deal longer, however, was the custom of executing humans by exposing them to the beasts or public incineration, and it is this practice that shows how little the tradition of martyrdom influenced the policy of Christian emperors, for those had been by far the most common fates for Christian victims of persecution. There is no distinction between Christian and non-Christian in the penal practices of the late empire, suggesting that Christian officials were minimally, if at all, bothered by doing unto fellow Christians what pagans had once done—and there was no insistence on the part of Church authorities that this was a bad thing.

The situation with athletic events is somewhat more complex. The decline stemmed from multiple causes. Some of these were financial, others were connected with changing tastes. On the financial side, important factors were the evaporation of endowments supporting many local festivals and the fact that pensions for successful athletes became increasingly burdensome for cities (Camia 2011: 74–75; Remijsen 2015: 305–308). The large-scale circuit of games, which linked competitions in smaller cities to those at major cities like Ephesus and Antioch or with the great festivals at Olympia and Delphi, largely collapsed by the middle of the fourth century, leaving only a few of the bigger contests in action (Remijsen 2015: 303–304; 311–312). Other reasons for the decline were connected with changes in audience preferences, with the result that people who might have founded new games in the second century might instead choose, in the third century, to fund gladiatorial combats (Nollé 1992/3; Remijsen 2015: 335–336). What there was not, was a single act of state that brought things to an end. Indeed, the tradition that the Roman state ordered an end to the Olympics is every bit as tendentious as the tradition that the games began in 776 BCE (Potter 2011: 40–44). George Cedrenus, writing in the eleventh century, asserted that Theodosius I ended the games in 393 CE; scholiastic notes on Lucian's *Teacher of Rhetoric* state that the games continued 'from the time of the Hebrew Judges' (one note helpfully specifies the ninth year of the judge Jair) 'until that of Theodosius the Younger' (Scholiast on Lucian, *Teacher of Rhetoric* 9). From these texts we may safely conclude that, in the view of the Byzantine chronicle tradition, the games were ended under the Theodosian dynasty. Evidence from the *Theodosian Code* and Olympia itself will simply suggest that a date in the fifth century is probably correct: the latest list of victors seems to date to the late fourth century, and at some point in the early fifth century a church was built over the workshop of Phidias (Remijsen 2015: 38–51). A rescript of 399 (albeit in the West) appears to have taken by the compilers of the *Code* as a legal mandate, as there is no subsequent correction of the point, which is as follows:

> Just as we have already abolished profane rites by a salutary law, so we do not allow the festal assemblies of citizens and the common pleasure of all to be abolished. Hence we decree that, according to ancient custom, amusements be furnished to the people, but without any sacrifice or any accursed superstition, and they shall be allowed to attend festal banquets, whenever public desires so demand (*Theodosian Code* 16.10.17).

It was the purpose of the imperial government to ensure the pleasure of its subjects, and that meant that old events should continue (Blänsdorf 1990: 262–263). On this view, Christianity should coexist with spectacle and that seems to have been the case at Olympia and Delphi where Christian buildings supplemented rather than replaced the old temples: the Temple of Zeus was untouched and included within a late defensive wall (Brown 2006). In 424, a rescript to Isidorus, the prefect of Illyricum, granted fiscal relief to the local councils compelled to make financial contributions to entertainments at Constantinople, a concession apparently connected with the continuing need of the Delphians to fund the Pythian games (*Theodosian Code* 15.5.4).

The obscurity surrounding the end of gladiatorial combat and traditional festivals stems from decline due to lack of money and/or interest. At the same time, other events were coming into being, attracting greater or lesser attention depending upon the enthusiasm they aroused. One such event was singing rope dancing, known from a papyrus programme for chariot-races at Oxyrhynchus (*Oxyrhynchus Papyri* 2707). Another seems to be a particularly violent combat sport known as *pammachon*; Hesychius says that it was 'an unsophisticated sport practiced outside the *palaestra*, since the people of Cyprus wrestle untechnically' (Hesychius, s.v. *Kypria pale*). Our best evidence for the sport, however, now comes from Egypt in a letter written by a practitioner who probably performed for Diocletian when he visited Alexandria in 300 CE. The author, who is writing to his sister, says:

> Above all I pray to [the lord] god that you are doing well and also that the best things in life may be yours. ...
> We are glad to be here. I will tell you everything that has happened to me in Alexandria. So when I arrived here, we didn't find the person who we came looking for (but) we did find our lord the emperor visiting. He ordered that athletes be brought from the Campus and, fortunately, I and the other five were selected, without the other athletes knowing. When I arrived there, I was at first paired up to do pankration and I had bad luck, as I do not know how to do pankration. So I was performing [poorly] for a long time [...] falling. The god was about to [...] I challenged the five to do *pammachon*. The emperor wanted to know whether I was [immediately] summoned to do it one man after the other. When I saw that [those who fell] were collecting dung from the contest, I challenged then to *pammachon*.
> The prize for us was a linen tunic and a hundred coins. The [linen tunic] is inexpensive and I received [...] and I made [...] debtors and I got a gold coin with the money, and the other five the tunic. This happened on the 2(?) of Choaik. And on the 26th of the same month he held a festival in the Lageion and we performed there. And I got a silver prize, a sleeveless tunic, and the money.
> ... Take care of your sister. God willing, we will come to meet you after Mecheir, making you happy. Your [...] sends you many greetings. I greet my father and all who love my soul (SB 3.6222; Remijsen 2010).

In general terms the spread of *pammachon* fits with a pattern in ancient entertainment as a whole in which there was constant pressure from audiences for things that were new and more extreme (Potter 2011: xxix). Extreme would also seem to be the word to describe another form of entertainment that spread outwards from Syria in the fourth and fifth century: a form of aquatic entertainment known as *maiouma*. It seems plausible that performances of *maiouma* could take a variety of forms; some, to judge from the surviving *maiouma* facility in Aphrodisias, in rather tight quarters (Roueché 1989 nos. 38–40). The *Theodosian Code* preserves memoranda to the praetorian prefects Caesarius and Aurelian in 396 and 399 respectively, the first restoring *maiouma* so long as decency was preserved and the second ordering that the 'foul and indecent' spectacle which 'frivolous eloquence' called *maiouma* should stop (*Theodosian Code* 15.6.1–2). This cannot be said to be a specifically Christian objection since the first person we know of who objected to the frivolity (in this case banquets) associated with *maiouma* at Antioch was the anti-Christian emperor Julian; nor can we be certain if some or all *maiouma* was connected with the nude water ballet that John Chrysostom deplored (Julian, *The Beard-Hater* 362d; John Chrysostom, *Homilies on Matthew* 7.6). The last attested performance of *maiouma* took place at Constantinople in 777 CE in the context of some sort of triumphal celebration (Theophanes 452; Mango and Scott 1997: 623).

Issues of Christian identity in these cases seem far less significant than simple issues of status, taste, and the fact that a great deal of money was involved. That actresses in Constantinople could be very wealthy is suggested by a ruling of Theodosius I in 393 stating that while they might wear gems, they should not wear silk adorned with images or gilded textiles and they should avoid purple dyed garments altogether although they are allowed to wear checkered or multi-coloured silks and gold without gems on their necks, arms, and girdles (*Theodosian Code* 15.7.11). John Chrysostom complained that members of his congregation spent money on clothes as elaborate as those of people of the stage, showing that the phenomenon was not limited to the capital. Indeed, a leading mime actress at Antioch in the early fourth century is said to have been fabulously wealthy, something that made her conversion to Christianity a major coup (Layerle 2001: 34–35; Reich 1903: 103).

While some members of the clergy vociferously reproached all activities in the theatre, there were others who took a less extreme approach. Both John Chrysostom and Gregory Nazianzen assert (accusingly) that rival ecclesiastics appeared on the stage. More significantly, there is some evidence for a bishop named Nonnus putting on a mime to explain Christian doctrine (Reich 1903: 104–108). Elsewhere we are told of mimes associated with the great persecutions in which pagans made fun of Christian rites (Reich 1903: 95–99), but we may also be entitled to wonder what might have inspired such narratives in fictional martyrologies when, in 394, Theodosius wrote that:

> We add to the foregoing [an order that pictures of actors and charioteers not be placed in public porticoes] that female mimes who make a living through the wantonness of their bodies should not appear in public in the dress of those women who are dedicated to God (*Theodosian Code* 15.7.12; see also Blänsdorf 1990: 267–268; Jürgens 1972: 205–208).

In dealing with matters of the theatre, it is perhaps best to admit that the theatrical arts had an ambivalent place in Christian identity, with some continuing to hold a line with which

Tertullian would have been sympathetic, and others staking out a position that Tertullian's rivals might have found congenial.

The realm of public spectacle where Christian identity was most strongly felt was in the circus, where were found the increasingly powerful chariot factions that transformed ancient entertainment. The starting point for this process may have been the establishment of imperial capitals at Nicomedia and Constantinople in the early fourth century. We know almost nothing about Nicomedia save that its development took place under Diocletian and the fact that there was a circus there (Lactantius, *Deaths of the Persecutors* 7.9). In the case of Constantinople, the arrival of circus factions must have been roughly contemporaneous with the construction of Constantine's new imperial palace and the completion of its attendant circus, while legislation of the late 320s set out the rules for financing the games, which, though directed to Rome, would also shape the development of state-financed chariot-racing at Constantinople (*Theodosian Code*, 6.4.1–2). By 426 there was a treasury official in charge of festivals and horses at Constantinople, and in 465 the presidency of major provincial games was transferred to imperial officials (*Theodosian Code* 6.4.6; Gascou 1976). In 381, a fine of a pound of gold is imposed upon people who seem to have been taking racehorses from the circus. It is unfortunate that we do not know the precise context for the statement that 'Your illustrious authority knows that no punishment shall be inflicted upon those who perform the service of driving chariots on account of a circus race' (*Theodosian Code* 15.7.7), but it suggests rather high-level intervention in a local scandal.

Whatever led to the exemption from punishment for actions on the track, the protection did not exclude charioteers from punishment for egregiously poor behaviour outside the circus. At least one charioteer had been caught up in a series of scandals connected with the upper classes at Rome in the 370s; the behaviour of another sparked riots that broke out in Thessalonica in 390 when an extremely senior official had him imprisoned for making what he regarded as illicit advances to a member of the imperial guard. The official himself was killed in the subsequent riot in the circus, to be later avenged by an angry Theodosius I who caused an empire-wide scandal by sending in a powerful military force to slaughter the inhabitants of the city (Potter 2004: 567–569). At Antioch, however, the fabled charioteer Porphyrius encouraged circus fans to violence against the local Jewish population on 9 July 507, after his victories in the circus, but seems to have evaded punishment, possibly because he was acting as a representative of the emperor; he went on to greater fame at Constantinople (Malalas 396; Cameron 1973: 123–124; Rouеché 1993: 147–152). The connection between Antioch and Constantinople also plays a significant role in the life of Theodora, the future empress, who went to Antioch with the child she had in the course of a failed relationship with an imperial official named Hecebolus. Here she met Macedonia, a dancer with the Blue Faction and also, apparently, an agent for Justinian, then the heir apparent; through Macedonia, Theodora was introduced to Justinian (Procopius, *Secret History* 12.29–30; Potter 2015: 80–82).

The increased political role of the circus factions followed upon the growth of their financial and institutional complexity; their growth into empire-wide organizations was connected with a number of the most important developments in fifth-century public life. The trends included the strengthening of ecclesiastical factions during the Christological controversies of the fifth century, the devolution of independent civic *curiae* into more restricted councils of imperially connected functionaries, and the evolution of public ceremonials in which public demonstrations through acclamation were instituted as regular features of government (Whitby 1997). Linked with these developments appears to have been an increasing incidence of violence in general, as communities defined themselves, in part, through their ability to abuse their rivals, as an outgrowth of their organization for government tasks (Liebeschuetz 2001: 276–283). Faction violence in the circus parallels violent demonstrations resulting in pogroms against non-Christian communities, as it does the occasional vandalism of public monuments, such as the desecration of pagan statues in public areas of cities or the mass castration of statues in bath houses. A striking example of this appears in the seventh-century text *The Teaching of Jacob the Recently Baptized*; here both Jacob and his interlocutor place his youthful career as a faction thug in an explicitly religious context, often referencing tensions between Jews and Christians that fired political volatility. The actions cited took place in 602/3, when Phocas, a vehement supporter of the Blues, seized power from the emperor in Constantinople, and in 609/10 at Antioch when Phocas' general, Bonosus, was trying to rally resistance against the forces of Heraclius, advancing from Africa in a counter-coup. The author, writing here in his own voice says:

> Jacob was a man of Oriens [the Eastern Empire] by birth. He did many bad things to the Christians, and when in Rhodes as a Green with the sail-makers, he did evil to the Blues who were fleeing from Oriens, and he delivered them to the sail-makers as supporters of Bonosus and they were badly beaten (*The Teaching of Jacob* 5.30).

Speaking in his own right about his youth, Jacob says:

> being misled by the Devil, brothers, and hating Christ and not wishing to heed the prophecies concerning him, I did evil to the Christians. When Phocas was ruling in Constantinople, I delivered the Christians to the Blues, pretending that they were Greens, calling them Jews and *manzirs* (bastards). Then when the Greens under Crosius burnt the Mese and had a bad time, again as a Blue, I brutalized the Christians, assailing the Greens, calling them incendiaries and Manicheans. When Bonosus massacred the Greens at Antioch, I was at Antioch, and, as a Blue and partisan of the emperor, I beat the Christians well, calling them Greens and traitors. In Constantinople, when the Greens dragged the body of Bonosus, I aided them with all my heart because he was a Christian. Thinking to serve God, I abused the Christians as if I were a Pagan (*The Teaching of Jacob* 1.40).

Jacob appears to be using the language of acclamation so familiar to the circus crowd, as the faction claque chanted in unison to declare their will and incite each other to action (Cameron 1976: 150–152; Dagron and Déroche 1991). The text specifically echoes the circus chants preserved from narratives of the Nika revolt in 532, as for instance in the following exchange:

GREENS: Whoever he is, he will share the fate of Judas. God will speedily exact a penalty from my oppressor.
HERALD: You have not come here to watch, but only to insult your rulers.
GREENS: Surely anyone who wrongs me will share the fate of Judas.
HERALD: Silence, you Jews, Manichaeans, Samaritans!
GREENS: Do you call us Jews and Samaritans? May the Mother of God be with everyone.
HERALD: How long are you going to curse yourselves?
GREENS: If anyone denies that our lord is orthodox, let him be anathema, like Judas.
HERALD: I am telling you: Get baptized in One [God].
    The Greens shouted above each other, and chanted, as Antlas demanded, [Antlas is probably the speaker for the Greens], 'I am baptized in One [God].'

HERALD: Surely, if you do not keep quiet, I shall behead you (Theophanes, *Chronicle* 182).

Seating at entertainments had always been an important feature of spectacle, with trade and religious groups seeking to sit together, and, as the account of Jacob's life suggests, choosing as a group which faction they might follow in the case of the circus. In the years after Theodosius II changed the seating arrangement in the circus at Constantinople so that he could face his favourite Greens, it appears that sense of community and group identity was enhanced, and as imperial patronage of one faction or another became more pronounced, fandom became an inherently political act (Malalas 351.5–352.7; Whitby 1997: 237–238). In this way the principal venue for spectacle remained a central ingredient in the structuring of a community within a city. It was not required, as the language of Jacob makes clear, that one be a Christian to be a fan, but the vast majority of people who went to the circus in the fifth through seventh centuries were. It was in the circus that Christians could define themselves against their opponents—Christian or otherwise.

REFERENCES

Amat, J. 1996. *Passion de Perpétue et de Félicité suivi des Actes*. Paris.

Barnes, T. D. 2010. *Early Christian Hagiography and Roman History*. Tübingen.

Baumeister, T. 1991. *Genese und Entfaltung der altkirchlichen Theologie des Martyriums*. Berlin.

Blänsdorf, J. 1990. 'Die spätantike Staat und die Schauspiele im Codex Theodosianus.' In *Theater und Gesellschaft im Imperium Romanum*. 261–274. J. Blansdörf, ed. Tübingen.

Bowersock, G. W. 1995. *Martyrdom and Rome*. Cambridge.

Bremmer, J. N. 1996. *The Apocryphal Acts of Paul and Thecla*. Kampen.

Brière, M. and Graffin, F. 1974. *Les Homélies cathédrales de Sévère d'Antioche. Homilies XXVI-XXXI. PO* 36.4. Turnhout.

Brown, A. R. 2006. 'Hellenic Heritage and Christian Challenge: Conflict over Panhellenic Sanctuaries in Late Antiquity.' In *Violence in Late Antiquity: Perceptions and Practices*. 309–319. H. A. Drake, ed. Aldershot.

Cameron, A. 1973. *Porphyrius the Charioteer*. Oxford.

Cameron, A. 1976. *Circus Factions: Blues and Greens at Rome and Byzantium*. Oxford.

Camia, F. 2011. 'Spending on the Agones. The Financing of Festivals in the Cities of Roman Greece.' *Tyche* 26: 41–76.

Dagron, G. and V. Déroche. 1991. 'Juifs et chrétiens dans L'Orient du VIIe siècle.' *T&MByz* 11: 17–273.

Davis, S. J. 2001. *The Cult of Saint Thecla: A Tradition of Women's Piety in Late Antiquity*. Oxford.

Gascou, J. 1976. 'Les institutions de l'hippodrome en Égypte Byzantine.' *BIAO* 76: 185–212.

Jonkers, E. J. 1954. *Acta et Symbola Conciliorum quae saeculo quarta habita sunt*. Leiden.

Jürgens, H. 1972. *Pompa diaboli: die lateinischen Kirchenväter und das antike Theater*. Stuttgart.

Layerle, B. 2001. *Theatrical Shows and Ascetic Lives: John Chrysostom's Attack on Spiritual Marriage*. Berkeley.

Liebeschuetz, J. H. W. G. 2001. *The Decline and Fall of the Roman City*. Oxford.

Mango, C. and R. Scott. 1997. *The Chronicle of Theophanes Confessor: Byzantine and Near Eastern History, AD 284–813*. Oxford.

Moretti, L. 1953. *Iscrizioni agonistiche greche*. Rome.

Moss, C. 1935. 'Jacob of Serugh's Homilies on the Spectacles of the Theatre.' *Mouseion* 48: 87–112.

Nollé, J. 1992/3. 'Kaiserliche Privelegien für Gladiatorenmunera und Tierhetzen Unbekannte und ungedeutet Zeugnisse auf städitschen Münzen des grieschischen Ostens.' *JNG* 42.3: 49–82.

O'Donnell, J. J. 1992. *Augustine: Confessions.* Oxford.

Potter, D. 2004. *The Roman Empire at Bay AD 180–395.* London.

Potter, D. 2010. 'Constantine and the Gladiators.' *CQ* 60: 596–606.

Potter, D. 2011. *The Victor's Crown: Ancient Sport from Homer to Byzantium.* London.

Potter, D. 2015. *Theodora: Actress, Empress, Saint.* New York.

Reich, H. 1903. *Der Mimus: ein litterar-entwicklungsgeschichtlicher Versuch.* Berlin.

Remijsen, S. 2010. 'Pammachon: A New Sport.' *BASP* 47: 185–204.

Remijsen, S. 2015. *The End of Greek Athletics in Late Antiquity.* Cambridge.

Robert, L. 1982. 'Une Vision de Pérpetue Martyre.' *CRAI*: 228–276.

Roueché, C. 1989. *Aphrodisias in Late Antiquity.* London.

Roueché, C. 1993. *Performers and Partisans at Aphrodisias in the Roman and Late Roman Period.* London.

Sallmann, K. 1990. 'Christen vor der Theater.' In *Theater und Gesellschaft im Imperium Romanum.* 243–259. J. Blänsdorf, ed. Tübingen.

Turcan, M. 1986. *Tertullien: Les spectacles.* Paris.

Ville, G. 1960. 'Les jeux de gladiateurs dans l'empire chrétien.' *MEFRA* 72: 273–335.

Whitby, M. 1997. 'The Violence of the Circus Factions.' In *Organized Crime in Antiquity.* 229–253. K. Hopwood, ed. London.

CHAPTER 15

··

THE DECLINE AND
FALL OF SPECTACLE

··

PAUL MILLIMAN

THE decline and fall of Roman spectacle in many ways mirrored the decline and fall of the Roman empire itself. In other words, while it did decline, it did not so much fall as transform into something else. Just as Rome cast a long shadow over the Middle Ages and early modern era in many parts of the former empire and beyond, so too were vestiges of Roman spectacle preserved and transformed in the Latin, Byzantine, and Islamic successor states of the Roman empire. In addition, scholars in the last few decades have challenged traditional assumptions regarding Christianity's central role in the decline and fall of Roman spectacle as well as the view that the end of some spectacles can be precisely dated using imperial decrees. Our understanding of when and why certain spectacles ceased to exist has been complicated by the discovery and publication of new sources as well as more nuanced readings of existing sources (Potter 2011; Potter 2010; Wiedemann 1992: 128–164; Roueché 2007; Roueché 1993; Hen 1995: 216–231; Dugast 2007; Lim 2009; Lim 1999; Lim 1997; Retzleff 2003; Webb 2008).

Religious, political, and economic factors as well as changes in the tastes of elites all contributed to the transformation of Roman spectacle. In particular a new relationship between public and private spectacle in the Middle Ages led to the exclusion of the masses from most medieval spectacles. Like the citizens of the Roman empire who participated in spectacles to enact a variety of identities, including their *Romanitas*, the sponsors of spectacles in the Middle Ages also used games to link themselves to their particular visions of a glorious past—Roman or otherwise—as well as to present concerns, both sacred and secular. These same concerns also preoccupied political leaders in the early modern era. But, whereas medieval nobles performed spectacles almost entirely for themselves alone, early modern rulers reincorporated the public into at least some parts of their spectacles so that their subjects could bear witness to their magnificence. Therefore, what follows is an analysis of the decline and fall of most forms of Roman spectacle in Late Antiquity, as the empire contracted in some places and collapsed in others; an exploration of the evolution and development of various other spectacles—especially equestrian games like tournaments, hunting, and *palii*—in Rome's medieval and early modern Latin, Byzantine, and Islamic successor societies, which shared many of the characteristics of ancient spectacle in terms of function if not necessarily form; and also an examination of the privatization of public spectacle and sites of spectacle in the Middle Ages and the enduring impact of the images of Roman spectacle—especially those associated with the hippodrome in Constantinople—as expressions of political power in medieval and early modern Europe.

THE DECLINE OF SPECTACLE IN THE WEST IN LATE ANTIQUITY

As other chapters in this handbook have demonstrated, spectacle was extremely expensive and its continued existence relied on wealthy and competitive patrons who sought glory and power through their sponsorship of events that would be attended by thousands of spectators. Such aspirations eventually disappeared in the former western empire, where changing views of nobility evolved among both the old Roman aristocrats and their new Germanic overlords. In the early sixth century, Cassiodorus—speaking for Theoderic, the Ostrogothic king of Italy and a great admirer of *Romanitas*—claimed that spectacles were intended solely for popular consumption and were beneath the dignity of elites. But spectacles were very soon to become the exclusive purview—as patrons, participants, and spectators—of the nobility of medieval Europe:

> We are compelled to support this institution by the necessity of humouring the majority of the people, who are passionately fond of it; for it is always the few who are led by reason, while the many crave excitement and oblivion of their cares. Therefore, as we too must sometimes share the folly of our people, we will freely provide for the expenses of the Circus, however little our judgment approves of this institution (*Letters* 3.51; Hodgkin 1886: 229).

In fact, Theoderic's nearly six-decade-long reign as Ostrogothic king—a period in which the last western emperor was deposed by Theoderic's predecessor as king of Italy, Odovacar, in 476—marks a transitional period in which some of the elites of the new Germanic-Roman world of Western Europe still saw it as their duty to provide public spectacles. As we learn from many of Cassiodorus' letters, as well as from other contemporary sources, spectacles were still viewed as an integral part of public life in the Italian peninsula during Theoderic's reign (Ward-Perkins 1984: 105–107). Later in the sixth century this Germanic-Roman synthesis gave way to a more fragmented political and economic landscape in which local elites—both Roman and Germanic—became less interested in investing their more limited resources in demonstrating their *Romanitas* through extravagant spectacles.

In fact, it was the Roman emperor Justinian who put an end to spectacles in the city of Rome through his attempts to reassert Roman authority in Italy. Justinian's wars devastated the Italian peninsula and eventually destroyed the very institution which had produced the spectacles of Rome—the senate and its *cursus honorum* (Lim 1999: 281). In the late fourth and early fifth centuries it seems that senators were already for the most part celebrating the commencement of praetorships and quaestorships far less frequently and far more frugally, although some—most famously Symmachus in 393 and 401—did still spend lavishly on quaestorian and praetorian games (Jennison 1937: 94–97; Ward-Perkins 1984: 98–101; Lim 1999: 278). At the turn of the sixth century, however, incoming consuls were still expected to provide suitable spectacles, and apparently did so quite willingly according to both literary and material evidence; but by the century's end, these positions had ceased being even honorific ones, as the Roman Senate itself ceased to function (Ward-Perkins 1984: 101–103; Olovsdotter 2005). Increasing the irony of the end of Roman spectacle in the former capital of the empire, the last recorded circus games in the city of Rome were given by the very barbarian that Justinian was trying to remove from power—Totila. According to Procopius, Totila used this spectacle to celebrate his recapture of Rome from the forces of Justinian, the same ruler who Procopius claims ended spectacles throughout the empire because he was too cheap to pay for them, which was for Procopius another example of Justinian's depravity and lack of interest in the well-being of his subjects (Dewing 1928: 12–13; Dewing 1935: 304–305; Ward Perkins 1984: 106).

Before turning to the provinces in Western Europe, it is worthwhile to examine the decline and fall of spectacle in the other part of the former western empire, North Africa; again relying on Procopius' account of Justinian's wars, the discontinuation of the games here was not a direct result of the Vandal invasions. Indeed, the Vandals allegedly appreciated some aspects of *Romanitas*, at least the parts that would appeal most to the basest motives of barbarians. This included spectacles:

> For of all the nations which we know, that of the Vandals is the most luxurious. ... For the Vandals, since the time when they gained possession of Libya, used to indulge in baths, all of them, every day, and enjoyed a table abounding in all things, the sweetest and best that the earth and sea produce. And they... passed their time ... in theatres and hippodromes and in other pleasurable pursuits (Dewing 1916: 257).

However, in contrast to the Ostrogothic king Theoderic, who seems to have looked to spectacles as a way to achieve a *modus vivendi* between his Arian Germanic and orthodox Roman subjects, it is likely that the Arian Vandal rulers had no such aspirations, based on the 'rough tolerance' they showed to their orthodox Roman subjects (Merrills and Miles 2010: 192–196).

Despite the social upheaval generated by the Germanic conquests and Byzantine reconquests along the Mediterranean littoral, political and economic transformations were already well under way throughout the current and former empire. In addition to the withdrawal of elites from the position of patrons of public games, we can also see the intrusion of private activities into formerly public spaces. Theatres, amphitheatres, and circuses were turned into residences or places of business or used as raw material for other building projects. It appears that by the fifth century, only a few of these buildings in North Africa continued to function as sites of spectacle, and by the turn of the seventh century, on the eve of the Muslim conquests and not as a result of them, these venues of spectacle had ceased to function even in important cities like Carthage (Leone 2007: 136–140). These changes took place throughout the former western empire, even in the city of Rome itself, where medieval and early modern inhabitants of the city found new uses for the former sites of spectacle (Mahler 2012; Karmon 2011).

The repurposing of parts of sites of spectacle or the removal of some materials to build new buildings is not necessarily, however, an indication that the original functions of these buildings were completely abandoned at that time (Klingshirn 1994: 175–176); and, in fact, parts of some large venues were converted into smaller sites of spectacle as they hosted less spectacular events for fewer spectators (Roueché 2007: 60). Archeological and documentary evidence can help to provide insights into when, where, and how spectacles continued into Late Antiquity, but this evidence is less useful in determining precisely when, where, and why those spectacles ceased. An *argumentum ex silentio* is always fraught with difficulties, but evidence for the continuation of spectacle also presents its own problems. In Late Antiquity different secular and ecclesiastical magnates used the idea of spectacle to advance their own political, social, and religious agendas, just as earlier emperors and senators had sponsored spectacles for their own purposes.

For example, one could conclude that in mid-fifth-century Gaul spectacles were still prevalent enough to be viewed as a threat to Christian morality, because Salvian dedicated the entire sixth book of his *On the Government of God* to 'the ruinous influence of circuses and spectacles' (Sanford 1930: 157). However, not much of this book actually concerns spectacles per se. In fact, the main argument Salvian makes is that those in Gaul still wanted spectacles, but the barbarian conquests and economic decline of the empire meant that they could not have them. Although the decline of spectacles pleases Salvian, he wishes it were due to the good intentions of Roman Christians rather than to circumstances beyond their control. In fact, he uses the idea of spectacles 'to return again to [his] oft-repeated contention' that this was just another example of how the Roman Christians behave worse than barbarians, because barbarians do not have circuses and theatres in their lands (Sanford 1930: 168).

The next century presents even more problematical evidence. Procopius claims that in 549 Arles' circus was still functioning; based on the archeological evidence, this does appear possible, but only just, as the circus was raided for building materials from the middle of the sixth century on (Hen 1995: 220–221). While Arles—located on the Mediterranean and the principal city in Gaul in Late Antiquity—had a long history of spectacle, making Procopius' statement plausible, it is difficult to believe Gregory of Tours' claim that Chilperic—grandson of Clovis, the first king of the Franks to convert to orthodox Christianity—tried to introduce Roman spectacle into northern France by ordering circuses to be built in Paris and Soissons in the 570s (despite the circus Constantine had built in Trier) and this may have reflected Chilperic's aspirations rather than acts (Thorpe 1974: 275; Hen 1995: 225–226; Humphrey 1986: 411, 430).

At the turn of the seventh century, Isidore of Seville's discussion of spectacles in his *Etymologies* appears even more anachronistic, as it mimics the stereotypical condemnations of some early Church Fathers. The description here of spectacles must have reflected their world far more than his own, although one would not know it by the way he thunders against them:

> Surely these spectacles of cruelty and the attendance at vain shows were established not only by the vices of humans, but also at the behest of demons. Therefore Christians should have nothing to do with the madness of the circus, the immodesty of the theater, the cruelty of the amphitheater, the atrocity of the arena, the debauchery of the games. Indeed, a person who takes up such things denies God, having become an apostate from the Christian faith, and seeks anew what he renounced in baptism long before—namely, the devil and his pomps and works (Barney et al. 2007: 370–371).

So, what are we to make of these references to Roman spectacle in places where it was unlikely for them to have existed? Even if we take these sixth- and seventh-century sources at their word, as some scholars have argued we should (McCormick 1986: 332–334), the spectacles these writers could have witnessed would have looked very different from the spectacles of the empire at its height or the spectacles that were still being performed in Constantinople's hippodrome. They and their audiences were living in a very different world. But the legacy of Rome persisted, and the imagery of Rome and its spectacles could be used to make claims to power and authority, both sacred and secular. This was the case throughout medieval and early modern Europe. It was the case for the Merovingian dynasty, the first Germanic rulers to convert to orthodox Christianity (Fanning 2002: 324). And such aspirations were even more apparent in their successors in Gaul, the Carolingians, especially in the man who revived the Roman empire in the West, Charlemagne.

As the first Roman emperor in the west in more than 300 years, it was only natural that Charlemagne would seek to legitimize his reign as emperor with symbols from Rome's past. This was evident during his lifetime in the scholarly and artistic achievements of his court, and it was also evident in his death. When he was laid to rest in the church he had built in Aachen with Roman *spolia*, his body was covered in objects displaying imperial imagery from both Rome's classical past and the current Byzantine empire. Charlemagne's antique marble sarcophagus shows the story of Persephone and may very well have been chosen by his daughters as 'a demonstration of female power as well as vulnerability' and also *Romanitas* (Nelson 2000: 153). In fact, the iconography of the story depicted on the sarcophagus includes a link with Roman spectacle—a four-horse chariot. Inside the sarcophagus as well, Charlemagne's body was wrapped in a brilliant blue and gold Byzantine silk depicting this same spectacular image of Roman power—a charioteer and *quadriga* (Muthesius 1997: 72–73; Brubaker and Haldon 2001: 93). Now it is necessary to return to the site of this textile's production—the Byzantine empire—to determine how Roman spectacle fared in the East during Late Antiquity.

The Transformation of Spectacle in the Eastern Empire

As David Potter's essay in this volume (Chapter 14) explains, gladiatorial combats and athletic competitions came to an end in the fifth century, but in their place new spectacles appeared in the East, and other previously existing spectacles grew in popularity. None was more popular than chariot-racing. Alan Cameron argues that this spectacle shot to prominence in Constantinople at the turn of the sixth century because it filled a void caused by Anastasius banning *venationes* in 498 and pantomime in 502. Even though the ban was not the end of either one of those spectacles, these imperial attacks on the amphitheatre and the theatre in rapid succession allowed the hippodrome to become the pre-eminent site of spectacle in the early sixth century (Cameron 1973: 232). With the rapid ascent to dominance of the chariot-races and the decline of other spectacles as stand-alone events, vestiges of these spectacles—athletic competitions, theatrical performances, and wild beast shows—were consolidated as part of circus experience to provide entertainment between the chariot-races (Potter 2011: 309, 313; Roueché 2007: 62; Roueché 2008).

Horse racing was popular throughout the Mediterranean and Middle East in the first millennium AD. During the reign of the Abbasid caliphs, Baghdad and Samara had specially built racecourses. Like the hippodromes in Constantinople, they were part of the palace complex; unlike the Byzantine hippodromes these Abbasid hippodromes were built—like both Byzantine and Abbasid polo grounds (more about this sport below)—primarily for the private entertainment of the caliph and his court and not for the general public (Northedge 1990; Ahsan 1979: 243–249, 252–254, 262–264). Also, whereas the Abbasids preferred horse-races with jockeys, the Byzantines preferred the ancient Roman form of this spectacle—chariot-racing. Because chariot-racing in Late Antiquity has already been analysed in such detail elsewhere (Cameron 1973; Cameron 1976; Giatsis 2000), instead of describing Constantinople's hippodrome in its heyday, this essay explores why the hippodrome in Constantinople remained one of the most enduring images of the Roman empire long after its decline and fall.

Constantinople's hippodrome symbolized the imperial aspirations of the successor states that emerged within the *limes* of the former empire and beyond. The example of Charlemagne and his revival of the western empire has already been analysed above, and the final section of this essay will analyse how this symbol of spectacle was used in late medieval and early modern Europe. But, first it is necessary to look far beyond the north-eastern frontiers of the Byzantine empire, to the city of Kiev, where the eleventh-century ruler of Rus', Iaroslav the Wise, chose to adorn the walls of the church of St Sophia with a nearly fifty-foot-long fresco depicting images of the hippodrome in Constantinople. This depiction of spectacle imbued his capital with some of the aura of authority derived from the centres of ecclesiastical and imperial authority in Constantinople—Hagia Sophia and the hippodrome—creating a 'simulacrum of the imperial capital, a "Constantinople-on-the-Dnieper"' (Boeck 2009: 295). The idea of decorating a church with scenes from the hippodrome might also have come from Constantinople, where several centuries earlier, during the Iconoclast controversy, Byzantine emperors who could no longer express their power and authority with sacred images turned to spectacle: 'In particular, hippodrome races and royal hunts operated as metaphors for imperial strength and valor' (Walker 2012: 21).

The main reason why Constantinople's hippodrome became such a potent image of im-perial power is because it was the centre of spectacle for the entire empire. Well over a dozen cities in the Byzantine empire had hippodromes, but by the seventh century all of these sites of spectacle, except for the one in Constantinople, had ceased to function (Mango 1981: 345; Mango et al. 1991). The declining economies, shrinking populations, and ebbing political power of cities in the east, as well as the conquest of many of them during the wars of the sixth and seven centuries, meant that they eventually suffered the same fate as those in the west, as sites of spectacle were abandoned, mined for materials, converted into places of business or residence, or used in or as fortifications. In fact, the sixth century saw both the zenith of chariot-racing's popularity as well as the beginning of its long decline in the east, as the emperor became the sole sponsor of expensive events which generated no revenue (Cameron 1973).

Chariot-races continued at Constantinople's hippodrome into the eleventh and twelfth centuries, as the poetry of Christopher Mytilene and Michael Hagiotheodorites as well as Nicetas Choniates' chronicle attest (Baldwin 1985: 81–90; Magoulias 1984: 67, 132, 160). And according to accounts from travellers from the Muslim world, wild beast shows were also staged there in the twelfth century (Ševčenko 2002: 75–76). But these spectacles had already been much diminished both in duration and frequency by the tenth century and most likely much earlier (Cameron 1973: 255–256; Mango 1981: 345–347). Alexius I moved the formal

Imperial residence to the Blachernai Palace in the late eleventh century; when he abandoned the Great Palace with its passageway to the imperial box (*kathisma*), the hippodrome no longer connected the emperor and his people (Mango 1991; Cameron 1973: 6).

FROM AMPHITHEATRES AND HIPPODROMES TO TOURNAMENT GROUNDS AND HUNTING PARKS: THE EXCLUSIONS OF THE MASSES FROM SPECTACLE

The decline of chariot-racing in Constantinople's hippodrome might also have been hastened somewhat by the rise in popularity of two sports which the Byzantine nobility imported from their neighbours (Giatsis 2007: 20). From the Muslim world came *tzykanion*, a form of polo, and from Latin Christendom came the tournament, a mounted combat sport which included jousts (single combat with lances) and mêlées (group combat with a variety of weapons). Although both of these new spectacles involved horses, that is where the similarities to chariot-races end, because *tzykanion* and the tournament were (usually) both played and watched only by nobles. The polo field (*tzykanisterion*), like the hippodrome, was adjacent to the Great Palace, but whereas the hippodrome linked the ruler and his people, the polo grounds excluded the public (Janin 1950: 119; Karpozilos and Cutler 1991). There was also a smaller, covered hippodrome adjacent to the palace, which was for the private use of the emperor and his court (Mango 1991; Giatsis 2000: 37). We can see this as an expression of the larger processes at work in the Byzantine empire. As the imperial court became the sole patron of spectacles and other entertainments and as the nature of rulership changed, emperors became less interested in expending vast sums of money on public entertainments, especially because spectacles could be sites of protest as well as of acclamation. Soon most forms of spectacle came to be enjoyed exclusively by the emperor and other nobles (Tougher 2010: 143; Mango 1981: 352). Even the bathhouse, a principal Roman public institution, became a private place of enjoyment for the imperial household during the Byzantine empire, as magnificent new facilities were built in the Great Palace, while the general populace was left to make do with baths that had been built centuries earlier (Mango 1981: 340–341).

In the west the public was not so much deliberately excluded from spectacle as simply ignored, as nobles ran roughshod over commoners' rights during their pursuit of pleasure. This can most clearly be seen in the tournament and the hunt. The twelfth-century tournament bore a striking resemblance to a real battle, in which knights on horseback laid waste to everything in their paths, including peasants' cultivated lands (Crouch 2005: 55). Peasants suffered even more from hunting, though, both because they were not allowed to hunt and because productive lands could be turned into hunting parks. One of the most striking examples of this comes from England, where before the Norman Conquest in 1066 anyone had the right to hunt on the land he possessed, but by the twelfth century as much as one-third of all the land of the kingdom had been 'afforested', i.e. turned into game preserves in which the inhabitants were subjected to particularly onerous laws or from which they were expelled (Griffin 2007: 16–19). All animals—not just the exotic and expensive ones kept in menageries or exchanged with other nobles as gifts—belonged to the nobility in most medi-eval European lands, and the hunting of wild beasts (and at times their wholesale slaughter) was their exclusive purview, except for certain designated huntsmen (Kiser 2007: 104–107; Ševčenko 2002; Ahsan 1979: 205–206; Loisel 1912: 140–182). The spectacle of hunting wild animals was for the private enjoyment of the nobility who took part both in the hunt and in the feasting that followed.

The spectacles of the Middle Ages were for the most part private pursuits of pleasure and expressions of excess meant to impress a very limited audience. This audience largely consisted of other noble participants, mostly because these elites performed for their peers, but also because spectatorship was difficult until adaptations made these spectacles more viewer friendly. The mêlée, the most popular part of the tournament in its early years, was eventually eclipsed by the part of the tournament which had initially been viewed merely as a preliminary—jousting—at least in part because this event lent itself more easily to spectatorship (Barber and Barker 1989: 7). Similarly, hunting lodges were constructed so that devotees could watch their beloved birds of prey or be seen by their peers performing heroics (Shearer 1961; Ševčenko 2002). These permanent and temporary structures enabled better noble spectatorship, although little effort was made to include the public. Yet these spectacles were not always private. Like ancient rulers, medieval rulers were cognizant of the symbolic power of spectacle. Important state events such as coronations, royal weddings, and diplomatic meetings were often celebrated with tournaments and other spectacles, like Henry VI's 1431 coronation 'hunt' through Parisian streets made to resemble a forest (Barber and Barker 1989: 169–173; Mileson 2009: 20). Henry's coronation was also an *adventus*, and just as in the ancient world, the arrival of a ruler in a town—especially a contested town—was often celebrated with spectacle. When Manuel I celebrated his *adventus* in Antioch in 1159 by defeating the Latin knights in a tournament after humiliating their leaders during his triumphal entrance, he used their own spectacle of nobility to demonstrate his superiority over them (Jones and Maguire 2002; Schreiner 1996). This diplomatic aspect of spectacle was further developed in the early modern era.

New Spectacles and the Remembrance of Rome: Hippodromes in Renaissance Italy and the Ottoman Empire

Spectacle continued to change in the late Middle Ages and the Renaissance. In particular spectacles once again came to be associated with diplomacy and governance. Whereas most medieval spectacles had been noble pursuits from which the public had been excluded, in early modern Europe many spectacles were once again made public (or at least included a public component) so that the subjects of emerging states could bear witness to their rulers' power. Medieval knights would have cared very little what non-nobles thought of their performance in tournaments. The audiences for which they were performing were their fellow knights and also noble non-combatants, like the women at court who would help judge the victors. Early modern spectacles on the other hand were often used to help build a civic or national identity and were also meant to demonstrate the power of these states to their neighbours, both enemies and allies. This survey of the decline and fall of spectacle ends, therefore, with an analysis of new hippodromes in Renaissance Italy and the legacy of Constantinople's hippodrome in the Ottoman empire, in order to demonstrate that while the forms of spectacle changed dramatically during the millennium between the fall of the western empire and the fall of the eastern empire, spectacles still retained some of the same functions they had in ancient Rome, and their promoters in many ways continued to channel their own interpretations of *Romanitas* for their own political purposes.

As Roy Strong has most forcefully demonstrated, early modern rulers understood the importance of spectacle—including triumphs, theatrical displays, and 'tableaux of imperial grandeur, enhanced by the forms of Renaissance classicism'—in demonstrating a variety of political programmes both at home and abroad (Strong 1973: 79). David Lee Bomgardner has also drawn attention to similarities between early modern and ancient spectacles 'in their desire to impress by the novelty, apparent impossibility, and extravagance of their special effects' (Bomgardner 2000: 225). These issues are far too complex to be discussed in any detail here. So, rather than try to analyse the debt early modern spectacle owed to Roman spectacle, this final section will focus on the one image which more than any other symbolized the power of imperial spectacle in medieval and early modern Europe—Constantinople's hippodrome—by briefly analysing the image and function of the idea of this hippodrome in Renaissance Venice and Florence and the ruins of this hippodrome in Ottoman Constantinople. Let us begin with the Italian hippodromes.

The Venetian hippodrome is not a hippodrome in the sense of a site of horse-races, but rather the site of some famous horses which were brought to Italy from Constantinople in the Middle Ages. One of the many items stolen during the sack of Constantinople in 1204 was a gilded bronze *quadriga* from the hippodrome, which the Venetians placed on top of the cathedral dedicated to their patron saint, Mark. Unlike many other northern Italian cities, Venice did not have *palii*, horse-races through town streets and squares (discussed in more detail below). Charles Freeman, however, has made a compelling case for the Piazza San Marco as a hippodrome, based on the link between the symbols of horse-racing in Constantinople and the projection of imperial authority, which has already been analysed above in both Western and Eastern Europe in the early Middle Ages. By placing the *quadriga* taken from Constantinople so prominently in the town's principal public space, the Venetian conquerors of the Roman empire (or at least the three-eighths of it they claimed according to their arrangement with the French crusaders) were able to use symbolically charged *spolia* from that conquest in much the same way that Roman emperors had used *spolia* from throughout the empire to decorate Constantinople's hippodrome (Freeman 2010: 105–120). And even though Constantinople and large parts of the Latin empire were reclaimed by the Greeks later in the thirteenth century, the Venetians still held many former Byzantine territories, including Crete, which rebelled against Venetian rule in 1364. After crushing that rebellion, the Venetians celebrated in the Piazza San Marco with festivities which Petrarch has described in detail (Petrarch 1992: 132–136).

From this metaphorical hippodrome of Renaissance Italy, we now travel to a real hippodrome in Renaissance Italy, the Piazza Santa Maria Novella in Florence. In the late Middle Ages many cities in northern Italy celebrated important feast days with a *palio*—a horse-race with jockeys through the streets or around a square—and among the most important patrons of this spectacle were the Medici of Florence (Mallett 1996). In 1563 Cosimo I introduced a new *palio* to his Florentine subjects—the Palio dei Cocchi—a revival of Roman chariot-racing, which reflected the imperial aspirations of its sponsor (Tobey 2005: 130–135; McClelland 2007: 108–110). In medieval western Europe, most people did not know what ancient chariots looked like, so medieval artists usually depicted them as 'the only vehicles known to them—farm carts or wagons' (Boyer 1990: 25). It was in this form that the *bigae* (two-horse chariots) of the new *palio* appeared. Even though horse-drawn carts—painted the colours of the factions—racing around wooden obelisks in a town square may seem a rather poor imitation of Roman chariot-races, it greatly impressed Montaigne, who observed the race in 1581 and remarked: 'I enjoyed this spectacle more than any other I had seen in Italy for its resemblance to the ancient type of race' (Tobey 2005: 131; McClelland 2007: 110).

Finally, this essay concludes by analysing the fate of the hippodrome in Constantinople after the Ottomans' conquest of the city in 1453. Although this once grand space had fallen into ruin long before Turks took the city, it once again became a public (or at least semi-public) site of spectacle in which state power was expressed. Pashas built their palaces overlooking this space, which Leslie Peirce characterizes as 'culturally and ceremonially an extension of the [imperial] palace, in a sense the most public of its courtyards,' because 'it was there that important dynastic events such as weddings and circumcisions were celebrated' (Peirce 1993: 203). Of all the spectacles acted out in the hippodrome during the reign of the Ottomans, the most spectacular—or at least it would seem so from the preserved records of both Ottoman and European spectators—was the celebration commemorating the circumcision of Mehmed, the son of Sultan Murad III, in 1582 (Terzioglu 1995). Diplomats from all over Europe witnessed the magnificence of the sultan and artists were employed by the Ottoman court to record the festivities in beautifully illustrated books (Atasoy 1997; Terzioglu 1995: 84). This nearly two-month-long spectacle included mock battles, horse-races, banquets, exotic animal shows, a variety of performances, and 'also served as a vehicle for various groups to convey messages to the public and to the sultan' (Terzioglu 1995: 87). Although there were no longer chariot-races in the hippodrome, both the form and the function of the spectacles acted out there would have been in many ways familiar to citizens of the Roman empire. And, most importantly for the sultan and his court, they were able to demonstrate the power of the state both to their own subjects and to visitors from foreign courts in a language that was easily comprehensible to both groups. Like the other groups analysed above, the Ottomans in many ways saw themselves as heirs to the Roman empire, and as such adopted and adapted Roman symbols and sites of spectacle for their own purposes.

Although Roman spectacles had indeed declined and fallen during Late Antiquity, the idea of the Roman empire and its symbols of power had not. Spectacles based on some real or imagined Roman past emerged in medieval and early modern Europe and were featured prominently in the discourses of power of several nascent states, many of which laid some claim to being new Romes. For people living in medieval and early modern Europe, Rome was alive and well, and among its most enduring symbols of power were its sites of spectacle—the hippodrome in Constantinople and (although it has not been analysed in much detail here) the Colosseum in Rome. According to a popular proverb attributed (most likely incorrectly) to Bede, who wrote in a monastery located near the northern *limes* of Roman Britain many centuries after the fall of the empire but in an environment still very much influenced by *Romanitas*: '*Quandiu stat Colisaeus, stat et Roma; quando cadet Colisaeus, cadet et Roma. Quando cadet Roma, cadet et mundus*' (Bayless and Lapidge

1998: 132). And even though exactly which monument the proverb refers to has been debated almost as much as its authorship (Canter 1930), the fact that most people since the Middle Ages have followed the same line of reasoning as Lord Byron is a testament to the enduring legacy of Roman spectacle:

> 'While stands the Coliseum, Rome shall stand;
> When falls the Coliseum, Rome shall fall;
> And when Rome falls—the World.'

(Childe Harold's Pilgrimage, IV.145)

REFERENCES

Ahsan, M. M. 1979. *Social Life under the Abbasids*. London.

Atasoy, N. 1997. *1582 Surname-I Hümayun: An Imperial Celebration*. Istanbul.

Baldwin, B., ed. 1985. *An Anthology of Byzantine Poetry*. Amsterdam.

Barber, R. and J. Barker. 1989. *Tournaments: Jousts, Chivalry and Pageants in the Middle Ages*. Woodbridge.

Barney, S. A., W. A. Lewis, J. A. Beach, and O. Berghof, trans. 2007. *The Etymologies of Isidore of Seville*. Cambridge.

Bayless, M. and M. Lapidge, eds. 1998. *Collectanea Pseudo-Bedae*. Dublin.

Boeck, E. 2009. 'Simulating the Hippodrome: The Performance of Power in Kiev's St. Sophia.' *ABull* 91: 283–301.

Bomgardner, D. L. 2000. *The Story of the Roman Amphitheatre*. New York.

Boyer, M. N. 1990 'The Humble Profile of the Regal Chariot in Medieval Miniatures.' *Gesta* 29: 25–30.

Brubaker, L. and J. Haldon. 2001. *Byzantium in the Iconoclast Era (ca 680–850): The Sources: An Annotated Survey*. Aldershot.

Cameron, A. 1973. *Porphyrius the Charioteer*. Oxford.

Cameron, A. 1976. *Circus Factions: Blues and Greens at Rome and Byzantium*. Oxford.

Canter, H. V. 1930. 'The Venerable Bede and the Colosseum.' *TAPA* 61: 150–164.

Crouch, D. 2005. *Tournament*. London.

Dewing, H. B., trans. 1916. *Procopius*, vol. 2: *History of the Wars, Books III and IV: The Vandalic War*. London.

Dewing, H. B., trans. 1928. *Procopius*, vol. 5: *History of the Wars, Books VII.36 to VIII: The Gothic War*. London.

Dewing, H. B., trans. 1935. *Procopius*, vol. 6: *The Anecdota, or Secret History*. London.

Dugast, F. 2007. 'Spectacles et édifices de spectacles dans l'Antiquité tardive: La mémoire prise en défaut.' *Antiquité Tardive* 15: 11–20.

Fanning, S. 2002. 'Clovis Augustus and Merovingian *Imitatio Imperii*.' In *The World of Gregory of Tours*. 321–335. K. Mitchell and I. Wood, ed. Leiden.

Freeman, C. 2010. *The Horses of St Mark's: A Story of Triumph in Byzantium, Paris, and Venice*. New York.

Giatsis, S. G. 2007. 'How Did Byzantine Authors Approach Sport?' In *New Aspects of Sport History*: 16–23. M Lämmer, E. Mertin, and T. Terret, ed. Sankt Augustin.

Giatsis, S. G. 2000. 'The Organization of Chariot-Racing in the Great Hippodrome of Byzantine Constantinople.' *International Journal of the History of Sport* 17: 36–68.

Griffin, E. 2007. *Blood Sport: Hunting in Britain since 1006*. New Haven.

Hen, Y. 1995. *Culture and Religion in Merovingian Gaul, A.D. 481–751*. Leiden.

Hodgkin, T. 1886. *The Letters of Cassiodorus*. London.

Humphrey, J. H. 1986. *Roman Circuses: Arenas for Chariot Racing*. Berkeley.

Janin, R. 1950. *Constantinople Byzantine: développement urbain et répertoire topographique*. Paris.

Jennison, G. 1937. *Animals for Show and Pleasure in Ancient Rome*. Manchester.

Jones, L. and H. Maguire. 2002. 'A Description of the Jousts of Manuel I Komnenos.' *Byzantine and Modern Greek Studies* 26: 104–148.

Karmon, D. 2011. *The Ruin of the Eternal City: Antiquity and Preservation in Renaissance Rome*. Oxford.

Karpozilos, A. and A. Cutler 1991. 'Sports.' In *The Oxford Dictionary of Byzantium*. 1939–1940. Alexander P. Kazhdan, ed. New York.

Kiser, L. J. 2007. 'Animal Acts: Animals in Medieval Sports, Entertainments, and Menageries.' In *A Cultural History of Animals*: 2. 103–126. L. Kalof and B. Resl, eds. Oxford.

Klingshirn, W. E. 1994. *Caesarius of Arles: The Making of a Christian Community in Late Antique Gaul*. Cambridge.

Leone, A. 2007. *Changing Townscapes in North Africa from Late Antiquity to the Arab Conquest*. Bari.

Lim, R. 2009. 'Christianization, Secularization, and the Transformation of Public Life.' In *A Companion to Late Antiquity*. 497–511. P. Rousseau, ed. Chichester.

Lim, R. 1999. 'People as Power: Games, Munificence and Contested Topography.' In *The Transformations of Vrbs Roma in Late Antiquity*: 265–281. W. V. Harris, ed. Portsmouth.

Lim, R. 1997. 'Consensus and Dissensus on Public Spectacles in Early Byzantium.' *ByzF* 24: 159–179.

Loisel, G. 1912. *Histoire des ménageries de l'Antiquité a nos jours*. Paris.

Magoulias, H. J. trans. 1984. *O City of Byzantium: Annals of Niketas Choniates*. Detroit.

Mahler, G. A. 2012. 'Afterlives: The Reuse, Adaptation and Transformation of Rome's Ancient Theaters.' PhD dissertation, New York University.

Mallett, M. 1996. 'Horse-Racing and Politics in Lorenzo's Florence.' In *Lorenzo the Magnificent: Culture and Politics*. 253–262. M. Mallett and N. Mann, eds. London.

Mango, C. 1991. 'The Great Palace.' In *The Oxford Dictionary of Byzantium*. 869–870. Alexander P. Kazhdan, ed. New York.

Mango, C. 1981. 'Daily Life in Byzantium.' *Jahrbuch der Österreichischen Byzantinistik* 30: 337–353.

Mango, C., A. Karpozilos, and A. Cutler. 1991. 'Hippodromes.' In *The Oxford Dictionary of Byzantium*. 934–936. Alexander P. Kazhdan, ed. New York.

McClelland, J. 2007. *Body and Mind: Sport in Europe from the Roman Empire to the Renaissance*. London.

McCormick, M. 1986. *Eternal Victory: Triumphal Rulership in Late Antiquity, Byzantium, and the Early Medieval West*. Cambridge.

Merrills, A. and Miles, R. 2010. *The Vandals*. Chichester.

Mileson, S. 2009. *Parks in Medieval England*. Oxford.

Muthesius, A. 1997. *Byzantine Silk Weaving: AD 400 to AD 1200*. Vienna.

Nelson, J. L. 2000. 'Carolingian Royal Funerals.' In *Rituals of Power: From Late Antiquity to the Early Middle Ages*. 131–184. F. Theuws and J. L. Nelson, eds. Leiden.

Northedge, A. 1990. 'The Racecourses at Samarra.' *Bulletin of the School of Oriental and African Studies, University of London* 53: 31–56.

Olovsdotter, C. 2005. *The Consular Image: An Iconological Study of the Consular Diptychs.* Oxford.

Peirce, L. P. 1993. *The Imperial Harem: Women and Sovereignty in the Ottoman Empire.* New York.

Petrarch, F. 1992. *Letters of Old Age: Rerum senilium libri I–XVIII*, vol. I: *Books I–IX.* A. Bernardo, S. Levin, and R. Bernardo, trans. Baltimore.

Potter, D. 2011. *The Victor's Crown: Ancient Sport from Homer to Byzantium.* London.

Potter, D. 2010. 'Constantine and the Gladiators.' *CQ* 60: 596–606.

Retzleff, A. 2003. 'Near Eastern Theatres in Late Antiquity.' *Phoenix* 57: 115–38.

Rouché, C. 2008. 'Entertainments, theatre, and hippodrome.' In *The Oxford Handbook of Byzantine Studies*: 677–684. E. Jeffreys, ed. Oxford.

Rouché, C. 2007. 'Spectacles in Late Antiquity: Some Observations.' *Antiquité Tardive* 15: 59–64.

Rouché, C. 1993. *Performers and Partisans at Aphrodisias in the Roman and Late Roman Period.* London.

Sanford, E. M., trans. 1930. *Salvian, On the Government of God.* New York.

Schreiner, P. 1996. 'Ritterspiele in Byzanz.' *JÖByz* 46: 227–241.

Shearer, C. 1961. 'The Castles and Hunting Lodges of Emperor Frederick II.' In *The Art of Falconry: Being the De arte venandi cum avibus of Frederick II of Hohenstaufen*: xc–cx. C. A. Wood and F. M. Fyfe, eds. Stanford.

Strong, R. 1973. *Splendor at Court: Renaissance Spectacle and the Theater of Power.* Boston, MA.

Ševčenko, N. P. 2002. 'Wild Animals in the Byzantine Park.' In *Byzantine Garden Culture.* 69–86. A. Littlewood, H. Maguire, and J. Wolschke-Bulmahn, eds. Washington, DC.

Terzioglu, D. 1995. 'The Imperial Circumcision Festival of 1582: An Interpretation.' *Muqarnas* 12: 84–100.

Thorpe, L., trans. 1974. *Gregory of Tours: The History of the Franks.* New York.

Tobey, E. M. 2005. 'The Palio in Italian Renaissance Art, Thought, and Culture.' PhD dissertation, University of Maryland.

Tougher, S. 2010. 'Having Fun in Byzantium.' In *A Companion to Byzantium.* 135–145. L. James, ed. Chichester.

Walker, A. 2012. *The Emperor and the World: Exotic Elements and the Imaging of Middle Byzantine Imperial Power, Ninth to Thirteenth Centuries C.E.* Cambridge.

Ward-Perkins, B. 1984. *From Classical Antiquity to the Middle Ages: Urban Public Building in Northern and Central Italy, AD 300–850.* Oxford.

Webb, R. 2008. *Demons and Dancers: Performance in Late Antiquity.* Cambridge.

Wiedemann, T. 1992. *Emperors and Gladiators.* London.

PART III

FORMS OF CONTESTS AND DISPLAY

....

CHAPTER 16

GREEK FOOTRACES AND FIELD EVENTS

....

DAVID GILMAN ROMANO

BASED on the available evidence, individual athletic events appear to have been introduced into Greek cult over the course of many centuries. The events are represented to us from a variety of sources and it is important to note that the competitive events of Greek athletics of the historical period were not the first examples of athletic events, nor were they the first athletic competition in the ancient world. Rather, they were, in some part, later developments of events that had been first introduced centuries and in some cases millennia earlier from neighbouring civilizations.

From the archaeological contexts of the Mycenaean and Minoan periods, the events of boxing, running, and chariot-racing are known (Younger, this volume Chapter 4). For example, boxing is clearly depicted on the *rhyton* from Hagia Triada from *c*.1500 BCE (Heraklion Archaeological Museum 409) as well as in the scene of the young boys boxing in the Thera frescoes of *c*.1650 BCE (Marinatos 1984). There are scenes of boxers that occur as decoration on Mycenaean painted pottery of the thirteenth century BCE (Swaddling 1980: 63; *BMC* C334) and there are representations of chariot teams that have been interpreted as from an athletic context: for instance, three grave stelai from Grave Circle A at Mycenae (Mylonas 1951: 134–147) that date from 1600–1510 BCE, as well as the later scene of a chariot-race from Tiryns from 1200–1100 BCE (Laser 1987 vol. 3 fig. 2). There are also a number of other athletic events for which there is archaeological evidence from Bronze Age Greece that have less prominence in the historical period, including bull-leaping and archery—although both are known from festivals of the classical and Hellenistic periods (Gallis 2002: 226–227).

There is substantial evidence to suggest that the earlier cultures of the Near East and Egypt influenced the origins and early development of some of the individual events of Greek athletics (Decker, this volume Chapter 3). Athletic training and competition are known from the Sumerian and Babylonian periods as early as the third millennium BCE, where the events of wrestling and boxing are documented. From the text of the *Epic of Gilgamesh* and the marriage of Mardu are athletic scenes and trials of strength that may be understood as a part of preparations for a wedding that take place in the courtyard of a temple (Sjoberg 1985: 7–9). Other literary texts from the Sumerian period attest to the athletic accomplishments of Shulgi, the second king of the famous dynasty of Ur, who boasts of his athletic accomplishments and mentions the site of his victories as the great courtyard of the temple. Shulgi is also known for his long-distance running exploits, and in one particular hymn that he was supposed to have sung, he boasts of taking part in two festivals, one in Ur and the other in Nippur on the same day. Furthermore, he ran between the two cities, making a round trip of some 200 miles (Kramer 1981: 284–288).

There are also Egyptian precedents for Greek athletics that include scenes of wrestling, as depicted in the wall paintings of Beni-Hasan from the Middle Kingdom c.1900 BCE (Newberry et al. 1893 Tomb 15 pl. V). Also known, of course, is the ritualistic run by King Djoser of the Third Dynasty in Egypt from c.2650 BCE. Djoser had an architect named Imhotep design a massive stone tomb in the shape of a step pyramid with surrounding buildings, temples, tombs, and altars as well as open spaces, known today as the Step Pyramid of King Djoser. A part of this complex of buildings has been identified as the cult racecourse on which Djoser ran in a ritual run during certain important religious occasions during his lifetime, for instance at the dedication of the temple precinct and at the thirtieth anniversary of the King's rule, known as the Heb-Sed Festival. Although a run, this does not appear to have been a race, as Djoser was apparently not competing against anyone (Decker, this volume Chapter 3).

From the archaeological record of the Geometric period in Greece, roughly 900–700 BCE, the same events are known from the archaeological evidence with the addition of wrestling. Other events are introduced in literature by the time of the late eighth century BCE. Footraces and field events are described in Homer's *Iliad* and *Odyssey*, including running, wrestling, boxing, discus, and javelin. Several events from Homer do not transfer to the historical period in the major Greek athletic festivals, including archery, throwing the *solos* (a lump of iron), and close combat in armour. It must be understood that athletics, which are included in the *Iliad* and the *Odyssey*, show what must be a part of a long tradition of athletic competition that had a substantial previous history and which may very well represent athletic competition from the Mycenaean period.

Although it is not clear from the archaeological remains of the Mycenaean and Minoan periods what the context for athletic competition was, this becomes much clearer by c.700 BCE when the texts of the *Iliad* and the *Odyssey* are written down. By this time it is known that footraces, equestrian events, and field events are common, as in the context of the funeral games of Patroklos (*Il.* 23.257–897) where a total of eight contests are undertaken: the two-horse chariot-race, boxing, wrestling, footrace, armed combat, weight throw, archery, and the javelin (Nagy, this volume Chapter 22). Athletic competition is also provided in an after-dinner context when Odysseus lands on the shores of Phaeacea and is entertained by Alcinoos (*Od.* 8.97). The following are the events: footrace, jump, wrestling, boxing, and the discus. On the other hand the recreational aspects of athletic activities can be illustrated by the way that the Achaeans throw the discus and practise archery as Achilles sulks in his tent (*Il.* 2.774).

From the Hymn to Apollo on Delos, written in the eighth century BCE, there is the mention of long-robed Ionians gathering together with their families to watch athletic contests in boxing and listening to groups of Delian girls singing and watching them dance. Hesiod writes that he competed in the funeral games for Amphidamos at Chalcis, winning a tripod that he dedicated to the Muses of Helicon (Hes. *WD* 655; Hesiod claims that he defeated Homer in the contest). From Archaic and Classical period texts we hear of athletic competitions as a part of weddings, as well as a part of celebrations of heroes, military leaders, victorious battles, and the death of military leaders, or some combination thereof. Sometimes athletic contests are added to an already established festival, as at Delphi, when athletics supplemented the already long-standing musical festival. The most celebrated of all the athletic festivals, the one at Olympia, was, according to the most popular of the myths, established to celebrate the marriage of Pelops and Hippodameia.

The historical Olympic Register provides the date of 776 BCE as the date of the 'first' victor at Olympia, discussed below. However, it is known from recent archaeological excavation at the Sanctuary of Zeus at Olympia that the earliest evidence associated with the cult of Zeus at the site, from the level associated with the ash altar of Zeus, appears around 1050 BCE (Kyrieleis 2002: 213–220; Sinn, this volume Chapter 5). In the immediate area of the ash altar of Zeus at Olympia there are the remains of Early and Middle Helladic houses, although the German Archaeological Institute (DAI) has not found evidence of continuity between the Bronze Age and the eleventh-century material (Eder 2001: 201–209; German 2007: 15–25; Sinn, this volume Chapter 5). Many hundreds of full-size and miniature bronze tripod cauldrons, together with terracotta and bronze human and animal figurines, including chariots and drivers, as well as two examples of bronze rings of women dancing, at Olympia probably dating from the tenth or ninth century BCE, show evidence for some enhanced cult activity at the site (Furtwängler 1890 pls. 15, 16, 27–34). These full-size and miniature tripod cauldrons have been found associated with the ash level beneath the foundations of the Temple of Hera and to the south of the building, in the area of the Pelopion and the Early Helladic houses. The black ash is also found to the north-west and east of the Temple of Zeus and at the west end of the Temple of Rhea. Miniature as well as full-size tripod cauldrons were found in the area of the southern embankment of the stadium, probably dumped there as a part of a later filling operation.

These dates would be generally in keeping with the earlier traditions of Olympic contests that were organized by the local king Iphitus before the series of games began c. 776 BCE as discussed by Pausanias many centuries later (Paus. 5.8.5).

New evidence from the ash altar of Zeus at the Sanctuary of Zeus at Mt Lykaion in Arcadia includes multiple miniature tripod cauldrons made of bronze, and the series probably begins from the tenth century BCE. At Mt Lykaion, however, there is evidence of continuous cult activity from at least the fifteenth century BCE from the LH IIB period through the Classical period, and the miniature tripod cauldrons are in the middle of this time-span (Romano and Voyatzis 2010: 9–21; Romano and Voyatzis 2014: 618-620). The significance of the introduction of these miniature tripod cauldrons at this time is currently under study.

STADION

According to the Olympic Register, the *stadion* was the first event at the ancient Olympic Games, introduced in 776 BCE, and the only event until the addition of the *diaulos* race in 724 BCE. The first Olympic *stadion* victor was Koroibos from Elis, who was said to be a cook. The word *stadion* first appears about the middle of the sixth century BCE in the context of a painted inscription on a Panathenaic amphora indicating the name of the race in which the amphora was won 'ΑΝΔΡΩΝ ΣΤΑΔΙΟ' ('stade race for men'; Metropolitan Museum of Art 1978.11.13). This use of the word *stadion* in a compound noun would imply that the word has an older origin; I have argued that the root of the word comes from the Greek verb to stand, ἵστημι (*histēmi*), meaning 'the standing place' (Romano 1993: 1–7). This would be appropriate since the early facilities for running races in Greece had low embankments of earth on the sides of the racecourse where it would have been more comfortable to stand than to sit, and it is likely that the spectators stood on these facilities. There were three meanings of the word in antiquity: as the linear distance of 600 feet, as the race of the same distance, and as the place where the athletic event took place. The fact that the distance of the *stadion* is 600 feet is probably related to Sumerian and Babylonian mathematics with a base-60 as well as a sub base-10 system. The actual linear measure of the 600 feet varied from *stadion* to *stadion* because the absolute length of the foot varied also from place to place. So, for instance, at Olympia, in the Sanctuary of Zeus, the length of the *stadion* was 192.28 m between starting lines, whereas at Halieis, in the Sanctuary of Apollo, the length, also between starting lines, was 166.50 m (Romano 1993: 34–36). The athletic race was always one length of the *stadion* and was the shortest footrace of Greek athletics, whereas the length of the race was always the same as 600 feet; the absolute measure of the foot differed from place to place. As a race it is the only event of Greek athletics that could be considered anaerobic, which meant that the runners could run the entire distance without taking a new breath of air. It was the only true sprint, but it was long enough in distance to provide the necessary *ponos* and *agōn*, 'labour' and 'struggle'. At the same time, the *stadion* race was 'longer' in absolute distance at Olympia than it was at Halieis, for instance. The stadium race was run in lanes from one end of the *dromos* ('course') of the stadium to the other. It is usually assumed that the stone starting-lines would also have served as the finish lines for all of the footraces, although there are also other possibilities. For instance, in the Nemea stadium, there is a square block with a cutting for a vertical post approximately 5.3 m to the north of the southern starting-line. Although this block for a post is usually interpreted as a turning post, it is possible that the post could also have been used for the finish of races (Miller 2001: 43–44; Romano 1981: 86). In the *stadion* race, judging finishes may have been challenging depending on the number of entries and the closeness of the race. The winner would have been selected by judges who were standing by the finish line and, at times, there was controversy about the outcome. There is the example of Eupolemus of Elis (Paus. 6.3.7) who won the men's *stadion* race in 396 BCE, although there was a controversial decision by the three judges.

   An important part of the race would have been the start itself, and we know that stone starting-lines to be used in the footraces, and perhaps some of the field events, were typically a part of the Greek stadium by *c.*500 BCE. Although the details of the starting arrangements are not given in the *Iliad* nor the *Odyssey*, only that the athletes lined up 'foot by foot', we can imagine that the arrangements were of the greatest simplicity. From the archaeological record, it is known that toeholds in stone starting-line blocks provided a basis for stability as well as location on the starting-line that was also defined by the location of wooden posts as lane dividers. The stone starting-lines that had an evolution from toe-holds to single groove to parallel grooves were later modified to include starting mechanisms, *husplēges* (ὕσπληγες), a device that was based on torsion, something that would have been spring loaded, and that regulated the start. Although the *husplēges* would have added to the fanfare of the start of the footraces, they would not necessarily have prevented false starts. (It is probable that athletes still 'jumped the gun' even with a barrier since athletes often try to anticipate the starting command of a race.)

   As the oldest of the events for which there is a record of victors from Olympia, and also probably because of the nature of the event, the *stadion* race took on greater importance than the other events at Olympia, and the winner of the *stadion* race became associated with the Olympic festival of a specific year. The earliest example of this comes from a history of Sicily written by Philistus of Syracuse, who mentions the Olympiad in which Oibotas of Dyme won the *stadion*. This evidence suggests that the first Olympic victor list appeared between 400 and 360 BCE (Christesen 2007: 48).

Philostratos, who wrote a physical training manual in the third century CE, gives the origin of the *stadion* race at Olympia as a competition by athletes who ran towards a priest holding a torch, the winner of which lighted the flame. Philostratos also states that the ideal *stadion* runner should have light, slender legs that work with athlete's hands as if they were wings (Philostr. *Gym.* 32). In 632 BCE, the boys' *stadion* race was introduced at Olympia and the winner was Polyneikes of Elis. In the same year boys' wrestling was also introduced at Olympia and the winner was Hipposthenes of Sparta.

Livy tells us that Greek athletic events were first held in Rome in 186 BCE by Fulvius Nobilior, and Suetonius tells us that Greek athletic events, the Neronian Games, were staged by the emperor Nero in the first century CE (Liv. 39.22.1–2; Suet. *Nero* 11–12). Nero became interested in Greek athletic competition, and in his tour of Greece in 67 CE he participated in and won victories at the Panhellenic festivals and, in all, he claimed 1,808 staged victories at festival sites in Greece (Dio 62.21). Later in the first century CE, the emperor Domitian had a large Greek stadium built in Rome in the Campus Martius (Suet. *Dom.* 5). During the reign of Sulla and at the time of his sack of Greece in the 80s BCE, he attempted to transfer the Olympic Games from Olympia to Rome (App. *BC* 1.11.99). There are relatively few *stadia* known from the Italian peninsula, although one recent one, of a Republican era date, has come to light at Cumae (Giglio 2009: 623–642).

During Alexander's campaigns to the east in the fourth century BCE, Athenaeus records, the soldiers brought with them the makings of a gymnasium for training purposes. It is likely that the specific length of a stadium of 600 feet as a training ground of the gymnasium was brought along, since that specific length was carried in goatskins to create a shady training ground (Athen. 12.539C).

Of course there were no times recorded for the running events from antiquity, nor were there many distances recorded in the field events, although it is interesting that some recorded distances have come down to us in the jump and in the discus. Comparative results between athletes must have been based on the results of competition, of one athlete having won over a competitor at a certain festival at a certain time. There were no standardized weights for the athletic implements, such as the discus or javelin or the jumping weights, nor were there standardized linear measures for the absolute length of the foot.

DIAULOS

The *diaulos* was a footrace of two lengths of the stadium, or 1200 feet, introduced at Olympia in 724 BCE. The name of the first victor was Hypenos of Pisa. The word *diaulos* means a 'double pipe', a musical instrument that is characterized by two roughly parallel pipes with a mouthpiece, and it must have suggested the course to be run by the competitors from the start, around a post at the distant end of the stadium and then a return to the starting-line. There are two different theories about the nature of the turn in the *diaulos* race. The first is that all of the competitors would have started in individual lanes and turned around a single post, centrally located at the distant starting-line. The other possibility is that the competitors would each have started in individual lanes and turned around their own turning-post at the distant starting-line. According to the first theory, if all the runners turned at the same post there likely would have been congestion and injuries resulting from collisions. According to the second theory, the runners would have run in lanes the entire race, and could possibly even have used two lanes per competitor, depending on the number of starting athletes and the width of the starting-line. The arrangements may have varied from festival to festival and stadium to stadium.

HIPPIOS

The *hippios* or *ephippios* was a footrace of four lengths of the stadium or 2,400 feet. It was only known from certain festival sites, for instance at Isthmia, Nemea, Argos, Athens, Epidauros, and Plataea. Its name comes from the Greek word for horse, ἵππος (*hippos*), and it may relate to the idea that the competitors had to be as 'strong as a horse' to run the race, which was typically *c*.800 m. The name could also have been a reference to the length of the hippodrome, the equestrian track. In the *hippios* race the same two possibilities exist for the turns as in the *diaulos* race. It seems most sensible that the competitors turned around their individual turning posts.

DOLICHOS

The *dolichos* was a distance race held in the stadium. The *dolichos* was introduced at Olympia in 720 BCE and the name of the first victor was Akanthos of Sparta. The number of lengths differed from site to site, from seven to twenty-four lengths. Although it is not known for certain why the number of lengths differed, it is possible that it may have been related to the absolute length of the racecourses that varied in length from sanctuary to sanctuary, because the length of the foot varied from site to site, so that, for instance, twenty lengths at one stadium could have been the equivalent of twenty-four lengths at another stadium. It may also have been related to local custom and practice. Philostratos mentions that the distances run in the *dolichos* had to do with distances that Arcadian day-runners ran, back and forth, to carry news about war (Philostr. *Gym.* 4).

HOPLITE RACE

The hoplite race, *hoplitodromos*, was introduced in 520 BCE at Olympia, where the first victor was Damaretos of Heraea. The race was characterized as a footrace by athletes wearing the armour of a hoplite: helmet, shield, and, in the beginning of the history of the race, also greaves, although their use was discontinued later. The athletes never carried spears. The distance of the race varied from two stadium lengths at Olympia and Athens to four stadium lengths at Nemea. Pausanias gives us the information that twenty-five bronze shields were kept in the Temple of Zeus at Olympia for the hoplite race (Paus. 5.12.8).

Philostratos comments on the introduction of the race and suggests that it came into being because of growing hostilities during the time of the athletic festivals at different sites (Philostr. *Gym.* 7). If true, this would suggest that the organizers of the Olympic Games were cognisant of local political difficulties and were trying to react to the situation, reminiscent of the earliest stories about the origins of the Olympic Games related to making peace between antagonistic regions.

PENTATHLON

The *pentathlon*, was composed of five events—jump, javelin, discus, running, and wrestling—and it must have been instituted as a kind of 'all-around athletic championship'. It was first introduced at Olympia in 708 BCE, although in Homer (*Od.* 8.100–103), during the after-dinner games in which Odysseus takes part on the island of Phaeacia, the five events (although not called the 'pentathlon') consist of boxing, javelin, discus, running, and wrestling, where boxing has replaced the jump. The first Olympic victor in the pentathlon was Lampis of Sparta in 708 BCE. Although the running and wrestling events were duplicated in individual events in Greek athletics, the jump, javelin, and discus were only a part of the pentathlon and were unique to this event. It seems likely that the origins of the event have to do with military preparedness in general. It is understood that the events of the pentathlon took place in the stadium, although it is known that at Olympia, during the festival of 364 BCE, the wrestling event of the pentathlon was held outside the *dromos* and closer to the Altar of Zeus (Xen. *Hell.* 7.4.29). In 628 BCE, the pentathlon event for boys was introduced at Olympia and the victor was Eutelidas of Sparta, although the event was subsequently discontinued. Philostratos says that the contestant in the pentathlon should preferably be heavy as opposed to a light athlete, tall and of good build (Philostr. *Gym.* 31).

JUMP

The jump, *halma*, of the pentathlon was a running long-jump that was characterized by the athletes carrying weights or *haltēres* and having the accompaniment of a flute player who provided a cadence for the jumper (Lee 2007: 153–165). Philostratos tells us that the weights were used to stabilize the jumper on landing and implies that they may have increased the distance of the jump (Philostr. *Gym.* 55). In addition, the landing needed to be clean in order for the jump to be counted. Numerous examples of *haltēres* have been discovered and they vary greatly in design, size, and weight, the implements being made of stone or metal. The weights of excavated *haltēres* vary between approximately 1 to 4.5 kg (Gardiner 1930: 146). At the Sanctuary of Zeus at Nemea, an archaic athletic deposit has been found dating to the third quarter of the sixth century BCE. It includes the metal equipment that a pentathlon athlete likely dedicated, including a lead jumping weight, the bronze tips of two javelins, an iron discus and the remains of a bronze strigil (Miller 1983: 78-82). This dedication was discovered in the area to the east of the later long altar, east of the fourth-century-BCE Temple of Zeus.

The jump required a runway of some kind and a line (*batēr*) behind which the jumper had to leave the ground. There would also need to be a soft jumping pit for the athlete to land in (*skamma*), although the pit has never been found in an excavated stadium. It is likely that the pit would have been located at one of the ends of the stadium or along one of its long sides. There are numerous vase painting scenes, as well as miniature bronze representations, showing the jumper in different stages of the jump, and there is no firm evidence to suggest that the jumpers did not hold the *haltēres* through the entire jump and landing. The jumps were marked with rods (*kanones*), as seen in numerous vase paintings. There is also some evidence from vase paintings and miniature bronzes for a standing jump, without a run, although it is not certain that this was a competitive event. It is not known how many jumps were allowed in the competition or whether there were groups of jumpers competing in flights as in the modern day. There are records of several celebrated jumps, including that of Phayllus, who is said to have jumped 55 feet (*Anth. Pal.* App. 297; Gardiner 1904: 70–80). There have been various suggestions to account for the length of the jump, one of which is that the jump may have been composed of multiple stages, something like the modern triple jump. There are several other explanations for such a long jump that include the idea that the distance of the three jumps was added together. Another possible explanation is that the length of the foot used to measure the distance of the jump could have been smaller than the 'typical' Greek foot length.

JAVELIN

The javelin, *akontion*, was a wooden spear that was thrown for distance. The ancient athletic javelin was typically made of elderwood and was tipped with bronze points. Pausanias mentions that three javelins were kept in the Treasury of the Sikyonians at Olympia (Paus. 6.19.4). The javelin was thrown with the assistance of a leather thong, *ankylē*, which was wrapped around the shaft of the javelin and ended in a loop that the athlete used to guide the implement with the first two fingers of his throwing hand. There are many vase painting scenes that show the *ankylē* and the athletes working to attach it to the javelin. The *ankylē*, which came off the shaft of the javelin during the motion of the throw, was used to propel the javelin by putting a spin on the shaft that would steady the throw and increase the distance. Philostratos mentions that the length of fingers was a great advantage to the javelin thrower (Philostr. *Gym.* 31). The javelin may have been the most dangerous event of ancient Greek athletics, as accidents were known to occur. There would have been a necessary run-up to the release of the javelin and a point behind which the throw had to be released. This would have necessitated a runway of some kind. Of course, care had to be considered in the design of the use of the stadium for the javelin for safety reasons.

DISCUS

The discus, *diskos*, was a flat or flattish metal or stone disc that was used for throwing. The weight and size could vary substantially, although it is likely that some of the preserved examples were votive discuses and perhaps not used for competition. Discuses have been found that vary in weight between 1.3 and 5.7 kg and in size between 0.17 and 0.35 m in diameter. The centre was often somewhat thicker than the edges. The discus was thrown from behind the *balbis*, which is also the name for the stone starting-line in the stadium. If this is the same line, then there was some space for an approach to the throw, between 5 and 10 m and, based on representations of discus throwers, there would have been at least a few steps before the throw. Although it is not known how many throws were allowed by each athlete in historical times, during the after-dinner games in Phaeacia there was only one throw per athlete. In the *Thebaid*, however, the Roman poet Statius gives an account of the first Nemean games in which Phlegyas of Pisa is the first to throw the discus and begins with a practice throw up in the air (*Od.* 8.83 ff.; Stat. *Theb.* 6.255). Pausanias relates that a specific discus at Olympia, stored in the Temple of Hera, commemorated the Olympic truce that included the name of the early king Iphitos (Paus. 5.20.1). Although this discus has never been found, it might suggest the possible early date of the discus and the pentathlon event. Like the javelin throw, the discus was a dangerous event, and Greek mythology gives us the story of Hyacinthos who was killed by a discus thrown by Apollo (Apollod. 1.3.3).

Running

The running event of the pentathlon was probably the *stadion* race, one length of the *dromos*. The *stadion* race was also run as an individual event in the schedule of the events of the Olympic Games.

Wrestling

The wrestling event, *palē*, was probably the last event of the pentathlon, and we know that it definitely was last during the Olympic Games in 364 BCE mentioned above, when the wrestling event of the pentathlon was being contested in the area near the altar (Xen. *Hell.* 7.4.29). Wrestling was also an individual event in the schedule of the events of the Olympic Games.

The subject of the scoring of the pentathlon has attracted a number of different explanations, several of them quite complicated (for an alternate explanation, see Kyle 2014). It is likely that the scoring was based on a simple and straightforward system and that the three unique pentathlon events—discus, jump, and javelin—would have been the first to be contested, followed by the footrace and then wrestling (Harris 1972: 34–35). The victor in the pentathlon would have had to win at least three of the five events in order to win overall. (Only this makes sense and is agreed on by virtually all the scholars who have studied the question.) If a single competitor won the first three events, he was the pentathlon victor. However, if there were more than one victor as a result of the first three events, as would be commonplace, then those victors would compete in the footrace. If there were still no winner of three events, then the remaining athletes would compete in the wrestling event, if necessary for several rounds.

BOXING

Boxing, *pugme*, is known from the funeral games of Patroklos in *Iliad* 23.651–699, where the contestants Epeios and Euryalos wear oxhide thongs around their hands and a belt around their waist. There is the mention of a 'circle' in this context, so it seems that the boxers were restricted in some way to a specific area. The belt is known from an earlier context from the boxing-boys fresco from Thera (sixteenth century BCE) and from earlier literary and archaeological contexts in the Near East (Sjoberg 1985: 7–9). From the historical period it is known that the oxhide thongs were used through the fifth century BCE. These thongs consisted of long strips of oxhide that were wound around the four fingers and the knuckles (leaving the thumb free), then passed diagonally across the palm and the back of the hand and around the wrist. In the Hellenistic period the oxhide thongs were superseded by gloves with more volume, known as 'balls' or *sphairai*. Later in the Roman period boxing gloves were further elaborated. In all historical periods boxing gloves were an attempt to protect the hands of the boxer and in later periods the gloves were more offensive. There were no rounds in Greek boxing, nor were there weight categories. The competitors fought until one of the competitors gave up.

PANKRATION

The pankration was a field event that combined aspects of wrestling and boxing. Unlike wrestling, the contest could continue once one or both of the competitors had fallen to the ground and, unlike boxing, the athletes did not wear oxhide thongs to protect their hands. Philostratos describes the event by saying that pankratiasts practise a hazardous style of wrestling that includes the necessary skills of strangling and backward falls, which are not safe for the wrestler; furthermore he says that only biting and gouging are prohibited in the event. The first Olympic pankration victor was Lygdamis of Syracuse in 648 BCE. Only much later, in 200 BCE, was the pankration for boys introduced at the Olympic Games. Perhaps the most famous pankration competitor was Theagenes of Thasos, who competed in and won 1,400 contests all over the Greek world.

HERAEA FOOTRACE FOR UNMARRIED
GIRLS AT OLYMPIA

It is known that at Olympia the same *dromos* that was used for the boys' and men's contests in honour of Zeus was also used for the footraces for unmarried girls at Olympia in honour of Hera. Our primary source for this information is Pausanias in the second century CE, but there is a good possibility that the Heraea festival was very old at Olympia and that the tradition was long-standing (Scanlon 2002: 98–120). The Hera temple at Olympia dates to the years around 600 BCE and the festival of Hera may have been at least this old. Pausanias (5.16.2) mentions that every fourth year there is a *peplos* woven for Hera by the sixteen women, and the same also hold footraces, called Heraea, for unmarried girls. Pausanias mentions three age-groups of unmarried girls and mentions that the costume they wear is a tunic that exposes the right breast and shoulder. He adds that the stadium at Olympia is reserved for these contests but that the *dromos* of the stadium is shortened for them by about one-sixth of its length. The winners received olive crowns and a portion of the ox that they dedicated to Hera. I have suggested elsewhere that the shortened length of the *dromos* of the stadium for the Heraea events may be related to a shorter foot being used for the measurement of the 600 feet (Romano 1981: 255–256; Romano 1993: 9–16); alternatively, it may have arisen from the girls' stride being shorter than those of boys and men (Scanlon 2002: 100). It is the mention of the Sixteen Women that organize the games in honour of Hera, in order to bring an end to the violence between several of the local communities, that is of interest, in the sense of being another reason to hold athletic contests. If this is the case, then the age of the Hera games could be considerably older than *c*.600 BCE.

Torch-Races

Torch-races, *lampadedromia*, are known from some festivals including several in Athens, the Panathenaia, the Hephaisteia, and the Promethea, as well as the festivals for Pan, Bendis, and Nemesis. In the Hellenistic period the Theseia and the Epitaphia also included torch-races (Kyle 1987: 190–193). The Isthmian games in honour of Poseidon included a torch-race. Some of these festivals in Athens—such as those to Prometheus, Hephaistos, Bendis, and Pan—were not athletic. Although it is not certain that all torch-races were relay races, at least some of them were. The runners ran with lighted torches from one altar to another. In Athens, for instance, according to Pausanias the torch-race was run as a part of the Panathenaia, starting in the Academy at the altar of Prometheus and being run towards the city. The objective was to run and keep the torch burning at the same time (Paus. 1.30.2).

References

Christesen, P. 2007. *Olympic Victor Lists and Ancient Greek History*. Cambridge.

Eder, B. 2001. 'Continuity of Bronze Age Cult at Olympia? The Evidence of the Late Bronze Age and Early Iron Age Pottery.' In *Potnia: Deities and Religion in the Aegean Bronze Age*. 201–209. R. Laffineur and R. Hägg, eds. Liège.

Furtwängler, A. 1890. *Olympia IV, Die Bronzen und ubrigen kleineren Funde aus Olympia*. Berlin.

Gallis, K. J. 2002. 'The Games in Ancient Larisa.' In *The Archaeology of the Olympics: The Olympics and Other Festivals in Antiquity*. 2nd edition. 217–235. W. J. Raschke, ed. Madison, WI.

Gardiner, E. N. 1904 'Phayllus and His Record Jump.' *JHS* 24: 70–80.

Gardiner, E. N. 1930. *Athletics of the Ancient World*. Oxford.

German, S. 2007. 'Politics and the Bronze Age Origins of Olympic Practices.' In *Onward to the Olympics: Historical Perspectives on the Olympic Games*. 15–25. G. P. Schaus and S. R. Wenn, eds. Waterloo, Ont.

Giglio, M. 2009. 'Lo stadio et le mura in eta repubblicana, Cuma.' *Atti del quarantottesimo convegno di studi sulla Magna Grecia*. 623–642. Istituto per la storia el'archeologia della Magna Grecia. Taranto.

Harris, H. A. 1972. *Sport in Greece and Rome*. Ithaca, NY.

Kramer, S. N. 1981. *History Begins at Sumer*. Philadelphia.

Kyle, D. G. 1987. *Athletics in Ancient Athens*. Leiden.

Kyle, D. G. 2014. 'Winning and Watching the Greek Pentathlon.' In *Sport in the Greek and Roman Worlds*. Vol. 1. 228–246. T. F. Scanlon, ed. Oxford.

Kyrieleis, H. 2002. 'Zu den Anfagen des Heiligums von Olympia.' In *Olympia 1875–2000, 125 Jahre Deutsche Ausgrabungen*. 213–220. H. Kyrieleis, ed. Mainz.

Laser, S. 1987. *Sport und Spiel: Archaeologica Homerica*, vol. 3. Gottingen.

Lee, H. M. 2007. 'The Halma: A Running or a Standing Jump.' In *Onward to the Olympics: Historical Perspectives on the Olympic Games*. 153–165. G. P. Schaus and S. R. Wenn, eds. Waterloo, Ont.

Marinatos, N. 1984. *Art and Religion in Thera: Reconstructing a Bronze Age*. Athens.

Miller, S. G. 1983. 'Excavations at Nemea, 1982.' *Hesperia* 52: 78–82.

Miller, S. G. 2001. *Excavations at Nemea II: The Early Hellenistic Stadium*. Berkeley.

Mylonas, G. E. 1951. 'The Figured Mycenaean Stelai.' *AJA* 55: 134–147.

Newberry, P. E., F. L. Griffith, and G. W. Fraser. 1893. *Beni Hasan II*. London.

Romano, D. G. 1981. 'The Stadia of the Peloponnesos.' PhD dissertation, University of Pennsylvania.

Romano, D. G. 1993. *Athletics and Mathematics in Archaic Corinth: The Origins of the Greek Stadion*. Philadelphia.

Romano, D. G. and M. E. Voyatzis. 2010. 'Excavating at the Birthplace of Zeus.' *Expedition* 52: 9–21.

Romano, D. G. and M. E. Voyatzis. 2014. 'Mt. Lykaion Excavation and Survey Project, Part 1, The Upper Sanctuary.' *Hesperia* 83: 569–652.

Scanlon, T. F. 2002. *Eros and Greek Athletics*. New York.

Sjoberg, A. 1985. 'Trials of Strength.' *Expedition* 27: 7–9.

Swaddling, J. 1980. *The Ancient Olympic Games*. British Museum.

....

CHAPTER 17

GREEK COMBAT SPORT AND THE BORDERS OF ATHLETICS, VIOLENCE, AND CIVILIZATION

....

MICHAEL B. POLIAKOFF

THE PARADOX OF THE GREEK COMBAT SPORTS

....

THE three Greek combat sports, wrestling, boxing, and pankration (a sport that allowed a broad variety of unarmed fighting tactics) appear in historical times as well-developed athletic events with established rules and procedures that distinguish these sports from simple unarmed fighting. The rules and conventions vary over time and place, but as is to be expected in a sport, the combat element is regulated and controlled, and the determination of victory differs, albeit slightly, from the resolution that might be expected in a contest outside the rules and structure of organized athletics. All three sports incorporate a significant level of violence, with the possibility of major injury present in all of them.

It is a remarkable paradox that the intensely individualistic and often violent combat sports were a central social institution of ancient Greece, but that the armed duels that characterized European society through most of its history were very rare in ancient Greece after the Mycenaean era, with a few battlefield exceptions (Glotz 1904: 271–287). (Nor, for different reasons, were they part of Roman civilization, again with a few battle-field exceptions.) The paradox appears yet deeper with the realization that Greek combat sports emerge from a context in their early history—as is evident in the Homeric poems—in which the boundaries between athletic contest and duelling with intent to harm are both unclear and permeable. Even in later, highly organized athletic contests, the combat sports slide easily into extreme violence: the goal of boxing and pankration was, after all, to render an opponent unable or unwilling to continue the contest, much like any ordinary physical confrontation. It is only the ever-present element in sport of the weaker competitor's prerogative to signal submission that establishes the difference between the resolution of the sporting contest and a fight between two rivals in which such an option might not be granted (or, when deadly weapons are in use, might quickly be irrelevant). Wrestling and boxing bouts in Greek mythology not infrequently end in death, and both archaeological evidence and the twenty-third book of Homer's *Iliad* bespeak a world in which duelling with weapons fits into a context of unarmed athletic events. Later, the Greek East found Roman gladiatorial combat interesting, if not attractive. Finally, contrary to the widely held view that the Greeks kept their boxing free of the dangerous spiked gloves that characterized Roman boxing, the evidence is that the Greek festivals at times did admit this destructive equipment, though its use appears not to have been widespread (see next section).

Gustave Glotz, in a few significant pages, engaged the question: 'Were the private quarrels between members of the same tribe or the same city never preserved to be seen?' (Glotz 1904: 276). This essay will serve as a preliminary exploration of this important frontier: why did the archaic culture of single combat described so vividly in Homer's *Iliad* not find expression in the type of duelling seen throughout European history? As Glotz suggested, the answer must lie in the evolution of the Greek concept of *agōn*, 'contest'. According to Glotz, the *agōn* held a role in legal process, namely, the judicial resolution of disputes by combat, which then vanished, replaced by the rationality of law, with its traces remaining in athletics. The thesis of this article goes further, arguing that the Greeks from their earliest history engaged and resolved through competitive athletics, in particular the combat events, issues of honour and status, and thereby negotiated quite well challenges that could easily slide into far more destructive manifestations. This appears to be the reason there is a vibrant legacy of Greek combat sport, while the Hellenic world remained an antitype, not a precedent, for the carnage of sword and pistol duels in latter-day Europe.

OVERVIEW OF THE COMBAT SPORTS

Wrestling, boxing, and pankration were contested at the Greek athletic festivals, with Olympic competition for men commencing in 708, 688, and 648 BCE and the competition for boys in 632, 616, and 200 BCE, respectively. There were separate categories in competitions for boys and men at Olympia, and, at some athletic festivals, also for an intermediate age group of youths. Since there were no weight classes, large competitors had a distinct advantage. It is significant that the Greeks apparently saw the inherent inequity of pitting boys against men but did not seek to create an opportunity for smaller competitors to compete more equitably. There were no time limits placed on the competition. Competitions continued without significant pause for rounds or rests. Since the stadia were not roofed, the midsummer heat and sunlight added to the discomfort and physical stress of the contests. Cicero noted that inexperienced boxers might be able to endure the blows they received at Olympia better than the heat (Cicero, *Brutus* 69): this observation was hardly unique (Poliakoff 1987: 9). The inscription from Olympia honouring Tiberius Claudius Rufus of Smyrna (*IvO* 54/55) records how the final round in the pankration competition continued beyond nightfall, and ended only when the judges determined to award first prize to both competitors: the inscription honouring him observes that he considered it 'finer to scorn life than the hope of a victor's crown.'

The rules of the contests and the organization of competition betray an unwillingness to make the combat events less dangerous or injurious. The absence of weight classes

or any conventions to permit the athletes to keep hydrated during competition and reduce the dangers of heat stroke suggest a convergence with the world of warfare, where the
combatants' ability to withstand harsh conditions was a determinant of victory. Wrestling
was by far the safest of the three events, yet through most of its history, it was apparently legal
to break an opponent's fingers (Siewert 1992: 111–117). A sixth century BCE inscription from
Olympia prohibits this practice, yet in 456 and 452 BCE Leontiscus won at Olympia using
this very tactic (Pausanias 6.4.3). Several Greek bronze figurines show one wrestler applying
pressure to his opponent's shoulder joint in a manner that would be illegal in modern amateur wrestling because of the imminent danger it creates of dislocating the joint (Poliakoff
1987: 47). Since pankration and boxing ended with the submission of one competitor or his
inability to continue the contest, these events incorporated a much greater level of violence.
Several authors, including Plato, describe padded gloves, *sphairai*, apparently much like
modern boxing gloves, but these were used only in practice, not competition. Plato's description of the preparation for a boxing match is particularly revealing: 'coming as close as possible to the same thing, we put on *sphairai* instead of thongs, so that blows and defences can
be practised as much as possible in a satisfactory way' (*Laws* 830 a–c).

In competition, Greek boxers wore strips of leather over their knuckles and wrists
(*himantes*), whose purpose was to protect the hand, not the opponent's face, from injury, and Greek art regularly depicts the blood flow from these contests. Shortly after the
middle of the fourth century BCE, Greek vase paintings show boxers using an even more
lacerative type of boxing thong, called by the Greeks the sharp thongs (*oxeis himantes*),
which had a thick strip of leather over the knuckles, clearly seen in Greek sculpture (Miller
2004: 51–57). Several literary sources referred to the thongs as hard and dry (Apollonius of
Rhodes, *Argonautica* 2.52–53; Nonnos, 37.507): the thick ridge would have served as a highly
damaging cutting edge.

The Romans introduced the most dangerous boxing equipment of the ancient world.
The Roman *caestus* frequently included metal spikes, lumps of metal, or a wide metal ridge.
Examples can be seen depicted in Roman mosaics as well as figurative sculpture. The poet
Virgil describes these devices as 'stiff with lead and iron sewn in' (*Aeneid* 5.404–405). Most
modern scholarship has regarded the use of such devastating boxing equipment as a purely
Roman phenomenon, but recent numismatic evidence suggests that the Greeks at least on
occasion escalated the violence of their contests from the use of sharp thongs to the metal
and leather Roman *caestus*. A bronze coin from Philippopolis in Thrace (Fig. 17.1) celebrating
the visit of the emperor Caracalla, depicts a boxer wearing a *caestus* with projections from
the fist, one an apparent cutting edge, the other at a right angle probably providing protection for the boxer's hand. The depiction on the coin seems similar to the *caestus* seen on
other monuments, most clearly on a bronze fragment in the Metropolitan Museum of Art
(Fig. 17.2).

Since the coin bears the inscription 'PYTHIA', indicating an isopythian contest (i.e.,
modelled after the games at Delphi) and the festival the coin commemorates is called the
Alexandria, it would be very hard to argue that the coin depicts a purely Roman rather than
a Greek event. At very least, the Greeks who held this festival at Philippopolis, even were it
specially designed to please Caracalla, did not shrink from using the Roman device in a contest they describe as following the model of the sacred crown games at Delphi. (A full publication by Anthony Milavic and Michael Poliakoff concerning this coin is forthcoming.) It is
also noteworthy, as pointed out by Hugh Lee, that the boxers depicted in Roman art wearing

FIGURE 17.1. Bronze Coin (Reverse), THRACE, Philippopolis, AE-30mm 19.48g. 198–217 CE. Legend: ΚΟΙΝΟΝ ΘΡΑΚΩΝ -ΑΛΕΞΑΝΔΡΙΑ ΕΝ ΦΙΛΙΠΠΟ[ΠΟΛΙΣ], in exergue ΠΥ-ΘΙΑ in left and right fields; boxer stepping left with left hand extended and both hands wrapped in Roman *caestus* (boxing glove)—as evidenced by projections from fist—rather than Greek sharp thongs. Obverse (not shown), wreathed bust of Caracalla, Legend: AUT(OKRATOR) K(AISAR) M(ARKOS) AUP(ELIOS) SEUE(ROS) ANTONEINOS. Collection of Anthony Milavic. Source: Edward J. Waddell Stock.

the dangerous *caestus* are typically shown naked, following the practice of Greek, not Roman athletes. The fact that they are shown adhering to Hellenic practice strongly suggests that the Romans viewed this form of boxing as part of Greek athletics, rather than a variation on Roman arena contests, in which the gladiators wore armour and clothing (Lee 1997: 164, 168).

As Louis Robert demonstrated in his seminal *Gladiateurs dans l'Orient grec*, Greeks participated with enthusiasm in gladiatorial contests (Robert 1940: 13–15). It should not be surprising that they did not deem the dangerous Roman boxing equipment off limits. Greek vocabulary such as *pygmē* ('boxing'), *pykteuein* ('to box') and *pyktēs* ('boxer'), which are properly athletic terms, moreover, were used to describe gladiatorial combat. Thus, the Greek vocabulary itself for what happened in the arena seems to show how the world of boxing and gladiatorial combat overlapped and how ambiguous the boundaries between athletics and deadly combat could be.

LETHAL CONTESTS IN GREEK MYTHOLOGY

In the world of mythological athletic encounters, it is noteworthy how often the outcome is death for one of the competitors. Ingomar Weiler observed in his study of mythological

FIGURE 17.2. Roman boxing *caestus*. A cord ties the projecting metal plate onto the boxer's forearm. First/second century CE. Metropolitan Museum of Art, 2001.219.

contests that it is difficult to draw a clear line between wrestling and a confrontation whose purpose is the destruction of the opponent (Weiler 1974: 146): in other words, it is unclear whether the contest is sport or an unarmed duel to the death. Hercules slays Antaeus in a wrestling match, lifting him in the air and crushing him to death (Lucan, *Civil War* 4. 589–660; Philostratus, *Imagines* 2.21). He breaks the ribs of Menoites, the herdsman of the underworld, in a wrestling bout and only stops when Persephone, the queen of the underworld, intervenes (Apollodorus 2.5.12). He kills the brothers Polygonus and Telegonus, who had challenged him to a wrestling match (Apollodorus 2.5.9). Eryx challenges Hercules to a wrestling match (or in Virgil, *Aeneid* 5.400–414, a boxing match) wagering his land against the hero's bull (Pausanias 3.16.4, 4.36.4; Apollodorus 2.5.10). He loses the contest and also his life. The ogre Amycus forces all strangers to box with him, but meets his death when he challenges Pollux (Apollonius of Rhodes, *Argo* 2.1–97). The Athenian hero Theseus slays Cercyon in wrestling. In most versions of the myth, Cercyon forced wayfarers to wrestle with him and killed them; Theseus, relying on his skill and technique, wrestles and slays Cercyon (Pausanias 1.39.3; Apollodorus ep.1.3). As we have seen above in the Greek vocabulary of boxing and gladiatorial combat, the various versions of mythological contests in combat sports show their ambiguous nature and how readily they blend into the world of the duel.

THE HOMERIC WORLD

The funeral games for Patroclus in the twenty-third book of the *Iliad* include boxing and wrestling, which were part of the athletic contests of historical times, as well as an armed single combat—a duel—which has no role in the Greek contests of historical times. Of these three contests, only boxing has a clear outcome: Epeius strikes Euryalus with such force that he is lifted off the ground before collapsing in semi-senselessness (*Iliad* 23.685–695). It is noteworthy that Epeius alone of all the competitors in these games is boastful and minatory. 'I will smash his skin apart and break his bones on each other. Let those who care for him wait nearby in a huddle about him to carry him out, after my fists have beaten him under' (*Il.* 23.672–675). He acknowledges that he is not distinguished as a soldier, and that deficiency makes him more determined to prove himself pre-eminent in boxing. That is to say, his athletic prowess is his surrogate for martial distinction. The event has the formalities of athletic competition: both boxers are girded and wear leather thongs on their hands.

The boxing match is the contest within the funeral games described in *Iliad* 23 in which the greatest damage is inflicted on an opponent. The boundaries between sport and a fight to the death are even less clear in the match that the suitors arrange between the beggar Irus and the disguised hero Odysseus in the eighteenth book of the *Odyssey*. There the combatants are girded, but they wear no thongs on their hands—there is no athletic convention or equipment in evidence. More significant yet is the outcome. Odysseus considers the option of killing Irus with a well-placed blow to the head but decides it might cause the suitors to see through his disguise; he delivers instead a blow that crushes bone and leaves the hapless Irus twitching on the ground, to be dragged off to a threatened demise at the hands of a mysterious King Echetus, who has a reputation for mutilating his victims.

The fight in armour in *Iliad* 23 has a far more innocent conclusion than either the boxing match in *Iliad* 23 or the one in *Odyssey* 18. Achilles initially sets out the armour that Patroclus had stripped from the fallen Sarpedon as the prize for an armed fight, but then states that the first prize is the sword he took from Asteropaius, and it will go to 'whichever one first reaches the fair flesh and touches the entrails, through the armour and black blood' (23.805–806). He seems confident that the contest will not end in death, since he adds, 'Let both men take away this armour as a common possession, and we will set a good banquet for them in our hut.' The great warriors Ajax and Diomedes step forward. The confusion over what represents the first prize is compounded by the manner in which the fight proceeds. Contrary to Achilles' confidence that there will be no serious injury, the rest of the Greeks fear for the safety of the competitors and call for the contest to end. Although neither combatant inflicted a wound, Diomedes gets the sword, presumably the first prize, anyway.

Thus the *Iliad* seems to reflect a historical context in which duelling in armour is known but perhaps not fully understood. (Duels of military champions in the course of warfare, on the other hand, are frequent and clearly understood, including the combat of Paris and Menelaus, Hector and Ajax, and the climactic duel of Hector and Achilles.) The funeral games of book 23 also introduce a theme that will be highly important for the social history of Greek athletics: the combat sport, in this case boxing, as a surrogate for warfare. It is dangerous, injurious, and, at least in the eyes of Epeius, a compensation for a lack of battlefield status.

Beyond *Iliad* 23, there is only scattered evidence of armed duelling. The juxtaposition of armed contest and athletics in Homer has an archaeological parallel in a Mycenaean *larnax* (sarcophagus) from the thirteenth century BCE, found in Tanagra in Boeotia. It depicts both bull-leaping and armed fighting, strongly suggesting funeral games in honour of the deceased. The armed fighting is of a particularly brutal variety in that the combatants have weapons, but have neither shield nor armour, as Ajax and Diomedes had in their fight in the *Iliad* (Decker 1982–3: 1–24). Plutarch, writing in the second century CE, believed that there was a contest in ancient Pisa, which at times controlled the site of Olympia, that involved fighting in armour, *hoplomachia* (Plutarch, *Quaest. Conv.* 5.2), and proceeded until the death of the vanquished. In historical times there is little evidence to suggest that *hoplomachia* contests were fights, rather than exhibition exercises (Saglio 1899; Jüthner 1913). The story of Dioxippus of Athens, an Olympic victor in pankration who, naked and oiled, defeated a heavily armed Macedonian in a duel before Alexander the Great and his army (Diodorus Siculus 17.100.2) stands out as an exceptional event.

COMBAT SPORT, THE DUEL, AND THE CONCEPT OF THE *AGŌN*

A characteristic of European duelling was a belief that the sense of honour that motivated such confrontations drew inspiration from classical antiquity. In *Boswell on the Grand Tour*, Boswell describes how the Corsican general Paoli told him that a man who would 'form his mind to glory' needed to read Plutarch and Livy, not contemporary authors (discussed in Kiernan 1988: 13). Yet Europeans were not unaware of the ahistorical nature of their claims. As one German proponent of duelling noted, 'In the Greek and Roman world individual honor paid too much deference to one's honor as a citizen' (McAleer 1994: 12). For those who invoked the Roman author Livy, it is ironic that among the elements of *Romanitas* that Livy describes is Titus Manlius Torquatus executing his son for fighting a single combat with an enemy champion contrary to orders (Livy, *Histories* 8.17). Similarly, in Plutarch's *Life of Sertorius*, Metellus rejects Sertorius' challenge to a single combat in front of the armies, ostensibly deeming it unseemly for generals. Neither Rome nor Greece had a place for the extra-legal, personal assertion of physical bravery that duelling represented. V. G. Kiernan aptly remarked: 'Wherever warfare is well-developed, battlefield habits will influence attitudes to private combat; the self-willed knight, not the well-drilled Greek or Roman, was the ancestor of the duellist.' It was the unusual brilliance of Greek civilization that, even in Homeric times, the Greeks saw the absurdity of jeopardizing an Ajax or Diomedes or any other soldier in an armed duel outside of the battlefield—and hence the Greek troops' clamour for an end to the contest: instead of private resolution of quarrels in armed aggression, Hellenic society cultivates a surrogate in athletics. Athletic competition, as both Greek and Roman strategists like Epaminondas, Philopoimen, and Alexander recognized, was not effective as a military drill, but as a social mechanism to channel aggression and individual wilfulness; it was a remarkable success. The hoplite phalanx moved forward in disciplined, locked ranks; maverick behaviour was welcomed and rewarded only in the stadium.

The European duel grows from a belief in personal honour and desire to maintain a behaviour identified with an aristocratic class. The medieval jousts and *pas d'armes* ('passage of arms'; a chivalric armed challenge) that were the real precedents for later European duelling were replete with a sense of class honour and status. The fact that many took place before the eyes of the king could only reinforce the belief that these demonstrations of martial courage were the emblems that differentiated the nobleman from others. In Germany from the seventeenth to the early twentieth centuries, where a particularly dangerous convention of duelling with pistols claimed many lives, the terms associated with duelling were *Ehre* ('honour') and *Standesehre* ('class or status honour') (McAleer 1994: 3–4). It was a class distinction to be *satisfaktionsfähig*, 'capable of giving satisfaction in a duel', a privilege initially restricted to an elite minority (Kiernan 1988: 4–5). German military thinkers were hardly oblivious to the cost of duelling among their officers, and both military and criminal codes attempted at various times to extirpate, or at least mitigate, the institution. Frederick the Great said, 'I love brave officers, but executioners are something my army does not need', and considered duelling 'this misplaced sense of honor, which has cut short the lives of so many respectable men from whom the Fatherland had expected the greatest service'. Yet Friedrich ultimately tolerated the behaviour among his soldiers (McAleer 1994: 20–21). The institution was deeply embedded in German aristocratic values and in particular, military codes of honour, and as the social upheavals of the industrial revolution threatened aristocratic identity, the ferocity of duelling increased. Remarkably, its trajectory was quite the opposite in mid-nineteenth-century England where an assertive middle class had more practical concerns—note the fulmination of nineteenth-century historian Heinrich von Treitschke: 'The old sense of honor and prejudices of the upper classes were scattering before the superior strength of money, while the German nobility remained poor but chivalrous' (McAleer 1994: 77). British pragmatism, combined with the rising popularity of boxing among the upper classes (Kiernan 1988: 213–215), supplanted the duel. The edict of Prime Minister Robert Peel in 1844, pronounced with the blessing of Queen Victoria, that the family of a man killed in a duel would not receive his pension, was tantamount to a *coup de grace* for British duelling (McAleer 1994: 95).

What is remarkable about the European duel as it develops from medieval into modern times is how much it is focused on courage (real or feigned) in the face of death and how little it was focused on competition. Whereas Greek aristocrats like Diagoras of Rhodes and his sons would seek the fame of an Olympic crown by their skill as pankratiasts or boxers (Pindar, *Olympian Odes* 7; Pausanias 6.7.1-7), the aristocratic duellists (and the bourgeoisie who imitated them) were principally distinguished by their willingness to accept disfigurement in sword-fighting and death in confrontations with firearms. The details are chilling. Fencing skill was minimized to accommodate the display of daring. Whereas inscriptions honouring athletes in combat sport record with pride when the athlete was *atraumatistos* ('unscarred') as a sign of superior skill (Poliakoff 1987: 10–11; 165), the German duelling corps member revelled in his *Renommierschmiss*, his 'bragging scar'. A Prussian inspector observed that student duellists scorned skilful defence as cowardice and rained blows on each other simultaneously (Frevert 1995: 105). A witness in 1888 wrote enthusiastically, 'Once someone has looked his opponent calmly in the eye a few times with rapiers clashing, once he has refrained from flinching while receiving one blow after another with warm blood flowing over his body, the easier he will be able to maintain his composure in other difficult situations in life' (Frevert 1995: 105). A remarkable sign of how little the competitive aspect of the contest mattered is that, despite the thousands of university sword fights held in the student duelling corps (a contemporary source estimated 8,000 per year during the 1890s; Frevert 1995: 106), Germany had very limited success in men's Olympic fencing until the 1970s. Although there were some strictures against intentionally structuring the confrontation to be a duel to the death, court and newspaper records tell of pistol duels at fifteen, ten, and even five paces with multiple exchanges of fire, often with highly accurate, rifled weapons (Frevert 1995: 160; McAleer 1994: 64–84). Ironically, some nineteenth-century German sources document the aristocratic horror at the idea of English boxing (Kiernan 1988: 77–78). Historian Kevin McAleer's sarcastic analysis is not misplaced: 'Bravery among German prewar stock was measured not by the exhibition of physical and mental agility, flexible response and active daring, but by a bovine impassivity that could trade shots at suicidal range' (McAleer 1994: 59).

While physical courage, endurance and pain tolerance are elements common to Greek combat sport, to the Roman arena, and to duelling, the features that distinguish the Hellenic combat sports are structured competition, a keen, almost obsessive focus on winning the contest, and the application of a high level of science and technique to the contest. For the victors in Pindar's *Odes*, courage and toil, along with athletic skill, are the tools of gaining the immortal honour of victory. Tiberius Claudius Rufus, discussed earlier in this chapter, and numerous other athletes known through texts or inscriptions, risked death *to achieve an athletic victory*. Success in the contest—which was open to all social classes—was what brought status, not the willingness to embrace self-destruction. To be denied a victory that the competitor believed he had earned was catastrophic—it was this that pushed Cleomedes of Astypalaia to madness and murder (Pausanias 6.9.6–8). When Theogenes of Thasos entered the Olympic festival in both pankration and boxing, defeating Euthymus of Locri in the boxing finals but defaulting to his opponent in pankration out of exhaustion, the judges laid an enormous fine on him for entering the boxing contest out of spite for Euthymus (Pausanias 6.6.5–6).

Honour and public reputation were as important for the ancient Greek as they were for the nineteenth-century European. K. J. Dover aptly pointed out that for the Greeks, 'goodness divorced from a reputation for goodness was of limited interest': this applied to civic life, as well as the battlefield (Dover 1974: 226–229). But the city-state depended upon and demanded a high level of cooperation in civic and military life. Amassing political power could lead to ostracism in Athens, with a ten-year mandatory exile, and often even successful generals were not given the privilege of commemoration on victory monuments, lest the military achievement of the city be seen as the achievement of an individual. It is not difficult to see how the Greek combat sports, which did indeed flirt with reckless endangerment of life and limb, represented an outlet for the aggression and ambition that had devastating consequences elsewhere. The element of sport, of athletic competition, channelled through the rough contests of the combat sports, made the Greek pursuit of honour far less destructive than the European duel and relatively safe for the cohesion of society.

CONCLUSION AND PROSPECTUS

What do we mean when we say 'sport'? At what point does the contest cross the line from a competitive activity bound by its own special rules and conventions, abstracted from the criteria that govern success or failure in everyday life, to an activity that more closely resembles acts of violence that are typically regarded as criminal behaviour? The controversy over whether the gladiatorial games qualify as sport or an armed spectacle deepens, as more evidence and scholarship demonstrate the frequency of gladiatorial games with blunted weapons (Carter 2006: 161–175). The line between a sword fight with blunt weapons and a boxing match with weighted and spiked gloves seems very thin indeed. But when one puts side by side the combat sports of the Greeks and the duelling culture of nineteenth-century Europe, especially that of Germany, the restraint of Greek civilization, even when it experimented with the Roman *caestus* and the world of the arena, stands in remarkable contrast.

Johan Huizinga himself hesitated to draw bright lines between the world of play and the serious; instead he bid mankind to listen to its moral conscience in determining whether an 'action to which our will impels us is a serious duty or is licit as play'. The decisions, informed by history, about what is licit or illicit as sport have real implications for contemporary policy. Full-contact karate tournaments, mixed martial arts, and the revival and popularity of pankration invite the historian's comment on what, as Huizinga would ask, is a sound, culture-producing force and what is not. The answers, which need to respect the free choices of individuals in a free society while looking to the norms and values that appropriately respect human life and dignity, are not easy. Huizinga will have to have the last word: 'As soon as truth and justice, compassion and forgiveness have part in our resolve to act, our anxious question loses all meaning. One drop of pity is enough to lift our doing beyond intellectual distinction. Springing as it does from a belief in justice and divine grace, conscience, which is moral awareness, will always whelm the question that eludes and deludes us to the end, in a lasting silence' (Huizinga 1955: 210–13).

REFERENCES

Carter, M. 2006. 'Gladiatorial Combat With "Sharp" Weapons.' *ZPE* 155: 161–175.

Decker, W. 1982–1983. 'Die mykenische Herkunft des griechischen Totenagons.' *Stadion* 8–9: 1–24.

Dover, K. J. 1974. *Greek Popular Morality in the Time of Plato and Aristotle*. Oxford.

Frevert, U. 1995. *Men of Honour: A Social and Cultural History of the Duel*. Anthony Williams, trans. Cambridge.

Glotz, G. 1904. *La solidarité de la famille dans le droit criminel en Grèce*. Paris.

Huizinga, J. 1955. *Homo Ludens: A Study of the Play Element in Culture*. Boston, MA.

Jüthner, J. 1913. 'Hoplomachie.' In *RE* 8. 2298–2299. Stuttgart.

Kiernan, V. G. 1988. *The Duel in European History: Honour and the Reign of the Aristocracy*. Oxford.

Lee, H. M. 1997. 'The Later Greek Boxing Glove and the "Roman" Caestus: A Centennial Reevaluation of Jüthner's "Über Antike Turngeträthe".' *Nikephoros* 10: 161–178.

McAleer, K. 1994. *Dueling: The Cult of Honor in Fin-de-Siècle Germany*. Princeton.

Miller, S. G. 2004. *Ancient Greek Athletics*. New Haven.

Poliakoff, M. B. 1987. *Combat Sports in the Ancient World: Competition, Violence, and Culture*. New Haven.

Robert, L. 1940. *Les gladiateurs dans l'Orient grec*. Paris.

Saglio. E. 1899. 'Hoplomachia.' In *Dar.–Sag*. 3.1. 248–249. Paris.

Siewert, P. 1992. 'The Olympic Rules.' In *Proceedings of an International Symposium on the Olympic Games*. 111–117. W. Coulson and H. Kyrieleis, eds. Athens.

Weiler, I. 1974. *Der Agon im Mythos*. Darmstadt.

CHAPTER 18

··

GLADIATORS

··

MICHAEL CARTER

> Do not think that I am sullying the dignity of history when I write about such
> things. Otherwise I would not have mentioned them.
>
> Dio Cassius 73.18.3

INTRODUCTION: AN EMBARRASSING FASCINATION

So Dio Cassius apologizes to us, his readers, for deigning to describe Commodus' gladiatorial infatuations. What Dio found embarrassing, Augustine would later find threatening. In a well-known passage from his autobiographical *Confessions*, he traces the rapid descent of his pious Christian friend, Alypius, into a sort of mindless intoxication brought on simply by witnessing gladiatorial combats. A good Christian, Alypius had never wanted anything to do with the violent spectacle and had always refused to attend whenever his fellow students urged him to go with them. He finally relented but said that he would keep his eyes closed and not watch. 'If only he could have closed his ears too!' laments Augustine, for an incident in the fight drew a roar from the crowd, and Alypius, overcome with curiosity, finally opened his eyes:

> As soon as he saw that bloodshed, he drank in its savageness. He did not turn away, but he
> fixed his gaze on the scene and drank in the frenzied madness without knowing what he was
> doing. He revelled in the wickedness of the fighting and became drunk on the gory pleasure.
> He was no longer that man who had come to the amphitheatre, but was now one of the mob
> which he had joined, a true companion to those who had brought him! (*Confessions* 6.8).

Clearly, the spectacle of gladiatorial combat had the power to engage the spectator and to elicit a strong emotional response: simply hearing the roar of the crowd and then witnessing the combat was enough to overcome all of Alypius' pious resistance. This image of murderous gladiators and their bloody combats is an enduring one. Though recent scholarship is moving us away from this view, many of us, both scholars and others, still see the combats as brutal and homicidal encounters and the gladiators themselves as especially desperate and murderous men. How else to explain the blood and gore of Augustine's account? Yet, while

Augustine does provide important testimony for the effect of the spectacle and insight into the reaction of the spectators, he expresses no interest in what the gladiators were doing or in the spectacle itself. What provoked the crowd's reaction? Augustine says only that there was an incident in the fight. Was a gladiator killed? Were the people reacting to the wounding of a gladiator? Or were they reacting to an especially thrilling match? We cannot know. The image of the gladiator here is entirely our own.

For a long time scholars would have sympathized with both Dio and Augustine. Though the importance of gladiatorial spectacles for the Romans has long been recognized (there is no ignoring an amphitheatre), they were nevertheless considered beneath contempt and offered the historian little of value other than a horrifying glimpse into the psyche of the old pagan Romans (Brown 1992; 1995). This has all changed in the last generation. Both sport and (increasingly) spectacles are now seen by many to occupy a place at or near the centre of Greek and Roman culture. The time, the money, the energy, and the enthusiasm that they invested in sports and spectacles has to be accounted for. As this volume itself attests, taking sport seriously has generated great insights into Greek culture, and scholarship is now benefiting from similar attention to Roman spectacles (see, for example, Kyle 2007). To understand the social and cultural significance of the spectacle of gladiatorial combats in Roman society, we must recognize what assumptions the Romans brought with them to the amphitheatre and what interested them as they watched. All depends on putting aside our own preconceptions and appreciating the reality of the spectacle in the context of Roman sentiments and practices. Rather than concerning ourselves with pious Alypius' soul, we should instead determine what so aroused the interest of the cheering thousands watching with him.

In this chapter, I wish to explore two connected areas. First, I consider the nature of gladiatorial combats. What in fact were the ancient Romans looking at? What does our evidence, read critically, tell us about how gladiatorial combats were fought and what about them was important to the Romans? Given the limitations and scope of this volume, this can be no more than a brief review. The second area emerges from the first and considers what role the spectacle might have filled in Roman society. The spectacles associated with the arena, specifically gladiatorial combats but also wild beast hunts and displays and executions, presented the spectators with several values and themes central to Roman culture. The shows might even have played a role in the creation and maintenance of a Roman sense of identity by helping to shape society's values and the community's perception of itself.

GLADIATORIAL COMBAT BY THE RULES

By the time Alypius ventured into the amphitheatre, gladiators had been a part of Roman life for several hundred years, and in that time the institution had evolved considerably. Since its first appearance in Rome, traditionally at the funeral of Decimus Iunius Brutus in 264 BCE and then throughout the republic, the spectacle of gladiatorial combat was found almost exclusively in connection with the funerals of great men (Servius, *Commentary on Vergil's Aeneid* 10.519: *viri fortes*) and became known as a *munus* (duty) offered to the community (see especially Ville 1981 on the institution's development). Due to its popularity, however, the spectacle became increasingly politicized during the later years of the republic

as ambitious politicians in Rome often waited to present *munera* until a politically oppor-
tune time. By the early imperial period it was removed from its strictly funerary context and
came to be presented primarily in association with wild beast hunts (*venationes*) and often
executions: the 'standard *munus*' (*munus legitimum*). Throughout Italy and the provinces,
where the spectacles rapidly spread, the *munera* became most intimately associated with the
celebration of the imperial cult (Robert 1940: 270–280; Futrell 1997: 79–93).

Originally, the gladiators themselves had been drawn exclusively from the ranks of
slaves or prisoners of war, both abundant due to Rome's continual wars of expansion.
By the later republic and imperial period, however, convicts condemned to the gladiatorial school (*damnati in ludum*) and even free volunteers made up a large proportion of
gladiators (Wiedemann 1992: 102–127). The institution's funerary origins made its cultural
significance suspect even to some contemporaries. Perhaps relying on other sources, the
Christian apologist Tertullian turned traditional Roman accusations of Christian human
sacrifice back on the Romans, charging them with this practice in the *munus*. Even he
admits, however, that those slaves and others who were to be killed at the tombs had first
been trained in the use of weapons (*On the Spectacles* 12.2–3). The admission is key. It hints
that what might have been important to the Roman spectators was something other than
the death of the combatants, even if at the time that was the eventual result. Another hostile Christian author, Cyprian, Bishop of Carthage in the mid third century CE, pointed to
gladiatorial spectacles as one of the most obvious examples of cruelty and suffering in the
world, yet he too acknowledges that the gladiators fought with skill, practice, and art (*To
Donatus* 7). All sources note the intense training that gladiators endured in preparation
for the combat spectacles. So disciplined were gladiators that their dedication could serve
as a model for the rhetorician in training (Cicero, *On the Orator* 3.86; Tacitus, *Dialogue on
Oratory* 34.5; Quintilian 5.12.17). Training was what distinguished gladiators from others
who appeared in the arena to be executed. Even those *damnati* condemned to the gladiatorial *ludus* received some instruction with weapons. A rescript of the emperor Constantine
in 315 CE condemned those guilty of kidnapping to the gladiatorial *ludus* if they were free
born (slaves and freedman were condemned to the beasts), but since Constantine really
wanted them executed, he had to stipulate that they were to do nothing by which they
might defend themselves, that is, they should receive no weapons training (*Theodosian
Code* 9.18; Potter 2010). As is clear in a rescript from the emperor Hadrian, all gladiators,
even those who had been condemned to fight, had the opportunity to win their freedom if
they survived (*Mosaicarum et Romanarum Legum Collatio* 11.7, citing Ulpian). Survival was
achieved by fighting well.

Intense weapons training was vital and this took place in the *ludus* (school) under a
professional weapons instructor, known as a *magister* or *doctor* in Latin and attested as an
epistates in Greek. Collectively a troupe of gladiators was known as a *familia*, the technical
term for an extended household body of slaves. Even free volunteers, known as *auctorati*,
were thought to have sold themselves to the gladiatorial school. Kathleen Coleman has
studied the *ludus*, focusing especially on the physical evidence from Pompeii, in particular
on the Casa dei Gladiatori, a house apparently converted (at least temporarily) to a barracks
for gladiators, and the Caserma dei Gladiatori, a portico behind the theatre converted to
serve as a gladiatorial school (Coleman 2005). A *familia* was typically owned and managed
by a *lanista*, though troupes belonging to magistrates or priests are known (Carter 2004;
Coleman 2005: 4–5), while the emperors controlled large *familiae* located around the empire,

managed by imperial *procuratores*. We know very little about how gladiators were trained, though we can say that they tended to practise blows against a post set in the ground (the *palus*) using both swords and shields, as soldiers were known to have done (Juvenal, *Satires* 6.247–249; Vegetius, *On Military Matters* 1.11; Coulston 1998; Junkelmann 2000b; Fagan 2015), and that they sparred with each other, sometimes using real weapons (Quintilian, *Institutes of Oratory* 10.5.20). More importantly, the instruction tended to be specific to armament type. The gladiators were divided into different armament classifications, such as *murmillo, secutor, retiarius, thraex*, among others, and there were specific *doctores* attested for each. For example, we know about a *doctor murmillonum* (instructor of *murmillones*), a *doctor secutorum* and others (Mosci Sassi 1992; Junkelmann 2000a; Shadrake 2005; Dunkle 2008; Mañas 2018). So central does the armature appear to be for gladiators, that Kathleen Coleman has referred to it as the basic 'unit of cohesion' in the *ludus* (Coleman 2005: 11). Certainly in the vast majority of gladiatorial epitaphs it is by this classification, as *secutor* or *retiarius*, that the deceased gladiator identifies himself.

Within each classification the gladiators were somehow ranked, if for no other reason than for the purposes of setting contracts to hire out their services: the better gladiators naturally fetched higher prices. I have argued that the numbered *palus* groupings referred to in many gladiatorial epitaphs (for example, first *palus* or second *palus*) may point to the ranking groups, though the existence of sixth and eighth *palus* groups may indicate a more complex hierarchy (Carter 2003). In most cases, someone expecting to present a gladiatorial *munus*, perhaps to fulfil part of the duties of a political office or priesthood, would have leased gladiators from a *lanista* or some other owner. The gladiators would have fought under a contract. It is impossible to know lease rates, but they were probably a small percentage of the gladiator's overall value. The real cost was incurred with the serious wounding or death of a gladiator, since at that point the lease would have converted to a sale. Our evidence indicates that the sale price was fifty times greater than the lease price (Gaius, *Institutes* 3.146). An imperial decree of Marcus Aurelius and his son Commodus sought to control the costs of gladiatorial spectacles, but even there the (purchase) costs of top-ranked gladiators were between 12,000 and 15,000 *sesterces* (Carter 2003; Edmondson 2016). We should think of this assessing the risk of the death of a gladiator in combat more as evidence of great expenditure than as evidence for a murderous inclination. The *munerarius* willing to spend so freely on the entertainment of the people could win enormous popularity.

But we should not assume that it was the death of a gladiator that the people came to see. Armament seems to have dictated tactics to some degree, as has become especially evident from studies attempting to replicate the specifics of combat (Junkelmann 2000a; Teyssier and Lopez 2005; Shadrake 2005). These tactics were known and appreciated by the people who came to watch. Supporters of gladiators tended to organize themselves according to armament type (for example, the *parmularii* or *scutarii*), indicating that they were interested in the particular tactics or fighting styles of the different types (Potter 1994: 231). The *parmularii* supported the Thracians, gladiators who fought with the *parma* (a small shield), while the *scutarii* supported the *murmillones*, who fought with the larger *scutum* (a longer shield). The people wanted their Thracians to fight like Thracians and their *murmillones* to fight like *murmillones*. That this appreciation extended to a greater familiarity with actual training tactics is indicated in our sources. While Petronius may satirize the commoner who criticized the gladiator for fighting *ad dictata*, 'according to his lessons' (*Satyricon* 45), Tertullian compares the advice he offers to those about to be martyred with the advice shouted to gladiators, noting how even the most accomplished gladiators can benefit from the *dictata* shouted not only by their *magistri*, but also by the crowd (*To the Martyrs* 1.2). Proper fighting skills and the courage displayed in dangerous single combat are what the people appreciated and came to see.

We have few ancient descriptions of actual gladiatorial combat in the arena and so what we do know must be cobbled together from a variety of ancient texts. Perhaps the most vivid is found in Pseudo-Quintilian's ninth *Major Declamation*, although it is entirely fictional. The text is in the form of a courtroom speech in which a son contests his father's decision to disown him. The son had previously been captured by pirates and then sold to a gladiatorial school, where he was eventually discovered and rescued by his best friend. This friend even took his place as a gladiator and died in combat in the arena. In the passage below, the disowned son describes that fatal combat for the court:

> After the attendants had departed, the fight was allowed to begin. How anxiously I watched! With what a terrified mind! How I imitated every move of his body! How often I ducked the stabbing sword as if it were aimed at me! How often I stood up when he made a try! Oh, my concern for him was distressing! Oh, how hard-hearted was the nature of my fear! Deservedly, my friend, did you prefer to fight. It is a shame that his spirit and fervour were not employed in the army, in the combat of soldiers, where real courage is not circumscribed by any *lex pugnandi*. With what vigour did he rush into the fight, enraged against his opponent as though he were still mine! But his every effort was adroitly intercepted by the skill of the veteran gladiator, and all his attempts were turned against himself. He should have had *missio* (release from the combat) without any difficulty, especially given the contract under which he fought (*auctoramentum*), but the gladiator did not want him to live. Therefore, offering now his bared body to his opponent's attack, so that he might pay my entire cost all at once, he died still standing up. (Pseudo-Quintilian, *Major Declamation* 9.9)

The speech is meant to appeal to the prejudices, preconceptions, and knowledge of the institution generally held by the jurors, so, although entirely fictional, it nevertheless had to be recognizable to them. The author's 'blow-by-blow' description of the combat gives life to the passion of a spectator's reaction to watching gladiatorial combats. It is easy to see why Alypius became so enraptured.

Even though the combat described by Pseudo-Quintilian may seem to confirm our worst suspicions about the nature of the spectacle—the novice gladiator dies in the end because his veteran opponent 'did not want him to live'—the passage nevertheless suggests the existence of rules. The author tells us that the defeated gladiator here had served under a contract (*auctoramentum*) and had fought well enough to earn release (*missio*) from the fight: he deserved to live, not to die. Moreover, the combats were not uncontrolled, homicidal encounters but were instead governed by a *lex pugnandi* ('rule of fighting'). Even the murderous drive of the veteran gladiator, that he 'did not want him to live', implies that the individual gladiator's will played some role in the outcome (Carter 2015).

So there were rules that governed the combats between gladiators. Most familiar is the opportunity for one gladiator to yield when defeated and so request *missio*. Numerous reliefs and mosaics depict a gladiator holding up a finger or hand to signal submission. Literally, gladiators fought *ad digitum*, 'to the finger' (Ville 1981: 412 n. 129; Mosci Sassi 1992: 70–72; Coleman 2006: 223–226; Kyle 2007: 315). When a gladiator yielded, an official supervising the contest would step in to stop the fight. This official is known to us as the *summa rudis*, though a *secunda rudis* is also attested and might also have been in the arena. A late first- or early second-century CE mosaic from Zliten in modern Libya provides clear examples of this practice: several gladiators are shown either in combat or in the act of submitting, with their shields lowered, weapons dropped, and their hands indicating submission to the officiating *summa rudis* (see, for example, Junkelmann 2000a: 103 fig. 142; Coleman 2006: 224–225). The *summa* (and *secunda*) *rudis* wore white tunics with purple stripes in front and carried a long stick, which they could use to signal to the gladiators from a safer distance. The question of whether the gladiator should be granted *missio*, however, was referred to the *munerarius*, who would then be expected to defer to the wishes of the people.

While *missio* may be better known to us, the existence of a *lex pugnandi* governing the fights is more interesting. Pseudo-Quintilian implies that this *lex* offered an advantage to the veteran gladiator. It was not that the novice lacked eagerness or bravery or even combat skill— we are told that the friend would have flourished as a soldier. Instead, he lacked experience fighting *as a gladiator*. Since gladiators were trained and fought in specific ways according to the tactics dictated by their armament type (*retiarius* or *secutor* etc.), this *lex* must have compelled gladiators to fight according to the standards and expectations of their armature. Advantage: veteran. What this *lex* also implies is the existence of someone to enforce it and this responsibility most probably fell also to the *summa rudis*, who was in the arena with the combatants. Louis Robert identified the *summa rudis* as 'un arbiter technique' to ensure that the gladiators fought bravely, skilfully and according to the rules (Robert 1982: 262–263), and I have argued that these officials were probably drawn from the ranks of ex-gladiators who would have had the requisite experience and knowledge (Carter 2006/2007: 102).

The veteran gladiator's desire to see the novice dead, however, would seem to support the stereotype of the murderous gladiator. Yet, the fact that the author draws our attention to it implies that the will of the gladiators is significant. This winner wanted his opponent dead, but could a victorious gladiator have wanted to let the other man live instead? Indeed, in another part of the same *Declamation*, Pseudo-Quintilian tells the court just that 'even gladiators spare their defeated opponents' (*Major Declamation* 9.18). There is more evidence of this behaviour. While Robert interpreted this sort of conduct as evidence of an informal camaraderie between gladiators (Robert 1940: 306), and Coleman saw it as evidence for the professionalism of gladiators (Coleman 2005: 14), I have proposed that it represented a more formal, though unwritten, 'code' of behaviour followed by most gladiators: to fight bravely, skilfully and according to the established rules, but not necessarily to kill their opponents (Carter 2006/2007: 106–112).

Of course, gladiatorial combat was dangerous and the risk of death in the arena was always present, and of course some gladiators no doubt intended to kill their opponents; but rules existed under which a gladiator might submit, and this meant that his life was not necessarily lost the moment he entered the arena. Indeed, David Potter argues that it was rare for a gladiator to face certain death in the arena: 'Despite common modern perceptions, gladiators rarely found themselves in a situation in which death was likely' (Potter 2004: 76). There is evidence for games in which gladiators were compelled to fight for their lives, but such games were the exception rather than the rule. For example, a priest of the imperial cult in Beroia in Roman Macedonia advertised a three day *munus* with wild beast hunts and gladiatorial combats, 'including on each day one pair who would fight for their lives (*peri psychēs*) in addition to the normal two pairs' (*AE* 1971 no. 431). Note, however, that the priest immediately proceeded to advertise (to boast?) that he had imperial permission to mount the special fights *peri psychēs*. That has to be exceptional. Even the use of sharpened weapons appears to have become more unusual in the imperial period, the inference being that usual combats were fought with blunted weapons (Potter 2004: 77; Carter 2006). Whatever 'normal' or usual combats were, they were clearly not necessarily fights to the death.

ROMAN ARENA, ROMAN SOCIETY

However real the risk of death undoubtedly was in the arena, it is becoming increasingly clear to scholars that the gladiators were expensive, well-trained professionals too valuable to be killed off on a whim, and that the people were knowledgeable aficionados who—generally speaking—appreciated the combats as displays of skill, bravery, and discipline. The fact that death was always a possibility just made the bravery all the more real and the level of skill all the higher. But the arena in the imperial period was a complex place. Gladiatorial combats were preceded by a number of other events, such as wild beast hunts and often spectacular executions. Even the people gathered to watch did so in an organized way, sitting in hierarchical placement: senators and important dignitaries up front, followed by equestrians, and then others, in decreasing status away from the arena (Edmondson 1996).

Though the institution naturally evolved over the course of the Roman republic and empire, its primary significance seems to have remained as a spectacle of courageous and skilled single combat. Even in its earliest centuries when the spectacle was connected with the funerals of great men, what was important about it was the extreme combat. The gladiatorial *munera* demonstrated and symbolized several of the key values in Roman society. The spectacles were presented for *great* men: *viri fortes*, said Servius (*Commentary on Vergil's Aeneid* 10.519). That these *exempla* were presented in association with the funeral of a great man suggests that gladiatorial combat was an edifying celebration meant more for the living than the dead, a demonstration of the values that had made Romans great and that would see them through the crisis created by the death of a leading man. Livy's description of the *munera* celebrated by the Seleucid king Antiochus IV in Syria in the second century BCE claims that this adopted cultural practice aroused an enthusiasm for arms and weapons-training in the youth (Livy 41.20). They were violent, but such violence is more a social concern for us than for the Romans (Wistrand 1992). It is because the combats presented examples of powerful military virtues that the institution spread out of Rome in the later republic. The amphitheatre at Pompeii, the earliest surviving stone amphitheatre, was erected by Roman veterans precisely to celebrate those martial virtues that they themselves knew and lived (Welch 1994; Welch 2007: 76–91).

The *munus*, as it had developed and spread in the imperial period, offered plenty of bloodshed: wild animals were hunted and killed and convicts were executed. Gladiatorial combats offered something different. They were displays of perfected and disciplined martial virtues: courage in combat, skill with weapons, and discipline, all done according to established rules and expectations. This is what the Romans came to see at the amphitheatre. What role, then, do such spectacles play in Roman society?

Thomas Wiedemann's important study, *Emperors and Gladiators* (1992), even while focusing on gladiatorial combats, considered the complex spectacle as a whole: wild beast hunts celebrated the triumph of Roman civilization over the hostile natural world; spectacular executions celebrated the triumph of justice over those who opposed or rejected

Roman civilization; and gladiatorial combats celebrated the display of pure Roman martial virtue. He extended this to explore the latent religiosity in the gladiatorial combats and proposed that they celebrated life rather than death, specifically the theme of rebirth: gladiators were socially dead, but could be socially reborn and earn release from the occupation by demonstrating perfect military virtues in the arena. For Wiedemann, the spectacle of two gladiators fighting in ostentatious single combat affected Roman spectators and presented them with a demonstration of some of the key values at the heart of what it meant to be a Roman (Wiedemann 1992: 1–54). Others have subscribed to similar views about the importance of the show to a sense of Romanness (e.g. Hopkins 1983; Plass 1995; Welch 2007) and the celebration of key Roman virtues in the arena (Potter 1999: 306). In another important work, Garrett Fagan has explored the Roman fascination with the arena from the vantage of social psychology, demonstrating that this was not just a Roman fascination: there is an important human dimension to the desire to witness such spectacles (Fagan 2011).

If the spectacles were important for cultivating a sense of Romanness among the Roman spectators, what impact did they have in the provinces, where the spectacles were presented and watched with equal pleasure? The significance of the spectacle as an element of the 'romanization' of the provinces is a critical issue (Mann 2009; Carter 2009). While the combats were clearly Roman, they could be seen as more culturally flexible: gladiators and gladiatorial combats, especially when understood to be rule-bound contests, display much that is recognizably athletic. Mark Golden has made the case to see these combats in the way (Greek) gladiators tended to present them: as a form of sport (Golden 2008: 68–104; Carter 2009). Though this might simply have been an attempt by Greek gladiators to assimilate athletic ideals that were culturally dominant in the East, it may also point to a problem in the way we understand 'sport'. Scholars have tended to exclude gladiatorial combats from studies of ancient sport for a variety of reasons: gladiators were not willing participants; they were slaves; their fights were a form of warfare for spectators; they killed their opponents; they belonged to showy Roman 'spectacle' rather than competitive Greek athletics. But it is becoming increasingly clear that Greek athletics are not as pure and unbloodied as we have long thought; there is much, likewise, that we have misunderstood about gladiatorial combats.

The spectacle made an impact in the provinces, including among the Greeks (Robert 1940). So ingrained within the culture of Greek society did the ideology of the spectacle become, that Glen Bowersock could argue that these Roman entertainment spectacles came to play a central role in the formation of civic ideology. For Bowersock, it is this civic ideology, expressed in arena spectacles, that the Christians later adopted to articulate the significance of martyrdom: 'the role of martyrs in dying is conceived as a kind of public entertainment offered by God to communities where it takes place as some kind of far more edifying transmutation of the traditional games' (Bowersock 1995: 52). The same Christian writers who could attack gladiatorial combats would enthuse over the blood of dying martyrs.

References

Bowersock, G. W. 1995. *Martyrdom and Rome*. Cambridge.

Brown, S. 1992. 'Death as Decoration: Scenes from the Arena in Roman Domestic Mosaics.' In *Pornography and Representation in Greece and Rome*. 180–211. A. Richlin, ed. Oxford.

Brown, S. 1995. 'Explaining the Arena: Did the Romans Need Gladiators?' *JRA* 8: 376–384.

Carter, M. 2003. 'Gladiatorial Ranking and the *SC de Pretiis Gladiatorum Minuendis* (CIL II 6278 = ILS 5163).' *Phoenix* 57: 83–114.

Carter, M. 2004. '*Archiereis* and Asiarchs: A Gladiatorial Perspective.' *GRBS* 44: 41–68.

Carter, M. 2006. 'Gladiatorial Combat with 'Sharp' Weapons (*tois oxesi siderois*).' *ZPE* 155: 161–175.

Carter, M. 2006/2007. 'Gladiatorial Combat: The Rules of Engagement.' *CJ* 102: 97–114.

Carter, M. 2009. 'Gladiators and *Monomachoi*: Greek Attitudes to a Roman Cultural Performance.' *International Journal of the History of Sport* 29: 298–322.

Carter, M. 2015. 'Bloodbath: Artemidorus, *Apotomos* Combat and Ps.-Quintilian's *The Gladiator.*' *ZPE* 193: 39–52.

Coleman, K. M. 2005. 'Bonds of Danger: Communal Life in the Gladiatorial Barracks of Ancient Rome.' The Fifteenth Todd Memorial Lecture. Department of Classics and Ancient History, University of Sydney.

Coleman, K. M. 2006. *M. Valerii Martialis Liber Spectaculorum*. Oxford.

Coulston, J. C. N. 1998. 'Gladiators and Soldiers: Personnel and Equipment in *ludus* and *castra*.' *JRMES* 9: 1–17.

Dunkle, R. 2008. *Gladiators: Violence and Spectacle in Ancient Rome*. Harlow.

Edmondson, J. C. 1996. 'Dynamic Arenas: Gladiatorial Presentations in the City of Rome and the Construction of Roman Society during the Early Empire.' In *Roman Theater and Society*. 69–112. W. J. Slater, ed. Ann Arbor.

Edmondson, J. C. 2016. 'Investing in Death: Gladiators as Investment and Currency in Late Republican Rome.' In *Money and Power in the Late Republic*. 37–52. H. Beck, M. Jehne, and J. Serrati, eds. Brussels.

Fagan, G. G. 2011. *The Lure of the Arena*. Cambridge.

Fagan, G. G. 2015. 'Training Gladiators: Life in the Ludus.' In *Aspects of Ancient Institutions and Geography*. 122–144. L. Brice and D. Slootjes eds. Leiden.

Futrell, A. 1997. *Blood in the Arena: The Spectacle of Roman Power*. Austin.

Golden, M. 2008. *Greek Sport and Social Status*. Austin.

Hopkins, K. 1983. *Death and Renewal*. Cambridge.

Junkelmann, M. 2000a. *Das Spiel mit dem Tod: So kämpften Roms Gladiatoren*. Mainz.

Junkelmann, M. 2000b. 'Gladiatorial and Military Equipment and Fighting Techniques: A Comparison.' *JRMES* 11: 113–117.

Kyle, D. G. 2007. *Sport and Spectacle in the Ancient World*. Malden, MA.

Mañas, A. 2018. *Gladiatores. El gran espectáculo de Roma*. Barcelona.

Mann, C. 2009. 'Gladiators in the Greek East: A Case-Study in Romanization.' *International Journal of the History of Sport* 29: 272–297.

Mosci Sassi, M. G. 1992. *Il Linguaggio Gladiatorio*. Bologna.

Plass, P. 1995. *The Game of Death in Ancient Rome*. Madison, WI.

Potter, D. 1994. 'Review of T. Wiedemann, *Emperors and Gladiators.*' *JRS* 84: 229–231.

Potter, D. 1999. 'Entertainers in the Roman Empire.' In *Life, Death, and Entertainment in the Roman Empire*. 256–325. D. Potter and D. Mattingly, eds. Ann Arbor.

Potter, D. 2004. 'Gladiators and Blood Sport.' In *Gladiator: Film and History*. 73–86. M. M. Winkler, ed. Oxford.

Potter, D. 2010. 'Constantine and the Gladiators.' *CQ* 60: 596–606.

Robert, L. 1940. *Les gladiateurs dans l'Orient grec*. Paris.

Robert, L. 1982. 'Une vision de Perpétue martyre à Carthage en 203.' *CRAI*: 228–276.

Shadrake, S. 2005. *The World of the Gladiator*. Stroud.

Teyssier, E. and B. Lopez. 2005. *Gladiateurs. Des sources à l'expérimentation*. Paris.

Ville, G. 1981. *La gladiature en occident des origines à la mort de Domitien*. Rome.

Welch, K. E. 1994. 'The Roman Arena in Late-Republican Italy: A New Interpretation.' *JRA* 7: 59–80.

Welch, K. E. 2007. *The Roman Amphitheatre: From its Origins to the Colosseum*. Cambridge.

Wiedemann, T. 1992. *Emperors and Gladiators*. London.

Wistrand, M. 1992. *Entertainment and Violence in Ancient Rome: The Attitudes of Roman Writers of the First Century A.D*. Gothenburg.

CHAPTER 19

···

GREEK HIPPIC CONTESTS

···

NIGEL NICHOLSON

In the Greek imagination the horse was a resonant symbol. Horses were the most human of animals—carefully tended by their owners, regularly given names, and considered capable of mourning their masters or languishing in love for them—and the ways that horses were perceived and judged were deeply intertwined with judgements about human behavior and social order (Griffith 2006: 200–205, 307–336). But if the horse served as a privileged symbol for conceptualizing the social order, the hippic contests at athletic festivals served as one of the primary sites where such conceptualizations received visible form. Even local festivals often featured lengthy equestrian programmes, and, by concretely embodying hierarchies that also structured Greek society, these programmes served to affirm the social order. At the same time, however, because of the close relationship between the social and equestrian orders, questions raised of the equestrian hierarchies were questions raised of the social hierarchies, and consequently hippic contests served as a platform for challenging as well as affirming these hierarchies.

Compared to the varied gymnastic programmes, hippic programmes may look bland: before 500 BCE the Olympics featured only a four-horse chariot-race and a horse-race. But at Olympia the programme soon grew: in 500 a mule-cart race was added, and in 496 the *kalpē*, a race for mares in which the rider dismounted and ran alongside the horse (Bell 1989: 170–174). Both were discontinued about fifty years later, but further additions followed: a two-horse chariot (the *sunōris*) in 408, a four-colt chariot in 384, a colt *sunōris* in 264, and a colt horse-race in 256 (Kyle 2007: 126–127). Delphi developed the same programme (Kyle 2007: 138–139), and Isthmia and Nemea likely followed suit, although athletic festivals did not follow a standard form. Being sacred to Poseidon, the Isthmia in particular may have featured more contests.

Local and regional festivals certainly featured greater diversity. A stele dedicated on the Spartan acropolis records the victories of one Damonon from around the end of the fifth century and mentions races for full-grown mares (Christesen 2019; Cartledge, this volume Chapter 28), while the Panathenaea in the early fourth century offered two events for a *zeugos* (some kind of two-horse chariot that may have been heavier than a *sunōris*), a race for armour-clad runners, who would ride on chariots and dismount (the *apobatēs* race depicted on the Parthenon; Nagy, this volume Chapter 22), a javelin-on-horseback contest, and perhaps a war-chariot race (Shear 2003: 92–103). Mule-cart races had been offered in the sixth century (Kyle 2007: 161), and the second-century programme included some 28 equestrian events for individual competitors (Tracy and Habicht 1991: 196–201).

Many local festivals featured equestrian programmes. Some, such as the Adrasteia at Sicyon, attracted competitors from far away, but others were barely known beyond their region. The Damonon inscription lists six obscure festivals in the southern Peloponnese with equestrian events (Christesen 2019: 10; Cartledge, this volume Chapter 28).

Hippic contests thus formed a complex system, but three hierarchies structured this system. First, hippic events as a whole enjoyed greater prestige than gymnastic contests. Second, a sequence of hierarchies ranked the different events: chariot above horse, horse above mule, four horses above two, full-grown horses above colts, stallions above mares, and the Olympian and Pythian games above the other festivals. Third, the seniority of the owner to driver and horse framed a particular understanding of the labour involved in the events.

HIERARCHIES OF ATHLETICS

One thing the horse symbolized was high class. Horses were a significant part of elite life, whether used for hunting, racing, or fighting, but the horse came to serve as a primary signifier of elite status. In various Greek cities, the elite were known as *hippeis* ('knights') because they had the resources to serve in the cavalry; in Athens, *hippeis* were contrasted with *zeugitai* ('yoke-men'), who held enough land to need a pair of oxen or mules. Many members of the interstate aristocracy bore horsey names such as Hippocleas or Hipponikos; this naming practice was so marked that the comic playwright Aristophanes was able to joke about an aristocratic mother wishing to name her son something horsey ('Xanthippos, Charippos or Kallippides') while the rustic father prefers Pheidonides ('Son of Thrifty') (*Clouds* 63–65; Griffith 2006: 201–202).

The elite was, in fact, identified as horses, not just with horses: just as horses were the aristocrats of the equine hierarchy, so aristocrats were the horses of the social order. When Semonides complains that a beautiful woman is 'an evil, unless [you are] a tyrant or sceptre-bearing king', he speaks of her as coming from a horse, and the chorus leaders in Alcman's *Great Partheneion* are compared to race horses of different breeds, perhaps Venetic, Celtic, and Scythian (Griffith 2006: 310–312; Semonides 7.68–69; Alcman 1.50–59). One ostrakon (pottery ballot for ostracism) calls not only for the exile of the powerful Athenian Megacles, but also his horses (Forsdyke 2005: 155–156). For the Athenian who scratched this potsherd, the horses themselves were as much a part of the elite as the owner.

Within this cultural context, hippic events easily assumed a superior position in athletic festivals simply because they involved horses. This is not to claim that the gymnastic competitors belonged to a lower class than equestrian ones. Athletics as a whole was the province of the elite (Kyle 2007: 211–216). Rather, the equestrian events themselves enjoyed a higher status than the gymnastic ones (Golden 1998: 5–6; Kyle 2007: 126–127).

The games themselves supported this hierarchy. The Panathenaea offered considerably larger prizes for the main equestrian events. In the early fourth century the men's *stadion* victor received perhaps 80 amphorae of oil, but the victor in the full-grown *zeugos* commanded 140, and the four-horse chariot must have commanded much more (Shear

2003: 95–96). At Olympia, the new temple constructed around 460 represented the chariot-race of Pelops and Oenomaus as the founding moment of the games. Moreover, equestrian competitors often entertained the whole gathering, thus presenting themselves as the senior competitors. Alcibiades, Dionysius I of Syracuse, and the mule-cart victors Anaxilas of Rhegion and Psaumis of Camarina did this, as well as Empedocles of Acragas, grandfather of the philosopher and victor in the horse-race. His entertainment was particularly memorable because he somehow created a vegetarian ox-substitute for all to share (Athenaeus 1.3e; Plut., *Alc.* 12.1; [Pind.], *Ol.* 5.5–6; Diod. 14.109).

Some victors publicly rated their equestrian victories above their gymnastic ones. Damonon's stele gives much greater prominence to his equestrian victories, listing them before the running victories and depicting a racing chariot in a relief (Hodkinson 2000: 304–305).

Finally, the status of the equestrian competitors was distinguished from that of the gymnasts in one respect: kings and tyrants almost wholly confined their competition to hippic events. Those tyrants and kings, and queens, who tried their hand at Olympic equestrian events include Cleisthenes of Sicyon; Pisistratus of Athens; Damaratus and Cynisca of Sparta; Gelon of Gela; Anaxilas of Rhegion; Theron of Acragas; and Hieron and Dionysius I of Syracuse; Arkesilas IV of Cyrene; Philip of Macedon; Ptolemy I and II; and their wives Berenice I and Arsinoe II (Moretti 1957; Thompson 2005: 273–274).

HIERARCHIES WITHIN THE EQUESTRIAN PROGRAMME

That there were different classes of event at athletic festivals reinforced the idea that in society more generally class was a natural fact and a proper basis on which to organize people and resources; indeed, just as the horse served as a metaphor for the elite, so did the hippic events. While all athletics drew animosity from the lower classes, particular vitriol was reserved for equestrian athletics, with Athenian ostraca occasionally citing an arisotcrat's horse-racing as a reason to ostracize him (Golden 1998: 157–175; Forsdyke 2005: 155–156). Yet, while hippic competition marked out a separable elite, it also distinguished different levels within that elite.

All equestrian events marked their competitors as members of the elite, but the four-horse chariot-race was superior to all other contests. While some of the rulers cited above competed in other events, all but Anaxilas certainly competed in the chariot (and Anaxilas probably did). Requiring twelve laps of the hippodrome, the chariot-race was also longer than the other equestrian contests (Miller 2004: 75–80).

Lesser events might be left to sons or commanders. Damonon competed in both racehorse and chariot events, but his son only competed in the racehorse. When Hieron of Syracuse entered the Olympic horse- and chariot-races, his lieutenant Hagesias won the mule-cart (Pind. *Ol.* 6). The mule-cart thus bore a markedly lower prestige than the single horse; among heads of state, only Anaxilas seems to have competed in the mule-cart. Similarly, the *kalpē* was probably ranked below the horse-race because of the restriction to mares.

It is likely that the expansion of the hippic programme was a response to the rise of a hyper-wealthy segment within the elite that was able to dominate the chariot and racehorse.

Largely shut out from victory, the less wealthy probably sought new arenas to gain prestige, while the hyper-wealthy probably welcomed the articulation of distinctions within the elite (cf. Golden 1998: 40–3). The institution of the mule-cart and *kalpē* should be correlated with the victory of the Spartan king Damaratus in 504 and the entrance onto the scene of rich Sicilians such as Empedocles of Acragas and Pantares of Gela (father of the tyrant Hippocrates and an equestrian victor likely before 505). The wider programme was certainly sustained by the great wealth of the Sicilian tyrants and the increasingly expensive competition for the chariot- and horse-race that they stimulated. Thus in the 440s, when the Sicilian tyrannies had collapsed, the Battiads of Cyrene had retreated and anonymous competitors such as Psaumis of Camarina and Diaktorides (of unknown provenance) had once again begun to win the crown (Moretti 1957: 99–101), the programme was reduced. At this point, it was not yet obvious that Sparta's elite would dominate racing for the next fifty years, but when they did, expenditure again ballooned; to maximize his chances, Alcibiades had to enter seven chariots in 416. The introductions of the *sunōris* and the four-colt chariot in 408 and 384 respectively were surely responses to this development, just as the next wave of introductions came at the time when the Ptolemies were dominating the contests. These lesser contests gave the rest of the elite a reasonable shot at success.

The introduction of both colt and *sunōris* races prevented a linear ranking of the races, but clearly the four-horse chariot was better than both the two-horse and the colt chariot. When Posiddipus praises Berenice I's Olympic chariot victory, he looks back only to the chariot victory of the Spartan queen Cynsica in the early fourth century; the subsequent victory of a second Spartan woman, Euryleonis, could be overlooked, since it was in the *sunōris* (Posidippus 87; Paus. 3.17.6). While the Ptolemies and their queens raced in the chariot as well as many other events, Ptolemy II's mistress, Bilistichē, seems to have been restricted to colt races; she won two of these, including the inaugural colt *sunōris*, and a satirical epigram that mocks her double life as courtesan and horse-racer features colts prominently (Golden 2008: 17–19; *Anth. Pal.* 5.202).

In the fuller programmes outside of the crown games, there were further distinctions. The Panathenaea gave smaller prizes for contests involving warhorses, and presumably also for those contests restricted to Athenian citizens.

As in gymnastic events, ranking also depended on where the victory was won, but, where gymnastic victories in the four Panhellenic contests carried special prestige, in equestrian competition the special cachet was limited to Olympia and Delphi. Nemea especially was left to subordinates, such as Chromius of Syracuse, one of Hieron's right-hand men, or Berenice the Syrian, the biological daughter of Ptolemy II, who won victories at Nemea and the Isthmus as a child (Pind. *N.* 1; Posidippus 79–82). Winning the period was not a concern; victories at other festivals were usually omitted from monuments and poems celebrating Olympic wins (Pind. *Ol.* 1, 3–6; Ba. 3; Posidippus 71–88; Pind. *Ol.* 2.48–51 and Ba. 5.37–41 are exceptions). Olympic chariot victors distinguished themselves by listing earlier family successes or garnering further victories. Winning those victories with the same horse brought additional cachet, and the pinnacle of equestrian success was to win three consecutive Olympic chariot crowns with the same team, a feat that the elder Cimon missed by trading his second win to Pisistratus (Hdt. 6.103).

Particular breeds brought no special glory in racing, despite the use of breeds to rank the chorus leaders in Alcman's *Great Partheneion*. Breeds pass almost unremarked in memorials before the Hellenistic period (the memorial of Leon of Sparta, from 440, is an exception; see

Nobili 2016: 52–54), and then they are tokens of national pride: a Thessalian uses a Thessalian horse, a courtier of the Ptolemies an Arab stallion (Posidippus 76, 83; Thompson 2005: 280). The sex of the horses seems to have been equally incidental. Posidippus' victory epigram for Berenice I is put in the mouth of the mares that won her Olympic victory, but the mares are not represented as enjoying a particular link to the queen because of their sex and the trope is used more emphatically elsewhere (Posidippus 87, 75; cf. 74).

The wide variety of hippic contests thus fell into certain clearly defined hierarchies, and was used to distinguish levels of seniority within the aristocracy. The symbolism of these distinctions was rather different in different cases, however. Whereas colts and two-horse chariots created only distinctions of quantity (of years, or horses), the mule-cart represented a qualitative distinction based on species, since mules were only half horse. Such a distinction reified the differences between levels within the elite—and more generally the differences between levels in a class system—in a way that distinctions of quantity did not. If the lower echelons of the elite were the mules, the *dēmos* was the donkeys, and each level was assigned to its place by the apparent facts of biology. Class mobility was not a question of getting more, but of becoming an entirely different being.

HIERARCHIES OF LABOUR

As a group, those who competed in the hippic contests were known as *hippotrophoi* ('horse-breeders'), because according to the elite view of such contests the primary work of victory lay in the provision of fine horses, not in the driving or riding. In the major festivals, and in the most prestigious events, owners did not have to drive or ride their horses, and as a rule did not do so. Accordingly, entrants could be syndicates, such as cities, brothers, or friends (Moretti 1957: 78–79, 88–92), and could make multiple entries. Only one Panhellenic victor is known to have driven his own chariot, Herodotus of Thebes, who won at the Isthmia around 470 (Pind. *Is.* 1.14–16). At minor games, owner-drivers were likely more common; Damonon drove in all the chariot wins preserved on his stele. Yet Damonon's pride in his driving indicates that this was far from normal. Even at these obscure Peloponnesian festivals, owners must have typically used drivers.

In at least some of the contests at local festivals, it seems likely that the owners were required to drive, ride, or run. Certainly the various citizen-only cavalry races in the Panathenaea of the second century BCE must have required the cavalrymen to ride, while the owner of the team in the *apobatēs* contest was surely the dismounting warrior (Neils and Schultz 2012: 196, 200).

In the open events, however, at larger or smaller festivals, dependents, slaves, or professionals were mostly employed to drive carts and chariots, and their work went largely unrecognized. The victor was, of course, the owner, but victory memorials typically did not even name the driver, and often left them out of sculptural groups depicting the victorious chariot. This was not because the work they performed was trivial; horsemanship was highly valued, and when the driving was done by the owner or by a friend or family member, such as Carrhotus, an in-law of the victor Arkesilas of Cyrene, the work was handsomely recognized (Pind. *Py.* 5.26–54; Nicholson 2005: 1–63). Rather, the worker was trivial. Aristocratic ideology disdained dependent labour, especially wage labour (Golden 1998: 146–157), and hippic athletics served as visible validation of this ideology. Drivers were present; they just did not count. Victory was won by hippotrophs' wise expenditure and favour with the gods.

This treatment of the drivers sharply contrasts with the treatment of the horses. Victors were described as winning 'with horses' rather than with a driver, and these horses were often named in victory memorials, and even described as winning the victory (Nicholson 2005: 95–116; Golden 2008: 6–16). The elder Cimon even gave his team of thrice-victorious horses an ostentatious burial on a road leading out of Athens (Hdt. 6.103). Such lionizing of the horses continued in the Hellenistic period: horses speak four of the epigrams in Posidippus' *Hippika* and are even said to have intervened with the judges when the race was too close to call (Posidippus 73–75, 83, 87; Golden 2008: 20–21).

The honour paid to the horses promoted the same ideology of labour. The horses' work could be recognized because of who the horses were. Typed as the aristocrats of the animal kingdom, they easily slipped into a role much like that of Carrhotus, Arkesilas' charioteer; rather than low-class dependents, they were friends, colleagues, and even family (Nicholson 2005: 95–116). In the *Iliad* Hector's horses Xanthus, Podargus, Aethon, and Lampus are fed before Hector by Andromache (8.186–190). The horses' labour thus counted, and served to eclipse the low labour of driver or jockey.

The rhetorical distinction between racehorse and driver seems to have sharpened as the drivers became increasingly professional, selling discrete services to different employers, and moving between Greek cities. Commodity exchange generated particular trouble within elite ideology, structured as it was around gift exchange, and the focus on the horses served to mask the (from this point of view) mostly unsavoury transactions that placed the driver in the chariot (Nicholson 2005: 42–63). Horses themselves were not immune to commodification, however, and the use of the horse as the symbol of aristocratic labour came under pressure in the late fifth century. Where earlier in the century it was assumed that an owner bred his own horses, memorials such as those of Damonon or the Olympic victor Kleogenes of Elis (Paus. 6.1.4) trumpet the fact that the owner has bred his own horses. Their competitors were clearly less principled or less successful at breeding, and, like Alcibiades, bought their racehorses from others (Kyle 1987: 211).

CHALLENGES TO THE HIERARCHIES

Hippic events thus form a surprisingly complex group, both because of the variety of the events and because of the number of personnel involved, but the group was organized by various hierarchies that located it within athletics generally and gave order to the events and the personnel. This equestrian order was intertwined with the social order; its hierarchies were drawn from the elite ideology of class and labour rather than from any kind of independent evaluation of skill, and served in turn to validate that ideology. And since athletics occupied a privileged place in the Greek imagination, the hierarchies that the hippic events promoted carried enormous cultural weight.

These hierarchies did not pass unchallenged. They were regularly and powerfully contested and the history of hippic athletics can be understood as a history of struggle over its ideologically loaded hierarchies. Indeed, hippic athletics offered not so much a vehicle for the promotion of aristocratic ideology as a particularly visible locus of ideological struggle.

The end of the fifth century saw a significant challenge to the hierarchy that ranked hippic over gymnastic events. At this moment a prominent Elean, Hippias, produced an Olympic chronology that, against the view of some other accounts, made gymnastic events, and particularly the *stadion*, the original events of the festival. The hippic events had enjoyed a strong fifth century—a chariot-race had been installed on the front of the temple of Olympian Zeus, several visually dominating chariot groups had been dedicated in the Altis (Smith 2007: 123–124), and new hippic events were added in 408 and 384— but Hippias' chronology represented a serious challenge to that dominance (Golden 1998: 37–45).

By the time this idea of the Olympics was institutionalized, hippic events faced an uphill battle, partly because of the new orthodoxy in the ideology of nudity. Nakedness had not always been positive, and the sixth century saw a tense conflict over its evaluation: gymnasts took pride in their nakedness, but hippotrophs took pride in their clothing. A Panathenaic prize amphora for a racehorse victor from the third quarter of the sixth century contrasts the naked jockey unfavourably with the richly clothed victor who obscures much of the horse and jockey (Nicholson 2005: 104–108). The Persian wars put an end to this conflict, however. Nudity emerged in the fifth century as a sign of strength, self-discipline and Greekness, while rich clothing signified effeminacy, barbarity, and extravagance (Bonfante 1989: 547– 557; Kurke 1991: 91–106; Kyle 2007: 85–90). One of the codes through which the superiority of hippic competition had been asserted had thus been reversed, and the pole with which hippotrophy was associated was now the negative pole. It was in this context that Xenophon could place in the mouth of the Spartan King Agesilaus the criticism that hippotrophy was proof of wealth, not manliness (Xen. *Ages.* 9.6).

Xenophon's choice of mouthpiece shows that the privileging of nudity and gymnastics did not promote democracy, but a different elite style, more attuned to the context of the polis (cf. Scanlon 2005: 68–70 and Kyle 2007: 85–90). Connections with the east had been rejected, but the players were still elite, and their equipment still luxury items: the luxury of hippotrophy had simply been replaced by the luxury of a carefully honed body.

The hierarchy of owner, horse, and driver was also challenged. Professional drivers were not allowed to make victory dedications at the festivals so that, even if they could afford to, they could not assert the value of their work in that context. Desirable drivers could, however, insist on being included in epinician poetry, as perhaps Nicomachus did (Pind. *Is.* 2; Nicholson 2005: 64–81), or make dedications elsewhere. One such example is likely the fine statue that was buried in Dionysius' sack of Motya, a Phoenician town off western Sicily, in 397 (Fig. 19.1; see also Raschke, this volume Chapter 35). Large stone statues make poor booty, so the statue was likely dedicated near where it was found. It represents a freestanding charioteer who was not part of a chariot group. The dedicant (who may have been Greek or Phoenician) was perhaps an owner-driver, but more likely drove chariots for one or more of the Sicilian tyrants of the 470s (for identification of the figure as a priest, see Palagia 2013). But while he helped them win their crowns, this statue asserts a novel hierarchy. With its erotic, closely contoured clothing and bulging veins it demands that the driver be seen as a significant actor in the victory, whether dependent or not (Nicholson 2005: 76–78; Smith 2007: 130–135).

The labour hierarchy was particularly fragile. In its service, victors could insist that equestrian victory was not about labour—Euripides praised Alcibiades for winning 'without toil' (Plut. *Alc.* 11.2)—but the labour imposed itself upon spectators. At some festivals, owners

FIGURE 19.1. Motya Youth, *c.*470 BCE. By permission, Regione Siciliana, Assessorato dei Beni Culturali e della Identità Siciliana, Dipartimento dei Beni Culturali e della Identità Siciliana, e Servizio Parco archeologico ed ambientale presso le isole dello Stagnone e delle eree archeologiche di Marsala e dei Communi limitrofi, Marsala.

were required to drive or ride in certain events. Other events, like the Olympic *kalpē*, distinguished the jockey's work from the horse's. (The jockey cannot have been the owner; a requirement that the owner take part would have been entirely anomalous at Olympia.) Typically, jockeys were belittled by memorials. Horses are described as winning without being whipped, and jockeys as 'pleasant weight' that needs to be 'guarded'; one piece of fanciful Olympic folklore celebrated a horse that had won after throwing its jockey (Pind. *Ol.* 1.21; Ba. 5.47; Posidippus 73.3; Paus. 6.13.9; Nicholson 2005: 95–116). But in the *kalpē* the contribution of the rider could not easily be scorned: he had to run alongside the mare as well as ride (Bell 1989: 170–174).

Individual victors also challenged the hierarchies that ranked the different events and, by implication, the different competitors. The city of Argos refused to leave the chariot- and horse-races to kings and very wealthy individuals; it won the former in 472 and the latter in 480, surely beating Hieron in both races. Anaxilas of Rhegion elevated his mule-cart victory of 484 or 480 by placing it on the huge coin issues of Messene and Rhegion (Fig. 19.2); Gelon of Syracuse had signalled his Olympic chariot victory on Syracuse's coins and Anaxilas' mule-cart coins were perhaps initially meant to challenge Gelon's supremacy, although after 480, when Gelon had humbled Anaxilas, they were surely reinterpreted as a sign of subordination (cf. Luraghi 1994: 218–222). But the most interesting challenge comes from Hagesias of Syracuse, the Syracusan who won the mule-cart race during Hieron's reign. He commissioned *Olympian* 6, one of Pindar's most beautiful and memorable odes, but also an extended interrogation of Olympic symbolic hierarchies.

In many ways, *Olympian* 6 displays a symbolic structure typical of Pindar's odes. Hierarchies of gender, topography, body, and class combine to reinforce the superiority of his Olympic and other successes. Through the central myth, which traces the ascent of Iamos, one of Hagesias' ancestors, to the mantic seat of Olympia, Olympic victory is represented as a lofty, masculine, regal and bright achievement. Iamos' journey proceeds from the 'bowels' (43) of his mother to his father, Apollo's voice, from limitless and damp vegetation to the 'steep rock of Kronos' high hill' (64), from the snakes that nursed him to a special relation with the Olympian gods, from illegitimacy and anonymity to fame, truth and kingship (Segal 1998: 105–132). Yet the parallel between Iamos' journey and Hagesias' is questioned. In an extraordinary move, the ode makes clear that Hagesias was not a king, but subordinate to Hieron's 'clear sceptre' (93). According to the usual hippic hierarchy, Hagesias' event also signals this subordination: Hieron won the horse- or chariot-race when Hagesias won the mule.

FIGURE 19.2 Olympic Mule-Cart Race, Tetradrachm of Rhegion, 484 or 480 to 462 BCE. Museum of Fine Arts, Boston, 04.407. Photograph © 2011, Museum of Fine Arts, Boston.

Yet the usual hierarchies are not respected in this ode. The family's chariot-racing is praised, but Hagesias' mules supplant horses: where a typical epic formula replaces 'horses' with 'strength of horses' (*sthenos hippōn*), just as Idomeneus, for example, becomes 'strength of Idomeneus', so Pindar terms the mules 'strength of mules' (*sthenos hēmionōn*); and, where typically Pindar figures his song as a chariot, here he figures it as a mule-cart. The mules lead the way on a path that is 'clear' (23) like Hieron's sceptre, and tell the story of the aristocratic family of Iamos. The hierarchy of owner and driver is also not respected. This ode is one of the few memorials to name a driver, Phintis, and the only one to name a mule-cart driver. Indeed, the fundamental structure of the ode is less the symbolic hierarchies described above than a sequence of oxymorons that oppose distinct hierarchies. The baby Iamos is 'drenched by the yellow and purple rays of violets' and fed by the snakes with honey described as 'the blameless poison of bees', and his mother's birth pangs are 'beautiful' (43–55). Far from being left behind, mothers continue to influence Iamos and the imagery of the ode. Although Iamos' father summons him to Olympia, he is, uniquely, named by his mother and speaks of kingship as a 'people-nursing honour' (60). Hagesias' town of birth, Stymphalis, may be in 'well-manned' (80) Arcadia, but Hagesias' ancestors who made it their home are referred to specifically as 'maternal men' (*matrōes andres*).

The elevation of the mule thus stands at the centre of a more general collapse of the usual Olympic hierarchies. Half-horse and half-donkey, the hybrid mule seems to have generated a hybrid symbolism that takes over the ode, privileging women as well as men, drivers as well as owners, mules as well as horses, the lower as well as the higher. Such a revision of the Olympic order draws support from more democratic discourses that accord the hardy mule a greater value than the fussy horse: Athenian urban legend praised a mule whose commitment to the building of the Parthenon did not dim with age, while Herodotus marks Cyrus as a mule not only because his parents belonged to different peoples, but also because he was hardy enough to defeat the horsey Lydians with their luxury and soft feet (Hdt. 1.55, 91; cf. 1.79.3; Griffith 2006: 342, 351–352). (Such discourses were also used by Herodotus to critique restrictive citizenship laws; see Strong 2010.) The importation of this alternative equine hierarchy into Olympia undermines the radical distinction of levels within the elite, just as it collapses the symbolic hierarchies of *Olympian* 6: if Hagesias is the mule to Hieron's horse, this distinction no longer marks a clear difference in status between the two (cf. Nicholson 2005: 82–94).

CONCLUSION

Equestrian competitors found themselves in the centre of a complex symbolic system that placed hippic athletics at the apex of elite achievement, and the elite at the apex of society. But this system of hierarchies was far from stable, and was contested from a number of angles. It is from this point of view that the *kalpē* and the mule-cart race, while at the margins in the history of hippic contests, are particularly illuminating. Both slotted into and supported the traditional hippic hierarchies, yet both also challenged those hierarchies, the *kalpē* by emphasizing the work of the jockey and the mule cart through the slippery value of the mule. These dynamics were surely a consideration when the Olympic programme was once again expanded around 400. The new events, the *sunōris* and the colt chariot, had limited symbolic potential: they were simply lesser four-horse chariots, with fewer horses in one case and younger horses in the other.

Suggested Reading

Golden (1998; 2008: 1–23) offers the best overview of the politics of equestrian competition. On class, wealth, and hippotrophy, see also Hodkinson (2000: 303–333), Mann (2001), and Kurke (1991: 163–256), and on the relations between owners and drivers, Nicholson (2005). Kyle (1987), Shear (2003), and Tracy and Habicht (1991) navigate the Panathenaic programme, while Bell (1989) traces a single event, the horse-race. Miller (2004: 75–82) and Crowther (2004: 177–179, 229–240, 323–327) discuss the mechanics of the races. Crowther (2004: 121–132) surveys hippic events in the imperial period. The best place to start, however, is the odes Pindar composed for equestrian victors.

References

Bell, D. 1989. 'The Horse Race (*kelēs*) in Ancient Greece from the Pre-Classical Period to the First Century B.C.' *Stadion* 15: 167–190.

Bonfante, L. 1989. 'Nudity as a Costume in Classical Art.' *AJA* 93: 543–570.

Christesen, P. 2019. *A New Reading of the Damonon Stele*. Newcastle Upon Tyne.

Crowther, N. 2004. *Athletika: Studies on the Olympic Games and Greek Athletics*. Hildesheim.

Forsdyke, S. 2005. *Exile, Ostracism, and Democracy: The Politics of Expulsion in Ancient Greece*. Princeton.

Golden, M. 1998. *Sport and Society in Ancient Greece*. Cambridge.

Golden, M. 2008. *Greek Sport and Social Status*. Austin.

Griffith, M. 2006. 'Horsepower and Donkeywork: Equids and the Ancient Greek Imagination.' *CPh* 101: 185–246, 307–358.

Hodkinson, S. 2000. *Property and Wealth in Classical Sparta*. London.

Kurke, L. 1991. *The Traffic in Praise: Pindar and the Poetics of Social Economy*. Ithaca, NY.

Kurke, L. 1992. 'The Politics of *Habrosune* in Archaic Greece.' *CA* 11: 91–120.

Kyle, D. 1987. *Athletics in Ancient Athens*. Leiden.

Kyle, D. 2007. *Sport and Spectacle in the Ancient World*. Malden, MA.

Luraghi, N. 1994. *Tirannidi arcaiche in Sicilia e Magna Grecia da Panezio di Leontini alla caduta dei Dinomenidi*. Florence.

Mann, C. 2001. *Athlet und Polis im archaischen und frühklassichen Griechenland*. Göttingen.

Miller, S. 2004. *Ancient Greek Athletics*. New Haven.

Moretti, L. 1957. 'Olympionikai. I vincitori negli antichi agoni olimpici.' *MAL* 8: 55–198.

Neils, J., and P. Schultz. 2012. 'Erectheus and the *Apobates* Race on the Parthenon Frieze (North XI–XII).' *AJA* 116: 195–207.

Nicholson, N. 2005. *Aristocracy and Athletics in Archaic and Classical Greece*. Cambridge.

Nobili, C. 2016. *Corone di Gloria. Epigrammi agonistici ed epinici dal VII al IV secolo a.C.* Alessandria.

Palagia, O. 2013. 'The Motya Charioteer: An Alternative View,' www.youtube.com/watch?v=f195T5lZhWE.

Scanlon, T. 2005. 'The Dispersion of Pederasty and the Athletic Revolution in Sixth-Century BC Greece.' *Journal of Homosexuality* 49: 63–85.

Segal, C. 1998. *Aglaia: The Poetry of Alcman, Sappho, Pindar, Bacchylides and Corinna.* Lanham, MD.

Shear, J. 2003. 'Prizes from Athens: The List of Panathenaic Prizes and the Sacred Oil.' *ZPE* 142: 87–108.

Smith, R. 2007. 'Pindar, Athletes and the Early Greek Statue Habit.' In *Pindar's Poetry, Patrons, and Festivals: From Archaic Greece to the Roman Empire.* 183–239. S. Hornblower and C. Morgan, eds. Oxford.

Strong, A. 2010. 'Mules in Herodotus: The Destiny of Half-Breeds.' *CW* 103: 455–464.

Thompson, D. 2005. 'Posidippus, Poet of the Ptolemies.' In *The New Posidippus: A Hellenistic Poetry Book.* 269–283. K. Gutzwiller, ed. Oxford.

Tracy, S. and C. Habicht. 1991. 'New and Old Panathenaic Victor Lists.' *Hesperia* 60: 187–236.

....

CHAPTER 20

ANIMAL EVENTS

....

DONALD G. KYLE

GLADIATORS were the stars of the Roman arena, but beast shows and hunts (*venationes*) were prominent, popular, and enduring Roman entertainments. These elaborate and bloody spectacles involved the display, performance, hunting, and (usually) killing of beasts within restricted areas. Although exact totals are impossible (Kyle 1998: 76–79), undoubtedly more animals than humans died in spectacles, and, for economic more than moral reasons, *venationes* were held more often than gladiatorial combats. Animal events played a major role in the festivals, social life, and public space of Rome, they spread Roman cultural values throughout a vast empire, and they outlasted the fall of gladiatorial combats and of Rome itself.

Historically, Rome's beast shows combined native traditions of rural hunts and animal abuse with imported traditions of staged hunts and beast displays. As the power of the Roman republic spread throughout the Mediterranean, increasingly exotic animals, from elephants to lions, were paraded and put on display, often by generals in triumphs. Over time, shows came to include combats of beasts against other beasts (sometimes they were chained together) and against 'hunters' (*venatores*) in the Forum and the Circus Maximus. Adapted for the comfort, security, and entertainment of viewers, the hunts became a Roman spectator sport. Under the empire even more elaborate beast spectacles were housed in amphitheatres, most famously the Colosseum, as well as in circuses. The ferocity, unpredictability, and deaths of exotic beasts, the skill, bravery, and risk of injury to human hunters, along with the engineering and stagecraft of shows, all added to the allure, suspense, and excitement for attentive and appreciative spectators from all levels of society.

This essay discusses the rise, expansion, and significance of the spectacular beast events. Why were *venationes* so violent, so alluring, so enduring, so 'Roman'? Were hunts perverse indulgences or rituals of power? While I do not endorse ancient or modern brutality to animals, Rome's abuse of animals is not unique or incomprehensible from a comparative ancient perspective. Humans find viewing wild animals inherently fascinating, frightening, and thrilling, due perhaps to instinctual stone-age memories of chasing and being chased by beasts. Watching animals being challenged, controlled, or killed by humans, or giving trained performances, has been entertaining—diverting, amusing, and comforting—for humans around the globe for millennia. It remained so in medieval traditions of beast baiting, and it persists today in blood sports, rodeo, and bull-, cock-, and dog-fighting.

Venationes were not inventions *ex nihilo* but variations and adaptations within an ancient Mediterranean discourse on nature, power, empire, and entertainment. Rome's expanding wars and imperialism are relevant; the assembly, display, control, and killing of beasts demonstrated Rome's territorial extent and imperial dominion over animals, peoples, lands, and even nature itself. Rome's imperial resources were deployed on every level to make the beast shows distinctive in terms of scale, scope, variety, and ingenuity of stagecraft. The social and political traditions of Rome enveloped the *venationes* as well, as opportunities for ostentatious patronage, consumption, and generosity within Roman spectacle practices. Animal events were richly symbolic in Roman culture (*Romanitas*). Entertaining but carefully staged hunts reassured Romans that they were empowered, privileged, and secure. As the patron and protector of his people, the emperor typically produced and attended shows with generosity and dignity.

EVIDENCE AND SCHOLARSHIP

The scale and longevity of Roman animal events left behind a wealth of material and written evidence that allows us to investigate their allure and history (Wiedemann 1992: 55–59). Without modern photography, taxidermy, or media to record and broadcast their conquests and hunts abroad, early Roman generals brought back live beasts to display, dominate, and defeat in shows. Soon officials and leaders, and emperors eventually, were expected to finance and produce such shows with regularity; naturally they wanted their efforts commemorated for publicity and posterity. Public inscriptions, painted notices, coins, and even graffiti announced or recorded details of such performances: what beasts could be seen, how many had been killed. Spectators wanted souvenirs of the exciting shows, and common objects (lamps, figurines) testify to their enthusiasm. Studies of facilities also help us understand the stagecraft and the spectatorship of hunts.

While shocking to moderns, Romans found images of hunts in art a source of wonder and pride (Brown 1992). Hunt mosaics and paintings with graphic, unapologetic scenes of suffering beasts were popular decorations at villas, especially in North Africa, where they memorialized the munificence of local hunt providers (Dunbabin 1978). A striking mosaic from Zliten in Libya combines hunts, executions, and gladiatorial combats—events that took place in sequence over time. Extensive mosaics from Piazza Armerina in Sicily associate rural hunting, procurement, and transport of beasts for shows with virtue and status.

One major literary source is Martial's *Book of Spectacles*; this collection of laudatory epigrams, while intended to ingratiate the poet with the Flavians (possibly Titus, or Domitian, or both), offers important contextual insights (Coleman 2006). Other authors (e.g. Livy, Cicero) present historical details, anecdotes, or commentary (Futrell 2006). Imperial historians, notably Suetonius and Dio Cassius, suggest the character of emperors through their spectacles, while the elder Pliny and Aelian combine zoological information with fables and anecdotes.

Like all Roman blood events, Rome's beast spectacles traditionally evoked moralistic, anachronistic condemnation from modern writers as alien and savage. Antiquarian handbooks nevertheless produced valuable detailed inventories of beast shows. From the 1980s on, probably stimulated by concerns about violence in modern society, sport, and media, studies of Roman blood spectacles became more sophisticated and interpretive. Scholars went beyond numbers and narratives to investigate the shows from the perspectives of both the arena and the stands. Recent ecological concerns and the animal rights movement have also increased interest and study in the abuse of animals in the ancient and modern world (Bomgardner 1992; Shelton 2007). New interdisciplinary perspectives indicate that Rome's violent spectacles are not unfathomable (Hopkins 1983; Wiedemann 1992; Barton 1993; Plass 1995; Kyle 1998; Futrell 2006).

ANCIENT ATTITUDES TO ANIMALS

As we learn more about animals' social instincts, emotions, language, tools, and culture, moderns are becoming more concerned about our relationships with non-human creatures. However admirable, this is a modern and not an ancient perspective. Ancient people valued domesticated animals but, as Aristotle said: 'The art of war is duly employed against wild animals' (*Politics* 1256a; Shelton 2007: 107 n. 42).

The Mediterranean world had long used animals for sport and spectacle. Beasts represented wildness, strength, and fertility, so leaders used animals as symbols of their fundamental defence of society and order from chaos and natural threats, and of their courageous conquest of foes and foreign lands. Near Eastern monarchs killed lions and bulls in staged 'royal hunts', Minoans and Thessalians had bull sports, and Greeks staged cockfights as martial inspiration (Morgan 1975; Kyle 2007: 33–37; Kalof 2007: 11–26; Shelton 2007: 98–116.)

Similarly, Romans admired wild, great beasts and they were intrigued by rare species, but they also regarded animals, wild or domesticated, as sub-human, non-sentient, soulless parts of nature. Animals lacked reason and so were to be used as objects (Marcus Aurelius, *Meditations* 6.23). They represented predators or game, threats and nuisances to be controlled or killed, economic resources of labour and food, or trophies won by virtue (Wiedemann 1992: 62–67).

Romans had few qualms about the abuse and death of humans in the arena, let alone about killing non-humans, so beast shows faced almost no opposition in Roman society (Wistrand 1992). Associating themselves with the victors, not the animal victims, Romans cheered for the hunter fighting against alien others and wild nature. They welcomed beast shows as entertainment, not as senseless cruelty.

THE REPUBLIC: EXPANSION AND BEASTS AS POLITICAL CAPITAL

Early Italians had long, indeed prehistoric, traditions of subsistence hunting of local wild animals (e.g. rabbits, boars, wolves) for food and to protect their farms, and elite Romans also came to hunt for sport, sometimes at rural estates with game preserves (Varro, *On Agriculture* 3.13.1–3; Anderson 1985: 83–100; Green 1996; Shelton 2007: 119–120). Early Rome also presented public hunting or torment of local wild animals in the Circus Maximus. In the *Ludi Cereales* foxes with burning brands tied to their tails were let loose, perhaps representing the elimination of vermin from cultivated fields. Games for the fertility goddess Flora included hunts of harmless roe deer and hares, and in the *Ludi Taurei* bulls were hunted or abused with fire (Kyle 1998: 41–43; Futrell 1997: 24–26). Along with the practice of public butchering and animal sacrifices, such customs in the Circus made Romans more open to carnage in arenas.

By the third century BCE, Rome controlled Italy and began expanding overseas, which brought a great increase in the volume, variety, and violence of beast shows. When battling Pyrrhus of Epirus (281–272 BCE) Romans first faced elephants, which remained awe-inspiring symbols of foreign threats. In 275 the consul Manius. Curius Dentatus exhibited four elephants, taken from Pyrrhus, in his triumph; many spectacular uses of elephants in processions and arenas followed (Scullard 1974).

With their wars against Carthage, expansion exposed Romans to more exotic African beasts and to older traditions of the symbolic use of animals in propagandistic processions and imperial iconography (Anderson 1985: 57–83; Coleman 1996). Roman generals soon adapted the practice of collecting and transporting large numbers of beasts to demonstrate imperial power and territorial control. In triumphal celebrations generals paraded for-eign animals like exotic prisoners of war. At first animals were just displayed as curiosities and symbols of conquest, sometimes in costumes or with coloured coats, but soon beasts were hunted by humans or forced to fight each other. In 252 BCE, the proconsul L. Caecilius Metellus exhibited some 140 captured elephants in the Circus Maximus and arranged a mock battle with slaves. Pliny wryly comments that those who say the elephants were not killed cannot explain what became of them (*Natural History* 8.16–17).

Wars in the Greek East brought more beasts and more shows. In his triumph in 186 BCE, M. Fulvius Nobilior held the first known *venatio* at Rome, with a hunt of lions and panthers (Livy 39.22.1–2; Rosivach 2006). Later the Senate ordered that animal events must be no costlier than Nobilior's extravagant show (Livy 40.44.8–12); but such sumptuary measures were doomed by the popularity and political advantages of shows, as likewise with the Senate's ban of 170 BCE on the importation of *Africanae* (probably any large feline; Pliny, *Natural History* 8.24.64). By 174, the censors themselves arranged for iron animal cages in the Circus (Livy 41.27.6). In 169, the aediles exhibited sixty-three African beasts (probably leopards), forty bears, and some elephants in the Circus (Livy 44.18.8), confirming that beast shows had become part of official circus games.

During the troubled LATE REPUBLIC, beast shows spread from festivals and triumphs to funeral games (*munera*) and they became larger and more elaborate. Generous and innova-tive shows were necessary political capital for seekers of office. Political leaders, especially ambitious aediles wanting to put on memorable shows in the *Ludi Romani* and *Megalenses*, needed wild animals to compete for popularity and promotion. Letters by M. Caelius Rufus to Cicero include appeals to him as governor of Cilicia (in 51 BCE) to send leopards for his aedilician games at Rome (Jennison 1937: 137–140; Ville 1981: 88–93). Cicero replied that he was trying, but there was a shortage from over-hunting (*Letters to his Friends* 2.11.2).

Among the many shows, those of Pompey the Great and Julius Caesar were spectacularly extravagant (Wiedemann 1992: 59–60; Beacham 1999: 11–13; Dunkle 2008: 207–214). After hunting elephants and lions in North Africa for his African triumph of 81 BCE, Pompey at the age of 25 wanted to enter Rome in a chariot drawn by elephants, but the entrance gate proved too narrow (Plutarch, *Pompey* 12.8). Pompey's games for the dedication of his theatre in 55 CE involved the deaths of 600 lions, 400 leopards, and the first rhinoceros at Rome, but the most famous episode was a combat of twenty elephants against Gaetulian hunters in the Circus on the last day (Dio Cassius 39.38.2; Jennison 1937: 51–55; Toynbee 1973: 22–23; Shelton 1999; 2004: 372–378; Wiedemann 1992: 139–141). In a letter consoling a friend who missed the spectacle, Cicero downplayed the show's appeal, claiming that the boring, excessive games offered nothing new (*Letters to his Friends* 7.1). Rhetorically, Cicero asks what pleasure a cultured man might find in watching a great beast overwhelming a man, or an elephant struck by a hunting spear. He adds that the spectators felt compassion (*misericordia*) with the elephants, which seemed rather like humans. Later sources claim that the elephants charged the barrier and seemed to cry and beg for mercy almost like humans, which turned the crowd against Pompey (Pliny, *Natural History* 8.121). Rather than sincere expressions of sympathy for the beasts—no beasts were spared—the authors and the crowd criticized Pompey's egotistical and botched show for its nearly disastrous lack of control and of safety and pride for spectators.

Like Pompey, Caesar had ambitions and resources from wars and conquered territories. Having captured sixty-four elephants at Thapsus, he issued coins with images of elephants and he included elephant fights in his spectacles. Outdoing Pompey, Caesar's quadruple triumphal games in 46 BCE included his procession to the Capitol escorted by two lines of elephants bearing lit torches in their trunks (Suetonius, *Caesar* 37.2; Dio Cassius 43.22.1). He put on beast shows for five days in a row, including the killing of 400 lions, a display of Thessalian bull-fighting, and the first display of a giraffe at Rome (Suetonius, *Caesar* 39; Jennison 1937: 55–59).

EMPERORS AND BEAST SHOWS IN AMPHITHEATRES

Attentive to traditions, the emperor Augustus realized the importance of animal shows. Pragmatic and demanding, Romans saw animals from the provinces and frontiers as imperial commodities to be supplied by the emperor for their amusement and Augustus proudly details his giving of twenty-six games in which 3,500 African beasts died ('*confecta sunt*': *Deeds of the Divine Augustus* 22.3). Augustus carefully institutionalized and monopolized violent shows (*munera*), so beast events came under imperial supervision and generally moved to the amphitheatre as morning shows (*matutina*) followed by executions at noon and gladiatorial combats in the afternoon (Wiedemann 1992: 8–9, 55, 60). Augustus personally set an example of generosity and attentiveness: emperors were to provide the beasts, produce a thrilling but safe and well-controlled show, pay attention to complaints or requests from the assembled Romans, and play their role of decorous spectator, since they themselves were on display before the crowds.

Parsimonious and reclusive, Tiberius courted bad feelings by not continuing the tradition of shows. Caligula's enthusiasm for violence and shows of all kinds was welcomed, but only for a time. Eager for legitimacy, Claudius sponsored chariot-races in Caligula's Vatican circus and sometimes he held *venationes* between every five events there (Suetonius, *Claudius* 21.2–4). He also staged a panther hunt using a cavalry squadron of the Praetorian Guard, as well as, like Caesar, Thessalian bull sports. Hardly unbiased, Suetonius links Claudius' supposed bloodthirstiness to his enthusiasm for *venationes*, for which he arrived at daybreak and stayed throughout (*Claudius* 34.2). The last Julio-Claudian, Nero was personally more inclined to Greek-style entertainments, but he still staged hunts with artificial scenery and exotic animals, including elk, hippopotamuses, and seals (Calpurnius, *Eclogues* 7.24).

Vespasian knew spectacles would harmonize the reign of the new Flavian dynasty with the people and he strategically started building a new, magnificent, and politically symbolic facility—the Flavian Amphitheatre or Colosseum —over the artificial lake of Nero's Golden House. The need to control growing numbers of beasts and to protect spectators already had contributed to the invention and careful design of a new purpose-built facility: the amphitheatre in the Late Republic (Welch 2007). Amphitheatres facilitated sylvan settings and stage effects and the Colosseum was designed to control wild beasts as well as humans (Coarelli 2001; Hopkins and Beard 2005).

Titus inaugurated the Colosseum in 80 CE with extravagant spectacles lasting a hundred days (Dio Cassius 66.25) in which 9,000 wild and tame animals perished; Suetonius (*Titus* 7.3) claims 5,000 beasts died in one day alone. Extolling the events, Martial in his *Book of Spectacles* pays more attention to beasts than to gladiators. He seems intrigued that a pregnant sow, though speared and dying, gave birth (14.6; Coleman 2006). In other wonders, unnatural enemies fight: a rhinoceros attacks and tosses a bull (*Book of Spectacles* 11); the same beast (probably) later tosses a bear and other animals (26); goaded by flames, a bull attacks an elephant, which kills him (22). Beasts revere the emperor's divine power over nature: having fought a bull, an elephant spontaneously worships the emperor (20); when a doe stops in supplication before the emperor, the hounds that were chasing it also desist because 'beasts know his sacred power' (33). The emperor upholds hierarchical order: when a trained lion attacks its trainer, it is killed (12). The hunter Carpophoros outdoes mythological hunters by killing a boar, a bear, a lion, and a leopard (17), killing some twenty beasts in one show (32). Two women also hunt beasts (7–8). (Dio Cassius 66.25.2 says non-elite women killed animals in the inaugural games, but Juvenal's remark, 1.22–23, that a woman costumed as an Amazon killed bears probably concerns Domitian's games.) Martial repeats the obvious messages of the games: wonders were staged, wildness tamed or destroyed, order sustained, and disobedience punished. Animals, humans, and nature itself must yield to the divine emperor's power.

THE HUNTED

As emperors strived to put on lavish shows to bolster their legitimacy and popularity, the numbers and variety of animals escalated. The more numerous and exotic the beasts, the more likely the show and its producer would be discussed and remembered. One of the 'good' emperors, the imperialistic Trajan had 11,000 beasts killed over the course of 123 days (roughly ninety beasts per day) in his Dacian triumph in 107 CE (Dio Cassius 68.15.1).

Constantly needing more beasts, the Romans applied their characteristic organizational talents to the capture and transport to Rome of animals from all over the empire MacKinnon 2006). Rome commodified and categorized beasts by ferocity and fodder: as wild (*ferae*) or domesticated, as carnivores (*dentatae*) or herbivores (Wiedemann 1992: 58–59), and according to performance potential (fierceness and rarity). Some beasts were native to Italy but most were foreign and exemplified untamed nature. Elephants were expensive but popular, as were large cats (lions, tigers, and leopards or panthers) in part because lions symbolized death (Toynbee 1973: 60–69). Even camels, giraffes, hippopotamuses, rhinoceroses, and crocodiles appeared, often with elaborate props, artificial pools, and woods. Bears, bulls, and boars were less exotic but predictably ferocious. Costly to keep, most beasts soon ended up in shows. Driven from cages in the basement of the amphitheatre, they were lifted up to the arena and forced before loud and excited crowds. They fought, fled, or attacked out of instinct or terror. No matter how big, fast, or fierce, the citizens of the animal kingdom were no match for Rome (Fig. 20.1).

Although most hunts were deadly, the early tradition of displaying exotic beasts continued with exhibits and imperial menageries. For example, on days without hunts, Augustus displayed exotic species—a rhinoceros, a tiger, a huge snake—in public sites (Suetonius, *Augustus* 43.11). Some beasts were trained to perform in the arena. Elephants were most easily schooled because of their intelligence; some danced in costume to music, sat at couches as if banqueting, or walked tightropes; one supposedly wrote a phrase in Greek in the sand (Dunkle 2008: 214–215). Such trained performances were not benign, light amusements, but rather less destructive (and more economical) demonstrations of Rome's mastery and humbling of nature and threats (Shelton 2004: 379–382). As with trained, exotic gladiators, Romans felt satisfaction and pride when trained, exotic beasts were controlled by—and performed for—them. Like expensive gladiators, costly trained beasts might be

FIGURE 20.1. Detail from mosaic with *venatores* and leopards, early fourth century CE, Galleria Borghese, Rome. Daderot, Wikimedia Commons. Public domain.

spared and recaptured for reuse—if they behaved. Big cats were harder to teach and unreliable: Martial (2.75) mentions that a trained lion killed two young arena attendants.

Though expected, enjoyed, and valuable for public relations, hunts ultimately declined. When the empire ceased to expand and to acquire new resources, finances and infrastructure for the supply of beasts diminished. Centuries of over-hunting in Africa and Asia had harmful ecological effects (Bomgardner 1992), so expensive animals were hard to replace. The letters of the statesman Symmachus demonstrate that by around 400 CE the challenges of arranging wild beasts had mounted steeply. With more use of trained and local beasts, the hunts continued into the sixth century in the West, but consular diptychs depict shows with acrobatic displays more like modern circus acts (Bomgardner 2000: 217–220; Rea 2001: 235–239).

THE HUNTERS

Usually of lowly or servile origins, hunters (*venatores*) were professionals who hunted wild prey in the arena, using specialized equipment and weapons (lances or spears), often assisted by hounds (Junkelmann 2000: 70–74). In early shows, foreign hunters were imported, often from North Africa, to restage exotic hunts as reminders of Roman conquests. For example, after the Jugurthine War, Sulla brought in Mauretanian hunters to kill 100 lions (Pliny, *Natural History* 8.53; Plutarch, *Sulla* 5.1). By the late republic and early empire, there were mock battles of soldiers against big cats and bears; some reliefs depict beast fighters with helmets, shields, and swords (Fig. 20.2), reinforcing the analogy of hunts to military battles. Later hunters wore tunics and sometimes leg wrappings but they had no armour. Under the empire *bestiarii* (beast handlers or fighters) assisted hunters and managed beasts in shows. Both probably trained at a special facility at Rome, the imperial Ludus Matutinus.

North African mosaics depict associations or 'families' of professional hunters (Blanchard-Lemée, M. et al. 1996). A third-century example from Tunisia, the Magerius mosaic depicts leopards and hunters of the venatorial family of the Telegenii, who provided both animals and hunters. Bags of money are shown and an inscription applauds the expenditure of the sponsor Magerius (Fig. 20.3; Brown 1992).

Just as gladiators set inspirational, even educational, examples of virtue, *venatores* impressed and pleased Romans with their skills and courage (Seneca, *Proverbs and Quotes* 2.8). Like gladiators, they often had vivid stage names; the numbers of their kills might be celebrated in art. They also shared in the glamour and sex appeal of the arena, but the ambivalence Romans felt about gladiators extended to them. They might win their release by facing danger courageously, but they retained the social stigma attached to performers.

EMPERORS AS HUNTERS

Venationes had symbolic analogies to Near Eastern royal hunts, but the proper role of the Roman emperor was fundamentally different from that of the king. Roman ideology and edicts dictated that citizens of status were not to perform in public shows like base slaves or

FIGURE 20.2. Relief with *venator* and *bestiarius* in the Circus Maximus. Museo Nazionale Terme, Rome. Erich Lessing/Art Resource, NY.

foreign entertainers. An emperor like Trajan might hunt virtuously outside the city (Pliny, *Panegyric to Trajan* 81.1–3), but at arena hunts the emperor was a powerful imperial patron, ordering that others bring home the prey of the empire to impress his people. Prominently placed at shows, the emperor's role was that of producer and host. Like Augustus, he was to remain appropriately Roman—attentive but composed.

Already supreme, an emperor would only disgrace himself by actually killing beasts in the arena with little personal risk, like the Near Eastern kings Rome had defeated. Indeed, Domitian was criticized for hunting from a safe platform at his country estate, killing beasts driven to him (Suetonius, *Domitian* 19); Caracalla later performed as a hunter (Augustan History, *Caracalla* 5.5; 9) but Commodus was the most notorious imperial *venator*. He personally killed animals both privately at his estate (Augustan History, *Commodus* 8.5) and publicly in the arena. A dilettante hunter in no real danger, in 192 CE he slew 100 bears by spearing them from a gallery built above the arena and shot other beasts at a distance with a bow and arrow. He very improperly demanded cash prizes and he even threatened spectators. As with the outrageous antics of Caligula and Nero, scholars debate whether Commodus was challenging social norms, fashioning a more popular imperial role, or simply indulging in megalomania (Wiedemann 1992: 177–178; Kyle 1998: 90, 94–95; 158–159; Hekster 2002: 154–162; Futrell 2006: 158–159).

FIGURE 20.3. Magerius mosaic from Smirat, Tunisia. Gilles Mermet/Art Resource, NY.

HUNTING GAME

Christians regarded the hunts, like all spectacles, as idolatrous sacrifices (Tertullian, *On the Spectacles* 4–13), but Roman spectators saw beasts in the arena as wild game, not domesticated, flawless, and ritually willing sacrificial victims. The elements of the chase (dogs, spears, hunters, even nets), the beasts' flight and resistance, the emphasis on using 'wild', often dangerous animals, and the care expended on elaborate sylvan scenery (pools, forests) all suggest re-creations of hunts in the wild.

What happened to the animal carcasses? Early studies speculated that the remains were dumped in pits, but arena animal meat probably was usually given to the people as food (Kyle 1998: 187–194). Christian sources accuse Romans of indirect cannibalism, saying they ate the flesh of boars, bears, and other wild beasts soiled with human blood from the arena (Tertullian, *Apology* 9.11). As political devices, public banquets and distributions of animal meat (*viscerationes*) often accompanied spectacles (Cicero, *On Obligations* 2.57; Kajava 1998).

At spectacles emperors often scattered tokens or wooden balls (*missilia*) redeemable for goods to the crowds. Domitian, Titus, Elagabalus, and others distributed foodstuffs and live birds and animals via tokens, for which spectators scrambled in the stands. In the third century CE, Gordian I and Probus went further by apparently letting the people come down from the stands into the arena to hunt and carry off great numbers of beasts (mostly herbivores) themselves as meaty trophies (Kyle 1998: 191–194). Recent finds of bones of exotic animals (leopards, ostriches, bears) in fifth- to seventh-century fill near the Meta Sudans fountain may suggest rough butchering of beasts near the Colosseum (MacKinnon 2006: 154–155).

Poor, hungry Romans were probably happy to get arena meat. Feasting meant incorporation, and emperors used hunts to assist their obligation—within the imperial 'moral economy'— to feed and amuse the people. The disposal of arena meat by distribution—not by pits but by pots—confirms the enduring perception of *venationes* as hunts to provide food and to protect the community and food supply of Rome.

References

Anderson, J. K. 1985. *Hunting in the Ancient World*. Berkeley.

Barton, C. A. 1993. *The Sorrows of the Ancient Romans: The Gladiator and the Monster*. Princeton.

Beacham, R. C. 1999. *Spectacle Entertainments of Early Imperial Rome*. New Haven.

Blanchard-Lemée, M. et al. 1996. *Mosaics of Roman Africa: Floor Mosaics from Tunisia*. New York.

Bomgardner, D. L. 1992. 'The Trade in Wild Beasts for Roman Spectacles: A Green Perspective.' *Anthropozoologica* 16: 161–166.

Bomgardner, D. L. 2000. *The Story of the Roman Amphitheatre*. London.

Brown, S. 1992. 'Death as Decoration: Scenes from the Arena on Roman Domestic Mosaics.' In *Pornography and Representation in Greece and Rome*. 180–211. A. Richlin, ed. Oxford.

Coarelli, F. and A. Gabucci. 2001. *The Colosseum*. Los Angeles.

Coleman, K. M. 1996. 'Ptolemy Philadelphus and the Roman Amphitheatre.' In *Roman Theatre and Society*. 49–68. W. J. Slater, ed. Ann Arbor.

Coleman, K. M. 2006. *M. Valerii Martialis Liber Spectaculorum*. Oxford.

Dunbabin, K. M. D. 1978. *The Mosaics of Roman North Africa*. Oxford.

Dunkle, R. 2008. *Gladiators: Violence and Spectacle in Ancient Rome*. Harlow.

Futrell, A. 1997. *Blood in the Arena: The Spectacle of Roman Power*. Austin, TX.

Futrell, A. 2006. *The Roman Games: A Sourcebook*. Malden, MA.

Green, C. M. C. 1996. 'Did the Romans Hunt?' *ClAnt* 15.2: 222–260.

Hekster, O. 2002. *Commodus: An Emperor at the Crossroads*. Amsterdam.

Hopkins, K. 1983. *Death and Renewal*. Cambridge.

Jennison, G. 1937. *Animals for Show and Pleasure in Ancient Rome*. Manchester.

Junkelmann. M. 2000. '*Familia Gladiatoria*: The Heroes of the Amphitheatre.' In *Gladiators and Caesars: The Power of Spectacle in Ancient Rome*. 31–74. E. Köhne and C. Ewigleben, eds. Berkeley.

Kajava, M. 1998. 'Visceratio.' *Arctos* 32: 109–131.

Kalof, L. 2007. *Looking at Animals in Human History*. London.

Kyle, D. G. 1998. *Spectacles of Death in Ancient Rome*. London.

Kyle, D. G. 2007. *Sport and Spectacle in the Ancient World*. Malden, MA.

MacKinnon, M. 2006. 'Supplying Exotic Animals for the Roman Amphitheatre Games.' *Mouseion* 6: 137–161.

Morgan, M. G. 1975. 'Three Non-Roman Blood Sports.' *CQ* 25: 117–122.

Plass, P. 1995. *The Game of Death in Ancient Rome: Arena Sport and Political Suicide*. Madison, WI.

Rea, R. 2001. 'Il Colosseo, teatra per gli spettacoli di caccia. Le fonti e i reperti.' In *Sangue earena*. 223–243. A. La Regina, ed. Rome.

Rosivach, V. J. 2006. 'The First *Venatio*.' *NECJ* 33: 271–278.

Scullard, H. H. 1974. *The Elephant in the Greek and Roman World*. Ithaca, NY.

Shelton, J. 1999. 'Elephants, Pompey, and the Reports of Popular Displeasure in 55 BC.' In *Veritatis Amicitiaeque Causa: Essays in Honor of Anna Lydia Motto and John R. Clark*. 231–271. S. N. Byrne and E. P. Cueva, eds. Wauconda, IL.

Shelton, J. 2004. 'Dancing and Dying: The Display of Elephants in Ancient Roman Arenas.' In *Daimonopylai: Essays in Classics and the Classical Tradition Presented to Edmund G. Barry*. 363–382. R. Egan and M. Joyal, eds. Winnipeg.

Shelton, J. 2007. 'Beastly Spectacles in the Ancient Mediterranean World.' In *A Cultural History of Animals in Antiquity*. 97–126. L. Kalof, ed. New York.

Toynbee, J. M. C. 1973. *Animals in Roman Life and Art*. Ithaca, NY.

Ville, G. 1981. *La gladiature en Occident des origines à la mort de Domitien*. Rome.

Welch, K. E. 2007. *The Roman Amphitheatre from Its Origins to the Colosseum*. Cambridge.

Wiedemann, T. 1992. *Emperors and Gladiators*. London.

Wistrand, M. 1992. *Entertainment and Violence in Ancient Rome: The Attitudes of Roman Writers of the First Century A.D.* Gothenburg.

CHAPTER 21

···

NAVAL EVENTS AND
AQUACADES

···

RABUN TAYLOR

SPECTACLES OF THE CONDEMNED

···

IT seems inevitable that ancient Romans, who took great pleasure and pride in their urban
waterworks, should have found creative and entertaining ways to combine them with their
celebrated taste for spectacle. Water entertainments of a purely theatrical kind seem to have
been popular in certain parts of the Roman world, especially Italy, the Near East, and Gaul.
But surviving literature, with its hard bias toward the centres of power, favours the far more
dangerous and sanguinary affairs that were inspired by the amphitheatre, not the theatre
or gymnasium. The participants in these were not professional entertainers or sportsmen,
but capital criminals and prisoners of war, all of them technically condemned to death
(*damnati*). We can only guess at the norms of justice or punishment they were subjected
to; but clear-cut incentives, ranging from reprieve to full clemency in exchange for a good
show of courage, animated their desperate performances. Treatment of *damnati* in Roman
spectacle fell along a sliding scale. A few were condemned to die violently with no chance
to resist, but others were given various degrees of autonomy in the outcome. Water spectacle offered the condemned an opportunity to save themselves with a redeeming display of
skill or physical courage. Such opportunities, of course, did not guarantee a better result for
participants (Coleman 1990). But one thing was certain: timidity invited a swift and igno-
minious death.

In the imperial period, a favourite treatment of the condemned was to present them to the
public as protagonists in parodic re-enactments of Greek myths, particularly episodes that
promised either physical humiliation, situational danger, or both. The usual venue for such
things was the arena. One mythological episode in particular, however, turns up in aquatic
venues: Leander's nocturnal swim across the Hellespont to visit his lover, Hero (Berlan-
Bajard 2006: 99–101, 105–106; Coleman 1993: 63; 2006: 202–211). In the story, Leander
drowns when his beacon on the shore is extinguished. How the drama was translated into
compelling spectacle starring a convict is unknown. The poet Martial provides the merest
hint of one staging at Rome. The crux of his reticent couplet is that the pretend Leander, to

his own surprise, survived the ordeal: 'Stop wondering, Leander, that the nocturnal wave spared you: it was Caesar's wave' (*On the Spectacles* 28 (25)).

Whatever trials 'Leander' faced during his public swim, they were potentially lethal. 'Caesar's wave', some kind of *deus ex machina* that stayed his execution, was issued at the pleasure of the emperor, presumably because the protagonist's courage merited the equivalent of a gladiatorial *missio*, or reprieve. Although theatre and sport were merged in this kind of spectacle, its quasi-accidental character—with an outcome contingent on the performance—relates it more closely to sport. In this respect the mythological enactment of the condemned closely resembles its more famous counterpart, the naval battle show.

Naumachiae

The staged naval battle was a Roman invention. In fact, the phenomenon was born, lived, and died at Rome itself, with little diffusion to other cities. The rarest of any identifiable genre of ancient spectacle, it was known more by hearsay than by direct experience: the total number of securely attested spectacles involving mortal combat on ships amounts to about nine. Of these, all but two took place in man-made structures at Rome. Other naval spectacles are known, but they were small-scale burlesques or *divertissements*: if blood flowed at all, it did so on a small scale. A single outlier, staged in 161 CE on a river at Gadara, south of the Dead Sea, is too poorly documented for us to judge its character (Meshorer 1966; Berlan-Bajard 2006: 51–52, 375).

The genuine article was blood sport on a titanic scale, its casualties numbering in the thousands. Very Roman, to be sure; yet the name the Romans gave to the genre and its artificial venues, *naumachia*, is Greek. From the time of its invention at the triumphal games of Julius Caesar in 46 BCE until its denouement in the second and third centuries, the *naumachia* was conceived as a parodic reimagining of famous episodes in Mediterranean naval history, most of them involving Greek fleets. The motif of Greek galleys at war was popular in Roman art from the first century CE (Jacobelli and Avilia 1989; Berlan-Bajard 2006: 303–310). Caesar's chosen scenario, however, was a battle between Egyptians and Tyrians. To accommodate this show, a huge basin was dug in the Campus Martius at Rome. Thousands of men in biremes, triremes, and quadriremes engaged in the battle (Suetonius, *Caesar* 39.6; Appian, *Civil Wars* 2.102; Dio Cassius 40.23.3–6). Like Leander's swim, these themed conflicts were not expected to unfold according to the story. Settled history could be reversed, as would happen in 80 CE, when the 'Athenians' defeated the 'Syracusans' in a re-enactment of a famous Syracusan victory in 414 BCE (Dio Cassius 66.25.4).

Most of the great *naumachiae* took place in the Julio-Claudian and Flavian periods. At least four purpose-built basins (also called *naumachiae*) were constructed to accommodate them. Caesar's was meant perhaps to be temporary, like other large venues for spectacle in Rome at the time. It probably occupied the area west of Piazza Navona (Coarelli 1997: 19–20; Cariou 2009: 31–39, 226–230). The excavated earth would likely have been mounded around the perimeter to serve as an embankment for the spectators. One of Rome's four existing aqueducts may have supplied it, but the basin was so low in the floodplain that the river itself could have supplied much of the water.

In 2 BCE Augustus introduced his own *naumachia*, complete with a dedicated aqueduct. In *The Deeds of the Divine Augustus*, a public summary of his achievements, the emperor says,

> I presented to the people the spectacle of a naval battle across the Tiber [i.e. in the Trastevere district], in the place that is now the Grove of the Caesars, having excavated an area 1,800 feet in length and 1,200 in width. In it roughly 30 beaked ships, triremes or biremes, along with many smaller craft, did battle with one another. About 3,000 men, not counting the oarsmen, fought in these fleets (*Deeds of the Divine Augustus* 23).

Unlike Julius Caesar's event, this one did not accompany a triumph; it was part of the games celebrated to mark the dedication of the Temple of Mars Ultor. The Grove of the Caesars came to commemorate Augustus' two heirs presumptive, Gaius and Lucius Caesar, who would predecease him a few years later. Their memorial monument was built on an islet in the basin that could be reached from the shore by a wooden bridge (Pliny, *Natural History* 16.190, 200). Despite numerous literary references to this *naumachia*, its physical topography remains elusive. On the basis of ancient cartographic evidence, I have proposed that it followed a north–south orientation (Fig. 21.1; Taylor 1997; 2000: 169–200). Cariou disagrees, noting the presence of an ancient east–west drain that notionally cut off the southern third of the basin as I proposed it. He suggests that this drain determined the southern limit of the basin, which he thus orients east–west, with rounded ends (2009: 48–109, 230–278). Cariou's reconstruction seems to thrust the west end of the *naumachia* into the Janiculum hillside, but admittedly we do not know the hill's precise contours in antiquity. The drain, however, is 6.2 m below *ancient* ground level and would have run comfortably underneath the shallow *naumachia*—which, in any event, was abandoned and subjected to gradual disintegration from the end of the first century CE (Taylor 1997: 471–472; 2000: 174–179).

The islet may relate to Augustus' decision to stage his *naumachia* as the battle between Athenians and Persians in 479 BCE at the island of Salamis (Dio Cassius 55.10.7–8). The next known spectacle involving the *naumachia* of Augustus, some eighty-one years later, brought the islet into greater prominence:

> And also in that place, on the first day there was a gladiatorial contest and a wild-beast hunt, the part of the lake fronting the statues [of Gaius and Lucius on the islet?] having been overbuilt with planks and surrounded by platforms; on the second day, there was a horse race; and on the third, a sea battle with three thousand men and after this an infantry battle. The Athenians, defeating the Syracusans (they used these names in the naval battle), went out onto the little island and attacked and captured a wall that had been built around the memorial (Dio Cassius 66.25.3–4).

As we have seen, the outcome contradicted history's verdict. But the geography at least had a small claim of authenticity by mimicking Ortygia, the well-defended island sector of the city of Syracuse (Coleman 1993: 67). Titus' emphasis on the island memorial of Gaius and Lucius also threw into relief the parallel dynastic status, but better fortune, that he and his younger brother Domitian were now able to enjoy in the wake of their father Vespasian's death the year before. They could fulfil, in essence, the unfulfilled promise of Gaius and Lucius.

Thereafter the *naumachia* of Augustus was abandoned, succumbing to urbanization of its neighbourhood and the failure of its water source (Taylor 1997: 477–480; 2000: 184–186). Domitian staged two *naumachiae* within the next decade, both at other venues: a miniature one in the Colosseum (probably that arena's last) and a full-scale one in a new basin excavated

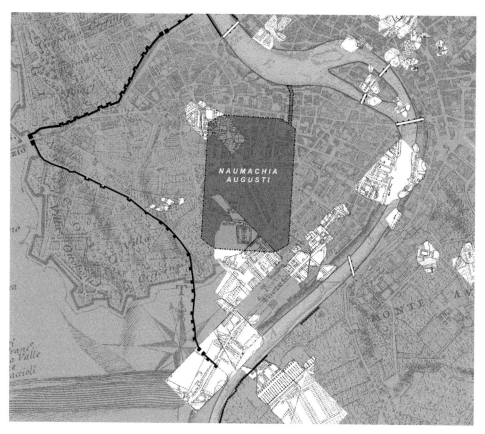

FIGURE 21.1. Map of the proposed location of Augustus' basin in Trastevere, Rome, superimposed on G.-B. Nolli's *Nuova pianta di Roma* of 1748. Areas in white represent fragments of the Severan marble plan of *c*.205–210 CE, indicating the overbuilding of Augustus' *naumachia* following the Flavian era. Source: R. Taylor.

'near the Tiber' (Suetonius, *Domitian* 4.1–2, 6; Dio Cassius 67.7.8). This event, celebrating the emperor's triumph in November 89, was infamous: 'almost all the combatants in it died, and many spectators too', Dio Cassius reports. During the spectacle a violent winter tempest arose but Domitian let nobody leave or even change clothes, consigning many to die of exposure.

Within a generation the new basin was ransacked for building material after a fire (Suetonius, *Domitian* 5), probably under Trajan. When this emperor introduced an abundant new aqueduct from the north-west, he erected Rome's fourth and final *naumachia* (Buzzetti 1968; Cariou 2009 111–178, 279–304). Situated in the Vatican, it is Rome's only *naumachia* to have been identified archaeologically (Fig. 21.2). Its precise date of dedication was 11 November 109 CE (*The Ostian Calendar* 22 [109] 14–17). Over six days it hosted a gladiatorial exhibition, with festivities continuing until the 24th. Strangely, the public document recording this information gives no record of a naval battle! But the opening was behind schedule; the aqueduct's grand inauguration had been in June. Trajan must have called off the marquee event to avoid any ominous comparisons with Domitian's November

FIGURE 21.2. Outline of Trajan's *naumachia* on a satellite map of the Prati neighbourhood in modern Rome. © Google 2020. After Buzzetti 1968.

debacle some years earlier. We may presume that later *naumachiae* at Rome, of which we have scattered testimony, were staged here.

Only one full-scale *naumachia* event seems to have been held in a natural setting. It took place on the Fucine Lake east of Rome in celebration of the completion of this crater lake's drainage works. The contestants were labelled 'Sicilians' and 'Rhodians', collectively accounting for the largest single spectator event in Roman history. Tacitus relates the event this way:

> Claudius armed triremes, quadriremes, and 19,000 men, and surrounded the perimeter with rafts to prevent random escapes, allowing enough space to display the strength of the oarsmen, the arts of the helmsmen, the momentum of the ships, and all things expected in battle. On the rafts stood maniples and squadrons of the praetorian cohorts behind bulwarks, from which they operated catapults and ballistae.... The battle, though between criminals, was carried out in a manly spirit, and after much bloodshed those remaining were exempted from death (*Annals* 12.56).

Suetonius' account, however, is less straightforward. Before the battle, the combatants hailed the emperor, crying, 'Those who are about to die salute you!' To this, Claudius responded ambiguously: 'Or not.'

> After these words, which were taken for clemency, nobody wanted to fight. He [Claudius] debated whether he should destroy them all by fire or sword; finally, leaping from his seat and running along the lakeshore with his contemptible waddle, he compelled them to fight, now with threats, now with encouragement (*Claudius* 21.6).

Dio Cassius' epitome also emphasizes the defiance of the combatants:

> When they saw ... that they would have to fight as they had been told, they resorted to *diekploi*
> and *aploi* ('breaking through' and 'not sailing'), wounding one another as little as possible,
> until they were forced to kill (61.33.4).

To add insult to injury, the culmination of the spectacle, the draining of the lake, was an utter
failure, forcing a second event to be held later. This is an instructive episode in Roman imperial history, not least because it exposes the fragility of the emperor's public persona when
confronting the prospect of humiliation on an epic scale.

PREPARING NAUMACHIAE

Most kinds of spectacle entertainment operated as a business or a trade within a perpetual economy of procurement, training, scheduling, transport, staging, and so forth.
Naumachiae, by contrast, were almost by definition one-off extravaganzas beyond the means
of mere magistrates. Extreme rarity fostered extreme expectations: novelty and scale were
not enough. Some degree of verisimilitude was also essential, and therein lies a difficulty.
How could these most complicated of productions avoid the infamy of disastrous ineptitude
when most of their principals were untrained and unwilling participants? Poor execution or
technical failures threatened an embarrassment far worse than collateral civilian damage: a
colossal entertainment that failed, colossally, to entertain.

The question remains, then, how and where convicts and prisoners of war could have
Since these battles granted survival to the fittest, nobody doubts that the incentive
for vigorous combat was present. But naval engagement was a team event, a game of skill
and coordination requiring precise manoeuvres among rowers (oars), seamen (sails and
steering), and marines (weaponry) (Casson 1971: 120–123, 278–280). The participants at the
Fucine Lake cannot have been entirely green. Their initial forays, described as *diekploos* and
aploos, were technical manoeuvres in themselves; but as Tacitus makes explicit, they were
expected to exhibit skill in engaging, not evading, the enemy. Training must have taken place
in advance of all major *naumachiae*, along with consultation in strategy and tactics. In the
spectators' interests, combatants were surely denied access to heavy artillery, though it was
common to outfit real navies with it (witness the superior firepower on the guards' rafts at
the Fucine Lake); even javelins may have been forbidden. Thus boarding and hand-to-hand
fighting played a larger role.

The question remains, then, how and where convicts and prisoners of war could have
trained for these once-in-a-generation events. The *naumachia* venue itself is one possibility.
But the logistics of controlling thousands of captives in the city were daunting. One source
may obliquely suggest a plausible alternative. In a passage of the *Mosella* of Ausonius, a late-
antique poem of praise to the eponymous river, a playful skirmish of boatmen on the river
prompts the poet to reflect on three earlier enactments of naval battles:

> Liber peers down at such games on the Cumaean swell when he walks along the cultivated
> ridges of sumptuous Gaurus and the vineyards of steaming Vesuvius, and when Venus, glad
> at Augustus' Actian triumph, orders lascivious Cupids to enact the kind of savage battles the
> fleets of the Nile and Latian triremes fought beneath the citadels of Apollonian Leucas; or

when Euboean skiffs re-enact the dangers of Mylae in the war with Pompey across resounding Avernus; or when the sky-blue sea under a verdant sheen reflects the harmless collisions of prows and the jesting battles of a *naumachia* such as was seen at Sicilian Pelorus (*Mosella* 208–219).

This enigmatic passage is sometimes thought to refer to an otherwise unattested event that Augustus held at Cumae (hence nearby Mt Gaurus) to celebrate his battle at 'Leucas', i.e. Actium (Berlan-Bajard 2006: 383). More probably, the enactments described were entertainments attached to the Sebasta—the quadrennial, Greek-style games founded in 2 CE at Naples to honour Augustus. (Naples lies between Gaurus and Vesuvius, both mentioned in close proximity here.) These skirmishes were of a playful, non-violent sort, involving 'Cupids' and 'skiffs' borrowed from the staffage of mythological tableaux in Roman art. Lake Avernus, however, is a particularly telling venue for a re-enactment of the victories against Sextus Pompey at Mylae and Naulochus ('Sicilian Pelorus'). Serving as the inner basin of Agrippa's provisional harbour built in 38–37 BCE, this lake had likely been a training venue for the very navy that would soon defeat Sextus (Dio Cassius 48.49–51). By the time of the founding of the Sebasta games, the Roman naval fleet had moved down to its new harbour at nearby Misenum, leaving the old harbour installations available for training sessions. The teams of desperadoes destined for Augustus' *naumachia* at Rome, held just three years before the founding of these games, may have taken advantage of the enclosed, militarized environment of Lake Avernus to develop the skills necessary to present a competent and plausible technique. Not only was there plenty of professional naval expertise immediately available on the Bay of Naples, but also—equally important—shipbuilding facilities that could produce custom craft for any event. These were not the premier galleys used by the navy, but 'fleets that were almost regulation' (Suetonius, *Domitian* 4). The city of Rome had sheds for its small naval fleet, but no shipyards; it was only natural that the logistical reach of every large *naumachia* extended down to the Bay of Naples, home of Italy's most important port facilities. All the battle venues of Rome were in the Tiber's floodplain so that the custom vessels could be floated up the river to their destinations.

Ephebic Aquatic Contests

The playful naval exhibitions on the Bay of Naples reported by Ausonius certainly owed a debt to Rome-centred blood spectacle. They may also have emerged in part from a much older tradition of ephebic contests at Athenian games, called in the fourth century BCE the 'competitions of boats' (*IG* 2² 2311). Staged as re-enactments of the Battle of Salamis of 480 BCE, these were elaborate races or manoeuvring contests that blended Attic youths' physical training with a ritual of collective memory (Viscardi 2013). By the Flavian period the contests had taken on a more western flavour, acquiring the name *naumachiai*. Now teams of ephebes in small boats competed in bloodless jousts that probably received inspiration from the mortal combats of Rome (Van Effenterre 1955; Oliver 1971; Berlan-Bajard 2006: 52–55, 375–377). Echoes of these kinds of youthful contests crop up occasionally in Roman literature, as when Horace evokes a mock re-enactment of the Battle of Actium on the pond of a villa, its contestants a pair of youths with teams of slaves manning small boats (*Letters*, 1.18.61–64).

Berlan-Bajard traces a particular taste for such affairs in late-antique Gaul, best exemplified by the tussle observed by Ausonius on the Moselle (Berlan-Bajard 2006: 374–383).

It goes unremarked, however, that ancient Naples had both strong ties to Athens and a robust tradition of training ephebes that seems to have gained new life with the establishment of the Sebasta games. Long after other Greek cities in Italy had shed the tradition, Naples maintained it (Strabo 5.4.7). Indeed, Capri, a longtime Neapolitan possession, was hosting ephebic training just days before the Sebasta were to begin in 14 CE (Suetonius, *Augustus* 98.3), and almost certainly in connection with the games. Ausonius, then, may well have been faithfully recording Sebasta exhibitions or contests held at Lake Avernus and other suitable natural venues nearby. We may conjecture that ephebes themselves, costumed in the guise of Cupids, undertook these harmless burlesques of famous naval battles as entertainments for the gathered crowds. Such lightness of heart, masking seriousness of ideological purpose, was perfectly attuned to Augustus' own wishes when he visited the bay to attend the games in August of 14 CE (Suetonius, *Augustus* 98).

HYDROMIMES

A more widespread form of water spectacle than naval combat, and easier to manage, was a kind of mythologically themed costume pageantry staged in smaller venues such as theatres and amphitheatres. In terms of production values it was perhaps not so different from the popular aquacades of 1930s America, but with fewer concerns about nudity. Lacking a convenient ancient descriptor, scholars have coined the term hydromime for this genre on the basis of its evident association with the art of mime, particularly the Roman variant of danced mime (D'Ippolito 1962; Berlan-Bajard 2006: 99–148). Hydromime may have featured short, gestural sketches or revues on 'watery' mythological themes and musical intervals with synchronized swimming (Coleman 1993). Its capacity to titillate seems to have induced withering condemnation from John Chrysostom in fourth-century Antioch (*Homilies on Matthew* 7.5).

John's passage has also been read as pure allegory with no grounding in theatrical practice (Retzleff 2003). Yet Antioch shows more evidence of enthusiasm for hydromime than any other city. The emperor Hadrian is said to have introduced water to a 'theatre of the sources' and a 'small theatre' at the suburb of Daphne, which enjoyed voluminous springs (Malalas 11.363–364). The theatre excavated there has a hydraulic feature in its orchestra (Wilber 1938; Traversari 1960: 91–103; Berlan-Bajard 2006: 120–122, 225, 458–466). The topographical border of a famous mosaic from Daphne represents two structures seen from a bird's-eye view watered by springs labelled 'Kastalia' and 'The Pallas' (Fig. 21.3; Çimok 2000: 274; Brands 2016). The Pallas flows into a rectangular structure containing a nude swimmer, waist-high in water. Beside it, under the Kastalia, stands an inundated theatre, within which appears a small boat. Antioch supposedly even hosted a miracle in a water-theatre: condemned to die *ad bestias* for her faith, St Thecla was said to have been plunged naked into a large basin full of vicious seals at the theatre. A burst of radiance killed the seals and shielded her nakedness from the crowd (*Acts of Paul and Thecla* 34).

Though they are not well attested in literary sources, hydromimes were probably as varied as they were widespread in the Roman world. Recent scholarship has retreated

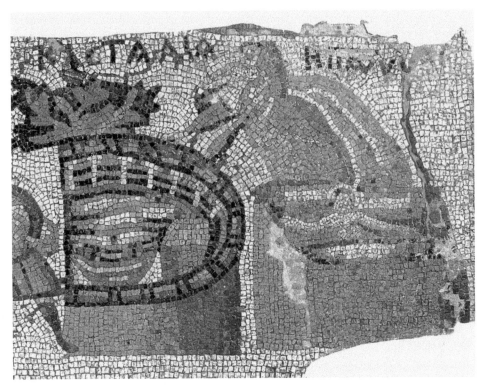

FIGURE 21.3. Detail of the Megalopsychia Mosaic from the Yakto Complex at Daphne depicting a hydromime venue and an allegory of the source spring. Antakya Archaeological Museum. Source: Çimok 2000, 274. Photo courtesy of A Turizm Yayınları.

from Traversari's hypothesis that they were derived from Syrian ritual bathing attached to the *maiouma*, a mysterious water festival of Semitic origin that achieved fairly wide popularity (Traversari 1960: 91–103; Belayche 2004; Berlan-Bajard 2006: 225–228). They may instead have originated as pure spectacle in Campania in the first century BCE, spreading later to theatres around the Roman world. A handful of amphitheatres—Verona and Mérida, for instance—acquired basins for this purpose too (Berlan-Bajard 2006: 217–273, 297–303, 444–553). Recent investigations have confirmed that the Colosseum at Rome was equipped to host aquatic spectacles in its central arena before the floor was permanently raised. Cascading from thirty-two adapted drainage shafts around the arena's edge, the water could rise to a metre in 22 minutes (Beste 2019). Water spectacles seem to have been hosted here at least twice in the structure's early life (Rea et al. 2000; Garello 2004: 118–120; Cariou 2009: 335–351; Dodge 2014: 646). At its inauguration in 80 CE, the flooded arena served as a venue for two events: a water show involving horses, oxen, and other terrestrial animals 'trained to do everything they do on land'; and a miniature *naumachia* pitting 'Corcyreans' against 'Corinthians' (Dio Cassius 66.25.2–3). One novelty of this event was the speed at which the conversion took place, allowing traditional arena spectacles to alternate with these marine events. At some point, conceivably at the very same games but probably some years later, Martial witnessed a water-ballet in which swimming 'Nereids' formed patterns in the water representing a trident, an anchor, and a ship with moving oars. We do not know where it took place, but the Colosseum's seating provided the best angle for this kind of spectacle (*Spectacles* 30 (26); Coleman 1993: 63–64; 2006: 212–214). Aquatic spectacle in theatres seems to have reached its peak of popularity in late antiquity, at least in abundantly watered cities like Antioch. In 399 CE, Claudian penned a couplet remarking on a similarly theatrical phenomenon at consular games in Milan: 'frolicsome boats contest on the sudden flood; a pond appears, its songful waters frothing from the oarsmen' (*On the Consulship of Mallius Theodorus* 331–332).

The Bay of Naples, famous for its culture of entertainment, preserves numerous venues that seem to have incorporated hydromime (Maiuri 1951: 362–364; Frézouls 1959: 202–208; Berlan-Bajard 2006: 228–231, 297–303, 444–457). The theatre at Pompeii had no fewer than seven water basins from various phases countersunk into its orchestra, the earliest probably dating to the Augustan period. At Baiae a circular tank was sunk into the floor of a miniature theatre (Fig. 21.4), and the entire orchestra of a small theatre at nearby Bacoli, which acquired an attached cistern, may have been fitted out as a basin (Maiuri 1955: 271; Iodice and Raimondi 1996). Even some of the coastal villa fishponds in the region featured theatrically inspired spaces from which the exotic sea creatures cultivated within them could be viewed. Just off the southern headland of the harbour of Baiae, a semicircular portico served as a theatre-like vantage point from which to observe the great aquarium within its orbit (Di Fraia 1993: 42).

FIGURE 21.4. Miniature theatre at Baiae with a basin embedded in the orchestra. Photo: R. Taylor.

FIGURE 21.5. Aerial view of the theatre at the imperial villa of Pausilypon. Wikimedia Commons CC BY-SA 2.0. Photo: Salvatore Capuano. Modified.

A particularly striking spectacle venue on the bay is at the coastal imperial villa of Pausilypon. Its hillside theatre had no permanent stage; instead, the spectator's viewshed was split axially by a long, narrow pool just wide and deep enough to accommodate a linear form of hydromime (Fig. 21.5; Varriale 2015: 242–243).

Hadrian would have known this theatre, and its form and function may have partly inspired the famous 'Canopus' complex at his villa near Tivoli (Aurigemma 1984). There, in place of the *cavea*, was a semicircular dining pavilion under a semidome. In front of the diners was a square basin suitable for shallow-water hydromime; beyond that extended a long, narrow pool shaped like a circus, complete with two island 'turning posts' crowned by statues of Skylla (Fig. [sing.] 21.6). Here one could stage the kind of sentimentalized marine tableaux that were so popular in Roman imperial art. Around this miniature Mediterranean—a veritable travelogue in hyperreality, peopled with marble figures from the Greco-Roman geographic imaginary (Kuttner 2003)—one can imagine boys tricked out as Cupid-charioteers racing skiffs drawn by swimming Tritons, churning and jostling to the dinner guests' delight.

FIGURE 21.6. Dining pavilion area of the 'Canopus' at Hadrian's Villa near Tivoli. Photo: R. Taylor.

CONCLUSION

As places for staged warfare, rough justice, and martial triumphalism, *naumachiae* presented a particular vision of sea power derived from Hellenistic victory propaganda. But the *naumachia* is also an apt metaphor of the Roman empire: an emperor and his great, oblong sea surrounded by throngs of his subjects, all attending to the terrors of his might and the cold wisdom of his justice. Through these rare spectacles the emperor could confirm his role as absolute arbiter of human affairs and master of the seas (Berlan-Bajard 2006: 326–336). The Roman imperial era produced no significant naval conflicts of its own; thus the concept of the sea battle gradually became a cultural relic almost as mythic as the tale of Leander. Its danger and menace could be sentimentalized: witness boatloads of adorable Cupids aping deadly encounters of the past. But the medium itself—water, the imponderable substance that flowed through all the regions of the dead, living, and divine, from underworld to sky— encouraged a certain distance between audience and performers, whatever they might be doing. As the embodiment of the boundary between the self and the other, it was the perfect element of Roman spectacle.

REFERENCES

Aurigemma, S. 1984. *Villa Adriana*, 2nd edn. Rome.

Belayche, N. 2004. 'Une panégyrie antiochéenne: le *maiouma.*' In *Antioche de Syrie: histoire, images et traces de la ville antique. Colloque Lyon 2001.* 401–415. B. Cabouret, P.-L. Gatier, and C. Saliou, eds. Lyon.

Berlan-Bajard, A. 2006. *Les spectacles aquatiques romains.* Rome.

Beste, H.-J. 2019. 'Rom, Italien. Neue Argumente zu einer Naumachie im Colosseum. Die Arbeiten der Jahre 2017 und 2018.' *e-Forschungsberiche des DAI* 1: 146–150.

Brands, G. 2016. 'Kastalia und Pallas: Zum Megalopsychia-Mosaik aus Daphne.' *Istanbuler Mitteilungen* 66: 257–291.

Buzzetti, C. 1968. 'Nota sulla topografia dell'Ager Vaticanus.' *Quaderni dell'Istituto di Topografia Antica della Università di Roma* 5: 105–111.

Cariou, G. 2009. *La naumachie: morituri te salutant.* Paris.

Casson, L. 1971. *Ships and Seamanship in the Ancient World.* Baltimore.

Çimok, F. 2000. *Antioch Mosaics: A Corpus.* Istanbul.

Coarelli, F. 1997. *Il Campo Marzio dalle origini alla fine della Repubblica.* Rome.

Coleman, K. M. 1990. 'Fatal Charades: Roman Executions Staged as Mythological Enactments.' *JRS* 80: 44–73.

Coleman, K. M. 1993. 'Launching into History: Aquatic Displays in the Early Empire.' *JRS* 83: 48–74.

Coleman, K. M. 2006. *M. Valerii Martialis Liber spectaculorum.* Oxford.

Di Fraia, G. 1993. 'Baia sommersa. Nuove evidenze topografiche e monumentali.' *Archeologia subacquea* 1: 21–48.

D'Ippolito, G. 1962. 'Draconzio, Nonno e gli idromimi.' *A&R* 7: 1–14.

Dodge, H. 2014. 'Venues for Spectacle and Sport (other than Amphitheaters) in the Roman World.' In *A Companion to Sport and Spectacle in Greek and Roman Antiquity.* 635–653. P. Christesen and D. P. Kyle, eds. Malden, MA.

Frézouls, E. 1959. 'Recherches sur les théâtres de l'Orient syrien.' *Syria* 36: 202–227.

Garello, F. 2004. 'Sport or Showbiz? The *Naumachiae* in the Flavian Amphitheatre.' In *Games and Festivals in Classical Antiquity: Proceedings of the Conference Held in Edinburgh 10–12 July 2000.* 115–124. S. Bell and G. Davies, eds. Oxford.

Iodice, S. V. and M. Raimondi. 1996 (2001). 'Il "sepolcro di Agrippina" a Bacoli: architettura e decorazioni.' *Bollettino di Archeologia* 37–38: 1–12.

Jacobelli, L. and F. Avilia. 1989. 'Le naumachie nelle pitture pompeiane.' *RSP* 3: 130–154.

Kuttner, A. 2003. 'Delight and Danger in the Roman Water Garden: Sperlonga and Tivoli.' In *Landscape Design and the Experience of Motion.* 103–156. M. Conan, ed. Washington, DC.

Maiuri, A. 1951. 'Terme di Baia. Scavi, restauri e lavori di sistemazione.' *BA* 36: 359–364.

Maiuri, A. 1955. 'Il teatro-ninfeo detto "sepolcro di Agrippina" a Bacoli.' In *Anthemon. Scritti di archeologia e di antichità classiche in onore di C. Anti.* 263–271. Florence.

Meshorer, Y. 1966. 'Coins of the City of Gadara Struck in Commemoration of a Local Naumachia.' *Bulletin of the Maritime Museum of Haifa* 1: 28–31.

Oliver, J. H. 1971. 'Athenian Lists of Ephebic Teams.' *AEph* 110: 66–74.

Rea, R., Beste, H. K., Campagna, P., and del Vecchio, F. 2000. 'Sotterranei del Colosseo. Ricerca preliminare al progetto di ricostruzione del piano dell'arena.' *MDAI(R)* 107: 311–339.

Retzleff, A. G. 2003. 'John Chrysostom's Sex Aquarium: Aquatic Metaphors for Theater in Homily 7 on Matthew.' *JECS* 11: 195–207.

Taylor, R. 1997. 'Torrent or Trickle? The Aqua Alsietina, the Naumachia Augusti, and the Transtiberim.' *AJA* 101: 465–492.

Taylor, R. 2000. *Public Needs and Private Pleasures: Water Distribution, the Tiber River, and the Urban Development of Ancient Rome.* Rome.

Traversari, G. 1960. *Gli spettacoli in acqua nel teatro tardo-antico*. Rome.

Van Effenterre, H. 1955. 'Cupules et naumachies.' *BCH* 79: 541–548.

Varriale, I. 2015. 'Pausilypon tra *otium* e potere imperiale.' *MDAI(R)* 121: 227–268.

Viscardi, G. P. 2013. '*In limine*. Religious Speech, Sea Power, and Institutional Change: Athenian Identity Foundation and Cultural Memory in the Ephebic *Naumachia* at Piraeus.' *SMSR* 79: 239–276.

Wilber, D. N. 1938. 'The Theater of Daphne: The Excavations (1933–1936).' In *Antioch-on-the-Orontes*, vol. 2: *The Excavations, 1933–1936*. 57–94. R. Stillwell, ed. Princeton.

PART IV

TEXTS, CONTEXTS, CONTESTS

CHAPTER 22

ATHLETIC CONTESTS
IN CONTEXTS OF EPIC
AND OTHER RELATED
ARCHAIC TEXTS

GREGORY NAGY

DEFINITIONS

THE term 'archaic' in the title refers to a period in the history of Greek-speaking people that extends from the eighth century to the second half of the fifth century BCE, to be followed by the so-called Classical period. The term 'epic' here refers to the primary representatives of Archaic poetry, the Homeric *Iliad* and *Odyssey*, together with the Homeric *Hymns*. The 'other related Archaic texts' include the poetry attributed to Hesiod, whom the ancients in the Classical period understood to be a contemporary of Homer, and the songmaking of the late Archaic period as represented especially by Pindar and Bacchylides. In general, it can be said that the verbal arts of poetry and songmaking in the Archaic period, grounded as they were in oral traditions, did not depend on the technology of writing for the actual composing and performing of the texts that have come down to us: writing was indispensable only for the recording of texts. The same kind of formulation applies to the visual arts of this period. In the case of black figure vase paintings, for example, the pictures that we see are not illustrations derived from set texts. Rather, they are visualizations grounded in oral traditions, just like the visualizations achieved in the verbal arts as recorded in the texts that have survived. Finally, in the case of recorded texts surviving from the Archaic period, they include not only pieces of poetry and songmaking but also inscriptions that record various athletic contests.

GREEK WORDS REFERRING TO ATHLETICS

In the Archaic period, athletic contests were a matter of *religion*, which I analyse here in anthropological terms as *a dynamic interaction of myth and ritual*; to that extent, an understanding of athletics as 'sport' in the modern sense of that word is historically inaccurate

(Nagy 1990: 118). A more accurate way of understanding athletic contests in their Archaic Greek historical contexts is to keep in mind the meanings of the ancient Greek words *āthlos* (epic *aethlos*) 'ordeal, contest', *āthlon* (epic *aethlon*) 'prize won in the course of participating in an *āthlos*', and *āthlētēs* 'athlete, one who participates in an *āthlos*'. To restate the concept of athletics in ancient Greek terms: an *āthlos* was the ritual 'ordeal' or 'contest' of an athlete engaging in athletic contests that were taking place in the historical present, but it was also the mythological 'ordeal' or 'contest' of a hero engaging in life-and-death contests that took place once upon a time in the heroic past; moreover, the ritual 'ordeals' or 'contests' of the historical present were viewed as *re-enactments* of the mythical 'ordeals' or 'contests' of the heroic past (Nagy 1990: 137). That is to say, the myths about the life-and-death 'ordeals' of heroes functioned as *aetiologies* for the rituals of athletic competition. When I say *aetiology* here, I mean *a myth that motivates an institutional reality, especially a ritual* (Nagy 1999: 279).

Besides *āthlos* and its derivatives, another ancient Greek word that proves to be essential for understanding the nature of athletic contests in Archaic contexts is *agōn*, derived from the root *ag-* of the verb *agō* as it is used in the compound formation *sun-agō*, which means 'bring together, assemble, gather' (Nagy 2013 8b§4). Basically, an *agōn* is a 'bringing together' of people; and the occasion of such a 'bringing together' is a 'competition'. This meaning, 'competition', is still evident in the English borrowing of a compound formation involving the word *agōn*, that is, *antagonism*. We can see a comparable idea embedded in the meaning of the Latin word that gives us the English borrowing *competition*: basically, the meaning of Latin *com-petere* is 'to come together', and to *come together* is to *compete* (Nagy 1990: 136). In the case of the Greek word *agōn*, the activity of *competition* to which it refers was understood to be a ritual ordeal, just as the Greek word *āthlos* meant 'ordeal' as well as 'contest', that is, *competition*. The concept of *ordeal* as embedded in the Greek word *agōn* is still evident in the English borrowing *agony*.

These words *āthlos* and *agōn* refer to the experience of a ritual ordeal not only in athletics but also in warfare (Nagy 2013 8b§5). For example, the expression *arēios agōn*, 'the *agōn* of Ares', as used by Herodotus (9.33.3) refers to the ritual experience of combat in war. Similarly, in the case of *āthlos*, epic *aethlos*, this word refers to the experience of warriors (Hdt. 1.67.1) as well as athletes (Hdt. 5.22.2). In epic, we find *aethlos* applying to the martial efforts, all considered together, of Achaeans and Trojans alike in the Trojan War (*Il.* 3.126), or, considered separately, to the efforts of the Achaeans in general (*Od.* 3.262) or of Odysseus in particular (4.170).

The Mentality of Re-enacting in Athletics the Experiences of Heroes in War

As we have just seen by observing the uses of the words *āthlos* and *agōn*, the ritual ordeals of humans fighting in war and the mythical ordeals of heroes fighting in war were not distinguished from each other. In our own terms of thinking, by contrast, when someone undergoes the real experience of war in the historical context of his or her own life and times, this experience is seen as distinct from the mythical experiences of heroes who fought in wars in mythical times. But the thinking is different in terms of ritual and myth, reflecting the mentality of the ancient Greeks in their own historical context: from their standpoint, a human who fights in war is undergoing a ritual ordeal that *re-enacts* the mythical ordeals of heroes. This way, the distinction between that human's ritual ordeal and the heroes' mythical ordeals is neutralized. And such a mentality of not distinguishing between human experience and heroic experience in the context of ritual and myth applies not only to the ordeals of war but also to the ordeals of athletics (Nagy 2013 8b§7).

It can be said in general that different aspects of athletics re-enact different aspects of warfare as experienced by heroes. Besides such obvious examples as the throwing of spears or javelins, however, there are other examples where it is not at all obvious how a given kind of athletic event is related to a given kind of event in warfare, even if these two kinds of events are defined by the same instrument of war. One such example is the athletic event of chariot-racing. The question here is this: how exactly is chariot-racing as an athletic event related to chariot-fighting as an event in warfare? The answer here is not obvious until we examine at a later point two different kinds of chariot-racing as attested at two different athletic festivals.

For now, however, it is enough to keep in mind a basic fact that we have seen by observing the uses of words like *āthlos* and *agōn*: just as the ritual ordeal of a human who fights in a real war and the mythical ordeals of heroes fighting in mythical wars are not distinguished from each other in the thinking we see reflected in the ancient Greek texts, so also the ritual ordeal of a human who competes in a real athletic contest is not distinguished from the corresponding mythical ordeals of heroes.

The Mentality of Re-enacting in Athletics the Experiences of Heroes in Contexts other than War

In terms of the argument so far, someone who competes in an athletic competition is undergoing a ritual ordeal that *re-enacts* the mythical ordeals of heroes. But the mythical ordeals of heroes may include any life-and-death experience, not only the experience of combat in war (Nagy 1990: 138–139). For example, a conventional way to refer to one of the labours of Herakles is to use the word *aethlos*: this word refers to the hero's life-and-death struggle with the Nemean Lion (Pind. *I.* 6.48; Bacchyl. *Ep.* 9.8). This same word *aethlos* is in fact a generic designation of all the labours of Herakles, as we see in epic usage (*Il.* 8.363; also *Il.* 19.133, *Od.* 11.622 and 624).

So the ritual ordeal of an athlete competing with other athletes in an athletic event re-enacts not only the ritual ordeal of a hero fighting to the death with other heroes in war: more than that, the ritual ordeals of athletes can re-enact any and all life-and-death experiences of heroes, not only their experiences in war.

The Mentality of Athletics as a Compensation for Death

The ritual ordeal of an athlete is not only a re-enactment: it is also a compensation for one single fact that is larger than life itself. And that fact is the hero's mortality. The hero, though he is larger than life, is subject to death. To make up for that prototypical death of the hero, which is understood to be larger than life just as the hero is larger than life, athletes must die ritually to their old selves. Unlike the prototypical death of the hero in myth, however, which can happen only once, the figurative death of the athlete in ritual is recurrent, taking place year after year at the right season, in the context of seasonally recurring festivals. And, since the prototypical ordeal of the hero is understood to be larger than life, the corresponding ordeals of athletes can fully compensate for heroic death only if the seasonal recurrence of these ordeals lasts for a notional eternity.

There is a clear example in the *Homeric Hymn to Demeter*, where we see a myth about the establishment of an athletic ritual in compensation for the ordeal of a hero's death. The queen of Eleusis, mother of the infant hero Demophon, had inadvertently ruined the plan of the goddess Demeter to make Demophon exempt from death, and the goddess angrily announces that the infant will now be subject to death, like all other mortals. But there will be a compensation for the ordeal of this hero's death, says the goddess to the mortal mother of Demophon:

> I [= Demeter] swear by the Styx, the witness of oaths that gods make, as I say this: immortal and ageless for all days would I have made your dear [*philos*] little boy, and I would have given him honour [*tīmē*] that is unwilting [*a-phthi-tos*]. But now there is no way for him to avoid death and doom. Still, he will have an honour [*tīmē*] that is unwilting [*a-phthi-tos*], for all time, because he had once sat on my knees and slept in my arms. At the right season [*hōra*], every year, the sons of the Eleusinians will have a war, a terrible battle among each other. They will do so for all days to come. (*HH* 13.259–267)

The death of the infant hero will be compensated by seasonally recurring athletic re-enactment, as expressed by the word *tīmē*, 'honour' (l. 263), which refers here to the honour conferred upon cult heroes in the rituals of hero cult. In this case, the rituals take the form of athletic competitions that overtly simulate warfare. And these rituals will have to recur seasonally, year after year, for a notional eternity. That is why the *tīmē* that the prototypical hero receives in compensation for his death is described as *a-phthi-tos*, 'unwilting', lasting forever.

We see in this passage a reference to a mock battle, an athletic event known as the *Ballētus*, which was evidently the ritual kernel of a whole complex of events known as the Eleusinian Games (Nilsson 1906: 414 n. 4; Nagy 1990: 121 n. 26; Pache 2004: 76–77; Nagy 2013 8b§19). Here is how the athletic event is defined in the Alexandrian lexicographical tradition named after Hesychius:

Βαλλητύς· ἑορτὴ Ἀθήνησιν, ἐπὶ Δημοφῶντι τῷ Κελεοῦ ἀγομένη ('*Ballētus* is a festival in Athens, celebrated in honour of Demophon son of Keleos'). For the moment, I translate the preposition *epi* (ἐπὶ) here as 'in honour of'. As we will see later, however, a more accurate translation is 'in compensation for [the death of]'.

This athletic event, the *Ballētus*, as featured in the Eleusinian Games, was understood to be a form of eternal compensation for the prototypical death of the cult hero Demophon, as we can see from the reference to this event as I quoted it from the *Homeric Hymn to Demeter*. And there are historical parallels, including the Nemean and the Isthmian games, which were seasonally recurring festivals featuring athletic competitions that were intended as an eternal compensation for the prototypical deaths of two other infant heroes, Arkhemoros and Melikertes respectively (Pache 2004: 95–180). I will have more to say presently about those two heroes.

RITUAL ORIGINS OF ATHLETICS

Here I invoke, as I have invoked in my earlier research on the ritual origins of Greek athletics (Nagy 1990: 118; Nagy 2013 8a§2), the relevant evidence assembled by Walter Burkert in his handbook on Greek religion, showing that the traditions of ancient Greek athletics evolved out of practices that originated from 1) rituals of initiation into adulthood and 2) rituals of compensation for death (Burkert 1985: 105–107).

These two kinds of rituals are actually related, since the ritual process of initiation, in and of itself, can be seen as a compensation for death. From an anthropological point of view, a common characteristic of initiation rituals is the figuring of death as a prerequisite for a rebirth from one given age class to another, as in the case of initiations from pre-adult into adult status; in terms of the mentality underlying such rituals of initiation, you must die to your old self in order to be reborn to your new self (Nagy 1990: 118–119, 121–122, with examples and references; Nagy 2013 8a§3).

Here is a salient example: in the case of athletic competitions at the festival of the Lykaia in Arcadia, these competitions are organically connected with rituals that re-enact the separations of pre-adult and adult age classes, and these rituals are in turn organically connected with a myth that tells about the death and regeneration of an infant hero named Arkas (Nagy 1990:126, following Burkert 1983: 86–87; Nagy 2013 8a§4). By contrast, in the case of athletic competitions held at the festival that we know as the Olympics, the Olympia, the existing patterns of separation between pre-adult and adult age classes are no longer overtly ritualized, though the myth that tells about the death and regeneration of the hero Pelops as an infant is still organically connected with an actual athletic competition. In this case, the ritual competition is a single-lap foot-race known as the *stadion*, which is motivated by an aetiological myth about the death of Pelops (Burkert 1983: 100; Nagy 1990: 125). In terms of myth and ritual, the single-lap and double-lap foot-races known respectively as the *stadion* and the *diaulos* at the Olympic Games need to be viewed together as an organic unity (Philostr. *Gym.* 5 and 6 respectively, as analysed by Nagy 1990: 123–127). The myth about the death and regeneration of Pelops is artfully retold in Pindar's *Olympian* 1 as an alternative narrative within an overall narrative about the origins of the Olympic Games (Nagy 1990: 121–135; Pache 2004: 84–94; Nagy 2013 8a§5).

By applying a comparative perspective, then, we have seen the initiatory aspects of athletics at work in the myth about the death and regeneration of the infant hero Pelops. In this case, the point of comparison was a corresponding myth about the death and regeneration of the infant hero Arkas, which, as we have seen, serves as an aetiology for the festival of the Lykaia. Such myths can be understood in terms of initiation from boyhood into manhood, for the purpose of preparing men for warfare. Such a ritualized purpose is evident also in such institutions as the seasonally recurring mock battle known as the *Ballētus*, which we have considered in the context of the Eleusinian Games. More famous examples include the mock battle of Spartan boys in a sacralized space known as the *Platanistās*, 'Grove of the Plane Trees' (Paus. 3.11.2, 3.14.8–9; at 3.20.8, we read that the boys sacrificed to the hero Achilles before they started their mock battle). On the basis of such rituals, we may infer that the institutionalized practices of athletics and warfare were originally viewed as parts of one single ritual continuum (Nagy 2013 8a§6).

Such an inference, I must note in passing, is not an attempt to essentialize warfare. Given the exponentially increasing horrors of war in modern times, most observers today (including myself) would be repelled by any such attempt. Still, there is no denying that warfare was a fact of life in pre-modern times—and that it was ritualized in different ways in different societies (Nagy 2013 8a§7).

Besides the narrative about the death and regeneration of the infant hero Pelops, there is also another narrative that serves as another aetiological myth for yet another athletic event at the Olympics. In this case, the narrative is about the victory of Pelops as an adolescent hero in a four-horse chariot-race. In fact, this narrative serves as the aetiological myth for the athletic event of four-horse chariot-racing at the Olympics, as we see from the artful retelling in Pindar's *Olympian* 1 (Nagy 1990: 199; Nagy 2013 8a§8).

From other retellings of this aetiological myth, we learn that the basic motivation for the athletic event of the four-horse chariot-race at the Olympics was the death of the hero Oinomaos while he was competing in a prototypical four-horse chariot-race with Pelops. We learn what the Delphic Oracle is reputed to have said about the consequences of this prototypical death when we read the reportage of the antiquarian Phlegon of Tralles (*FGH* 257 F 1 ll. 8–9): θῆκε δ' ἔπειτα ἔροτιν καὶ ἔπαθλα θανόντι | Οἰνομάῳ ('then he [Pelops] established a festival and contests for prizes [*ep-āthla*] in honour of the dead Oinomaos'). In terms of this extended narrative, not only the chariot-race but the entire festival of the Olympics was founded by Pelops. Moreover, in the words of the Delphic Oracle as reported by Phlegon (ll. 6–7), Pelops was in fact only the second founder of the Olympics: the Oracle says that the first founder was Pisos, the eponymous hero of Pisa, a place closely associated with the Olympics. As for the third founder, it was Herakles, as we read further in the words of the Oracle as quoted by Phlegon (lines 9–11): τρίτατος δ' ἐπὶ τοῖς πάϊς Ἀμφιτρύωνος | Ἡρακλέης ἐτέλεσσ' ἔροτιν καὶ ἀγῶνα ἐπὶ μήτρῳ | Τανταλίδη Πέλοπι φθιμένῳ ('after them [= the first two founders of the Olympics] the third was Herakles son of Amphitryon: he established the festival and the competition [*agōn*] in honour of [*epi*] his maternal relative, the dead Pelops, son of Tantalos' (Nagy 2013 8a§9)).

Here we see the same syntactical construction that we saw in the compressed retelling of the aetiological myth that motivated the foundation of the athletic competition 'in honour of' the infant hero Demophon. I repeat here the wording as we found it in Hesychius: Βαλλητύς· ἑορτὴ Ἀθήνησιν, ἐπὶ Δημοφῶντι τῷ Κελεοῦ ἀγομένη ('*Ballētus* is a festival in Athens, celebrated in honour of [*epi*] Demophon son of Keleos'. Once again, I have translated the preposition *epi* (ἐπὶ) here in combination with the name of Demophon in the dative case as 'in honour of the dead Demophon'). But this translation, as I have noted already, is inadequate, and it would be more accurate to word it this way: 'in compensation for [the death of] Demophon'. After all, as we saw in the *Homeric Hymn to Demeter*, the athletic competition of the *Ballētus* is overtly described as an act of compensation, recurring at the right season into all eternity, and this competition is understood to be an eternal compensation for one single all-important fact: that the hero Demophon must die (Nagy 2013 8a§10).

The necessity of this death, of this primal ordeal of the hero in myth, is what motivates in aetiological terms the corresponding necessity of the seasonally recurring ordeals of participants in the ritual athletic competition of the *Ballētus*. And we have just seen, a corresponding expression in the words of the Delphic Oracle as quoted by Phlegon (ll. 10–11): Ἡρακλέης ἐτέλεσσ' ἔροτιν καὶ ἀγῶνα ἐπὶ μήτρῳ | Τανταλίδη Πέλοπι φθιμένῳ ('Herakles established the festival and the competition [*agōn*] in honour of [*epi*] his maternal relative, the dead Pelops, son of Tantalos'). And again, it would be more accurate to reword the translation: 'in compensation for the death of his maternal relative, Pelops, son of Tantalos'. A parallel translation is needed for the wording attributed to the Delphic Oracle's description of the competitions in honour of Oinomaos as instituted by Pelops. I repeat here the wording as quoted by Phlegon (ll. 8–9): θῆκε δ' ἔπειτα ἔροτιν καὶ ἔπαθλα θανόντι | Οἰνομάῳ ('then he [Pelops] established a festival and contests for prizes [ep-āthla] in honour of the dead Oinomaos'). I now retranslate this way: 'then he [Pelops] established a festival and contests for prizes [-āthla] in compensation for the death of [ep-] Oinomaos'. In this case, the myth makes it clear that the compensation was needed because Pelops himself had caused, wittingly or unwittingly, the death of Oinomaos in the course of their chariot-race with each other (Apollod. *Epit.* 2.7).

This kind of aetiology is typical of athletic contests. A case in point is the *Tlēpolemeia*, a seasonally recurring festival of athletic contests held on the island of Rhodes and named after Tlepolemos, son of Herakles and founder of Rhodes (Nilsson 1906: 462–463). In the words of Pindar, this athletic festival was founded by the hero Tlepolemos as a *lutron*, 'compensation', for a 'pitiful misfortune' (*O.* 7.77 λύτρον συμφορᾶς οἰκτρᾶς). The 'misfortune' or catastrophe to which Pindar's wording refers is the hero's deranged slaying of a maternal relative (7.27–32, with commentary by Nagy 1990: 140; Nagy 2013 8a§13).

It can be said in general that athletic festivals were aetiologically motivated by myths that told of a hero's catastrophic death (Roller 1981a: 107 n. 4; an extensive set of examples is collected by Pfister 1912: 496–497; see also Brelich 1958: 94–95). In the case of the three other most prestigious athletic festivals besides the Olympic Games in the Peloponnesus, that is, in the region recognized by all Hellenes as the cradle of their ancient Hellenic civilization, the relevant foundation myths are (Roller 1981a: 107 n. 5; Nagy 1990: 120; Nagy 2013 8a§13):

- the Pythian Games, founded by the Amphiktyones in compensation for the killing of the Python by Apollo: ἐπὶ τῷ Πύθωνος φόνῳ, ('in compensation for the killing of the Python [by Apollo]'; Aristot. F 637.16);
- the Isthmian Games, founded by the hero Sisyphus in compensation for the death of the infant hero Melikertes, who was also known as Palaimon: τὸν ἀγῶνα ἐπ' αὐτῷ ('the competition [agōn] in compensation for [epi] him'; Paus. 2.1.3);
- the Nemean Games, founded by the heroes known as the Seven against Thebes in compensation for the death, by snakebite, of the infant hero Arkhemoros, who was also known as Opheltes: ἄθλησαν ἐπ' Ἀρχεμόρῳ ('they [= the Seven] endured ordeals [āthloi] in compensation for Arkhemoros'; Bacchyl. 9.12). In poetic terms, the antidote for the prototypical snake-bite is the singing of *ep-aoidai*, 'incantations' (Pind. *N.* 8.49), and such songs (*aoidai* means 'songs') counteract the deadly venom by celebrating athletic victories that are won at the Nemean Games in compensation for the prototypical death (*N.* 49–53).

As we have seen, then, the idea of athletics as a ritual activity that compensates for the death of a hero in myth can be expressed by combining the prefix/preposition/preverb *epi-* ἐπι-) with the dative case referring to that hero. So far, we have seen this usage in the context of athletic competitions that are aetiologically motivated by the death of a hero in myth, as in the case of the Eleusinian Games as well as the Olympic, Pythian, Isthmian, and Nemean Games. But the aetiological motivation of compensating for a death can extend from mythical times to historical times as well. For example, I cite the evidence of dedicatory inscriptions that memorialize various prizes won at athletic competitions held in honour of persons who died in historical times: from a study of eight such inscriptions (collected by Roller 1981b: 2–3), ranging in date from the early seventh to the middle-fifth century BCE, we can see that the texts of seven of these eight inscriptions show a combination of the preposition *epi* with the dative case of the name of the dead person who is being honoured by way of the competitions (Nagy 1990: 120–121). The same combination can also be found in inscriptions on gravestones where the gravestone itself is notionally speaking by way of the letters inscribed on the gravestone, saying that 'I am' here as a compensation for the death of the person whose dead body is marked by 'me' (for example, *IG* VII 605 επι Φαεινιδι ειμι ['I am (here) in compensation for (the death of) Phaeinis']; examples collected by Häusle 1979: 130 n. 330).

Conversely, the aetiological motivation of compensating for a death can extend from historical times to mythical times. That is to say, ritual competition in athletics can be performed not only by athletes in historical times but also by heroes who compete as athletes in mythical times. A case in point is the hero Herakles, who, as we saw, was considered to be a founder of the athletic festival of the Olympics. Here again are the words of the Delphic Oracle as quoted by Phlegon (*FGH* 257 F 1 l. 10–11): Ἡρακλέης ἐτέλεσσ' ἔροτιν καὶ ἀγῶνα ἐπὶ μήτρῳ | Τανταλίδῃ Πέλοπι φθιμένῳ ('Herakles established the festival [of the Olympics] and the competition [*agōn*] in compensation for [*epi*] his maternal relative, the dead Pelops, son of Tantalos'). In terms of this myth, as we see from a retelling by Diodorus of Sicily (4.14.1–2), the hero Herakles not only founded this major athletic festival but also competed in every athletic event on the prototypical occasion of the first Olympics: on that occasion, he won first prize in every Olympic event.

THE HERO'S ENGAGEMENT IN ATHLETICS

As we have seen by examining the relevant interactions of myth and ritual in ancient Greek thinking, athletes who participate in athletic competitions are undergoing a ritual ordeal that re-enacts the mythical ordeals of heroes. This way, the distinction between the ritual ordeals of athletes and the mythical ordeals of heroes is neutralized. And this is why heroes in their heroic past can compete as athletes in their own right, thus showing the way for humans in the historical present who compete as athletes. As athletes, heroes compensate for the deaths of other heroes, just as athletes in historical times compensate for the deaths of heroes. A case in point, as we have just seen, is the aetiological myth about the engagement of the hero Herakles in the athletic competitions at the Olympics, which he organizes in compensation for the death of his maternal relative, the hero Pelops.

In the *Alcestis* of Euripides, we find a most evocative example of heroic engagement in athletics. To compensate for the death of Alcestis, the hero Herakles engages in a wrestling match with Death personified, Thanatos. After he has defeated Thanatos and thus won back the life of Alcestis, Herakles declares his victory over death by cryptically referring to his struggle with Thanatos as an athletic event: ἀθληταῖσιν ἄξιον πόνον ('a worthy exertion for athletes [*āthlētai*]'; Eur. *Alc.* 1027). In the wording of his declaration of victory, Herakles does not reveal that he has struggled with Thanatos but prefers to represent his life-and-death ordeal as a wrestling match that took place in a 'competition' at a 'local' festival, described as an *agōn pan-dēmos* (ἀγῶνα πάνδημον, *Alc.* 1024; commentary by Nagy 1990: 138). In this context, the festive mood that Herakles displays after his victory over death reflects what can best be described as an *epinician* celebration. In what follows, we will consider the meaning of this term *epinician*.

ATHLETICS AND THE EPINICIAN

There was a form of poetry and songmaking that explicitly coordinated the ritualized experiences of athletes with the mythical experiences of heroes. Modern literary historians commonly refer to this form as the *victory ode*. Most surviving examples of the victory ode were composed by the poets Pindar and Bacchylides, who both flourished in the first half of the fifth century BCE, toward the end of the Archaic period. In the words of Pindar himself, victory odes are *epinīkioi aoidai*, or 'epinician songs' (*N.* 4.78 ἐπινικίοισιν ἀοιδαῖς). On the basis of such poetic self-references, literary historians sometimes describe the victory ode simply as the *epinician* or, in Hellenized spelling, the *epinīkion*.

The adjective *epinīkios*, which for the time being has been translated here simply as 'epinician', is derived from a combination of the prefix *epi-* with an adjectival form of the noun *nīkē*, meaning 'victory'. As we have seen, when this same form *epi* is used as a preposition in combination with the dative case of a noun or a pronoun referring to a dead person who is being honoured at an athletic event, it has the specialized sense of 'in compensation for', with reference to the death of that given person. But this specialized use of the preposition *epi* combined with the dative in the sense of 'in compensation for' extends beyond references to a death that has to be compensated. As we will now see, it can be argued that the same sense of 'in compensation for' can refer to a celebration of a victory, and that this celebration notionally compensates for the ordeal that went into the winning of the victory.

There are numerous attestations of the preposition *epi* combined with the dative of *nīkē*, 'victory' (so, ἐπὶ + νίκη), in contexts relating to public celebrations held in compensation for individual victories in athletic events (for example, Paus. 5.21.4, 6.13.11, 6.15.2, 6.20.19, 10.7.8) or for collective victories in war (6.2.8, 10.11.5). Of particular interest is a reference made by Plutarch (*Dem.* 1.1) to an epinician song composed for a public celebration of Alcibiades in compensation for his sponsoring victorious chariot-teams at the Olympics: Ὁ μὲν γράψας τὸ ἐπὶ τῇ νίκῃ τῆς Ὀλυμπίασιν ἱπποδρομίας εἰς Ἀλκιβιάδην ἐγκώμιον, εἴτ᾿ Εὐριπίδης ὡς ὁ πολὺς κρατεῖ λόγος, εἴθ᾿ ἕτερός τις ἦν ('the person who wrote the encomium [*en-kōmion*] for Alcibiades in compensation for [*epi*] his victory [*nīkē*] in the chariot-racing at the Olympics, whether that person was Euripides, which is what most people say, or someone else'; I will have more to say later about the use of the word *en-kōmion*, 'encomium', with reference to the epinician). Also of interest is the ritual shout *epi nīkēi* (ἐπὶ νίκη) as attested in poetry dating back to the Classical period (Aristoph. *Lys.* 1278, *Eccl.* 1182; we may compare also Aesch. *Lib.* 868).

The linguistic evidence of such attestations, we should note, does not require us to interpret the adjective *epi-nīkios* only in the specialized sense of 'compensating for the victory'. We may also interpret *epi-nīkios* in the more general sense of 'marking the occasion of the victory'. Still, this linguistic evidence does show that there was a built-in idea of compensation in the semantics of *epi-nīkios*. So, such attestations of the preposition *epi* combined with the dative of *nīkē*, 'victory', weaken the argument (made by Rodin 2009: 315, disputing Nagy 1990: 142) that the adjective *epi-nīkios* does not express the idea of compensation. And these same attestations strengthen the argument that epinician song serves the function of compensating for victories won by athletes (as we shall see later, Rodin 2009: 315 n. 71 offers a different explanation).

In terms of the underlying meaning of the adjective *epi-nīkios*, 'epinician', I offer this working definition of the expression *epinīkioi aoidai*, 'epinician songs', as used by Pindar (again, N. 4.78 ἐπινικίοισιν ἀοιδαῖς): *an epinician song compensates for the competition of the athlete whose competitive ordeal leads to victory, just as the ordeal of the athlete compensates for the prototypical ordeal of the hero as he struggles to achieve victory over death itself.* This definition is based on an extended analysis of the relevant wording used in the songs of Pindar and Bacchylides in referring to their medium of songmaking in the contexts of their victory odes (Nagy 1990: 140–142). Here I sum up the essentials of that analysis:

> In the end, of course, all heroes must die, just as all mortals must die, and so the prototypical struggle with death is ultimately lost. But this struggle is then taken up anew, year after year, in the seasonally recurring competitions of athletes at festivals. These ritual events of athletic competition, linked as they are with mythical events of heroic regeneration as in the case of the infant hero Pelops, dramatize the ultimate victory of life over death. And a notionally eternal series of such victories in the course of seasonally recurring athletic ordeals can then compensate for the one-time heroic ordeal of a death that is primordial and therefore larger than life. In these terms, then, an epinician song is required as a compensation for each one of these seasonally recurring athletic victories. And, as we can see from the actual wording of epinician songs composed by Pindar and Bacchylides, the effort that it takes to compose and to perform such a song is imagined as a ritualized ordeal in its own right—an ordeal that becomes the last link in a sacred chain of compensation that goes all the way back to the idea of a first ordeal, which is a primordial heroic struggle with death.

Having explained the victory ode or epinician song as a ritualized compensation for the victory of the athlete, I note that there have been other explanations offered. Here is an example (Rodin 2009: 315 n. 71): 'A different explanation for the use of the vocabulary of recompense in the *epinikia* is advanced in Kurke (1991: 108–116): inasmuch as *apoina* [this Greek word refers to a set of compensatory gestures conceptualized as a unitary system] "protects the community from the threat of a destructive past", Pindar's use of this concept serves to "depict the whole community's well-being as contingent on the smooth workings of aristocratic exchange" [Kurke 1991: 108].'

As a genre, epinician song was a complex form, and there is good reason to think that this form had to keep on adapting itself to the historical vicissitudes of the first half of the fifth century, which was the era when poets like Pindar and Bacchylides were composing their songs for public performances in a wide variety of political situations (Kurke 1991: 1, 134). Still, the simple fact remains that the basic form of epinician song was at its core deeply conservative (Currie 2005: 18).

Granted, epinician song cannot be described as the most ancient attested form of Greek poetry. That kind of description applies only to the epic poetry of the Homeric *Iliad* and *Odyssey*, the formation of which can be dated as far back as the eighth century BCE. But the epinician, as a form, is remarkably ancient nonetheless. In fact, the actual form of epinician lyric poetry can be considered to be in some ways more ancient than the corresponding form of epic poetry (Nagy 1990: 416–418, applying the methods of comparative linguistics in analysing the relevant poetic diction and metre). And the wording of epinician song even claims that it is more ancient than epic. In Pindar's *Nemean* 8 (50–52), for example, where the epinician lyric poem celebrates the prototypical athletic feats of the heroes known as the Seven against Thebes, the claim is made that the poetic medium for celebrating these feats was even more ancient than the poetic medium for celebrating the prototypical martial feats of these same heroes. Just as the athletic feats happened earlier than the martial feats in the case of the myths about the Seven against Thebes, so also the epinician poetic medium for celebrating the athletic feats was supposedly more ancient than the epic poetic medium for celebrating the martial feats (as attested in the surviving fragments of the epic *Thebaid*). In the logic of the poetry here, the victory ode of Pindar claims that its epinician lyric poetry was praising heroes even before the events recorded by epic poetry (Nagy 1990: 192–194; 1999: 227–228). Here is the actual wording:

ἦν γε μὰν ἐπικώμιος ὕμνος | δὴ πάλαι καὶ πρὶν γενέσθαι | τὰν Ἀδράστου τάν τε Καδμείων ἔριν.

But the *epi-kōmios humnos* has been in existence since ancient times. It was there even before the war between Adrastos and the Thebans ever happened. (Pind. *N.* 8.50–51)

The adjective *epi-kōmios* here, combined with the noun *humnos*, 'song', refers to epinician singing, that is, to a form of song that is sung and danced in a victory revel or *kōmos*, and such a description is relevant to the fact that Pindar's epinician songs conventionally refer to their own occasion of performance as a *kōmos*, 'victory revel' (Nagy 1990: 142). Accordingly, we may translate *epi-kōmios humnos* here as 'the song marking the occasion of a *kōmos*'.

The prefix *epi-* in the adjective *epi-kōmios* seems at first to be semantically less specialized than the corresponding prefix *epi-* in the adjective *epi-nīkios*. In the case of *epi-nīkios*, as we have seen, *epi-* has the specialized sense of 'compensating for'; in the case of *epi-kōmios*, on the other hand, *epi-* seems at first to have only the more general sense of 'marking the occasion of'. But the general sense of *epi-* is not excluded in the meaning of *epi-nīkios*. As we have already noted, this adjective *epi-nīkios* can be interpreted not only in the specialized sense of 'compensating for the victory' but also in the more general sense of 'marking the occasion of the victory'. Conversely, as we may now also note, the specialized sense of *epi-* is in fact included in the general sense of *epi-kōmios*, which can be interpreted not only in the general sense of 'marking the occasion of a victory revel' but also in the more specialized sense of 'compensating for a victory revel', since the revelling that takes place at a *kōmos* presupposes a victory. By implication, then, every new *kōmos* will compensate for every previous *kōmos*.

In the passage just quoted from Pindar's *Nemean* 8, the epinician song is claiming to be the same thing as a prototypical epinician song that keeps on renewing itself every time it celebrates athletic victories won at the seasonally recurring Nemean Games. As we noted earlier, myth has it that these Nemean Games were begun in the heroic age by the Seven against Thebes in compensation for the death, by snake-bite, of the infant hero Arkhemoros. And, as we also noted earlier when we first considered this same epinician song of Pindar, the antidote for the prototypical snake-bite is imagined metaphorically as the singing of *ep-aoidai*, 'incantations' (*N.* 8.49). In terms of such a metaphor, these 'incantations' are a succession of self-renewing epinician songs (*-aoidai*) that compensate (preverb *ep-*) for that prototypical snakebite, counteracting its venom of death by celebrating athletic victories that are won every two years, into eternity, at the seasonally recurring Nemean Games (*N.* 49-53). By implication, the genre of epinician songmaking is a form that will keep renewing itself forever by eternally compensating for previous forms of itself.

The adjective *epi-kōmios*, 'marking the occasion of a *kōmos*', which refers to the prototypical form of epinician song in Pindar's *Nemean* 8, is related to the adjective *en-kōmios*, to be translated as 'having its occasion in a *kōmos*' or 'taking place in a *kōmos*', which can likewise refer to epinician songmaking. Here is an example we find in another epinician song, Pindar's *Olympian* 2 (47): ἐγκωμίων τε μελέων λυρᾶν τε τυγχανέμεν ('to win [*tunkhanein*] melodies [*melea*] that are *en-kōmia*, sung to the tune of the lyre'). So these *melea,* 'melodies', described by the adjective *en-kōmia*, 'taking place in a *kōmos*', are epinician melodies. In the wording of this kind of songmaking, the primary prize for the athlete to win must be the epinician song itself. A derivative of the adjective *en-kōmios*, 'having its occasion in a *kōmos*', is the noun *en-kōmion,* 'encomium', which as we have already seen can also refer to the epinician (in the case of the song celebrating the chariot-victories of Alcibiades).

Another striking example of the epinician as a prototypical song is a mythical encomium sung to Herakles on the occasion of that hero's athletic victories at a prototypical scene of Olympic celebration—an encomium re-enacted in the poetry of Archilochus (F 324). And this encomiastic re-enactment is recognized as the wording of Archilochus himself in the poetry of Pindar at the beginning of his *Olympian* 9 (τὸ μὲν Ἀρχιλόχου μέλος φωνᾶεν Ὀλυμπίᾳ ['the song of Archilochus, sounding forth at Olympia']).

Of particular interest is the historical fact that Pindar's epinician songs were transmitted in the form of four scrolls canonically arranged to match the four most prestigious festivals celebrated in the Peloponnesus:

- the Olympic Games, operating on a four-year cycle, was celebrated at Olympia in the summer of every fourth year of the calendar as we number it, starting at 776 BCE;
- the Pythian Games, starting at 586 BCE, also operating on a four-year cycle, was celebrated at Delphi in the summer of every second year after the Olympics;
- the Isthmian Games, starting at 582 BCE, operating on a two-year cycle, was celebrated at the Isthmus of Corinth in the spring of each even-numbered year of the calendar as we number it, before the summer festivals of the Olympia and the Pythia;
- the Nemean Games, starting at 573 BCE, operating on a two-year cycle, was celebrated at Nemea on odd-numbered years of the calendar as we number it, one year before and one year after the festival of the Olympia.

The four scrolls of Pindar's epinician songs, the *Olympians*, *Pythians*, *Isthmians*, and *Nemeans*, originally followed the order that is given here, though the ordering of the *Nemeans* and the *Isthmians* was accidentally switched at a later point in the course of their textual transmission (Irigoin 1952: 100).

These four festivals are known as the *Panhellenic Games*. The Panhellenic prestige of these four festivals, headed by the Olympics as notionally started in 776 BCE, was rivalled, however, by the newer Panhellenic prestige of the festival of the Great Panathenaia as notionally started in 566 BCE. This newer festival, operating on a four-year cycle, was celebrated at Athens in the late summer after the earlier summer celebration of the Pythian Games in that same year, which, as we have seen, took place every second year after the Olympics (Bell 1995: 18).

The seasonally recurring celebration of the Great Panathenaia, which lasted several days and required several months of preparation, was evidently designed to rival the four most prestigious older festivals celebrated in the Peloponnesus. And, as in the case of the Olympic and the Pythian, Isthmian, and Nemean games, the Panathenaic Games were likewise ritually motivated by an aetiological myth about the death of a prototypical hero. In this case, as we can see from what we read in Hesychius (s.v. ἐπ᾽ Εὐρυγύῃ ἀγών) with reference to the testimony of Amelesagoras (FGH 330 F 2), the combination of the preposition *epi* with the dative of the name *Euruguēs* indicates that the death of the hero who was called by this name led to the founding of the Panathenaia (Nagy 1990: 121 n. 26).

Here are two indications of the rivalry between the Great Panathenaia and the other four Panhellenic games:

- the parallelism between the athletic competitions (*agōnes*) at the Great Panathenaia and at the Olympics.
- the parallelism between the 'musical' competitions (*agōnes*) at the Great Panathenaia and at the Pythia.

As we will now see, the idea of 'musical' competitions here will be key to understanding the correlation of epic and athletics.

ATHLETICS IN EPIC AND BEYOND

Having considered the epinicians of Pindar, which celebrate mostly the *agōnes*, 'competitions', of athletes at the four Panhellenic games, we noted that the epinician song can refer to itself as an *agōn*, 'competition'. This kind of self-reference, as we will now see, is relevant to competitions in the performance of epic at the fifth of the Panhellenic Games, the Panathenaia. These competitions, as we will also see, are likewise known as *agōnes*. So the question is, how are the athletic competitions related to the epic competitions?

In epic, we find clear examples of athletic events where heroes compete as athletes. In the *Iliad*, there are the Funeral Games for Patroklos (23.257–897), for Amarynkeus (23.629–642) and for Oedipus (23.677–680). In the *Odyssey*, there are the funeral games for Achilles (24.85–92). A most telling feature of the narrative about the funeral games for Achilles is the expression *epi soi* (ἐπί σοι 91) with reference to the prizes to be won in the competitions: once again we see here the preposition *epi* in combination with the dative case referring to the hero who died and whose death is being compensated by way of athletic competitions for prizes. And the setting for the competitions that take place at the funeral games for Achilles is called an *agōn* (86), while the prizes to be won in these competitions are called *aethla* (85, 89, 91).

Examples of such athletic competitions in lyric include the funeral games for Pelias (Stesichorus *PMG* F 178), for Adrastos (Pind. *I.* 4.26), for Protesilaos (*I.* 4.58), and for Tlepolemos (*O.* 7.80).

In vase paintings, most illustrations of athletic competitions among heroes centre on the Funeral Games for Patroklos and the funeral games for Pelias, all dating no earlier than the early sixth century BCE (Roller 1981a: 108–113; Scanlon 2004: 79). In the case of the athletic competitions held in honour of Patroklos, there are two black figure paintings attested: 1) on a fragment of a *dinos* by Sophilos, dating from about 580 BCE (*ABV* 39.16) and 2) on the 'François Krater' by Kleitias and Ergotimos, dating from about 570 BCE (*ABV* 76.1). On the *dinos* we see an inscription that identifies a scene of chariot-racing: ατλα Πατροκλυϲ = āt(h)la Patrokl(o)us ('prizes to be won in the contests of Patroklos'; Roller 1981a: 108–109). In the case of the athletic event for Pelias, the two most important pieces of evidence are depictions on two precious artefacts, both now lost: 1) the chest of Kypselos, dating from before the second quarter of the sixth century BCE, as described by Pausanias (5.17.5–11) and 2) the throne of Apollo at Amyklai, dating from shortly after the middle of the sixth century BCE, again as described (though much more briefly in this case) by Pausanias (3.19.16). In the case of the chest of Kypselos, it also depicts the chariot-race between Oinomaos and Pelops, who is shown riding with Hippodameia on his chariot (Scanlon 2004: 71).

Just as heroes in epic, as also in lyric, can compete as athletes to compensate for the deaths of other heroes who lived in heroic times, humans in historical times can compete as athletes to compensate for the deaths of other humans in their own times—if and when such other humans are deemed worthy of heroic honours. Examples include the athletic festivals established in honour of historical figures like Miltiades (Hdt. 6.38), Brasidas (Thuc. 5.11), and Leonidas (Paus. 3.14.1). And, in such cases, we can see further attestations of a combination of the preposition *epi* with the dative case in expressing the idea that the athletic competition is meant as a compensation for the deaths of such historical figures (Nagy 1990: 121 n. 27). A salient example is the expression ἐπ᾽ αὐτοῖς ... τιθέασιν ἀγῶνα ('they organize a competition [*agōn*] in compensation for [*epi*] them'; again, Paus. 3.14.1), with reference to seasonally recurring competitions held near the cenotaph of Brasidas and the tomb of Leonidas (along with the tomb of another Spartan king, Pausanias).

As for the actual athletic events described in poetic contexts, they closely resemble the athletic events that we see attested in historical contexts. For example, in the Funeral Games for Patroklos (*Il.* 23.257–897), the setting for which is described overall as an *agōn*, 'competition' (258) for *aethla*, 'prizes' (259), the premier event is two-horse chariot-racing (262–652), followed by boxing (653–699), wrestling (700–739), a foot-race (740–797), mock combat in full battle gear (798–825), tossing a lump of iron (826–849), archery (850–883), and the casting of spears (884–897).

A notably archaizing detail in this narrative about the Funeral Games for Patroklos is the reference to the tossing of a lump of iron instead of a discus (Scanlon 2004: 63). Another archaizing detail is the fact that the racing chariots in the narrative about the chariot-race at these funeral games are drawn by two horses instead of four (Scanlon 2004: 67). A two-horse chariot team, known by its Latin name as the *biga*, was more suitable for warfare than a four-horse chariot team, known as the *quadriga*, and there is evidence for the active use of the *biga* in the Mycenaean era (again, Scanlon 2004: 67). As for the *quadriga*, visual representations of its use for racing are poorly attested before the seventh century BCE but there are clear traces in the seventh; by the early sixth century the visual evidence is amply attested (Scanlon 2004: 67–69). According to Pausanias (5.8.7), the athletic event of racing in the *quadriga* at the festival of the Olympics was introduced already in the twenty-fifth Olympiad, that is, in the year 680 BCE (Scanlon 2004: 67 finds this dating plausible).

In the text of Homeric poetry as we have it, there are two references to a racing chariot drawn by a team of four horses. In one case (*Od.* 13.81), we find the reference in the context of a Homeric simile. In the other case (*Il.* 11.699–702) it has been argued that the narrative is making a veiled reference to the competition in chariot-racing at the Olympics (Scanlon 2004: 63–89). In terms of this argument, the dating of such a reference could be explained as follows:

> There can, of course, be no certainty in determining when the *Iliad* 11 *quadriga* passage was composed, but given the ... evidence on iconography and popularity of themes, we can reasonably conjecture that it was a product of the evolving Iliadic tradition between 680 [BCE], when the *quadriga* first appeared in the Olympic program, and 580-40 [BCE], when epic depictions on vases enjoyed great popularity and four-horse chariots were first widely evident in art. More precisely, ... the passage was likely an invention of the first half of the sixth century, the period when the other Panhellenic games and the Panathenaic games are founded or reorganized. (Scanlon 2004: 79)

(For a similar explanation, see also Frame 2009: 727–6, who argues that the passage we see in *Il.* 11.689–672 derives from a version of the *Iliad* that used to be performed at the festival of the Panathenaia; see especially Frame 2009: 733.)

Now I proceed to consider another relevant example of an epic narration of athletic events: in this case, the competition takes place in the public gathering space of the Phaeacians (*Od.* 8.100–101). Here again, the word *agōn*, 'competition', applies to the overall set of athletic events (259). The first event is the foot-race (120–125), followed by wrestling (126–127), jumping (128), discus-throwing (129), and, finally, boxing (130).

There are also references in epic to forms of athletic competition that are only rarely attested in the historical evidence. A striking example is the Homeric mention of a kind of ballgame (*Il.* 12.421–423) that dramatizes 'the negotiation of competing territorial claims' (Elmer 2008: 420). The fighting between the Achaeans and the Trojans over the possession of the Trojan Plain is implicitly being compared here to this game, the basic rules of which can be summarized as follows:

> The team that acquired possession threw the ball toward their opponents' half of the field, while the opposing team had the task of retrieving the ball ... and of casting it back, in turn, toward the opposite side. The object of the game was to force one's opponents across the base line, thus claiming possession of the entire field. As far as we can tell, the game ended when the field was gained. (Elmer 2008: 414)

What appears at first to be radically different about epic narrations of athletic events, as we see most clearly in the case of the Funeral Games of Patroklos, is that the events themselves seem to happen only once, by contrast with historical attestations of corresponding athletic competitions. Those competitions, as we have already seen, were not one-time events in their historical settings. Rather, they were seasonally recurring events that took place at festivals held year after year, notionally for all eternity. When we take a closer look at epic narrations of athletic competitions, however, we find that first appearances are deceiving. Such competitions as narrated in epic are not really one-time events, since they were narrated again and again at festivals held year after year, notionally for all eternity. And, as we will now see, these recurring epic narrations took place in the form of poetic competitions that were being held at these festivals. Moreover, as we will also see, these festivals were the same festivals at which athletic competitions were being held, and the poetry of the poetic competitions that were being held at these same festivals could even be coordinated with these athletic competitions.

Such a coordination of poetic and athletic competitions can best be understood if we take a second look at the epic narrative about the athletic competitions held in the public gathering space of the Phaeacians (*Od.* 8.100–101), where the word *agōn* applies to the overall set of events (259). As we saw earlier, the athletic events are the foot-race (120–125), followed by wrestling (126–127), jumping (128), discus-throwing (129) and, finally, boxing (130). But the events are not only athletic (Nagy 2010: 91): there is also choral dancing and perhaps singing (370–380), and the setting is described as an *agōn*, 'competition' (380). The same word *agōn* occurs at an earlier point as well, where it refers to the setting for the singing of the court poet Demodokos when he performs his second song (259, 260). Still earlier, *agōn* refers to the athletic competition (200, 238).

There is a striking parallel to be found in the *Homeric Hymn to Apollo* (146–155), which is a passage describing the Delia, a seasonally recurring festival of Ionians who come from all over the Ionian world to gather together on the island of Delos. I highlight the fact that the occasion of this Delian festival is described as an *agōn*, 'competition' (149). The competitive events at this festival include athletics—boxing is the example that is highlighted—as well as dancing and singing (149). In this case, the poetry that underlies the dancing and singing is overtly coordinated with the athletics. There is a comparable occasion described in the Hesiodic *Works and Days* (654–659), where the figure of Hesiod himself claims to have won a victory in a competition for *aethla*, 'prizes' (454, 456); the form of this competition is said to be a *humnos*, 'song', whereas the other forms of competition on this occasion appear to be athletic events (Roller 1981b: 1–6).

Thucydides (3.104.2–6) quotes and analyses the passage in the *Homeric Hymn to Apollo* (146–150) that describes the seasonally recurring festival of the Delia. In his analysis, he refers to this festival as an *agōn*, 'competition', that combines athletic and 'musical' events: ἀγὼν ἐποιεῖτο αὐτόθι καὶ γυμνικὸς καὶ μουσικός, χορούς τε ἀνῆγον αἱ πόλεις ('a competition [*agōn*] was held there [= at Delos] that was both athletic [*gumnikos*] and musical [*mousikos*]; also, the cities brought choral ensembles'; 3.104.3). Having said this, Thucydides goes on to explain what he means when he says that 'musical' competitions took place along with athletic competitions at the seasonally recurring festival of the Delia: he now goes on to say that the 'musical' competitions involved the 'art of the Muses [*mousikē*]' (3.104.5), and he makes it clear that he has in mind primarily the art of Homer, that is, the art of performing the Homeric *Iliad* and *Odyssey* as well as the *Homeric Hymns* (Nagy 2010: 15–18).

During the fifth and the fourth centuries BCE, the most important context for competitions in performing the poetry of the Homeric *Iliad* and *Odyssey* was the seasonally recurring festival of the Panathenaia in Athens, featuring a grand *agōn*, 'competition', in *mousikē tekhnē*, 'the art of the Muses' (Aristot. *Const. Ath.* 60.1). At the Panathenaia, there were separate sets of competitions in performing separate kinds of *mousikē*, and those who competed with each other in performing the Homeric *Iliad* and *Odyssey* were called *rhapsōidoi*, 'rhapsodes' (Plat. *Ion* 530a–b, 533b–c; Isoc. 4.159; and Plut. *Per.* 13.9–11). It can be argued that these rhapsodic competitions in performing Homeric poetry at the festival of the Panathenaia in Athens stemmed ultimately from earlier performance traditions that evolved at the festival of the Panionia as celebrated in the late eighth and early seventh centuries BCE at the Panionion of the Ionian Dodecapolis in Asia Minor (Nagy 2010: 22, following Frame 2009: 551–620).

So by now we have seen that the one-time athletic events as described in the epics of the Homeric *Iliad* and *Odyssey* were transformed into seasonally recurring events by virtue of being retold year after year at the seasonally recurring rhapsodic competitions that were held at festivals like the Panathenaia in Athens.

A DIRECT LINK BETWEEN AN ATHLETIC EVENT AND A HEROIC EXPERIENCE

Besides the poetic competitions of rhapsodes and of other kinds of specialists in poetry and song, there were also seasonally recurring athletic competitions that were held at that same festival of the Panathenaia. And, in one such athletic competition, the experiences of the athletes were directly linked with the experiences of heroes in mortal combat. That is because these experiences were being narrated in the Homeric poems as performed by the rhapsodes. This athletic competition was known as the *apobatōn agōn*, which means 'competition of the *apobatai*' (Phot. *Lexicon* α 2450, see also α 2449 and *Suda* α 3250), where competing athletes wearing full battle gear and standing next to their charioteers on the platforms of their speeding chariots would suddenly leap to the ground (the word *apobatēs* means literally 'one who steps off') and then race with each other, thus ritually re-enacting the leaps executed by warriors in the battle narratives of the Homeric *Iliad* as retold by rhapsodes competing with each other at the same festival.

Here is how I describe the experience of the *apobatēs* as re-enacted at the Panathenaia:

> Weighted down by his hoplite armor, the *apobatēs* must literally hit the ground running as he lands on his feet in his high-speed leap from the platform of his chariot. If his run is not broken in a fall, he continues to run down the length of the racecourse in competition with the other running *apobatai*, who have made their own leaps from their own chariots. (Nagy 2010: 172)

The execution of such an apobatic leap by a heroic warrior was a climactic moment in the Homeric narrative, as we see from this example:

Ἕκτωρ δ' ἐξ ὀχέων σὺν τεύχεσιν ἆλτο χαμᾶζε

Hector leapt out of his chariot, armour and all, hitting the ground. (*Il.* 11.211)

In other climactic moments as well, Hector is described as leaping out of his chariot:

αὐτίκα δ' ἐξ ὀχέων σὺν τεύχεσιν ἆλτο χαμᾶζε

Straightaway he leapt out of his chariot, armour and all, hitting the ground. (*Il.* 5.494, 6.103, 12.81, 13.749)

Four other warriors are described in comparable wording at moments when they too leap out of their chariots: Menelaos (*Il.* 3.29), Diomedes (4.419), Sarpedon (16.426), and Patroklos (16.427). In the case of Menelaos (3.29), he leaps out of his chariot and hits the ground running as he rushes toward Paris to fight him in mortal combat on foot. Paris does not meet him head-on but keeps backing up until he melts into a crowd of foot soldiers who are massed behind him (3.30–37). In the case of Diomedes (4.419), he leaps off his chariot as he hits the ground running, while his bronze breastplate makes a huge clanging sound upon impact as he rushes toward the enemy, who all shrink back to avoid encountering him in mortal combat on foot (4.420–421).

Similarly, in a scene already cited (12.91), Hector leaps out of his chariot and hits the ground running as he rushes to fight the enemy on foot, and, in this case, his fellow chariot fighters follow his lead and dismount from their chariots, since they too are now ready to fight on foot (12.82–87). In the case of Sarpedon and Patroklos, we see these two heroes simultaneously leaping out of their chariots and hitting the ground running as they rush toward each other to fight one-on-one in mortal combat on foot—a combat that is won here by Patroklos (16.428–507). Later on, when Patroklos is about to engage in mortal combat with Hector, he once again leaps out of his chariot:

Πάτροκλος δ' ἑτέρωθεν ἀφ' ἵππων ἆλτο χαμᾶζε

Then Patroklos, from one side, leapt from his chariot, hitting the ground. (*Il.* 16.733)

What happens next is that Patroklos throws a rock at Kebriones, the charioteer of Hector, which hits Kebriones on the forehead, smashing his skull (*Il.* 16.734–754). Meanwhile, Hector leaps out of his chariot:

Ἕκτωρ δ' αὖθ' ἑτέρωθεν ἀφ' ἵππων ἆλτο χαμᾶζε.

Then Hector, from the other side, leapt from his chariot, hitting the ground. (*Il.* 16.755)

Patroklos and Hector proceed to fight one-on-one in mortal combat on foot—a combat that is won here by Hector (16.756–863).

From this collection of apobatic moments in the *Iliad* (I offer a more detailed survey in Nagy 2013 7c§§7–9), it is evident that Hector is featured far more often than any other Homeric hero in the act of leaping out of his chariot to fight in mortal combat on foot. It can be argued, then, that Hector's virtuosity in his feats of apobatic bravura is relevant to the fact that this hero is exceptionally described as having a four-horse chariot (*Il.* 8.185). As we have seen, four-horse chariots are more suitable for racing than for warfare (Scanlon 2004: 67). And we know for a fact that the athletic event of apobatic racing at the Panathenaia involved four-horse chariots (Shear 2001: 48, 55, 301, 303, 309). A prime illustration comes from the representation of the Panathenaic Procession on the Panathenaic Frieze of the Parthenon, where we see twenty-one apobatic chariot-teams on display, with eleven chariots featured on the north side (North XI–XXIX) and ten on the south side (South XXV–XXXV); in each case, the chariot is shown with four horses, a driver, and an *apobatēs* (Shear 2001: 304–305).

The apobatic leap in heroic warfare is also attested in the wording of Pindar. Here is his description of the hero Achilles himself in the act of leaping out of his chariot as he rushes ahead to kill his mortal enemy, the hero Memnon:

καὶ ἐς Αἰθίοπας | Μέμνονος οὐκ ἂν ἀπονοστή|σαντος ἔπαλτο· βαρὺ δέ σφιν | νεῖκος Ἀχιλεύς | ἔμπεσε χαμαὶ καταβαὶς ἀφ' ἁρμάτων, | φαεννᾶς υἱὸν εὖτ' ἐνάριξεν Ἀόος ἀκμᾷ | ἔγχεος ζακότοιο.

And it [= the name of the lineage of the Aiakidai, especially the name of Achilles] leapt at the Aethiopians, now that Memnon would not be coming back safely [to his troops]. Heavy combat fell upon them [= the Aethiopians] in the person of Achilles hitting the ground as he stepped down [*kata-bainein*] from his chariot. That was when he killed [Memnon] the son of the luminous dawn-goddess, with the tip of his raging spear. (Pind. *N.* 6.48–53)

There is a vivid reference to the athletic event of the *apobatai* in a work attributed to Demosthenes (61.22–29). The speaker here refers to the event as an *agōn*, 'competition', that is highlighted by the act of *apobainein*, 'stepping down' (61.23 τοῦ δ' ἀποβαίνειν ... ἐπὶ τοῦτον τὸν ἀγῶν‹α›). This athletic event of 'stepping down' from a speeding chariot is singled out as the most similar, among all *agōnismata*, 'forms of competition', to the experiences of warriors in the life-and-death struggles of combat warfare (61.24). As a spectacle, the event of the *apobatai* is described as matching most closely the grandeur of the gods themselves (61.24–25), and thus it is deserving of the greatest of all *āthla*, 'prizes won in contests' (61.25 μεγίστων δ' ἄθλων ἠξιωμένον). The speaker views this kind of competition as closest not only to combat warfare in general but also, in particular, to the scenes of combat as narrated in Homeric poetry, and that is why, the speaker goes on to say, only the greatest cities of the Hellenic world preserve the tradition of such *agōnes*, 'competitions' (61.25–26). The speaker then goes on to tell about a spectacular feat once performed by the athlete whom he is praising (61.27–29). Though it is difficult to reconstruct the details of this compressed narration, it appears that our athlete, having leapt from his speeding chariot and running with all his might, was almost run over from behind and trampled to death by horses drawing the chariot of a rival team that was heading full-speed toward him; instead of losing his nerve, our athlete somehow managed to surpass the momentum of this oncoming chariot-team (Nagy 2013 7b§§8–10).

Here is the original Greek text of the climax of the narration (Ps.-Dem. 61.28):

Τῶν γὰρ ζευγῶν ἀφεθέντων, καὶ τῶν μὲν προορμησάντων, τῶν δ' ὑφηνιοχουμένων, ἀμφοτέρων περιγενόμενος ὡς ἑκατέρων προσῆκε, τὴν νίκην ἔλαβες, τοιούτου στεφάνου τυχὼν ἐφ' ᾧ, καίπερ καλοῦ τοῦ νικᾶν ὄντος, κάλλιον ἐδόκει καὶ παραλογώτερον εἶναι τὸ σωθῆναι. φερομένου γὰρ ἐναντίου μέν σοι τοῦ τῶν ἀντιπάλων ἅρματος, ἁπάντων δ' ἀνυπόστ ατον οἰομένων εἶναι τὴν τῶν ἵππων δύναμιν, ὁρῶν αὐτῶν ἐνίους καὶ μηδενὸς δεινοῦ παρόντος ὑπερηγωνιακότας, οὐχ ὅπως ἐξεπλάγης ἢ κατεδειλίασας, ἀλλὰ τῇ μὲν ἀνδρείᾳ καὶ τῆς τοῦ ζεύγους ὁρμῆς κρείττων ἐγένου, τῷ δὲ τάχει καὶ τοὺς διηυτυχηκότας τῶν ἀνταγωνιστῶν παρῆλθες

This passage has been translated by N. J. DeWitt (London 1949). I offer revisions, highlighting with strikethrough/italics the wording that I have subtracted/added:

When the [*chariot*] teams had ~~been~~ started and some had ~~leaped~~ *rushed* to the fore and some were being reined in, you, prevailing over both [*the faster and the slower teams*], first one and then the other, ~~in proper style~~ [*surpassing each team*] *in a way that was most appropriate* [*for each situation*], seized the victory, winning that envied ~~crown~~ *garland* in such fashion that, glorious as it was to win it, it seemed the more glorious and astounding that you came off safely. For when the chariot of your opponents was bearing down upon you ~~head-on~~ and all thought the momentum of ~~your~~ *their* horses beyond checking, you, aware that some ~~drivers~~ [*runners*], ~~though~~ *even when* no danger ~~should~~ threaten*s*, become overanxious for their own safety, not only did not lose your head or your nerve, but by your courage ~~got control of~~ *overcame* the impetus of ~~your~~ *their* [*chariot*] team and by your speed passed even those contenders [= *the other runners*] whose luck had suffered no setback.

This athletic event of the *apobatai* as held at the festival of the Panathenaia in Athens was in some ways more conservative than the athletic event of the chariot-race as held at a festival like the Olympics. For example, whereas only the chariot driver was standing on the platform of the speeding chariot in the Olympic chariot-race, there was also a chariot rider standing next to the chariot driver in the Panathenaic race of the *apobatai*, and this chariot rider or *apobatēs* would then leap off the speeding chariot and back on it in death-defying manoeuvres that re-enacted the leaps executed by chariot fighters like Hector in the epic. Even in comparison with the chariot-race at the Funeral Games for Patroklos as narrated in our *Iliad*, the apobatic chariot-race at the Panathenaia is more conservative—at least with regard to the pairing of a chariot rider with the chariot driver. Further, the event of the *apobatai* at the Panathenaia was in some ways also more conservative than the event of the chariot-race at the Funeral Games of Patroklos as depicted on the 'François Krater', where we see that the heroes driving their racing chariots are wearing the ankle-length costume of professional chariot drivers, not the full armour of apobatic chariot fighters.

In some other ways, however, the relevant black figure vase paintings are most conservative. A case in point is the composite picturing of Achilles in two roles: he is depicted simultaneously as an epic chariot fighter and as a Panathenaic athlete participating in an apobatic competition (Nagy 2010: 170–177, following Stähler 1967). From the standpoint of these paintings, Achilles will keep on riding on his speeding chariot, ready at any moment to leap to the ground and rush into mortal combat on foot, so long as his heroic feats as a chariot fighter are being re-enacted again and again by competing apobatic athletes on each new occasion of the seasonally recurring festival of the Panathenaia—and so long as his story is being re-performed again and again by competing rhapsodes at that same festival.

In the narrative of the Homeric *Iliad* as we have it, by contrast, Achilles is featured only as a chariot fighter, not as an apobatic athlete. Even at the Funeral Games for Patroklos as retold in the *Iliad*, Achilles delegates the role of the athlete to his fellow heroes. Instead of engaging in any athletic event, Achilles here reserves for himself the role of the one hero whose death must be compensated by way of athletic competitions. That one hero is Patroklos. And so Achilles becomes the ritual representative of Patroklos, his other self, by presiding over the athletic competitions at the funeral games for his dead friend. His chosen role as presider here is a substitute for the role that he chooses in the vase paintings, where he engages directly in the athletic competition of the *apobatai* (Nagy 2010: 175–176).

No matter which hero is shown as engaging in athletic events, whether it be Achilles or only his fellow heroes, the fact remains that heroes who engage in these events become models for athletes who compete in these same kinds of events. And they are models because they are shown as competing in athletic ordeals that are instituted explicitly in compensation for the death of one of their own kind, a hero.

This is not to say that the modelling is consistently positive. We have already seen that the actions of heroes may be negative models—even when they serve as aetiologies for existing institutions like athletic festivals, as in the case of the *Tlēpolemeia*. Moreover, the models for heroes who compete in athletics may be their very own selves in other phases of their own lives as narrated in epic. For example, the heroes who compete in athletic events at the Funeral Games for Patroklos in the *Iliad* can unwittingly re-enact corresponding heroic events, either positive or negative, that they will experience at some point in their actual lives as characters in the heroic narration (Whitman 1958: 169; Nagy 1990: 193; Frame 2009: 170–172, 205–216).

I close by recalling the *tīmē a-phthi-tos*, 'unwilting honour', of the seasonally recurring athletic event that the hero Demophon receives as an eternal compensation for his death in the *Homeric Hymn to Demeter* (l. 263). We may now compare that seasonal recurrence with the seasonal recurrence of the *kleos a-phthi-ton*, 'unwilting glory', that the hero Achilles receives as a likewise eternal compensation for his own death in the *Iliad*:

> My mother Thetis tells me that there are two ways in which I may meet my end [*telos*]. If I stay here and fight, I shall not have a return [*nostos*] alive but my glory [*kleos*] will be unwilting [*aphthiton*]: whereas if I go home my name [*kleos*] will perish, but it will be long before the end [*telos*] shall take me. (*Il.* 9.410–416)

Just as the *tīmē a-phthi-tos*, 'unwilting honour', awaiting the hero Demophon is equated with the hero's cult, which is understood as lasting for eternity by virtue of being renewed year after year in the form of seasonally recurring athletic competitions, so also the eternal *kleos a-phthi-ton*, 'unwilting glory', awaiting the hero Achilles is being equated here with the hero's epic, which is Homeric poetry itself, and which is likewise understood as lasting for eternity. In the case of epic, as we have seen, its notional eternity is achieved by virtue of being renewed year after year in the form of seasonally recurring rhapsodic competitions at the Panathenaia, which are coordinated with the seasonally recurring athletic competitions at the same festival.

REFERENCES

Bell, M. 1995. 'The Motya Charioteer and Pindar's *Isthmian 2*.' *Memoirs of the American Academy in Rome* 40: 1–42.

Brelich, A. 1958. *Gli eroi greci. Un problema storico-religioso.* Rome.

Burkert, W. 1983. *Homo Necans: The Anthropology of Ancient Greek Sacrificial Ritual and Myth.* P. Bing, trans. Berkeley.

Burkert, W. 1985. *Greek Religion.* J. Raffan, trans. Cambridge, MA.

Currie, B. G. F. 2005. *Pindar and the Cult of Heroes.* Oxford.

Elmer, D. F. 2008. '*Epikoinos*: The Ball Game *Episkyros* and *Iliad* 12.421–3.' *CPh* 103: 414–422.

Frame, D. 2009. *Hippota Nestor.* Hellenic Studies 34. Cambridge, MA.

Häusle, H. 1979. *Einfache und frühe Formen des griechischen Epigramms.* Commentationes Aenipontanae 25. Innsbruck.

Irigoin, J. 1952. *Histoire du texte de Pindare.* Paris.

Kurke, L. 1991. *The Traffic in Praise: Pindar and the Poetics of Social Economy.* Ithaca, NY.

Nagy, G. 1990. *Pindar's Homer: The Lyric Possession of an Epic Past.* Baltimore.

Nagy, G. 1999. *The Best of the Achaeans. Concepts of the hero in Archaic Greek poetry.* Baltimore. Second ed. of orig. 1979.

Nagy, G. 2010. *Homer the Preclassic.* Berkeley.

Nagy, G. 2013. *The Ancient Greek Hero in 24 Hours.* Cambridge, MA.

Nilsson, M. P. 1906. *Griechische Feste.* Leipzig.

Pache, C. O. 2004. *Baby and Child Heroes in Ancient Greece.* Urbana, IL.

Pfister, F. 1912. *Der Reliquienkult im Altertum*, II. Giessen.

Rodin, B. P. 2009. 'Pindaric Epinikion and the Evolution of Poetic Genres in Archaic Greece.' PhD dissertation. University of California, Berkeley.

Roller, L. E. 1981a. 'Funeral Games in Greek Art.' *AJA* 85: 107–19.

Roller, L. E. 1981b. 'Funeral Games for Historical Persons.' *Stadion* 7: 1–17.

Scanlon, T. F. 2004. 'Homer, the Olympics, and the Heroic Ethos.' In *The Olympic Games in Antiquity: 'Bring Forth Rain and Bear Fruit'*. 61–91. Maria Kaïla G. Thill, H. Theodoropoulou, and Y. Xanthacou, eds. Athens; reprinted with footnotes added in *Classics@* 13, https://chs.harvard.edu/classics13-scanlon/. Accessed March 15, 2021.

Shear, J. L. 2001. 'Polis and Panathenaia: the History and Development of Athena's Festival.' PhD dissertation, University of Pennsylvania.

Stähler, K. 1967. *Grab und Psyche des Patroklos: Ein schwarzfiguriges Vasenbild*. Münster.

Whitman, C. H. 1958. *Homer and the Heroic Tradition*. Cambridge, MA.

CHAPTER 23

EPINIKION, KUDOS, AND CRITICISM

LESLIE KURKE

THE COMMEMORATION OF VICTORY: *EPINIKION* AND VICTOR STATUES

WHAT we call '*epinikion*' [plural, *epinikia*] (following the Hellenistic scholars who organised the corpora of archaic lyric poets) is a particular subspecies of poetic encomium, composed on commission to celebrate the victory of an individual at one of the circuit of great Panhellenic games or at a lesser, local contest. The poems we have preserved in this genre are highly circumscribed in time; we have titles for some individual poems and books of *epinikia* by Simonides; forty-five poems organized into four separate books by Pindar that range in date from 498 to 446 BCE (forty-four of which are actually *epinikia*); and fourteen more or less fragmentary poems by Bacchylides. In addition, patchy papyrus finds have led some scholars to suggest that *epinikia* were already composed by Ibykos (probably in the second half of the sixth century BCE); but given the fragmentary state of the remains, it is impossible to tell whether Ibykos' compositions were real *epinikia* or sympotic encomia designed for solo performance (see Barron 1984; but note the cautious remarks of Page 1970: 94–95, Rawles 2012). Even if we tentatively include Ibykos in our time-reckoning, this gives us a window of a mere hundred years (*c*.550–450 BCE) for the heyday of *epinikia* composed by first-rank poets of Panhellenic reputation.

We must of course imagine this brief efflorescence against a background of an enormous outpouring of ephemeral compositions by local poets—amateurs who were friends, family members, or admirers of victors—a continuing tradition of one-off celebratory songs. We find a good (fictional) representation of this latter tendency in the opening scene of Plato's *Lysis*, where one elite youth, Ktesippos, complains that his friend Hippothales, smitten by the beautiful boy Lysis, is constantly sounding his praises in speech and song. The text cues us to the likely sympotic context of these speeches and songs when Ktesippos tells Socrates, 'He's made us deaf pouring the name "Lysis" into our ears; and especially when he's had something to drink, it's easy for us, even wakened from sleep, to think we hear the name of Lysis'

(Plat. *Lysis* 204c7–d3). When Socrates asks about the content of these songs, Ktesippos really lets loose:

> Indeed, it's ridiculous, Socrates! For how is it not ridiculous if, being an admirer of the boy and exceptionally beyond all the rest paying attention to him, he has nothing distinctive to say about him that a child couldn't say? But the things the entire city is buzzing with, about [his father] Demokrates and his grandfather Lysis, and about all his ancestors—their wealth and their raising of horses (*hippotrophias*) and their victories at Pytho and at the Isthmus and at Nemea with four-horse chariots and single horses—these things he puts in poems and speeches, and in addition, things still more outmoded than these. For just the other day he was narrating to us in some poem the hosting of Herakles, how on account of the kinship of Herakles, their ancestor received Herakles hospitably, himself sprung from Zeus and the daughter of the deme founder—the kind of stuff old women sing, and many other such things, Socrates. (Plat. *Lysis* 205b6–d3)

It is striking here that what Ktesippos regards as the hackneyed themes of the infatuated Hippothales' sympotic encomia precisely overlap with the conventional content of Pindaric *epinikion*—the family's noble lineage, their wealth, *hippotrophia*, victories at Panhellenic contests, even stories of an early ancestor hosting a god or hero (for this theme, cf. *N*.10.49–51).

In contrast to this presumed background of ephemeral composition and performance, what makes 'epinikion' anomalous within the system of archaic Greek lyric genres is that, for the first time ever, a living, named individual was publicly celebrated by a singing, dancing chorus—probably an amateur chorus of his fellow citizens (but possibly also, on occasion, paid performers; see Carey 2007: 206–208). In archaic Greek terms, it is the choral element that is extraordinary, since otherwise choral performance is entirely circumscribed within religious worship, as choruses sing and dance in unison to honour gods and heroes; to sanctify the ritual of marriage; and to commemorate the dead at funerals. Epinikion as we have it preserved in Pindar and Bacchylides is thus a latecomer to the Greek lyric system, an odd hybrid genre that merges elements of sympotic encomium for living, named individuals with other elements of sacred choral song (what we call 'hymn' for the gods; perhaps also elements drawn from *threnos* and marriage song).

It is this odd—even transgressive—merging of monodic and choral, sympotic and public ritual elements in *epinikion* that accounts, I would contend, for a further anomaly that scholars have noted and worried over: that Pindar and Bacchylides never call the group performing the *epinikion* a *choros*, but only a *kōmos* (the unstructured, rowdy group that spills out drunk from the symposium into the public streets, singing, carousing, and often making trouble). But it is not just that the *kōmos* is one source for the *en-com-iastic* song *epinikion* represents, but that in the archaic period at least the term *choros* is still hedged round with religious and ritual associations that make it unsuitable as a designation for the unified singing group praising a living contemporary (on *kōmos*, see Cole 1992: 11–32; Agócs 2012; on *choros*, see Bremer 1990: 51–55).

How are we to account for this strange choral mutation that lies somewhere behind the hundred-year vogue for lavish *epinikia* by famous poets? It should be noted that, especially if we date the first *epinikia* to Ibykos, we have a precise synchronicity with the first great period of the dedication of victor statues at the sites of the games and in the victors' home cities. For the earliest known victor statue dedicated at Olympia is 544 BCE, even if these life-size images continue well into the Roman period all over Greece and the Hellenized East (see Herrmann 1988; Rausa 1994; Smith 2007; Raschke, this volume Chapter 35). And just as *epinikion* represents the first choral, public praise of a living individual, victor statues (as far as we can tell) were the first publicly erected images of named, living individuals; before victor statues, there were only images of gods, dedications, and funerary monuments (see Stewart 1986; Smith 2007).

At one level, this great period of lavish display and self-promotion in different media follows pretty closely on the expansion of locations and programs of athletic contests in the Greek world in the first half of the sixth century BCE, which we might in turn plausibly connect with a significant shift in military tactics and the development of new ways of fighting. Thus, the rise and standardization of hoplite tactics made the aristocratic elite more or less irrelevant—or at least, the same as everybody else—in the domain of warfare. In response, Greek elites sought new venues in which to distinguish themselves and win personal glory, so that the domain of intra-elite conflict shifted from war to athletics (see Rose 1992: 143–151).

But even this does not fully account for the boom in choral *epinikia* and victor statues from the mid-sixth to the mid-fifth century BCE. Why, after all, these particular forms of elite commemoration and display rather than others? And even if victor statues continue, why do lavish epinikian performances suddenly disappear (with one significant exception) after a hundred years? We must set these developments against the background of intense social and political contestation over values, models of leadership, and forms of community throughout the sixth century BCE. The characteristic Greek institutional structure of the *polis*, the city-state with urban centre and attached territory, had emerged in the early archaic period and, in the sixth century, the *polis* with its attendant egalitarian ideology began to centralize and assert its authority in such domains as coinage, the reorganization of public space, and significant building programmes (see Hölscher 1991; Kurke 1999). Most *poleis* in this period were of course still led by elites, but there was a significant trend toward greater democratization in many parts of the Greek world (see Robinson 1997). In some cases, the interests of the demos, the people at large, were promoted by rogue aristocrats who mobilized popular support to set themselves up as unconstitutional rulers or 'tyrants' (in its original Greek meaning). Thus we might say that in the sixth century, much in the political sphere was up for grabs—the elite no longer enjoyed an unchallenged monopoly of wealth and power, as the wider demos became more of a significant political actor and as superwealthy elites might vie with each other for tyrannical pre-eminence.

In addition, Catherine Morgan has noted that already in the last quarter of the eighth century we see a shift in the patterns of dedication of prestige objects, from funerary contexts within emerging states to conspicuous interstate sanctuaries like Olympia and Delphi (Morgan 1990; 1993). This pattern continues throughout the archaic period, leading Morgan to suggest that one important function of these interstate sanctuaries was to provide a neutral extra-territorial venue for elite display and competition (in the form of dedications and athletics) as these were becoming more problematic within the elites' home states. And yet, at the same time it is clear that athletic victory at the great Panhellenic games could translate into palpable political prestige at home. Witness the case of the Athenian Olympic victor Kylon who attempted a coup in Athens in the 630s. This attempt famously failed, but what is significant for our purposes is that Kylon himself seems to have regarded his Olympic victory as a sure stepping-stone to tyrannic power at home—even mounting his coup attempt to coincide with the celebration of the Olympic Games (Thuc. 1.126). Herodotus preserves the story of another archaic Athenian aristocrat that bespeaks the same (potentially dangerous) political potency attached to Olympic victory as the example of Kylon. The elder

Cimon, father of the Marathon general Miltiades, was driven out of Athens by the sixth-century tyrant Peisistratus. But when Cimon won his second Olympic chariot victory and was willing to 'hand it over' to Peisistratus (so that the tyrant was announced as the victor in his stead), he was allowed to return to Athens 'under truce'. Cimon went on to win yet a third Olympic chariot victory, whereupon the sons of Peisistratus (who had inherited the tyranny from their father) arranged to have him killed (Hdt. 6.103).

Thus success at the great athletic games could be a source of useable symbolic capital, but could also be a threat to political stability at home. For athletic victory produced a tension between the extraordinary prestige and aura it conferred on the individual victor and his proper integration within various communities—within the group of Panhellenic elites who were his peers and direct competitors, and within the notionally egalitarian community of his home city. There was, as Ian Morris observes, 'a crisis of praising' (Morris 2000: 187). The casual, ephemeral praise of other elites at parties was no longer enough; instead elite victors sought permanent memorials of victory via magnificent statues by Panhellenic artists and ornate, highly wrought *epinikia* composed by professional poets.

To understand these phenomena, we must treat victor statues with their identifying inscriptions and choral *epinikia* as parts of a single coherent system: both serve as long-lasting commemoration of individuals and as spaces or sites for negotiation between the victor and his various communities. Indeed, victor monuments and *epinikia* alike work to forge ideological consensus about the shared value of victory, thereby crystallizing an imagined community of the victor's family, the Panhellenic elite, and his fellow citizens. To do this, both forms of commemoration proliferate at the significant endpoints of the victor's journey—at the site of his success at the games, and in his home city, to which he returns resplendent with victory. In the case of victor statues, we know that there were massive numbers of them set up, especially in the Altis on the south side of the sanctuary at Olympia, for which the second-century-CE tour-guide Pausanias offers us a wealth of information, much of it confirmed by archaeological finds of inscribed statue-bases (Paus. 6.1–18; see Herrmann 1988; Rausa 1994; Smith 2007; Raschke, this volume Chapter 35). The statues in this early period are not individual portraits so much as generic types of the youthful and re-splendent *kouroi* that represent the Greek aristocratic ideal; they are individuated only by the attached inscriptions. By setting up his image in this forest of victor statues, the individual victor becomes, as Richard Neer notes,

> one of the *homoioi*, the 'peers' or 'interchangeables', dwelling permanently in the shrine. Uniting past victors and present ones, Greeks from the mainland and those from distant colonies, the army of *kouroi* is a veritable instantiation of the imagined community of the Hellenic elite. (Neer 2007: 230)

And while the image integrates the victor into the Panhellenic elite, the terms of the inscription (which reprise the original victory announcement) draw his family and his city also into the halo of victory. Thus, in an inscription from the first half of the fifth century preserved in Pausanias (Paus. 6.9.9 = Ebert 1972 no. 11):

> My homeland Corcyra, Philon my name, I am Glaukos's
> son and victor in boxing at two Olympiads.

Short and simple as it is, the epigram gives pride of place to the victor's homeland Corcyra, while it encircles his own name with those of his city and father, so that they participate equally in the permanent commemoration of his glorious achievement. In addition, a special perk of being an athletic victor was being allowed to set up a life-size image of oneself in one's home city (or even to have one's city set up such an image at public expense); here the visible monument set up in a prominent place simultaneously glorifies the victor and (via the inscription) redounds to the glory of the whole city.

Like the statues, epinikian performance clustered at the endpoints of the victor's journey; thus *epinikia* were performed immediately at the site of the games, or much more elaborately back in the victor's home city. In several cases, we have two *epinikia* preserved, by the same or different poets, articulating both ends of the victor's journey with celebration (thus Pind. *O.* 4–*O.* 5; *O.* 10–*O.* 11; Bacchyl. 2–1; Bacchyl. 6–7; Bacchyl. 4-Pind. *P.* 1; see Gelzer 1985: 97–98). In these different settings, *epinikion*'s hybrid form enabled different kinds of negotiation. At the site of the games, one might imagine a more informal celebratory *kōmos* of young elites who accompanied the victor, while at home, a full-scale epinikian performance co-opted the multiple voices of the victor's fellow citizens to celebrate his achievement in unison—a veritable enactment of the ungrudging community of praise the poems advocated. In content too, *epinikia* combined praise of the victor with a multilayered rhetoric of inclusion, working in performance to reintegrate the extraordinary individual back into his various communities with his new status (Crotty 1982: 104–138; Kurke 2013). Thus the poems interweave invocation and thanks to the patron gods of the games and the victor's home city; commemoration of his family's virtues and past athletic achievements; and praise of his city with the implicit assertion that the victor's athletic success redounds to the greater glory of the whole civic community. All these different themes are caught up in a weave of complex imagery, wise aphorism, and (in the longer odes) ornate and allusive mythic narrative that often associates the individual victor and his fellow citizens with their local heroes of myth and cult.

And after the original lavish performance, it seems likely that individual families preserved the texts of these poems as precious heirlooms—these local family treasures may indeed have been the source of the Hellenistic collections of *epinikia* from which our own texts ultimately derive (Irigoin 1952: 8–9; Hubbard 2004). More significant perhaps for the immortality conferred by song that these poems consistently promise was their afterlife in re-performance; thus the fame and skill of a Panhellenic poet might enable individual *epinikia* to spin free of their local surround and become part of the symposium repertoire performed by cultured elites all over the Greek world. Pindar seems to embed a vignette of just such imagined re-performance in one of his *epinikia* (*N.* 4.13–16). Likewise, the old-fashioned father in Aristophanes' *Clouds* of 423 BCE bids his Sophist-trained son 'after the feasting to take up the lyre and sing Simonides' tune about Krios [the ram], how he was shorn', referring to one of our earliest certain *epinikia*, composed by Simonides for an Aeginetan wrestling victor (*Cl.* 1354–1356). And the elite Athenian characters in the dialogues of Plato frequently quote or allude to bits of Pindar's poetry as common cultural resources, with Plato's Socrates in one instance even invoking the beginning of an epinikian ode for a private citizen of Thebes (Plat. *Phaedrus* 227b, quoting Pind. *I.* 1.1–3; cf. Irigoin 1952: 18). Here again, the hybrid form of *epinikion* (with its constant references to symposia and *kōmoi*) as well as its pervasive avoidance of the specifics of the contest in favour of the extreme generality of myth and gnome can be seen to serve and facilitate the poems' desired transubstantiation into an afterlife of sympotic re-performance.

I offer this as a general, schematic model of the social and political work done by *epinikion* in performance; the exact contours of the negotiation of individual and group achieved of course varied from community to community, and with the status of individual victors. Thus poems composed for tyrants diverge significantly from those composed for private citizens. The latter regularly assert that athletic victory served the common good, glorifying the whole city, while they work to reassure the victor's fellow citizens that he does not aim at excessive political power through the prominence and charismatic authority gained by athletic victory. These poems for private citizens carefully craft a portrait of the victor as an ideal middling citizen whose values can be expressed through a generalizing first person, as in these lines written for a victor in oligarchic Thebes:

> I would desire beautiful things from god,
> Striving for things that are possible within my age class.
> For finding the middle ranks blooming with more enduring prosperity throughout
>   the city,
> I blame the lot of tyrannies;
> And I am strained over common achievements. And the envious are fended off,
> if a man, having taken the peak of achievement, plies it in peace and avoids dread
>   hubris . . .

(Pind. P. 11.50–58)

The 'I' here is nominally the poet's persona, but the values and choices it espouses, sung in unison by a chorus of the victor's fellow citizens, are meant to represent or mirror the victor's own. Thus the victor's civic contribution is affirmed and the envy of his fellow citizens allayed (Young 1968: 1–26; Kurke 2013: 185–189).

In contrast, the *epinikia* composed for victorious tyrants and dynasts make no effort to allay envy; in one poem addressed to Hieron, tyrant of Syracuse, for example, Pindar asserts 'envy is better than pity' (*P.* 1.85; cf. Hdt. 3.52.5 for the same sentiment in a tyrannic context). Instead, the tyrant odes embrace a rhetoric of the superlative, showcasing all that is exceptional about the victor's wealth, military prowess, athletic success, and scope of rule. These poems simultaneously laud the victor's political virtues, fashioning a portrait of him as an ideal ruler—a portrait aimed both at the victor's own citizen-subjects and at the wider community of the Panhellenic elite.

At this level, we can trace out patterns in the frequency and shared content of epinikian commissions from different polities and different parts of the Greek world. The single largest group of Pindaric and Bacchylidean *epinikia* (twenty altogether) celebrate Western Greeks—victors from Sicily and (occasionally) southern Italy. Of these, nine are commissions from Hieron and Theron, the fantastically wealthy Deinomenid and Emmenid tyrants who dominated much of eastern and southern Sicily, with another five poems commissioned by these tyrants' kin and henchmen (all fourteen for hippic victories; see Luraghi 1994; Mann 2001: 236–248; Antonaccio 2007; Morgan 2015; Nicholson 2016). What all these commissions, especially those of the tyrants and their entourages, suggest is that these Western Greeks sought maximum presence and visibility on the Greek mainland, competing in great numbers at the most prestigious games at Olympia and Delphi, making lavish dedications to commemorate their victories, and hiring poets of international reputation to celebrate them at home and at the site of the games. These Western Greeks (tyrants and private citizens alike) seemed thereby to be aiming for acceptance and integration as members of the Panhellenic elite, even as the tyrants' unprecedented displays of prestige expenditure in all these different media put them in another class entirely (see Dougherty 1993: Ch. 5; Kurke 1999: 131–142; Mann 2001: 248–288; Neer 2007: 236–239; Morgan 2015).

Different again is the pattern of commissions from Aegina, the second largest group of Pindaric and Bacchylidean *epinikia* (eleven plus a fragmentary twelfth of Pindar, two of Bacchylides). Inhabiting a small, rocky island, the Aeginetans had no interest in equestrian events; all but two of the Aeginetan odes celebrate athletes in the heavy contests of wrestling and pankration. Other ancient evidence (especially Herodotus) suggests that the wealthy elite of Aegina made its money from trade, importing, exporting, and serving as carriers for foreign traders and merchandise as well (Figueira 1981; Mann 2001: 220–225). In content, the *epinikia* of Pindar and Bacchylides conform to this model, speaking to and promoting the values and ideology of a shipping elite. Thus over and over again, these poems single out for praise Aegina's 'hospitality' and 'justice to strangers', while the myths of Aiakid heroes the poems pervasively narrate emphasize the Aiakids' far-flung adventures, and especially their interconnectivity and collaborative expeditions with foreign heroes like Herakles and the Atreidai (see Pind. *O.* 8, *N.* 3, *N.* 4, *N.* 5, *N.* 7, *I.* 5, and *I.* 6, and Bacchyl. 13; on the ideology of the Aeginetan odes, see Figueira 1981: 322–331; Mann 2001: 192–235; Hornblower 2007; Kowalzig 2010). It is also intriguing that none of these Aeginetan odes is composed for performance at the site of the games; all fourteen seem to have been performed at home on Aegina, apparently often integrated into public festivals celebrating Aiakos and other Aiakid heroes (Mann 2001: 227–234).

This pattern in turn represents a marked contrast with the commissions for Aegina's old enemy Athens. We have preserved very few *epinikia* commissioned for Athenians—just two short odes of Pindar (*P.* 7, *N.* 2) and one longer fragmentary poem by Bacchylides (Bacchyl. 10). Gelzer (1985) has argued that both of Pindar's brief odes were composed for immediate performance at the site of the games, with (apparently) no pendant longer ode performed at home in Athens. Was such choral epinikian performance at home regarded as too naked a form of aristocratic display in post-Kleisthenic Athens? Or was it rather that the negotiation of mass and elite through choral performance was finessed in Attica by other genres like tragedy and dithyramb (see Wilson 2000)? However that may be, we find a similar shape of absence in the statue record: while (smaller?) victor statues could be dedicated on the Acropolis, the fourth-century orator Lycurgus could boast that in other cities, 'athletes are set up in the agoras; among [the Athenians] only good generals and those who killed the tyrant' have images dedicated there (Lyc. 1.51; cf. Dem. 20.70; Smith 2007: 100).

KUDOS, CROWNS, AND CRITICISM

I have suggested that we must understand epinikian performance and athletic monuments in the archaic and classical periods as parts of a single coherent cultural system; we might describe that system as a ritual economy of *kudos* and crowns. For *epinikion* and the monuments alike participated in and perpetuated a belief that victors at the great games were endowed by their victories with talismanic power or magical potency in battle, and that they were able to share that charisma with their civic communities. Such a belief in the talismanic power of athletic victors is suggested by the frequency with which crown victors show up in the archaic and classical periods as military commanders or leaders of colonial expeditions, and by an odd report in Plutarch that victors at the crown games were traditionally stationed beside the Spartan king in the battle line (Plut. *Quaes. Conv.* 2.5.2; *Lyc.* 22.4). We can offer rationalistic explanations for these phenomena: in this period, crown victors were almost certainly wealthy aristocrats who were also most likely to be military commanders and oikists (founders of colonies), while Plutarch's Spartan custom is predicated on athletics as good training for war. But such a rationalistic account doesn't seem entirely adequate; why, for example, is it only *crown* victors who accompany the Spartan king? And such an account gives us no purchase on a remarkable story preserved in the first-century-BCE historian Diodorus of Sicily, about the great sixth-century athletic victor Milo of Croton leading his countrymen in battle against the aggression of the neighbouring city of Sybaris:

> With Milo the athlete commanding and, on account of the superabundance of his bodily force, first having routed those stationed against him. For this man, a six-time Olympic victor and having the courage to go with his bodily nature, is said to have entered into battle crowned with his six Olympic crowns and wearing the garb of Herakles with lion skin and club. And [it is said] that he was marvelled at by his fellow citizens as being the cause of victory. (Diod. 12.9.5–6).

Milo here seems to wield a numinous *mana* or charisma, making him invincible in battle, and that talismanic potency is somehow connected with his Olympic victory crowns.

The native Greek term for such talismanic potency, I would contend, is *kudos*. Analysing the Homeric evidence, the linguist Emile Benveniste observed,

> The gift of *kudos* ensures the triumph of the man who receives it: in combat the holder of *kudos* is invariably victorious. Here we see the fundamental character of *kudos*: it acts as *a talisman of supremacy*. We use the term talisman advisedly, for the bestowal of *kudos* by the god procures an instantaneous and irresistible advantage, rather like a magic power, and the god grants it now to one and now to another at his good will and always in order to give the advantage at a decisive moment of a combat or some competitive activity. (Benveniste 1973: 348; cf. Fränkel 1973: 80 n. 14)

In Homer, such *kudos* attaches specifically to two spheres of activity—battle and the assembly-place where men compete in speeches or athletic contests. This pattern endures in Greek usage: from the archaic period to late antiquity, the term *kudos* shows up most frequently in agonistic inscriptions and those that commemorate military victory. We should also note that in *epinikion* and the agonistic inscriptions alike, we often find a collocation between the victor's crown and *kudos* for his city. Thus in one poem, Pindar prays to Zeus,

> Receive this Olympic-victory *kōmos* by the grace of the Charites,
> the longest-lasting light of achievements broad in strength. For it comes from
> the carts of Psaumis who, crowned with olive from Pisa, is eager to awaken *kudos*
>   for Kamarina. (*O.* 4.8–12)

Again, in *Isthmian* 1, Pindar affirms that he will celebrate the Isthmus, 'since it bestowed six crowns from contests on the people of Kadmos, victorious *kudos* for the fatherland' (*I.* 1.10–12). Similarly Bacchylides, in an address to an Athenian victor, links his crowns to *kudos* for his city: 'however many times by the grace of Victory having bound your blond head with flowers you established *kudos* for broad Athens and glory for the Oineidai' (Bacchyl. 10.15–18). In the agonistic inscriptions, one traditional formula for victory is that the athlete has 'crowned his city' (*stephanoun tēn polin*; see Ebert 1972 nos. 12, 19 [suppl.], 35, 67, 71, and Robert 1967: 17–27). But sometimes we find a variation of this formula: the victor is said to 'bestow *kudos* upon his city' (*kudainein tēn polin*; see Ebert 1972 no. 76B, and cf. nos. 36, 74, 75; Pind. *O.* 10.66). The functional equivalence of these two verbs with the city as object bespeaks the same association of *kudos* with the victor's crown that we find in Pindar and Bacchylides.

To account for the persistent association of the victor's crown with special talismanic power in the diction of *epinikion* and the inscriptions, as in the later anecdotes of Diodorus and Plutarch, I would suggest that the victor's *kudos* inheres in the crown, and that this is what makes the 'crown games' of the *periodos* so special. There is evidence that, on his re-turn home from the games, the athletic victor would dedicate his crown on the altar of a local god or hero (Pind. *O.* 9.110–112, *N.* 5.50–54). It is this ritual act that lies behind the for-mula that the victor has 'crowned his city', suggesting also that the dedication of the crown is a means by which the returning victor could share his *kudos*, his talismanic potency, with the whole civic community. The city reciprocated with specifically *civic* honours that could include large money payments, front-row seating at festivals, *sitēsis* or a lifetime of meals in the Prytaneion, sometimes even the erection of a victor statue at public expense (Neer 2007: 231).

Within such a symbolic economy of *kudos* and crowns, we can re-conceive both *epinikia* and victor monuments as machines for the perpetual renewal of the victor's *kudos* and as conversion mechanisms to ensure the safe transfer to the civic community of the victor's dangerous potency. Since agonistic inscriptions (as I noted) reprised all the elements of the original victory announcement, the victor statue with attached epigram co-opted the voice of every passer-by who read the inscription to re-enact the moment at which the victorious athlete was announced at the games and simultaneously crowned (see Day 1989; 2010 on epigrams as re-enactments of ritual). In like manner, *epinikion* obsessively linked the terms of the original victory announcement—the name of the victor, his event, patronymic, and ethnic—with the imagery of crowning, real and metaphorical (see Nisetich 1975). By these strategies, both media reanimated the ritually significant moment of victory announcement and crowning with a living voice or voices, but did so within the frame of public space and community celebration.

It is this ritual economy that helps us understand the historically localized phenomena of choral *epinikion* and the first appearance of victor statues, and we need to ground this sudden efflorescence of elite display in a particular political context. J. K. Davies has observed that in Athens, aristocratic participation in chariot-racing at the great games increased dramat-ically in the sixth and fifth centuries BCE, and then dropped off again in the fourth (Davies 1981: 88–131; see Golden 1998: 171–175 for supplements to Davies's thesis). Davies explained this phenomenon as the deployment of property-power as a substitute for the aristocracy's waning cult power within the city, to be replaced, in turn, toward the end of the fifth cen-tury, by rhetorical skill. Indeed, charismatic authority is involved in both the first two forms of power Davies chronicles; as the institutionalized form of charisma represented by cult power recedes in the face of the rational order of the *polis*, aristocrats seek to renew their power and prestige within the city by personal charisma won at the great games. Davies's model applies specifically to Athens, but we might extend it *mutatis mutandis* to aristocrats and dynasts throughout the Greek world. The ideology of *kudos* represented a serious bid for renewed talismanic power by members of the Greek elite, justifying their pre-eminence and distinctive status while claiming to benefit the wider civic community by sharing their special potency.

But even with this shared ideology powerfully and repeatedly conjured by victor statues and epinikian performances, the communal value of athletic victory was not uncontested in the archaic and classical periods; we can detect a strand of civic or middling critique running through our fragmentary sources. Thus in what may be a complete poem, Xenophanes (c.560–470 BCE) directly challenges the civic value of athletic victory:

> But if someone should win victory by the swiftness of his feet,
> or in the pentathlon, where the precinct of Zeus [is]
> beside the streams of Pisa in Olympia, or wrestling,
> or even having the grievous boxing,
> or the terrible contest they call the pankration,
> then he would be more prestigious (*kudroteros*) for his fellow citizens to look upon
> and he would have a visible front-row seat in the assemblies,
> and food from public property,
> and [even] a gift from the city to be a treasure for him.
> —or also [if he should win] with horses—he would be alloted all these things,
> though he is not deserving as I am. For better than the strength
> of men and horses is our *sophiē*.
> But this is now conventionally organized very much at random, nor is it just
> to prefer strength to good *sophiē*.
> For not even if a good boxer should be among the people,
> or one who is good at the pentathlon or wrestling
> or in the swiftness of his feet, the very thing which is most honoured
> of all the works of strength of men in the contest,
> would the city on that account be well ordered by law (*en eunomiēi*).
> But there would be small joy for the city in this—
> if someone competing win beside the banks of Pisa—
> for these things do not fatten the city's coffers. (fr. B2 DK)

Xenophanes was born in Kolophon in Ionia, but spent much of his life travelling the world, including the Greek colonies of southern Italy, so we may take his sentiments here as a response to phenomena observed in many different cities. It is noteworthy that Xenophanes makes no attempt to deny the charismatic prestige acquired by athletic victors (for this is conceded by the adjective *kudroteros* in line 6). Instead he first contrasts the physical strength of athletes unfavourably to his own *sophiē*—both poetic skill and political know-how—and then, in the last lines of the poem, he opposes the symbolic exchange of *kudos* and civic rewards with the good order and material prosperity of the city. Modern scholars have read Xenophanes' poetry as an attack on aristocratic values, and we may apply that interpretation to fr. 2 as well (see Fränkel 1973: 328–330). In response to a serious aristocratic bid for renewed talismanic authority within the community, Xenophanes counters with a very different model of civic good, consciously rejecting charismatic power in favour of political wisdom, good government, and material well-being.

We find a somewhat different challenge to the value of athletic victory in a fragment of the seventh-century Spartan poet Tyrtaios. And this is just what we might expect, since (as I have noted) athletic victory and its celebration had different meanings within different

Greek polities. Thus in an extended priamel in one of Tyrtaios' elegies, which is presumably a poem of military exhortation:

> I would not mention, nor would I put in account a man
> neither for the virtue of his feet nor for wrestling,
> nor if he should have the size and strength of the Kyklopes
> nor if he should beat Thracian Boreas at running,
> nor if he should be lovelier in form than Tithonus,
> or richer than Midas or Kinyras,
> nor if he should be more kingly than Pelops, son of Tantalos,
> or have the honey-voiced tongue of Adrastos,
> nor if he should have every glory except thrusting courage.
> For he would not be a man good in war
> unless he could endure seeing bloody slaughter,
> and fight, taking a firm stand near the enemies. (fr. 12 W, ll. 1–12)

Here the speaker rejects a whole series of culturally valued qualities and possessions (including athletic prowess; mythic speed, strength, and beauty; and the wealth and royal power of Eastern dynasts) in order to valorize the ideal of the hoplite warrior who stands his ground fighting for his city. Such a deliberate sundering of the usually closely paired honourific domains of warfare and athletic victory, while extreme, seems appropriate to the relentlessly militaristic culture of Sparta.

Such civic or middling attacks on the value of athletic victory continue in the classical period. So for example, Euripides in a fragment of a satyr play bemoans the uselessness of athletes and asserts that 'one should crown instead ... whoever leads the city best ... and he who puts an end to fights and internal strife with words' (Eur. fr. 282 N²). Likewise on several occasions, the speech-writer and teacher of rhetoric Isocrates echoes Xenophanes in questioning the lavish civic rewards conferred on athletic victors, contrasting their physical might unfavourably with those who (like himself) 'toil in private for the public good and train their souls so as to be able to benefit others' (Isoc. 4.1–2; cf. Isoc. 15.250, 301–302; Plat. *Apol.* 36d).

The End of an Era?

All these challenges strongly suggest that the prestige and material rewards of athletic victory endured unabated. So what happened to *epinikion* after its hundred-year efflorescence (550–450 BCE)? As I have noted, with a single exception (to which I'll return), we know of no more choral *epinikia* composed by professional poets after Pindar's *Pythian* 8, datable to 446 BCE. It is not an adequate historical explanation to peg this to the death of individual poets (Pindar, Bacchylides). There is also an issue of radically changed historical circumstances in individual cities. For example, the Sicilian tyrannies, whose members and henchmen had accounted for fourteen epinikian commissions, had all fallen by the mid-fifth century; likewise in 431, the Aeginetans, formerly so committed to athletic competition and epinikian celebration, were expelled from their island by imperial Athens (Thuc. 2.27; see Figueira 1991; Mann 2001: 235).

But even beyond these local upheavals, we may suggest a more pervasive set of changes. After the mid-fifth century, with the rise of the Athenian empire, more radical democracies in Athens (and elsewhere?), and the intellectual revolution fostered by the Sophists, the performance of *epinikion* seems to have been perceived as hopelessly old-fashioned as a space for the negotiation of individual and community. We might take the character of the son, Pheidippides, in Aristophanes' *Clouds* of 423 BCE as in himself emblematic of these shifts. Thus we are told at the start of the play that he is an Alkmeonid on his mother's side, crazy for horses and chariot-racing, who, through these expensive hobbies, has landed his father Strepsiades deep in debt (*Cl.* 12–80). Over the course of the play, Strepsiades prevails on his reluctant son to become a student of Socrates (here portrayed as an arch-Sophist), so he can learn the new rhetoric that will make father and son invincible against their creditors. But Pheidippides absorbs Sophistic values and attitudes (along with speaking ability) all too well. At this point, when his father asks him to take up the lyre and sing an *epinikion* of Simonides ('Krios, how he was shorn', quoted above), Pheidippides rejects the practice of such sympotic solo performance as 'old-fashioned' (*archaion*)—'like a woman grinding barley' (*Cl.* 1356–1357). Scholars have seen in this moment a shift in musical styles (the rise of the 'New Music'), but it is also the content and world of values *epinikion* represents that the Sophist-trained son scornfully rejects. (And here we might recall the complaint of the character Ktesippos in Plato's *Lysis*, which I quoted at the beginning of this essay; in spite of the elite pedigree suggested by his 'horsey' name, Ktesippos finds the epinikian themes of his besotted friend's encomia to Lysis and his family embarrassingly 'outmoded' [*kronikōtera*]— 'the kinds of things old women sing'.)

Given that the dedication of victor statues at interstate sanctuaries continued robustly, we might take the contrasting fates of *epinikion* and victor statues to mean that the elite persevered in their rivalry and negotiation with their peers at the Panhellenic sites of the games, but had more or less given up their efforts to integrate themselves into the *polis* order (thus Golden 1998: 84–86; Thomas 2007). I would say rather that other spaces for such mass-elite negotiation rose to prominence within the city. With the rationalizing training provided by the Sophists and the development of professional rhetoric, prose speeches in the assembly and the law courts replaced the negotiations enacted by choral song, just as professional logographers (speech-writers) replaced professional poets (see Ober 1989).

We do know of one more chorally performed *epinikion* (I leave out of account here the genre experiments of the Hellenistic poet Callimachus which combine the content of *epinikion* with the metrical form of agonistic inscriptions; see Fuhrer 1993; Golden 1998: 86– 88). In 416 BCE, the flamboyant Athenian aristocrat Alcibiades (nephew and ward of Pericles) entered seven four-horse chariots at the Olympic Games and came in first, second, and fourth (according to Thucydides 6.16). Staging a debate before the Athenian democratic assembly, Thucydides has Alcibiades boast that he 'prepared everything else in a way worthy of the victory'; this included feasting all those assembled at Olympia (Isoc. 16.34, Ath. 1.3e), and commissioning an *epinikion* from the poet Euripides. Plutarch preserves a few lines of this poem, which combine conventional elements of *epinikion* with one or two *outré* Euripidean touches (Eur. frs. 755, 756 PMG; see Bowra 1970: 134–148). But perhaps most remarkable is the simple fact of this poem's existence, thirty years after Pindar's last *epinikion* and seventy years after his last datable poem for an Athenian (*P.* 7 for the Alkmeonid Megakles, dated to 486 BCE). Christian Mann has suggested that in the act of commissioning and mounting a choral epinikian performance, Alcibiades was consciously archaizing, in order to imitate and evoke Pindar's and Bacchylides' most famous patrons—Hieron and Theron, the tyrants of Sicily (Mann 2001: 102–113). This certainly makes sense in the context of Athens' foreign policy; just a year later, in 415, the Athenians would mount their grandiose expedition to Sicily, with Alcibiades as one of the three commanders. But this conscious evocation of the Sicilian tyrants also conforms to what we are told about Alcibiades' own lifestyle and possible ambitions. Thus Thucydides has Alcibiades boast that in entering seven chariots he has done 'what no private citizen (*idiōtēs*) had ever done before'—the implication being that only the tyrants of old could match Alcibiades' lavish displays of *hippotrophia* and other prestige expenditure. Alcibiades, it seems, did not hesitate to identify himself with tyrannic pre-eminence—the very thing, according to Thucydides, that later led to his downfall, as the Athenians came to fear and distrust his undemocratic excess and lawlessness (Thuc. 6.15.3-4)—and his epinikian commission participated in such fearless tyrant-style self-aggrandisement. We are thus faced with a paradox: this last choral *epinikion* does not serve the genre's traditional goal of reintegrating the victor into his community; just the opposite (Mann 2001: 110–111). In Alcibiades' hands, this *unicum* of literary history functions to assert his own spectacular uniqueness. The end of an era indeed.

References

Agócs, P. 2012. 'Performance and Genre: Reading Pindar's *kōmoi*.' In Agócs, Carey, and Rawles. 191–223.

Agócs, P., C. Carey, and R. Rawles, eds. 2012. *Reading the Victory Ode*. Cambridge.

Antonaccio, C. M. 2007. 'Elite Mobility in the West.' In Hornblower and Morgan. 265–85.

Barron, J. P. 1984. 'Ibycus: *Gorgias* and Other Poems.' *BICS* 31: 13–24.

Benveniste, E. 1973. *Indo-European Language and Society*. E. Palmer, trans. London.

Bowra, C. M. 1970. *On Greek Margins*. Oxford.

Bremer, J. M. 1990. 'Pindar's Paradoxical *egō* and a Recent Controversy about the Performance of his Epinicia.' In *The 'I' in Archaic Poetry*. 41–58. S. Slings, ed. Amsterdam.

Carey, C. 2007. 'Pindar, Place, and Performance.' In Hornblower and Morgan. 199–210.

Cole, A. T. 1992. *Pindar's Feasts, or the Music of Power*. Rome.

Crotty, K. 1982. *Song and Action: The Victory Odes of Pindar*. Baltimore.

Davies, J. K. 1981. *Wealth and the Power of Wealth in Classical Athens*. Salem, NH.

Day, J. W. 1989. 'Rituals in Stone: Early Greek Grave Epigrams and Monuments.' *JHS* 109: 16–28.

Day, J. W. 2010. *Archaic Greek Epigram and Dedication: Representation and Reperformance*. Cambridge.

Dougherty, C. 1993. *The Poetics of Colonization: From City to Text in Archaic Greece*. New York.

Ebert, J. 1972. *Griechische Epigramme auf Sieger an gymnischen und hippischen Agonen*. Abhandlungen der Sächsischen Akademie der Wissenschaften zu Leipzig. Berlin.

Figueira, T. J. 1981. *Aegina: Society and Politics*. Salem, NH.

Figueira, T. J. 1991. *Athens and Aegina in the Age of Imperial Colonization*. Baltimore.

Fränkel, H. 1973. *Early Greek Poetry and Philosophy*. M. Hadas and J. Willis, trans. New York.

Fuhrer, T. 1993. 'Callimachus' Epinician Poems.' In *Callimachus*. Hellenistica Groningana I. 79–97. M. A. Harder, R. F. Regtuit, and G. C. Wakker, eds. Groningen.

Gelzer, T. 1985. '*Mousa Authigenēs*: Bemerkungen zu einem Typ pindarischer und bacchylideischer Epinikien.' *MH* 42: 95–120.

Golden, M. 1998. *Sport and Society in Ancient Greece*. Cambridge.

Herrmann, H.-V. 1988. 'Die Siegerstatuen von Olympia.' *Nikephoros* 1: 119–183.

Hölscher, T. 1991. 'The City of Athens: Space, Symbol, Structure.' In *City States in Classical Antiquity and Medieval Italy*. 355–80. A. Molho, K. Raaflaub, and J. Emlen, eds. Stuttgart.

Hornblower, S. 2007. '"Dolphins in the Sea" (*Isthmian* 9.7): Pindar and the Aeginetans.' In Hornblower and Morgan. 287–308.

Hornblower, S. and C. Morgan, eds. 2007. *Pindar's Poetry, Patrons and Festivals: From Archaic Greece to the Roman Empire*. Oxford.

Hubbard, T. K. 2004. 'The Dissemination of Epinician Lyric: Pan-Hellenism, Reperformance, Written Texts.' In *Oral Performance and its Context*. 71–93. C. J. Mackie, ed. Leiden.

Irigoin, J. 1952. *Histoire du texte de Pindare*. Paris.

Kowalzig, B. 2010. 'Musical Merchandise "on Every Vessel": Religion and Trade on Aegina.' In *Aegina: Contexts for Choral Lyric Poetry*. 129–171. D. Fearn, ed. Oxford.

Kurke, L. 1998. 'The Economy of *Kudos*.' In *Cultural Poetics in Archaic Greece: Cult, Performance, Politics*. 131–163. C. Dougherty and L. Kurke, eds. Oxford.

Kurke, L. 1999. *Coins, Bodies, Games, and Gold: The Politics of Meaning in Archaic Greece*. Princeton.

Kurke, L. 2013. *The Traffic in Praise: Pindar and the Poetics of Social Economy*. 2nd ed. Berkeley, CA.

Luraghi, N. 1994. *Tirannidi arcaiche in Sicilia e Magna Grecia: da Penazio di Leontini alla caduta dei Dinomenidi*. Florence.

Mann, C. 2001. *Athlet und Polis im archaischen und frühklassischen Griechenland*. Göttingen.

Morgan, C. 1990. *Athletes and Oracles: The Transformation of Olympia and Delphi in the Eighth Century B.C.* Cambridge.

Morgan, C. 1993. 'The Origins of Pan-Hellenism.' In *Greek Sanctuaries: New Approaches*. 18–44. N. Marinatos and R. Hägg, eds. London.

Morgan, K. A. 2015. *Pindar and the Construction of Syracusan Monarchy in the Fifth Century B.C.* Oxford.

Morris, I. 2000. *Archaeology as Cultural History*. Oxford.

Neer, R. T. 2007. 'Delphi, Olympia, and the Art of Politics.' In *The Cambridge Companion to Archaic Greece*. 225–264. H. A. Shapiro, ed. Cambridge.

Nicholson, N. 2016. *The Poetics of Victory in the Greek West: Epinicia, Oral Tradition, and the Deinomenid Empire*. Oxford.

Nisetich, F. J. 1975. '*Olympian* 1.8–11: An Epinician Metaphor.' *HSPh* 79: 55–68.

Ober, J. 1989. *Mass and Elite in Democratic Athens: Rhetoric, Ideology, and the Power of the People*. Princeton.

Page, D. L. 1970. 'Fragments of Greek Lyrical Poetry: *P.Oxy.* 2637.' *PCPhS* n.s. 16: 91–96.

Rausa, F. 1994. *L'immagine del vincitore: L'atleta nella statuaria greca dall' età arcaica all' ellenismo*. Rome.

Rawles, R. 2012. 'Early Epinician: Ibycus and Simonides.' In Agócs, Carey, and Rawles. 3–27.

Robert, L. 1967. 'Sur des inscriptions d'Éphèse.' *RPh* 3rd s. 41: 7–84.

Robinson, E. W. 1997. *The First Democracies: Early Popular Government outside Athens*. Stuttgart.

Rose, P. W. 1992. *Sons of the Gods, Children of Earth: Ideology and Literary Form in Ancient Greece*. Ithaca, NY.

Smith, R. R. R. 2007. 'Pindar, Athletes, and the Early Greek Statue Habit.' In Hornblower and Morgan. 83–139.

Stewart, A. F. 1986. 'When is a Kouros not an Apollo? The Tenea "Apollo" Revisited.' In *Corinthiaca: Studies in Honor of Darrell A. Amyx.* 54–70. M. del Chiaro and W. Biers, eds. Columbia.

Thomas, R. 2007. 'Fame, Memorial, and Choral Poetry: The Origins of Epinikian Poetry—an Historical Study.' In Hornblower and Morgan. 141–166.

Wilson, P. 2000. *The Athenian Institution of the Khoregia: The Chorus, the City and the Stage.* Cambridge.

Young, D. C. 1968. *Three Odes of Pindar: A Literary Study of Pythian 11, Pythian 3, and Olympian 7.* Leiden.

CHAPTER 24

THEMATIC TEXTS
Ovid, Martial, Tertullian

KATHRYN CHEW

THE early imperial period was the age of spectacle. By this time, not only had theatres and amphitheatres become permanent structures in Rome and in other major cities, but the control over the spectacles themselves had also passed into the hands of the emperor. In this chapter we will examine both spectacles and the concept of spectacle in the writings of three authors whose works span this period: Ovid (Publius Ovidius Naso, 43 BCE–17 CE), Martial (Marcus Valerius Martialis, *c.*40–104 CE), and Tertullian (Quintus Septimius Florens Tertullianus, *c.*160–240 CE). The analysis will cover aspects both synchronic, comparing the authors' attitudes toward spectacle, and diachronic, studying the three authors within their social and political contexts. The result of this examination will be an understanding of spectacle not only as a tool of imperial power but also as a device that any group with something worth seeing to display can appropriate.

We will distinguish between spectacles, meaning the games and shows at the theatre and amphitheatre, and spectacle, the use of visually stimulating media or description. Actual public performances, then, are spectacles, and spectacle is the idea of public display.

THE AUTHORS: OVID, MARTIAL, AND TERTULLIAN

It is rare to find literary treatments that embrace these three authors together, but they make a provocative group because of the similar thread that runs through their writings.

Ovid grew up under Augustus and witnessed the elevation of imperial spectacle to social and political importance. In his *Ars Amatoria* (*The Art of Love*), a treatise that counsels both men and women on how to seduce the opposite sex, Ovid recommends the theatre and the games as fertile hunting grounds for amorous encounters: *spectatum veniunt, veniunt spectentur ut ipsae* 'women come to be spectators, they come to be inspected themselves' (1.99; all translations are the author's). Ovid's enthusiasm for spectacle imbues his most famous work, *Metamorphoses*, stories of mortals' encounters with gods that prove to be life- and form-changing (Solodow 2002; Segal 1998). Ovid describes these episodes in detail, such as Actaeon's unfortunate transformation by Diana into a deer, to be torn apart by his dogs, transforming them from private experiences into spectacular events.

Martial, author of books of epigrams satirizing contemporary Roman life, dedicates his first extant book, *Liber Spectaculorum* (*Book of Spectacles*), to the shows celebrating the games inaugurating the Flavian amphitheatre, the Colosseum, given by Emperor Titus. Martial celebrates the power of spectacle even as he mocks its degradation of the divine:

> *Iunctam Pasiphaen Dictaeo credite tauro:*
> *vidimus, accepit fabula prisca fidem.*
> *Nec se miretur, Caesar, longaeva vetustas:*
> *quidquid fama canit, praestat harena tibi.* (*Book of Spectacles* 5)

> Believe that Pasiphae mated with the Cretan bull:
> we've seen it, the old story has earned belief.
> Don't let hoary antiquity boast, Caesar:
> whatever fame sings of, the arena shows you.

Tertullian, the first Latin Church Father and an early Christian apologist, wrote his treatise *On the Spectacles* (*de Spectaculis*) as a warning to Christians to avoid attendance at the spectacles at the cost of their souls, for the spectacles are sheer idolatry:

> *dubitas illo enim momento, quo diabolus in ecclesia furit, omnes angelos prospicere de caelo et singulos denotare, quis blasphemiam dixerit, quis audierit, quis linguam, quis aures diabolo adversus deum ministraverit?* (*On the Spectacles* 27.3)

> For do you doubt at that moment at which the devil rages about the assembly that all the angels look down from heaven and mark down each person, who spoke blasphemy, who listened to it, who lent his tongue, who lent his ears to the devil against God?

These writers' attitudes toward the spectacles and the idea of spectacle are as varied as their social positions within the Roman empire. Hailing from a town in northern Italy, Ovid abandoned a political career in favour of writing poetry. Success came quickly and Ovid adored the life and culture of Rome, which made his exile to Tomis on the Black Sea in 8 CE all the more painful, a move that seems to have ended his work on *Metamorphoses* (Oliensis 2004; Gibson 1999). The *carmen* (poem)—perhaps *The Art of Love?*—*et error* (and mistake) to which he attributes his misfortune have been the cause of much speculation (see e.g. McGowan 2009). Martial, a Spaniard by origin, wears his outsider status like a badge of honour. A late-blooming poet, he published *Book of Spectacles* after his fortieth year (Coleman 2006; Fitzgerald 2007); his subsequent books of epigrams, though humorous and witty, are tinged with bitterness, perhaps for his underappreciated genius, perhaps for the elusive spectre of success. Although he received many imperial favours, Martial struggled financially while in Rome, living in poverty for much of the time and relying on his patrons for subsistence. Unlike Ovid, Martial was not enamoured of city life and yearned to return to his ancestral home, a dream that would become a disappointment. Tertullian was born and appears to have spent his life in Carthage, in the Roman province of Africa. Little can be surmised about his life from his writings, beyond his classical and legal education. The first major Latin Christian author, Tertullian wrote extensively on theological, dogmatic, and apologetic topics, staying on the right side of orthodoxy until his conversion at around forty years of age to the Christian sect of Montanism, a Pentecostal movement professing that both men and, amazingly, women could be inspired by the Holy Spirit (Barnes 1985). Tertullian may never have visited Rome, but he was very conscious of living in the shadow of the empire.

THE POWER OF THE VISUAL

From the dedication of Pompey's permanent theatre in Rome in 55 BCE, it became clear that the power of the visual had gained a stronghold in Roman culture. More than any other means, visual display could impress more people in less time.

The powerful in Rome had always been aware of this. Before the imperial era, public spectacle was carefully controlled. Theatres were temporary structures, made of wood so that they could be put up and taken down, to discourage mobbing (see e.g. Kyle 2007, Beacham 1999; Welch 2007; Humphrey 1986). During the republican period, only the senate could grant triumphal processions, in which the victorious general would be given near-divine rights for a day and would parade down the main streets of Rome with his unarmed soldiers, the senators and magistrates, carts full of the spoils of war, the enemy leaders, and white bulls for sacrifice. Part of this procession involved dedicating a wreath to Jupiter, the triumphator's acknowledgement that he was surrendering his power and would not seek kingship. Many sumptuary laws passed during the republican period constrained even lesser displays. For instance, the *lex Oppia* in 215 BCE restricted for years the amount of jewellery and colourful clothing that women could wear and banned carriage-riding aside from religious transport. Other laws limited the amount of money that could be spent on entertainments, such as at weddings. This enforced modesty of appearance was a means of preventing an individual from gaining notoriety and power. In the last decades of the republic as oligarchic coups weakened the state, spectacle became a tool of political power (Potter and Mattingly 2010; Köhne, Ewigleben, and Jackson 2000; Futrell 1997). With the imperial age, the emperor used spectacle to aggrandize himself through the shows that he provided to the populace at large (Wiedemann 1995). The triumphal procession as well ironically became the privilege solely of the imperial family.

Fascination with the power of spectacle also characterizes the literature of this period and informs most of the major writings from this time, such as those of the historian Livy (59 BCE–17 CE), the epic poet Lucan (39-65 CE), the historian Tacitus (55–117 CE), the satiric poet Juvenal (*c*.55 CE–*c*.140 CE), and the historian Suetonius (*c*.69–130 CE), as well as those of Ovid, Martial, and Tertullian, who were chosen for closer analysis in this chapter not only because of the overt connections to the spectacles in their works, but also because their dates nicely frame discussion of spectacle during the Principate (27 BCE–312 CE), and their social positions present a variety of perspectives (König 2008; Slater 1996).

Recent monographs examine the power and use of spectacle in the works of single authors from the early imperial period. For instance, Feldherr argues that Livy adopts the language of public spectacle to give authority to his history, depicting crucial actions in the form of public spectacles, as if eyewitnessing begets validation (Feldherr 1998: 223). Leigh explores the power of spectacle over the spectator, positing that in Lucan's *On the Civil War* spectacle is 'the narcotic through which dissent is lulled into forgetfulness' (Leigh 1997: 306; see also Henderson 1987). Santoro L'Hoir argues that Tacitus' use of words like *spectaculum* connotes deception in Tiberius' reign (2006: 98–99), and that the Stoic outlook of Seneca, wherein humans are as performers in the universe's *spectaculum*, informs Tacitus' portrayal of the Julio-Claudians, their appropriation of spectacle, and the Great Fire of Nero (2006: 204–220). These works both acknowledge the sway of spectacle over the common person and hold spectacle as the tool of the emperor or person in command to wield over his subjects.

SPECTACLES AND SPECTACLE IN OVID

From the very beginning of *The Art of Love* Ovid emphasizes the importance of seeing and sight for his disciple of love:

> *Haec tibi non tenues veniet delapsa per auras:*
> *Quaerenda est oculis apta puella tuis.* (*The Art of Love* 1.43–44)

> This girl will not fall through thin air into your lap:
> your eyes must seek out a fitting femme.

Ovid introduces a hunting metaphor, which he wittily extends both to love as the object of the hunt and to the theatre as not only a place for conducting an amorous conquest but also where actual hunting games are performed (*The Art of Love* 1.89–134). All spectacular venues in Rome make suitable hunting grounds for lovers—the Circus, the forum, triumphal processions, as well as other public areas, such as colonnades, temples, synagogues, and beach resorts (Henderson 2002; Johnson and Malamud 1988). Rome's beauties of all ages are offered as spectacles for lovers of all tastes:

> *Quot caelum stellas, tot habet tua Roma puellas:*
> *Mater in Aeneae constitit urbe sui.*
> *Seu caperis primis et adhuc crescentibus annis,*
> *Ante oculos veniet vera puella tuos:*
> *Sive cupis iuvenem ...* (*The Art of Love* 1.59–63)

> However many stars has the sky, your Rome has girls:
> mother Venus stands in the city of her own Aeneas.
> If you are taken by the very young and still blossoming in years,
> before your eyes the exact girl will appear,
> or if you want an adolescent ...

Ovid also likens love to an athletic contest, and again employs the metaphor doubly, as viewing such contests as opportunities to court love and in turn be vanquished by love:

> *Saucius ingemuit telumque volatile sensit,*
> *Et pars spectati muneris ipse fuit.* (*The Art of Love* 1.169–170)

> He felt the weapon fly and bellowed at his wound,
> and became himself a part of the show he was watching.

Further examples are legion. Ovid also encourages women to make displays of themselves, in the hopes of attracting a man:

> *Utilis est vobis, formosae, turba, puellae.*
> *Saepe vagos ultra limina ferte pedes.*
> *Ad multas lupa tendit oves, praedetur ut unam,*
> *Et Iovis in multas devolat ales aves.*
> *Se quoque det populo mulier speciosa videndam:*
> *Quem trahat, e multis forsitan unus erit.* (*The Art of Love* 3.417–422)

> Crowded places are useful for you, pretty girls.
> Let your steps wander often out of the house.
> The wolf attacks many sheep so that it will seize just one,
> and Jupiter's eagle dives into the midst of many birds.
> So too let a woman worth seeing give herself to the public for viewing.
> Perhaps there will be one out of the whole crowd whom she attracts.

Once again, irony haunts his hunting metaphor, as the distinctions between hunter and prey are blurred: by making a [passive] spectacle of herself, does a woman control the situation or surrender her will? Or is Ovid deceitfully encouraging women to join the parade of Rome's beauties that he extols to the male hunter above (*The Art of Love* 1.59–63)?

This begs the obvious question: who wields the control in spectacles, the viewer or the viewed? Ovid artfully seems to argue both ways, that the viewer holds the advantage of directing his gaze, and the viewed can manipulate the gaze of her viewers. Erotic behaviour is clearly gendered in Ovid; men actively do the choosing, women passively attract. There is power in attracting, but it cannot be directed, or at least Ovid does not assert that it can.

In *Metamorphoses* there is less ambiguity about the power of sight and spectacle. With rare exception (for instance, Narcissus, who is both viewer and viewed), the viewer maintains the advantage of power and control over the viewed. A few examples will suffice. Ovid presents a range of viewers: Mercury surveying a group of maidens (2.710), Apollo seeing Leucothea from his heavenly vantage (4.196), Perseus watching the sea monster approach Andromeda (5.22), Cephalus watching the spectacle of the hunt (7.780), the spectators' seats resounding with applause for Hippomenes (10.668), and Nestor's great age making him the spectator of great things (12.187). He also depicts those being viewed: Actaeon becoming a spectacle for his friends (3.246), Pentheus spotted by the Bacchants (3.709), Niobe conspicuous in her purple (6.166), and Cyparissus seen as a tree (10.140).

SPECTACLES AND SPECTACLE IN MARTIAL

According to Martial, spectacles are more powerful than traditional mythology (*Book of Spectacles* 5, 8), and the home of the spectacles, the Colosseum, is the greatest wonder of the world (*Book of Spectacles* 1). Lack of interest in the spectacles is a sign of barbarity:

> *Quae tam seposita est, quae gens tam barbara, Caesar,*
> *ex qua spectator non sit in urbe tua?* (*Book of Spectacles* 3.1–2)

> What race is so remote or so barbarous, Caesar,
> that its spectator does not sit in your city?

Martial repeatedly proclaims that the spectacles surpass stories from mythology or tradition. For instance, Carpophorus, a celebrated *bestiarius* or hunter of wild beasts, outdoes the labours of Hercules and Meleager in a single show (*Book of Spectacles* 15; also 27). In the *Book of Spectacles* 7, a mime about a condemned criminal from the time of Caligula finds its real-life representation in the combination of crucifixion and offering to the wild beasts of an actual petty thief. After comparing this convict to Prometheus, Martial closes the poem:

> *Vicerat antiquae sceleratus crimina famae,*
> *in quo, quae fuerat fabula, poena fuit.* (*Book of Spectacles* 7.11–12)

The wicked man had topped the crimes of ancient lore,
for whom that which had before been a play became his punishment.

This convict, Martial claims, has outdone not only a tale of recent mint, but also one of the foundational Greek myths. The irony here lies in the parallel between Prometheus' life, in which he is punished for benefiting humans to the detriment of the gods, and the convict's death, which provides delightful entertainment for humans even as it degrades the divine.

Martial continues his subtle assault on traditional myth, and by extension on the imperial regime that seeks self-glorification, with several references to myths that have been 'proven' by the spectacles of the arena. In each case, the assertion is highly ironic for its juxtaposition of the epic and the banal: the birth of Bacchus is validated by the sight of piglets tumbling forth from the slashed belly of a wild sow (*Book of Spectacles* 12.7–8), the power of the goddesses Lucina and Diana is likewise confirmed by a similarly dying sow (*Book of Spectacles* 13.4–6), as is the mating of Pasiphae with the bull in the quotation above (*Book of Spectacles* 5). The power of the spectacles, Martial implies, is creating a new kind of mythology, one not told or read about, but one that can be seen.

The *Book of Spectacles* culminates with the praise of Caesar as the architect of these transformations, who has designed the shows to exceed the accomplishments of Jupiter, the king of the gods (*Book of Spectacles* 16, 20), and, indeed, to surpass all of history itself: *haec tantum res est facta* **par' historian** 'this thing alone was done beyond the bounds of history' (*Book of Spectacles* 21.8). Martial's final proof of Caesar's divinity, however, is tinged with the irony discussed above, that is highlighted by the contrast in register: the animals in the shows bow to the emperor:

Quod pius et supplex elephas te, Caesar, adorat
hic modo qui tauro tam metuendus erat,
non facit hoc iussus, nulloque docente magistro,
crede mihi, nostrum sentit et ille deum. (*Book of Spectacles* 17)

How the elephant adores you, Caesar, as devoted suppliant,
that just now was an object of fear for the bull.
He does this unbidden, under the direction of no teacher,
believe me, even he senses the presence of our god.

and also:

Numen habet Caesar: sacra est haec, sacra potestas,
credite: mentiri non didicere ferae. (*Book of Spectacles* 30.7–8)

Caesar has divinity: believe that his power
is sacred: the beasts have not been taught to lie.

SPECTACLES AND SPECTACLE IN TERTULLLIAN

Tertullian operates upon quite different assumptions from Ovid and Martial. Sight and seeing, in his view, god gives to people to employ in his service: *Neque enim oculos ad concupiscentiam sumpsimus* 'for we have not received eyes for lust' (*On the Spectacles* 2.10) and:

si ergo gulam et ventrem ab inquinamentis liberamus, quanto magis augustiora nostra, et aures et oculos, ab idolothytis et necrothytis voluptatibus abstinemus, quae non intestinis transiguntur, sed in ipso spiritu et anima digeruntur, quorum munditia magis ad deum pertinet quam intestinorum (On the Spectacles 13.5)

If therefore we keep our gullet and belly free of defilement, how much more should we protect our nobler parts, our ears and eyes, and abstain from the pleasures of sacrificing to idols or to the dead, which pleasures pass not into our intestines but are borne in our very spirit and soul, whose cleanness is more important for God than that of our intestines.

It is clear that Tertullian has read his Ovid, for he condemns spectators thus: *nemo denique in spectaculo ineundo prius cogitat nisi videri et videre* 'no one in the end thinks of anything in going to a spectacle except being seen and seeing' (*On the Spectacles* 25.3). Tertullian does not emphasize spectacular venues as lusty locales, but he acknowledges this potential (*On the Spectacles* 10.6–8). What is particularly corrupting about seeing spectacles, he reiterates, is the pleasures (*voluptates*) they bring the viewers. Demonizing pleasure has pre-Christian roots: compare the moralizing tale of the 'Choice of Herakles' in Prodicus and Xenophon, poetically transformed by Silius Italicus into Scipio Africanus' choice between Virtue (*Virtus*) and Vice (*Voluptas*), where vice is synonymous with pleasure (*Punic War* 15.20–30). Tertullian argues for the connection between lust and spectacles:

nam sicut pecuniae vel dignitatis vel gulae vel libidinis vel gloriae, ita et voluptatis concupiscentia est; species autem voluptatis etiam spectacula. opinor, generaliter nominatae concupiscentiae continent in se et voluptates, aeque generaliter intellectae voluptates specialiter et in spectacula disseruntur. (On the Spectacles 14.2–3)

For just as there is lust for money or position or gluttony or sex or glory, there is also a lust for pleasure. Yet the spectacles are also a type of pleasure. Lusts named as a class, I think, also include pleasures, similarly too pleasures understood as a class are analysed by type into spectacles.

Attendance at spectacles abuses God's gifts of the senses and nature, we learn from Tertullian, because such activities presume upon God's right to be the principal viewer in the universe and the master of all spectacle, for at the end of the world God will bring about the most amazing spectacles, not the least of which will be the conflagration of this world, and all those who have disobeyed him will be liquefied in fire (*On the Spectacles* 30).

utinam autem deus nulla flagitia hominum spectaret, ut omnes iudicium evaderemus. sed spectat et latrocinia, spectat et falsa et adulteria et fraudes et idolatrias et spectacula ipsa. et idcirco ergo nos non spectabimus, ne videamur ab illo, qui spectat omnia. comparas, homo, reum et iudicem, reum, qui, quia videtur, reus est, iudicem, qui, quia videt, iudex est. (On the Spectacles 20.3–4)

Would that God looked at no sins of humans, so that we all might escape judgement. But he does look upon robbery, and he does look upon lies and adulteries and fraud and idolatry and the spectacles themselves. And for that reason we will not therefore look upon them, lest he who sees all see us. Are you putting defendant and judge on the same level, man? The defendant, because he is seen, is the defendant; the judge, because he sees, is the judge.

What seems to bother Tertullian is when sight is taken for an end in itself, rather than as a means to serve God. It is God's privilege to be the ultimate viewer and all people's place to be in his purview, to be objects of his and his angels' viewing and ultimately objects of his judgement, as the quote above from *On the Spectacles* makes clear.

Thus we can surmise why Tertullian would abhor Ovid's and Martial's attitudes towards spectacle. Ovid's blurring of boundaries between viewer and viewed is like 'putting defendant and judge on the same level', and anyone who presumes upon God's right as principal viewer, as is rampant throughout *Metamorphoses*, 'uses his eyes for lust'. Martial's dubious praise of the emperor for reducing lofty mythology to the level of humans through the spectacles would be yet another example of 'putting defendant and judge on the same level'. To believe a myth because one has seen it performed in the amphitheatre is an outright perversion of scripture, in which Jesus praises those who believe without seeing (John 20:29). Tertullian is ever on the watch for such perversions of nature, because they must be the work of the devil, that *aemulator dei* who perverts creation.

This is the foundation of Tertullian's lengthy proof in *On the Spectacles* that every aspect of the spectacles derives from worship of pagan gods or ancient hero cult, and thus any Christian not wanting to pollute his body must shun the spectacles. An adroit apologist, though sometimes his logic defies reason, Tertullian addresses theoretical objections, from the argument that creation is good and thus each element of spectacles—horses, lions, strength of body, and such—should necessarily be good (*On the Spectacles* 2), to the argument that using eyes and ears, which are God's gifts, cannot be evil (*On the Spectacles* 17), to the argument that abstention is not scriptural (*On the Spectacles* 20). For those who find breaking the habit of attending spectacles difficult, Tertullian offers Christian equivalents: for the Circus, the race of time toward the end and the great conflagration; for the theatre, Christian books, poems, and songs that offer not fable, but truth, not artifice, but simplicity; for the spectacles of the amphitheatre, the moral contests of Christians, impurity overthrown by chastity, perfidy slain by faith, cruelty crushed by pity; for those with a taste for blood, the blood of Christ (*On the Spectacles* 29).

Spectacles and Spectacle in Early Imperial Literature

As mentioned above, much recent scholarship has focused on the spectacles as the tool of the emperor to control and subjugate the masses through entertainment. This, of course, was the opinion of Juvenal:

> *nam qui dabat olim*
> *imperium, fasces, legiones, omnia, nunc se*
> *continet atque duas tantum res anxius optat,*
> *panem et circenses. (Satires 10.78–81)*

> for [the people], who used to grant
> the right to rule, the symbols of power, legions, all that, now
> hold themselves back and anxiously desire only two things,
> bread and circuses.

Complementarily, other scholars have examined how the institution of the games was used to co-opt the masses by giving them the illusion of power through their participation in this conspicuous consumption (Hammer 2010; Plass 1995; Keane 2003). Ovid hints at this reading in his ambivalence about the relative power of the viewer and the viewed. The word *spectaculum* also contains this duality in its very definitions: it can refer either to the sight or show itself, or to the view from the spectators' seats. This implies that there is a reciprocal relationship between seeing and being seen, that one cannot happen without the other. In this case, the viewed could potentially have as much, or as little, power as the viewer. Consider, for instance, the spectators, who are viewing the spectacles that the emperor has arranged for them. Their objectivity, in being the recipients of Caesar's powerful display, is countered by their subjectivity, in commenting upon and judging not only the performance but also the director of the performance, Caesar himself (Bartsch 1994).

Dean Hammer likens the games to modern reality television: viewers see a microcosm of the world, within which people live epic fantasies (Hammer 2010: 66). As the emperors' tastes create an increasing demand for more outrageous spectacles, the line between reality and fiction gets blurred. According to Martial, by breaking the boundaries of nature, the emperor undermines his own authority. If one can watch the birth of a god onstage, then what prevents any person from becoming divine? It is this easy familiarity with power, prestige, privilege, and authority that deludes viewers into thinking that they actually participate in that which they observe and that the spectacles they observe have any relation to reality as it must be lived outside of the amphitheatre. The actual power of the people had become wholly symbolic long before the imperial age (Mouritsen 2001: 14–15; Barton 1993).

If the emperor loses any prestige or authority for his presentation of the games, it must be *apparent* prestige or authority. Though spectators are allowed access to a privilege, they can in no way influence or direct that programme; they are at the mercy and whim of the emperor's taste. Clearly, passive participation in spectation in no way compares with active control of human vicissitudes, hence the association of this pattern of behaviour by modern spectacologists with imperialistic and colonial domination (Baudrillard 1995; Benjamin 1999).

There are many avenues open for further scholarly exploration. Much more critical work can be done examining individual writers' ambivalent attitudes toward spectacle. Occupying a position outside the conventional political schema of emperor versus people, writers can be revealing for how they assert themselves as masters of their own literary spectacles as well as how they critique the accrual of power through spectacle. Another fruitful area of investigation is the idea of competition, the *raison-d'être* of sport and spectacle, and how the many levels of competition—among and between contestants, spectators, genders, emperor, writer—interact and reveal assumptions about the nature of power. By engaging this topic, writers also compete with the visual and thus become appropriators of spectacle.

The emperor's control over spectacle is eventually appropriated, albeit literarily, in the stories of the early Christian martyrs who conquer the engines of torture in the spectacles and triumph over their persecutors. These martyrs are made to co-opt imperial power, as shown by the mockery or destruction of the presiding official, the conversions of observers to Christianity that occur at the end of the accounts, and the reception of the martyr in heaven, where, as Tertullian pronounces, all spectacles are given final judgement. The Christian usurpation of Roman power could only have been achieved in the age of spectacle (Bowersock 1995).

Through spectacle the Roman Empire achieved its own legacy to rival that of the Greeks. To the extent that Greek writers are in dialogue with Homer, so too must imperial writers gauge their own work in relation to spectacle.

References

Barnes, T. D. 1985. *Tertullian: A Historical and Literary Study*. Oxford.

Barton, C. A. 1993. *The Sorrows of the Ancient Romans: The Gladiator and the Monster*. Princeton.

Bartsch, S. 1994. *Actors in the Audience: Theatricality and Doublespeak from Nero to Hadrian*. Cambridge, MA.

Baudrillard, J. 1995. *Simulacra and Simulation*. Ann Arbor.

Beacham, R. C. 1999. *Power into Pageantry: Spectacle Entertainments of Early Imperial Rome*. New Haven.

Benjamin, W. 1999. 'The Work of Art in the Age of Mechanical Reproduction.' In *Illuminations*. 217–252. H. Arendt, ed. Schocken.

Bowersock, G. W. 1995. *Martyrdom and Rome*. Cambridge.

Coleman, K. M. 2006. *M. Valerii Martialis Liber Spectaculorum*. Oxford.

Feldherr, A. 1998. *Spectacle and Society in Livy's History*. Berkeley.

Fitzgerald, W. 2007. *Martial: The World of the Epigram*. Chicago.

Futrell, A. 1997. *Blood in the Arena: The Spectacle of Roman Power*. Austin.

Gibson, B. 1999. 'Ovid on Reading: Reading Ovid. Reception in Ovid *Tristia 2*.' *JRS* 89: 19–37.

Hammer, D. 2010. 'Roman Spectacle Entertainments and the Technology of Reality.' *Arethusa* 43: 63–86.

Henderson, J. 1987. 'Lucan/The Word at War.' *Ramus* 16: 122–164.

Henderson, J. 2002. 'A Doo-Dah-Doo-Dah-Dey at the Races: Ovid *Amores* 3.2 and the Personal Politics of the Circus Maximus.' *CA* 21: 41–65.

Humphrey, J. H. 1986. *Roman Circuses: Arenas for Chariot Racing*. Berkeley.

Johnson, P. and M. Malamud. 1988. 'Ovid's *Musomachia*.' *Pacific Coast Philology* 23: 30–38.

Keane, C. 2003. 'Theatre, Spectacle, and the Satirist in Juvenal.' *Phoenix* 57: 257–275.

Köhne, E., C. Ewigleben, and R. Jackson. 2000. *Gladiators and Caesars: the Power of Spectacle in Ancient Rome*. Berkeley.

König, J. 2008. *Athletics and Literature in the Roman Empire*. Cambridge.

Kyle, D. G. 2007. *Sport and Spectacle in the Ancient World*. Malden, MA.

Leigh, M. 1997. *Lucan: Spectacle and Engagement*. Oxford.

McGowan, M. M. 2009. *Ovid in Exile: Power and Poetic Redress in the Tristia and Epistulae ex Ponto*. Leiden.

Mouritsen, H. 2001. *Plebs and Politics in the Late Roman Republic*. Cambridge.

Oliensis, E. 2004. 'The Power of Image-Makers: Representation and Revenge in *Metamorphoses* 6 and *Tristia* 4.' *CA* 23: 285–321.

Plass, P. 1995. *The Game of Death in Ancient Rome: Arena Sport and Political Suicide*. Madison.

Potter, D. S. and D. J. Mattingly. 2010. *Life, Death, and Entertainment in the Roman Empire*. Ann Arbor.

Santoro L'Hoir, F. 2006. *Tragedy, Rhetoric, and the Historiography of Tacitus' Annales*. Ann Arbor.

Segal, C. 1998. 'Ovid's Metamorphic Bodies: Art, Gender, and Violence in the *Metamorphoses*.' *Arion* 5: 9–41.

Slater, W. J. 1996. *Roman Theatre and Society*. Ann Arbor.

Solodow, J. B. 2002. *The World of Ovid's Metamorphoses*. Chapel Hill.

Welch, K. 2007. *The Roman Amphitheatre: From its Origins to the Colosseum*. Cambridge.

Wiedemann, T. 1995. *Emperors and Gladiators*. London.

....

CHAPTER 25

CONTESTS IN CONTEXT
Gladiatorial Inscriptions and Graffiti

....

ANNE HRYCHUK KONTOKOSTA

KNOWLEDGE of Roman gladiators comes from a variety of ancient evidence. Perhaps most influential for popular conceptions of *munera* (gladiatorial shows) are the remains of evocative spectacle buildings, such as the Flavian Amphitheatre, and the accounts of Roman authors. While informative, ancient literary sources often focus on either the experiences of spectators or the intellectual responses of elite Romans to these events. Literary texts rarely address the viewpoints of the gladiators themselves, which are more difficult to ascertain. In many cases, inscriptions, particularly those that can be analysed within the context of their original monuments, best illuminate the daily lives of Roman gladiators and the organization of the *munera* in which they participated.

Despite some regional differences in scale, rate, and production, the vast majority of surviving inscriptions in the Roman world come from the imperial period, peaking in the late second and early third centuries CE (MacMullen 1982). This timeframe corresponds to the bulk of evidence for inscribed gladiatorial monuments set up in Italy and throughout the provinces. A variety of these inscribed texts, including examples on public and private monuments as well as commissions by both elite Romans and gladiators themselves, are analysed here to offer an overview of the multivariate ways gladiators and their sponsors were memorialized. A study of this evidence provides new perspectives that augment our understanding of Roman gladiators, ranging from the personal life experiences and values of individual gladiators to the official, empire-wide organization of their competitions.

IMPERIAL LETTERS AND DECREES

....

Inscriptions recording official imperial views on matters directly related to the workings of Roman *munera* are not very common. However, two second-century examples that do exist offer insight into the costs and benefits of staging gladiatorial games. These represent a very public type of gladiatorial inscription and one that is concerned exclusively with elite members of Roman society who had the requisite political connections and sufficient financial means to sponsor the games.

In 1994, excavations at Aphrodisias in Caria uncovered a large, marble inscription, originally displayed on a wall, but found reused on a street leading from the city's basilica to its Hadrianic bath complex (Chaniotis 2005: 58–59; Reynolds 2000). The inscription recorded at least four letters that the emperor Hadrian had sent to the magistrates, city council, and people of Aphrodisias. One of these letters, dated to 125 CE on the basis of the emperor's titles, discusses the reluctance of local priests to contribute cash to pay for the construction of an aqueduct in place of putting on a *munus*, a duty traditionally associated with priests of the Imperial Cult (Price 1984; Robert 1940). For the priests, gladiatorial shows offered widespread popularity as well as the freedom to determine how—and how much of—their money was spent on the games. A contribution to the city's new aqueduct, on the other hand, would have been a fixed and presumably onerous cost, given the complaints to which the emperor was responding. A particularly interesting feature of this inscription is the personal involvement of the emperor in the *munera* of a free city. The fact that Aphrodisias even referred this matter to the emperor underscores the scale of the local controversy that such a proposal engendered (Coleman 2008 has an alternate reading of this inscription).

Two copies of another important imperial inscription also refer to the costs of presenting gladiatorial *munera* during the latter half of the second century CE (Carter 2003; Gómez-Pantoja 2009: 44–66). These inscriptions document an *oratio* of the co-emperors Marcus Aurelius and Lucius Commodus in 177 CE on reducing the rising costs of gladiatorial games throughout the Roman world and the *sententia prima* (first opinion) of an unidentified senator. The most complete version of the inscription was found on a large bronze panel in the city of Italica in Baetica. Although only part of the inscription is extant, it preserves almost sixty-three lines of text and offers insight into the contemporary logistics of presenting gladiatorial games. A second copy of the inscription, found at Sardis in the province of Asia, largely overlaps with the text from Italica, providing little new information regarding the specifics of the decree. The copy does, however, underscore that this was a topic of universal significance, given the wide circulation of the decree. Since the ancient name of the decree is not preserved, these inscriptions are known respectively as the *Aes Italicense* or *Senatus Consultum de Pretiis Gladiatorum Munuendis* (*CIL* 2.6278) and the *Marmor Sardianum* (*CIL* 3.7106).

The two inscriptions record that, in order to mitigate the growing economic burden on the high priests of the Imperial Cult, the senate should abandon imperial revenues collected on *munera* and institute price controls limiting the cost of obtaining gladiators. Under the new legislation, a calculation of the price of gladiators would be based on a combination of the overall cost and size of a *munus* and the quality of the gladiator. A pre-existing hierarchy of gladiators may have been used to determine the maximum price that a *lanista* (owner) could charge for the appearance of a gladiator. Within a gladiatorial troupe, fighters were organized and trained according to their armament type and then ranked according to their skill level or *palus* (originally the word for a post against which gladiators practised their sword blows). For a gladiator, a high *palus* ranking (first or second *palus*) was a source of pride (Robert 1940: 30). Not all gladiators achieved such status and epigraphical evidence attests to a large number of lower rankings, including a seventh *palus* at Ephesus and an eighth *palus* at Aphrodisias and Stratonikeia (Aydas 2006: 106; Roueché 1993: 65). While it is not clear from the *Aes Italicense* and *Marmor Sardianum* inscriptions that *palus* designations were being used to regulate the cost of gladiators (the specific term is not used), it is apparent that the emperors and senate assumed the existence of a standardized ranking system. By decreasing the price of gladiatorial spectacles, this legislation both promoted the presentation of *munera* and encouraged eligible men to run for office and hold priesthoods by reducing the economic burden of the positions. The direct involvement of Marcus Aurelius and Commodus in this issue underscores the popularity of gladiatorial shows and their importance to the Imperial Cult and municipalities throughout the empire.

FAMILIA MONUMENTS

Ancient authors such as Suetonius, Dio Cassius, and Martial famously document lavish gladiatorial spectacles sponsored by the emperor in Rome. Comparatively less is known about the local magistrates and priests who played a critical role as patrons of smaller-scale games throughout the provinces (Ville 1981: 211–213). In the Greek East, high priests of the Imperial Cult owned *familiae* (troupes) of gladiators that performed in annual spectacles associated with the cult. Frequently, these men were commemorated with a specific type of inscribed *stelae* that acted as the centrepiece of larger gladiatorial monuments.

Stelae with inscriptions celebrating *familiae* and their patrons have been widely recorded throughout the Greek East, including at Amisos, Aphrodisias, Cyzicus, Ephesus, Hierapolis, Kos, Miletos, and Phrygia (Ritti and Yilmaz 1998: 448–453; Robert 1940: 55–58). The extant examples are epigraphically similar, following a formula that identifies the monument as a memorial to a *familia*, enumerates the various members of the troupe (this might include gladiators, *venatores*, convicts, and bull-catchers, among others), and identifies the owner as a high priest. The lack of parallels from the Roman West suggests that this type of gladiatorial monument was a product of distinct traditions that developed around the Imperial Cult in Asia Minor. Although usually less chronologically secure than inscriptions recording imperial missives or decrees, in many cases *familia* monuments can be dated by their association with specific high priests who, as local elites, left an epigraphical record as patrons of other buildings and monuments throughout their respective cities (Roueché 1993: 63–64).

The function of *familia* inscriptions is a topic of debate, in part because the original contexts of many of the *stelae* are unknown. Since the language chosen for these inscriptions was clearly distinct from that typically used for an epitaph, Louis Robert argued that a *familia* monument would have been erected in a city to commemorate a particular *munus* and its patron, the high priest (Robert 1940: 55–58). Archaeological evidence from the North Necropolis at Hierapolis, however, suggests that this type of monument, if not an actual tombstone, could also be set up within elite funerary contexts. There, a *familia* inscription was found with a series of gladiatorial panel reliefs that had been incorporated into a low wall surrounding the tomb complex of an imperial high priest, the reliefs providing a visual counterpart to the inscribed commemoration (Ritti and Yilmaz 1998: 448–453).

Inscribed altar or panel-shaped *stelae* decorated with reliefs are another common type of gladiatorial monument. Often found in groups that are uniform in style and dimension, they sometimes functioned as a parapet wall (altar-shaped) or were affixed as wall decoration (panel-shaped). The standard iconography usually includes a relief of a single gladiator (altar-shaped) or combat scenes with multiple figures (panel-shaped). While the associated inscriptions can vary, they are often short and simple. The most basic type includes only the name, or in many cases the stage-name, of the gladiator written in large letters and using the nominative case, pointing to a non-funerary function for these *stelae* as the nominative was not used for epitaphs in this period (Fig. 25.1) (Kurtz and Boardman 1971: 260).

A slightly more complex epigraphic formula that is frequently found on altar and panel-shaped *stelae* references the depicted gladiator not only by name, but also by his *palus*. The formula is as follows: the name of a gladiator listed in the nominative with the number of his

FIGURE 25.1. Altar-shaped *stela* from Aphrodisias depicting a *murmillo* named Εὐρώτας, his stage name taken from a powerful river near Sparta, a city known for the prowess of its soldiers. Photo courtesy of the Aphrodisias Project.

palus followed by the preposition υπο ('by') and the name of a second gladiator in the genitive with the number of his *palus*. Together, the inscriptions and their reliefs can be understood as a monument to a victorious gladiator (depicted on the relief and named second) that celebrated a defeat over a particular foe (named first), for example 'Gladiator Y [defeated by] Gladiator X' (Roueché 1993: 65). Archaeologically attested groups of such *stelae* at Cibyra and Aphrodisias suggest that both altar and panel-shaped *stelae* were used to decorate larger gladiatorial monuments, including the grand tombs dedicated to patrons of the cities' games (Berns and Ekinci 2015; Kontokosta 2008).

Gladiatorial monuments erected in the Greek East frequently use words transliterated from Latin to reference terms associated with the staging of *munera*. In addition to the common πάλος (*palus*), Greek inscriptions directly transliterate φαμιλία (*familia*), λούδος (*ludus*), fighting styles (σεκούτωρ for *secutor*, προβοκάτωρ for *provocator*, etc.), as well as stage names of many of the gladiators themselves; for example, Καίστιλλος took his name from *caestus*, the Latin term for 'boxing glove'. This dependency on Latin is striking in part because of the almost complete absence of Latin loanwords in Greek literature from the imperial period. Here, it underscores a recognition of the foreign nature of gladiators in the Greek East as well a certain level of universal renown that the gladiatorial profession must have assumed throughout the Roman world (Carter 2009).

Epitaphs

Epitaphs account for a large proportion of extant Roman inscriptions, perhaps as much as seventy per cent (Saller and Shaw 1984: 124); accordingly, tombstones inscribed with epitaphs memorializing gladiators constitute a rich source of information. These monuments offer a different, sometimes idealized viewpoint on gladiators from those commissioned by elite Romans, recording and commemorating the fighters as individuals and revealing personal information regarding their aspirations, accomplishments, affiliations, and identities. In-depth studies of gladiatorial epitaphs (Garcia y Bellido 1960; Hope 1998; Hope 2000) and collections of gladiatorial inscriptions, such as *Epigrafia anfiteatrale dell'occidente romano* (*EAOR*) and *Les gladiateurs dans l'Orient grec*, show that there was surprising consistency in the type of information included in epitaphs and the ways that gladiators were represented in death throughout the Roman world (*EAOR* Robert 1940). Nevertheless, we do see some regional variations in epigraphic formula and decoration. For example, allusions to the beauty of gladiators, the fame they brought their home city, comparisons with mythological figures, and even the occasional use of hexameter in epitaphs from the Greek East likely were rooted in long-established frameworks of Homeric ethics and Greek athletics (Carter 2009; Mann 2009).

Unfortunately, the preservation of gladiatorial tombstones is haphazard and uneven. At the carefully excavated site of Aphrodisias, for example, there is archaeological evidence for the presence of a large number of gladiators, frequent *munera*, and a thriving Imperial Cult, yet only two stone grave *stelae* have been discovered. This discrepancy may be explained by both the low social status of gladiators who were tainted by the legal stigma of *infamia* (*Digest of Justinian* 3.2) and the relatively high cost of stone tombstones. And while the very existence of gladiatorial tombstones suggests that some gladiators' corpses could be claimed and accorded funerary rites, it is likely that others were buried anonymously or in mass graves (Hopkins 1983: 207–211). Inexpensive and perishable materials that are not preserved in the archaeological record, such as wood or terracotta, may also have been regularly used as gladiatorial grave markers (Toynbee 1971: 101–103).

The greatest challenge to studying gladiatorial epitaphs is reconstructing their original contexts. In many cases, tombstones have been preserved only in secondary circumstances, reused as building blocks when Roman cemeteries were destroyed. There are only a few groups of *in situ* gladiatorial tombstones that have been scientifically excavated or studied in depth (Cambi 1987: 260; Hope 1998; Kanz and Grossschmidt 2005; 2009), but even this limited evidence suggests that gladiatorial burials were often segregated in cemeteries. The reason for the isolation of gladiatorial tombstones is not entirely clear. As members of a stigmatized profession and victims of violent death, it is possible that the interment of gladiators in regular cemeteries was officially or socially prohibited (Hopkins 1983: 23; Ville 1981: 462–463). Alternatively, gladiators, who were part of a tight-knit and collegial community while alive, may have chosen to be buried separately as an expression of group affiliation, possibly in land donated by the troupe leader or a generous patron (Hope 1998: 183–184; Wiedemann 1992:117–118).

Greg Woolf has attributed the inclusion of detailed information that clearly defined the deceased's identity on inscriptions, like epitaphs, to be a reaction to the 'expansion and complexification' of Roman society in the early imperial period; individuals felt the need to assert a place for themselves in a diverse and often difficult world (Woolf 1996: 29). Certainly, the corpus of extant gladiatorial tombstones includes many detailed epitaphs that share remarkable consistencies in the type and amount of information conveyed, including name, fighting style, age, and commemorator. Aside from his, or occasionally her, name, a gladiator's fighting style (such as *thraex*, *retiarius*, or *murmillo*) is the most important element of an epitaph. The emphasis placed on gladiatorial type suggests a sense of pride in distinctive combat skills, as well as a degree of personal identification. The importance of fighting styles confirms what we know about the communities fostered by the *palus* system, where gladiators of different types were trained separately by specialized *doctores* or trainers (Wiedemann 1992: 117).

The inclusion of the deceased's age in many epitaphs corroborates that gladiators, as expected, did not live into old age. While a few individuals seem to have survived the arena, retired, and lived into their forties (e.g. *CIL* 6.33983, 10177), most gladiators died in their twenties or thirties. In numerous cases, the recorded age at death is divisible by five, a feature characteristic of semi-literate cultures (Harris 1989: 271). In addition to documenting age, additional emphasis is often placed on the number of appearances and victories in the arena. This apparent interest in recording statistics might indicate that gladiatorial troupe leaders kept such records and were involved in commissioning the epitaphs (Hope 2000: 103). It is noteworthy that epitaphs listing the number of victories, appearances in *munera*, or providing details about a gladiator's demise do not always present a picture of the games as brutal events. In fact, evidence from epitaphs indicates that in the first century CE only ten per cent of gladiatorial duels ended in a death, although fatalities seem to have become much more common later in the imperial period (Ville 1981: 318–321). This suggests that *munera* were governed by rules of behaviour that encouraged displays of martial excellence, while limiting both the lethality of the spectacle and its associated costs (Carter 2006/2007).

Roman tombstones bore the names not only of the deceased but also the names of those who had dedicated the memorial (Saller and Shaw 1984). According to their epitaphs, gladiators were commemorated by a wide variety of individuals, including wives, family members, friends, and fellow gladiators. Despite the fact that gladiators led a transient life-style, surrounded by mostly male colleagues and stigmatized by their legal status, it is notable that a large number of epitaphs were set up and paid for by women. It is unclear, however, whether some gladiators set aside money to pay for their own commemoration, or if others, perhaps even the *familia*, contributed to the cost. There is limited evidence that gladiators were able to form *collegia* (professional associations), societies that here, as elsewhere in the Roman world, may have had a funerary function (Wiedemann 1992: 117–118).

Although it is not consistently part of a gladiatorial epitaph, tombstones sometimes include mention of the home town, province, or ethnic origin of the deceased gladiator. Epitaphs of gladiators of Syrian, Thracian, Egyptian, and Greek origin (to name a few) found in Spain, Gaul, Italy, or Asia Minor illustrate the geographic mobility of gladiatorial troupes. It seems that the desire to claim a distinct regional background was important enough that the home town of an Italian gladiator from Florence was emphasized in his epitaph even though he died in nearby Milan (*CIL* 5.5933). For individuals whose defining characteristic was a set fighting style, the recognition of ethnicity might have offered an increased sense of individualism. This also explains why the names and locations of gladiatorial training schools, where gladiators may have lived for an extended period of time, are sometimes added to their epitaphs.

The type of information included in gladiatorial tombstones is generally consistent across the empire. However, the style and decoration of the tombstones varied considerably. In Italy, pictorial reliefs were conventional and representations of weapons and equipment were the norm for gladiators (Hope 2000). In Gaul and Spain, gladiatorial tombstones rarely displayed any sculptural decoration and most were left unadorned, often with rounded or semi-circular upper boundaries (García y Bellido 1960; Hope 1998: 188). Since these tombstones lacked a sculpted figural reference to *munera*, an abbreviation of the gladiator's fighting style—for example *TR* for *thraex* or *M* for *murmillo*—was often placed prominently at the beginning of the epitaph to act as a visual symbol. By reducing the gladiatorial type to a shorthand of one or two characters, the gladiator's occupation would have been decipher-able even to semi-literate or illiterate viewers (Woolf 1996: 28; Woolf 2009).

In general, tombstones with gladiatorial epitaphs from the Greek East incorporate more re-lief decoration than examples from Italy or the western provinces. The combination of images and words helped to convey a meaning that was less ambiguous, while also challenging viewers to make sense of a composite message (Newby and Leader-Newby 2007: 2). In some cases, the reliefs greatly enhance our reading of the epitaphs. For example, two tombstones found in the excavations at Mylasa and Aphrodisias depict an *essedarius*, a gladiator previ-ously known only from literary evidence, who fought others of the same type armed with a short sword, large oval shield, brimless helmet, and high greaves (Petronius, *Satiricon* 36, 45; Seneca, *Letters* 29.7; Suetonius, *Caligula* 35.3; *Claudius* 21.5). The secure identification of this type of gladiator is made possible only by the epitaphs' specific references to the gladiatorial type in concert with corresponding depictions of its armour (Kontokosta 2008: 201–202). These two tombstones can now be used to link the iconography of the *essedarius* to images of previously unidentified gladiators in various media throughout the empire.

GRAFFITI AND *DIPINTI*

The English word graffiti comes from the Italian verb *graffio* meaning 'to scratch'. The study of graffiti analyses texts, images, or a combination of both that were scratched, inscribed, or painted (also called *dipinti*) on surfaces not intended for this function. Graffiti is a unique source for historians as it is one of few forms of writing that always preserves the material context of its production. Perhaps owing to its generally informal nature, however, graffiti has traditionally received less attention than other types of epigraphic documentation, often relegated to a subcategory of inscriptions. Despite this, evidence for graffiti is abundant and exists within a variety of geographical and chronological contexts across the Roman world (Bagnall et al. 2016; Baird and Taylor 2011; Benefiel and Coleman 2013; Chaniotis 2009; Langner 2001; Milnor 2014). The ubiquity of ancient graffiti implies a potential audience significantly larger than other forms of writing and, by its very nature, offers the opportunity for scholars to study texts and images in context.

Graffiti has often been interpreted as an artefact of less educated, 'common', or 'ordinary' members of ancient society (Garrucci 1856; Mouritsen 1988; Tanzer 1939). Throughout the twentieth century, associations with urban graffiti in contemporary cities propagated negative views about ancient graffiti and contributed toward an approach that decoded graffiti as an inherently subversive product of Rome's lower classes. Unlike more formal forms of writing, no concrete prerequisites of money, skill, or even literacy exist for either the production or consumption of graffiti; however, the discovery of graffiti in contexts inhabited by elite Romans, such as inside wealthy houses in Pompeii and Dura Europus, indicate that this was, in fact, a type of writing that transcended class, education, and geography (Baird 2011; Benefiel 2011; Benefiel and Keagan 2017).

The study of Roman graffiti has been dominated by the city of Pompeii, where the eruption of Mount Vesuvius in 79 CE preserved an unparalleled number of examples (over seven thousand), which have been transcribed in Volume Four of the *Corpus Inscriptionum Latinarum* (*CIL*) and its supplements. At Pompeii, graffiti is found in a wide variety of contexts, including areas of public and private encounters that were accessible to both elite and non-elite Romans. Most of the graffiti from Pompeii belongs to the years immediately preceding the volcanic eruption, which falls within the highest period of epigraphical activity in Italy (between 50 and 250 CE). Graffiti at Pompeii may not be typical of cities throughout the Roman empire; its strong economy and easy connection to the Greek world might, for example, have augmented its literacy levels (Harris 1989: 265). Nevertheless, the preservation of the city—which includes an extant amphitheatre, a *ludus* where gladiators trained and lived, and an armoury, as well as the houses and tombs of organizers (Jacobelli 2003)—offers a unique opportunity to study a large and varied corpus of graffiti and *dipinti* specifically associated with Roman gladiators, spectators, and the patrons of *munera*.

The preservation of *dipinti*—painted signs—is unique to the city of Pompeii. *Dipinti* most relevant to the study of Roman gladiators are *edicta munerum*, official communications to announce upcoming games, posted by magistrates who by law were obligated to offer gladiatorial spectacles during their year in office (Sabbatini Tumolesi 1980; Weeber 1994). Professional sign painters wrote the painted *edicta* and their work was generally characterized by formality, competence, and correct orthography (Harris 1989: 260). The care with which these notices were presented to the public underscores the political signifi-cance of hosting a local spectacle.

Throughout Pompeii the contents of *edicta* are almost identical, including the name of the *editor muneris* (magistrate) in large letters and the genitive case at the top, the number of gladiatorial pairs to be shown, the occasion for the spectacle, and also its time and place. Sometimes additional inducements to attend were included, such as whether *venationes* (wild beast shows) were planned, a particularly famous gladiator would be fighting, or a *velum* (awning) would be provided. At Pompeii, *edicta munerum* usually advertised twenty gladiatorial pairs (forty gladiators total) that would fight over either one or four days. Occasions celebrated by the games could vary from the inauguration of a monument, public building, or painting, to spectacles honouring the emperor. Most of the notices preserved at Pompeii concern games held in the local arena, although a few examples announce games to be held in nearby cities, such as Nuceria, Nola, and Puteoli. Although the *edicta* are some-times difficult to date (see Mouritsen 1988), a study of the evidence by Patrizia Sabbatini Tumolesi (1980: 113–116) found that most of the notices belonged to the period prior to the earthquake of 62 CE. This suggests that the incidence of gladiatorial shows may have declined after 62 CE as a consequence of the economic burden of rebuilding the city.

The inscribed graffiti from Pompeii offers a different view of gladiators from that found in official *edicta munerum*. For graffiti, context is critical as it can help to identify who may have written the text or inscribed the image as well as a potential reader. A large corpus of graffiti from Pompeii comes from two gladiatorial barracks, one in Region 5.5.3 that was occupied until the reign of Nero, and the other in the quadriporticus behind the theatre, which was converted into a new barracks after the earthquake of 62 CE (Garrafoni and Funari 2009; Jacobelli 2003: 52). Since gladiators and their trainers occupied these areas, the graffiti found here can be attributed to actual gladiators, as opposed to spectators, which is more common throughout the Roman world (Langner 2001: 45–54). Like gladiatorial epitaphs, the graffiti always identifies a gladiator not only by name or stage-name, but also by his fighting style. While *retiarii, essedarii, murmillones, equites,* and *hoplomachi* all appear in the Pompeian corpus, the most frequently mentioned and depicted type of gladiator is the *thraex,* which may also have been the most popular type of gladiator during the early empire.

The graffiti from the barracks at Pompeii offers interesting perspectives into the lives of Roman gladiators. Some reference the popularity of gladiators with women, a subject that is also mentioned by ancient literary texts (Juvenal, *Satires* 6.82–113). For example, a *thraex* named Celadus calls himself the 'heartthrob of the girls' (*suspirium puellarum*; CIL 4.4342), while the *retiarius* Cresces claims to be a 'physician to night-time girls, morning girls, and all the rest' (*Cresces retiarius puparum nocturnarum mattinarum aliarum ser[.]atinus [..] medicus*; CIL 4.4353). Others refer to the unusual skills of some gladiators, such as a gladiator named Albanus (Fig. 25.2) who is described as left-handed (*sc[aeva]*; CIL 4.8056; Coleman 1996). Graffiti incorporating both text and image show scenes of gladiatorial combat and frequently reference the outcomes of the pairings using the abbreviation V for *vicit* (vic-torious), M for *missus* (defeated but spared), or P for *perit* (dead). Once again, this type of evidence contradicts a brutal view of Roman *munera* as almost all of the Pompeian examples record that the defeated gladiator was discharged from the arena alive (*missus est*). Indeed, in the thirty-two competitions chronicled by the graffiti at Pompeii, only seven gladiators were killed. Moreover, graffiti indicating that individuals participated in large numbers of

FIGURE 25.2. Graffito from Pompeii published by M. Della Corte (*CIL* IV 8056) showing a left-handed gladiator (*Albanus*) identified as *sc* (*scaeua* or left-hander). Drawing by C. McClarty, after Coleman 1996: 194.

contests—sometimes more than one hundred—signifies the value of keeping well-trained and popular gladiators in the arena (Ville 1981: 321).

The long-standing study of gladiatorial graffiti at Pompeii is now augmented by new research from other sites. At Aphrodisias, for example, pictorial and textual graffiti concentrated in the city's Urban Park (formerly the 'South Agora') attests to the significant impact of *munera* on a local audience who frequented this area in the public heart of the city (Chaniotis and De Staebler 2018). At Smyrna, in the exceptional corpus of graffiti incised on plaster walls and piers in a cryptoporticus below the city's basilica, an impressive thirty-one per cent of the graffiti relates to gladiators and *munera* (Bagnall et al. 2016). As more graffiti is being studied and published, this epigraphic tradition attests vividly to the exceptional popularity and pervasive culture of gladiators throughout the Roman world.

Although the inscriptions and graffiti discussed here are only a small portion of the inscribed monuments celebrating and recording Roman gladiators, they illustrate how this type of evidence can convey a variety of unique perspectives on gladiators and the organization of Roman *munera*. Inscribed records of imperial decrees and letters shed light on the financial burdens placed on magistrates and priests who were responsible for the production of local games throughout the empire; *familia* monuments and grand tombs that celebrated the local patrons of games emphasize the political and social currency this role engendered; painted *edicta munerum* illustrate how gladiatorial games in small municipalities were organized and advertised; and epitaphs and graffiti tell more personal and varied stories about gladiators as individuals. The study of such inscriptions and graffiti—particularly in concert with associated imagery and archaeological evidence—is an important tool for better understanding of the world of Roman gladiators.

References

Aydas, M. 2006. 'Gladiatorial Inscriptions from Stratonikeia in Caria.' *EA* 39: 105–110.

Bagnall, R. S., R. Casagrande-Kim, A. Ersoy, and C. Tanriver. 2016. *Graffiti from the Basilica in the Agora of Smyrna.* New York.

Baird, J. A. 2011. 'The Graffiti of Dura-Europos: A Contextual Approach.' In *Ancient Graffiti in Context.* 49–68. J.A. Baird and C. Taylor, eds. New York.

Baird, J. A. and C. Taylor, eds. 2011. *Ancient Graffiti in Context.* New York.

Benefiel, R. B. 2011. 'Dialogues of Graffiti in the House of the Four Styles at Pompeii (*Casa Dei Quattro Stili*, I.8.17, 11).' In *Ancient Graffiti in Context.* 20–48. J. A. Baird and C. Taylor, eds. New York.

Benefiel, R. B. and K. M. Coleman, 2013. 'The Graffiti.' In *Excavations at Zeugma Conducted by Oxford Archaeology.* 178–191. W. Aylward, ed. Los Altos, CA.

Benefiel, R. B. and P. Keagan. 2017. *Inscriptions in the Private Sphere in the Greco-Roman World.* Leiden.

Berns, C. and H. A. Ekinci. 2015. 'Gladiatorial Games in the Greek East: A Complex of Reliefs from Cibyra.' *AS* 65: 143–179.

Cambi, N. 1987. 'Salona und seine Nekropolen.' In *Römische Gräberstraeszettsen. Selbstdarstellung, Status, Standard.* 251–280. H. von Hesberg and P. Zanker, eds. Munich.

Carter, M. J. 2003. 'Gladiatorial Ranking and the *SC de Pretiis Gladiatorum Minuendis* (*CIL* II 6278 = *ILS* 5163).' *Phoenix* 57: 83–114.

Carter, M. J. 2006/2007. 'Gladiatorial Combat: The Rules of Engagement.' *CJ* 102: 97–114.

Carter, M. J. 2009. 'Gladiators and *monomachoi*: Greek Attitudes to a Roman "Cultural Performance".' *IJHS* 26.2: 298–322.

Chaniotis, A. 2005. 'Macht und Volk in den kaiserzeitlichen Inschriften von Aphrodisias.' In *Popolo e potere nel mondo antico.* 47–61. G. Urso, ed. Pisa.

Chaniotis, A. 2009. 'Graffiti in Aphrodisias: Images, Texts, Contexts.' In *Roman Portraits from Aphrodisias.* 201–215. R. R. R. Smith and J. Lenaghan, eds. Istanbul.

Chaniotis, A. and P. D. De Staebler. 2018. 'Gladiators and Animals: New Pictorial Graffiti from Aphrodisias and their Contexts.' *Philia* 4: 31–54.

Coleman, K. 1996. 'A Left-Handed Gladiator at Pompeii.' *ZPE* 114: 194–196.

Coleman, K. 2008. 'Exchanging Gladiators for an Aqueduct at Aphrodisias (*SEG* 50.1096).' *AClass* 51: 31–46.

Garrafoni, R. S. and P. P. A. Funari. 2009. 'Reading Pompeii's Walls: A Social Archaeological Approach to Gladiatorial Graffiti.' In *Roman Amphitheatres and Spectacula: A 21st-Century Perspective.* 185–194. T. Wilmott, ed. Oxford.

Garcia y Bellido, A. 1960. 'Lápidas funerarias de gladiadores de Hispania.' *AEA* 33: 123–144.

Garrucci, R. 1856. *Graffiti de Pompeii.* Paris.

Gómez-Pantoja, J. 2009. *Epigrafia anfiteatrale dell'Occidente Romano, VII: Baetica, Tarraconensis, Lusitania Vetera 17.* Rome.

Harris, W. V. 1989. *Ancient Literacy.* Cambridge, MA.

Hope, V. 1998. 'Negotiating Identity and Status: The Gladiators of Roman Nîmes.' In *Cultural Identity in the Roman Empire.* 179–195. R. Laurence and J. Berry, eds. London.

Hope, V. 2000. 'Fighting for Identity: The Funerary Commemoration of Italian Gladiators.' In *The Epigraphic Landscape of Roman Italy.* 93–113. A. E. Cooley, ed. London.

Hopkins, K. 1983. *Death and Renewal.* Cambridge.

Jacobelli, L. 2003. *Gladiators at Pompeii.* M. Becker, trans. Los Angeles.

Kanz, F. and K. Grossschmidt. 2005. 'Stand der anthropologischen Forschungen zum Gladiatorenfriedhof in Ephesos.' *JÖAI* 74: 103–123.

Kanz, F. and K. Grossschmidt. 2009. 'Dying in the Arena: The Osseous Evidence from Ephesian Gladiators.' In *Roman Amphitheatres and Spectacula: A 21st-Century Perspective*. 211–220. T. Wilmott, ed. Oxford.

Kontokosta, A. H. 2008. 'Gladiatorial Reliefs and Elite Funerary Monuments at Aphrodisias.' In *Aphrodisias Papers 4: New Research on the City and Its Monuments*. 190–229. C. Ratté and R. R. R. Smith, eds. Portsmouth.

Kurtz, D. and J. Boardman. 1971. *Greek Burial Customs*. Ithaca, NY.

Langner, M. 2001. *Antike Graffitizeichnungen. Motive, Gestaltung und Bedeutung*. Wiesbaden.

MacMullen, R. 1982. 'The Epigraphic Habit in the Roman Empire.' *AJPh* 103: 233–246.

Mann, C. 2009. 'Gladiators in the Greek East: A Case Study in Romanization.' In *Sport in the Cultures of the Ancient World: New Perspectives*. 124–149. Z. Papakonstantinou, ed. London.

Milnor, K. 2014. *Graffiti and the Literary Landscape in Roman Pompeii*. Oxford.

Mouritsen, H. 1988. *Elections, Magistrates and Municipal Élite: Studies in Pompeian Epigraphy*. Rome.

Newby, Z. and R. Leader-Newby, eds. 2007. *Art and Inscriptions in the Ancient World*. Cambridge.

Price, S. R. F. 1984. *Rituals and Power: The Roman Imperial Cult in Asia Minor*. Cambridge.

Reynolds, J. 2000. 'New Letters from Hadrian to Aphrodisias: Trials, Taxes, Gladiators and an Aqueduct.' *JRA* 13: 5–20.

Roueché, C. 1993. *Performers and Partisans at Aphrodisias in the Roman and Late Roman Periods*. London.

Ritti, T. and S. Yilmaz. 1998. 'Gladiatori e venationes a Hierapolis di Frigia.' *MAL* 10: 443–542.

Robert, L. 1940. *Les gladiateurs dans l'Orient grec*. Paris.

Sabbatini Tumolesi, P. 1980. *Gladiatorum Paria. Annunci di Spettacoli Gladiatorii a Pompeii*. Rome.

Saller, R. P. and Shaw, B. D. 1984. 'Tombstones and Roman Family Relations in the Principate: Civilians, Soldiers and Slaves.' *JRS* 74: 124–156.

Tanzer, H. 1939. *The Common People of Pompeii: A Study of the Graffiti*. Baltimore.

Toynbee, J. M. C. 1971. *Death and Burial in the Roman World*. Baltimore.

Weeber, K.-W. 1994. *Panem et circenses: Massenunterhaltung als Politik im antiken Rom*. Mainz am Rhein.

Wiedemann, T. 1992. *Emperors and Gladiators*. London.

Ville, G. 1981. *La gladiature en Occident des origins à la mort de Domitien*. Rome.

Woolf, G. 1996. 'Monumental Writing and the Expansion of Roman Society in the Early Roman Empire.' *JRS* 86: 22–39.

Woolf, G. 2009. 'Literacy or Literacies in Rome?' In *Ancient Literacies: The Culture of Reading in Greece and Rome*. 46–68. W. A. Johnson and H. N. Parker, eds. Oxford.

CHAPTER 26

CURSE TABLETS

ALEXANDER HOLLMANN

In Graeco-Roman antiquity the intense competition (*agōn*) between opponents in the sporting arena was echoed by an equally fierce competition of magical materials inside and outside the venue. Curse tablets, thin sheets of lead inscribed with binding spells (Gr. *katadesmoi*, L. *defixiones*) calling for the failure of an opponent and buried secretly in or near the sporting arena or in graves and wells nearby, phylacteries (protective magical texts worn on or near the person), and other magical materials, symbols and rituals all competed with each other to advance or retard the performance of the competitors in the event.

The earliest curse tablets on lead relating to sport so far uncovered come from the second century CE and the latest from the sixth century CE, but it is quite likely that they were also used in the Classical and Hellenistic periods, since curse tablets connected with other, non-sporting events at Greek festivals such as choral competition and acting are attested from these periods (Gager 1992 nos. 1, 2), and the general use of such tablets for erotic, business, and judicial magic in these periods is well documented (e.g. Gager 1992 nos. 25, 49). That sport-related tablets from the earlier period have not yet appeared may thus be purely a question of chance and new finds could change this. In addition, we know that materials other than lead were also used as media upon which to inscribe binding spells: curses on papyrus have been found but, except under exceptional circumstances (as in the arid conditions of Egypt), these have generally not survived.

It has been suggested that already in Pindar's victory ode (476 BCE) in honour of Hieron of Syracuse (*O.* 1) we may find a reference to the use of binding magic to alter the outcome of competition (Faraone 1991). In a mythical excursus, Pelops addresses a prayer to the god Poseidon to 'fetter' the bronze spear of King Oenomaus (whom he must beat in a chariot-race to win his daughter, Hippodamia, and who will however attempt to kill him if he does so) and to grant him speed in the upcoming race.

The extant sport-related tablets contain curses relating to wrestling and running in Greek-style athletics from both mainland Greece and Egypt, gladiatorial combat and beast-hunting (*venatio*) in the arena of Roman Carthage, and chariot-racing in the circuses of Rome, Roman North Africa, and the provinces of Syria and Palestine. Tablets relating to the latter predominate by far.

The overriding concern of the curses and spells found on such tablets is the binding of the victim so that he or she (or it, since horses may also be the objects of such curses) be rendered bound or immobile in some fashion. The generic term in antiquity for such a binding spell is *katadesmos* in Greek (attested already in Plat. *Rep.* 364C), from *katadeō* ('I bind down'), and *defixio*, from *defigo* ('I fasten down'), or *devotio* in Latin. Sometimes the binding effect is presented as a physical binding of the victim: thus a tablet in Latin from Hadrumetum in North Africa (Audollent 1904 no. 295 = Tremel 2004 no. 45) calls upon infernal demons to 'bind' (*obligate*) the feet of the victims' horses so that they cannot run in the circus, while another tablet from Carthage (Audollent 1904 no. 234 = Tremel 2004 no. 53) calls upon the underworld powers to prevent the horses of the Green faction from even leaving the starting gates. On many tablets, the binding effect is presented as restraining or paralysing both body parts and mental functions, which are often catalogued, as in the following curse against runners (Gager 1992 no. 8 = Tremel 2004 no. 10) from Oxyrhynchus in Egypt and dated to the third or fourth century CE: 'Bind, bind down the sinews, the limbs, the mind, the senses, the thought, the three hundred and sixty five limbs and sinews of [name not preserved] and those around him.' The same binding effect is sometimes shown in a drawing of the victim inscribed on the tablet in which the victim is shown bound by ropes or even snakes (e.g. Gager 1992 figs. 6, 9). Some tablets (though none so far relating to sports) have been found deposited together with 'voodoo'-doll type figures made of clay or wax similarly bound (e.g. Gager 1992 nos. 28, 30, 41). Both drawings and dolls seem designed to work in a parallel fashion to the words inscribed on the tablet, which would have been recited aloud when activating and depositing the spell, accompanied by ritual actions.

Binding spells are prayers addressed largely to underworld deities, who are invoked, entreated, and sometimes compelled, to carry out the petitioner's request. The naming of these gods is important: although sometimes they may be referred to using a general expression such as *khthonioi theoi* ('chthonic gods'), they are generally named with great care and deliberation, using epithets and names sometimes described as 'secret'. This precision is a characteristic of ancient Greek and Roman prayer in general and seems to reflect a concern to obtain the ear of the god best able to carry out the request. Knowledge of the god's true names and epithets and praise of his or her attributes is also more likely to obtain his or her favour and cooperation. Thus the underworld gods Hermes, Hades, Kronos, Persephone, Demeter, and Hecate, well-known from mainstream civic religion, appear frequently on curse tablets, often with strings of epithets attesting to the god's nature and power: cf. the following epithets of Hecate from a tablet from the hippodrome at Antioch (Hollmann 2003 = Tremel 2004 no. 11): 'dragon-shaped', 'snake-holding', 'mortal-destroying'. These and other divinities become increasingly identified syncretistically with Egyptian, Babylonian, or Hebrew gods (e.g. Hekate with the Egyptian goddess Isis or Babylonian Ereshkhigal, Typhon with the Egyptian Seth). A large number of the names and epithets of gods that appear in these documents from about the second century CE on are in fact non-Greek (or non-Roman), and attest both to the kind of magical *koinē* that developed around the Mediterranean, drawing on magical practices and language from Egypt and the Near East, and to magic's tendency to create a language that is 'other' and distinct from everyday speech or mainstream religious discourse. Some typical names are Thoth, Osiris, Seth, Abrasax, Iao (the Greek version of the name Yahweh). Adonai (Hebr. 'Lord') also appears and is treated as the name of a separate deity. Magical formulae (*logoi*) containing strings of 'secret' divine epithets, names, and invocations, often based on original Egyptian, Coptic, Aramaic, Hebrew, and Persian elements, become increasingly more common in the Roman period.

Sometimes a lesser divine or supernatural being is constrained to act as a go-between to bring the petitioner's message to a more powerful god, or sometimes addressed as an agent in his or her own right. One such figure is the *nekudaimōn*, literally 'corpse-demon', or one of the *ahōroi*, 'untimely dead', spirits of those that have died before their time, often because of violence. These restless spirits may be constrained by the words and actions of the petitioner to do his bidding: 'I adjure you, *nekudaimōn*, whether male or female ... do not turn a deaf ear to these commands and names, but awaken yourself from the rest that holds you, whoever you are, male or female, and go into every place, street, house ... and drag X by her hair ... If you do this for me, I shall soon allow you rest.' (*PGM* IV.361–384)

PLACEMENT OF THE TABLET

Once inscribed, the tablet is rolled or folded up, occasionally being secured with a nail. The function of the latter, like the action of rolling or folding itself, was more than simply to seal the contents and to prevent them from being viewed and exposed, but rather to further bind or fix the victim. The rolled or folded tablet is then hidden from sight: magical practice in the Greco-Roman tradition is a secret act, partly perhaps because of the nocturnal and mysterious atmosphere with which it surrounded and defined itself but likely also for practical reasons: aggressive magic enjoyed a negative reputation in the eyes of the authorities and in some places and times could be severely punished.

Prime locations for the deposition of tablets are graveyards, wells, drains, or a place associated with the competition that the curse is designed to influence. In the case of graveyards, where tablets are often slipped into graves, or inserted into tubes used for libations, the presence of the dead, especially the unhappy and restless dead (see the 'untimely dead' above), may further facilitate the contact with the underworld that is already implicit in the location. Wells and drains, places equally dark and unseen as the grave, have a connection to the underworld through water (Heintz 1998). Placement of the tablet near the place of competition clearly brings the tablet and spell close to the intended victim. Thus in the circus at Antioch curse tablets were found buried near the further *meta*, the rounded end of the barrier running down the centre of the arena, about which the charioteers would execute a hazardous turn, bringing their chariots as close as possible to the barrier, so as to steal the lead from their competitors. As several narrative descriptions and mosaics showing chariot-racing attest (see Humphrey 1986 figs. 36, 112, 119, 120), terrible collisions often happened here, making it an ideal spot for a tablet to wreak havoc. A tablet from Carthage calls on the *nekudaimōn* of the grave into which it has been deposited to prevent the victim from successfully rounding this spot (Audollent 1904 no. 234 = Tremel 2004 no. 53, discussed below).

EXTANT TABLETS: CURSE TABLETS RELATING TO *STADION* EVENTS

We have only a few extant examples of curse tablets related to sporting competition in the Greek *stadion*, specifically wrestling and running, which all date from the second century CE or later. This paucity of evidence may simply be a matter of chance: as has been noted above, literary evidence suggests that the practice of using magic to influence outcome in competition goes back at least to the fifth century BCE, and curses may have been written on materials other than lead which have simply not survived.

A well just outside the south-western edge of the Athenian agora has yielded a cache of lead tablets, five of which relate to a wrestling competition. Of these five, three are directed against the same wrestler (*palaistēs*), Eutykhianos (Jordan 1985 nos. 1–3 = Tremel 2004 nos. 1–3). This gives us an opportunity to see how clients and practitioners target their victim using multiple curses. These appear to be the work of the same practitioner, being in the same competent and professional hand and having roughly the same formulae. The 'mighty' god Betpu is invoked, and the victim is handed over to him so that the divinity can 'chill' him and his companions. This imagery of chilling is combined with idea of general inability to act in order to paralyse and bind the victim.

> I hand over to you Eutykhianos, slated to wrestle against Secundus, in order that you may chill Eutykhianos and his judgement and his ability, his strength, his wrestling, and into your gloomy air also those with him. Bind into the lightless eternity of forgetfulness and chill and destroy also the wrestling of Eutykhianos the wrestler. If you chill him in respect to Secundus and do not let him wrestle, so that he may fall and disgrace himself, Morzounē Alkheinē Pepertharōna Iaia, I hand over to you Eutykhianos. Mighty Typhon Kolkhloikheilōps, let the wrestler Euthykhianos be chilled. Just as these words/names are chilled, so let Eutykhianos' names and soul, his passion, his triumph, his knowledge, his reason, his knowledge be chilled. Let him be deaf and dumb, without sense, stupid, wrestling against nobody. (Jordan 1985 no. 2 = Tremel 2004 no. 2)

The attack is aimed at Eutykhianos but more specifically his wrestling: qualities associated with success in the sport are catalogued in order to ensure that every aspect is covered by the spell. In a technique known to scholars as *similia similibus*, the practitioner calls upon these qualities of the victim to be chilled in precisely the same way as the words and names written on the lead tablet are chilled by the cold water of the well. Thus here the properties of both the material on which the curse is inscribed and the environment in which it is placed form an essential part of the magical technique of the spell.

Of the three tablets directed against Eutykhianos, two are on behalf of different named individuals (Secundus, Hegoumenos), while one mentions no name, but does specify the time ('this coming Friday') and place (imperfectly preserved) of the upcoming bout. It is also interesting that Eutykhianos is here identified not only through his mother (a striking method of identification characteristic in magical texts from the first century CE onward) but also by his trainer ('the pupil [*mathētēs*] of Aithales'): the standard form of magical identification has been tailored to the specific context of wrestling competition, where the wrestler's affiliation with his trainer is important.

The other two tablets from the same well, also directed against wrestlers (Attalos the ephebe and Petres the Macedonian, the pupil of Dionysios), show much the same formulae.

Five tablets against runners are preserved. Two (Jordan 1985 nos. 6, 7 = Tremel 2004 nos. 6, 7) come from wells in the Athenian agora, and are dated to same period as those against wrestlers. One of these (Jordan no. 6 = Tremel 2004 6), which was found in the same well as the tablets against the wrestlers mentioned above and calls upon the same god, Betpu, uses identical magical formulae, so that it appears to be from the same magical workshop. The god is asked not to let Alkidamos

> leave the borders/starting lines of the Athenians/Athenaia. But if he does so, in order that he veer off course and disgrace himself, I hand him over to you ... Just as these names/words are

chilled, so let the name/reputation, soul, drive/anger, knowledge, and reason of Alkidamos be chilled. Let him be deaf and dumb, unable to speak, senseless, stupid, hearing nothing about Apollonianos and without anger towards Apollonianos.

The provisions of the curse are also similar to those on the wrestling tablets, with some that are specific to running, although it is not entirely certain that this tablet relates to this sport, since the key terms 'runner' (dromeus) or 'running' (dramein) do not appear here as they do on the others. In my translation 'borders/starting lines' and 'Athenians/Athenaia' reflect the ambiguity of the Greek words: the general meaning of horos is 'border', but it is possible that it is used here as a (so far unparalleled) technical term for starting-line. Likewise, Athēnaiōn could refer to the Athenian people or more specifically to the festival of the Athenaia, attested from the late second to mid-third century CE as a venue for ephebic games, or Panathenaia (an attested usage). The term translated as 'veer off course' (apokampsēi) is usually attested in the context of equestrian competition, though it can be used of humans leaving a path.

The third tablet (Jordan 1994 no. 5 = Tremel 2004 no. 8) is from Isthmia, site of the Isthmian Games, and has been dated to roughly the same date as the tablets relating to wrestling and running mentioned above. Like them it was also discovered in a well. Four victims are named, three of whom are depicted in a drawing. The figures are not obviously dressed as runners; the clearest of them wears a tunic-like garment. They are also not shown as bound, unlike many figures on curse tablets. In comparison to the tablets so far mentioned, this one uses the simplest possible formula: on side A, Eulamo (often invoked on curse tablets from all over the ancient world but still not satisfactorily identified) is called upon to 'bind down' (the verb used is the same as the root of katadesmos, the Greek term for binding spell) each of the victims. Then follows the command, 'Let them have no strength for running on the day before the Sabbath but ..', so that, as on the wrestling tablets from the Athenian agora, we find specification of the time of the contest. The fourth tablet (Gager 1992 no. 8 = Tremel 2004 no. 10), from Oxyrhynchus in Egypt and dated to roughly the same period as the others, also contains the Eulamo formula. Like the tablets against the wrestlers, it uses the typical cataloguing of body parts and centres of thought and action that seems both to aim at completeness and to serve as a kind of fracturing and breaking down of the victim:

> Bind, bind down the sinews, the limbs, the mind, the senses, the thought, the three hundred and sixty five limbs and sinews of those around [the name is unfortunately lost here], whom Taeias gave birth to, and Ephous, whom Taeias gave birth to, of the runners, that they [not be able] ... to be strong but suffer insomnia the whole night and that they lose all nourishment, to the detriment of their ... so that they have no strength for running, but fall behind ... and restrain their ... the ones around ..., whom Taeias bore, and around Aphous, whom Taeias bore ... hinder and darken their vision, so that they have no strength for running ... through your power, lord Abrasax.

A fifth tablet (Tomlin 2007), almost certainly from Egypt and likely dating to the fourth century CE, is directed against three competitors in the stadion. Though they are not named specifically as runners, this is likely from the context and from the striking lines at the end of the curse:

> Bind their feet, sinews, legs, spirit, excellence, the three hundred and fifty-five limbs of their bodies and souls, that they be not able to proceed in the stadium, but remain like stones, unmoving, un-running.

These few tablets represent more or less the sum total of tablets concerning Greek-style athletic games. The bulk (approximately ninety per cent) of sport-related tablets is connected with the Roman-style sporting venues of the circus and the amphitheatre. Of these, the tablets related to the circus and chariot-racing are in the majority, with a few pertaining to competition in the amphitheatre. Before surveying the numerous tablets involving chariot-racing, I will discuss the tablets relating to gladiatorial combat and beast-hunting in the amphitheatre.

These come mainly from the amphitheatre at Carthage. Aggressive magic using curse tablets was certainly used in other amphitheatres in the Graeco-Roman world, as references in literary texts attest. The amphitheatre at Carthage was an impressive structure that may have held as many as 30,000 spectators. The tablets were found as a cache in the arena of the great amphitheatre in what the excavators described as a square subterranean passage ending in a cul-de-sac (Audollent 1904: 333). Their location seems deliberately close to the action they were attempting to influence. There may have been another factor, if certain scholars (e.g. Audollent 1904: 334) are correct in associating the location of the cache of tablets with a structure known from literary sources as the *spoliatorium* (contra Bomgardner 1989: 99). Here the dead or dying were brought from the arena before being disposed of elsewhere (Kyle 1998: 158–159). As we have seen above, the spirits of those dying an untimely or violent death were sometimes sought to carry out the requests and commands of the magical practitioner, and one magical text includes gladiators among the category of those dying a violent death (*PGM* IV.1394). On this interpretation, the curses recovered from the Carthage amphitheatre may have been placed precisely in or near the *spoliatorium* in order to harness the restless spirits of violently dispatched gladiators, beast hunters, and criminals forced to fight in these spectacles (Audollent 1904: 334). In any case, the fact that tablets relating to multiple events at different times and with different victims were found together might suggest that this place was habitually used by practitioners and their agents as a place to deposit their materials. Was this location an open secret, tacitly tolerated by the officials responsible for the maintenance of the amphitheatre?

The curses on these tablets contain, on the one hand, a mixture of general commands to bind and retard the physical and mental strength and acuity of the victim, often accompanied by a catalogue of the parts to be affected (e.g. Audollent 1904 no. 252 = Tremel 2004 no. 98: 'Bind him and ... his power, heart, liver, mind, senses'). They thus resemble the general curses found on tablets relating to other sports and indeed those found in love or business magic. On the other hand, they also contain provisions highly specific to contests in the amphitheatre. Most of the published tablets from Carthage relate in fact to the spectacle of *venatio*, where 'hunters' (*venatores*), distinct from gladiators, were pitted against wild animals. On the tablets bulls, boars, lions, and bears are mentioned, with a great deal of attention given to the latter. It seems from other types of evidence that Carthage may have been something of a centre for spectacles involving bears: a considerable number of mosaics from the area that depict *venationes* feature 'catalogues of bears' (Dunbabin 1978: 73–74), while the epigrams of Luxorius, the court poet of the Vandalic kings at Carthage, especially celebrate *venationes* involving bears (*Anthologia Latina* 48, 49). A common provision in the tablets is that the victim not be able to use a *lacinia* (rag) to bait bears but himself become entangled in it (e.g. Audollent 1904 no. 253 = Tremel 2004 no. 99), an interesting elaboration of the general imagery of binding found on most curse tablets. Also interesting is the bilingual nature of these texts: Greek (sometimes written in Roman letters) and Latin (written with both Greek and Roman letters) may be found on the same tablet (e.g. Audollent 1904 no. 252 = Tremel 2004 no. 98). Sometimes the invocations of the underworld gods and general curses appear in Greek, while the curses specifically related to action in the arena and the technical terms are in Latin (e.g. Audollent 1904 no. 250 = Tremel 2004 no. 96 side B). This may be evidence of the use of magical pattern books written in Greek and widely used throughout the empire and copied and adapted by local practitioners.

Roughly thirty tablets dating to the fourth and fifth centuries CE were found in the Trier amphitheatre, of which seventeen were found in a subterranean chamber similar to that described above in the Carthaginian amphitheatre. But unlike the Carthaginian tablets, those that can be deciphered do not seem to be directed against gladiators or to refer to activity in the arena (Wünsch 1910: 4). They relate to concerns and victims outside the amphitheatre and were likely deposited there, perhaps after gladiatorial games were no longer offered, in order to use the restless spirits of those who had died there to convey their requests to the underworld gods.

To the tablets from Carthage and Trier can be added tablets from the Roman amphitheatre at Eleutheropolis, now Bet Guvrin in southern Israel. One of these was found in the arena and three (possibly four) in the *sacellum* or cult-room under the western tribunal (Kloner and Hübsch 1996: 101). The tablets have not yet been published or deciphered, so it is not yet clear whether they relate directly to activities in the arena or whether, as with the Trier tablets, they have no relationship to gladiatorial competition but were deposited there to harness the power of the restless dead, possibly even after the structure ceased to be used for staging games.

Curses from the Circus

The greatest number of sport-related curse tablets is connected with the circus or hippodrome and the chariot-racing that took place there. Some eighty are listed in Tremel's collection (nos. 11–90), drawn from the great circuses in Rome, in North Africa (Carthage, Hadrumetum, Leptis Magna), and in the Near East (Syrian Antioch, Beirut, Tyre, Damascus, Apamea). To these can now be added a large collection from Caesarea, of which eighteen have been deciphered and edited (Daniel and Hollmann, forthcoming 2022). As a sport that drew tens of thousands of spectators, whose actions when displeased threatened to bring down emperors and high officials, it is not surprising that chariot-racing figures so prominently in our extant tablets. The charioteers, one of the closest equivalents in the ancient world to modern footballers or rock stars, were some of the highest paid and most adored (and correspondingly hated) performers of their day. This fact and the inherent uncertainties and dangers of the sport together with the anxiety of their handlers and supporters for them to win also ensured that magic was resorted to as a means to damage opponents, guard against accidents, and counteract the aggressive magic of the opposing side. One fourth-century-CE Christian writer goes so far as to describe chariot-racing as 'a contest of magicians, not of the speed of horses' (Amphilochius of Iconium, *Iambi ad Seleucum* 179). Not only magic but the accusation of magic could be used as an effective tool against rivals (Brown 1970).

Curses relating to the circus differ from those relating to other sports in that they involve the activities, skills, and abilities not only of humans but also of horses. These were an equally vital part of the team and could be stars in their own right, and this is reflected in the fact that many tablets name not only the charioteers and the factions they belong to but also the horses. Sometimes the names of the charioteers are simply ignored, while those of the horses are exhaustively listed, as on a lengthy tablet from Antioch (Hollmann 2003 = Tremel 2004 no. 11), where thirty-six horses of the Blue faction are targeted, probably the entire stable. The horse names are often indicative of speed, light, and victory, and sometimes overlap with charioteer names: thus Pherenikos ('Victory-bringer') appears apparently as a human name on a tablet from Apamea (Tremel 2004 no. 18) but as a horse name on the above-mentioned Antioch tablet. This is perhaps another indication of the equal importance of man and beast in this sport. A tablet from Hadrumetum in North Africa (Audollent 1904 no. 273 = Tremel 2004 no. 23) lists twenty-six names without distinguishing charioteer from horse, referring to them jointly at the end of the tablet as 'the names of men and horses'.

As with the tablets relating to the amphitheatre, those connected with the circus combine general provisions of binding and restriction of movement and thought with more specific directives which refer to the particular conditions of chariot-racing and the structure of the circus. A lengthy tablet (Audollent 1904 no. 234 = Tremel 2004 no. 53), found in the grave of a Roman official in a cemetery in Carthage, is a perfect example of this, referring the critical areas of the racetrack, the starting gates and turning posts (*kamptēres*):

> I conjure you, whosoever you are, untimely spirit of the dead [*nekudaimōn*], according to ... the names ... [here follow magical names and formulae], in order that you bind the horses of the Blue faction and their partner, the Green faction ... for you [*sc.* spirit of the dead] I have deposited in this vessel [these names] written on seashells, Vittatus, Derisor, Victor, Armenius, Nimbus, Tyrius, Amor, Praeclarus (also known as Tetraplas), Virilis, Paratus, Victor, Imbutrium, Phoenix, Licus, and from their partner, the Green faction, Darius, Agilis, Cupidinus, Pugio, Pretiosus, Prunicus, Dardanus, Inachus, Floridus, Pardus, Servatus, Fulgidus, Victor, Proficius. ... Bind their running, power, soul, onrush, speed, take away their victory, hobble their feet, chop them, unstring their tendons, take apart their limbs, so that they be unable tomorrow in the hippodrome when they come either to run, or walk, or win, or go beyond the gates of the starting boxes, or advance into the arena or the track [*spatium*], or circle the turning posts, but let them fall with their charioteers, Dionysius of the Blue faction and Lamyrus and Restutianus and from their partner, the Green faction, Protus and Felix and Narcissus ... Bind their hands, rob them of victory, success, sight, so that they be unable to see their opponents when they are driving their chariots, but rather snatch them from their own chariots and bend them to the ground, so that they fall and be dragged in every part of the hippodrome, especially by the turning posts, together with their own horses. Now, now, quick, quick, quickly!

All evidence suggests that from at least the fifth century BCE to the seventh century CE, magic was a constant feature of sporting competition, despite expressions of disapproval and legal provisions that threatened practitioners and users of aggressive magic with dire consequences, including death (Gager 1992: 23–24, 258–259). This suggests that this type of magic may have functioned not as a desperate, last-ditch attempt to dispose of a superior opponent, but was *de facto*, if not *de iure*, recognized as a means of optimizing and regulating performance (Heintz 1999). In a way, the persistence of the practice of magic in sports over this lengthy period answers the question 'Did magic really work?' in the affirmative (Gager 1992: 22–23).

References

Audollent, A. 1904. *Defixionum tabellae*. Paris.

Bomgardner, D. 1989. 'The Carthage Amphitheater: A Reappraisal.' *AJA* 93: 85–103.

Brown, P. 1970. 'Sorcery, Demons, and the Rise of Christianity: From Late Antiquity into the Middle Ages.' In *Witchcraft: Confessions and Accusations*. 17–45. M. Douglas, ed. London.

Daniel, R. and Hollmann, A. 2022 (forthcoming). *Magica Levantina*. Paderborn.

Dunbabin, K. 1978. *The Mosaics of Roman North Africa: Studies in Iconography and Patronage*. Oxford.

Faraone, C. 1991. 'The Agonistic Context of Early Greek Binding Spells.' In *Magika Hiera: Ancient Greek Magic and Religion*. 3–32. C. Faraone and D. Obbink, eds. New York.

Gager, J. 1992. *Curse Tablets and Binding Spells from the Ancient World*. Oxford.

Graf, F. 1997. *Magic in the Ancient World*. F. Philip, trans. Cambridge, MA.

Heintz, F. 1998. 'Circus Curses and their Archaeological Contexts.' *JRA* 11: 337–342.

Heintz, F. 1999. 'Agonistic Magic in the Late Antique Circus.' PhD dissertation, Harvard University.

Hollmann, A. 2003. 'A Curse Tablet from the Circus at Antioch.' *ZPE* 145: 67–82.

Humphrey, J. 1986. *Roman Circuses: Arenas for Chariot Racing*. Berkeley.

Jordan, D. 1985. '*Defixiones* from a Well near the Southwest Corner of the Athenian Agora.' *Hesperia* 54: 205–255.

Jordan, D. 1994. 'Inscribed Lead Tablets from the Games in the Sanctuary of Poseidon.' *Hesperia* 63: 111–126.

Kloner, A. and Hübsch, A. 1996. 'The Roman Amphitheater of Bet Guvrin: A Preliminary Report on the 1992, 1993, and 1994 Seasons.' *Atiqot* 30: 85–106.

Kyle, D. 1998. *Spectacles of Death in Ancient Rome*. London.

Tremel, J. 2004. *Magica agonistica. Fluchtafeln im antiken Sport*. Hildesheim.

Wünsch, R. 1910. 'Die Laminae litteratae des Trierer Amphitheaters.' *Bonner Jahrbücher* 119: 1–12.

CHAPTER 27

COINS

NATHAN T. ELKINS

INTRODUCTION

THIS handbook provides an opportunity to explore the ways that coins referred to games or festivals in different periods and places, as the numismatic evidence has a role to play in grappling with questions about identity, perception, and political expediency in ancient games. The ancient world produced tens of thousands of distinct images on its coins, many of which referred to games and festivals (for exhibition catalogues on coins and ancient games, see Mannsperger 1984; Klose and Stumpf 1996). It is, therefore, the aim of this contribution to survey how sport and spectacle iconography was typically used on the coinage.

GREEK COINS

Most images on archaic and classical Greek coins were of a civic character; they referred directly to the identity of the state by depicting the chief god or goddess of the city as at Athens, a local nymph or hero as at Thebes, local myths as at Corinth, or commodities for which a city was famous as at Metapontum or Cyrene (e.g., Franke and Hirmer 1964; Kraay 1976; Carradice and Price 1988: 56–61; Ritter 2002). But some Greek cities overtly showcased festivals and athletics as a means of announcing their identity to the Greek world.

Elis usually controlled the sanctuary at Olympia and organized the Olympic Games. The coinage of Elis for Olympia appears to have been issued irregularly and probably in conjunction with the Panhellenic festival every four years (Seltman 1921; Kraay 1976: 103–107). The iconography of Elis's coinage, which began in the late sixth century BCE, celebrated the cult of Zeus at Olympia. References to the Olympic Games are more direct on types that show Nike carrying a crown. Since so many votive figures of thundering Zeus have been discovered at Olympia, the standing Zeus wielding a thunderbolt in his right hand and holding an eagle in his left on some coins may, like the votives, represent the archaic cult statue before it was replaced by Phidias' chryselephantine statue around 435 BCE (Schwabacher 1962). This Zeus is accompanied by the legend ΟΛΥΜΠΙΚΟΝ, which is a genitive plural that denotes the festival. As Pausanias (5.11.1) recounts, the head of Phidias' Zeus wore a crown of olive and thus it is this Zeus depicted on the coins of 416 BCE (Seltman 1951: 45–46). Around 420 BCE, a second Elean mint at Olympia opened; its coinage is distinctive through the depiction of Hera, who also possessed a temple there.

Local sporting events are depicted on the coins of Larissa in Thessaly (Gallis 1988). It is unsurprising that equestrian events were popular in Thessaly, because of the horses raised on its plains. Reverses of fourth-century BCE drachms of Larissa (with the head of a nymph on the obverse) depict a galloping horse with a man running beside it; presumably they illustrate a horse-mounting competition. Bull sports are also attested by textual and visual evidence in Thessaly. Some drachms show a competitor wrestling a bull by the horns on the obverse (Fig. 27.1) with either a horse or bull on the reverse.

While some cities referred to Panhellenic or local festivals on their coins, others used the medium to advertise their victories in such events. In the second quarter of the fifth century BCE, Kos produced silver tetradrachms featuring a *diskobolos* in action next to a tripod on the obverse and a crab, the 'civic badge' of Kos, on the reverse. The athletic scene recalls the festival of Apollo at Triopion, participation in which was restricted to the cities of Kos, Knidos, Ialysos, Lindos, and Kameiros (Barron 1968: 76). According to Herodotus (1.144), athletic victors in this festival were awarded bronze tripods that were in turn dedicated in the Temple of Apollo at Triopion. The coins, therefore, celebrate Koan victories in the *diskos*. The athlete on the coin is nude with his left leg crossed behind his weight-bearing right leg; his upright torso is twisted to the right as he holds the *diskos* above his head with his right hand in the moment before releasing it. Athletes in Greek art are often depicted in the midst of dynamic action, as in Myron's famous sculpture of the *Diskobolos*, although the moment captured on the coin differs from the one selected by Myron and his many copyists.

Croton in Magna Graecia actively recruited and trained athletes to compete in the Olympic Games and boasted many Olympic victories (Garello 2004). A complete study of

FIGURE 27.1. Silver drachm of Larissa, Thessaly. Yale University Art Gallery, The Ernest Collection, in Memory of Israel Myers, 2007.182.247.

Croton's highly varied coinage has yet to be undertaken, but from *c.*425 to *c.*350 BCE they produced silver coins that depicted an eagle, sometimes standing on an Ionic capital or grasping prey. These are very similar to some coins of Elis at Olympia. The resemblance may have been to deliberate showcase Croton's Olympic success (Kraay 1976: 181; Rutter et al. 2001: 170).

Although most images on Greek coins are civic in character, the individual prerogatives of minting authorities sometimes came through on the designs. This is especially true in the Hellenistic world. But even in archaic Greece, some coins *might* have symbolized individual accomplishments. The earliest Athenian coins, produced in the second half of the sixth century BCE, are the so-called *Wappenmünzen* or 'heraldic coins', as the different emblems on the obverses were often understood as the badges of the leading aristocratic houses responsible for the minting of coins. This interpretation, however, has been largely abandoned; it is more likely that the different designs on the *Wappenmünzen* served as administrative control marks for particular officials responsible for the production of coin or denoted annual issues. Some silver didrachms and fractions from this series depict the distinctive form of a Panathenaic prize amphora. If the meaning of the images on the *Wappenmünzen* is properly understood as an emblem of a minting official, this anonymous moneyer might have used the Panathenaic amphora to indicate his own successes. It may also be that the amphora simply functioned as a civic symbol of Athens herself.

Sicilian tyrants, such as Gelon, immortalized their own Olympic victories on the coins of Syracuse and Gela. At Gela, for example, the reverses on his coins show a charioteer driving a four-horse chariot with a crown-bearing Nike flying above; later types at Gela omit Nike and insert an Ionic column in the background to denote a turning post (Jenkins 1970: 53–55). Victorious charioteers remained popular subjects on the coins of Syracuse and Gela into the fourth century BCE.

Philip II of Macedon was particularly adept at exploiting games for his own political purposes (Miller 2004: 223–224); as the Sicilian tyrants, he publicized his many victories on coinage. In the Olympics, Philip was victorious in the *keles*, a race on horseback. Tetradrachms of Philip from mints in Macedonia depict a head of Zeus on the obverse and a jockey on horseback holding the palm branch awarded to winners. The design is accompanied by the legend ΦΙΛΙΠΠΟΥ to underscore his victory. Gold staters of Philip II, struck both during his lifetime and posthumously, depict a head of Apollo on the obverse and a charioteer driving a two-horse chariot with the same legend. These celebrate Philip's victory in that event, the *synoris*. Since Philip won *synoris* victories at both Olympia and Delphi, some scholars have been uncertain which victory is celebrated, but the presence of Apollo must indicate the Pythian Games at Delphi.

Some coins may also illustrate the association of Greek athletics with military training. Silver staters of Aspendus from the mid-fifth century BCE (after 467) depict a hoplite or hero with a round shield and sword on the obverse and a *triskeles* of running human legs on the reverse. Kraay (1976: 277) hypothesized that the design may indicate the coins were used as military pay, since coins from Tarsus showing a Persian soldier were struck to pay soldiers. In the later fifth century BCE, a new series of Aspendian staters began to depict two naked wrestlers grappling with one another on the obverse and a clothed slinger preparing to fire, with the *triskeles* in the field, on the reverse (Fig. 27.2). Early staters of this type show the feet of the two wrestlers crossed as if one were trying to trip the other, while later types show them simply grasping one another by the arms. It is unknown whether or not Aspendus was

FIGURE 27.2. Silver Stater of Aspendus, Pamphylia. Yale University Art Gallery, from the Peter R. and Lenore Franke Collection, 2004.6.3144.

particularly proud of its wrestlers, but their depiction opposite the slinger (and *triskeles*) may be read in a martial context. Many athletic contests in the Greek world were born from military training and practised to maintain the readiness of young men for battle (e.g., Golden 1998: 23–28; Crowther 2004: 313–321). The iconographic change from the hoplite/*triskeles* type to the later wrestlers/slinger type may not, however, have significantly altered the meaning or intent of the designs, as both can be understood in military contexts.

Roman Provincial Coins

Some cities in the eastern Mediterranean continued to strike coins, or began to do so, under Roman domination. In specialist literature, these coins are often termed 'Greek imperial', although 'Roman provincial' is preferred today (Butcher 1988; Howgego, Heuchert, and Burnett 2005). Roman provincial coinage in the western Roman empire disappeared in the reigns of Tiberius and Caligula; from that time, the western provinces relied instead on the centrally issued imperial coinage. In the eastern Roman empire, however, locally produced bronze coinage persisted until the late third century CE. The height of Roman provincial coinage production was in the reign of Septimius Severus when approximately 400 cities were striking their own coins.

The character of designs on Roman provincial coinage in the east was largely civic, as it had been in the Greek world before Roman domination. The most significant change was that the portrait of the emperor typically dominated the obverses. Reverses most frequently referred to local cults, myths, or monuments, or privileges bestowed upon the city by the emperor. Some also showcased local games and festivals, especially as a means of promoting the city over its neighbours (e.g., Klose 2005; Nollé 2012).

The most common provincial coins that refer to games do so by depicting various prizes, such as oil amphorae, money purses, or prize crowns, often set upon tables (e.g., Klose 2005: 128–130; Dunbabin 2010; Nollé 2012). Often the accompanying legend announced the games for which the prize was awarded, as on a coin of Commodus from Nicaea; a table supporting two prize crowns with palms also has a legend denoting the *Kommodia* festival, held in honour of the emperor. Sometimes representing athletes referred to the victory. An example is a third-century coin of Volusian from Aspendus that illustrates three nude athletes standing frontally; the athlete in the middle stands next to an amphora and holds a palm branch while crowning himself.

Coins that depict actual athletic events are much more uncommon. Under Elagabalus, Laodicea ad Mare struck coins showing two wrestlers in a manner similar to the earlier Greek coins from Aspendus. Rare coins of Gallienus from Synnada in Phrygia depict amphitheatre events and attest the popularity of Roman-style entertainments there. Some show animal spectacles; in the foreground a *venator* spears a boar, in the middle ground a lion chases a gazelle, and in the background a trainer stands next to a performing bear. Others depict in the foreground two gladiators, a Thracian and a *retiarius*, in combat; in the background are two palms flanking a *cippus* or doorway on the arena floor (Fig. 27.3).

Depictions of spectacle buildings on Roman provincial coins are most uncommon. Bronze coins of Athens, perhaps dating to the third century CE, have an obverse bust of Athena and a reverse depicting the *cavea* of the Theatre of Dionysus below the Acropolis. Coins from the mid-third century CE from Heraclea in Bithynia show a three-quarter aerial view of the stadium there; the execution of the image is clearly based on imperial *sestertii* of Trajan and Caracalla that represented the Circus Maximus in a similar way (see below). Inside the stadium stands a nude athlete who crowns himself before a seated Herakles, the eponymous hero of the city.

FIGURE 27.3. Bronze coin of Gallienus from Synnada, Phrygia. Bibliothèque nationale de France.

ROMAN REPUBLICAN AND IMPERIAL COINS

Greek cities used the iconography of athletics on coins as a means to proclaim their identity, either as hosts of important festivals or as the proud homes of victorious athletes. The coins of Sicilian tyrants and Philip II of Macedon were more political in the sense that they celebrated the accomplishments of the individual head of state, rather than the state itself. Roman provincial coinage tended to follow the pattern established by coins of the Greek world prior to Roman conquest. In contrast, Roman republican and imperial coins consistently referred to games to communicate a specific ideological message about the issuing official or the emperor to the viewer (e.g. Burnett 1987).

During the Republic, three appointed moneyers oversaw annual coinage production. In the 130s BCE, designs on republican coins began to be more varied than in previous decades and the iconography became more politicized or commemorative. The *lex Gabinia* of 139 BCE may have brought about this change; it allowed for a secret ballot in elections and, thus, young moneyers might have relied less on noble patronage and more on the prestige of their families or their own promises to be elected to future offices (Wiseman 1971: 4; Crawford 1974: 710–711, 728). In essence, the coinage became a medium through which they might 'campaign' for elected offices. But the new images also developed in a cultural background of familial commemoration (Meadows and Williams 2001).

Several republican coins refer to games that would be organized if the moneyer were elected aedile (Crawford 1974: 286, 308, 399–402, 729). The first Roman coins to depict games were *denarii* of a Cn. Domitius in 128 BCE, the reverses of which show a *venator* fighting a lion below Victory driving a *biga*. A grain stalk appears behind Roma's head on the obverse; games and grain distribution were two important duties of curule aediles. Another allusion to spectacles appears on the reverses of *denarii* of T. Didius of 113/112 BCE that show two gladiators, one armed with a shield and whip and the second with a whip and spear, in the midst of combat; since gladiatorial events were not yet part of the regularized religious calendar, they were more reliant on individual initiative.

The intent to hold games is also the theme of the five *denarii* issued by M. Volteius in 78 BCE. The obverse and reverse combinations for these are a head of Jupiter/Temple of Jupiter Optimus Maximus, head of Hercules/boar, head of Liber/Ceres driving a *biga* of snakes, head of Attis(?)/Cybele driving a *biga* of lions, and a head of Apollo/tripod with a snake coiled around one leg. The types respectively refer to deities honoured at the *ludi Romani*, the *ludi Plebeii*, the *ludi Cereales*, the *ludi Megalenses*, and the *ludi Apollinares*, representing major festivals for which the curule aediles (*Romani, Megalenses, Apollinares*) and the plebeian aediles (*Plebeii, Cereales*) were responsible. Crawford interprets the letters SC DT on either side of the tripod on the Apollo type as *Stipes Collata Dei Thesauro*, which proclaims the funding of the *ludi Apollinares* by popular contribution (Crawford 1974: 402; Livy 24.12.14; Festus, *Games of Apollo*).

In 42 BCE, coins of the moneyer L. Livineius Regulus, presumably the son of the *praetor* with the same name who was Cicero's friend (*To Atticus* 3.17.1; *Letters to his Friends* 13.60.1), depicted the bust of the *praetor* on the obverse and a *venatio* on the reverse. In the foreground, a *venator* spears a lion and in the background a *venator* spears a panther while a boar or bear looks on. The coin was seemingly issued to commemorate an animal hunt held by the moneyer's father.

Desultores who performed in the Circus Maximus also appeared on republican coins. The first representation is on *denarii* of 112/111 BCE minted by Ti. Quinctius upon which a *desultor* is shown riding two horses. A similar depiction adorns reverses of *denarii* of C. Marcius Censorinus in 88 BCE. These may have alluded to the *ludi Apollinares*, as the moneyer claimed descent from the seer Marcius, whose prophecies advised the founding of those games (Livy 25.12). Coins of 44 BCE, struck by P. Sepullius Macer after the death of Caesar, have an obverse portrait of a veiled Caesar or Marc Antony (bearded) with a reverse showing a *desultor* on two horses and a crown in the field. Issued just after the assassination, these commemorate the games held during the *Parilia* that year in which Caesar's memory was honoured (Dio Cassius 45.6.4).

In the late Republic, coin iconography began to revolve around the ideology of the *triumviri*, and after the establishment of the principate, designs dealt with the rhetoric of the imperial regime. In 42 BCE, Octavian struck *denarii* that showed his bearded portrait on the obverse and a laurel wreath upon a curule chair inscribed CAESAR DIC(TATOR IN) PER(PETVO) on the reverse. This must be the honorary chair for Caesar placed among those for the gods in the *orchestra* of theatres both during his lifetime and after his death (Dio Cassius 44.6.3). Caesar's chair on the coin reaffirmed Caesar's status as *divus*, especially since placing his chair in the theatres had apparently become dangerous after his assassination (Dio Cassius 45.6.5).

In addition to his chair in the theatres, Caesar was honoured with a cart drawn along-side those for the gods in the *pompa circensis*. Under the emperors, chairs in the theatres and carts bearing images or attributes to be placed on chairs or couches in the *pulvinar*, the viewing platform for the gods, of the Circus Maximus were typically awarded to deified emperors and deceased members of the imperial house who had not been deified. These carts are depicted on imperial coins of the first and second centuries CE.

Attributes upon chairs or thrones appeared on coins into the Antonine period. One of the most extensive series of coins showing chairs or thrones were *aurei* and *denarii* struck by Titus and Domitian early in their reigns. Types included a wreath upon a curule chair, per-haps symbolizing the emperor, and thrones supporting triangular or semicircular *struppi*, crowns woven from laurel branches, perhaps indicating the *divi* and *divae*; other thrones bore a thunderbolt for Jupiter and a Corinthian helmet for Minerva. Belonging to this series are coins that show attributes of other gods: a dolphin coiled around an anchor (Neptune), a tripod (Apollo), and a small lighted altar (Vesta). Taylor (1935) advanced the hypothesis that they depicted the chairs carried in the *pompa theatralis*. The coins are better associated with the *pompa amphitheatralis* since the opening of the Colosseum was the biggest event in Titus' reign (Damsky 1995; Elkins 2004: 155–157; Elkins 2014; Elkins 2019: 54–58); other coins of Titus show an elephant that appeared in the Colosseum's inaugural games and *sestertii* of Titus and Domitian feature a three-quarter aerial view of the Colosseum itself, the first spec-tacle building to be depicted on coins (Fig. 27.4).

The *sestertii* of Titus and Domitian celebrated the dedication of the Colosseum in 80 CE, accompanied by a lavish set of games. The reverse shows a three-quarter view of Titus seated and surrounded by the spoils of the Jewish War. The only numismatic prototypes for the peculiar reverse type are *sestertii* of Claudius that had an obverse bust of his father, Nero Claudius Drusus, and a reverse of Claudius seated on a curule chair and surrounded by the spoils of war to mark his conquest of Britannia. The allusion to Claudius was delib-erate; Divus Claudius was a member of the Julio-Claudian Dynasty with whom the Flavians

FIGURE 27.4. Bronze sestertius of Domitian for Divus Titus from Rome. American Numismatic Society, 1954.203.170

closely associated themselves ideologically (e.g., Elkins 2019: 75–85 and *passim*). Indeed, his temple—adjacent to the Colosseum—was completed by Vespasian. A reference to Claudius may also be present on the obverses. Some coins depict the Colosseum in isolation, others show it with the Meta Sudans on its right and the porticus of the Baths of Titus to the left, but most have the porticus on the right and the Meta Sudans on the left. This latter vantage point could only be achieved by viewing the amphitheatre from the area of the Temple of the Deified Claudius. In any case, the appearance of the flanking structures is notable because they were all part of Flavian efforts to reclaim the area of Nero's Domus Aurea. Martial (*Book of Spectacles* 2) places the Colosseum alongside the Baths of Titus and Claudius' colonnade as he speaks about Rome being restored to herself. It is also remarkable that while imperial bronze coins were typically produced in vast numbers, only five obverse dies have been counted for the Flavian Colosseum *sestertii*. This suggests that their production was limited for a special occasion; perhaps they were distributed by Titus at time of the dedicatory games and early in Domitian's reign (Elkins 2006). The Colosseum appeared again on rare gold, silver, and bronze coins of Severus Alexander to celebrate the building's reconstruction following the fire of 217 CE. Another appearance, on medallions of Gordian III, depicts a fight between a bull and an elephant on the arena floor; the legend MVNIFICENTIA indicates that they celebrated lavish games held there by the emperor (Rea 1988).

The Circus Maximus was featured in a three-quarter aerial view on *sestertii* of Trajan (Fig. 27.5). It was difficult to depict a massive and irregularly shaped monument like the Circus on coins, and so it was reduced to its most fundamental elements. At the centre of the coin is the *spina*, the track's central barrier, adorned with various monuments, most conspicuously the *metae* at either end and the obelisk. Amidst the rows of spectators at the back is the Temple of Sol and Luna. The wall curves towards the viewer at the left of the temple to indicate the eastern bend of the Circus. Below that is an arch, perhaps the Arch of Titus in the Circus. This view of the Circus can only be achieved from the Palatine Hill and the residence of Rome's emperors (Humphrey 1986: 104; Elkins 2015: 86–87). This vantage point may be significant, as it refers to Trajan's patronage. It is certain that the coins were struck

FIGURE 27.5. Bronze sestertius of Trajan from Rome. Yale University Art Gallery, Promised Gift of Ben Lee Damsky, TR2007.13938.418.

to mark Trajan's rebuilding of the Circus; a recent study of Trajan's coins has demonstrated that these coins date to the second half of 103 CE (Woytek 2010: 113). An inscription indicates that Trajan's reconstruction of the Circus was completed in that year (*CIL* 6.955). Associated *sestertii* show the emperor standing on a platform with attendants in the Circus, next to a *meta*, addressing the people. Caracalla issued *sestertii* showing a panoramic view of the Circus that was clearly modelled on Trajan's prototype. The only conspicuous difference is the addition of a prominent depiction of the *carceres*, which were the focus of Caracalla's reconstruction (Humphrey 1986: 117; Elkins 2015: 103).

While some references to games or the building of entertainment venues can provide insight into imperial ideology, attention to the coins might also help researchers better understand texts and the visual world that Latin authors encountered. Although it has been generally accepted that Titus' inaugural games in the Colosseum were the subject of Martial's *Book of Spectacles*, the identity of the vague 'Caesar' to whom the poems are addressed has been debated (Coleman 2006: xlv–lxiv). One point of controversy regards the *quadrantes* of Domitian minted in c.83 CE that depict a rhinoceros; games were often commemorated on coins with the representation of exotic animals. Appearances of rhinoceroses in spectacles were, however, very rare. Martial (*Book of Spectacles* 9 [11] and 26 [22 + 23]) also describes the exhibition of a rhinoceros in the Colosseum. Domitian's *quadrantes* could be evidence that it is Domitian's games that were the subject, wholly or partly, of the *Book of Spectacles* (Buttrey 2007).

Great festivals were also celebrated on imperial coins. The *ludi saeculares*, held approximately every 110 years to commemorate the turn of an era, figured prominently in the coinages of Augustus, Domitian, and Septimius Severus. Domitian's *ludi saeculares* coins have attracted the most attention, as they depict some of the different rituals held at various venues. The most common types are *asses* showing the emperor making a bloodless offering of ritual cakes before a temple, images that could be understood by a broad audience. Types depicting a blood sacrifice, the *fruges* (collection of grains and legume offerings), and the *suffimenta* (distribution of substances to be used in sacred fires) are rarer and may reflect the fact that the images are a bit more arcane; perhaps they were reserved for some special distribution to a limited group (Grunow-Sobocinski 2006). *Aurei* and *denarii* of Septimius Severus with the legend LAETITIA TEMPORVM (happiness of the times) depict a famous spectacle from the Saecular Games in 204 CE in which parts of the Circus were disguised as a ship and rigged to fall apart suddenly so that animals would jump out (Dio Cassius 76.1.4–5). The coins show this event in process: the barrier of the Circus is the hull, with the obelisk as its mast, and on the track/sea around it are lions, leopards, bears, oxen, asses, and ostriches (Humphrey 1986: 115–116). Septimius Severus also struck *aurei* that show a three-quarter aerial view of the Stadium of Domitian with athletes on the arena floor; these too may have been issued in conjunction with the *ludi saeculares*. The extreme rarity of the coins suggests they were produced for a special distribution and not as regular currency (Damsky 1990). Claudius had also established a sequence for the *ludi saeculares* that departed from the Augustan system (or returned to an earlier scheduling) and coincided with the centennial anniversaries of Rome's founding. In 248 CE, on Claudius' system, Philip II struck an extensive series of coins to celebrate the one thousandth anniversary of Rome's founding. The coins depicted the Temple of Venus and Roma or various animals with legends denoting the *Ludi Saeculares*.

Originally an agricultural festival, the *Parilia* had become an annual celebration of Rome's foundation by the end of the republic; Hadrian called the festival the *Romaia*. On Hadrianic *aurei* and *sestertii* of 121 CE, the Circus Maximus is represented by means of a reclining figure who holds a wheel and leans against a *meta* (Elkins 2015: 91). The legend is ANN DCCCLXXIIII NAT VRB P CIR CON. The type celebrated the 874th birthday of Rome and the games given to the people on the occasion.

In the later Roman empire, references to games on coins became much less common, as the resources to sustain them diminished and were refocused. Notable exceptions include a series of late third- and fourth-century CE coins for the Festival of Isis (Alföldi 1937). Although most of these emperors were Christian, the coins were struck in Rome where worship of the traditional gods was able to survive longer than it did in the East. The so-called contorniate medallions of the fourth and fifth centuries CE depict pagan themes, deceased emperors, and famous charioteers or other performers and events pertaining to the Circus Maximus (Alföldi 1943; 1976; Mittag 1999). Emperors who were great patrons of the Circus, such as Nero and Trajan, frequently adorn their obverses. The function of contorniates is uncertain. They may have been gaming tokens, souvenirs from spectacles in the Circus Maximus, or served as gifts for the New Year.

Conclusions

Coins that refer to athletics on Greek coins, and the related series of Roman provincial coins, do not merely illustrate what scholars already know from history but are a testament to the importance of festivals and athletics in the self-perception and identity that cities wished to disseminate to their neighbours. Roman republican and imperial coins speak to the individual provisioning for games, festivals, and venues and, therefore, provide insights into the importance of spectacle in Roman life and politics. Although this contribution does not presume to provide any definitive answers to the question of games and coins, coins are an important source material and are as deserving of attention as other documentary or visual sources. Arguably, they are more important, since coins provide a more copious and consistent visual record than any other form of ancient art.

The great variety in the Roman series and the range of individual historical personages responsible for the issuing of coins provides many fruitful opportunities for research. For instance, it seems probable that emperors who lavished games upon the people tended to strike more coins that reminded viewers of their generosity. And the particular vantage points from which the Colosseum and the Circus Maximus are depicted may have bearing on the semantic value of the images. Some Roman coins that refer to games or the construction of entertainment buildings were issued for special occasions and in limited quantities. It would be useful to explore these phenomena in greater detail and probe the extent and purpose of these targeted issues produced for special occasions, such as games or festivals.

REFERENCES

Alföldi, A. 1937. *A Festival of Isis in Rome under the Christian Emperors of the IVth Century.* Budapest.

Alföldi, A. 1943. *Die Kontorniaten. Ein verkanntes propagandamittel der stadtrömischen heidnischen Artistokratie in ihrem Kampfe gegen das christliche Kaisertum.* Leipzig.

Alföldi, A. 1976. *Die Kontorniat-Medallions.* Berlin.

Barron, J. P. 1968. 'The Fifth-Century Diskoboloi of Kos.' In *Essays in Greek Coinage Presented to Stanley Robinson.* 75–89. C. M. Kraay and G. K. Jenkins, eds. Oxford.

Burnett, A. 1987. *Coinage in the Roman World.* London.

Butcher, K. 1988. *Roman Provincial Coins: An Introduction to the Greek Imperials.* London.

Buttrey, T. V. 2007. 'Domitian, the Rhinoceros, and the Date of Martial's *Liber de Spectaculis.*' *JRS* 97: 101–112.

Carradice, I. and M. Price. 1988. *Coinage in the Greek World.* London.

Coleman, K. M. 2006. *M. Valerii Martialis Liber Spectaculorum.* Oxford.

Crawford, M. H. 1974. *Roman Republican Coinage.* Cambridge.

Crowther, N. B. 2004. *Athletika: Studies on the Olympic Games and Greek Athletics.* Hildesheim.

Damsky, B. L. 1990. 'The Stadium Aureus of Septimius Severus.' *AJN* 2nd series 2: 77–105.

Damsky, B. L. 1995. 'The Throne and Curule Chair Types of Titus and Domitian.' *Schweizerische numismatische Rundschau* 74: 59–70.

Dunbabin, K. M. 2010. 'The Prize Table: Crown, Wreaths and Moneybags in Roman Art.' In *L'argent dans les concours du monde grec: Théâtres du monde.* 301–345. B. Le Guen, ed. Saint-Denis.

Elkins, N. T. 2004. 'Locating the Imperial Box in the Flavian Amphitheatre: The Numismatic Evidence.' *NC* 164: 147–157.

Elkins, N. T. 2006. 'The Flavian Colosseum *Sestertii*: Currency or Largess?' *NC* 166: 211–221.

Elkins, N. T. 2014. 'The Procession and Placement of Imperial Cult Images in the Colosseum.' *PBSR* 82: 73–107.

Elkins, N. T. 2015. *Monuments in Miniature: Architecture on Roman Coinage.* New York.

Elkins, N. T. 2019. *A Monument to Dynasty and Death: The Story of Rome's Colosseum and the Emperors Who Built It.* Baltimore.

Franke, P. R. and M. Hirmer. 1964. *Die griechische Münze.* Munich.

Gallis, K. J. 1988. 'The Games in Ancient Larisa: An Example of Provincial Olympic Games.' In *The Archaeology of the Olympics*. 217–235. W. J. Raschke, ed. Madison, WI.

Garello, F. 2004. 'La scuola atletica di Crotone.' In *Agonistica in Magna Grecia. La scuola atletica di Crotone*. 59–76. A. Teja and S. Mariano, eds. Calopezzati.

Golden, M. 1998. *Sport and Society in Ancient Greece*. Cambridge.

Grunow-Sobocinski, M. D. 2006. 'Visualizing Ceremony: the Design and Audience of the Ludi Saeculares Coinage of Domitian.' *AJA* 110: 581–602.

Howgego, C., V. Heuchert, and A. Burnett, eds. 2005. *Coinage and Identity in the Roman Provinces*. Oxford.

Humphrey, J. 1986. *Roman Circuses: Arenas for Chariot Racing*. London.

Jenkins, G. K. 1970. *The Coinage of Gela*. Berlin.

Klose, D. O. A. 2005. 'Festivals and Games in the Cities of the East during the Roman Empire.' In *Coinage and Identity in the Roman Provinces*.125–33. C. Howgego, V. Heuchert, and A. Burnett, eds. Oxford.

Klose, D. O. A. and G. Stumpf. 1996. *Sport, Spiele, Sieg. Munzen und Gemmen der Antike*. Munich.

Kraay, C. M. 1976. *Archaic and Classical Greek Coins*. Berkeley.

Mannsperger, D. 1984. *Olympischer Wettkampf. Sportdarstellung auf antiken Münzen und Medaillen*. Tübingen.

Meadows, A. and J. Williams. 2001. 'Moneta and the Monuments: Coinage and Politics in Republican Rome.' *JRS* 91: 27–49.

Miller, S. G. 2004. *Ancient Greek Athletics*. New Haven.

Mittag, P. F. 1999. *Alte Köpfe in neuen Händen: Urheber und Funktion der Kontorniaten*. Bonn.

Nollé, J. 2012. 'Stadtprägungen des Ostens und die "explosion agonistique": Überlegungen zu Umfang, Aussagen und Hintergründen der Propagierung von Agonen auf den Prägungen der Städte des griechischen Ostens.' In *L'organisation des spectacles dans le monde romain*. 1–46. K. Coleman, P. Ducrey, and J. Nelis-Clement, eds. Geneva.

Rea, R. 1988. 'Le antiche raffigurazioni dell'anfiteatro.' In *Anfiteatro flavio. Immagine, testimonianze, spettacoli*. 23–46. Rome.

Ritter, S. 2002. *Bildkontakte. Götter und Heroen in der Bildsprache griechischer Münzen des 4. Jahrhunderts v. Chr*. Berlin.

Rutter, N. K., A. M. Burnett, M. H. Crawford, A. E. M. Johnston, and M. J. Price. 2001. *Historia Numorum: Italy*. London.

Schwabacher, W. 1962. 'Olympischer Blitzschwinger.' *AK* 5: 9–17.

Seltman, C. T. 1921. *The Temple Coins of Olympia*. Cambridge.

Seltman, C. T. 1951. 'The *Katoché* Hoard of Elean Coins.' *NC* 11: 40–55.

Taylor, L.R. 1935. 'The *Sellisternium* and the Theatrical *Pompa*.' *CPh* 30: 122–130.

Wiseman, T. P. 1971. *New Men in the Roman Senate*. Oxford.

Woytek, B. 2010. *Die Reichsprägung des Kaisers Traianus (98–117)*. Vienna.

PART V

CIVIC CONTEXTS

SECTION 1

SOME LOCAL CONTESTS AND FESTIVALS

CHAPTER 28

SPARTA'S CONTRIBUTIONS TO GREEK SPORT

PAUL CARTLEDGE

PROBLEMS OF DEFINITION AND METHOD

IT is indeed the case that 'every culture's sport is fashioned by its traditions and needs' (Kyle 2007: 180), but ancient Sparta was one of those—few—societies in which traditions (indeed, the very notion of tradition as such) were exceptionally strong and gave at the least a very powerful direction and impulse to the fashioning of the city's communal needs (Christesen 2012, 2014). There is a question, perhaps, and one not limited to the case of Sparta by any means, whether the ancient Greeks practised 'sport' at all, as we might want to define that term today (Sansone 1992; Golden 1998; 2004; 2008; Miller 2004a; 2004b; Kyle 2007: 180; Potter 2011). Their own emic term *agōn*, meaning contest, which via the ancient Greek noun *agōnia*, 'competitiveness', gives us our word 'agony', is much nearer the mark. In ancient Greece, not only but perhaps especially in Sparta, such athletic competitiveness could be a life and death affair, literally. 'Sport', however, is a time-honoured word and will be retained here, used alternately and interchangeably with 'games'.

A further, methodological problem confronts us at the outset—that of Sparta's exceptionality, which is itself linked with the extra problem created by the fact that the ancient written sources for Sparta in the archaic and classical periods (roughly 700 to 300 BCE) are so significantly skewed. That is, they tend to be either massively positive or 'pro', or equally massively negative or 'con'. Since so many of these writings were filtered through an Athenian lens, Sparta tends as a result to come out looking like either a (e)utopia or a dystopia. The literary evidence for Spartan sport or games begins in the seventh century, with a very rare example of an internal Spartan source—Tyrtaeus, the patriotic elegist. Normally, the sources, beginning not before Herodotus in the third quarter of the fifth century and followed soon after him by the Athenian extreme oligarch Critias, are non-Spartan outsiders.

Xenophon the Athenian exile was an exception of a different kind. For, as a client of King Agesilaus II and beneficiary of official Spartan largesse in the shape of an estate near Olympia, and a devoted philo-Spartan who sent his two sons to be put through the Spartan educational cycle (see the next section), he was not exactly an outsider—but then he was hardly an unbiased witness, either. One of the questions that his extant writings—including a biography of Agesilaus (cf. Cartledge 1987) and a cultural essay on the Spartan way of life as well as works of more 'straight' historiography—most pertinently raise is whether or not Sparta was a more or less 'normal' Greek *polis* (city, citizen-state). This is not a question that can be addressed properly within the scope of this chapter—I happen to believe it was quite abnormal, but the opposite case has been firmly put, against the run of the sources (Hodkinson); but it has to be borne in mind constantly throughout. Facets of Spartan society and culture that are especially vulnerable to the potential for distortion on this account are collective and individual piety, the city's usually overriding commitment to the communal and the collective interest, including a formal and compulsory public education system, its possession of huge numbers of unfree Greeks held down in hereditary subjection (as 'Helots') and, finally, the public and civic role the city accorded to the female half of the Spartan population. Only to a quite limited extent and degree can the weaknesses of the literary sources—chiefly anachronism, ethnocentricity, and political-ideological bias—be mitigated or offset by other written texts and by the relatively jejune extant archaeological record.

PUBLIC EDUCATION

Exactly when and how Sparta acquired the societal, civic feature that certainly did make it unique among the one thousand or so Greek cities—namely its public, centrally directed and comprehensive educational cycle compulsory for all legitimate Spartan proto-citizen boys from an early age until the age of civic manhood—is not known. The pamphlet of Xenophon mentioned above, datable probably somewhere in the first quarter of the fourth century and certainly no later than 350, offers the *terminus post quem*. So striking a feature was it that Plato took it as a starting point for his own, radically antinomian social-utopian prescriptions and Aristotle ascribed to it a good deal of the responsibility for Spartans' boorish behaviour and performance, at least abroad. But the ancient name by which it is now often known—*Agōgē* or Raising/Upbringing—is not attested in a literary source until some two centuries later than they, and an alternative title—*paidikos agōn* or Boys' Contest—appears epigraphically later still. Scholarly debate continues, fairly enough, over exactly what the stages and components of the cycle were at any one time, and in particular over the balance struck as between public and private instruction (Ducat 2006). But compelling agreement subsists that, all the way through, the education on compulsory offer was as much or more a matter of socialization, the internalization of Sparta's dominant social values, as of technical instruction of any sort, and that such technical instruction as was imparted was far more heavily physical than strictly intellectual.

Thus basic literacy was taught, and a good deal of 'literature', not least locally produced Spartan work, was memorized for purposes of communal recitation, but the chief aim of the education overall was to produce the ideal Spartan hoplite infantryman, ready to take his place as soon after the age of 20 as required in his assigned platoon and regiment in the phalanx. Indeed, successful passage through the educational cycle was a prerequisite for a Spartan male's attaining, by way of his election to a communal mess-group, the status of citizen and thus citizen-warrior in the first place. No doubt it was not unhelpful to be able to run fast, at least under armour, but a premium will have been placed rather on strength and endurance, the sorts of qualities that would enable a Spartan to shine in the 'heavy' field sports rather than on the running track.

NUDITY

And in a sense to shine literally, not only metaphorically, since, according to Thucydides (1.6), it was the Spartans who first introduced what by his day (second half of the fifth century) was universal Greek athletic practice, namely the anointing themselves with olive oil both before and after an athletic event (for mainly though not necessarily entirely practical reasons; cf. Sansone 1992). How Thucydides could have been so sure that it was indeed the Spartans who were the pioneers of this practice is a bit of a puzzle, but inferential reasoning allows us to note that the oil was something the Spartans possessed in superabundance thanks to both environmental and socio-political reasons, and had done so probably since as early as the eighth century BCE. Archaeology further reveals that local potters and painters had made a speciality, at least from the later seventh century, of the type of oil-flask (*aryballos*) in which athletes (and others of course) carried the oil around. Anointing with olive oil went with— and probably was initially designed specifically to complement—the again characteristic- ally Hellenic practice of competing at athletics stark naked (*gumnos*, whence *gumnasion*). Rival tales—or myths—were told of when and how and why nudity in competition was introduced at the Olympic Games, at a time when the sole event was the *stadion* or (roughly) 200-metre dash. But the practice was not confined to the Olympics, even if it may have been that contest's supreme authority which secured its universal acceptance.

Whatever the actual sequence, or chain of causation, there is every reason for thinking that the Spartans, with their exceptionally toned bodies, might have been unusually keen both to accept it and promote it. That possibly accounts for what can be read as an implied protest against the overvaluation of athletic as opposed to military success, as expressed in a poem of the martial poet laureate of early (and much later) Sparta, Tyrtaeus (*fl. c.*650 BCE):

> I would not rate a man worth mention or account | either for speed of foot or wrestling skill/ … unless he can endure the sight of blood and death | and stand close to the enemy, and fight. | This is the highest worth (frag. 12, trans. M. L. West)

It may also account at least in part for a possible case of the granting of heroic—super- human—post mortem status to one extraordinarily successful athlete: three-times *Olumpionikēs* Chionis (Young 2010 [1996]: 277–278; but see also Christesen 2010). Sparta was as a society particularly keen on posthumous heroization and the paying to such heroes of the appropriate religious worship (Cartledge 1988), but mostly those so honoured were of divine or semi-divine descent and royal status in life, and no other athlete besides Chionis is known to have been even a possible candidate.

OLYMPICS

Nothing succeeds like success, and Sparta is on record as being an exceptionally successful producer of successful athletic competitors in the first two to three centuries of documented competition at the international (that is, between Greeks from different cities) level. Prime among such competition was that organized at Olympia in north-west Peloponnese in honour of Zeus of Mount Olympus, traditionally from 776 BCE but probably from a date nearer 700. The origins of what became the quadrennial Olympic Games are shrouded in mystery, but at least as far as the location is concerned it is perhaps not irrelevant that in later times there was a permanent oracular shrine of Zeus onsite. The mystery is at any rate not dissipated by the Greeks' own typically rival myths of origin. Among the attributed human founders one—probably not entirely human, if human at all—Spartan called Lycurgus was given a place of special honour, credited with being a signatory to some sort of truce or cessation of warfare that enabled the Games to get going. Indeed, a discus with the actual terms of the truce inscribed thereon could be pointed to, and Lycurgus' 'signature' there duly noted (Lämmert 2010: 39—a manifest forgery). If any history can be rescued from such a myth-historical farrago, it would be the inference that Sparta from early on became a champion and sponsor of the Olympic Games, an inference that is at least quite compatible with the exceptional success at the Games of citizens of Sparta during its earliest century and a half or so.

Down to the mid-sixth century almost thirty Spartans are accredited with forty-five Olympic victories between them, and in a form of contest where the winners took all, and there were no prizes—or documentary records—for coming even second or third, this was no mean statistic. That the Spartans took the winning of an Olympic victory deadly seriously is shown by their symbolic, non-rationalistic practice of stationing a crown Olympic victor near or around a commanding king in battle formation, as 'a talisman of victory' like the king himself (Kurke 2010: 206–207, 208–209, cf. 211). The adopted Spartan seer Teisamenus, originally of Elis, thus proved himself more Spartan than the Spartans by wrongly interpreting an oracular prediction that he would win five 'victories' for his new state to mean that he would become a victorious pentathlete and trained vigorously accordingly—only to discover that the five victories would be battles the Spartans would win with his indispensable mantic aid (Hdt. 9.35). War and athletic games were two spheres for the winning of *kudos* (glory) (Kurke 2010) that ran parallel in ancient Greece but nowhere more winningly than in Sparta.

Athletics and Heavy/Combat Sports

Strikingly, all the earliest Spartan victors were competitors in athletic contests broadly interpreted—running, wrestling, throwing, or jumping: *stadion, diaulos, dolichos, palē, pentathlon*, discus, javelin, standing long-jump (Christesen 2018). Emblematic is the self-proclaimed 'Akmatidas the Spartan (Lakedaimonios)' who 'winning in the pentathlon dedicated' [*sc.* this inscribed jumping-weight to Zeus] around 550 BCE (Whitley 2011: 169). Yet for the next couple of centuries after that there were only a half-dozen or so known Spartan athletic victors at Olympia, and none at all apparently between 448 (or possibly 468) and 316 (De Ste. Croix 1972: 354–355; Hodkinson 1999: 161–167, 161 fig. 1 graph).

For whatever reason—and there could be many, apart from a possible loss of Spartan interest or fall-off in athletic dedication—thereafter for the next two centuries what is striking rather is the Spartans' exceptional success in a very different kind of equestrian competition, which took place over a quite separate track or course. Here victory was gained by proxy, since owners and trainers were not normally also riders or charioteers, and it might even be gained by a significant part of the human species otherwise banned not only from competition in but even from spectatorship of the athletic events at Olympia: women.

Hippics

Between about 548 and about 368, thirteen or fourteen Spartans (records are patchy and not altogether reliable: Christesen 2007) won between them seventeen or eighteen victories in chariot-races. One Spartan, Euagoras, achieved the staggering and almost unique feat of winning three times in a row (over a span of eight years) with the same team of four mares (Hdt. 6.103; Paus. 6.10.8). Victory especially in the four-horse chariot-race, the 'blue riband' event, conferred huge prestige, and even political influence (Kurke 2010 [originally 1993]). That helps to explain why a Spartan visiting Phigaleia in south-west Arcadia towards the end of the sixth century, was keen to make an offering to 'Poseidon the driver' (Cartledge 2000); and much more conspicuously why, when in 420 all Spartans were banned from competing at the Olympics by the organizing state of Elis (then almost at open war with its one-time alliance leader, Sparta), one unusually passionate and arrogant Spartan chariot-racer, Lichas son of Arcesilaus, entered his team under foreign (Boeotian) colours and was even prepared to throw off the disguise and claim the prize for victory in his own name (Hornblower 2000; Lämmert 2010: 48–50). For his pains he was publicly flogged—a mark both of his formal disqualification and of his gross dishonouring. At the following Olympics the Spartans had to endure the even more shaming spectacle of an Athenian with Spartan connections, Alcibiades, carrying off the supreme equestrian prize—and possibly also gaining second and third (or at least fourth) place into the bargain.

Soon enough, though, Spartans were back competing legitimately, but in 396 it was again Sparta that notched up another 'famous first'—the first woman to win the four-horse chariot Olympic crown was the Spartan princess Cynisca (Valavanis, this volume Chapter 9; Raschke, this volume Chapter 35). Cynisca, clearly, was no ordinary Spartan woman. Apart from being extremely wealthy—as all indulging in equestrian sports had to be (Hodkinson 2000: 312–317)—she was also the full sister of the dominant Spartan king of the day, Agesilaus II. Indeed, thanks to his confidant Xenophon (*Ages.* 9.6), we happen to be given the official royal version of how and why Cynisca came to be involved with chariot-racing in the first place: which is that any success of hers would demonstrate that such was no mark or test of manly courage (the sort of virtuous courage required for success in war) but rather—and merely—one of the possession of great wealth (not best applied, we infer). Cynisca, however, probably did not see things the way her brother wanted her to: on a still extant stone statue-base at Olympia she loudly proclaimed her pioneering priority as 'the only woman in all Hellas to have won this crown'—a feat she repeated probably in 392 (Kyle 2003; 2007: 188–191, 194–196; cf. further Valavanis, this volume Chapter 9). Cynisca of course had not driven the chariots in person, but we will return to the question of Spartan women's participation in sport later in this chapter.

OTHER PANHELLENIC OR HELLENIC FESTIVALS

Olympia was the pre-eminent Panhellenic (all and at first only Greeks) athletics festival. It was the first, it stayed first (Spivey 2004). The Spartans maintained a close relationship with the sanctuary, choosing to use it rather than Delphi to mark or celebrate some specially momentous occasions, such as their victory over the Athenians in the battle of Tanagra in 458 or 457—which they commemorated visually and extremely visibly by the placing of a golden shield on the ridge of the roof of the recently completed temple of Zeus (later to contain a Wonder of the Ancient World, master-crafted by Phidias). The display here of Spartan athletic prowess was not in itself something remarkable. What is, is the seemingly total absence of Spartan success in any other of the other three major Panhellenic festivals that together since the 570s constituted the Periodos or Circuit: the Pythian Games at Delphi (where Sparta was not shy of self-presentation by any means: Palagia 2007), the Isthmian at Corinth, and the Nemean at Nemea (later Argos) (Valavanis 2004). We know the names of some 670 victors at these three—not one is a Spartan (Scanlon 2002: 79–80).

On the other hand, there is some evidence for Spartan interest—and success—in a quadrennial games that ranked only just below the Circuit Big Four: the Panathenaic Games at Athens, which were instituted very soon after the Circuit, in the 560s, and in obvious emulation of it. Here, somewhere about 500 BCE perhaps, a Spartan king, Damaratus, won a victory in—unsurprisingly—the four-horse chariot-race, and there is a well-preserved prize oil-amphora excavated in the sanctuary of Sparta's patron goddess Athena that may conceivably represent a—small—part of Damaratus's winnings (cf. 'Athletics and Interstate Rivalries', Valavanis, this volume Chapter 9); at any rate, as its external signature image shows, it was part of the prize for this particular race. It may therefore not be merely coincidental that in c.505 Damaratus had effectively stymied an intended Spartan and allied invasion of Athens—a decision that in due time was to cost him his throne.

Apart from in the near- or quasi-Panhellenic Panathenaea, Spartans are known to have competed and won in much lesser festivals—the Lycaia in Arcadia (fourth century), the Eleutheria at Larissa in Thessaly (second/first century BCE), and the Amphiareia at Oropus (first century BCE) (Scanlon 2002: 80). These serve to introduce the normally hidden side of Spartan athletic and hippic competition—at home, in 'Lacedaemon', which was one of the names of the extraordinarily hypertrophied state territory of the Spartans: some 'two fifths of the Peloponnese' (Thucydides), or in modern terms about 3,000 square miles or 8,000 square kilometres of land embracing both Messenia (on the west side of the Taygetus mountain range) and Laconia (on the east of it).

Local 'Lakonian' Athletic and Hippic Festivals

Damonon's Stele

One single inscribed pillar datable either in the third quarter of the fifth century or, more likely, the first quarter of the fourth throws huge swathes of light on what it was to be a player, a competitor, in games held at the local, intra-state level of Spartan politics and society (Christesen 2019). This document is usually known for short as the stele of Damonon (as in Hodkinson 2000: 303–307 figs.18–19), but it should really be of Damonon *and* Enymakratidas, for below a relief of a four-horse chariot, now much damaged, the almost 100-line (as preserved) text lists the no fewer than seventy victories (fifty chariot-racing, twenty running) won by this extraordinarily agonistic, self-promoting—and markedly un-laconic—father and son duo. And all of them were won within the bounds of 'Lacedaemon'. Does this mean that the standard of competition within Lacedaemon was relatively low—that father and son would have stood little or no chance of winning outside Lacedaemon, even at the Arcadian Lycaea? Or is it rather the case that they chose to concentrate their efforts locally, that in so doing they were fully expressing, if in a different way from Akmatidas, what it was to be a 'Lacedaemonios', a member of a master-race, lording it over other Greeks, indeed, but in this case other Greeks, both free and enslaved, who were subordinate denizens of their own—vast—*polis*? Of course, we'll never know the answer, but I rather prefer to think in terms of the latter alternative.

Roughly speaking, this is how the inscription is disposed (I follow Tillyard 1908): lines 1–5 a metrical dedication ('Damonon dedicated this to Athena Poliachos ('City-Holder'), having gained these victories in a manner unparalleled among those now living'); lines 6–34 Damonon's victories in chariot-races; lines 35–49 victories of Enymakratidas; lines 49–65 victories of Damonon as a *pais* (sub-adult); lines 66 to end victories of both father and son at the same games/festivals. I shall adopt (since I am less interested than Damonon in his obviously Freudian competitiveness with his own son) an alternative reading—by location.

Nine games sites may be identified—and here I shall be a little dogmatic, based on my own extensive researches over many decades into the political topography of Sparta and what I have called 'Lakonia' (Cartledge 2002). The sanctuary of Poseidon (in local spelling Pohoidan) 'Earth-holder' was situated in Sparta itself. Both father and son won here, the son interestingly achieving success in both the sprints and the 'long' race (probably only middle-distance by our standards); and the family seems to have owned a racehorse that also won here. The relevant sanctuary of Athena was again probably in or near Sparta itself, though hardly on what passes for the city's acropolis. Damonon here won both a running race (the short sprint) and chariot victories, his son both the short sprint and a horse-race (twice). The sanctuary of Demeter of Eleusis was located several kilometres south of Sparta in the basin of Sparta, at modern Kalyvia Sokhas; here at the Eleusinia (Eleuhinia in the local dialect) festival, Damonon seems to have won eight chariot victories, himself driving his own teams. He won the same number at the Pohoidaea games, which were held at Thouria in south-east Messenia, a town of the Perioeci ('Outdwellers'), who though free were not full Spartan citizens and once at least rebelled (in *c*.464, in company with a mass of the unfree Helots, both Messenian and Laconian). At the Pohoidaea games at Helos (the area at the mouth of the Eurotas where most of the Helots of Laconia lived and worked) he won one fewer chariot-race but no fewer than seven horse-races. Next, and politically of immense significance, both father and son won at the Parparonia games, held in the Thyreatis (also known as Cynouria), an area of north-east Laconia taken permanently from Argos in the mid-sixth century in a war made famous by Herodotus (1.82). In this permanently contested frontier zone, inhabited by Perioeci and used by the Spartans opportunistically as a dumping-ground for congenial refugees such as the Aeginetans, the games served to give a pious religious veneer to the Spartans' possession by brute conquest. Next comes the Lithesia in honour of Apollo Lithesius and held apparently somewhere near the south-easternmost cape of Laconia, the dreaded Cape Malea. Penultimately, there is cited the Maleateia, given in honour of Apollo Maleatas, who was worshipped also in north-east Laconia just south of the Thyreatis. Here Damonon won the two shorter running races as a boy. Finally, the site of one games listed, the Ariontia, remains uncertain; if the connection with the poet Arion is correct, this could conceivably have been staged at the foot of the central prong of the Peloponnese, where Arion's visit *c.*600 BCE was commemorated in a sanctuary of Poseidon. This was a special scene of glory for both father and son, the former only hippically, the latter with his own feet as well as those of a quadruped.

Between them father and son seem to have had pretty well all bases in Laconia and Messenia (excepting only west and north Messenia) covered. The Perioeci and Helots presumably got sick of the sight of them after a while, but to their Spartan peers they surely ranked as legends in their own lifetimes. Athena the City-Holder, also known as Chalcioikos ('of the Brazen House'), will no doubt have been gratified to receive this stele in her sanctuary as a dedication betokening the true competitive—and pious—spirit of her favoured people.

Leonidaea

A festival not mentioned in the above stele, for the good reason that it hadn't yet been invented, began in earnest probably in the third century BCE, a time when Sparta had been forcibly confined to the role of modest Peloponnesian struggler and found itself trying to compete in a new world of Hellenistic territorial monarchies. A time, in other words, to reach back into the golden past, to the book of heroes, and pull out the great Leonidas. To him and to Regent Pausanias, the victor of Plataea but whose memory was less golden, was dedicated an annual festival involving athletic games of some kind open only to Spartan competitors (Robert 2010 [1982]: 109–110 speaks of 'xenophobia'). In the reign of Roman emperor Trajan the festival was re-endowed and revivified, a suitably nostalgic note on which almost to end (Cartledge and Spawforth 2002 esp. 192–193; cf. Van Nijf 2010: 186 for the 'rich agonistic life of Roman Sparta').

VIRGINEUM GYMNASIUM?

One of Sparta's most notorious quirks, at least as perceived and retailed by outside observers and commentators, was the special place accorded to the female half of the citizen population under the 'Lycurgan' dispensation—literally 'order' (*kosmos*: Hdt. 1.65). Spartan girls, young unmarried women, and married women allegedly did all sorts of things that decent Greek women were supposed not to be allowed to do. Indeed, if one was to believe Aristotle, they actually ruled their menfolk, the world turned upside down (Cartledge 2001a). Prominent among the oddities of a Spartan female's existence as thus represented was a devotion to athletic prowess, including training in public and with members of the opposite sex. Many of the sources for this thrillingly antinomian narrative are well post-classical, of the Roman period, deriving from the theme-park Sparta alluded to in the previous section. But some are contemporary, most prominently Xenophon, and his presumably eyewitness testimony to the Spartan female diet and physical exercise is at least not contradicted by a humorous passage of Aristophanes' *Lysistrata* (411 BCE) and is seemingly supported by the totally serious evidence of a series of Archaic, sixth-century bronze figurines depicting adolescent girls or young married women in a state of total nudity (deeply shocking to non-Spartans—even Aphrodite was represented clothed until the fourth century BCE), with slim, shapely and toned bodies and in a couple of cases actually caught in the act of running—or possibly dancing (Cartledge 2001b: 180–181).

The very late source Pausanias (second century CE) speaks of a running race held actually at Olympia and over the same Olympic track for females only, organized by a committee of women. The context, appropriately, was the Heraea, or festival of Hera, to whom principally the earliest temple at Olympia had been dedicated, well before the monumental temple to her consort Zeus (Scanlon 2008). Almost certainly, such feminine running was typically a matter not of practical athletics, in a masculine sort of secular competition, but of ritual and doubtless also eugenic preparation of females for their appointed tasks of childbearing and childrearing (Scanlon 2002: 104–105, 134–135, 287–290; Golden 127–129). Except that in Sparta that was not all a woman was supposed or allowed to be or do, by any means (Cartledge 2001a), and I think we have to allow that here women were in the Spartan sense educated to be not just homemakers but also physically vigorous counterparts to their male partners.

A SPECIAL CASE: BRASIDAS

I end with the case of a Spartan individual, who flourished in the later fifth century, a commoner but one who achieved the highest distinction attainable by a Spartan born outside the two royal families.

I noted above that the heroization of mortal males was a Spartan predilection. The process affected Spartans abroad too, as when Brasidas, victor over Athens in the battle of Amphipolis in 422, was made retrospectively the founder-hero of that in fact Athens-founded city and granted the religious honours appropriate to his new station (Thuc. 5.11). But the way had been prepared in 423 by the people of Scione in Chalcidice, who, having been as they saw it liberated by Brasidas from Athenian control, collectively and officially crowned him with a golden crown as 'Liberator of Greece'. But individual Scionaeans festooned him rather with ribbons, *as if he were* a victorious athlete (Thuc. 4.121): they knew the way to a Spartan's—and Sparta's—heart. To conclude, Sparta was indeed a place apart, exceptional in what passed for sport in ancient Greece, as in many other respects.

REFERENCES

Cartledge, P. A. 1987. *Agesilaus and the Crisis of Sparta*. London.

Cartledge, P. A. 1988. 'Yes, Spartan Kings were Heroized.' *LCM* 3: 43–44.

Cartledge, P. A. 2000. '"To Poseidon the Driver": An Arkado-Lakonian Ram Dedication.' In *Periplous: Papers on Classical Art and Archaeology Presented to Sir John Boardman*. 60–67. G. R. Tsetskhladze, A. J. N. W. Prag, and A. M. Snodgrass, eds. London.

Cartledge, P. A. 2001a [1981]. 'Spartan Wives: Liberation or Licence?' Repr. in *Spartan Reflections*. 106–126. London.

Cartledge, P. A. 2001b. 'The Mirage of Lykourgan Sparta: Some Brazen Reflections.' In *Spartan Reflections*. 169–184. London.

Cartledge, P. A. 2002. *Sparta and Lakonia: A Regional History 1300–362 BC*, 2nd edn. London.

Cartledge, P. A. and A. Spawforth. 2002. *Hellenistic and Roman Sparta: A Tale of Two Cities*, new edn. London.

Christesen, P. 2007. *Olympic Victor Lists and Ancient Greek History*. Cambridge.

Christesen, P. 2010. 'Kings Playing Politics: the Heroization of Chionis of Sparta.' *Historia* 59: 26–73.

Christesen, P. 2012. 'Athletics and Social Order in Sparta in the Classical Period.' *ClAnt* 31: 193–255.

Christesen, P. 2014. 'Sport and Society in Sparta.' In *A Companion to Sport and Spectacle in Greek and Roman Antiquity*. 146–158. P. Christesen and D. G. Kyle, eds. Malden, MA.

Christesen, P. 2018. 'Sparta and Athletics.' In *A Companion to Sparta*, 2 vols. 2: 543–564. A. Powell, eds. Malden, MA.

Christesen, P. 2019. *A New Reading of the Damonon* Stele. *HISTOS* Supp. 10. Newcastle Upon Tyne. https://research.ncl.ac.uk/histos/documents/SV10.ChristesenDamononStele.pdf.

De Ste. Croix, G. E. M. 1972. *The Origins of the Peloponnesian War*. London.

Ducat, J. 2006. *Spartan Education: Youth and Society in the Classical Period*. Swansea.

Golden, M. 1998. *Sport and Society in Ancient Greece*. Cambridge.

Golden, M. 2004. *Sport in the Ancient World from A to Z*. London.

Golden, M. 2008. *Greek Sport and Social Status*. Austin, TX.

Hodkinson, S. 1999. 'An Agonistic Culture? Athletic Competition in Archaic and Classical Spartan Society.' In *Sparta: New Perspectives*. 147–187. S. Hodkinson and A. Powell, eds. London.

Hodkinson, S. 2000. *Property and Wealth in Classical Sparta*. London.

Hornblower, S. 2000. 'Thucydides, Xenophon, and Lichas: Were the Spartans Excluded from the Olympic Games from 420 to 400 B.C.?' *Phoenix* 54: 212–215.

König, J., ed. 2010. *Greek Athletics*. Edinburgh.

Kurke, L. 2010 [1993]. 'The Economy of *kudos*.' In König. 204–237.

Kyle, D. 2003. '"The Only Woman all Greece": Kyniska, Agesilaus, Alcibiades and Olympia.' *JSH* 30: 183–203.

Kyle, D. 2007. 'Spartan Sport and Physical Education.' In *Sport and Spectacle in the Ancient World*. 180–197, 364–366. Malden, MA.

Lämmert, M. 2010. 'The So-called Olympic Peace in Ancient Greece.' (German original 1982–3). In König. 36–60.

Miller, S. G. 2004a. *Ancient Greek Athletics*, 2nd edn. New Haven.

Miller, S. G., ed. 2004b. *Arete: Greek Sports from Ancient Sources*, 3rd edn. Berkeley.

Palagia, O. 2007. 'Spartan Self-presentation in the Panhellenic Sanctuaries of Delphi and Olympia in the Classical Period.' In *Athens–Sparta: Contributions to the Research on the History and Archaeology of the Two City-States*. 32–40. N. Kaltsas, ed. Athens.

Potter, D. S. 2011. *The Victor's Crown*. New York.

Robert, L. 2010. 'Opening Address: Eighth International Congress of Greek and Latin Epigraphy.' (French original 1982) In König. 108–119.

Sansone, D. 1992. *Greek Athletics and the Genesis of Sport*. Berkeley.

Scanlon, T. F. 2002. *Eros and Greek Athletics*. New York.

Scanlon, T. F. 2008. 'The Heraia at Olympia Revisited.' *Nikephoros* 21.9: 159–196.

Spivey, N. 2004. *The Ancient Olympics: A History*. Oxford.

Tillyard, H. J. W. 1908. 'Laconia I. Excavations at Sparta, 1907 § 10–Inscriptions.' *ABSA* 14: 174–182.

Valavanis, P. 2004. *Games and Sanctuaries in Ancient Greece: Olympia, Delphi, Isthmia, Nemea, Athens*. Malibu.

Van Nijf, O. M. 2010 [1999]. 'Athletics, Festivals and Greek Identity in the Roman East.' In König. 175–197.

Whitley, J. 2011. 'Hybris and Nike: Agency, Victory and Commemoration in Panhellenic Sanctuaries.' In *Sociable Man: Essays on Ancient Greek Social Behaviour, in Honour of Nick Fisher*. 161–192. S. D. Lambert, ed. Swansea.

Young, D. C. 2010 [1996]. 'First with the Most: Greek Athletic Records and "Specialization." ' In König. 267–283.

....

CHAPTER 29

IMPERIAL SPECTACLE IN THE ROMAN PROVINCES

....

GUY CHAMBERLAND*

INTRODUCTION AND DEFINITIONS

....

CIRCUSES, theatres, amphitheatres, and other entertainment facilities where Roman spectacles were produced are attested in the hundreds in the provinces of the Roman empire. Hundreds or even thousands of spectacles must have been organized in each of these buildings in the course of the decades and centuries. Likewise gladiators, charioteers, stage performers, *venatores*, and athletes are known from hundreds of funerary monuments. The iconographic evidence is pervasive, from single gladiators depicted on domestic oil lamps to full event programmes tessellated on the dining room floors of the wealthy and powerful. It may, therefore, seem rather puzzling that fewer than 200 provincial honorary, dedicatory, and funerary inscriptions (out of over 100,000) record the organization of any spectacle by the provincial municipal elites in the Latin part of the empire, on which this chapter will mostly focus. Nevertheless, epigraphy is the best source of knowledge for the mounting of spectacles in the provinces. The number of men who assumed any title as organizer of a spectacle is, at first sight, surprisingly small as well; there are altogether barely forty provincial *munerarii* and *curatores muneris* (respectively, givers of a statutory or private *munus*, i.e. of an amphitheatrical spectacle, and organizers of a statutory or at least state-administered periodic *munus*), and we know of only a single uncertain case of a *curator lud[orum?]* (organizer of games). We therefore have many more buildings than we have organizers and their spectacles. This chapter will provide an explanation for this fundamental problem, which must be addressed if we are to make sense of the inscriptions and other artefacts which do record spectacles in some or other way.

'Imperial spectacles' are here defined as Roman spectacles (so excluding e.g. Greek agonistic festivals) of the period from the perpetual dictatorship of Caesar (for the virtual lack of earlier evidence) to the end of Roman rule in the West (though little will be said about the late empire for lack of space). I apply the term 'statutory' to spectacles which were constitutionally *required* from office holders, while privately sponsored spectacles could be organized

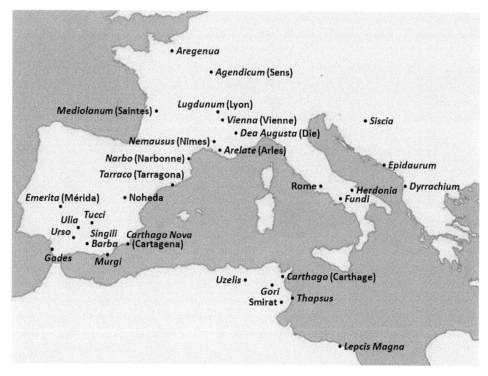

FIGURE 29.1. Map with selected sites where Roman spectacles were organized, especially outside Italy. Source: G. Chamberland.

not only by magistrates and priests, but by private individuals as well, even freedmen. Some inscriptions, as we are about to see, bring the two categories together but without confusing them. Figure 29.1 shows all sites mentioned in this chapter.

THE MUNICIPAL CHARTERS AND THE DISTRIBUTION OF THE EVIDENCE

So far as we can tell from our lacunose sources, the earliest Roman spectacles organized outside Italy are irrelevant to our purposes here, because they were mounted not by local magistrates or other notables, but by Roman military and political figures sent by the Senate on overseas missions. Thus in 206 BCE P. Cornelius Scipio (the future Africanus) mounted a *munus gladiatorium* in Carthago Nova to honour his deceased father and uncle while the city still belonged *de iure* to Carthage (Livy 28.21). In the same city, an inscription was set up by four Roman citizens (possibly *quattuorviri*) who had erected a column and provided for a procession and *ludi*; this they did even before the town gained the status of a colony in 45 BCE, since they dedicated their endeavours to the Genius of the *oppidum* (*CIL* 2.3408: ... *Genio op(p)idi columnam, pompam ludosq(ue) coiraverunt*). A few years later, however, G. Asinius Pollio, then governor of Nearer Spain, records the earliest known spectacle that is at once

Roman, provincial, and municipal (Cicero, *Letters to His Friends* 10.32). In 44 or 43 BCE, his *quaestor*, L. Cornelius Balbus (the same person who later built a theatre in Augustan Rome), organized *ludi scaenici* in Gades, in Further Spain, probably because they were required of him as *quattuorvir* in that Caesarean *municipium*, his birthplace. Interestingly, he also mounted a gladiatorial show; Pollio's wording leaves uncertain whether this, too, was required of Balbus *ex officio*, but he mentions the local gladiatorial school (*ludus*), whose presence indicates that gladiatorial spectacles (*munera*) were already well integrated into the local system of public entertainments.

In *c.*45 BCE, Caesar granted the status of Roman colony to the town of Urso in Further Spain. We happen to have much of the colonial charter in a slightly updated version datable to the Tiberian–Vespasianic period (*CIL* 2²/5.1022). Sections 70 and 71 prescribe that the *duumviri* 'must organize a *munus* or scenic representations for Jupiter, Juno, Minerva, and the (other) gods and goddesses, during four days, for the most part of the day' and that 'each one of them must spend at least 2,000 *sestertii* of his own money on those representations and that *munus*, and it is lawful for each *duumvir* to take and spend up to 2000 *sestertii* of public money' (*ei in suo mag(istratu) munus ludosve scaenicos Iovi Iunoni Minervae deis deabusq(ue) quadriduom m(aiore) p(arte) diei … faciunto inque eis ludis eoque munere unusquisque eorum de sua pecunia ne minus (sestertium bina milia) consumito et ex pecunia publica in sing(ulos) IIvir(os) d(um)t(axat) (sestertium bina milia) sumere consumere liceto*). As for the *aediles*, they 'must organize a *munus* or scenic representations for Jupiter, Juno, and Minerva during three days, for the most part of the day, and one day for Venus in the circus or forum' (the forum was used for the display of gladiators and beasts where no amphitheatre was available). Like the *duumviri*, each of them must spend at least 2,000 *sestertii* of his own money, but he can receive no more than 1,000 *sestertii* from the public treasury.

We happen to know of two *duumviri* from Urso. Gaius Vettius was twice *duumvir* in the Triumviral or early Augustan period, presumably after he had been aedile and, therefore, was three times *ex officio* organizer of statutory spectacles (*CIL* 2²/5.1025). Sometime in the second century CE, the *duumvir* M. Valerius Sabinus must have organized those same spectacles twice (*CIL* 2²/5.1032). Even though neither inscription says anything about spectacles, the important fact remains that both men were legally required, *ex officio*, to mount spectacles. The same logic applies to thousands of higher Italian and provincial municipal magistrates—mostly *duumviri*, *aediles*, and *quattuorviri*—whose inscriptions likewise do not explicitly mention any spectacles. The scale and programme may have varied greatly, but everywhere the organization of statutory spectacles was one of the main functions of upper magistrates.

A remarkable case of epigraphic silence is provided by Nemausus (Nîmes), a large Latin colony in Narbonensis equipped with a theatre, an amphitheatre, and, probably, a gladiatorial school and cemetery too, with some fourteen recorded gladiators' epitaphs (Hope 1998; *EAOR* 5 *passim*). It may seem surprising that only four of the 2,000 local inscriptions record actual spectacles (*EAOR* 5.6 and 9; *AE* 1982, 680 and 681; perhaps also a Greek *agon*: *AE* 1992, 1216), and that none of those spectacles can be attributed to any of the thirty-two attested *duumviri* and prefects of the vigils and arms (the second highest magistracy in Nemausus' peculiar *cursus honorum*). What is more, one of the four inscriptions indirectly honours a probable freedman (through his freeborn daughter) because, among other benefactions, he had bequeathed 300,000 *sestertii* to secure the future organization of *ludi sevirales*: *ob liberalitates [p]atri[s] eius qui praeter c[e]tera CCC (milia sestertium) rei pub(licae) (se)virorum reliquit ad ludos seviral(es) in perpet(uum) celebrandos (AE* 1982, 680). These were theatrical representations mounted by the *seviri Augustales*, a board of priests, mostly freedmen, who performed the rituals of the Imperial Cult. None, however, of the seventy local *seviri Augustales* is documented for his spectacles.

Perhaps the most extreme case is provided by the Danubian provinces: Raetia, Noricum, the two Pannoniae, the two Moesiae, and Dacia (Bouley 2001). Besides some Hellenistic and Roman theatres (but no known circuses), there are a good number of amphitheatres and many household objects which depict gladiators and amphitheatrical events. Roman spectacles were meaningful to the inhabitants of these provinces as they were elsewhere, but one looks in vain for any organizer of a spectacle; the sole exception is a clumsy graffito from Magdalensberg (Noricum) of a head with the word *EDIT(or)* above it, i.e. 'game-giver' (Bouley 2001: 138–139 with pl. 34.1), but the context is military, not municipal. Incidentally, the evidence for *munera castrensia*, the 'arena spectacles of the military camp', is largely limited to the presence of amphitheatres on the frontier, but one such spectacle, mounted in 203 CE in Carthage for the birthday of Geta Caesar, is known in unusual detail thanks to the vivid account in the *Passion of Saints Perpetua and Felicity*, written in part by Perpetua herself (or at least presented as such) before she was exposed to the beasts.

This is not to claim that statutory spectacles were never commemorated in inscriptions, for they occasionally were, but never as the direct object of praise. Not very far from Urso, in Singili Barba, Marcus Valerius Proculinus was publicly honoured in 109 CE, at the end of his remarkable duumvirate (*CIL* 2²/5.789 = *EAOR* 7.16). Among his benefactions were 'the same number of days of public and private games' (*publicos ludos et totidem dierum privatos dedit*). The distinction here between 'public' and 'private' is certainly to be understood in terms of statutory vs privately sponsored, for a spectacle presented in the private sphere only to acquaintances would not be deserving of public praise. We are not actually told how many days of games there were, but everyone knew the regulations. The mention of Proculinus' public games, therefore, provided a context to assess the importance of the private programme. It is to be noted, however, that the verb used for both is *dedit* ('he gave'), though *curavit* would be more correct for the public programme; it seems likely that Proculinus did not ask for any subvention from the public treasury and, therefore, that his public games deserved some praise as well, but a modest savings of 2,000 *sestertii* for the city treasury (if we take the figure from Urso as representative) would not on its own be worthy of commemoration on a public honorary monument. At some point in the year the praiseworthy *duumvir* also opened the gymnasium and baths to men and women free of charge 'on the day he gave the Games of the Youth in the theatre' (*quo die ludos iu(v)enum in theatro dedit gymnasium et balinea viris et mulieribus gratuita praestitit*). These *ludi iuvenum* serve, here, a temporal function for the 'real' benefaction, and only incidentally document Proculinus' generosity; hence these games were probably required *ex officio* from *duumviri* in Singili Barba and, no doubt, elsewhere.

Sometimes spectacles in the public arena were mounted by officials with the title of *curator muneris publici*. Such officials may have been created to complement the magistrate in his guise as '*curator ludorum*'. Some cities, therefore, relied on a special fund to provide for these spectacles; evidence suggests that a private bequest was the source of many such special funds. At Lepcis Magna, in Tripolitania, Plautius Lupus was 'elected curator to mount the public *munus* in accordance with the testament of Iunius Afer' (*IRT*2009.601: *cum ad munus publ(icum) [e]x t(estamento) Iuni Afri... edendum curator ele[c]tus esset*). Likewise, at

Dea Augusta (Narbonensis), two priests (*flamines*) held at the same time the title of curator of the public *munus* in one case, and curator of the gladiatorial *munus* of Villius in the other. These are probably two instances of the same public honour: a periodic gladiatorial spectacle instituted thanks to the bequest of a Villius (*EAOR* 5.2 and 3: *flamini divi Augusti, item flamini et curatori muneris gladiatori Villiani*). Interestingly, no other city is known to combine the flaminate and *cura muneris* in this way.

There is no exact parallel to Proculinus' *ludi privati* at Singili Barba. Most privately sponsored spectacles, which form the bulk of our evidence, can be identified only by the circumstances in which they were mounted. The largest category is that of spectacles offered for the dedication of a building or statue. Most were *ludi scaenici*, as in Uzelis (Numidia) where in 221 a *quaestor* promised to erect a statue to Unconquered Hercules, protector of the emperor Elagabalus, using his own funds; the monument was dedicated early the following year accompanied by a day of stage representations (*AE* 1917–1918, 44: ... *statuam cum base quam ... sua liberalitate pollicitus est ... et ob eius dedicationem edito die ludorum scaenicorum, sua pecun(ia) fecit idemq(ue) dedicavit*). There were few *munera* offered 'ob dedicationem', but they include twelve pairs of gladiators organized for the dedication of a library at Dyrrachium in Macedonia (Robert 1940: 75 no. 2). Statues were dedicated with a spectacle of boxers at Epidaurum in Dalmatia (*CIL* 3.1745: *pugilum spectaculum*) and with chariot-races at Murgi in Baetica (*CIL* 2.5490).

COMMEMORATION IN THE PUBLIC SPACE

The evidence for the actual mounting of spectacles, therefore, is not only scarce but distributed unevenly both geographically and in terms of their statutory or private nature. A tentative explanation can be drawn at this point: that spectacles organized *ex officio* by municipal magistrates were not considered true benefactions but rather payments for their office and, therefore, not usually worthy of, or even appropriate for, public commemoration. This is supported by some observations about our evidence which may seem puzzling at first sight. Most striking is the fact that the title of *curator ludorum*, often used in modern accounts, is not once securely attested outside Rome (where the games were such a huge undertaking that the magistrate or emperor needed to rely on an appointed official to assist him, e.g. Tacitus, *Annals* 13.22). The only possible case of a *curator lud[orum]* is in an inscription found at Nemausus, but the omnipresence of the gladiatorial institution makes the reading *curator lud[i gladiatorii]*, or manager of a gladiatorial school, just as likely (*CIL* 12.3290). As a matter of fact, a number of local gladiators' epitaphs record their specific school or troupe by name, such as the *murmillo* Columbus who was 'Serenianus' and, therefore, belonged to one owned by a Serenus or Serenius (*EAOR* 5.20). Our evidence is therefore biased in favour of the title of *curator muneris*, which, unlike *duumvir* or *aedilis*, is self-explanatory.

This assumes that magistrates were by definition *curatores ludorum*. It is probable that in the majority of Italian and provincial cities, the less expensive *ludi scaenici* were set as the minimum required spectacle (as at Urso); very few men, especially in the smaller communities, were wealthy enough to afford the more expensive chariot-races or gladiators and wild beasts. In the more ancient communities, too, constitutions that predated the introduction of *munera* as well as the force of tradition may have worked against the im-position of *munera* on magistrates. As a matter of fact, most *curatores muneris* are attested in central and southern Italy, regions populated with ancient communities (e.g. *EAOR* 3.17, at Herdonia). On the other hand, many provincial communities were neither small nor par-ticularly ancient. In cities such as Nemausus and its neighbour Arelate (Arles), Augusta Emerita (Lusitania), or Siscia (Pannonia), where amphitheatres are attested as well as plenty of other evidence for *munera*, it seems probable that magistrates were required to mount these costly spectacles. It is to be noted that almost everywhere the same number of four higher magistrates were elected every year; in larger communities this meant more competi-tion and, therefore, greater expectations.

The data presented so far suggest that local systems for the organization of spectacles reflected or were conditioned by local history, traditions, and economic capability. Perhaps this flexibility, so typical of Roman institutions, is best demonstrated through an exam-ination of the chariot events or *ludi circenses*. The evidence is very unevenly distributed (Humphrey 1986). In the Gallic provinces, for example, circus buildings are securely attested only at Narbo (Narbonne), Arelate, Vienna (Vienne), Lugdunum (Lyon) and Mediolanum Santonum (Saintes). These large cities are epigraphically rich; the fact that only three inscriptions, from Narbo (*EAOR* 5.1), Arelate (*CIL* 12.670; also Ammianus Marcellinus, 14.5.1), and Lugdunum (*CIL* 13.1921) mention circus spectacles, all privately sponsored, is probably evidence that such sponsorship was institutionalized as part of the regular responsibilities of the higher magistrates. The Hispanic provinces have produced much more evidence. Circus spectacles are attested at some twenty sites, many of which were small communities where no circus building has been found, such as Tucci (*CIL* 2²/5.69 and 93) and Ulia (*CIL* 2²/5.492) in Baetica. This suggests that such sites were not equipped with monumental circuses but rather used open fields minimally adapted for chariot-racing. One should not assume, therefore, that races were on the same scale as in the 1959 Hollywood classic *Ben-Hur*. In fact, the small scale and modest price of such events, some of which were mounted for the dedication of a statue, may explain why they were organized privately as one-time events and made their way into the epigraphic record. By contrast, two large pro-vincial capitals, Tarraco and Carthage, each equipped with a monumental circus structure, have produced not a single formal inscription commemorating a circus spectacle. But one can almost hear the pounding of the horses when reading the vividly detailed curse tablets buried in Carthage just before races were to take place. One tablet conjures the spirit of a dead person to bind the horses of the Red and Blue teams: 'Bind their running, their power, their soul . . . hobble them, so that tomorrow morning in the hippodrome they are not able to run . . . may they fall with their drivers' (Gager 1992: 61; Tremel 2004: 158–160 no. 56).

Other indications suggest that local spectacles were often a much more modest affair than in Rome. At Gori in Proconsular Africa, an annual return as small as sixty *denarii* (= 240 *sestertii*) on a private bequest was sufficient to provide for a display of boxers (*pugiles*), an oil distribution, and a banquet for the *decuriones* (*CIL* 8.12421). The amount is by any standard so small that the prizes, if any were awarded, must have appealed only to local amateurs, not professional athletes.

The spectacles of the provincial priests were much grander affairs. Thanks to yet another bronze document from southern Spain, the so-called *Aes Italicense*, we know that the main expense incurred by provincial priests (*flamines* or *sacerdotes provinciae*) was the mounting of a gladiatorial *munus*. The inscription records the efforts of the Senate and the emperors

Marcus Aurelius and Commodus, in 177 CE, to come up with a table of prices for gladiators according to their rank in order to stop the inflation that had made gladiatorial spectacles ruinous for those who were required to mount them, particularly the provincial priests whose spectacles had to be worthy of their capital. Says one relieved senator (quoted by the orator) who had previously appealed his appointment: 'What do I have to gain with an appeal now? The most sacred emperors have removed the whole burden which crushed my patrimony. Now I want and look forward to being a priest, and the mounting of a *munus*, which we used to abhor, now I embrace' (*EAOR* 7.3). In the Tiberian age a priest of Rome and Augustus for the Three Gauls, C. Iulius Rufus, built much of the amphitheatre at the federal sanctuary in Lugdunum (*EAOR* 5.75). Presumably gladiatorial spectacles were already being mounted by the priests, hence the need for such a building. Two centuries later, Titus Sennius Sollemnis' tenure must have been remarkable, for he was quite unusually honoured by the Concilium of the Three Gauls with a statue back in his home town of Aregenua (*EAOR* 5.58). The inscription records his *munus*, composed of thirty-two pairs of gladiators, eight of which fought to the death (*sine missione*)—an expensive potlatch. Otherwise, we know little of such spectacles since they were required of the appointees, and none of the federal priests' inscriptions found in Lyon records any, though one of them had previously been priest of Augustus and *munerarius* in Agendicum, his home town (*EAOR* 5.55: *flamen Aug(usti) munerarius*). We know even less of the significance of those spectacles for the imperial cult since game-givers were never honoured for their piety but for being generous with their money. Still, it is worth pointing out that much thought was given to imperial symbolism and ideology in the insertion of the amphitheatre into such sanctuaries (Ville 1981: 212–213; Futrell 1997: 79–93).

COMMEMORATION IN THE PRIVATE SPHERE

Spectacles were highlights in the life of those who mounted them. If this statement were not already obvious enough, it is splendidly illustrated by the archaeological evidence. Although very little wall painting has survived, floor mosaics in villas and *domus* of the powerful and wealthy document scenes from the amphitheatre and circus throughout Italy and the provinces (Dumasy 2004; Dunbabin 1978; Brown 1992; Kondoleon 1999; Papini 2004). Since there is no reason to suppose that the same rules applied in the private as in the public sphere, it is difficult, not to say almost impossible, to determine whether any given depiction is about a spectacle that was statutory or privately sponsored, or even, in many cases, whether the mosaic illustrates a real or imagined spectacle. Sometimes the owner of the house—the *dominus*—instructed the mosaicists to identify the performers by name, including gladiators, horses, and other trained animals such as bears, and even animals to be killed; this strongly suggests that the depiction presents a real event, or at the very least real performers and animals (Dunbabin 1978: 72–73). Otherwise, there is little that is inscribed. Pictorial mosaics belonged to the more public areas of the house, such as the dining room, and served as conversation pieces; a *dominus* did not need any written reminder as he described the spectacle he had organized to his guests.

Nevertheless, one such *dominus* commissioned a mosaic with an exceptionally long tessellated text (Fig. 29.2). From Smirat, a village in the Tunisian Sahel about midway

FIGURE 29.2. The Mosaic of Magerius, from Smirat, Tunisia. Gilles Mermet/Art Resource, NY.

between Thapsus and several other cities, comes a mosaic which belonged to the villa of one Magerius and dates to about the middle of the third century (Beschaouch 1966; *AE* 1967, 549; Dunbabin 1978: 67–69; Brown 1992: 198–200; Vismara 2007: 107–112). It depicts a 'hunt' (*venatio*) with four hunters and four leopards, all individually named, presumably in an amphitheatre; the hunters belong to the *Telegenii*, one of the corporations of such performers which thrived in Africa (Vismara 2007). Four other figures are depicted which seem to be Diana (or perhaps a man disguised as the goddess?) on the left, Dionysus in the centre-right, possibly the leader of the troupe of hunters in the upper right-hand corner (rather than Magerius himself, based on his abbreviated garb: K. M. D. Dunbabin, pers. comm.), and an attendant in the centre, displaying four money bags of 1,000 *denarii* each. On each side of this last figure is a long inscription, unique of its kind, that records the dialogue between participants and attendees at this spectacle. A herald (not shown) asks the wealthy and privileged (*Domini mei*—'My lords!') for 500 *denarii* per leopard. The audience (not shown either but obviously looking down towards the lower *cavea* where Magerius is sitting) begs him to come forward and pay for the show; if (or when) he does, they claim, he will outdo the forefathers and be the model for future benefactors. The fact that Magerius had four money bags ready to be displayed and delivered suggests that the whole event was staged. He waited for the acclamations to take shape and be directed towards him (possibly the inscribed shouts *Mageri Mageri*—'Magerius! Magerius!'—started at this point) and only then fulfilled his part of the agreement. It is most unlikely that this staging happened at the end of the show, as several scholars believe, with Magerius remaining virtually anonymous through it all. It must have taken place *before* the show started for Magerius to take on his role as presiding *munerarius* (even though the word is not used, but *munus edes*, 'you will give the *munus*!' suggests the equivalent title of *editor muneris*). Probably few were fooled by the 'spontaneity' of the whole staging, but all would have agreed that Magerius was performing a true *liberalitas*. A *curator muneris* could be praised for his good management of public funds (e.g. *EAOR* 4.21 from Fundi); Magerius was praised for spending his patrimony.

The most popular forms of stage productions are seldom depicted in the western provinces (while new scenes of comedy keep on turning up in the East). This may be due to a preference for depicting the myths themselves rather than their staging, since mosaics with mythological scenes are numerous. Still, in addition to some spectacular late fourth-century mythical scenes discovered in 2005 at Noheda in Spain, there are two panels which show stage performers: mimes, a pantomime, and even at such a late date, tragic actors in their high shoes; there are musicians as well, including an organ player and a *scabillarius*, who stomped a rhythm with cymbals strapped to his feet. One of the scenes is inscribed MIMV ZELOTIPI NVMTI (or more correctly: *mimus zelotypi nupti*), i.e. 'The mime of the jealous bridegroom', one of the many versions of a popular theme known from several sources, including Juvenal (8.197) and the Fathers of the Church (W. J. Slater, pers. comm.; Lancha and Le Roux 2017).

CURRENT SCHOLARSHIP AND FUTURE DIRECTIONS

Current scholarship strongly favours the study of Roman spectacle along the lines of individual categories or 'disciplines'. Gladiators and gladiatorial shows have received the most attention (Ville 1981; Wiedemann 1992; Futrell 1997; Papini 2004; Coleman 2008; Carter 2009; Hugoniot 2010). The series *Epigrafia anfiteatrale dell'Occidente Romano*, as its title indicates, (re)publishes only inscriptions that are relevant to the study of *munera*. There has been some interest in chariot-racing (Horsmann 1998; Nelis-Clément and Roddaz 2008), and a number of studies have improved our understanding of athletics in the Roman West (Caldelli 1997; Newby 2005). Less attention has been paid to the mounting of *ludi scaenici*, especially in the provincial context where the evidence is poor, but Roman theatres were (and remain) among the most visible markers of *Romanitas* from Lusitania to Syria (Polverini and Malavolta 1977–1978; Leppin 1992; Slater 1996; Sear 2006). There *are* studies which encompass the different categories, but most are limited to a specific geographical area or narrow period, such as the reign of an emperor, and tend to be descriptive, probably because the boundaries they set for themselves are not particularly relevant to the investigation of the sociocultural significance of public spectacle (among the more successful is Weiss 1999). However, given that money and wealth were so defining in classical antiquity, the study of spectacle as payment-for-office vs spectacle as gift has received much less attention than it deserves (cf. Chamberland 2012). Of the second category, Magerius articulates it remarkably well in his mosaic inscription commemorating the *munus* he sponsored for his community: *hoc est habere! hoc est posse!*—'That is to be wealthy! That is to be powerful!' These are the spectators' shouts, or so he frames them, but no monument erected in public would have allowed him such boasts, and a writer such as the Younger Pliny would have outright disapproved (*Letters* 1.8; unless Magerius were a friend: *Letters* 6.34). Such spectacles, however, were exceptional moments in the life of the Italian and provincial notables who mounted them, hence their urge to immortalize them. Spectacle as payment was the norm, a reality distorted by our surviving sources.

NOTE

* This chapter was written in March–April 2011 and was only very slightly revised in February 2021.

REFERENCES

Beschaouch, A. 1966. 'La mosaïque de chasse à l'amphithéâtre découverte à Smirat en Tunisie.' *CRAI*: 134–157.

Bouley, E. 2001. *Jeux romains dans les provinces balkano-danubiennes*. Paris.

Brown, S. 1992. 'Death as Decoration: Scenes from the Arena on Roman Domestic Mosaics.' In *Pornography and Representation in Greece and Rome*. 180–211. A. Richlin, ed. Oxford.

Caldelli, M. L. 1997. *Gli agoni alla greca nelle regioni occidentali dell'Impero. La Gallia Narbonensis*. Rome.

Carter, M. J. 2009. 'Gladiators and *Monomachoi*: Greek Attitudes to a Roman "Cultural Performance".' *International Journal of the History of Sport* 26: 298–322.

Chamberland, G. 2012. 'La mémoire des spectacles: L'autoreprésentation des donateurs.' In *L'organisation des spectacles dans le monde romain* (Fondation Hardt: Entretiens sur l'Antiquité classique 58). K. M. Coleman and J. Nelis-Clément, eds. Vandœuvres–Genève.

Coleman, K. M. 2008. 'Exchanging Gladiators for an Aqueduct at Aphrodisias (*SEG* 50.1096).' *AClass* 51: 31–46.

Dumasy, F. 2004. 'L'autocélébration des élites gallo-romaines dans la peinture murale.' In *Autocélébration des élites locales dans le monde romain*. 345–361. M. Cébeillac-Gervasoni, L. Lamoine, and F. Trément, eds. Clermont-Ferrand.

Dunbabin, K. M. D. 1978. *The Mosaics of Roman North Africa*. Oxford.

Futrell, A. 1997. *Blood in the Arena: The Spectacle of Roman Power*. Austin.

Gager, J. G. 1992. *Curse Tablets and Binding Spells from the Ancient World*. Oxford.

Hope, V. M. 1998. 'Negotiating Identity and Status: the Gladiators of Roman Nîmes.' In *Cultural Identity in the Roman Empire*. 179–195. R. Laurence and J. Berry, eds. London.

Horsmann, G. 1998. *Die Wagenlenker der römischen Kaiserzeit*. Stuttgart.

Hugoniot, C. 2010. 'La disparition de la gladiature en Afrique romaine.' In *Des déserts d'Afrique au pays des Allobroges: Hommages offerts à François Bertrandy I*. 207–231. F. Delrieux and F. Kayser, eds. Chambéry.

Humphrey, J. H. 1986. *Roman Circuses: Arenas for Chariot Racing*. Berkeley.

IRT2009 = J. M. Reynolds and J. B. Ward-Perkins. *The Inscriptions of Roman Tripolitania*. Enhanced electronic reissue, G. Bodard and C. Roueché. 2009. http://irt.kcl.ac.uk/irt2009/.

Kondoleon, C. 1999. 'Timing Spectacles: Roman Domestic Art and Performance.' In *The Art of Ancient Spectacle*. 321–342. B. Bergmann and C. Kondoleon, eds. New Haven.

Lancha, J. and P. Le Roux. 2017. 'MIMUS ZELOTIPI NUMTI: À propos de la mosaïque de Noheda (Villar de Domingo García, Cuenca).' *Conimbriga* 56: 201–216.

388   GUY CHAMBERLAND

Leppin, H. 1992. *Histrionen: Untersuchungen zur sozialen Stellung von Bühnenkünstlern im Westen des Römischen Reiches zur Zeit der Republik und des Prinzipats.* Bonn.
Nelis-Clément, J. and J.-M. Roddaz, eds. 2008. *Le cirque romain et son image.* Bordeaux.
Newby, Z. 2005. *Greek Athletics in the Roman World: Victory and Virtue.* Oxford.
Papini, M. 2004. *Munera gladiatoria e venationes nel mondo delle immagini.* Rome.
Polverini, L. and M. Malavolta. 1977–1978. 'Ludi.' *Dizionario Epigrafico* IV: 2005–2098.
Robert, L. 1940. *Les gladiateurs dans l'Orient grec.* Paris. (repr. 1971. Amsterdam.)
Sear, F. 2006. *Roman Theatres: An Architectural Study.* Oxford.
Slater, W. J., ed. 1996. *Roman Theater and Society.* Ann Arbor.
Tremel, J. 2004. *Magica agonistica: Fluchtafeln im antiken Sport.* Hildesheim.
Ville, G. 1981. *La gladiature en Occident des origines à la mort de Domitien.* Rome.
Vismara, C. 2007. 'Amphitheatralia Africana.' *AntAfr* 43: 99–132.
Weiss, Z. 1999. 'Adopting a Novelty: the Jews and the Roman Games in Palestine.' In *The Roman and Byzantine Near East: Some Recent Archaeological Research* 2. 23–49. J. Humphrey, ed. Portsmouth.
Wiedemann, T. 1992. *Emperors and Gladiators.* London.

ARCHITECTURE OF GAMES AND COMPETITIONS

CHAPTER 30

GREEK SANCTUARIES AND STADIA

DAVID GILMAN ROMANO

INTRODUCTION

ATHLETIC competitions were an important part of religious cult, and Greek stadia were frequently a part of the Greek sanctuary. From the earliest evidence of the appearance of athletics, it is clear that the *dromos* of the stadium was constructed adjacent to the altar in the sanctuary in whose honour the athletic contests were held; often the temple of the god or goddess was nearby. Specifically it was the *dromos*, the racecourse itself, which was of importance as the site of the athletic contests. Technically, the word 'stadium' referred to the structure comprising the *dromos*, the track, together with the spectator facility, and as such, was very likely a later development (Romano 1993: 9–16). The stadium was clearly designed to provide somewhere near the racecourse for spectators to stand to watch the contests: the word 'stadium' likely derives from the Greek verb *histēmi*, 'to stand'. The contests were also religious in the sense that the athletes were competing to please the god or goddess.

'Stadion' eventually came to have three meanings in antiquity: as an absolute measure of distance of 600 feet; as the foot race of 600 feet; and as the place of athletic competition. While the popularity of athletic competition at sanctuaries grew, stadia were expanded, enlarged, and rebuilt to accommodate more spectators. Eventually the standing room that existed in the early days of the history of the stadium evolved into facilities with modest, and then at times large, and even extensive, seating areas.

It is safe to say that in the beginning, when athletic contests were fairly simple, the *dromos* existed with no formal spectator facilities. Spectators would have stood informally near the racecourse or along the sides where they would have watched the contests within the area of the *temenos*, or sacred area, of the sanctuary. It is likely that there would have been very few seats, but, if there existed a naturally sloping embankment that could be used for spectators, this would have been utilized.

STADIUM CONSTRUCTION

An early method of creating stadia was to build up artificial embankments of earth on relatively flat land, as spectator areas, along one or both long sides of the *dromos*. The early *dromos* required relatively little work to construct since it was merely a level stretch of land, 600 feet long, 50–100 feet wide. The principal task involved in the building of these early stadia of the sixth and fifth centuries BCE was the construction of the artificial embankments that required retaining walls and foundation curbs as well as the movement of large quantities of earth. Examples of this form of stadium include the examples at the Sanctuary of Zeus at Olympia in the sixth century BCE, the Sanctuary of Poseidon at Isthmia and at the Sanctuary of Apollo at Halieis, both examples of the fifth century BCE (Romano 1993: 17–42).

There were several later methods of stadium creation to accommodate larger numbers of spectators; one was to employ a natural hollow that utilized the slopes of a hill or hills for the spectator areas on three sides of the *dromos*. Examples of this type of stadium include those at the Sanctuary of Zeus at Nemea, the later stadium at the Sanctuary of Poseidon at Isthmia, and the Panathenaic Stadium in Athens. Both examples at Nemea and Isthmia are from the late fourth century BCE and the stadium at Athens is Roman. Another method of constructing a stadium was to utilize the side of a hillside to build a terrace for the *dromos* of a stadium, often but not always built in connection with a theatre for dramatic events. Examples of this type of construction with a theatre are found at Pergamon, Sardis, Tralles, Rhodes, and possibly Pessinus. An example of a stadium built on a mountain terrace without the theatre is at Delphi (though the earlier hippodorome may have been in a hillside below the sanctuary; Valavanis 2019).

At the Hellenistic city of Pergamon the large and steep theatre was built on the western side of the acropolis linking the Athena sanctuary above with the long and narrow terrace below. The terrace, 250 m in length and 25 m in width, was situated immediately in front of, and to the west of, the theatre *cavea*. The terrace served as a *dromos* of a stadium and the seats in the theatre could have been utilized to watch either the dramatic or the athletic events. The stage building of the theatre, built on the terrace, was constructed of wood and was portable, so that it could be erected for the dramatic and musical events and disassembled for the athletic contests to free the terrace for the foot races. The stadium–theatre complex was likely built as the result of the victory of Eumenes II over Prusias in 182 BCE when he established musical and athletic contests in honor of Athena Nikephoros. The games were 'crown games', that is awarding crowns but not value prizes; the musical contests were the equal of the Pythian games, and the athletic contests were the equal of the Olympic games. It is likely that the Ionic temple at the north end of the terrace was dedicated to Athena Nikephoros (Romano 1982: 586–589; Kohl 2002: 227–253).

An earlier example of the combination of theatre with stadium is found in Athens where on the Pnyx Hill during the rule of Lykourgos in the fourth century BCE the theatral area, known to be the location of the meeting of the political assembly of Athens, was enlarged, and at the same time a long terrace was created, bordered by two long foundations for spectators. These foundations were likely to have been built to retain artificial earth embankments for spectators to watch the athletic contests of the Panathenaic Games. The assembly area, used as a theatral area, would have been the location of the musical contests of the Panathenaic Games (Romano 1985: 441–445; Romano 1996: 71–85).

In the Hellenistic city of Messene, an elaborate stadium was constructed in the southern part of the city abutting the city wall. The northern half of the stadium was characterized as having a colonnade around the closed end of the stadium with gymnasium-like rooms leading off from the colonnade. Below the colonnade were stone seats. In the southern half of the stadium there were no seats but sloping embankments to the west and east of the racecourse. At the southern end of the stadium was a *hērōon*, a funerary monument of the Saithidai, attached to the city wall probably in the first century BCE (Themelis 2003: 40–51, 61–72).

A yet more developed example of stadium construction is at the city of Aphrodisias where a stadium was built of stone from the ground up and had seats on all sides, not using natural embankments on any of the sides. The stadium at Aphrodisias was constructed in the first century CE (Welch 1998: 547–569) and was 270 m long and composed of thirty rows of stone seats. The track surface measures 238 m in length, 31 m wide at its narrowest and 40 m wide at its widest. The stadium located at the northern limit of the city was closed on both ends and, as such, is one of the best-preserved stadia in the ancient world. It was used for Greek athletic contests as well as for Roman spectacles, gladiatorial events, and *venationes*. An inscription from Rhodes mentions the Aphrodisias Isolympia in the first century CE although it is possible that there was a Hellenistic predecessor on the site.

Architectural Characteristics of the Stadium

There were a number of common architectural characteristics of a stadium. The surface of the racecourse floor was typically composed of a hard-packed clay that would have been carefully prepared and rolled in preparation for the contests. At Nemea, bands of red and white coloured earth have been discovered within the central lanes of the racecourse floor, along its long axis, suggesting that certain areas of the track surface were highlighted for running events, and also possibly relating to the spaces for the long jump, javelin, or the discus (Romano 1981: 86–87; Miller 2001: 37–40).

Starting lines, *balbides*, at either end of the *dromos* limited the length of the *dromos* or track itself. These starting lines were typically composed of stone blocks and were characterized by having starting positions and single or parallel starting grooves for the toes of the front (left) and rear (right) feet of the starting athlete. Typically there would also be vertical posts as lane dividers in the starting line that could also be used as turning posts (Valavanis 1999: 57–141). The characteristics of the starting lines vary somewhat over time, but the basic concept was to provide a starting position for each athlete in the foot races. The grooves guaranteed that before the start the athlete would stand stationary in a specific place, with both feet grounded. During the Hellenistic period an additional apparatus was added to starting lines, known as a *husplex* (plural, *huspleges*), a spring-loaded mechanism that automatically raised or lowered a bar or a cord to allow the athletes to start the race. From an inscription found at Epidauros (*IG* IV² 1.98) it is known that a *husplex* mechanism was being installed in the mid third century BCE. Typically there was a closed area of the racecourse floor found at either one or both of the short ends of the stadium. This would have been the area behind the starting line and in front of the beginning of the spectator area. In some cases, and depending on available space, this area could have been used for the wrestling, *pankration*, or boxing events.

Water facilities are often found in a stadium. They usually comprise a series of stone water channels at the level of the *dromos*, typically punctuated by stone settling basins limiting the racecourse on the sides and sometimes at the short ends. Although it is commonly assumed that this water would have been for drinking, it is much more likely that it was used to maintain the track surface during the course of the athletic events. It would have been necessary to periodically lightly water down the track, especially during the hot summer days, to prevent the surface from drying out and becoming too hard and uncomfortable for the athletes. Moreover, spectators would not want to drink water that was at the level of the track surface and had been circulating around a track and sitting in settling basins at track level. Water for drinking by athletes and spectators alike would have been brought in clean containers, much as in the modern day. Sometimes, as at Delphi and Halieis, there is a convenient spring nearby the stadium, and consequently there are no water channels on the sides of the *dromos*, but more frequently water needed to be brought in by means of a pipeline as at Olympia, Nemea, Isthmia, and Epidauros.

Some Greek stadia have *plethron* steles, 100-foot markers, found on the side of the *dromos*, marking the measure of the racecourse. Usually these would be erected very close to the water channel blocks and the settling basins and immediately adjacent to the *dromos*. It is likely that spaces within the *dromos* floor, for instance the area between the 100 and 200 foot areas, could have been used specifically for one or more of the athletic events. This is suggested by the evidence at Olympia where the restricted zone for the judges, according to Pausanias 6.20.8, was opposite the altar of Demeter Chamyne. The judge's area is located between the 100-foot and 200-foot *plethron* markers on the track and was characterized by a series of benches that were constructed within a restricted rectangular space. This area of the track surface was likely to have been one *plethron* square (32.4 m², as at Olympia 100 feet = 32.4 m): it could have been utilized for specific field events, and the size might have related to the area (approximately the same) of the central courtyard of the *palaistra* at Olympia, and also to the training facility in Elis that we hear about from Pausanias 6.23.1–7, known as the *plethrion* (Romano 2007: 95–113). Pausanias also tells us that the altar of Endymion was located at the east end of the racecourse at Olympia, although it has not been located. The *plethron* markers could also have been used in connection with the measurement of discus or javelin throws.

Although each stadium in the Greek world was 600 feet in length, not all stadia were the same length. Each city-state, and by extension each sanctuary, used its own foot measure; the resulting stadium lengths, as racecourse lengths, therefore varied considerably. The absolute measurement of 600 feet varied as shown through the following examples.

Olympia = 192.28 m
Delphi = 177.80 m
Epidauros = 181.18 m
Nemea = 178.02 m
Halieis = 166.50 m

Formal entrances were an important aspect of the ancient stadium and over several centuries these took a variety of different forms. The approach of the athletes to the stadium was of significance in the design of the sanctuary as it appears from the archaeological evidence. From the fifth century there are examples of entrances that were open air and would have served the purpose of channelling the athletes toward the track. One is found at Isthmia, where an 11-metre ramp with low walls leads from near the south-east corner of the Temple of Poseidon to the northern corner of the curved end of the stadium. Another open-air corridor may be found at the Sanctuary of Zeus at Mt Lykaion, between the Administrative Building and the direction of the stadium and hippodrome (Romano and Voyatzis 2015: 216–228). Later, in the Hellenistic period vaulted entrances were constructed to the stadia at Olympia, Nemea, Delphi, and Epidauros, to create an artificial formal and dramatic entrance for athletes to arrive into the stadium. They were larger and more elaborate constructions: at Olympia the vaulted entrance was 32.10 m long and at Nemea 36.35 m (Miller 2001: 62–89).

The spectator facilities could vary considerably from stadium to stadium and from period to period. The embankments included only very few seats for VIPs, as at Olympia where two seat blocks are known from the sixth century BCE (see the next section). The stadium at Olympia was rebuilt in the fifth century BCE creating artificial embankments on all four sides of the *dromos* and, subsequently, was able to accommodate about 45,000 spectators; this stadium was used through the fourth century CE without the addition of seats.

HISTORY OF THE STADIUM: EXAMPLES

Olympia

Although the evidence for the cult of Zeus at Olympia dates to the second half of the eleventh century BCE (Kyrieleis 2002: 213–220), the earliest evidence for the stadium from Olympia is the archaeological remains for a part of an archaic stadium—a retaining wall and an artificial earth embankment—that is dated to about 540 BCE. Numerous archaic shields and helmets were found on the embankment, having been set up as dedications during the use of the stadium. Two stone seats of *proxenoi* are associated with this stadium, the seats of Gorgos and Euwainos, dated by letterforms to the middle of the sixth century BCE (Romano 1993: 19–21; Mallwitz 1972: 180–194). The earth embankment of the archaic stadium was likely to have had a very low slope of earth that faced the *dromos* of the stadium, similar to the situation of the two successive Olympia stadiums, where the earth embankments created a slope between 4 and 7 degrees. It is the low slope of the earth embankments that suggests that the spectators who used the embankments probably stood rather than sat to view the contests. The archaic stadium at Olympia used the natural slope of the Kronos Hill to the north as the northern spectator embankment and the *dromos* opened into the *altis* to the west and towards the ash altar of Zeus.

The *dromos* surface of the archaic stadium at Olympia was not found during excavation since the later stadia on the same site dug below the floor of the earlier structure. Stone starting line blocks characterized by two parallel grooves on their top surfaces and made of the local limestone, likely to be associated with the early Classical stadium at Olympia, were found reused in a drain nearby. By the Roman period the stadium at Olympia was used for the athletic contests in honor of Zeus as well as for the girls' games in honour of Hera (Pausanias 5.16.1–8). The Hera games may have been introduced at Olympia from early times, possibly as early as the construction date of the Temple of Hera at Olympia *c.*600 BCE, and, if so, the archaic stadium at Olympia could also have been used for the Hera festival from that time.

Corinth

A *dromos* of a stadium was discovered in the Upper Lechaion Road Valley at Corinth dating to the very late sixth century BCE around the year 500. This is one of two partially excavated racecourses that have been found in Corinth beneath the area of the later Roman forum. The later racecourse dates to after 270 BCE. The deity in whose honour the contests were held at Corinth is not known for certain, although scholars have suggested that the cult was that of Athena Hellotis or Artemis Hellotia (Morgan 1937: 549; Herbert 1972: 70–76). The area of the Upper Lechaion Road valley where the racecourses were found was characterized in the Greek period by the presence of many hero shrines (Williams 1978). Evidence of the earlier of the two racecourses has been found principally at its two extremities (Williams and Russell 1981: 2–19). At the east end has been discovered an early form of a stone starting line that is characterized by being in the form of a curve. The starting line is composed of rectangular porous blocks set between a cement mix. Toe grooves for the front (left) and the rear (right) foot are cut into the porous blocks. Blue-black paint covers the surface of the starting line, on which were painted red letters labelling the seventeen starting positions. The first five positions were destroyed by the later Hellenistic starting line. The preserved letters include, from south to north, tau, zeta, the next position has no letter, eta, theta, iota, kappa, lambda, mu, nu, omicron, and pi. The letter xi does not appear. The racecourse floor associated with the curved starting line is composed of a crushed porous surface; the same kind of surface has been found at the south-west end of the racecourse, where there is also associated a simple stone altar. The earlier of the two starting lines at Corinth is curved—unique in the Greek world—indicating that it was used as the start of a distance race in which each starting athlete had an equal distance to run to a specific point on the racecourse floor.

Halieis

At Halieis in the Argolid, the rural sanctuary of Apollo is located some 600 m to the northeast of the city, outside the circuit walls, and today is totally submerged beneath the Bay of Porto Cheli (Romano 1993: 34–42). The stadium is located to the south of the Temple of Apollo, a second temple, an altar, and associated buildings. The axis of the stadium is approximately north–south, agreeing generally with the axis of the two temples and long altar. Now under water, the stadium was originally located near the shoreline. It comprises a rectangular *dromos* with spectator facilities on the east and west sides for the northern one-third of the track. Stone starting lines are found at both the north and south ends of the stadium, 166.50 m apart. The *dromos* of the stadium may have been built in the sixth century BCE but the architectural features of the stadium likely date to the fifth century BCE. The athletic contests held in this stadium were local games and the facility was very modest, but worthy of the city of Halieis.

Mt Lykaion

An unusual example of a stadium is found at the Sanctuary of Zeus at Mt Lykaion in Arcadia. Recent excavation at this mountaintop site by the Mt Lykaion Excavation and Survey Project under the direction of the Ephoreia of Antiquities of Arcadia in Tripolis, in collaboration with and under the auspices of the American School of Classical Studies at Athens, has greatly enhanced our knowledge about the site (see http://lykaionexcavation.org). Located in a mountain meadow about 1,180 metres (3,870 ft.) above sea level, this stadium is found as a part of a stadium–hippodrome complex and is unique. The two facilities were constructed side by side on two broad terraces, each approximately 50 m wide and 250 m long. Whereas the dromos of the stadium occupied only 2/3s of this space at a higher elevation, the hippo-drome was likely the full length and width of the terrace at a lower elevation (Romano 2019: 27–43). The hippodrome is the only example in the Greek world that can be visualized and measured. Although there are no artificial seats adjacent to the stadium or the hippo-drome, there are the slopes of the mountain nearby that could have been utilized for spec-tator accommodation (Romano and Voyatzis 2015: 245–258). Although the earliest use of the hippodrome and stadium is yet undetermined, it is clear that there was a construction phase in the second quarter of the fourth century BCE.

Approximately 200 m above the area of the hippodrome is the southern peak of Mt Lykaion, the location of the ash altar and *temenos* of Zeus. Recent work at the altar has revealed archaeological evidence as early as the Final Neolithic period in the fifth millen-nium BCE, followed by activity in the Early, Middle, and Late Helladic periods, and with a large cache of Mycenaean kylikes and terracotta human and animal figurines indicating the likelihood of a Mycenaean shrine from the sixteenth century BCE. Although it is not known how early organized athletics began at the site of Mt Lykaion, according to Pliny the Elder (*Natural History*, 7.205) the earliest gymnic contests in Greece were held at Mt Lykaion, not at Olympia. Immediately to the south of the altar of Zeus at the southern peak of the moun-tain is a flat natural hollow between two hills, 155 m long, that could have served as the early location of a *dromos* at the site. It is not yet known when athletic competition began at Mt Lykaion (Romano and Voyatzis 2014: 629–630).

Rome

The Stadium of Domitian in Rome was built by 86 CE when Domitian held the first Capitoline Games in the facility. Located in the Campus Martius next to the Baths of Agrippa and north of the Theatre of Pompey, the site today is the location of the Piazza Navona. The stadium was characterized by a closed northern end and an open southern end, with spectator ac-commodation for approximately 15,000 along the sides and at the end (Platner 1929: 495–496). This was the first permanent facility for Greek athletics in the city of Rome, although there had been, earlier, a temporary facility built by Augustus in the Campus Martius that had been used for displays of Greek athletics (Suetonius, *Augustus* 43.2).

Panhellenic Sanctuaries

The great Panhellenic sanctuaries of Olympia, Delphia, Isthmia, and Nemea were regarded as the 'crown' festivals since wreaths of leaves were offered to the victors of the athletic contests; olive at Olympia, laurel at Delphi, celery or pine at Isthmia, and wild celery at Nemea. Each of these major festival sites had an important stadium and in each case there were several generations of stadium construction. The early stadia of Olympia and Isthmia have been described above.

By the fifth century BCE the stadium at Olympia had been greatly enlarged with the creation of artificial embankments on three of the sides of the facility, east, south, and west, utilizing the natural sloping embankment to the north. Although there were very few seats in this stadium, the facility could accommodate approximately 45,000 standing spectators. The racecourse floor was long and wide, a total length of 212 m and 192.28 m between the starting lines. The long sides of the *dromos*, including the water channels and basins and the spectator embankments bowed out in a convex curve increasing the width of the *dromos* toward the centre of the track. This design feature undoubtedly was related to the optimum visibility for the spectators standing on the low embankments and it is also known from a number of other stadia in the Greek world, including the Hellenistic stadia at Isthmia and Nemea. Water channels lined the floor of the *dromos* with water basins at regular intervals. Two stone starting lines were excavated by the Deutsches Archäologisches Institut (German Archaeological Institute) and are characterized by two parallel grooves. The preserved starting line blocks provide lanes for eighteen starting positions on the west and twenty positions at the east. The starting positions were used in different ways for each of the running events (Mallwitz 1972: 180–186).

At Isthmia, two successive stadia exist, the earlier dating to the fifth century BCE although there are some remains of an archaic phase. The latter dates to the Hellenistic and Roman periods. The earlier stadium located near the Temple of Poseidon is characterized as having two parallel long sides and a gradual curved western end. The earliest starting line is characterized as a triangular stone pavement with postholes to receive vertical wooden posts also serving as starting gates for sixteen starting positions. Later, in the early fourth century BCE, the triangular platform was covered and a simple single groove starting line installed in the stadium for twelve starting athletes. The later stadium at Isthmia is built into a natural hollow between two hills 200 m away from the earlier stadium, and, although the structure has never been fully excavated, it is known to have accommodated larger numbers of spectators (Broneer 1973: 49–52).

The Early Hellenistic Stadium at Nemea, built in the late fourth century BCE, is located in a hollow between two projecting hills about 450 m to the south-east of the temple of Zeus at Nemea. The stadium is characterized by a closed, almost semicircular end to the south and an open end that creates an artificial tongue of land projecting to the north. There were very few seats found in the stadium although some stones were found suitable for standing. There also exist ledges cut into the clay bedrock that could have been utilized by spectators. A stone water channel fed by water coming from the south-east borders the *dromos* on all sides with water basins spaced at intervals along the sides of the track. A stone starting line at the southern, closed end of the stadium is punctuated at each end by a stone statue base. The starting line has two parallel grooves with two sets of vertical postholes, the earlier ones for twelve lanes, with an additional central lane, and the later ones for ten lanes, also with an additional central lane. With the second phase, there is evidence of the addition of the *hysplex* for a mechanical start. A vaulted entrance approaches the stadium from the west (Miller 2001: 12–89). An earlier stadium has been discovered close to the sanctuary of Zeus and to the excavated shrine of Opheltes (Miller 2002: 239–250).

At Delphi the stadium is found high above the sanctuary of Apollo on a terrace of Mt Parnassos (Aupert 1979). Pausanias (10.32.1) tells us that Herodes Atticus was responsible for paying for the stone seating that exists in the stadium. The stadium is characterized by seats on three sides of the *dromos* with a curved closed end (*sphendonē*) towards the west. Stone starting lines have been found at both ends of the *dromos*; in the area beyond the east starting line there was built a Roman monumental arch. In the north-west corner of the stadium there is a small spring.

Civic and Rural Sanctuaries

Stadia and *dromoi* would have been common in local sanctuaries all over the Greek world. The sanctuaries could be found in cities, in suburbs of cities, or in the countryside and they would have been associated in each case with a hero or a god or goddess. In certain cases a stadium could be used by multiple cults, as was the case at Tegea, where the stadium near the Temple of Athena Alea was used for the Alea festival as well as for the Halotia festival to commemorate the capture of the Lacedaimonians alive in the battle of Dipaia (Pausanias 8.47.4). In large cities it is likely that there would have been multiple stadia, or at least *dromoi*, in different parts of town associated with different cults. For instance in Athens where there was the Panathenaic festival and the Panathenaic stadium, there were also other festival sites all over Athens that would have included athletic contests and facilities, and sometimes equestrian events as well—for instance the Theseia, Epitaphia, Anthesteria, Olympieia, Herakleia, Eleusinia, and the Oscophoria (Kyle 1987: 32–48). Pausanias mentions one in Mantineia, on the road leading to Tegea, a hippodrome and stadium where games in honour of Antinous are celebrated, another, near one of the roads to Orchomenos—the stadium of Ladas, where Ladas practised his running—and by it a sanctuary of Artemis (Pausanias, 8.10.1, 8.9.10, 8.12.5). Pausanias (3.14.6–8) has a long description of the *dromos* in Sparta where the young men of the day trained. He describes it as being located between shrines, sanctuaries, and tombs and being the location of two gymnastic schools. He also describes a place called '*platanistas*' as a ring of plane trees surrounding an area where the youths fight, and a road leading off from the agora that takes its name from a footrace run along the road for Penelope's suitors (Pausanias 3.12.1). The name of the road comes from the word for starting line of a racecourse, *aphesis*.

In Elis, Pausanias (6.23.1–2) gives us information about *dromoi* that were found in a gymnasium used for the training of athletes in preparation for the Olympic Games. High plane trees grew between the *dromoi* inside a wall and the whole area was called *xystos*. As mentioned earlier in this chapter, Pausanias explains that there is a separate racecourse for the competing runners, called the '*hieros dromos*', or sacred racecourse, and also another area called the '*plethrion*' that is the place where the judges match the competitors based on age and skill. At Olympia, the well-known third-century-BCE gymnasium includes a *dromos* as a covered practice track: this was a 600-foot long training area with starting lines at both ends.

Civic control of rural sanctuaries was typically in the hands of the city-state in whose territory the sanctuary was found, although there could be disputes about the control of the festival itself. For instance there are accounts suggesting that at Olympia there were controversies over the control of the Olympic festival as early as the seventh century BCE. Pausanias (6.22.2) gives us the information that—probably in 688 BCE—Pheidon, a powerful tyrant of Argos, was asked by the town of Pisa, near Olympia, to help capture the Sanctuary of Zeus at Olympia from Elis. Pheidon with his army of well-trained hoplites helped to secure the sanctuary for Pisa. Herodotus (6.127) says that Pheidon himself presided over the conduct of the games in that year. By the year 364 BCE Elis had again lost control of the sanctuary to Pisa, which together with its allied forces from Arcadia was directing the festival and the Olympic Games. It was at this time that Elis decided to attack the sanctuary. Xenophon, who was an eyewitness (*Hellenica* 7.4.29–31), tells us that the attack occurred after the horse race and during the wrestling event of the pentathlon, and that an all-day battle ensued with the participation of thousands of hoplites. Eventually Elis regained control of the sanctuary; according to the Eleans the Olympic Games of 364 BCE lost their legitimacy since the Pisans had been in control.

Conclusion

In conclusion, stadia were an integral part of many ancient Greek sanctuaries and they contribute to what we know about the workings of Greek cult. Stadia were often the largest and most conspicuous element of a Greek sanctuary (except for the hippodrome), and, of course, the modern counterpart has influenced our civilization in countless ways. Architecturally, the stadium had a very modest beginning, usually in the heart of the sanctuary, and then grew to great size and importance, sometimes moving to the outskirts of the sanctuary. Stadia could be found in urban as well as in rural sanctuaries; their use was related to the religious purpose of the facility as the place where athletes would compete to please the hero, god, or goddess. The winner of the contest was one who pleased the god the most.

References

Aupert, P. 1979. *Fouilles de Delphes*, vol. II : *Topographie et Architecture. Le Stade*. Paris.

Broneer, O. 1973. *Isthmia: Topography and Architecture*, vol. II. Princeton.

Herbert, S. C. 1972. 'Corinthian Red Figure Pottery.' Dissertation, Stanford University.

Kohl, M. 2002. 'Das Nikephorion von Pergamon.' *RA* 2: 227–253.

Kyle, D. 1987. *Athletics in Ancient Athens*. Leiden.

Kyrieleis, H. 2002. 'Zu den Anfängen des Heiligtums von Olympia.' In *Olympia 1875–2000, 125 Jahre Deutsche Ausgrabungen*. 213–220. H. Kyrieleis, ed. Mainz am Rhein.

Mallwitz, A. 1972. *Olympia und seine Bauten*. Munich.

Miller, S. G. 2001. *Excavations at Nemea: The Hellenistic Stadium*, vol. II. 37–40. Berkeley.

Miller, S. G. 2002. 'The Shrine of Opheltes and the Earliest Stadium of Nemea.' In *Olympia 1875–2000, 125 Jahre Deutsche Ausgrabungen*. 239–250. H. Kyrieleis, ed. Mainz am Rhein.

Moretti, J.-C. and P. Valavanis, eds. *Les hippodromes et les concours dans la Grèce antique*. BCH supplement 62. Athens.

Morgan, C. H., II. 1937. 'Excavations at Corinth, 1936–37.' *AJA* 41: 459.

Platner, S. B. 1929. 'Stadium of Domitian.' In *A Topographical Dictionary of Ancient Rome*. 495–496. T. Ashby, ed. Oxford.

Romano, D. G. 1981. 'The Stadia of the Peloponnesos.' Dissertation, University of Pennsylvania.

Romano, D. G. 1982. 'The Stadium of Eumenes II at Pergamon.' *AJA* 86: 586–589.

Romano, D. G. 1993. *Athletics and Mathematics in Archaic Corinth: The Origins of the Greek Stadion*. Philadelphia.

Romano, D. G. 1985. 'The Panathenaic Stadium and Theater of Lykourgos: A Re-examination of the Facilities on the Pnyx Hill.' *AJA* 89: 441–454.

Romano, D. G. 1996. 'Lykourgos, the Panathenaia, and the Great Altar of Athena: Further Thoughts concerning the Pnyx Hill.' In *The Pnyx in the History of Athens*. 71–85. B. Forsén and G. Stanton, eds. Helsinki.

Romano, D. G. 2007. 'Judges and Judging at Olympia.' In *Onward to the Olympics: Historical Perspectives on the Olympic Games*. 95–113. G.F. Schaus and S.R. Wenn, eds. Waterloo, Ont.

Romano, D. G. 2019. 'The hippodrome and the equestrian contests at the Sanctuary of Zeus on Mt. Lykaion, Arcadia.' In Moretti and Valavanis. 27–43.

Romano, D. G., and M. E. Voyatzis. 2014. 'Mt. Lykaion Excavation and Survey Project, Part 1: The Upper Sanctuary.' *Hesperia* 83: 569–652.

Romano, D. G. and M. E. Voyatzis. 2015. 'Mt. Lykaion Excavation and Survey Project, Part 2: The Lower Sanctuary.' *Hesperia* 84: 207–276.

Themelis, P. G. 2003. *Heroes at Ancient Messene*. Athens.

Valavanis, P. 1999. *Hysplex: The Starting Mechanism in Ancient Stadia*. Berkeley.

Valavanis, P. 2019. 'Ο ιππόδρομος, το αρχαϊκό στάδιο και τα δυτικά όρια της ιεράς χώρας των Δελφών.' In Moretti and Valavanis. 197–215.

Welch, K. 1998. 'The Stadium at Aphrodisias.' *AJA* 102: 547–569.

Williams, C. K., II. 1978. 'Pre-Roman Cults in the Area of the Forum of Ancient Corinth.' Dissertation, University of Pennsylvania.

Williams, C. K., II, and P. Russell. 1981. 'Corinth: Excavations of 1980.' *Hesperia* 50: 2–19.

CHAPTER 31

GYMNASIUM AND BATH

GARRETT G. FAGAN

GREEK GYMNASIA

IN ancient Greece, the gymnasium and the *palaestra* were the locations par excellence for the athletic training and education of freeborn young men (Delorme 1960; Tzachou-Alexandri 1989; Kyle 2007: 83–90). They were also, as their mature forms developed across the Greco-Roman Mediterranean, important locations for the display of athleticism and the athletic body. More than just public spaces dedicated to bodily health and exercise, they provided an arena for the spectacle of youth, physical prowess, and athletic competition.

The gymnasium (literally 'the naked place') emerged in the archaic age as little more than a natural woodland clearing with very few facilities. In the classical age it had evolved a rudimentary architectural form organized around a large open space, usually square or rectangular in shape. This space could be walled off, or lined with trees, and provided with separate running tracks, as at the Academy in Athens (Plutarch, *Cimon* 13.8). Scenes painted on contemporary vases show athletes oiling up under trees, their tunics hanging from the branches above (Yegül 1992: 19, fig. 20). By the fourth and third centuries BCE, the gymnasium had become a more elaborate but still essentially simple structure. Arrayed around the sides of the central open space were porticoes and rooms for various functions connected with education and physical training. In some cases, indoor running tracks and baths were located nearby, or integrated right into the structure, as at Priene or Nemea. The links between the final, monumental form of the gymnasium and its natural antecedents seem clear: the porticoes offered to patrons the shade and shelter formerly afforded by trees lining a clearing.

A good example of the development of the gymnasial form is to be found at Olympia (Pausanias 6.21.2; Mallwitz 1972: 284–289; Herrmann 1989: 63–64; Günther 2004: 147–152), although others are known from all over the Greek world. Set adjacent to the Kladeos River, much of the original area has been eroded away, but the main features of the complete gymnasium at Olympia are clear. The archaic and classical forms of the area remain obscure. In keeping with Peloponnesian conservatism, it may have long remained an undeveloped open space along the riverbank. It was not until the third century BCE that the rectangular space at the heart of the structure was delineated by porticoes on all sides, at least one of which featured a double colonnade. At some 220 metres long, it corresponded in length to the Stadium, thus allowing runners and discus- and javelin-throwers to practise there. On the south side, and attached to it, stood a smaller, square *palaestra*, also of the third century BCE (Fig. 31.1). The *palaestra* was a related building type that was used primarily for training in combat sports, such as boxing or wrestling. It too had porticoes and rooms on all four sides for changing clothes and for oiling before practice.

Standing nearby was a bathhouse, which dated originally to the fifth century, but was developed and refined in the fourth through first centuries BCE. The proximity between the bathhouse and the gymnasium constitutes good evidence that this area of the sanctuary, although undeveloped in the archaic and classical periods, was used as a training ground. The Greek bathhouse (*balaneion* or *loutron*), marked by hot-water bathing in individual hip-bath tubs where users sat, was not itself associated with exercise and training and was usually found as a stand-alone structure (as at Olympia) (DeLaine 1989; Fagan 2001; Hoffmann 1999; Ginouvès 1959; 1962; Trümper 2009; Yegül 1992: 6–29). A revealing passage in Aristophanes' comedy *Clouds* (ll. 1045–1054), first performed in 423 BCE, illustrates the differences between the *balaneion* and the gymnasium/*palaestra*:

> WORSE ARGUMENT: Now what's your reason for scorning hot baths (*therma loutra*)?
> BETTER ARGUMENT: Because they are utterly bad and turn a man into a coward.
> WORSE ARGUMENT: Stop right there! I've already got you in an unbreakable hammerlock. Pray tell me which of Zeus' sons you consider the heartiest he-man and the doer of the doughtiest deeds? Speak up!

FIGURE 31.1. The *palaestra* at Olympia. Photo: G. Fagan.

BETTER ARGUMENT: In my opinion, no he-man outclasses Heracles.

WORSE ARGUMENT: But where have you ever seen Heraclean cold baths? And yet who was ever manlier?

BETTER ARGUMENT: That there, that's just the sort of thing the teenagers spend day after day chattering about, that fills up the bathhouse (*balaneion*) and empties the wrestling schools (*palaestrae*)!

The *balaneion* here stands in sharp moral contrast to the virtuous gymnasium/*palaestra*: the former is a place of idle gossip, the latter a place of praiseworthy exercise. The evidence for hot-water bathing in Greek gymnasia or *palaestrae* before the first century BCE is precarious, resting mainly on Vitruvius' description of the ideal design for such a structure (Vitruvius, *On Architecture* 5.10–11) rather than on any solid archaeological evidence. It seems possible that heated spaces to induce sweating were installed in gymnasia and *palaestrae*, as that would have helped the process of removing the oil and grime from the athletes' bodies after exercise. Such rooms (termed *laconica* in Latin, *pyriateria* in Greek) were usually round with narrow entrances to retain heat, and can be tentatively identified in such gymnasia as those at Eretria or Assos. But it is not until the first centuries BCE and CE that fully fledged hot baths were built right into gymnasia in the Greek East, and that was likely a result of Roman influence on the region (see below on the Roman bath).

The administration of gymnasia was entrusted to an official, the *gymnasiarch*, and of *palaestrae* to officials called *paidotribai*. Both were drawn from the elite. These men were expected to maintain the buildings, regulate admission, and occasionally provide oil for the trainees. Although formal and competitive athletic events per se were not typically part of the gymnasium's regular agenda (though lists of victors occasionally mention gymnasia as a contest's setting), it does seem that some liked to attend gymnasia and *palaestrae* to watch the trainees at work (Delorme 1960: 269–315; Gardiner 1930: 82–93). In addition to physical exercise, intellectual instruction would also take place in the gymnasium, usually in large rooms termed *exedrai*, with professors and lecturers on hand to stimulate learning. Artistic endeavours (music, poetry, rhetoric) were encouraged and competitions among the students were staged. These events too likely attracted spectators. To this end, the porticoes provided shade and shelter for them.

BATH AND GYMNASIUM IN THE ROMAN WORLD

The Roman bath integrated the hot-water bathing establishment with the exercise ground, as exemplified by the early example of the Stabian Baths at Pompeii (Fig. 31.2), which date to around 120 BCE with additions in the Augustan era.

Here an open exercise area (Pa in Fig. 31.2) is flanked on three sides by a portico and bathing rooms, and on the western side by a suite of rooms that include a changing room (A), two *exedrae* (E), and an open-air pool (N). Access to the *palaestra* is denied to the women's section, which occupies the northern half of the main bathing wing, so it appears at this early stage that exercise was the preserve of male patrons (unless, after exercise, women walked around the outside of the establishment to enter their dedicated wing of the bathing wing, which seems unlikely). In the Forum Baths at Pompeii, dating to 80 BCE, the exercise yard is small and located in the middle of the *insula* occupied by the baths. By the time the Central

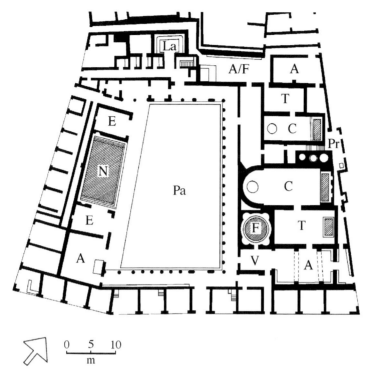

FIGURE 31.2. Stabian Baths at Pompeii. G. Fagan after F. Yegül.

Baths were being built—they were unfinished at the time of the eruption in 79 CE—separate male/female bathing suites had been abandoned and a very large *palaestra* with an open-air pool introduced. This was likely a result of influences from the larger imperial bathhouses at Rome.

The first large-scale 'imperial'-style set of baths built at Rome were those of Agrippa, which stood in the Campus Martius (Hülsen 1910; Yegül 1992: 133–137). Dio (53.27.1), writing two centuries later, states that Agrippa first opened a 'gymnasium' in 25 BCE and then dedicated the Aqua Virgo in 19 BCE. The problem here is that a large bathhouse such as that of Agrippa would require aqueduct water to function properly. It is possible that Agrippa opened a Greek-style gymnasium in 25 BCE and then added to it a bathing wing in 19 BCE. Given, however, the largely negative contemporary attitudes of the Roman elite toward Greek athletics in general and gymnasia in particular (Crowther 2004: 375–422; Ferrary 1988: 517–526), this would be a politically risky thing for Agrippa and Augustus to do. The difficulty here is more likely a product of terminological uncertainty. In Greek 'gymnasium' was used interchangeably with *balaneion* to denote a Roman-style bath (as Dio does in his notice about Agrippa's baths). So what Dio probably reports is that Agrippa opened some sort of bath in 25 BCE, which was then expanded when the aqueduct was introduced six years later. Little or nothing of the building remains to be studied today; outlines of it in a fragment of the Severan Marble Plan (*Forma Urbis Romae*) and in drawings by the sixteenth-century architect Palladio show open spaces that may well have been porticoed *palaestrae* (Yegül 1992: 135, fig. 147; Rodríguez Almeida 1981: fragment 38).

More interesting still is the building opened in Rome by the philhellene emperor Nero between 60 and 66 CE. Suetonius (*Nero* 12.3) states that in 60 Nero dedicated both a gymnasium and a set of *thermae* (large baths); he also appeared in person to distribute free oil to the senators and knights. In other words, Nero was playing the role of the traditional *gymnasiarch*. This is strong testimony, as Suetonius separates the gymnasium from the baths, and Nero's love of things Greek makes his opening of a gymnasium in Rome conceivable. In this same year, for instance, he inaugurated a Greek-style festival at Rome, named after himself (the *Neronia*), featuring gymnastic, athletic, musical, and equestrian events. Tacitus, a more reliable source than Suetonius, states (*Annals* 14.47.3) that Nero dedicated a gymnasium in 61 CE (he does not mention baths), but that it burned down the following year after being hit by lightning (Tacitus, *Annals* 15.22.3). He makes no mention of the opening of Nero's Baths, which we know to have been operational some decades later (Martial, *Epigrams* 7.34). Tacitus' notices reinforce the impression gained from Suetonius that we are dealing with two separate structures, a gymnasium (opened in 60 or 61 CE) and set of baths (opened sometime after 62 CE). Other ancient testimony only furthers the confusion (see Fagan 1999: 110–111 n. 21), and the archaeology offers little clarity, since the whole area of the Campus Martius that was occupied by the baths remains built-up to this day. Modern scholars tend to the view that the gymnasium and the *thermae* were one and the same building, with 'gymnasium' possibly used to denote only a part of the larger bath complex (see e.g. Tamm 1970; Yegül 1992: 137–139); this conflicts, however, with Tacitus' clear statement that the gymnasium was destroyed by fire the year after it opened.

Whatever the case about these details, the ancient sources seem clear that Nero's innovation was to dedicate, in the heart of Rome, a building of a sufficiently distinctive Greek character to justify the label 'gymnasium' among Latin writers, who normally would not use that word to describe a Roman-style bathhouse. Palladio's schema of Nero's Baths shows a twin set of *palaestrae*, which was to become a standard feature of subsequent imperial *thermae*. But since the building was heavily renovated by the emperor Severus Alexander in the third century CE, to the extent that its name was changed to *Thermae Alexandrinae*, it is not certain that the double *palaestrae* were an original design feature. That said, the fact that twin *palaestrae* were incorporated in the Baths of Titus (dedicated in 80 CE), which was arguably a private bathing suite of the Esquiline wing of Nero's Golden House that Titus expanded and elaborated for public use, and likewise in the Baths of Trajan (opened in 109 CE), may suggest that the innovation went back to Nero's Baths. After the Baths of Trajan, all subsequent imperial baths included twin *palaestrae* (Nielsen 1993: i.43–59; Yegül 1992: 139–173). In this way, the gymnasium and the bath came to be fully integrated in the Roman world in the first and second centuries CE, as dedicated space for exercise was fully incorporated into bathhouse design.

In Asia Minor, a region that had inherited the Greek traditions of the gymnasium, a hybrid bath-gymnasium form emerged in the first century CE and continued in use down to the fourth (Yegül 1992: 250–313). Found mostly in the large urban centres along the Aegean coast (or slightly inland), they combined very large *palaestrae* with Roman-style bathing suites. The most basic form was to add Roman bathing rooms to existing Hellenistic gymnasia, as at Pergamum, where baths were installed at the east and west end of the gymnasium's elongated *palaestra*. In other structures, built from scratch in the Roman era, the *palaestrae* are larger than is normal for a regular Roman bath and often have elaborately marbled halls opening onto them, as well as other rooms that served a variety of functions, as at the bath-gymnasium at Sardis (Yegül 1986). Another variation (best illustrated by the bath-gymnasium at Alexandria Troas) was to have the *palaestra* accessible to the bathing block via a U-shaped covered walkway that ran around the outside of the bathing block. Such a covered spaced could function as the covered running tracks (*xystoi*) of traditional Greek gymnasia, or as places to house educational activities. Inscriptions and other written evidence make it clear that these bath-gymnasia served precisely this dual function: the bathing wings, introduced by the Romans, served the needs of the bathing public, but the conjoined *palaestrae*, halls, and walkways catered to the traditional functions of the Greek gymnasium. Associations of youths (*neoi*) and older men (*gerousia*) are attested, as are gymnasiarchs, athletic clubs and competitions, and lists of *ephebes* (trainees). In this way, the gymnasial culture of old Greece survived well into the Roman period, housed in a building that perfectly expressed the hybrid Greco-Roman culture of imperial Rome.

EXERCISING IN THE ROMAN BATH

In most Roman baths, a light workout in the *palaestra* was part and parcel of the regular bathing routine and was regarded as healthful by ancient medical writers (Celsus 1.1.2–4; Pliny, *Letters* 9.36.4). By the imperial era, both men and women took part in exercise at the baths. Bathers could wrestle, box, exercise with swords at wooden stakes, lift weights, or run with hoops. In the larger baths, swimming pools (*piscinae* or *natationes*) were available, though they were typically little more than a metre deep. Patrons would apply oil and dust to their skin before their exertions, and then have it strigiled off afterward. To these ends, rooms for oiling (*unctoria*, *aleipteria*) and strigiling (*destrictoria*) could be on hand, though more often than not the strigiling took place in the medium-hot room (*tepidarium*).

The most common type of exercise at the bath was to play ball games (Balsdon 1969: 163–167; Yegül 1992: 33–38; 2010: 14–17). The doctor Galen composed a short treatise 'On Exercise with the Small Ball'. Several ball games find mention in the *Epigrams* of Martial: 'no *pila*, no *follis*, no *paganica* prepares you in the baths ... nor running about do you snatch the dusty *harpastum*' (*Epigrams* 7.32). So far as we can tell from other sources, the *pila* was a small hard ball that could be tossed back and forth between two people. If a third joined them, the game became *trigon*. In this version, three players stood in a rough triangle and threw balls at each other (several could be in play at once, it seems). The object appears to have been to catch the balls as they came to you, since missed catches were counted and skilful left-handed catches were much admired (Martial, *Epigrams* 7.72). The winner was presumably the player with the lowest score, that is, the fewest dropped catches (Martial, *Epigrams* 12.82). *Harpastum* was another form of hard ball game and it appears to have been played in teams. While its rules remain unclear, it was the most strenuous ball game played in the Roman baths, favoured more by the younger bathers than the older (Athenaeus 1.14f–15a). Martial, for instance, lampoons the manly woman Philaenis for playing *harpastum* (rather than the lighter ball games, more suitable for women) and lifting weights (*Epigrams* 7.67), and associates *harpasta* balls with the trained athlete (*Epigrams* 14.48). A form of wall ball or handball could also be played with the *pila*, and to such ends special ball courts (*sphaeristeria*) were installed in some baths (*AE* 1928.2 = Fagan 1999: 234, no. 5). In addition to the hard ball activities, there was the game played with the *follis*, a ball filled with air and thus very light (Martial, *Epigrams*

4.19, 14.47). This was an activity preferred by the very young and the elderly. Another lighter ball was the *pila paganica*, stuffed with feathers (Martial, *Epigrams* 14.45). The rules of the games played with these balls remain unclear to us.

The whole ball playing culture of the Roman bath is evoked in Petronius' *Satyricon* (27.1–3), when we first encounter Trimalchio at the baths:

> We ordered Giton, who up to this point had been serving us most willingly, to follow us to the baths. Meanwhile, we began to stroll about clothed ... or rather to joke and mix with the little groups, when suddenly we saw an old bald man, dressed in a red tunic, playing ball (*pila*) among long-haired boys. The boys didn't lure us to watch, though they were worth it, so much as the master of the house himself who, in his shoes, was engaged with a green ball. He never retrieved it when it hit the ground, but a slave had a bag full of them and supplied the players. We noted some innovations. Two eunuchs were standing at different spots in the group. One of them carried a silver chamber pot, the other counted the balls, not as they shimmered among the hands throwing them out, but as they fell to the ground.

The passage nicely captures the vibrancy of ball playing in the exercise yard of the Roman bathhouse. It also raises another issue: to what degree were exercise and athletics staged in baths in front of spectators? Martial (*Epigrams* 7.72; cf. 12.82) mentions an 'oiled circle' (*uncta corona*) of other bathers watching and approving of ball play at the baths, which seems to suggest at least informal observers in the *palaestra*. The matter deserves closer attention.

Athletics and Spectacle in Roman Baths

Martial's comment demonstrates that some of the better ball players were watched by their fellow bathers as they exercised. An interesting inscription from Rome provides more detailed information (*CIL* 6.9797 = *ILS* 5173 = Fagan 1999: 326, no. 283):

> Ursus am I, who was the first citizen to play gracefully the glass ball game with my fellow players, while the people approved with clamorous applause in the Thermae of Trajan, in the Thermae of Agrippa and of Titus, and frequently in Nero's (if only you believe me). Come together rejoicing, ballplayers, and lovingly cover the statue of your friend with blossoms, roses, and violets and many a leaf, and with languid perfume; pour forth the dark Falernian wine, or Setian, or Caecuban, from the master's cellar to one who is alive and willing; and sing with harmonious voice of the old man Ursus, a merry fellow, full of jest, a ballplayer, a scholar, who surpassed all of his predecessors in tact, dignity, and subtle skill. Now let us old men speak the truth in verse: I have been defeated, I confess it, by the patron Verus, thrice consul—not once but many times; I am gladly called his clown.

This inscription is strange in many ways, not least in the very notion of a glass ball game, which is attested nowhere else, and in the injunctions to treat one stated to be alive as if he were dead (by decorating his statue or pouring libations). It has been read literally by many scholars, as if a glass ball game were indeed played in the baths mentioned (e.g. Balsdon 1969: 167; Busch 1999: 406–408). An ingenious interpretation of the text reads it as an allegory (Champlin 1985). The Ursus of the inscription is L. Julius Ursus Servianus (consul in 91 and 102 CE) and Verus his political rival, M. Annius Verus (consul in 98, 121, and 126 CE). The glass ball represents the subtle game of court politics—once dropped, the ball shatters.

Ursus, though alive, has seen the death of his political career at the hands of Verus, hence the funerary references. Even if one accepts this analysis (and some do not, see Courtney 1995: 331), the inscription surely demonstrates that people habitually observed skilful ball-players in the *palaestrae* of the baths.

If fellow-bathers could watch ball-players informally, were the baths used to stage more professional athletic spectacles? Set into the surrounding precinct wall (the *peribolos*) of the imperial baths, beginning with those of Trajan and continuing down to the Baths of Constantine, was a large stadium or 'theatre' area, usually a hemicycle, equipped with seating. The scale of these *stadia* can be gauged from the Piazza della Repubblica in Rome, built atop the former location of the Baths and more or less following the contours of its hemicycle (Fig. 31.3).

The provision of such viewing areas in baths strongly suggests that formal athletic events were staged there, even if direct written evidence for such events is lacking (Yegül 1992: 172–179). Aside from the *stadia*, the *palaestrae* of the larger baths may also have been used for athletic displays. In the Baths of Caracalla, at least, there were upper galleries around the *palaestrae*, which were open to the sky and may have been used as viewing areas. In the hemicyclular *exedrae* of the *palaestra* in these baths were found large mosaics depicting athletes, some of them professionals (as marked by the distinctive ponytail called the *cirrus*), along with their trainers (or judges) and their equipment. Some of the athletes carry palm fronds or crowns of victory (Insalaco 1989; Newby 2005: 67–70). Bath mosaics from Ostia also show athletic scenes; one such from a room near the *palaestra* in the Porta Marina Baths

FIGURE 31.3. Piazza della Repubblica, Rome. Photo: G. Fagan.

(of Hadrianic date) features a table in the centre bearing a crown and palm frond while athletic competitions take place around it (Newby 2002; 2005). Assuming the depictions are meant to connect to activities in or near the areas housing them, these images can be read as evidence for competitions staged in the baths; this is far from certain, since they could also show (or evoke) competitions staged during festivals or as public spectacles in other locations. None of the mosaics feature spectators, though it may be that their very presence in the baths invites the viewer to adopt the persona of someone watching the events depicted.

Greek inscriptions from the Baths of Trajan (*CIG* 3.5906–5913) testify to the establishment there of a club (*synod*) of professional athletes, calling themselves the College of Herculean Athletes. Playing on the increasing popularity of the cult of Hercules in the second century, on the piety of the emperors, and on the political connections of their patron, M. Ulpius Domesticus, the club was expressly assigned permanent space in the baths by Hadrian, a space that has not been definitively identified in the surviving (very ruinous) remains. But any of the halls or *exedrae* in the *peribolos* wall are likely candidates for club headquarters. Another inscription from the baths (*CIL* 10.154 = *ILS* 5164) comments on the participation of one club member in athletic contests around the empire—and so not in the baths themselves—but a letter from Antoninus Pius recorded in the Greek texts appears to show that the Capitoline Games could be staged there, since the emperor grants space to the club in the baths 'for the storage of sacred objects and for documents . . . and specially for the celebration of the Capitoline Games'. That statues of victorious members of the club were set up in the fourth century in the *curia acletarum* [*sic*] of the baths may well corroborate this inference (*CIL* 6.10153 and 10154 = *ILS* 5164 and 5165). Of course, there is no reason to think that the athletes could not compete in contests both abroad and in the baths.

All in all, although the evidence is indirect, there is good reason to suppose that bath structures served as spectacle venues in the Roman world. Not only did bathers pause and linger to watch their fellows exercise or play ball games in the *palaestrae* of Roman baths, but guilds of professional athletes seem to have participated in formal competitions, either in the *stadia* or the *palaestrae* of the larger baths in Rome. The architecture and decorative schemes of the structures likewise encouraged spectation habits, in visual and physical references to the official events and practices of games and shows.

References

Balsdon, J. P. V. D. 1969. *Life and Leisure in Ancient Rome*. London.

Busch, S. 1999. *Versus Balnearum: Die antike Dichtung über Bäder und Baden im römischen Reich*. Stuttgart.

Champlin, E. 1985. 'The Glass Ball Game.' *ZPE* 60: 159–163.

Courtney, E. 1995. *Musa Lapidaria: A Selection of Latin Verse Inscriptions*. Atlanta.

Crowther, N. B. 2004. *Athletika: Studies on the Olympic Games and Greek Athletics*. Hildesheim.

DeLaine, J. 1989. 'Some Observations on the Transition from Greek to Roman Baths in Hellenistic Sicily.' *MedArch* 2: 111–125.

Delorme, J. 1960. *Gymnasion: Étude sur les monuments consacrés à l'éducation en Grèce*. Paris.

Fagan, G. G. 1999. *Bathing in Public in the Roman World*. Ann Arbor.

Fagan, G. G. 2001. 'The Genesis of the Roman Public Bath: Recent Approaches and Future Directions.' *AJA* 105: 403–426.

Ferrary, J.-L. 1988. *Philhellénisme et impérialisme: Aspects idéologique de la conquête romaine du monde hellénistique*. Rome.

Gardiner, E. N. 1930. *Athletics of the Ancient World*. Oxford.

Ginouvès, R. 1959. *L'établissement thermal de Gortys d'Arcadie*. Paris.

Ginouvès, R. 1962. *Balaneutikè: Recherches sur le bain dans l'antiquité grecque*. Paris.

Günther, R. 2004. *Olympia: Kult und Spiele in der Antike*. Darmstadt.

Herrmann, K. 1989. 'Olympia: The Sanctuary and the Contests.' In *Mind and Body: Athletic Contests in Ancient Greece*. 47–68. O. Tzachou-Alexandri, ed. Athens.

Hoffmann, M. 1999. *Griechische Bäder*. Munich.

Hülsen, Ch. 1910. *Die Thermen des Agrippa in Rom: Ein Beitrag zur Topographie des Marsfeldes in Rom*. Rome.

Insalaco, A. 1989. 'I mosaici degli atleti dalle Terme di Caracalla: Una nuova indagine.' *ArchClass* 41: 293–327.

Kyle, D. G. 2007. *Sport and Spectacle in the Ancient World*. Malden, MA.

Mallwitz, A. 1972. *Olympia und seine Bauten*. Munich.

Nielsen, I. 1993. *Thermae et Balnea: The Architecture and Cultural History of Roman Public Baths*, 2nd edn. 2 vols. Århus.

Newby, Z. 2002. 'Greek Athletics as Roman Spectacle: The Mosaics from Ostia and Rome.' *PBSR* 70: 177–203.

Newby, Z. 2005. *Greek Athletics in the Roman World: Victory and Virtue*. Oxford.

Rodríguez Almeida, E. 1981. *Forma Urbis Marmorea. Aggiornamento Generale 1980*. Rome.

Tamm, B. 1970. *Neros Gymnasium in Rom*. Stockholm.

Trümper, M. 2009. 'Complex Public Bath Buildings of the Hellenistic Period: A Case-study in Regional Differences.' In *Le bain collectif en Égypte*. 139–179. M.-F. Boussac, T. Fournet, and B. Redon, eds. Cairo.

Tzachou-Alexandri, O. 1989. 'The Gymnasium: An Institution for Athletics and Education.' In *Mind and Body: Athletic Contests in Ancient Greece*. 31–40. O. Tzachou-Alexandri, ed. Athens.

Yegül, F. 1986. *The Bath-Gymnasium Complex at Sardis*. Cambridge, MA.

Yegül, F. 1992. *Baths and Bathing in Classical Antiquity*. Cambridge, MA.

Yegül, F. 2010. *Bathing in the Roman World*. New York.

CHAPTER 32

··

THE COLOSSEUM

··

HAZEL DODGE

'As long as the Colosseum stands, Rome will stand. When the Colosseum falls, Rome will fall. When Rome falls, the world will fall.'

—prophecy by the Venerable Bede, *c.*700 CE (Migne 94.543)

THE Colosseum has fascinated scholars, visitors, and the general public alike for centuries, and in modern times has become a popular icon of Rome, not just the city, but also the mighty empire of which it was once capital (Conforto 1988; Futrell 1997: 9–11; Bomgardner 2000: 1–31; Gabucci 2001). Traditionally, the building is the place where gladiators fought to the death and numerous Christian martyrs met a grisly end. As a result, early Christian writers such as Tertullian and Augustine condemned the Roman games as immoral and cruel, with many of them expressing major concern for their negative effect on the spectators, turning them into a blood-lusting, drunken rabble (Tertullian, *On the Spectacles* 2 and 19; Augustine, *Confessions* 6.8). Tradition, however, overlooks the fact that the games in general continued to be popular into the sixth century in Rome, with the Colosseum enjoying persistent use even after the fall of Rome to the Goths. The size and scale of the Colosseum has also always awed observers; as befitting the imperial capital, it is the largest amphitheatre constructed in the Roman world. It was not referred to as the 'Colosseum' until well after the fall of the western Roman empire. Indeed, it is thought that it was this building that the Venerable Bede was referencing in his famous prophecy (see above), preserved in translation in Byron's *Childe Harold* (Hopkins and Beard 2005: 1–26). However, it has also been suggested that he was in fact referring to the Colossus, the great statue originally set up by Nero that stood nearby (Canter 1930). The statue may, of course, have transferred its name to the amphitheatre in popular usage much earlier, perhaps even from the latter's inauguration.

The Romans referred to the building as the 'Amphitheatrum Flavium', the Flavian Amphitheatre, after the dynasty of emperors responsible for its construction (*LTUR* 1: 30–35). Since the 1990s, a number of important studies have been published which have helped in particular to clarify the building's environmental and geological setting, the process of its construction, and the form and function of the arena substructures, although there is still extensive scholarly debate about the interpretation of the new evidence (for example, Lancaster 1998; 2005; Beste 2000; Connolly 2003).

BACKGROUND

In modern perceptions, the amphitheatre is first and foremost associated with Roman gladiatorial displays, but as a permanent building type it was a development only of the late republic (Futrell 1997: 40–44; Bomgardner 2000: 32–60; Welch 2007: 72–101; Dodge 2014a; 2014b). In republican Rome, gladiatorial displays were an important element of aristocratic funerary rituals, and as such were usually staged in the political and symbolic heart of the city, the Forum Romanum. It is highly probable that the ovoid plan of early permanent amphitheatres was derived from the design of the wooden audience seating that came to be erected for these displays around the open area of the Forum (Golvin 1988: 45–49; Coleman 2000: 227–228; Welch 2007: 43–55; Dodge 2014b: 548–549). In the mid first century BCE, a central subterranean corridor with four bisecting lateral arms was constructed under the paving, with twelve shaft openings giving access from below. Traces of installations in these galleries are reminiscent of the system of cages and pulleys that would later be installed beneath some of the more developed amphitheatres of the imperial period, including the Colosseum, for winching performers and animals up into the arena (Carettoni 1956–58; Welch 2007: 39–42). To further improve facilities for the spectators, Julius Caesar stretched awnings over the whole Forum on several occasions, according to Pliny the Elder (*Natural History* 19.23). Pliny also provided an alternative explanation for the permanent amphitheatre's elliptical form, with his description of the extraordinary building put up in Rome by C. Scribonius Curio in 52 BCE for funeral games in honour of his father (*Natural History* 36.116–120). This structure took the form of two very large wooden theatres that somehow could pivot to form one building when the need arose (Golvin 1988: 30–32; Schultze 2007). Modern scholars are unsure how this dangerous-sounding manoeuvre was actually achieved, but if true, it must have been a spectacle in its own right!

During the later second and first centuries BC, a number of towns in Italy, many of them Roman colonies in origin, were provided with a permanent amphitheatre, usually in a marginal or extramural location because of the space required. Outside Italy, amphitheatres were also built at Carmona and Ucubi (Spain), Antioch on the Orontes (Syria) and Corinth (Greece) at this time (Welch 2007: 192–198; Dodge 2014b: 548–549). Although several of these structures still survive, only the one at Pompeii in Campania, built 70–65 BCE, can be specifically dated (*CIL* 10.852). By comparison, the first permanent amphitheatre in Rome was not constructed until 30 or 29 BCE by T. Statilius Taurus, one of Augustus' generals (Suetonius, *Augustus* 29.5; *LTUR* 1. 36–37; Welch 2007: 108–126). This was located in the southern Campus Martius and was financed by *manubiae* (spoils of war) awarded to Taurus from the triumph he celebrated in 34 BCE for securing the province of Africa for Octavian (Dio Cassius 51.23.1). Little is known about this structure except that it was small and built of stone and wood. Dio referred to it as a hunting theatre (*theatron kunēgetikon*), possibly because it was more often used for animal displays. It was destroyed in the great fire of 64 CE (Dio Cassius 62.18.2). Several other amphitheatres were built in the city, but they were all temporary in nature: Julius Caesar's in the Forum Romanum, built probably in 46 BCE (Suetonius, *Caesar* 37; Dio Cassius 43.22.3), and a particularly sumptuous structure constructed by Nero in 57 CE on the Campus Martius where it is claimed he even held aquatic displays (Suetonius, *Nero* 12; Tacitus, *Annals* 13.31; Golvin 1988: 52–59; Coleman 2000: 228–229). It was not until the construction of the

Colosseum by the Flavian emperors that Rome finally had a venue befitting the centre of empire for that quintessentially Roman type of spectacle, gladiatorial combat (Golvin 1988: 173–175; Welch 2007, 128–162).

CONTEXT OF THE COLOSSEUM

The instigation of large building programmes in Rome as a means of bolstering political status was well established by the time the emperor Vespasian came to power. The Colosseum provides a good example of Vespasian's political manipulation of public imagery (Martial, *Book of Spectacles* 2; Golvin 1988: 173–174; Welch 2007: 128–162). The site chosen was the drained lake in the grounds of the Domus Aurea, Nero's Golden House, effectively returning to the people the land taken by Nero for his private domain (Elsner 1994: 119–122). In a valley formed by the slopes of the Palatine and Caelian Hills, south of the slopes of the Esquiline Hill, the Colosseum dominated the area by its sheer size, as it still does today. It was not, however, an ideal location from a constructional point of view and presented major environmental and architectural challenges to its planners. Positioned in the heart of the city, it was in an unusually urban location, rather than on the edge of town as was more typical (Welch 2007: 128–162); this made the transport and delivery of the building materials more difficult, let alone the movement and accommodation of performers once the building was up and running. Ideologically this was perfect, from a Flavian point of view. Not only had Augustus apparently intended to build a centrally located amphitheatre (Suetonius, *Vespasian* 9.1; Coleman 2003), but it also provided a very public focus in an area previously enclosed and cut off from the rest of the city. Studies have shown that as part of the preparation of the site and before the foundation trenches were dug, a number of Neronian period structures had to be cleared away (Lancaster 2005: 59).

Anderson suggested that the ideological benefit was emphasized even more with the construction of public baths by Titus on the slopes of the Esquiline nearby and with the great fountain, the Meta Sudans, constructed by Domitian, creating a set of monuments forever connected with Flavian munificence (Anderson 1997: 218–219). Furthermore, the Colosseum was close to the Forum Romanum and had a prime position on the triumphal route as it turned north-west to ascend the Velia and then descend into the Forum. As well as the amphitheatre itself, ancillary buildings added to the visibility and size of the overall complex (Coleman 2000: 235–237; Coarelli 2001; Welch 2007: 131). Of these, only the Ludus Magnus, the main gladiatorial training school, can be seen today, to the south-east of the Colosseum, to which it was connected by a tunnel giving direct, secure access to the area under the arena (*LTUR* 3: 196–197). There were other training schools on the south-east, including the Ludus Matutinus, for the training of animal fighters, the Ludus Dacicus, and the Ludus Gallicus. There were also storage areas, such as the Summum Choragium (*LTUR* 3: 195–198).

It is not known exactly when work started on construction, but it must have been early in Vespasian's reign as the building was sufficiently completed to be dedicated by his son and successor Titus in 80 CE (Suetonius, *Titus* 7.3; Dio Cassius 66.25). The dedicatory inscription, identified in the early 1990s on a block reused in the early fifth century CE, is particularly instructive (Alföldy 1995). The bunching of the letters in the imperial titles shows that Titus had his name inserted so that he could claim the major glory associated with its construction; the inscription also records that the Colosseum was funded from *manubiae*, like a victory monument, in this case using presumably the spoils of war carried off from the sack of the Temple in Jerusalem (Coleman 2000: 229). Thus, the direct physical relationship to the triumphal route and the close association with victory in a 'foreign' war, coming on the heels of civil conflict in 68–69 CE, were particularly significant features of the Colosseum's origin.

CONSTRUCTION AND DESIGN

As Lancaster has pointed out, much of the constructional history of the original building is masked by the extensive rebuilding work necessitated by the fire following a lightning strike in 217 CE (Lancaster 1998; 2005a; 2005b: 186). There is no doubt, however, that the building was an astonishing feat of planning and engineering; the scale of construction was unprecedented, with outer dimensions of approximately 188 by 156 metres, and an arena measuring 80 by 54 metres (Golvin 1988: 173–179; Wilson-Jones 1993; Bomgardner 2000: 1–32; Connolly 2003: 30–63; Rosin and Trucco 2005; Welch 2007: 128–130). (It is worth noting that there is a surprising degree of variation in the measurements given in the modern literature, particularly for the arena). Furthermore, the hydrology of the area is quite complex, and while this would have greatly facilitated the creation of the lake Nero installed in the Domus Aurea, it did mean that the Colosseum required a proper drainage system to deal not only with the groundwater but also with run-off water when it rained. Such arrangements, integrated into the foundations from the outset, were crucial as the whole building would have acted as a great water-collector (Gabucci 2001: 234–235; Lancaster 2005a).

A range of materials was used for the construction of the building: concrete (*opus caementicium*), fired brick, travertine, and tufa. These, in conjunction with the use of vaulting techniques, allowed the resolution of the structural problems inherent in its design (Lancaster 2005a). It was a grand and monumental edifice rising over 50 metres in height, standing on an elliptical ring of concrete foundations 12 metres (40 feet) deep; it has been estimated that digging the initial foundation trench alone would have taken a year (Rea et al. 2002: 347–354; Connolly 2003: 42–43).

The exterior of the building was formed by a four-storey facade, constructed using an estimated 100,000 cubic metres of travertine and 300 tons of iron to clamp the blocks together (Fig. 32.1) (Cozzo 1971; Connolly 2003: 41–42).

The interior of the structure was built around a framework of travertine load-bearing piers, connected by radial walls; these were of tufa in the first two storeys and brick-faced concrete in the upper parts of the building (Fig. 32.2) (Lancaster 1998; 2005a; Connolly 2003: 42–43). At each level, the eighty arches of the facade were framed by engaged columns, as on the Theatre of Marcellus, the bottom storey being of the Doric order (sometimes referred to as Tuscan because the columns have bases), the second Ionic, and the third Corinthian. The fourth storey was a plain wall with Corinthian pilasters and square windows alternating with bronze *clipea* (Welch 2007: 136–144). It is at this level that the corbels for the awning-masts are preserved (see below). There are suggestions, mainly based on a rather garbled passage in the *Chronographer of 354*, that at the time of Titus' inauguration the facade was only completed to the third level. A coin of Titus seems to depict the fourth storey already in

FIGURE 32.1. Colosseum. Exterior facade. Photo: H. Dodge.

place (*BMC* 190; Coleman 2000: 231); the Trajanic relief from the Tomb of the Haterii shows the building with only three storeys, but this may simply have been for artistic reasons. The arcuated design of the facade helped to relieve the visual heaviness of the building and this was further aided by the innovative display of sculpture within the arcades; statues are also indicated on the Haterii relief. These statues were necessarily colossal (at least five metres in height) in keeping with the size of the building (Welch 2007: 137–138; Elkins 2014). It is uncertain whether these statues were created specifically for this purpose, or whether they were removed from elsewhere to be put on display in the Colosseum, as was the case with the redisplay of Greek sculptures, originally looted by Nero, in the Flavian Templum Pacis (Pliny, *Natural History* 34.84; 36.27). The Haterii relief also depicts a monumental entrance surmounted by a *quadriga*, which marked the access to the imperial box located on the west side of the building on its shorter axis. As Welch has pointed out, this is the first instance of the use of Greek architectural orders to articulate an amphitheatre's facade (2007: 138–139). Combined with the decorative use of statues and shields, it represents an important innovation in the architecture of Roman amphitheatres (Legrottaglie 2008: 39–61).

Beneath the *cavea* was a series of passages, corridors, and staircases with piers of travertine forming the framework (Fig. 32.2). The two outer corridors were covered by concrete barrel vaults, each seven metres high. One further ring corridor closer to the arena was constructed of brick-faced concrete and veneered with marble. This particularly grand passageway gave access to the ringside seats set aside for the elite. The radial passages accommodated staircases, specifically organized for ease and control of access. Although a similar access

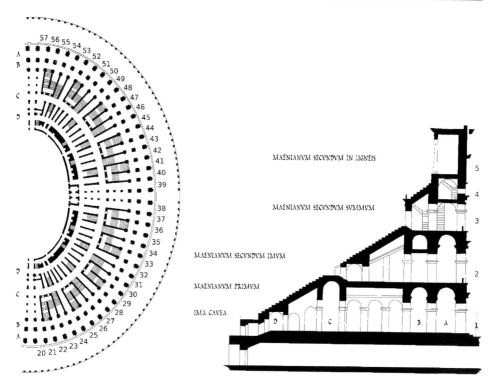

FIGURE 32.2. Colosseum. Plan and cross-section of *cavea*. Source: H. Dodge.

system was used in the theatres of Marcellus and Pompey, here in the Colosseum it was perfected so that the building superbly incorporated the functional demands of a highly stratified and segregated society into its fabric (see the section below on Seating and Spectators).

ARENA SUBSTRUCTURES (THE *HYPOGEUM*)

The arena originally had a wooden floor. The area beneath is 6 metres deep with a concrete platform at its base; over time it came to accommodate an elaborate system of subterranean passages and chambers (Beste 2000; 2003; Connolly 2003: 185–206). There has been much debate about the nature, development, and date of these facilities, and it is difficult to disentangle the archaeological and architectural evidence to achieve a clear picture. What is visible today (see Fig. 32.3) was heavily reconstructed and modified in the third to fourth century CE, an indication of the use of the building extending into late antiquity (Lancaster 1998; Schingo 2000; Beste 2003; Gabucci 2001: 148–159; 161–201). Archaeological evidence suggests that in the earliest phase the basement was essentially a brick-lined pit with no internal structures; timber uprights would have supported the arena floor. This first arrangement was only temporary (Beste 2000; Beste 2003: 373–374; Connolly 2003: 185–206) and certainly by the end of the first century CE the basement area had been much modified so that the timber supports were replaced by more permanent ones of tufa.

FIGURE 32.3. Colosseum. View of the arena substructures. Photo: H. Dodge.

These created a series of galleries with chambers beneath the arena floor. Four passageways gave access from outside the building; each one accommodated water drainage conduits, although the specific arrangements varied (Connolly 2003: 185). The south-east tunnel connected the basement with the Ludus Magnus, opening out into a fan-shaped area which lay outside the Colosseum at basement level; evidence of removable capstan wheels has been identified here (Beste 2003; Connolly 2003: 185). The north-west tunnel is far less well-preserved, but seems to have followed the same design. Excavations in the nineteenth century revealed that it eventually opened to the level of the external piazza outside (*LTUR* I: 30–35).

The interpretation of the arena basement is further complicated by the discussion of whether it was ever flooded for *naumachiae*, the displays involving large-scale sea-battle re-enactments. It has been suggested that the timber supports of the original design could have been easily removed (along with the arena flooring) to accommodate the *naumachiae* apparently attested by Suetonius and Dio (Suetonius, *Domitian* 4.1; Dio Cassius 66.25.15). Even though the archaeological evidence shows this design was only temporary, there is still much debate about the feasibility of such a process (Coleman 1993: 58–60; Connolly 2003: 188–194; Cariou 2009: 335–351). Predictably, discussion has tended to start with the major literary sources that focus on Titus' inauguration of the Colosseum in 80 CE (Martial, *Book of Spectacles*; Suetonius, *Titus* 7; Dio Cassius 66.25). According to the ancient authors, there was a wide range of different types of spectacles staged, not only in the Colosseum itself, but also at other venues. These included several large aquatic displays at Augustus' basin or *stagnum* on the other side of the Tiber River (Suetonius, *Titus* 7.3; Dio Cassius 66.25.2–4). Martial's relevant epigrams, collectively known as the *Liber Spectaculorum*, were published in 80 CE, not to provide accurate documentation of the games but as eulogistic poetry to commemorate the inauguration of this important Flavian building. Despite this, a great deal of reliance has been placed on the details provided. Martial did not specify the location of the sea battles, nor indeed the other aquatic displays, but he was definite that this location could be flooded and drained at will, leading modern scholars to identify that location as the Colosseum. Suetonius (*Titus* 17) gave only a brief and slightly confused account, stating that Titus provided an elaborate spectacle of gladiatorial combat in the Colosseum while also staging sea-battles on the artificial lake (*naumachia*) of Augustus. The latter was then drained for further gladiatorial combat and animal displays. Dio, writing some 150 years after the events he described, mentioned performances of single combat followed by a sudden and swift change to 'this same theatre', apparently meaning the Colosseum, when a large amount of water was introduced for a major naval display. He provided more detail about a similar show that was held the following day at the *stagnum* of Augustus; this display also involved gladiatorial combat and a horse race.

These conflicting details have resulted in heated debate amongst scholars about whether or not the Flavian amphitheatre really was capable of supporting large-scale water spectacles at the time of inauguration. There are serious objections to taking the literary sources at face value (Coleman 1993: 58–60; 2000: 234–235; Gabucci 2001: 148–159; Connolly 2003: 139–161, 185–206; Crapper 2007; Cariou 2009: 335–351).

The area beneath the arena was much remodelled by Domitian and later emperors (Beste 2000; Connolly 2003: 179–182). It is true that it was lined with waterproof mortar (*opus signinum*) from the outset and that drains were constructed to allow the evacuation of water in some quantity (Gabucci 2001: 234–240; Beste 2003). However, no permanent supply system large enough to provide the necessary volume of water to flood the whole arena has been identified. Equally, there have been no adequate estimates of the amount of time it might have taken to both fill and empty the arena. The smaller displays referred to by Martial during the inauguration (*Book of Spectacles* 25, 26) could have been accommodated in a smaller temporary pool or basin involving far less water volume and movement time.

Contemporary authors indicated that there was a sudden transition from dry land to water and back again. Recent engineering studies have suggested that if water could be provided in the necessary quantities, then the arena could only have been flooded to a depth of 1.5 metres (Crapper 2007). This limitation was due to four radial service passages at that height above the basement floor, which, although sealed now, slope downward to the exterior of the building (Beste 2000; Connolly 2003: 185–194). Flooding to this depth would have required approximately 17,000 cubic metres of water, which could have been achieved in two to five hours, depending on flow-rate and water source. A system of lead pipes was accommodated in thirty radial conduits, triangular in cross-section, beneath the lowest part of the seating. These pipes seem to have fed into a channel which ran around the edge of the arena and connected with a series of drop shafts 2 metres deep; these opened directly into the *hypogeum*. However, there is still the problem of where the water was supplied from; likewise, it would have been a substantial task to remove not only the wooden floor but also the large wooden uprights which supported it. Further, there would have been a huge problem with visibility for any naval displays; the 1.5 metre depth of water meant that the surface of the water would have been 4 to 5 metres below the lowest seating. Those seated further back in the stands would have been able to see very little.

The drainage of this water would have been a considerable process. The four main drainage culverts, mentioned above, apparently drain from the *hypogeum* to the outside of the building and thence into sewers. These conduits could have been intended for the drainage of water run-off from the fountains and from rainwater—today, it can rain up to 40 millimetres in twenty minutes, requiring a system that could drain off 750 litres per second. Again engineering estimates suggest that the *hypogeum* could be drained in two to five hours, although it would still be very sodden and might have taken a further ten or so hours to drain completely; the wooden supports would then have been needed to be replaced before the floor was put back (Crapper 2007). Thus, any discussion of the flooding of the arena of the Colosseum for aquatic displays must remain conjectural at this stage, and indeed, on balance, seems highly doubtful.

Water certainly was supplied to the Colosseum, if only for the drinking fountains for which evidence has been identified on the first, second, and third levels (Gabucci 2001: 235–237). These would have been vital, particularly in the height of summer, as spectators could potentially spend all day at the games. There are close to 3,000 linear metres of tunnels and channels for the delivery and drainage of water. Latrines have been suggested at various locations in the building; several such facilities in tunnels between the second and third levels would have been accessible to all spectators in the upper seating and the attic. Latrines for the elite seating in the lower level may have been located in the tunnelling beneath the arena podium; this was veneered with marble, which suggests that it was not a mere service corridor. Some of these facilities, however, may have been later additions (Gabucci 2001: 239–240; Connolly 2003: 196–206).

By the end of the first century, the area beneath the floor had been substantially remodelled and continued to be refashioned over subsequent centuries, making it difficult to separate out the details of any one point in time (Beste 2000; Connolly 2003: 196–202; Lancaster 1998; 2005a). The Domitianic remodelling is relatively clearer because it employed blocks of soft brownish tufa for the walls that effectively divided the area up into a series of straight and elliptical corridors. These were set on very shallow foundations, and within ten years the tufa walls required shoring up with brickwork. Evidence from brick stamps demonstrates that this started before the end of the first century CE and the process had to be repeated several times during the second century. The original elevator shafts, set into the perimeter wall and accessing the arena from the basement, were abandoned and new ones, possibly as many as thirty-two, were built next to the new curved walls. Ramps were constructed, giving access from the elevator to the arena floor through trapdoors; traces of these ramps can be seen in a series of grooves which remain in some of the well-preserved tufa piers in the northeastern sector (Connolly 2003: 200–201). The central corridors seem to have at one time been used to lift scenery and props to the arena, something referenced by several ancient authors (Connolly 2003: 203–204).

These complex substructures and their access points can be more fully appreciated elsewhere, such as the amphitheatres at Capua and Pozzuoli in Campania where they are better preserved (Golvin 1988: 180–185, 204–205). In both these examples, the arena floors of concrete (*opus caementicium*) are still in place and the trapdoor openings for hauling up animal cages can still be clearly seen. Outside Italy such arrangements are also visible at Pula in northern Croatia (Golvin 1988: 159, 171–173).

AWNINGS (*VELARIA*)

One of the most enigmatic features of the Colosseum is the provision of awnings to create shade for the spectators. Awnings at spectacles are mentioned in a number of literary sources. Lucretius (4.71–84) described the fluttering of yellow, red, and dark purple awnings 'over a great theatre', and Pliny the Elder (*Natural History* 19.6.23–24) describes awnings stretched over the Forum in 78 BCE using some kind of cable system. The techniques required to erect such awnings most likely paralleled the development of permanent stone theatres and amphitheatres in Italy during the late republic. The best preserved physical evidence for *velaria* comes from the Colosseum. Two rows of projecting corbels, 240 pairs in all, are preserved on the attic storey of the Colosseum (Fig. 32.1). The upper ones are pierced by a hole, through which wooden masts were inserted to rest on the lower brackets. Ropes were attached to these masts to support the awnings (*velarium/velaria, velum/vela*). Exactly how this was done, and how the awnings were extended out over the spectators, remains controversial: modern attempts at reconstruction have met little success (Montilla 1969; Barnes 1996). A number of ancient artistic depictions of awnings survive; the clearest is the famous amphitheatre fresco from a house in Pompeii (1.3.23) (Graefe 1979). In Rome the *velaria* were operated by a detachment of marines from the fleet at Misenum on the bay of Naples (Historia Augusta, *Commodus* 15.6); an estimated 1,000 men were required to operate the equipment that enabled the awnings to be unfurled and retracted. It has often been suggested that the stone bollards set into the pavement outside both the Colosseum and the imperial amphitheatre at Capua were part of the capstan system (Sear 1982: 19–28). However, this cannot have been the case without seriously obstructing the flow of spectators as they entered and exited the building. The bollards most likely provided some form of channelling as crowd control, such as a rope line or barrier, as seen in many modern sports venues (Connolly 2003: 63–65). The imperial period amphitheatres at Pula, Nîmes, and Arles (France) and the theatres at Orange (France) and Aspendus (southern Turkey) have similarly extensive surviving evidence for awnings.

THE SEATING AND SPECTATORS

The seating capacity of the Colosseum is another issue which has long been debated, with modern scholars now settling for a figure somewhere between 50,000 and 80,000 (Fig. 32.2). This is a problem shared with other ancient entertainment buildings, arising partly from the fact that the seating took the form of tiered, broad stone steps without seat divisions; there is little evidence for individualized seats outside the imperial box and some of the elite seating areas at the front. Seating capacities do not seem to have been a major concern of ancient sources and available evidence is contradictory. Much of the seating of the Colosseum is no longer preserved, but the fourth century *Regionary Catalogues* list the Colosseum with a seating capacity of 87,000 (Nordh 1949: 78 See also Hanson and Ortmann 2020).

The structural design of the Colosseum not only facilitated seating of the spectators, but also their movement within the building (Dodge 2014b: 551–554). There were eighty entrances; of these, seventy-six were public access points, all numbered, so that the entrance a particular spectator used depended on where he or she was seated, just as in modern sports venues. Of the other four entrances, those on the north-east and south-west sides led respectively to the consuls' box and emperor's box, above either end of the arena's short axis. The public entrances opened onto radial passages that housed stairways to access to the various seating zones. Stone balustrades lined the staircases to prevent people from falling at busy times; in some places there was as much as a three metre drop alongside. These balustrades were decorated in a variety of ways, with flowers, palmettes, acanthus leaves, and hunting dogs (Connolly 2003: 50–52). There were also inscriptions listing spectators allowed in a particular area (Orlandi 2004: 171–183; CIL 6.32098a–f). The corridors and stairways themselves were originally stuccoed and painted in bright colours (Connolly 2003: 50–51). After the fire of 217 CE, the finishing was replaced in more muted colours, as was noted in eighteenth-century excavations. Ease of access and directed mobility to seating arrangements demonstrated the tension between spectacles as opportunities to create social unity and the segregated regulation of society. In many ways, the design of the Colosseum rigidly reinforced the hierarchy of Roman life (Edmondson 1996; 2002) (Fig. 32.2).

Martial described the amphitheatre as a 'place for all the peoples of the world to unite' (*Book of Spectacles* 2), but there was no effort here at social levelling. From the second century BCE, there is increasing evidence of efforts to segregate the seating arrangements in the theatre in Rome, as a reflection and reaffirmation of social hierarchy (Edmondson 2002; Fagan 2011: 97–120). The legislation was renewed and reinforced under Augustus (*lex Iulia theatralis*) and from this time men and women were separated (Suetonius *Augustus* 44.1; Dio Cassius 53.25.1; Rawson 1987; Schnurr 1992). By the time the Colosseum was built, arrangements were even more rigid. By the end of the first century CE, audiences in the Colosseum were seated in a hierarchical fashion, segregated by social rank and gender, confirmed by the divisions in the *cavea* and by extensive epigraphic evidence from the seats (for example CIL 6.2059; 3207–3222; 32099–32151; 32152–32250; Orlandi 2004: 167–521; Edmondson 2002: 15–18). There were five levels of seating in the Colosseum overall. The *ima cavea*, also known as the podium, was at the very front and reserved for senators and other dignitaries, including the Vestal Virgins. It consisted of four broad terraces on which chairs were placed. The next level up, the *maenianum primum*, was much bigger and reserved for members of the equestrian class. The third level, *maenianum secundum imum*, had an even greater capacity, and above them, in the *maenianum secundum summum*, the lowest-status spectators were seated. At the very top was the *maenianum secundum in ligneis* where the seats were of wood to help reduce the thrust on the exterior wall; here were seated women and slaves (Edmondson 1996; 2002).

THE POST-IMPERIAL COLOSSEUM

The Colosseum continued to be used as a major venue for public entertainment into the fifth century; the last recorded display, a *venatio*, took place in 523 (Connolly 2003: 160). Restorations to the upper parts of the building as a result of earthquake damage in the fifth century were only partial repairs (*CIL* 6. 32091–32094). In the later sixth century, the arena floor was raised with the wide deployment of re-used materials (Gabucci 2001: 190). However, not long after this the building started to function as a quarry for building materials, particularly marble seating, travertine blocks, and metal; epigraphic evidence points to the possibility of senatorial involvement in these actions, at least initially (Gabucci 2001: 192). From the ninth century, there is evidence of dwellings both inside the building and in the surrounding area; deeds for these properties are still preserved in the Church of Santa Maria Nova (Gabucci 2001: 197; Wickham 2016: 292–299). In the late eleventh and twelfth centuries, part of the building was fortified by the Frangipane family in the form of the *palatium Frangipanis*. The earthquake of 1349 was particularly destructive; already considerably weakened by the removal of blocks, parts of the *cavea* on the west and south sides collapsed (Rea 1993). Spoliation continued under papal supervision until 1743, when the Senate of Rome began restoration work and legislation was passed to stop further removal of building materials. The brick buttresses at either end of the remaining outer circuit were constructed in the early nineteenth century and helped to stabilize and consolidate what was remained of the travertine façade (Gabucci 2001: 200–224).

In the first edition of *Murray's Handbook to Central Italy* (1843), it was asserted that 'there is no monument of Rome which artists and engravers have made so familiar to readers of all classes ... and there is certainly none of which the descriptions and drawings are so far surpassed by reality'. The Colosseum still stands today as a testimony to Roman technology, culture, and organization.

REFERENCES

Alföldy, G. 1995. 'Eine Bauinschrift aus dem Colosseum'. *ZPE* 109: 195–226.

Anderson, J. C. 1997. *Roman Architecture and Society*. Baltimore.

Barnes, M. 1996. *Secrets of Lost Empires*. London.

Beste, H.-J. 2000. 'The Construction and Phases of Development of the Wooden Arena Flooring of the Colosseum'. *JRA* 13: 79–92.

Beste, H.-J. 2003. 'Foundations and Wall Structures in the Basement of the Colosseum in Rome'. *Proceedings of the First International Congress on Construction History*. 373–380. Madrid.

Bomgardner, D. 2000. *The Story of the Roman Amphitheatre*. London.

Canter, H. V. 1930. 'The Venerable Bede and the Colosseum'. *TAPA* 61: 150–164.

Cariou, G. 2009. *La naumachie: morituri te salutant*. Paris.

Carettoni, G. 1956–1958. 'Le gallerie ipogee del Foro romano e i ludi gladiatori forensi'. *Bullettino della Commissione Archeologica Comunale di Roma* 76: 23–44.

Coarelli, F. 2001. 'Ludus Gladiatorius'. In *Sangue e Arena*. 147–151. A. La Regina, ed. Rome.

Coleman, K. 1993. 'Launching into History: Aquatic Displays in the Early Empire'. *JRS* 83: 48–74.

Coleman, K. 2000. 'Entertaining Rome'. In *Ancient Rome: the Archaeology of the Eternal City*. 210–258. J. C. Coulston and H. Dodge, eds. Oxford.

Coleman, K. 2003. 'Euergetism in Its Place: Where Was the Amphitheatre in Augustan Rome?' In *'Bread and Circuses'. Euergetism and Municipal Patronage in Roman Italy*. 61–88. K. Lomas and T. Cornell, eds. London.

Conforto, M. L. 1988. *Anfiteatro Flavio: immagine, testimonianze, spettacoli*. Rome.

Connolly, P. 2003. *Colosseum: Rome's Arena of Death*. London.

Cozzo, G. 1971. *L'Anfiteatro Flavio nella tecnica edilizia e nella storia delle strutture nel concetto esecutivo dei lavori*. Rome.

Crapper, M. 2007. 'How Roman Engineers Could Have Flooded the Colosseum.' *Proceedings of ICE: Civil Engineering* 160.4: 184–191.

Dodge, H. 2014a. 'Building for an Audience: the Architecture of Roman Spectacle.' In *A Companion to Roman Architecture*. 281–296. R. B. Ulrich and C. K. Quenemon, eds. Oxford.

Dodge, H. 2014b. 'Amphitheatres in the Roman World. In *A Companion to Sport and Spectacle in Greek and Roman Antiquity*. 545–560. P. Christesen and D. G. Kyle, eds. Oxford.

Edmondson, J. C. 1996. 'Dynamic Arenas: Gladiatorial Representations in the City of Rome and the Construction of Society during the Early Empire.' In *Roman Theater and Society*. 69–112. W. J. Slater, ed. Ann Arbor.

Edmondson, J. C. 2002. 'Public Spectacles and Roman Social Relations.' In *Ludi Romani: Espectáculos en Hispania Romana*. 43–63. T. Nogales Basarrate and A. Castellanos, eds. Mérida.

Elkins, N. 2014. 'The Procession and Placement of Imperial Cult Images in the Colosseum.' *PBSR* 82: 73–107.

Elsner, J. 1994. 'Constructing Decadence: the Representation of Nero as Imperial Builder.' In *Reflections of Nero: Culture, History and Representation*. 112–127. J. Elsner and J. Masters, eds. London.

Fagan, G. 2011. *The Lure of the Arena: Social Psychology and the Crowd at the Roman Games*. Cambridge.

Futrell, A. 1997. *Blood in the Arena: The Spectacle of Roman Power*. Austin, TX.

Gabucci, A. 2001. *The Colosseum*. Los Angeles.

Golvin, J.-C. 1988. *L'amphithéâtre romain: Essai sur la théorisation de sa forme et ses fonctions*. Paris.

Graefe, R. 1979. *Vela erunt: Die Zeltdächer der römischen Theater und ähnlicher Anlagen*. Darmstadt.

Hanson, J. W. and Ortmann, S. G. 2020. 'Reassessing the Capacities of Entertainment Structures in the Roman Empire.' *American Journal of Archaeology* 124.3: 417–40.

Hopkins, K. and M. Beard. 2005. *The Colosseum*. London.

Lancaster, L. C. 1998. 'Reconstructing the Restorations of the Colosseum after the Fire of 217.' *JRA* 11: 146–174.

Lancaster, L. C. 2005a. 'The Process of Building the Colosseum: The Site, Materials, and Construction Techniques.' *JRA* 18: 57–82.

Lancaster, L. C. 2005b. *Concrete Vaulted Construction in Imperial Rome. Innovations in Context*. Cambridge.

Legrottaglie, G. 2008. *Il Sistema delle Immagini degli Anfiteatri Romani*. Rome.

Montilla, R. B. 1969. 'The Awnings of Roman Theatres and Amphitheatres.' *Theatre Survey* 10.1: 75–88.

Nordh, A. 1949. *Libellus de Regionibus Urbis Romae*. Lund.

Rawson, E. 1987. 'Discrimina Ordinum: The *Lex Iulia Theatralis*.' *PBRS* 55: 83–114.

Rea, R. 1993. 'Il Colosseo e la valle da Teodorico ai Frangi[ane: note di studio.' In *La storia economica di Roma nell'alto Medioevo alla luce dei recenti scavi archeologici*. 71–88. Florence.

Rea, R., H.-J. Beste, and L. C. Lancaster. 2002. 'Il Cantiere del Colosseo.' *MDAI(R)* 109: 341–375.

Rosin, P. L. and E. Trucco. 2005. 'The Amphitheatre Construction Problem.' *Incontro Internazionale di Studi Rileggere L'Antico*. 1–10.

Schingo, G. 2000. 'A History of Earlier Excavations in the Arena of the Colosseum.' *JRA* 13: 69–78.

Schnurr, C. 1992. 'The *lex Julia theatralis* of Augustus.' *LCM* 17: 155–160.

Schultze, C. 2007. 'Making a Spectacle of Oneself: Pliny on Curio's Theatre'. *BICS* 100: 127–145

Sear, F. 1982. *Roman Architecture*. London.

Torelli, M. 1980. 'Innovations in Roman Construction Techniques between the First Century BC and the First Century AD.' In *Studies in the Romanization of Italy*. 213–233. M. Torelli, ed. Edmonton.

Welch, K. 2007. *The Roman Amphitheatre from its Origins to the Colosseum*. Cambridge.

Wickham, C. 2016. *Medieval Rome. Stability and Crisis of a City, 900–1150*. Oxford.

Wilson-Jones, M. 1993. 'Designing Amphitheatres.' *MDAI(R)* 100: 391–442.

CHAPTER 33

CIRCUSES AND HIPPODROMES

PETER J. HOLLIDAY

THE circus was the grandest of all venues for entertainment in antiquity, the site of public games (*ludi circenses*) that were among the earliest held in association with Rome's most venerable religious festivals. It was essentially a long, narrow racetrack designed primarily for chariots drawn by teams of two (*biga*) or generally four horses (*quadriga*), but it could accommodate all manner of other spectacles, including public executions, gladiatorial contests (*munera*), and wild animal hunts (*venationes*). A fully developed Roman town featured such an arena for athletic contests and chariot-racing, in addition to a forum for commercial and political functions, baths, a theatre, and a gymnasium. Such public buildings, usually erected by rich locals encouraged by the state and closely following established architectural norms, signified cultural unity throughout the empire. The canonical form of the circus, known today from archaeological excavations and ancient literary sources, fulfilled perfectly the practical requirements and social objectives of those who used it—the competitors, spectators, and sponsoring officials—thus exemplifying that essential Roman fusing of utility with striking design stipulated by Vitruvius (*On Architecture* 1.3.2). An examination of the development of that form reveals the Roman circus's dependence on earlier practices, how it served specifically Roman religious and political purposes, and sheds light on the unrivalled role the circus played in the public life of ancient Rome.

ORIGINS AND DEVELOPMENT

It is generally agreed that the origins of the Roman circus lie in the Greek hippodrome and Etruscan arenas for equestrian competitions; none of these has yet been fully excavated, especially as they were never as fully realized a building type as the Roman circus. The tradition for chariot-races reaches back to the funeral games for Patroclus (*Iliad* 23), where Homer recounts features found in later Greek and Roman races, including the layout of the makeshift course and drawing of lots to determine starting positions. Improvised courses on relatively level land near slopes for spectators probably served as temporary hippodromes throughout classical Greece, including the four main athletic competitions at Delphi, Isthmia, Nemea, and Olympia. With the exception of Olympia (Pausanias 6.20.10–21.1), Greek hippodromes never became permanent architectural structures, instead varying in shape and size, with the only fixed elements being the straight and the turning posts. Pausanias asserts that upwards of sixty chariots could race at a time at Olympia, dwarfing later Roman courses, and Pindar (*Pythian* 4.49) reports that in a single race at Delphi forty chariots crashed. Although prizes for equestrian events at Greek festivals were the same as for athletics, the expenses incurred by breeding and training thoroughbreds restricted direct participation in chariot-racing to the rich. In Aristophanes' *Clouds*, Pheidippides' wild expenditures on horses and chariots are ruining his father; Athenian audiences may have discerned here a caricature of Alcibiades, who entered seven teams at Olympia in 416 BCE. Although chariot-racing was well regarded, a class-conscious feeling among Greek spectators may have dampened their interest in equestrian events, in contrast to the frenzied fanaticism of Roman audiences (Harris 1972: 173–183).

Tacitus claims that equestrian contests came to Rome from the Greek colony of Thurii (*Annals* 14.21); however, since Thurii was only founded in the second half of the fifth century, the Roman popularity of the sport was probably stimulated by contacts with other Greek cities in Italy, which had long been sending teams to Olympia (Humphrey 1986: 64). Terracotta plaques from Murlo indicate that horse-racing was popular in Etruria shortly after 600 BCE and Herodotus (1.167) describes the existence of equestrian competitions at the Etruscan city of Caere in around 540 BCE. The Etruscans also held horse-races at Veii as early as the sixth century BCE (Pliny, *Natural History* 8.161), which supports the tradition that the Circus Maximus at Rome was established around 600 BCE by the Etruscan king Tarquinius Priscus, in conjunction with draining the valley between the Palatine and Aventine Hills south of the Capitol (Livy 1.35.8); further improvements were made by Tarquinius Superbus in the late sixth century (Livy 1.56.2). Livy (1.35.9) credits Tarquinius Priscus with bringing horses and boxers from Etruria and seems to suggest that the earliest races seen at Rome were with ridden horses rather than chariots. However, other sources (Plutarch, *Life of Publicola* 13.4; Pliny, *Natural History* 8.161; Festus 340L) state that in the late sixth century the aristocrat Ratumenna drove a winning *quadriga* at Veii; his horses bolted and threw him at the site of the Roman gate subsequently named for him. Pliny (*Natural History* 28.16, 35.157) notes that Tarquin ordered the four-horse chariot group for the Capitoline Temple from a workshop at Veii. Thus there is compelling evidence for Romans adopting chariot-racing from Etruria, mediated by Greek practice, including the custom by which nobles competed.

Since neither the Greek hippodrome nor the Etruscan racetrack was an established monumental type, it is difficult to detect any direct architectural influences on the Roman circus. Yet other material evidence—primarily tomb paintings, reliefs, and vase paintings—suggests some Etruscan derivation. Sixth-century paintings in the Tomba delle Bighe at Tarquinia depict a cross-section of four stands in two pairs, probably analogous to the structures called *fori* built in the Circus Maximus by the Etruscan kings (Livy 1.35.8). Represented in the tomb are two rows of wooden seats for spectators that face two arenas featuring both athletes and charioteers. Spectators include men and women, young and old, seated closely, while slaves (?) lounge on the ground between the supports. The paintings suggest hierarchical seating and confirm that women regularly attended athletic games, a Roman practice not followed in Greece. The same type of arena seems to serve for both equestrian and athletic contests, which accords with the tradition that during the regal and republican periods Roman circuses also featured diverse entertainments. A fifth-century *cippus* from Chiusi now in

Palermo shows a wooden platform resembling the Roman *tribunal* with portable seats of a type similar to the *sella curulis* for magistrates. These were probably judges who held priestly rank, as distinguished by their curved batons (*lituus*), indicating that the Roman custom of awarding seats of honour for officials at the circus games also goes back to Etruria.

THE CIRCUS MAXIMUS IN ROME

Circus races, theatrical performances, and gladiatorial and wild animal shows in arenas comprised the three great sources of Roman public entertainment. The Circus Maximus exemplifies how imperial munificence enshrined such spectacles in public buildings of increasing size and grandeur. The oldest and largest in Rome, it became the dominant model for circus buildings throughout the empire. Its original form was probably close to improvised Greek and Etruscan courses, marked with some shrines and sacred spots. In 329 BCE, the first starting gates (*carceres*) were built of wood (Livy 8.20.1); a barrier to protect the spectators may also have been added. Lucius Stertinius added an honorary arch in 196 BCE (Livy 33.27.3–4), which was replaced by the *fornix* in honour of the emperor Titus in 80–81 CE. Renovations in 174 BCE saw the addition of seven eggs for counting laps (Livy 41.27.6). Competitive generals in the late republic vied to sponsor spectacles in the Circus to curry favour with the Roman multitude in their pursuit of glory and political dominance. In 55 BCE Pompey sought to glorify himself and ingratiate the masses by staging a variety of performances there, including athletic contests, music, *munera*, and *venationes*: this last featured exotic creatures that delighted the crowd and symbolized the distant lands Pompey had subdued.

Caesar undertook the monumentalization of the Circus (Pliny, *Natural History* 36.102; Suetonius, *Caesar* 39.2), seeking both to dwarf Pompey's work on his magnificent theatre and to create an even grander space to assemble and influence the public. He provided seating for 150,000 and circled the track with a moat (*euripus*) to help drain the area and protect spectators from animals during *venationes*. Augustus is credited with completing the work begun by his adoptive father (Cassiodorus, *Letters* 3.51.4; cf. Livy 1.56.2). These renovations, probably under the direct control of Agrippa, established the canonical Roman circus (Fig. 33.1).

Dionysius of Halicarnassus gives a relatively detailed description of the Circus Maximus for this period (*Roman Antiquities* 3.68.1–4). It was one of Rome's most splendid buildings, with a continuous sweep of seating (*cavea*) around both long sides and the semicircular end, absent only at the other short end where the *carceres* stood. Augustus built a monumental stone tribunal (*pulvinar*) into the *cavea* on the long left (Palatine) side directly opposite the finish line from which to watch the competitions (*Deeds of the Divine Augustus* 19; cf. Cassiodorus, *Letters* 3.51). Augustus carefully maintained the trappings of the republic in his new monarchy. Wearing his toga and seemingly seated among other citizens, the emperor presented himself as the highest magistrate (*princeps*) to the senate and Roman people; later rulers who did not follow this acquiescence to republican sensibilities often alienated the senate and were ultimately deposed (Caligula, Nero, Domitian, Commodus). More than a mere theatre box, the *pulvinar* was also a shrine that accommodated thrones for the images of the gods carried in the opening circus procession (Festus 500L), underscoring Augustus' role as reorganizer and head of the Roman state religion. A wall (*podium*) was

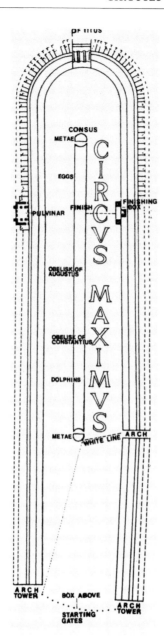

FIGURE 33.1. Plan of the Circus Maximus. Source: P. Holliday.

added to Julius Caesar's *euripus*. Three conical pillars (*metae*) on a platform marked the starting point, and three similar *metae* marked the turning point. Between them extended a low axial wall around which the chariots raced (*spina*), embellished with altars, shrines, and statues of gods. Pillars carried sets of seven eggs and seven dolphins to count laps. About 10 BCE Augustus replaced a mast on the *spina* with an Egyptian obelisk (now at the Piazza del Popolo).

FIGURE 33.2. Circus Mosaic, Carthage. Wikimedia Commons. Public domain.

In the first century CE, the amphitheatre of Statilius Taurus and the Colosseum became the preferred venue for wild-beast shows. Since the Circus Maximus' protective moat was now unnecessary, its decorative functions were transferred to the *spina*, which was embellished with a grander *euripus* with several pools and fountains. This building phase is that shown on most pictorial representations (Figs. 33.2 and 33.3; Marcattili 2009: 241–283). The arena was surrounded on the two long sides and the semicircular short end by rows of seats consisting of several tiers, possibly topped by a gallery, all resting on substructures in the same manner as in theatres and amphitheatres.

A great fire burned the Circus in the time of Domitian (Suetonius, *Domitian* 5), who subsequently planned and began extensive reconstruction, completed by Trajan in 103 (*CIL* 6.955) using more fireproof stone taken from the demolished *naumachiae* of Domitian. The Younger Pliny describes the new façade of the Circus as rivalling the beauty of Rome's temples, a monument equal to the spectacles presented therein (*Panegyric* 51.2–5). It featured vaulted entrances leading to steps and staircases as well as to shops housed on the ground floor, all topped with an attic, probably comparable with the Colosseum. From this time forward the building stood isolated, surrounded by a wide road in order to facilitate access. The boxes of the sponsoring magistrates were above the *carceres*; seats for the judges were posted along the track at the starting line, turning points, and the finishing line. The old *pulvinar* was raised up and built into the third zone of seats so that it dominated the long Palatine side.

FIGURE 33.3. Sarcophagus from Aquino representing the Circus Maximus. Photo: P. Holliday.

Pliny praised Trajan who, in contrast to Domitian's practice of watching the games from a private apartment in the new palace on the Palatine, once again sat and watched the games among the people, significantly visible to them on their level, thus linking himself to the esteemed Augustan model (*Panegyric* 51.4–5).

Later alterations included a second obelisk erected by Constantius II in 357 (now in the Piazza S. Giovanni in Laterano). At the same time towers were added beside the *carceres*, which probably influenced the construction of similar towers at the Circus of Maxentius on the Via Appia outside the city walls. Built together with the palace of Maxentius, this is the only other circus preserved in Rome; others, including the Circus Flaminius built by the censor C. Flaminius on the southern Campus Martius in 221 BCE, the Circus Vaticanus (Circus Gaii et Neronis), partially built over by St Peter's Basilica and Square, and the Circus Varianus built by Elagabalus at his Villa Sessorianum, have been completely destroyed. The last official races in the Circus Maximus were organized in 549 by the Ostrogothic king Totila. During the Middle Ages the site reverted to fields and by the nineteenth century was covered with various industrial enterprises. The whole area was cleared in the 1930s and is today a public park in modern Rome. The tradition of circus spectacles was so integral to the Roman *res publica* that when he refounded Byzantium as the new capital of his empire, Constantine laid out a vast hippodrome on the model of the Circus Maximus. Today that site remains a vast open space, some 3 metres above the level of Constantinople's ancient course, marked by monuments that once decorated its *spina*.

The overall length of the Circus Maximus racetrack was about 580 metres, the external length about 620 metres. The total width of the arena at the far turning post was nearly 80 metres, and somewhat less at the end near the starting gates. The banks of seating around the outside were 30 metres deep; thus the overall width reached about 140 metres. The position of the *carceres* at the west (Tiber) end was fixed by the discoveries of E. Bigot (1903–1908); they were partly excavated and then reburied (Humphrey 1986: 124). The richly ornamented *spina* now lies about 9 metres below the present ground level, but detailed representations of such features appear in mosaics and reliefs (Figs. 33.2 and 33.3). Sources vary in their estimates of the capacity of the Circus: Dionysius (3.68) gives the capacity as 150,000 in the reign of Augustus, while Pliny (*Natural History* 36.102) cites 250,000 during the reign of Trajan. The even larger figures given by the regionary catalogues of Rome in the late empire (often cited by modern guidebooks to the city) are dubious.

THE CIRCUS SPECTACLE

The origins of the circus games may lie in triumphal celebrations. The oldest events staged at the Circus were the *ludi Romani*, a festival of chariot-races and military displays held annually for fifteen days in September in honour of Jupiter Optimus Maximus, but by the time of the emperors, about twenty other annual games featured at least one day in the Circus.

The *ludi* opened with a grand procession (*pompa circenses*), which recalled their religious origin and gave the spectacle a sacred aura (Latham 2016). It began at the Temple of Jupiter Capitolinus, descended to the Forum and proceeded to the Circus Maximus, where it circled the entire length of the arena around the *spina*, presaging the races to follow (Dionysius of Halicarnassus, *Roman Antiquities* 7.72). Although sharing many features with the triumph, the sacred rite reversed the route and opened rather than closed the spectacle. At the head the sponsoring magistrate drove a *biga* and wore the decorative triumphal costume of the *tunica Iovis* (Juvenal 11.193–196, 10.36–40); a slave supported a gold crown (*corona aurea*) above his head: all Etruscan vestiges with religious significance (Pliny, *Natural History* 21.4; Tertullian, *On the Spectacles* 7) that glorified the sponsor. Romans in military formation on horseback and on foot followed, trailed by young men equipped for the weapon dance, musicians, and then the competitors, their horses, and chariots. Dancers dressed as sirens and satyrs came after them, performing boisterous dances for the gods, whose images (including those of deceased emperors and empresses who received divine honours) were borne on richly decorated litters and carriages escorted by *collegia* and priestly corporations (Hönle 2003: 359–60; Dodge 2011).

Throughout the republican period, circus contests could include foot-races, boxing, and wrestling (Cicero, *On the Laws* 2.38; Dionysius of Halicarnassus, *Roman Antiquities* 7.73). Because of its size and sightlines, the Circus was also the most frequent location for animal events and *venationes*, but eventually less commonly used for *munera* and theatrical entertainments. It remained the preferred site for military reviews, such as the cavalry manoeuvres of six divisions of equestrians (*ludi sevirales*), with their six leaders (*seviri*) and an imperial prince as *princeps iuventutis* at their head. Caesar staged the Troy Games (*ludus Troiae*) in the Circus Maximus. Traditionally introduced by Aeneas, this spectacle celebrated Rome's (and Caesar's) Trojan origins. Under Augustus young Roman *nobiles* performed the pageant's elaborate equestrian manoeuvres in light armour in separate divisions, one of the few respectable entertainments performed by freeborn Roman participants; although elites learned the difficult art of steering a chariot, their *dignitas* prevented them from entertaining a mixed festival audience. Following Greek and Etruscan custom, leading citizens had once raced their own horses in the Circus. Indeed, a branch of the *gens Claudia* bore the cognomen *Quadrigarius*, suggesting that an ancestor had won renown for his chariot skills. But the practice was abandoned: senators were forbidden to participate as competitors, and were eventually also banned from providing horses for most of the games. Consequently the state contracted with professional agents to provide the horses and charioteers, who were of humble, even servile, origin (Cameron 1976; Letzner 2009; Meijer 2010). The senatorial elite now competed for esteem by organizing and presiding over the races. The sponsor had to pay the entire expense; for the *ludi publici* in Rome this was still the praetor in the fourth century CE. The emperor paid for additional games that were free to spectators.

The presiding magistrate started the race by dropping a white napkin (*mappa*) into the arena. The chariots emerged from the *carceres* at the right of the *spina*, charged along the straight, rounded the further post, and raced back down the left side to the starting post. There were thirteen turns for seven laps, a distance of five miles that enabled spectators to watch more of the spectacle. (The counterclockwise direction can be explained by its easier manoeuvring for right-handed charioteers.) Seven laps constituted one heat (*missus*), after which the chariots drove off the course through the barriers to the left of the *spina*. During the republic there might be ten to twelve heats; after Caligula the number rose to twenty-four, taking up the entire day. Victory went to the first chariot that crossed a chalk line. Enumerating the various kinds of chalk, Pliny notes 'The cheapest is that with which they mark out the winning-line at the Circus' (*Natural History* 35.199; cf. Isidore of Seville, *Etymologies* 18.37).

INFRASTRUCTURE AND AMBIENCE

The increased number of contests raised the standards of competition among an ever higher calibre of horses and drivers, resulting in a professional sport dominated by four politically allied service companies (*factiones*), called by the names of the colours worn by their drivers. In the early imperial period the Blue and Green factions joined the original White and Red (Cameron 1976). With their growing financial strength, the *factiones* invested huge sums to acquire pedigree horses from Sicily, Calabria, Apulia, North Africa, and Spain (Hyland 1990). They employed numerous trained specialists to cover each aspect of the games (cf. *CIL* 6.10074–6). Despite his lowly status, a charioteer (*auriga* or *agitator*) of exceptional skill became the focus of adulation. Numerous monuments commemorated popular drivers and even horses; horses could win great fame and after a hundred victories attained the honorific title *centenarius*. Scirtus, a driver for the Whites, was a celebrated star under Tiberius (*CIL* 6.10051), while Martial (10.53) praised the Reds' Scorpus for having all the fame, money, and honorary statues that he himself desired. Traditional prizes had been palms and crowns, but with the professionalization of the races, charioteers were often awarded large amounts of money. These prizes allowed ambitious drivers to become contractors, or even directors of a company of contractors; nevertheless, they remained listed among the legally sanctioned *personae inhonesti* (*Theodosian Code* 15.7.2).

Graffiti in Pompeii indicate gamblers bet heavily on their favourite teams (cf. Harris 1972: 223–226). The factions were brought from Rome to the new Hippodrome at Constantinople, where the fanaticism of the populace surpassed that at Rome itself. As at Rome, partisanship extended outside the Hippodrome into the political life of the day; at Constantinople it even intruded into contemporary theological controversies, which were intimately connected with politics. In January 512, rioting broke out in the Hippodrome between Blues and Greens and nearly brought down the regime of the emperor Justinian I; the Nika Revolt lasted several days and ended in a massacre of 30,000 to 40,000 people (Procopius, *Wars of Justinian* 1.24; Theophanes 158; Zonaras 14.6.28; cf. Meijer 2010).

Both the factions and the gambling spectators pressed officials to ensure that races be made as fair as possible. Architects designed courses with the same distance from start to finish so that all competitors had an equal chance at victory. Whereas the Greeks had staggered the start of chariots temporally, the Romans adopted the simpler stratagem of staggering them spatially. Placed at the one short end, marble *carceres* (closed with bolts or bars opened by a torsion-sprung mechanism), eight or more usually twelve in number, were divided into two groups on either side of the central entrance and arranged in slanting lines creating a shallow arc so that the distance from them to the starting point was spread out, giving each charioteer an equal start, a geometry probably influenced by that for athletics in Greek stadia (Humphrey 1986: 132–174). The curving of the starting line may have made the start fairer, but it also increased the risk of crashes as drivers converged on the desirable inner position. According to Cassiodorus (*Letters* 3.51.7), to lessen the danger 'not far from the *carceres* a white line is marked right across the track from side to side, so that as the chariots race forward, the real fray may not start before that point; otherwise, if they tried too early to cause one another to crash, they might rob the spectators of the most compelling part of the spectacle'. Whether Cassiodorus' break-line was also the finish line described by Pliny is uncertain (Humphrey 1986: 84–91).

Neither the competitors nor the betting public believed that all the starting positions were equally favourable, no matter what mathematical or engineering solutions architects introduced. Hence drivers drew lots to determine their starting positions (Tertullian, *On the Spectacles* 16; Symmachus, *Official Dispatches* 9.6), a procedure retained from the Greeks when no gates existed in the hippodromes (cf. Lucian, *The Rival Philosophies* 40). An official rolled the lots in an urn where it was visible to all the spectators (atop the *carceres*?); each charioteer chose the stall he preferred, indicating that no one stall was generally agreed to give an obvious advantage (Humphrey 1986: 154–156). Although the skill of the drivers and quality of their horses were vital, Roman spectators believed the outcome also was swayed by fortune, the lot drawn, and the curses invoked by competitors and fans upon their rivals.

Like gladiatorial *munera*, some aspects of chariot-racing had military applications (Plass 1995: 40). It was dangerous and involved great skill on the part of the charioteers; the risks for man and horse were acute. Also like the *munera*, this peril seems originally to have linked racing with the cyclical renewal of human life (related also to the religious roots preserved in the opening procession). The spectacle of speeding teams manoeuvring for advantage down the long narrow arena generated considerable excitement, which only increased as they made their sharp turns around the *metae*, the most treacherous point on the track. Colliding with the turning posts could be fatal to both the driver himself and to the driver immediately behind him. In Rome, the shrine of the Etruscan deity Consus at that point underscored the underworld association (cf. Varro, *On the Latin Language* 6.20). In making turns, charioteers aimed to come as close to the *metae* as possible, even grazing them, while avoiding real contact (Ovid, *Loves* 3.2.12; Silius Italicus, *Punic War* 16.361; Humphrey 1986: 255–259). To overtake on the inside when approaching the turn was especially admired (Horace, *Odes* 1.1.4; Statius, *Thebaid* 6.479). As direct connection with funeral rites weakened, the entertainment and potential political value of circus games grew. During their term in office, republican leaders sought favour among the masses by sponsoring entertainments to celebrate important days and to demonstrate their munificence (Plass 1995: 30). The popularity of such shows greatly increased in the imperial period when emperors funded more and far greater spectacles.

The monumentalization of the circus, progressive use of stone and marble with each remodelling, and increasingly rich ornamentation joined with more elaborate spectacles to demonstrate imperial power and munificence to a vast audience. Nevertheless, the crowding of so many people in one place could be problematic. Augustus sought to enforce decorum at the spectacles through a series of decrees. Seats were reserved for senators, equestrians, and youths in the *toga praetexta*, the toga being the prescribed formal dress for men. The aediles made sure that nobody was admitted except those wearing undyed togas and without a cloak (Suetonius, *Augustus* 40.5); anyone who did not have light-coloured clothes was banned to the upper tiers (Suetonius, *Augustus* 44.2, Calpurnius, *Eclogues* 7). In the republic, senators had enjoyed special seats in the Circus, and although Claudius reserved a section of new stone seats for them, he allowed senators the option of sitting wherever they wished. Nero added stone seats for the *equites*. Seats for women were not isolated, unlike the theatres where they were segregated. On the inscription *CIL* 6.955 the thirty-five tribes thank Trajan for adding seats, which suggests that citizens may have sat in sections according to their tribes at the Circus (Humphrey 1986: 77); within sections seating was probably generally by rank, echoing Etruscan practice.

The individual seats themselves were narrow and uncomfortable. Many people used a cushion (*pulvinum*) to counter their hardness; the upper seats were so steep some resorted to footstools (*cava scamna*). The audience sat tightly packed together in narrow rows, the knees of spectators in one row jabbing the backs of those in front of them. Such proximity engendered the sense of solidarity and collective energy found in any mass audience, but in the circus, the audience's size and diversity suggested that the entire Roman people were assembled, a potentially explosive situation that could yield either spontaneous or organized political expression, yet one that also had the power 'to direct and bestow a great deal of popular goodwill and gratitude upon those politicians, patrons, and presiding officials responsible for the event' (Beacham 1999: 42–43). In their sheer numbers and fanaticism, the ancient Roman audience surpassed the spectators at a modern sporting event or rock concert.

Juvenal was famously disgusted by the circus both as a site of political manipulation of the masses and the entertainment found there: 'The people that once used to bestow military commands, high office, legions, everything, now limits itself. It has an obsessive desire for two things only—bread and circuses' (*Satire* 10.79–81). The Younger Pliny wrote to a friend how he relished the tranquility throughout Rome when the masses attended the *ludi circenses*; he loathed their furious partisanship and preferred to concentrate on his papers (*Letters* 9.6). Such writers represent that strand of Roman intellectual who despised the circus as the site of spectacles of death. But it was the affluent literati, not the impoverished masses, who scorned the arena. In fact, the plebs hated Tiberius for his meagre shows, while they loved Caligula for his extravagant games and distributions of food (Kyle 1998: 194). In the republic, ordinary citizens could nominally participate in the political life of the city, but the empire gradually forced them to transfer their ambitions to the private sphere. Although this large mass of people did not represent a serious threat to imperial authority, it was in the state's best interests that it was kept reasonably content and free from any inclination to riot (Harris 1972: 213). With all classes sharing together in the spectacle of the circus, chariot-racing became embedded in the city's life, with individuals, including emperors, devoting themselves to one faction or another.

Despite the occasional moralizing by some writers, there is little to refute the immense enthusiasm with which Romans embraced such exciting spectacles. Ammianus Marcellinus (28.4.28) describes Rome in the fourth century CE: 'Now consider the idle and indolent commons ... The Circus Maximus is their temple, home, assembly and the fulfilment of all their hopes. You can see them quarrelling fiercely about the races throughout the city... Before dawn on a race day they all rush recklessly to secure a place at such speed that they could almost outpace the chariots themselves.' Nor was the excitement of the race the only attraction. Since men and women intermingled in the stands, Juvenal (11.202) informs us that some men found it delightful to sit beside a well-dressed young woman, a *culta puella*. Ovid describes how the blurring of social barriers engendered celebratory relaxation and festivity among the throng, presenting remarkable opportunities for playful flirtation (*The Art of Love* 1.135–164; *Loves* 3.2). Sulla met his last wife Valeria at the Circus when she pulled a thread from his toga (Plutarch, *Sulla* 35).

The Roman circus developed into the most magnificent and effective venue for staging state-sponsored spectacles, a matchless juncture of sacred occasion, thrilling entertainment, fervid partisanship, and festive amusement, all in proximity to the major players on the political stage. With the largest assemblies in antiquity—competitors, spectators, and officials—pursuing their diverse agendas, it fulfilled a pivotal function in the social and political life of ancient Rome.

References

Beacham, R. C. 1999. *Spectacle Entertainments of Early Imperial Rome*. New Haven.

Cameron, A. 1976. *Circus Factions: Blues and Greens at Rome and Byzantium*. Oxford.

Dodge, H. 2011. *Spectacle in the Roman World*. London.

Harris, H. A. 1972. *Sport in Greece and Rome*. New York.

Hönle, A. R. 2003. 'Circus.' *Brill's New Pauly Encyclopaedia of the Ancient World*, vol. 3. 353–362. Leiden.

Humphrey, J. H. 1986. *Roman Circuses: Arenas for Chariot Racing*. Berkeley.

Hyland, A. 1990. *Equus: The Horse in the Roman World*. London.

Kyle, D. G. 1998. *Spectacles of Death in Ancient Rome*. London.

Latham, J. A. 2016. *Performance, Memory, and Processions in Ancient Rome: The 'pompa circensis' from the Late Republic to Late Antiquity*. New York.

Letzner, W. 2009. *Der römische Circus: Massenunterhaltung in römischen Reich*. Mainz am Rhein.

Marcattili, F. 2009. *Circo Massimo: Architetture, funzioni, culti, ideologia*. Rome.

Meijer, F. 2010. *Chariot Racing in the Roman Empire*. Baltimore.

Plass, P. 1995. *The Game of Death in Ancient Rome: Arena Sport and Political Suicide*. Madison, WI.

SECTION 3

REPRESENTATIONS AND MATERIAL CULTURE

....

CHAPTER 34

COMBAT SPORTS AND GLADIATORIAL COMBAT IN GREEK AND ROMAN PRIVATE ART

....

SHELBY BROWN

INTRODUCTION: GOALS, CONTEXT, AND LIMITATIONS

....

IN order to make representations showing ancient sport and spectacle manageable, I focus primarily on Classical Greek combat sports and Roman gladiatorial duels of the Late Republic and Empire. My primary goal here is to identify what the images can tell us about viewers' enjoyment of violent competition and its compelling moments. Did imagery in less expensive media resemble that of the wealthy or elite? Did private images share themes with public art? Violent sports and gladiatorial combat overlap as entertainment, and I view them both as competitive performances (Kyle 2015: 9–11; Kyle 2017). For convenience, I call the representations, whether practically useful or decorative, cheap or expensive, 'art'. Together, Greek and Roman images of violent competition appeared in public and private art in a full range of media, from cheap clay souvenirs to costly mosaics, and appealed to all levels of society. Since the topic of private art is dauntingly large, even when limited to violent competition, and relevant images span the sixth century BCE to the fourth century CE across a wide geographical range, generalizations are inevitable. One assumption I make here is that ancient artists produced private art for buyers and consumers who enjoyed the real competitions and combats and understood their internal rules. The art shows us how events were reimagined and helps us understand the relationships and roles of competitors, spectators, and sponsors.

Why did Greeks and Romans enjoy violent combat? Why do we? Biologists and anthropologists still debate whether humans simply have a biological imperative for violence (Gabbatiss 2017). Classicists, historians, psychologists, and sociologists sometimes apply the interdisciplinary approaches of modern sports theory (Giulianotti 2015) to the interpretation of ancient combat sports and gladiatorial games (Fagan 2011; Guttmann 1983; Kyle 2017), but scholarly views of violent entertainment remain conflicted. Even considering cultural context, there is little agreement about why watching violence was appealing in antiquity, or how it affected spectators (Hammer 2010: 64–65, n. 5; Coleman 2019). Theatricality, stagecraft, and novelty can contextualize brutality as diversion (Fagan 2016), and many scholars believe that watching violence desensitizes the viewer and reduces empathy (Goldstein 1998; Grimes et al. 2008; Zillmann 1998). Greeks and Romans clearly were desensitized to bloody, painful competition, but an answer (especially a single one) to the appeal of violent spectacle is elusive and undoubtedly more complicated than sometimes stated by one camp or another.

Combat entertained audiences with an exciting and unpredictable—but controlled and regulated—struggle that reinforced masculine values. Women were not heavy athletes, and female gladiators were rare (Brunet 2013; Kyle 2015: 209–218; McCullough 2008). Violent sport and combat involved serious physical damage or death, and audiences admired a skilful competitor who persisted even when badly hurt. Athletes fought nude, while gladiators wore specialized armour (evolved from that worn by early Roman captives) appropriate to different fighting styles. Both athlete and gladiator fought until one competitor collapsed or admitted defeat by raising a finger or hand. The winners could earn fame and prize money. The voluntary, free athlete won or lost on his own merit, whereas the slave gladiator had to impress the spectators, and the loser needed audience support to survive. However, a gladiator was not inevitably expected to die, like criminals condemned 'to the beasts' (*ad bestias*). Romans valued duels between men with an equal chance to win, and a trained gladiator was not to be wasted unnecessarily (Fagan 2011: 215–219). The system allowed for losers to walk away if they had fought well.

Approaches to evaluating visual images have evolved enormously in the past fifty years under multiple influences (Christesen and Kyle 2014: 2–3; Scanlon 2014: 7–21). Early semiotic studies and psychoanalytical, feminist, and Marxist theories of looking influenced artists, classicists, art historians, and—eventually—classical archaeologists to consider the social meaning and consequences of art and to ask who made it and who looked at it (Clarke 1998: 11; Koloski-Ostrow and Lyons 1997; Rabinowitz and Richlin 1993; Stansbury-O'Donnell 2011). Unfortunately, we often know little or nothing about individual makers or owners of ancient art. Many surviving representations are damaged, incalculable numbers are lost, and the statistical frequency of types of scenes within our pool of images is probably hopelessly skewed. Keeping these limitations in mind, however, we can still glean a great deal from art. In the absence of other evidence, we can loosely identify 'wealth' through expensive media and scale of decoration. 'Elite' implies tastes and attitudes (or mimicry of them) stemming from education, birthright, wealth, and social or political position or ambition. Smaller, affordable images, often mass-produced, represent mementos and souvenirs for 'ordinary' spectators. I consider 'private' the paintings, mosaics, reliefs, and portable objects and art in domestic contexts, from poor apartments to wealthy villas, and in some tombs. 'Private' is a flexible term when private monuments are visible to all or some, and especially in Hellenistic and Roman houses. Domestic imagery in a house was intended not just for personal enjoyment, but also to convey status and taste, and rooms and their decoration often served multiple functions, public and private (Bergmann 2007; Clarke 1991; 2003; Nevett 2007; Tuori 2015; Trümper 2012). The message of private narrative art, as of portraits, was thus politicized (Fejfer 2008: 16–17, 73).

GREEK COMBAT SPORT

The world of Greek athletics was centred on men, although women sometimes watched games and also competed against one another (Kyle 2015: 209–216; Miller 2012: 149–162). Competitions were held at religious festivals, and women could participate in aspects of religious performance. Greeks associated athletic victory with glory to the individual, family, and *polis*, and athletic training was an essential aspect of educating free young men in proper behaviour and good citizenship. The 'heavy' competitions (*barea athla*), later adopted by the Romans, comprised wrestling, boxing, and pankration, an 'all power' event (Pausanias, *Description of Greece* 6.24.1) that employed techniques of both (see Poliakoff, this volume, Chapter 17). At the most prestigious festivals, the only win in these events was first place, achieved after multiple combats. Most male citizens would have wrestled, but not all would have engaged seriously in pankration or boxing, which could be brutal. These events had only a few rules (biting and eye gouging were forbidden) and no weight divisions or time limits, so they favoured larger, heavier competitors. Boxing blows were largely aimed at the head, and severe damage to the face was common. In pankration, kicking as well as punching was legitimate.

Archaic and Classical representational art emphasizes symmetrical designs, idealized human bodies, and calm, expressionless faces. Athletes preparing, grooming, or fighting are carefully posed and reflect appreciation of aesthetically staged male bodies. That the toned, youthful nude male eventually became a complex symbol of moral and physical excellence is reflected in depictions of nude or partially nude males not just in athletic or mythological, but also in civic and military contexts. There were frequent references to the athletic male body in both public and private art. The sexual allure of watching male bodies at their peak was incorporated into the educational ideal, and sexual relationships were accepted between older men, positioned as mentors, and pubescent boys in the context of athletic training (Fisher 2014; Lear and Cantarella 2008: 91–97; Scanlon 2002; Shapiro 2015). Most nude athletes were slender, and heavy fighters were not singled out as different from other competitors. However, some heavy combatants fighting on private vases had noticeably protruding posteriors and bellies, sometimes meant to be funny, as was the portly, un-athletic boy shown next to a fit athlete on a drinking cup (Miller 2004 fig. 271; Poliakoff 1987: fig. 82). Philostratus (third century CE) noted a positive effect of a big belly: it could get in the way of strikes to the face (*Gymnasticus* 34; Miller 2004: 33, fig. 80).

The best private artistic sources for pre-Hellenistic Greek sports and male–male relationships are Black and Red Figure vases, primarily Attic, of the sixth and fifth centuries BCE (Brendle 2019; Stansbury-O'Donnell 2011: 125–128). Their decoration probably reflected the interests of both ordinary and elite citizens. While women were not protected from seeing images of naked athletes, the vases reveal male values since they were used at dinner and drinking parties (*symposia*) of male citizens that included women, but not respectable wives and daughters. The vessels were used to entertain males from outside the household. Non-athletic imagery depicted daily life, *symposia*, male–male courtship, mythology, and more. In scenes of athletes, heavy competitors were depicted alongside other athletes, and vases show buyers' interest in a variety of sports. Repeated poses reveal painters' use of templates, but few exact copies of scenes survive, and we cannot tell how often patrons

FIGURE 34.1. Black Figure amphora of the late sixth century BCE: two boxers with big bellies and posteriors are aligned in axial symmetry with two wrestlers above. Blood spurts from one boxer's nose. © Trustees of the British Museum.

commissioned a unique image. They did sometimes add a name to commemorate a love interest or personalize a gift. Related to such *symposion* vases are Panathenaic amphorae, decorated storage jars commissioned by event organizers. Filled with olive oil, they were given as prizes to victors, who treasured (but could also sell or gift) them (Bundrick 2019: 217–218; Kyle 2015: 153–157; Neils 1992). Athena, as symbol of the city and the games, was depicted on one side, the athletic event on the other. Both drinking and prize vessels shared themes, and while victory was sometimes indicated by ribbons, wreaths, branches, the victor, and the presence of personified Nike (Robertson 1992: figs. 284b, 289, 295, 299), vases most often showed heavy competitors in action.

Frontal poses and symmetrical, aesthetically posed limbs sometimes impede our interpretation of real fighting techniques (Poliakoff 1987: 5–6). Boxers are identified by their leather thongs, *himantes*, with which they wrapped their hands; they hold their elbows high as they protect their own faces and bloody those of opponents (Fig. 34.1). Vases document wrestlers' defensive and offensive moves and highlight pankratiasts' kicks and punches. Other fighters sometimes look on, reminding the viewer that the ultimate victory came only after a series of combats. Artists often depicted a blow that gave one man an advantage, as in a late sixth-century scene of two big-bellied fighters, both dripping blood, one covering his face as the other lands a punch to his chin (Miller 2004 fig. 80). In another late sixth-century scene, a fighter still being pummelled raises a finger to a referee to end the fight (Swaddling 2008: 72). Clothed trainers or referees identified by a staff or forked stick (*rabdos*) enforced the rules during training and competition. If a fighter gouged or bit in the heat of action, the referee could beat him with the stick (Fig. 34.2; Miller 2004 figs. 96–98; Swaddling 2008: 75).

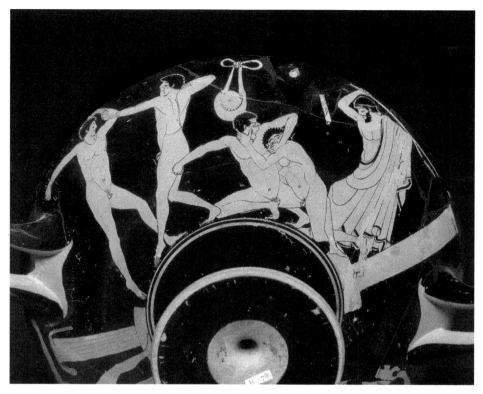

FIGURE 34.2. Red Figure kylix of the early fifth century BCE: two pankratiasts gouge as an arbiter brings his stick down to punish them. Two boxers punch one another to their left. The artist has arranged horizontal arms/stick and vertical bodies/column in a symmetrical pattern. © Trustees of the British Museum.

Most surviving public combat art, in contrast to private representations of the conflict itself, was an honorific or victory image of the winner, often a nude bronze statue erected by him or his city. However, the fighting techniques and standard poses of heavy events do appear in public mythological narratives. Heroes such as Theseus and Herakles, sometimes shown in sculpture with a cauliflower ear, fought like combat athletes. The brawling of centaurs with Lapiths at the wedding of Peirithoos shown on the west pediment of the Temple of Zeus at Olympia included wrestling and shoving—and a centaur biting—under the gaze of Apollo. The visual connection with scenes on private vases is marked (Barringer 2005; Raschke 2002: 43). A modern martial artist comparing modern and ancient techniques has even identified a 'horizontal outside elbow strike' executed by a Lapith maiden—a fascinating if unlikely idea (Dervenis and Lykiardopoulos 2005: 92). Other combats of Lapiths and centaurs on the southern Parthenon metopes reflect heavy fighting as well (including choking and groin-kneeing; Fig. 34.3). In such Classical sculpture, humans rarely show emotion, and then only faintly; subhuman opponents like centaurs are more expressive. Vase painters indicated fighters' effort or pain by a faintly downturned mouth or facial lines (Fig. 34.2). In the Hellenistic period, a general trend in representational art toward depicting complex three-dimensional poses and dramatic suffering influenced athletic

FIGURE 34.3. Metope from the south side of the fifth century BCE Parthenon, Athens: a centaur and Lapith fight like pankratiasts. © Trustees of the British Museum.

art. Small bronze groups reveal buyers' interest in elegant, sometimes erotic depictions of intertwined wrestlers or pankratiasts. Images of heavy athletes can now reveal pain, exhaustion, and the damage to face and body, and they may incorporate individualizing attributes (Stewart 2014: 124–132). The impact of colour for a viewer's understanding of physical trauma has largely been lost, but it must have been significant in all media. The Hellenistic life-sized bronze Terme Boxer from Rome, of debated date and context, has bodily and facial damage: cauliflower ears, scars, bruises and blood drops inset in reddish copper, and even a contusion in a different alloy under one eye (Boddy 2008: 22–23; Daehner and Lapatin 2015 no. 18; Ridgway 2002: 86).

When the Romans began to take an interest in (and admire, and deplore) Greek culture and athletics in the ate Republic and early empire, they borrowed both calm Classical and more dramatic Hellenistic styles to represent athletes. In Roman boxing, an evolved 'glove' (*caestus*), modified with metal, leather, and dangerous-looking protrusions carefully depicted in art, perhaps inflicted new levels of harm (Poliakoff, this volume Chapter 17); however, no major increase in facial damage has been preserved in Roman images (Junkelmann 2000: 76–80; Miller 2004: 32–33; Newby 2005 cover art). Romans considered public performers such as actors and gladiators *infames*, outside proper society, like prostitutes, and athletes too were tainted (Epictetus, *Discourses* 2.18; Tacitus, *Annals* 14.20; Potter 1999: 283). Nevertheless, Greek athletic competition did retain its status, especially in Greece and the

Greco-Roman east, and success in the major Greek crown festivals was valued even by Roman elites and emperors. Romans who wanted to Hellenize their private houses imported or copied victory statues to decorate gardens or baths (Kousser 2008: 146–148; Swaddling 2008: 49, 90), while figurines and decorated lamps of clay and bronze met the needs of those who could not afford larger marbles and bronzes. Many figurines show heavily muscled men with scarred faces fighting, or resting after combat. Athletes in both Classical and Hellenistic styles appeared together in private and public art (König 2005: 115–124; Newby 2005: 92–95). Greek-style athletic victors, whether idealized or physically damaged, symbolized persistence, courage, and success (Newby, this volume Chapter 10).

ROMAN GLADIATORS

In the late republic and empire, skilled and more deadly gladiatorial combat claimed public interest. The Roman arena was centred on male appreciation of fighting valour in a context of social hierarchy and identity (Dunbabin 2016: 171). Gladiatorial duels originally took place in the context of private funerals at Rome, but they eventually became included among the games (*munera*) presented at festivals by officials throughout the empire (for a concise description of all that a duel entailed, see Potter 1999: 235–240). The patron who paid for the games was the official judge of the event, although he deferred to the majority opinion of the audience. *Munera* came to include beast fights, animal hunts (*venationes*), and executions. Games, which included music, processions, and dramatic rituals, were held at first in temporary facilities, but eventually under the empire in permanent amphitheaters or (in the east) in modified theatres or stadia. Since gladiators were drawn from the ranks of captives, criminals, and slaves, the context was partly punitive, but audiences appreciated volunteers (*auctorati*) who could be expected to put on a good show (Petronius, *Satyricon* 45). These too became slaves while serving as gladiators. Although elite Romans considered the games vulgar and debased, they still enjoyed the skilled duels of courageous fighters and thought them edifying (Wistrand 1992). Rulers needed to provide games and seem interested in them as well, since the arena was a place to show themselves to and hear from the populace. Wise emperors like Titus, who favored Thracian fighters, showed that they were fans (Suetonius, *Titus* 8). Seating at spectacles was organized by social rank, and Augustus also regulated seats by gender, requiring even women of high status to sit in the upper sections (Suetonius, *Augustus* 44; Futrell 2006: 80–83). Sponsoring gladiatorial shows was a source of prestige, and producers (*editores* or *munerarii*) heralded events ahead of time in public flyers and paintings (Pliny, *Historia Naturalis* 35.52), and sometimes recapped them afterward, listing such information as gladiators' names, fighting styles, and win–loss records. How frequently gladiators fought per year, how long their bouts lasted, and how often combat ended in death is debated, but gladiators were valuable assets and it was not financially desirable for too many of them to die (Futrell 2006: 143–144). Sometimes a successful fighter was commemorated by name in artworks and souvenirs (Cassibry 2018; Jacobelli 2003: 78; Petronius, *Satyricon* 52.3), but since gladiators probably traveled to different venues, audiences often focused on favourite types of fighters employing armature that became standardized throughout the Empire (although chronological and regional variations can make secure identification difficult).

Private gladiatorial imagery was widespread on utilitarian objects (knives, lamps, dinnerware) of clay, bronze, glass, and ivory, and in more expensive paintings and mosaics. Figurines abounded; some even had removable helmets like those of 'action figure' toys today (Junkelmann 2000: figs. 29, 62, 63). Mass-produced, moulded terracotta lamps and drinking cups, prevalent throughout the Roman world in the first four centuries CE, were affordable souvenirs. Themes included the arena, daily life, mythology, athletics, sexual acts, and circus races. Non-gladiatorial arena images referenced *venationes* (skilled animal hunts), *damnatio ad bestias* (execution by beasts), and even public sexual punishments, as in a tableau of a donkey having intercourse with a woman (Apuleius, *Metamorphoses* 10.29–34; Golvin and Landes 1990: 191; Welch 2007: fig. 93). On pottery and glass vessels with bigger panels or longer registers, artists sometimes included subsidiary spectacles or a gladiatorial referee with a staff (Jacobelli 2003: fig. 65a), but lamps usually focused on one or two gladiators 'up close', emphasizing their equipment. This was only partly due to the small size of the decorative field, since circus scenes of enormous scope and detail could be squeezed onto a lamp, for example an entire circus, audience, and chariot-race (Junkelmann 2000: fig. 95). Lone fighters strike offensive and defensive poses, gesture with a finger to signal defeat (at which point fighting stops), or kneel awaiting a death blow, implying an unseen victor. If condemned, defeated gladiators were expected to submit to death with dignity, kneeling and bowing their heads (Augenti 2001 fig. 75; Junkelmann 2000: fig. 19). Possible gladiator burials from York, Ephesus, and London suggest that the men ate a specific diet, trained intensely, and followed rules of combat: ceasing to inflict wounds after a winning strike, and accepting a death blow (Hunter-Mann 2015; Kanz and Grossschmidt 2009; Redfern and Bonney 2013).

Types of paired gladiators were recognizable across the Roman world. Very common are scenes of two fighters in action or at the moment of or just preceding defeat. Palms or wreaths could signify victory, but these survive mostly on funerary reliefs, where fighters also recorded their win-loss-tie statistics. These and other written records suggest that many gladiators did not survive more than ten games; but many fared better, gained experience and popularity, and survived until they retired or transitioned to management (Futrell 2006:143–145). Sometimes two combatants of the same type competed, such as horse-riding equites who dismounted to fight. However, usually two different types were shown using different offensive and defensive weapons, such as the *murmillo* with angled, rectangular crest, large shield, and straight blade versus the Thraex (Thracian) with a griffin-headed crest, smaller shield, and a curved or angled blade (first century CE lamp, Fig. 34.4; second century CE mosaic from Zliten, second pair, Fig. 34.5), or the helmetless, net and trident-wielding *retiarius* ('net man') versus the *secutor* ('pursuer'), whose helmet had small eyeholes and a low, smooth metal crest to deflect the trident's prongs (Zliten mosaic, first pair, Fig. 34.5). Helmets probably encouraged the dramatic body language and gestures important for all masked performers (Schwarzmaier 2010: 35), and only the *retiarius* did without. Even the fighters themselves were unnecessary; an image of greaves, shields, weapons, and helmets alone signified a duel (Junkelmann 2000: fig. 20).

The games fascinated the crowd as both sport and violent spectacle (Goldstein 1998; Fagan 2011; Scanlon 2014: 21–23; Toner 2013). Cicero saw gladiators' discipline and willingness to be hurt as setting a good example (*Tusculan Disputations*, 2.17). Gladiators slammed their shields upward to stun an opponent or knock his shield or weapon aside (lamp, Augenti 2001 figs. 68, 71; figurines, Junkelmann 200 fig. 43; mosaic, Golvin and Landes 1990: 154). To

FIGURE 34.4. Clay lamp of the first century CE showing a Thraex standing over a fallen murmillo, who has dropped his shield and scrambles away as he gestures with his right hand. © Trustees of the British Museum.

FIGURE 34.5. Second century CE mosaic from Zliten (Bar Duc Ammera) showing gladiatorial combats and damnatio ad bestias. With permission of the National Museum, Tripoli. Photo courtesy of the Deutsches Archaeologishes Institut.

drop a shield or weapon was the beginning of the end, and at that point many fingers were raised in submission. On the Zliten mosaic, a *retiarius* who has dropped his trident and a *murmillo* who has lost his shield submit (first and sixth gladiators from left; Fig. 34.5). Blades stabbed vulnerable spots; in one typical but dramatic strike from above a fighter aims for a gap in the defensive armour at his opponent's neck (Zliten mosaic, fourth gladiator from left; Fig. 34.5). A common blow was to an exposed thigh or calf; artists emphasized the wounds, and a fighter spouting blood from the leg often admitted defeat, especially if he had lost his shield or weapon (Zliten mosaic, first and sixth gladiators from left; Fig. 34.5). The worst predicament was to fall and also drop one's shield or weapon; a downed man almost always signaled submission, even while scrambling away on hands and knees (Fig. 34.4).

While specific colours cannot be associated with types of gladiators, the colours and patterns of clothing, non-metal gear, and helmet crests and feathers must have helped spectators in the arena and viewers of art identify a fighter. Re-enactments of combat using equipment recreated from images and archaeological finds illuminate the effectiveness and visibility of gear (Coleman 2010: 656; Junkelmann 2000; 2008; 2010; Shadrake 2005; Teyssier and Lopez 2005). We gain some sense of the use of colour from rare wall paintings: the tomb of the first-century CE aedile Vestorius Priscus preserves shadowy crests on gladiators' metal helmets. Figurines and reliefs sometimes retain traces of paint (Jacobelli 2003: 102–103). Mosaics, although often faded, preserve colourful details, skin tones, and spurting blood and reveal regional variations in equipment (Dunbabin 1999: 81–82). Painted glass offers excellent evidence for colour. A third-century CE glass jug from Egypt shows two *secutor-retiarius* pairs overseen by referees (Hope and Whitehouse 2003: pls. 6 a–d, p. 298; the colour has been enhanced). The painting documents a wealth of decoration on belts and shields, and the faceplates and low metal crests of the helmets are carefully distinguished from the skull covering. A fragment of a glass beaker of probably the second century CE, now in the Metropolitan Museum (22.2.36, 37), shows two similarly equipped equites, one in a red tunic carrying a blue shield, the other in a blue tunic bearing a red shield. As with the uniforms of athletes today, the colourful armour and equipment of gladiators served to identify 'different sides'.

The surviving private art of the wealthy (actual or aspiring) provides the most thorough documentation of shows and personnel. The wealthy commemorated their own munificence in paying for games, or they recreated or mimicked a known performance put on by someone else (Petronius, *Satyricon* 29.9). Sometimes images of gladiators simply implied benefaction, as in the tomb chamber of Vestorius Priscus. His wall paintings, including a duel of two gladiators (one down and signalling), sent a general message of elite achievement (Augenti 2001 fig. 73; Clarke 2003: 187–203). The message is often one of largesse. The private mosaic from Zliten illustrates musicians, carts for the wounded, arena personnel, *venationes*, and *damnatio ad bestias* as well as gladiators overseen by referees (Fig. 34.5; Hönle and Henze 1981 fig. 8). A public necropolis relief of the first century CE from the Stabian gate similarly includes details of a parade, personnel, *venatio*, beast fights, and gladiatorial duels (Jacobelli 2003 fig. 77). Although gladiators generally fought in succession, elite images may show them in rows, emphasizing their numbers. Thus the public and private mosaics and reliefs of game sponsors (eventually, emperors) reflect a *munerarius*'s desire to document everything he had paid for. We may, by archaeological chance, be missing scenes of gladiators being paid; payment is emphasized elsewhere in private arena art, as in a mosaic showing a sponsor, Magerius, paying for a *venatio* while being acclaimed by the crowd (Brown 1992: 198–200; Futrell 2006: 49–51).

Surviving gladiator art emphasizes the relationship of sponsor and crowd in another way. As with Greek combat sports, competition ended with a fighter's incapacity or his signal of defeat, yet for gladiators this was not the end. A referee (or two) with a staff was present—not primarily to validate victory, but rather to encourage vigorous fighting during a bout and to enforce a pause following its legitimate end. Combatants and referees in art looked to the *munerarius*; in real life, so did the audience. Taking the crowd's judgement into consideration, he decided the fate of the loser and the final status of the winner. (There is no clear indicator in art or literature that the crowd actually signaled with thumbs 'up' or 'down'.) Gladiators sometimes fought to a draw and were 'sent away standing' (*missi stantes*).

A skilled combatant who lost but won the viewers' approval was 'sent away' (*missus*), a sort of honourable discharge recorded in his statistics. The loser could also be killed. In a mosaic now in Madrid, a referee turns away from two fighters, one dead, toward the unseen *munerarius*, Symmachius, who is imagined outside the border. He takes credit for the win and declares, 'Neco', 'I kill (him)', written above the referee's head. In turn Symmachius is directly addressed by the audience ('Symmachi') in an inscription above the dead man. The crowd's acclaim shows the patron's role in deciding the result of combat (Brown 1992: 204–205; Futrell 2006: 101–103). In the Zliten mosaic, a victorious hoplomachus and his opponent, a bleeding *murmillo* gesturing defeat, look out of the frame to the right toward the *munerarius*, as does the referee (third pair from the left; Fig. 34.5). In the left half of the same frieze, one of a pair of equites is down; a referee restrains the victor as both look to the left. The *munerarius* is imagined in each case as closest to the nearest vertical border (Brown 1992: 205–207). Gladiators in art could even look across real space toward a *munerarius*: on the tomb of Lucius Storax, a sevir of the first century CE from Chieti, several gladiators look out of the frieze and upward, seeking the eye of Storax, who appeared higher up in a pediment (Augenti 2001: figs. 48–50; Clarke 2003: 145–152, figs. 84–85). Thus gladiatorial artworks, especially of the wealthy, aligned spectators of the games and the art with the sponsor in judging the combatants. Although a fan urged his favourite fighter or fighting type to victory, the win was mediated.

Circus races provide an interesting contrast with gladiatorial bouts, since both involved dramatic and dangerous action (although at a different scale) and had comparable stars, fans, and sponsors (Matz 2019). In circus art, viewers and support staff identified more directly with winners of chariot-races, since a sponsor did not intervene before the final outcome. Palms, symbols of imminent as well as actual victory, were often depicted during and not just after the race. In artworks of all sizes, when a circus team and its colour won, multiple people basked in the victory, as seen on a first century CE lamp: a jubilant group holding boastful signage and victory palms leads a winning lead horse (Fig. 34.6). Sponsors do not dominate. Interestingly, in a subsequent evolution in art in Late Antiquity (after gladiators had fallen out of favour, but animal events and circus races had not), sponsors became extremely visible. On consular diptychs of the late fourth through sixth centuries CE they began to overshadow, by their enormous size and central position, the shows they provided (Lim 1999, Olovsdottor 2011).

While much of the evidence is still missing, we can identify some key elements that buyers appreciated in artworks showing violent conflicts. The image of a single victor in the funerary art and honorific statues of heavy fighters and gladiators—removed from conflict by victory—served to elevate a valorous combatant to heroic or martial status. These images represented the athlete or gladiator at his peak as he or his family, fans, or city wished him to be remembered. Combat art itself focused mostly on an ongoing fight or on the moments before the final outcome. Physical injury and blood were reminders of the high stakes. In gladiatorial art, differences in equipment and related combat styles were especially significant. But the portrayal of two proficient competitors pursuing victory, whether naked athletes or colourfully equipped gladiators, drew upon shared motifs that crossed social and status boundaries and served private and public purposes. Violent representations inevitably meant different things to different people, from sports fans and promoters to the politically motivated sponsors of gladiatorial events, who commemorated their magnanimity in art. The degree to which viewers of an artwork or a competition analysed their feelings about it is, of course, highly debatable, but watching fighters persist through pain

FIGURE 34.6. Roman lamp of the first century CE: jubilant supporters carrying victory palms and an explanatory placard parade with the lead horse of a victorious chariot team. © Trustees of the British Museum.

and risk was educational. Opposing views of fighters expressed by modern authors and artists echo dichotomies found in Greek and Roman literature: beauty/disfigurement, hero/villain, person/fetish, elevation/debasement, force/technique (Boddy 2008: 371–388, 391). However we explain its attraction, the core of combat sports and gladiatorial duels—as of competitions today such as boxing and mixed martial arts—was a dangerous fighting pair skilfully inflicting (and avoiding) serious harm. As sports art does today, the artworks and mementos of classical antiquity allowed buyers to relive excitement, fans to express allegiance, and sponsors to take credit.

IMAGES

Although representations of sport and spectacle are limited in general books on art history, some focused publications allow the interested reader to find images and relevant ancient texts fairly easily.

Thematic compilations (largely black and white): Brown 1992; Miller 2004; Newby 2005; Poliakoff 1987; Robertson 1992. Arenas: Tosi 2003; Welch 2007.

Colour images: Augenti 2001; Bergmann and Kondoleon 1999; Dunbabin 1978; 1999; Golvin and Landes 1990; Hönle and Henze 1981; Köhne and Ewigleben 2000; Jacobelli 2003; Lissarrague 2001; Neils 1992; Nossov 2009; Swaddling 2008; Shadrake 2005.

REFERENCES

Alcock, S. E. and R. Osborne., eds. 2007. *Classical Archaeology*. Blackwell Studies in Global Archaeology 10. Oxford.

Augenti, D. 2001. *Spettacoli del Colosseo nelle Cronache degli Antichi*. Rome.

Barringer, J. M. 2005. 'The Temple of Zeus at Olympia, Heroes and Athletes.' *Hesperia* 74.2: 211–241.

Bergmann, B. and C. Kondoleon., eds. 1999. *The Art of Ancient Spectacle*. Washington, DC.

Bergmann, B. 2007. 'Housing and Households: The Roman World.' In Alcock and Osborne. 224–243.

Boddy, K. 2008. *Boxing: A Cultural History*. London.

Brendle, R. 2019. 'The Pederastic Gaze in Attic Vase-Painting.' *Arts* 8(2), 47: 1–14.

Brown, S. 1992. 'Death as Decoration: Scenes of the Arena on Roman Domestic Mosaics.' In *Pornography and Representation in Greece and Rome*. 180–211. A. Richlin, ed. Oxford.

Brunet, S. 2013. 'Women with Swords: Female Gladiators in the Roman World.' In Christesen and Kyle. 478–491.

Bundrick, S. D. 2019. *Athens, Etruria, and the Many Lives of Greek Figured Pottery*. Wisconsin.

Cassibry, K. 2018. 'Spectacular Translucence: The Games in Glass.' *Theoretical Roman Archaeology Journal* 1(1). 5: 1–20.

Christesen, P. and D. Kyle, eds. 2014. *A Companion to Sport and Spectacle in Greek and Roman Antiquity*. Oxford.

Clarke, J. R. 1991. *The Houses of Roman Italy, 100 B.C.–A.D. 250: Ritual, Space, and Decoration*. Berkeley.

Clarke, J. R. 1998. *Looking at Lovemaking: Constructions of Sexuality in Roman Art 100 B.C.–A.D. 250*. Berkeley.

Clarke, J. R. 2003. *Art in the Lives of Ordinary Romans: Visual Representation and Non-Elite Viewers in Italy, 100 B.C.-A.D. 315*. Berkeley.

Coleman, K. 2010. 'Spectacle.' In *The Oxford Handbook of Roman Studies*. 651–670. A. Barchiesi and W. Scheidel, eds. Oxford.

Coleman, K. M. 2019. 'Defeat in the Arena.' *G&R* 66(1): 1–36.

Daehner, J. M. and K. Lapatin, eds. 2015. *Power and Pathos: Bronze Sculpture of the Hellenistic World*. Los Angeles.

Dervenis, K. and N. Lykiardopoulos. 2005. *The Martial Arts of Ancient Greece: Modern Fighting Techniques from the Age of Alexander*. M. J. Pantelides and K. Dervenis, trans. Rochester, VT.

Dunbabin, K. M. D. 1978. *The Mosaics of Roman North Africa: Studies in Iconography and Patronage*. Oxford.

Dunbabin, K. 1999. *Mosaics of the Greek and Roman World*. Cambridge.

Dunbabin, K. 2016. *Theater and Spectacle in the Art of the Roman Empire (Cornell Studies in Classical Philology, 66)*. Ithaca, New York.

Fagan, G. 2011. *The Lure of the Arena: Social Psychology and the Crowd at the Roman Games*. Cambridge.

Fagan, G. 2016. 'Manipulating Space at the Roman Arena.' In *The Topography of Violence in the Greco-Roman World.* 349–379. W. Reiss and G. Fagan, eds.

Fejfer, J. 2008. *Roman Portraits in Context.* Berlin.

Fisher, N. 2014. 'Athletics and Sexuality.' In *A Companion to Greek and Roman Sexualities.* 244–264. T. K. Hubbard, ed. Malden, MA.

Futrell, A. 2006. *The Roman Games: A Sourcebook.* Oxford.

Gabbatiss, J. 2017. 'Nasty, Brutish, and Short: Are Humans DNA-Wired to Kill?' *Sapiens,* July 19.

Giulianotti, ed. 2015. 'Sport and Violence.' In *Routledge Handbook of the Sociology of Sport.* London.

Goldstein, J. H., ed. 1998. *Why We Watch: The Attractions of Violent Entertainment.* Oxford.

Golvin, J.-C. and C. Landes. 1990. *Amphithéâtres et gladiateurs.* Paris.

Grimes, T., J. A. Anderson, and L.A. Bergen. 2008. *Media Violence and Aggression: Science and Ideology.* Thousand Oaks, CA.

Guttmann, A. 1983. 'Roman Sports Violence.' In *Sports Violence.* 7–20. H. H. Goldstein, ed. New York.

Hammer, Dean C. 2010. 'Roman Spectacle Entertainments and the Technology of Reality.' *Arethusa* 43: 63–86.

Hönle, A. and A. Henze. 1981. *Römische Amphitheater und Stadien: Gladiatorenkämpfe und Circusspiele.* Lucern.

Hope, C. A. and H. V. Whitehouse. 2003. 'The Gladiator Jug from Ismant el-Kharab.' In *The Oasis Papers 3: Proceedings of the Third International Conference of the Dakhleh Oasis Project.* 290–310. G. E. Bowen and C. A. Hope, eds. Oxford.

Hunter-Mann, K. 2015. *Driffield Terrace: An Insight Report.* York Archaeological Trust for Excavation and Research. https://static1.squarespace.com/static/5c62d8bb809d8e27588adcco/t/5d039456ab311a00011ad2bc/1560515684591/Driffield+Terrace+-+Kurt+Hunter+Mann.pdf.

Jacobelli, L. 2003. *Gladiators at Pompeii.* M. Becker, trans. Los Angeles.

Junkelmann, M. 2000. 'Familia Gladiatoria' and 'Greek Athletics in Rome.' In Köhne and Ewigleben. 31–85.

Junkelmann, M. 2008. *Gladiatoren: Das Spiel mit dem Tod.* Darmstadt.

Junkelmann, M. 2010. 'Gladiators in Action: Recent Work on Practical Aspects of Gladiatorial Combat.' *Journal of Roman Archaeology* 23: 510–532.

Kanz, F. and K. Grossschmidt. 2009. 'Dying in the Arena: The Osseous Evidence from Ephesian Gladiators.' In *Roman Amphitheatres and Spectacula: A 21st Century Perspective.* 211–220. T. Wilmott, ed. Oxford.

Köhne, E. and C. Ewigleben, eds. 2000. *Gladiators and Caesars: The Power of Spectacle in Ancient Rome.* Berkeley.

Koloski-Ostrow, A. and C. Lyons, eds. 1997. *Naked Truths: Women, Sexuality, and Gender in Classical Art and Archaeology.* London.

König, J. 2005. *Greek Athletics in the Roman Empire: Literature, Art, Identity and Culture.* Cambridge.

Kousser, R. M. 2008. *Hellenistic and Roman Ideal Sculpture: The Allure of the Classical.* Cambridge.

Kyle, D. G. 2015. *Sport and Spectacle in the Ancient World,* 2nd edn. Malden, MA.

Kyle. D. G. 2017. 'Ancient Greek and Roman Sport.' In *The Oxford Handbook of Sports History.* 79–100. R. Edelman and R. Wilson, eds. Oxford.

Lear, A. and E. Cantarella. 2008. *Images of Ancient Greek Pederasty: Boys Were Their Gods.* London.

Lim, R. 1999. 'In the "Temple of Laughter": Visual and Literary Representations of Spectators at Roman Games.' In Bergmann and Kondoleon. 343–365.

Lissarrague, F. 2001. *Greek Vases: The Athenians and their Images*. K. Allen, trans. New York.

McCullough, A. 2008. 'Female Gladiators in Imperial Rome: Literary Context and Historical Fact.' *Classical World* 101.2: 197–209.

Matz, D. 2019. *Ancient Roman Sports, A–Z: Athletes, Venues, Events and Terms*. Jefferson, NC.

Miller, S. G. 2004. *Ancient Greek Athletics*. New Haven.

Miller, S. G. 2012. *Arete: Greek Sports from Ancient Sources*. Los Angeles.

Nevett, L. 2007. 'Housing and Households: The Greek World.' In Alcock and Osborne. 205–223.

Newby, Z. 2005. *Greek Athletics in the Roman World: Victory and Virtue*. Oxford.

Neils, J. 1992. 'Panathenaic Amphoras: Their meaning, Makers, and Markets.' In *Goddess and Polis: The Panathenaic Festival in Ancient Athens*. 29–51. J. Neils, ed. Princeton.

Nossov, K. 2009. *Gladiator: Rome's Bloody Spectacle*. Oxford.

Olovsdottor, C. 2011. 'Representing Consulship: On the Conception and Meaning of the Consular Diptychs.' *Opiscula* 4: 99–123.

Poliakoff, M. B. 1987. *Combat Sports in the Ancient World. Competition, Violence, and Culture*. New Haven.

Potter, D. S. 1999. 'Entertainers in the Roman World.' In *Life, Death, and Entertainment in the Roman Empire*. 256–325. D. S. Potter and D. J. Mattingly, eds. Ann Arbor.

Potter, D. S. 2012. *The Victor's Crown: A History of Ancient Sport from Homer to Byzantium*. Oxford.

Rabinowitz, N. S. and A. Richlin, eds. 1993. *Feminist Theory and the Classics*. New York.

Raschke, W. J. 2002. 'Images of Victory: Some New Considerations of Athletic Monuments.' In *The Archaeology of the Olympics: The Olympics and Other Festivals in Antiquity*, 2nd edn. 38–54. W. J. Raschke, ed. Madison, WI.

Redfern, R. and H. Bonney. 2013. 'Headhunting and Amphitheatre Combat in Roman London, England: New Evidence from the Walbrook Valley.' *Journal of Archaeological Science* 43: 214–226.

Ridgway, B. S. 2002. *Hellenistic Sculpture III: The Styles of ca. 100–31 B.C.* Madison, WI.

Robertson, M. 1992. *The Art of Vase-Painting in Classical Athens*. Cambridge.

Scanlon, T. F. 2002. *Eros and Greek Athletics*. New York.

Scanlon, T. F., ed. 2014. *Sport in the Greek and Roman Worlds*, vol. 2: *Greek Athletic Identities and Roman Sports and* Spectacle. Oxford.

Schwarzmaier, A. 2010. 'Theater Masks.' In *The Art of Ancient Greek Theater*. 42–45. M. L. Hart, ed. Los Angeles.

Shadrake, S. 2005. *The World of the Gladiator*. Stroud.

Shapiro, J. 2015. 'Pederasty and the Popular Audience.' In *Ancient Sex: New Essays*. 177–207. R. Blondell and K. Ormand, eds. Columbus, OH.

Stansbury-O'Donnell, M. 2011. *Looking at Greek Art*. Cambridge.

Stewart, A. 2014. *Art in the Hellenistic World: An Introduction*. Cambridge.

Swaddling, J. 2008. *The Ancient Olympics*. Austin.

Toner, J. 2013. 'Trends in the study of Roman Spectacle and Sport.' In Christesen and Kyle. 451–462.

Teyssier, E. and B. Lopez. 2005. *Gladiateurs: des sources a l'experimentation*. Paris.

Tosi, G., ed. 2003. *Gli Edifici per Spettacoli nell'Italia Romana*. Rome.

Trümper, M. 2012. 'Gender and Space, "Public" and "Private".' In *A Companion to Women in the Ancient World*. 288–303. S. L. James and S. Dillon, eds. Malden, MA.

Tuori, K. 2015. 'Introduction: Investigating Public and Private in the Roman House.' In *Public and Private in the Roman House and Society*. Journal of Roman Archaeology Supplement 102. 7–16. K. Tuori and L. Nissan, eds. Portsmouth, RI.

Welch, K. 2007. *The Roman Amphitheatre: From Its Origins to the Colosseum*. Cambridge.

Wistrand. M., 1992. *Entertainment and Violence in Ancient Rome: The Attitudes of Roman Writers of the First Century A.D.* Gothenburg.

Zillmann, D. 1998. 'The Psychology of the Appeal of Portrayals of Violence.' In *Why We Watch: The Attractions of Violent Entertainment*. 179–211. J. H. Goldstein, ed. Oxford.

....

CHAPTER 35

ATHLETIC IMAGES AND THE MONUMENTALIZATION OF VICTORY

....

WENDY J. RASCHKE

INTRODUCTION

ANYONE who has visited the Acropolis Museum in Athens will have some appreciation of the experience of an ancient visitor to the sanctuary at Olympia. The main floor of the museum has been arranged, as the Acropolis itself once was, with a mass of statues and other monuments standing freely so that the visitor can see them from all angles and can also gain an impression of them as a group. This must have been the experience of Pausanias as he followed the route(s) recorded in his *Description of Greece* (6.1.16 and 6.1.17–18) in the 'much-seen precinct of Zeus' (6.3.14). Pausanias is a vital (though not the only) source for our knowledge of the monuments at Olympia (on Pausanias, Arafat 1996: 8–11; Smith 2007: 95–97); other ancient writers also help to reconstruct for us an idea of the Altis, Olympia's sanctuary, in antiquity. The statues themselves are long since gone, but many bases survive with inscriptions which expand our knowledge by providing names and city affiliations (Moretti 1953; Herrmann 1988).

In any major Greek sanctuary there was a broad variety of monuments; they were designed to celebrate successes of many kinds—in war, in politics, or for salvation from danger. The Stoa of the Athenians at Delphi records the completion of the Persian War by removal of Xerxes' cables from the bridge over the Hellespont (Hdt. 9.121; Walsh 1986 for a different date). At Epidauros in the sanctuary of Asklepios there are testimonies to the healing of various parts of the body. At the sites of the major Panhellenic games, Olympia, Delphi, Isthmia, and Nemea, there were also monuments to individual effort for the athletes who were victorious in the Games. These are the focus of the present examination.

WHAT *IS* A MONUMENT?

This apparently simple question raises the issue of what it meant *to the Greeks*, for the monuments are their work and it is *their* perception of their goal in establishing them which is important for our appraisal. The Greeks had several terms for 'monument': those used by Pausanias, our main source for Olympia, are *eikōn, andrias, agalma, anathēma,* and *mnēma.* These have discrete meanings:

- *eikōn* is a figure or likeness, a characterization (on *eikon* replacing the archaic *sēma,* see Smith 2007: 91);
- *andrias* is the image of a man;
- *anathēma* is a more general term meaning 'something which is set up, especially as a votive offering' (Lattimore 1988: 248–254). Pausanias (5.21.1) explains the distinction between *andrias* (statue) and *anathēma* (dedication);
- *agalma* may be used to connote an image of a god or in honour of a god, but its fundamental meaning is that of anything which brings joy or pleasure (LSJ s.v.1; Frontisi-Ducroux 2001: 165; Kurke 1991: 95–96, 104–105);
- *mnēma* is a memorial or monument, a marker of a grave or of a victory, which may in some cases be dedicated to a god (*LSJ*; Boedeker and Raaflaub 1998: 4).

The existence of a specialized vocabulary raises the question of its application by Pausanias: does he, for example, draw any distinction between *eikōn* and *andrias* as representations of humans? Does his choice of term reflect any qualitative judgement of the individual portrayed? A preliminary survey suggests that he uses either term indifferently to describe the images of three-time and other Olympian victors alike.

THE CHARACTER OF THE ATHLETIC MONUMENTS

In the sixth century BCE, like the *kouroi* of the period, these images were rather stiff and unrealistic and were probably largely votive in nature. They were fashioned out of stone or wood. Some may have become the object of cult, which suggests that a degree of identification between athlete and image was already being made (Harris 1964: 30, 115–121; Lattimore 1988: 247–248; Steiner 1998: 131; Currie 2002: 25; cf. Lucian, *Anach.* 11).

Since there are scarcely any extant original works from the Archaic and Classical Greek periods, much of what we know comes from the work of ancient writers or from Roman copies of renowned Greek originals. The latter are largely poor substitutes for their models, but we can gain some, if imperfect, impression from them. (On the negative view of many scholars regarding copies and a reappraisal of their usefulness, Hallett 1995: 121–123).

The choice of form must have been made by honouree and/or sculptor. Clearly it would have to be appropriate for the victory and usually athletic in orientation. Not infrequently well-known sculptors were commissioned for the purpose. Some control by the *Hellanodikai* (supervisors) at Olympia is conveyed by Lucian (*Pro imag.* 11), who states that even at the Olympic Games the victors are not allowed to set up statues larger than life size, or which go beyond the truth, and that 'the scrutiny of the statues is more strict than the examination of the athletes' (Herrmann 1988: 129; Hölscher 1998: 169 on Delphi). Lucian is, of course, writing at a relatively late point in the history of the Games (2nd cent. CE).

An athletic victor monument could take one of a number of forms. It could be an individual free-standing statue capturing the spirit of the victorious contestant, not necessarily a portrait per se, discussed below. The athlete would be represented at his peak, either at some point in the performance of his event, or at the moment of victory, tying his prize fillets on his head or with forearms extended forward to receive the ribbons or, quite literally, the fruits of victory, often apples.

Groups of statues were also found: these could represent participants in an athletic event, such as wrestlers. They could also be a family group, as in the fourth-century Daochus monument at Delphi. Daochus, a Thessalian of some status who was Alexander the Great's amanuensis at the sanctuary, established two group monuments, one in Delphi and one in Pharsalus. Each group comprised nine statues including an image of his ancestor, Agias, a pancratiast and victor in all four Panhellenic games in the early fifth century (Hyde 1921: 286–293; Stewart 1990: 187; Christesen 2007: 124, 183; Cummins 2009: 328–330). Such group monuments could have a potent effect on the viewer (Smith 2007: 99).

For hippic events, the image was frequently of the winning horse, with or without the rider (Figs. 35.1a and 35.1b). One of the finest examples from the middle of the second century BCE is the so-called 'Jockey of Artemision'. In the case of chariot-racing it was customary to have a chariot 'driven' by the owner rather than the victorious driver, who might appear beside the owner or might not be represented at all, the so-called 'absent charioteer' (Nicholson 2003: 101–128; see further below).

WHICH ATHLETES QUALIFIED FOR VICTORY MONUMENTS?

Ancient sources disagree as to which athletes were permitted to erect a public statue. According to Pausanias not all victors had one (6.1.1); but Pliny asserts that they did so

> especially at Olympia, where it was the custom to dedicate statues of all victors, while in the case of those three times victorious the actual features were portrayed. Such statues are called 'iconic' [iconicas]. (NH 34.16)

It is clear from this text that not all statues were actual portraits of the athlete. However, the subsequent identification in many cases between the sculpture and the athlete suggests that some were virtually so (Lattimore 1988: 248; Steiner 1998: 131). How far these images can be described as 'iconic' [portraits] in the modern sense of 'exact likeness' is a question not easily answered (Hyde 1921: 54–57; Steiner 1998: 125). The artist of the Classical period, unlike that of the Archaic period, was employing what has been termed a 'selective mimesis that now aims to present the world, divine and human, as directly and credibly as possible'(Stewart 1990: 149, fuller discussion: 73–83).

Equestrian victories were also monumentalized, but in chariot-racing the driver of the chariot was seldom celebrated since he was perceived as a hireling. The owner of the chariot would take the credit, just as in modern horseracing it is the owner, not the jockey, who carries off the trophy. Markers of women's victories were painted plaques dedicated on the Temple of Hera (Paus.5.16.2; on the use of the temple for display, Eckstein 1969: 85; Scott 2010: 153) (Figs. 35.1a and 35.1b).

FIGURE 35.1. The Jockey of Artemision. 150–100 BCE from a shipwreck off Cape Artemision, c.150–125 BCE. Athens, NM Br.15177. Photo: W. Raschke.

THE COST OF A MONUMENT

The cost of the monument could be undertaken either by the athlete himself or, in the case of an impecunious victor, by his native city (or the city which he chose to represent) (Nielsen 2004: 108; Barringer 2005: 237–238 and n.103; Christesen 2007: 138). The financial outlay for such an image has been assessed as perhaps three thousand drachmas (Smith 2007: 101–102); by comparison, skilled workers on public buildings were being paid one to two and a half drachmas a day in the fifth to fourth centuries BCE (Markle 2004: 125–131).

Sometimes two statues were erected, one in the sanctuary, the other in the native city. The latter may have been an attempt to re-accommodate a hero who, through his victory, had become superhuman and had outgrown his city (Raschke 2002a; Kurke 2010: 213). In the extraordinary case of Theagenes of Thasos three statues were erected, one each at Olympia, at Delphi, and in the city of Thasos. Such hybris aroused hatred against him (Steiner 1998: 144 on popular hatred of successful athletes). One equally presumptuous contestant is known to have come to the games prepared for victory. The renowned wrestler Milo of Croton supposedly arrived at the Altis carrying his own statue in anticipation of his victory (Paus. 6.14.6).

CHRONOLOGY OF VICTOR STATUES AND EARLIEST FORMS

The oldest (but *not extant*) victor statue seen by Pausanias is supposedly that of Eutelidas of Sparta, who was a champion in both wrestling and pentathlon for boys in 628 BCE. Pausanias (5.9.1; 6.15.8) describes the image (*eikōn*) as ancient and the letters on the base as dim with age. Such a work would be contemporary with the earliest *kouroi* (Richter's Sounion group, mid 7th cent. BCE). However, Pausanias elsewhere (6.18.7) asserts that the first statues of athletes dedicated at Olympia were those of Praxidamas of Aegina and Rexibios of Opous, victors in the fifty-ninth and sixty-first Olympiads (544 and 536 BCE). They were made of fig and cypress wood respectively. The root of Pausanias' inconsistency is unclear; in the absence of the statues themselves we cannot say certainly the date of the earliest, though Olympia is likely the originator of the 'statue habit' (Smith 2007). The latest victor monument for an athlete is that of Theopropos, who won in horseracing in 197 CE (Ol. 244); but an inscription records a later victory for Valerius Eklektos in the heralds' contest in 261 CE (Moretti 1957 no. 895; Herrmann 1988: 139 no. 10).

The earliest *extant* example is the statue of Arrachion, identified in an archaic stone image which was found approximately two miles from the Temple of Apollo Epikurios at Bassae (Hyde 1914; Harris 1964: 108; Richter 1970: 77 and figs. 14–16, who is sceptical of the identification, as are Lattimore 1988: 250; Steiner 1998: 125; Nielsen 2004: 93). (Fig. 35.2). Arrachion (or Arrichion) was a pancratiast and triple victor in the Olympic Games (Olympics 52–54 = 576–564 BCE; Brophy 1978; disputed by Hollenback 2010). Though he was an Olympic victor, Arrachion's statue was not erected in the Altis; rather it was placed nearby in his hometown of Phigaleia. Pausanias (8.40.1) describes a kouros-like figure with feet not far apart and hands by the sides extending to the buttocks. The inscription was already illegible in Pausanias' time and this is similarly true of the inscription on the identified statue.

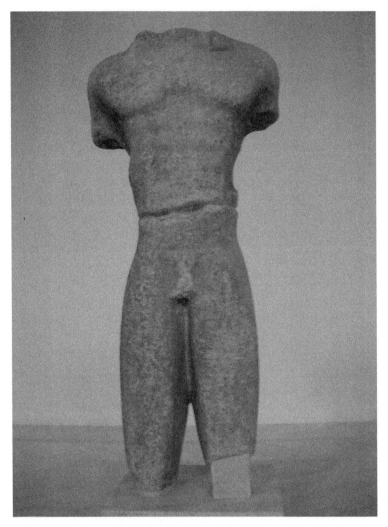

FIGURE 35.2. Statue of Arrachion. Erected at Phigaleia, mid sixth century BCE. Olympia Museum Λ 257. Photo: W. Raschke.

THE FIFTH AND FOURTH CENTURIES

Many renowned Greek sculptors were commissioned to make these monuments. Among these was Myron of Eleutherae, artist of the Diskobolos (e.g. Roman copy of Greek original c.450 BCE, Rome, Museo Nazionale delle Terme 126371). This work, with its most readily recognizable pose, represents the discus thrower initiating his throw (Fig. 35.3). Though the pose is athletically unlikely and actually two-dimensional, it is successful in its appeal to the viewer. Quintilian understood this when, in describing the figure as *distortum et elaboratum* ('twisted and overwrought'), he nevertheless asserted:

> Yet if anyone should disapprove of the figure for not being upright, surely he would demon-strate his lack of understanding for an art in which the most praiseworthy element is the very novelty and difficulty of execution.

(Quintilian 2.13.10)

Perhaps best known is the Sicyonian artist, Polycleitus. It is very likely that his works were victory monuments, though no specific athlete can be connected with them. Located at Argos, he was well positioned to serve the needs of the Panhellenic communities at Isthmia, Nemea, Delphi, and Olympia. His works are extant to us only in Roman copies

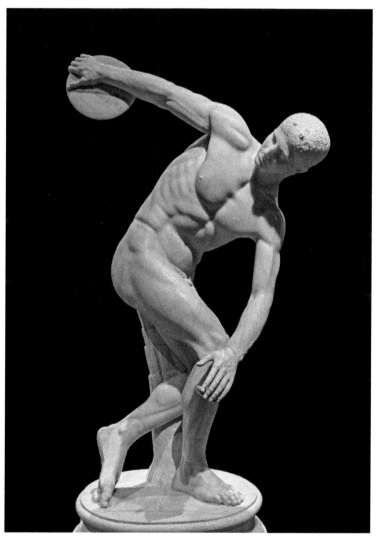

FIGURE 35.3. The Diskobolos by Myron. Roman copy of Greek original *c*.450 BCE. Rome, Museo Nazionale delle Terme 126371. Photo: Wikimedia Commons. Public Domain.

and the discussions of ancient writers. Polycleitus specialized in athletic sculpture; working largely in bronze—perhaps to reflect more closely the glistening sweat on an athlete's body (Steiner 1998: 133), he fashioned sturdy, muscular forms portraying his subject either at a calm point in his activity or at the moment of victory. His *Doryphoros* shows the athlete walking with his javelin leaning against his shoulder; in this work Polycleitus is believed to have exemplified his own theories of proportion (e.g. the Roman copy of a bronze original *c.*440 BCE, Naples, Museo Nazionale Archeologico 6146). Anatomically virtually perfect, it is also known for its *contrapposto* stance (Fig. 35.4). This characteristic

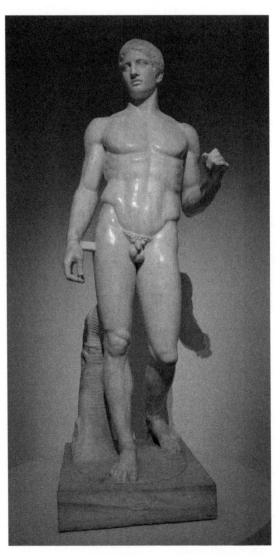

FIGURE 35.4. The Doryphoros of Polykleitos. From the palaestra at Pompeii. Roman copy of a bronze original *c.*440 BCE. Naples, Museo Nazionale Archeologico 6146. Photo: Wikimedia Commons. Public Domain.

FIGURE 35.5. The Diadumenos of Polykleitos. Roman copy of Greek original *c.*430 BCE. Athens. Athens, NM 1826. Photo: W. Raschke.

pose is also to be seen in his *Diadumenos*, a portrayal of an athlete tying around his head the ribbons of victory (Fig. 35.5).

MONUMENTS FOR VICTORIOUS CHARIOTEERS

The Delphic charioteer is a familiar illustration of this type (Fig. 35.6). What remains of the original group is the figure of the charioteer and fragments of the team. An engaging but emotionless work, it was erected in the sanctuary at Delphi to celebrate the victory of the Syracusan Polyzalos in the Pythian Games of 478 or 474 (Smith 2007: 126–130; Antonnacio

FIGURE 35.6. The Charioteer of Delphi. Part of a chariot group dedicated by Polyzalos of Gela (Sicily) at Delphi for a victory in 478 or 474 BCE. Delphi Museum inv. nos. 3484 and 3540. Wikimedia Commons. Public Domain. Photo: David Monniaux 2004.

2014: 198–199). By contrast, a more recent discovery in this category, the so-called 'Motya charioteer', appears to have been a single figure rather than part of a group, probably originally erected *c*.470 in Akragas, Sicily (Antonnacio 2014: 199–200). It has elicited much discussion, particularly on account of its 'transparent', somewhat form-revealing drapery and supposed sexual allure (Smith 2007: 130–135; Steiner 1998: 134–135; Nicholson, this volume Chapter 19 fig. 1. Not all scholars agree in the identification of this figure as a charioteer (e.g. Palagia 2013), but compelling arguments by Bell (1995) indicate that it represents Nikomachos, an Athenian charioteer who raced at Isthmia, Olympia, and the Panathenaia in the 470s BCE and who is celebrated by Pindar (*Isthm.* 2).

FIGURE 35.7. Base of Cyniska's victory monument. Early fourth century BCE. Olympia Museum Λ529. Photo: W. Raschke.

One unusual example is the chariot group of Cynisca, daughter of Archidamus II of Sparta (Valavanis, this volume Chapter 9; Cartledge, this volume Chapter 28). Pausanias informs us that

> she longed to do well in the Olympic Games, and was the first woman to own racehorses and the first woman to win an Olympic victory. Women after Cynisca's time, and particularly Spartan women, have won Olympic victories, but no woman is more famous as an Olympic winner than Cynisca. (Paus. 3.8.1)

Her victory—or rather victories, since she achieved two—in the four-horse chariot-race (*tethrippon*) date to the beginning of the fourth century BCE. These successes were memorialized in the Altis by one or perhaps two monumental groups: Pausanias records a group of chariot horses in front of the Temple of Zeus 'not so big as real horses' which 'stand on the right as you go into the porch'; and, at another point in his narrative, that 'beside the statue of Troilos is a stone ledge with a chariot and team and a driver and a portrait of Cynisca herself by Apelles and there are inscriptions about Cynisca' (5.12.5; 6.1.6; cf. Raschke 1994: 170–172). The base of the monument and the inscription have survived (Fig. 35.7); the latter reads:

Σπάρτας μὲν βασιλῆες ἐμοὶ πατέρες καὶ ἀδελφοί,
ἅρματι δ'ὠκυπόδων ἵππων νικῶσα Κυνίσκα
εἰκόνα τανδ' ἔστασε μόναν δ' ἐμέ φαμι γυναικῶν
Ἑλλάδος ἐκ πάσας τόνδε λαβεῖν στέφανον. (Ebert 1972: 110, no. 33)

Kings of Sparta were my fathers and brothers,
and I, Cynisca, erected this statue, winning the race
with my chariot of swift-footed horses. I assert that I am
the only woman in all Greece who won this crown.

Negative Images

Not all statues in the Olympic sanctuary reflected positive ideas. Remarkable were the so-called Zanes, figures of Zeus financed by the fines exacted from athletes who used bribery to achieve success.(Miller 2004 nos.103, 236; Christesen 2007: 83). Rather than being an image of the athlete, they were statues of Zeus, to whom they were dedicated. Most images at Olympia were not dedications to Zeus (Paus. 5.21.1; 5.25.1). Pausanias describes the Zanes as located on a terrace beneath the Hill of Kronos. (5.21.2). Sixteen bases have been found in this location; the position of the feet within these bases suggests a pose not unlike that of the Zeus of Artemision, in which the god strides forward to cast his thunderbolt (Stewart 1990: pls. 287–289). The location of these statues was clearly chosen carefully: they would be easily visible to athletes approaching the entrance to the stadium and would thus serve as an admonition to competitors that, as Pausanias says, 'you win at Olympia with the speed of your feet and the strength in your body, not with money' (5.21.4).

Monument and Metaphor

In his travelogue Pausanias uses famous cities and monuments as metaphors for the decline of the past into the (Roman) present (Elsner 1994: 250). He envisages Greece as only someone living in the age of the Roman domination can do, that is, as a political unit. In earlier periods Greece with its linguistic and cultural unity was paradoxically never a political unit, torn as it consistently was by strife among city states. Only in the myth of Panhellenism was such unity envisaged. Within the context of the Panhellenic sanctuaries and games then, as now, the appearance of peace is sustained, but internecine strife lies close to the surface; this is clear from the necessity of declaring a truce for the period of the games.

It is hardly surprising, then, that the buildings and images within the sanctuaries become 'potent political metaphors' (Elsner 1994: 249; Steiner 2001: 222 and following; Raschke 2013). The sculptural embellishment of the buildings resonates with meaningful messages for the viewer. The treasuries at Delphi, the site of the Pythian Games, are a good example: each is not only 'a way of diverting elite display in the interests of the city-state' (Neer 2003: 129) but also a statement of the superiority of the resources of the city. Treasuries are placed in prime locations, along the Sacred Way at Delphi or on the terrace beneath the hill of Kronos at Olympia. If the Minyan Treasury in Boeotia is typical, they are designed to be objects of admiration (*thaumata*) (Paus. 9.38.2; Elsner 1994: 245–249).

While I am not here primarily concerned with architectural sculpture, some of which I, among others, have discussed elsewhere (Raschke 2002b; Barringer 2005; also Tersini 1987), similar considerations come into play for victor statues at Olympia. Pausanias' protracted account of these monuments can appear rather uninspired—'eine ... recht trockene Beschreibung' (Herrmann 1988: 122, 'a truly dry description'), yet it raises questions about Pausanias' purpose. Herrmann saw it as a means of bringing back the past, but also recognized the pre-eminence of the Games and believed that the statues communicate an agonistic spirit not witnessed in Pausanias' own day. The inscriptions on the bases of the images suggest more: each records the victor, the event in which he was victorious, and the name of his native city. The formulation of the inscriptions drew attention to the city of origin of the victor. The choice of monument and its location within the sanctuary could make a strong political statement in a context open to a large number of visitors. Settings close to main arteries or temples were most desirable (Ridgway 1971: 340; cf. Barringer 2005: 237; Neer 2003: 129 and *passim*; cf. Vermeule 1968: 545–546).

Public monuments in antiquity played an essential part in the relationship between commissioned object, buyer, and audience. (Smith 2002: 65, 73). They are a reflection of contemporary concerns and do not represent, as in subsequent eras, some idealistic vision of the artist. In antiquity function is primary, and artists and stylistic development are secondary considerations. Ancient images are active expressions of the agenda of the buyer (Smith 2002: 96). In some cases this buyer could be a city rather than an individual and this inevitably led to the use of images in enhancing political agendas.

INTER-CITY RIVALRY

Because of the form of the inscriptions (detailed above), victor statues are inevitably identified with the athlete's city of origin or the city which he has chosen to represent (Nielsen 2007: 92). As a result the Panhellenic sanctuaries clearly became the focus of rivalry between the Greek states. Most city-states were represented in the sanctuaries through architecture, statues and other votives (Hintzen-Bohlen 1998:12–13); at Olympia and elsewhere cities vied for supremacy not only in the field of athletics but in the politicization of the monuments they established in the Altis. Hölscher (1998: 156; 174–182) speaks of 'a veritable war of monuments' between Athens and Sparta. As we have seen, such rivalry can be illustrated at Delphi, where the Greek states strived to surpass each other in the use of exotic materials and the richness of the decorative schemes of their treasuries (*pace* Hölscher 1988: 157).

In another section of his account Pausanias also relays how, as a form of insult, the Thebans and the Athenians deliberately used money taken from their enemies in war to erect respectively a treasury and a stoa at Delphi (Paus. 10.11.4–5; Miller 2004 no. 232).

VIEWERS AND VIEWING

The Panhellenic sanctuaries, and all Greek sanctuaries of any size, are anchored by major temples for the pertinent god or gods. The decorative schemes of such buildings have been the focus of consistent scholarly discussion and interpretation and there is no need to rehearse it here. What *is* of consequence for the present purpose is how the typical ancient Greek visitor to the sanctuary might have viewed these images and those of individual athletes. For this we have a modest amount of contemporary evidence, whose value has only relatively recently piqued the interest of classicists and art historians.

One source is a frequently quoted fragmentary satyr play by Aeschylus, *Theoroi*, in which the chorus of satyrs is portrayed, interestingly, at the sanctuary of Poseidon at Isthmia, site of one of the four Panhellenic games. They comment on images of themselves which they carry and intend to present as votives, virtual antefixes, on the temple, calling attention to the striking similarity between the images and their own appearances. Scholars have called attention to the parallelism here between drama and the visual arts and to the metatheatrical aspects of this scene (O'Sullivan 2000: 360–366; 2005: 101–102; Zeitlin 1994: 138–139 and n. 2). It also raises questions about the iconic nature of contemporary art, particularly the portrayal of human figures: the satyrs' emphasis is on the viewer and his response.

This idea is reinforced by the second source, Euripides' *Ion*. At lines 184–218 the female companions of Creusa who have come to Delphi from Athens wander around the Temple of Apollo, marvelling at its decorative scheme. Their pleasure is not only in the artistry but also in the mythological stories it recalls, as they recognize their patron deity Athena. As Ridgway has perceived, the significance of this scene is that

> It engendered a sense of recognition, a reinforcement of beliefs, even a diffusion of culture that can only be compared to the impact of present-day television, videos and billboards. (Ridgway 1999: 8).

However, what certainly would have attracted the average viewer would have been the colours of the pedimental sculpture and the glistening bronze of the free-standing statues. The 'shining' always draws the eyes of the crowd (Dreyfus and Kelly 2011). Homer saw this when he endowed his heroes with a shining aura at the moment of climax, as when Odysseus confronts Nausikaa (*Od.* 6.235–243) or, at last, his own persevering wife (*Od.* 23.156–163, with allusion to sculpture). The concept is perpetuated in the athletic sphere by Pausanias (6.1.1), who speaks of athletes who 'even have distinguished themselves *brilliantly* in the competition' (*kai apodeichamenoi lampra es ton agōna*) and yet have not received a statue.

Pindar speaks of 'the Zeus-given gleam' which accrues to the victorious athlete: 'When the brightness comes, and God gives it, there is a shining of light on men, and their life is sweet' (*Pyth.* 8.96–97). The victor is Aristomenes of Aegina, and his island is given due credit for his success; Pindar recognizes that the honour belongs to both. Victory brings with it 'fame imperishable', fame which can be conferred by song (Nagy 1979: 114–116; Segal 1985: 200, 209; Barringer 2005: 237–238); it can also be achieved by having a statue in the sanctuary where the games took place.

Recent analysis of the system of prizes has induced consideration of material and non-material forms of reward, and has led to comparisons between the athletic statuary and Pindar's Odes for the victors of the Panhellenic contests, particularly by scholars such as Kurke (1991 and 1999; cf. Nicholson 2003: 103). Pindar is conscious that sculptural recognition poses competition for his Odes, and he protests elsewhere (*Nem.* 5.1–5) that song is preferable in its greater mobility (O'Sullivan 2005 for a different interpretation). Pindar's description of the 'Zeus-given gleam' may well be a poetic reminiscence of the bronze victor monuments shining in the light of the sun in the Panhellenic sanctuaries of the gods.

REFERENCES

Antonnacio, C. 2014. 'Sport and Society in the Greek West.' In *A Companion to Sport and Spectacle in Greek and Roman Antiquity*. 192–207. P. Christesen and D. G. Kyle, eds. Malden, MA.

Arafat, K. W. 1996. *Pausanias' Greece: Ancient Artists and Roman Rulers*. Cambridge.

Barringer, J. M. 2005. 'The Temple of Zeus at Olympia, Heroes and Athletes.' *Hesperia* 74.2: 211–241.

Bell, M. 1995. 'The Motya Charioteer and Pindar's *Isthmian 2*.' *Memoirs of the American Academy in Rome* 40: 1–42.

Boedeker, D. and K. A. Raaflaub, eds. 1998. *Democracy, Empire and the Arts in Fifth Century Athens*. Cambridge, MA.

Brophy, R. H. 1978. 'Deaths in the Pan-Hellenic Games: Arrachion and Creugas.' *AJPh* 99.3: 363–390.

Christesen, P. 2007. *Olympic Victor Lists and Ancient Greek History*. Cambridge.

Cummins, M. F. 2009. 'The Praise of Victorious Brothers in Pindar's *Nemean* Six and on the Monument of Daochus at Delphi.' *CQ* 59.2: 317–334.

Currie, B. 2002. 'Euthymos of Locri: A case study in heroization in the Classical period.' *JHS* 122: 24–44.

Dougherty, C. and L. Kurke, eds. 2003. *The Cultures within Ancient Greek Culture: Contact, Conflict, Collaboration*. Cambridge.

Dreyfus, H. and S. D. Kelley. 2011. *All Things Shining: Reading the Western Classics to Find Meaning in a Secular Age*. New York.

Ebert, J. 1972. *Griechische Epigramme auf Sieger an gymnischen und hippischen Agonen*. Abhandlungen der Sächsischen Akademie der Wissenscheften zu Leipzig, Phil.hist. Kl. 63.2. Berlin.

Eckstein, F. 1969. *ΑΝΑΘΗΜΑΤΑ. Studien zu den Weihgeschenken strengen Stils im Heiligtum von Olympia*. Berlin.

Elsner, J. J. 1994. 'From the Pyramids to Pausanias and Piglet: Monuments, Travel and Writing.' In Goldhill and Osborne. 224–254.

Fontenrose, J. 1968. 'The Hero as Athlete.' *CSCA* 1: 73–104.

Frontisi-Ducroux, F. 2001. 'Living Statues.' In *Antiquities*. Postwar French Thought, vol. 3. 164–175. N. Loraux, G. Nagy, and L. Slatkin, eds. New York.

Goldhill, S. and R. Osborne, 1994. *Art and Text in Ancient Greek Culture*. Cambridge.

Hallett, C. H. 1995. 'Kopienkritik and the Works of Polycleitus.' In *Polycleitus, the Doryphoros, and Tradition*. 121–176. W. S. Moon, ed. Madison.

Hansen, M. H. and Nielsen, T. H. 2004. *An Inventory of Archaic and Classical Poleis*. Oxford.

Harris. H. A. 1964. *Greek Athletes and Athletics*. London.

Herrmann, H. V. 1988. 'Die Siegerstatuen von Olympia.' *Nikephoros* 1: 119–183.

Hintzen-Bohlen, B. 1998. *Herrscherepäsentation in Hellenismus*. Vienna.

Hölscher, T. 1998. 'Images and Political Identity: The Case of Athens.' In *Democracy, Empire and the Arts in Fifth Century Athens*. 153–183. D. Boedeker and K. A. Raaflaub, eds. Cambridge, MA.

Hollenback, G. M. 2010. 'Deaths in the Pan-Hellenic Games: The Case of Arrachion Reconsidered.' *Nikephoros* 23: 95–104.

Hyde, W. W. 1914. 'The Oldest Dated Victor Statue.' *AJA* 18.2: 156–164.

Hyde, W. W. 1921. *Olympic Victor Monuments and Greek Athletic Art*. Washington, DC.

Kurke, L. 1991. *The Traffic in Praise*. Ithaca, NY.

Kurke, L. 1999. *Coins, Bodies, Games and Gold: The Politics of Meaning in Archaic Greece.* Princeton.

Kurke, L. 2010. 'The Economy of Kudos.' In *Greek Athletics.* Edinburgh Readings on the Ancient World. 204–237. J. König, ed. Edinburgh.

Lattimore, S, 1988. 'The Nature of Early Greek Victor Statues.' In *Coroebus Triumphs. The Alliance of Sport and the Arts.* 245–256. S. J. Bandy, ed. San Diego.

Markle, M. M. 2004. 'Jury Pay and Assembly Pay at Athens.' In *Athenian Democracy.* 95–131. P. J. Rhodes, ed. Oxford.

Miller, S. G. 2004. *Arete: Greek Sports from Ancient Sources*, 3rd edn. Berkeley.

Moretti, L. 1953. *Iscrizioni agonistiche greche.* Rome.

Moretti, L. 1957. *Olympionikai: I vincitori negli antichi agoni olimpici.* Rome.

Nagy, G. 1979. *The Best of the Achaeans.* Baltimore.

Neer, R. T. 2003. 'Framing the Gift: The Siphnian Treasury at Delphi and the Politics of Architectural Sculpture.' In Dougherty and Kurke. 129–149.

Nicholson, N. 2003. 'Aristocratic Victory Memorials and the Absent Charioteer.' In Dougherty and Kurke. 101–128.

Nielsen, T. H. 2004. 'Victors in Panhellenic Games as Evidence for *polis* Identity.' In *An Inventory of Archaic and Classical Poleis.* 107–110. M. H. Hansen and T. H. Nielsen, eds. 2004. Oxford.

O'Sullivan, P. 2000. 'Satyr and Image in Aeschylus' *Theoroi.' CQ* 50.2: 353–366.

O'Sullivan, P. 2005. 'Pindar and the Statues of Rhodes.' *CQ* n.s.55.1: 96–104.

Palagia, O. 2013. 'The Motya Charioteer: An Alternative View,' www.youtube.com/watch?v=f195T5lZhWE.

Raschke, W. J. 1994. 'A Red Figure Kylix in Malibu.' *Nikephoros* 7: 157–179.

Raschke, W. J. 2002a. 'Images of Victory: Some New Considerations of Athletic Monuments.' In Raschke 2002b. 38–54.

Raschke, W. J., ed. 2002b. *The Archaeology of the Olympics: The Olympics and Other Festivals in Antiquity*, 2nd edn. Madison.

Raschke, W. J. 2013. 'Contest, Unity and Marriage in the Sanctuary of Zeus at Olympia. In *Kultur(en) Formen des Alltäglichen in der Antike.* Festschrift für Ingomar Weiler zum 75 Geburtstag. 101–119. P. Mauritsch und C. Ulf, eds. Graz.

Richter, G. M. A. 1970. *Kouroi: Archaic Greek Youths.* London.

Ridgway, B. S. 1971. 'The Setting of Greek Sculpture.' *Hesperia* 40.3: 336–356.

Ridgway, B. S. 1999. *Prayers in Stone: Greek Architectural Sculpture ca. 600 – 100 B.C.E.* Berkeley.

Scott, M. 2010. *Delphi and Olympia: The Spatial Politics of Panhellenism in the Archaic Classical Periods.* Cambridge.

Segal, C. 1985. 'Messages to the Underworld: An Aspect of Poetic Immortalization in Pindar.' *AJPh* 106.2: 199–212.

Smith, R. R. R. 2002. 'The Use of Images: Visual History and Ancient History.' In *Classics in Progress: Essays on Ancient Greece and Rome.* 59–102. T. P. Wiseman, ed. Oxford.

Smith, R. R. R. 2007. 'Pindar, Athletes, and the Early Greek Statue Habit.' In *Pindar's Poetry, Patrons and Festivals From Archaic Greece to the Roman Empire.* 83–139. S. Hornblower and C. Morgan, eds. Oxford.

Stampolidis, N.C. and Y. Tassoulas, eds. 2004. *Magna Graecia. Athletics and the Olympic Spirit on the Periphery of the Hellenic World.* Athens.

Steiner, D. 1998. 'Moving Images: Fifth-century Victory Monuments and the Athlete's Allure.' *ClAnt* 17.1: 123–150.

Steiner, D. 2001. *Images in Mind: Statues in Archaic and Classical Greek Literature and Thought.* Princeton.

Stewart, A. F. 1990. *Greek Sculpture.* New Haven.

Tersini, N. D. 1987 'Unifying Themes in the Sculptures of the Temple of Zeus at Olympia.' *ClAnt.* 6.1: 139–159.

Vermeule, C. 1968. 'Graeco-Roman Statues: Purpose and Setting - I.' *Burlington Magazine* 110. no. 787: 545–559.

Walsh, J. 1986. 'The Date of the Athenian Stoa at Delphi.' *AJA* 90.3: 319–336.

Zeitlin, F. 1994. 'The Artful Eye: Vision, Ekphrasis, and Spectacle in Euripidean Drama.' In Goldhill and Osborne: 138–196.

SECTION 4

URBAN CONTEXTS
OF LOCAL FESTIVALS

CHAPTER 36

....

LOCAL FESTIVALS

....

ONNO VAN NIJF

In the early decades of the third century CE an honorific monument was set up by a successful athlete in the small city of Termessos, high up in the mountains of Roman Pisidia (in Asia Minor):

PRIEST FOR LIFE OF THE GOD POSEI-
DON MARCUS AURELIUS
MOLES SON OF HOPLES
SON OF MOLES SON OF HOPLESIS
SACRED VICTOR
EXTRAORDINAIRE
VICTOR IN THE PRIZE-
CONTEST IN MEN'S
WRESTLING THAT WAS HELD
OUT OF THE HONOURABLE AMBITION OF TITUS
AELIUS AGRIPPINUS. WHEN
MARCUS AURELIUS ORESTIANOS PERIKLES WAS CHIEF MAGISTRATE
(TAM III, 168)

Hundreds of similar monuments were found throughout the Roman East, commemorating victors in obscure local contests. How should we interpret this phenomenon?

Greeks had always had a love for athletic competition as is evidenced by literary sources from Homer onward. The numerous material remains of gymnasia, stadia, and running tracks throughout the Greek world are testimony to a widespread and strikingly homogeneous athletic culture. Athletic competition was a major element in Greek self-definition: Greeks differed from barbarians by their keenness on athletic training (in the gymnasia) and competition (in the many athletic contests) (Golden 1998).

One would perhaps expect athletics to have declined when Greek cities were conquered by Hellenistic kings and Roman generals, but nothing could be further from the truth. Archaeological and epigraphical sources reveal the names of hundreds—thousands—of athletes who competed in countless festivals through the *oikoumenē*, the 'inhabited world'. Throughout the Hellenistic and Roman periods Greek cities equipped themselves with elaborate gymnasia, training places, and athletic stadia, as well as the rest of the athletic infrastructure. Literary, archaeological, and above all numismatic and epigraphical evidence suggests that by the Roman period this traditional Greek festival was popular as never before.

In the entire Greek world, and especially in Roman Asia Minor, old festivals were revived or reorganized, and new ones were founded in large numbers. (Louis Robert describes this as an 'athletic explosion'; Robert 2010: 111.)

The most prestigious athletic festivals were undoubtedly the Panhellenic crown contests at Olympia, Delphi, Isthmia, and Nemea, which for centuries had been the high points of the Greek festival calendar with a virtually unchanged programme. Their number even increased: Roman emperors added a small number of 'Panhellenic games' in the same style, such as the Actia in Nikopolis (Augustus) and the Panhellenia at Athens (Hadrian), and some cities strove to have their own games recognized as crown games as well (see below; on the foundation of imperial games see Guerber 2009: 215–301). However, the great majority of the festivals were local affairs. No Greek city of the Roman period was complete without one or more traditionally styled festivals that were celebrated in honour of Greek gods and Roman emperors, or important citizens. The exact number of such games is unknown, but a reliable estimate puts it in the hundreds (Leschhorn 1998a; Pleket 1998). This number is of the same order as the number of Greek cities under Roman rule, which suggests that Greek contests were an important marker of Greek city status under Roman rule.

Festive life developed its own dynamics. Small festivals, for locals only, were 'upgraded': disciplines were added, and prizes increased, to attract competitors from further afield. The more successful festivals attracted the top performers of their time: (Professional) athletes and artists from all over the Greek world. However, most contests would be lucky to attract a handful of top athletes, who could command a hefty appearance fee (just as modern tennis-stars do). Their heroes were normally local—or regional—champions. Yet, all contests shared in a common Greek festival culture. But these games were not mere athletic events. They were just one (important) element in a wider package that included civic processions, sacrifices, distributions, and banquets for all members of the community, and in this sense they were part of a wider political culture as well, but they were also an integral part of the self-representation of Greek cities under Roman rule. Finally, agonistic festivals must have had a major impact on economy and society at a local level.

CIVIC RITUALS

Public ceremonies came in many forms, and there are of course many ways in which one could try to explicate or 'read' them. The approach which I shall adopt here sees ceremonies as 'part of the symbolic expression of civic concerns and as a difficult to read, but ultimately eloquent text about the nature of civic life' (Connor 1987). Medieval and modern historians have over the last decades turned their attention to the study of public ceremonial. The inhabitants of Mediaeval and Renaissance cities lived through a perpetual series of periodic and occasional civic rituals and festivals, seen as lying at the core of a city's identity. The importance of these rituals is indicated by the fact that they were strictly controlled by the authorities and could be the subject of detailed regulation (Muir 1997; 1981; Trexler 1980). This approach is also of use in ancient history.

Greek cities were rightly proud of their festivals. Even if each festival took up no more than a few days a year, together they must have made a tremendous and lasting impact on the city and its institutions, on built-up space, and on the very rhythm of urban life. Large sums of money were invested in order to build proper facilities (stadia, theatres, gymnasia), while political time was dedicated to proposals for setting up new foundations, special magistrates appointed to oversee the events, and coinage issued to commemorate and advertise new contests. The ritual calendar had to be adapted to accommodate new or expanded celebrations. And of course, hundreds if not thousands of inscriptions were set up in public spaces to commemorate victors and festival organizers, or simply to mark the successful completion of yet another contest.

Agōnes and Themides

Local games were organized in honour of traditional gods, Roman emperors, and local benefactors and magistrates. A handful were set up in commemoration of (pre-)deceased elders or children (Pleket 1998). They are known to us mainly through the medium of inscriptions; but many are only known through rich numismatic records, as Greek cities were allowed under the empire to mint their own coins (coinage: Leschhorn 1998b; Harl 1987).

The normal word for a contest was *agōn*, but in southern Asia Minor a common term seems to have been *themis*. Why these cities opted for this term is not completely clear. The expression could be used, however, in combination with *agōn*, in which case it simply seems to have indicated the particular celebration or edition of contests—as in the Nth *themis* of a particular *agōn* (Strasser 2001; Farrington 2008). The term *themis* seems to refer more openly to the cash or value prizes (*themata*) that were on offer, but *agōnes* had prizes too. There were *agōnes thematitai*, *argyritai*, or *chrēmatikai*, which all put similar emphasis on the prizes (Farrington 2008; Pleket 2004). In some inscriptions set up for or by victorious athletes, victories in local games could be lumped together under this heading, but the expression was also used by the organizers themselves (van Nijf 2012). In other cases we find that the contest title specifically mentioned the level of prize money available, when they were dubbed *talantiaioi* or *hēmi-talantiaioi agōnes* (i.e. games worth a talent or half a talent; a talent was worth 6,000 *drachmae* or *denarii*). Cities would also display the value of cash prizes on their own local coinage, which may well have served to bring the attractions of the local contest to the attention of potential contestants (Harl 1987).

Of course, the terminology set these events apart from the sacred crown games (*agōnes hieroi kai stephanitai*) that were considered more prestigious and had a wider appeal and catchment area. But we should not conceive of these games as fundamentally different types, and even less as immutable categories. Contests could move from one category to another, as they were declared (and recognized) as isolympian or isopythian (i.e. equal to the Olympic or Pythian games). This may have meant no more than that they cautiously adapted the programme, and copied prizes and styles and titles of Olympic officials (Farrington 1997; Robert 1974; 1938: 53–62). In the Roman period, when the emperor became the obvious arbiter of all things Greek, granting of stephanitic status was his gift (such festivals were technically known as a *dōrea* [gift] of the emperor). Cities aiming to outdo each other accumulated imperial games, and their titles could change with each regime change (cf. Hall and Milner 1994).

Distinctions were permeable anyway: crown games could offer prizes or valuable gifts alongside the crowns, and some were even officially styled as 'sacred crown and prize games' (*thematitai stephanitai agōnes*); on the other hand, on inscriptions, victories in prize games may be indicated by forms of the verb *stefanoō* (to crown) (Pleket 2004).

FESTIVALS AND BENEFACTORS

We should not want to distinguish sharply between public and private contests either. There were of course the traditional festivals that had a long civic history. Such contests would have been funded mainly—or exclusively—from civic funds; they were sometimes described as *politikoi agōnes* (Roueché 1993: 176; cf. Pleket in *SEG* 43: 698). But private money was also used. In the early Principate many existing festivals were revived, or upgraded. Here benefactors stepped in—which may have been welcome—especially in the cities of Greece and western Asia Minor that suffered heavily in the Roman civil wars (e.g. IG VI. 2712; Robert 1935). But benefactors did not limit themselves to restoration: many new contests were directly paid for by wealthy benefactors.

We know this phenomenon as euergetism (from *euergesia*, the Greek word for benefaction) and it is one of the defining characteristics of civic life of the Roman period. It should be understood that the regime of the notables, as it is often called, did not rely on a formal constitutional position. Most cities were formally democracies, while on the other hand real power lay in the hands of the Roman governor, his taxmen, the army and ultimately the emperor. Yet, integration into the empire also strengthened a pre-existing tendency towards oligarchization. There was immense competition for status among the elite, and euergetism (benefactions by the wealthy) provided them with an opportunity to shine. In this context it important to note, with Gordon, that their choices were not neutral; the benefactions 'construct an image of what is needful to the community, an idea constructed by the élite in terms of their own values' (Gordon 1990; for a discussion of the political culture: van Nijf and Alston 2010.).

The members of the leading oligarchies funded most of the amenities of urban culture and civic life from their own pockets, in return for which they received a symbolic reward in the form of public honours—thousands of honorific inscriptions stand testimony to this symbolic exchange. Euergetism took many different forms. Magistrates often paid for the costs connected with their offices from their own pockets. Benefactors arranged for distributions of food, wine, oil, and money; they constructed lavish civic buildings, and they provided for the imperial cult. But contests and agonistic life in general seem to have been particularly attractive to them. Benefactors spent on athletic training facilities; they built or decorated the gymnasia, paid for the expenses of running the baths, they paid for teachers and instructors, and provided the oil with which athletes rubbed their bodies. But most importantly, benefactors organized or subsidized the contests in which the athletes competed: they provided the funds, set up the prize money, and hired other performers (the classic study is Veyne 1976; see also Zuiderhoek 2009).

Their modus operandi could differ, and not all festivals are known in equal detail. But even the most laconic victory inscriptions—through which the vast majority of local contests is known to us—may offer clues towards the organization. Many contests simply state that they were funded *ek philotimias* (i.e. out of honorable ambition, public generosity) (Robert 1940: 276–280). Other common expressions emphasize that this was private money (*ek tōn idiōn; ek oikeiōn chrēmatōn*), or that the money was really offered as a gift (*ek dōreas*) (Pleket 1998: 156–162). In such cases the normal road was to set up a foundation either by life, by making a promise (*hyposchesis*) in the *ekklēsia* or council, or on the other hand by setting up a testamentary foundation. Scholars have been able to reconstruct the legal niceties involved in these processes. A striking and uniquely detailed example is found in a long text from the small city of Oinoanda in Lycia, where a local benefactor offered to set up a main capital fund to endow his city with a quadrennial theatrical festival (Wörrle 1988: 151–171; the classic study of foundations remains Laum 1914).

The donor specifies how much money he and his heirs are to invest, and how exactly the money is to be spent. The text even stipulates the exact amount of the prize money for different categories of competitors. Such lists were common, and they may have been set up to ensure that money was not to be diverted by cash-starved city councils to other purposes. (Other examples in Roueché 1993: 164–174 with discussion of the problems that might arise.) On the other hand, we also hear about endowments that were set up so generously that a surplus was to be expected. Demosthenes wanted the surplus money to be used for distributions; other benefactors used to money to set up statues or to supply the oil to the gymnasia (Wörrle 1988: 6–7, lines 24–26; *IG* V.1, 550; *I.Ephesos* 3420).

The reasons behind this festive euergetism may be surmised. Modern experience suggests that contests, festivals, and spectacles are popular with the wider public, but what about the elites? There is some evidence to show that some members of the elite—and also intellectuals—were not always keen on organizing festivals. Philosophers were ready to point out the deleterious effect (for the benefactors!) of giving in to popular tastes, and even emperors could lend their weight to efforts to invest in other 'good causes'; but it would seem that most individual benefactors were more than willing to supply their cities with *agōnes* (Quet 1981; *I.Ephesos* 1493). We cannot simply assume that all notables shared this intellectual distaste for festive life—and that their generosity was a case of cynical populism to be written off as 'bread and circuses'.

Euergetism was not a form of altruism; one of its main purposes was to create social distance—to establish the benefactors as a superior stratum in society. It is not hard to understand how festivals fitted in. Each festival offered the prospective donor immense prospects of individual glory. The proposals put the proposers at the centre of political deliberation. They had to propose their plans to their peers in the *boulē* (council) and to the *ekklēsia* (assembly), which spent considerable political time in debating the merits of each proposal, and deliberated on the appropriate answer to the benefactor. Once accepted, the festivals often immortalized the name of the wealthy benefactor on a yearly or quadrennial basis. The advertisements, embassies, and coins that were to draw foreign visitors to a festival were thus an opportunity to add to the fame of the founder (Rogers 1991; Zuiderhoek 2009). The high point was undoubtedly the festival day itself. A passage of John Chrysostom captures the atmosphere neatly:

> The theatre is filling up, and all the people are sitting aloft presenting a splendid sight and composed of numberless faces ... You can see neither tiles nor stones but all is men's bodies and faces. Then as the benefactor who has brought them together enters in the sight of all, they stand up and as from a single mouth cry out. All with one voice call him protector and ruler of the city that they share in common, and stretch out their hands in salutation ... they liken him to the greatest of rivers ... they call him Nile of gifts ... and say that he is in lavish gifts what the Ocean is among waters ... What next? The great man bows to the crowd and in this way shows

his regard for them. Then he sits down amid the congratulations of his admiring peers, each of whom prays that he himself may attain the same eminence. (Chr. *de Inani Gloria* 4–5)

After the event permanent memorials remained: the coins, the public inscriptions, and the monuments for the athletic victors that all recycled the benefactor's name until the next instalment of the festival. The provision of festivals was a means for individual notables to obtain social and political prominence that legitimated their high, but potentially unstable, position on top of the civic hierarchy.

Festivals had other advantages, however. The text just quoted presents the civic festival as a dramatization of the city's social and political structure. Of course, the attention was focused on the benefactor, but when he looked around him he would see the theatre or stadium as an image of the city. It was a striking feature of the theatres and stadia of the Roman era that the seating order was modelled upon the social hierarchy. (Whereas the seating order in classical Athens, for example, had reflected a more democratic world view). Inscriptions on the seats in theatres and stadiums marked the places for various civic subgroups: members of professional associations, religious groups, members of youth associations, and lesser officials all sat in clearly demarcated areas (van Nijf 1997: 209–240). But on the best seats, in front of the others, we find the magistrates and councillors seated together with their families and their peers. This set-up was an integral part of a theatrical style of government: all spectators were part of a ritual performance designed to construct a hierarchical view of the city that put the benefactors and their families right on top. Festivals offered the class of benefactors an opportunity to stage manage a mass-participation ritual that served as an idealized representation of their own hierarchical world-view or—to borrow a phrase—offered an opportunity 'to put their world in order' (for the expression, see Darnton 1984).

GREEK AND ROMAN IDENTITIES

The political relevance did not stop at the borders of the city territories. In most cases the inhabitants of neighbouring cities would attend these orchestrated displays of civic identity, but envoys could also be sent out to invite Greek cities further afield that were linked through treaties, friendship or fictive kinship relations. (For examples of contests 'open to all Lycians' in Oinoanda see Hall and Milner 1994; on fictive kinship: Jones 1999 and Curty 1995.) Formal observers (*theōroi*) received seats of honour in the theatres and stadia, and special envoys were sent to share in the sacrifices (*synthytai*) (Roueché 1993: 182–187; Hall and Milner 1994 no. 22). The organization of a traditional Greek festival allowed cities (and their organizers) to claim their place in a global (oikoumenic) network of Greek cities. This would of course be important to 'old' Greek cities that looked back nostalgically to their past as a time of glory. But the importance of being Greek would perhaps be more keenly felt by the numerous cities whose Greek credentials were not at all secure, and whose status as a *polis* was in fact closely tied up with the *Pax Romana*. For one of the paradoxical effects of Roman rule was the spread of Greek cities in areas that had been not heavily urbanized before. Greek cities could not be envisaged otherwise than as integrated into the empire at large, and the relationship between the Greek and Roman aspects of their identities became an important ingredient of their political experience.

It is no surprise, then, that festive culture proved sensitive to such matters, of which the introduction of the Roman imperial cult is only the most obvious example (Price 1984). Many contests were celebrated in honour of the Roman emperors, and it has been suggested that the imperial cult—or at least the need to produce massive displays of loyalty to the Roman cause—was one of the most important elements behind the spectacular rise of festivals in the first three centuries CE (Mitchell 1990). Even modest *themides* could be named after the ruling emperor, only to have their titles altered at the next regime change. This was not one-way traffic: the emperors themselves promoted and intervened where necessary. Even a benefactor like Demosthenes of Oinoanda had to enlist the support of Hadrian to convince his fellow citizens to accept his offer of a theatrical festival, and the emperor's fingerprints can be found all over the foundation (Wörrle 1988, esp. 172–182). Hadrian, as a staunch Philhellene, was renowned for his interest in Greek festive culture, but other emperors were also prepared to use the festivals to prop up their dominance over the Greeks. That individual benefactors who offered such games also stood to benefit is clear; it cannot be an accident that C. Julius Demosthenes, and other benefactors who turned their contest into a mass display of loyalty to the emperor, enjoyed Roman citizenship.

WHO WERE THE ATHLETES?

Here we touch upon one of the old chestnuts of sport history. The traditional view is that Greek athletics of the Roman empire were dominated by specialists, lower class professionals, uncultured musclemen who used their athletic success (and the prize money they gained) as a vehicle of social mobility. This image has the attraction of familiarity: many of our modern sports stars followed exactly this road—but for the Roman empire the image seems inadequate. It has been demonstrated conclusively that the Graeco-Roman elite was 'never absent' from the athletic field (Pleket 1992; 2001; 2010), and it has by now become increasingly accepted that athletic competence was a major ingredient of the Greek elites under Rome. Local festivals needed local champions (Farrington 2008; van Nijf 2001; 2002; 2010a).

The large numbers of festivals were only possible because they rested on a widely shared gymnasium culture. All cities must have had one or more gymnasia, where civic education was offered as a mix of traditional Greek *paideia* and physical culture (van Nijf 2003; Kah and Scholz 2004; Farrington 1995). There is no doubt that the gymnasium crowd was socially selective, consisting mainly of the sons of local notables and of the wealthier craftsmen and traders with time and money to spare. Boys, ephebes, and young men would be trained and prepared for athletic competitions. But adults—and even old men—continued to frequent the gymnasia (elders in the *gymnasion*: I.Iasos 87; SEG 30, 546; OGIS 764). However, they did not merely go to the gym for their health: physical fitness was required of politicians too, and had to be put to the test in the many local contests under the gaze of their fellow citizens. If we look back briefly at our athlete from Termessos, we may note that he can be identified with one of the leading families of this local town, members of which performed the most important offices and priesthoods of the town. As a priest of Poseidon he was not of mean status himself. (The genealogies of the Termessian families were established by Heberdey 1929; see also his indices in *TAM* III. Marcus Aurelius Moles belonged to family O 13 [generation 7].)

Nor was he unique: his case can be paralleled in Termessos and elsewhere. More than 50 per cent of the known athletes in Termessos can be identified as members of the local elite. This does not imply that athletes from outside the elite did not compete—they did, of course—but that they were less successful in achieving permanent commemoration of their successes. The epigraphic record of Termessos shows that members of the elite were able to commemorate their athletic victories in the city centre (Fig. 36.1).

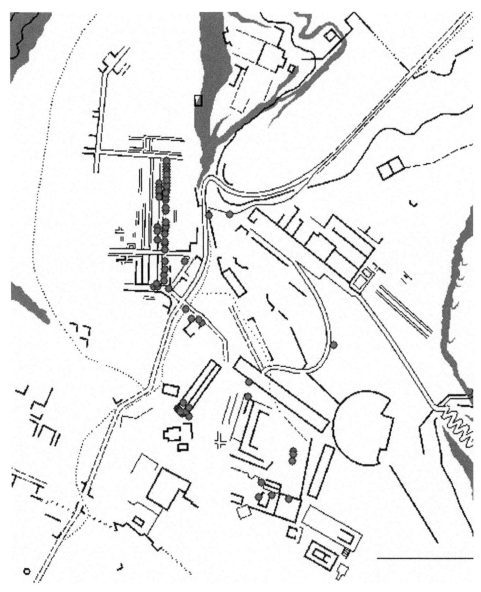

FIGURE 36.1. Map of Termessos showing locations of inscriptions of athletic victors. Map by O. van Nijf.

This juxtaposition of statues and inscriptions performed several functions at once. At one level it emphasized the civic importance of athletics, by presenting the athletes as the equals of civic officials and benefactors. Athletic successes and civic benefactions were praised in similar terms, and commemorated by similar monuments. They presented athletic victory as a benefaction to the city. Moreover, the honorific epigraphy served as an ideological underpinning of the oligarchic regimes. The display of statues repeating the names and faces of a few families presented them as the repositories of all the qualities of the ideal citizen. Judging by numbers, athletic success was one of the most popular elements of this representative strategy (van Nijf 2010b).

Of course, this was the same pool from which the top athletes of the day were recruited (Pleket 2004). Successful athletes were able to go out to provincial contests, or even to the more prominent Panhellenic games; and some even became full-time athletes and members of the synods. It should be stressed, however, that the distinctions between these categories are only relative. The successes of these star performers in these circuits would still be publicly commemorated by their proud fellow-citizens and family members. (Roueché 1993: 191–212 shows how 'international victors' of Aphrodisian stock were commemorated alongside boy-victors in local contests; cf. Hall and Milner 1994.) Moreover, they may have provided local athletes with an inspiring example. The Lycian athletes who claimed to be *themioneikai*, i.e. *themis* victors, may have been dreaming of bigger things (*TAM* II 688; *MAAL* 23 [1914] 170, 120 = *RWKIL* Ada 10).

THE ECONOMIC IMPACT OF FESTIVALS

The impact of festivals was felt in many different ways. Local festivals had a major impact on economic life. Even competitions in small cities could attract many visitors: athletes and other performers and their entourage (trainers and coaches and other assistants), official observers and other visitors, spectators, and of course the inevitable number of street performers, philosophers, tradesmen, and even prostitutes that would be attracted to festival markets (*panēgyris*) (de Ligt and de Neeve 1988). The population of a given city may have easily been doubled at the occasion of the festival, which presented challenges for the authorities and organizers, as well opportunities for enterprising types.

Public ceremonies and civic festivals were frequent interruptions to the daily routine, but they did not necessarily imply any slackening in the city's economic life. Civic and religious ceremonies did not mark out general 'holidays' in a modern sense. The contest of Demosthenes of Oinoanda took up twenty-three days during a 'period of intense harvest activities', but was itself interrupted by the scheduled monthly agora (Wörrle 1988, esp. 209–215). Many festivals were accompanied by an 'accessory festal market' (*panēgyris*), the main purpose of which appears to have been to provide the festival crowd with foodstuffs, sacrificial animals, and votives, and it may have attracted large numbers of visitors and traders. Dio Chrysostom observes that 'many [*panēgyreis*] bring in merchandise of all sorts, the tradespeople that is; and some display their own arts and crafts while others show off their accomplishments, many of them declaiming poems, both tragedies and epics, and many other prose works' (Chr. 27.5). In another speech he shows awareness of the economic benefits of such events: 'not only can those who sell goods obtain the highest prices, but also nothing in the city is out of work, neither the teams nor the houses nor the women. And this contributes not a little to prosperity; for wherever the greatest throng of people comes together, there necessarily we find money in greatest abundance, and it stands to reason that the place should thrive' (Chr. 35.15–16).

Ancient authors seem to have thought mainly about the services—although there is some evidence that local craft production may have benefited from selling mementoes. There is, however, no suggestion that such festival markets played the part of medieval trade fairs (de Ligt and de Neeve 1988; de Ligt 1993).

In any pre-industrial context, such large fluctuations of the population would have had an immediate effect on the food situation. The supply of grain, the main staple, was something that civic authorities had to supervise at the best of times, but the dramatic rise in demand during a festival presented some acute problems. First, adequate supplies had to be secured well in advance, to meet prospective demand. *Agoranomoi* had to ensure supplies, and private benefactors stepped in. The grain-funds that are occasionally found in the cities of Asia Minor may have been set up especially with festivals in mind. But even if the foundations were of a structural nature, we may assume that their existence would have been particularly necessary in a festival context (Strubbe 1987: 1989; cf. Zuiderhoek 2008).

A related problem would be the inevitable rises in the price of grain and other foodstuffs at the event itself. It is generally agreed that local authorities were unwilling, or unable, to set maximum prices under normal circumstances, but there is sufficient evidence that a festival context offered the occasion for more interventionist policies. It is surely no coincidence that the evidence for price-fixing and other measures such as *paraprasis* (selling below cost price) can often be connected to festival contexts (Garnsey and van Nijf 1998; cf. Migeotte 1997).

The dossier on Demosthenes of Oinoanda provides us with an example: the founder arranges for the appointment of three panegyriarchs selected among the councillors, 'in order to take charge of the market and the supply of provisions at the festival, with the power to write up the prices for the purchase of provisions and to inspect (60) and organize the things which are offered for sale, and to punish those who disobey'. The expression 'write-up' (*epigraphein*) shows that we have to think of official price-lists on wooden boards or stone. Evidence from other cities also points at the existence of such lists (Wörrle 1988: 209–215; de Ligt 1993: 42–45), as in Ephesos, where a number of the so-called *agoranomos* inscriptions on the gate of the South agora show the bread prices that were kept during Ephesian festivals (Garnsey and van Nijf 1998).

Conclusion: Contests and the City

I have argued that athletics were a defining element of civic life in the Greek cities of the Roman empire. Many if not all cities seem to have organized one or more festivals on a yearly or quadrennial basis. Such festivals were an immense source of civic pride, and it would seem that cities competed to have the most prestigious, sophisticated, or lavish celebrations. A lot of political time must have been taken up by the preparations and arrangements of the civic festivals, and not in the last place the food supply. The world of athletics had also a place in the built city. Gymnasia, stadia, and other athletic facilities dominated the urban landscape; walking about in the city centre you could see everywhere the honorific statues that the proud city set up for its athletes. Finally, the members of the ruling oligarchies, the councillors and their families, were deeply involved in athletics and athletic festivals. They were the benefactors who paid for the training facilities and who funded the festivals. Their social importance was underlined by the hierarchical set-up of the processions and sacrificial banquets, and they often had the front seats in the stadia, from where they could watch their sons as the intended star performers of the games. Summing it up: local festivals were much more than an innocent pastime. Greek contests were a strikingly civic phenomenon.

REFERENCES

Connor, W. R. 1987. 'Tribes, Festivals and Processions: Civic Ceremonial and Political Manipulation in Archaic Greece.' *JHS* 108: 40–50.

Curty, O. 1995. *Les parentés légendaires entre cités grecques: Catalogue raisonné des inscriptions contenant le terme SUGGENEIA et analyse critique.* Geneva.

Darnton, R. 1984. 'A Bourgeois Puts his World in Order: the City as a Text.' In *The Great Cat Massacre and other Episodes in French Cultural History.* 105–140. R. Darnton. Harmondsworth.

De Ligt, L. 1993. *Fairs and Markets in the Roman Empire: Economic and Social Aspects of Periodic Trade in a Pre-Industrial Society.* Amsterdam.

De Ligt, L. and P. W. de Neeve. 1988. 'Ancient Periodic Markets: Festivals and Fairs.' *Athenaeum* 66: 391–416.

Farrington, A. 1995. *The Roman Baths of Lycia: An Architectural Study.* Ankara.

Farrington, A. 1997. 'Olympic Victors and the Popularity of the Olympic Games in the Imperial Period.' *Tyche* 12: 15–46. Revised and reprinted in Scanlon 2014: 158–205.

Farrington, A. 2008. 'Θέμιδες and the Local Elites of Lycia, Pamphylia and Pisidia.' In *Pathways to Power: Civic Elites in the Eastern Part of the Roman Empire. Proceedings of the International Workshop Held at Athens, Scuola Archeologica Italiana di Atene, 19 December 2005.* 241–249. A. D. Rizakis and F. Camia, eds. Athens.

Garnsey, P. and O. M. van Nijf. 1998. 'Contrôle des prix du grain à Rome et dans les cités de l'Empire.' In *La mémoire perdue: Recherches sur l'administration romaine.* 303–315. C. Moatti, ed. Rome.

Golden, M. 1998. *Sport and Society in Ancient Greece.* Cambridge.

Gordon, R. 1990. 'The Veil of Power: Emperors, Sacrificers and Benefactors.' In *Pagan Priests.* 199–231. M. Beard and J. North, eds. Oxford.

Guerber, E. 2009. *Les cités grecques dans l'Empire romain: les privilèges et les titres des cités de l'orient hellénophone d'Octave Auguste à Dioclétien.* Rennes.

Hall, A. and N. Milner. 1994. 'Education and Athletics: Documents Illustrating the Festivals of Oenoanda.' In *Studies in the History and Topography of Lycia and Pisidia in Memoriam A. S. Hall.* 7–47. D. French, ed. Oxford.

Harl, K. W. 1987. *Civic Coins and Civic Politics in the Roman East A.D. 180–275.* Berkeley.

Heberdey, R. 1929. *Termessische Studien.* Vienna.

Jones, C. P. 1999. *Kinship Diplomacy in the Ancient World.* Revealing Antiquity 12. Cambridge, MA.

Kah, D. and P. Scholz, eds. 2004. *Das hellenistische Gymnasion.* Berlin.

Laum, B. 1914. *Stiftungen in der griechischen und römische Antike, ein Beitrag zur antike Kulturgeschichte.* Leipzig.

Leschhorn, W. 1998a. 'Die Verbreitung von Agonen in den Östlichen Provinzen des römischen Reiches.' *Stadion* 24: 31–57.

Leschhorn, W. 1998b. 'Griechische Agone in Thrakien und Makedonien. Ihre Verbreitung und politisch-religiöse Bedeutung in der römischen Kaiserzeit.' In *Stephanos nomismatikos. Edith Schönert-Geiss zum 65. Geburtstag.* 399–415. U. Peter, ed. Berlin.

Migeotte, L. 1997. 'Le contrôle des prix dans les cités grecques.' In *Economie antique: Prix et formation des prix dans les économies antique.* Entretiens d'archéologie et d'histoire. 33–52. St. Bertrand-de-Comminges.

Mitchell, S. 1990. 'Festivals, Games, and Civic Life in Roman Asia Minor.' *JRS* 80: 183–193.

Muir, E. 1981. *Civic Ritual in Renaissance Venice.* Princeton.

Muir, E. 1997. *Ritual in Early Modern Europe.* Cambridge.

Pleket, H. W. 1992. 'The Participants in the Ancient Olympic Games: Social Background and Mentality.' In *Proceedings of an International Symposium on the Olympic Games, 5–9 September 1988.* 147–52. W. Coulson and H. Kyrieleis, eds. Athens.

Pleket, H. W. 1998. 'Mass-Sport and Local Infrastructure in the Greek Cities of Roman Asia Minor.' *Stadion* 24: 151–172.

Pleket, H. W. 2001. 'Zur soziologie des antiken Sports.' *Nikephoros* 14: 157–212. Revised and and translated into English in Scanlon 2014: 29–84.

Pleket, H. W. 2004. 'Einige Betrachtigungen zum Thema: Geld und Sport.' *Nikephoros* 17: 77–89.

Pleket, H. W. 2010. 'Games, Prizes, Athletes and Ideology: Some Aspects of the History of Sport in the Graeco-Roman World.' In *Greek Athletics.* 145–174. J. König, ed. Edinburgh.

Price, S. 1984. *Rituals and Power: The Roman Imperial Cult in Asia Minor.* Cambridge.

Quet, M.-H. 1981. 'Remarques sur la place de la fête dans les discours de moralistes grecs et dans l'éloge des cités et des évergètes aux premières siècles de l'Empire.' In *La fête, pratique et discours, d'Alexandrie hellénistique à la mission de Besançon.* Centre de recherches d'histoire ancienne. Annales littéraires de l'Université de Besançon, vol. 42. 41–84. Paris.

Robert, L. 1935. 'Etudes sur les inscriptions et la topographie de la Grèce centrale.' *BCH* 471–488 [= OMS 2, 740–757].

Robert, L. 1938. 'Fêtes, musiciens et athlètes.' In *Études épigraphiques et philologiques.* 7–112. L. Robert, ed. Paris.

Robert, L. 1940. *Les gladiateurs dans l'Orient grec.* Paris.

Robert, L. 1974. 'Les femmes théores à Éphèse.' *CRAI* 118: 176–181 [= OMS V, 669–674].

Robert, L. 2010. 'Opening Address: Eighth International Congress of Greek and Latin Epigraphy.' In *Greek Athletics.* 108–119. J. König, ed. Edinburgh. [Translation of: Robert, L. (1984). 'Discours d'ouverture' In Πρακτικά του Η΄ διεθνούς συνεδρίου Ελληνικής και Λατινικής επιγραφικής. Αθηνα, 3-9 Οκτωβρίου 1982, Τόμος Α΄. Athens: 35–45.]

Rogers, G. M. 1991. 'Demosthenes of Oenoanda and Models of Euergetism.' *JRS* 81: 91–100.

Roueché, C. 1993. *Performers and Partisans at Aphrodisias in the Roman and Late Roman Periods: A Study Based on Inscriptions from the Current Excavations at Aphrodisias in Caria.* London.

Scanlon, T. F. ed. 2014. *Sport in the Greek and Roman Worlds* I. Oxford.

Strasser, J.-Y. 2001. 'Études sur les concours d'Occident.' *Nikephoros* 14: 109–155.

Strubbe, J. 1987. 'The *Sitonia* in the Cities of Asia Minor under the Principate, i.' *EA* 10: 45–81.

Strubbe, J. 1989. 'The *Sitonia* in the Cities of Asia Minor under the Principate, ii.' *EA* 13: 99–121.

Trexler, R. C. 1980. *Public Life in Renaissance Florence.* New York.

Van Nijf, O. M. 1997. *The Civic World of Professional Associations in the Roman East*. Amsterdam.

Van Nijf, O. M. 2001. 'Local Heroes: Athletics, Festivals and Elite Self-Fashioning in the Roman East.' In *Being Greek under Rome*. 306–334. S. Goldhill, ed. Cambridge.

Van Nijf, O. M. 2002. 'Athletics, Andreia and the Askesis-Culture in the Roman East.' In *Andreia: Studies in Manliness and Courage in Classical Antiquity*. 263–286. I. Sluiter and R. Rosen, eds. Leiden.

Van Nijf, O. M. 2003. 'Athletics and *Paideia*: Festivals and Physical Education in the World of the Second Sophistic.' In *Paideia: the World of the Second Sophistic*. 203–228. B. E. Borg, ed. Berlin.

Van Nijf, O. M. 2010a. 'Athletics, Festivals and Greek Identity in the Roman East.' In *Greek Athletics*. 175–97. J. König, ed. Edinburgh.

Van Nijf, O. M. 2010b. 'Public Space and Political Culture in Roman Termessos.' In *Political Culture in the Greek City after the Classical Age*. 215–242. O. M. van Nijf and R. Alston, eds. Leuven.

Van Nijf, O. M. 2012. 'Athletes, Artists and Citizens in the Imperial Greek City.' In *Patries d'origine et patries électives: les citoyennetés multiples dans le monde grec d'époque romaine*. A. Heller and A.-V. Pont-Boulay, eds. Bordeaux.

Van Nijf, O. M. and R. Alston. 2010. 'Political Culture in the Greek City after the Classical Age: Introduction and Preview.' In *Political Culture in the Greek City after the Classical Age*. 1–26. O. M. van Nijf and R. Alston, eds. Leuven.

Veyne, P. 1976. *Le pain et le cirque: Sociologie historique d'un pluralisme politique*. Paris.

Wörrle, M. 1988. *Stadt und Fest in kaiserzeitlichen Kleinasien: Studien zu einer agonistischen Stiftung aus Oenoanda*. Munich.

Zuiderhoek, A. 2008. 'Feeding the Citizens: Municipal Grain Funds and Civic Benefactors in the Roman East.' In *Feeding the Ancient Greek City*. 159–180. R. Alston and O. M. van Nijf, eds. Leuven.

Zuiderhoek, A. 2009. *The Politics of Munificence in the Roman Empire: Citizens, Elites and Benefactors in Asia Minor*. Cambridge.

CHAPTER 37

··

POMPEII AND GAMES

··

LUCIANA JACOBELLI

THE city of Pompeii offers an extraordinary vantage point for learning about urban games in Roman times. Surviving there are not only the buildings where the athletes trained, performed, and sometimes lived, along with the houses and tombs of the organizers, but also notices announcing the events, graffiti drawn by the gladiators themselves or by their fans, paintings, reliefs, and objects attesting to the organization and popularity of the games.

In the Roman world, games were not merely a form of entertainment: they had a much more complex function than similar modern events, involving a range of profound religious, political, and social implications. City life was punctuated by the *ludi* or games that were often an integral part of religious festivals and offered an important opportunity for the manifestation of political power. Responsibility for the costs and organization of performances in the provincial cities resided with the local magistrates, who were statutorily obliged during their year of tenure to disburse a fairly hefty sum of money (*summa honoraria*) for the sponsorship or *editio* of games (*ludi* or *munera*) or, more rarely, for the construction of public works (Garnsey 1971: 309–325). The local council could fund part of these, but public coffers were generally insufficient and frequently the magistrates shouldered the costs of the performances in their entirety. Clearly, their munificence in organizing lavish games was a means of displaying their power and, at the same time, winning over the goodwill of the people so that they could count on their support in the acquisition or maintenance of political positions. On the other hand, for the majority of the population the games represented an opportunity for diversion and entertainment and even offered material advantages, since it was quite common for foodstuffs or money to be distributed during such events.

As in other Greek-influenced cities of Campania, permanent edifices for performances were built in Pompeii long before they were in Rome. The Large Theatre, constructed in the second century BCE, is one of the oldest buildings of its kind to have survived (Fig. 37.1). A decisive factor in the choice of the site was the closeness to the earlier Doric Temple, dedicated to Hercules and later to Minerva (de Waele 2001). When the Theatre was built, this sacred area was renovated also: porticoes were constructed around the terrace on which the Temple stood and the entire area was opened to the city via a splendid entrance colonnade leading to both the Temple and the Theatre. There was another connection between the sacred area and the Theatre in the form of a magnificent flight of steps, probably used for sacred processions during the festivals (Van Andringa 2009: 181). Dating to the same period is the

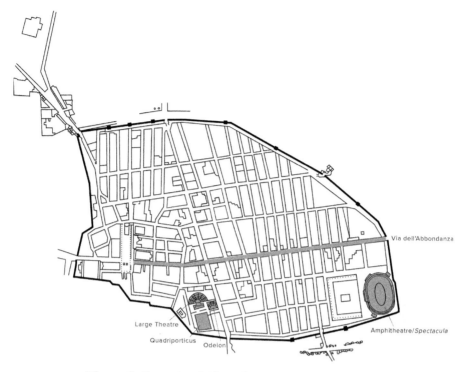

Large Theatre

Quadriporticus   Odeion

Via dell'Abbondanza

Amphitheatre/*Spectacula*

FIGURE 37.1. Plan of Pompeii. Wikimedia Commons. CCA SA 3.0 License. Source: M.violante. Modified K. Kuxhausen.

construction, in the area of the Triangular Forum, of a gymnasium or *palaestra* for the young of the most important Samnite families, where they underwent physical training to prepare for military careers (Guzzo 2007: 100 with bibliography). In the early years following the foundation of the Roman colony in 80 BCE, a smaller, roofed theatre (*Odeion*) was also built next to the Large Theatre, through the munificence of the duovirs Caius Quintus Valgus and Marcus Portius, the same magistrates who, a few years later when they held the office of *quinquennales*, also built for the citizens of Pompeii the Amphitheatre, the oldest building of its kind to have survived. Evidence of its antiquity can be seen even in the dedicatory inscription, where the term *spectacula* (*CIL* 10.852) is used to refer to the structure; the word 'amphitheatre' would not appear until later (Coarelli 2001: 43). This magnificent edifice was built by the two magistrates at their own expense in the south-eastern area of the city, which was relatively underdeveloped at the time. It was erected in the immediate vicinity of one of the city gates, in order to facilitate the entry and exit of the masses on the days of performance without obstructing the normal life of the city (Fig. 37.1). The impact of the flow of spectators was far from insignificant, if we consider that the amphitheatre could seat 20,000 people, who were clearly not all from Pompeii but came also from neighbouring cities. The relative antiquity of the amphitheatre also explains the absence of the underground areas below the arena in which cages for the animals and storerooms for the scenery were usually located in later structures. Other unusual elements include the access pathways to the upper seating levels, the *summa cavea*, which were reached by steps built against the exterior of the building. The best seats (reserved for magistrates on the lower levels) and these spaces, the *ima cavea*, were reached by means of a covered gallery, accessible from two passageways located on the western side. Another two passageways, positioned respectively to the south and north, led directly into the arena.

We are particularly well informed about the gladiatorial *munera* in Pompeii, since the sudden burial of the city as a result of the eruption of Vesuvius in 79 CE has left us extraordinary evidence of them. Particularly fascinating is the series of eighty-six *edicta munerum*, the inscriptions painted on city walls in the form of programmes announcing forthcoming events to the population (Sabbatini Tumolesi 1980; Fora 1996). These provide extraordinary documentation in many respects: the chronological homogeneity (most of these posters date to the reigns of Claudius, Nero, and the Flavians), the ephemeral nature of the messages, and the details they provide about the type of performances organized in the city. The wording was almost identical in each notice: the name of the specific *editor muneris* appeared in big letters at the top, followed by the number of gladiator pairs competing (*gladiatorum paria*). Sometimes notices specifically mentioned the occasion for which the show was being organized (*causa muneris*). Indeed, a magistrate might decide to offer a performance for reasons unconnected with his municipal and statutory obligations. The events might serve to inaugurate a public building or a monument, as in the case of an altar (*CIL* 4.1180), or for the presentation of paintings (*CIL* 4.1177; 1178; 3883; 7993), or even for a funeral, though this would have been rare during the empire. Among the most frequently recorded shows in Pompeii were the spectacles presented in honour of the emperor, the *munera pro salute imperatoris* (*CIL* 4.7989 a, c; 1181; 1196; 1197; 1198; 7986 a; 7988 b–c; 3822; 9971 a); by making such an ostentatious gesture, the magistrates hoped to win the emperor's favour. The time and place of the performance were almost always announced in the *edicta*. Thus we know that the majority of the spectacles took place either on a single day (*CIL* 4.1180; 1190; 9986; 1193; 1989; 1201; 10161), or over the course of four days (*CIL* 4.1199; 9970; 9972; 9979; 9981 a). Spectacles lasting two (*CIL* 4.7988 b, c; 1183; 9973; 9977; *CIL* 10.1074d) or three days (*CIL* 4.1179; 1187; 3881; 9976) were not as common. Although performances are recorded throughout the year, spring was preferred, likely in view of the weather. There are also numerous records of events held in the early months of the year, when the organization of the games functioned to win votes for the imminent elections. The choice of dates must also have been affected by the calendar of agricultural activities, since farming was one of the major sources of income in the Pompeii economy and could not be interrupted in crucial periods by the staging of shows (Tuck 2008: 30–33). Another even more important factor affecting the programming schedules of Pompeiian games appears to have been coordinating them with the dates of the most important festivities and fairs in Rome. More specifically, the available data indicate that the games organized in Pompeii never conflicted with the performances held in the Circus Maximus in Rome (Tuck 2008: 30–33). Movement between the two cities was frequent, and the absence of a venue for chariot-racing in Pompeii would suggest that some of the inhabitants were in the habit of travelling to Rome to attend this very popular type of event. In the same way, care appears to have been taken to avoid organizing performances on the days when events were being held in other important cities in Campania, such as Puteoli and Nuceria. The fact that the games attracted spectators from neighbouring cities is confirmed not only by the famous episode of the brawl that broke out between supporters from Pompeii and Nuceria (see below) but also by the inscriptions posted in Pompeii advertising performances in other cities of

Campania (*CIL* 4.1184; 1187; 3881; 3882; 4299; 9970; 9972; 9978; 1204; 7994; 9983 a; 9984 a, b; 9976; 9968 a; 9977).

The *edicta munerum* also detail the extra amenities offered during the games, such as the *velarium* stretched over the top of the building to protect the audience from the sun, or the use of *sparsiones* (*CIL* 4.7989 a, c; 1177; 1180; 1181; 1184; 3883; 9984 a, b). According to certain scholars, these *sparsiones* consisted of the distribution of small sums of money or foodstuffs, while others are of the opinion that they refer to the system whereby sprays of fragrant water offered spectators relief from the heat or mitigated the stench of the animals (Jacobelli 2003: 22, 36–37, 64, 118 with bibliography). A spectacle in its own right was offered by the illumination, making the amphitheatre as bright as day and enabling the organization of spectacular night-time events. In Pompeii these *lumina* actually became a requirement specifically laid down in the law of the colony (*CIL* 10.857 a, c, d).

As we have seen, the *edicta* placed great emphasis on the *editores munerum*, the sponsors who were responsible for paying all or part of the expenses of the gladiatorial contests. Inscriptions testify to the existence of about ten specific *editores*, all belonging to the local magistracy. Almost all of them were duovirs, the chief executive magistrates, with only one instance of a sponsor holding the lower office of aedile (*CIL* 4.1189–1190). It has been suggested that this disparity depends on the fact that the municipal legislation of Pompeii, as was the case elsewhere, laid down a distinction whereby the duovirs were obliged to offer *munera* **and** *ludi* but the aediles sponsored **either** *munera* **or** *ludi*, and that the latter more frequently chose the *ludi* because they were less costly (Sabbatini Tumolesi 1980: 131). Performances were also offered by priests, especially the *flamines* or the *augustales* of the Imperial Cult. In any case, anyone who wished to organize an event had to apply to the *lanista*, who was the professional gladiatorial entrepreneur, the names of some of whom are preserved in the *edicta* (Sabbatini Tumolesi 1980: 128–129). The job of the *lanista* was quite demanding: finding the requisite number of gladiators to participate in each contest called for considerable recruitment efforts. Agents were always looking out for new talents to replace the gladiators who had been killed or had retired. Often they would recruit in the forum, where they could buy slaves or find daring young men or idlers who would do anything to earn money. The agents also had to deal with the city authorities to arrange for the use of the amphitheatre and pay the fees for the spectacles. Finally, they maintained relations with the officials of the judiciary and the prison, since they needed access to prisoners who had been condemned to death (*noxii*) (Sabbatini Tumolesi 1980: 143). All of this intense activity must have taken place in some kind of office, which in Pompeii was situated close to the forum, now no longer in existence (Angelone 1989: 339–359). The *lanista* accommodated his troupe of gladiators (*familia gladiatoria*) in special schools (*ludi*), where they were subjected to very strict discipline. To keep in optimal shape for fighting, they trained daily, followed a diet aimed at increasing their muscle mass and weight, and underwent medical check-ups. Two *ludi* are known in Pompeii: the barracks situated in Region 5.5.3, which were occupied by gladiators up until the earthquake that devastated the city in 62 CE. Following this event the old *ludus* was abandoned and the gladiators moved to the *quadriporticus* adjacent to the theatres (Jacobelli 2003: 65–66, 68, 117) (Fig. 37.1). The installation of a gladiatorial *ludus* in a public building has led to the suggestion that it belonged to the city. In this case it would not be the quarters of *familiae gladiatoriae* managed by *lanistae*, but would instead have been run by the municipal authorities, a practice confirmed also in other cities such as Este (*CIL* 5.2529) and Praeneste (*CIL* 14.3014).

The epigraphic documentation from Pompeii has also offered us greater insights into important aspects relating to the various phases of a typical performance in the context of the city. First there was the *pompa*, the official parade in which all the persons involved in the contest moved in procession to the site of performance, after which the day of the games began with the *venatio*, or beast hunt. From the information provided by the inscriptions and the analysis of the amphitheatre itself, it can be ruled out that wild animals such as tigers or lions were exhibited at Pompeii. The safety parapet around the arena in Pompeii's amphitheatre was only 2.18 metres high, too low to contain the rush of a wild animal, unless nets were raised as in other amphitheatres; in Pompeii, however, no trace of such equipment has been found. Nor is there any mention of big cats in the inscriptions announcing the contests, which refer only to animals of the local fauna, such as bears (*CIL* 4.1989), wild boars (*CIL* 10.1074d), and bulls (*CIL* 10.1074d). The situation of Pompeii appears to reflect that of other cities of the empire too, where the scope of the hunts proves to have been fairly limited (Fora 1996: 45). The recruitment of wild animals was very expensive, and although the coffers of the emperor could stretch to it, those of the municipal magistrates were much less well furnished.

The most eagerly awaited part of the *munus* consisted of the gladiatorial contests that took place in the afternoon. The same modesty observed in the *venationes* organized by the municipality also characterized the gladiatorial contests, in which generally only a couple of dozen pairs of gladiators performed. The most widely recorded number in Pompeii was twenty pairs, that is forty gladiators (*CIL* 4.1187; 1193; 1201; 3881; 3882; 7986 a; 9963; 9968; 9968 a–c; 9970; 9973; 9977; 9979; 9980; 9981 a; 9982; 9983 a; 3884; 7995; 7991; 7992); less frequently ten (*CIL* 4.3884; 7995; 7992; 1185; 9985 b), thirty (*CIL* 4.1179; 1200; 1204), and forty pairs (*CIL* 4.9986; D'Ambrosio and De Caro 1987: 206). The highest recorded number is forty-nine pairs, in an *edictum* painted on a tomb outside Porta Nocera advertising a contest in Puteoli (*CIL* 4.7994). Precisely because they were meant to give only general information, the *edicta munerum* list the type and names of gladiators to appear without going into detail. Rather than the announcements, it is the graffiti that help to cast light on the world of the gladiators. Some were scrawled by the gladiators themselves, and some by their supporters and friends (Jacobelli 2003: 47–52). Thanks to the graffito etched by 'Florus', for example, we learn that the gladiators moved around a lot: Florus writes that he was victorious in Nuceria on the 28th of July and again on the 15th of August in the arena of Herculaneum (*CIL* 4.4299; Angelone 1989–1990: 217–223).

The graffiti in which the gladiators' names are accompanied by the outcome of the contest are of particular interest (Fig. 37.2): the letter V means victorious (*vicit*); M means *missus*, or defeated but spared; P (*perit*) or O (*obiit*) means dead. These documents appear to belie the common beliefs perpetrated by literary sources and films about the outcome of gladiatorial contests: at least in Pompeii, the number of deaths is quite small in comparison to the number of gladiators who were spared (Jacobelli 2003: 52). The number of contests in which each individual gladiator participated is also minutely recorded in the Pompeian documents: sometimes the total exceeded seventy. These contests did not therefore necessarily end in death—after all, the training of a gladiator cost time and money.

The graffiti, along with the painted and sculpted spectacle illustrations, found in Pompeii have yielded considerable information about the different types of gladiators engaged in the games: *equites*, *samnites*, *murmillones*, *thraeces*, *retiarii*, *hoplomachi*, *essedarii* and *pontiarii* (a type of gladiator who fought on a platform) (Mosci-Sassi 1992: 130–131). A figured graffito

FIGURE 37.2. Drawing of graffiti from Tomb 14 in the Porta Nocera necropolis. Source: L. Jacobelli.

on the front of a tomb from the Porta Nocera necropolis (Fig. 37.2) recalls the combat of a young gladiator named Marcus Attilius, who as a *tiro* was making his debut in the arena and emerged as the star, even defeating Hilarus, a gladiator from the most prestigious Neronian *ludus* of Capua, belonging to the emperor (*CIL* 4.10236–10238).

The notices for gladiatorial contests are particularly numerous on the fronts of the tombs outside the Porta Nocera, where the major road connecting Pompeii with the towns and cities of the Campania hinterland entered the city, and along the Via dell'Abbondanza, the main street of Pompeii. It is even possible that, on special occasions, processions took place along this street leading from the forum to the amphitheatre (Fig. 37.1). This could explain the large number of 'religious' paintings on the exterior of the buildings, some of them directly related to the *pompae*, such as the image of Venus on a chariot or on a *ferculum* (9.7.5–7), or the procession of the *Magna Mater* on the exterior of a shop (9.7.1) (Spinazzola 1953: 163–242). These images indicate the involvement of the major guilds in the religious festivals, and at the same time symbolize their official integration within the city (Van Andringa 2009: 183).

The fact that the forum was originally a typical venue for hosting religious festivals and even gladiatorial contests is confirmed by the sources (Vitruvius, *On Architecture* 5.1.1). There is evidence of this practice in Pompeii too, provided by an important tomb inscription, rediscovered and copied in the seventeenth century and now lost (*CIL* 10.1074d; Sabbatini Tumolesi 1980:18–21). The inscription commemorates the *ludi* and the *munera* that had been offered by Aulus Clodius Flaccus while holding three magistracies during the Augustan age. During his first term as duovir (around 20 BCE), for the festival of Apollo he orchestrated a solemn procession (*pompa*) through the forum of all the participants in the games. He presented bulls and bullfighters, boxers, and three pairs of *pontiarii*. He also staged theatrical productions with clowns and mimes, including the well-known Pylades, the (possible) freedman of Augustus who became famous for creating the pantomime genre (Sabbatini Tumolesi 1980: 20). In his second magistracy (when he held the *quinquennalis*, the most prestigious elected office), Aulus Clodius Flaccus offered entertainments again to coincide with the *ludi Apollinares*. Again he organized a *pompa* in the forum and displayed bulls, bullfighters, and boxers. This time, the theatrical productions were replaced by a day of contests between thirty pairs of wrestlers and forty pairs of gladiators in the amphitheatre. There was also a hunt with wild boars and bears, along with bullfights. For his third term (3–2 BCE), Flaccus only presented theatrical performances, but the inscription is careful to note that first-rate actors were used.

This inscription deserves comment. In the first place we should note the connection between the games given by the magistrate and the *ludi Apollinares*, which were among the most important festivals of the Roman world, celebrated every year between 5 and 13 July. There were probably various reasons for the solemn celebration of these *ludi* in honour of Apollo, but the most important appears to have been as homage to the political and religious ideas of Augustus, with the implicit inclusion of the emperor in the worship of his patron deity (Sabbatini Tumolesi 1980: 21). Further, the decision to use two different sites for the games appears to indicate different spectacular and ritual demands. The use of the forum area for the Apolline games, when specifically theatrical premises had already been available for some time, is justified by the proximity to the Temple of Apollo (Fig. 37.1); indeed, originally the sanctuary was connected to the forum by ten gates. It seems plausible that the *pompa* started from the Temple of Apollo, where the sacrificial rite proper had already taken place, and then continued on to the forum, involving all the citizens in the performances and games. On the next day there was probably a procession along the Via dell'Abbondanza that culminated in the amphitheatre, where it was followed by the commencement of the gladiatorial events.

A marble relief from the mid first century CE (Fig. 37.3), found in the necropolis of the Stabian Gate and considered by certain scholars to come from the tomb of Aulus Clodius Flaccus himself, illustrates the three crucial phases of a *munus* as it is described by this and other Pompeiian inscriptions (Maiuri 1947: 491–510). The representations are arranged in three separate horizontal spaces of different heights, one above the other. In the upper section, we see the opening ceremonial procession (*pompa*). The front of the parade is on the right side with two lictors and three musicians. Following them is a group carrying a *ferculum*, or litter, on their shoulders, upon which two blacksmiths are seated, one in front of the other. According to Bianca Maiuri, this display of craftsmanship offered good publicity

FIGURE 37.3. Tomb relief from the Porta Stabia necropolis. Photo: L. Jacobelli.

for those who produced the weapons (Maiuri 1947: 496–498). Next come *harenarii*, the arena professional staff; the first carries a board that would have indicated the date of the spectacle and the name of its *editor*, the second brings the palm destined for the victor. A figure in a toga follows, perhaps the *editor* of the games himself, and behind him is a line of *harenarii* bearing the helmets and shields to be used by the gladiators. The procession closes with a horn player and two *harenarii* holding the reins of horses, harnessed for the festivities. In the middle section, five groups of gladiators engage in combat, supported by arena assistants. The lower area of the relief portrays scenes from a *venatio* with combats between *bestiarii* pitted against a bull and a wild boar, as well as fights among animals (dogs, deer, bulls, wild boars). In the last scene, on the right, a bear that has just come out the door into the arena has already taken a bite out of a *bestiarius* (La Regina 2001: 359; Jacobelli 2003: 94–96; Papini 2004: 146–148). The animals portrayed in these *venatio* vignettes are likely those that actually fought in the amphitheatre at Pompeii and were mentioned in the *edicta*. Similar to others, the relief appears to portray a typical and realistic local spectacle, very probably offered by the owner of the tomb in his role as *editor*. The importance of the *munera* in the political and social life of the city generated a multiplication of such images on funeral monuments, perpetuating memory of the munificence of the deceased for the future (Jacobelli 2003: 90–99).

The quantity of graffiti, of notices of performances and of images of gladiatorial contests demonstrates the extraordinary popularity of this type of entertainment and the fanatic following of the champions by their supporters. In effect the zeal of the fans, fomented by the ancient rivalry between the cities of Pompeii and Nuceria, led in 59 CE to the outbreak of a terrible brawl in the amphitheatre of Pompeii between the local hooligans and the Nuceria supporters, a riot so notorious as to deserve a mention in Tacitus' *Annals* (14.17; Maiuri 1958: 35–40; Moeller 1970: 84–95). The Pompeian fans, being more numerous given that the game was held at home, came off the better. Many Nucerians were carried home either dead or mutilated. In view of the gravity of the episode, Pompeii was banned from holding games in the amphitheatre for the next ten years. Despite this it appears that the emperor Nero revoked the ban after the earthquake of 62, deciding to allow the restoration of their favourite games as relief to the people of Pompeii who had been hit so hard by the disaster. Extraordinary figurative evidence of this tragic event has been preserved: the fresco found in house 1.3.23. It represents the crucial moment of the clash: riotous groups are fighting in the arena and in the seats but the brawl has already moved outside, onto the walls and around the amphitheatre, where itinerant vendors and ordinary passers-by appear to carry on with their ordinary business, oblivious to the violence.

In addition to the gladiatorial *munus*, which continued to be far and away the most popular of the games, the festivals of the citizens of Pompeii were also enlivened by athletic contests. Although these events never achieved the popularity that they had in Greece, they nevertheless aroused a certain enthusiasm, particularly as a result of the major promotion undertaken by the emperors themselves and by the civic authorities. For example, a graffito on a wall in Pompeii (*CIL* 4.8325 a) references the Sebasta of Naples, the famous competition festival set up in honour of the emperor Augustus in 2 CE and held every five years like the Olympic games. Athletic disciplines included track and field events such as running, long jump, javelin and discus throwing, and horse-races. Heavy athletics consisted of wrestling, boxing, and the *pancratium*, the fighting event in which everything was permitted: kicking, boxing, twisting of the joints, with the exception of biting and scratching.

There are numerous illustrations in Pompeii of athletes engaged in various disciplines. These images are to be found above all in the bath structures. In fact athletics was not restricted to professional competitors; the passion for sports was widespread among the citizens and was commonly associated with the practice of bathing. The two oldest bath complexes of Pompeii, the Stabian and the Forum Baths, had a small adjacent gymnasium where anyone could train. The large *palaestra*, situated opposite the amphitheatre, was built during the Augustan age under the impetus of imperial policy, designed to promote physical exercise together with traditional virtue or *virtus* among the youth. A similar stimulus gave rise to youth associations called *collegia iuvenum*, where, together with the training of the body, a consciousness of traditional social virtue and political loyalty were forged in the children of bourgeois citizens. Documentation of one of these youth associations, the *Iuventus Pompeiana*, comes from Pompeii, where boys and girls met to exercise and organize games (*ludus iuvenum* or *iuvenalia*) in honour of the goddess *Iuventus*, the patron deity of youth. During these festivals the young offered proof of their prowess, performing in a series of spectacles comprising athletic contests as well as hunting and simulations of gladiatorial contests. Another specialization was the Troy Game, the *ludus troianus*, consisting of an elaborate and complex series of exercises which the youths performed on horseback, one of which involved a serpentine movement (*lusus serpentis*). The great popularity of this event with the public is testified in Pompeii too by a bizarre inscription in the shape of an 'S' praising the *lusus serpentis* and the expertise of a certain young *Septumius* in performing it (*CIL* 4.1595).

The extraordinary amount of epigraphic material, graffiti, and illustrations originating from Pompeii relating to the games—especially the gladiatorial contests –is useful not solely for the purpose of demonstrating the importance that they had in the daily life of the Romans. This evidence also allows us to glimpse, in embryo, the initial processes of meditation on such spectacles and the development of certain customs that are deeply engrained in our social life today (Lattuada 2003: 108). The gladiators' rise to stardom, in the midst of so many fans and opposing allegiances, transferred the weight of their public personae into their lives as individuals. The gladiatorial contests were popular in the broadest sense of the word: the combat between famous gladiators was a duel between stars, and their mode of fighting was, in itself, an exercise in style and taste—if one may apply such terms to physical combat.

REFERENCES

Angelone, R. 1989. 'L'agenzia di un lanista in Pompei all'insegna di un famoso combattimento gladiatorio.' *AAP* 38: 339–359.

Angelone, R. 1989-1990. 'Spettacoli gladiatori ad Ercolano e gli edifici da essi postulati.' *RAAN* 62: 215–243.

Coarelli, F. 2001. 'Gli anfiteatri a Roma prima del Colosseo.' In *Sangue e Arena*. 43–47. A. La Regina, ed. Milan.

D'Ambrosio, A. and S. De Caro. 1987. *Un impegno per Pompei: La necropoli di Porta Nocera*. Milan.

De Waele, J. A. K. E. 2001. *Il tempio dorico del Foro Triangolare a Pompei*. Rome.

Fora, M. 1996. *I munera gladiatoria in Italia*. Naples.

Garnsey, P. 1971. 'Honorarium decurionatus.' *Historia* 20: 309–325.

Guzzo, P. G. 2007. *Pompei: Storia e paesaggi della città antica*. Milan.

Jacobelli, L. 2003. *Gladiatori a Pompei*. Rome.

La Regina, A., ed. 2001. *Sangue e Arena*. Milan.

Lattuada, R. 2003. 'Dai Gladiatori a Tiger man: Conoscenza, confronto e morte nello spettacolo del duello.' In *Gladiatori a Pompei*. 107–114. L. Jacobelli, ed. Rome.

Maiuri, A. 1958. 'Pompei e Nocera.' *RAAN* 33: 35–40.

Maiuri, B. 1947. 'Rilievo gladiatorio di Pompei.' *RAL* 2: 491–510.

Moeller, W. O. 1970. 'The Riot of A.D. 59 at Pompeii.' *Historia* 19: 84–95.

Mosci Sassi, M. G. 1992. *Il linguaggio gladiatorio*. Bologna.

Papini, M. 2004. *Munera Gladiatoria e venationes nel mondo delle immagini*. Rome.

Sabbatini Tumolesi, P. 1980. *Gladiatorum paria: Annunci di spettacoli gladiatorii a Pompei*. Rome.

Spinazzola, V. 1953. *Pompei alla luce degli scavi nuovi di via dell'Abbondanza*. Rome.

Tuck, S. T. 2008. 'Scheduling Spectacle: Factors Contributing to the Dates of Pompeian Munera.' *RSP* 19: 25–34.

Van Andringa, W. 2009. *Quotidien des dieux et des hommes: La vie religieuse dans les cités du Vésuve à l'époque romaine*. Rome.

CHAPTER 38

....

GYMNASIUM AND POLIS

....

NIGEL KENNELL

SHORTLY after the Treaty of Apamea in 189, Eumenes II of Pergamum awarded the status of *polis* to Tyriaion, a community in Phrygia (*IK* 62 393). In the first of two royal letters authorizing the city's creation, the king offered the inhabitants of the new city a set of laws 'suitable for establishing a council and other offices, and for dividing up and distributing the people into civic tribes, and for setting up a gymnasium and providing oil for the young men'. In the second he simply referred to the two elements as 'a constitution and a gymnasium'. That Eumenes considered a gymnasium essential to a city's proper functioning could not be clearer. The juxtaposition of constitution and gymnasium, implying their equivalence, points to an even more important place for the gymnasium in the Greek city than the much-quoted passage of Pausanias on Panopeus in Phocis, whose claim to *polis*-status he questioned because it had 'neither government offices, nor a gymnasium, nor theatre, nor agora, nor water flowing down into a fountain house' (10.4.1).

Gymnasia in Pausanias' time were large, multi-use venues fully integrated into the institutional fabric of the city. The gymnasium, however, was originally a private institution that gradually, at different times in different places, became public. Derived from *gumnazesthai*, 'to exercise in the nude' (*gumnos*), *gumnasion* properly means exercise, either physical or mental of any type, but more commonly designated a place or an institution for exercise rather than a particular building (Isid. *Etym.* XV ii 30, 40–41). The earliest gymnasium discovered so far is at Delphi (Fig. 38.1), constructed in the final third of the fourth century BCE (Delorme 1960: 76–78), but the institution was much older. The earliest gymnasia were just large areas, sometimes enclosed, outside the city walls where young members of the upper classes met to pass the time in exercises and other amusements (Glass 1968: 58–62; Glass 2002). As development during the later archaic period of a *polis*-centred mentality among the population at large made it increasingly difficult to keep monopolizing at will civic space for display in athletic contests as they had done previously (e.g. Hom. *Od.* 8.97–110), the elite apparently established gymnasia away from the city centre as exclusive venues for their own activities (Mann 1998). That the gymnasium began as an institution of 'the great and the good' suggests that it was not originally intended as a training ground for hoplite infantry, as proposed earlier (Delorme 1960: 28–30). Indeed, now that the history of hoplite tactics has been reassessed, a sixth-century date for the introduction of mass military training of citizens becomes anachronistic (Krentz 2002; van Wees 2004: 81, 89–91).

FIGURE 38.1. Gymnasium at Olympia with *xustos* on left. Photo N. Kennell.

The gymnasium soon became a recognizable feature in the landscape. Scenes of athletic activity on Attic red-figure pottery from the late sixth and early fifth centuries BCE sometimes contain architectural elements representing its essential features—tracks for running (*dromoi*) (e.g. *CVA* Deutschland 21 Berlin 2 pls. 63.3, 4 and 124.2, 6; pls. 97.1, 2, 3 and 130.3, 7) and a building to shelter the equipment and practising athletes (*palaistra*) (e.g. *CVA* Greece 2 National Museum 2 pl. 13.4; *ARV²* 322 no. 37). Infrastructure was rudimentary: apart from the *dromoi* and *palaistra*, the sole purpose-built elements, only trees for shade and a water source were considered essential (*CVA* Netherlands 3 Leiden 1 pl. 13; E. *Tr.* 833–835). Gymnasia were usually near shrines, as in the well-known cases of the Athenian Lyceum (Apollo), Academy (the hero Academus), and Cynosarges (Heracles), which gave them a sacred character they kept throughout antiquity. Later in the fifth century, Euripides' audience needed no explanations of references to gymnasia and the associated ideology of virile excellence (*Ph.* 366–368; cf. *El.* 528–529), while a grasp of boxing was essential for appreciating the humour in a poetic description of the drinking game *kottabos* (Dionysius Chalcus F3 West 1972 cited in Athenaeus 15.668e–69e; Borthwick 1964).

Earlier, Cimon had the Academy landscaped to make it a more appealing place to spend time, balancing this benefaction to the higher echelons of society with beautification of the agora in central Athens (Plut. *Cim.* 13.7). By the end of the century this exclusivity was under attack: some complained that while certain rich men still enjoyed their own gymnasia, the *dēmos* was building its own *palaistrai* and deriving more enjoyment from them than its betters ([Xen.] *AP* 2.10). Democratization was probably behind Alcibiades' decision to devote himself to chariot-racing rather than athletics because he met a better class of people in the hippodrome than in the *palaistra* (Isoc. 16.32–33).

In the meantime, Athenian gymnasia had also become places to marshal citizens for unpopular military reviews (Hesych. sv *Lykeion*; Ar. *Pax* 353–356), thus signalling an association with military affairs that would to a great extent shape the institution throughout the rest of its history. Military reform was behind the transformation of Athens' gymnasia from leisure facilities into vital components of the city's defence system. In the early fourth century, Athenians scrapped their inefficient system of conscription in favour of one that, like the Spartans', was based on annual age groups (Christ 2001: 409–422), at the same time introducing a two-year training period for young Athenians. Athens was not the first city to put gymnasia to military use. Already in the fifth century, Argos had trained up at public expense a cadre of 'athletes of war' only to have them (perhaps) participate in a coup against the democratic government (Thuc. 5.67.2, 76.2; Diod. Sic. 12.75.7, 80.2). Sparta, of course, had long devoted much time and effort in producing physically and mentally conditioned warriors, but such training was uncommon even in the fourth century (e.g. Xen. *Hell.* 6.1.5). By about 300, however, the situation had changed, influenced partly by Athenian practice. Athens was probably the inspiration for Eretria's establishment of an ephebate first attested between 315 and 305 BCE (*IG* XII.9 191; Chankowski 1993). On Ceus, an island with long-standing ties to Athens, a reform at Coresia at around the turn of the fourth to third centuries saw the founding of a festival with contests for boys (*paides*) and youths (*neōteroi*) along with regular training of the latter in the javelin, archery, and catapult (*IG* XII.5 647).

Once the idea of utilizing the gymnasium to train citizen soldiers began to spread at the end of the fourth century, all its elements, exemplified by the gymnasium at Delphi, were in place: a *palaistra*, where combat sports could be practised, surrounded by a quadrangular colonnade behind which were rooms for lectures (*exedra*), undressing (*apodutērion*), storage of equipment and olive oil (*aleiptērion*), and a bathing facility (*loutron*), along with a spacious area for running, javelin- and discus-throwing, and archery, along one side of which was a covered stoa (*xystos*) long enough for a full stade race in the event of bad weather (Fig. 38.2). The gymnasium's physical plant remained remarkably stable over time and geography (Skaltsa 2008: 2), but the dimensions and arrangement of its elements could vary widely (Skaltsa 2008: 17–24), from the split-level complex at Delphi with its 'boutique' *palaistra* and the almost canonical arrangement at Olympia, famously recalling Vitruvius' description (Vitr. 5.11.3–4; but see Wacker 2004: 354–356), to the multiple gymnasia of cities like Pergamum and Priene and the unique gymnasium-stadium combination at Messene (Fig. 38.3). In addition to buildings, the gymnasium had a complex administrative infrastructure of slaves, trainers, teachers, and managers of various sorts. In its developed form, this package of buildings and staff could be found all over the Greek world in the next centuries, from the Ukraine to North Africa and from Marseilles to Babylon and even Afghanistan.

The most important users were the ephebes, freeborn citizen males in their late teens who undertook regular training there in mainly athletic and military subjects, usually for one or two years; their older counterparts, the 'youth' (*neoi*), the core of the civic defence forces, generally in their twenties; and the boys from about twelve to ephebic age who, when not learning their letters and music, came for physical education. Anyone not belonging to these official groups faced access restrictions that must have varied from city to city. Those at Beroea were stringent: entry to the city's single gymnasium was denied to slaves, freedmen and their sons, prostitutes, drunks, anyone engaged in commercial activity, and *apalaistroi*, who were probably prevented by some disability from engaging in athletic activity (Gauthier and Hatzopoulos 1993: 79). On the other hand, free foreigners and others not explicitly

FIGURE 38.2. Gymnasium at Delphi. Photo N. Kennell.

FIGURE 38.3. Stadium–Gymnasium complex at Messene with later amphitheatre conversion. Photo N. Kennell.

excluded might visit occasionally and, depending on the generosity of the presiding official, be included in the distributions of oil and other benefactions (e.g. Michel 1900 no. 544; *IK* 19, ll. 62, 72–74; Chankowski 1993: 22–25).

Contests and festivals were frequently held in a city's gymnasium and were open to all enrolled there. The youth of Hellenistic Samos contended amongst themselves in bimonthly military and athletic competitions (*IG* XII.6 179, 182, 183). Such regular contests, known collectively as *diadromai* ('races'), were widespread. In fact, few institutions better exemplify the agonistic element in Greek culture than the constant round of competition in various disciplines that youths underwent during their years in a citizen training system. In addition to the skill and physical excellence displayed by the participants themselves, such events also afforded officials associated with the gymnasium an opportunity to display their status and their commitment to the welfare of the city's youth. In this instance too the gymnasium justifies the appellation 'another agora' (Robert 1966: 422 [= *OMS* 6, 46]), because the *diadromai* and festivals mirrored the gymnasium's overall function as a venue for public and private display, where benefactions from individuals or royals could be seen in tangible form, where statues of the city's gods and heroes, and memorials of great men of the past, could excite patriotic piety and emulation, and where gymnasial youth and citizens generally might assemble for athletic competitions and enjoy feasts.

Although special *diadromai* were sometimes held to honour royals (Holleaux 1906: 357), 'races' not necessarily linked to any particular cult or political observance were a regular feature of life in the gymnasium. A well-endowed gymnasium might host many *diadromai* (Michel 1900 no. 544). The events at Samos were predominantly military: catapult, javelin, archery, heavy and light weapons handling (*hoplomachia* and *thureamachia*), foot-race and discipline (*eutaxia*) (*IG* 12.6 179). Programmes elsewhere remain largely unknown, except that in some places the *diadromē* seems to have retained its original character as a foot-race (*IK* 35.909.15–19; *IGR* 4.1692; cf. Antiph. *Tetr.* 2.4.4). Along with *diadromai*, competitions in arms were held at Pergamum (Jacobsthal 1908: 381 no. 3); Mylasa had stand-alone competitions in wrestling, boxing, and pankration for boys as well (*IK* 35 909). Such competitions, which like *diadromai* evidently existed independently of any festival, were not uncommon. In the month of Geraestus, Coan boys ran in a foot-race called a 'mini-contest' (*agonarion*) (*ICos* ED 45 A, ll. 5–7). Eretrians liked long-distance races (*dolichoi*) in their gymnasium and praised those who presented lots of them (*IG* 12.9 234, ll. 14–15; Supp. 554). A contest (*athlon*) held in the gymnasium at Tralles had competitions for the young citizens in racing, javelin, archery, and good physique (*euexia*) (*IK* 36.1 106), while the people of Priene noted that a prominent benefactor had established 'contests of competition in literary subjects and athletic activity' (*I.Priene* 113 xxxviii).

The most common gymnasial festival was the Hermaea honouring Hermes—with Heracles, one of the institution's tutelary deities—a festival with which the gymnasial year traditionally closed (*IG* II² 2980; Gauthier and Hatzopoulos 1993: B45; *I.Histria* 1 59, ll. 9–10, 13–16). While the Hermaea's elements were different in each *polis*, the festival's celebrations had some common features. Usually the gymnasiarch (*gumnasiarchos*), the magistrate in charge of the gymnasium, officiated at sacrifices and honorific announcements, which were followed by competitions including a long-distance race (*dolichos, makros dromos*) and events peculiar to gymnasium-centred contests, such as the *euexia, eutaxia,* and *philoponia* (diligence), evaluation in which was based on monitoring throughout the year. An indispensable adjunct to the Hermaea was a torch-race, an event commonly associated with ephebes. Victors in the Hermaea were awarded prizes—weapons, very often shields, for those of ephebic age and older, and 'valuable prizes' for the younger competitors (Gauthier and Hatzopoulos 1993: 100–101). Contests concluded, the feasting began, which sometimes resulted in discipline problems among the graduating ephebes. For instance, Beroea banned the hiring of risqué dancers for the banquet, probably because of previous troubles (Gauthier and Hatzopoulos 1993: 113–114). Finally, as required by law, the victors dedicated their prizes, sometimes with the outgoing gymnasiarch's financial help.

As the official in charge of training, the gymnasiarch (*gumnasiarchos*) headed the gymnasial hierarchy. Gymnasiarchs are known at Athens from as early as the fifth century, but the Athenian office was a competitive tribal liturgy whose holder was expected only to fund teams in training for torch-relay races (Andoc. 1.132; Antiph. *Tetr.* 2.1; Dem. *Phil.* I 36.3). Elsewhere, the gymnasiarch was the gymnasium's chief administrator, responsible for maintaining order and discipline among its users (Aristot. *Pol.* 1322b). Since the two inscriptions from Troezen (*IG* IV 749, 753 add.) often cited as very early evidence for gymnasiarchs (e.g. Delorme 1960: 68; Schuler 2004: 172) actually date to the second half of the third century BCE (Swoboda 1912: 45 n. 1), the earliest explicit evidence for gymnasiarchs comes from Camirus on Rhodes (*IK* 38 141) and Pherae, where locals returning from Alexander's campaigns probably built a gymnasium and established the office in 330/329 BCE (Helly et al. 1979: 227–228). A few decades later, the Coresians used their new festival to justify establishing an annual gymnasiarchy to supervise the training of the young (*IG* XII.5 647, ll. 21–25).

Before this, Coresia may well have had a gymnasium that was privately run. This was not uncommon (Gauthier 1995: 7–8). At Xanthus in Lycia, the gymnasium's users were so impressed by a popular gymnasiarch's performance during one year that, on their own initiative, they invited him back for the next (Gauthier 1996: 3, ll. 25–28). We can expect that such independent gymnasia functioned in many cities to serve local needs. However, the gymnasiarchical law from Beroea indicates serious discipline problems among the youth, and peculation by officials provided the rationale for 'nationalizing' the gymnasium and putting the gymnasiarchy, in particular, under public control (Gauthier and Hatzopoulos 1993: A ll. 5–16).

During the Hellenistic period, the gymnasiarchy developed into one of the most prestigious (and financially onerous) civic offices. At Regium it was even the eponymous magistracy (*SEG* 1 418; Iamb. *vita Pyth.* 130). The post's normal financial and administrative duties were enough for most gymnasiarchs, however: they were expected to hire suitable military and athletic instructors, subject to the city's approval (*SIG*³ 578, ll. 21–23), arrange for sacrifices (*IG* XII.7 234, ll. 21–24; *IGR* IV 1692 ll. 55–58), and hold the sometimes numerous athletic contests normal in a Hellenistic gymnasium—as many as forty-one in certain years at Sicilian Tauromenium (*IG* XIV 422 III a.93–95). In addition to duties within the gymnasium, gymnasiarchs were expected to participate with their charges in major public ceremonies, usually in parades at festivals (e.g. *IG* XII.7 515, l. 45; *I. Cos* ED 82, ll. 20–24), public funerals of distinguished benefactors (e.g. *I.Priene* 104, ll. 9–11; *SEG* 33 1039, ll. 45–51), ceremonies celebrating good relations with the prevailing powers (e.g. *Milet* 6.1 203b, ll. 19–27; Holleaux 1906: 357, ll. 11–14), official greetings of foreign visitors (e.g. *I. Perg.* 1 246, ll. 33–37), and other displays with which the wheels of Hellenistic diplomacy were lubricated.

Gymnasiarchs handled considerable sums, and financial probity was prized, with accounts (sometimes quite detailed) expected of them annually (*IG* XII.9 236, ll.

60–65; *IGBulg* 1 45, ll. 21–26). Apart from the public fund (*to gumnasiarchikon*) available for expenditures relating to the gymnasium (Migeotte 2000: 153), a number of other endowments existed, especially in major cities. At Eretria, for instance, a single foundation to pay for the distribution of olive oil had a principal of 40,000 dr. (*IG* XII.9 236, ll. 60–65). Antiochus III earmarked a portion of the harbour dues at Heraclea ad Latmum for the city's purchase of oil to use in the gymnasium (Wörrle 1988: 460–462). Prominent locals, dynasts, kings, and eventually emperors all used donations to gymnasia as a means of raising their profile in life or perpetuating their memory posthumously. Gymnasial endowments might sometimes be named after their founders (*IK* 60 43, ll. 28–29), but were all considered their eternal memorials (e.g. *IG* XII.9 236, ll. 16–24). Indeed, the title 'eternal gymnasiarch' came to be bestowed on founders of funds for oil distribution in the Roman period (*TAM* III.1 21; Robert 1960: 294–298). Financial aid to such a prominent *polis* institution had propaganda value at an international level. Among the donations the Sicilian tyrants Hieron and Gelon made to Rhodes after the devastating earthquake of 224 BCE was a considerable amount of silver coin for the distribution of oil in the gymnasium (Polyb. 5.88.5–8). In the next century, King Herod of Judaea showed his philhellenism by establishing funds to purchase olive oil at Cos and in several other Greek cities (Joseph *BJ* 1.423). The foundations were usually either straight cash donations or gifts of real estate—either arable land or commercial property— the revenue from which was used to purchase oil, sacrificial victims, prizes for festivals, and any extra expenses, including distributions to citizens, that would serve to perpetuate the donor's memory. Philetaerus of Pergamum gave both sorts of benefaction to Cyzicus in the 270s BCE—a monetary grant of 26 silver Alexandrian talents for oil and the corporation (*sunagōgē*) of the youth, along with land which he dedicated to the gymnasial god Hermes (*OGIS* 748, 749). In such a situation, the gymnasium would profit from the income generated by leasing the land (*IK* 5 102). Leonidas of Halicarnassus chose a slightly different approach in making his benefaction to the gymnasium of Pharsalus in Thessaly. Instead of land, he donated a stoa and the shops within, earmarking the income to purchase oil throughout the year, with the sum of two minas to be spent on a torch-race and an athletic contest (*gumnikos agōn*) called the Leonidea (Decourt 1995: 52).

The regular expenses of a gymnasium will have differed little from place to place: wood to heat the rooms of the *palaistra* (*IG* V.1 1390, l. 107; *I.Priene* 112 xxv, ll. 95–100) and cook meat at sacrifices (*SEG* 11 256, ll. 3–7); towels and strigils for the athletes (*SEG* 11 492, l. 12; *SEG* 37 1675; *IK* 19 1, l. 77); and salaries for the regular staff of trainers (*paideutai*) (Ameling 2004: 154–155). Dwarfing these, however, was the cost of olive oil, the gymnasium's essential fuel. Gymnasium users were called collectively *hoi aleiphomenoi* ('those who are oiled up'), since exercising without first being anointed with oil was unthinkable (Gauthier and Hatzopoulos 1993: 11–13), and provision of olive oil later so overshadowed the gymnasiarch's other duties that the word *gumnasiarchia* came to mean simply 'distribution of oil' (Robert and Robert 1983 no. 84). Each day, the gymnasiarch would signal the availability of oil for a set period of time by raising a flag (Robert 1962: 143) or sounding a gong (Wilhelm 1932: 45–47). Some idea of the amounts involved can be gleaned from an inscription from Roman Sparta, where the daily allowances at a local athletic festival for men, youths, and boys were about 182, 136, and 91 millilitres (1 litre = 4.2 US cups) respectively (*IG* V.1 20, ll.6– 7), and from Magnesia on the Maeander, where about 27 litres were considered sufficient for the gymnasium's use every day (Kern 1900 no. 116, ll. 10–21). Gymnasiarchs were naturally expected to supplement these oil rations at their own expense. They might subsidize gymnasium users by selling them oil below the purchase price (e.g. Papazoglou 1988: 238 no. 5, ll. 7–12), but the more ambitious would provide the oil free of charge, and copiously. An Erythraean gymnasiarch made high-quality oil available from vats as opposed to the more moderate ladles (*IK* 1 85); one gymnasiarch at Magnesia ad Sipylum did not lower his flag over the gymnasium for an entire year to show that oil was always freely available (*IK* 8 4, ll. 7–9); and at Smyrna, the orator Heraclides installed a fountain in the gymnasium that literally gushed olive oil (Philostr. *VS* 2.26.2).

Although the gymnasiarchy was, properly speaking, a public office (*archē*) in the late Hellenistic and Roman periods, it also possessed a marked liturgical character, most visible in its jurisdiction over oil distribution, which made it far more dependent than other offices on the incumbent's financial well-being. Very wealthy gymnasiarchs might take on responsibility for larger numbers of gymnasium users, a phenomenon often reflected in their various titles, for example, gymnasiarch of *ephēboi* and *neoi* (*IG* 12.2 134); gymnasiarch of *neoi* and *presbuteroi* (*IK* 28.2 250); of *gerousia* and *neoi* (*Milet* 6.1 309); of *neoi, gerontes,* and *paides* (*IK* 8 34); and of *neoi, ephēboi,* and *polis* (*I. Cos* EV 87).

Gymnasiarchs were sometimes aided by an assistant, the 'under-gymnasiarch' (*hupogumnasiarchos*), about whom little is known. This was an unelected post, to which gymnasiarchs could appoint their sons or other relatives (*IG* XI.4 1151; *IG* XII.7 421, 423; *TAM* II.3 552). Hypogymnasiarchs might replace incapacitated gymnasiarchs in their daily duties (*TAM* V.2 100, ll.16–19; *IG* XII.2 258), aid them in such tasks as compiling the official list of graduating ephebes (*IG* XII.3 339, 342), or oversee their honours at the end of their term in office (*IG* XII.7 235). Sometimes hypogymnasiarchs were honoured in their own right (Fränkel 1895 no. 468), suggesting that the office was not always a sinecure. This impression is strengthened by an inscription from Messene, in which former ephebes and a military officer praise 'their hypogymnasiarch for his excellence and for the support (*aretas heneken kai eunoias*) he continually had for them' (*SEG* 43 401), though how this was manifested in practice is unclear.

Instruction was normally in the hands of itinerant teachers. Athens, with its permanent cadre of athletic and military specialists (elected until the late second century BCE)—the *paidotribēs* (wrestling school trainer), *akontistēs* (javelin instructor), *toxotēs* (archery instructor), *hoplomachos* (weapons instructor), and *katapaltaphetēs* (catapult instructor)— was the prominent exception to this rule. Usually, instructors were hired on a per-course basis for limited periods of time, as at Teos where *hoplomachoi* were only required to teach for two months in the year (*SIG*[3] 578, ll 21–27). An inscription from Thespiae granting proxeny to an Athenian arms instructor indicates that a law of the Boeotian League in the early third century required all the youth to be trained in weapons-handling and manoeuvres (*SEG* 32 496). Gymnasiarchs themselves might hire scholars to present lectures (*akroaseis*) or even courses of study (*scholai*) on subjects in the liberal arts. For example, an Eretrian gymnasiarch brought a Homeric philologist from Athens (*IG* XII.9 235, ll. 9–13), while a generous gymnasiarch at Priene provided his charges with a grammar teacher (*I.Priene* 112 xxiv, ll. 73–74). Sometimes instruction appears to have been at the scholar's own initiative, as when the grammarian Cassopaeus offered courses in the Delphic gymnasium (*FD* III.3.2 338) or at Samos, where a travelling philosopher was awarded with citizenship for benefiting the citizen youth with his learning and teaching anyone free of charge who could not pay his fees (*IG* XII.6 128). Academic freedom was limited, however, with the gymnasiarch authorized to inflict corporal punishment on speakers whose lectures he deemed not conducive to the ephebic good ([Pl]. *Eryx.* 398e; Diog. Laert. 6.90).

There was a ubiquity and a remarkable consistency of training programme of the gymnasium through space and time: the Hermaea held in Sarmatian Gorgippia (*IOSPE* 4 432) and in the Greco-Macedonian community in Babylon under the Parthians (Haussollier 1909: 352–353, 360–362) featured the same events as in the Greek heartland of the Aegean. This uniformity made it an extraordinarily successful vehicle for transmitting Hellenic values and identity from one generation to another and for representing Hellenism to non-Greek cultures. That prominent members of non-Greek communities aspired to share in what the gymnasium could offer their young men beyond athletic and ethical training— acceptance into the dominant culture and unsurpassed networking opportunities (Plut. *praecepta* 816b)—is clear from the indigenous names occurring in gymnasial contexts in places like Cyzicus, Pergamum (Özlem-Aytaçlar 2010: 516), Tyana (*SEG* I 466), Termessus (*TAM* 3.1 146, 205–213), and Thracian Odessa (*IGBulg* 1 47, C l. 29). On the other hand, not all local elites unanimously viewed gymnasial culture as an unadulterated good (Groß-Albenhausen 2004). One particular community was profoundly split. Jewish ephebes are to be found in Corone (*IG* V.1 1398, ll. 91–92), Cyrene (*SEG* 20 741 I l. 34, II ll. 47–49) and Iasus (*IK* 28.2 284, l. 4), despite the idolatrous implications of their participation ('Abodah Zarah 18b). At Damascus, Jews might avail themselves of special funds to purchase their own unpolluted oil (Joseph., *AJ* 12.3.1 [120]), and Jewish entry into the Alexandrian gymnasium was apparently a problem only for non-Jews in the Roman era (*CPJ* II, 153 col. 5). But among religious scholars, the gymnasium, with its materialistic emphasis on physicality and its connotations of idolatry and immorality, was anathema, while *epispasmos*, the operation to reverse circumcision, was the breaking of Abraham's covenant (Harris 1976; Hall 1992). Traces of their deep antipathy are visible in the characterization of the gymnasium built at Jerusalem under Antiochus IV as the 'pinnacle of Hellenism and an advance in the adoption of alien ways' and its builder as 'the impious anti-high priest Jason' (II Macc. 4.13). The subsequent successful revolt of the Maccabees was in reaction to this and even more serious threats to the Jewish way of life (Ameling 2003; Kennell 2005).

The gymnasium was a locus of display: for youths in athletic ability and military discipline; for scholars in academic and rhetorical excellence; for the elite in their civic-mindedness and generosity. It was at once a place where young males trained in strict segregation and a venue for mass gatherings of all citizens to watch contests or participate in public banquets. Above all, it was a place of competition where ephebes were led by physical training to personal excellence, where young citizens were prompted to outdo the great deeds of the men whose statues lined the stoas, and where the gymnasiarch was eager to be the first and only to confer some benefaction on his charges and his city. As Eumenes and Pausanias recognized, the gymnasium, by tangibly manifesting the agonistic spirit, was essential to the Greek city.

References

Ameling, W. 2003. 'Jerusalem als hellenistische Polis: 2 Makk 4, 9–12 und eine neue Inschrift.' *ByzZ* 47: 105–111.

Ameling, W. 2004. 'Wohltäter im hellenistischen Gymnasion.' In *Das hellenistische Gymnasion*. 129–161. D. Kah and P. Scholz, eds. Berlin.

Borthwick, E. 1964. 'The Gymnasium of Bromius: A Note on Dionysius Chalcus, fr.3.' *JHS* 84: 49–53.

Chankowski, A. 1993. 'Date et circonstances de l'institution de l'éphébie à Érétrie.' *DHA* 19: 17–44.

Christ, M. 2001. 'Conscription of Hoplites in Classical Athens.' *CQ* n.s. 51: 398–422.

Decourt, J.-C. 1995. *Inscriptions de Thessalie I: Les cités de la vallée de l'Énipeus*. Études Epigraphiques 3. Athens.

Delorme, J. 1960. *Gymnasion: Étude sur les monuments consacrés à l'éducation en Grèce (des origines à l'Empire romain)*. BEFAR 196. Paris.

Fränkel, M. 1895. *Die Inschriften von Pergamon*. Altertümer von Pergamon VIII.2. Berlin.

Gauthier, P. 1995. 'Notes sur le rôle du gymnase dans les cités hellénistiques.' In *Stadtbild und Bürgerbild im Hellenismus*. 1–11. M. Wörrle and P. Zanker, eds. Munich.

Gauthier, P. 1996. 'Bienfaiteurs du gymnase au Létôon de Xanthos.' *REG* 109: 1–34.

Gauthier, P. and M. Hatzopoulos. 1993. *La loi gymnasiarchique de Beroia*. Meletemata 16. Athens.

Glass, S. 1968. 'Palaistra and Gymnasium in Greek Architecture.' PhD dissertation, University of Pennsylvania.

Glass, S. 2002. 'The Greek Gymnasium: Some Problems.' In *The Archaeology of the Olympics: The Olympics and other Festivals in Antiquity*, 2nd edn. 155–173. W. Raschke, ed. Madison, WI.

Groß-Albenhausen, K. 2004. 'Bedeutung und Funktion der Gymnasien für die Hellenisierung des Ostens.' In *Das hellenistische Gymnasion*. 313–322. D. Kah and P. Scholz, eds. Berlin.

Hall, R. 1992. 'Epispasm: Circumcision in Reverse.' *Bible Review* 8.4: 52–57.

Haussollier, B. 1909. 'Inscriptions grecques de Babylone.' *Klio* 9: 352–363.

Harris, H. A. 1976. *Greek Athletics and the Jews*. Cardiff.

Helly, B., G. Te Riele, and J. van Rossum. 1979. 'La liste des gymnasiarques de Pheres pour les années 330–189 av. J.-C.' In *La Thessalie: Actes de la Table-Ronde, 21–24 Juillet 1975, Lyon*. 221–255. Lyon.

Holleaux, M. 1906. 'Note sur une inscription de Colophon Nova.' *BCH* 30: 349–358 (= *Études d'épigraphie* II: 51–60).

Jacobsthal, P. 1908. 'Die Arbeiten zu Pergamon 1906–1907, II: Die Inschriften.' *MDAI(A)* 33: 375–420.

Kennell, N. 2005. 'New Light on 2 Maccabees 4:7–15.' *JJS* 56: 10–24.

Kern, O. 1900. *Die Inschriften von Magnesia am Maeander*. Berlin.

Krentz, P. 2002. 'Fighting by the Rules: The Invention of the Hoplite Agon.' *Hesperia* 71: 23–39.

Mann, C. 1998. 'Krieg, Sport und Adelskultur: Zur Entsehung des griechischen Gymnasions.' *Klio* 89: 7–21.

Michel, C. 1900. *Recueil d'inscriptions grecques*. Brussels.

Migeotte, L. 2000. 'Les dépenses militaires des cités grecques: Essai de typologie.' In *Économie antique: La guerre dans les économies antiques. Entretiens d'archéologie et d'histoire*. 145–176. Saint-Bertrand-de-Comminges.

OMS = Robert, L. *Opera minora selecta: Epigraphie et antiquités grecques*. Amsterdam 1969.

Özlem-Aytaçlar, P. 2010. 'An Onomastic Survey of the Indigenous Population of North-Western Asia Minor.' In *Onomatologos: Studies in Greek Personal Names Presented to Elaine Matthews*. 506–529. R. Catling and F. Marchand, eds. Oxford.

Papazoglou, F. 1988. 'Les stèles éphébiques de Stuberra.' *Chiron* 18: 233–270.

Robert, L. 1962. *Villes d'Asie Mineure*. 2nd edn. Paris.

Robert, L. 1960. 'Recherches épigraphiques.' *REA* 62: 276–361 (= *OMS* II, 792–877).

Robert, L. 1966. 'Inscriptions d' Aphrodisias I.' *AC* 35: 377–432 (= *OMS* VI, 1–56).

Robert, L. and J. Robert. 1983. 'Bulletin Épigraphique.' *REG* 96: 246–361.

Schuler, C. 2004. 'Die Gymnasiarchie in hellenistischer Zeit.' In *Das hellenistische Gymnasion*. 163–192. D. Kah and P. Scholz, eds. Berlin.

Skaltsa, S. 2008. 'Hellenistic Gymnasia: The Built Space and Social Dynamics of a Polis Institution.' DPhil thesis. Oxford.

Swoboda, H. 1912. 'Studien zu den griechischen Bunden II.' *Klio* 12: 17–50.

Van Wees, H. 2004. *Greek Warfare: Myths and Realities*. London.

Wacker, C. 2004. 'Die bauhistorische Entwicklung der Gymnasien von der Parkanlage zum Idealgymnasion des Vitruv.' In *Das hellenistische Gymnasion*. 349–362. D. Kah and P. Scholz, eds. Berlin.

West, M.L. 1972. *Iambi et elegi Graeci*, vol. 2. Oxford.

Wilhelm, A. 1932. *Neue Beiträge zur griechische Inschriftenkunde*, vol. 5. 45–47. Vienna.

Wörrle, M. 1988. 'Inschriften von Herakleia am Latmos I: Antiochus III, Zeuxis und Herakleia.' *Chiron* 18: 421–476.

SECTION 5

GAMES AND COMMUNITY

CHAPTER 39

....

ECONOMIC ASPECTS OF ATHLETIC COMPETITION IN THE ARCHAIC AND CLASSICAL AGE

....

LUCIA D'AMORE

INTRODUCTION

....

THE theme of the economic aspects of the Panhellenic games in the archaic and classical age may be defined through analysis of the relations between economy and political life in the Greek cities, considered from a diachronic perspective and in terms of the interaction among the categories of the private (*idios*), public (*dēmosios*), and sacred (*hieros*), with 'economy' understood as all the activities of production, exchange, and consumption of material goods in the intersection of the hoarding–exchange duality (Migeotte 2002). Athletic competition was an integral part of Greek life, culture, and economy, expressing the different social strata and classes of various eras. The economic and social status of the athletes is a complex problem that has divided modern criticism.

In the Homeric poems, athletic competition is a way of honouring people of equal social origin, and is restricted to the heroes and *aristoi*, while the *laos* is remote from this type of contest, although not excluded from athletic exercises clearly connected to military training.

In the past it was commonly thought that athletic contests in the archaic period were the prevalent and characteristic element of a milieu that was first heroic and then aristocratic, while later there was a progressive democratization of competitive sport. The extension of athletics to the less-affluent classes and their participation in the Panhellenic games was said to correspond to a sort of decadence that led to athletic professionalism (Gardiner 1930; Biliński 1959). This vision has now been partly superseded by the understanding that participation in sport was not closed to representatives of the lower class, as the fundamental study of Young (1984) has shown. Nevertheless, there is no doubt that in the archaic period rich aristocrats enjoyed greater opportunities to devote themselves to athletic competition and, in fact, to dominate the sporting scene in the first centuries of the Panhellenic games (Pleket

2005; Kyle 1997). Equestrian competitions, which required a greater financial investment on the part of their participants, remained for centuries the prerogative of aristocrats, as is demonstrated by the *Epinikia* of Pindar, which express the exaltation of aristocratic *aretē*. On the other hand, forms of athletic 'professionalism' are already recognizable in the archaic age. Such is the case of Theogenes of Thasos, a contemporary of Pindar's, who in the course of 22 years competed in more than 1,300 events (Moretti 1957 no. 201). Present-day studies have therefore for some time abandoned the terms 'amateur' and 'professional' in regard to archaic Greek sport, since it is clear that these modern concepts had little meaning for the ancients: 'Amateurism is a strictly modern concept born in England not much more than a century ago' (Young 1984: 14).

In the eighth century BCE, an epoch that saw the first Olympiads in Greece, athletic competition was still an expression of the dominant classes of the warrior and landowning aristocracy. The lengthy and costly athletic preparation for the Olympic Games, taking at least a year before each meet, was—like the expensive journey to Olympia—a burden so heavy that only members of the wealthiest classes could easily bear it. The literary sources, as well as the data furnished by archaeology and epigraphy, serve to illuminate our understanding of the characteristics of the phenomenon. A large number of bronze tripods of the early archaic period have been found in the excavations of the sanctuary at Olympia, implying the possibility that they were *anathēmata* dedicated by victors in the Panhellenic games, according to aristocratic custom (Papakonstantinou 2002). In fact, the victors in Panhellenic contests, who in the classical era received the prize of a simple wreath with symbolic value, were rewarded by their cities not only with formal honours for having brought renown to their communities of origin, but also with prestige goods (tripods, hydria, etc.) consecrated in the civic sanctuaries (Kyle 1996). In this regard the dedication of Cleombrotus of wealthy Sybaris is instructive. After having won in the Olympic Games, he dedicated one-tenth of the prize in the local sanctuary of Athena (Guarducci 1967: 110–111). The ancient sources indicate that this phenomenon should be seen from the perspective of the predominantly pre-monetary, hoarding economy of the archaic and aristocratic *polis*, in which the public and the sacred are not yet distinct.

The seventh century, the epoch of the birth of the *polis*, saw the formation of new social classes that, through the development of craftsmanship and commerce, brought about a crisis for the bases archaic aristocracy by introducing the new value of monetary wealth. The law-making activity of Solon in the Athens of the sixth century BCE was a response to the needs of the emerging social classes. The new conception of the timocratic *polis* also found expression in the money prizes offered to victors in the Panhellenic contests (Plut. *Sol.* 23.5; Diog. Laert. 1.55).

In the fifth century, the affirmation of the ideals of *isonomia* and *isotēs* ('equality') on the part of the Athenian democracy (which, for example, provided access to the gymnasia for all free men and introduced the liturgies), meant that athletic competition could be practised with greater freedom by all social classes. We must understand as democratic developments the introduction at Athens of the figure of the gymnasiarch—a rich citizen who saw to the financing of a *trophē* ('maintenance') for the young men of his own tribe in preparation for the *lampadēdromiai* ('torch race') at the Panathenaic Games (Xen. *Vect.* 4.51–52)—and the introduction of liturgies and *chorēgiai* (chorus financer) that permitted the redistribution of private wealth for public purposes. Contrary to past belief, the gradual democratization of athletics, which in fact became accessible to all, was not related to a moral decline in the athletes, who were once thought to have been attracted only by the profits and economic advantages connected with the contests rather than inspired by the ideals of aristocratic *aretê* ('excellence'). It is undeniable, however, that the advent of the Hellenistic kingdoms and the transfer of citizen interest from the agora to the arenas and gymnasia increased the practice of athletics, multiplied the meets and competitions throughout the Greek world, and gave rise to private associations of 'professional' athletes.

THE HOMERIC WORLD

The Homeric poems, in the view of most scholars, reflect the historical conditions of the Greek communities at the end of the ninth century and the beginning of the eighth century BCE. The economy of the Homeric world was essentially one of aristocratic and warrior communities, before the advent of states and cities, and it was intended to satisfy the necessities of the large family groups around which the community was organized. The basis of the early archaic economy was primarily agricultural, but it was above all a natural economy: coinage did not exist, the talent and half-talent of gold were measures of weight, exchanges were made through barter, and value was expressed in oxen. Homeric communities were little inclined to commerce, being based on self-rule and self-sufficiency. But Homeric society did possess alternative ways for goods to circulate: war, with its attendant raiding, and the economy of hospitable giving. Both systems permitted the acquisition and transmission of land, cattle, slaves, metals, and prestige goods.

It is in this aristocratic economic and social context that we must place the first Greek competitions of which we have a record. These athletic contests were organized according to a private ritual and were expressions of relations among private individuals, not yet institutionalized events. Although Homer several times represents the Achaean army as engaged in sporting activities, the athletic contest was a privilege reserved to the *aristoi*, used to honour a guest or a fallen member of the same social rank. The prizes offered (*aethla*) were personal prestige goods, and their awarding belonged to the exchange of gifts among aristocrats (*xenia*). They were considered expressions of honour (*timē*), a central conception in Homeric ethics; they had a value not only material but above all symbolic, expressing a status and an aristocratic custom. Therefore the *aethla* were not objects of consecration or of hoarding, but could be converted back into *xenia*, as is shown by the story of the silver cup of Sidon (*Il.* 23.740–747), an object that belonged first to Thoas and then to Patroclus before being offered by Achilles to the victor in the race in the funeral games. The victor, therefore, did not receive objects produced for the purpose of being prizes, but already-existing prestige goods, as in the funeral games for Patroclus, during which Achilles awards tripods and cauldrons of bronze, talents of gold, iron, horses, mules, and slaves (*Il.* 23.259–261).

Proof that this aristocratic practice persisted comes from Hesiod (*Works and Days* 654–659), who came to Chalcis to compete in the funeral games in honour of King Amphidamas, given by his sons with the offer of many prizes. At Chalcis the poet won a handled tripod that he dedicated in the sanctuary of the Muses of Helicon, the place where he had learned the art of poetry. In comparison with the Homeric evidence, Hesiod's account reveals an important novelty: the consecration of the prize or prestige object and its hoarding in the sanctuary, a clear indication of the transition from the Homeric to the archaic economy. The practice recorded by Hesiod finds a precise correspondence in archaeological finds from the seventh century BCE in the sanctuaries of Attica, the north-eastern Peloponnese and Boeotia: bronze cauldrons bearing a double inscription in two different dialects. The first inscription, as one would expect, concerns the agonistic context in which the cauldrons were offered as prizes, while the second records their consecration in a sanctuary venerated by the victor in the funeral games. These documents furnish extraordinary evidence of the circulation of prizes or prestige goods in different parts of the Greek world (De Polignac 2005: 20).

THE ARCHAIC PERIOD
(EIGHTH–SIXTH CENTURY BCE)

The distinctive traits of this era are the transformation of aristocratic society, the birth of the *polis*, and the establishment of the Panhellenic games. The transition towards the *polis* was accomplished through the collective management of power by the civic community and through the establishment of magistracies charged with administering goods in the name of the whole community. Initially, the management of power, of civil defence, and of religion remained the privilege of the landed and warrior aristocracy, while the lower classes of the population were excluded from these duties. From an economic point of view, however, new phenomena arose between the eighth and sixth centuries. Land remained the fundamental element of the archaic economy, but different elements of development, artisanal and mercantile, came into play. Closely related to them was the introduction of coined money, an instrument of normative progress for the civic community of the sixth century BCE, which saw the consolidation of the chrematistic economy: a new vision of material goods, *chrēmata*, whose value was measured by coins, according to the Aristotelian definition (*Eth. Nic.* 1119^{b}26–27). To the political and economic context thus articulated belong the mechanisms that led the *polis* to establish a festival in honour of a god, a hero, or an illustrious figure of the past, celebrating it with public games (Lévêque 1996). The institutionalization of religious festivals brought with it their removal from the private sphere and their assignment to the public: the organization of the contests and the rewarding of the victors was no longer a privilege of rulers or aristocrats, but became the role of the entire community, of the *polis*. From the end of the sixth century, rules of competition were developed, as is shown by the fragmentary remains of a *nomos enagōnios* found at Olympia (Minon 2007 no. 5). Among the various duties undertaken by the *politai*, we find those of the *agōnothetai* (*epimelētai*, *Hellanodikai*, *panēguriarchai*, *athlothetai*, etc.), charged with the whole organization of the contests, with the awarding of prizes, with the setting up of honorary inscriptions and with the erection of statues of the victors. The establishment of Panhellenic festivals in the Peloponnese and central Greece from the eighth to sixth centuries BCE is therefore evidence for the formation of a model of a common culture of the *polis*.

If we turn to analysis of the economic aspects of the introduction of public athletic contests, we may state without exaggeration that the Panhellenic games must have been the driving force of the ancient Greek economy, since they were part of an economic system highly articulated according to the categories of circulation and hoarding. They allowed for the circulation of money, of prestige goods and of labour, but also for the hoarding of valuable goods and of monetary reserves in the sanctuaries, accessible in case of emergency not only by the sanctuary itself but also by the whole community, for civil and military purposes (Musti 1981).

As has been noted, the ancient economy included the category of *hiera*, sacred property, consisting of movable and immovable goods. Although the Greeks did not distinguish between the sacred and the profane (in the sense that festivals and religious observances were considered public and organized by the magistrates of the cities, and the possessions of sanctuaries were administered by citizens elected or selected by lot), the *polis* did distinguish clearly between the fortune of the god and that of the city (Migeotte 1998).

The gods and heroes of the *polis* possessed lands, buildings, vineyards, woods, and other property, leased to private citizens for substantial returns, as well as objects of value and sums of money (*hiera chrēmata*), consecrated by individuals or by communities as a tenth of the booty of war. The economic administration of the sanctuaries also was founded on an interrelationship between hoarding and circulation: the revenues from the exploitation of real property—for example, the leasing of sacred lands—permitted not only the development of normal cultural life, but also the organization of contests and the awarding of symbolic or valuable prizes, the construction and restoration of structures intended for athletic exercise (palaestae and gymnasia) and the offering of sacrifices and public banquets during the festivals. This was a way of redistributing the wealth of the sanctuaries among the population and of putting the sacred revenues back into circulation. For this reason, the organization of contests in the sanctuaries was advantageous to the entire community, and also because, on the occasion of the *panēgureis* ('public festivals'), it was customary to organize large markets that permitted the mobility of goods and persons.

During this first period, the participants in the Olympic Games were probably of local origin or were visitors to the sanctuary, but as time passed, athletes gradually gathered at Olympia from different parts of the Greek world, including Sicily and Magna Graecia, especially at the end of the sixth and the beginning of the fifth centuries BCE, with the specific intent of participating in the contests. For almost two centuries the Olympic Games were the only Panhellenic festival, until the establishment or reorganization of the festivals of Delphi (586/585 BCE), Isthmia (582 BCE), and Nemea (573 BCE). The sixth century saw the definition of an athletic circuit (*periodos*) with its potential victors (*periodonikai*), a circuit that in this era attracted athletes from every part of the Mediterranean, to the great economic benefit of the whole host community and the sanctuaries. At Olympia, for example, access to the sanctuary was granted to foreigners if they respected its internal rules, on pain of paying a penalty to Zeus, as is suggested by the fragment of a *lex sacra* ('sacred law') from the end of the sixth century BCE (Minon 2007 no. 3). The Panhellenic games favoured political relations among the *poleis* (city states) to the entire advantage of the sanctuaries, as is proven by the dedication of 'treasuries' (*thēsauroi*) by cities and peoples at Olympia and Delphi.

Another notable aspect of the economy of the contests is the assignment of prizes to the victors and of the fines they had to pay to the sanctuaries. As is well known, ancient athletic contests were divided into *agōnes stephanitai* and *agōnes thematikoi* ('crown games') or *chrēmatitai* ('money games'). The former, usually Panhellenic and connected with festivals in which the wreath better corresponded to the sacred character of the event, rewarded victors only with a symbolic wreath of leaves from the sacred grove of the sanctuary. In the latter category were contests of more recent establishment, which attracted participants by awarding money prizes along with wreaths, compliments of the presiding god. For example, in the

Diïa at Pellene the victors received a woollen cloak, in the *Heraia* at Argos a metal shield, in the *Lykaia* in Arcadia a metal tripod, in the *Herakleia* at Marathon a silver cup, etc.: all prizes provided by drawing on the funds of the sanctuary (Mezger 1880: 1–6).

The winning athletes who received only a prize of symbolic value were substantially rewarded in their homeland, since the *timē* (honour) no longer applied only to the winner of the games, but to the whole community he represented. The athlete's home *polis*, in fact, awarded prizes in money and in material privileges. It is well known that cities such as Athens, Sparta, Croton, and Sybaris gave much importance to the athletic successes of their citizens and rewarded them with money and special honours (Buhmann 1972; and Pleket 1975: 49–89).

Already by the sixth century BCE, Xenophanes tells us (referring probably to the *poleis* of Magna Graecia), the winners of athletic contests received *timai* (honours) such as *sitēsis* (meals) at the expense of the *polis*, *proedria* (special seats) at public spectacles, and a *dōron* or reward (Xen. Fr. 2; West 1992: 186–187). Special rewards were also granted by tyrants to athletes who had competed in the name of their fellow citizens. Astylos of Croton, who lived in the first half of the fifth century BCE, received for his Olympic victories in the name of the Syracusans a substantial *dōron* from the Deinomenid Hiero of Syracuse (Paus. 6.13.1; Moretti 1957 nos. 178–179). His victory poem was commissioned from Simonides (Fr. 10), and his statue at Olympia from the famous sculptor Pythagoras of Samos (Paus. 6.13.1). Similar arrangements are found elsewhere, according to the testimony of Plutarch (*Sol.* 23) and Diogenes Laertius (1.55). Solon fixed at 500 drachmas the *timē* paid by the Athenians to *Olympianikai* and at 100 drachmas the reward for victors in the Isthmian and other games. Furthermore, an Attic decree of the fifth century BCE records the granting of *sitēsis* (meals) in the Prytaneum to all Athenian winners at Olympia, Delphi, Isthmia, and Nemea (*IG* I³ 131.11–17).

Athletic prizes given in money or in goods of monetary value were not the object of hoarding on the part of their owners, but were quickly put back into circulation. A part of the monetary prize was destined to be used in consecrating goods of value in the sanctuaries that had hosted the competition or in the homeland of the athlete. The consecrated objects were primarily of bronze, such as those recorded in inscriptions or found in archaeological excavations. One of the earliest known donors is the already-mentioned Cleombrotus, son of Dexilaos of Sybaris (sixth century BCE), who consecrated in the sanctuary of Athena at the Timpone della Motta—a Sybarite sanctuary outside the city—an object, perhaps a statue, as a tenth of the prize from his Olympic victory (Moretti 1992: 123). There is debate as to whether the archaic bronze tripods found in the sanctuary of Zeus at Olympia are really *anathēmata* ('dedications') consecrated after victories or generic ex-voto offerings, but it is certain that the first votive dedications at Olympia with the express mention of a victory date to the end of the sixth century BCE (consecrated by Pantares and by Akmatidas; Moretti 1957 nos. 151 160), and that the *Olympionikai* consecrated statues of Zeus called *Zanes* in the sanctuary (Paus. 6.21.2). Moreover, a review of the principal collections of archaic sacred dedications will suffice to show the type of objects consecrated: particularly *haltēres* (jumping weights), disks of metal, tripods, cauldrons, statues, etc. (Lazzarini 1976: 109, nos. 827–839, 842–865). An exceptional treasury was the *thēsauros* of the Sicyonians dedicated to the tyrant Myron after his equestrian victory in the thirty-third Olympiad (648 BCE) (Moretti 1957 no. 52). Finally, the fines levied from athletes served to enrich the coffers of the sanctuary. The above-mentioned Theogenes of Thasos, for example, was once made to pay two fines of a talent each to the sanctuary of Olympia for irregularities in the course of the games (Moretti 1957 no. 201).

The dedicated objects contributed to the formation of a considerable reserve of metals in the sanctuaries, usable and convertible to currency to help the city in difficulty, as the ancient sources often demonstrate (Migeotte 1998: 181–185). According to Thucydides, the military and financial situation of the opposing forces at the beginning of the Peloponnesian War confirms that the *chrēmata* ('money'; 'value prizes') of the sanctuaries at Delphi and Olympia were extensive enough to allow the Lacedaemonians to equip a fleet and to pay the *misthos* ('salary') of the sailors (Th. 1.121.3, 1.143.1)—further evidence of how sacred goods were easily convertible to money in emergencies (Musti 1981). In conclusion, the Panhellenic aspect of the games increased the renown and importance of the sanctuary, the size of its treasury, and, in consequence, its reserves of disposable wealth.

The scale of the economic machine represented by the Panhellenic competitions can be fully understood if we think of the auxiliary industries associated with them. The victors commissioned sculptors to create statues and portraits (a privilege at Olympia conferred on victors as a prize; Paus. 5.21.1), bronze-workers to make *anathēmata* ('dedications'), stonecutters to produce honorary or votive inscriptions to be attached to goods dedicated in the sanctuaries; they might entrust poets with the composition of victory poems and celebratory epigrams. In the fifth century BCE, the wealthier victors had their virtues immortalized in the verses of Simonides (who the ancient sources tell us was the first poet to be paid for his poetry; Schol. Aristoph. *Pax* 695; *Suda* s.v. Simonides), of Pindar, and of Bacchylides. The work of artists, artisans, and writers thus received an extraordinary impulse from the *hieronikai* (victors in the sacred Panhellenic games) and the victors in other contests.

THE CLASSICAL ERA (FIFTH CENTURY BCE)

The fifth is par excellence the century of *dēmokratia*, and it is in this light that we must understand certain innovations in the organization of the games. The first difference from archaic practice was the introduction of the system of the liturgies: personal contributions of individual citizens, required in different measure of the richest among the *pentakosiomedimnoi*, that is, all those possessing at least twenty talents, who could not escape this duty imposed in the name of pride in citizenship. The system of liturgies was established first at Athens, but in the following centuries it was introduced gradually at all the democratically governed *poleis*. It allowed the redistribution of private wealth for the use of the whole community, in the name of *isototēs*.

It was in the fifth century, in fact, that Athens saw the introduction of the gymnasiarchy (office of overseer of gymnasium activities), which with the subsequent *agōnothesia* ('game sponsorship'; fourth century) involved heavy expenses for the preparation of the Athenian athletes, divided into tribes, participating in the *lampadēdromiai* ('torch races') of the Great Panathenaea, of the *Hephaisteia*, of *Prometheia*, and of the festivals in honour of Pan (Xen. *Vect.* 4.51–52; and *DNP* 5, 1998, cols. 19–20, *s.v. gumnasiarchia*). Other liturgies were the well-known *chorēgiai*, which financed the equipping of choruses in the dramatic competitions (the Dionysia, the Lenaia, and the Thargelia). The burden of organizing the competitions may be reconstructed by means of certain literary and epigraphic evidence.

According to a fragment attributed to Simonides (Fr. 43 Page 1982; Fr. 155 Bergk 1843), the first prize in the *pentathlon* for *andres* in the Panathenaea at the beginning of the fifth century was 60 amphorae of oil. The financial scope of the organization of the Great Panathenaea is illustrated by a fragmentary catalogue of the prizes awarded to victors at the beginning of the fourth century (*IG* II² 2311; and shear 2003; Pritchard 2013: 96–99). The winners of the individual gymnastic and equestrian contests were given oil amphorae bearing the inscription *tōn Athēnēthen athlōn* ('of the games at Athens'). These prizes ranged from a minimum of one amphora to a maximum of 140. Winners of musical contests were awarded crowns of gold and sums of money between 100 and 1,000 drachmas, while the tribes that were victorious in the Phyrric dance, the *euandria* ('male beauty contest'), the *lampadēdromia* ('torch race'), and the boat race won oxen and sums of money. The oil came from groves sacred to Athena and was probably dispensed by the *tamiai* ('treasurers') of the goddess to the *athlothētai* ('contest sponsors'). It seems that the athletes were able to export the oil won in contests without paying the usual customs duty, a privilege that undoubtedly increased the value of the prizes (Young 1984: 126 n. 16). The amphorae must have contained little less than one *metrētēs* of oil, normally estimated at 39.396 litres (10.4 US gallons; 8.66 UK gallons). It has been calculated that in the fourth century, the *polis* of Athens awarded around 2,000 amphorae of oil to victors at the Panathenaea, for a total of little less than 2,000 *metrētai*. Since an amphora of oil was estimated in the fourth century at approximately 12 drachmas in monetary value, Athens gave out prizes in amphorae of oil to a value totalling about 24,000 drachmas. Wages for a skilled worker or a hoplite soldier were about one drachma per day in the classical period (Thuc. 3.17.4). The money prizes alone, apart from the value of the wreaths, which was not listed in the catalogue, amounted to about 7,000 drachmas, according to the remains of the fragmentary inscription.

The introduction of the liturgies, like the creation of gymnasia open to all free inhabitants, increased participation in competitive events at Athens and then in the rest of the Greek world. But it was especially in the fourth century, after the golden period of radical democracy, that the Greek townsman's lack of interest in public affairs drove him to frequent gymnasia and arenas at an ever-increasing rate. Numerous *koina* of athletes are attested in the Hellenistic era, such as those of the *aleiphomenoi*, habitués of gymnasia who were concerned to assure themselves a provision of oil for the normal course of sporting activities. A different purpose, in the Hellenistic era, impelled the formation of true associations of athletes, intended to support athletic training and to finance travel to the most varied destinations in order to multiply meets and contests (Pleket 1973), although it would be wrong to state that this tendency corresponded to a moral decline in sport. In comparison with the past, and because of changed historical conditions determined by the formation of the Hellenistic kingdoms, there was a decline in the civic sense of belonging to the *polis* and consequently in the communitarian aspect of participation and victory in the contests, along with the emergence of a more markedly individualist spirit in the athletes.

Principal Studies of the Subject

Studies of the economy of the Greek world have appeared under the names of Austin and Vidal-Naquet (1972), Musti (1981), and Migeotte (2002). Systematic studies of the principal problems connected with the economic and social status of athletes have been undertaken from a traditional viewpoint by Gardiner (1930) and Biliński (1959), and from newer perspectives by Crowther (2004), Young (1984), Pleket (1975, 1992, 2001 [2014], 2004, 2005), and Pritchard (2013). On the prizes won in the Panhellenic games and in other athletic competitions, useful references are Patrucco (1972), Buhmann (1972), and Kyle (1996), while for the dedication of prizes in the sanctuaries the findings of Lazzarini (1976) and Jeffery (1990) are fundamental. For the contests and prizes of the Homeric world, see Sheid-Tissinier (1994), and for the civic role of athletic competition, Mann (2001).

REFERENCES

Austin, M. and P. Vidal-Naquet. 1972. *Economies et sociétés en Grèce ancienne.* Paris.

Bergk, T. 1848. *Poetae lyrici Graeci.* Reichenbach, Germany.

Biliński. B. 1959. *L'agonistica sportiva nella Grecia antica: Aspetti sociali e ispirazioni letterarie.* Rome.

Buhmann, H. 1972. *Der Sieg in Olympia und in anderen panhellenischen Spielen.* Munich.

Crowther, N. B. 2004. *Athletika: Studies on the Olympic Games and Greek Athletics.* Hildesheim.

De Polignac, F. 2005. 'Usage de l'écriture dans les sanctuaires du haut archaïsme.' In Ἰδίᾳ καὶ δημοσίᾳ: *Les cadres 'privés' et 'public' de la religion grecque antique. Actes du IXe Colloque du Centre International d'étude de la Religion Grecque Antique tenu à Fribourg du 8 au 10 septembre 2003.* Liège: 13–25.

Gardiner, E. N. 1930. *Athletics of the Ancient World.* Oxford.

Guarducci, M. 1967. *Epigrafia Greca,* vol. I. Rome.

Jeffery, L. H. 1990. *The Local Script of Archaic Greece,* 2nd edn. Oxford.

Kyle, D. G. 1996. 'Gift and Glory: Panathenaic and Other Greek Athletic Prizes.' In *Worshipping Athena: Panathenaia and Parthenon.* 106–136. J. Neil, ed. Madison, WI.

Kyle, D. G. 1997. 'The First Hundred Olympiads: A Process of Decline or Democratization?' *Nikephoros* 10: 53–75.

Lazzarini, M. L. 1976. *Le formule delle dediche votive nella Grecia arcaica.* Rome.

Lévêque, P. 1996. 'Anfizionie, comunità, concorsi e santuari panellenici.' in *I Greci: Storia, cultura, arte, società,* vol. 2: *Una storia greca;* Part I: *Formazione.* 1111–1139. S. Settis, ed. Turin.

Mann, C. 2001. *Athlet und Polis in archaischen und frühklassischen Griechenland.* Göttingen.

Mezger, F. 1880. *Pindars Siegeslieder.* Leipzig.

Migeotte, L. 1998. 'Finances sacrées et finances publiques dans les cités grecques.' In *IX Congreso Español de Estudios Clásicos, Madrid, 27 al 30 de septiembre de 1995,* vol. VI: *Historia y Arqueología.* 181–185. J. F. González Castro, ed. Madrid.

Migeotte, L. 2002. *L'économie des cités grecques de l'archaïsme au Haut-Empire romain.* Paris.

Minon, S. 2007. *Les inscriptions éléennes dialectales (VIe–IIe siècle avant J.Ch.),* vol. I: *Textes.* Geneva.

Moretti, L. 1957. *Olympionikai: I vincitori negli antichi agoni olimpici.* Rome.

Moretti, L. 1992. 'Nuovo supplemento al catalogo degli Olympionikai.' In *Proceedings of an International Symposium on the Olympic Games, 5–9 September 1988.* 119–128. W. Coulson and H. Kyrieleis, eds. Athens.

Musti, D. 1981. *L'economia in Grecia.* Rome.

Page, D. L. 1982. *Further Greek Epigrams.* Cambridge, UK.

Papakonstantinou, Z. 2002. 'Prizes in Early Archaic Greek Sport.' *Nikephoros* 15: 51–67.

Patrucco, R. 1972. *Lo sport nella Grecia antica.* Florence.

Pleket, H. W. 1973. 'Some Aspects of the History of Athletic Guilds.' *ZPE* 10: 197–227.

Pleket, H. W. 1975. 'Games, Prizes, Athletes and Ideology: Some Aspects of the History of Sport in the Greco-Roman World.' *Stadion* 1: 49–89.

Pleket, H. W. 1992. 'The Participants in the Ancient Olympic Games: Social Background and Mentality.' In *Proceedings of an International Symposium on the Olympic Games, 5–9 September 1988.* 147–152. W. Coulson and H. Kyrieleis, eds. Athens.

Pleket, H. W. 2001. 'Zur Soziologie des antiken Sports.' *Nikephoros* 14: 157–212. Repr. and revised with English translation. 'On the Sociology of Ancient Sport.' In *Sport in the Greek and Roman Worlds*, vol. 1: 29–81. T. F. Scanlon, ed. Oxford, 2014.

Pleket, H. W. 2004. 'Einige Betrachtungen zum Thema "Geld und Sport".' *Nikephoros* 17: 77–89.

Pleket, H. W. 2005. 'Athleten im Altertum: Soziale Herkunft und Ideologie.' *Nikephoros* 18: 151–163.

Pritchard, D. M. 2013. *Sport, Democracy and War in Classical Athens.* Cambridge.

Shear, J. L. 2003. 'Prizes from Athens: the List of Panathenaic Prizes and the Sacred Oil.' *ZPE* 142: 87–108.

Sheid-Tissinier, E. 1994. *Les usages du don chez Homère: Vocabulaire et pratique.* Nancy.

West, Martin L. 1992. *Iambi et Elegi Graeci ante Alexandrum Cantati.* Volume 2, 2d ed. Oxford.

Young, D. C. 1984. *The Olympic Myth of Greek Amateur Athletics.* Chicago.

CHAPTER 40

··

'PROFESSIONAL' ORGANIZATIONS IN THE HELLENISTIC WORLD

··

INGOMAR WEILER

Two preliminary remarks: 1. The professional athlete is a person who is able or would be able to earn his living from the material prizes for contests, regardless of his aristocratic, plutocratic, or lower-class origins. Normally the professional athlete is highly specialized and focused on maximizing his efficiency through a strict training programme. 2. The concept of Hellenism in this paper follows the traditional division of Greek history into periods: archaic, classical, Hellenistic. In other words: Hellenism covers the three centuries from Alexander to Actium; it is not understood in Arnold J. Toynbee's sense, for instance, where it designates Greek civilization from Homer to the Byzantine era (Bichler 1983: 33–54).

In his treatise *Thrasbulus sive utrum medicinae sit an gymnasticae hygieine* (*Thrasybulus, or Is Health a Part of Medicine or Gymnastics?*) Galen (33 [870]) writes that the art or the craft of the coaches (*technē tōn gymnastōn*) had appeared shortly before Plato's time and that the calling and the profession of the athletes (*to tōn athlētōn epitēdeuma*) had appeared at that time (Pleket 2001: 182). While in ancient times an athlete could compete and win in various disciplines, in later times everything was separated in agonistic disciplines. Galen says that from then on—i.e. from the close of the 5th century BCE—there emerged a class of specialists in athletics who were unable to do everyday work like ploughing or digging, not even walking any distance, who were therefore unfit for daily life.

Euripides criticized this new class of athletes in a cynical fashion: of the ten thousand evils in the Greek world (*kakōn murioi*) the species of athletes (*athlētōn genos*) is the worst. Slaves of their jaws and servants of their belly, they acquire more wealth than their fathers (*olbon eis huperbolēn patros*). They cannot bear poverty and they are bad soldiers (*Autolycus*, Fr. 282 Nauck; Collard and Cropp 2008: 284–285). A few decades later Plato (*Res Publica* 403c–404b), in his description of the aims of gymnastic training of the *phulakes*, contrasts simple, healthy living and the ascetic style of life required with the dissipated life of professional athletes. Their poor diet, their consumption of alcohol, and their great need of sleep were the reason that they were unfit for war service and harmed the state rather than being useful to it. In this point Plato and Euripides have similar views, as had Xenophanes (Fr. 2 DK) in the late sixth century BCE.

The nub of this ancient critique of civilization is a concept of decadence that in the perspective of sport history separates an idealized early period from the present, which appears decadent. In these ancient texts the idea is expressed that in the social structure of the Greek polis there developed a group of people who defined themselves through sport: the professional athletes (Crowther 2007: 4, 10, 37, 112–113, 165, 167). (In his book *Sport in Ancient Times*, which is conceived as a universal history, Crowther has examined twenty different societies from five continents and established that professionalism in sport is not a phenomenon restricted to Greece. Professionals existed in the Far East—China—and the Middle East, in Mesoamerica, in the Minoan culture, and of course in the Roman world.) It is this group we shall first consider. Here the questions arise: from what date were there professional athletes in Greece, and what do modern historians of sport have to say about them? What ancient authors thought about them we have already seen in the quoted texts of Galen, Euripides, Plato, and Xenophanes. The second topic of my chapter will be the genesis of associations formed by the professional athletes and victors in *agōnes* ('contests').

Professionalism and Class

Older standard works of research by classicists into agonistics and gymnastics, such as those by E. Norman Gardiner and H. A. Harris, see the criteria of decadence in the secularization of everyday life, as proposed by the sophists, together with the social change from the participants at the Panhellenic 'crown games' (the Olympic, Pythian, Isthmian, Nemean, Actian, and Capitolian festivals), a group predominantly aristocratic and plutocratic in character, to a broader group including middle- and lower-class citizens. According to Gardiner and Harris these changes were also supposed to have caused corruption to appear in sport (Golden 1998: 20). One result of this social change, for which the high level of specialization by the athletes is held responsible, was the proliferation of professional athletes in the ancient world. This development, according to M. Golden, implies the thesis 'that archaic Greek sport was marked by the love of competition for its own sake' and that 'the great panhellenic festivals were the crowning glories of this spirit of amateurism because their wellborn winners were satisfied with a wreath as a reward; prizes of value and the predominance of lower class professionals who wanted to win them were later developments' (Golden 1998: 141). Gardiner associated with this developing professionalism the cases of corruption listed by Pausanias (5.21.2–18) in his description of the Zanes, 'decline of the old ideal', the degeneration of the physical type of athlete, even brutality: 'The evil effects of professionalism are worst in those fighting events, boxing, wrestling, and pankration, where the feeling of *aidōs* or honour is most essential.' The *rise of professionalism* is dated in the late classical and early Hellenistic periods, and Gardiner names as the determining factors of this process the specialization in sport, new methods of training and a special diet (Gardiner 1930: 101–105). H. A. Harris, who argues in a similar way, suggests a slightly later date for this change in mentality; he says: 'It is true that even before Greece became part of the Roman empire, athletics had become almost wholly professional and were mounted solely for the entertainment of spectators' (Harris 1972: 184).

A modified interpretation of this partial change in Greek athletics is given by Julius Jüthner. The contestants who wished only to win the victor's wreath were to be 'designated amateurs in the modern sense, but, as they were able to devote themselves entirely to training and exercised no other profession, were professional athletes according the concepts of the ancient world' (Jüthner 1965: 90). Jüthner uses the expression *idiōtēs* ('individual') for those who aspired only to the victor's wreath, and *athlētēs* for professional athletes. He distinguishes between three kinds of athletes: 1) the boy trained physically in the gymnasium; 2) the adult who practises sport for reasons of health and therefore also occasionally takes part in contests; and 3) the professional athlete, the retired athlete, who in later life also earns his living as a *paidotribēs*, *gumnastēs*, or *aleiptēs*. This terminology is thought by Jüthner to have been used from about 400 BCE. This dating and interpretation is supported by the fact that in the pseudo-Platonic dialogue *Alcibiades* (145E) the athletes are designated *technitai* and are listed together with other professions (Pleket 2001: 182).

The two models of decadence proposed by Gardiner and Harris, who operate with the concepts of amateurism versus professionalism, have attracted the attention of several critics. H. W. Pleket has refuted the antithesis of aristocratic amateurism versus professionalism of the lower-class athletes with a number of arguments, and has classed Gardiner's and Harris's theses as idealistic, classicistic positions. Pleket characterizes the classicist ancient historian who 'prefers to work with rigorous schemata in which the development necessarily goes from the pure and high-minded sports mentality of the aristocracy of the archaic Greek period into the base professionalism of the lower-class athletes of post-classical times'. In his discourse, Pleket shows that negative characteristics like vulgarity, brutality, and lack of fairness were already present in pre-Hellenistic agonistics. According to Pleket 'the first true "professional athletes"' came from the ranks of the aristocracy; Theogenes of Thasos with his 1,200 to 1,400 victories represents a prototype of this category (Pleket 2001: 157–171, 160, 176, 180). Nigel Crowther, too, declared Theogenes from the early fifth century BCE 'the first of the so-called professionals'. His athletic success brought him wealth from the organizer of the games and from his home town, where he gained honours, privileges, and financial benefits (Crowther 2007: 141). There was also an 'indirect professionalizing of sport' (Pleket 2001: 167–168, 182–183, 194) with the democratization of the gymnasium, promoted through the public institution for the *ephēboi*. In the Hellenistic era, when armies of mercenaries determined military events, the training of *ephēboi* lost some of its original essential competencies and functions. Alongside the *jeunesse dorée*, poorer, talented youths were now given the chance of being trained in the gymnasium, and hence a springboard to a career as an athlete in top-level sport.

David Young deserves credit for producing a critical analysis of the research into Greek athletics published by John Mahaffy (1839–1919), Percy Gardner (1846–1937), and the sport historians H. A. Harris and above all E. Norman Gardiner, both still often quoted today. Gardiner distinguishes between two types of athletes, the 'amateurs from the Greek Archaic period' with a noble social background, and from the end of the classical period, lower-class professionals. Young's criticism of Gardiner's concept of amateurism shows inconsistency. For Gardiner the term 'genuine or professional amateur', 'by which he means an upper class athlete who trains and makes money from sport', is a representative of the 'sons of the noble families'. On the other hand the author speaks about the 'true professional', the 'lower class athlete who trains and makes money from sport'. From the fifth century 'the excessive prominence given to bodily excellence and athletic success had produced specialization and professionalism' (Gardiner 1910: 4; quoted by Young 1985: 78). Gardiner associates corruption with the professional athletes. ('When money enters into sport, corruption is sure to follow.') Another important outcome of Young's discourse is the demonstration that Gardiner's concepts of 'amateur' and 'professional' stem from the spirit and vocabulary of the nineteenth century, and were transferred to the athletics of the Greeks. In the Victorian era in the United Kingdom there was a contrast between sporting activities of gentlemen, which served purposes of amusement, and those of mechanics, artisans, and labourers, whose primary goal was to earn their living as athletes (Young 1985: 77–81; a more moderate critique of Gardiner than Young's is found in Kyle 1998: 109). This concept of amateurism was taken over by Pierre de Coubertin and later International Olympic Committee presidents for the ideological concept of Olympism (Young 1985: 82–88; see also Scanlon 2002: 40–41 about the 'unhistorical view that an ideal period of amateurism preceded the late Classical and Hellenistic "decline" of professionalism'). The projection of modern ideologies onto the world of Greek sport has caused numerous misunderstandings, as is generally recognized.

Rightly, M. Golden has therefore remarked on the adaptation of this concept that 'ancient Greek amateurism is a nineteenth-century invention, a conspiracy of shoddy scholarship and the desire to exclude working-class athletes from vying with (and perhaps emerging victorious over) their social superiors' (Golden 2004: 140).

Questions of professionalism in the ancient world have also occupied Hugh Lee. In his study (Lee 2003), the anachronistic adaptation of the professionalism–amateurism antithesis to ancient agonistics is rejected. Lee examines the sport-historical genesis of the concept of professionalism. He is able to demonstrate firstly that even before the English 'Victorian' sport historians, the German pioneer and scholar of Greek athletics Johann Heinrich Krause (1800–82) noted the fundamental change in Greek athletics, and also in the way professional athletes and their social origins were seen. Secondly, he noted that the dating of these changes, 'shortly before Plato', corresponds to the chronology that Plato himself and Galen had already proposed. Lee is also able to demonstrate that the concept of professionalism already occurs in the treatise *Dissertation on the Olympick Games* (1749) by the English poet Gilbert West (1703–56), and bears a clearly negative connotation. Tellingly, West invokes Galen (*Thrasybulus* 33).

One of the most recent contributions to this discussion of terminology comes from the pen of Donald G. Kyle. Here too the point of departure is Gardiner's 'Victorian world-view' and his concept of sport and professionalism (excessive popularity, rewards, specialization). Kyle comments:

> A fifth-century shift from an elitism of birth to an elitism of wealth in athletics was possibly aided by increased athletic opportunities at lower level and tribal contest [...]. Social change influenced sport more than sport influenced social change (Kyle 2007: 209).

In the fourth century BCE and especially from the time of Alexander III 'financial professionalism was not far off' (Kyle 2007: 176; see also 240). Kyle adduces convincing arguments against the popular view, also supported by Gardiner, that Hellenism was a decadent period in which the world of sport, too, was prey to decadence. Clearly this does not preclude the idea that significant changes had taken place. The agonistic market with hundreds of festivals, the foundation of a special infrastructure for sports in the civilized Greek world in the period of the Third Colonization after Alexander, the construction of *stadion*, *hippodromos* ('horse-race course'), *gumnasion*, and *palaistra* in many Greek and Hellenized cities, the awarding of material prizes and cash to victors, the mobility of athletes, and the theoretical treatises about training methods, about diet and health are far from being criteria for a decline. They show the high prestige of sporting events and the increase of athletic professionalism. The development of the athletic games towards a more professional manner of conducting sport is occasioned by several further factors. Kyle sees professionalization 'in terms of more athletes spending more time in preparation and competition, and profiting more from victory'. He discusses also the sponsoring of talented young citizens by private benefactors, monarchs, city-states, who finance the local athletic festivals, the training, and the equipment in the gymnasium, and subsidize athletes. There is no doubt that these measures create professionalism in athletics (Kyle 2007: 215, 229–230, 245–246).

In the light of this overview of the history of research, there can be no doubt that alongside athletics continuing in a traditional manner from the fourth century BCE, a group of athletes who saw sport as a life's occupation emancipated themselves and went their own way. These athletes all came from the free bourgeois class. The only new thing about this is that owing to the democratization of sport there had also been a greater inclusion of the middle and lower classes. The assumption by N. Crowther that 'the guild of athletes was a significant factor in assisting athletes, especially those of the lower-class' (Crowther 2004: 27) is doubtless correct, but it is hard to substantiate it with ancient sources. The changes in sport, some of them very significant, cannot be explained by a single cause. In addition to the factors listed above, which contributed to a partial change in athletics in the late classical and pre-Hellenistic ages, two concrete events may be quoted by way of example: an inscription from Ephesus (around 300 BCE) relates that a trainer requested financing of the training for a young *nemeonikēs* (a victor at the Nemean Games) in his polis and travelling expenses for a period spent 'abroad'. About one hundred years later a second epigraphic document tells us about a decision by the people of Miletus that the *paidotribēs* (athletics teacher) employed by the city, who accompanied a talented young athlete to the sacred crown games 'abroad', should find a replacement for the time of his absence from the gymnasium (Pleket 2001: 186). Whether these two epigraphs are sufficient to allow us to assume general support of athletes of low social origin, and what proportion of the participants at the Panhellenic and local contests they represented, are questions which can only be answered by *non liquet* (not clear), in my opinion.

The often-quoted passage from Isocrates (*De bigis* [*On the Team of Horses*] 33), that Alcibiades 'disdained the gymnastic contests, for he knew that some of the athletes were of low birth, inhabitants of petty states, and of mean education', and therefore he favoured horse-breeding (*hippotrophein*) and only participated in the *agōnes hippikoi* ('equestrian events') at Olympia, in my opinion supports the hypothesis that the number of athletes from the lower classes increased from the fourth century BCE on. An indication of this development is given by an inscription found at Olympia (*IvO* 56. 2 CE). The decree provides that during the month of preparatory training that participants in the *Sebasta Italika* in Naples were required to do, the athletes should be paid a *per diem* (*opsōnion*). The regulations provided that 17 to 20 year-old *paides* (boys) and *ageneioi* (youths) as well as the *andres* (men) should receive one drachma from the first to the fifteenth day. For the second half of their training period, the youths then received two and a half drachmae, and the men three. This *per diem* financing, paid to each contestant, facilitated participation at the Isolympic *agōnes* (contests like those in Olympia) in Naples for the poorer athletes (Weiler 2018: 309–321).

Further help for the representatives of the middle and lower classes was available, at least to successful athletes, in the chance to win value prizes and cash in the *agōnes chrēmatitai* (money games). How an indigent athlete could manage to produce top-level performances is a question that we cannot answer, owing to the lack of sources. It is sufficiently well known that from Homeric times victors in competitions could count on receiving valuable prizes. (The word for athlete, *athlētēs*, derives from *athlon*, the 'prize' in a competition.) Though the victors at the sacred Panhellenic contests officially received only a wreath, in their home cities they were given valuable gifts and privileges. In addition, successful athletes received prize money, honours, and privileges in local contests. Alongside the 'big four' (or 'big seven' from the late Hellenistic and Roman periods onwards) an extensive games culture developed from the fourth century BCE, comprising more than five hundred regular sport festivals. The mere contrast between the crown games (*agōnes hieroi, stephanitai, phullinai*) and the contests for value prizes (*agōnes chrēmatitai, thematitai, arguritai, [hēmi-]talantiatioi*) where the victors, and sometimes the place-getters too, could get money and other material rewards, stresses the partly commercial character of the sporting events. A factor in the blossoming of contests may also be seen in the fact that the political independence of the polis in monarchic times caused it to seek a source of income. The attitude that money gives prestige is admittedly not a Hellenistic concept—it is attested in archaic and early classical times in proverbs: *chrēmat'anēr* ('money is the man') says Alcaeus (*Fr.* 360 Lobel and Page; Campbell 1982: 392–393), and Pindar writes 'Money makes the man' (*Isthmia* 2.17).

ATHLETES' ORGANIZATIONS

Athletes devoted their life more or less entirely to training and competition; their desire for financial security, if possible after the end of their career as well (if it was not assured a priori by their elite social status), and for guarantees of the privileges granted, was most likely a dominant motive for the founding of professional organizations. Admittedly it is only towards the end of the Hellenistic period that we find the first references to the existence of guilds (*sunodoi*), which professional athletes had formed. The beginnings and continuing history of these organizations have not been elucidated at all by scholarship. Decades ago, Louis Robert already talked of an *histoire obscure et changeante des associations d'athlètes* ('obscure and changing history of the associations of athletes'; quoted by Pleket 2001: 196), an assessment which, if we leave minor detail out of account, is still valid today for the Hellenistic age. As to the dating of the foundation of the first guilds, Stephen G. Miller, who assumes the beginnings were 'during the time of Alexander', and Ulrich Sinn, who speaks of local societies of athletes 'as early as the fourth century BCE', have proposed plausible hypotheses, but concrete evidence is still lacking (Miller 2004b: 197; Sinn 2004: 130). This assumed date seems plausible because guilds of artisans, *hoi peri ton Dionuson technitai* ('The Dionysiac Artists'), which administratively and organizationally encompassed the categories of musicians, actors, poets, and other artists, are attested in the early Hellenistic age. Franz Poland (1909) gives extensive documentation and analysis of the existence and popularity of these Dionysiac artists' societies from the fourth century BCE onwards. The sources attest that individual guilds of artisans, for instance the Attic *sunodos* ('guild') and the Isthmic and Nemeic *koinon* ('association'), communicated with each other—it seems irrelevant to attempt a distinction between the designation of the societies here. These organizations were concerned with guarantees and the extension of their privileges, the nomination of functionaries, the society's funds and members' subscriptions, and also the foundation or reorganization of new *agōnes mousikoi* and the structure of an umbrella organization and the individual synods. Peter Frisch (1986) has treated the further development of these *sunodoi* in imperial Roman times. Here, too, requests for confirmation of privileges were among the main concerns of the artists' societies.

As to the existence, aims, and structures of the athletes' societies in the Hellenistic age, we have only general ideas and conclusions based on analogy to shed light on these questions, given the shortage of evidence. They are based on a comparison with (1) the Hellenistic artisans' guilds (*sunodoi tōn peri Dionuson technitōn*) which probably for certain periods also included athletes and (2) the 'international' and regional athletic *sunodoi* of imperial times. Here it must be noted that apart from Dionysiac and athletic societies, there also existed a *sunodos tōn apo tēs oikoumenēs hieronikōn kai stephaneitōn*, i.e. a guild in which victors in crown games of both categories, athletic and *agōnes mousikoi* (contests of music, poetry, and performing arts), were gathered (see Poland 1909: 150–152). In my opinion it is possible to reconstruct a speculative picture of the professional organizations in the Hellenistic world. This dual approach and the comparative view promote better understanding of the athletes' guilds in Hellenism, but admittedly it leads only to hypothetical results.

It is even more rewarding to direct our attention to two late Hellenistic documents. The earliest Hellenistic evidence attesting the existence of an athletes' society—according to a suggested dating by Josef Keil it is from the first century BCE—is an inscription from which we gather that a plebiscite of the Ionian Erithreans most probably honoured a successful athlete with a wreath. The honoured athlete had already been given a wreath by the *dēmos* of the Eleans, which means that at least one of the victories was won at Olympia. Other laurel wreaths adorning the stone come from two societies, *hoi apo tēs oikoumenēs athlētai* ('The Worldwide Athletes') and *hoi apo tēs oikoumenēs hieronikai* ('The Worldwide Sacred Game Victors') (Keil 1910: 70–71; Pleket 1973: 199–200; Forbes 1955: 239). Keil wrote in his commentary on 'the earliest certain attestation of athletic guilds [...] in the late Hellenistic inscription at Erythrae':

> 'The honoree was to all appearances an athlete and had received the wreath from the *dēmos Ēleiōn* ['people of Elis'], and probably also the wreaths from *hoi apo tēs oikoumenēs athlētai* and *hoi apo tēs oikoumenēs hieronikai* on the occasion of his participation in the Olympic games. For the history of both the last named organizations, which are to be sharply distinguished, even if their members were necessarily identical in part, our text [...] might be important' (trans. C. A. Forbes/I. Weiler).

The two associations mentioned here have in common that they saw themselves as 'international', as worldwide federations of athletic guilds. The inscription at Erythrae distinguishes between two categories: (1) the athletes' guild and (2) the guild of prominent *hieronikai*, a 'permanent, official elite association of sacred victors', who could be artists or athletes, but in this particular case must be counted among the second category (Pleket 1973: 200). In the programme of contests at Olympia there were no *agōnes mousikoi*, as is well known.

The second important piece of evidence for the existence of a late Hellenistic association is a letter by Marc Antony, which was written immediately before the battle of Actium around

33/32 BCE (*PLond* 137). The triumvir sent a rescript to the Asian *koinon*, which confirmed privileges of the *sunodos tōn apo tēs oikoumenēs hieronikōn kai stephaneitōn* ('Guild of the Worldwide Victors in the Sacred and Crown Games'), which had already been granted at an earlier time on the occasion of a visit to Ephesus (Deininger 1965: 16; Pleket 1973: 200–203). The fact that this ecumenical organization was an athletes' guild is confirmed by the terminology which was customary in agonistic inscriptions of imperial times, above all in the case of Dionysiac artisans' guilds. Marc Antony, who was active in the east of the empire, and whose affinity to agonistics is attested (Plutarch, *Antonius* 33.7), writes (*PLond* 137; Pleket 1973: 200–201; Forbes 1955: 239–240; Miller 2004a no. 209):

> I willingly grant the earlier appeal to me in Ephesos by Markos Antonios Artemidoros, my friend and *aleiptēs* ('trainer'), who was acting in concert with Charopeinos of Ephesos, the eponymous priest of the *synodos* of Worldwide Victors of Sacred Games and Crowns (*synodou tōn apo tēs oikoumenēs hieronikōn kai stephaneitōn*) that I agree to write to you immediately concerning the honours and benefits (*timiōn kai philanthrōpōn*) which were asked of me for exemption from military service (*astrateusia*), from all public duties (*aleitourgia pasē*), and from the billeting of troops (*anepistathmeia*), a truce during the festival (*peri tēn panēgyrin ekecheiria*) of Ephesos, invulnerability and personal security (*asylia*), and the right to wear purple (*porphyra*) and I grant this appeal because of my friendship for Artemidoros and in order to oblige their priest for the glory and advancement of the *synodos*. And now that Artemidoros has appealed to me again to allow them to put up a bronze plaque and to incise on it the benefits written (*peri tōn progegrammenōn philanthrōpōn*) above, I, not wishing to hinder Artemidoros in any respect, have granted that the plaque be put up as he requested. Thus I have written to you concerning these matters. (trans. St. G. Miller/I. Weiler).

This *synodos* is an association of 'sacred victors in athetics, originating from all over the world', as is rightly stressed by the use of *aleiptēs* or 'trainer'. The friend of the triumvir, who was addressed as *aleiptēs*, was thus either a trainer or masseur, in any case a member of the athletic community. This interpretation is further supported by the fact that *aleiptēs* was in Roman times also a 'title for functionaries in athletes' guilds' (Pleket 1973: 200; Jüthner 1909: 6).

Apart from these two decrees from Erythrae and Ephesus, we have no concrete information about professional Hellenistic athletes' organizations. In view of the high prestige that athletics and professional associations in general enjoyed in Greek society, this dire shortage of sources is rather surprising. The situation is quite different with artisans' guilds, which are attested from the fourth century BCE through epigraphic documents. This does not mean, of course, that there were no professional athletes before the first century BCE. Poland already tried to offer an explanation for this difference in the availability of source for artisans' and athletes' guilds and for the late beginning of the widespread, or 'ecumenical', organization of the athletes. The reason for this discrepancy, according to Poland, who speaks of one of the 'most conspicuous phenomena' in his history of Greek societies, may be found in the fact 'that in early times the athletic accomplishments were restricted to the floor of the gymnasium, and only later did the cult of the virtuoso establish itself more independently' (Poland 1909: 147). A further reason might also be the integration of successful athletes in the associations of artisans (*technitai*) and sacred crown game victors (*hieronikai*).

The structure of their guilds, which, similarly to Roman *collegia*, were organized on the pattern of the Greek polis, meant that artists and athletes had an instrument which, 'on an equal basis with cities, rulers and magistrates', could negotiate privileges, honours such as the right to wear purple, and exemptions such as personal protection on journeys and in-demnity from service to the state (Harmon 2002: 75). Details of these forms of organization and their aims are generally known mainly from the *sunodoi* of professional athletes of im-perial times. Membership of the *sunodos tōn apo tēs oikoumenēs hieronikōn kai stephaneitōn* ('Guild of Sacred and Crown Game Victors') naturally had as a prerequisite victory at the crown games. In one single case an ancient source mentions a membership fee of 100 *denarii*. The assumption by N. Crowther that 'the guild of athletes was a significant factor in assisting athletes, especially those of the lower-class' is surely correct, but cannot be confirmed by an-cient sources (Crowther 2004: 27).

After the eastern Greek athletes had joined together to form associations, they presum-ably made their first headquarters at Ephesus (or Sardis), which was moved in the first cen-tury CE to Rome in the course of the Roman tendency to centralize. H. W. Pleket says in this connection: 'we have no ideas as to where the organizations of the ecumenical athletes and the sacred visitors had their home-base in late Hellenistic and early imperial times' (Pleket 1973: 213). With the creation of the *athletarum curia* (Latin for 'Headquarters of the Organized Athletes' [Greek term: *xustikē sunodos*]) in imperial Rome around the middle of the first century BCE the *sunodos xustikē peripolistikē* (full title: *hiera xustikē peripolistikē sunodos tōn peri ton Hēraklea*—'Sacred Guild of Itinerant Athletes Devoted to Herakles') was given an organizational centre about which *PLond* 1178 gives extensive information and which under the philhellenic adoptive emperors was given its own building (*oikēma*) and a *temenos* near the Baths of Trajan in Rome (Remijsen 2015: 240–241). Details about the *nomos* and the function of this centre, which had an archive and probably also a schedule of the athletic festivals, are given by inscriptions and papyri. They present details about the associations, and about their different subdivisions: for instance, (1) the temporary assemblies of athletes from all over the world: the *sumpas xustos* (entire portico), and (2) the 'permanent ecumenical guild of athletes' (*hiera xustikē sunodos*) (Pleket 1973: 207–208). They also discuss the dissolution (*katalusis*) of associations and describe the titles and competence of the *prostatēs* [president], *archōn* [magistrate], *prōtos tōn apo tēs oikoumenēs* [leader of the world members], *xustarchēs* [guild magistrate], and *archiereus* [chief priest]. Some of them were former *hieronikai* (sacred victors) or *periodonikai* (circuit games victors), the hierarchy in the association and the other functionaries—*argurotamias* (treasurer), *grammateus* (sec-retary), *archiatros* (chief doctor), *iatros* (doctor), *gumnastēs* (coach), *aleiptēs* (trainer)—who are responsible for the administration.

For the history of the administrative centre under the patronage of the emperors in Rome and of the imperial athletic associations, there are some noteworthy publications by M. L. Caldelli (1992), C. A. Forbes (1955), H. W. Pleket (1973; 1975; 2001; 2008), Remijsen (2015), and W. C. West (1990). Frequently the *sunodoi* then added the name of the emperor who had fostered the association to their title. In various cities of the Roman empire there existed local *sunodoi*, sometimes with the epithet *peripolistikē* ('itinerant') or *olumpikē* ('Olympic'), as was the case in Ephesus, Aphrodisias, Tralles, Smyrna, Thyatira, Miletus, Hierapolis, and Alexandria. Ulrich Sinn has put up the hypothesis that a complex of buildings also existed at Olympia, south of the Leonidaion, which was probably built by one of Nero's and Domitian's teams of builders, and whose function was connected with the organized profes-sional athletes (Forbes 1955; Pleket 1973: 197–227; Caldelli 1992: 75–87; Sinn 1998; 2004: 130–131, 241). Possibly they were also subsidiary associations cooperating with an 'umbrella organization' (Golden 2004: 73). The source material for all these institutionalized athletes' associations begins with Augustus, who extended the privileges for athletes (Suetonius, *Augustus* 45.3), and extends as far as Constantine I. To draw conclusions from it about the professional organizations in the Hellenistic world remains historical speculation, however. Nevertheless it throws light on the situation of the guilds in the centuries before the imperial era.

The central concern of the athletes, pursued by the imperial associations, was the granting and maintaining of privileges, exemptions, and honours by state and private authorities. As is well known, the tradition of these privileges goes back to the sixth century BCE. Apart from the honours at the site of the festival, the victors' statues and coins, and the *epinikia* ('victory odes'), the victor could be given numerous privileges in his home city which provided a festive reception for its successful athlete—the privileges could be cash, free meals at the prytaneion (*sitēsis*), a place of honour at festivals and *agōnes* (*prohedria*), and exemption from taxes (*ateleia*). In addition, in the Hellenistic and Roman ages some cities gave successful athletes an honorary citizenship (*politeia*, *proxenia*) and honorary membership in the *boulē* ('assembly') (Pleket 2001: 186–190; Buhmann 1975: 111–114). It was of course in the interests of the athletes' guilds to preserve these privileges and receive guarantees to this effect from the authorities. This greed for 'glory and garlands, prizes and plaudits' (Forbes 1955: 250) on the part of the athletes' representatives was not in any way diminished during imperial Roman times. On the contrary, it seems to have increased. This emerges from the decrees of the *sunodoi tōn apo tēs oikoumenēs hieronikōn kai stephaneitōn* ('Guild of the Worldwide Victors in the Sacred and Crown Games') and those of the *tōn peri Dionyson technitōn* ('Dionysiac artists'). Thus it is not surprising that Diocletian and Maximian set limits to the sometimes inappropriate and excessive demands. The *Codex Iustinianus* (10.54) says:

> It is the custom to exempt from civil duties those athletes who are proved to have won not less than three crowns in formal contests during their entire lives (one of which must have been obtained at Rome, or in ancient Greece), and who have not been defeated, and deprived of their crowns by their competitors.

The giving of privileges to athletes, criticized by Greek intellectuals, did not stop in Hellenistic times, and the athletes formed guilds to preserve this elite status—an assumption that rings true all the more as ancient historians have painted a clear picture of the foundation and activities of Greek associations in other segments of social and economic life. The athletes' guilds attested only in the later Hellenistic era must be seen in a social context which is associated with the changes in political life as a whole in the Greek *poleis* from the fourth century BCE. Permanent or temporary associations of persons with particular cultural or economic interests and defined aims—a universal sociological phenomenon—naturally also existed in ancient Greece. The aims pursued by these associations and the recruiting of their members changed considerably in the course of the centuries, changes which corresponded and correlated with the social changes of the citizenry. In contrast to the traditional social organizations and associations of persons like the *phulai*, *phratriai*, and *dēmoi*, or the political clubs like those of the oligarchs of the fifth century BCE, forms of associations developed from the fourth century BCE which brought together people according to age (*neoi*, *ephēboi*), religious or cult activities (*orgeōnes*, *thiasoi*, *eranoi*), or vocational categories like shipowners, merchants, and artisans (*technitai*). In a similar way, and also associated with the gymnasia, local *sunodoi* were formed, dedicated to Herakles, one of the patrons of this educational institution.

One of the special forms that arose in the Hellenistic age was constituted by the members of the Ptolemaic gymnasium, the so-called *hoi ek tou gumnasiou* ('Those from the Gymnasium'). This form of organization, which seems comparable to the modern associations of alumni, was concerned with the honouring of teachers and the commemoration of dead comrades. Amongst the functions of these associations was also the financial support of the gymnasium, as well as endowments, and ultimately also the exercise of military functions. Therefore they were given important privileges by rulers (Habermann 2004: 339–340; Rostovtzeff 1955–1956: 2, 840).

Most of the Hellenistic organizations were no longer political corporations; rather, they primarily served private interests. They were able to take up contact with the polis or directly with the monarch and wealthy benefactors. This development has been described by M. Rostovtzeff, following Max Weber's sociological categories with a gradual transition from *homo politicus* to *homo oeconomicus* and *homo technicus* (Rostovtzeff 1955–1956: I. 330, II. 854; about the status and function of imperial professional associations which were obviously similar to the Hellenistic ones, see Pleket 2008: 535–544). As specialization increased, individual merchants and business people organized themselves into professional associations. Among the earliest societies to be founded were, tellingly, the merchants and travelling dealers (*nauklēroi, emporoi*) (Poland 1909: 106; see also Pleket 2008: 533–544), who had to deal with the dangers of travel, in a similar way to the athletes. Other professional groups also organized themselves into guilds, like the weavers, dyers, fullers, or the gold- and silversmiths. The Roman equivalents were the *collegia* and *corporationes*, which were given a legal framework in the *tabulae duodecim* (8.27); allegedly these had been taken over from a law of Solon (*sed haec lex videtur ex lege Solonis translata esse*), an assertion for which there is no evidence. A constant concern of these professional associations was to request *privilegia et honores* from state authorities. The professional athletes' associations must also be seen in the socio-historical and economic-historical context briefly sketched here. The term *sunodos* was one used mainly in the context of private associations and hardly ever in a political sense.

It seems important to me to make a closing comment concerning the fundamental discussion in Classical Studies, namely the almost unending controversy over terminology between modernists and minimalists. It has to do with the use without comment of modern concepts like money, work, trade, but also sport, training, professionalism/amateurism, or, as in the concrete case of 'professional organizations' (German *Berufsvereine*), for similar phenomena in earlier, above all, pre-industrial societies (see Pleket 2008: 533–544). Modern concepts and vocabulary cannot be transferred to earlier historical periods, according to the minimalists. This rigorous point of view, evidenced particularly by Moses I. Finley's attitude to M. I. Rostovtzeff's terminology, has gained more acceptance in German than in Anglo-American classics, and I think it is worth considering. It therefore seems inevitable in the use of modern concepts that we must adduce the necessary reservations, as in the case of adapting the professionalism/amateurism antitheses, where reference was made to the ideology of the nineteenth century. Only in this way can new perceptions and insights be gained productively by investigation. Otherwise, in the final analysis it would mean that one could write only in Ancient Greek or Latin about contests and athletics in the ancient world.

REFERENCES

Bichler, R. 1983. 'Hellenismus': Geschichte und Problematik eines Epochenbegriffs. Darmstadt.

Buhmann, H. 1975. Der Sieg in Olympia und in den anderen panhellenischen Spielen. 2nd edn. Munich.

Caldelli, M. L. 1992. 'Curia athletarum, iera xystike synodos e organizzazione delle terme a Roma.' ZPE 93: 75–87.

Campbell, D. A., ed. and trans. 1982. Greek Lyric I. Sappho and Alcaeus. Cambridge, MA and London.

Collard, C. and M. Cropp, eds. 2008. Euripides Fragments. Aegeus-Meleager. Cambridge, MA and London.

Crowther, N. B. 2004. 'Athlete and State: Qualifying for the Olympic Games in Ancient Greece.' In Athletika: Studies on the Olympic Games and Greek Athletics. 23–33 Hildesheim.

Crowther, N. B. 2007. Sport in Ancient Times. Westport.

Deininger, J. 1965. Die Provinziallandtage der römischen Kaiserzeit von Augustus bis zum Ende des dritten Jahrhunderts. Munich.

Forbes, C. A. 1955. 'Ancient Athletic Guilds.' Classical Philology 50: 238–252.

Frisch, P. 1986. Zehn agonistische Papyri. Opladen.

Gardiner, E. N. 1910. Greek Athletic Sports and Festivals. London.

Gardiner, E. N. 1930. Athletics in the Ancient World. Oxford.

Golden, M. 1998. Sport and Society in Ancient Greece. Cambridge.

Golden, M. 2004. Sport in the Ancient World from A to Z. London.

Habermann, W. 2004. 'Gymnasien im ptolemäischen Ägypten—eine Skizze.' In Das hellenistische Gymnasion. 335–348. D. Kah and P. Scholz, eds. Berlin.

Harmon, R. 2002. 'Technitai.' In Der Neue Pauly 12.1: 74–75.

Harris, H. A. 1972. Sports in Greece and Rome. London.

IvO = Dittenberger, W. and K. Purgold. 1896. Die Inscriften von Olympia. Berlin.

Jüthner, J. 1909. Philostratos: Über Gymnastik. Leipzig.

Jüthner, J. 1965. Die athletischen Leibesübungen der Griechen, vol. 1. F. Brein, ed. Vienna.

Keil, J. 1910. 'Forschungen in der Erythraia.' JDAI 13: 70–71.

Kyle, D. G. 1998. 'Games, Prizes, and Athletes in Greek Sport: Patterns and Perspectives (1975–1997).' CB 74.2: 103–127.

Kyle, D. G. 2007. Sport and Spectacle in the Ancient World. Malden, MA.

Lee, H. M. 2003. 'Galen, Johann Heinrich Krause, and the Olympic Myth of Greek Amateur Athletics.' Stadion 29: 11–20.

Miller, S. G. 2004a. Ancient Greek Athletics. New Haven.

Miller, S. G. 2004b. Aretē: Ancient Writers, Papyri, and Inscriptions on the History and Ideals of Greek Athletics and Games. 3rd edn. Berkeley.

Pleket, H. W. 1973. 'Some Aspects of the History of Ancient Athletic Guilds.' ZPE 10: 197–227.

Pleket, H. W. 1975. 'Games, Prizes, Athletes and Ideology.' Stadion [=Arena] 1: 49–89.

Pleket, H. W. 2001. 'Zur Soziologie des antiken Sports.' Nikephoros 14: 157–212. Repr. and revised with English translation 'On the Sociology of Ancient Sport.' In Sport in the Greek and Roman Worlds, vol. 1: 29–81. T. F. Scanlon, ed. Oxford, 2014.

Pleket, H. W. 2008. 'Berufsvereine im kaiserzeitlichen Kleinasien: Geselligkeit oder Zünfte?' In Antike Lebenswelten. Konstanz—Wandel—Wirkungsmacht. 533–544. P. Mauritsch, W. Petermandl, and R. Rollinger, eds. Wiesbaden.

Poland, F. 1909. Geschichte des griechischen Vereinswesens. Leipzig.

Remijsen, S. 2015. *The End of Greek Athletics in Late Antiquity*. Cambridge, UK.

Rostovtzeff, M. 1955–1956. *Gesellschafts- und Wirtschaftsgeschichte der hellenistischen Welt*, vols. I–III. Tübingen.

Scanlon, T. F. 2002. *Eros and Greek Athletics*. New York.

Sinn, U. 1998. 'Olympia und die Curia Athletarum in Rom.' *Stadion* 24.1: 129–135.

Sinn, U. 2004. *Das antike Olympia: Götter, Spiel und Kunst*. Munich.

Weiler, I. 2018. Überlegungen zum opsonion bei den Sebasta in Neapel. In *Emas non quod opus est, sed quod necesse est. Beiträge zur Wirtschafts-, Sozial-, Rezeptions- und Wissenschaftsgeschichte der Antike*. 309–321. K. Ruffing and K. Droß-Krüpe, eds. Wiesbaden.

West, W. C. 1990. 'M. Oulpios Domestikos and the Athletic Synod at Ephesus.' *AHB* 4: 84–89.

Young, D. C. 1985. *The Olympic Myth of Greek Amateur Athletes*. Chicago.

CHAPTER 41

....

LUDI AND *FACTIONES* AS ORGANIZATIONS OF PERFORMERS

....

STEVEN L. TUCK

THE major performers in Roman spectacle entertainments—charioteers, animal hunters, and gladiators—were not independent contractors, but members of organizations of performers. These organizations were in many cases far-reaching in their social, political, and economic activities and influences. In some cases, they stretched across the empire and offered an identity not only to their performers, but to the fans who followed them. Given the ubiquity of spectacular entertainments, these organizations came to be integral parts of the Roman world. Their links to local as well as imperial political life are without doubt. Their complex economic roles also extended beyond the narrow confines of their spectacles and into a range of activities. This chapter will paint a portrait of these groups. Given the disparate surviving evidence and their varying importance, that portrait for some, such as the animal hunters, is necessarily less detailed and possibly an impressionist image. For the chariot-racing factions, the portrait is more akin to a painting by Lucien Freud, unromantic and hyper-realist.

The first difficulty in study and analysis of the organizations is one of vocabulary and the related issue of comparability among them: how parallel were these groups of performers? Both *venator* and *bestiarius* are found in the sources in reference to a hunter of animals at spectacles. The precise distinction between them is unclear, but by convention we refer to *venatores* when meaning the animal hunters and *bestiarii* as their assistants, support staff, or even those who were thrown to the beasts as punishment. For gladiators' organizations, two terms were used, each with their own ambiguities. Local groups of gladiators are referred to in the sources as *familiae*, while the city of Rome was dominated by the four large *ludi*, schools for gladiators. The term *ludus* therefore can refer to games, to the building complex that housed the gladiators in Rome, and to the organization. For the chariot-racing associations, the term *factiones* is used universally for the four major collectives. The assumption implicit in most scholarship that they are equivalent to the *ludi* and the groups of *venatores* seems imprecise; the *factiones* were far more complex institutions, broader in their reach. There seem, however, to be notable parallels in the personnel of these organizations that deserve brief mention. All of the performers share commonalities of overwhelmingly lower-class and non-citizen status. Although elite Romans ran the organizations through much of the period and some even appeared as performers, these are a demonstrable minority. There is also a common potential trajectory of advancement, money, and celebrity as motivators for performers, whether citizen or non-citizen. Finally, it is clear that the organizations shared the common role to recruit, train, and provide performers for games.

A famous passage in a letter by Seneca (*Letters* 7) gives the sequence of events in a day's games in the arena, from the *venationes*, animal hunts, to prisoner executions, and then moving to the main event, gladiatorial combat. This might serve as a structure to our considerations as we start with the animal hunters, the first event in a day of games in the arena.

VENATORES: ANIMAL HUNTERS OF SPECTACLE

We know almost nothing about the individual performers who hunted animals professionally in the Roman world. Lacking the celebrity status of top gladiators or the prize money of successful charioteers, they are not the typical subjects of moralistic essays, satire, or panegyric. The best evidence for the individuals and organizations of professional animal hunters, the *venatores*, is found in Roman Africa. An example is the third century mosaic discovered in 1966 at the site of Smirat (Fig. 41.1), which portrays a specific hunting show; it features a long inscription documenting the action in the arena, the dialogue between the spectators and the patron of the games, Magerius, and his act of extraordinary beneficence in providing a bonus to the *venatores* (Dunbabin 1978: 65–70).

In addition to the inscription, the mosaic depicts a central figure holding a tray with bags of money, the deities Diana and Bacchus, Magerius himself, and four *venatores* fighting four leopards. The *venatores* are each named as individuals, but all have what we can conclude are stage names: Bullarius, Hilarinus, Mamertinus, and Spittara. For our purposes the key importance of the mosaic is found in the central inscription, which names the performers as part of a group called the Telegenii; the dialogue makes clear they are the recipients of the generous bonus Magerius provides to the *venatores*. These hunters are not named as individual recipients: the troupe receives the money collectively (Bomgardner 2009). The Telegenii are the best understood of the organized *venatores*, documented in inscriptions across Roman North Africa. This professional guild of animal hunters was organized as a *sodalitas venatorum*—i.e. a formal association of this particular kind of performer. As was true for other professional guilds, it had a patron deity and symbol; the Magerius mosaic shows both with the images of Diana and Bacchus, divinities notable for their control of animals, and the crescent symbol. The extent of activities of these sodalities is uncertain. They definitely recruited, trained, named, and supplied animal hunters to the games as stipulated in contracts between the group and *editores* of various games. It seems certain that they also served a social function, operating to provide appropriate burial rites for their *venatores*. There were at least five prominent *sodalitates venatorum* known for Roman Africa.

A mosaic from El Djem (Fig. 41.2) shows representatives or personifications of such groups reclining at a banquet prior to a set of games in the presence of the five bulls to be killed in the arena the next day. Each of the figures bears or wears the iconography of a *sodalitas*; on

FIGURE 41.1. Magerius mosaic from Smirat, Tunisia. Mid third century CE. Gilles Mermet/ Art Resource, NY.

the far right is the representative of the Telegenii, holding a crescent-moon tipped staff like the one in the Magerius mosaic, while others wield an ivy leaf and a millet stalk (possibly for the Taurisci and Leontii corporations). Symbols are also visible on the rear flank of the cattle, branded or tattooed marks that may be linked to each sodality. There is additional evidence that at least the Telegenii and the Leontii were involved in other activities: olive oil amphorae marked with the symbol of the Telegenii and mosaics with shipping imagery associated with ancient Sullecthum suggest that these two groups at least participated in the profitable trade that supplied African commodities to other parts of the Roman world (Bomgardner 2009; Beschaouch 1977). One valuable commodity to which they are not directly linked would be the wild animals for spectacles. It is possible that the associations arranged for the beasts as well as the *venatores*; the best evidence for this is found in the distinctive marks on each of the bulls in the banquet mosaic that may indicate *sodalitas* property. If the hunting corporations did not deal in beasts, other groups must have filled that void, as the references in literature to hunters, handlers, and shippers who captured and transported animals for the games make clear (Kyle 2007: 325). While the artistic representations and epigraphical sources, notably announcements of games from Pompeii (Cooley and Cooley 2004: 48–50), demonstrate that there was tremendous variety and specialization among *venatores*, there is no evidence of any hierarchy of hunters as there was for gladiators.

One parallel to imperial gladiatorial schools is the Ludus Matutinus in Rome. Known from a few inscriptions (*CIL* 6.352, 10171–3, 14.2922; *IG* 14.1330) and apparently named for the fact that *venationes* occurred in the morning (*matutinus*) of a day of games, this imperial

FIGURE 41.2. Mosaic from El Djem; five hunting sodalities at banquet. Wikimedia Commons. CCA SA 3.0 License. Photo: Pascal Radigue.

school was probably located close to the Colosseum and was one of the four gladiatorial training schools in Rome established under Domitian. Details of the *venatores'* training here are not known, but that the hunters were cared for and that the treatment was considered valuable is suggested by inscriptions honouring their *medicus* or physician; a similar inscription was found at Corinth having been dedicated by *venatores* there, reinforcing the conclusion that regional schools for *venatores* existed across the Roman world (*CIL* 6.10171–3; *IG* 4.365; Wiedemann 1992: 117). On some occasions, the *venatores* were freed for great achievements in the arena just as gladiators were, suggesting strong parallels in how they were viewed as performers (Fagan 2011: 126–127). In fact, however, gladiatorial schools and families are far better documented and understood.

GLADIATORS

Like the animal hunters in the arena, gladiators were armed and armoured professional entertainers facing not certain death, but the real possibility of it in spectacular
performances. They often represented significant investments, having been recruited,
trained, armed, and prepared to fight against other gladiators by their *ludi*, the gladiatorial
schools. These schools date back to the late Roman republic and are best documented in
Campania, notably at Capua where Spartacus was trained and from where he started his
revolt in 73 BCE. His school belonged to a man named Lentulus Batiatus, the earliest *lanista*,
owner and operator of a gladiatorial school, whose name comes down to us from antiquity
(Plutarch, *Crassus* 8; Livy, *Summaries* 95).

LOCAL SCHOOLS AND ORGANIZATIONS

Some of the ancient textual references to gladiatorial schools are very brief asides,
establishing, at most, the practice and its lucrative nature. Atticus, for example, bought a
troupe of gladiators in 56 BCE and recouped his investment after just two matches (Cicero,
Letters to Atticus 4.49.2; 8.2). Local gladiatorial schools provide our best surviving evidence
for the names of *lanistae*, the organization of schools, the names of the gladiators in them,
the processes by which they came to perform in local games, and the careers and deaths of
gladiators. Pompeii and Ephesus have given us the best material on these local matters. At
Pompeii the *edicta munerum*, the painted announcements of upcoming games found on the
walls of buildings, provide the names of three *lanistae*. Notably they refer to their gladiators
as a *familia*, suggesting not only an organizing principle, but probably the social role they
fulfilled. The heads of these *familiae* at Pompeii are Numerius Festinus Ampliatus, Marcus
Mesonius, and Pomponius Faustinus (Jacobelli 2003: 45–46). The announcements generally call for ten pairs of gladiators per day of games, which we should be able to take as a
minimum size for the *familia*, although it probably represents only a portion of the group,
considering the inevitability of injuries and deaths at any given time.

The graffiti and *edicta* at Pompeii also provide evidence that each *familia* contained a
range of gladiatorial types; there is no indication that individual schools specialized in a
specific armature. Rather, each trained gladiators in certain standard categories of armament and offered a variety of these to the officials paying for the games. Only one trainer
is documented in these *dipinti* and graffiti: Telephus is designated a *summa rudis*, meaning
that he earned the wooden sword of a freed gladiator and now works as an instructor (*CIL*
4.7991). The listing of gladiatorial types found at Pompeii does not convey the organization or ranking system of a *familia gladiatoria*. For that, an inscription from Centumcellae
provides a more complete picture (*CIL* 6.631). This inscription, dated to 177 CE and so contemporary with the *Senatus Consultum de Pretiis Gladiatorum Minuendis* discussed in the
next section, may in fact document the structure of a *familia* under imperial control. The
two caretakers (*curatores*) were Marcus Aurelius Hilarus, a freedman of the emperor Marcus
Aurelius, and Coelius Magnus, who was in charge of the practice ground (*cryptarius*). They

oversaw a group of thirty-two gladiators and other staff of various categories and ranks, divided into four groups of ten, each labelled a *decurion*. In addition to the gladiators, who range from three novice recruits to eight trained beginning performers to eleven veterans, there is an armourer (*manicarius*), a masseur (*unctor*), and two non-combatants.

IMPERIAL SCHOOLS AND ORGANIZATIONS

The *edicta munerum* at Pompeii point to the existence of groups of imperial gladiators, perhaps in their own schools in the first century CE: the Iuliani and Neroniani, the former founded by Julius Caesar at Capua (*CIL* 4.1189–1191, 7987). Beyond the names nothing is known of their size, organization, or personnel. The best-documented gladiatorial *ludi* were the imperial ones in Rome, thought to have held about 1,000 gladiators in the late first century (Teyssier 2009: 399). Domitian founded, or perhaps more accurately re-founded in new facilities, four schools: in addition to the Ludus Matutinus discussed above, these were the Ludus Dacicus, the Ludus Gallicus, and the Ludus Magnus. The former were probably named for the ethnic origins of the prisoners of war who made up the core of trainees when they were founded. The last, the 'great' school, was located immediately adjacent to the Colosseum in Rome and has been the focus of several excavations. The remains of the structure reveal few details about the training or organization of the school; the gladiators lived in small cells, built in at least two storeys around a central practice arena where they trained, watched and assessed by as many as 3,000 peers and select spectators. Inscriptions indicate that the gladiators were tended by physicians (*medici*) and taught by specialist instructors, *doctores* and *magistri*, some of whom were themselves former gladiators, as attested at Pompeii and other communities across the Roman world (Carter 1999).

Other specialists such as armourers supported the performers, but little is known of them other than their names. An epitaph from Rome (*CIL* 6.10164) records the name of Marcus Ulpius Callistus, freedman of the emperor Trajan, who was in charge of the *armamentarium* of the Ludus Magnus. He was wealthy enough to have his own extensive household; the burial inscription makes provisions for his freedmen and freedwomen. Other staff positions were necessary but details are few. The Ludus Magnus employed a *dispensator* and a *cursor*, who may have been an accountant and a message runner, respectively (*CIL* 6.10165–10166). Reliefs depicting the procession or *pompa* prior to a set of gladiatorial games show assistants or attendants carrying gladiatorial armour into the arena. Of these assistants, including the referees of the bouts, those who carried away the bodies of the injured and deceased, and so forth, none are known by name or job title. Based on the inscriptions, the size of a *familia gladiatoria* is estimated at twenty-four trained gladiators, twelve in training, five instructors, five kitchen staff, three armourers, three physicians and masseurs, and a *lanista* with a staff of seven for an average of sixty persons per *familia* (Teyssier 2009: 435, 439).

Placement of the imperial *ludi* in the centre of the city suggests that gladiators might have had more personal freedom and been more integrated into their communities than might be imagined from their servile status. Some active gladiators were even married and had families, more among the veterans and freedmen (*CIL* 12.3323, 3327, 5836 in Futrell 2006: 152). These *ludi* were not managed by the entrepreneurial *lanistae* known from Campania, but by imperial *procuratores* of equestrian rank.

The internal organization of the schools must be extrapolated largely from epigraphical sources. Graffiti and the epitaphs of gladiators reveal that someone, probably an official in each *ludus*, was keeping careful track of their number of fights, wins, losses, and times granted *missio*, appeals to mercy. Along with these are indicators of rank that are reinforced by the *Senatus Consultum de Pretiis Gladiatorum Minuendis* (*CIL* 2.6278), which applied cost controls on gladiators beginning in 177 CE. From these sources it is clear that gladiators of whatever armament category in the *ludi* were structured in a hierarchy named after the *palus*, the heavy vertical post set in the ground that was the foundation of sword training. This ranking system developed by the later first century CE (*CIL* 6.10189) and may be associated with the *ludi* founded by Domitian. Separated by armature type, all gladiators above the level of *tiro*, the trained beginner who had not yet fought in the arena, were divided into five ranks: *primus palus* at the top, followed by *secundus palus* and so on. The process of assigning rank is not spelled out, although years of experience, win record, number of bouts, and popularity with fans were likely part of the calculation. The *palus* hierarchy was the basis for the cost charged to the patron of a set of games by the *lanista* or procurator of the *ludus*; the higher the rank, the more expensive the gladiator would be (Carter 2003: 87). The ranks seem to cross armature categories so that, for example, a *primus palus secutor* would cost the same as a *primus palus essedarius*. There seems to be no overarching authority assigning ranks. Rather, the market might serve as a check on the inclination of a *familia* to inflate a particular gladiator's rank, as that would risk pricing him out of reach of a patron who might go with a cheaper gladiator or even to a competing *ludus* for his performers. The *palus* ranking system may have been empire-wide, judging by epigraphical evidence from Aphrodisias, Cyzicus, and several other communities in Asia Minor (Carter 2003: 90). The *palus* system had a practical impact on training and housing; there are some indications that gladiators were housed hierarchically by rank as well as type within the *ludus* (Seneca, *Natural Questions* 7.31.3; Juvenal, *Satire* 6.07–13; Dio Cassius 73.22.2). Friendship, or at least collegiality, seems to have developed among the gladiators. An epitaph (*CIL* 6.10169) of a *retiarius* from the Ludus Magnus was dedicated by a *murmillo* from the same school, who refers to the deceased as his 'co-victor' (*convictor*). What is missing from the evidence of the *palus* system is any link to the origins of the gladiators. There is no distinction between gladiators who came to the *ludus* as prisoners of war, condemned criminals, or free volunteers (*auctorati*). It seems that the *ludus* and *palus* system represented a true meritocracy, where, no matter their origins, each gladiator had the chance to survive and excel.

CHARIOTEERS AND THEIR *FACTIONES*

The *factiones* of chariot-racing are the most important of these performer organizations, owing to their widespread fan base, the vast organization needed to raise horses and recruit and train drivers and, most specifically, their political connections which made them influential institutions in the later Roman world. The fanatical appreciation of circus factions had its origins in a variety of factors. First, the fact that there were only four factions during almost all of Roman history meant that the populace divided their fan loyalties among a relatively small number of options, as opposed to, for example, the countless choices among modern soccer or football teams. In addition, the circus itself was the largest venue for spectacular performance in a Roman city: more members of the community thus had direct exposure to the races than to *venationes* or gladiatorial matches.

From the middle republic until the sixth century CE, there were four major *factiones*, the professional stables and charioteer organizations of circus racing. These companies eventually worked under the emperor's patronage, supplying teams to the *editores* giving games and collecting revenue from the prize money. Each faction was associated with the colour worn by its charioteers: white for the Albata, red for the Russata, blue for the Veneta, and green for the Prasina. Domitian's two new *factiones* were identified by purple for the Purpurea and gold for the Aurata (Suetonius, *Domitian* 7; Dio Cassius 67.4.4).

Indicative of the substantial organization of the *factiones* were the elaborate stable complexes (*stabulae*) that each maintained near the major circuses in larger communities. The best evidence for the structure and staffing of a faction is provided by an inscription which details the jobs and titles for a stable of the Red faction at Rome (*CIL* 6.10046; *ILS* 5313):

> The association for four-horse chariot racing (*familia quadrigaria*) of Titus Ateius Capito of the Reds, for which Chrestus was treasurer, distributed oil to the decurions who are inscribed below: ... Docimus the overseer (*vilicus*), Chrestus the *conditor*, Epaphrus the *sellarius*, Menander the charioteer, Apollonius the charioteer (*agitator*), Cerdo the charioteer, Liccaeus the charioteer, Helletus the assistant *conditor*, ..., Hyllus the *medicus*, Anterotes the *tentor*, Antiochus the blacksmith (*sutor*), Panaces the *tentor*, ..., Hilarius the charioteer (*aurigarius*), Nicander the charioteer, Epigonus the charioteer, Alexander the charioteer, Nicephorus the *sparsor*, Alexion the *morator* ... the messenger (*viator*).

Capito is the faction master and is clearly a Roman citizen, probably related to the slightly earlier senator Gaius Ateius Capito. The *conditor* Chrestus probably oversaw stable operations with his assistant, a *succonditor*. *Sellarius* may be an error for *cellarius*, a person in charge of a storeroom or *cella*. The *tentor* operated the mechanism of the starting gates; one was probably needed for each team the faction ran in a race. The *morator* ('delayer') held the horses prior to and after the race. The *sparsor* ('sprinkler') is believed by some to have thrown water at the racing horses to cool them down. This seems most unlikely given the difficulty of such an act, coupled with the expected result of startling the horses. Instead I associate him with a figure seen in some circus images who seems to be sprinkling water on the track itself to cut the dust stirred up in the race, particularly on the turns. The *hortator* ('encourager') is probably the figure seen on horseback in circus scenes either preceding or following the team, although whether he is urging on the driver or the team and how he did so is unknown. The eight charioteers might represent the number needed for a day's racing or a fraction of that. If these are *decuriones* as the inscription says, they might be ten per cent of the personnel of the *stabula*, indicating a total staffing of 240 or 250. And this was only one stable of one faction in Rome. The total personnel employed by the *factiones* in Rome alone was probably in the thousands. Notably missing from among the jobs listed are trainers or coaches of the horses or charioteers, along with stable attendants and others who maintained or guarded the facilities, as well as a variety of low-status positions that one would expect in a stable. Finally, the names are almost all ethnically Greek; likewise, the single names indicating non-Roman citizens predominate among the personnel of the stable (Dodge 2010: 294–295). The arguably elite status of Titus Ateius Capito is not unusual for the first century as a faction master, but by the third century it would have been. By then the *domini* of the factions seem to have been largely former charioteers rather than high-status Roman citizens, although whether this change resulted from the higher merit given to the lower classes or to legislation forbidding the upper from such positions is debated (Cameron 1976: 7). Either way, the result was tighter and more direct imperial control of the *factiones* and their resources by the fourth century. By the sixth century the factions had been condensed to two, the Greens and Blues, who operated as massive, government-sponsored corporations responsible for every element of public spectacular entertainment (Cameron 1976: 15).

These corporations, however, attracted powerful and intense followings among the people of the Roman world. The abundant curse tablets or *defixiones*, through which fans attempted to summon cosmic forces to bind and hurt specific competitors of hated *factiones*, provide evidence that the names of charioteers and horses were well known and perhaps known in advance for major races (Gager 1990; Futrell 2006: 204). It is clear, however, that the focus of attention was not on the personnel, but on the *factio* itself. Romans were fans or bitter enemies of the faction while the charioteers could move from faction to faction in the manner of modern professional sports stars. Still, rivalries and fandom stayed with the team, not even the star player. Pliny the Younger makes that point with derision in a letter (*Letters* 9.6) in which he says that if the colours of the charioteers were to be switched in the middle of a race, the crowd would stick with the colour, switching over their favour and enthusiasm as well. The best example of the movement of charioteers as well as their success is the epitaph of Gaius Appuleius Diocles (*CIL* 6.10048; *ILS* 5287), whose name seems to indicate a freed slave who had become a Roman citizen. Born in Lusitania, he drove chariots for twenty-four years until his death at age forty-two, appearing in 4,257 races, taking first place in 1,462 of them, and amassing career winnings of 35,863,120 *sesterces*. Diocles drove for three different factions, starting his career with the Whites, ending with more than a decade for the Reds. The process of his movement between these companies is not described; we do not know if he could be considered the equivalent of a modern free agent athlete or if his career is the result of being traded between organizations. The question is complicated still further by Diocles' legal status: when, and under what circumstances, did he gain his freedom? What is clear is that, as with gladiators, someone was keeping careful record of the career statistics of charioteers and their horses, including such details as how many races were won by leading from the start, versus those won by coming from behind. In addition careful attention is paid to the circumstances of each race and when it fell in a day's racing—initial races to start the day's events were apparently particularly prestigious—and how many other chariots competed. In some of these races, two or three chariots from a faction might work together to ensure that one of them would win, a strategy familiar from modern car and bicycle racing. Given the number of races in a day, which by some accounts could be as many as twenty-five in the morning, the need for multiple teams of charioteers and horses was acute.

The pattern of recruiting charioteers and other personnel for the *factiones* is not clear. The names of most of the staff are non-Roman and heavily Greek, but their places of origin are not explicit. That is not the case for the horses that the *factiones* bred, transported, and trained. From literary as well as epigraphical sources we can compile a list of regions for desirable horses in the imperial period. Such a list would include Spain, Sicily, Thessaly, North Africa, Cappadocia, and the region of Hirpinum in Italy (*CIL* 6.10053, 10056, 37834; Horsmann 1998: 294–296). Such a geographical spread gives us an excellent sense of the reach of the *factiones* and their widespread organizations. Each faction must have employed agents in these locations to find the strongest and fastest horses, to purchase and transport them before their rivals could do so. There is no evidence that they operated their own stud farms, instead perhaps purchasing from breeders directly or in local auctions as Juvenal seems to suggest (*Satires* 8.57–63). Juvenal's poem also notes that some people judge horses on bloodlines and pasturage, so those must have been important considerations; and perhaps the *factiones* kept track of bloodlines as they recorded the successes of charioteers and winning horses.

In the Late Roman world, notably the fifth and sixth centuries, *factiones* are known as important organizations, particularly at Constantinople. It is critical to distinguish these from the earlier organizations of performers. These later factions were social groups, often organized around geographical areas that provided the circus fans and others in the community a visible and influential social identity. Their place as a component of the political sphere demonstrates how far they are from the professional organizations of the past centuries (Futrell 2006: 210–211). As such their actions fall outside the limits of this chapter.

The structure and extent of these performer organizations reflects a number of important elements of the Roman world. The key role of spectacle entertainments in both small communities and imperial politics is evident from the evidence of organizations of *venatores*, gladiators, and charioteers across the Roman world. Their vital role in religious and political ritual and festivals ensured their dominant place in the public life of ancient Rome. In many cases these groups, no matter which sport they represented, also illustrate Roman values of individual achievement and collective identity that permeated the entire class structure and served as a route of social and economic mobility for hundreds of years. Far more than mere entertainment, their performers exemplify much that held the Roman world together during its height.

References

Beschaouch, A. 1977. 'Nouvelles recherches sur les sodalités de l'Afrique romain.' *CRAI*: 486–503.

Bomgardner, D. 2009. 'The Magerius Mosaic Revisited.' In *Roman Amphitheatres and Spectacula: A 21st Century Perspective*. 165–178. T. Wilmott, ed. Oxford.

Cameron, A. 1976. *Circus Factions: Blues and Greens at Rome and Byzantium*. Oxford.

Carter, M. 1999. 'A *Doctor Secutorum* and the *Retiarius* Draukos from Corinth.' *ZPE* 126: 262–268.

Carter, M. 2003. 'Gladiatorial Ranking and the *SC de Pretiis Gladiatorum Minuendis* (*CIL* II 6278 = *ILS* 5163).' *Phoenix* 57: 83–114.

Cooley, A. E. and M. G. L. Cooley. 2004. *Pompeii: A Sourcebook*. London.

Dodge, H. 2010. *Spectacle in the Roman World*. London.

Dunbabin, K. M. D. 1978. *The Mosaics of Roman North Africa*. Oxford.

Fagan, G. G. 2011. *The Lure of the Arena: Social Psychology and the Crowd at the Roman Games*. Cambridge.

Futrell, A. 2006. *The Roman Games: A Sourcebook*. Malden, MA.

Gager, J. G. 1990. 'Curse and Competition in the Ancient Circus.' In *Of Scribes and Scrolls*. 215–228. H. W. Attridge, J. J. Collins, and T. H. Tobin, eds. Baltimore.

Horsmann, G. 1998. *Die Wagenlenker der römischen Kaiserzeit*. Stuttgart.

Jacobelli, L. 2003. *Gladiators at Pompeii*. M. Becker, trans. Los Angeles.

Kyle, D. G. 2007. *Sport and Spectacle in the Ancient World*. Malden, MA.

Teyssier, E. 2009. *La mort en face: Le dossier gladiateurs*. Arles.

Wiedemann, T. 1992. *Emperors and Gladiators*. London.

CHAPTER 42

....

ANIMAL SUPPLY

....

MICHAEL MACKINNON

ANIMALS of all types, be these domestic or wild, native or exotic, were routinely required for spectacles and events in the Graeco-Roman world, most notably, perhaps, in the context of the amphitheatre and circus games of Roman antiquity. Accounts of beasts pitted against one another or matched with gladiators are chronicled in ancient Greek and Latin texts and inscriptions; images of exotic animals and spectacles exist in works of Greek and Roman art; remains of ancient amphitheatres and circuses survive, while bones of exotic animals, presumably associated with such spectacles, have been recovered from various archaeological contexts. Scholarly attention, however, traditionally has been directed towards chronicling and detailing the spectacles themselves and the structures wherein they were staged, with less concern about the processes that underlie the acquisition, supply, and transport of animals for such events. What animals were obtained, and from which regions? Who acquired the wild beasts? How were they captured and transported? The integration of ancient textual, iconographical, archaeological (including zooarchaeological), and ethnographical evidence provides the requisite data to investigate aspects of animal supply for ancient spectacles. Each is not without its concerns, however. Investigations of ancient texts, for example, invite questions about reliability and embellishment of the events portrayed, in light of the audience to which such texts are directed. Archaeological and iconographical remains inevitably carry biases associated with recovery and preservation of materials. Extrapolation of ethnographical evidence to past populations may draw criticism of contextual and cultural variation. Nevertheless, the use of all these sources helps reduce biases that may be tied to assessments based on any single category of evidence, when researching the topic.

Although human interest in exotic beasts presumably dates far back, arguably to prehistoric periods in representations of wild animals in Upper Paleolithic cave art, the history of their capture and use during antiquity is rather piecemeal and ambiguous. As early as 2500 BCE, groups of elephants were being assembled in India, some even being trained to haul cargo (Luoma 1987: 5). Concurrently, zoo-type collections and sacred animal 'parks' were noted in Egypt (Luoma 1987: 5; Kisling 2001: 12–15). One thousand years later, Thutmose III is said to have maintained a palace 'zoo', stocked with exotic beasts acquired from trading expeditions to Ethiopia (Luoma 1987: 5). Kings in Assyria and Babylon also sponsored royal zoos (Gold 1988: 2), while accounts of the ancient Greeks collecting exotic animals filter in from the eighth and seventh centuries BCE onwards. By the fourth century BCE, enough was known to prompt Aristotle to write the first systematic zoological survey, entitled *The History of Animals*. Greek 'zoos' reached a pinnacle during the third century BCE when Ptolemy I established a grand menagerie at Alexandria. His successor, Ptolemy II, added to the collection with scores of beasts captured from Ethiopia and Arabia, which paraded through the streets as components of potent royal display (Athenaeus 5.201b, c).

The demand for exotic beasts escalated immensely during Roman times, coincident with the popularity of amphitheatre and circus games (Aymard 1951; Epplett 2013, 2015; Jennison 1937; Sparreboom 2016). As early as the third century, but first recorded in Rome in 186 BCE (Livy 39.22.2), *venationes*, or wild beast exhibitions, were staged across the Roman world, continuing into late antiquity in some areas (Historia Augusta, *Probus* 19; Symmachus, *Letters* 2.75.2; 10.117). The list of species showcased was extensive—lions, leopards, bulls, elephants, tigers, giraffes, hyenas, rhinoceroses, apes, crocodiles, gazelles, ostriches, among other *taxa*—gathered chiefly from Africa and Asia. The larger geographic extent of the Roman world coupled with widespread demands for goods across the entire empire brought new opportunities and challenges. The Roman economy intensified with new technological developments, trade linkages, and production and supply networks for numerous materials and resources. Exotic animals were acquired and transported over vast distances, often in tandem with other resources and products, as the empire conquered, exploited, and developed new areas. Rome's conquest of the North African provinces of Mauretania, Numidia, Africa Proconsularis, and Cyrenaica opened up closer sources of exotic animals for Rome but also ushered in new complications since, with no truly navigable rivers in these areas, animal collectors had to roam overland, often over great distances and at great expense, to acquire the beasts. Certainly these exotic animal supply systems needed organization; but just how was this accomplished?

ORGANIZATION

Little evidence survives on which to reconstruct aspects of exotic animal supply during Greek antiquity. Alexander recruited elephants in some of his military campaigns in the east, some of which may have been transported afterward to other areas of the Hellenistic world (such as Alexandria and Athens) as part of the special animal parks, parades, or menageries being developed (Scullard 1974: 254–255; Toynbee 1973: 32). India and Ethiopia, for example, supplied the great Processions of the Ptolemies, although details surrounding any such movements are lacking (Athenaeus 5.201b, c; Scullard 1974: 123–125). Elephants figure occasionally in Greek art; both Indian and African varieties were known and used. Still, there is often great variation in their depiction, some more accurately rendered than others, which raises questions about the degree to which elephants were commonly seen or recalled in the Greek world. Presumably acquisition networks for elephants, be they for military and/or show purposes, were interconnected, although specific details about such networks do not survive. Currently, no excavated elephant bones have been reported from ancient Greek sites.

The evidence for supplying lions in ancient Greek culture is also somewhat vague. Like elephants, lions were presumably known to the larger populace; they are the most frequently mentioned wild animal among Greek texts (Bartosiewicz 2009: 275), and fairly commonly represented in iconography, chiefly in depictions of the Nemean Lion. Scattered lion bones from Bronze and Iron Age sites in Greece have been reported; however, the bulk of these are isolated teeth, suggesting secondary deposition, perhaps lion's teeth used as curio objects or 'show-pieces' (Bartosiewicz 2009: 281). Nevertheless, lions originally inhabited areas of south-east Europe, including Greece, to be extirpated from the northern border areas of present-day Greece sometime in the first century CE. Thereafter, Africa and Asia would be the principal supply destinations for lions. Indigenous European lion populations were never very numerous, however, and given their elevated symbolic and cultural role for the Greeks, it is doubtful that they were viewed in the same manner as other localized wild animals such as bears and deer. Still, the few zooarchaeological materials found at ancient sites could represent lions captured or hunted locally.

In general, the scale of exotic animal acquisition in the ancient Greek world appears extremely specialized and limited, with ad hoc supply schemes drawn up as required. No specific details of exactly who did this work or of any formalized mechanisms or organizations in place to hunt, trap, and transport these beasts are recorded in the ancient sources available. The evidence for exotic animal supply during Roman times is equally vague in parts, especially during earlier periods. Exotic beasts, notably large felids, are depicted in various Etruscan tombs (e.g. Tomb of the Leopards, c.480–450 BCE), which may suggest some sort of early wild animal trade (Strong 1968: 121–123). Conclusive connections, however, are tenuous; depictions of these animals need not imply that the physical animal was imported as well. Some of these representations may reflect adaptation or copying of Greek artistic types, rather than actual Etruscan capture of exotic cats. The first beast shows in Roman Italy are hypothesized to have occurred during the third and early second centuries BCE and these were likely supplied predominantly with indigenous Italian fauna, such as wild boars, bulls, deer, and bears, with only a few foreign exotic beasts (Beacham 1999: 12). Details regarding acquisition of animals, scale of operations, and care and feeding regimes are sparse, with little ancient textual or iconographical evidence on which to draw for these early games, but a total absence of exotic animal bones from archaeological sites of the early republican period in Italy provides some support for early preference for local animals to be used in relatively impromptu and localized shows. Consequently, supply networks were presumably somewhat informal or ad hoc, with little in the way of the infrastructure that developed with subsequent *venationes* of the late republican and imperial periods. Acquisitions were probably facilitated by local contacts; where available, overseas, 'contacts' might have been established on a needs basis by the republican magistrates and officials sponsoring the events. Roman troops stationed in different areas, in Italy and abroad, may have assisted in early exotic animal capture, but specific evidence of such activity in the republican period does not survive (Epplett 2001: 210). Nevertheless, foreign animals were not unknown to the early Romans. Elephants were among the first exotics displayed in Italy—originally, it seems, as parade animals, and later as show beasts in amphitheatre and circus games. Their use on two occasions, 275 BCE and 251 BCE, is recorded in Seneca (*On the Shortness of Life* 12.3; 14.2), Eutropius (2.2.14), Varro (*On the Latin Language* 7.389.39), and Florus (1.18.26). Once introduced and established, however, demands for foreign animals appear to increase quickly in Rome. A Senate-issued ban around 179 BCE (Pliny the Elder, *Natural History* 8.17.64) on the use of imported beasts in *venationes* seems to have had little impact on their popularity, leading to subsequent, and apparently swift, modification of this legislation to permit African animals for show purposes in Rome by at least 169 BCE (Beacham 1999: 12).

As the demand for exotic beasts spread with the expansion of the Roman empire, so also did the networks and scales of operations in supplying such animals augment and develop during late republican and imperial times. Available data point to a number of groups involved in capture of these wild beasts. Representations in mosaics show a mix of soldiers and what appear to be professional hunters undertaking these tasks. One key example from the site of Hippo Regius, dating to the fourth century CE, depicts armed men with shields (presumably soldiers) and torches, forming a corral around trapped exotic beasts, in turn driving them into nets and other enclosures. Soldiers were likely involved; in fact, capturing wild beasts could be regarded as a military exercise of sorts (Epplett 2001: 211). Exotic goods were acquired as tribute from subject states of the Roman empire and Roman soldiers stationed in these areas could help in the capture and transport of requisitioned animals. The degree to which these commodities were formalized under tax collection regimes, which could and did have military support, however, is not specifically detailed in the ancient sources.

Although infrequently noted in ancient texts or portrayed in art, media which often catered to or reflected the social and political interests of the elite, no doubt some civilians and indigenous peoples were also recruited (or coerced) into exotic animal capture. Indigenous hunters, in fact, may have conducted the brunt of the work. Comparable ethnographic accounts note that many of the animal collectors hired in Central America in more recent times are local 'peasants who turn to catching now and then in the slack season' (Hahn 1967: 365). Some ancient references imply native involvement. Aelian (*On the Nature of Animals* 3.93) reports upon the skill of the Moors of North Africa in hunting leopards, while troupes of local Laodicean, Ethiopian, and Mauretanian hunters, noted in the specific context of hunting and capturing exotic beasts, are mentioned by Cicero (*Letters to his Friends* 2.11.2), Pliny the Elder (*Natural History* 8.54.131; 6.25.185, 191), and Plutarch (*Customs and Mores* 972b), respectively. Darker skin tones on some of the figures depicted among available hunting mosaics, moreover, may suggest participation of indigenous Africans, but in no case are these individuals dressed dissimilarly from other workers depicted to suggest any distinct ethnic or cultural differentiation being made by the artist.

That ancient animal hunting, for some, was professionalized also finds some support in literary and inscriptional references to dealers and merchants of wild beasts (Bertrandy 1987: 227–233; Auguet 1972: 114; Bomgardner 2000: 139, 212–213). Guilds of *venatores* (specialized gladiators who fought wild animals in ancient games), including the Pentasii, the Synematii, the Tauriscii, and the fairly popular Telegenii in North Africa, are also known from ancient sources, including inscriptions and mosaics (Auguet 1972: 114). Although their specific roles are uncertain, it seems plausible that *venatores* were involved in initial capture of these animals, to gain some familiarity in battling them in the amphitheatre and circus games. Some, such as the Telegenii, are by implication active both in the supply of their own animals and also likely as middlemen in coordinating transport of other captured exotics (Bomgardner 2000: 213). Indigenous hunters may have worked alongside members from guilds of professional hunters and trappers, such as the *venatores*, in the actual capture of exotic beasts or may have been commissioned by such groups to execute certain tasks, such as fashioning and preparing hunting equipment, including wooden cages (Claudianus, *On the Consulship of Stilicho* 3.323–325; Epplett 2001: 212), or to supply certain beasts for use within the process. Extrapolating from modern accounts of wild animal capture, a range of participants, including Roman soldiers, civilians, and professional hunters, may have participated in trapping comparatively smaller, timid creatures, such as deer, gazelles, and ostriches; more probably indigenous hunters caught the bulk of the more ferocious, massive, and deadly creatures, such as large felids and elephants (MacKinnon 2006: 145).

CAPTURE AND TRANSPORT

Although opinions varied among ancient philosophers about the manner in which to treat different kinds of animals, in general most beasts destined for ancient spectacles were viewed as commodities for exploitation; their welfare was typically inconsequential in that their ultimate economic value, and use by humans outweighed any pressing need to attend too assiduously to the animals' well-being. Similar attitudes historically have prevailed across many cultures until relatively recently. For example, before opening his zoo, Carl Hagenbeck (a late nineteenth and early twentieth century merchant of wild animals) had been responsible for killing countless animals in their pursuit and capture for various zoo and personal collections, professing that young elephants and rhinos 'cannot as a rule be secured without first killing the old ones' (Luoma 1987: 12–13). Catching animals that are too young has been a constant problem; many are too weak to survive the rigours involved in trapping and transport, let alone any trauma associated with separation from their parents (Hahn 1967: 367). Animal capture of the recent past has more often involved ambush, deceit, baiting, hiding, trapping, and sneaky behaviour. Extrapolating from such concepts provides a basis from which to debate whether the Romans employed similar tactics, even though literary and iconographical accounts are more likely to present a 'noble warrior' image (MacKinnon 2006: 145–148). Closer inspection of the ancient sources provides some clues to this effect. The Elder Pliny mentions an elephant's fear of ambush (*Natural History* 8.5.9) and the use of pit-traps in its capture (*Natural History* 8.8.24). Camouflaged pits are noted as a means to catch other wild beasts (*Natural History* 8.21.54), while the tactic of baiting a tigress by stealing her cubs is also outlined as a good means to catch this animal (*Natural History* 8.25.66). Methods to trick and bait animals also appear in Roman iconography. One scene from a mosaic at Piazza Armerina shows a large felid mesmerized by her reflection in a shiny disk (Fig. 42.1), presumably a technique to distract her and allow close approach. Nets, pits, traps, and other basic equipment of animal capture likewise can be seen in ancient images of exotic animal capture and were probably more commonly used, even if the ancients chose to depict debatably bolder methods of capture—such as chasing with a spear—with greater frequency in artistic media.

Certainly dangers accompanied animal capture, and no doubt some hunters were killed in the process. Arguably many more animals, however, died en route than might be extrapolated from the vast numbers of animals appearing in the games as reported by ancient texts, a fact that must be stressed in developing a more balanced account of exotic animal capture during antiquity. Injuries from falls or traps, or wounds from weapons and other equipment, as occur today, would certainly compromise the survival of those taken.

Neglectful and insensitive attitudes towards animals continued in transport. Confined and cramped into tiny cages (drawn by oxen or carried by hand) or forced to walk on foot, the beasts (principally the more docile and submissive babies and juveniles, if one extrapolates from modern practices) were paraded to ports for further shipment (Fig. 42.2). Claudian

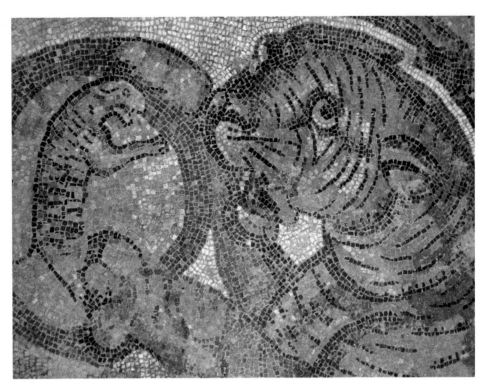

FIGURE 42.1. Tigress caught by image in reflective globe. Mosaic from Villa del Casale, Piazza Armerina. Wikimedia Commons CC BY-SA 2.0 License. Photo: psub.

(*On the Consulship of Stilicho* 3.327–328) notes that some of these processions reached such great lengths as to block roadways. Journeys may have taken weeks, depending on distances involved: special encampments close to the roads were required for accommodations and supplies (Robinson 1992: 207). Conditions for both human workers and the transported animals may have been arduous. Many injured or suffering animals were probably unlikely to receive care, and constant vigilance was required to keep animals in line and to avoid conflicts between various species, as well as aggression toward humans. Hagenbeck commented that sheep and goats are driven along with modern versions of these animal trains, the ewes and nanny goats providing a constant supply of milk for the young animals and the remainder being used as food for the carnivores (Luoma 1987: 14); there is no guarantee, however, that provisions were in adequate supply during antiquity. Water would have been especially important if the animal train had to cross any desert terrain. Moreover, as cities and their agricultural hinterlands grew in North Africa, the Near East, and other capture territories throughout the Roman period, the natural habitat for any native exotic animals within these regions would diminish, pushing the beasts into farther and more remote zones. The increased distances now needed to procure these remaining beasts from such distant regions would add significantly to the associated costs, even if the security and connectivity of the Roman empire helped ease some transport difficulties. Nonetheless, details of how transport expenses and needs were met are not fully articulated in the ancient sources. Costs of provisions (including livestock and fodder) seem to have been borne partly

FIGURE 42.2. Overland transport of captured animals. Mosaic from Villa del Casale, Piazza Armerina. Wikimedia Commons. Public domain.

by the Roman government and partly by those municipalities through which the animal trains passed or sheltered temporarily (Bomgardner 2000: 213). Such maintenance could be quite expensive to some communities. An official petition to the emperor Theodosius II in 417 CE, for example, complains about the extended stay of one transport caravan in Hierapolis (the capital of the province of the Euphrates), which was unfairly draining resources and burdening local citizens (*Theodosian Code* 15.11.2).

Conditions appear no better for overseas transport of animals (Fig. 42.3). Sea voyages had to be swift to combat potential losses en route. The fastest ships departing North Africa could reach Ostia in two days (Pliny the Elder, *Natural History* 19.4); routes from other regions would require more time. Presumably ships stocking wild animals were also equipped with extra oars to hasten journey times (Bertrandy 1987: 226). Claudian acknowledges that some rowers were fearful of the beasts they were transporting, presumably nervous the animals might escape (*On the Consulship of Stilicho* 3.325–327). Complications and delays associated with poor weather and mechanical or logistical problems added extra levels of stress onboard and for anxious waiting officials. The younger Pliny bemoans how bad weather impeded a shipment of African beasts for a show at Verona (*Letters* 6.4.3); Claudian notes that the added weight of elephants on a vessel could cause travel delays (*On the Consulship of Stilicho* 3.354–355); Symmachus laments the loss of exotic animals in a shipwreck of the late fourth century CE (*Letters* 9.117, 2.76). Onboard, there would be concerns over limited food supplies and other complications. Prolonged exposure in cramped, caged conditions might provoke behavioural changes, with some animals more vicious and territorial and others

FIGURE 42.3. Overseas transport of animals. Mosaic from Villa del Casale, Piazza Armerina. Wikimedia Commons CC BY-SA 3.0 License. Photo: suwa.

withdrawn from the shock of habitat displacement and exhaustion (Berggren 1969: 29–30). Mortality among young animals that were separated from their mothers was probably high. Moreover, diseases and other infectious ailments could spread rapidly on board, especially if animals were malnourished, weakened, and uncomfortable.

Modern comparisons may again be useful. Early twentieth-century animal shippers did not always feed their cargo. They did not care because they could still secure a good profit from the sale of even a few beasts out of an original cargo of many more (Hahn 1967: 366). Such risk assessment underlies the ultimate economic payoff of such ventures—both past and present. There are examples of exotic animals dying en route to zoos even today; many zookeepers even stipulate to dealers that the purchased animals must survive a two-week period after transport in order for the sale to be valid (Hahn 1967: 366). Undoubtedly, the ancient journey to the final destination harboured as many difficulties, for exotic beasts and humans alike, as surrounded the actual initial hunting and capture of the animals. Despite the complications, however, the high prices of some exotics, and the enormous inflation rate at which such costs escalated throughout antiquity (Bomgardner 2000: 211), likely assured Roman hunters and trappers a good profit on delivery of only a few quality animals.

MAINTENANCE

Exotic animals destined for Rome were initially unloaded at the port in Ostia, then barged up the Tiber or carted overland to the city. Other docking points may also have been used. Pliny mentions elephants disembarking at Pozzuoli, probably a distribution centre for supplying games in the Bay of Naples area (*Natural History* 8.3). Transfers did not always go smoothly: Pliny tells of a sculptor at the docks who was attacked by an escaped leopard (*Natural History* 36.40). Once at their final destination, however, animals would require short- or long-term storage, depending on the schedule of games. In Rome, some animals could be kept in subterranean rooms and pens at the Colosseum itself, but these seem designed to provide only temporary housing immediately prior to the shows (Bomgardner 2000: 85). *Vivaria*, or stockyards, furnished longer-term storage. In Rome such compounds may have been located outside the *Porta Praenestina* (*CIL* 6.130) or the *Porta Labicana* (Procopius, *Gothic Wars* 1.22.10; 1.23.13–23), although no uncontested archaeological traces of such stockyards have yet been found in Rome or elsewhere (Bertrandy 1987: 230; Auguet 1972: 112). Circular enclosures have been identified at several Roman sites in Germany and Britain (notably the forts at Zugmantel, Dambach, and Lunt); it may be argued that these are *vivaria* on the basis of structural dimensions to corral animals, but the connection is far from certain (Epplett 2001: 219). Zookeepers, or *custodes vivari* (*CIL* 6.130), are occasionally noted in the ancient sources but typically in connection with Roman amphitheatres and similar entertainment venues and not specifically animal care and maintenance during capture and transport. Without supplementary details it is difficult to determine their exact role. It seems likely that some keepers were involved in the logistics of animal care throughout the whole process.

What about the animals themselves? Is there zooarchaeological evidence for exotic beasts from excavations in Roman cities with amphitheatres, circuses, or arenas? Scattered bones of gazelle, wild boar, deer, camel, bear, ostrich, wild goat and sheep, and hartebeest have been found at a number of late antique Roman sites in North Africa, especially Carthage (MacKinnon 2006: 151). Two isolated elephant bones were noted from first-century CE excavation levels at the Magon Quarter in Carthage (Nobis 1999: 583), but bones of other traditionally 'exotic' fauna such as lions, panthers, tigers, giraffes, and so forth are absent across deposits. The lack of big cats is especially noteworthy since it contrasts with their apparent popularity in both the ancient textual and iconographical sources (Bomgardner 2000: 35).

As for Rome, there are accounts of nineteenth-century and early twentieth-century CE antiquarian excavations in and around the Colosseum, where supposedly remains of lions, tigers, and other exotics were retrieved (Lanciani 1979: 373, 385); however, these cannot be verified in the absence of these bones or of detailed reports discussing them. Only one site, that of the Meta Sudans, located about 50 metres south-west of the Colosseum, provides unambiguous information. Here, sixteen bear bones, two leopard bones, an ostrich fragment, and several red deer, roe deer, wild boar, and fox remains were recovered and identified from excavations of a fifth to seventh century CE fill of a drain (De Grossi Mazzorin 1995: 309–318). It seems logical to relate these materials to the games in the amphitheatre; their location suggests that the remains of some exotic beasts, at least, were deposited near the venue. Other carcasses may have been buried in pits, either within or outside the city, or perhaps even distributed to spectators (Kyle 1995), but there is currently no unambiguous zooarchaeological evidence from Rome or its environs that might identify such locations or practices.

Secure identification of exotic animal remains in other areas of the Roman world is equally problematic. The occasional bone or tooth of an arguably 'exotic' beast does occur sporadically across sites, but never in sufficient quantities or in ideal contexts to argue a secure connection with supplies for *venationes* or other spectacles (MacKinnon 2006: 150–155). Many may simply represent curio-, charm- or talisman-type objects (especially teeth, given that these preserve well, are visually impressive, and are easily portable). In total, the available pool of exotic animal bones retrieved and reported from ancient archaeological sites hardly carries the extensive numbers or species diversity one might expect to find, even factoring in retrieval and preservation biases that can severely reduce a zooarchaeological assemblage. Most of these reported finds date to Late Antique contexts, when changes in spectacle led to the decline of *venationes*, so reduced numbers might be expected. Indeed, Bomgardner (1992: 161) has argued that increasing environmental degradation and poor wildlife management practices, from the latter part of the second century CE onward, jeopardized stocks of exotic animals, leading to modified games that relied on relatively more common species (e.g. bulls, boars, and deer), less arena slaughter, and a gradual shift toward animals performing clever tricks, forebears of modern European circus practices. Nevertheless, this still leaves a real dearth of exotic animal bones reported for sites throughout the Roman world that date to late republican and imperial times, the peak of traditionally bloody *venationes* and animal spectacles; this in turn casts some doubt on both the vaunted magnitude of *venationes* and on the successes of the supply systems providing for such games, as presented through the media of ancient texts and art. This is not to say that such events could not have taken place in the manner in which they are reported in the ancient texts, for indeed, given its wealth and impact, the Roman world could and likely did marshal the resources required to capture, transport, and display vast numbers of exotic animals, perhaps even into the thousands claimed by some accounts for a single event. The mechanisms to conduct these operations were indeed impressive for the time. And some events, especially imperial-sponsored games, were quite spectacular and extraordinary in this respect. Nevertheless, in light of the somewhat sobering zooarchaeological and ethnographic evidence, it is important not to normativise these grandiose events as standards across the wider context for the capture, trade, and use of exotic beasts in antiquity.

CONCLUSIONS

Assessment of ancient textual, iconographical, archaeological, and ethnographical evidence yields key information about the processes involved in animal supply for spectacle events during antiquity. The use of these categories of information in such reconstructions, moreover, creates a more balanced account of this topic and helps expose and temper biases associated with reliance on any single line of evidence. Although interest in exotic animals dates back to Egyptian, Assyrian, and Greek times, Roman demand for show and spectacle purposes increased significantly and prompted professional and organized systems of animal supply. Textual and iconographical data allude to the use of Roman soldiers and other imperial administrative officials in these campaigns, probably aided by indigenous collectors and hunters contracted in the areas exploited. A range of equipment and techniques, including nets, pits, traps, and cages, was used in animal capture, followed in turn by often long, complex, and arduous journeys by land and sea to transport the beasts to their final destinations for amphitheatre and circus games. Acceptance of the numbers of exotics displayed in these spectacles, as outlined in some ancient texts, should be considered with caution and scepticism, notably when contrasted with the far more limited archaeological and zooarchaeological evidence for such beasts from Roman sites, considering as well the practical difficulties in capturing, transporting, and maintaining such animals as reconstructed from historical information. Certainly, the wealth, power, and influence of the Roman world was capable of sponsoring exceptional events involving considerable numbers of wild beasts, but a larger appreciation of the complexities entailed in supplying, conducting, and operationalizing these events deepens our critical understanding of the more widespread and typical practice of spectacle in antiquity.

REFERENCES

Auguet, R. 1972. *Cruelty and Civilization: The Roman Games*. New York.

Aymard, J. 1951. *Essai sur les chasses romaines des origines à la fin du siècle des Antonins*. Paris.

Bartosiewicz, L. 2009. 'A Lion's Share of Attention: Archaeozoology and the Historical Record.' *AArchHung* 60: 275–289.

Beacham, R. 1999. *Spectacle Entertainments of Early Imperial Rome*. New Haven.

Berggren, S. 1969. *Berggren's Beasts*. New York.

Bertrandy, F. 1987. 'Remarques sur le commerce des bêtes sauvages entre l'Afrique du nord et l'Italie.' *MEFRA* 99: 211–241.

Bomgardner, D. L. 1992. 'The Trade in Wild Beasts for Roman Spectacles: A Green Perspective.' *Anthropozoologica* 16: 161–166.

Bomgardner, D. L. 2000. *The Story of the Roman Amphitheatre*. London.

De Grossi Mazzorin, J. 1995. 'La fauna rinvenuta nell'area della Meta Sudans nel quadro evolutivo degli animali domestici in Italia.' In *Padusa Quaderni I: Atti del 1° Convegno Nazionale di Archeozoologia. Rovigo, March 5–7, 1993*. 309–318. R. Peretto and O. De Curtis, eds. Rovigo.

Epplett, C. 2001. 'The Capture of Animals by the Roman Military.' *G&R* 48: 210–222.

Epplett, C. 2013. 'Roman Beast Hunts.' In *A Companion to Sport and Spectacle in Greek and Roman Antiquity*. 505–519. P. Christesen and D. G. Kyle, eds. Malden, MA.

Epplett, C. 2015. *Gladiator and Beast Hunts: Arena Sports of Ancient Rome*. Barnsley, UK.

Gold, D. 1988. *Zoo: A Behind-the-Scenes Look at the Animals and the People Who Care for Them*. Chicago.

Hahn, E. 1967. *Animal Gardens*. Garden City, NY.

Jennison, G. 1937. *Animals for Show and Pleasure in Ancient Rome*. Manchester.

Kisling, V. N. Jr. 2001. 'Ancient Collections and Menageries.' In *Zoo and Aquarium History: Ancient Animal Collections to Zoological Gardens*. 1–47. V. N. Kisling Jr., ed. Boca Raton.

Kyle, D. G. 1995. 'Animal Spectacles in Ancient Rome: Meat and Meaning.' *Nikephoros* 7: 181–205.

Lanciani, R. 1979. *The Ruins and Excavations of Ancient Rome*. New York.

Luoma, J. R. 1987. *A Crowded Ark*. Boston, MA.

MacKinnon, M. 2006. 'Supplying Exotic Animals for the Roman Amphitheatre Games.' *Mouseion* 6: 137–161.

Nobis, G. 1999. 'Die Tierreste von Karthago.' In *Die deutschen Ausgrabungen in Karthago* III. 575–632. F. Rakob, ed. Mainz am Rhein.

Nobis, G. 1992. 'Karthago: Eine antike Weltstadt im Blickfeld der klassischen Archäozoologie.' *Tier und Museum* 3: 1–11.

Robinson, O. F. 1992. *Ancient Rome*. London.

Scullard, H. H. 1974. *The Elephant in the Greek and Roman World*. London.

Sparreboom, A. 2016. *Venationes Africanae: Hunting Spectacles in Roman North Africa: Cultural Significance and Social Function*. PhD Thesis, University of Amsterdam.

Strong, D. 1968. *The Early Etruscans*. New York.

Toynbee, J. M. C. 1973. *Animals in Roman Life and Art*. Ithaca, NY.

CHAPTER 43

....

GLADIATORS AS A CLASS

....

VALERIE M. HOPE

INTRODUCTION

....

> When recently Caesar, in mock naval battle,
> Brought on Greek and Persian vessels,
> Why, young men and girls came from either sea,
> And all the vast wide world was in the City.

Ovid, *The Art of Love* 1.171–174

THE amphitheatre has been described as a microcosm of Roman society (Edmondson 1996: 82). In Rome (and the cities of the empire) the amphitheatre was filled with a large and varied crowd which came from far and wide; here the social divisions and distinctions that defined Roman society were exposed to all. From the worst seats to the best seats, from slaves to the emperor, from dirty clothes to regal purple, society was brought together and put on show. At the heart of this was the arena itself, where the gaze of all fell upon the victims and the performers—condemned criminals and trained gladiators. The gladiators were, in principle, the lowest of the low; despised and hated, they were debased outcasts from society. In reality the place of gladiators in Roman society, and their relationship to and with those who gazed upon them, was more complex. This chapter will investigate how gladiators (of the late Republic, but mainly the Imperial period) were viewed both by others and by themselves, and the extent to which gladiators were regarded, and regarded themselves, as a cohesive group or even a 'class'. To what extent can we understand and reconstruct the experiences and expectations of both the performers and spectators in Rome's arenas?

INFAMOUS AND DESPISED: FAMOUS AND ADMIRED

Roman society was hierarchical, but understanding the place of gladiators in this hierarchy is not as straightforward as it may appear. On the one hand gladiators were disreputable outsiders. Gladiators were frequently recruited from slaves and criminals; they were forced to sell their bodies for the entertainment of others; they were debased and dispensable performers. Gladiators had limited legal rights and were considered deserving of dishonourable treatment; they were 'men of the worst type' (Florus, *Epitome of Roman History* 2.8.3). In literature the gladiator was often made to symbolize what was abhorrent and lowly, what existed on the fringes of decent society: 'There is no meaner condition among the people than that of the gladiator', claimed Calpurnius Flaccus (*Declamations* 52). To call someone a gladiator or to suggest that they took too keen an interest in the ways of the arena was a common form of invective: 'From the time when Rufinus put on the adult toga, he abused adult freedom by attending gladiatorial training. He knew all the gladiators by name and knew all the details of their former contests and their wounds. He even trained under the supervision of a professional gladiator, although he came from a good family.' (Apuleius, *Apology* 98.7)

On the other hand, gladiators were skilled and trained combatants; symbols of Rome's military prowess, they could be regarded as strong, brave, and heroic. Gladiators could be admired for looking death unflinchingly in the face: 'Look at gladiators, who are either ruined men or foreigners, and see what blows they endure! Watch how they, who have been well trained, prefer to receive a wound rather than avoid it like a coward.' (Cicero, *Tusculan Disputations* 2.17.41; see also Seneca the Younger, *Letters* 30.8; *Dialogues* 2.16.2; and Cagniart 2000; Edwards 2007: 46–77.) These men may not have lived well, but they knew how to die well. Gladiators could be praised for their courage and noted for their fame, popularity, and sexual allure. Images of gladiators filled people's homes, to be found on mosaics and wall-paintings, or adorning lamps and mirrors (Jacobelli 2003: 69–105; Coulston 2009; Newby 2015; Dunbabin 2016). Graffiti from the gladiatorial barracks at Pompeii promoted gladiators as sex symbols: Celadus, a Thracian gladiator, made all the girls sigh, while Crescens, a net-fighter, held the hearts of many (*CIL* 4.4342, 4356). Gladiators were part of everyday life, conversation, and imagery (cf. Garraffoni and Funari 2009).

This ambivalent attitude and contradictory perspective toward gladiators has often been highlighted in scholarship (Hopkins 1983; Wiedemann 1992; Barton 1993; Kyle 1998: 80–81; Dunkle 2008: 8–29; Kyle 2015: 269–273). To put it very simply, many Romans (especially elite Romans) just did not know what they thought or believed about gladiators, or at best were inconsistent in how they spoke of and described them. As the early Christian Tertullian noted, 'They love whom they lower; they detest whom they approve; the art they glorify, the artist they disgrace' (Tertullian, *On the Spectacles* 22). To note, however, that gladiators evoked complex reactions and attitudes is to privilege the perspective of the arena audience (or, even more, a certain male elite segment of that audience), and to some degree to separate gladiators from Roman society. It is indeed easier, even if often full of contradictions, to investigate how gladiators were perceived by spectators and literary commentators than to investigate how gladiators perceived themselves; but by viewing gladiators as somehow 'other' (Gunderson 1996: 135), there is a danger of overlooking that gladiators were a part of and a product of Roman society, integral and even integrated with its day-to-day functioning.

There is also a tendency to consider all gladiators together and as the same, when gladiatorial schools or troupes had their own hierarchies, and each gladiator his own story. The gladiatorial identity, as with other Roman identity groups (such as slaves or freed slaves, senators or equestrians), may have been underpinned by legal realities, but was also awash with ambiguities, inconsistencies, and tensions, and marked disjunctions between ideals and reality.

CLASSES, STIGMAS, AND HIERARCHIES

The 'Thracian', the *retiarius*, the *murmillo*, and the many other types of gladiators, easily codified by their weapons and/or armour, were and remain readily recognizable figures. When we picture or reimagine the arena contests, details of combat techniques and how gladiators were paired are doubtless important, but this can prioritize fighting over the wider context of gladiatorial life. Time spent in the amphitheatre may have been life-defining and limiting, yet also may have been relatively brief. It has been suggested that the average fight lasted for just ten to fifteen minutes (Potter 1999: 314), and, as expensive professionals, gladiators may have rarely fought to the death, instead sometimes using blunted weapons (Carter 2006a; 2006b). There was a life outside the arena and there was more to distinguish gladiators than different styles of fighting. There were gladiators from different backgrounds, geographic origins, legal status, family standing, age, and even gender (McCullough 2008; Brunet 2013). The term 'class' or 'classes of gladiators' is often used to denote different fighting skills, but much else contributed to gladiatorial identity and could help both to unite and structure gladiators as a social group.

Gladiators, along with others such as prostitutes and actors, were marred by *infamia*, a moral stigma with practical legal limitations impacting court appearances, the right to stand for election, and the types of punishment which could be inflicted; if you were labelled *infamis*, you were not a full Roman citizen (Ville 1981: 339–345; Wiedemann 1992: 28–29; Gardner 1993: 135–140; Edwards 1997). For those who were enslaved these legal disabilities may have had little practical impact, although we should not assume from this that all gladiators were slaves. Many may have started gladiatorial life as enslaved persons, purchased for the arena, but some subsequently gained their freedom. Other gladiators were free men who chose to fight (literally selling themselves to the *lanista*, the gladiatorial trainer). This may have been an act of desperation and extreme poverty, but it suggests that for some the potential financial rewards were worth dishonour, *infamia*, and possible death. Free gladiators may have been able to claim a larger stake of any prize money than those who were enslaved (Oliver and Palmer 1955: 343); it is also worth remembering that stigmas of law and honour probably concerned the moralizing, intellectual, and wealthy elite considerably more than the majority of the urban population. We can also note that such was the allure of gladiatorial fame and fighting skills that some members of the elite wished to or were forced (by 'bad' emperors) to fight as gladiators, providing grist to the mill of commentators on the morality of certain times and certain characters (e.g. Juvenal 6.82–113; Tacitus, *Annals* 15.32; Suetonius, *Nero* 12; Dio Cassius 61.17; Futrell 2006: 156–157; McCullough 2008: 205). Indeed, in literature the arena and gladiators were often used as a gauge of Roman morals, a device 'to diagnose the ills of Roman society' (Gunderson 1996: 115).

The men (and women) of the arena, then, were not homogenous in their background, legal status, or reasons for fighting. What they did share was a certain loss or lack of autonomy over their bodies and many aspects of their lives. To become a gladiator, including for those sold into the profession, was to see the disappearance of certain features of the pre-gladiatorial life. This is illustrated, if in a somewhat superficial way, by the use of stage-names for and by some gladiators. These names, often derived from martial qualities, heroes, animals, or precious stones, symbolized the change in status to gladiator, and in many cases stayed with the gladiator to the grave, any previous name seemingly abandoned. Was the 'free' *murmillo* and *hoplomachus* called Smaragdus ('Emerald'), who was commemorated by his unnamed wife in Brescia (Italy), always known as such (*EAOR* II 41)? Did he select this name or accept it? In becoming Smaragdus, what did he lose and what did he gain? The details of Smaragdus' choices (or lack of power to make them) may escape us, yet his life as a gladiator would not have been a solitary one and may have afforded some opportunities, not only disadvantages.

It is probably inappropriate to speak of a gladiatorial 'career'. For many this was not a job of choice and the real risks meant that for some at least it was a short-lived profession. Yet for other gladiators there may have been a sense of progression hinging on experience and relative success. Gladiators could be graded, from the trained but untried (a *tiro*) to the well experienced (*primus palus*; a *palus* was a post set in the ground against which soldiers and gladiators practised sword work) and whether gladiators fought singly or as a team also affected their relative value (Oliver and Palmer 1955: 341–342; Kyle 1998: 84; Potter 1999: 318–319; Bomgardner 2000: 208; Carter 2003; Futrell 2006: 49). It may have been up to the *lanista* who managed the gladiatorial troupe to rank the gladiators (Carter 2003: 89). Presumably the successful gladiator could expect improved treatment from his owner and trainer: better rations, better living conditions, perhaps fewer arena appearances, and the prospect of freedom and/or retirement. High flyers and great champions were extremely valued. Regardless of their style of fighting, gladiators could accumulate victories, gain a reputation, and become admired, attracting followers and thus financially benefiting their owners or trainers, and probably also themselves.

In the gladiatorial barracks or schools there were undoubted hierarchies (Fagan 2015). Some of these hierarchies were forced upon the gladiators. We can note, for example, that some types of gladiator were considered more debased and despicable than others. The *retiarius*, who fought scantily clad and without a helmet, may have been seen as a particularly bad moral example (Carter 2008), although whether such external stigmas and judgements affected the *retiarius* away from the arena is impossible to judge. Within the gladiatorial school or barracks a gladiator's standing was probably affected by experience, his cost, and his earning potential, aspects over which the gladiator had some, if clearly finite, influence. Gladiators of similar grades and skills level may have been quartered together, separated from inferior gladiators; with the rigid hierarchy reinforcing discipline (Juvenal, *Satire* 6.7–13; Carter 2003; Fagan 2015: 131–136). Simultaneously, the differences between gladiators in terms of ability, experience, and ethnic origin may have created an intentional mix, designed by the trainers and owners to minimize any sense of social cohesion (Wiedemann 1992: 113). The gladiator owed his loyalty to his master and might have to fight his colleagues. Gladiatorial troupes, or individual fighters, may have moved between different venues, further disrupting life and connections, although also perhaps creating extended networks (Campbell 2019). By the early principate, however, there is evidence to suggest that, at least within some troupes and schools, gladiators were more akin to comrades than enemies; this may have been particularly true of gladiators of the same type, who shared basic skills, experiences and training, and were less likely to be pitted against each other in the arena. In a predominantly male militaristic environment, friendship bonds may have developed between these fighters. More experienced gladiators may have trained, mentored, and supported their inexperienced colleagues (Carter 2003: 94; Fagan 2015: 130–131) and the gladiators could organize themselves (or were organized) into clubs or societies, some of which might be based on shared fighting skills (Coleman 2005: 11). Epitaphs and other inscriptions sometimes mention *collegia* (clubs or guilds) and friendship networks (*sodalites*). The *collegium* dedicated to the god Silvanus, based in Rome, listed its thirty-two gladiatorial members and on one occasion restored a statue of its patron deity (*CIL* 6.631 and 632; *EAOR* I: nn. 45 and 46). In Rome, the 'Thracian' Macedo was commemorated by his fellow 'Thracian' gladiators (*CIL* 6.10197; *EAOR* I: n. 97). In Telmessasin (Turkey), the epitaph of the gladiator Hermes was set up by his 'cell-mates', emphasizing bonds created through shared sleeping and living quarters (Robert 1940: n. 109). Whether formal or informal, these groupings may have had internal hierarchies which gave some gladiators roles and responsibilities toward their comrades, and these groups provided a social and support network which might assist with, for example, the cost of burial.

For many gladiators these friendship networks, and the gladiatorial troupe in general, may have acted as a pseudo family, the equivalent of the slave *familia* found within many Roman households (Coleman 2005: 4). Epitaphs do indicate, however, that some gladiators did have wives and children. In Cos (Greece), Zeuxis was commemorated by his wife and child (Robert 1940: n. 191); Ingenua, from Brescia (Italy), lived with her *retiarius* husband for five years and two months (*CIL* 5.4506; *EAOR* II 45); in Milan (Italy), the *secutor* Urbicus was commemorated by his wife of seven years, who also mentioned two daughters, one just five months old (*CIL* 5.5933; *EAOR* II 50). The gladiatorial barracks may have been a precarious environment for fostering family life and these cannot always have been legally acknowledged families, but for the more experienced gladiators and veterans of the arena, some of the fundamentals of family life were not beyond their reach.

Numerous features then could contribute to gladiatorial identity. Some of these factors can appear contradictory and, like many other people in Roman society, a gladiator could have multiple roles in a complicated life. The same man could be a *murmillo*, an ex-slave, from Gaul, a father, husband, friend, and member of a *collegium*. Gladiators were not just defined by the ambivalent attitudes of others, but by various factors, some of which were beyond the gladiator's control, some within it.

OBJECTIFIED OR ORGANIZED;
SEPARATED OR UNITED?

Gladiators were often objectified and it is challenging for us to break from this mould. In the main surviving literary and visual sources, gladiators are the viewed and are not the viewers. Through these sources we look into the arena; we do not look out from the arena floor. It is therefore difficult to gain the perspective of the gladiators on their life, or how they understood, reacted to, or rationalized their place in society. Nevertheless we can piece together aspects which suggest that gladiators were far from the mindless rabble that the elite sources would often have us believe. There is evidence to suggest that the gladiators created their own structures and hierarchies, that they could function as a group, and thus as a part of Roman society. The importance of *collegia, familiae,* and friendship networks, staple building blocks throughout the Roman world, has been noted above. These would have fulfilled practical and emotional needs, and helped to unify the gladiators as a group. Gladiatorial tombstones and cemeteries also suggest that, despite segregation and stigma, gladiators could be proud of their individual and group identity, even if this pride was inculcated by enforced training and discipline.

Some of those killed in the arena, such as executed criminals (*noxii*), were generally excluded from formal burial rites; their bodies continued to be punished and defiled after death and in Rome may have been unceremoniously dumped in the river Tiber (Kyle 1998). This fate may have befallen some dead gladiators, but generally, despite his debasement, the gladiator could earn the right to a humane and decent burial; this is supported by the survival of epitaphs and tombstones that commemorate gladiators. These memorials were often set up by fellow gladiators, family, and friends. The inscriptions and designs of these tombstones drew the gladiators together as a group and celebrated, rather than suppressed, gladiatorial identity. The epitaphs entailed similar information: the name of the gladiator, his fighting type (e.g. Thracian), his age at death, the number of victories achieved, and the name of the commemorator. These brief, factual, and often tersely inscribed details united the gladiators through shared content and vocabulary. In some epitaphs from the south of France and Spain, the gladiatorial title took precedence, being placed in isolation on the first line of the epitaph, before the name of the deceased (Garcia y Bellido 1960; Hope 1998). This unusual layout emphasized the gladiatorial profession: it was the key element of the identity of the dead man. A similar impression could be created through the use of sculpted images of weapons, victory crowns, or wreaths, and portraits of armoured gladiators, found on some gladiatorial tombstones in Italy and the eastern empire (see for example *EAOR* I: nn. 59, 69, 83, 89, 91, 92, 97; *EAOR* II 40, 44, 45, 50; Robert 1940; Coulston 2009: 197–199).

The memorials of gladiators may have often been small and relatively inexpensive, but they effectively conveyed the identity of the deceased through the associated words and pictures. What is particularly exciting is that these epitaphs and tombstones were not elite constructs and interpretations of gladiators, but were created, or at least commissioned and purchased, by those who were associated with the arena—including fellow gladiators. The commemorators emphasized gladiatorial identity, finding esteem rather than shame in this, and this identity was framed by the conventions (for the poor often aspirational conventions) of Roman funerary practices: proper burial in a marked grave. Society may have rejected gladiators, yet at death gladiators (and the comrades that commemorated them) were defined by the conventions of that society and presented themselves as heroes rather than as victims of the arena. Tombstones and funerary monuments involved an act of self-presentation for the commemorated, commemorator, or both, and in death gladiators were presented positively. It has been noted that in the west tombstones of gladiators shared similar characteristics with those of soldiers (Hope 2000a: 111) and in the east with those of athletes (Robert 1940: 22–23; Golden 2008: 77–79; Mann 2009). Despite their debasement gladiators drew on a commemorative vocabulary of respectability and honour.

Gladiators may have also expressed shared identity and unity through burial in distinct gladiatorial cemeteries. At Salona (Solin, Croatia) a group of funerary urns inscribed with gladiatorial epitaphs was found to the west of the amphitheatre (Cambi 1987: 260); in Nîmes (France) four tombstones erected to gladiators were discovered close together in the area to the south of the amphitheatre (Haon 1969; Hope 1998); at Patras in Greece several gladiatorial tombstones were located in what may have been a communal tomb (Papostolou 1989); and in Ephesus the remains of at least sixty-eight individuals found 300 metres to the east of the amphitheatre are believed to have been gladiators (Kanz 2006; cf. Redfern and Bonney 2014). These grouped graves suggest a sense of community in death; shared life and ultimately a similar death brought and kept these gladiators together. By being placed in the same cemetery area, any associated tombstones or grave markers would also have gained increased visibility and prominence. For comparison, Roman military personnel serving in civil communities, such as the Praetorian Guard, were often buried together at death, suggesting both their social cohesion and personal investment in their profession (Durry 1938; de Caro 1979). An alternative interpretation, however, is to view these potential gladiatorial cemeteries as yet another factor indicating the debasement and segregation of the gladiators. Stigmatized by their profession and polluted by the blood they had shed, gladiators may have been excluded from the Roman cemetery and interred separately; who would want to be buried next to or with the lowest of the low? An inscription from Sarsina (Italy) recalls the donation of land to the town for the burial of its citizens by a certain Horatius Balbus (*CIL* 11.6528). The inscription stated that this cemetery was for the respectable only; those who hanged themselves or profited from immoral earnings were excluded. The inscription also specifically prohibited those described as *auctorati*, the free, contract gladiators. Those who chose to become gladiators, who deliberately elected to sell their bodies, may have been particularly reprehensible, but in general, as noted above, like prostitutes, actors, pimps, and undertakers, all gladiators were marred by *infamia*. For some gladiators this shame may have followed them to their graves, while others may have been buried in marginal cemetery zones for social and economic reasons. Like so much about gladiators, their burial is enigmatic. Gladiatorial cemeteries may suggest unity, a sense of pride in identity, and are paralleled by other professions including Rome's military; alternatively, these same cemeteries may be seen as representing isolation and the social rejection of gladiators. In the end these two possible interpretations can perhaps co-exist; how the gladiatorial cemetery was viewed and understood depended on the perspective of the viewer: whether they were a fellow gladiator, an ardent fan, or a member of the local elite.

Conclusion

The arena played 'an important role in the moralizing and maintenance of Roman social roles and hierarchical relations' (Gunderson 1996: 115). This was not just entertainment, but a violent enactment of Roman values, ideals, and power (Carter 2009; Hammer 2010; Fagan 2011; Toner 2014; Kyle 2015: 269–272). The amphitheatre brought together the people of Rome (and its many cities) and celebrated both what they shared in common and the social, financial, and legal differences that divided them. The ultimate division, or social barrier, was the edge of the seating, as those 'who performed down in the arena were socially dead or, at best déclassé' (Edmondson 1996: 83). All performers were stigmatized and could be grouped together: it was not only gladiators who sold their bodies for the entertainment of others; gladiators were members of a wider underclass. In terms of morality, however, because of their association with blood and death, gladiators were also in a class of their own; they were almost inhuman, non-Roman, separate, and isolated.

Roman society was undoubtedly hierarchical and gladiators were at the very bottom of the social heap, in principle even off the social and legal radar. The identity of individuals in the Roman world was in practice, however, more complex and made up of varied, sometimes competing factors; there was also a degree of flexibility and social mobility (Hope 2000b). It may have been difficult for a gladiator to become a social climber as such, yet some gladiators could move from slavery to freedom, from poverty to comfort, and even potentially become rich and famous. Employing the terminology of class and class distinctions can be problematic in the Roman world; legal distinctions were recognized, status mattered, family honour was crucial, and personal reputations were esteemed, but there were no exact equivalents of bounded upper, middle, and lower classes. In many ways, this is well illustrated by gladiators who were, on the one hand, unrecognized, not a part of society, and thus definitely not a 'class'; and, on the other hand, a group that served a distinct function and were very much a part, however denied and contested by some, of the society that created them.

In the face of this marginalization, the gladiators moulded their own hierarchies and support networks (and for the sake of control and stability may have been encouraged so to do by their owners), and thus gained some cohesion and overall identity as a distinct social group. To some degree the gladiators created their own society on the edges of more respectable society. Yet to view the gladiators as separate, as completely 'other', risks removing them from those who created them, exploited them, and needed them. Gladiators served Rome, they served society and the community, and were rewarded, despite their debasement, 'with, at least, an honourable death, and, at best, riches and freedom' (Kyle 1998: 84). Gladiators may well have been on the fringes of acceptability, but many aspects of their lives were framed by the principles, expectations, and conventions of the wider culture. Gladiators may have been regarded as outsiders, outcasts, and misfits, but this was not how they saw themselves. The evidence from their funerary monuments and cemeteries suggests that at least some gladiators identified with their allocated lot, and did their best to turn the negatives of their lives into positives; this evidence highlights the central dichotomy that faced gladiators and defined their life and marked their death: that they were both isolated from but integral to Roman society.

References

Barton, C. A. 1993. *The Sorrows of the Ancient Romans: The Gladiator and the Monster*. Princeton.

Bomgardner, D. L. 2000. *The Story of the Roman Amphitheatre*. London.

Brunet, S. 2013. 'Women with Swords. Female Gladiators in the Roman World.' In *A Companion to Sport and Spectacle in Greek and Roman Antiquity*. 478–491. P. Christensen and D.G. Kyle, eds. Oxford.

Cagniart, P. 2000. 'The Philosopher and the Gladiator.' *CW* 93: 607–618.

Cambi, N. 1987. 'Salona und seine Nekropolen.' In *Römische Gräbertrassen: Selbstdarstellung, Status, Standard*. 251–280. H. von Hesberg and P. Zanker, eds. Munich.

Campbell, V. 2019. 'Casting a Wide Net: Searching for Networks of Gladiators and Game-givers in Campania.' In *From Document to History. Epigraphic Insights into the Greco-Roman World*. 246–259. C. Noreña and N. Papazakadas, eds. Leiden and Boston.

Carter, M. 2003. 'Gladiatorial Ranking and the *SC de Pretiis Gladiatorum Minuendis* (*CIL* II 6278 = *ILS* 5163).' *Phoenix* 57: 83–114.

Carter, M. 2006a. 'Gladiatorial Combat with 'Sharp' Weapons (*tois oxesi siderois*).' *ZPE* 155: 161–175.

Carter, M. 2006b. 'Gladiatorial Combat: The Rules of Engagement.' *CJ* 102: 97–114.

Carter, M. 2008. '(Un) Dressed to Kill: Viewing the *retiarius*.' In *Roman Dress and the Fabrics of Roman Culture*. 113–135. J. Edmondson and A. Keith, eds. Toronto.

Carter, M. 2009. 'Gladiators and Monomachoi: Greek Attitudes to a Roman "Cultural Performance."' *International Journal of the History of Sport* 26: 298–322.

Carter, M. 2018. '*Armorum Stadium*: Gladiatorial Training and the Gladiatorial *Ludus*.' *BICS* 61: 119–131.

Coleman, K. 2005. 'Bonds of Danger: Communal Life in the Gladiatorial Barracks.' *The Fifteenth Todd Memorial Lecture*. Department of Classics and Ancient History, University of Sydney.

Coulston, J. 2009. 'Victory and defeat in the Roman Arena: The Evidence of Gladiatorial Iconography.' In *Roman Amphitheatres and Spectacula: A 21st-Century Perspective*. 195–210. T. Wilmot, ed. Oxford.

De Caro, S. 1979. 'Scavi nell'area fuori Porta Nola a Pompeii.' *Cronache Pompeiane* 5: 85–95.

Dunbabin, K. 2016. *Theatre and Spectacle in the Art of the Roman Empire*. Ithaca.

Dunkle, R. 2008. *Violence and Spectacle in Ancient Rome*. Harlow.

Durry, M. 1938. *Les cohortes prétoriennes*. Paris.

Edmondson, J. C. 1996. 'Dynamic Arenas: Gladiatorial Presentations in the City of Rome and the Construction of Roman Society during the Early Empire.' In *Roman Theater and Society*. 69–111. W. Slater ed. Ann Arbor.

Edwards, C. 1997. 'Unspeakable Professions: Public Performance and Prostitution in Ancient Rome.' In *Roman Sexualities*. 66–98. J. Hallet and M. Skinner, eds. Princeton.

Edwards, C. 2007. *Death in Ancient Rome*. New Haven.

Fagan, G. 2011. The Lure of the Arena. Social Psychology and the Crowd at the Roman *Games*. Cambridge.

Fagan, G. 2015. '*Training gladiators: Life in the* Ludus.' *In* Aspects of Ancient Institutions *and* Geography. Studies in Honor of Richard J.A. Talbert. 122–144. L. L. Brice and D. Slootjes, eds. Leiden.

Futrell, A. 2006. *The Roman Games*. Malden, MA.

Garaffoni, R. and P. Funari. 2009. 'Reading Pompeii's Walls: A Social Archaeological Approach to Gladiatorial Graffiti.' In *Roman Amphitheatres and Spectacula: A 21st-Century Perspective*. 185–193. T. Wilmot, ed. Oxford.

Garcia y Bellido, A. 1960. 'Lapidas funerarias de gladiators de Hispania.' *AEA* 33: 1–14.

Gardner, J. 1993. *Being a Roman Citizen*. London.

Golden, M. 2008. *Greek Sport and Social Status*. Austin.

Gunderson, E. 1996. 'The Ideology of the Arena.' *ClAnt* 15: 113–157.

Hammer, D. 2010. 'Roman Spectacle Entertainments and the Technology of Reality.' *Arethusa* 43: 63–86.

Haon, A. 1969. 'Les gladiateurs à Nîmes.' *Bulletin de l'École Antique de Nîmes* 4: 83–99.

Hope, V. M. 1998. 'Negotiating Identity and Status: The Gladiators of Roman Nîmes.' In *Cultural Identity in the Roman Empire*. 179–195. J. Berry and R. Laurence, eds. London.

Hope, V. M. 2000a. 'Fighting for Identity: The Funerary Commemoration of Italian Gladiators.' In *The Epigraphic Landscape of Roman Italy*. 93–113. A. Cooley, ed. London.

Hope, V. M. 2000b. 'Status and Identity in the Roman World.' In *Experiencing Rome: Culture, Identity and Power in the Roman Empire*. 125–152. J. Huskinson, ed. London.

Hopkins, K. 1983. *Death and Renewal*. Cambridge.

Jacobelli, L. 2003. *Gladiators at Pompeii*. M. Becker, trans. Los Angeles.

Kanz, F. 2006. 'Head Injuries of Roman Gladiators.' *Forensic Science International* 160: 207–216.

Kyle, D. G. 1998. *Spectacles of Death in Ancient Rome*. London.

Kyle, D. G. 2015. *Sport and Spectacle in the Ancient World*. Chichester.

Mann, C. 2009. 'Gladiators in the Greek East: A Case Study in Romanization.' *International Journal of the History of Sport* 26.2: 272–297.

McCullough, A. 2008. 'Female Gladiators in Imperial Rome: Literary Context and Historical Fact.' *CW* 101: 197–209.

Newby, Z. 2015. 'Roman Art and Spectacle.' In *A Companion to Roman Art*. 552–568. B. Borg, ed. Chichester.

Oliver, J. and R. Palmer. 1955. 'Minutes of an Act of the Roman Senate.' *Hesperia* 24: 320–349.

Papostolou, I. A. 1989. 'Monuments de gladiateurs à Patras.' *BCH* 113: 351–401.

Potter, D. S. 1999. 'Entertainers in the Roman Empire.' In *Life, Death and Entertainment in the Roman Empire*. 256–325. D. S. Potter and D. J. Mattingly, eds. Ann Arbor.

Redfern, R. and H. Bonney. 2014. 'Headhunting and Amphitheatre Combat in Roman London, England: New Evidence from the Walbrook Valley.' *Journal of Archaeological Science* 43: 214–226.

Robert, L. 1940. *Les gladiateurs dans l'Orient grec*. Paris.

Toner, J. 2014. *The Day Commodus Killed a Rhino. Understanding the Roman Games*. Baltimore.

Ville, G. 1981. *La gladiature en Occident des origins à la mort de Domitien*. Rome.

Wiedemann, T. 1992. *Emperors and Gladiators*. London.

CHAPTER 44

....

CULT AND COMPETITION

....

MATTHEW J. P. DILLON

Festive crowds welcome the god with the piping of the flute,
competing with the courageous strength of their limbs.

Pindar *Nemean Ode* 5.37–39

LEGITIMIZING aetiological ('explanatory') mythologies for cult practices were a feature of archaic but particularly of classical Greek religious practice. Yet Pelops' contest for Hippodameia's hand—the major myth attached to the Olympic festival held by the Eleans—was nevertheless not merely a convenient 'shorthand' means with which Elis established the Olympic festival and appropriated control thereof. This myth was a constituent part of the identity of the local people and had almost an autochthonic character: Pelops and Hippodameia were intrinsic to Peloponnesian and particularly Eleian culture and ethnic identity. Not mere utilitarian myths justifying the celebration of the athletic contests but rather an integral part of the Olympic festival, the myths of its various founders and re-founders (Pisos, Pelops, then Herakles) all constituted vital animating religious motives for Eleian organization of the festival and wider Panhellenic participation in it. (The festival was said to then have been re-established (for a fourth time) by Iphitus of Pisa in 776 BCE; aetiologies: see Nagy 1986: 71; religion and the athletic contests at festivals: Gardiner 1930: 28–52; Burkert 1985: 105–107; Nagy 1986: 73–75; Golden 1998: 10–23; Scanlon 2002: 25–39; Mikalson 2007.)

Notwithstanding Strabo's comment that the ancient accounts of the founding of the temple at Olympia and the institution of the *agōnes* (contests) there should be put to one side as there were many versions and they could not be trusted, these *agōnes* took place within a mythical framework (Strab. 8.3.30). Disjointed as the various myths of the establishment of the Olympic *agōnes* were (as Strabo critically comments)—with three heroes involved at different times—they eventually solicited a systemizing mythography. Not an editorial redaction in the biblical sense but nevertheless a reorganizing 'aetiologicalism' or search for the origins, this probably took place in the third century BCE, with the mythographer Apollodorus as a prime candidate for compiling the synthesis. Several 'historical' phases of the establishment and re-establishment of the festival did not constitute a mere further embellishment of the myths but rather strengthened the basic aetiology of divine sanction for the contests, as a celebration of Zeus, and to a lesser extent Pelops.

Rohde's older thesis that the various stephanitic *agōnes* (crown games) were funerary rites for heroes that transformed themselves into gods' festivals is still encountered in modern scholarship. *Agōnes* for heroes do have an aetiological role for three Panhellenic festivals (Sisyphus: the Isthmia; the Seven against Thebes: the Nemea; while Pisus, Pelops, then Herakles (re-)founded the Olympia). Yet these chthonic myths sit commodiously with Olympian ownership and custodianship of these *agōnes*, and the heroic connections are clearly accretions on the original Olympic festival. Nemea will always have been Zeus' festival as the region's main deity, but the Seven against Thebes' foundation saga for this festival accounted in Greek terms for the presence of *agōnes*, and did so in a mythologizing 'historical' fashion, and provided indigenous contextualization for the festivals and justificatory proprietorship of them for their host cities. Heroes had localized cults associated with their tombs and altars, and festivals associated with them could not therefore be moved to and celebrated at other places (Rohde 1925: 117; modern scholarship: Burkert 1985: 106 ('from the Chthonic to the Olympian'); Nagy 1986: 73–76; Golden 1998: 12–14).

Announcing Sacred Contests

Preparations for festival celebrations of major significance in ancient Greece commenced with an initial invitation to participate from the host state to other Greek states. Major Panhellenic festivals, and not simply those that included athletic events, were covered by the provisions of sacred truces, which are now often misunderstood. Prior to festivals involving athletics, heralds (*theōroi*) were sent out by the states organizing these festivals to announce truces (*spondai*). These *theōroi* would travel from festival sites such as Olympia, Nemea, Delphi, Corinth, and Athens to announce, respectively, the Olympic, Nemean, Pythian, Isthmian, and Panathenaic festivals. Only for the Olympia (and the Eleusinian Mysteries at Athens) were these truce-bearing heralds given the less generic and more specific title of *spondophoroi*, meaning 'truce bearers', indicating the religious pre-eminence of the Olympic festival and Eleusinian Mysteries amongst the Greeks. At Olympia the *spondophoroi* were chosen from amongst the sons of the *theokoloi* ('servants of the god') indicating not only that they proclaimed the sacred truce but were connected to the god in this capacity. How they were chosen elsewhere is unknown but the positions may well have been hereditary: this was certainly the case for the Eleusinian Mysteries. When they reached the cities to which they were travelling, these *spondophoroi* or *theōroi* would have been provided with accommodation, food, and entertainment by individuals known as *theōrodokoi* ('*theōroi*-receivers').

In this way the *spondophoroi* made their way throughout the greater Greek world. Inscriptions erected at Olympia recorded the names of *theōrodokoi* for the Olympic festival and honour them for carrying out their duties (*IvO* V 36, 39.9; Pind. *I*. 2.23–24; Dillon 1997: 5–6, bibliographic references at 229 n. 3, to which add Perlman 2000). These heralds were sacred and on the gods' business (Dillon 1997: 9–11). They carried the special herald's wand or sceptre, the *kerykeion* (as Hermes did), and like all Greek heralds were inviolate. Several such bronze *kerykeia* survive. One from Sicily has a length of 45.7 centimetres with the typical circle rising to two 'heads' that do not touch (Fig. 44.1; British Museum Bronze

319; Walters 1899 no. 319; see Hornbostel 1988: pl. 8 for a similar example with inscription from Syracuse).

Panhellenic festivals were religious celebrations held in honour of gods and, as such, were announced by sacred personnel. When the Aetolians seized the *spondophoroi* announcing the Eleusinian Mysteries, something akin to a modern diplomatic crisis took place (*SEG* 15.90; a similar incident is recorded at Aeschin. 2.133–134). Heralds proclaiming the Pythian festival swore an oath to Apollo to carry out their duties properly and these involved ensuring the success of his celebration (Dillon 1997: 7). In turn, states sent official ambassadors, also known as *theōroi*, on a *theōria* to festival celebrations. At Olympia some of the members of these *theōriai* were housed in the Leonidaion building (Mallwitz 1972: 246–253), while at Delphi, the *theōroi* sent by Thebes to participate in the Pythia had their own special accommodation, 'The House of the Thebans' (Dillon 1990). Andros, an Aegean island state, passed a detailed decree in the fifth century BCE regulating the behaviour of the members of

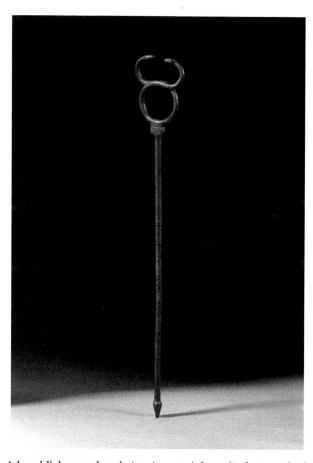

FIGURE 44.1.   A herald's bronze kerykeion (sceptre) from Sicily, inscribed, 'I am the property of the Longenaiai'; 450-420 BC; height: 45.7 cms. These sceptres were used by heralds on their various missions. Spondophoroi carried these, as did Hermes in his connection with agonistic contests (British Museum Bronze 319). © The Trustees of the British Museum.

its official *theōria* to Delphi, including particulars concerning the sharing out of sacrificial meat. Naturally it was a concern that those members of the religious delegation behave properly, and that the god—and his priests—receive their sacrificial due (*LSCG Suppl.* 38 [*CID* 1.7]; translated in Dillon and Garland 2011 doc. 3.25).

Religious activity of this kind affirmed the identity of the state via its participation in Panhellenic athletics. Newly created states, such as Megalopolis and Messene, founded in the wake of the collapse of Spartan power in the 360s BCE, sent *theōriai* to Delphi to worship at Apollo's Panhellenic festival (*CID* 2.4, 2.5–6, with Rutherford 2004: 108, 110–111). Theoric activity served as a legitimizing mechanism—the Messenians articulated their newly revived ethnicity through theoric participation at Delphi. After centuries of Spartan domination, this involvement affirmed the Messenians' separate ethnic identity and this religious activity reasserted their independence. The last Messenian victors at Olympia are known from the seventh century, and their participation at this festival ceased after their enserfment by the Spartans; engagement in Panhellenic *agōnes* re-established their status amongst the states of Greece. (For *theōroi* to festival sites, see Dillon 1997: 11–20, 22–24; Perlman 2000; Rutherford 2007.)

Sacred Truces

Sacred truces at Olympia were known as *spondai Olympiakai* or *ekecheiriai* (Dillon 1997: 1–2; Lämmer 1982–1983; Crowther: 2007: 72–76; cf. Golden 2008: 136–138). For other festivals there was a sacred month, the *hieromēnia* (also used for Olympia: Dillon 1997: 2–3). These *hieromēniai*, sacred months, also indicated that the city conducting the festival was safe from attack during this month, allowing it to celebrate the festival in peace. This did not always work out, and Olympia was the site of bitter fighting in 364 BCE, during the celebration of the festival itself—but this was highly unusual. Clearly, political and territorial interests and, in particular, the status involved in the control of Zeus' pre-eminent sacred site, overcame any scruples about offending the divine (Xen. *Hell.* 7.4.12–32; Diod. 15.78.1–3; Popp 1957: 135–137; Sordi 1984: 27–29, and *passim* for the fate of sanctuaries in war; Goodman and Holladay 1986: 154; Crowther 2003).

Iphitus of Pisa, who was said to have re-established (again) the Olympic festival in 776 BCE, revived both the festival and the truce on the advice of the Delphic oracle, as a renewal of the truce Herakles had established. Herakles as founder and Delphi as the source of Apollo's oracles were a legitimating force for the festival and its *agōnes*, interconnected to establish divine credentials for this truce (Olympic truce: Paus. 5.4.5–6, 5.8.5, 5.20.1, 8.26.3–4; *FGrH* 257.1; Luc. *Icar.* 33; Weniger 1905 esp. 184–189; Finley and Pleket 1976: 98; Dillon 1997: 2–3; Bollansée 1999; Syrigos 2009; Crowther 2001: 42).

These Olympic and other Panhellenic truces did not mean peace for the duration of the festival throughout the Greek world (e.g. Plut. *Ages.* 18.1–19.4). Rather, such truces guaranteed that travellers (official representatives of states, spectators, and the competitors themselves) could travel safely throughout the Greek world to athletic festivals without molestation, even if they were from cities that were at war with states through whose territory they passed on their way to the Panhellenic festivals. Diplomatic scandals erupted over the capture and holding of pilgrims journeying to sacred festivals. When an Athenian citizen named Phrynon was travelling to Olympia he was captured by Philip II's soldiers during Olympia's *hieromēnia*; Philip apologized for the incident, claiming his soldiers were ignorant of the regulations for the sacred month. Famously, the Peace of Nikias indicates the importance of these truces and participation in these festivals: the treaty between Athens and Sparta allowed all Greeks to travel safely to Panhellenic sites, and particularly to attend the *agōnes* (Phrynon: Aesch. 2.12–13; Scholiast to Dem. 19, hypothesis 2.3; Dillon: 1995; 1997: 32; Miller 1991 no. 67; Peace of Nikias: Thuc. 5.18.2; cf. Thuc. 4.118.1–2; sacred truces and months: Weniger 1905; Rougemont 1973 esp. 83–86; Goodman and Holladay 1986: 153; inviolability of pilgrims: Dillon 1997: 27–29, 39).

ALTAR OF ASH

Olympic *agōnes* definitely took place under the aegis of Zeus, as did the *agōnes* of other festivals and their respective gods. On the third day of the festival, there was a major sacrificial ritual, involving numerous sacrifices by Elis, official delegates from Greek states, and private individuals (trainers and their companions) to the god Zeus at his main altar (he had another ten subsidiary ones at the site). Unusually, this altar was not of stone as elsewhere but made up of the ashes of previous sacrifices: it stood about seven metres high, and the first 'course' had a diameter of about thirty-eight metres, with a second course of eleven metres in diameter. This quantity of ash had built up over the years, though of course this would not only have been the result of Panhellenic sacrifices at the time of the Olympia. With so much sacrificial activity, no wonder the Eleans prayed to 'Zeus, Averter of Flies', a practice that Herakles purportedly started (Paus. 5.13.8, 5.14.1, 5.15.9; Ael. *NA* 5.17; Burkert 1972: 111–113; Mallwitz 1998: 91–92).

Yet the altar became a mark of devotion to and piety towards the major Greek deity, and the Panhellenic gathering there on the third day of the contest marked the inextricable link between cult and sport. In like manner, the altars at both Nemea and the Isthmia were very large: at least some forty-one metres long at Nemea, while it had been extended several times (Miller 1990: 148–154), and about forty at the Isthmia (Broneer 1971: 98–101). Given the sheer size of these altars, several sacrifices must have been conducted at the same time, with competitors conducting sacrifices coming and going at a great rate. Clearly athletic competition was not divorced from religious practice but was concomitant with it, and the crowning of the victors could be said to have taken place, as in the phrase inscribed on one victor's statue base, 'beside the rich altar of Zeus' (Ebert 1972 no. 74). Similarly sacrifices were made to Hera before the *agōnes* began at the festival in her honour at the Argive Heraia (Pind. *N.* 10.21–24).

OATHS AND OATH-SWEARING

Pausanias provides information about an oath sworn by competitors before they participated in the Olympia. In the *bouleuterion* (council-chamber) at Olympia stood a statue of Zeus, 'the one most particularly to arouse fear in wrong-doers'. This was Zeus Horkios, and he held a thunderbolt in each hand, not simply as his usual iconographic shorthand descriptor but as a threat to those who broke their oaths. Athletes, and their fathers and brothers (who are to be imagined as accompanying them to Olympia), as well as their trainers, swore the oath that they would behave appropriately and ethically during the festival.

Recording that the oath was sworn over pieces of boar flesh, which had presumably been sacrificed beforehand to Zeus Horkios, Pausanias regrets that he forgot to ask what happened to the flesh after the oath was taken. He adds that the athletes took a further oath, swearing that they had for the last ten months followed the prescribed training regulations, while another oath was taken by those who scrutinized the boys (presumably as to their age category), and the horses, to the effect that their decisions would be just and they would not accept bribes. Such oaths presupposed the existence of cheating and bribery, which were obviously tempting given the glories associated with victory, and they tied all the oath-swearers to a pact with Zeus Horkios himself. In front of the statue's feet there was an inscribed bronze tablet in elegiac verse, the intention of which was strike terror into any would-be cheats and perjurers. This presumably gave poetic advice about the justice and retribution of Zeus, and any divine punishments to be inflicted on those who marred Zeus' festival through cheating. While it has been suggested that the verses referred to actual rather than divine punishments for those detected (Crowther 2008: 487), it is unlikely the poem would have detailed secular penalties (Olympic oath: Paus. 5.24.9–11; quote from §9, cf. 6.24.3; Finley and Pleket 1976: 63–65; Weiler 1991: 55–64; Crowther 1996: 42; 2008: 486–488; Dillon 1997: 105; Swaddling 2000: 25, 39, 50; Spivey 2004: 78; Perry 2007; Golden 2008: 122).

Fines for Cheating

Secular authority prescribed public humiliation for those who cheated in the contests; the existence of specific inscribed rules about cheaters and cheating supports the notion that Zeus' elegiac verses threatened divinely induced punishments. Two fragmentary Olympian laws of the sixth century BCE prohibit wrestlers from breaking their opponents' fingers, for which they will be punished by the judge (*diaitatēr*) striking them on the body (not the head); wrongdoers are referred to as bringing something and making a promise: perhaps some sort of compensatory gift was involved (Dillon 1997: 225; Siewert 1992: 114–116; Ebert and Siewert 1997; Crowther 2008: 487). No specific regulations against corruption at other festival sites survive, but an incident of bribery in which a youth swore on oath that he had paid the other to yield the victory in wrestling to him at the Isthmia created something of a scandal (Philostr. *Gym.* 45). At the contests of the Epidauria in honour of Asklepius at Epidaurus sometime in the third century BCE, an inscription records that three athletes were fined the substantial sum of 1,000 staters each as they had 'corrupted the *agōnes*' (*SIG³* 1076).

At Olympia in particular, cheating was an offence against Zeus as was made clear by the Zanes: those caught cheating paid a fine which was used to dedicate a statue of Zeus (such statues were called Zanes by the Eleans), with an inscription naming the offender and his offence. Clear connections were made between the fact that the contests were celebrated under Zeus' authority, and that the offence was against the god himself. These bronze statues of Zeus were placed outside the sanctuary itself on a stone platform and were paid for from the fines which were levied against athletes who flagrantly broke the rules of the contests. In the ninety-eighth Olympiad (384 BCE), the first of these was erected, when one Eupolus bribed his fellow contestants in the boxing event. Pausanias reports that he was told that this was the first time any competitor had broken Olympic regulations, but of course the archaic sixth-century-BCE laws mentioning punishments for foul play in the wrestling indicate that this was not the case. The change in 384 BCE must have meant that it was the first time the Eleans decided to have these statues erected. Inscriptions on the statue bases warned others against bribery, and stressed that victory came through skill, not money (i.e. bribes). According to Pausanias, the inscription on the second statue read that the statue was erected to the honour of the god, the piety of the Eleans, and as a warning ('reason for fear') to other athletes. The statue was in honour of Zeus, who had been dishonoured by this corruption of his contests, and like the inscription on the statue base of Zeus Horkios was intended to strike fear into any would-be cheating miscreants. Fear of the god and piety itself, as well as the promise of public humiliation through being named on stone, were the main restraining instruments against malpractice at Olympia.

Victors could and did erect statues of themselves at Olympia; cheats were forced to erect by proxy statues of Zeus instead: one type of statue glorified and immortalized victors, while the Zanes shamed their publicly named culprits, and stood outside the sanctuary, while victors' statues had pride of place within: liminal and central spaces were juxtaposed. Pausanias notes his astonishment that competitors could have so little piety for the god that they would give or take bribes. How the officials at other states dealt with corruption is not known: the Zanes appear to have been a purely Olympic phenomenon. (Zanes and fines: Paus. 5.21.2–17; Gardiner 1910: 134–135; Forbes 1952: 171; Mallwitz 1972: 74–75; Finley and Pleket 1976: 66; Dillon 1997: 106, 223–224; Crowther 2004: 149; Golden 2008: 123.)

Fines imposed on Olympic competitors became 'sacred to Zeus': Theagenes wanted to win both the boxing and pankration at Olympia, and entered the boxing where he defeated Euthymus of Locri, but then in the pankration was defeated because he was exhausted from the boxing. The *Hellanodikai* fined him one talent, on the grounds that he only entered the boxing because of animosity towards Euthymus; Theagenes paid the talent which he 'owed to the god' at the next Olympia and refrained from entering the boxing, which Euthymos then won (Paus. 6.6.5–6).

Apollo, as Zeus' prophetic mouthpiece at Delphi, was also seen as taking an active interest in athletic misdemeanours. When in 332 BCE the Athenian Callippus was convicted of bribing the other competitors in the pentathlon at Olympia so that he could win, he was fined by the Eleans—as were the bribed. Hyperides, one of the foremost of Athenian orators, was sent to plead on his behalf that the fine be waived, but the Eleans refused to rescind their decision. Athens refused to pay and in fact boycotted the *agōnes*. Delphi intervened and the god Apollo through the medium of his priestess, the Pythia, refused to grant them any further oracles until they paid up (Hyperides frs. 32.111, 32.112; Paus. 5.21.5–7; Plut. *Mor.* 850b).

GODS OF VICTORY

'Victory in the contest loves song above all else' (Pind. *N.* 3.7); Pindar's odes celebrating victories in the Olympian, Pythian, Nemean, and Isthmian contests not only extol the victors and often their ancestors, but celebrate the divine support granted to specific individuals in these contests. Sweat and toil were important but it was the gods who were the actual source of inspiration and victory. Zeus made the boy wrestler Alcimedon of Aegina victorious at the Nemean festival celebrated in his honour, and granted him another victory at the Olympia in 460 BCE; in fact he had thirty victories to his credit, all won with 'divine favour' (Pind. O. 8.15–18, 67, cf. l. 8: for the prayers of pious men are answered; cf. O. 8.67; Kurke 1991: 20). These festivals which included athletic events were, after all, the 'sacred contests' (Pind. O. 8.63). For Pindar, victory was a gift from Zeus, but it was granted in return for the piety and the prayers of the individual. Sacrifices made prior to the Olympia would be rewarded: Psaumis of Camarina in 448 BCE, before the contests, had sacrificed oxen at the six double altars established there by Herakles near the tomb of Pelops (Pind. O. 5.5–6; cf. O. 10.24–25, N. 6.13). Athletes needed the assistance of the god if they were to enjoy a victory, as did the poet who celebrated it in an ode (Pind. O. 8.10).

Pisa (i.e. Olympia) belongs to Zeus, Pindar proclaims, and he records that Herakles established the contests there as a 'first-fruit' offering to this god for victory in war (Pind. O. 2.2–4, 6.68–70). Each historical Olympic celebration, re-established by Iphitus in 776 BCE, was therefore a renewal of these first-fruit offerings, and the exertions of each competitor were like an offering to the god. Pindar's odes for Olympic victors were in themselves not just a commemoration of the victor's glory but honoured Zeus himself (O. 10.78–85), and Pindar asks Zeus to receive one of his odes as a celebration of victory (O. 13.29). In praising the chariot victory of Arcesilas of Cyrene, Pindar attributes this success to both Apollo and Pytho who granted him this glory (Pind. P. 4.66–67). Arcesilas of Cyrene won the Pythian chariot-race in 462 BCE through the divine favour of 'Castor, of the Golden Chariot', Castor, together with his brother Polydeuces, being a favourite Dorian deity, while Apollo is also said to delight in the victory kōmos: Arcesilas must not forget to give the god the credit. At the very end of this ode Pindar prays that Zeus grant Arcesilas another victory, this time at Olympia (Pind. P. 5.9, 23, 25, 124–152). In 446 BCE, Aristomenes of Aegina had his ode for a wrestling victory at the Pythia dedicated by Pindar to Hesychia, goddess of peace, while Apollo is said to have granted Aristomenes 'the greatest of delights', victory, just as he had when Aristomenes was successful in the pentathlon at the local Aeginetan festival of the Delphinia (Pind. P. 8.1–5, 66–67 with schol.). Pindar similarly attributes Hippokleas' victory in the boys' diaulos to Apollo's plans (Pind. P. 10.11–12); a victory comes by divine favour (Pind. O. 8.67).

Gods were present at and enjoyed spectacles: on the Parthenon frieze their sculptures occupy the central panel of the eastern side, where they are shown waiting and watching the procession of Athenians at the Panathenaia. So too they enjoyed agonistic festivals: Pindar sings of Poseidon, who often travelled to the Isthmus, where 'festive crowds welcome the god with the piping of the flute, competing with the courageous strength of their limbs' (Pind. N. 5.37–39). Delos too was graced by divine presence when the Ionians celebrated games and music there in honour of Apollo, who delighted in these events (HH 3.140–150). Zeus' statue in his temple at Olympia was not simply a visible reminder of the god but an actual manifestation of his presence at the contests, while Herakles also attended the Olympic contests (Pind. O. 3.34).

Prayerful Victories

Bacchylides' ode for Liparion from the island of Ceos praises him for having gained more victories than anyone else in the span of time in which he had been successful at Delphi, Nemea, and the Isthmus: may Zeus also answer Liparion's prayers for fame that is great, 'god-given', and accede to his wish to bind his head with the olive in the contests of Pelops at Olympia (Bacchyl. 8). A prayer for victory, answered with success, glory, and the olive crown for Liparion: all are within the perquisite of the god. Similarly, Automedon was granted victory by Zeus (Bacchyl. 10.25–26), and the association between victory and the presiding god was also celebrated at Nemea where victors were proclaimed by Zeus' altar (Bacchyl. 10.29–30).

Pausanias notes that the statue of Anaxander shows him as praying to the god, but it is not clear whether the act of praying depicted an initial prayer before victory or a thanksgiving afterwards: probably the latter (Paus. 6.1.7). Pausanias describes numerous victor statues at Olympia, but the catalogue is disappointing in terms of references to the gods or divine assistance (6.1–18). This might be thought significant except that he notes that the statues are dedications (6.6.2), and it probably seemed superfluous for statue inscriptions to state this explicitly, when all readers of the statue bases would understand this. Inscriptions generally listed events won and at which festivals (e.g. Ebert 1972 no. 37 [Theagenes]). Even for the famous competitors, such as Milo of Croton, these inscriptions could be surprisingly brief: just a bald two-line statement in this case (Ebert no. 61, cf. 62). But some victors paid tribute to the role of the gods: Philippus of Arcadia's statue base from the turn of the fourth century BCE recorded that he had won the boxing at Olympia, and asks Zeus again (*palin*) to grant Arcadia glory, so attributing his boxing victory to the god (Ebert 1972: 55). Callistratus at the end of the second century BCE attributed his victory to divine assistance in the chariot-race, for 'Poseidon himself held his hand from above on your ever-to-be-remembered chariot' (Ebert 1972: no. 75).

This god did have chariot-racing in his portfolio and had to be thanked for Herodotus of Thebes' victory in that event at the Isthmia (Pind. *I.* 1.52–54), as for Xenocrates' success in the same event (Pind. *I.* 2.14). But Zeus also was at work here, despite these being Poseidon's games, and was also responsible for Herodotus' victory and crown (Pind. *I.* 6.1–4). Hieron of Syracuse was victorious in the chariot-race because Artemis (as goddess of the island Ortygia off Syracuse), along with Hermes, harnessed the horses, while Hieron had called upon Poseidon to grant him victory. Artemis is included here as a local deity, while Poseidon was lord of the horse (Pind. *P.* 2.9). Hermes, too, frequently attended agonistic festivals and also had his part in Herodotus' victory (Pind. *I.* 1.60). The presence of this god at the Panathenaia is shown by the Athenian vases recording victories at this festival. Hermes and Athena are paired on at least three Panathenaic amphoras which were awarded to victors (*ABV²* 307.58; *ARV²* 197.5; *ARV²* 198.24; and on one Nolan amphora: *ARV²* 201.71). An association of Hermes with athletics is not surprising in that his heraldic wand announced truces and upcoming agonistic events and signalled the awarding of victory which he announced as messenger of the gods; he served in this role as presiding deity over these contests alongside Athena.

NIKE

Victory therefore did not come without divine support. While the various victory scenes on vases and coins showing an athlete being crowned or adorned with ribbons (*tainiai*) by a winged Nike ('Victory') may seem a little generic, such iconographic episodes are an explicit visual acknowledgement of the power of Nike. She stands beside Zeus on Mount Olympus and she judges the contests—for both immortals and mortals—while through her judging Alexidamus won victories and his city Mentapontion, thanks to her, was overflowing with *kōmoi* (revels) and celebrations in his honour for his victories at Delphi. Victory too at Olympia in the same event, boys' wrestling, would earlier have been his, for he threw many other boys to the ground, but either a god, or some twisted mortal judgement, robbed him of first place. Yet Artemis (Apollo's brother) has now granted him the Pythian victory (Bacchyl. 11.1–39). Bacchylides even has Nike commanding him to go to Aegina to sing the praises of Teisias of Aegina for his wrestling victory in the Nemean contests (Bacchyl. 12.1–7), and, at the Isthmia, Nike granted the foot-race to an athlete (whose name is now lost) (Bacchyl. 10.15–16).

Iconographically, Nike's role as divine judge finds expression in numerous scenes both on coins and on vases of the goddess hovering over victors in chariot-races and crowning them, or bestowing ribbons on stationary athletic victors. On a (rather neglected) Athenian red-figure bell-krater of about 420–410 BCE by the Nikias Painter, a winged Nike stands beside a bearded athlete at an altar (Fig. 44.2). He holds a torch; there are two other, younger men present: Beazley identifies all three as torch-racers. These three have high crowns as worn by torch-race participants and are presumably place-getters in the Panathenaia or perhaps the Dionysia; the bearded man is apparently the winner as he has the torch and stands closest to the altar and is at the centre of the composition. Nike holds part of a flowing victory ribbon while the athlete holds the other end. The ribbon originates with her and she is bestowing it on him, while her hand and his arm appear to touch. Present too is an older man with a white beard, wearing a festival wreath, who raises his eyes upward, thereby thanking the gods—specifically Athena, Dionysus, or Nike—for the victory and a sacrifice is about to take place at the altar in thanksgiving for success (British Museum 98.7-16.6 [*ARV²* 1333.1; Reinhardt 1957: 122–125, with pl.; Yalouris 1977: 249 fig. 144; *LIMC* I.678; the identity of the old man need not detain the reader here]; cf. *ARV²* 1041.10).

Polycleitus' life-size bronze statue Diadoumenos with the youth tying a ribbon around his head was enormously popular in the Hellenistic and Roman periods (described by Plin. *Nat.* 34.55–57; Luc. *Philops.* 18). Less well known is the small, superb Athenian terracotta vessel of a kneeling boy with his hands raised up, in the act of tying a ribbon (now missing). Inside would have been olive oil for athletic anointing (Agora Museum P1231; ed. pr. Vanderpool 1937 pl. X; Thompson 1957: 58 no. 23; Harris 1964: 231 no. 22a; Kyle 1992: 99 fig. 62). These ribbons, as the Panathenaic amphora of the Nikias Painter indicate, were awarded by mortal judges on the earthly plane, but came from Nike. Magnificent Syracusan coins of galloping four-horse chariots have a sedate Nike hovering above with crown in hand, for victories in this event at the stephanitic *agōnes* (crown games). On a magnificent dekadrachma (ten drachma) silver coin from Syracuse and dating to about 400 BCE, Nike holds the crown between her hands in an open formation, so that the crown can be seen as clearly circular in shape, the charioteer leans forward with his goad (the *kentron*) to urge the horses, and the horses are in full speed: the end of the race is to be imagined and rider and horses are striving for the finish post, while Nike appears to indicate the winner as determined by the gods. In the exergue of the coin (the scene below the horizontal line on which the action is presented) there is a panoply of armour: a cuirass has one greave on either side, with a helmet on the right; on the left the slight horizontal convex shape represents a shield (this is more

FIGURE 44.2. An Athenian red-figure bell-krater of about 420–410 BCE by the Nikias Painter: a winged Nike stands beside a bearded athlete at an altar and prepares to adorn him with a victory fillet (British Museum 98.7-16.6). © The Trustees of the British Museum.

pronounced on other coins, in the same place on the left); the word *athla* (prizes) appears under the armour (Fig. 44.3; *athla* is not quite clear on this example but is so on others; Evans 1892: 53 pls 1.5, 8). So this is not a victory in a crown contest, but in one of the lesser *agōnes* in the Greek world. Several coins from Syracuse, especially by the die-cutter Euainetus, and from elsewhere in the Greek world, have a similar presentation by Nike (but not with this exergue). The reverse of this coin shows the goddess Arethusa of Syracuse; on her headband appear the letters 'KI', an abbreviation for the master craftsman Cimon who cut several of the dies for Syracuse's coins.

The most detailed discussion of the word *athla* and the accompanying exergueal armour on such coins is still Evans, who suggests that the armour could in fact reflect prizes for a local Syracusan chariot-racing contest, with the coins actually awarded as part of the prizes along with a suit of armour (Evans 1892: 133–143). A mainland Greek *agōn* is also a possibility given the fact that armour was a prize at the Argive Heraia, quite a prestigious contest and well worth memorializing on a coin celebrating such a victory (Pind. *N.* 10.22–24, *O.* 7.83 [see below]; *IG* II² 3145). The 'bronze' prizes from *agōnes* at Cleitor, Tegea, Achaia, and Arcadia which Theaius of Aegina, winner of the wrestling at Nemea, had previously carried off for victories on these occasions, may well have been armour, as Pindar elsewhere refers to the bronze prize of the Heraia as simply 'bronze'; the festival was in fact sometimes called

FIGURE 44.3. A silver Syracusan dekadrachma coin, *c*.400 BCE, showing Nike crowning a victorious charioteer as he and his team complete the race. There are several Syracusan coins with a similar representation. Diameter: 35 mms (British Museum inv. no 1841,0726.288). © The Trustees of the British Museum.

'The Bronze Shield' (Pind. *N.* 10. 45–47 (this ode is quite a catalogue of prizes from festivals celebrated with athletic events); *O.* 7.83: 'the bronze in Argos'; Arnold 1937: 436).

Arcesilas dedicated the chariot equipment used in his Pythian victory of 462 BCE to Apollo in his Delphic sanctuary (Pind. *P.* 5.34–42). This was a typical type of dedication: to give the god either the instrument by which something had been awarded, or a part of the booty of profit or spoils of war. Apollo at Delphi often received dedications of tripods, as Zeus at Olympia did helmets and shields. In praying for victory, a competitor would naturally address the presiding god of the agonistic centre involved. Xenophon of Corinth, however, provides evidence for another phenomenon—prayers to the deity of the competitor's city—which was probably widespread but which has left no trace in the epinician (victory ode) or epigraphic records. Before competing in the Olympia in 464 BCE, he vowed to Aphrodite of Corinth that he would dedicate to her one hundred women as *hierodouloi* (sacred slaves) for her temple. After victory in the foot-race and pentathlon (Pind. *O.* 13), he delivered to her sacred grove 'a hundred-bodied herd of grazing girls, rejoicing in his fulfilled vows'. These, as Pindar makes clear were, literally, 'sex-slaves' owned by the goddess, not just for the financial benefit of her temple, but also through his donation, an act of piety and thanksgiving to her (Pind. Fr. 122 [Ath. 573–574b]; Kurke 1995; contra Budin 2008 [for which see Dillon 2012b]: 112–152, cf. 153–209, Pindar and other ancient authors provide incontrovertible proof of the existence of sacred prostitution at Corinth and other Greek cities).

CONTESTS TO HONOUR THE GODS

'With their long robes trailing', Ionian men, women, and children gathered on Delos celebrating Apollo in a festival including contests in boxing, dancing, and singing (*HH Apollo* 146–150, 165–172, quoted by Thuc. 3.104.4–6). Many cultic ceremonies focused on a sacrificial ritual and community feasting to honour and propitiate a deity. But it was also the case that there would be many attendant ceremonies as well to honour the gods: for example, processions, such as the one depicted on the Parthenon frieze, could be extremely large and involve many members of the community. Yet numerous festivals also involved the participation of athletes—or in some instances simply those who could run—who competed in a variety of events in honour of and to delight the gods, such as at the Delia festival on Delos in Apollo's honour. Here all genders of the Ionic community gathered in festive dress (with their 'long robes trailing') and the author of the hymn makes the contests the principal source of honour for the god.

Thucydides (3.104, cf. 1.8.1, 5.1, 5.32.1, 8.108.4), in writing about the revival of this festival by the Athenians in 425 BCE, chooses these very lines to indicate that it was primarily religious considerations that prompted the Athenians—who had had a long connection with the island—to renew the festival, which had ceased to be observed, presumably because of the Persians and their activities in Asia Minor. Peisistratus in the sixth century had purified the temple area, removing the graves within sight of it; now the Athenians repatriated all the graves and forbade women to give birth on the island or for anyone to die there. The festival with its musical and gymnastic events was fully revived, and horse-races were added. Athens had been prompted to the restoration by an oracle, whether a specific Delphic one or one in oral circulation that now struck people as being relevant, much as the 'floating' oracle about the Pelargikon now found applicability (Thuc. 2.17.1–2; Powell 1979: 26; Marinatos 1981: 139–140; the oracle concerning Delphi as coming from an oracular collection at Athens, such as that of Bakis: Brock 1996: 321–325). Athenian control of Delos as a sacred site extended to creating a body of Athenian *amphiktyones* (representatives), just like those at Delphi, but the Athenians alone were Delian *amphiktyones*, while those of Delphi were drawn from several neighbouring states (Delos: *ID* 89, 92, 93, 94, 97, 98 [an interval with five Andrian *amphiktyones*], 100, 103, 104; Athenaeus 437a; Rhodes 1991: 693–694; Constantakopoulou 2007: 70).

Thucydides' quotations of the *Homeric Hymn*—for there is a second one—are usually seen as his own explanation of the revival, his way of intellectualizing the events to complement what he knew of this *Hymn*. (The second extract from the hymn is an admonition by the author of the *Homeric Hymn* to the Ionian maidens to remember him always.) But Thucydides is reporting a decision made in the Athenian *ekklēsia* (assembly), and the lines about the Ionians honouring Apollo with athletic and musical competitions must reflect an expression of Athenian communal piety towards the deity in that debate. A very probable assumption is that the *ekklēsia* discussed the oracle with the supporting evidence of the *Homeric Hymn*: Thucydides is quoting two hymnal extracts which were probably crucial to the assembly debate (the assembly in 480 BCE discussed the two Delphic oracles concerning the invasion, and in 415 BCE discussed the views of diviners concerning the success of the Sicilian expedition: Hdt. 7.140–141; Thuc. 8.1). Impetus for reinvigorating the Delia came from a divine oracle and what constituted a sacred text for the Athenians (the hymn): the very real primary motivation of the Athenians was to revive Ionian worship of Apollo, with sporting and musical contests (Delia, the 425 BCE revival, and the Athenian *theōria*: *HH Apollo* 146–150, 165–173; Thuc. 3.104; Plat. *Phaedo* 58a–c, Xen. *Mem.* 3.3.12, 4.8.2; [Arist.] *Ath. Pol.* 54.7, 56.3 [with Rhodes 1991: 606, 626]; Callim. *Hymn* 4 (Delos) 312–315; Plut. *Thes.* 23.1; Semos *FGrH* 396 F12; Poll. *Onom.* 8.113; cf. Bacchyl. 17; Jordan 1986: 122–123, 137–139; Hornblower 1991: 517–531; 1992: 194–196; Parker 1996: 149–151, 222–225; Mikalson 1998: 214–216; purification: Parker 1983: 276–277).

HEROIZED ATHLETES

Cult could arise from stephanitic success or—more correctly in this case—its revocation when Cleomedes of Astypalaia killed Iccus of Epidaurus in the boxing *agōn* at Olympia. Technically he was the winner as he had defeated his opponent, but the *Hellanodikai* would not crown him as such because of the death; he went mad with grief and returned to his island home. There he attacked a school with some sixty children inside, all of whom were killed when he removed the column supporting the roof. Stoned by the citizens, he took refuge in the shrine of Athena, getting into a chest and closing it from the inside. No attempt to open the lid worked; they then broke the chest up and—there was nothing inside. An enquiry to Delphi as to what had happened to Cleomedes met with the response that he was 'the last of the heroes', and was to be honoured with sacrifices. If this was an attempt by Delphi to stop the creation of new hero cults, it was a failure (Paus. 6.9.6–7; Moretti 1957 no. 174 [with ancient source references]; Fontenrose 1968: 73–74, cf. 76–79 [overly schematic] ancient sources: 74 n. 1, his emendation of Paus. 6.6.7, from 'last' to 'most recent' is not necessary; Brophy and Brophy 1985: 177–182).

Euthymus is himself an interesting case, believed in his lifetime to be the son of a local river god, whose physical prowess overcame a local hero of Temesa who took a virgin in marriage each year to propitiate his spirit, and so earned heroization for himself on the command of a Delphic oracle (to make sacrifices to him) during his own lifetime; the Olympic victory is the starting point of the story, because it establishes Euthymus' physical credentials (Paus. 6.6.4–11; Callimachus F99; Strab. 6.1.5; Ael. *VH* 8.18; Suda *s.v.* Euthymus; Currie 2002, esp. 24–25; athletes and hero-cults: Fontenrose 1968 [Euthymus: 79–81]; cf. Currie 2005).

Theagenes of Thasos was also heroized: he was an incredibly successful athlete, with 1,400 victories to his credit in numerous events all over Greece. He was said to have been the son of a priest of Herakles, who took the form of his father Timosthenes one night and so was his father. On the way home from school one day he took a fancy to the statue of a god in the market-place and carried it home, but returned the statue after public protest. The deed won him fame throughout Greece. After his death, a statue was erected in Theagenes' honour on Thasos. One of his enemies came each night and flogged the statue and when eventually Theagenes' statue tired of this it fell on him with fatal consequences. In line with Athenian practice the statue was prosecuted, found guilty of murder, and cast into the sea. A blight then ensued on the island, Delphi was consulted, and the oracle commanded the 'restoration of exiles'. Doing this brought no relief, so a second journey to Delphi yielded the more explicit instruction that they had forgotten to restore Theagenes. The restoration of the statue ended the 'wrath of the gods' and sacrifices were then made to it 'as to a god'. Both amongst the Hellenes and the *barbaroi* there were many statues of him, and he became a healing deity among the latter. Several divine intersections are evident here: the relationship with Herakles, the gods' interest in his statue being returned, and the two commands of the Pythia. His theft and return of a god's statue are reflected in the removal and return of his own statue, while his numerous superhuman victories, particularly at Olympia, are all ingredients in his heroization (Paus. 6.6.5, 6.11.6; Fontenrose 1968: 75–76, cf. 76–79; Hornblower and Morgan 2007: 26). The heroization of triumphant historical athletes was an Olympian phenomenon, entirely absent for victors at other festivals; only victory in the greatest of *agōnes*, the Olympian, secured posthumous sacrifice and cult (see also Euthykles, Kleomedes, and Oibotas: Fontenrose 1968: 73–76). Theagenes was not the only one with a Heraklean dimension: Milo never gained heroization, but he did go into battle and defeated the enemy wearing his six Olympic crowns and dressed as Herakles (lion skin and club) (Diod. 12.9.5–6).

Defeated athletes might sneak into their cities at night, but successful competitors made quite an entry: it was a custom to tear down part of the city walls and receive the victor or victors in a victory procession: the festivals which permitted this were known as eiselastic ones. In 412 BCE Exaenetus of Acragas won the *stadion*, or foot-race, at Olympia (as he had in 416 BCE), and on his return the city demolished part of its walls and escorted his triumphal return with a procession of three hundred chariots, each drawn by two white horses. Diodorus indicates that this was just one feature of the procession, but does not elaborate further. Plutarch misinterprets such incidents: that a city does not need walls anyway if it has men capable of fighting and winning. Rather, such processions should be seen as potential precursors to posthumous divination for the victorious entrants. Processions were for gods: Exaenetus and others were being likened to divine beings (Diod. 13.82.7 and Aelian *VH* 2.8 [Exanaitus]; Plut. *Mor.* 639e; Suet. *Nero* 25; Dio 63.20).

Heroes could arise for other reasons, and the most common of those who were honoured with festivals and agonistic events were the *oikistai* (singular *oikistēs*), the 'founders' of colonies. Tlapolemus, *oikistēs* of the Rhodians, was worshipped 'as a god' with a sacrificial procession and athletic contests: Diagoras was pelted with flowers there as a victor (Pind. *O.* 7.77–82; Dougherty 1993: 191–193). When the people of Amphipolis changed their *oikistēs* from the Athenian Hagnon, who had actually founded the colony, to Brasidas who brought it over to the Spartan side but was killed in the battle over the city in 422 BCE, the city built an enclosure around his tomb and honoured him as a hero, with sacrifices and athletic competitions. Now that the city had gone over to the Spartans the city felt it could no longer honour Hagnon, the Athenian founder, and this heroization of Brasidas was also a manifestation, Thucydides notes, of the city's desire to have the Spartans as allies.

With his customary meticulous attention to religious details, Thucydides articulates a crucial principle of Greek religion, which is more often implicit than explicit in the ancient sources: neither Pindar nor Bacchylides, nor numerous other ancient sources writing about the agonistic competitions, comment on this aspect. It is Thucydides alone who propounds the reciprocal nature of the worship offered in agonistic cult in Greek religion. Hagnon, as an Athenian founder, could no longer give Amphipolis any posthumous assistance as the city had gone over to the enemies of his own city, Athens. Therefore contests and sacrifices in Hagnon's honour would be futile (and Hagnon might well have still been alive at the time, which was probably also a consideration). In adopting Brasidas instead as *oikistēs*, the Amphipolitans destroyed every single physical reminder that Hagnon had ever been associated with their city; this is probably the Greek world's first example of an official cult suppression and extirpation. To make Brasidas work solely for them meant the eradication of the memory of Hagnon. Fundamental to this, of course, was the grave of Brasidas at Amphipolis, which, as with all hero cults, acted for the localization of the benefits he would bring the city (Thuc. 5.11; Malkin 1987: 228–232; overlooked by Jordan 1986 and Hornblower 1992). In the same way Pelops, as the hero of Olympia, was worshipped there, and his altar was crowded with visitors at the time of the festival (Pind. *O*. 1.90–93).

Divine beings—gods or heroized mortals—were honoured with festivals of processions, sacrifices, and sports contests. This in fact was a major definition of the divine and semi-divine; competitions held in honour of someone or some god were a principle of delineation between the ordinary mortal and divinity. Cultic athletic activity was also gendered: there were no female heroes—heroines—who received such honours for physical prowess. Cynisca was the classic exception but not for any brute strength which she possessed. Sister of the Spartan king Agesilaus II, she financed chariots in the Olympia and won victories in 396 and 392 BCE (but herself, of course, could not be present at the race itself). There was a *hērōön* ('hero-shrine') dedicated to her at Sparta, and a statue of her at Olympia, by none other than Apelles himself. Other Spartan women went on to win races but none received the attention Cynisca did: she was the first woman victor and also of royal lineage; she foreshadowed the heroization of women in the Macedonian court and Hellenistic kingdoms (Xen. *Ages*. 9.6; Paus. 3.15.1, 5.12.5, 6.1.6; *IG* V.1 235; her epigram: *IvO* 160; Moretti 1953 no. 17; Ebert 1972: 33; *CEG* 1.820; *Anth. Pal*. 13.16; in this volume see Mari and Stirpe [Chapter 7], Valavanis [Chapter 9], Nicholson [Chapter 19], Cartledge [Chapter 28], and Raschke [Chapter 35]).

WOMEN RACING FOR THE GODS

Running and women's ritual were commonly intertwined in ancient Greece. While often seen as a man's domain, athletic activity in fact was also possible for girls and women. This could be at small local festivals or Panhellenic ones. In male events, the religious ideology was implicit rather than explicit: the wrestling, pankration and boxing, and other events took place, for example, under the aegis of Poseidon at the Isthmia, but individual events were not linked into direct worship of a god or the gods. Women-specific cultic activity involving competition—to be specific, the running of races—employed altogether another paradigm.

At Orchomenos in Boeotia (central Greece), a stronghold of the worship of the god of ecstasy and possession Dionysos, women celebrated the festival of the Agrionia. An annual event, it commemorated the myth in which the daughters of Minyas (the Minyai) refused to acknowledge the divinity of the young god and were sent mad by him, after which they ripped apart and then consumed one of their sons raw (Ael. *VH* 3.42; Lib. *Met*. 10 [*The Minyai*] 3). The sisters' descendants, called the *Oleiai* ('Murderesses'), were pursued each year in the Agrionia by a sword-wielding priest of the god, who technically was allowed to kill any of the women he caught. This detail is known because Plutarch, the sole authority, records that in his own time an over-zealous priest called Zoilus caught and fatally stabbed one of the women: he died from a trifling infection and Orchomenos was also punished. This running recalls women's maenadic activities through the hills and here becomes a cultic race in which they had to exert themselves, 'encouraged' by a male in pursuit, in order to honour the god: an event 'sponsored' and of interest to a single specific deity (Plut. *Mor.* 299 e–f, cf. 717a; Dillon 2012a; Müller 1844: 166; Burkert 1972: 189–200; 1985: 164–165).

Emphasis on the physical fitness of girls and women at Sparta achieved through training is quite well known and attributed by the Spartans themselves to their lawgiver Lykourgos (Xen. *Const. Lc.* 1.3–8; Plut. *Lyk.* 14; Kritias F15; cf. Aristoph. *Lys.* 82; Poll on 4.102; Cartledge 1981: 90–97; Scanlon 1988; 2002: 121–138; Dillon 2007: 154–155 with bibliography at n. 21). Girls did not undergo the boys' systematic training in the *agōgē* system, and they did not have their own similar regime despite incorrect modern assumptions (Cartledge 1981: 93 [2002: 141 n. 39]; Garland 1990: 138; Fantham 1994: 59; cf. Kennell 1995: 45–46; Ducat 1999: 57–58). Not surprisingly, Spartan females both pre- and post-adolescent were fit. Euripides indicates that there were no segregated training grounds but that the boys and girls shared both running tracks and wrestling places: the girls left home wearing loose clothing with their thighs exposed. Athenaeus reports that on Chios it was pleasant to watch the boys and girls wrestling together, and Plutarch has girls dancing and racing on the island of Keos while their suitors watched, which makes the competitions seems very much like a prenuptial rite, probably in honour of a goddess, perhaps Aphrodite or Hera (Eur. *Andr.* 599–600; Ath. 566e; Plut. *Mor.* 249d). Spartan girls were known to other Greeks as 'thigh flashers' (*phainomēridas*): as they ran in their short dresses, they held one hem up high to allow the greatest mobility as they ran (*phainomēridas*: Ibycus 339 (*PMG* 58); Poll. *Onom.* 2.187, 7.55 (cf. 54); Prop. 3.14.1–4; Scanlon 1988: 208; 2002: 125; Dillon 2000: 460–461).

Several Greek bronze statuettes of girls and young women running in a 'miniskirt' tunic revealing their thighs are believed, unnecessarily, to be of Spartan origin (examples at Serwint 1993: 410 n. 35). In particular there is a very fine piece of the archaic period, of about 560–550 BCE, which shows a young woman hitching up her skirt (BM 208, *c.*520 BCE: Walters 1899 no. 208; Arrigoni 57; Serwint 1993: 407 fig. 1; Fantham 1994: 60 fig. 2.1; Scanlon 2002 fig. 4.1). While the literary evidence for girls hitching up their skirts to run comes only from Sparta, when girls from other states ran they will have presumably also have done so, and these statuettes do not necessarily represent Spartan girls, particularly as numerous Greek states allowed their girls to compete in races. (For Spartan girls running see also Thommen 1999: 137–138; Dillon 2000; Kyle 2007: 184–185.)

This commitment to exercising and running is always seen by both ancient writers and modern scholars as part of Lykourgos' eugenic scheme. But there is another dimension as well. Spartan girls raced ritually: complementing the Agrionia at Orchomenos, eleven girls (known as Dionysiades; why specifically eleven cannot be determined) honoured Dionysos at Sparta with both sacrifices and running. Pausanias notes that the Spartans took the practice from Delphi, which indicates that races for girls also existed there, but whether they were in a similarly religious context is not made clear, and the connection to Delphi is presumably incorrect (but part of a legitimizing aetiology for the practice) as there is no need to assume that these races were not an indigenous Spartan practice (Paus. 3.10.7; cf. 3.16.1; Hesychius *s.v.* 'Dionysiades'; Pettersson 1992: 34, 40; Larson 1995: 64–69; Calame 1997: 149–156; Dillon 2000: 465; Dillon 2002: 213; Dillon 2013). Plato's races for girls in the *Laws* could be presumed to be modelled on Sparta, according to the commonplaces of modern scholarship, but he divorces them from any religious context (Plat. *Laws* 833c–d).

Only males—the categories being boys, youths, and adults—could compete at the Olympic festival held every four years. Married women were prohibited from attending and watching the events: this could be in line with several Greek religious prohibitions against women participating in certain male-only cults (Dillon 2000: 469–471). As women were spectators at—as far as is known—all other festivals involving athletics and nude athletes, this prohibition is unique to the Olympic *agōnes*. Death through being thrown alive from Mt Typaion was the punishment, but no woman had been convicted except for the widow Callipateira (also known as Pherenike) who was exempted after she disguised herself as a male trainer and brought her son to Olympia; she was so excited when he was victorious that she jumped out of the enclosure from which the trainers watched. Pardoned on account of the number of Olympic victors in her family, henceforth trainers had to strip naked, as the athletes themselves did (Paus. 5.6.7–8, 6.7.2; Dillon 2000: 459–460; cf. Philostr. *Gym.* 17; Crowther 1982; training and trainers, cf. Philostr. *Apoll.* 5.43; Crowther 1991; Dillon 1997: 221; Nicholson 2005: 117–210 [not Kallipateira]).

Girls and young unmarried women, however, could compete at Olympia at their own festival. For every Olympic celebration, sixteen women wove a *peplos* (dress) for the goddess Hera, and also organized contests called the Heraia in the form of races for the goddess. Girls were divided into three age categories and competed after the Olympia itself had ended, and had exclusive use of the racetrack. Winners received an olive crown, just like male Olympic victors, marking a certain equality with them, as well as a portion of the sacrifice to Hera, confirming the cultic orientation of their *agōnes*. What is interesting to note is that Pausanias described their dress: hair let down, a tunic just above knee length, and the right shoulder bared as far as that breast. Clearly they would in appearance have been very similar to the famous Spartan 'thigh-flashers'. This has led to a misconception amongst some scholars that it was Spartan girls who competed at these Olympic races, but a similarity of dress cannot clinch this. Rather it needs to be imagined that some girls accompanied their brothers or even fathers to Olympia and after the all-male five-day festival, then competed in their own games.

There is no specific mention of Spartan girls in Pausanias' account and no reason to consider that this festival was even a priority for Spartan girls in terms of attendance and participation; the races may indeed even have been only for local girls (but it can readily be postulated that sisters of athletes attended). Winners dedicated statues of themselves with their names inscribed, just as male victors could; statues in the girls' case would doubtless be dedicated to Hera. Aetiologically, Pausanias explains that Hippodameia, the wife of Pelops, established the races in appreciation to Hera for her marriage. These girls, consequently, were participating in a prenuptial rite. These races for Hera were probably very ancient in origin, with Zeus and Hera the most ancient deities of Olympia, and became more formalized as the Olympic events for males became transformed from local contests to Peloponnesian and then Panhellenic ones (Paus. 5.16.2–3; Dillon 2000: 460–462; 2002: 131, 213, 243; Scanlon 1984; 2002: 98–120; Bouvrie 1995; Spivey 2004: 117–121; Crowther 2007: 148; Scanlon 2008; as if for Spartan girls: Kunstler 1987: 36; Fantham 1994: 59). Girls competed in other races in ritual contexts, in other festivals both Panhellenic and local. At the Brauronia festival at Athens they honoured Artemis with races, not as a transition rite to womanhood—many of the girls shown on vases and in statues at the sanctuary are far too young for this—but to worship the goddess in a kourotropic ('child-raising') sense, namely fostering growth and childbirth.

What is interesting is that girls competed very much in foot-races at local festivals in honour of various deities—and not simply kourotrophic or marriage-oriented deities, but also Dionysos. The races for Dionysus juxtaposed their maenadic meanderings in the hills with a formal structured racing event, while those for Hera reflected her interest in young girls as a patron of marriage. Similarly, the races for Helen at Sparta were specifically to assist girls with undertaking marriage. While men did compete in a variety of races and other competitions in honour of gods, these in fact tended to be at major Panhellenic or *polis* events, very much within the formal public gaze where the competitive aspect was stressed through crowns, monetary awards, and glorification through victory odes and victory scenes on magnificent vases. For males (men and boys) it was the physical prowess which they exhibited and what they wanted from the gods was the victory of a first place, which only one of them could obtain; their cult expression was individualistic in that sense, whereas the girls' was collective. Even if the winner in the three races of the Heraia was especially honoured, clearly each girl wanted not only to worship the goddess, but also to gain a favourable marriage for herself. Races for Dionysus at Sparta and Orchomenos had the same focus: it was a collective experience rather than an egocentric one. This reflects the individualistic and agonistic nature of male culture in ancient Greece. Women's festivals, such as the Thesmophoria and the Adonia, were much more communal expressions of gender identity amongst women. They came together in secret or semi-public gatherings and joked and laughed about their sexuality and their sexual desires, expressed their solidarity as a gender group with specific concerns relating to marriage, fertility, and childbirth (Dillon 2002). This was in contrast to the male or male-dominated festivals, in which the men might have worshipped together but did not express a specific gender identity or celebrate a specific male sub-culture.

Generally, men dominate the Athenian vase-image records for athletics and charioteering: men wrestle, box, struggle in the pankration, long-jump, and throw javelins (the visual evidence for Greek sport is nearly almost all Athenian). While some agonistic festivals included events for girls and women, these do not find iconographic expression. Atalanta in myth is the exception. She is shown on vases wrestling with and defeating Peleus in the contests for Pelias; she is the first to hit the beast, with an arrow, in the Calydonian boar hunt. Running was a speciality—she was to marry whoever defeated her. Hippomenes distracted her with golden apples, so he won, they had intercourse in a temple, and were then turned into lions for this offence. Some versions of the myth record her marriage and a child. She combines the roles of hunter, athlete, wife, and mother. But she does not appear to have been a role model for the Greek girl or woman athlete. Certainly she did not receive heroic honours or cult from women for her athletic prowess, and there is no evidence that girls and women participating in events such as the Olympic Heraia worshipped Atalanta; her own main devotion at any rate was to Artemis as huntress. By distorting gender conventions and combining male and female attributes, she was singled out for uniqueness, and found no historical female equivalent (Atalanta: esp. Hes. frs. 72–76; Theognis 1287–1294; Apollod. 3.9.2; *LIMC* II s.v. Atalante nos. 60–89; cf. Scanlon 2002: 175–198).

OF PANOPLY AND COW

While control of Delos was part of Athens' aspirations to be a religious and political leader of the Ionians, highlighted by the ethnocentric character of the Delia, the generally secular modern interpretation of these events in 425 BCE stresses the political and imperial benefits accruing to Athens from celebrating a Panionian celebration, tying in the greater promotion of the Panathenaia as a so-called 'empire festival' (with the allies bringing a cow and panoply of arms to dedicate at Athens: *IG* I³ 46.17–18 [Brea]; *IG* I³ 34. 41–43, *IG* I³.56–57; schol. Aristoph. *Cl.* 386) and the bringing of the *phoros* (usually mistranslated as 'tribute') by the allies to the Great Dionysia along with a larger-than-life model phallus (*IG* I³ 46 [Brea]; Krentz 1993; Dillon 1997: 144–145). It is primarily the religious aspect which interested the Athenians, who in their assemblies routinely made religious decisions, such as the introduction of the worship of new gods to the Athenian pantheon and what sort of doors Athena would like for the Parthenon. The extra-civic identity of the Athenians as leaders of the Ionians was obviously important, but did not necessarily compete with religious piety and was not an obstacle to it. This piety was not merely complementary to political considerations but existed in its own right. At the very least they were intertwined (extra-civic activities and cult). More probably, in the consciousness of the Athenian citizen, the athletic, equestrian, and musical contests honouring the gods, and the communal participation in the festival were central to the construction of Athenian religiosity. It was not so much the case that the allies were obligated to send gifts to the Panathenaia and the Dionysia, but that Athens in a very real sense had to ensure that all the communities of Athens—and the allies were these—joined in the communal worship of the gods by participating and bringing gifts. One can only imagine the religious awe allied embassies felt when arriving with their gifts in Athens and partaking in the magnificent Panathenaia and fecund Dionysia, both in honour of major deities.

Nikias led the Athenian *theōria* to Delos at some unknown date between 425 and 415 BCE, but conducted a more than usually sumptuous celebration or, if Plutarch is to be understood correctly, seems to have done so on more than one occasion. His piety is well known, and one of his most ardent admirers, Thucydides, criticizes him for being 'over-given' to divination (Thuc. 7.50.4). It is tempting to interpret this as a further manipulation of Ionionism serving his own need for popularity (Plut. *Nik.* 3.1) and as a natural outcome of Athenian religious imperialism. Plutarch described the event and in a manner so detailed that his account can only have come from a fourth-century-BCE Atthidographer (historian of Attica; *Nik.* 34–36). While Plutarch provides his own editorial comments, the basic narrative is a confirmation of Nikias' own *eusebeia*. Instead of an impromptu choral performance as the ships landed and the disembarking performers were met by the crowds bidding them to sing before they had even put on their sacred robes, Nikias reorganized the festival: the ships pulled into port at Rheneia, the nearby island, and then on the next day the choirs set off along a boat-bridge he had brought from Athens, singing as they went, followed by the sacrificial victims. That is, he transformed an impromptu worship into a formal one, involving a procession honouring the god with song (Plut. *Nik.* 3.4–6; Furley 1995: 32–33; Dillon 1997: 127).

Conclusion

While it might seem too subtle a distinction, it is perhaps a little erroneous to make general statements such as '[there was] a combination of religious rites and spectacular athletics' (Kyle 1992: 101, writing of the Panathenaia). *Agōnes* occurred within religious contexts.

Panathenaic celebrations included a spectacular procession to the Acropolis in honour of Athena: cavalry, sacrificial victims, young women and the like; *agōnes* were subsumed within the pattern of organized worship and calendrical precision (Athena's birthday was celebrated in the Panathenaia on the twenty-eighth day of the month Hekatombaion). Inscribed on marble, the fourth-century-BCE Panathenaic programme lists numerous contests and their prizes, perhaps in the order in which the contests were held (*IG* II² 2311: incomplete; cf. Neils 1992a: 15–17). While the Panathenaia played a large role in the development of the construction of the Athenian identity (commencing with Peisistratus), it was also important for gender identity and confirming status within the civic body: the old woman who notes how she had been a *kanēphoros* for Athena (as well as a bear at the Brauronia) uses this fact to claim a role for herself in the state (Aristoph. *Lys.* 641–646; Dillon 2002: 37–52). Though striving for Panhellenic attention, the Panathenaia never joined the stephanitic contests, and the necessity of attracting non-Athenian competitors led to the awarding of prizes, in particular jars of olive oil, presented to victors as the 'Panathenaic' *amphorai* (*IG* II² 2311; Neils 1992b). These *amphorai* always depict Athena on the obverse: the *agōnes* were celebrated as part of her festival and birthday, the oil symbolized the sacred olive tree she presented to Athens, and the terracotta amphora image left no doubt that the contests were in honour of Athena and that it was she who had granted the victory (Athena as 'the canonical obverse decoration': Neils 1992b: 30).

While the four great Panhellenic festivals provided no monetary gain for their athletic participants, those of all the other festivals did. So the athletes themselves at these prize contests presumably had a motive which was, if not primarily, at least partially monetary in attending and competing, rather than a religious one involving piety towards the gods— though this situation might have arisen because host cities wished to attract as many good competitors as possible for the entertainment of their deities. Modern celebrations of the Olympic Games are spectacularly secular, being primarily celebrations of national rivalry and reflecting the consumeristic, commercial nature of modern sport and western capitalist ideologies. By contrast, the religious context for the ancient Greek games cannot be neglected; the emphasis should not be on these spectacles as sports, but on the close association of sports with festival and worship. The intertwining of sports and cult with which the Greeks themselves were preoccupied was primarily intended to delight and entertain their gods, gaining their favour for both states and individual competitors.

REFERENCES

Arnold, I. R. 1937. 'The Shield of Argos.' *AJA* 41: 436–444.

Bollansée, J. 1999. 'Aristotle and Hermippos of Smyrna on the Foundation of the Olympic Games and the Institution of the Sacred Truce.' *Mnemosyne* 52: 562–567.

Brock, R. 1996. 'Thucydides and the Athenian Purification of Delos.' *Mnemosyne* 49: 321–327.

Broneer, O. 1971. *Isthmia I. Temple of Poseidon.* Princeton.

Brophy, R. and M. Brophy. 1985. 'Deaths in the Pan-Hellenic Games II: All Combative Sports.' *AJPh* 106: 171–198.

Bouvrie, S. des. 1995. 'Gender and the Games at Olympia.' In *Greece and Gender.* 55–74. B. Berggreen and N. Marinatos, eds. Bergen.

Budin, L. 2008. *The Myth of Sacred Prostitution in Antiquity.* New York.

Burkert, W. 1972. *Homo Necans: Interpretationen altgriechischer Opferriten und Mythen*. Berlin.

Burkert, W. 1985. *Greek Religion: Archaic and Classical*. J. Raffan, trans. Oxford.

Calame, C. 1997. *Choruses of Young Women in Ancient Greece: Their Morphology, Religious Role, and Social Function*. J. Collins and J. Orion, trans. London.

Cartledge, P. 1981. 'Spartan Wives: Liberation or Licence?' *CQ* 31: 84–105 (= 2002, Whitby, M. [ed.] *Sparta* [Edinburgh]: 131–160).

Constantakopoulou, C. 2007. *The Dance of the Islands: Insularity, Networks, the Athenian Empire, and the Aegean World*. Oxford.

Crowther, N. B. 1982. 'Athletic Dress and Nudity in Greek Athletics.' *Eranos* 80: 163–168.

Crowther, N. B. 1991. 'The Olympic Training Period.' *Nikephoros* 4: 161–166.

Crowther, N. B. 1996. 'Athlete and State: Qualifying for the Olympic Games in Ancient Greece.' *JHS* 23: 34–43.

Crowther, N. B. 2001. 'Visiting the Olympic Games in Ancient Greece: Travel and Conditions for Athletes and Spectators.' *IJHS* 18: 37–52.

Crowther, N. B. 2003. 'Power and Politics at the Ancient Olympics: Pisa and the Games of 364 B.C.' *Stadion* 29: 1–10.

Crowther, N. B. 2004. *Athletika: Studies on the Olympic Games and Greek Athletics*. Hildesheim.

Crowther, N. B. 2007. 'The Ancient Olympics and Their Ideals.' In *Onward to the Olympics: Historical Perspectives on the Olympic Games*. 69–80 (= 2004, *Athletika* 1.2: 11–22). G. Schaus and S. Wenn, eds. Waterloo, Ont.

Crowther, N. B. 2008. 'Nothing New under the Olympic Sun? The Swearing of Oaths at the Ancient and Modern Games.' In *Pathways: Critiques and Discourse in Olympic Research: Ninth International Symposium for Olympic Research*. 485–497. R. K. Barney et al., eds. London, Ont.

Currie, B. 2002. 'Euthymos of Locri: A Case Study in Heroization in the Classical Period.' *JHS* 122: 24–44.

Currie, B. 2005. *Pindar and the Cult of Heroes*. Oxford.

Dillon, M. P. J. 1990. 'The House of the Thebans (*FD* iii.1 357–58) and Accommodation for Greek Pilgrims.' *ZPE* 83: 64–88.

Dillon, M. P. J. 1995. 'Phrynon of Rhamnous and the Macedonian Pirates: the Political Significance of the Sacred Truces.' *Historia* 44: 250–254.

Dillon, M. P. J. 1997. *Pilgrims and Pilgrimage in Ancient Greece*. London.

Dillon, M. P. J. 2000. 'Did Parthenoi Attend the Olympic Games? Girls and Women Competing, Spectating, and Carrying out Cult Roles at Greek Religious Festivals.' *Hermes* 128: 457–480.

Dillon, M. P. J. 2002. *Girls, Women, and Cult in Classical Greece*. London.

Dillon, M. P. J. 2007. 'Were Spartan Women Who Died in Childbirth Honoured with Grave Inscriptions? Whether to Read ἱερῶν or λεχοῦς at Plutarch *Lykourgos* 27.3.' *Hermes* 135: 149–165.

Dillon, M. P. J. 2012a. 'Agrionia.' *Encyclopedia of Ancient History*. R. Bagnall, ed. Oxford.

Dillon, M. P. J. 2012b. 'Book Review: *The Myth of Sacred Prostitution in Antiquity*. By Stephanie Budin.' *European Legacy* 17.6: 839.

Dillon, M. P. J. 2013. 'Engendering the Scroll: Girls' and Womens's Literacy in Classical Greece.' In *The Oxford Handbook of Childhood and Education in the Classical World*. 396–417. J E. Grubbs and T. Parkin, eds. Oxford.

Dillon, M. P. J. and L. Garland. 2011. *Ancient Greece: Social and Historical Documents from Archaic Times to the Death of Alexander the Great*. 3rd edn. London.

Dougherty, C. 1993. 'It's Murder to Found a Colony.' In *Cultural Poetics in Archaic Greece: Cult, Performance, Politics*. 178–198. C. Dougherty and L. Kurke, eds. Cambridge.

Ducat, J. 1999. 'Perspectives on Spartan Education in the Classical Period.' In *Sparta: New Perspectives*. 43–66. S. Hodkinson and A. Powell, eds. London.

Ebert, J. 1972. *Griechische Epigramme auf Sieger an gymnischen und hippischen Agonen*. Berlin.

Ebert, J. and J. Siewert. 1997. 'Eine archaische Bronzeurkunde aus Olympia mit Vorschriften für Ringkämpfer und Kampfrichter.' In *Agonismata*. 200–236. M. Hillgruber, R. Jakobi, and W. Luppe, eds. Stuttgart.

Evans, A. J. 1892. *Syracusan 'Medallions' and Their Engravers in the Light of Recent Finds, With Observations on the Chronology and Historical Occasions of the Syracusan Coin-Types of the Fifth and Fourth Centuries B.C. and an Essay on Some New Artists' Signatures on Sicilian Coins*. London.

Fantham, E. 1994. 'Spartan Women: Women in a Warrior Society.' In *Women in the Classical World: Image and Text*. 56–67. E. Fantham et al., eds. New York.

Finley, M. I. and H. W. Pleket. 1976. *The Olympic Games: The First Thousand Years*. London.

Fontenrose, J. 1968. 'The Hero as Athlete.' *CSCA* 1: 73–104.

Forbes, C. A. 1952. 'Crime and Punishment in Greek Athletics.' *CJ* 47: 169–173, 202–203.

Furley, W. D. 1995. 'Praise and Persuasion in Greek Hymns.' *JHS* 115: 29–46.

Gardiner, E. N. 1910. *Greek Athletic Sports and Festivals*. London.

Gardiner, E. N. 1930. *Athletics of the Ancient World*. Oxford.

Garland, R. 1990. *The Greek Way of Life*. Ithaca, NY.

Golden, M. 1998. *Sport and Society in Ancient Greece*. Cambridge.

Golden, M. 2008. *Greek Sport and Social Status*. Austin, TX.

Goodman, M. D. and A. J. Holladay. 1986. 'Religious Scruples in Ancient Warfare.' *CQ* 36: 151–171.

Harris, H. A. 1964. *Greek Athletes and Athletics*. London.

Hornblower, S. 1991. *A Commentary on Thucydides*, vol. 1: *Books I–III*. Oxford.

Hornblower, S. 1992. 'The Religious Dimension to the Peloponnesian War, or, What Thucydides Does Not Tell Us.' *HSCPh* 94: 169–197.

Hornblower, S. and C. Morgan, eds. 2007. 'Introduction.' In *Pindar's Poetry, Patrons, and Festivals: From Archaic Greece to the Roman Empire*. 1–44. S. Hornblower and C. Morgan, eds. Oxford.

Hornbostel, G. W. 1988. 'Syrakusanische Herolde.' In *Beiträge zur Architektur und verwandten Künsten Bathron*. H. Buesing and F. Hiller, eds. Saarbücken.

Kennell, N. M. 1995. *The Gymnasium of Virtue: Education and Culture in Ancient Sparta*. Chapel Hill, NC.

Jordan, B. 1986. 'Religion in Thucydides.' *TAPhA* 115: 119–147.

Krentz, P. 1993. 'Athens' Allies and the Phallophoria.' *AHB* 7: 12–16.

Kunstler, B. 1987. 'Family Dynamics and Female Power in Ancient Sparta.' In *Rescuing Creusa: New Methodological Approaches to Women in Antiquity*. 31–48. M. Skinner, ed. Lubbock, TX.

Kurke, L. 1991. *The Traffic in Praise: Pindar and the Poetics of Social Economy*. Ithaca, NY.

Kurke, L. 1995. 'Pindar and the Prostitutes, or Reading Ancient "Pornography".' *Arion* 4: 49–75.

Kyle, D. G. 1992. 'The Panathenaic Games: Sacred and Civil Athletics.' In *Goddess and Polis: The Panathenaic Festival in Ancient Greece*. 77–101. J. Neils, ed. Princeton.

Kyle, D. G. 2007. *Sport and Spectacle in the Ancient World*. Malden, MA.

Lämmer, M. 1982–1983. 'Der sogennante Olympische Friede in der griechischen Antike.' *Stadion* 8–9: 47–83.

Larson, J. 1995. *Greek Heroine Cults*. Madison, WI.

LSCG Suppl.: Sokolowski, F. 1962. *Lois sacrées des cités grecques: Supplément*. Paris.

Malkin, I. 1987. *Religion and Colonization in Ancient Greece*. Leiden.

Mallwitz, A. 1972. *Olympia und seine Bauten*. Munich.

Mallwitz, A. 1988. 'Cult and Competition Locations at Olympia.' In *The Archaeology of the Olympics: The Olympics and Other Festivals in Antiquity*. 79–109. W. Raschke, ed. Madison, WI.

Marinatos, N. 1981. 'Thucydides and Oracles.' *JHS* 101: 138–140.

Mikalson, J. 1998. *Religion in Hellenistic Athens*. Berkeley.

Mikalson, J. 2007. 'Gods and Athletic Games.' In *The Panathenaic Games*. 33–40. O. Palagia and A. Chroemi-Spetsieri, eds. Oxford.

Miller, S. G. 1990. *Nemea: A Guide to the Site and Museum*. Berkeley.

Miller, S. G. 1991. *Arete: Greek Sports from Ancient Sources*. 2nd edn. Berkeley.

Moretti, L. 1953. *Iscrizioni agonistiche greche*. Rome.

Moretti, L. 1957. *Olympionikai: I vincitori negli antichi agoni*. Rome.

Müller, K. O. 1844. *Orchomenos und die Minyer*. Breslau.

Nagy, G. 1986. 'Pindar's *Olympian* 1 and the Aetiology of the Olympic Games.' *TAPhA* 116: 71–88.

Neils, J. 1992a. 'The Panathenaia. An Introduction.' In *Goddess and Polis: The Panathenaic Festival in Ancient Athens*. 13–27. J. Neils, ed. Princeton.

––––– 1992b. 'Panathenaic Amphoras: Their Meaning, Makers, and Markets.' In *Goddess and Polis: The Panathenaic Festival in Ancient Athens*. 29–51. J. Neils, ed. Princeton.

Nicholson, N. J. 2005. *Aristocracy and Athletics in Archaic and Classical Greece*. Cambridge.

Parker, R. 1983. *Miasma*. Oxford.

Parker, R. 1996. *Athenian Religion*. Oxford.

Perlman, P. J. 2000. *City and Sanctuary in Ancient Greece: The Theorodokia in the Peloponnese*. Göttingen.

Perry, J. S. 2007. '"An Olympic Victory Must Not Be Bought": Oath-Taking, Cheating and Women in Greek Athletics.' In *Horkos: The Oath in Greek Society*. 81–88, 238–240. A. Sommerstein and J. Fletcher, eds. Exeter.

Pettersson, M. 1992. *Cults of Apollo at Sparta: the Hyakinthia, the Gymnopaidiai and the Karneia*. Stockholm.

Popp, H. 1957. *Die Einwirkung von Vorzeichen: Opfern und Festen auf die Kriegürhung der Griechen im 5. und 4. Jahrhundert v. Chr*. Würzburg.

Powell, C. A. 1979. 'Religion and the Sicilian Expedition'. Historia. *Zeitschrift für Alte Geschichte* 28: 15–31.

Reinhardt, K. 1957. 'Zum neuen Aischylos.' *Hermes* 85: 123–126.

Rohde, E. 1925. *Psyche: The Cult of Souls and Belief in Immortality among the Greeks*. 8th edn. London.

Rhodes, P. J. 1991. *A Commentary on the Aristotelian Athenaion Politeia*. Oxford.

Rougemont, G. 1973. 'La hiéroménie des Pythia et les "trêves sacrées" d'Éleusis, de Delphes et d'Olympie.' *BCH* 97: 75–106.

Rutherford, I. 2004. 'The Keian Theoria to Delphi: Neglected Data From the Accounts of the Delphic Naopoioi (CID 2.1–28).' *ZPE* 17: 107–114.

Rutherford, I. 2007. 'Network Theory and Theoric Networks.' *Mediterranean Historical Review* 22: 23–37.

Scanlon, T. F. 1984. 'The Footrace of the Heraia at Olympia.' *Ancient World* 9: 77–90. Revised with addendum as 'Racing for Hera: A Grils' Contest at Olympia.' In *Sport in the Greek and Roman Worlds*. Vol. 2. T. Scanlon, ed. 2014: 108–150.

Scanlon, T. F. 1988. '*Virgineum Gymnasium*: Spartan Females and Early Greek Athletics.' In *The Archaeology of the Olympics: The Olympics and Other Festivals in Antiquity.* 185–216. W. Raschke, ed. Madison, WI.

Scanlon, T. F. 2002. *Eros and Greek Athletics.* New York.

Scanlon, T. F. 2008. 'The Heraia at Olympia Revisited.' *Nikephoros* 21.9: 159–196.

Serwint, N. 1993. 'The Female Athletic Costume at the Heraia and Prenuptial Initiation Rites.' *Journal of American Archaeology* 97: 403–422.

Siewert, P. 1992. 'The Olympic Rules.' In *Proceedings of an International Symposium on the Olympic Games.* 111–117. W. Coulson and H. Kyrieleis, eds. Athens.

Sordi, M. 1984. 'Il santuaro di Olimpia e la guerra d'Elide.' In *Il santuari e la guerra nel mondo classic.* 20–30. M. Sordi, ed. Milan.

Spivey, N. 2004. *The Ancient Olympics.* Oxford.

Swaddling, J. 2000. *The Ancient Olympic Games.* 2nd edn. Austin, TX.

Syrigos, A. 2009. 'Olympic Truce: From Myth to Reality.' In *Olympic Truce: Sport as a Platform for Peace.* 22–25. K. Georgiadis and A. Syrigos, eds. Athens.

Thommen, L. 1999. 'Spartanische Frauen.' *Museum Helveticum* 56: 129–149.

Thompson, D. B. 1957. *Miniature Sculpture from the Athenian Agora Athens.* Athens.

Vanderpool, E. 1937. 'The Kneeling Boy.' *Hesperia* 6: 426–441.

Weiler, I. 1991. 'Regel und Regelbruch bei den antiken Olympischen Spielen.' In *The Olympic Games through the Ages: Greek Antiquity and its Impact on Modern Sport.* 55–64. R. Renson et al., eds. Athens.

Walters, H. B. 1899. *Catalogue of the Bronzes in the British Museum: Greek, Roman and Etruscan.* I–II. London.

Weniger, L. 1905. 'Das Hochfest des Zeus in Olympia, III: Der Gottesfriede.' *Klio* 5: 184–218.

Yalouris, N. 1977. *Athletics in Ancient Greece: Ancient Olympia and the Olympic Games.* Athens.

CHAPTER 45

....

LAW, LITIGATION, AND
SPORT IN ANCIENT GREECE

....

ZINON PAPAKONSTANTINOU

LAW as a hegemonic, state-imposed set of rules has been traditionally considered by many scholars as a prerequisite of orderly civic life. This belief has been partially challenged in recent years on the basis of the realization that law (hereafter understood as comprising legally binding rules, legal institutions, and administration of justice as well as perceptions of what law is and does) can be both a constitutive and a constituent of social relations and political conditions. Hence some recent trends in historical and cultural analysis of law go beyond law as a monolithic category which unilaterally articulates the concerns of an established civic authority. Instead, more emphasis is placed on the multiple ways law operates as it affects modes of thought and shapes social relationships while at the same time being subjected to the respect, challenges, and often abuses of social agents.

Rules with legal force existed in Greece from at least the late Bronze Age, but are more fully documented for the communities of the Archaic and later periods. The Homeric epics and Hesiod's poems (Gagarin 1986: 19–50) contain fairly detailed descriptions of legal procedures as well as allusions to orally transmitted community rules. In some communities, texts of legal import (statutes, decrees) were promulgated, inscribed, and publicly displayed from the second half of the seventh century BCE (Gagarin 2008; Papakonstantinou 2008). Late literary sources preserve echoes of comprehensive overhauls of the legal systems of some archaic cities implemented by 'lawgivers' (Hölkeskamp 1999). During the same period, and especially during the sixth century BCE, the evidence suggests a gradual expansion, specialization, and sophistication of the legal apparatus of Greek polities. For the Classical and later periods the evidence allows an in-depth study of the legal systems of some Greek *poleis* (Athens, Gortyn) and Hellenistic kingdoms (Ptolemaic Egypt), but it is frustratingly silent or lacunose about others. It is also worth noting that during the Hellenistic and Roman Imperial periods many Greek communities preserved and operated select legal institutions of bygone eras even though in most cases they had surrendered their political autonomy to the encroaching empires that dominated the eastern Mediterranean.

In the Greek world, most aspects of social, political, familial, and religious life were regulated by laws or decrees with legal force. Sport is an innately competitive activity that inevitably necessitates some form of regulation. City-states often promulgated laws that regulated aspects of civic athletic training, games, and victory. Moreover, the Panhellenic games were conducted within the framework of a detailed set of legal regulations that were meant to be applicable to participants from the entire Greek world. The remainder of this chapter will examine in more detail select facets of the interaction between law and sport in ancient Greece. More specifically, we shall explore the law of Solon on athletic rewards as an instance of legislation prescribing aspects of the relationship between athletes and their communities; examples of the legal framework governing the conduct of athletic contests, with particular emphasis on the Olympic games; and finally, rules concerning the management of athletic facilities as well as regulations germane to the institution of citizen training (*ephebeia*). We shall also explore facets of the reception of sport regulations by athletes and the authorities that enacted them, including their impact on sport perceptions and practices.

Solon's Legislation on Athletic Rewards

Sport was in the Greek world a popular, yet somewhat ambivalent activity. In the account of the funeral games of Patroclus (*Il.* 23.257–897) Homer portrays a massive, involved, and passionate group of spectators who watched a set of well-regulated games. Such games to commemorate special occasions were largely contrasted with institutionalized, periodic games. Among the latter, the Olympic games grew in popularity during the Archaic period, and competitive athletics really took off in the sixth century BCE when the number of other Panhellenic and local contests sharply increased. Yet the prestige of athletic victory was at times abused for personal political objectives, as in the case of Cylon in late seventh-century Athens (Hdt. 5.71; Thuc. 1.126.3–5). Moreover, critics begun voicing their concerns and resentment over what they perceived as exaggerated adulation and remuneration of athletic victors (Tyrt. fr. 12 West; Xenoph. fr. 2 West).

In the early sixth century BCE Solon was appointed archon with extraordinary powers in Athens, with the objective of mediating in the acute social and economic crisis afflicting the city. Briefly, the evidence suggests that Solon's legislative reforms had short- and long-term objectives without unilaterally favouring a particular social group. A number of measures aimed at quickly resolving some of the most pressing problems, while other measures were introduced with the goal of overhauling institutions and practices. Among the numerous laws attributed to Solon there is a regulation, originally perhaps a clause of a statute, stipulating the rewards to be granted to victors in the Olympic (500 drachmas) and Isthmian (100 drachmas) games (Plu. *Sol.*, 23.3 = Leão and Rhodes 2015 Fr. 89/1a; D. L. 1.55-56 = Leão and Rhodes 2015 Fr. 89/1b). Moreover, some sources attribute to Solon laws pertaining to athletic morality and the management of athletic facilities, but these are usually discounted as anachronistic (Kyle 1984: 95).

In evaluating Solon's law on athletic rewards, one has to keep in mind wider trends in early sixth-century athletics and politics as well as particular Athenian conditions. Even though individuals of modest backgrounds had opportunities to practise sport, the evidence suggests that for a number of reasons social elites dominated the most prestigious athletic contests in Archaic Greece, and that they used athletic victory as a token of social distinction and political advancement. To the extent that we know, this picture fits well with the state of affairs of Athenian sport at the time of Solon's reforms (Kyle 1993: 156–9). But traditional elite signifiers of power were increasingly coming under attack, and there were attempts to re-negotiate and rearticulate the meaning and influence of elite lifestyles and practices (Morris 2000). Hence Solon's law on athletic rewards appears to be in keeping with the wider trend, attested in other parts of the Greek world as well, to introduce 'sumptuary' laws, i.e. legislation that aimed at regulating forms of elite material extravagance. Solon's law on victory rewards in all likelihood curtailed the amounts that victors had previously received from the state (Mann 2001: 68–81). The value of the rewards was still pretty high; but if we accept that in most cases it was citizens of the most well-heeled backgrounds who could achieve prestigious Panhellenic victories, then for them the exact amount they received was not of primary importance. It is most likely, therefore, that the real objective of Solon's law was to legally standardize the rewards in an attempt to appropriate and thus redefine on behalf of the community (without however completely abolishing) elite perceptions of sport as a power discourse, including the association between sport, material wealth, and claims to social and political ascendancy (Papakonstantinou 2019: 36–37, 69–70).

Moreover, Solon's law could be associated with discontent and opposition, evinced in some quarters, towards some Athenian aristocratic athletes and their rich rewards, sentiments which were perhaps shared by Solon as well. If that were the case, then one might link Solon to outspoken critics of athletics (Papakonstantinou 2014) as well as to wider debates on the civic, educational, and moral value of sport conducted in late Archaic Greece.

Following the enactment of Solon's laws, it is documented that Athenian elites continued to achieve prestigious victories throughout the sixth century (Kyle 1993: 195–228). Yet since it seems that it was not one of the law's objectives to engineer a radical shift in the social origin of Athenian athletic victors, the dominance of social elites in sixth-century Athenian victors' lists should not be perceived as a failure of Solon's law. Furthermore, it is hard to assess with certainty whether the law succeeded in promoting an alternative paradigm of aristocratic sport and its dissociation from social entitlement and political privilege. But extant clues are suggestive. For instance, according to Herodotus (6.126–130), two pre-eminent Athenian aristocratic youths participated in the year-long Agariste betrothal contests, with a significant athletic component, in Sicyon. Moreover, the same author (Hdt. 6.103) relates the story of Cimon allowing Peisistratus to take credit for the former's *tethrippon* Olympic victory of 532 BCE. Such incidents suggest that, for some sixth-century Athenian aristocrats, sport and victories were in some ways still thought of as exclusive elite privileges or as prestigious, transferable, and exploitable tokens of *kudos*.

THE LEGAL FRAMEWORK OF ATHLETIC CONTESTS

In addition to laws pertaining to athletes of particular communities, there existed from the Archaic period a corpus of legal regulations which governed the conduct of periodic athletic contests. These regulations were usually enacted by the body which controlled the sanctuary associated with the games in question, but were applicable to all participants at the games regardless of their city of origin. Nonetheless, the earliest evidence for regulations of an athletic meeting can be found in connection with a different type of athletic contests, the funeral games of Patroclus (*Il.* 23.257–897). Funeral games for private individuals existed in the Greek world until the Hellenistic period (Roller 1981). Such games were by necessity one-off occasions that had certain sponsors who provided the required resources and frequently also acted as organizers/supervisors of the actual competitions. In *Il.* 23.566–613 Achilles, in his capacity as sponsor and supervisor of the games, was faced with a dispute between two contestants (Menelaus and Antilochus) in the chariot race (Gagarin 2008: 23–6; Papakonstantinou 2008: 29–31). The issue at hand was deciding the runner-up of the race: Antilochus had finished second but Menelaus argued that he did so by driving his chariot recklessly and hence endangering the life of both competitors. Following a fiery speech by Menelaus, Antilochus accepted Menelaus' superiority and agreed to give up his prize. The arrangement met with the approval of the organizer Achilles who was presented as the ultimate authority in distributing the prizes, often on a whim and not always on the basis of athletic performance, but in keeping with the Homeric aristocratic code of hierarchy and reciprocity. Other evidence, such as the athletic contests for the betrothal of Agariste, daughter of the tyrant of Sicyon Cleisthenes (Hdt. 6.126–130), corroborates the impression that such extempore or non-institutionalized games were often treated by their organizers as platforms for promoting particular agendas. As a result, these games were regulated chiefly by their organizers on the basis of their personal objectives as well as some widely shared notions of morality and justice.

The emergence and consolidation during the Archaic period of periodically held athletic contests, including most notably what became known as the *periodos* games, radically altered the athletic landscape of the Greek world (Christesen 2007; Kyle 2015: 107–146). Moreover, beginning in the sixth century BCE specialized facilities for athletic training, most notably the *gymnasion* and the *palaistra*, were constructed in cities as well as at the sites of panhellenic athletic festivals (Glass 2002; Mann 1998). The increasing proliferation and specialization of athletic practices inevitably led to the articulation of detailed, formal regulations governing the administration of games and facilities. But growth alone cannot account for the context of enactment, format, and content of the regulations for athletic contests. The promulgation of legal frameworks for sport practices corresponds in many respects to the emergence and development of laws which regulated other aspects of life in the Greek world. Many of the rules germane to athletics are encountered, either identical or with slight variations, in communities and other sites of athletic activity across the Greek world. Correlatively, some of the rules in question (e.g. the Olympic *ekecheiria*) were endowed with interstate or even Panhellenic validity. On the other hand, local conditions often led the appropriate authorities to adopt specific, regionally applicable rules. Finally, for the most part laws regulating athletic practices appear to be after-the-fact responses to actual troublesome situations, not pre-emptive provisions on envisaged cases of rule infringement.

The rules regulating the organization and conduct of the Olympic games are fairly adequately documented, and constitute a convenient starting point. Much of the evidence dates from the Roman imperial or even the Byzantine periods. Whenever possible, variations over time are duly noted. The *Hellanodikai*, a board of Elean officials who were selected by lot and served for one Olympiad, were the major executive force charged with supervising the games, especially with regard to the enforcement of Olympic rules before and during the festival (Crowther 2004: 53–64; Romano 2004). The very title '*Hellanodikai*' strongly suggests the appeal–for the Elean authorities at least–of the Panhellenic status of the Olympics. It is quite likely that the title was invented in the wake of the Persian wars, and that the board was known by other names (*agonothetai, diaitetai*) before 480 BCE (Paus. 5.9.4–6; Siewert 1992; 2005; Romano 2004: 96–9). Although references to the *Hellanodikai* initially occur in some fifth-century inscriptions and literary texts (Minon 2007: 532–5), their functions and responsibilities are attested primarily by authors of the Roman period. Before the festival, the *Hellanodikai* superintended the athletes' month of training in Elis (Crowther 2004: 65–70), led the procession to Olympia, and administered the oaths of the athletes, their trainers, and their relatives in the *bouleuterion*. Moreover, they adjudicated on whether athletes were qualified, both physically and in terms of ethnic origin (Philostr. *Gym.* 25; Hdt. 5.22), to compete, and assigned them to age groups. During the games, they acted as umpires and enforced the rules of each event. Furthermore, they awarded the wreaths to the victors (Pi. *O.* 3.12–13) and presided over the final feast.

Epigraphic evidence suggests that the rules pertaining to specific Olympic events had been written down since at least the late sixth century BCE. A fragmentary bronze tablet of the last quarter of the sixth century BCE (Ebert and Siewert 1999; Minon 2007: 38–47; Siewert and Taeuber 2013: no. 2) prescribed that a wrestler should not break his opponent's fingers, and outlined the penalties to be imposed on transgressors. Moreover, the law quite probably laid down the conditions for readmission of an offender to a future Olympic festival. The interpretation of the last four lines is quite uncertain, but the language suggests provisions against corruption and clauses regarding compensation through payment of monetary sums. By analogy with other late archaic laws (Koerner 1989; Papakonstantinou 2008: 121–123), it is quite likely that the last provisions concern negligent officials (*thearoi*, l. 8; perhaps also umpires) and hence stipulate the sanctions to be inflicted in cases of duty infringement.

It is very likely that the preceding law, as well as other laws pertaining to the Olympic festival and athletic contests, were publicly displayed. During his visit to Olympia, Pausanias (5.20.2) claims to have seen the 'disposition of the games'. Thucydides (5.49.1) also refers to the 'Olympic law'. These references should not be understood as referring to a comprehensive code of Olympic rules, but most probably to a series of individual written statutes on specific issues, such as the law regulating the attendance of women at the games (Paus. 5.6.7–8) or the regulations for the Olympic *ekecheiria* (Paus. 5.20.1; Plut. *Lyc.* 1.1). The Olympic truce (*ekecheiria*) is a good example of the Panhellenic appeal and legally binding nature of some (if not all) Olympic rules. During the late Archaic and Classical periods, the Olympic *ekecheiria* consisted of a status of sanctity for the sanctuary of Zeus in Olympia as well as the inviolability of the territory of Elis during the duration of the truce. Moreover, it provided immunity and safe passage from all territories for Olympic delegations, prospective athletes, and their companions, as well as spectators (Lämmer 2010). As the dispute between Elis and Sparta in 420 BCE suggests (Thuc. 5.49.1–50.4; Xen. *Hell.* 3.2.21), clauses prescribed the exact procedure and timetable for the official start of the *ekecheiria* as well as the penalties to be imposed on individuals who violated these procedures. This level of detail can only mean that a written statute on the Olympic *ekecheiria* existed at least by 420 BCE.

It is not known who exactly drafted and enacted the written laws germane to Olympic matters. It is possible that the *nomophylakes*, officials who instructed the *Hellanodikai*-elect (Paus. 6.24.3) and the Olympic Council, were involved. Lawmaking was an ongoing dynamic process, and we must assume that laws regulating aspects of the Olympic festival were often revised, as well as that new laws which supplemented the existing legal framework were promulgated until the demise of the festival in late antiquity (e.g. Siewert 2000: 31–7). At any event, athletes and other persons of interest (e.g. trainers, umpires, fans) would have been thoroughly familiar with the specific rules of athletic events and the penalties

stipulated in statutes. The Olympic oath provided an additional layer of deterrence for potentially corrupt athletes, trainers, and umpires (Lämmer 1993; Crowther 2008). Pausanias
(5.24.9–11) provides a summary of the procedure and content of the oath. It was sworn in
the *bouleuterion* in Olympia, in front of the statue of Zeus Horkios. The athletes as well as
their fathers, brothers, and trainers swore that 'in nothing will they commit any offence
against the Olympic games' (Paus. 5.24.9). Athletes in the men's age group also swore that
they had trained for ten months. Moreover, Pausanias refers to the oath of the *Hellanodikai*
in connection with their review of athletes and horses and their allocation to the appropriate
age groups. The *Hellanodikai* also swore to decide fairly and without bribes, as well as not to
disclose information about athletes.

Scholars have commented on the 'generic' wording of the oath, especially the clause
against offences committed during the Olympic games quoted above, and many feel that
Pausanias is summarizing the contents of a more detailed set of oaths for the different groups
of oath-takers involved (Lämmer 1993: 144–146; Perry 2004: 60; Crowther 2008: 486).
However, the terse yet unambiguous formulation of the oath recorded in Pausanias, especially the invocation of the legally comprehensive term 'offence' (κακούργημα), might have
been deliberately introduced by the Olympic authorities in order to minimize the danger of
distorting the meaning and import of the oath, e.g. through the exploitation of a potential
gap in the provisions for a particular violation. The oath as recorded by Pausanias would
adequately cover the Olympic authorities who would have had to decide whether an offence
has been committed.

All the written regulations and oath-taking did not deter rogue athletes from cheating in
the ancient Olympics (Weiler 1991a and 1991b; Perry 2004). This inference is in keeping with
what we know about the reception of law and legal procedures in general in the Greek world.
Perjury, for instance, which is assumed in any violation of Olympic laws, was a common
occurrence in the Greek world since the Archaic period (Papakonstantinou 2007: 101–
110). In Olympia the Zanes, the statues paid for and dedicated by offending athletes, stood
near the entrance of the Olympic stadium from 388 BCE, and were a palpable reminder of
the punishments and the ignominy incurred by Olympic rule breakers (Paus. 5.21.2–8).
Besides the erection of the Zanes statues, fines (Paus. 5.21.2–8; 5.21.16–17; 6.6.5–6), flogging
(Crowther and Frass in Crowther 2004: 141–168), and expulsion from the games (Paus.
5.21.12–14) were in some cases meted out to violators of the Olympic rules.

As the account of the oath-taking ceremony in Pausanias and possibly the law containing
wrestling rules suggest, negligent *Hellanodikai* were also liable to sanctions. Moreover, their
decisions were open to appeals. During the second quarter of the fifth century BCE it was
probably the board of *mastroi*, magistrates with powers to review the decisions of other
officials, that heard appeals to the judgments of *Hellanodikai* (IvO 2). However, by the early
fourth century BCE the Olympic council had taken over the right to hear such appeals. In the
Olympics of 396 BCE, two of the judges assigned to the *stadion* race, which ended in a dead
heat between Leon of Ambracia and Eupolemus of Elis, declared Eupolemus as the winner,
while one judge voted for Leon (Paus. 6.3.7; Crowther 2004: 71–81). The latter appealed the
decision, perhaps first to the board of the *Hellanodikai* and then to the Olympic council. The
council ruled in favour of Leon and fined the two *Hellanodikai* who had awarded the victory to Eupolemus, but did not overturn the latter's victory. Similarly, it was most likely the
Olympic council–and not, as it has been claimed (Weiler 1991b: 91), the *boule* of Elis–which

heard the appeal of Athens in the case of the Athenian athlete Callippus who was fined in the Olympics of 322 BCE for bribing his opponents (Paus. 5.21.5; Plut. *Mor.* 850b).

According to Thucydides (5.49.1–50.4) and Xenophon (*Hell.* 3.2.21), in 420 BCE the Eleans claimed that Sparta had violated the Olympic truce, and a court imposed a fine of 2,000 *mnai* (200,000 drachmas) and a ban from competitions and sacrifices at Olympia. The Spartans sent delegates and pleaded against the decision but Elis, despite Spartan demurrals, sustained the original verdict. The identity of the court involved in the events of 420 BCE and its possible links to other Elean institutions, including the Olympic Council, remain in doubt. The assumption that the court in question consisted exclusively of Elean judges is in keeping with the particulars of the events as described in the sources (Roy 1998: 362). Moreover, there is no compelling reason to believe (following Siewert 1981 and 2005: 93–6) that a c. 475 BCE inscription from Olympia referring to an arbitration is somehow related to an 'Olympic' tribunal, the *Hellanodikai*, or to a violation of the Olympic *ekecheiria* (Minon 2007: 108, 112). The question of the identity and number of tribunals empowered to adjudicate Olympic matters is further complicated by the fact that court voting tokens of the Hellenistic period have been discovered both in the vicinity of the theatre in Elis and in the area near the *bouleuterion* in Olympia (Baitinger and Eder 2001). This suggests, if not two different tribunals, at least two different meeting venues. If one tribunal is assumed, then the choice of location could have been determined on the basis of the content of the case heard and its relevance to the Olympic games.

Rules often evolved and were modified, in practice or *de jure*. If Pausanias (6.4.3) is to be believed, a few decades after the promulgation of the late sixth-century BCE statute which prohibited finger breaking in wrestling, Leontiskos of Messene won two Olympic wrestling victories by breaking his opponents' fingers. This can be accounted for either as a result of the modification of the sixth-century law or as a case of ingenious foul play that went undetected by the judges. Taking into account the need for modifications, it can be safely assumed that, at least since the late Archaic period, rules of engagement for the various athletic events were fairly standardized across the Greek world. A certain degree of standardization was a de facto precondition for the increasing participation of athletes in the elaborate network of Panhellenic and local games. Moreover, it is likely that the regulations governing the conduct of the Olympic games served as a blueprint for other athletic contests, especially those claiming 'isolympic' status. One should not, however, assume an absolute overlap between the regulations and procedures of the Olympics and the various isolympic games. A case in point is *IvO* 56, which outlines the rules of the Sebastan Olympic Games at Naples (Crowther 2004: 93–96; Miranda De Martino 2014).

A fair amount is also known about patterns of organization, officials, and the rules governing the conduct of other Panhellenic and local games. For instance, civic authorities often decreed the regulations of local athletic contests (e.g. Vanderpool 1984; *IG* II² 2311) and appointed the officials responsible for supervising them (Nagy 1978). Furthermore, truces of varying durations and content are attested in connection with other Panhellenic and local festivals (Rougemont 1973; Lämmer 2010). Punishments such as flogging, fines, and expulsion were common (e.g. Crowther and Frass in Crowther 2004: 141–168). Cases of rule infringement and other mischief are widely attested beyond Olympia, to the extent that in the early third century CE Philostratus (*Gym.* 45), with a touch of rhetorical exaggeration, presents corruption and foul play as endemic attributes of Greek athletics (Papakonstantinou 2016).

REGULATIONS OF ATHLETIC FACILITIES

There is a significant body of evidence germane to the administration of athletic facilities in the Greek world. *Gymnasia* and *palaistrai* existed in urban areas and inter-state sanctuaries until late antiquity. They were widely used for a variety of cultural and athletic purposes, including training for contests and physical education regimes (e.g. as part of the *ephebeia*). Some *palaistrai* were privately owned and operated, but there were several public ones, often built in a complex with a *gymnasion*. Civic authorities to a significant extent legally regulated the administration, operation, and activities of these facilities, especially in the Classical and early Hellenistic periods. The method of appointment and responsibilities of the gymnasiarchs and other officials associated with *gymnasia* and *palaistrai* varied across the Greek world (Cordiano 1997). The individuals who supervised athletic complexes were often public officials who managed state funds and were accountable for their actions. By contrast, in the late Hellenistic and Roman imperial era, the upkeep and operation of athletic complexes and the activities they hosted, including the *ephebeia*, although still subject to civic regulation and intervention, to a great extent depended on the generosity of wealthy patrons, and as a result the various positions associated with the *gymnasion* essentially became voluntary benefactions (Kennell 2010; Papakonstantinou 2019: 89–188).

Two laws and one edict from Hellenistic and Roman Macedonia exemplify these trends. First, a second-century BCE law from Veroia regulates in detail various activities of the *gymnasion* of the city (Gauthier and Hatzopoulos 1993; *SEG* 43.381). The gymnasiarch and his assistants were responsible for supervising the training of the youths, enforcing the rules, and maintaining order. Furthermore, the law prescribes the categories of persons who did not have access to the *gymnasion*, outlines the arrangements for the Hermaia festival and other *gymnasion* contests, and stipulates procedures for prosecuting offenders, especially negligent officials, as well as penalties for a number of infractions. Moreover, a law dated to 24/3 BCE and set up in the *gymnasion* of Amphipolis contains extensive provisions for the local *ephebeia*, and illuminates various aspects of the life of the local *gymnasion* and *palaistra*, the conduct of *ephebes*, their contests and training, as well as the responsibilities of their supervisors/trainers (*ephebarchos, paidotribes*) (Lazaridou 2015; *SEG* 65.420).

The picture of bustling athletic activity in the Veroia *gymnasion* adumbrated by the law of the second century BCE contrasts sharply to the conditions alluded to in a late first-/early second-century CE proconsular edict from the same city (Nigdelis and Souris 2005; *SEG* 48.742 and 55.678). The document in question records the attempts of Memmius Rufus, proconsul of Macedonia, to reach a permanent solution to the periodic closure of the *gymnasion* of Veroia. The edict suggests that the main causes of this state of affairs were the shortage of immediately accessible financial resources as well as the inability of the city's elite to reach a satisfactory arrangement. The latter corroborates the importance of elite munificence in maintaining the operation of the *gymnasion*, the *ephebeia*, and civic athletics in the Greek-speaking parts of the empire. In the case of Veroia; the proconsul's solution was to create a permanent gymnasial fund, and to finance the workings of the city's *gymnasion* from the fund's annual return.

Conclusion

Laws and other texts of legal import (e.g. decrees and edicts) illustrate the challenges faced by the organizers of athletic contests and the overseers of athletic facilities. Moreover, as the case of Solon's law on athletic rewards demonstrates, sport legislation can be intertwined with wider social issues. In any case, the text of a law contains only half of the story. The other half is to be found in how the law is implemented, received, negotiated, accepted, neglected, or abused, as the case may be. Extant Greek laws on sport, and the evidence for their reception and use, articulate the realities and dynamism of athletic practices as well as something of the popularity, excitement, and at times ambivalence that accompanied Greek sport. As such, laws open up a valuable vantage point from which to evaluate the wider social and cultural ramifications of sport in the Greek world.

References

Baitinger, H. and B. Eder. 2001. 'Hellenistische Stimmarken aus Elis und Olympia. Neue Forschungen zu den Beziehungen zwischen Hauptstadt und Heiligtum. Mit einem Beitrag von K. Herrmann.' *JDAI* 116: 163–257.

Christesen, P. 2007. 'The Transformation of Athletics in Sixth-Century Greece.' In *Onward to the Olympics: Historical Perspectives on the Olympic Games*. 59–68. G. P. Schaus and S. R. Wenn, eds. Waterloo, Ont.

Cordiano, G. 1997. *La ginnasiarchia nelle 'poleis' dell'Occidente mediterraneo antico*. Pisa.

Crowther, N. 2004. *Athletika: Studies on the Olympic Games and Greek Athletics*. Hildesheim.

Crowther, N. 2008. 'Nothing New Under the Olympic Sun? The Swearing of Oaths at the Ancient and Modern Games.' In *Pathways: Critiques and Discourse in Olympic Research*. 485–97. R. K. Barney et al., eds. London, Ont.

Ebert, J. and P. Siewert. 1999. 'Eine archaische Bronzeurkunde aus Olympia mit Vorschriften für Ringkämpfer und Kampfrichter.' In *XI Bericht über die Ausgrabungen in Olympia*. 391–412. A. Mallwitz, ed. Berlin.

Gagarin, M. 1986. *Early Greek Law*. Berkeley, CA.

Gagarin, M. 2008. *Writing Greek Law*. Cambridge.

Gauthier, P. and M. B. Hatzopoulos. 1993. *La loi gymnasiarchique de Beroia*. Athens.

Glass, S. L. 2002. 'The Greek Gymnasium: Some Problems.' In *The Archaeology of the Olympics*, 2nd ed. 155–173. W. J. Raschke, ed. Madison, WI.

Hölkeskamp, K.-J. 1999. *Schiedsrichter, Gesetzgeber und Gesetzgebung im archaischen Griechenland*. Stuttgart.

Kennell, N. M. 2010. 'The Greek Ephebate in the Roman Period.' In *Sport in the Cultures of the Ancient World: New Perspectives*. 175–94. Z. Papakonstantinou, ed. London.

Koerner, R. 1989. 'Beamtenvergehen und deren Bestrafung nach frühen griechischen Inschriften.' *Klio* 69: 450–498.

Kyle, D. G. 1984. 'Solon and Athletics.' *AncW* 9: 99–105.

Kyle, D. G. 1993. *Athletics in Ancient Athens*. Leiden.

Kyle, D. G. 2015. *Sport and Spectacle in the Ancient World*, 2nd edn. Malden, MA.

Lämmer, M. 1993. 'The Nature and Significance of the Olympic Oath in Greek Antiquity.' In *The Institution of the Olympic Games: A Multidisciplinary Approach.* 141–148. D. P. Panagiotopoulos, ed. Athens.

Lämmer, M. 2010. 'The So-Called Olympic Peace in Ancient Greece.' In *Greek Athletics.* 36–60. J. König, ed. Edinburgh.

Lazaridou, K. D. 2015. Ἐφηβαρχικὸς νόμος ἀπὸ τὴν Ἀμφίπολη.' *AEph* 154: 1–48.

Leão, D. F. and P. J. Rhodes 2015. *The Laws of Solon: A New Edition with Introduction, Translation and Commentary.* London.

Mann, C. 1998. 'Krieg, Sport und Adelskultur. Zur Entstehung des griechischen Gymnasions.' *Klio* 80: 7–21.

Mann, C. 2001. *Athlet und Polis im archaischen und frühklassischen Griechenland.* Göttingen.

Minon, S. 2007. *Les inscriptions éléennes dialectales (VIe–IIe siècle avant J.-C.).* 2 vols. Geneva.

Miranda De Martino, E. 2014. 'Les Sebasta de Naples à l'époque de Domitien. Témoignages épigraphiques.' *CRAI*: 1165–1188.

Morris, I. 2000. *Archaeology as Cultural History: Words and Things in Iron Age Greece.* Malden, MA.

Nagy, B. 1978. 'The Athenian Athlothetai.' *GRBS* 19: 307–313.

Nigdelis, P. M. and G. A. Souris. 2005. Ἀνθύπατος λέγει. Ἕνα διάταγμα των αυτοκρατορικών χρόνων για το γυμνάσιο της Βέροιας. Thessaloniki.

Papakonstantinou, Z. 2007. 'Legal Procedure in the Homeric *Hymn to Hermes.' RIDA* 54: 83–110.

Papakonstantinou, Z. 2008. *Lawmaking and Adjudication in Archaic Greece.* London.

Papakonstantinou, Z. 2014. 'Ancient Critics of Greek Sport.' In *A Companion to Sport and Spectacle in Greek and Roman Antiquity.* 320–31. P. Christesen and D. G. Kyle, eds. Chichester.

Papakonstantinou, Z. 2016. 'Match Fixing and Victory in Greek Sport.' *RhM* 159(1): 13–27.

Papakonstantinou, Z. 2019. *Sport and Identity in Ancient Greece.* London.

Perry, J. 2004. '"An Olympic Victory Must Not Be Bought": Women, Cheating and the Olympic Ethos.' In *Cultural Relations Old and New: The Transitory Olympic Ethos.* 57–65. K. B. Walmsley, S. G. Martyn, and R. K. Barney, eds. London, Ont.

Roller, L. E. 1981. 'Funeral Games for Historical Persons.' *Stadion* 7: 1–18.

Romano, D. G. 2004. 'Judges and Judging at the Ancient Olympic Games.' In *Onward to the Olympics: Historical Perspectives on the Olympic Games.* 95–113. G. P. Schaus and S. R. Wenn, eds. Waterloo, Ont.

Rougemont, G. 1973, 'La hiéroménie des Pythia et les trêves sacrées d'Éleusis, de Delphes et d'Olympie.' *BCH* 97: 75–106.

Roy, J. 1998. 'Thucydides 5.49.1-50.4: The Quarrel between Elis and Sparta in 420 B.C., and Elis' Exploitation of Olympia.' *Klio* 80: 360–368.

Siewert, P. 1981. 'Eine Bronze-Urkunde mit elischen Urkunden über Böoter, Thessaler, Athen und Thespiai. In *X. Bericht über die Ausgrabungen in Olympia.* 228–48. Berlin.

Siewert, P. 1992. 'The Olympic Rules.' In *Proceedings of an International Symposium on the Olympic Games, 5–9 September 1988.* 113–117. W. Coulson and H. Kyrieleis, eds. Athens.

Siewert, P. 2000. '"Due iscrizioni giuridiche della città di Elide.' *Minima epigraphica et papyrologica* 3: 18–37.

Siewert, P. 2005. '"Richter über der Hellenen" (Hellanodikas) und andere überstaatliche Gemeinschaftsbezeichnungen in Olympia.' In *Il cittadino, lo straniero, il barbaro, fra integrazione ed emarginazione nell' antiquità.* 93–104. M. Gabriella, A. Bertinelli, and A. Donati, eds. Rome.

Siewert, P. and H. Taeuber. 2013. *Neue Inschriften von Olympia. Die ab 1896 veröffentlichten Texte*. Vienna.

Vanderpool, E. 1984. 'Regulations for the Herakleian Games at Marathon.' In *Studies Presented to Sterling Dow on his Eightieth Birthday*. 295–296. Durham, NC.

Weiler, I. 1991a. 'Regel und Regelbruch bei den antiken Olympischen Spielen.' In *The Olympic Games Through the Ages: Greek Antiquity and its Impact on Modern Sport*. 55–64. R. Renson et al., eds. Athens.

Weiler, I. 1991b. 'Korruption in der Olympischen Agonistik und die diplomatische Mission des Hypereides in Elis.' In *Achaia und Elis in der Antike*. 87–93. A. D. Rizakis, ed. Athens.

CHAPTER 46

SPECTATORSHIP, CONTROL, AND COLLECTIVE GROUPS

GEOFFREY SUMI

There was a horse-race on, and as the horses were about to contend for the seventh time, a crowd of children ran into the Circus [Maximus], led by a tall maiden of grim aspect, who, because of what happened afterwards, was thought to have been a divinity. The children shouted in concert many bitter words, which the people took up and then began to bawl out every conceivable insult; and finally the throng leaped down and set out to find Commodus (who was then in the Quintilian villa), invoking many blessings on him and many curses upon Cleander. The latter sent some soldiers against them, who killed and wounded a few; but, instead of being deterred by this, the crowd, encouraged by its own numbers and by the strength of the Praetorians, pressed on with all the greater determination. They were already drawing near to Commodus ... who was so terrified ... that he at once ordered Cleander to be slain, and likewise his son ... (Dio Cassius 72.13.3–6; Loeb trans., slightly adapted; cf. Herodian 1.12.3–13.6; Augustan History, *Commodus* 14.1–3).

INTRODUCTION

THIS episode illustrates in striking fashion conflicting axioms about spectatorship and public spectacles in Rome. Through the imperial ideology of 'bread and circuses' the emperor attempted to exercise some control over the Roman people (Juvenal, *Satires* 10.81; Fronto, *Elements of History* 18). Indeed, the feeding of the city populace was one of the most pressing obligations of the emperor and his court, the 'bread' of bread and circuses (Garnsey 1988: 240–243; Mattingly and Aldrete 1999; Virlouvet 1985). Yet the people also expressed their collective will at events where, even as spectators, they were active rather than passive participants (Hopkins 1983: 15; Bergmann 1999: 11–12). The riot that culminated in the death of Cleander, Commodus' *cubicularius* and commander of the cavalry guard, shows that spectators could be the agents of political interaction at public spectacles, indeed, that public spectacles could be organizing events for the non-elite population.

A number of elements of this episode deserve closer examination. What, for instance, was the relationship between the circus games on this occasion and the riot that ensued? It has been argued that crowds find the motivation for their collective action through a 'notion of legitimation': the crowd believes it is preserving the traditional customs and values of its society and that its actions are an expression of community consensus; this is the crowd's 'moral economy' (Thompson 1971: 79; Cameron 1976: 183–184). It is the aim of this chapter to demonstrate that the crowd at Cleander's riot acquired its notion of legitimation in part from the conventions of spectatorship at Roman public spectacles. These conventions include the fact that spectacles had long been a venue for the expression of popular will and protest. In the imperial period they were also an opportunity for the people to interact productively with the emperor; this was enabled by the custom of arranged seating in the theatre, amphitheatre, and circus, as well as the kind of collective behaviour (chants and acclamations as well as rhythmic clapping) that was characteristic of the crowd at public spectacles. As I will argue further below, these conventions had the effect of encouraging the collective action that culminated in the riot that brought down Cleander.

PUBLIC SPECTACLES AND THE WILL OF THE PEOPLE

According to Dio, the spectators at the circus in 189 CE needed only slight prompting from a group of children before they began a protest that erupted in violence. Public spectacles as a venue for the expression of popular will and political protest originated in the Roman republic with the best attested examples occurring, not surprisingly, in the tumult of the late republic. The Roman republican constitution required the participation of the people in many of its fundamental political institutions. In particular, laws were promulgated and debated in public meetings (*contiones*) while magistrates were elected and laws passed by popular vote at assemblies of Roman citizens (*comitia*) (Taylor 1966; Pina Polo 1996 and 2012; Mouritsen 2001). Importantly for our purposes, Cicero claims that in addition to *comitia* and *contiones*, the people expressed their collective will at *ludi* (circus games and theatrical performances) as well as gladiatorial shows (Cicero, *For Sestius* 106; *Letters to Atticus* 2.19.3). He thus could meaningfully parody *senatus populusque Romanus*, 'the senate and people of Rome', the famous slogan that was a distillation of Roman political culture in this period, by referring to *theatrum populusque Romanus*, 'the theatre and people of Rome' (Cicero, *For Sestius* 116).

A famous example of what Cicero had in mind occurred in July of 59 BCE at the games in honour of the god Apollo. At the time, Caesar as consul had put through a legislative programme favourable to Pompey's interests; these two, along with Marcus Licinius Crassus, were attempting to control politics in the city: this was the three-headed political monster that in modern history books is often called the 'First Triumvirate'. When Caesar entered the theatre, he received only a smattering of applause, while the younger Curio on the same occasion was loudly cheered. During the performance itself, an actor on stage uttered the line 'Because of our misfortune, you are Great!' The spectators immediately seized on this line, taking it to refer to Pompey (the Great), and demanded several encores. Cicero was delighted to interpret the whole episode as a sign of popular dissatisfaction with the informal political arrangement struck by the three men (Cicero, *Letters to Atticus* 2.19.3; Valerius Maximus, *Words and Deeds of Famous Men* 6.2.9).

Many such incidents are documented for the late republic, triggered no doubt by the political unrest of the period (Vanderbroeck 1987). But similar incidents occurred in the imperial period; indeed, it is a longstanding contention that the elimination of *comitia* and the fading importance of *contiones* made public spectacles an even more important venue for the expression of popular will (Hopkins 1983: 15; Cameron 1976: 157–192). Suetonius, for example, describes one such occasion as evidence of the unpopularity of Nero's successor, Galba: during the performance of an Atellan farce, an actor's particular refrain was interpreted as a reference to Galba's unwelcome return to Rome. The audience chimed in and chanted the familiar line repeatedly, even using the accompanying gestures (Suetonius, *Galba* 13). Such a performative response indicates how the spectators in the theatre were culturally conditioned to respond to actors' lines that they deemed politically relevant: it was one way to express their displeasure at the actions of a ruling authority.

As is evident from these incidents, the principal change from the late republic to the imperial period was that the focus of the spectators at public spectacles shifted to the person of the emperor and members of his court. The people came to expect the emperor's presence at these games, indeed, they anticipated active interaction with him. When during Augustus' principate, for instance, a member of the equestrian order agitated at a public show for the abolition of Augustus' marriage legislation, Augustus responded by summoning his great-grandchildren to his side as a visual example of lawful progeny, communicating with gestures and facial expression that all should try to emulate their father Germanicus' example (Suetonius, *Augustus* 34.2). Other emperors were even more specific. Claudius granted an honourable retirement to a gladiator at the behest of the gladiator's children; he then circulated a placard among the cheering spectators encouraging them to have children who could advocate for them (Suetonius, *Claudius* 21.5; Aulus Gellius, *Attic Nights* 5.14.29). A similar incident in a later period shows how the engagement between emperor and people at the games took the form of a negotiation. In 176 CE, the emperor Marcus Aurelius readily acquiesced to the people's demand that a certain man-eating lion be brought into the arena; but he subsequently refused their request to free the lion's trainer, on the grounds that, as he declared in a proclamation, the trainer had done nothing to earn his freedom (Dio Cassius 72.29.4). Theatrical licence had its limits: the manumission of a slave, which constituted a change in his legal and social status, could not be granted willy-nilly. In some ways, public spectacles were a conservative political venue, reminding the spectators of their social status and denying attempts to usurp a higher status without due cause.

SEATING AND SOCIAL STATUS

Members of the senatorial aristocracy at the games in Rome were an easy target for the lower orders, as we have seen illustrated above, in part because of the principle of arranged seating, which also may have had the effect of encouraging the kind of participatory crowd behaviour that was so characteristic of Roman spectacles (Parker 1999). It is important to bear in mind that the arranged seating was both vertical—dividing the larger social orders (senatorial, equestrian, plebeian, servile)—and horizontal—dividing these orders into subgroups. Arranged seating reified social distinctions and imposed a kind of control over the spectators at the games, yet it also, as we have already seen, encouraged a divisiveness that might have been present in society at large (Edmondson 1996: 100–102).

The first reference to the practice of arranged seating in the historical period dates to 194 BCE, when seats at performances for the *ludi Romani* began to be set aside for members of the senatorial order (Livy 34.44.5; Briscoe 1981: 118; cf. Livy 34.54.3–8). It took more than a century for the equestrian order to be allowed a similar privilege; Lucius Roscius Otho, who was tribune of the plebs in 67 BCE, promulgated a law, eventually passed by the tribal assembly, that allowed the next fourteen rows after the senatorial seats to be set aside for members of the equestrian order (Broughton 1951: 2.145; Slater 1994: 130–131).

Popular opposition to stratified seating, however, was concerted and long-standing. In 62 BCE, at a performance in the Theatre of Apollo, Roscius, now holding the office of praetor, was roundly hissed by the people and warmly applauded by the equestrians as he entered the theatre. The hissing and applause continued back and forth and ultimately escalated to a riot that was quelled only by Cicero's soothing words (Plutarch, *Cicero* 13). At the previously discussed Apolline Games of 59 BCE, the reaction of the spectators was similarly divided: the younger Curio was warmly applauded especially by the equestrians, which prompted Cicero's comment that the people despised the Roscian law (Cicero, *Letters to Atticus* 2.19.3). Even in the imperial period such division persisted. The emperor Gaius, we are told, used vouchers for free merchandise to tempt the plebs to usurp the seats reserved for equestrians (Suetonius, *Caligula* 26.4). The story endures as an example of Gaius' depravity in that he encouraged the violation of social distinctions that the custom of arranged seating was meant to preserve. Livy's account of the origin of this custom in 194 BCE recounts similar displeasure on the part of the people, who viewed these innovations as diminishing their privilege and status by elevating the elite (Valerius Maximus 2.4.3; Livy 34.54).

Despite these existing laws, as well as long-standing tradition, additional enactments were necessary over time. The best attested and most thorough arrangement of seating at public games is ascribed to the emperor Augustus who was motivated, we are told, by the lack of order among spectators; a particular catalyst, Suetonius claims, was when a single senator failed to obtain a seat in a crowded theatre at games in Puteoli. The implication, of course, is that someone of lower social status failed to give up a seat to this senator (Suetonius, *Augustus* 44.1). Augustus' resulting legislation, the *Lex Julia Theatralis* (probably to be dated after 20 BCE), not only reaffirmed the first rows for members of the senatorial and equestrian orders but went a step further to separate civilians from soldiers, to set aside seats for married men, a section for young men and their tutors, and to restrict women at gladiatorial combats to the seats furthest from the action (Rawson 1987; Slater 1994: 130 n. 54). It is worth emphasizing that the original impetus for Augustus' legislation seems to have been to replicate within the *cavea* of the theatre the distinction between the social orders that he tried to institute in society at large. Hierarchical seating was primarily a matter of distinction and honour; crowd control appears to have been a secondary consideration. In fact, as we have seen, separate sections for the equestrian order and the people fostered a rivalry between these two orders that resulted in occasional confrontations at public spectacles (Edmondson 1996: 102).

The passage from Suetonius, while invaluable for our understanding of the custom of hierarchical seating in the theatre and amphitheatre, does not tell the whole story; in particular, it leaves unanswered questions about seating in the circus. It is probable that senators had their own section in the circus by the time of Claudius (Suetonius, *Claudius* 21.3; Dio Cassius 61.16.4), perhaps near the finish line (Humphrey 1986: 101-2); members of the equestrian order were similarly honoured by the time of Nero (Suetonius, *Nero* 11.1; Tacitus, *Annals* 15.32; Humphrey 1986: 102 n. 240). Archaeological and epigraphical evidence—which, admittedly, is more abundant for locations outside Rome—when used with caution may further illuminate the picture (Roueché 1993: 119–120; Kolendo 1981). At Aphrodisias, for instance, inscriptions at the three principal venues for public games (the stadium, theatre, and odeon) indicate that some seats were reserved for various groups in society, such as the butchers' and tanners' guilds, as well as age groups, in particular the young men of the city, the *ephēbes* (aged 18–19) and *neotēroi* (aged 19 and up) (Roueché 1993: 90, 94, 97, 112). Similar arrangements can be found at other cities in the empire.

The reserved seats for members of trade guilds are especially intriguing, for these organizations structured the lives of much of the population in Rome. Members of certain occupations belonged to the same guilds (*collegia*) and even lived in the same neighborhoods (*vici*) because of this close association (Lott 2004: 52–53). These *collegia* also had a political history: they were briefly outlawed in 64 BCE, as instigators of violent political unrest. Publius Clodius Pulcher, a prominent tribune of the plebs in this period, relied heavily on the support of the *collegia* for his political advancement and might have offered them special seats at his aedilician games in 56 BCE (Rawson 1987: 87–88). Seating at games may thus reflect important social bonds that linked spectators outside the shows; tanners or butchers worked together, belonged to the same guilds, lived in the same neighbourhoods, and then sat together at the theatre, amphitheatre, and perhaps also the Circus Maximus (Meijer 2010: 99–100). Cleander's riot, in fact, makes more sense if we allow for guilds at the circus (see Whittaker 1964 and below).

The spectators at public spectacles, even those of the lowest orders, valued the connection between seating and social status, and therefore sitting out of one's accustomed order was noteworthy. The emperor Trajan, for example, as a way of distinguishing himself from his more despotic predecessor Domitian, sat among the spectators in the circus rather than in the imperial box, a practice in keeping with his avowed *civilitas* (Pliny, *Panegyric* 51.4–5; Edmondson 1996: 104). In this instance, the emperor 'lowered' his social status by sitting among the lower orders, a politic gesture and an acceptable modification of standard seating practices. An incident during the reign of the emperor Claudius, on the other hand, demonstrates the spectators' disapproval for 'raising' one's status in like fashion. At a theatrical show, when an actor on stage uttered the line 'A prosperous whipping-boy is intolerable', the spectators at once turned to stare at Polybius, Claudius' imperial freedman, whose swift ascent to a position of great influence in Claudius' court was a source of resentment (Dio Cassius 60.29.3). The spectators used the actor's line as a way of pointing out the social aberration inherent in Polybius' position. Despite his real social status as an ex-slave, he likely was sitting in close proximity to the imperial seats, which contravened the long-standing tradition of arranged seating. The spectators, many of whom were freeborn citizens and therefore legally of higher social status than Polybius, likely relished the opportunity to rebuke him publicly in this fashion.

FACTIONS AND CLAQUES

As I mentioned above, the seating at public spectacles in Rome was arranged both horizontally and vertically, and one of the organizing principles that cut across social distinctions was the grouping of spectators by their support for individual theatrical performers or chariot-racing teams. Chariot-racing in Rome was organized into four racing stables or teams, often called factions, which were identified by four colours: red, white, green, and blue (Cameron 1976; Meijer 2010: 52–64). Fans of chariot-racing similarly identified themselves with the colour of the team they supported (Blues and Greens, in particular), with certain *collegia* supporting certain circus factions (Roueché 1993: 128, 131). These fans were often rabid in their devotion. The younger Pliny disparagingly informs us that fans cared little for the skill of the drivers or the speed of the horses but paid attention only to the colour of the charioteer's jersey (*Letters* 9.6). Moreover, curse tablets survive that record the ill wishes of fans of one team for their opponents: 'I charge you demon, whoever you are, and demand of you from this hour, from this day, from this moment, that you torture the horses of the Greens and Whites. Kill them! The charioteers Glarus and Felix and Primulus and Romanus, kill them! Crash them! Leave no breath in them!' (Audollent 1904 no. 286; trans. Sherk 1988 no. 168H). An extreme example of this kind of devotion is the story of the over-zealous fan of the Red faction who threw himself on the funeral pyre of his favourite charioteer (Pliny, *Natural History* 7.186). Emperors, too, had their allegiances: Gaius (Caligula), Nero, and Commodus, for instance, were fans of the Greens, while Vitellius and Caracalla rooted for the Blues. The devotion of these emperors is recorded in the ancient sources as a mark of their excess and is intended to impugn their character. Gaius, for instance, regularly spent the night and dined with the charioteers of the Green stables (Suetonius, *Gaius* 55). Better, more politic, emperors, such as Marcus Aurelius, kept above the fray, it seems, and avoided committing themselves to a single faction (M. Aurelius, *Meditations* 1.5; Meijer 2010: 120–127).

In the theatre, spectators focused not on a corporate colour but an individual performer. The performances of pantomime dancers, in particular, provoked intense emotional responses and fierce rivalries among spectators that frequently escalated into rioting (Jory 1984; Slater 1994). These rivalries were stoked by the presence of claques, groups of spectators who led the cheers for their favourite performers; in some cases they were hired to do so (Roueché 1993: 28–29). These claques were known to form retinues that accompanied their favoured performers in processions winding through the streets of Rome (Pliny, *Natural History* 29.9; Slater 1994: 129). The most famous, or notorious, example is the *Augustiani*, recruited applauders (*plausores*) who accompanied Nero in procession with rhythmic chants and clapping (Suetonius, *Nero* 25.1; cf. 20.2–3; Tacitus, *Annals* 14.15). These claques are another example of groups formed for the purpose of public spectacles that spilled into the streets.

The organization of spectators at public spectacles into these subgroups fostered the most common kind of participatory actions in the form of acclamations and other chants, as well as the rarer attested instances of rhythmic clapping. Many acclamations in the Roman world originated in a religious context and tended to follow a standard formula (Roueché 1984: 181–188; Potter 1996). A famous example is Paul's visit to Ephesus recorded in the Acts of the Apostles (19.21–40). The silversmiths, whose livelihood depended on the manufacture of images of Artemis, showed their opposition to Paul's preaching through the acclamation 'Great is Artemis of the Ephesians!' The hostile crowd grew, flowing into the theatre where the chant was taken up by the spectators. Of interest to us is the role of members of a trade guild in provoking the demonstration and ultimately its conclusion in a public entertainment venue.

Several other demonstrations in the circus and theatre occurred around the time of Cleander's riot. A horse named Pertinax won a race at Rome, while Pertinax, the future emperor, was still in Britain. The fans of this horse shouted 'It is Pertinax!' in honour of his victory. Commodus' opponents, thinking of the prominent then-governor Pertinax, responded in kind: 'Would that it were so!' (Dio Cassius 73.4.1–2). After Commodus' death the people twisted to new purposes the acclamations that they had been compelled to raise to the emperor in the amphitheatre; rhythmic chants now were directed to the senators who had been living in terror under Commodus: 'Cheers! You are saved! You have won!' (Dio Cassius 73.2.3). Of special interest for our purposes was a chariot-race in 196 CE during the reign of Septimius Severus that occurred before the Saturnalia festival (in December). The circus crowd suddenly fell silent and then clapped in unison, at the same time praying for good fortune for the public welfare and lamenting the suffering entailed by a long period of warfare. Dio was so struck by their chants in unison—like a carefully trained chorus, as if they had rehearsed—that he attributed this demonstration to divine inspiration (Dio Cassius 75.4.4–5). Dio must have witnessed numerous such occasions in the public entertainment venues while resident in Rome, and yet was taken aback by the remarkable unity of these acclamations.

CLEANDER'S RIOT, SPECTATORSHIP, AND THE MORAL ECONOMY OF THE CROWD

We can now return to the riot at the circus with which we opened this chapter and examine the connection between the conventions of spectatorship in Rome and the moral economy of the crowd. Of crucial importance was the crowd's notion of legitimation: the crowd had to believe that it had a right to assemble and was operating under the aegis of a community consensus. Achieving that unity of will likely required the methods of communication typical of urban masses, especially those assembled for spectacles. We have already seen how silversmiths' chants on the streets of Ephesus made their way into the theatre, and how chants from the arena moved into the streets after Commodus' death. Important in each of those cases, as well, is the perceived grievance or threat that charged the communication with urgency. A famine endangered Rome in 189 CE, its effects allegedly exacerbated by official tampering with the grain supply. Vulnerability to this specific kind of danger may help explain the involvement of a group of children in sparking the riot; their unison chanting in the circus spread quickly among the spectators at large. The acclamations turned ugly, with hostility directed against Cleander in particular. What were these chants? An example from a much earlier famine is described by Cicero; using a call-and-response model to dominate the public meeting, Clodius asked the crowd: 'Who is responsible for the famine?' Clodius' well-trained thugs (his own claque) led the comeback: 'Pompey!' (Cicero, *Letters to his brother Quintus* 2.3.2). We can envision a similar question in 189 CE, but this time with a response of 'Cleander!' The acclamations, whatever precisely they were, had the effect of uniting the crowd in its resentment against Cleander, making them realize their common cause.

This belief in a community consensus was based on a larger sense of purpose that arose out of the ideology of the circus. All public spectacles in the imperial period—whether in the theatre, amphitheatre, or circus—were essential to the emperor's public image and his relationship with the people, as we have already seen. But the circus was arguably the most important venue for creating this demonstration of unity between *princeps* and populace. The proof of this was the proximity of the Palatine, the location of the imperial palace, to the Circus Maximus; here was the meeting place for emperor and people, to share in the excitement and satisfaction of the races, the distribution and enjoyment of imperial generosity, where the people could petition the emperor and he would respond. So close was this connection that the architectural combination of palace and circus (or hippodrome) became a regularized feature of imperial capitals in the later empire (Cameron 1976:178–183). The spectators in the circus, riled up with concerns about the food shortage, turned to the emperor to demand ameliorative action in 189 CE. Since Commodus wasn't present, the crowd left the circus to seek him out, thus ensuring Cleander's downfall. This crowd perceived it as their right, legitimized by long habit, to find and demand action from the emperor because of the relationship between emperor and people established in the circus.

Our sources claim that the food shortage was caused by the manipulation of the grain supply, although Herodian's account portrays the machinations as much more sinister and devious (1.12.4). It is not surprising that the portion of the city's population which depended upon the grain dole would have blamed the authorities in these circumstances. Cleander was clearly the target of the crowd's wrath and he was the one whom Commodus eventually sacrificed, whether he had truly been responsible for the food crisis or was simply a convenient scapegoat. The crowd's animosity toward Cleander might also have been provoked by his rise from Phrygian slave to Commodus' *cubicularius*, one of his closest courtiers; this leap in social status ran counter to the careful social hierarchy on exhibit in the seating arrangements at public spectacles. Even the more loosely organized circus had seats by this time set aside for the senate and members of the equestrian order. Cleander was a target of the spectators just as Claudius' freedman, Polybius, had been. Ensuring Cleander's downfall was another aspect of the crowd's notion of legitimation, for by doing so, social order was restored.

One of the most unusual aspects of Dio's account is the role played by the group of children under the apparent direction of a tall maiden, who initiated the acclamations that were taken up by the spectators at large in the circus and ultimately precipitated the rioting that led to Cleander's downfall. This young woman may have been a mime actress, leading a performance during an intermission between races (Potter 2018: 259; Futrell 2006: 198 [*P. Oxy.* 34.2707]). As we have already seen, Roman spectators were primed to respond to such performances in the theatre. Perhaps on this occasion this mime actress played on the emotions of the spectators, likely high to begin with (cf. Popkin 2016: 116–125), and further exploited an aspect of theatrical licence to evoke a response among the spectators in the circus.

As for the children, were they members of families dependent on the grain dole? Or were they fed at public expense in the *alimenta* programme (Eck 1979: 146–189)? In either case, they would have been striking and sympathetic examples of the failure of the imperial authorities to fulfil their fundamental obligation of providing for the population.

The task of the children and mime performer, namely to rile up the crowd against Cleander, was made more difficult by the venue, for the Circus Maximus was the largest public entertainment building in Rome, seating some 150,000 spectators in a *cavea* that stretched about 650 metres. A single mime performer accompanied by a group of children in such a large venue could have provoked the crowd with acclamations only if they targeted a select segment of the spectators, such as *collegia*. While it is true that direct evidence for separate seating for *collegia* in the Circus Maximus is lacking, the fact that senators under Claudius (Suet. *Claud.* 21.3; cf. Dio 60.7.4; 62 [61]. 16.4) and members of the equestrian order under Nero (Suet. *Nero* 11.1) were allotted separate seats in the circus suggests that seating in this venue had already come to resemble the more rigidly arranged seating of the theatre or ampthitheatre. The silversmiths in Ephesus, who had an economic stake in the spread of Christianity and began the acclamations that the rest of the population echoed, provide a possible analogy. The children in the circus could have targeted certain guilds that were most at risk during a food crisis: the private shippers (*navicularii*) who transported the grain, for example, or the bakers (*pistores*) who made the bread (Garnsey 1988: 239). These were groups who used their corporate organization to their political advantage, and in some cases, had enjoyed the emperor's patronage. In Arelate (modern Arles), the shippers threatened to withdraw their services if abuses from authorities did not cease (Rickman 1980: 92); at Arles, these *navicularii* had reserved seats at the amphitheatre (*CIL* 12.697). Both the greater privileges bestowed on bakers by Trajan (*Digest of Roman Law* 50.6.6.3; Rickman 1980: 90) and the dedicatory inscription by the guild of *pistores* for Antoninus Pius (*CIL* 6.1002) point to specific imperial cultivation of this occupation. Trajan, in fact, may have been the emperor who licensed the bakers' *collegium* (Aurelius Victor, *On the Caesars* 13.5). This connection between emperor and *collegia* was likely also an attempt to control these associations whose history of sometimes violent collective action dated back to the late republic. In any case, it stands to reason that the bakers and the shippers would have been anxious to alert Commodus to alleged abuses in the grain supply system, especially if they felt that their own livelihoods hung in the balance.

CONCLUSION

The crowd at the circus on that day in 189 CE communicated its displeasure at the failure of the imperial authorities to provide for the sustenance of the city's population. In so doing, the crowd took its notion of legitimation from the customs and conventions of spectatorship that informed their behaviour at Roman public shows. Of fundamental importance was the circus itself, a venue that came to represent a key component of imperial ideology, a place where the people could expect to interact with the emperor. Equally important was the tradition of public spectacles as opportunities for the expression of popular will and protest. Moreover, the crowd was instigated by the acclamations chanted first by a group of children—acclamations that were instantly repeated and quickly spread through the circus, a display of community consensus that lay at the heart of the crowd's notion of legitimation. These acclamations transformed into insults against Cleander, the ex-slave now occupying a seat in the emperor's inner circle, whose rise to power problematized the notion of order created by the strict seating at public spectacles. His downfall thus righted a social wrong. This incident draws together in striking fashion 'bread' and 'circuses', key elements of imperial ideology, and demonstrates how the conventions of spectatorship at Roman public spectacles spilled beyond the entertainment venue itself and triggered collective action with serious political consequences.

References

Audollent, A. 1904. *Defixionum tabellae. Quotquot innotuerunt tam in Graecis orientis quam in totius occidentis partibus praeter Atticas in Corpore Inscriptionum Atticarum editas.* Paris.

Bergmann, B. 1999. 'Introduction: The Art of Ancient Spectacle.' In *The Art of Ancient Spectacle.* 9–35. B. Bergmann and C. Kondoleon, eds. New Haven.

Briscoe, J. 1981. *A Commentary on Livy Books XXXIV–XXXVII.* Oxford.

Broughton, T. R. S. 1951. *Magistrates of the Roman Republic.* New York.

Cameron, A. 1976. *Circus Factions: Blues and Greens at Rome and Byzantium.* Oxford.

Eck, W. 1979. *Die staatliche Organisation Italiens in der hohen Kaiserzeit.* Munich.

Edmondson, J. C. 1996. 'Dynamic Arenas: Gladiatorial Presentations in the City of Rome and the Construction of Roman Society during the Early Empire.' In *Roman Theater and Society.* 69–112. W. J. Slater, ed. Ann Arbor.

Futrell, A. 2006. *The Roman Games: A Sourcebook.* Malden, MA.

Garnsey, P. 1988. *Famine and Food Supply in the Graeco-Roman World: Responses to Risk and Crisis.* Cambridge.

Hopkins, K. 1983. *Death and Renewal.* Cambridge.

Humphrey, J. 1986. *Roman Circuses: Arenas for Chariot Racing.* Berkeley.

Jory, J. 1984. 'Early Pantomime Riots.' In *Maistor: Classical, Byzantine and Renaissance Studies for Robert Browning.* 57–66. A. Moffatt, ed. Canberra.

Kolendo, J. 1981. 'La répartition des places aux spectacles et la stratification sociale dans l'empire Romain apropos des inscriptions sur les gradins des amphithèâtres et theaters.' *Ktema* 6: 301–315.

Lott, J. B. 2004. *The Neighborhoods of Augustan Rome.* Cambridge.

Mattingly, D. J. and G. Aldrete. 1999. 'Feeding the City: The Organization, Operation, and Scale of the Supply System for Rome.' In *Life, Death, and Entertainment in the Roman Empire.* 171–204. D. S. Potter and D. J. Mattingly, eds. Ann Arbor.

Meijer, F. 2010. *Chariot Racing in the Roman Empire.* Baltimore.

Mouritsen, H. 2001. *Plebs and Politics in the Late Roman Republic.* Cambridge.

Parker, H. N. 1999. 'The Observed of All Observers: Spectacle, Applause, and Cultural Poetics.' In *The Art of Ancient Spectacle.* 163–179. B. Bergmann and C. Kondoleon, eds. New Haven.

Pina Polo, F. 1996. Contra Arma Verbis. *Der Redner vor dem Volk in der späten römischen Republik.* Stuttgart.

Pina Polo, F. 2012. 'Contio, Auctoritas and Freedom of Speech in Republican Rome.' In *Rome, a City and its Empire in Perspective: The Impact of the Roman World through Fergus Millar's Research.* 45–58. S. Benoist, ed. Leiden/Boston.

Popkin, M. L. 2016. *The Architecture of the Roman Triumph: Monuments, Memory, and Identity.* Cambridge.

Potter, D. S. 1996. 'Performance, Power, and Justice in the High Empire.' In *Roman Theater and Society.* 129–159. W. J. Slater, ed. Ann Arbor.

Potter, D. S. 2018. *Ancient Rome: A New History,* 3rd edn. New York.

Rawson, E. 1987. 'Discrimina Ordinum: The Lex Julia Theatralis.' *PBSR* 55: 83–114.

Rickman, G. 1980. *The Corn Supply of Ancient Rome.* Oxford.

Roueché, C. 1984. 'Acclamations in the Later Roman Empire: New Evidence from Aphrodisias.' *JRS* 74: 181–199.

Roucché, C. 1993. *Performers and Partisans at Aphrodisias in the Roman and Late Roman Periods.* London.

Sherk, R. K. 1988. *The Roman Empire: Augustus to Hadrian.* Cambridge.

Slater, W. J. 1994. 'Pantomime Riots.' *ClAnt* 13: 120–144.

Taylor, L. R. 1966. *Roman Voting Assemblies: From the Hannibalic War to the Dictatorship of Caesar.* Ann Arbor.

Thompson, E. P. 1971. 'The Moral Economy of the English Crowd in the Eighteenth Century.' *P&P* 50: 76–136.

Vanderbroeck, P. 1987. *Popular Leadership and Collective Behavior in the Late Roman Republic (ca. 80–50 B.C.).* Amsterdam.

Virlouvet, C. 1985. *Famines et émeutes à Rome des origines de la République à la mort de Néron.* Rome.

Whittaker, C. R. 1964. 'The Revolt of Papirius Dionysius A.D. 190.' *Historia* 13: 348–369.

PART VI

....

BODY AND
INDIVIDUAL

....

SECTION 1

HEALTH AND TRAINING

....

CHAPTER 47

TOO MUCH OF
A GOOD THING
The Health of Olympic Athletes in
Ancient Greece

....

LESLEY DEAN-JONES

REASONS FOR EXERCISE IN ANCIENT GREECE

....

In the ancient world every town and city that considered itself Greek made gymnasia and *palaestrae* available to its citizens; physical exercise was thought to be essential both for the good life of the individual and for the maintenance of an effective citizen army. But not everybody made equal use of these facilities. The orator Aeschines remarks (Aeschin. 1.189) that those who exercise are recognizable from the good condition of their bodies even by those who do not visit the gymnasium, a remark which implies that exercisers and non-exercisers were meaningful categories in ancient Greece. The Hippocratic author of *Prorrhetic* II 1 says that other doctors claim to be able to detect small departures from normal regimen both in athletes and in those who are exercising 'on account of diseases', showing that the category 'exercisers' can be further subdivided. But these two groups clearly do not exhaust the category. The term 'athlete' is used on only one other occasion in the Hippocratic Corpus, at *Aphorisms* I 15, where the author remarks that people generally need more food in the winter and spring because that is when their innate heat is greatest, and then points to the young and athletes for proof that greater heat requires more food, clearly indicating that most people do not fall under the rubric 'athlete'. The adjectival form of the word is used at *Nutriment 34* which states, 'The athletic condition is not natural. A healthy state is better in everybody.' In both *Aphorisms* and *Nutriment* the term 'athlete' clearly refers to those who exercise beyond the norm and this is a norm set by ordinary healthy men, not those who are exercising 'because of diseases'. The author of *Prorrhetic* II conjoins athletes with those who are exercising on account of diseases because both groups would be following a more strictly controlled regimen than a normal healthy man. Of the large category of individuals that are neither patients nor athletes the same author remarks in chapter 4:

> From the same amount of food most stools are passed by those who exert themselves least and a small amount by those exerting themselves most, if they are both healthy and following a judicious regimen.

It is not that medicine and training had nothing to say to the healthy non-athlete about what might be a 'judicious' regimen, but the parameters did not need the close attention of a professional.

We might expect that elite athletes who underwent rigorous training in preparation for competition at both the local and Panhellenic level were thought to be the healthiest individuals and by dint of this the finest soldiers. But in the classical period the peak of physical fitness was thought to be a very treacherous state of health. *Aphorisms* I 3 declares:

> In those who exercise being in peak condition is dangerous if they are at the very pinnacle of health. For they cannot remain in the same state and they cannot be stable. And although they cannot remain stable they can no longer improve to a better state; and so it remains to deteriorate to a worse. On this account it is for the best to reduce the good condition quickly, so that the body may again begin the process of building-up.

The Greek maxim 'Nothing to Excess' reverberates throughout Greek literature, but it is surprising to modern readers to see it applied even to health. To understand why this is so we need to consider the Greek conceptions of health and disease and how the regimen followed by athletes was thought to affect their bodies.

Greek Conceptions of Health and Disease

The earliest medical theory of which we are aware, that of Alcmaeon of Croton *c*.500 BCE, held that health resulted when the powers of the body were in a state of balance. For Alcmaeon these powers are such things as the moist and dry, the hot and cold, the sweet and bitter. If any one element begins to preponderate, sickness results. The preponderance can come about through an excess or deficiency of nourishment or of exertion. The idea that health resulted from a balance of bodily constituents that were increased or depleted by nourishment and exertion was the basis of almost all rational medicine for the rest of Greco-Roman antiquity, though there was a variety of theories on what the constituents themselves were. *On Ancient Medicine*, probably written about 430 BCE, argues that humans, unlike animals, did not originally know instinctively what was needed for them to retain a constitutional balance and tried to subsist on the same raw foods as other animals. These untreated foods were too 'strong' for humans and in the early periods of human history the majority of mankind was sickly or downright ill until trial and error by some individuals (the earliest doctors) found the foods most suited to the human constitution and the most advantageous ways to prepare them. The knowledge of what foods in general a human should eat to remain healthy, *On Ancient Medicine* says, is now an everyday affair and has become the province of cooks. However, the expertise of a doctor is needed both to oversee the diet of individuals who fall ill and can no longer digest ordinary food, and to advise on what types of food from the range offered by cooks would be most beneficial for different human body types and environmental conditions.

In fulfilment of this latter remit, the author of *Regimen in Health* (probably a work of the last quarter of the fifth century BCE) proffers advice to laymen (*idiōtas* in Greek) on diet and exercise with reference to individual constitutions (fleshy and soft, lean and sinewy, etc.) and time of year. In winter, the general aim is to stop the body from getting too moist and cold, so individuals are advised to eat as much as possible (specifically bread, roast meats, and few vegetables) and drink as little as possible (preferably very lightly diluted wine). In summer individuals should drink diluted wine as copiously as possible and in lesser amounts eat barley-cake, raw or boiled vegetables, and boiled meat. Spring and autumn were respectively periods of gradual increase or decrease.

Regarding exercise, the author of *Regimen in Health* initially offers advice (in chapters 3 and 4) only to those who wish to change their physique, advising stout people who wish to become thin to exercise while fasting and to eat highly seasoned food. Thin people who wish to gain weight should, he says, adopt the opposite regimen. Note that this advice deals primarily with the diet to be followed while exercising, not the exercise itself. The only exercise mentioned at this stage is walking, which stouter people should do faster than thinner.

In the final chapter of the treatise the author proceeds to give advice on exercise to 'those who exercise' (*tous gumnazomenous*). W. H. S. Jones (1931: 55) sees this chapter as directed to 'athletes in training' in contrast to the laymen addressed in the earlier part of the treatise, but as I have just argued, the earlier advice was directed at a very specific subgroup of laymen—those who wished to change their physique—and dealt more with diet than exercise. Remember also that Aeschines' remark implies that not all citizens chose to avail themselves of the gymnasium, and that *Prorrhetic* II, *Aphorisms*, and *Nutriment* all use the term 'athlete' to demarcate those in training from the rest of the populace. Furthermore, the advice in the last chapter of *Regimen in Health* seems unsuitable for those aiming at Panhellenic or even local competition. The initial advice on exercise, as with nutrition, is determined by the seasons of the year—for example, running and wrestling should both be undertaken in winter, but in summer no running at all and only a very little wrestling, walking being the preferred exercise. The author is operating on the assumption that if an individual has moderated his intake of food as advised in the dietetic part of the treatise, walking would be sufficient exertion to keep the body's constituents in balance. But this does not smack of the sort of training undertaken by competitive athletes who would be gearing up for the Panhellenic festivals in the early summer. When the term 'those who exercise' occurs in the Hippocratics it does not refer to elite athletes for whose custom the Hippocratics were in competition with trainers.

The role that the author of *Regimen in Health* does see a doctor playing in the training of elite athletes is suggested by the latter part of his last chapter. This is dedicated to therapeutic measures that should be taken to counter the deleterious consequences of rigorous exercise such as excessive fatigue, diarrhoea, vomiting, swollen hypochondria, and stomach-aches. For example:

> Those who develop diarrhoea when exercising and who pass undigested food in their stools should cut their exercise by at least a third and their food by a half. For it is clear that their stomach is not capable of heating up the amount that they eat so that they can digest it. Let them eat well-baked bread crumbled up into wine, and let them drink as little as possible, and undiluted liquids, and they should not walk after food. During this period they should eat once a day, for in this way the stomach will heat up very well and master the incoming food.

> This kind of diarrhoea afflicts especially those whose flesh is compact when a man with this constitution is forced to eat meat, for compacted veins cannot take in the incoming food.

The advice to reduce exercise by at least one third has no meaning unless the exercise is structured to a greater extent than is suggested by the advice earlier in the chapter to 'walk in the summer'. The reference to being under a compulsion to eat meat also indicates that the situation is unlikely to arise in an individual undertaking exercise for prophylactic purposes. Ordinary exercise was meant simply to ensure that any excess of nourishment was used up. Meat was not normally a large part of the ancient Greek diet (Sweet 1987: 200). To consume large amounts of food, especially meat, merely increases the need to exercise and would be an expensive zero sum game for normal levels of health. This sort of diarrhoea, then, is likely to afflict an individual in training at the competitive level. The doctor's advice could help such an individual moderate his regimen to restore his health, but the need for such advice might well signal a less-than-successful athletic career. On the Greek model of physiology, anyone who has to limit his intake of nourishment drastically because of the nature of his flesh will not be able to build up the resources needed to fuel the exertion expended at an elite level. Our extant medical sources suggest that calibrating the minutiae of such a regimen for the exceptional individual who could compete at these levels is not part of a doctor's expertise, though he would be needed to treat athletes for injuries incurred in the gymnasium such as broken noses, dislocated shoulders and internal wounds (e.g. *Diseases* I 15 and 21).

The type of nourishment and exertion needed to develop the body's physical potential beyond the parameters of ordinary health was left to gymnastics trainers. Their methods are in many ways a continuation of the therapeutic advice given by the Hippocratic doctors. The author of *On Ancient Medicine* 4 states this explicitly:

> And still even now, those who concern themselves with gymnastics and training (*askēsis*) are constantly making discoveries by following the same method as doctors in the earlier period as to what food and drink are most easily assimilated and make a man stronger than he was.

Places in Man 35, however, describes gymnastics not as the continuation but as the opposite of medicine:

> Gymnastics and medicine are by nature opposites, for gymnastics ought not to produce changes while medicine has to; for it does not benefit a healthy person to change from his existing condition, but it does an ill person.

The apparent contradiction between the two statements arises because, whereas *Places in Man* is contrasting medicine to exercise that simply aims to maintain a healthy status quo, *On Ancient Medicine* is commenting on the activity of trainers who deal with elite athletes and whose aim is to make the body stronger, as doctors try to do for those who are ill.

Prorrhetic II, *Places in Man*, and *Regimen in Health* all suggest that neither trainers nor doctors played an active role in the exercise routine of healthy adults if they were not training at a competitive level, but trainers do seem to have had a much higher profile in dealing with young males, and this may be precisely because they are engaged in bringing about bodily changes as they guide the physical development of young males through youth to adulthood. Their aim was not simply to maintain health or to produce a prize-winning athlete but to develop a body that could fulfil its duty as a citizen soldier. One vase from the fifth century BCE can be read as showing the beginning and end product of the trainer's efforts (Athens,

National Archaeological Museum 18797; see Tzachou-Alexandri 1989: 171, pl. 57). The very young boys on one side of the vase, engaged in cleaning themselves off after some exercise, are clearly on the pudgy side; the young men on the other side of the vase (which is unpublished) are well-toned but not depicted in an athletic context, indicating that the aim of the training was to produce ephebes rather than Olympic victors.

Once grown, the average Greek citizen understood the basics of diet and exercise and did not need a trainer to maintain a healthy physique. So, too, the Hippocratic authors needed to give only the most general advice on diet and exercise to adult males in good health who had grown up under a trainer.

How Exercise Affected Bodies

We have less advice about exercise than about nutrition in the Hippocratic Corpus because, whereas patients usually (though not always) continue to need some sort of sustenance when they fall ill, this is very often a time they take to their beds. *Prorrhetic* II 3 comments that it is not easy to recognize mistakes in the regimen of patients because they stay in bed, and although in chapter 4 the author divides individuals in his care into three groups (those who stay home, those who exercise and all others) the only exercise he specifies is walking. Recommending arduous running drills or strenuous wrestling bouts to patients feeling too ill to continue with their normal daily round is simply not practicable. There is, however, a treatise written for people who are *about* to become sick which gives detailed advice on diet and exercise that could only be followed while they are still healthy. This treatise is *Regimen*, and the author claims to be able to diagnose an illness before it manifests itself in bodily symptoms by means of the patient's dreams. In these cases what is needed is often not just a rebalancing of the fluids in the body but the compacting, dissolution, and reconstitution of the flesh itself. In line with the statement in *On Ancient Medicine* that trainers were continuing the discoveries of early medicine, we can extrapolate from *Regimen*'s therapeutic advice to how trainers aimed to improve the performance of elite athletes in the classical period, and what it was about peak conditioning that seemed so threatening to the ancient Greek psyche.

The first condition discussed as being amenable to correction by physical exercise is excess weight (*Regimen* II 62). Walking could be used to help reduce and dry out a fat belly, but if done immediately after eating dinner it also helped to fill out the rest of the body. It does this by causing the flesh to heat up and draw to itself the moisture from the food that has just been eaten. Most of the purest part of this is consumed by the body's innate heat and the residual fluids are purged by increased respiration and perspiration. The nourishment drawn into the flesh that is not used stays there and does not return to the belly but fills out the body. Notice that this is a general filling out of the body; the nourishment does not accumulate in any one body part. For those who are congested both in bowel and head, walks in the early morning are particularly advantageous. From various places in the Hippocratic Corpus it is clear that early morning walks were taken before any food was consumed, so there is no moisture from recent meals in the stomach. The inspired cool morning air rushes into the bowels from above (because there is nothing in the stomach to hold it up), causing the heat to give way before the cold; the bowels empty themselves and then draw the moisture down from the rest of the body, thereby purging the head so that sight and hearing become clearer.

Walking is an exercise a doctor could recommend to his older or more infirm patients, but most of the exercise discussed in *Regimen* is more vigorous. For example, when the body needs to be made lean, says the author (II 63), the best exercise is the *trochos*. This type of running is contrasted with long runs and the *diaulos* and, of the three types of run, is described as causing the most panting. It should therefore be identified as sprinting. In his Loeb edition, W. H. S. Jones (1931: 353) translates *trochos* as 'circular running', but it is hard to see how the shape of the track would cause runners to pant more or affect the physiological results of the exercise. I assume the author used the term *trochos* rather than *stadion*—the word used to refer to the shortest race or the sprint in athletic sources—because if an individual was not in training for a specific event, short, fast sprints could be of any distance and were run round the palaestra rather than in the stadium. The author describes the effect of the *trochos* as reducing and contracting the flesh with the least amount of dissolution. To fuel these concentrated bursts of speed the runner needed only to draw the moisture out of the flesh and this he did by rapid respiration, leaving the flesh compact, but not dissolved (i.e. muscular). Depictions of sprinters show a lithe torso with well-developed chest and thighs (Panathenaic amphora (460 BCE), Bologna, Museo Civico; see Yalouris 1976: 162, pl. 69). The compacting of the flesh is unproblematic if it is the aim of the exercise, as in the case of therapy or prophylaxis; but a trainer preparing a runner for the *stadion* would need to devise a regimen that would ensure that the compact flesh could still store sufficient fluid to be drawn on for a competitive race. His task would be made difficult by the fact that the more a runner ran sprints, the more compact his flesh would become, and the less easily would it hold fluids, resulting in the diarrhoea described in *Regimen in Health 7*. Practising the sprint develops flesh that is least amenable to supporting that event.

Another form of vigorous exercise is less intense but longer runs. The author of *Regimen* again uses a non-technical term to refer to long runs, 'flexible and long' (*kamptoi kai makroi*), rather than the technical term for a long race in athletic competitions, *dolichos*; *kamptoi* may refer to any runs at least two stades (about 200 m.) in length, alluding to the stadium turning-post, *kamptēr*, used in races that length or longer. Although the *dolichos* was even less standardized than the *stadion* (between one and three miles, more a middle-distance race in our terms), there is obviously still greater latitude in the term 'flexible and long'. Run outside of the palaestra these races can follow a route of any shape; and somebody undertaking a long run for therapy is not concerned to cover any specific distance associated with competitive racing. In later chapters patients are advised to increase the length of 'flexible' runs gradually (e.g. III 68 and 79). Unlike sprinting, long runs cannot be fuelled simply by the moisture drawn from the flesh. To provide the nourishment it needs for continuous exertion the body heats flesh to the point where it dissolves and becomes fluid itself. One would therefore expect a long-distance runner to have less flesh on his body than a sprinter (as is the case in modern middle- and long-distance runners). Surprisingly, though, the author of *Regimen* says that long runs cause the body to become stockier (*pachuteros*) than do sprints. A vase painting generally agreed to show runners in the *dolichos*, because of their gait and distancing, does depict bodies decidedly stockier than those shown sprinting (Panathenaic amphora (333 BCE), London, British Museum; see Yalouris 1976: 167, pl. 75). In his *Symposium* 2.17, Xenophon has Socrates say that it is only the legs of long-distance runners, *dolichodromoi*, which thicken up while their shoulders become thin. Socrates is here exaggerating the discrepancy between the upper and lower bodies of *dolichodromoi* to make a point about the need for symmetry in true beauty, but the point remains that an exercise which *Regimen* says dissolves flesh was generally thought in ancient Greece to make a body stockier than sprinting.

The reason for this is that dissolved flesh did not necessarily leave the body. In *Regimen* II 66 the author discusses the problems of fatigue pains that arise after exercise in those who are generally unused to exertion and those who do exercise regularly but perform some unaccustomed activity. In these cases, either the whole body or a part of the body is overly moist to start with, due to not being exercised, and therefore dissolves readily. However, the untrained body or body part cannot use up all this liquefied material, which then reconstitutes itself in the fleshy parts of the body where, says the author, it is 'not advantageous' (*ou sumpheron*). *Regimen* advises gentle walks, hot baths, restricted diet, and other reducing methods to break up the reconstituted flesh. However, for competitive long-distance runs, an increase in flesh-fuel would be advantageous. Elite athletes would be accustomed to this exercise, so in order to keep their bodies at the requisite level of moistness they would have to eat a lot. Wherever the nourishment settled in the body, during their practice runs it would dissolve, be drawn to their legs, and any that was not consumed would reconstitute itself in the fleshy parts, the muscles of thigh and calf.

'Flexible' and long runs, says the author of *Regimen*, are good for those who eat a lot, those who have excess flesh, and those who are older. The author is prescribing suitable exercise for certain types of bodies, not advising athletes how to build up the body to be able to perform better at the *dolichos*. Once again, a trainer would be the one who would calibrate the bodily economy for his charges. The flesh of a long-distance runner did not become as compact as a sprinter, so diarrhoea from force-feeding might be less of a concern; but in building up the reservoirs of flesh needed for the *dolichos*, the trainer would have to steer a fine course between providing food that was too easily passed by stool and having the athlete consume a large quantity of food that could cause constipation.

Between the long run and the sprint *Regimen* II 63 mentions the *diaulos*. This is a technical term used to refer to a double *stadion*—there and back again—basically an extended sprint. It is unclear why the author would use the name for an athletic distance here when he avoided it in discussing sprinting and long runs. It may be there was no other way to readily identify what for the Greeks would be a middle-distance run. Like the *trochos*, this run needs to call immediately on the body's fluids (which are drawn *away from*, not *to* the flesh as in the case of the *dolichos*) to be expended in the labours of the psyche:

> The *diaulos*, run in the open air, dissolves the flesh less than long runs but makes the body leaner; this is because the exertions, insofar as they have to do with the interior parts of the psyche, draw the moisture away from the flesh causing the body to become thin and dry.

Coupled with the author's citation of the rapid panting caused by sprinting as the reason for sprinting producing the leanest bodies, it is clear that he sees what we might refer to as high-intensity running as being driven by the vital force of the body rather than the body itself. However, the *diaulos*, like long runs, also has an element of duration for which the fuelling of the psyche by fluids is insufficient and the body itself needs to be fuelled by dissolving flesh, though not as much dissolved flesh as the *dolichos*. Because the *diaulos* was a sprint it is difficult to distinguish differences in body-type between *stadion* and *diaulos* runners on vases, but the turning-post on one vase identifies the event as a *diaulos* (Panathenaic amphora [480–470 BCE], Northampton, Castle Ashby; see Yalouris 1976: 167, pl. 74). Whether this would be the hardest or the easiest run for which to formulate a diet is hard to say. It would not have to deal with the problem of inducing extremely compacted flesh to retain fluids for at least short periods of time as with the *stadion,* or of maintaining large reservoirs of easily dissolvable flesh on an active body as with the *dolichos,* so it might seem that the diet could be more flexible—but then again it would have to calibrate food for both types of exertion and they might work against one another.

The other main form of exercise *Regimen* recommends to ward off oncoming disease is wrestling. The particular benefit of wrestling is that it causes the flesh to harden but the veins that feed it to grow. This is because the rubbing of wrestling compresses solid flesh while causing the hollow vessels to expand. Holding the breath also forces open the passages and makes the skin thin, which means moisture is then easily expelled from the flesh. This brings to mind the anecdote of the wrestler Milo who proved his strength by holding his breath till he snapped the bands encircling his head (Pausanias 6.14.7). However, further comments show that in wrestling as in running, the author of *Regimen* is not addressing his advice to competitive athletes. He views wrestling in oil and wrestling in dust as alternatives, with wrestling in dust the colder of the two; wrestling in oil is to be avoided in the summer because it melts the flesh too much (*Regimen* II 65). All competitive wrestling used oil, though it was sometimes deliberately overlaid with dust. Apart from making it more difficult for an opponent to get a grip, oiling may have been viewed as advantageous precisely because it helped melt the flesh quickly to provide the nourishment the athlete needed.

Although the author occasionally advises sparring (*anakinēmata*) and the use of the punch ball (*kōrukomachiē*), he does not suggest boxing, pankration, *diskos,* javelin, long-jump, or any equine pursuits as therapeutic exercise. Regarding sparring, *Regimen* says that it is the exercise that heats the flesh least, which may mean it was not thought to provide enough exertion for most therapeutic purposes, though it does stimulate the body and soul and empty the body of breath, *pneuma* (*Regimen* II 64). *Pneuma* is an essential component of life; to drain it from the body while at the same time stimulating the body and soul was perhaps seen as having limited therapeutic value. There are probably two additional reasons why the more intense boxing is not recommended as prophylactic or therapeutic exercise. As represented on vases the body-type of the typical boxer seems rather larger than the Greek ideal (Panathenaic amphora (336/335 BCE), London, British Museum; see Yalouris 1976: 223, pl. 125). A vase contrasting the bodies of a young runner, a young boxer, and two young pentathletes implies that boxing and a stocky body-type were thought to go hand in hand from an early age (Red-figure Athenian drinking cup (475 BCE), London, British Museum, inv. 1846,0512.2; Spivey 2004: 61, fig. 9). Maintaining such a physique without allowing the excess material to upset the body's balance would require extreme vigilance, and such dangers may be illustrated in portrayals of slightly older boxers in which the material seems to have drifted south (Munich, Staatliche Antikensammlungen 1541; see Tzachou-Alexandri 1989: 139, pl. 31). The second reason boxing, and pankration, would not be popular with doctors is that they were more likely than other exercise to result in injury and permanent scarring.

The lack of reference in *Regimen* to the other three events that besides wrestling and running make up the pentathlon—*diskos,* javelin, and long-jump—is perhaps to be explained by the fact that the performance of these pursuits relied more heavily on technique than the type of exertion which could avert impending illness. At the elite level, technique is important in running and wrestling also, but not so much if winning is incidental or irrelevant to the exercise. It is not clear that horse-riding was ever a great pastime of most male citizens in Greece, and in fact continued horse-riding was seen as responsible for varicose veins in the legs among the Scythians (*Airs, Waters, Places* 22). It is, then, not surprising that *Regimen* does not number it among its recommended exercises.

FRAILTY OF THE ATHLETIC CONSTITUTION

Military service must have been the most gruelling exercise that most ordinary Greek citizens undertook, and we might expect that the bodies of athletes, accustomed as they are to extreme exertion, would be the best prepared for the rigours of campaign, but from a military point of view athletes are often treated with contempt. In Euripides' *Autolycus*, produced *c*.420 BCE, a character is made to say:

> What man has ever defended the city of his fathers by winning a crown for wrestling well or running fast or throwing a *diskos* far or planting an uppercut on the jaw of an opponent? Do men drive the enemy out of their fatherland by waging war with *diskoi* in their hands or by throwing punches through the line of shields? No one is so silly as to do this when he is standing before the steel of the enemy. (fr. 282, trans. Miller 2004: 198)

The implication, obviously, is not just that athletics is different from war but that excessive attention to athletics does not function well as *preparation* for warfare. A soldier's body could not be totally untrained, for such bodies suffer the pain of fatigue after the slightest exercise (*Regimen* II 66); the character is not advocating complete inactivity. But a soldier has to be adaptable to periods of quiescence as well as activity, to fasting as well as eating, and to eating whatever is available. The carefully calibrated regimen of excessive eating and exertion necessary to prepare for specific athletic events did not promote this adaptability. For this reason, the strength of highly trained athletes was not viewed as a reserve that they could call on to help them withstand adverse conditions. An Olympic sprinter would not have enough fluid in his flesh to fuel a long march; the flesh of a *dolichos* champion would not melt quickly enough in situations where speed was of the essence, and inopportune periods of forced rest could cause all sorts of trouble. This may be why one vase contrasts pairs of overweight wrestlers and boxers on one side of its body with pairs of muscular hoplites in combat on the other (Thera, Archaeological Museum AK 1725; see Tzachou-Alexandri 1989: 282, pl. 169). The latter, not the former, were the bodies that the state really wished to inculcate in its citizens.

This explains why elite athletes do not make the best soldiers, but as long as they can continue with their training regimen, why should they not be able to maintain their peak condition? In modern training it is recognized that peaking too early is problematic because an organic body cannot physically maintain that level of performance. The ancient concept of a body's intake and performance, however, is much closer to that of a car; put the right fuel in, carry out scheduled maintenance and it should continue to run. In principle, there seems no reason an ancient athlete should not have expected to be able to maintain peak condition if he and his trainer geared his event and training to his underlying body-type and the prevailing weather conditions, selected the right foods, prepared them correctly, expended just the right amount of exertion after eating, and rested the right amount of time before eating again. There is no indication in the texts that the ancient authors had any concept of the body becoming stressed by this process. However, there is one text that states explicitly why athletes cannot remain in peak condition. *Aphorisms* I 5 declares:

> In a restricted regimen those who are ill make mistakes, and on this account become more indisposed; for everything that happens is magnified compared to what happens in slightly more relaxed regimens. For this reason, even for the healthy, restricted and tightly controlled regimens are dangerous, because they deal with mistakes less readily.

In *principle*, an athlete could maintain an extreme regimen indefinitely, but in *practice* men are fallible and mistakes are made; to attempt to extend peak condition longer than necessary is dangerous.

For modern athletes a miscalculation in training regimen might be expected to adversely affect performance, but it is not usually thought to result in disease. Disease was a constant spectre for the ancient elite athlete at the top of his game because of the Greek conception of the bodily economy of fluids. The flesh of a man satisfied with a human level of health can handle a slight accidental excess or deficiency of fluid on any given day. But the extremely compact flesh of a sprinter cannot absorb even a slight unforeseen increase in fluid; the excess flows to his bowels, causing diarrhoea. And for the *dolichodromos*, an unplanned decrease could lead to him using up all the moisture from his food to build his flesh, leaving none to flow to his bowels, thereby causing an excess of heat there and constipation. So, once its usefulness has passed, an athlete must descend from his exalted peak of health in a controlled way and follow a less finely tuned regimen. It is not that reaching the summit of health is to be sick, any more than reaching the summit of wealth is to be poor. In itself, the achievement is worthy of admiration, but insofar as it surpasses the normal state of humans, the extreme health of a competitive athlete places him in danger.

NOTE

Citations from the text and chapter divisions of the Hippocratic treatises *On Ancient Medicine, Airs, Waters, Places, Nutriment, Regimen in Health, Aphorisms,* and *Regimen* are those of Jones 1923 and 1931; of *Diseases* I, *Prorrhetic* II and *Places in Man* those of Potter 1988 and 1995. All translations are my own.

REFERENCES

Jones, W. H. S. 1923. *Hippocrates*, vol. I. Cambridge, MA.
Jones, W. H. S. 1931. *Hippocrates*, vol. IV. Cambridge, MA.
Miller, S. G. 2004. *Ancient Greek Athletics.* New Haven.
Potter, P. 1988. *Hippocrates*, vol. V. Cambridge, MA.
Potter, P. 1995. *Hippocrates*, vol. VIII. Cambridge, MA.
Spivey, N. 2004. *The Ancient Olympics: A History.* Oxford.
Sweet, W. E. 1987. *Sport and Recreation in Ancient Greece.* New York.
Tzachou-Alexandri, O., ed. 1989. *Mind and Body: Athletic Contests in Ancient Greece.* Athens.
Yalouris, N. 1982. *The Olympic Games in Ancient Greece.* Athens.

CHAPTER 48

....

ATHLETIC PARTICIPATION, TRAINING, AND ADOLESCENT EDUCATION

....

DAVID M. PRITCHARD

INTRODUCTION

....

THE class background of Greek sportsmen has been hotly debated (Kyle 2007: 205–210; Pritchard 2013: 35–46). One group of ancient historians has argued that upper-class citizens dominated or even monopolized athletic competition in Archaic and Classical Greece (e.g. Golden 1998: 141–175; Kyle 1987; Poliakoff 1989; Pritchard 2003), while another has argued just as forcefully that the lower class competed as athletes in ever-increasing numbers (e.g. Fisher 1998; Pleket 1975; 1992; Young 1984). Within this second group there have been further disagreements over the extent, timing, and causes of the proposed taking up of athletics by non-elite citizens. Forty years of debate, which at times has been acrimonious, have failed to produce a consensus. In an attempt to move this controversy forward this chapter shifts the focus of the debate from competition to training for athletic *agōnes* ('contests'). The Classical Athenians believed that an athlete could only perform creditably, not to mention win, at one of the recognized Panhellenic games, if he had devoted large amounts of his time to regular athletic training (e.g. Aeschin. 3.179–180; Isoc. 16.32–33; Plat. *Laws* 807c). Likewise, for local games at home, they held that it was sustained training alone that turned boys and young men into competent *athlētai* or athletic competitors (e.g. Aristoph. *Frogs* 1093–1094; Isoc. 15.183–185; Plat. *Stat.* 294d–e.) Against them the *idiōtai* or untrained had little chance of success (e.g. Plat. *Rep.* 422b–c; Xen. *Hiero* 4.6). Competing as an athlete was clearly dependent on appropriate preparation. As a consequence, those of the city's boys and young men who lacked access to athletic training would have performed poorly in sporting competitions and would have been greatly disheartened about entering a race or bout in the first place.

Athletic training may be a promising avenue for investigating afresh the class position of Classical Athenian athletes, but working out who had access to it is a surprisingly complex business. At the outset it is necessary to establish what relationship, if any, existed between this preparation for sporting *agōnes* and the physical education classes that were considered to be a normal part of adolescent education. This will clarify whether athletic participation required specialized instruction or was a function of the larger phenomenon of education. Once we have done so, we can consider closely the economic and social costs of preparing for competition, which social classes or class fractions could have met these demands, and any evidence about who exactly trained for, and competed in, sporting contests. Classical Athens is, of course, the only *polis* for which enough testimonia have survived to support such detailed social history. Nevertheless, its sporting scene still sheds light on the likelihood of lower-class participation in the Greek world more generally. As this city had the most fully developed democracy of pre-modern times, and was the centre of long-distance trade in the Aegean and probably wealthier per capita than any other *polis* (Pritchard 2010: 1–5), its free inhabitants enjoyed substantial social mobility. If lower-class Greeks, therefore, did take up athletics in increasing numbers before the close of the Classical period, we can anticipate finding clear evidence of broadening sporting participation in this socially progressive and prosperous city.

Before we begin, we must clarify the structure and character of social classes under Classical Athenian democracy (Rosivach 1991; 2001; Pritchard 2013: 2–9; Vartsos 1978). Classical Athenians are known to have divided up the citizen-body on the basis of military roles, the Solonian income classes, occupation, or place of residence. But the distinction which they used much more often than others and which demarcated the most important social cleavage was between *hoi plousioi* ('the wealthy') and *hoi penētes* ('the poor'). According to surviving comedies and public speeches, the wealthy were marked out primarily by their lives of *scholē* ('leisure') and hence lack of the necessity to work, distinctive clothing and footwear, exclusive pastimes, and particular but not-always-highly-regarded attitudes and actions (Pritchard 2020: 110–116). They were also expected to undertake expensive public services, paid the *eisphora* or extraordinary war-tax, and furnished the city's political and military leaders. Their lifestyle and significant contributions to public life made them conspicuous amongst the city's residents. They most probably numbered close to, but less than, five percent of the citizen-body (Hansen 1991: 90–94, 115). While it contrasts markedly with how contemporary societies habitually divide up their populations into gradations of upper, middle, and lower classes, the classical Athenians classified the rest of their citizen-body—from the destitute to those sitting just below the elite—as 'the poor' (Pritchard 2020: 116–120). Classical sources suggest what the varied members of this social class had in common was a lack of leisure—and hence a need to work—and a way of life that was frugal and moderate.

ATHLETICS AND ADOLESCENT EDUCATION

To understand the preparations which Athenian athletes undertook for competition, we need to investigate what relationship, if any, existed between training of this sort and the traditional physical education of free males up to the age of seventeen years, whom the Athenians called *paides* or boys (Golden 1990: 12–22). Typically, the later-fifth-century comedy *Clouds* by Aristophanes is taken as evidence that the city's young had abandoned the *palaistra* ('wrestling school') and *gumnasion* ('athletics field') for the 'new education' of the

so-called sophists with their lessons in *hoplomachia* ('weapons training'), oratory, and philosophy (961–1054). However, a wide range of surviving literature, including a close reading
of this comedy, suggests otherwise: although opportunities for male adolescents to learn
new disciplines did proliferate in the second half of the fifth century (de Romilly 1992), physical education manifestly remained an established element of the normative and traditional
paideia ('education') of young Athenians throughout the Classical period (e.g. Aeschin.
1.10; Aristoph. *Frogs* 727–730; Plat. *Lach.* 184e). This branch of what Aristophanes calls the
archaia paideia or 'old education' (961) was taught by the *paidotribēs* or athletics teacher (e.g.
Aristoph. *Cl.* 973; *Kn.* 490–492, 1238–1239; Plat. *Lach.* 184e), whose lessons were not one-
on-one but for groups of students (e.g. Isoc. 15.183–185; Plat. *Stat.* 294c–d). The verb normally used to describe the attendance of boys at his lessons—*phoitaō*, which literally means
to go back and forth frequently—indicates how his classes were just as regular and ongoing
as those of the other traditional disciplines (e.g. Isoc. 15.183; Plat. *Gorg.* 456d–e). It is a historical irony that, while Athens-based sophists of the late fifth and fourth centuries assimilated
their newfangled lessons to traditional education or even argued for the superiority of what
they were teaching (Tarrant 2003), they were the first to describe the 'old education' system-
atically and to invent an abstract terminology to do so.

How this *gumnastikē* related to training for athletic competition and what the
circumstances of the latter were have been largely overlooked by the historians of ancient
Greek sport, who are usually content to write of 'training' or 'coaching' without providing
any details (e.g. Fisher 1998: 94, 96; Golden 1998: 143, 160; Nicholson 2005: 5–7). A com-
mendable exception is Donald Kyle, who, after several pages of discussion in his *Athletics in
Ancient Athens*, concludes (1987: 143): 'To a certain extent the activities of athletics and physical education overlapped but the degree of involvement and specialization differed'. Taking
his definitions from two authors of the late Roman period, Kyle suggests that the *paidotribēs*
was 'a wrestling school teacher with his own *palaestra* where he instructed boys in basic
gymnastics and also where athletes trained' (1987: 141–142). He was, in short, 'more of a
preliminary physical trainer'. The so-called *gumnastēs*, by contrast, was a 'more specialized
trainer, hired to prepare an athlete for competition, supervising his exercises and diet'. The
gumnastēs, then, was 'the 'coach' or 'athletic expert', whose services were sought out by an individual in training for competition. 'The distinction between these two', Kyle writes, 'arose
in practice in the fifth century and was established in terminology by the fourth'. The division
of tasks Kyle proposes might be logical and plausible, but it is not, unfortunately, one that
is corroborated by Classical Athenian sources. Instead they suggest that it was the regular
school classes of the *paidotribēs* that were the means by which young Athenians prepared for
athletic competition and that *gumnastēs*, far from describing a specialist athletics coach, was
simply one of a few philosophical synonyms for *paidotribēs* (Pritchard 2013: 46–53).

The critical text for understanding the relationship between physical education and athletic competition in Classical Athens is the *Antidosis* of Isocrates (15.181–185). In the course
of what is actually a justification of his own classes in oratory, which he confusingly calls
philosophy, Isocrates details how athletics teachers instruct their students (*mathētas,
tous phoitōntas*) in 'the moves devised *for competition* (*ta schēmata ta pros tēn agōnian
heurēmena*)' (15.183). Once he has accustomed them to 'the moves', the *paidotribēs* trains
them in athletics, gets them used to toil (*ponein*) and compels them to combine each of the
lessons that they have learnt (184). According to Isocrates, this teaching and training turns
students into competent athletic competitors as long as they have sufficient natural talent

(185). The picture drawn here of the *paidotribēs* teaching groups of students competitive athletics *and* overseeing their training is confirmed by other Classical Athenian authors. A few, for example, have pupils learning athletics under a *paidotribēs* (Aristoph. *Kn.* 1238–1239; Plat. *Gorg.* 456c–e), several have him supervising those in athletic training (e.g. Aristoph. *Kn.* 493; Plat. *Crito* 47b; *Rep.* 389c), while one, like Isocrates, puts the teaching (*paideuō*) and training (*askeō*) of an athlete into his hands (Plat. *Lach.* 184e).

Athletics teachers are most frequently represented in classical texts or on red-figure pots giving lessons in the 'heavy' events of Greek athletics: wrestling (*palē*), boxing, and the *pankration* (e.g. Aristoph. *Kn.* 490–492, 1238–1239; Plat. *Gorg.* 456d–e; Beck 1975). This comes as no surprise, as each of these events was technically demanding and many *paidotribai* owned their own *palaistrai*, while some, when they were young, had been famous Panhellenic victors in these events. But the so-called track-and-field *agōnes* required athletes to be no less proficient in 'the moves devised for competition' (Isoc. 15.183; Golden 2008: 26; Nicholson 2005: 124). This was obviously the case with the throwing of the discus or the javelin, but the long-jump too demanded real technique and timing: in contrast to the modern event, Greek jumpers held *haltēres* or hand weights, which, while airborne, they carefully swung backwards and then dropped in order to extend the distance of their jump.

Thus on finely painted pots and in Athenian literature we also find athletics teachers training groups in the non-combat events. In his *Statesman* Plato, for example, outlines how there are in Athens 'very many' supervised 'training sessions for groups' where instructions

FIGURE 48.1. An athletics teacher supervises two students who are practising the *skhēmata* or moves for throwing the discus and jumping with hand weights. Attic red-figure kylix, *c.*490–480 BCE, attributed to Antiphon Painter. Sydney, Powerhouse Museum, inv. no. 99/117/1. Collection: Powerhouse Museum, Sydney. Photo: Penelope Clay.

and *ponoi* ('toils') take place not just for wrestling but also 'for the sake of competition in the foot-race or some other event' (294d–e). Plato also writes of an athletics teacher receiving a wage for running lessons (*Gorg.* 520c–d) and Antiphon has one conducting a class in javelin-throwing for a group of Athenian boys in a *gumnasion* (3.1.1; 3.2.3, 7; 3.3.6; 3.4.4, etc.). By contrast, red-figure pots show *paidotribai* supervising not only running and javelin-throwing but also discus-throwing and the long-jump (Beck 1975; Nicholson 2005: 245 n. 25, 246 n. 38). A good example is a red-figure kylix attributed to the Antiphon Painter in Sydney: it depicts a young *paidotribēs*, who is distinguished from the other figures by his cloak and staff, watching over one adolescent who is practising with jumping weights and another with a discus (Fig. 48.1). That all of these events are the standard ones of local and international games underlines how the school classes of the *paidotribēs* were geared to turn pupils into *athlētai* ('athletic competitors'). This important point is also borne out by the frequent use of *agōnia* ('competition') as a synonym for *gumnastikē* (e.g. Plat. *Lach.* 184e; *Laws* 765c; *Meno* 94b).

Fourth-century works by Athens-based intellectuals employ not only '*paidotribēs*' but also '*gumnastēs*', along with a few other newly invented words, to describe teachers or coaches of athletes. Critically, as these neologisms are often used for those performing duties traditionally associated with the *paidotribēs*—such as, for example, a *gumnastēs* or *tis gumnastikos* supervising athletes in training (Plat. *Laws* 720e; *Stat.* 295c) or a *gumnastikos* with wrestling expertise (Aristot. *Eud. Eth.* 1217b39–40)—they appear to be synonyms for the more common and better established word for athletics teacher (Pritchard 2003: 304–306). The athletes of Classical Athens, then, received the training which they needed to compete creditably in the group classes of the *paidotribēs*. For most of the Classical period technical instruction in the standard athletic events was given only in his classes, which were also the only attested opportunity for practising these sports. Thus we can see that athletics in Classical Athens consisted of two closely related activities: festival-based competitions and the physical-education classes of the *paidotribēs* (e.g. Plat. *Laws* 764c–d). In terms of the overall number of participants and the total amount of time that they spent participating, athletics in Classical Athens was probably more of an educational than a festival-based activity. Thus taking part in athletic contests was indeed a function of the larger phenomenon of adolescent schooling in Classical Athens.

ORGANIZATION AND AIMS OF ADOLESCENT EDUCATION AND BARRIERS TO FULL PARTICIPATION

Physical education was one of the three disciplines of traditional *male* education in Classical Athens (e.g. Plat. *Cleit.* 407b–c; *Prot.* 312b, 325e, 326c). The other widely agreed disciplines were *mousikē* ('music') and *grammata* ('letters'), to which were occasionally added choral lessons in singing and dancing dithyrambs (e.g. Aeschin. 1.9–11; Aristoph. *Frogs* 727–730; Pritchard 2004). The discipline of music was the preserve of the *kitharistēs* or lyre teacher, who taught students how to play the *kithara* and sing lyric poems (e.g. Aristoph. *Cl.* 962–972; Plat. *Prot.* 326a–b), while that of letters was overseen by the *grammatistēs* or 'letters teacher' (Beck 1964: 111–129). He instructed students in literacy and probably also numeracy and made them memorize and recite edifying passages of epic poetry, principally that of Homer (e.g. Plat. *Protagoras* 325e–326a).

Although the term *grammatistēs*, like others concerning Greek education, was coined only in the early years of the fourth century, comedy and finely painted pottery bear out this specialist teacher's presence at Athens throughout the fifth century (Harris 1989: 57–64; Robb 1994: 184–186). Aristophanes brings on stage in *Peace* a boy whose effortless recitation of Homer and an epic poem that is no longer extant points towards the drills of the letters teacher (1265–1299). Ceramic evidence indicates that the letters teacher was already active in Athens several decades before the birth of Aristophanes. From the turn of the fifth century painted pots sport school scenes, which frequently include a teacher supervising a youth who either reads from a scroll or gives a recitation without reference to the scroll included in the image (Immerwahr 1964; 1973). Furthermore, when the pottery painters actually include legible letters on these book rolls, invariably they form lines from the two works of Homer or other epic poems (Fig. 48.2). The instruction of the young in this genre of poetry was of course the chief role of the *grammatistēs*.

As classes in each of the three main disciplines were taken concurrently, students travelled from one *didaskaleion* or school room to another throughout the day (e.g. Aristoph. *Cl.* 963–964), probably spending only a few hours at each (Beck 1964: 81–83; Golden 1990: 62–63). This schooling of boys was a predominantly private affair in Classical Athens (e.g. Aristot.

FIGURE 48.2. A *didaskalos* or teacher checks the recitation of a student against a scroll of epic poetry. The text scans as hexameter and reads: 'Muse to me. I begin singing about wide-flowing Scamander.' Attic red-figure kylix, *c.*490–480 BCE, attributed to Douris. Berlin, Staatliche Museen zu Berlin, inv. no. 2385. © Bildagentur für Kunst, Kultur und Geschichte, Berlin. Collection: Antikensammlung, Staatliche Museen zu Berlin. Photograph: Johannes Laurentius.

Pol. 1337a22–33; Xen. *Cyrop.* 1.2.2). Admittedly, laws were passed, probably in the mid-fourth century, to regulate school hours, class sizes, and the minimum age of pupils (Aeschin. 1.9–11). But the democracy did not license teachers, determine the curricula for their lessons, nor subsidize their wages. Thus it was fathers or guardians who decided what disciplines their boys should study, who the good teachers were, and how long they should be at school.

For the Classical Athenians the solitary goal of education was not the teaching of practical skills but the forming of boys into *agathoi andres* or courageous men (e.g. Eur. *Supp.* 911–917; Plat. *Prot.* 325d–e; *Meno* 94b). Precise ways in which each of the three disciplines of traditional Athenian education contributed to this moral end are postulated by Protagoras in the Platonic dialogue bearing his name (325a–6c). The physical education of the *paidotribēs*, he suggests, guarantees that bodily weakness will not be the cause of a young man playing the coward on the battlefield (326b–c). Protagoras isolates the source of moral fortification that is provided by the lessons in *mousikē*, not in the content of lyric poetry, but in the practising of scales and rhythms on the *kithara*, which helps foster in young men a gentleness of character and an effectiveness in word and deed (326a–326b). However, this sophist's musings reveal that Athenian boys received the lion's share of their instruction in morality sitting at the school benches of the letters teacher (325e–326a):

> when the boys understand their letters and are on the point of comprehending the written word..., the teachers set before them on the benches poems of good poets to read, and they are compelled to learn by rote these works, which contain many admonitions and numerous descriptions, eulogies and commendations of virtuous men of long ago, so that the boy out of a sense of jealousy imitates them and yearns to be this sort of man himself.

When using such a dialogue there is always some concern that Plato might be presenting distortions of Athenian sentiments in support of his at times novel theses or the minority points of view of his predominantly upper-class readers (Ober 1989: 43–52; Pritchard 1998: 38–40). Fortunately, these comments of Protagoras correspond not only with other sources written for an elite audience but also with the so-called popular literature of Classical Athens (Pelling 2000: 5–9; Pritchard 2009: 216). Admittedly texts of this second class, which includes comedy, tragedy, and oratory, were also written by members of the city's upper class. But their plays and speeches were judged by vocal audiences of predominantly lower-class citizens, which compelled them to tailor their offerings to the dramaturgical or rhetorical expectations, morality, politics, and points of view of the Athenian *dēmos* (Pritchard 2019: 112–115).

Thus the clear parallels between what Protagoras suggests and other surviving texts point to Plato doing no more than articulating conventional thoughts on the role of poetry in Athenian education. A variety of authors agree, for example, that boys learned poetry by heart, especially passages of Homer (e.g. Aristoph. *Frogs* 1038–1039; Xen. *Sym.* 3.5–6), for education in moral behaviour (e.g. Aeschin. 3.135; Isoc. 1.51, 2.3; Plat. *Laws* 810e–811a). And, like Protagoras, Aristophanes makes the didactic content of Homeric poetry its gallant and morally upstanding heroes, when he has the dead Aeschylus claim in *Frogs* (1040–1042):

> In imitation of him, my purpose was to represent in poetry the many excellences (*pollas aretas*) of Patrocluses and lion-hearted Teucers, in order to induce the citizen to become a rival of these men, whenever he heard the trumpet of war.

The citizens of Classical Athens believed, then, that the rote learning and recall of poetry, principally that of Homer, was the chief method for instructing boys and youths in morality. Within the three traditional branches of Athenian education these instructive passages of epic poetry were encountered and studied only in the lessons of the *grammatistēs*.

Classical Athenians understood that a family's resources dictated the number of disciplines a boy could take up and the length of his schooling. This inequality of educational opportunity is again expressed very clearly by the Platonic Protagoras, who explains that the three subjects of the 'old education' are taken by those 'who are most able; and the most able are the wealthiest (*hoi plousiōtatoi*). Their sons begin school at the earliest stage, and are freed from it at the latest' (Plat. *Prot.* 326c). Likewise, Xenophon acknowledges how education depends on money (*Hunt.* 2.1). Aristotle sometimes presents education as one of the preserves of the upper class (*Pol.* 1291b28–30, 1317b38–41); and Aristophanes makes out that education beyond the three disciplines of the 'old education' is the preserve of *kaloi te k'agathoi* or upper-class gentlemen (*Cl.* 101, 797–798).

An obvious way in which wealth impacted on education was that a family had to have enough cash to cover the fees of three teachers, which together could be expensive (Beck 1964: 130; Golden 2008: 36). To be educated in letters, music, and athletics, a boy also needed to be free of other daytime obligations, as he would be attending classes in two or more disciplines each day (e.g. Isaeus 9.28). Critically such *scholē* was only guaranteed for the boys of upper-class families: most poor citizens could not afford enough or any household slaves, as Aristotle explains (*Pol.* 1323a5–7), and so needed their children and wives to help run family farms or businesses (Golden 1990: 34–36; Harris 1989: 19–20, 102). The negative impact of such child labour on the education of poor boys was appreciated by contemporaries (e.g. Isoc. 14.48; 7.43–45; Xen. *Cyrop.* 8.3.37–39). Lysias, for example, notes how a wealthy boy goes to the city to be educated, while poverty forces another to be a shepherd (20.11–12), while Demosthenes contrasts the comprehensive education that he enjoyed as an upper-class adolescent with the impoverished childhood of Aeschines, who had to perform the menial tasks in his father's letters school that were normally done by slaves (18.256–267).

LETTERS

In light of these perceived barriers to a comprehensive adolescent education, scholars have usually argued that poor families passed over *gumnastikē* and *mousikē*, athletics and poetic arts, and sent their sons only to lessons in *grammata*, writing and literacy, (e.g. Beck 1964: 79–80, 83, 94, 111; Golden 1990: 63–64). This discipline, they suggest, would have been 'more strictly useful' for non-elite involvement in politics and commerce (Beck 1964: 83). However, as the role of writing in the Athenian democracy, not to mention literacy itself, has become extremely controversial, their assessment of this discipline's utility is no longer secure. Thus working out which Athenian boys went to the classes of the *grammatistēs* requires us to reconsider the case for widespread literacy in Classical Athens

A long-standing argument for near universal literacy among Classical Athenians is that reading and writing were basic prerequisites for involvement in the democracy. In this vein an important handbook on Classical Greek education suggests that the institution of ostracism 'presupposes the widespread knowledge of writing among the citizen body and therefore the existence of schools for its introduction' (Beck 1964: 77). This argument has several problems. Firstly, although the capacity to scratch out the name of another person shows some writing capacity, it does not demonstrate the highly developed ability to read and write fluently. Secondly, Athenians who lacked even a limited writing ability could still take part in these institutional expulsions; for they could always ask an educated fellow to incise a potsherd for them (e.g. Plut. *Arist.* 7.5–6).

Others have posed the necessity of literacy for political participation in more general terms. Josiah Ober for one suggests (1989: 158): 'In order to function as a citizen, and certainly in order to carry out the responsibilities of many of the magistracies, the Athenian citizen needed a basic command of letters.' Certainly there were two small groups of Classical Athenians who did need high levels of literacy and numeracy. Politicians were expected to have a confident grasp of public finances, which depended on their close scrutiny of the public accounts of financial boards (e.g. Aristot. *Rh.* 1.4.7–8; Xen. *Mem.* 3.6.5–6; Pritchard 2015: 21–22). As adolescents and young men they would also have honed their public speaking and leadership skills by studying with the sophists, whose most popular lessons were in oratory (Joyal et al. 2009: 59–87; Yunis 1998). As these lessons required students to consult handbooks of oratorical technique and model speeches (Ford 2001), upper-class parents, who were eager for their sons to be famous leaders one day, would have made sure that their sons were well schooled by a *grammatistēs*. The second small group manifestly able to read and write fluently were the non-elite functionaries of the democracy (Pritchard 2015: 80–82). These secretaries and heralds of individual magistrates, magisterial boards, and the city's deliberative and legal organs were required to keep written records and accounts, read out relevant documents and make proclamations (e.g. Dem. 19.249).

Lower-class Athenians would most probably have perceived literacy and numeracy to be useful for taking part in the public affairs of the city. A hoplite or naval petty officer, for instance, would have found it more convenient to search a posted list of conscripts for his name himself than to rely on another person's reading ability (Pritchard 2019: 43–46, 92–94). And a minor financial magistrate would presumably have been far more relaxed and comfortable during his scrutiny at the end of his term of office if he was able to consult his financial accounts without the mediation of a secretary. However, such skills were in no way a precondition for participating in the major deliberative and judicial organs of the democracy (Thomas 1989: 61–64; 1992: 3). Literacy and numeracy were simply not necessary for passive participation in the jury courts, the council of five hundred, and the assembly. The debates of these institutions were conducted orally, with documents and testimonies relevant to them read out by undersecretaries (e.g. Aristot. *Const. Ath.* 54.5). Finally, the decisions of the council and assembly, along with the instructions of the city's chief magistrates, were made known through proclamations (e.g. 62.2). Thus the operation of Athenian democracy did not depend on anything approaching universal literacy.

Likewise, the existence of publicly displayed inscriptions recording decisions of the council and assembly cannot be taken as evidence that the Athenian *dēmos* wanted records that they could read at their leisure; for if we take as a guide the ways in which speakers of the first half of the fourth century used such records, inscriptions appear to have been produced for very different reasons (Harris 1989: 73–80; Hedrick 1994: 165–174). Citizens saw them, not as texts to be read, but as physical memorials of a decision or law and as concrete emblems of the democratic ideals of accountability, open government, and legal equality (Hedrick 1999).

Proponents of widespread literacy have also presented some ancient references that supposedly show how most citizens could read and write (e.g. Beck 1964: 83; Golden 1990: 64; Thomas 1992: 155). The first of two passages allowing such an interpretation comes from the *Laws* of Plato (689d). The Athenian interlocutor of this dialogue argues that only those harmonizing their emotions and reasoning ability will be judged wise in his ideal city, 'even if, as the saying goes, they know neither letters nor how to swim (*mēte grammata mēte nein epistōntai)*'. This aphorism is usually interpreted as evidence that the Athenians thought illiteracy was very strange indeed. A similar conclusion is drawn from the opening scene of *Knights* by Aristophanes where the sausage-seller, objecting to the unlikely prediction of his leadership of the city, explains (188–189): 'my good fellow I do not even know music, except letters (*oude mousikēn epistamai plēn grammatōn*), and these I actually do very badly'. This character, of course, is not an average Athenian but is a criminally inclined and underemployed individual from a deprived background (296–297, 1242, 1397–1401). Thus, it is argued, if a marginal individual, such as the sausage-seller, can read and write, then a majority of Athenians, who were certainly much better off, must have been able to do so as well.

A common problem with the interpretation of these two passages is the assumption that the phrase *epistasthai grammata* ('knowing one's letters') denotes nothing less than the capacity to read and write easily. This assumption pays too scant regard to the fact that different levels of literacy exist, ranging from the ability to sign one's own name and the sounding out of words syllable by syllable, to the highly developed skills of reading and writing without conscious effort (Thomas 1992: 8–9). In addition, two other passages by Plato and Aristophanes suggest that 'to know one's letters' must be placed much lower down the scale of literary levels than the advocates of near universal literacy assume. As already noted, the Platonic *Protagoras* details how the teachers of letters get their students to read (325e 326a):

> when the pupils understand letters (*grammata mathōsi*) and are on the point of comprehending the written word (*sunēsein ta gegrammena*), just as when they are about to understand the spoken word, the teachers set before them on the benches poems of good poets to read (*anagignōskein*)....

What is striking here is the distinction drawn between learning and understanding the alphabet (*manthanein grammata*) and the act of reading itself (*sunienai ta gegrammena, anagignōskein*). As *manthanein* is semantically very close to *epistasthai*, the phrase *epistasthai grammata* most probably refers (as the phrase *manthanein grammata* certainly does) to a pre-reading familiarity with the alphabet.

This new interpretation of 'knowing one's letters' backed up by a fuller consideration of the educational attainment of Aristophanes' sausage-seller. Towards the end of *Knights* an exchange between him and Paphlagon makes plain his complete lack of schooling (1235–1238):

> PAPHLAGON: When you were a boy, which teacher's establishment (*eis tinos didaskalou*) did you attend?
> SAUSAGE SELLER: I was trained with knuckles in the swine-singeing yards.
> PAPHLAGON: At the school of the athletics teacher (*en paidotribou*) what wrestling technique did you learn?
> SAUSAGE SELLER: How to swear falsely and to steal while saying the opposite.

As the generic term *didaskalos* can describe a lyre teacher just as easily as a letters teacher (e.g. Plat. *Prot.* 325d, 326c), these witty responses of the sausage-seller suggest that he lacked schooling, not just in athletics, but in *mousikē* and *grammata* as well (Joyal *et al.* 2009: 52–53). It would have been hard for any Athenian, not to mention an impoverished seller of small goods, to have acquired any competency in reading and writing without formal schooling (Kleijwegt 1991: 78). Thus the sausage seller's earlier claim about 'knowing letters' (188–189) denotes, not an ability to read and write, but a pre-reading knowledge of the alphabet. In view of the most likely meaning of the phrase *epistasthai grammata*, scholars have been mistaken, then, to present these two passages as good evidence for near universal literacy in Classical Athens.

It is left to archaeology to provide the decisive evidence that literacy was not confined to upper-class Athenians. Small finds from the American excavations of the Athenian Agora or civic centre as well as finely painted pottery suggest that many lower-class residents of Athens, in addition to the functionaries of the democracy, were reasonably literate and numerate. This presupposes that the classrooms of the letters teacher also included good numbers of lower-class boys. The Agora excavators have unearthed and inventoried over three thousand sherds of pottery with incised or painted texts, ranging in date from the early Archaic period to the eighth century of our era. More than eight hundred of these pieces whose preserved texts are long enough to determine their original functions have been catalogued by Mabel Lang (1976).

Far and away, the largest group in Lang's catalogue are ownership marks for pottery vessels (1976: 23–51). Admittedly, sixty per cent of these marks do not demonstrate any significant level of literacy: they are no more than an abbreviated name or a complete name in the nominative case. Nonetheless over twenty per cent of them have names in the genitive or dative cases, while more than six per cent consist of short sentences. Classical-period examples of the latter consist of *eimi* ('I am/belong to') plus the owner's name in the genitive case, to which is often added the adverb *dikaiōs* or 'rightly' (e.g. nos. F 131–132, 139, 154). These simple sentences and names in oblique cases demonstrate a level of writing skill that is higher than a simple knowledge of the alphabet or an ability to write one's own name. However, while the large number of proprietary marks points to a widespread capacity to write a personal name, the archaeological context of nearly every piece is too ambiguous or not sufficiently documented to determine the social backgrounds of those incising these pieces. As a result, it is not possible to say in which section(s) of the Attic population this writing skill predominated. Nevertheless, enough is known of the taphonomy (archaeological context) of two classical pots with proprietary marks to show that name-signing literacy existed among the city's craftsmen. A black-glaze base of a cup from the second quarter of the fifth century which has the name Simon in the genitive case most probably came from the workshop and home of a cobbler (no. F 86). Similarly a black-glaze *kantharos* or drinking cup of the fourth century, which was found in the house of a family of marble workers, was incised with the name Menon (no. F 164; Pritchard 1999: 14–21).

In addition, the functions of several other types of marks in Lang's catalogue point to the socio-economic identity of those who made them. The largest group providing this valuable information are the records of capacity, tare weight, date, and contents that were originally inscribed onto ceramic containers (Lang 1976: 55–81). Of these it is the capacity marks that exemplify most clearly the variations possible in this class of commercial notations. Among capacity indications of the Classical period, the simplest consists of tally marks alone (e.g. nos. Ha 3–4). More sophisticated texts display the first letter of the name of a standard measure followed by tally marks or numerals (e.g. nos. Ha 5–7, Ha 9–12). The most complex of capacity notations have complete words. For example, one black-glaze *olphē*, or wine jug, of the fifth century has *mēetrio*, a misspelling of the name of a middle-sized measure (*metrion*), while a partially glazed juglet predictably bears the name *khos*, or jug, the capacity measure, *khous* (nos. Ha 1, 8). Other types of commercial notations also have full words and phrases. Two *amphorae*, for example, record dates by means of the preposition *epi* and the name of a late fourth-century eponymous archon in the genitive case (nos. Hc 1–2), while a fifth-century wine *amphora* bears the painted label *okhos*, meaning ordinary wine (no. Hd 1). Several other pieces classified by Lang as numerical notations are of a commercial nature as well (21–23). Most notable among the Classical-period objects is a tag recording the batch size of some ceramic product, which gives the word *keramos* and numerals (no. E5).

Other archaeological evidence confirms that a good number of Athenian craftsmen were similarly literate. In the so-called house of Mikion and Menon a bone stylus, bearing the inscription *ho Mikion epoiese* ('Mikion made [me]'), was found on a fifth-century floor (inv. no. BI 818; Pritchard 1999: 17). Whether this tool was made by a marble-worker living in this abode or a different craftsman, its inscription points again to a reasonably high level of writing dexterity on the part of its maker. Certainly some painters of black- and red-figure pots possessed no more than a pre-reading knowledge of the alphabet because they could include only gibberish words and phrases in their paintings. But others were literate enough to paint in the names of characters in mythological scenes or an inscription next to an image of a comely boy describing him as beautiful (Vickers and Gill 1994: 163–164). Other pots reveal even higher writing competencies on the part of their painters. Around one per cent of surviving examples have inscriptions recording that a certain craftsman painted (*egraphsen*) the scene and that another manufactured (*epoiēsen*) the actual pot (100, 154–171). More impressive still are the book-scrolls in depictions of classes of the letters teacher, on which sometimes appear actual lines of epic poetry (Fig. 48.2).

As Athenian gentlemen abhorred direct contact with selling and the trades, these inscribed artefacts from Attica could only have been the work of non-elite craftsmen and retailers. As a consequence, they prove that literacy and numeracy existed far below the city's upper class. Indeed the obvious utility of these skills in the world of Attic business would have been a powerful motivation for lower-class businessmen to send their sons to the lessons of the letters teacher (Aristot. *Pol.* 1338a15–19).

Archaeology confirms that many lower-class Athenians had quite high levels of literacy and numeracy, and hence must have attended the classes of a *grammatistēs* as boys. On closer inspection, it appears that attending lessons in letters was not prohibitively expensive nor something that prevented boys from helping out with family farming or business concerns. The school fees that Athens-based *grammatistai* charged were most probably very low. Third-century inscriptions, for example from Miletus and Teos, indicate that letters teachers received between 1 and 2 drachmas per day (*SEG* 43.381; *SIG* I³ 577; cf. Dem. 19.249), which was no more than the wage of a skilled labourer. What figures we have for class sizes outside of Athens suggest that classes were normally large, consisting of several dozen or more students (Hdt. 6.27; Paus. 6.9.6). In these circumstances school fees would have been far from prohibitive (cf. Theophr. *Char.* 30.14). Moreover, as classes in each discipline of the 'old education' lasted no more than a few hours (see the previous section on Athletics and Adolescent Education), lower-class boys who only attended the classes of the *grammatistēs* had plenty of time out of school when they could help secure the livelihood of their families.

It is striking that the complex poetry of Homer was introduced to Athenian boys very early in the course of their studies at the letters school. We have seen that the Platonic *Protagoras* describes that pupils received copies of epic poetry to read and memorize, when they had just mastered the alphabet and were about to begin reading. Nevertheless, they were initially using copies of Homer simply as a mnemonic aid and hence required only so-called phonetic literacy, which is the ability to decode texts syllable by syllable and to pronounce them orally (Thomas 1992: 9, 92). Letters-school students seem not to have been made to complete the time-consuming tasks of learning to read and write fluently before being introduced to Homeric poetry. Consequently, even a pupil whose family's difficult economic circumstances prevented him completing his studies with the letters teacher would have been assured of encountering passages of Homer during his student days.

This certainty of learning by heart stories of the heroes would have been another major motivation for Athenian fathers to send male offspring to the classes of the *grammatistēs*. Indeed for those humble Athenians not associated with the trades, selling, or state administration it might have been the only motivation. After all, the solitary goal of education in the extant literature of Classical Athens was the moral improvement of young males, while the chief means to achieve this was universally understood to be the memorization and recall of Homeric poetry (see the previous section). Therefore, their certain and extended introduction of boys to the poetry of Homer made the letters school appear to non-elite fathers, who were worried about the waywardness of contemporary youth, the surest and easiest of ways to guarantee the rectitude of their sons. We can say with some certainty that the classes of the *grammatistēs* did contain good numbers of Athenian boys from lower-class backgrounds.

ATHLETICS AND MUSIC

Some scholars have suggested a similar level of lower-class participation in athletic competition. Harry Pleket for one has long argued that while the upper class originally monopolized Greek athletics, from the early fifth century athletes of hoplite status increasingly entered sporting contests (Pleket 1975: 71–74; 1992: 148, 151–152; 1998: 317). By contrast, David Young suggests there were always good numbers of lower-class athletes before and after the early fifth century (1984: 107–163). Focusing on Classical Athens specifically, Nick Fisher maintains that involvement in local athletic contests reached down to, and included, not just hoplites but even some Athenians of sub-hoplite status (Fisher 1998: 86–94). The extent of athletic participation which these scholars advocate presupposes that large numbers of non-elite families sent boys to the regular lessons of the *paidotribēs*; for, as we have seen, his lessons alone provided the athletic training which was recognized as essential for satisfactory performance in a race or bout.

Yet, the education of non-elite boys in this discipline in Classical Athens seems far from likely. The limited means of poor families and their reliance on child labour would have made it very difficult to send their sons to lessons in letters *and* athletics. Nor is it likely that they would have had their boys give up the practical and moral lessons of the *grammatistēs* in favour of athletics. Without this training in athletics, which everyone recognized as necessary for creditable performance, boys and youths would have been greatly disheartened about entering a race or bout in the first place. If they were unable to undertake preparations that were widely considered to be indispensable, they could not have met the other costs of athletic participation either. Ideally an athlete-in-training had an expensive and unusually meat-rich diet to help build up his bodily strength and a hired *iatros* or doctor whose medical advice extended to dietary matters (Pritchard 2003: 301). In order to compete away from home, an athlete also needed free time to attend foreign games and to train (as was the case with the Olympics) in the host city beforehand (e.g. *IvO* 56) as well as enough cash to cover related travelling expenses (Miller 2003: 5–6). What literary evidence we have confirms these doubts: schooling in *gumnastikē* and *mousikē*, athletic and musical expertise, and participation in sporting contests, appear to have been predominant or even exclusive preserves of the Athenian upper class.

This limited direct experience of athletics and music among lower-class citizens is reflected very clearly in a final scene of Aristophanes' *Wasps* where Bdelycleon struggles to teach his father, Philocleon, how to be an upper-class symposiast (1122–1264). The humour of this scene depends primarily on the unexpected difference in the social-class position of father and son: as a lower-class citizen Philocleon is naturally wary of the upper class and its exclusive pursuits, such as the *sumposion* or drinking party (Murray 1990: 149–150), and is ill-equipped to assimilate the lessons of his upper-class son. Bdelycleon initially finds it very difficult to persuade his father to exchange his *embades* ('felt slippers') and *tribōn* ('coarse cloak'), which are the standard attire of lower-class citizens (Aristoph. *Wasps* 33, 115–117; *Pl.* 842–843; Isaeus 5.11), for imported shoes and gown, and to ape 'the walk of the wealthy' (1122–1173). Next, Bdelycleon asks his old man whether he knows any 'posh stories' suitable for relating to 'well-educated and clever men' (1174–1175). We quickly learn that Philocleon does not and so his son suggests he speak perhaps of an embassy in which he may have participated (1183–1187). However, as only wealthy citizens with their overseas guest-friends could be ambassadors (e.g. *Ach.* 607–11; *Birds* 1570–1571; Dem. 19.237–238), the best Philocleon can do is to bring up his service as a rower on an expedition to Paros (Aristoph. *Wasps* 1188–1189). Instead of this, Bdelycleon encourages him to talk about a famous 'heavy' athlete (1190–1194): 'you need to say, for example, that although he was grey and old, Ephoudion continued to fight well in the *pankration* with his very strong sides, hands and flank as well as his very fine torso (*thōrak' ariston*)'. Philocleon interrupts his son's extemporizing (1194–1195): 'Stop! Stop! You're speaking nonsense. How could he fight in the *pankration* wearing a suit of armour (*thōrak' ekhōn*)?' Philocleon's confusing of the two established meanings of *thōrax* reveals his unfamiliarity with what North Americans call 'jock talk' and suggests that he had spent no time as a boy with a *paidotribēs* or in athletic competition (Golden 1998: 160; Thiercy 2003: 145).

Undeterred, Bdelycleon tells his father he will have to relate 'a very manly exploit of his youth' (1197–1199) and, in response to Philocleon's inability to do even this (1200–1201), suggests he talk about 'how once you chased a wild boar or a hare, or you ran a torch race, after you have worked out your most dashing youthful exploit' (1202–1205). His father's experience of such things again seems unlikely. Hunting was clearly an exclusively upper-class pursuit (e.g. Xen. *Cyn.* 2.1; 12.1–13.18; Men. *Dys.* 39–44), while joining a tribal team of torch-racers—before the reform of the *ephēbeia* in 335—would have been possible for only a small minority of Athenian youths (Pritchard 2013: 76–80, 214–216). Thus it is a surprise to find Philocleon relating what seems an anecdote about athletics before, that is, we realize that he is talking about something quite different (1205–1207): 'Well I certainly know the most impetuous and youthful deed of early years: while still a boy, the runner Phayllus I overtook (*heilon*), pursuing (*diōkōn*) him for slander, by two votes.' The joke here rests on two more double entendres: *haireō* (aorist form, *heilon*) and *diōkō* are commonly used in discussions of sporting *and* legal contests (Campagner 2001: 57, 119). Therefore, while Philocleon, at first, seems to be recalling a race against a famous Olympic victor of a previous generation, Phayllus of Croton (cf. Aristoph. *Ach.* 214; Paus. 10.9.2), his last three words dash this impression: this addict of the jury courts has been reminiscing about a legal prosecution all along. His lack of athletic *nous* is revealed again when, the demonstrations of his son notwithstanding, he botches reclining on a symposium couch *gumnastikōs* or athletically (1208–1213).

Aspects of this scene's treatment of athletics and music occur in other Classical texts. In the famous *parabasis* of *Frogs*, for example, Aristophanes links athletics, music, and political leadership with the upper class (727–730), while wrestling schools for Euripides belong to the 'well-born man' (*Electra* 528). Alternatively, Athenian authors group athletics with other activities, such as hunting and philosophy, which were clearly preserves of wealthy Athenians (e.g. Isoc. 7.45).

In his defence speech against the charge of treason, Aeschines not only couples athletics and other upper-class pursuits, but proffers his family's practising of sport as proof of its belonging to this social class (Golden 2000: 169–171). In the speech for the prosecution Demosthenes had made a big issue out of his political opponent's humble background: his father had been a poor *grammatistēs* (19.249), and he and his brothers had worked as minor undersecretaries or even a painter of tambourines and boxes, before their elevation to positions of political and military leadership (19.237–238, 249, 287). Aeschines responds directly to these comments, not just as he was 'sensitive to such slurs' (Golden 2000: 170), but because they provided plausibility to the main accusation against him, namely that as an ambassador he had taken bribes from Philip of Macedon (e.g. Dem. 19.127, 248, 313, 343). Lower-class Athenians, from whose ranks jurors were predominantly drawn, believed that poor political leaders were especially susceptible to bribes and that newly rich politicians had most probably gained their social elevation by accepting such payments (Ober 1989: 233–238).

Aeschines never explicitly denies that he and his brothers were self-made. But he skillfully insinuates that his family is now and had once been upper class. His father, he claims, had actually been an athletic competitor, before the Peloponnesian War destroyed his property, and was linked with a traditionally prestigious religious group or *genos*, the Eteoboutadai (2.147). Aeschines also points out how his eldest brother is not, as Demosthenes slanderously suggests, a man of 'ill-born pastimes' (*agenneis diatribas*), but spends his time at athletics fields (*en gumnasiois diatribōn*, 2.149). He has also been a general now for three years, whereas his youngest brother has been an ambassador to the king of Persia (2.149). Aeschines, finally, reinforces his own claim to membership of the upper class by dropping in here and in other speeches athletic metaphors and details (e.g. 1.10, 26, 33; 2.183; 3.179–180, 206, 246). As Ober explains (1989: 283), 'Apparently he hoped to be perceived as the sort of man who spent a good deal of time in *gumnasia* and so naturally used athletic turns of phrase'.

Admittedly a few other texts from Classical Athens (as proponents of a broader-based sporting culture point out) do refer to lower-class athletics (e.g. Hubbard 2008: 384; Pleket 1975: 73; 1992: 151; Young 1984: 156). Pseudo-Xenophon's *Constitution of Athens*, for one, suggests that while wealthy citizens have privately owned *gumnasia* or athletics fields, the Athenian people have built for their own enjoyment 'many wrestling schools' (2.10, cf. 1.3). Sometimes Pseudo-Xenophon is a reliable source for imperial Athens. More often than not, however, his political partisanship and prejudice against lower-class citizens cause him to exaggerate or misrepresent realities of Athenian society (Ceccarelli 1993: 446; Harding 1981: 41). This chapter seems a clear example of his regularly falsifying commentary, as the other Classical testimonia on sporting facilities present the *gumnasia* rather as publicly owned and stand-alone wrestling schools as belonging to individual athletics teachers (see the section above on Athletics and Adolescent Education). Additionally, this chapter directly contradicts what Pseudo-Xenophon asserts at 1.13: 'The people have destroyed those practising athletics there and pursuing music because they do not believe this is a good thing and know that they themselves are unable to practise these things.' This too egregiously misrepresents the reality of athletics under the Athenian democracy; for the people, in fact, assiduously deliberated about, and spent public funds on, sporting contests and athletics fields, esteemed athletes above every other public figure, and rewarded them lavishly when they returned home victorious (Pritchard 2009: 212–216; 2013: 84–138). Thus Pseudo-Xenophon's testimony here is clearly unreliable and must be discounted in favour of other testimonia on Athenian athletics.

Lower-class athletes were also mentioned in a jury-court speech of 397 in which the son of Alcibiades had to defend himself against a *dikē*, or private prosecution, which had arisen out of his father's extraordinary winning of first, second, and probably fourth place in the *agōn* for four-horse chariots at the Olympic games of 416 (Isoc. 16). Once again, however, there are good reasons for questioning the reliability of this testimony for broader sporting participation (Pritchard 2013: 71–74). This action for damages had been brought by another citizen, who was demanding five talents from Alcibiades' son on the grounds that one of the seven teams that his father had entered into the chariot-race had, in fact, been stolen from him (1, 46). As the controversy that still surrounded his late father (e.g. 3–4, 10–11, 43; [Andocides] 4), along with his obviously burning ambition to be victorious at the Olympics of 416, lent plausibility to the allegation of theft, Alcibiades the Younger hired a gifted young *logographos* or speech-writer, who would go on to found his own school of oratory. Isocrates deftly overcame this problem by providing a glowing account of his victory which completely suppressed the personal advantages that he gained from it, suggesting instead that he was only motivated by the unimpeachable motivation of patriotism (Isoc. 16.32–33). Alcibiades, he asserts, competed as lavishly as he did because he knew that he was doing so as a representative of Athens and hence that any victory of his would enhance the power of his *polis* on the international stage.

Isocrates was no less careful with his explanation of Alcibiades' choice of chariot-racing at the Olympics of 416. Although he had, the *logographos* writes, the natural talent and bodily strength to be an athletic competitor, he saw that 'some of the *athlētai* were ill-born, lived in small cities and were poorly educated' (Isoc. 16.33). Thus he overlooked 'the athletic contests' and took up chariot-racing, which, he knew, was the preserve 'of the most wealthy' and hence beyond the reach of a *phaulos* or vulgar man. Proponents of broad sporting participation have understandably relied on this explanation. It does not, however, necessarily contradict what we know of athletic participation under Athenian democracy. The lower-class athletes of Isocrates 16 do not come from Athens, and an Athenian gentleman refuses to compete with them out of a concern for his own standing and that of his city. Athenian jurors would have only accepted this justification if they too viewed athletic competition as an upper-class pursuit that required school-based training. In addition, other scholars have questioned the veracity of the entire passage (e.g. Golden 1998: 170; Kyle 1987: 136–137; 2007: 172, 214). Kyle explains (1987: 137): 'Despite Isocrates, chariot-racing was the obvious choice for Alcibiades, not something he was forced to pursue.' In 416, Alcibiades was in his mid-thirties and so at the age by which even the greatest athletic victors of the Olympics had retired. As participation in athletic *agōnes* would have pitted him against much younger competitors, who had trained intensively for years, it would have given him only a very small chance of victory (Golden 2008: 9–10). For an older competitor, chariot-racing offered much better odds, especially if he was able, like Alcibiades, to enter multiple teams.

Obviously Isocrates had to stop jurors thinking about these dangerous facts, which could have easily supported the idea that Alcibiades had been prepared to do anything to be victorious and hence was not above stealing an opponent's team of horses. Thus the *logographos* introduced 'a very convenient rationalization' for Alcibiades' choice of chariot-racing over athletics (Kyle 1987: 137), which was clearly very unlikely. This economy with the truth probably extended to his claim that some of the Panhellenic athletes were lower class. Certainly this claim goes against the weight of evidence that this chapter has gathered. In light of the egregious falsifications of political history in which Isocrates engaged in defence of his client's father (e.g. Isoc. 16.5–8, 10–11, 20–21, 24–28, 36–37), a useful fib about some sportsmen from some cities being lower class seems very plausible.

Reliable sources from Classical Athens strongly suggest that athletics and music were upper-class activities. As they are mainly examples of popular literature, they attest both to the reality of athletic participation and to the popular perceptions of athletics as an elite pursuit and hence a marker of membership of this social class. Although scholars of Greek athletics have not done so, these widely held beliefs about athletics also need to be factored into any assessment of sporting participation. When it comes to modern sporting choices, the need to do this was well established by Pierre Bourdieu in his classic study of sport and social class in France of the 1970s. What Bourdieu shows, with respect to 'the most distinctive sports, such as golf, riding, skiing or tennis', is that 'variations in economic and cultural capital or spare time' only ever provide a partial explanation why different classes or 'class fractions' take up or ignore different leisure pursuits (1978: 838). For there are always 'hidden entry requirements, such as family tradition and early training, and also the obligatory clothing, bearing and techniques of sociability' that help to keep such sports closed to the working and middle classes. Still more important for Bourdieu is that 'economic constraints' only ever determine 'the field of possibilities and impossibilities' for the members of different classes and not their 'positive orientation towards this or that practice'. Instead, inclinations and disinclinations towards this or that sport rest on how each class calculates its 'immediate' and 'social' profits (835).

For most of the non-elite families of Classical Athens, calculating the profits of physical education for their sons would have been superfluous; for economics alone would have put athletics out of their reach. Yet there was most probably a small number of families, sitting just below the elite, who could have sent their sons to the classes of the athletics teacher, because of their better financial services. We should not, however, assume automatically that they would have been inclined to do so. Indeed, these prosperous families of the lower class probably judged athletics to be something, on balance, which was *not* profitable for their sons to pursue. Poor Athenians may have believed athletics helped turn boys into virtuous men (see the section above on Organization and Aims of Adolescent Education). They also thought positively of athletics, devoted public funds to athletics facilities, and saw a positive relationship between athletics and soldiering. But the popular perception of sports as a marker of elite membership would most probably have made athletics a risky proposition for genuinely lower-class citizens.

Poor Athenians may have longed one day to escape poverty but they were well aware of the drawbacks of being wealthy under their democracy. The rich were under heavy moral and legal pressure to perform trierarchies and other expensive public services (e.g. Aristoph. *Frogs* 1066–1067; *Lys.* 652–654; Dem. 21.151, 208). They were also obliged to pay the *eisphora* or extraordinary war-tax. Popular culture also associated this social class with a range of highly objectionable attitudes and actions. Poor citizens believed that the wealthy were more likely than others to commit *hubris*, that is, the violent or verbal assault of another citizen, conspire with the city's enemies, and plot against the democracy (Pritchard 2009: 218–219). Finally, wealthy individuals were frequently criticized for squandering their patrimonies on dissolute activities instead of vital public services (e.g. Aristoph. *Frogs* 431–433, 1065–1068; *Lys.* 14.23–24; 19.9–11). Critically, as Davidson explains (1997: 242–243), 'Despite the importance of the contribution the rich made to the state, the state did very little to assess accurately or even record who owned what.' Instead, being identified as rich and hence liable for liturgies and war-taxes was a matter of perception: a citizen was a rich man as he and his family did the things the rich normally do (Gabrielsen 1994: 43–73; Vartsos 1978: 239).

This subjective identification of upper-class citizens most probably made athletics unprofitable to an economically comfortable but lower-class family. Because it was considered proof of elite membership, for a non-elite father the danger of sending a son to a *paidotribēs* was that he would be marking himself out as an elite citizen, regardless of his actual financial resources or his own perception of his class position. As a result, he could be pressed into being a liturgist or payer of *eisphora* and would begin to be suspected of the stereotypical crimes and misdemeanours of the upper class by his lower-class relatives and (one-time) friends (e.g. Aristoph. *Pl.* 335–385). These negative implications may very well have discouraged lower-class families from having their sons attend athletics and take part in athletic *agōnes*. As lower-class Athenians were also reluctant to interact privately with upper-class fellow citizens, whom they contradictorily continued to see as socially superior, they and their *paides* would have no doubt felt uneasy too about hobnobbing with them at sporting venues (Kyle 1997: 73; 2007: 212–215). Athletics was consciously taken up not by those families which were getting close to elite status, but by those which had recently arrived at the top and hence wanted to advertise their hard-won membership of the elite (Kyle 1987: 113–121, 123, 149–151).

Conclusion

Under Athenian democracy athletics consisted of two closely integrated activities: the physical-education classes of the athletics teacher and athletic contests at local and Panhellenic festivals. Formal lessons in the standard athletic events were given only as part of these classes, which were also the only attested opportunity for practising them. As athletic training was essential for a competitive performance in a race or bout, being an athlete was a direct function of participation in adolescent education. However, wealthy and poor Athenians did not enjoy equal access to education. This was mainly due to socio-economic barriers: poor families struggled to pay school fees and needed to have their sons at home in order to keep farming or business interests going. As a result, lower-class fathers could only afford to send their sons to classes in one discipline of traditional education. They judged the discipline of letters to be the most valuable for teaching morality and practical skills, and hence sent their boys to the classes of the letters teacher. It was only the sons of upper-class families who received instruction in each of the three disciplines of adolescent education: athletics, music and letters. Therefore, without school-based training in athletics, which everyone recognized as necessary, poor boys simply did not enter athletic competition. In the most prosperous and democratic of the cities of the ancient Greek world athletics most probably remained an exclusive pursuit of the wealthy.

REFERENCES

Beck, F. A. G. 1964. *Greek Education, 450–350 BC*. London.

Beck, F. A. G. 1975. *Album of Greek Education: The Greeks at School and at Play*. Sydney.

Bourdieu, P. 1978. 'Sport and Social Class.' *Social Science Information* 17: 819–840.

Campagner, R. 2001. *Lessico agonistico di Aristofane*. Rome.

Ceccarelli, P. 1993. 'Sans thalassocratie, pas de démocratie?: Le rapport entre thalassocratie et démocratie à Athènes dans la discussion du V et IV siècle av. J.-C.' *Historia* 42: 444–470.

Davidson, J. N. 1997. *Courtesans and Fishcakes: The Consuming Passions of Classical Athens*. New York.

De Romilly, J. 1992. *The Great Sophists in Periclean Athens*. Oxford.

Fisher, N. 1998. 'Gymnasia and the Democratic Values of Leisure.' In *Kosmos: Essays in Order, Conflict and Community in Classical Athens*. 84–104. P. Cartledge, P. Millett, and S. von Reden, eds. Cambridge.

Ford, A. 2001. 'Sophists without Rhetoric: The Arts of Speech in Fifth-Century Athens.' In *Education in Greek and Roman Antiquity*. 85–109. Y. L. Too, ed. Boston.

Gabrielsen, V. 1994. *Financing the Athenian Fleet: Public Taxation and Social Relations*. Baltimore.

Golden, M. 1990. *Children and Childhood in Classical Athens*. Baltimore.

Golden, M. 1998. *Sport and Society in Ancient Greece*. Cambridge.

Golden, M. 2000. 'Demosthenes and the Social Historian.' In *Demosthenes*. 159–180. I. Worthington, ed. London.

Golden, M. 2008. *Greek Sport and Social Status*. Austin.

Hansen, M. H. 1991. *The Athenian Democracy in the Age of Demosthenes: Structure, Principles and Ideology*. J. A. Crook, trans. Cambridge, MA.

Harding, P. 1981. 'In Search of the Polypragmatist.' In *Classical Contributions: Studies in Honour of M. F. McGregor*. 41–50. G. S. Shrimpton and D. J. McCargar, eds. New York.

Harris, W. V. 1989. *Ancient Literacy*. Cambridge, MA.

Hedrick, C. W. 1994. 'Writing, Reading, and Democracy.' In *Ritual, Finance, Politics: Athenian Democratic Accounts Presented to David Lewis*. 157–174. R. Osborne and S. Hornblower, eds. Oxford.

Hedrick, C. W. 1999. 'Democracy and the Athenian Epigraphical Habit.' *Hesperia* 68.3: 387–439.

Hubbard, T. 2008. 'Contemporary Sport Sociology and Ancient Greek Athletics.' *Leisure Studies* 27.4: 379–393.

Immerwahr, H. R. 1964. 'Book Rolls on Attic Vases.' In *Classical, Mediaeval, and Renaissance Studies in Honour of Berthold Louis Ullman*. 17–48. C. Henderson, ed. Rome.

Immerwahr, H. R. 1973. 'More Book Rolls on Attic Vases.' *AK* 16: 143–147.

IvO = Dittenberger, W. and K. Purgold. 1896. *Die Inscriften von Olympia*. Berlin.

Joyal, M., I. McDougall, and J. C. Yardley. 2009. *Greek and Roman Education: A Sourcebook*. London.

Kleijwegt, M. 1991. *Ancient Youth: The Ambiguity of Youth and the Absence of Adolescence in Greco-Roman Society*. Amsterdam.

Kyle, D. G. 1987. *Athletics in Ancient Athens*. Leiden.

Kyle, D. G. 1997. 'The First Hundred Olympiads: A Process of Decline or Democratization?' *Nikephoros* 10: 53–75.

Kyle, D. G. 2007. *Sport and Spectacle in the Ancient World*. Malden, MA.

Lang, M. 1976. *The Athenian Agora*, vol. XXI: *Graffiti and Dipinti*. Princeton.

Miller, S. G. 2003. 'The Organization and Functioning of the Olympic Games.' In *Sport and Festival in the Ancient Greek World*. 1–40. D. J. Phillips and D. Pritchard, eds. Swansea.

Murray, O. 1990. 'The Affair of the Mysteries: Democracy and the Drinking Group.' In *Sympotica: A Symposium on the Symposion*. 149–161. O. Murray, ed. Oxford.

Nicholson, N. 2005. *Aristocracy and Athletics in Archaic and Classical Athens*. Cambridge.

Ober, J. 1989. *Mass and Elite in Democratic Athens: Rhetoric, Ideology, and the Power of the People*. Princeton.

Pelling, C. 2000. *Literary Texts and the Greek Historian*. London.

Pleket, H. W. 1975. 'Games, Prizes, Athletes and Ideology: Some Aspects of the History of Sport in the Greco-Roman World.' *Stadion* 1: 49–89.

Pleket, H. W. 1992. 'The Participants in the Ancient Olympic Games: Social Background and Mobility'. In *Proceedings of an International Symposium on the Olympic Games (5–9 September 1988)*. 147–152. W. Coulson and H. Kyrieleis, eds. Athens.

Pleket, H. W. 1998. 'Sport and Ideology in the Graeco-Roman World.' *Klio* 80: 315–324.

Poliakoff, M. B. 1989. Review of Young, 1984. *AJPh* 110: 166–71.

Pritchard, D. M. 1998. '"The Fractured Imaginary": Popular Thinking on Military Matters in Fifth-Century Athens.' *AH* 28: 38–61.

Pritchard, D. M. 1999. 'Fool's Gold and Silver: Reflections on the Evidentiary Status of Finely Painted Attic Pottery.' *Antichthon* 33: 1–27.

Pritchard, D. M. 2003. 'Athletics, Education and Participation in Classical Athens.' In *Sport and Festival in the Ancient Greek World*. 293–349. D. J. Phillips and D. Pritchard, eds. Swansea.

Pritchard, D. M. 2004. 'Kleisthenes, Participation, and the Dithyrambic Contests of Late Archaic and Classical Athens.' *Phoenix* 58: 208–228.

Pritchard, D. M. 2009. 'Sport, War and Democracy in Classical Athens.' *IJHS* 26.2: 212–245.

Pritchard, D. M. 2010. 'The Symbiosis between Democracy and War: The Case of Ancient Athens.' In *War, Democracy and Culture in Classical Athens*. 1–62. D. M. Pritchard, ed. Cambridge.

Pritchard, D. M. 2013. *Sport, Democracy and War in Classical Athens*. Cambridge.

Pritchard, D. M. 2015. *Public Spending and Democracy in Classical Athens*. Austin.

Pritchard, D. M. 2019. *Athenian Democracy at War*. Cambridge.

Pritchard, D. M. 2020. 'The Social Structure of Democratic Athens.' In *Morte e Vida na Grécia Antiga: Olhares interdisciplinaires*. M. A. de Oliveira and C. D. de Souza, eds. Teresina.

Robb, K. 1994. *Literacy and Paideia in Ancient Greece*. New York.

Rosivach, V. J. 1991. 'Some Athenian Presuppositions about "The Poor"'. *G&R* 38: 189–198.

Rosivach, V. J. 2001. 'Class Matters in the *Dyskolos* of Menander'. *CQ* 51: 127–134.

Tarrant, H. 2003. 'Competition and the Intellectual.' In *Sport and Festival in the Ancient Greek World.* 351–363. D. J. Phillips and D. Pritchard, eds. Swansea.

Thiercy, P. 2003. 'Sport et comédie au Ve siècle.' *Quaderni di Dioniso* 1: 144–167.

Thomas, R. 1989. *Oral Tradition and Written Record in Classical Athens.* Cambridge.

Thomas, R. 1992. *Literacy and Orality in Ancient Greece.* Cambridge.

Vartsos, J. A. 1978. 'Class Division in Fifth-Century Athens.' *Platon* 30: 226–244.

Vickers, M. and D. W. J. Gill. 1994. *Artful Crafts: Ancient Greek Silverware and Pottery.* Oxford.

Young, D. C. 1984. *The Olympic Myth of Greek Amateur Athletics.* Chicago.

Yunis, H. 1998. 'The Constraints of Democracy and the Rise of the Art of Rhetoric.' In *Democracy, Empire, and the Arts in Fifth-Century Athens.* 223–240. D. Boedeker and K. A. Raaflaub, eds. Cambridge, MA.

SECTION 2

GENDER AND SEXUALITY

CHAPTER 49

GENDER AND SEXUALITY IN GREEK SPORT

THOMAS F. SCANLON

PRELIMINARIES

FOR the sake of this discussion, gender is taken to mean the characteristics assigned to masculinity and femininity, including biological sex, social structures, and gender identity; gender can also be understood as a construction that is enacted or 'performative' (Rosen and Sluiter 2003: 22, 78, 92; Ormand 2005). Sexuality may be understood as the human experience of erotic desire, including physical sexual actions as well as psychological, emotional, and spiritual responses to it. Sport we will define as competitive, physical activity undertaken formally or informally, for health, entertainment, or status-demonstration, usually with the aim of victory, and often with spectators. For Greek sport, we include not only public contests but also the activities of the gymnasium. This essay will offer some thoughts about how gender and sexuality relate to sport in ancient Greece, and will do so in a chronological survey from the Archaic period (the eighth century BCE) to the Roman imperial era. Since sex and gender are obviously interconnected in complex ways, a diachronic approach will allow observations and pose questions about the changes of practice and representation of these phenomena over time.

There are certain generic, virtually universal aspects of sport in relation to sexuality and gender that have held true, so far as evidence indicates, beyond the Greek and Roman world, and these are important to note as phenomena that we share with the ancients and may have been fostered by them in Western culture. First, in the realm of gender, sport has been for most of history and globally a performance overwhelmingly by and for males. This is attested by all indices, including media broadcasts, attendance, and coverage in print media and on web blogs (McGinnis et al. 2019). The phenomena of women's sports will be noted below, but we observe that in the modern Olympics there was no women's marathon race until 1984, almost ninety years into the games. Even then, in 1984, only 25 per cent of all Olympic participants were female; today it is still fewer than half (45 per cent in 2016). The first Olympic women's boxing events came in 2012. Pierre de Coubertin, the founder of the modern Olympic movement, wrote in 1934 that 'women will always be imperfect copies.

There is nothing to learn from watching them; so those who assemble for this purpose have other things in mind' (Campbell Warner 2006: 102; Henson Leigh 1974: 82). Coubertin's bias, voiced near the end of his life, suggests one reason why the incorporation of women's events came so slowly. But it also conveys two opinions that some still maintain, namely that women's sport is a less competitive version of men's and that the only attraction is the sexiness of the performance. Women's participation in sports at all venues and events has slowly improved over the last thirty years, thanks to gender equality movements as a whole.

Still, males have been the majority participants in and the most avid audiences for competitive sports globally throughout history. Is it tradition and culture (military associations, gender identities, etc.) or nature (testosterone and men's greater muscle bulk) that has driven this trend? Testosterone levels are five to ten times higher in men than women, and testosterone levels have generally been linked with aggressive behaviour. Notably testosterone levels aid in building muscle, correlate with dominance rank, and increase libido (McDermott at al. 2007). Groups with higher testosterone levels performed better in competition: testosterone provides 'an adaptive neurobiological response to competition' (McDermott et al. 2007: 18). Scholarly disagreement continues on the balance in and nuances of the nature/culture controversy. The answer obviously involves both nature and culture, with nature perhaps establishing certain fundamentals of muscle, build, chromosomes, etc., and individual personality and cultural context guiding the decisions of how to respond to nature. Whatever the mix of motivations over recent decades, the attempts to put women's sports on an equal footing with men's, economically and in terms of audience interest, have largely not succeeded.

The close identification of males with sport, does not, however, imply that male identity has been similarly constructed in human societies across time and place (Roisman 2005; Van Nortwick 2008; Foxhall and Salmon 1998a; 1998b; Foxhall 2013). Bassi (2003) gives a convincing overview of the meaning of 'manliness' from Homer to Aristotle by looking at the term *andreia* and cognates. The present study helps contextualize the concept in sport. Essentially, the term *andreia* moves from the 'individual martial ethos' of early epic to 'a collective political one' of the fifth-century polis, *andreia politikē*, 'manliness of the polis', as Plato and Aristotle call it. In the *Iliad* troops are frequently told by their leaders to 'Be men' (*aneres este*), occurring ten times in the epic, eight in conjunction with the term 'strength' (*alkē*) (Bassi 2003: 33 and n. 24). The term 'masculinity' (*ēnoreē*) is several times paired with terms for might and strength (*alkē, sthenos, kartos*) in Homer, related to acting as a man should do. Success in combat is the aim (Bassi 2003: 6). Though Thucydides describes the slippery shift of meanings of virtues during civil strife, the concept of *andreia* is associated closely with 'boldness', *tolma* (3.82.4; Bassi 2003: 28–32). Plato's Laches fails to define manliness, but Socrates at one point suggests that the endurance itself (*karterēsis*) of the dialogue may exemplify manliness (*Laches* 194a; Bassi 2003: 51–52). So although the term becomes more 'relativist' in Classical literature and philosophy, it plays there against the Homeric sense of it. For participants in Greek sport of the Archaic period and later, on the other hand, manliness is not ironized; athletes seek to assimilate directly to the Homeric ethos. Not surprisingly, the conventional Homeric virtues of strength, might, endurance, and boldness are those praised in Pindar, Philostratus, athletic inscriptions, and elsewhere in the ancient literature of sport. Sport for men may be described as a refuge from the political manipulation of virtues. It is essentially meritocratic, and therefore egalitarian. Yet the virtues are evocative of the hierarchical heroic age, and can exist in tension with that image (Pleket 1975).

In the sphere of ancient sports, even within ancient Greece, each polis had different institutions, practices, and even strict laws relating to men's role in participation in sport as sponsors and athletes. Sport was frequently a system to help construct masculinity for the ancient Greek polis. By the fifth century BCE, boys and youths of elite and middle classes went through training, sometimes public, often private, that taught physical, mental, and spiritual strength, and fostered in the endurance of citizens-to-be, their resourcefulness, readiness for challenge, patriotism, and devotion to the family. Sport also activated a sense of individuality that may seem in tension with devotion to the polity, but is crucial in building citizenry that seek the ideal 'always to be best and excel the others' (*Iliad* 6.208). Sport was the most peaceful and, excluding equestrian events, the most egalitarian means to establish male status and identity: fathers took pride in victorious sons and vice versa; relations among male friends were validated through the homosocial bonding of training and competing; sports complemented military activities (the Athenian *ephēbeia* ('youth corps') is a prime example from the fourth century BCE and later); men learned the need for restraint (*sōphrosynē*) of appetites during training; and after their 'sporting days' veteran athletes could reapply their skills to civic business. Though many of these athletic-related aspects of male identity find analogies in later cultures and even today, the Greek mix of ideals and realities serves as an informative contrast to our own, not least in its erotic associations.

And so in our second main concern, the sphere of sexuality, we note that eroticism has long been associated with sport, often obliquely in the centuries before the last forty years but of late much more openly, the most overt example of which is the famously liberal sexual atmosphere in the Olympic villages over the decades (Alipour 2013).

It is no surprise that fit youth also pursue erotic liaisons when they can, usually after their events are over. So the question here is how these more generic phenomena are crucially given their own character within an ancient context, and how that character reflects its unique social and political contexts. A chronological survey of the Greek phenomenon of eros and sport is offered below.

HOMER, SPORTS, SEXUALITY, AND MASCULINITY

The *Iliad*, we noted above, virtually performs heroic masculinity and models strength and boldness. Homeric heroes compete to be 'best', but they also sometimes display strong respect and affection for one another. Rivalry and friendship can be in tension. In this culture the quality of male *timē* ('honour' or 'respect') is of great social importance, indexed by birth and status, but also by achievement (Christesen 2012: 119–134; Scanlon 2002: 9–12). This results in a society highly driven by the *agōn* ('contest'). The heroes enact masculine might not only in battle, but also on the playing field in the Funeral Games for Patroclus (*Iliad* 23). The warrior culture of the *Iliad* also displays devotion and affection among males, most famously the homosocial bonding between Achilles and Patroclus, though the erotic relationship is not made evident in Homer (Dover 1989: 197–203; Skinner 2014: 52–53; Fantuzzi 2012). Neither Patroclus nor Achilles, despite his 'swift-footed' epithet, appears as an athlete per se in the epic. But the major sports contests in the *Iliad*, the Funeral Games for Patroclus, involve both the one honoured and the host, Achilles (*Il.* 23). A display of male devotion among warriors motivates the holding of the games, and within the contests, normal rules for winning by are overridden by Achilles' patronage. The bestowing of gifts, particularly the final gesture of Achilles to his political antagonist throughout the epic, presents the Greek heroic paradigm for the use of sports patronage as a mode of male status demonstration. The Iliadic model inspired Pindar who, in his ode *Olympian* 10 (476 BCE), compares the victorious athlete's thanking of his trainer to Patroclus' thanking of Achilles, putting both athlete and trainer vicariously in the company of the Homeric heroes (Hubbard 2003b: 1).

Performances of status are again the rule for the *Odyssey*, primarily on three occasions. Odysseus on Phaeacia, his true identity not known to the locals, avoids shame when Euryalos, judging by appearances, challenges him, saying 'you are no athlete'; whence the hero hurls the weight further than anyone (*Od.* 8.159–185). Back at his palace in Ithaca and in a beggar's disguise, Odysseus is compared to 'an old baker woman' (18.27) by the resident beggar, Iros (*Od.* 18.50–116) whereupon Odysseus defeats him in an impromptu boxing match and wards off the slight to his manhood and status. Finally in the climactic contests of *Odyssey* 21 Odysseus defeats the suitors in the contest of stringing the bow and shooting an arrow through axe heads, followed by the slaughter of the suitors and his regaining his kingship. In all three contests, the hero claims honour among the other men, at first symbolically, and finally to attain real power.

Homer's contests provide a model for manly virtue (*aretē*) that is available to men pursuing sports and warfare in the historical period (Pleket 1975: 165). The 'heroic ethos' that embodied the Homeric male warrior and athlete was, I have argued, a vital spur to the success of the Olympics and the rise of athletic festivals and athletic training among Greek cities generally (Scanlon 2004). Though the athletic contests and custom of funeral games in Homer may well partly reflect earlier Bronze Age traditions, this discussion takes the eighth-century epics primarily as narratives mirroring their own time. They include otherwise unattested contests such as armed combat, to engage Homer's audience, but they mostly validate familiar sports and a similar male-warrior spirit most famously formalized in the Olympic Games begun in that same century (776 BCE is the traditional foundation date of the Olympics; but some say later in the 700s, some say even a century earlier).

THE ARCHAIC AGE

Economy and Classes

First, social history gives a context for the changes. Economically speaking, the time was ripe for the spread of athletics festivals and gymnasia in the sixth century. The major mainland Greek colonization of the eastern Aegean, of northern Greece, and of the Adriatic and Italy and Sicily in the west, had largely abated by 580 BCE. Established connections could be exploited by trade and civic alliances (Hall 2007: 246–247). In these conditions the Greek polis flourished and with it a more egalitarian form of polity arose. It signalled the transition from the dominance of the wealthy classes (*plousioi*) to the greater inclusion of the prosperous but not wealthy middle class (*penētēs*); the very poor (*ptōchoi*) were de facto still marginalized. This meant essentially a greater demand for games and training among those classes than had been the case before the late seventh century (Christesen 2014: 211–235). The term 'training' is perhaps too evocative today of formal gymnasia and routines for keeping fit. As we will discuss below, we should rather see the gymnasium experience as an enormous opportunity for both older and younger males to socialize, to 'network', and sometimes to form erotic ties. In sum, the Archaic Age remains a contest society still deeply concerned with demonstration of status in wealth, in deeds in war, in athletic achievements, and in sexual politics.

Regarding access to sports, others have argued that athletics, along with the symposium and the custom of pederasty, began as an elite activity, and remained so well into the fifth century (Pritchard 2013: 66–82, 130–133; this volume Chapter 48). The argument essentially emphasizes the money needed to finance education and training in gymnasia. Yet it is diffi-cult, with the sparse evidence, to be certain about what percentage of each class (insofar as classes are definable) enrolled in gymnasia, participated in festival contests, or were involved in pederastic liaisons. On the other hand, despite the disputes over evidence here, it seems clear that there was a gradual opening up of athletics, and of pederastic relationships, to middle classes in Athens and elsewhere from the mid-sixth to the late fifth centuries, and even further access to these institutions in the fourth centuries and thereafter.

PEDERASTY, NUDITY, AND THE GYMNASIUM

The Greek 'sexual system' was something less rigid and formal than the term may imply, but was generally characterized by bisexuality for citizen males and monogamous relations for women. Generally within this system, it was illegal or strongly censured for citizen males or females to prostitute themselves, and for males to act as the effeminate or passive partner, a *kinaidos*, an image diametrically opposite to the manly hoplite, and to the heroic athlete (Winkler 1990: 45–46). Allowance has to be made also for changes to sexual mores over the time and place of the 900 years considered here, from the 700s BCE to the 200s CE, beginning with the 200 years of the archaic period. We will focus here on the connections between the specific form of Greek male same-sex relations known as *paiderastia*, or pederasty, literally 'boy love', issues of masculinity, and Greek sport. The reasons for the public emergence of pederasty are complex and disputed, but in brief we here follow the Greek textual tradition that sees the origin in the Dorian cultures of Crete and Sparta. Athletic nudity widely appears by the early sixth century (Scanlon 2002: 208–209; Christesen 2014: 211–235). Homeric texts depict athletes such as wrestlers wearing loincloths. This may be archaizing, or it could be an actual eighth-century practice. Some have argued that athletic nudity was adopted at least in some city-states, e.g. Sparta and Megara (Theognis' polis; see below), by 650–600 BCE (McDonnell 1991).

Pederasty comes 'out of the closet' in the sixth century, coinciding with the surge in popu-larity of athletic festivals. Is there a connection? Some have used a demographic explan-ation for the newly open sexual trend, based on a hypothetical population explosion after 800 BCE that put a strain on agriculture and food supplies, resulting in an enforced delay in marriage, and in pederasty practised as a quasi birth-control measure that segregated males from females, notably at Crete and Sparta (Skinner 2014: 82, citing Sallares 1991: 166–171). Skinner correctly notes that 'we would do well, following Foucault, to inquire how the col-lective ideology is responding to broad social trends by adjusting sexual protocols so as to retain some control over personal lives' (2014: 83). Davidson (2007: 484–486) argues that 'the training-ground' (gymnasium or palaestra) 'was probably the place where Greek homosexuality largely took place', including courting youths, mingling with them, sacrificing to Eros, and giving gifts; possibly even the sex itself (see also Davidson 2007: 418–445; Buffière 1980: 561–573; Percy 1996: 92–121; Hawhee 2004: 109–132; Fischer 1998: 94–104). The root cause may well be related to the emergence of overt pederasty with the simultaneous rise of the polis fostering individual self-assertion and the 'expansion of a sympotic culture' (Skinner 2014: 84). To which we should add another root cause, even more crucial than the symposium, namely the culture of the gymnasium and athletics.

Athletic nudity had already been present as an option since the late eighth century at Olympia, even if it was not broadly adopted until much later, and the erotic dimension should be allowed even for that early date. The *kouroi* statues of nude males (*c*.650– *c*.550; discussed below) also carry an erotic force, since that genre appears after Spartan athletic nudity and, I argue, pederasty had already been generalized to its male citizens by the mid-seventh century. Late *kouroi* production overlaps with the earliest appearance of vases with naked athletes, the same time when the Spartan version of an eroticized athletic nudity was spreading to other states (Scanlon 2005).

The evidence for the origin of widespread pederasty in Greece points generally to a gradual process between the early seventh to mid-sixth centuries. The Spartan *agōgē* and possibly also the Cretan system of *paideia* appear to have been largely formally established in the early seventh century with pederasty being an essential part of both (Scanlon 2005). A critical Athenian speaker in Plato's Laws claims that pederasty arose at Crete and Sparta: 'For these two customs [gymnastic exercises and communal dining which give rise to pederasty], your two states may well be the first to be blamed, as well as any others that make a particular point of athletic exercises' (*Laws* 636b–d; Skinner, trans. adapted; Skinner 2014: 75–76). The harsh critique may be related to Plato's aim of discouraging any sex purely for pleasure and not also producing children, yet it certainly goes contrary to the contemporary popularity of pederasty in Athens. In any case Plato does assert a Dorian pedigree for pederasty that likely reflects a fourth-century popular view, but also one that also seems historically credible. The early practice of nudity in athletic training and contests in Sparta, for example in the Gymnopaediae, undoubtedly fostered a Greek male-body centrism and further explains the inclination to see the open practice of pederasty as spreading from there.

Possibly the earliest use of the terminology of athletic nudity appears in Theognis (*c*.600– *c*.550) and is notably tied to a lover who 'returning home after exercise enjoys the whole day with a handsome youth' (*Theognidea* 1335–1336; Hubbard 2003a: 45; Scanlon 2002: 208–209; Christesen 2014: 211–235). In the words of Plutarch, pederastic *erōs* came later than heterosexual *erōs*, entered the gymnasium, slowly 'grew wings', and became bolder as a presence there (Plutarch *Amatorius* 751f–752a). Lactantius (*Divine Institutions* 1.20) attributes to Cicero a statement that the fusion of *erōs* with the gymnasium was a 'bold plan'. More probably it was the natural and inexorable movement of complementary seventh- to sixth-century practices. The 'athletic revolution', whereby once disparate Greek cities felt a new unity with one another in their sharing of festivals and training practices, called for a new and visible expression of the spirit. Athletic nudity that appears to have been inspired by the Spartan model of undress was adopted as a free expression of Hellenic confidence, aesthetic inclination, and a movement of erotic liberation. Since the Bronze Age, the athletes of Greece and of other eastern Mediterranean cultures had worn little. By abandoning all vestiges of clothing, the costume of nudity now made Greek athletes resemble their statues of the gods. Athletic nudity simultaneously attested to the self-sufficiency of individuals and the freedom of a civilization easily distinguished from 'the barbarians'. It also, and in a more mundane but no less crucial way, served the physical and social needs of homosocial desire within the city-state.

The growth of pederasty in this context was probably fundamentally fostered by erotic desire from the visual and tactile stimuli of the gymnasia and simultaneously shaped by cultural and political agendas of the day. The classic text for this is Plato's narrative of Alcibiades' failed attempt to seduce Socrates by wrestling with him in the gymnasium (*Symposium* 217; Hubbard 2003a: 205). Pederastic *erōs* was of course not literally 'invented' in the gymnasium, but it was given a focus there and, under the restrictions of various formal and informal conventions, allowed to flourish there.

The crucial new phenomena of the early sixth century noted in this study are as follows: 1) the increase in athletic festivals, both Panhellenic and local; 2) the rise of training practices and venues (gymnasia and palaestrae; often interchangeable terms); 3) the custom of nudity among athletes; and 4) the acceptance of pederastic networking at training sites. We should note that there is no archaeological evidence for a gymnasium (or palaestra) earlier than the fourth century BCE, though they certainly existed in some simple form, probably an open space bordered by walls or markers, sometimes with altars and sacred spaces within, perhaps some covered tracks, and rudimentary spaces for gathering, socializing, and sometimes dining (Kennell, this volume Chapter 38; Foxhall 2013: 127–129; Glass 2002: 155–173). The image of boys sitting on the ground in such simple venues, and easily evoking leers from onlookers, is vividly sketched in a speech in Aristophanes' *Clouds* in which the Just Argument describes the proper decorum of the gymnasium: 'in the place of the trainer, boys while seated were expected to put their thighs forward so that they reveal nothing ungentle to the those outside; accordingly they had to smooth the ground when they stood up and take care not to leave behind an image of young manhood for their would-be lovers' (ll. 793–796). The three earliest, and most famous, public gymnasia in Athens, the Academy, Lyceum, and Cynosarges, are outside the city walls or on the edge of town. The locations were more likely due to available space than trying to avoid women's gazes (*pace* Foxhall 2013: 127–128)—women could easily see naked boys and men at public contests—but the long walks to the gymnasia would usually require escorts for youths vulnerable to unwelcome advances of men.

Solon and the Gymnasium

Solon, the famous lawgiver and chief archon at Athens in 594/593 BCE, is alleged to have instituted two pieces of moral legislation in Athens pertaining to homosexuality in the gymnasium (Kyle 1984). The first prohibits slaves from activities of the gymnasium and from having freeborn boys as lovers:

> The law prohibits a slave from frequenting the gymnasium (*gumnazesthai*) and from anointing themselves in the palaestrae ... [and it prohibits] a slave from loving or following a freeborn boy on the penalty of being given fifty lashes with a whip. (Solon fr. 74e Ruschenbusch = Aeschines *Against Timarchus* 138–139; Hubbard 2003a: 148–149)

Slaves were thus forbidden from doing what normal free citizens were encouraged to do. The concurrence of sources, all fourth century BCE or later, can be taken as an indication that some regulation of this sort was proposed and instituted by Solon *c.*580 BCE, and that homosexual *erōs* in gymnasia was a reality in early sixth-century Athens (Scanlon 2002: 212–214; Hubbard 2003b: 5; Christesen 2014: 216–217). As often, this seems to be a policy written post facto to sanction a prevailing norm and to keep it under control.

Solon was probably therefore responsible for institutionalizing pederasty to some extent at Athens in the early sixth century. He notably did not attempt to set up obligatory pederasty or kidnapping of boys by lovers, as may have been the case at some places in early Crete; nor did he adopt the 'herds' of boys as in Crete and Sparta of his day. Pederasty no doubt existed at Athens in less formalized contexts, and he maintained it as a freer practice associated inter alia with gymnasia and symposia. We cannot say for certain whether Solon himself or some aristocratic group of his day first introduced public or private gymnasia with nude athletic training to Athens. In any case, the date of Solon's pederastic regulations corresponds neatly to our earlier hypothesis that athletic nudity and pederasty began to see more widespread acceptance *c.*600 BCE.

A second 'Solonian' law, this probably dating to the late fifth century, prescribes hours for opening and closing schools and palaestrae to discourage homosexual liaisons from taking place there in the dark or without the presence of the proper supervisors:

> [Solon] forbade teachers from opening schools and *paidotribai* [pl. of *paidotribēs*, a wrestling school trainer] from opening the palaestrae before sunrise, and he ordered that they shut them before sunset, holding the deserted and dark places in very great suspicion. (Aeschines *Against Timarchus* 10; Hubbard 2003a: 132)

The law goes on to state ages and qualifications for *neaniskoi*, bridging the categories of the older young men (*paides*) or younger adults (*neoi*), possibly anywhere between 18 and 30 years of age according to various sources. It later calls for the exclusion of males from the Hermaea ('Contests of Hermes'), or else the head of the gymnasium would be subject to the law concerning corruption of youth; anyone older than the boys, other than relatives of the teacher, caught entering the palaestra will be punished with death (Aeschines, *Against Timarchus* 12). The restrictions on attendance at the Hermaea is enlightening since it implies that the games themselves, and not just the gymnasia, furnished real opportunities for men to 'pick up' a young beloved. Though these last aspects of the law (and chapter twelve of the speech generally) have rightly been judged as unauthentic in view of anachronisms and errors (Kyle 1984: 101), the earlier parts concerning opening and closing times and age regulations appear to be authentically Solonian. Solon's laws thus seem to reflect an early concern about the gymnasia becoming the site of illicit trysts (e.g. between slaves and freeborn youths) which could not be openly observed by supervisors.

'Revolutions' in Sports and Sexuality

With the first quarter of the sixth century, the picture changed dramatically. Between 586 and 573, three other major Panhellenic games were instituted in Greece: the Pythia at Delphi (582/581 or 586/585), the Isthmian Games near Corinth (582/581), and the Nemean Games at Nemea in the Peloponnese (573). These were joined by the major local games at

Athens, the Panathenaia, reorganized in 566. And an inscribed law from Olympia from the last quarter of the sixth century (on infractions in wrestling) suggests that a bureaucracy with written records did not arise at Olympia until the first half of the sixth century (Siewert 1992). The early sixth century, then, was marked by an intense institutionalization of athletic festivals, the very period when pederasty and nakedness blossomed in gymnasia, in art, and in symposia. The athletic 'revolution' was accompanied by a sexual 'revolution' of sorts, no doubt fostered by the increasingly egalitarian polis and greater prosperity of the elite and 'middle' classes. Nudity is an emblem of this equality and an incentive to greater socialization of the community (Christesen 2012: 135–183; Christesen 2014). To envision how such sudden and deep cultural changes take place, we can analogize with the rapid 'sexual revolution' of the 1960s in North America and Western Europe, a movement clearly made possible by the new birth control methods, and complexly bound with the 'liberated' spirit among post-World War II nations, an economic boom, a baby boom, and greater leisure allowing for the cliché cocktail of 'sex, drugs, and rock and roll'. In Greece's case there was no great war of the mid-sixth century to explain the changes (as the Persian Wars later further fostered a cultural acme in Athens), but polis structure and relative prosperity with new colonies laid the foundation for systems of sex and sports to become much more visible.

Women's Sports Begin

Contemporaneous with the athletic and sexual transformations in early sixth-century Greece was the appearance of contests for girls, of a much more limited scope and with entirely different aims. At Sparta the famous education system for boys, the *agōgē*, established by the legendary Lycurgus, had its counterpart in a physical training programme for girls (Scanlon 2002: 121–138). This programme may be hinted at in the *Parthenion* ('Maiden Song') of Alcman of Sparta (*c*.650–*c*.600), a song to accompany a choral dance and offering homoerotic comments on female beauty (Calame 2001). Aristophanes alludes to the clichéd muscularity of Spartan women (*Lysistrata* 78–81; 411 BCE); Ibycus calls them 'thigh-flashers' with their skimpy athletic attire (fr. 58 Page; sixth cent. BCE), echoed in Euripides' overstated lines about Spartan girls who 'go out with young men, with their thighs bared and robes ungirt as they hold races and wrestling contests with them' (*Andromache* 595–602; 430–424 BCE). Xenophon attests to 'contests of running and strength' required of Spartan girls, following Lycurgus' educational system (*Constitution of Sparta* 1.3–4; 396–383 BCE). This custom is amplified later by Plutarch (100–120 CE) who says that Lycurgus instituted 'running, wrestling, and the throwing of discus and javelin, so that the root of these born might better mature by taking a strong beginning in strong bodies' (*Lycurgus* 14.2; see 14.1–15.1; see Talbert 2009 on the need for scepticism on Plutarch's views on Lycurgus). Eugenics are therefore represented, plausibly, to be the primary motive for female contests at Sparta, and they seem to have lasted for centuries.

The other girls' athletics of note in the sixth century is the Heraia or Festival of Hera at Olympia, which included foot-races for girls, probably instituted in the 580s BCE (Scanlon 2002: 98–120; Scanlon 2008). Pausanias is the only literary source and he describes the contestants as unmarried girls of three age-groups who run a race of one stadium length, shortened by one sixth from the men's length (Pausanias 5.16.2–3; *c*.150 CE). The costume was a short, single-strap chiton having one breast uncovered, a pose exactly mirrored in two representations. One is a bronze statuette from about 580 BCE (British Museum Br. 208; Scanlon 2002: 102 fig. 4-1; Scanlon 2008: 164–169 and Tafel 12/2; Scanlon 2014: 114 and fig. 4.1) and the other a marble statue including a victory palm, dated to the Julio-Claudian era (about 30 BCE to 68 CE) but stylistically evocative of an early fifth-century statue (Rome, Vatican City, Vatican Museum Galleria dei Candellabri, XXXIV.36.1, inv. no. 2784; Scanlon 2002: 103 fig. 4-2; Scanlon 2008: Tafel 2; Scanlon 2014: 115 fig. 4.2). The evidence is sparse but strikingly congruent, and it indicates that the event went on for centuries with a generally quiet obscurity. The phenomenon recalls the famous adage of Pericles that '[women's] renown is great ... if [their] fame is least circulated among men, either for excellence or blame' (Thucydides 2.45.2). Participation was probably Panhellenic, open to any daughters of Greek citizens, and it was only for unmarried girls. Participants in the Heraia, likely mainly from the elite, travelled there with their mothers, who watched the Heraia but encamped south of the Alpheus River during the Olympics. Unmarried girls, who were 'not barred from watching [the Olympic Games]' (Pausanias 6.20.9) could attend that festival with their fathers, who used the venue to arrange marriages for their daughters, as famously evident in the story of Cleisthenes of Sikyon and in other examples (Herodotus 6.126; Scanlon 2008: 184–192; Scanlon 2014: 145–17). Pausanias (5.16.4–8) gives us the only direct testimony of the Heraian origin to mythical times when Hippodameia, out of gratitude to Hera for her marriage to Pelops, assembled the Sixteen Women (organizers) and inaugurated the Heraia. The festival is one of thanksgiving for the mythical marriage to honour the goddess of women as maidens and wives. Thus the historical race encouraged girls to seek a similarly successful union. I have argued that the races took place at the time of, probably just before, the men's Olympics, not least for the practical reasons of furnishing a safe escorts for girl participants and of having the stadium ready without special preparations (Scanlon 2008: 184; Scanlon 2014: 145). In sum, the Heraia and the Olympics together provided a significant opportunity for arranging marriages among Greek families.

The sixth century programmes of contests for girls in Sparta and at the Heraia each highlight, in different ways, the roles of women to be the best mothers and to seek the best marriages. The female games mirror the men's in the events practised, in prizes, and in intense competition for high repute. Yet they avoid tension with the men's sports by keeping a 'low profile' (no victory hymns, few statues, few literary mentions), and in fact complement the men's games reflecting heroic warrior culture in their essentially female, sanctioned aims of producing good wives and mothers. As the sports contest became more widely open to men in the sixth century, so too the format suggested itself to women's rites and activities, beginning with the Heraia and the Spartan games for girls, but continuing for centuries thereafter in those locations, and only occasionally appearing elsewhere through the Roman period.

Images of Masculinity and Eros

The conjunction of sports, sexuality, and gender is also widely reflected in the visual evidence of the Archaic Age. Athletic sculpture flourished mid-sixth to mid-fifth century, and with it the visual ideals of masculinity were on display, to emulate, to admire as a mother, a teacher, a possible wife, or a male lover (Kurke, this volume Chapter 23; 1993: 141–149; Raschke, this volume Chapter 35; Steiner 1998; 2001: 259–264). As mentioned above, statues of nude, muscled young men (sometimes possibly gods), life-sized or larger, called *kouroi*, abounded in this period as monuments of masculinity in Athens (Osborne 1998). While the *kouroi* were sometimes in sanctuaries and sometimes used as grave markers, the ones in cemeteries commemorated the happy lives of the men playing ball, performing sports, or hunting (Osborne 1998: 26, 27 pl. 3). Images of athletic nude men from the same period appear on other slab-shaped grave markers, *stelai*, celebrating the youth holding a discus, oil flasks for pre-training anointment, and the armour and weapons of the hoplite warrior. The male images persisted in Athenian graveyards only until about 500 BCE, after which for half a century women dominated on the *stelai* as the fashion changed, perhaps due to the egalitarian male-citizen ethos (in the cemeteries at least) of the new, democratic polis (Osborne 1998: 29). But from the mid to late fifth century on, the naturalistic sculptural style of male, free-standing sculptures appeared in abundance in home towns or sanctuaries, a style most famously exemplified by Myron's Discobolos ('Discus-Thrower'; 470–440 BCE). The piece has to be imagined in its original gleaming bronze, like the oiled tan of the athlete, poised in mid-throw that epitomizes the balance of the golden mean and yet showcases male virtue (*andragathia*) of the active hero (Jenkins 2012). The stiffer archaic statues seem more distant and august, though they are undoubtedly impressive images of masculinity. The athlete statues of the Classical period and later, through to the Roman era, are at first highly idealized, strong, and yet sensual, as with works of Myron and Praxiteles. The 'Getty Bronze' (Getty Villa 77.AB.30) is a rare, original, life-sized bronze athletic statue of a youth crowning himself at the moment of victory, possibly by Lysippus (fourth century BCE), and it conveys the pride, confidence, and sensuous curved stance of a victorious youth. The other glimpse at a rare, life-sized bronze athlete is that of the Therme Boxer ('Boxer of the Quirinal'; Rome, Palazzo Massimo, Inv. 1055), perhaps from 330 BCE, and it shows an almost deliberately unidealized, yet noble and moving portrait of an older boxer, seated and resting, perhaps between rounds. The weariness from intense violence is palpable, and it is remarkable for its depiction of vulnerability and strength, ending in victory: a broken nose, swollen ears, a thick beard, creased face, wounds and scars, monstrous sharp gloves on his hands, and even blood on his skin represented by trickles of copper. If the Getty youth seems like a perfect, all-round elite athlete, this veteran of combat sport evokes the image of a professional, non-elite, a different model of mature, well-muscled masculinity, capable of great violence and yet sympathetic.

Athletic scenes on vase paintings greatly increase in the first half of the sixth century but continue well into the fifth and fourth centuries (Christesen 2014: 217; Goossens and Thielemans 1996). Vases inscribed 'beautiful [male]' (*kalos*) begin from about 550 to 450, and those with pederastic scenes are most numerous from 550 to 475 (Lear 2008; Scanlon 2002: 205–206 and fig. 8-2; Skinner 2014: 101–138, esp. 111–114 with gym scenes). In this same period, Attic vases 'repeatedly associate scenes of homosexual courtship and play with gymnastic settings and accessories' (Fisher 2010: 75; cf. Kilmer 1993: 81–86).

Hubbard (2003a) illustrates gymnasium courting scenes in a series of figures in his sourcebook: fig. 11, three pairs of older men with boys: one pair kissing and one boy with a discus being given a ribbon by his man friend; figs. 16 and 19 again 'courting' men and boys with strigils hanging in the background; fig. 24b and c, a cup showing seemingly coeval youths in a scene in which clothed ones admire the nude athletic ones who hold discuses or a javelin. Hubbard (2003b: 7–16) adduces the evidence of vase painting from about 520 to 420, showing young trainers with young men or boy athletes, to argue from the body language (position of the gaze, eye contact, visibility or covering of genitals, etc.) that the two may be lover and beloved. Hubbard argues that love relations between trainers and athletes were common (2003b: 4–6), citing the relation of Kallias with Autolycus in Xenophon's Symposium (see also Fisher 2010: 79). Pindar *Pythian* 10 of 498 BCE praises the victor Hippocleas, whose patron, Thorax, may well have also been his lover (Hubbard 2003b: 6–7). The poem brims with praise for the boy's beauty in the eyes of other youths, maidens and older men (ll. 55–60). The most widely praised trainer in Pindar is the wealthy Athenian Melesias (*O*. 8, *N*. 4, and *N*. 6), culling at least thirty victories; Hubbard (2003b: 7) adduces erotic motivation.

Some early fifth-century vases show 'a money pouch being offered by the *erastēs* ['lover'] and the *paidika* ['boys'] in gymnastic contexts' (Fisher 2010: 77–78; see von Reden 1995: 195–216; Neils 1994: 154–159). Are these the gymnasiarchs (gymnasium directors) financing the youths? Or the trainers getting paid by the youths? Fisher suggests that the representations disappear in 470 when training became 'more widespread among wider circles of Athenians and more problematized, both morally and in terms of legal proceedings, and so representations of them came to be avoided' (Fisher 2010: 78). Or was training per se not the problem, but financing that became more public, more legitimate, and less underhanded? Or did the pederastic relations themselves become more widely accepted and less frowned upon, hence less interesting as subjects? The questions are left open with many attractive possibilities. What is clear is that the representations of pederastic courting in athletic contexts are never the object of satire on vases, and so visual evidence maintains a noble visage for the practice, whatever critique athletes faced in the literature of the day (Pritchard 2013: 113–120).

The god Eros himself first appears on vases with athletes in gymnasia in the early fifth century, further endorsing the practice. About 490–480 BCE a red-figure kylix attributed to Douris depicts gymnasium scenes of wrestling and undressing on one side, and Eros flying in and boys fleeing on the other (Berlin V.I.3168; 500–466 BCE; Stafford 2013: 187–189 and fig. 5; Scanlon 2002: 239–242 and fig. 8.10). An Attic red-figure kylix (*c*.470; Munich 2669) shows on the interior Eros putting a fillet on an altar, and on the exterior Eros once on each side [or possibly Pothos and Himeros?] in a gymnasium context, possibly even the Academy itself (Stafford 2013: 185–187 and fig. 4)! Is Eros a stand-in for the would-be lover/viewer of the vase (this author's view), or is Eros himself the lover and a symbol of the love among the boys themselves (Stafford 2013: 188–189 following Shapiro 1992: 69–70)? The figure of Eros appeared most frequently on vases (mainly from Attica) from 450 to the 300s BCE, possibly replacing explicit pederastic scenes found earlier (Lear 2014: 252; Kilmer 1993; Skinner 2014: 101–138). The switch is more likely due to a change of style than from de facto censorship. But the style choice may have been influenced by the increasing democratization of Athens, when citizens had an ambiguous relationship with activities tinged previously with elitism, hence critiqued in Athenian drama (Pritchard 2013: 131; this volume Chapter 48).

THE CLASSICAL PERIOD

The Classical period, broadly speaking from about 480 to 323 BCE, was a time of magnificent cultural achievements, notably at Athens, but also a time of virtually continual fierce strife among Greek states. After the Persian Wars (490–478), Greek city-states from Asia Minor and the whole Aegean coast to the mighty cities of South Italy and Sicily shared in the culture of athletics, drama, literature, and variations on egalitarian forms of government, but they also shifted constantly in political alliances for their own benefit. Athletics was unquestionably one of the shared, Panhellenic, and unifying cultural forces, as were the mostly stable images of masculinity, womanhood, and sexuality inherited from the Archaic Age.

The prominent role of the gymnasium as the locus of pederasty continues in this century, but opens up further with more options of public and private training centres and more opportunities for lovers finding their beloved. Gymnasia and *palaestrai* were often democratized by the fifth century, then privatized to an extent by the fourth (Plato Lysis 203A–204A; the wealthy may have had their own gyms: [Xenophon] *Constitution of Athens* 2.10; Fisher 2010: 70). Pseudo-Xenophon, an Athenian author of a fifth-century tract, rants about the problems with democracy, including how the wealthy build gymnasia and the Athenian people build 'many wrestling schools [*palaestai*]' ([Xenophon], *Constitution of Athens* 2.10; Pritchard 2013: 70; this volume Chapter 48). In the fourth century, publicly appointed trainers (*paidotribai*) reflected the further democratization of athletic training, and also perhaps a desire to distance training from the role of private patronage and pederastic influence which may have been increasingly marginalized by Athenian democracy (Hubbard 2003b: 5). In any case, erotic attraction among young athletes and older onlookers continued, as we observe in a speech written on the occasion of the athletic victory of a certain Epikrates (Demosthenes 61, *c*.350–325 BCE; Worthington 2006; Foxhall 2013: 80–83). The writer praises the youth's natural beauty (61.11), and his masculinity (*andreia*) is celebrated at length (61.22–29).

If the gymnasium is the site of liaisons, looking, and even leering at other males, then athletic contests, as Demosthenes 61 evidences, are the perfect venue to display the body's manly virtues in peak performance (Osborne 2011: 27–36). Striking evidence of the stadium as a place of beauty on display is found in the six preserved erotic *kalos* inscriptions found on the walls inside the entrance tunnel to the stadium at Nemea: '[so-and-so is] beautiful' (Miller 2001: 86–89, 313–340; inventory numbers GRAF 2c, 7, 9, 11b, 14c, 15d, 19a). These seem to be the work of athletes 'waiting in the wings' for their contest, prompting one suggestion that they evidence the attraction of one competitor to another (Lear 2014: 250). But they may also be self-boasts. Admiration or attraction among coeval athletes is attested in Plato's *Lysis* and Xenophon's *Symposium* (Davidson 2007: 86–90; Hubbard 2003b: 11), yet some say the evidence for same-age relations among males is 'rare and problematic' (Lambert 2004: 440).

Further evidence of the conjunction of male beauty and contests is the *euandria*, a 'Contest in Being a Good Man'. This was a team event, mostly for Athenian tribes, but sometimes admitting non-Athenians, that took place at the Panathenaia and at the Theseia festivals in Athens attested to first in the fourth century BCE (van Nijf 2003: 263–286). Though the criteria for judging the *euandria* are unclear, it is thought that it involved beauty exemplified in size and strength, perhaps including some quasi-military show of strength (van Nijf 2003: 273; Crowther 2004: 333–339). Inscriptions show that the *euandria* was also held at festivals outside Athens in the Hellenistic and Roman period, including at Rhodes, Sestos, and Sparta (Crowther 2004: 335). Along with other male 'beauty' contests of the same period in comportment (*euexia*), discipline (*eutaxia*), and endurance (*philoponia*), the *euandria* may be understood as an award for most successful training of young men, rewarding the group or individuals whose overall training seemed most successful for healthy and fitness (Crowther 2004: 333–344; Remijsen 2015: 255). It may have served as a consolation prize (with sincere respect) to those who did not excel in a particular athletic context, but were the most handsome, best behaved, most hard-working, and most impressive in training-related achievements. These contests collectively highlight masculine ideals as marks of high civic achievement. We note that there were no such 'beauty contests' for females among the Greek cities.

The manliness (*andreia*) openly celebrated by Homer and lyric poets like Tyrtaeus becomes subject to interrogation in the fifth century, notably in tragedy and comedy where the ascription of 'manliness' at times to women and, ironically, to obviously cowardly comic figures, shows that the concept has become manipulated in political and poetic usage (Bassi 2003: 44–46). Strong female figures of myth and legend like Medea and Clytemnestra challenge stalwart males, while Herakles complains of being murdered by Deianeira (Euripides' *Medea*; Aeschylus' *Agamemnon*; Sophocles' *Women of Trachis*). The comic character Lampito shines forth as a parody of Spartan muscularity (Aristophanes' *Lysistrata*). Even in *The History* of Herodotus, we find the Greek woman Artemisia, allied to Persia, praised for her *andreia* (7.99.1; cp. 8.88.1–3). In Pericles' Funeral Oration, *andreia* is described as a contested virtue, in the Spartan form compelled by external custom and in the Athenian by internal character (Thucydides 2.39.4). Aristotle once defined manliness as a reasoned and moderate negotiation between boldness and fear; it is the moderation that makes *andreia* a virtue (Aristotle *Eudemian Ethics* 1228a26–30a37; 1230a26–33; Bassi 2003: 50). The fifth-century parsing of masculinities can directly relate to the male image of the athlete, which is not monolithic, but flexible and challenged. Athletic manliness is in part measured by the traditional terms and values, established since Homer, of valour, endurance, and strength, but it is also now judged differently by different critics with regard to degrees of violence and restraint that define a man.

A remarkable development in women's participation in sports arose in the case of Cynisca of Sparta (see Mari and Stirpe, Valavanis, Nicholson, Cartledge, Raschke, and Dillon, Chapters 7, 9, 19, 28, 32, and 44 respectively in this volume). Women were excluded from competing in the Olympics, except for the chariot- and horse-race events where, like today, the owner was honoured as victor. The first such female victor was Cynisca who won in the four-horse chariot race at Olympia *c.*390 BCE. Regarding her, we have the testimonia of Xenophon, Plutarch, Pausanias, and her victory epigram, preserved both in the Palatine Anthology and on an inscription found at Olympia (Xenophon *Ages.* 9.6–7; Plutarch, *Ages.* 20.1 and *Spartan Sayings* 212B; Pausanias 3.8.1–2, 3.15.1, 15.12.5, 6.1.6–7; *Anth.Pal.* 13.16; *IG* V.1564 a):

> My fathers and brothers were kings of Sparta.
> I, Cynisca, having won with a team of swift-footed horses,
> dedicated this statue. I assert that I am the only woman
> in all Greece to have taken this crown.

This epigram displays what is the only athletic victory dedication claiming distinction on the basis of gender. A few other women did follow Cynisca as Olympic chariot victors, and most of these were also daughters of wealthy nobles or rulers: Berenike I wife of Ptolemy I; Arsinoë, sister of Ptolemy II; also Belistiche of Macedonia, courtesan of Ptolemy II (268 and 264 BCE); Berenike II, wife of Ptolemy III (248 BCE). Certainly each won some political capital for their fatherland, but visibility for them as women was also an incentive to enter the competition, as Cynisca's proud epigram attests.

Yet an intriguing anecdote told by Xenophon and Plutarch about Cynisca's entry into Olympic fame seems to undercut her pride in her sex:

> [King Agesilaus] persuaded his sister Cynisca to breed horses for chariot-racing, and showed by her victory that this breed is not an example of manly valour (*andragathias*), but of wealth. (Xen. *Ages*. 9.6)

The assumption here is that if a woman can accomplish this deed, it is therefore not a deed of *aretē*, but of some other quality, namely, in this case, possession of wealth (Plut. *Ages*. 20.1). It was doubtless as true then as it is today that any individual, male or female, could raise prize-winning horses, since that requires only the money with which to feed, stable, hire trainers, own land for training, etc. The fact that Agesilaus had to use a woman to make this point suggests that, for ancient Greek males, 'excellent accomplishments' in public competition were considered a male prerogative, and that when or if a woman equalled a normally male achievement, the excellence of that achievement was at once called into question. As mentioned above, this anecdote would seem to be at odds with Cynisca's victory epigram.

The public inscription was written under a very impressive bronze sculpture by Apelles showing an almost life-sized team of horses, driver, and Cynisca herself. Such an impressive monument would of course not have been the place for Agesilaus to make his point about excellence versus wealth. That would have impugned the excellence not only of his sister, but of every Greek who ever won in the hippic events at Olympia! Yet Agesilaus must have been tempted to make his point once and for all in writing 'to the Greeks' at Olympia, as the anecdote relates. Ironically, Cynisca herself became the most famous woman Olympic victor of all time (Paus. 3.8.1); her epigram and monument at Olympia no doubt contributed to her fame. Even today a sourcebook on women in the ancient world records the victory epigram, but omits the anecdote about Agesilaus (Lefkowitz and Fant 2005: 161 no. 202).

So Cynisca resides in that ambiguous middle ground between male and female athletic values, achieving and not achieving *aretē* and fame usually reserved for males. Perhaps Cynisca's problematic athletic fame is balanced by another, less well-publicized monument which displays her concurrent devotion to a role which is clearly female. A small Doric capital with her name on it, apparently set up as a base for a dedication to Helen, was found at Sparta (IG V (i) 235). Cynisca was, therefore, a devotee of the heroine/goddess who was admired by Spartan girls gathered at their racecourse and had 'the role of conducting Lacedaimonian adolescent girls to full sexual maturity' (Theocr. *Idyll* 18.39–42). To Cynisca we may compare another woman of the first century CE, Damodica of Cyme in Asia Minor, whose epitaph states that she died 'not without fame since she left a son and the glory of victory in a four-horse chariot' (Mantas 1995: 133). Like Cynisca, Damodica both obtained traditional female fame and had a share in the male version as well.

THE HELLENISTIC AND ROMAN ERAS

After the defeat of Athens in the Peloponnesian War (404) came the long series of struggles between Sparta, Corinth, Thebes, and Athens in the fourth century, culminating in the rise of Macedon, thanks to Philip II and his son Alexander the Great. First Persia loomed large to the East, then, after the death of Alexander (323), the Ptolemies in Egypt and the Seleucids in the Near East held sway for a time. Greek athletic festivals spread farther than ever in the fourth to early second centuries BCE. Gymnasia as formal buildings and with serious academic training became standard fixtures from the eastern Mediterranean to the Greeks in the West. And the legacy of the Greek sexual practice of pederasty remained strong across the Greek world. The Roman overlordship started seriously in the second century and was marked by the sack of Corinth and defeat of the Achaean League in 146 BCE. Ironically, Roman laissez-faire policy toward Greek culture allowed athletic festivals and gymnasia to flourish, injecting them with new capital. Alongside Greek leisure facilities there arose Roman baths and arenas for gladiator games. Greek sexuality and athletic nudity were not condoned by strict Roman *gravitas* and *severitas*, but they were tolerated with an amused glance to their eastern neighbours (Crowther 1980; 1982).

From the mid-second century BCE, the Gymnasiarchal Decree of Beroia (Macedonia) records many regulations for gymnasium officials, management of the young male students, and the holding of their most important annual festival, the Hermaea (Miller 2012: 137–142, no. 185; see also Papakonstantinou, this volume Chapter 45). The Hermes festival is similar to the Athenian one mentioned by Solon, since the god ushered youths to manhood. This Hellenistic law from northern Greece is also in the tradition of the Solonian laws 450 years earlier, listing those prohibited from entering the gymnasium, including slaves, freedmen, the infirm, male prostitutes (*hetaireukōtes*), peddlers, drunkards, and lunatics. As in Solon's gymnasium laws, only the undesirables who might exercise a bad influence on the citizen youth are excluded, and there is even a similar clause forbidding the 'youths' (*neaniskoi*) to speak with the 'boys' (*paides*). We can only speculate whether the surveillance was to discourage these different age classes from having sexual relations with one another rather than with a sanctioned older man, or simply to stop squabbles among different groups.

In the first to second century CE, we can recall the remark of Plutarch quoted earlier about pederastic Eros entering the gymnasia and crowding out conjugal Eros (Plut. *Amatorius* 751f–752a). Even allowing for comic parody here, it is significant that there exists in the Greek world of the high Roman empire 1) an explicit tension between boy-love and wife-love that is not evident in earlier periods (perhaps arising here due to the nudge of Roman values) and 2) a narrative of pederastic origins linked solely to training venues that epitomizes earlier Greek associations since Theognis.

A high esteem for manliness persisted into the Julio-Claudian, Flavian, and Nervan dynasties, if we can take a monument, a sculptural image, and two inscriptions as testimonies for that value's broader importance. Tiberius Claudius Rufus, a pancratiast from Smyrna in Asia Minor, sometime between 43 and 123 CE was honoured with a monument as one who 'stood out among the pancratiasts of his own day on account of his *andreia* and *sōphrosynē* ('manliness' and 'self-control/moderation') (van Nijf 2003: 263–264; Poliakoff 1987: 127–128). Van Nijf suggests that 'moderation' was singled out since he was appointed as a games commissioner (xystarch) that required moral restraint. But that quality could also be an athletic one, showing his self-control in training and perhaps even in the contest where manly aggression without restraint can cause mistakes. Second, a sculptural representation of the divinity Andreia as an armed warrior with helmet, sword, and spear is found in ancient Hieropolis (Syria) carved as a Roman era theatral decoration alongside figures representing the union of athletes (*Synodos*, in goddess form) and the long-distance race (*Dolichos*, a naked male running) (van Nijf 2003: 274 and fig. 1). This image literally associates military *andreia* with athletics. *Andreia* is also closely linked to athletics in the Roman-era inscription in which Ephesus honours a certain athlete, Aurelius Achilles, who, though not an Ephesian, competed twice in the Olympics for Ephesus and won (event unspecified), 'competing impressively and with full manliness (*diaprepōs kai meta pasēs agōnisamenos andreias*) ... his manliness and enthusiasm are numbered among the most distinguished of contests' (van Nijf 2003: 275–276). Finally, another inscription of this period praises the *andreia* and the wisdom (*sophia*) of a pancratiast, Kallikrates, from Oenoanda in Asia Minor, suggesting that intellectual achievement can be valued, even though it is not a conventional part of athletic masculinity (van Nijf 2003: 282–283). So still alive in the Greek east of the Roman empire is the concept of Homeric manliness, in association still with martial valour.

In the wake of the Heraia at Olympia and Spartan athletics for unmarried girls, we find sporadic evidence that the anomaly of games for girls was, if not consistently and robustly practised, at least revived from time to time. The Julio-Claudian era in particular witnessed some games for girls. A contest for girls (*certamen virginum*; uncertain in nature) at the imperial festival for the emperor Tiberea Caesarea Sebasta is mentioned in a Latin inscription from Corinth dating to about 2 BCE (Kyle 2015: 217). A foot-race for girls was held at the Augustalia (Sebastea) games in Naples in 2 CE. A one-off foot-race was held in Sparta by Tiberius or Claudius to honor Livia (*SEG* 11.830; Mantas 1995: 134). An important inscription on a monument from Delphi from about 45 CE records the several victories achieved by three daughters of Hermesianax of Tralles (Asia Minor inland from Ephesus) (Kyle 2015: 217–218; Mantas 1995: 132–133; Miller 2012: 109–110 no. 162). These three girls won at Panhellenic and other major games: the Pythia, the Isthmia, the Sebastea in Athens, and the Asclepieia at Epidaurus. Their events included foot-races presumably against other girls, a chariot in armour (possibly competing against males, but also possibly as sponsor using a male driver), and the kithara singing (likely against boys; Lee 1988). In 154 CE, the husband of Seia Spes commemorated her victory in a foot-race for daughters of the local magistrates held in Naples (Mantas 1995: 132,135; Kyle 2015: 217). Current evidence suggests that athletic contests for young females in the Roman period were scattered, random, and short-lived. Or else there was a more contiguous and widespread tradition, but public mention of the events or commemoration of girl victors was not supported by custom or economics.

Some, perhaps most, of the recorded events for girls certainly may have been one-time events, to honour the daughters of the elite and, by reflection, their families. An enigma is posed by the inscription for the daughters of Hermesianax, in which the girls competed in the major, regular festivals. This implies training, travelling in a circuit for girls in which a number of other girls competed, and presumably competing in contests and festivals beyond the ones listed on the monument. The time span for the victories of the girls is estimated to have been from 39 to 45 or 47 CE (West 1928: 259). The agonothetes, those in charge of the games, and the circle of elite who controlled them were connected with the imperial cult (West 1928: 268). The period of the victories falls under the end of the reign of the emperor Caligula and the early years of Claudius. Emperors could and did take an interest in the programme of the Panhellenic games. We know, for instance, that the emperor Domitian ruled on a proposed change to the Pythian games (West 1928: 265). If the radical inclusion of females in three of the four traditional Panhellenic games was decided by an emperor (or by local elite Greeks seeking the emperor's favour), the originator would have been Caligula, after which the custom would have continued into the reign of Claudius. Though imperial support for a circuit of girls' games must remain conjecture, it is difficult to imagine how else a coordinated cluster of such events across festivals over a few years could be ordained entirely by local Greek officials, since each festival had separate governing bodies and separate authority for their sanctuaries. The only other, less likely explanation is that for some unknown reason there arose a fad for inclusion of girls' games in regular festivals in this period, echoing the occasional one-off contests before and after the phenomenon of Hermesianax's daughters.

Concluding Observations

We can make several broad observations in this survey covering a millennium of phenomena related to Greek sport, gender, and sexuality. We first note some of the general characteristics of these phenomena before suggesting the possibly greater motivations behind them:

1) Greek sport was in its earliest forms and predominantly thereafter a male activity;
2) masculinity and its virtues were a consistent motif in Greek texts discussing sport from Homer onward;
3) sport and war were regular points of reference in characterizing and evaluating the athlete in relation to the warrior; the athletic and the martial spheres were often in tension regarding how greatly success in sport was valued as a measure of male excellence;
4) the Greek gymnasium and athletic nudity were factors that fostered the Greek male sexual system of pederasty, consistently at least from Solon and seventh-century Sparta onward;
5) material culture in the form of sculpture, inscriptions, and vase paintings reflects the androcentrism of Greek sport, frequently and fairly uniformly from the Archaic period to the Roman era;
6) female participation in Greek sport has a historical existence much less consistent and widespread than that of males: it begins historically in the early sixth century BCE (in Sparta and at the Heraia at Olympia), continues with female victories in Olympic chariot racing from the fourth century BCE to the Hellenistic period, and is finally evidenced in a series of female contests in the Roman imperial period.

Many of the reasons behind these phenomena are actively discussed by scholars without uniform agreement. The predominance of male participation in Greek sport seems to arise from a combination of biological and cultural factors, and these factors are reflected in general terms in the sporting history of western modernity. Notably higher levels of testosterone, as mentioned above, have been linked to greater physical aggression and to sexual libido, at times to demonstrate social rank and to excel in contest situations. These characteristics of male physiology and behaviour are not surprising as they occur globally and across time. Again, scholars of ancient Greece, and indeed those of sport in modern cultures, debate without resolution regarding the degree to which sport is a 'safety valve' for physical aggression or a force that contributes to it. Or to what degree sport feeds or curbs the libido. There are no simple answers, since circumstances and individual character determine biological responses, though the current consensus is that sport does not divert human aggression (Pritchard 2013: 20–30; Christesen 2014: 104–105). And yet the Greek construction of sport does achieve certain positive advances for each state and its citizens.

It is remarkable to observe how the Greeks, without any known close models from earlier Mediterranean cultures, converted male inclinations to aggression and competition into a sophisticated system of contests, *agōnes*. The contests served for the Greeks as a formal demonstration of social rank parallel to or as an alternative to other outlets in military, political, hunting, and economic competition. In the Greek gymnasium the competitive impulses, mainly those of elite males, were regulated and channelled to specific activities. In the gymnasia men were afforded a space to give rein to the libido, but sexual liaisons were also monitored and regulated by the community. The success of the regulations cannot be inferred from the evidence, but the restrictions continued over the centuries, and apparently so did the reputation of the gymnasium as a sexual hot spot. By the sixth century BCE, the nexus of sport, masculinity, and sexuality was thoroughly integrated into Greek culture through widespread agonistic festivals and gymnasia. Though the venues and formats changed over the centuries, the nexus of male sport remained rooted in Greek states until the late Roman empire. Few cultural constructions of the Greeks were so persistent and successful. Sport in each polis was a way to escape the vicissitudes of daily life, but it also served to control masculine drives with civic sanction. Political and civil strife was not entirely averted, but citizens were offered an occasional game-like diversion that was essentially a non-destructive way to perform masculinity and to watch it being performed. Sport modelled masculine excellence without loss of life or limb, it endorsed a relatively harmless means of allotting honour without vicious public debate, and it fostered civic unity through peaceful social interactions in the gymnasium and stadium. In sociological terms, Greek sport contains in itself divisive, hierarchical aspects, but these are counterbalanced and arguably contained by a stronger force within each polis of democratic 'horizontal' meritocracy (Christesen 2014).

If Greek sport is from its origins a masculine enterprise that fosters an image of manly virtue (*aretē*), then sport for women is modelled primarily on men's sport. It is an epiphenomenon, a secondary occurrence, such as the Heraia at Olympia which formally resembles the men's Olympic foot-race closely. It is beyond this study to sketch out more fully the many non-sporting activities of ancient Greek women that are genuinely and uniquely female, including, in general, physical activities like female participation in rituals and choruses, and their singing, dancing, and weaving. These more commonly female pursuits arguably better represent the core aspects of Greek female identity. Yet the fact that female sport is epiphenomenal to men's does not deny its having its own separate and rich importance in the formation of women's identity. A few examples are mentioned above: the Heraia festival honouring Hera in hopes of a successful marriage; Spartan female athletic training that aims to enhance their childbearing strength; and a girls' contest in the Roman era honouring the empress Livia. Yet the relative paucity of evidence for Greek female sport in material culture and in literature suggests that it is a distant second to male athletics in public recognition.

To what extent does modern sport continue the gender and sexuality practices of the Greeks? Current western sport is largely an invention of the nineteenth and twentieth centuries, in both the private and public spheres. The same masculine domination of sport, the performance of 'manly virtues', and the assimilation to military events can easily be observed, though space here does not permit specifics. Guttmann (1991) offers a good, balanced overview of women's sport from antiquity to the present, demonstrating that women were almost consistently at the margin of the universal sporting scene. As mentioned above, the media attention to and general public spending for women's sports globally has for decades been a consistent index of the lesser interest in watching or reading about women's sport, even though the actual practice of it has increased manifold in the same time. It has been over four decades since the Title IX law of 1972 passed in the US, a comprehensive federal law that prohibits discrimination on the basis of sex in any federally funded education programme or activity. Female participation in sport in US high schools jumped from under 300,000 in 1972 to 3.2 million in 2011; in US NCAA Division I college sports in 2010, women constituted less than 46 per cent of the schools' student athletes, and got about 40 per cent of the funding for coaching and recruiting (Dusenbery and Lee 2012). Sport media networks in the US devote only about 5 to 10 per cent of their coverage to women's sport (Messner 2002: 95). There are of course bursts of interest in women's sports, as has happened in the US when the US women's teams won the world soccer championships in 1999 and again in 2015. But these phenomena are still occasional and unfortunately do not signal broad new interest, as a rule not anywhere internationally.

The twenty-first century is an age of increasing equality for women economically, politically, and socially. Though it is not where it should be in the US or elsewhere, there have been massive strides in the last forty years. Messner has his own suggestions for future improvements with a 'social justice model' allowing broader participation and putting women closer to the male centre, but not by being co-opted into the industry of men's sport nor being ghettoized into something separate (Messner 2002: 152–166). Governments can formalize more just and less exploitative sports, and can require equal funding for women's participation in sports in the educational sector, as Title IX has tried to do. But there persists a general, popular lack of interest on the part of audiences, both male and female, globally, in either watching or following women's sport. This begs the question why so, and again no easy answer is at hand. The Greek model that has partly shaped modern sport shows us that the androcentric model has endured for millennia, and has been tied to that other huge area of continued male predominance, namely fighting wars on the battlefront. Here again, modern forms of warfare are changing and they increasingly allow women to participate in combat. There is a desire to shield women from injury arising from physical violence, but there is also a default image of the fierce soldier as a male. To this extent the Homeric warrior-athlete is an archetype with continuing resonance. The construction of masculinity that we sketched for ancient Greece as a foundational image of the athlete is one that is still very much alive in the Western imagination. This is a cultural image that is more difficult to displace than it is to regulate through requiring equity in funding for sports for both sexes. Women's sport is every bit as compelling to watch as men's, and as challenging as men's to perform well. To the extent that masculinity is a cultural construction in which sport is implicated, it is possible slowly to educate the public to watch and participate with equal interest, as seems to have happened even during the Roman empire. But it will probably be a lengthy process that only gradually alters the trends engrained since Classical antiquity.

REFERENCES

Alipour, S. 2013. 'Will You Still Medal in the Morning? The Real Games in the Olympic Village Will Not Be Televised.' *ESPN The Magazine*, 15 April 2013: http://espn.go.com/olympics/summer/2012/story/_/id/8133052/athletes-spill-details-dirty-secrets-olympic-village-espn-magazine.

Bassi, K. 2003. 'The Semantics of Manliness in Ancient Greece.' In Rosen and Sluiter 2003. 25–58.

Buffière, F. 1980. *Eros adolescent: La pédérastie dans la Grèce antique*. Paris.

Calame, C. 2001. *Choruses of Young Women in Ancient Greece: Their Morphology, Religious Role and Social Functions*, rev. edn. D. Collins and J. Orion, trans. Lanham, MD.

Campbell Warner, P. 2006. *When the Girls Came out to Play: The Birth of American Sportswear*. Amherst.

Christesen, P. 2012. *Sport and Democracy in the Ancient and Modern Worlds*. Cambridge.

Christesen, P. 2014. 'Sport and Democratization in Ancient Greece.' In Christesen and Kyle 2014. 211–235.

Christesen, P. and D. Kyle, eds. 2014. *A Companion to Sport and Spectacle in Greek and Roman Antiquity*. Malden, MA.

Crowther, N. 1980. 'Nudity and Morality: Athletics in Italy.' *CJ* 76.2: 119–123.

Crowther, N. 1982. 'Athletic Dress and Nudity in Greek Athletics.' *Eranos* 80: 163–168

Crowther, N. 2004. *Athletika: Studies on the Olympic Games and Greek Athletics*. Hildesheim.

Davidson, J. 2007. *The Greeks and Greek Love: A Radical Reappraisal of Homosexuality in Ancient Greece*. London.

Dover, K. J. 1989. *Greek Homosexuality*, 2nd edn. Cambridge, MA.

Dusenbery, M. and J. Lee, 'Charts: The State of Women's Athletics, 40 Years after Title IX.' *Mother Jones*. 22 June 2012. http://www.motherjones.com/politics/2012/06/charts-womens-athletics-title-nine-ncaa.

Fantuzzi, M. 2012. *Achilles in Love: Intertextual Studies*. Oxford.

Fisher, N. 1998. 'Gymnasia and the Democratic Values of Leisure.' In *Kosmos: Essays in Order, Conflict, and Community in Classical Athens*. 84–104. P. Cartledge, P. Millet, and S. von Reden, eds. Cambridge.

Fisher, N. 2010. 'Gymnasia and the Democratic Values of Leisure.' In König 2010: 66–86.

Foxhall, L. 2013. *Studying Gender in Classical Antiquity*. Cambridge.

Foxhall, L. and J. Salmon, eds. 1998a. *Thinking Men: Masculinity and its Self-Representation in the Classical Tradition*. London.

Foxhall, L. and J. Salmon, eds. 1998b. *When Men were Men: Masculinity, Power and Identity in Classical Antiquity*. London.

Glass, S. 2002. 'The Greek Gymnasium: Some Problems'. In *The Archaeology of the Olympics*, 2nd edn. 155–173. W. Raschke, ed. Madison, WI.

Goossens, E. and S. Thielemans. 1996. 'The Popularity of Sports Scenes on Attic Black and Red Figure Vases.' *Bulletin Antike Beschaving* 71: 59–94.

Guttmann, A. 1991. *Women's Sports: A History*. New York.

Hall, J. M. 2007. *A History of the Archaic Greek World ca. 1200–479 BCE*. Oxford.

Hawhee, D. 2004. *Bodily Arts: Rhetoric and Athletics in Ancient Greece*. Austin, TX.

Henson Leigh, M. 1974. 'The Evolution of Women's Participation in the Summer Olympic Games, 1900–1948.' Doctoral dissertation, Ohio State University.

Hubbard, T. K., ed. 2003a. *Homosexuality in Greece and Rome: A Sourcebook of Basic Documents*. Berkeley.

Hubbard, T. K. 2003b. 'Sex in the Gym: Athletic Trainers and Pedagogical Pederasty.' *Intertexts* 7: 1–27.

Jenkins, I. 2012. *The Discobolos*. British Museum Objects in Focus. London.

Kilmer, M. F. 1993. *Greek Erotica*. London.

König, J. ed. 2010. *Greek Athletics*. Edinburgh Readings on the Ancient World. Edinburgh.

Kurke, L. 1993. 'The Economy of Kudos.' In *Cultural Poetics in Archaic Greece: Cult, Performance, Politics.* 131–163. C. Dougherty and L. Kurke, eds. Cambridge.

Kyle, D. G. 1984. 'Solon and Athletics.' *Ancient World* 9: 99–102.

Kyle, D. 2015. *Sport and Spectacle in the Ancient World*, 2nd edn. Malden, MA.

Lambert, M. 2004. Book review: 'T. K. Hubbard (ed.): *Homosexuality in Greece and Rome. A Sourcebook of Basic Documents.*' *CR* 54.2: 439–441.

Lear, A. 2008. '*Kalos* Inscriptions.' In *Images of Ancient Greek Pederasty: Boys were their Gods.* 164–173. A. Lear and E. Cantarella, eds. London.

Lear, A. 2014. 'Eros and Greek Sport.' In Christesen and Kyle 2014: 246–257.

Lee, H. M. 1988. '*SIG* 802: Did Women Compete against Men in Greek Athletic Festivals?' *Nikephoros* 1:103–117.

Lefkowitz, M. R. and M. B. Fant, eds. 2005. *Women's Life in Greece and Rome: A Sourcebook in Translation.* Baltimore.

Mantas, K. 1995. 'Woman and Athletics in the Roman East.' *Nikephoros* 8: 125–144.

McDermott, R., D. Johnson, J. Cowden, and S. Rosen. 2007. 'Testosterone and Aggression in a Simulated Crisis Game.' *Annals of the American Association of Political and Social Science.* 614: 15–33.

McDonnell, M. 1991. 'The Introduction of Athletic Nudity: Thucydides, Plato, and the Vases.' *JHS* 111: 182–193.

McGinnis, L., R. Robinson, and D. Weingarten. 2019. 'More women are Playing Sports. Why is No One Watching?' *CS Monitor* 9 September 2019 https://www.csmonitor.com/The-Culture/2019/0909/More-women-are-playing-sports.-Why-is-no-one-watching

Messner, M. A. 2002. *Taking the Field: Women, Men, and Sports.* Minneapolis.

Miller, S. 2001. *Excavations at Nemea II: The Early Hellenistic Stadium.* Berkeley.

Miller, S. 2012. *Arete: Greek Sports from Ancient Sources*, 3rd edn. Berkeley.

Neils, J. 1994. 'The Panathenaia and Kleisthenic Ideology.' In *The Archaeology of Athens and Attica Under the Democracy.* 151–161. W. D. E. Coulson et al., eds. Oxford.

Ormand, K. 2005. Book Review: '*Andreia: Studies in Manliness and Courage in Classical Antiquity*, ed. R. M. Rosen and I. Sluiter, 2003.' *Phoenix* 59: 379–381.

Osborne, R. 1998. 'Sculpted Men of Athens: Masculinity and Power in the Field of Vision.' In Foxhall and Salmon 1998a: 23–42.

Osborne, R. 2011. *The History Written on the Classical Greek Body.* Cambridge.

Percy, W. A. 1996. *Pederasty and Pedagogy in Archaic Greece.* Urbana, IL.

Pleket, H. W. 1975. 'Games, Prizes, Athletes and Ideology: Some Aspects of the History of Sport in the Greco-Roman World.' *Stadion* (formerly *Arena*) 1: 49–89; reprinted in König 2010: 145–174.

Poliakoff, M. B. 1987. *Combat Sports in the Ancient World.* New Haven.

Pritchard, D. 2013. *Sport, Democracy and War in Classical Athens.* Cambridge.

Remijsen, S. 2015. *The End of Greek Athletics in Late Antiquity.* Cambridge.

Roisman, J. 2005. *The Rhetoric of Manhood: Masculinity and the Attic Orators.* Berkeley.

Rosen, M. and I. Sluiter, eds. 2003. *Andreia: Studies in Manliness and Courage in Classical Antiquity.* Leiden.

Sallares, R. 1991. *The Ecology of the Ancient Greek World.* London.

Scanlon, T. F. 2002. *Eros and Greek Athletics.* New York.

Scanlon, T. F. 2004. 'Homer, The Olympics, and the Heroic Ethos.' In *The Olympic Games in Antiquity: 'Bring Forth Rain and bear Fruit'.* 61–91. Maria Kaïla et al., eds. Athens; reprinted with footnotes added in *Classics@* 13, http://chs.harvard.edu/classics13-scanlon/.

Scanlon, T. F. 2005. 'The Dispersion of Pederasty and the Athletic Revolution in Sixth-century BC Greece.' *Journal of Homosexuality* 49.3/4: 63–85.

Scanlon, T. F. 2008. 'The Heraia at Olympia Revisited.' *Nikephoros* 21: 159–196.

Scanlon, T. F. 2014. 'Racing for Hera: A Girl's Contest at Olympia.' In *Sport in the Greek and Roman Worlds*, vol. 2: *Greek Athletic Identities and Roman Sport and Spectacle*. 108–147. T. F. Scanlon, ed. Oxford.

Shapiro, A. 1992. 'Eros in Love: Pederasty and Pornography in Greece.' In *Pornography and Representation in Greece and Rome*. 53–72. A. Richlin, ed. Oxford.

Siewert, P. 1992. 'The First Olympic Rules.' In *Proceedings of an International Symposium on the Olympic Games, 5–7 September 1988*. 113–117. W. Coulson and H. Kyrieleis, eds. Athens.

Skinner, M. 2014. *Sexuality in Greek and Roman Culture*, 2nd edn. Walden, MA.

Stafford, E. 2013. 'From the Gymnasium to the Wedding: Eros in Athenian Art and Cult.' In *Erôs in Ancient Greece*. 175–208. E. Sanders, C. Thumiger, C. Carey, and E. Lowe, eds. Oxford.

Steiner, D. 1998 'Moving Images: Fifth-Century Victory Monuments and the Athlete's Allure.' *CA* 17: 123–149.

Steiner, D. 2001. *Images in Mind*. Princeton.

Talbert, R. 2009. 'Plutarch's Sparta: *Lieux de mémoire, tous de mémoire*.' In *Athens-Sparta: Contributions to the Research on the History and Archaeology of the Two City-States*. 61–65. N. Kaltsas, ed. Athens.

Van Nijf, O. 2003. 'Athletics, Andreia and the *Askēsis*-Culture in the Roman East.' In Rosen and Sluiter 2003. 263–286.

Van Nortwick, T. 2008. *Imagining Men: Ideals of Masculinity in Ancient Greek Culture*. Westport, CT.

Von Reden, S. 1995. *Exchange in Ancient Greece*. London.

West, A. B. 1928. 'Notes on Achaean Prosopography and Chronology.' *CPh* 23: 258–269.

Winkler, J. J. 1990. *The Constraints of Desire: the Anthropology of Sex and Gender in Ancient Greece*. New York.

Worthington, I. 2006. *Demosthenes: Speeches 60 and 61, Prologues, Letters*. Austin, TX.

CHAPTER 50

....

SEX IN THE ARENA

....

ALISON FUTRELL

FOR centuries, Rome has been imagined as a realm of extremes, an empire in which fabulous power, unfettered by later moral strictures, could realize an astonishing array of pleasures, indulge appetites fed on a global level. A key component of this excess was *surely* their sexual depravity, the institutionalized orgies that overflowed the Forum, the Circus, the Palace, and the Colosseum. Hollywood Technicolor attempted to do it justice: Peter Ustinov's Nero peered owlishly through a green lens at the debauchery made safe for an American general audience by the Hays Code. Changing legal and social standards for the expression of sexual desire and the consumption of explicit creative products have reconfigured modern expectations about sex in the public realm. And in Rome?

The following selectively explores sex in Rome's popular entertainments through specific lenses both analytical and categorial. There is some consideration of gender, the roles played by human beings in any given society that are broadly considered more appropriate for men or for women; sometimes these roles are allocated on the basis of reproduction, but also aligned with perceptions of what the body *can* do, or what it *should* do. In Rome, gender is best understood as a continuum rather than a binary: phenotypically male humans could be feminized for a number of reasons (Edwards 1993: 63–97). There is some effort to investigate spectacularized sexual activity, performed for a mass audience, the evidentiary basis for the imagined Roman orgy. Women as performers, or as the focus of the audience's gaze, are also probed, as are the meanings they may have assigned to the way that performance impacted their gender.

Rome's spectacles were sponsored by political leaders, in order to please, persuade, and woo constituents; to impress spectators with their generosity; to enhance their public reputation; and to secure the social contract underpinning the continuity of the Roman state. A range of performances were organized by the state, from chariot-races to gladiatorial combats, theatrical events and pageants inspired by mythology, from executions to synchronized dances. Much was at stake. Sponsors therefore determined a positive outcome by controlling the actions, the attention, and the perceptions of others. They made the performers commit their bodies to the evocation of desired responses from the audience. That essential ability, the capacity to command and to order, is at the heart of elite masculine authority in Rome; as Aemilius Paulus pointed out, the same proficiency was needed for successful military conquest and for the organization of spectacle (Livy 45.33). This is understood as a male virtue and it has strong sexual overtones.

Those who defer to that power are gendered on the feminine side. This includes certain categories of people that some might find surprising, such as Roman legionaries and gladiators, who both take oaths to submit to discipline, to yield to commands (Walters 1997; Alston 1998). The gladiatorial oath or *sacramentum* notoriously binds a gladiator to let himself be beaten and wounded, thus giving up a free citizen's right to bodily autonomy, reducing him in important ways to the physical vulnerability of the slave (Edwards 1997: 73–75).

Roman spectacle is a highly visible demonstration of gendered authority: the emperor or sponsor, dominating the venue from the focally placed imperial box, represents the far end of masculinity's continuum. His will has contrived the scenarios that play out in the arena. His nod, his slightest gesture, determines the life or death of the performers. He wields the fundamental sword.

In the arena, gladiators' bodies are on display, exposed to the gaze of the masses, swayed by their screams and their demands; the crowd watches them being penetrated. This is how the action was understood from the perspective of elite male Roman tradition (Edwards 1997: 83–85). There were other ways of reading this, of course, and hints of those alternative points of view are embedded in our sources. But this dominant and normative interpretation is apparent in the lion's share of the surviving literature.

GLADIATORS AND GENDER

The gladiator belonged to a category of non-men, inherently subject to the power of the editor of the games, his body physically positioned in the arena below, unable to escape the optimized sightlines of those above him (Walters 1998: 264). Not all gladiators were alike, however; fighters specialized in different armatures, assemblages of weapons and techniques that kept the contest interesting. Usually, gladiators in the same armature were not pitted against each other; instead, 'heavy' and 'light' combinations were paired, each with their assets and disadvantages. One frequent combat set the lightly armed *retiarius* (net-man) against the heavily armoured *secutor* ('follower'), as is depicted in Fig. 50.1.

This is one of several critical moments featured on the Borghese Mosaic, probably representing a particular spectacle, with the participants individually labelled and the outcomes, typically fatal, documented visually and textually. Most of the pairs are like this one: a *retiarius/secutor* combination. Alumnus, the victor, vaunts over his fallen opponent, raising his blood-smeared dagger over Mazicinus, who is meant to be read as lying prostrate on the sands, blood pooling around him. The gladiators wear the *manica* or arm protector, the loin-covering *subligaculum*, belted by the *balteus*, with padded bands or *fasciae* wrapped around the feet and ankles. Mazicinus is covered by the hefty oblong shield of the *secutor* and wears the smooth helmet also typical of that armature. Alumnus as a *retiarius* wears no helmet, although his *galerus* offers some protection to neck and shoulder. His trident lies on the sands to the left; the net is not clearly represented, but is referenced in the net-like surface of Mazicinus' shield.

Aside from the practical utility of the different toolsets, armatures took on a certain social and moral weight as well: not all armatures were equally honourable. In fact, some were coded as specifically dishonorable (i.e. feminized) along gender lines. Seneca bemoans tendencies in his contemporaries to harm virility, to transform masculinity; some men go

FIGURE 50.1. Detail, mosaic with *retiarius* Alumnus, early fourth century CE. Borghese Gallery. SEF/Art Resource, NY.

so far as to 'flee into the offensive or impure part of the gladiatorial school and ... take up a disreputable kind of armature, with which they put their disorder into training' (*Natural Questions* 7.31).

The *retiarius* seems to have been regarded as this distinctively base, unmanned gladiatorial type. Further evidence of this special status can be traced in Juvenal, scattered across three of the *Satires*, his snarky commentaries on first-century urban society in Rome. Juvenal introduces us in *Satire* 2 (117–148) to the young Gracchus, a degraded contemporary representative of an ancient elite family, whose social choices include diverging expressions of gender alignment. One example that Juvenal highlights is shown in the young man's entry into the arena: indeed, when Gracchus hit the sands, he took up the trident, becoming a *retiarius* in motion. In *Satire* 8, Juvenal reinforces his assessment of the *retiarius* as lowest in the hierarchy of gladiatorial armatures (199–210). Gracchus is 'the disgrace of the city' (200) because of his specific selections: he scorns the shield, the blade, and the face-covering helmet, i.e. the weaponry of heavily armed fighters like the *murmillo* or the *secutor*. Instead Gracchus brandishes the trident and spins his weighted net, face bared to the crowd. Some practical consequences of this hierarchy are hinted at in the 'Oxford' manuscript fragment interpolated into *Satire* 6; the *lanista* in charge of the gladiatorial school houses the *retiarius*, the 'naked' fighter who wields trident and net, separately from other gladiators, thus demonstrating a 'better' and 'purer' sensibility. This parallels Seneca's mention of quarters notorious for their impurity (Oxford 7–13; Braund 1996: 159–160; Gunderson 1996: 145–146; Williams 1999: 140–141, 249–250, 364; Carter 2008: 113–115, 120–126; Courtney 2013: 118–122, 263–266, 364–365).

Why the net-men? Why perceive this armature as 'degraded'? Juvenal does seem intent on the weaponry and its meaning and indeed, the *retiarius* differs in this way from the others. The *secutor*, as represented on the Borghese Mosaic, is equipped with sword, shield, and helmet; so are the majority of the armatures. (As indeed are Rome's legions.) The *retiarius* would thus lack some of the potent resonance of Rome's martial culture. And admittedly, on a basic level, the trident lacks the overtly phallic quality of the sword, a weapon designed for thrusting penetration. This may be an important factor in the *retiarius'* particularly diminished masculinity.

Instead of weapons of war, the *retiarius'* arena toolbox is, literally, a toolbox; he wields the tools of a fisherman, a manual labourer. There was a long tradition in the ancient Mediterranean of elite contempt for those who worked with their hands: they were *banausoi*, 'mechanicals', who bent their bodies to scrabble for sustenance. This deformed the physique, literally bringing it lower to the ground; the body was also feminized by this degrading work, toil inappropriate, perhaps, for a citizen (Xenophon, *Economics* 4.2–3; Aristotle, *Politics* 1278). The social standing of a fisherman, in particular, was low; his labour was considered unskilled, rendered for poverty-level returns (Plautus, *Rudens* 283–296; Oppian, *Fishing* 1.36). Worse, the long hours, the scrambling over rocks, the endurance in bad weather, still might not result in a good catch; the fisherman's life was believed to be burdened with unproductive and exhausting toil (Petronius, *Satyricon* 3; Plautus, *Rudens* 898–899; Silius Italicus, *Punic War* 5.581; Corcoran 1963: 101–102).

Juvenal references the 'nudity' of the *retiarius* (Oxford 12), a descriptor that merits some consideration. In what sense are these gladiators particularly naked? In Fig. 50.1, Alumnus wears the same belted loincloth, the same padded shin protectors, the same armguard as the *secutor* standing next to him. The main distinction lies in the face: the *retiarius* wears no helmet.

The face, particularly the eyes and the eyebrows, was understood as a main indicator of emotion, of sadness, pity, contempt, love, and hatred; here were revealed as well the character and consciousness of the individual (Pliny, *Natural History* 11.51, 54). The *retiarius* was thus conceivably better able to woo the crowd, could potentially win their support and empathy and enhance his chances of success in a way that a competitor whose humanity was thoroughly concealed by a helmet could not; Alumnus' direct gaze in Fig. 50.1 still engages the viewer, even after all these hundreds of years. On the other hand, the face could also reveal an unidealized truth behind the discipline and focus required of the best gladiators; *retiarii* were thus at a significant disadvantage in maintaining the appearance of courage and selflessness that was demanded by the crowd (Edwards 2007: 59–63). Their enhanced risk of involuntary negative emotional reactions may be why Claudius insisted on watching the dying faces of certain *retiarii*; focus broken by an accidental stumble brought their pain to the cruel attention of the emperor (Suetonius, *Claudius* 34).

Reasons for the segregation of *retiarii* alleged by Juvenal may be traced in the context of that passage, embedded as it is in Juvenal's diatribe about the polluting qualities of wavering gender performances, the social and moral taint carried by those whose movements, clothing, expressions, vocalizations, and penetrative sexual practices veer from the normative gender binary idealized in conservative Roman tradition. Many Romans believed that the way the body moved was an indicator for the spirit within; Seneca suggests that shamelessness can be detected by paying close attention to small signs, such as the gait, the movement of the hand, the turning of the eye (*Letters* 52.12). Cicero also registers the importance of scrutinizing the deportment of fellow Romans, as external markers like posture and gesture would reveal whether an individual deserved respect or contempt; the honourable man must project propriety from face and form, must avoid the effeminate (*On Duties* 1.128–129). Members of the ruling class secured their dominance through performance, displaying in public spaces a body in motion that was coded as 'superior', 'virtuous', 'dignified', and 'manly'. Their pace was stately and measured, the torso kept still and straight, the arms close to the body. Rapid motion, of hands or eyes or feet, was to be avoided. Visible strain or exertion signalled that control was out of reach (Corbeill 2002: 185–191, 198–202; Gleason 1990: 399–400, 408). By these measures, movement routinely deployed by the *retiarius* would be accorded very different meanings.

Distinctively, the net-man attacked from a distance, circling his opponent, spinning and throwing the net; indeed, to be effective the *retiarius* cannot close with his foe in using either *rete* or trident. These circling steps and shifting balance were more characteristic of a dancer, a prancing *saltatrix* or a mincing, effeminate *cinaedus*, the latter specifically connected with a range of gender deviance with social and political valence (Corbeill 2002: 194–196; Taylor 1997: 338–340). Fast-paced agility was an essential asset of this lightweight armature; speed, however, marked the movements of slaves and on the battlefield revealed cowardice (Quintilian, *Institutes of Oratory* 11.3.112). For Juvenal, speed is a specific point of criticism of Gracchus (*Satire* 2.44, 8.206). Swift movement also led to fast breathing, a gaping mouth that distorted the face in a manner undignified and unbecoming (Cicero, *On Duties* 1.131). The technique of the *secutor*, in contrast, was based on calculated forward movement, as he literally followed his opponent. The arms were kept close to the body, to defend against attack and to maximize the power of the thrust, with either shield or sword. The *secutor* would track, externally, much more closely with the comportment that read as traditionally masculine.

To be sure, not everyone shared the focused concerns of the aristocratic minority; the net-men had their fans, as individuals and as a type. This approval registered as sexual attraction as well, be they ever so deviant in the eyes of some. Famously, several graffiti at Pompeii tout the sexual dominance of the *retiarius* Crescens, the 'master of the dolls in the night', the 'master of the girls' (*CIL* 4.4353, 4356, 8915).

SEX AS SPECTACLE

A sex-saturated production was presented under imperial auspices during the reign of Nero, organized in the summer of 64 CE, to share with the people the emperor's private pleasures. Tacitus describes the event (*Annals* 15.36), designating this as a representative sample of Nero's excesses and abuse of the principate. Tigellinus, Nero's chief henchman and Praetorian Praefect, organized this as a water-borne feast; an ornately outfitted pontoon, bedecked with the luxurious trappings appropriate to Nero's refined tastes, was launched on the Stagnum Agrippae, the artificial lake just west of Agrippa's Baths on the Campus Martius. The open-air spaces of the Baths were reconfigured as groves, inhabited by exotic birds and beasts; the pool was stocked with marine animals, creating a sort of wilderness in the midst of the city. Tigellinus also removed social constraints in this space; the barge was towed by *exoleti*, adult men whose flexible sexual skills primarily qualified them for this responsibility. On opposite sides of the water feature were two groups of women, displayed in defiance of social expectations: on one flank, hidden inside a *lupanaria* or brothel, were high-born women assembled for the evening, the type of women who might normally be guests at such banquets. Across from them were prostitutes, their bodies naked, shamelessly cavorting in the open air, instead of skulking in the seamier parts of town. Obscene gestures and movements could be seen, illuminated by lamps that turned day into night as the music rang out.

Dio Cassius' later version of the event intensifies the sexually transgressive impression of the banquet (Dio Cassius, *Epitome* 62.15). A mass of beautiful women, he says, have been brought poolside, including slaves and freeborn, prostitutes, plebeians, elite ladies, virgin girls, and mature matrons, all available for sexual use by Nero's guests, men also drawn from all stations in society. In this telling, the party breaks down into a deadly riot of debauchery marked especially by violations across status lines.

Accounts of the event emphasize the decadence of Nero's court, his wasteful expenditure of resources, his disrespect for traditional Roman order. Some of this critique is of long standing in Roman polemic; similar rhetoric about hubristic leadership, about elites trying to remake nature in their arrogance, was marshalled by contemporaries during the late republic (Woodman 1992: 177). Like other youthful emperors, Nero's public image portrays a less traditional Roman masculinity and his habits, as various authors allege, cross into behaviours that many identified as soft, self-indulgent, undisciplined, feminine. On the other hand, one can recognize Nero's preference for styles of authority routinized in the eastern Mediterranean, established by the Hellenistic kings of earlier generations. Indeed, this event recalls the leisurely recreation of Ptolemaic kings, well known for their extravagant ceremonial barges and palaces that contained pleasure groves and menageries (Strabo, *Geography* 17.8–10; Athenaeus, *Dinner Sophists* 5.204F, 14.654C; Woodman 1992: 180–183; Thompson 2013). Similar facilities could, of course, be found in the Bay of Naples area, and even closer to Rome: Caligula, Nero's uncle, cruised in two large and well-appointed vessels on Lake Nemi.

The spectacle element, staged to be viewed from the emperor's barge, involved rehearsed movements and gestures of enticement, performed to musical accompaniment and lit to effect; the sex workers hired for the performance were visibly nude, as Tacitus notes. Did the show get raunchier than this? And the noblewomen? Conscription of high-born ladies into performances, inappropriate to their status, is an accusation levelled against Nero and other 'bad' emperors elsewhere. Dio's account certainly details sexual assaults against elite (and non-elite) women, but his abbreviated surviving text does not suggest these are intended as shows.

SEX AND ANIMALS

Nero arranged for a display of bestiality in the arena (Coleman 1990: 68–69; Welch 2007: 146–147). What the audience saw was a bull penetrating a wooden heifer, like the one constructed by Daedalus for doomed Queen Pasiphae in the story. They were told that a woman was in-side, but she was apparently not visible. Indeed, Suetonius indicates some scepticism among the crowd: 'many of the spectators believed' that the human Pasiphae re-enactor was there (*Nero* 12); others, presumably, did not. The spectacle context may be significant: this was one of a series of vignettes presented by a troupe of pyrrhic dancers in Nero's deluxe tem-porary arena, built in 57 CE at great expense in the Campus Martius (Beacham 1999: 202–203). The structure housed sensational special effects, intended to awe the audience and to provide for their lavish comfort and enjoyment. 'Pasiphae' and the bull, along with the flight of Icarus, may be among the ingenious technology produced by Nero's engineers (Seneca, *Letters* 88.22, 95.15). Though a catastrophic mechanical failure doomed the Icarus per-former, this myth-flavoured event seems designed to impress attendees with the scale of his world-building rather than so much to titillate (Elsner 1994).The games were also marked by some of Nero's signature status transgression, as he conscripted hundreds of senators and equestrians to participate in the armed combats (Edwards 1997: 85–90). Suetonius points out, however, that the emperor had no one killed, not even criminals (*Nero* 12).

Pasiphae's tale was re-enacted in more lurid and deadly form during the inaugural spectacles organized for the Flavian Amphitheatre, as the sexual joining of the bull and the Cretan queen was reconfigured as one of multiple executions that literalized gruesome episodes from mythology (Coleman 1990: 63–64; Coleman 2006: 62–68; Welch 2007: 145–147). That said, we have few details about the condemned woman; no name is left to us, no notion of the nature of her offence. It seems that she was exposed to the view of spectators, unlike the Neronian event; as Martial says, 'we have seen' (*vidimus*) (Martial, *Book of Spectacle* 6). Martial's abbreviated epigrams take a formulaic approach to this type of event, hailing them as marvels commanded by the emperor: amazing legends of yesteryear come to life in his staging and special effects. The audience is shocked and yet believes, and both reactions are important.

The 'shock' (and other emotions) generated by the graphic realism of these reenactments was a major part of the incentive to present them. Roman theatrical tastes seem to be shifting toward the sensational and hyperreal in the later first century CE, reflecting perhaps audi-ence preferences for exposure to darker features of the human experience. The arena, with its regularized element of capital punishment, offered a distinct opportunity to capitalize on that drive toward intense encounters by providing 'real' suffering and death, rather than imitation.

The mythological referent also provided a meaningful framing device for the audience, creating memory more effectively than the shock value alone, through association with com-munal narratives that linked spectators together. There was some moral value transmitted as well; the original Pasiphae's passion for the bull was not motivated by an extreme focus of her particular sexual desires, but rather inflicted on her as divine punishment. In the arena, the emperor, represented as earthly agent of righteous ire, could benefit from the salutary reminder. The shared narrative reinforced the restoration of shared values that had been shaken by disruptive criminality.

Public punishment aims to disempower the criminal, however it may be shaped. Amphitheatrical penalties enhanced this effect through the visible, extended suffering inflicted on the condemned. Application of the mythic narrative in the arena would in-crease the hubristic quality of the criminal, on the one hand, while likewise diminishing the individualized context of their crime, the specific motivations, and impact on society.

Instead, the focus is on their failure, often with an innovative and bloody twist (Coleman 1990: 69).

The prominence of these 'fatal charades' in Martial's contemporary text may be no co-incidence. Welch suggests that this kind of execution is developed under the Flavians spe-cifically for the new venue of the Colosseum; what had previously been only simulated in mime or other theatrical settings, now was reified, visibly, within the all-encompassing amphitheatrical ambience (Welch 2007: 145–147). The Pasiphae story may also link us to specific image construction on the part of the Flavians, embedded in the contrast between the Neronian enactment and the version at Titus' dedicatory events, suggesting that Nero's games, in which 'not even criminals' were killed, were a mark of his Hellenized stance to-ward performance and toward empire. Nero was all show. Titus' executions were meant as a political corrective, their intensity giving them a Roman moral and cultural flavour that would enhance the public image of the new Flavian dynasty. In Titus' amphitheatrical uni-verse, criminals received due punishments and the legendary past came to life, or death, as the case may be.

Another account of a Pasiphae simulation enfolded into public spectacle can be found in Apuleius' second-century CE novel *The Golden Ass* (10.17–34); here, the protagonist, Lucius, is transformed into an ass, whose misadventures take him eventually to Corinth. His owner there, Thiasus, was a candidate for the city's chief executive magistrate and organized a set of games, combining gladiatorial bouts, synchronized dances, and elaborate pageantry, to sway the voters to his election. He learns of Lucius-the-ass's remarkable (and lucrative) skills in putting on improvised shows of human behaviour; these had recently extended to include the mimicry of bedsports, on hire to an elite matron who, captivated by his tricks, yearned ardently to become Lucius' 'asinine Pasiphae' (*Golden Ass* 10.19).

The Golden Ass is, of course, fictional; it is, however, generally understood to be a fairly authentic depiction of day-to-day life in the Roman provinces, transformations into quad-rupedal ungulates aside. A notable shift here has to do with the high-born lady, Lucius' bed-room hook-up. Apuleius devotes some description to the specific arrangements made to ease the interaction: the balsam oil liberally deployed by the woman, along with carefully placed cushions, soft covers, perfume, and mood lighting. She takes the initiative in rousing the donkey to performance, caressing him and breathing honeyed phrases in his ears, urging him on to the culmination of the process (*The Golden Ass* 10.21–22). In other words, the author presents this as a risky but survivable activity for both participants. Lucius, who is the first-person narrator of the novel, is both excited and terrified in this encounter, lest his brutal clumsiness be fatal to his partner and have him condemned to the beasts at his owner's show.

Inspired by these successes, Thiasus decides to add an animal–human sex show compo-nent to his games. He encounters some difficulty in adding the new event to his planned spectacle; he cannot book the woman's part. The lady's respectable status precludes her legal performance in public spectacle. Thiasus, therefore, acquires from the governor a crim-inal, one *damnata ad bestias*. This condemned woman, we are informed, manifestly merits the death penalty, having been driven by misplaced jealousy to murder her husband, her daughter, and her secret sister-in-law, along with her poison supplier and his wife. The sordid nature of the crime, involving as it did the betrayal of family bonds and the killing of innocents, was thought to merit a truly terrible punishment, something worse than execu-tion (*Golden Ass*, 10.28), hence an elaborate wedding to be staged and the murderer joined in connubial intimacy with an ass, indeed, with Lucius.

The protagonist donkey is far more concerned about the impact this notorious exposure will have on him. Lucius articulates the messages of this particular type of sexualized narrative execution: the forced copulation, played out in public view, conveys intense shame upon a woman whose nefarious character represents a terrifying source of contamination (*Golden Ass* 10.34). Lucius, however, perceives himself as the primary sufferer of pollution and shame. He's also especially afraid of being killed: that some ferocious beast, sent in to end her, will not be able to recognize the innocence of her unfortunate bedmate. He is thus oblivious to his own role as the penetrative tool of highly gendered coercive political power (Coleman 1990: 64). Indeed, Connors suggests that this is the function of Lucius' transformation into animal form: to experience first-hand the vulnerability to Roman power that profoundly shapes the lives of those not protected by status, wealth, and class (Connors 2008: 177–178).

How often did imperial authority deploy sexual assault by animals to carry out capital penalties? A number of terracotta lamps that depict women abed with equine partners may suggest some regularity for these productions (Welch 2007: 146). On the other hand, they may represent the popularity of the story of Lucius; Greek texts survive that parallel Apuleius' telling of the carnal misadventures of the man-turned-ass. Then too, the challenges presented by arranging performances that involve sexual congress between humans and animals likely disincentivized too frequent appearances in the arena (Coleman 2006: 65–66).

There is interesting evidence connecting animal sexual performances to the early career of the empress Theodora, a controversial figure who rose from humble roots to tremendous power at the side of her husband, Justinian I (reigned 527–565 CE). The specific evidence is a hostile source, Procopius' *Secret History*, a text which emerged after the deaths of the imperial pair and represents them quite differently from the histories Procopius published while they still lived. That said, rumours about Theodora's unconventional backstory seem to have been circulating during her lifetime, prior to the composition of *Secret History* (Evans 2002: 16–19; Potter 2015: 25–26).

Secret History fits into a pattern of political invective, aimed at undermining an emperor's political authority by suggesting he cannot control his natural subordinates, in the family and household; a Roman elite whose wife and children stray beyond the bounds of decent behaviour obviously cannot provide proper leadership in the political realm. Procopius' Theodora certainly evades Justinian's control, demonstrating the impropriety of a woman holding such power by her habit of inverting the ideals of womanly virtue. Theodora does private things in public (like the sex acts) and, behind closed doors, works in secret, shamelessly deploying her sexual wiles to usurp the decisions and powers that should be in the hands of public officials, working for the public good (Brubaker 2004: 89). Worse, she sets a model for other women; soon all the matrons followed Theodora's path, becoming abusers of their husbands' trust in pursuing their own sordid and selfish ends (Brubaker 2004: 92). Whether or not Procopius' allegations are true, Theodora is hardly the only sixth-century woman of influence tarnished by lurid stories of murder and seduction; indeed, the stories follow a fairly predictable pattern used against women in the political sphere.

In book nine, Procopius turns to Theodora's youth. The story goes that the empress began her life as the daughter of Acacius, the Bear Keeper for the Greens entertainment faction in Constantinople. When the family encountered economic difficulties, her mother started her three daughters on a stage career; like many others, Procopius elides the theatre with prostitution, dropping allegations about Theodora's appetite for abundant penetration and her lack of discrimination in selecting clients. He also offers some details about her experience in public performance: Theodora joined a theatrical troupe, demonstrating a special talent for mime. Theodora's use of humour is key to her rising success: she was good at imitation and skilled at whacking her fellow performers with sticks, while being bonked on the head in return. She was known for her comically exaggerated hip-wiggling and penchant for lifting her skirts, to 'reveal feminine secrets, both front and back' (*Secret History* 9.14), inspiring great hilarity in the spectators. A particularly famous sketch of hers skirted the edge of the legal limits: performers were required to wear at least a *subligaculum* on stage and hers was apparently the slimmest of loin ribbons. Dressed in that, Theodora would lean way back (she was known for her flexibility, especially her backbends) while an attendant scattered grains of barley on the 'calyx of the passion flower' (9.21); a trained goose then nibbled the grains, one by one, from her body. A strange performance, says Procopius, in which she gloried without a blush (9.22). Her fame grew and she soon caught the eye of powerful men.

How shall we understand this? Was the future empress a fowl Pasiphae? Did the young Theodora perform live sex acts on stage, with a goose? Probably not, or at least not with the primary intent to provoke a libidinous charge.

Theodora was a professional mime, performing in a deeply rooted theatrical genre that improvised comic farces with standardized plots and standardized targets for their humour, larded with ludicrously exaggerated stage violence, farts, and chamber pots. Plot parodied mythological episodes, for example. The Adultery Mime milked the tension between a young wife and her older husband; the Jealous Mistress variant emphasized the female owner's desire for the male slave. Dialogue in mime was fast and clever, with plenty of play on words and innuendo; verbal byplay was a skill in which Theodora had some talent (Webb 2008: 118–119; Procopius, *Secret History* 9.13).

Procopius was not alone in his reductive presentation of mime; for centuries, critics had derided the genre, fixating on its lurid content, supposedly meant to inflame the lusts of unwary spectators. The performers likewise were highly suspect; this was not acting, these were sexual deviants, living out their true selves onstage (White 2013: 50–51). Choricius of Gaza wrote his *Defence of the Mimes* to challenge this pervasive view. He emphasized the professionalism involved: the individual performer trained in multiple roles, multiple character types, each with different social backgrounds and motivations. The actor studied vocal technique and projection, along with dance, movement, and how to persuade with a look (*Defence of the Mimes* 124).

Beyond the castigation of performers, Choricius addresses the social value of mime. Because of their brevity, because of their improvisational structure, mimes could be more responsive to current events. Their plots could serve as vehicles for the exposure and probing of social and political tensions (Webb 2008: 129–131). The humour depended on exposing the human truth behind social hierarchy, revealing that the power of the *paterfamilias* is not, in fact, all-encompassing, that the dutiful wife is an unchaste schemer. It arose from undermining, in the comic world, the coercive violence that underpinned imperial power: fists and clubs bounce off stage bodies, indeed, they bounced off the body of the young Theodora (Procopius, *Secret History* 9.14; Webb 2008: 119–123).

The Adultery Mime was more than sexy titillation; it enacted the subversion of social and political order, revealing that all parties were hip-deep in trickery and counter-trickery, deceit, physical flexibility, inspiration, and 'cunning intelligence' (Webb 2008: 132–136). Consider the Mythological Adultery plotline of Leda and the Swan, or not-Leda and the

Goose. This is a story about submission to divine power, about women's ambition, about the unequal power distribution between sexual partners. It's also about the resilience and adaptation necessary to survive the human experience.

How naked were Theodora's shows? How sexy? The surviving evidence is pretty thin and open to interpretation; a modern translator may approach the ancient text of Procopius a bit differently from their counterpart in the nineteenth century. Nudity for example: was Theodora clad only in a G-string? Maybe more like a bikini? Boy shorts? Even if she was naked, is the naked body all she was? Choricius points out that actors merely living their authentic degradation on stage would not delight and engage the audience's humanity as mime clearly did; as, indeed, Theodora clearly did (*Defence of the Mimes* 80; White 2013: 55–56).

WOMEN IN THE ARENA

Women performed in public spectacle. A handful of mentions document their participation in a small number of imperial events in Rome, inserted into larger texts for different narrative ends. Elite women are pressured into participation by a boundary-breaking Nero (Tacitus, *Annals* 14.14; 15.32; Dio Cassius 61.17). Women menace fearsome beasts and cavort as Nereids among the marvels of the age at the Colosseum's inauguration (Suetonius, *Titus* 7.7; Dio Cassius 66.25; Martial, *Book of Spectacle* 7, 8, 30). They appear alongside other distinctive participants in Domitian's night-time games, the dark events of a dark *Dominus* (Suetonius, *Domitian* 4; Dio Cassius 67.4). Other fragmentary and allusive evidence may suggest that outside the centre of empire, female *venatores* and combatants were, if not precisely common sights, then not utterly extraordinary either (Brunet 2004; Briquel 1992; Cébeillac-Gervasoni and Zevi 1976; Frei-Stolba 2000; McCullough 2008; Schäfer 2001; Vesley 1998).

Women were likely more consistent performers in the interstices of spectacle, as musicians and dancers creating the pageants and displays that filled out the programme. They appear in this role on the lower range of the marble base of the Obelisk of Theodosius, erected as part of the central barrier of the Hippodrome of Constantinople around 390 CE (Fig. 50.2). The south-eastern face of the monument depicts the emperor in the *kathisma*, the imperial loge at the games; he is the centre of attention, represented as substantially taller than anyone else, in recognition of his overweening authority. Behind him rises the palace that adjoins the circus structure. Flanked by sons and courtiers, Theodosius holds a wreath ready to declare the victor, in circus games as in the Roman world. Two rows of smaller-scale sub-elites, depicted primarily as a series of heads, sit underneath the balustrade of the prestige seating, sharing the experience of the games with their social superiors in the ordered hierarchy dominated by Theodosius. Below them, and at an even smaller scale, are female dancers, flautists, harpists, and organists; clearly captured mid performance, each figure is carefully individuated, in posture, movement, and features. This is the side of the monument that faced the actual imperial box and seems the most carefully rendered, the most attentively detailed, of the four (Safran 1993).

Women did, however, enter the arena as combatants. Intriguing details can, perhaps, be extracted from the second-century relief from Halicarnassus, now in the British Museum, that hails the achievement of a pair of female gladiators (Fig. 50.3).

FIGURE 50.2. Dancers and musicians on the Theodosian Obelisk Base, late fourth century CE. Vanni Archive/Art Resource, NY.

Facing off against each other are two women. Each grips a *gladius*, point forward, in her right hand, her right arm fully protected by a *manica*. Each wears a rectangular shield on the left, protecting the leading side; the left leg wears a greave as well. This is the armature of a 'heavy'. Each is clad only in a belted loincloth, a version of the *subligaculum* worn by gladiators. They stand on a platform, their helmets behind them on the ground. On the platform are inscribed, apparently, their arena names: Amazon, Achillia. Above them is the Greek word *apeluthesan*, 'they were released'; in the bout celebrated by this small monument, Amazon and Achillia were both granted *missio*, in recognition, perhaps, of their equal technical skill and effort (Coleman 1990; Robert 1940: 188–190). It is clear from their posture that neither was disarmed, neither yielded in submission. The performance names selected by each woman point to narratives that legitimize and complicate the gendered meanings of their actions in the arena.

One referenced the female-dominated society of the Amazons, famed for their abilities in war, both fascinating and thoroughly alien, functioning, in many ways, as the polar opposite of normative human behaviour (DuBois 1982; Tyrrell 1984). This ancient imagined people was located in legendary interactions with heroes of days long gone, in the distant time of early foundations and the Trojan War. The Amazons were thought to live on the peripheries of the known world, far to the east or south. Some sources claim they dwelt apart from men

FIGURE 50.3. Relief of female gladiators from Halicarnassus, second century CE. British Museum. © The Trustees of the British Museum/Art Resource, NY.

and contacted them only for reproduction (Strabo 11.5). Others depict an inversion of gender norms known elsewhere in the Mediterranean: Amazon women were leaders and citizens, while their men lived quietly at home, barred from participation in war and politics (Diodorus Siculus 3.53). In some accounts, they mark their bodies in dedication to their lifestyle, cutting or searing to remove one or both breasts in order to better wield their weapons; this excision of a key sexual feature is alleged to be the etymology of their Greek name, the *a-mazos*, the breastless. Representations of the Amazons often depict them in abbreviated hunting tunics, well suited to their dynamic mobility, with, notably, no sign of body modification. As a people, they gloried in battle, their queen excelling above all others (Diodorus Siculus 2.45; Apollonius Rhodius, *Argonautica* 2.989–991). One such queen, Penthesileia, led her people to fight on the side of Troy, where a fateful showdown took place between Achilles and the Amazon leader.

Achilles was famously the bravest of the Greeks at Troy, the protagonist of Homer's *Iliad* whose rage at the violation of his honour presents a terrible threat to Greek success. In addition to his well-known martial valour and impressive warrior skill set, stories of Achilles also preserve a motility of gender. His divine mother, Thetis, in an attempt to protect him from the doom awaiting him at Troy, hid the youthful Achilles among the women of King Lycomedes of Skyros, disguised as a beautiful girl. His attraction to weaponry eventually exposed the true masculinity of Achilles, in a stratagem devised by wily Odysseus. Among the trinkets and gewgaws brought as gifts to the royal ladies of Skyros, Odysseus hid weapons; when his men outside blew horns to simulate an attack, Achilles leapt to take up arms and was revealed.

Achilles' coming of age was a popular literary topic in the Roman period, with an extended treatment of the Skyros episode in Statius' unfinished epic *Achilleid* (1.25–396). Achilles, to become the hero of destiny, undergoes an extended period of destabilized gender. Thetis tells Lycomedes that her 'daughter' has been reared as an Amazon; the time on Skyros will cultivate the domestic habits appropriate to respectable women. Even before he takes on the accoutrements of women, Achilles is said to possess a feminized physicality: he has a sweetness of form, shining hair, the look of his mother in his face, characteristics of both male and female visibly perceptible in him (Statius, *Achilleid* 1.158–165; McAuley 2010: 43). Clothing further enhances the effect, softening his neck and shoulders like heated wax (Statius, *Achilleid* 1.325–327; McAuley 2010: 45–47). Apparel, gait, posture, gesture here re-make the inner reality of Achilles, even as his *virtus*, his core masculinity, resists the transition. His female identity reaches a crisis point during a set of women-only Bacchant rituals, when the gorgeously arrayed 'female' Achilles, stunningly beautiful, takes a crucial step toward sexual maturity, and the realization of his heroic destiny, with his rape of Deiadamia (Statius, *Achilleid* 1.609–618; Cyrino 1998: 235–237).

One of the most frequently depicted moments in the Achilles myth is his duel against the Amazon Penthesileia outside Troy; as he delivered the mortal blow, he fell in love. The instant is immortalized in the ancient artistic repertoire as a lovers' clinch, eyes locking as Achilles' sword or spear penetrates the falling Amazon; each connects profoundly and horrifyingly briefly to their other self. There's a slight shift in the Roman period, with a number of pieces focusing on the moment after Penthesileia's death and Achilles' realization of agonizing loss. Achilles was simultaneously Amazon lover, Amazon slayer, and a remnant 'Amazon' himself. Achillia and Amazon, in second-century Halicarnassus, were spared the painful fate of their eponymous forebears, even as their experience found, perhaps, some resonance in the legendary past.

Female Christian martyrs, condemned on the capital charge of Christianity, were women whose arena performances had significant social impact on the development of early Christian identity. Their stories were circulated among Christian communities, who perceived them as models of faith, strength, and authority. Their female bodies and their defiance of gender normatives are central features of these texts and fundamental to their importance for the target audience.

Blandina was caught up in a persecution that took place in Lugdunum (modern Lyons) in 177 CE (Eusebius, *Church History* 5.1). Blandina was a female slave, a person who would have no autonomy, no agency at all in the Roman system, her body constantly vulnerable to exploitation and use by others. The endurance required to sustain such an existence is reconfigured here as masculine and as worthy of honour: what is considered worthless and despicable among humans is truly worthy of great glory (5.1.17; Shaw 1996). Her strength astonishes her torturers, who admit that they have been worn out by their efforts. Her body is broken and mangled, but she is insensible to the pain, drawing strength from her repeated simple confession of faith. The physical torments continue in the arena, where she is eventually mounted on a post, assuming the form of Christ crucified. This is described as a literal transformation and a sign of divine promise for her fellow martyrs (5.1.41). Blandina's female body is tiny and weak, and physically she has no significance in Roman society. Her faith, however, has made it a vessel for powerful cosmic truth (Shaw 1996: 307–309)

The *Passion of Perpetua and Felicitas* focuses on a smaller persecution enacted in Carthage around March of 203 CE. The text relates that Perpetua, identified as a respectable, educated, well-born young woman, is herself the author of the central first-person portion of the narrative, purportedly written by her own hand while incarcerated and awaiting her formal hearing and execution. The *Passion* as a whole pays much attention to female social roles and relationships, to the bodily experiences of female human beings. Both martyrs reshape and reject the normative feminine, asserting for themselves a different gender role in preparation for their entry into the arena.

Perpetua progressively sheds all ties to her social identity, removing herself from her obligations as mother, wife, and daughter. Physically, she is positioned as male: she is the stable entity repeatedly supplicated by her increasingly feminized father, who lowers himself before her. He weeps and rages, losing his emotional control, claiming the family's safety and well-being depend on *her* choices, not his (Cobb 2008: 94, 97–101; Gold 2011: 239–241). The tension climaxes at Perpetua's public hearing, when her father is publicly shamed, beaten on the order of the procurator (*Passion* 6.5; Cooper 2013: 204). She pities him, but remains distant, constant in her Christian adherence.

Perpetua's sacred authority increases, as she takes on the power to request visions and to affect the spiritual realm. This culminates in her fourth vision, set in an amphitheatre that serves as a spiritual precursor of the earthly arena to which they are condemned. Christ looms above it as the heavenly *lanista*. Perpetua is stripped down and 'made masculine' to take on the Devil (*Passion* 10.7), achieving victory as a *pankratiast* in a cosmic showdown against forces of evil. She realizes that this spiritual combat is the fight that matters, that what happens in the arena at Carthage will have no effect on the true combat that she has already won.

Felicitas was a slave and eight months pregnant at the time of her arrest, but determined to share the arena with her fellow Christians. The group prayed that this be possible, groaning together in hopeful anticipation of early labour (*Passion* 15.4). When the pains began, Felicitas committed to the suffering of a difficult childbirth, embracing the pain as a gateway to the joy of martyrdom, where she would be released from the suffering of her female body. The parallels are made explicit in the text in gendered terms: Felicitas moves from one bloodbath to another, from *obstetrix* ('midwife') to *retiarius* (*Passion* 18.3).

The comportment of Perpetua as the condemned enter the venue is a challenge to audience assumptions: she walks with dignity and confidence, not like a criminal. The power of her gaze, we are told, diminishes the capacity of the spectators to humiliate her, *damnata* though she may be. She is now the *matrona* of Christ, the plaything of God (*Passion* 18.2; Shaw 1993: 4). Even the end of her life is shaped by Perpetua: she seizes the trembling hand of the youthful inexperienced tyro, her designated executioner, and herself guides the phallic *gladius* to her throat; it is *her* will, the text claims, that determines her death (*Passion* 21.9–10; Gold 2011: 248–249; Cobb 2008). The self-determined execution deployed here by Perpetua is praised as a noble and elevating death for defeated gladiators (Seneca, *Letters* 30.8; Edwards 2007: 61, 67; Shaw 1996: 272–274; Potter 1993: 63–66).

These martyr tales function as such arena stories do in building early Christian identity. In a context where the condemned, humiliated social and legal outcasts, are compelled to submit to spectacularized force of Roman power, the arena instead becomes a place where Christians assert the universal power of their faith, victorious over the empire. Women martyrs become powerful exemplars of this. They're not just Christian social and legal outcasts; as women, as slaves, freshly postpartum, they are persons whose social and legal identity is profoundly attached to and limited by the body and its reproductive functions. And yet they choose to disrupt the system, to remove themselves from Roman law, Roman social norms, and gender assumptions, their spiritual strength enabling them to overcome the physical and reproductive weakness of their sex. As elsewhere, the arena context impacts the gender of the person, catalysing shifts in the sexualized body and its social and political meaning.

REFERENCES

Alston, R. 1998. 'Arms and the Man: Soldiers, Masculinity and Power in Republican and Imperial Rome.' In *When Men were Men: Masculinity, Power, and Identity in Classical Antiquity*. 205–223. L. Foxhall and J. B. Salmon, eds. London.

Beacham, R. C. 1999. *Spectacle Entertainments of Early Imperial Rome*. New Haven.

Braund, S. H. 1996. *Juvenal: Satires Book 1*. Cambridge.

Briquel, D. 1992. 'Les femmes gladiateur: examen du dossier.' *Ktèma* 17: 47–53.

Brubaker, L. 2004. 'Sex, Lies and Textuality: The Secret History of Prokopios and the Rhetoric of Gender in Sixth-Century Byzantium.' In *Gender in the Early Medieval World: East and West, 300–900*. 83–101. L. Brubaker and J. M. H. Smith, eds. Cambridge.

Brunet, S. 2004. 'Female and Dwarf Gladiators.' *Mouseion* 4.2: 145–170.

Carter, M. J. 2008. '(Un) Dressed to kill: Viewing the *retiarius*.' In *Roman Dress and the Fabrics of Roman Culture*. 113–135. J. Edmondson and A. Keith, eds. Toronto.

Cébeillac-Gervasoni, M. and F. Zevi. 1976. 'Révisions et nouveautés pour trois inscriptions d'Ostie.' *MEFRA* 88.2: 612–620.

Cobb, L. S. 2008. *Dying to Be Men: Gender and Language in Early Christian Martyr Texts*. New York.

Coleman, K. M. 1990. 'Fatal Charades: Roman Executions Staged as Mythological Enactments.' *JRS* 80: 44–73.

Coleman, K. M. 2000. 'Missio at Halicarnassus.' *HSPh* 100: 487–500.

Coleman, K. M. 2006. *M. Valerii Martialis: Liber Spectaculorum*. Oxford.

Connors, C. 2008. 'Politics and Spectacle.' In *The Cambridge Companion to the Greek and Roman Novel*. 162–181. T. Whitmarsh, ed. Cambridge.

Cooper, K. 2013. 'A Father, a Daughter and a Procurator: Authority and Resistance in the Prison Memoir of Perpetua of Carthage.' In *Gender and the City before Modernity*. 195–212. L. Foxhall and G. Neher, eds. Malden, MA.

Corbeill, A. 2002. 'Political Movement: Walking and Ideology in Republican Rome.' In *The Roman Gaze: Vision, Power, and the Body*. 185–215. D. Fredrick, ed. Baltimore.

Corcoran, T. H. 1963. 'Roman Fisherman.' *CW* 56.4: 97–102.

Courtney, E. 2013. *A Commentary on the Satires of Juvenal*. Berkeley.

Cyrino, M. 1998. "Heroes in D(u)ress: Transvestism and Power in the Myths of Herakles and Achilles.' *Arethusa* 31: 207–241.

DuBois, P. 1982. *Centaurs and Amazons: Women and the Pre-History of the Great Chain of Being*. Ann Arbor.

Edwards, C. 1993. *The Politics of Immorality in Ancient Rome*. Cambridge.

Edwards, C. 1997. 'Unspeakable Professions: Public Performance and Prostitution in Ancient Rome.' In *Roman Sexualities*. 66–95. J. P. Hallett and M. B. Skinner, eds. Princeton.

Edwards, C. 2007. *Death in Ancient Rome*. New Haven.

Elsner, J. 1994. 'Constructing Decadence: The Representation of Nero as Imperial Builder.' In *Reflections of Nero*. 112–127. J. Elsner and J. Masters, eds. London.

Evans, J. E. 2002. *The Empress Theodora: Partner of Justinian.* Austin, TX.

Frei-Stolba, R. 2000. 'Le donne e l'arena.' *Labeo* 46.2: 282–288.

Gleason, M. W. 1990. 'The Semiotics of Gender: Physiognomy and Self-Fashioning in the Second Century c.e.' In *Before Sexuality: The Construction of Erotic Experience in the Ancient Greek World.* 389–416. D. M. Halperin, J. J. Winkler, and F. I. Zeitlin, eds. Princeton.

Gold, B. K. 2011. 'Gender Fluidity and Closure in Perpetua's Prison Diary.' *EuGeSta* 1: 237–251.

Gunderson, E. 1996. 'The Ideology of the Arena.' *ClAnt* 15: 113–151.

McAuley, M. 2010. '*Ambiguus Sexus*: Epic Masculinity in Transition in Statius' *Achilleid.*' *Akroterion* 55: 37–60.

McCullough, A. 2008. 'Female Gladiators in Imperial Rome: Literary Context and Historical Fact.' *CW* 101: 197–209.

Potter, D. S. 1993. 'Martyrdom as Spectacle.' In *Theater and Society in the Classical World.* 53–88. R. Scodel, ed. Ann Arbor.

Potter, D. S. 2015. *Theodora: Actress, Empress, Saint.* Oxford.

Safran, L. 1993. 'Points of View: The Theodosian Obelisk Base in Context.' *GRBS* 34.4: 409–435.

Schäfer, D. 2001. 'Frauen in der Arena.' In *Fünfzig Jahre Forschungen zur antiken Sklaverei an der Mainzer Akademie, 1950–2000: Miscellanea zum Jubiläum:* 243–268. H. Bellen and H. Heinen, eds. Stuttgart.

Shaw, B. D. 1993. 'The Passion of Perpetua.' *P&P* 139: 3–45.

Shaw, B. D. 1996. 'Body/Power/Identity: Passions of the Martyrs.' *JECS* 4.3: 269–312.

Taylor, R. 1997. 'Two Pathic Subcultures in Ancient Rome.' *JHSex* 7.3: 319–371.

Thompson, D. J. 2013. 'Hellenistic Royal Barges.' In *Ptolemies, the Sea and the Nile.* 185–196. K. Buraselis, M. Stefanou, and D. J. Thompson, eds. Cambridge.

Tyrrell, W. B. 1984. *Amazons: A Study in Athenian Mythmaking.* Baltimore.

Vesley, M. 1998. 'Gladiatorial Training for Girls in the *Collegia Iuvenum* of the Roman Empire.' *EMC* 17: 85–93.

Walters, J. 1997. 'Soldiers and Whores in Pseudo-Quintilian Declamation.' In *Gender and Ethnicity in Ancient Italy.* 109–114. T. Cornell and K. Lomas, eds. London.

Walters, J. 1998. 'Making a Spectacle: Deviant Men, Invective and Pleasure.' *Arethusa* 31.3: 355–367.

Webb, R. 2008. *Demons and Dancers: Performance in Late Antiquity.* Cambridge, MA.

Welch, K. E. 2007. *The Roman Amphitheatre From Its Origins to the Colosseum.* Cambridge.

White, A. 2013. 'Mime and the Secular Sphere: Notes on Choricius' *Apologia Mimorum.*' *Studia Patristica* 60: 47–59.

Williams, C. A. 1999. *Roman Homosexuality: Ideologies of Masculinity in Classical Antiquity.* Oxford.

Woodman, A. J. 1992. 'Nero's Alien Capital: Tacitus as Paradoxographer (*Annals* 15.36–7).' In *Author and Audience in Latin Literature.* 137–188. A. J. Woodman and J. Powell, eds. Cambridge.

INDEX